OUR SUNDAY VISITOR'S

CATHOLIC ENCYCLOPEDIA

REVISED EDITION

Reverend Peter M.J. Stravinskas
Ph.D., S.T.D.
Editor

Our Sunday Visitor Publishing Division
Our Sunday Visitor, Inc.
Huntington, Indiana 46750

Editor

The Rev. Peter M. J. Stravinskas, editor of the *Catholic Encyclopedia*, holds a bachelor of arts degree in classical languages and French and a master's degree in school administration from Seton Hall University, a master of arts degree in biblical theology from Immaculate Conception Seminary, a doctorate of philosophy in school administration from Fordham University, and a licentiate of sacred theology from the Pontifical Faculty of the Immaculate Conception in Washington, D.C. He possesses a doctorate in sacred theology from the Marian Institute at the University of Dayton and the Marianum in Rome.

Father Stravinskas is the author of eleven books and more than five hundred articles. He is the founding editor of *The Catholic Answer* and the administrator of St. John the Baptist Church in Bayonne, New Jersey. He likewise serves as adjunct professor of education at Seton Hall University in South Orange, New Jersey.

(Note: The information on the contributors below is based on data received for the 1991 edition of this work.)

Contributors

The Rev. Leonard F. Badia, a priest of the Diocese of Brooklyn, holds a master's degree in theology from St. John's University and a doctorate in theology from New York University. He is the chairperson of the Philosophy/Theology Division on the Staten Island Campus of St. John's University, New York.

The Rev. Robert Barry, O.P., has a master's degree in political science from the University of Wisconsin at Madison and a doctorate in moral theology from The Catholic University of America. Father Barry was a Fellow of the National Endowment for the Humanities and is now professor of Religious Studies at the University of Illinois, Champaign-Urbana.

The Rev. Robert Batule received his master of divinity degree from Immaculate Conception Seminary in Lloyd Harbor, New York, and a master of arts degree in sociology from Adelphi University in Garden City, New York. He serves as parochial vicar at St. Martha's Church in Uniondale, New York, and is widely published in the Catholic press.

The Rev. John Michael Beers, a priest of the Diocese of Allentown, received his licentiate in Sacred Scripture from the Pontifical Biblical Institute in Rome and holds a doctorate in classical languages from The Catholic University of America, as well as a diploma from the Hebrew University of Jerusalem. Father Beers is assistant professor of Scripture and patristics, as well as director of seminary research and planning at Mount St. Mary's Seminar in Emmitsburg, Maryland.

Professor Ronda Chervin holds a doctorate in philosophy from Fordham University and is currently associate professor of philosophy at St. John's Seminary in Camarillo, California.

Sr. M. Scholastica Crilly, O.S.B., is a nun of St. Scholastica Priory in Petersham, Massachusetts. She has studied at Rutgers University and Weston School of Theology and is presently the director of St. Bede Publications.

The Rev. Stephen M. DiGiovanni holds a doctorate in Church history from the Pontifical Gregorian University in Rome. He currently serves as the director of vocations for the Diocese of Bridgeport.

The Rev. Giles Dimock, O.P., holds degrees from Providence College, the Dominican House of Studies in Washington, D.C., and the Pontifical University of St. Thomas in Rome. Father Dimock is a professor of theology at Holy Apostles Seminary in Cromwell, Connecticut, and a visiting professor of theology at the University of St. Thomas in Rome.

The Rev. Joseph A. DiNoia, O.P., holds a doctorate in philosophy from Yale University. He is associate professor of theology at the Dominican House of Studies in Washington, D.C., and is also the editor of *The Thomist*.

The Rev. Timothy Dolan, a priest of the Archdiocese of St. Louis, has earned degrees from Cardinal Glennon College in St. Louis, the Pontifical University of St. Thomas in Rome, and a doctorate in Church history from The Catholic University of America in Washington, D.C. He currently serves as a secretary to the Apostolic Pro-Nuncio in Washington, D.C.

The Rev. Thomas P. Doyle, O.P., holds degrees in philosophy, political science, theology, canon law and Church administration from the Aquinas Institute of Philosophy, University of Wisconsin, University of Ottawa and The Catholic University of America. Father Doyle has served as secretary canonist to the Apostolic Pro-Nuncio, presiding judge for the Metropolitan Tribunal of Chicago, consultant for the Canonical Affairs Committee of the National Conference of Catholic Bishops and judge for the Archdiocese for the Military Services. At present he is a chaplain for the United States Air Force.

The Rev. Joseph M. Egan studied at the Pontifical Gregorian University in Rome and earned both a master's degree and a doctorate in sacred theology from St. Mary of the Lake Seminary in Mundelein, Illinois. He formerly served as professor of dogma at St. Bernard's Seminary in Rochester, New York, where he is now engaged in pastoral work.

Dr. David Ruel Foster holds degrees from the University of Notre Dame and the Dominican House of Studies in Washington, D.C., as well as a doctorate in philosophy from The Catholic University of America. He is currently professor of philosophy in the School of Theology at Seton Hall University in South Orange, New Jersey.

Dr. Mark E. Frisby has a master's degree in theology from Loyola University of Chicago and a doctorate in philosophy from DePaul University. He serves as assistant professor of philosophy at St. John's Seminary College in Camarillo, California.

The Rev. Robert Fuhrman has received degrees from Seton Hall University and Immaculate Conception Seminary. He is the vice-rector of Immaculate Conception Seminary, South Orange, New Jersey.

The Rev. Robert J. Hennessey, O.P., is professor of systematic theology at Mount St. Mary's Seminary in Emmitsburg, Maryland. He holds a doctorate in sacred theology from the Dominican House of Studies in Washington, D.C., and the rank of lector of sacred theology from the Dominican Studium Generale in Rome.

The Rev. Msgr. Thomas J. Herron possesses a licentiate in Sacred Scripture from the Pontifical Biblical Institute and a doctorate in theology from the Pontifical Gregorian University, both in Rome. For six years, he served as a secretary in the Congregation for the Doctrine of the Faith and now teaches Scripture and dogmatic theology at St. Charles Seminary in Philadelphia.

The Most Rev. Mark J. Hurley received a doctorate in education and psychology from The Catholic University of America, a canon law degree from the Lateran University in Rome, and a doctorate of letters from the University of Portland. He is the former bishop of Santa Rosa and is now a consultor for the Congregation of Catholic Education and a member of the Secretariat for Non-Believers in Rome.

The Rev. Kevin W. Irwin, a priest of the Archdiocese of New York, has a master's degree in liturgy from the University of Notre Dame and a doctorate in sacramental theology from the Pontifical University of San Anselmo in Rome. He is associate professor of liturgy and sacramental theology at The Catholic University of America.

The Rev. Carlton Jones, O.P., a convert from Anglicanism, holds degrees from Yale University, Episcopal Theological School and the Pontifical Faculty of the Immaculate Conception in Washington, D.C. He is pursuing a doctorate in theology at the Pontifical University of St. Thomas in Rome.

Sr. Mary Joseph McManamon, O.S.B., is a nun of St. Scholastica Priory in Petersham, Massachusetts, with a degree in political science from Xavier College in Chicago and another in library science from the University of Hawaii. She is the editor of *Word and Spirit*.

Dr. Marianne Mahoney holds a master's degree and a doctorate in philosophy from the University of Chicago. She is a lecturer in philosophy at Loyola University of Chicago.

The Rev. Charles M. Mangan, a priest of the Diocese of Sioux Falls, holds a master's degree in theology from Mount St. Mary's Seminary in Emmitsburg, Maryland. He is parochial vicar at the cathedral parish and writes extensively for the Catholic press.

Dr. Stephen Miletic is the academic dean for the Notre Dame Apostolic Catechetical Institute in Arlington, Virginia. He holds advanced degrees from the University of Windsor in Ontario, Canada, and Marquette University in Milwaukee. He is the former director of the National Office of Religious Education for the Canadian Conference of Catholic Bishops.

Mr. Jay Scott Newman, a seminarian for the Diocese of Charleston, has studied at Princeton University and Belmont Abbey College. He is presently pursuing his theological studies at the Pontifical Gregorian University in Rome.

The Rev. Hector Perez holds a doctorate in theology from the Pontifical University of St. Thomas in Rome. He writes for the Catholic press and is engaged in parochial work in the Diocese of Pensacola-Tallahassee.

Mr. Edward Peters holds a civil law degree from the University of Missouri at Columbia and a licentiate of canon law from The Catholic University of America, where he is currently a candidate for a doctorate in canon law. He serves as vice chancellor and associate judge for the Diocese of Duluth.

The Rev. Christopher Phillips, a convert from Anglicanism, is a priest of the Archdiocese of San Antonio. He is a graduate of Salisbury and Wells Theological College in England. He is a prolific writer and lecturer, as well as a parish priest.

The Rev. Jean-Pierre Ruiz, a priest of the Diocese of Brooklyn, holds both a licentiate and a doctorate in sacred theology from the Pontifical Gregorian University in Rome. He is a professor of biblical studies at Pope John XXIII Seminary in Weston, Massachusetts.

The Rev. Peter J. Scagnelli is the director of worship for the Diocese of Providence. He holds degrees from the University of Connecticut and St. John's Seminary in Boston. He serves on the International Commission on English in the Liturgy.

The Rev. Msgr. John T. Sekellick, a priest of the Ruthenian Diocese of Passaic, possesses degrees from Duquesne University, the Pontifical Gregorian University in Rome, and The Catholic University of America. Msgr. Sekellick is a judge of the Passaic Diocesan Tribunal and also serves as a pastor.

Sr. M. Trinitas Sullivan, O.P., holds degrees in music and education from Manhattanville College, Villa Schifanoia in Florence, Italy, and Rutgers University. She has served as executive secretary for the Music Commission of the Archdiocese of New York and has administered and taught in the New York School of Liturgical Music. Sr. Trinitas is now a school administrator in the Diocese of Metuchen.

The Rev. Msgr. James C. Turro teaches New Testament at Immaculate Conception Seminary in South Orange, New Jersey. He holds advanced degrees from The Catholic University of America, Columbia University, the Pontifical Biblical Institute in Rome and New York University. Msgr. Turro is the author of several books on biblical themes and was a contributor to the *Jerome Biblical Commentary.*

The Rev. Brian VanHove, S.J., belongs to the Missouri Province of the Society of Jesus and has degrees in philosophy and theology from St. Louis University and the University of Toronto. He is engaged in doctoral work in Church history at The Catholic University of America in Washington, D.C.

Mother Mary Clare Vincent, O.S.B., is the prioress of St. Scholastica Priory in Petersham, Massachusetts. She is widely known as a teacher, author, lecturer and retreat mistress, holding degrees from Radcliffe College, Harvard University and Weston School of Theology.

The Rev. Robert Wister, a priest of the Archdiocese of Newark, is the executive director of the Seminary Department of the National Catholic Educational Association. He has a master's degree in theology from Union Theological Seminary in New York and a doctorate in Church history from the Pontifical Gregorian University in Rome.

The Most Rev. Donald Wuerl, Bishop of Pittsburgh, studied philosophy at The Catholic University of America and holds a doctorate in sacred theology from the Pontifical University of St. Thomas in Rome. He has written extensively on theological and patristic themes.

Sr. Mary Frances Wynn, O.S.B., is a nun of St. Scholastica Priory in Petersham, Massachusetts, where she serves as the director of education and liturgy. She holds degrees from Magdalen College and Harvard Divinity School.

Acknowledgments

"Soli Deo gloria" (To God alone be the glory) is a line which appropriately comes to one's lips upon the completion of a project such as this. At the same time, it is good to recall that God's greatest works are usually accomplished through the efforts of his human collaborators, who endeavor to make His glory shine forth.

The concept of the encyclopedia was the brainchild of Mr. Robert Lockwood; he honored me by asking me to spearhead the project. The Board of Directors of Our Sunday Visitor demonstrated their confidence in both Mr. Lockwood and me by committing financial resources and personnel to what lesser visionaries might have considered merely a pipe dream. Mrs. Jackie Lindsey and Mr. Henry O'Brien were most helpful in bringing this project to fruition.

This second edition was envisioned, even as the first edition was being completed, for the simple reason that a living organism like the Church must be possessed of a living faith, which calls for ever-deeper insights into that "faith which was once for all delivered to the saints" (Jude 3). Beyond that, the period between these two editions has been one of almost incredible vitality in terms of Church teaching, most especially thanks to the publication of the *Catechism of the Catholic Church* and the prodigious writings of Pope John Paul II. Hence, the revision team reviewed each and every article to determine its suitability in light of the new ecclesiastical documents; reworking was needed for many, while totally new entries were required in other instances. I am intensely grateful to these fine scholars for their capable and timely completion of the project.

Yet others should be mentioned. The artwork for the present volume came from the talented Mrs. Margaret Bunson. Computer input was handled by the proficient Mr. Christopher Clay, a seminarian for the Diocese of Lincoln.

So, while one must be conscious of the need to give God the glory, it is also good for the inspired thought of St. Paul to arise in the heart: "We give thanks to God for all of you, remembering you in our prayers, unceasingly calling to mind your work of faith and labor of love" (1 Thes 1:3).

The Rev. Peter M. J. Stravinskas, Editor

Preface

Our Sunday Visitor's Catholic Encyclopedia is a timely publication that meets the need for a handy and scholarly resource on the many facets of Catholic life and thought. It is evident that it is the result of a great deal of scholarly research and collaboration, and the timing of its publication seems to me ideal. We have long lacked just such a work which can place at the disposal of everyone, Catholic or not, succinct and helpful information on an immense array of important topics of Catholic interest.

This volume provides a needed resource on the Catholic Faith. It presents the beliefs and teachings of the Church in a clear and concise manner, contains valuable information on the history of the Church, explains the sacramental and prayer life of the Church, and conveys a wealth of information on the practical aspects of the Catholic Faith. This work achieves the commendable goal of offering information on the Catholic Church in a way that presents both a depth and breadth of knowledge.

Catholics will find this work to be an invaluable and current resource in helping them to understand their faith and explain it more clearly to others. Those who are not Catholic will find this volume to be an accessible and clear means for readily gaining concise and insightful information on the beliefs and workings of the Church.

Our Sunday Visitor's Catholic Encyclopedia is the fruit of the work of a team of thirty-nine contributing scholars. We owe them and the editor, Father Stravinskas, our gratitude for producing such a complete, handy and informative resource on the Catholic Church.

Anthony Cardinal Bevilacqua
ARCHBISHOP OF PHILADELPHIA

Foreword

Just a little more than a quarter-century ago, that special grace for the Church and the human race which was the Second Vatican Council came to an end. The Council Fathers, as they left the Eternal City of Rome, knew that they had spoken to the world of today with the voice of the Holy Spirit. But the work of the Council had just begun. Over the past twenty-five years so much has been written about the documents of that great assembly. Many men and women in the Church have sought to plumb the rich depths of its teaching. It reminds all of us of the vast scope of knowledge and information that make up the complex life of the Church in this modern world.

It is precisely within this context that I find the appearance of *Our Sunday Visitor's Catholic Encyclopedia* so timely, for there can be no true following of Christ without knowledge of His Body, which is the Church. Nor can there be any sharing of His Person or message without the understanding which comes from a catechesis built on solid teaching.

Pope John Paul II established this linkage very clearly in his landmark document on the transmission of the faith when he wrote: "Catechesis is one of [the] moments — a very remarkable one — in the whole process of evangelization. The specific character of catechesis . . . has the twofold objective of maturing the initial faith and of educating the true disciple of Christ by means of a deeper and more systematic knowledge of the Person and the message of our Lord Jesus Christ" (*Catechesi Trandendae*, nn. 18-19).

This new *Catholic Encyclopedia* should be a most worthwhile contribution to that ongoing catechesis necessary for all members of the Church.

I am sure that this volume will be of use in homes, in Catholic school classrooms and libraries and in rectory offices as a handy and reliable reference tool for information on the various aspects of Catholic teaching and practice. I hope that it will also serve as an invitation to non-Catholics to learn and appreciate the truth of the Catholic Faith which St. Augustine heralded centuries ago as beauty ever-ancient, yet ever-new.

The postconciliar era has seen changes in the life of the Church in different parts of the world. In the western nations like our own, some of these new phenomena give rise to concern, such as the decline in religious observance. How often this is caused by religious misinformation or even religious illiteracy in the lives of modern men and women. I applaud Our Sunday Visitor's effort to help dispel that religious ignorance with this new work. Father Peter Stravinskas is to be congratulated for accepting the editorial challenge of such a major undertaking and for bringing it to so impressive a conclusion. I am truly pleased by the wide support and endorsement this work has received from so many brother bishops from dioceses large and small around the country — another testimony to this volume's usefulness and necessity but also to its fidelity to the basic truths of Catholicism put into a contemporary key.

Vatican II and all the Popes since it have called the entire Church to be servants of the whole truth of Jesus Christ by hearing His Word and by sharing it. This is the Gospel call to evangelize. Recently in a beautiful ad limina address to bishops from the Philippines, Pope John Paul put it this way: "The evangelizer is a servant of the truth about God, about man and his mysterious destiny, and about the world. He should not neglect to study this truth; he should serve it generously, without making it serve him. Above all, the evangelizer should be filled with love for those to whom he is sent — a love that consists in transmitting the genuine truth of the Gospel and not doubts and uncertainties born of an erudition poorly assimilated; a love that respects the freedom of conscience and the spiritual situation of others but does not hesitate to engage them in serious dialogue concerning the deeper questions facing individuals and society" (*L'Osservatore Romano*, December 1, 1990). Every Catholic encyclopedia should serve to help in that process.

As the Catholic world delves ever more deeply into the rich treasure of the recently published *Catechism of the Catholic Church* and meditates on the towering encyclicals of Pope John Paul II, may *Our Sunday Visitor's Catholic Encyclopedia* serve as a fitting tribute to the continuing implementation of the Second Vatican Council. May it bear witness that missionary zeal for the teaching of the truth lives on in the hearts and minds of the faithful of the New World as it prepares with joyful hope for the Third Millennium of Christianity.

Theodore E. McCarrick
ARCHBISHOP OF NEWARK

Abbreviations

AA: *Apostolicam Actuositatem*: Decree on the Apostolate of Lay People.

A.A.: *Augustiniani Assumptionis*: Augustinians of the Assumption (Assumptionists).

AAS: *Acta Apostolicae Sedis*: Acts of the Apostolic See.

A.B.: *Artium Baccalaureus*: Bachelor of Arts.

Abb.: Abbacy.

Abp.: Archbishop.

A.D.: *Anno Domini*: in the year of Our Lord.

ad lib.: *ad libitum*: at your own choice.

AG: *Ad Gentes*: Decree on the Church's Missionary Activity.

A.M.: *Artium Magister*: Master of Arts.

A.M.D.G.: *Ad majorem Dei gloriam*: to the greater glory of God.

Ap.: Apostle.

A.U.C.: *Ab Urbe Condita*: from the founding of the City [of Rome].

A.V.: Authorized Version (of the Bible).

b.: born.

B.A.: Bachelor of Arts.

B.C.: Before Christ.

B.C.L.: Bachelor of Canon (Civil) Law.

Bl.: Blessed.

Bp.: Bishop.

Bro.: Brother.

B.S.: Bachelor of Science.

B.V.M.: Blessed Virgin Mary.

c.: *circa*: about.

CARA: Center for Applied Research in the Apostolate.

C.E.: Common or Christian Era.

CCCB: Canadian Conference of Catholic Bishops.

CCD: Confraternity of Christian Doctrine.

CD: *Christus Dominus*: Decree on the Pastoral Office of the Bishops in the Church.

CEF: Citizens for Educational Freedom.

cf.: *confer*: compare.

C.F.A.: *Congregatio Fratrum Cellitarum seu Alexianorum*: Alexian Brothers.

C.F.X.: *Congregatio Fratrum S. Francisci Xaverii*: Xaverian Brothers.

C.I.C.: *Codex Iuris Canonici*: Code of Canon Law.

C.I.C.M.: *Congregatio Immaculati Cordis Mariae*: Congregation of the Immaculate Heart of Mary (Missionhurst; Scheut Missionaries).

C.J.: *Congregatio Josephitarum Gerardimontensium*: Josephite Fathers (of Belgium).

C.J.M.: Congregation of Jesus and Mary (Eudists).

C.M.: Congregation of the Mission (Vincentians or Lazarists).

C.M.F.: *Cordis Mariae Filii*: Missionary Sons of the Immaculate Heart of Mary (Claretians).

C.M.M.: *Congregatio Missionariorum de Mariannhill*: Missionaries of Mariannhill.

CMSM: Conference of Major Superiors of Men.

CNS: Catholic News Service.

C.O.: *Congregatio Oratorii*: Oratorians.

COCU: Consultation on Church Union.

C.P.: Congregation of the Passion (Passionists).

CPA: Catholic Press Association.

C.P.M.: *Congregatio Presbyterorum a Misericordia*: Congregation of the Fathers of Mercy.

C.PP.S.: *Congregatio Missionariorum Pretiosissimi Sanguinis*: Society of the Precious Blood.

C.R.: Congregation of the Resurrection.

C.R.M.: Clerics Regular Minor (Adorno Fathers).

CRS: Catholic Relief Services.

C.R.S.P.: Clerics Regular of St. Paul (Barnabites).

C.S.: Missionaries of St. Charles (Scalabrinians).

C.S.B.: Congregation of St. Basil (Basilians).

C.S.C.: *Congregatio Sanctae Crucis*: Congregation of the Holy Cross.

C.S.P.: Congregation of St. Paul (Paulists).

C.S.S.: Congregation of the Sacred Stigmata (Stigmatine Fathers and Brothers).

C.SS.R.: *Congregatio Sanctissimi Redemptoris*: Congregation of the Most Holy Redeemer (Redemptorists).

C.S.Sp.: *Congregatio Sancti Spiritus*: Holy Ghost Fathers.

C.S.V.: Clerks of St. Viator (Viatorians).

C.Y.O.: Catholic Youth Organization.

D.C.L.: *Doctor Canonicae (Civilis) Legis*: Doctor of Canon (Civil) Law.

D.D.: *Divinitatis Doctor*: Doctor of Divinity.

DH: *Dignitatis Humanae*: Decree on Religious Liberty.

D.N.J.C.: *Dominus Noster Jesus Christus*: Our Lord Jesus Christ.

D.O.M.: *Deo Optimo Maximo*: To God, the Best and Greatest.

DS: *Denzinger-Schönmetzer, Enchiridion Symbolorum*.

DV: *Dei Verbum*: Dogmatic Constitution on Divine Revelation.

D.V.: *Deo volente*: God willing.

e.g.: *exempli gratia*: for example.

Er.Cam.: *Congregatio Monachorum Eremitarum Camaldulensium*: Monk Hermits of Camaldoli.

et al.: *et alii (aliae, alia)*: and others.

f., ff.: following.

F.D.P.: *Filii Divinae Providentiae*: Sons of Divine Providence.

F.M.S.: *Fratres Maristarum a Scholis*: Marist Brothers.

Fr.: Father, or Friar.

F.S.C.: *Fratres Scholarum Christianarum*: Brothers of the Christian Schools (Christian Brothers).

GE: *Gravissimum Educationis*: Declaration on Christian Education.

GS: *Gaudium et Spes*: Pastoral Constitution on the Church in the Modern World.

I.C.: Institute of Charity (Rosminians).

ICEL: International Committee on English in the Liturgy.

i.e.: *id est*: that is.

IHS: Jesus (from Greek IHSOYS).

IM: *Inter Mirifica*: Decree on the Means of Social Communication.

I.M.C.: *Institutum Missionum a Consolata*: Consolata Society for Foreign Missions.

I.N.R.I.: *Iesus Nazarenus, Rex Iudaeorum*: Jesus of Nazareth, King of the Jews.

J.C.D.: *Juris Canonici Doctor*: Doctor of Canon Law.

J.C.L.: *Juris Canonici Licentiatus*: Licentiate in Canon Law.

J.M.J.: Jesus, Mary and Joseph:

J.U.D.: *Juris Utriusque Doctor*: Doctor of Both (Civil and Canon) Laws.

KJV: King James Version (of the Bible).

K. of C.: Knights of Columbus.

K.H.S.: Knight of the Holy Sepulchre.

K.M.: Knight of Malta.

K.P.: Knight of Pius IX.

K.S.G.: Knight of St. Gregory.

K.S.S.: Knight of St. Sylvester.

LCWR: Leadership Conference of Women Religious.

LG: *Lumen Gentium*: Dogmatic Constitution on the Church.

LL.B.: *Legum Baccalaureus*: Bachelor of Laws.

LL.D.: *Legum Doctor*: Doctor of Laws.

LWF: Lutheran World Federation.

M.Afr.: Missionaries of Africa.

MCCJ: *Missionarii Comboniani Cordis Jesu*: Comboni Missionaries of the Heart of Jesus (Verona Fathers).

M.E.P.: *Société des Missions Étrangers de Paris:* Paris Foreign Missions Society.

M.H.M.: Mill Hill Missionaries.

M.I.C.: *Congregatio Clericorum Regularium Marianorum sub titulo Immaculatae Conceptionis Beatae Mariae Virginis*: Marian Fathers and Brothers.

MM.: Martyrs.

M.M.: Catholic Foreign Mission Society (Maryknoll Missioners).

M.S.: Missionaries of Our Lady of La Salette.

M.S.C.: Missionaries of the Sacred Heart.

M.S.F.: *Congregatio Missionariorum a Sancta Familia*: Missionaries of the Holy Family.

Msgr.: Monsignor.

n., nn.: number, numbers.

NA: *Nostra Aetate*: Declaration on the Relations of the Church to Non-Christian Religions.

NAB: New American Bible.

NCCB: National Conference of Catholic Bishops.

NCCC: National Council of Churches of Christ.

NCCM: National Council of Catholic Men.

NCCW: National Council of Catholic Women.

NCEA: National Catholic Educational Association.

NCRLC: National Catholic Rural Life Conference.

NEB: New English Bible.

NFPC: National Federation of Priests' Councils.

NOBC: National Office for Black Catholics.

N.T.: New Testament.

O.A.R.: Order of Augustinian Recollects.

O.Carm: *Ordo Carmelitorum*: Order of Carmelites.

O.Cart.: *Ordo Cartusiensis*: Carthusian Order.

O.C.D.: *Ordo Carmelitorum Discalceatorum*: Order of Discalced Carmelites.

O.Cist.: *Ordo Cisterciensis*: Cistercian Order.

O.C.S.O.: Order of Cistercians of the Strict Observance (Trappists).

O. de M.: *Ordo Beatae Mariae de Mercede*: Order of Our Lady of Mercy (Mercedarians).

OE: *Orientalium Ecclesiarum*: Decree on the Eastern Catholic Churches.

O.F.M.: Order of Friars Minor (Franciscans).

O.F.M. Cap.: Order of Friars Minor Capuchin (Capuchins).

O.F.M. Conv.: Order of Friars Minor Conventual (Conventuals).

O.H.: *Ordo Hospitalarius S. Joannis de Deo:* Hospitaller Order of St. John of God.

O.M.I.: Oblates of Mary Immaculate.

O.P.: Order of Preachers (Dominicans).

O.Praem.: Order of Premonstratensians (Norbertines).

O.S.A.: Order of Hermits of St. Augustine (Augustinians).

O.S.B.: Order of St. Benedict (Benedictines).

O.S.B.M.: *Ordo Sancti Basilii Magni*: Order of St. Basil the Great (Basilians of St. Josaphat).

O.S.C.: *Ordo Sanctae Crucis*: Order of the Holy Cross (Crosier Fathers).

O.S.Cam.: Order of St. Camillus (Camillians).

O.S.F.: Order of St. Francis: Franciscan Brothers; also various congregations of Franciscan Sisters.

O.S.F.S.: Oblates of St. Francis de Sales.

O.S.J.: Oblates of St. Joseph.

O.S.M.: Order of Servants of Mary (Servites).

O.S.P.: Order of St. Paul the First Hermit (Pauline Fathers).

O.SS.T.: *Ordo Sanctissimae Trinitatis Redemptionis Captivorum*: Order of the Most Holy Trinity (Trinitarians).

OT: *Optatam Totius*: Decree on the Training of Priests.

O.T.: Old Testament.

P.A.: Protonotary Apostolic.

PC: *Perfectae Caritatis*: Decree on the Up-to-Date Renewal of Religious Life.

Ph.D.: *Philosophiae Doctor*: Doctor of Philosophy.

P.I.M.E.: *Pontificium Institutum pro Missionibus Externis*: Pontifical Institute for Foreign Missions; Missionaries of SS. Peter and Paul.

PO: *Presbyterorum Ordinis*: Decree on the Ministry and Life of Priests.

Pont. Max.: *Pontifex Maximus*: Supreme Pontiff.

PP., Pp.: *Papa*: Pope.

R.C.: Roman Catholic.

R.I.P.: *Requiescat in pace*: may he (she) rest in peace.

RNS: Religious News Service.

R.P.: *Reverendus Pater*: Reverend Father.

R.S.V.: Revised Standard Version (of the Bible).

S.A.: *Societas Adunationis*: Franciscan Friars of the Atonement.

S.A.C.: *Societas Apostolatus Catholici*: Society of the Catholic Apostolate (Pallottines).

SC: *Sacrosanctum Concilium*: Constitution on the Sacred Liturgy.

Sch.P. or **S.P.:** *Ordo Clericorum Regularium Pauperum Matris Dei Scholarum Piarum*: Order of Regular Poor Clerics of the Mother of God of the Pious Schools; Piarists.

S.C.J.: *Congregatio Sacerdotum a Corde Jesu*: Congregation of the Sacred Heart; Sacred Heart Fathers and Brothers.

S.D.B.: Salesians of Don Bosco.

S.D.S.: Society of the Divine Savior (Salvatorians).

S.D.V.: Society of Divine Vocations (Vocationists).

S.F.: *Congregatio Filiorum Sacrae Familiae*: Sons of the Holy Family.

S.F.O.: Secular Franciscan Order.

S.J.: Society of Jesus (Jesuits).

S.M.: Society of Mary (Marists or Marianists).

S.M.A.: *Societas Missionum ad Afros*: Society of African Missions.

S.M.B.: *Societas Missionaria de Bethlehem*: Society of Bethlehem Missionaries.

S.M.M.: *Societas Mariae Montfortana*: Company of Mary (Montfort Missionaries).

S.P.: Servants of the Paraclete.

Sr.: Sister.

S.S.: Society of St. Sulpice (Sulpicians).

SS.CC.: *Congregatio Sacrorum Cordium*: Fathers of the Sacred Hearts (Picpus Fathers).

S.S.E.: Society of St. Edmund.

S.S.J.: *Societas Sancti Joseph SSmi Cordis*: St. Joseph's Society of the Sacred Heart (Josephites).

S.S.L.: *Sacrae Scripturae Licentiatus*: Licentiate in Sacred Scripture.

S.S.P.: Society of St. Paul for the Apostolate of Communications.

S.S.S.: *Congregatio Presbyterorum Sacerdotes Sanctissimi Sacramenti*: Congregation of the Blessed Sacrament.

S., St.; SS., Sts.: Saint; Saints.

S.T.: *Missionarii Servi Sanctissimae Trinitatis*: Missionary Servants of the Most Holy Trinity (Trinity Missions).

S.T.B.: *Sacrae Theologiae Baccalaureus*: Bachelor of Sacred Theology.

S.T.D.: *Sacrae Theologiae Doctor*: Doctor of Sacred Theology.

S.T.L.: *Sacrae Theologiae Licentiatus*: Licentiate in Sacred Theology.

S.T.M.: *Sacrae Theologiae Magister*: Master of Sacred Theology.

S.V.D.: *Societas Verbi Divini*: Society of the Divine Word.

S.X.: *Societas Xaveriana*: Xaverian Missionary Fathers.

T.O.R.: Third Order Regular of St. Francis.

UR: *Unitatis Redintegratio*: Decree on Ecumenism.

USCC: United States Catholic Conference.

v., vv.: verse, verses.

V.A.: Vicar Apostolic.

Ven.: Venerable.

V.F.: Vicar Forane.

V.G.: Vicar General.

V.T.: *Vetus Testamentum*: Old Testament.

WCC: World Council of Churches.

Key to Abbreviations of Biblical Books

(In Alphabetical Order)

Old Testament Books

Am — Amos
Bar — Baruch
1 Chr — 1 Chronicles
2 Chr — 2 Chronicles
Dn — Daniel
Dt — Deuteronomy
Eccl — Ecclesiastes
Est — Esther
Ex — Exodus
Ez — Ezekiel
Ezr — Ezra
Gn — Genesis
Hb — Habakkuk
Hg — Haggai
Hos — Hosea
Is — Isaiah
Jer — Jeremiah
Jb — Job
Jdt — Judith
Jgs — Judges
Jl — Joel
Jon — Jonah
Jos — Joshua

1 Kgs — 1 Kings
2 Kgs — 2 Kings
Lam — Lamentations
Lv — Leviticus
Mal — Malachi
1 Mc — 1 Maccabees
2 Mc — 2 Maccabees
Mi — Micah
Na — Nahum
Neh — Nehemiah
Nm — Numbers
Ob — Obadiah
Prv — Proverbs
Ps — Psalms
Ru — Ruth
Sg — Song of Songs
Sir — Sirach
1 Sm — 1 Samuel
2 Sm — 2 Samuel
Tb — Tobit
Wis — Wisdom
Zec — Zechariah
Zep — Zephaniah

New Testament Books

Acts — Acts of the Apostles
Col — Colossians
1 Cor — 1 Corinthians
2 Cor — 2 Corinthians
Eph — Ephesians
Gal — Galatians
Heb — Hebrews
Jas — James
Jn — John
1 Jn — 1 John
2 Jn — 2 John
3 Jn — 3 John
Jude — Jude
Lk — Luke

Mk — Mark
Mt — Matthew
Phil — Philippians
Phlm — Philemon
1 Pt — 1 Peter
2 Pt — 2 Peter
Rom — Romans
Rv — Revelation
1 Thes — 1 Thessalonians
2 Thes — 2 Thessalonians
Ti — Titus
1 Tm — 1 Timothy
2 Tm — 2 Timothy

A Capella • The style of choral music which is unaccompanied by instruments. From the Italian meaning "in chapel style."

A.D. • The abbreviation for the Latin "Anno Domini," meaning "in the Year of Our Lord." It is used in dating events following the birth of Christ.

Abaddon • The word is from the Hebrew *abhaddon,* meaning "destruction." It is associated with death and is referred to as the dwelling place of the dead (Ps 88:11-12; Jb 28:22). It is a synonym for Sheol (Prv 15:11) and the generic Hebrew term for "underworld" or region of the dead (Jb 26:6; Prv 27:20). In postbiblical Judaism it is associated with Gehenna. In the New Testament it occurs only at Revelation 9:11 and represents the name of the angel or ruler of the abyss whose Greek name is *Appolyon* ("destroyer").

For further reading: Herbert G. Grether, "Abaddon," *Anchor Bible Dictionary,* 1:6.

Abba • An Aramaic word meaning father, *abba* appears in the New Testament in Mark 14:36, Romans 8:15 and Galatians 4:6. In each of these three instances, the Aramaic word is accompanied by its Greek equivalent, *pater.*

In the Old Testament, God is often identified as a father to Israel (cf. Jer 31:9) and as father to the anointed king (cf. Ps 89:27). Jewish prayer includes the litany "Our Father, Our King," a series of forty-four invocations, each of which begins by calling on God by those titles.

All three New Testament occurrences of *abba* are in the context of prayer. In Mark 14:36 Jesus prays, "Abba, Father, all things are possible to thee. Remove this cup from me; yet not what I will but what thou wilt." *Abba* is not found in the Synoptic parallel texts (Mt 26:42 and Lk 22:42).

In Romans 8:15 and Galatians 4:6, "Abba, Father" is the inspired outcry of believers who have received the spirit of adoption, the Spirit of the Son in whose relationship to God the Father we have been given a share.

Although the Aramaic word *abba* itself is found only infrequently, the New Testament frequently refers to God as Father. Many scholars believe that Semitic usage underlies the opening words of the Lord's Prayer, "Our Father who art in heaven" (Mt 6:9) and "Father" (Lk 11:2).

For further reading: John Ashton, "Abba," *Anchor Bible Dictionary,* 1:7-8.

Abbacy Nullius • An ecclesiastical territory that is set apart from any diocese, although it is equivalent to a diocese in many ways. Historically, abbacies nullius were attached to monastic abbeys with the abbot as the ordinary of the clergy and faithful within the abbacy.

Abbé • A French title used originally for abbots of a monastery. Today, an abbot is addressed as *Père l'Abbé,* while any diocesan priest or seminarian is called *Monsieur l'Abbé.* A religious priest is properly addressed as *Mon Père.*

Abbess • Dating back to the sixth century, this title is the feminine form of "abbot" and designates the spiritual and temporal superior elected by a community of nuns. The Rite for the Blessing of an Abbess in the *Pontifical* issued after the Second Vatican Council prays that "her manner of life show clearly that she is what she is called, a mother," seeking "to help her sisters rather than to preside over them." According to a monastic tradition repeated in the post-Vatican II *Pontifical*, the abbess is to be the living embodiment of the community's Rule of life, teaching her monastic family "to grow in love of [God] and of their neighbor" and "to hold in high esteem the Divine Office and sacred reading." Referring originally to superiors in the Benedictine tradition, the title was later extended to Poor Clares and other communities which profess or observe the monastic ideal of stability to a particular place.

In former times, though not after the 1917 Code of Canon Law, abbesses exercised considerable ecclesiastical jurisdiction over territories associated with their abbeys. While obviously not possessing priestly powers, nor exercising prelatial authority (as some abbots still do in virtue of the 1983 Code of Canon Law, Canon 370), some abbesses formerly used various pontifical insignia. The new rite, however, mentions only the conferral of a ring, and this only if the abbess has not received it on the day of her profession. In many communities the use of a simple pectoral cross visually designates the abbess but the formal bestowal of the Rule at the blessing emphasizes the essentially spiritual nature of the abbess's jurisdiction.

Abbey Church of St. Denis

Abbey • A monastery of monks or nuns governed respectively by an abbot or abbess elected by the community. According to the constitutions proper to each order, an abbey may be virtually independent while maintaining an association with other abbeys of the same order in a "federation" or "congregation"; or the abbey may be completely independent under the jurisdiction of an abbot primate or the supreme governing body of the order. The principal components of an abbey are the abbey church, monastic refectory, chapter hall, and "dormitory," though in modern usage the common dormitory has been replaced by individual rooms called "cells." Depending on the size of the abbey and the community's apostolic or contemplative nature, the abbey complex may also include an infirmary, workshops, schools, guest house or retreat center. Although specific legislation may vary according to various orders, a monastery usually must have a minimum of twelve solemnly professed religious to be "elevated" to the rank of abbey and granted canonical independence. Smaller "daughter" houses of an abbey are usually called priories and remain dependent upon the "motherhouse" or founding abbey to which the religious have vowed monastic stability and at which the novices generally receive their monastic profession.

Abbey Nullius • An abbey which, according to the literal Latin term *nullius*, belongs to no diocese. It is separated territorially and jurisdictionally from surrounding dioceses by boundaries which are set up by the Holy See, just as in the case of a diocese. The abbey *nullius* has its origin in the large and influential monasteries of Europe during the Middle Ages. Around the ninth and tenth centuries, these monasteries which exercised pastoral care of the faithful living in the territories adjacent to the monasteries and their land holding were first exempted from the jurisdiction of the local bishop or ordinary. The powers of the local ordinary were thus transferred to the abbot of the monastery in question. The abbot or *abbas nullius* may or may not be a bishop, but he always has the ordinary authority and jurisdiction similar to a bishop within his own territory (Canon 381.2).

In regard to the inhabitants of the territory over which the abbot has jurisdiction, he has the power and authority over them of an ordinary, even if he is not a bishop. He also shares some of the prerogatives and privileges of a bishop. For instance, he may wear the violet skullcap or

zucchetto, in addition to the other distinctive signs of the office of abbot. His name is said during the Canon or Eucharistic Prayer of the Mass in place of the bishop's name. He may confirm, consecrate churches, chalices, etc. When a bishop, he has all the added powers that come with that share in the fullness of the priesthood. Abbots of abbeys *nullius* are usually named by the Supreme Pontiff, except in cases where the monks of a particular abbey have been given the right to elect him. In these cases, the Pope may give them a list from which to choose or they may present the Pope with their choice. If the Holy Father is in agreement on the candidate proposed or elected by the monks, he then confirms the election and makes the appointment. If the abbot is also to be a bishop, he is then consecrated.

Following the Second Vatican Council, Pope Paul VI issued a *motu proprio*, *Catholica Ecclesia*, on October 23, 1976, in which he decreed that in the future there should be no more such abbeys erected except for very special reasons. Henceforth, they would also receive a new name, "territorial abbey," which the new Code of Canon Law adopts as well (cf. Canon 370). Examples of abbeys *nullius* are the Benedictine monasteries of Monte Cassino and Subiaco, which were both founded by St. Benedict in the early sixth century. Belmont Abbey in North Carolina is the only abbey *nullius* or territorial abbey in this country.

Abbot • The historical term abbot ("father") is used to denote the head of a religious community of men. While several large religious institutes, for example, the Benedictines, have preserved the title, others, such as the Dominicans and Jesuits, use other terms (prior and rector, respectively) to describe the same office. Most abbots are not bishops, but over the centuries canon law and tradition have accorded them several quasi-episcopal powers, especially in matters of governance and worship within their community.

Abdication • An older term for resignation of ecclesiastical office. As such, the rules on resignation apply to abdication. If the Pope were to abdicate the papal throne (as did St. Peter Celestine), his abdication would be announced to the College of Cardinals, but not being his superior, they could not technically accept it, nor do they have the power to refuse it. (Cf. Canon 332.2.)

Abduction • One of the canonical impediments to a valid marriage. It means the forcible retention of a woman against her will for the purpose of marriage. The impediment applies only to the situation of a *man* kidnapping or forcibly retaining a *woman* and not vice versa. An attempted marriage is invalid because the law presumes that the woman is unable to give her free consent. The impediment ceases to exist only when it can be established that the woman has been released and is able to choose marriage of her own free will (cf. Canon 1089).

Abel • Described as the second son of Adam and Eve and the younger brother of Cain in Genesis 4, Abel was a shepherd and his brother Cain was a farmer. Both brothers offered sacrifices to God, with Cain presenting "an offering of the fruit of the ground" and Abel bringing an offering "of the firstlings of his flock and of their fat portions." In doing this, Abel anticipated the sacrificial offerings by which Israel would acknowledge God's ultimate ownership of all created things, including the products of human labor. The offerings by Cain and Abel are the first sacrifices mentioned in the Bible. According to Genesis 4:4-5, "the LORD

had regard for Abel and his offering, but for Cain and his offering he had no regard." No reason whatsoever is supplied for God's preference of Abel's offering over Cain's; nothing is said either about the worthiness of either brother's offering or about the quality of either brother's intention in presenting it. Neither is there any evidence that God's selection indicated a preference for Abel's pastoral, seminomadic way of life over Cain's settled, agricultural way of life.

We are told of Cain's anger at the rejection of his offering, an anger that earns him a divine admonition in Genesis 4:7, "if you do not do well, sin is crouching at the door; its desire is for you, but you must master it." Tragically, it is sin that masters Cain, for we learn in Genesis 4:8 that Cain lured his brother Abel into the field and killed him there. The crime goes neither unnoticed nor unpunished. When God interrogates Cain, "Where is Abel your brother?" (Gn 4:9) and Cain denies responsibility for his brother, "I do not know; am I my brother's keeper?" God tells him, "The voice of your brother's blood is crying to me from the ground. And now you are cursed from the ground, which has opened its mouth to receive your brother's blood from your hand" (Gn 4:10-11).

In the New Testament, the blood of Abel is mentioned in Luke 11:50-51. There Jesus invokes divine wisdom against "this generation," guilty of killing prophets and Apostles. As a result, "the blood of all the prophets, shed from the foundation of the world, may be required of this generation, from the blood of Abel" on forward. In the Synoptic parallel, Matthew 23:35, the blood is further qualified as "righteous" and Abel as "innocent."

In the Epistle to the Hebrews, Abel is the first among the great Old Testament heroes of faith to be mentioned in Chapter 11. In Hebrews 11:4, the acceptance of Abel's sacrificial offering is attributed to his faith:

"By faith Abel offered to God a more pleasing sacrifice than Cain, through which he received approval as righteous, God bearing witness by accepting his gifts; he died, but through his faith he is still speaking." Emphasizing the one perfect sacrifice of Jesus on the cross, Hebrews 12:24 declares that the blood of Christ "speaks more graciously than the blood of Abel." It is this emphasis on the sacrifice of Abel that carries over into the mention of Abel in Eucharistic Prayer I (the Roman Canon) of the Mass, in which the priest prays: "Look with favor on these offerings and accept them as once you accepted the gifts of your servant Abel, the sacrifice of Abraham, our father in faith, and the bread and wine offered by your priest Melchisedech," recalling the sacrificial offerings made by these three Old Testament figures.

For further reading: Richard S. Hess, "Abel," *Anchor Bible Dictionary*, 1:9-10.

Abib • The original Canaanite name of the first month of the Hebrew calendar. Later known as Nisan, it corresponds to the period within March-April.

Abjuration of Heresy • Under Canon 2314 of the 1917 Code of Canon Law, most converts from apostasy, heresy or schism were required to offer an abjuration of their earlier opinions, prior to being received into full communion with the Church. In light of the fact, however, that so many adherents of such movements were simply born into them, the formal abjuration over the years came to emphasize more the Profession of Faith (which was always a part of the ceremony) of the new member.

Canon 2314 of the 1917 Code was not carried over into the 1983 Code. In the event, though, that a person who culpably fell into apostasy, heresy or schism and later wished to seek reconciliation with the Church, it would seem within the authority of the competent superior to seek a manifestation of repudiation of past errors as part of the reintegration process, albeit without the formal trapping of the older forms of abjuration.

Ablution • Comes from the Latin *abluo*, and refers to a washing or cleansing. In liturgical language it refers principally to the washing of the hands at Mass by the celebrant, the purification of his fingers which have touched the Sacred Species after Communion, and the purification of the sacred vessels at the same time. Usually this is done by pouring wine and/or water over the index fingers and thumbs of the celebrant into the chalice. It may also be done by inserting these fingers into the water found inside the ablution cup. This witnesses to the Church's great reverence for the Body and Blood of Christ and her concern that no remains or particles of that heavenly food be lost or unintentionally profaned. It is also a reminder that the Church's Magisterium has defined (at the Council of Trent, for one) that even the tiniest particle of the Sacred Species is the Body and Blood, Soul and Divinity of Our Lord Jesus Christ, substantially present in this sacrament (cf. *Mysterium Fidei* of Pope Paul VI).

The term "ablution" is also given to the wine/water which has been poured into the chalice and drunk or consumed by the celebrant or the one who purifies the sacred vessels. The term "ablution cup" is used to signify the small bowl-like container with a cover which should always be kept next to the tabernacle and in which anyone who for reasons of office or apostolate needs to touch the Sacred Host dips his thumb and index finger for the above-mentioned reasons (cf. *Institutio Generalis Missalis Romani*, n. 237; "Letter to All the Bishops of the Church on the Mystery and Worship of the Holy Eucharist," February 24, 1980, n. 11).

Abomination of Desolation • The phrase "abomination [sacrilege] of desolation" occurs with slight variation in Mark 13:14 and Matthew 24:15 (cf. Lk 21:20; 2 Thes 2:3). It probably refers to the desecration of the Jerusalem Temple which signals the nearness of the end of "this world" and the second coming of Christ (*parousia*). The New Testament usage is informed by two principal Old Testament witnesses. In 1 Maccabees 1:48, the phrase carries with it the notion of desecration and false worship or idolatry. A small altar dedicated to a pagan god (probably Zeus) was placed upon the Jerusalem Temple altar where the God of Israel was worshiped. In Daniel 11:31 (cf. Dn 12:11 and 9:27), the Temple of Jerusalem is defiled by the Syrian monarch Antiochus IV, who erected an altar to Zeus, thus driving Jewish worshipers and even God from that now-desecrated place. The defilement is an "abomination" which God momentarily leaves, resulting in "desolation."

For further reading: David Wenham, "Abomination of Desolation," *Anchor Bible Dictionary*, 1:28-31.

Abortion • Either the removal of a nonviable embryo or fetus from the womb or the deliberate killing of a nonviable embryo or fetus in the womb. On December 5, 1989, the Pontifical Commission for the Authentic Interpretation of the Code of Canon Law broadened the definition of abortion to include any killing of an immature fetus. This was approved by Pope John Paul II on May 23, 1988, a change which has come about primarily because of the development of abortifacient drugs.

Abortion can be direct, when the death of the infant is intended as an end in itself or as a means to another end; or it can be indirect when it is a side effect of another intended, morally good action. If there is any moral teaching of the Catholic Church that is nearly absolute, it is the teaching on the immorality of abortion, which has been condemned with remarkable consistency in every age of the Church. No bishop or teacher has ever taught that direct abortion is morally permissible, and the condemnation of abortion is remarkably consistent. Abortion is particularly malicious because the unborn child is innocent of any offense against either the mother or father and is defenseless against any attack.

Abortion is mortally sinful and may incur further penalty of excommunication for those connected with an abortion by ordering it or cooperating in it. Catholics who have been involved in seeking abortions or implementing them, however, should not despair of God's forgiveness but should seek absolution in the sacrament of Penance and healing through counseling and penance.

Abortion not only kills the baby but is sometimes followed by serious physical conditions affecting the mother, such as infection, hemorrhage, sterility and blood-clotting.

The fact that millions of abortions have been performed since their legalization does not change the moral law forbidding them. Scripture that points to the living reality of the child in the womb in a graphic way is: ". . . thou didst knit me together in my mother's womb" (Ps 139:13). The salutation to Jesus by John the Baptist while in the womb of Elizabeth also confirms the personhood of infants before birth (cf. Lk 1:41). "You shall not kill" (Dt 5:17) is a commandment that has reference to the taking of any innocent human life. The Second Vatican Council, in *Gaudium et Spes* (n. 51), calls abortion "an unspeakable crime." (Cf. Canon 1398.)

For further reading: R. Huser, "The Crime of Abortion in Canon Law," *Studies in Canon Law*, No. 162 (Catholic University of America, 1942).

Abraham • The Hebrew patriarch, the son of Terah (Gn 11:26) and the father of Ishmael (Gn 16:15) and Isaac (Gn 21:1-3; and cf. Gn 25:1-2). Abraham's story is presented in Genesis 12-25. The collection of Abraham stories in Genesis 12-25 can be outlined as follows:

12:1-9: Abram's call and migration from Ur

12:10-20: Abram and Sarai in Egypt

13:1-18: Abram and Lot

14:1-24: Abram and the kings

15:1-21: God's promise to Abram

16:1-16: The birth of Ishmael

17:1-27: The covenant of circumcision with Abraham

18:1-16a: Abraham and the three guests at Mamre

18:16b-33: Abraham intercedes on behalf of Sodom

19:1-29: Sodom and Gomorrah are destroyed

20:1-18: Abram and Abimelech

21:1-7: The birth of Isaac

21:8-21: Hagar and Ishmael are expelled and rescued

21:22-24: The agreement between Abraham and Abimelech at Beersheba

22:1-19: Abraham's sacrifice of Isaac

22:20-24: Nahor's descendants

23:1-20: The death and burial of Sarah

24:1-67: Isaac and Rebekah

25:1-11: Abraham's death

The name Abra(ha)m itself is a theophoric name meaning "God [*Ab*, Father, a divine title] is exalted [*ram*]." Abram and Abraham are actually two variants of the same name. Genesis 17:5 provides a popular folk etymology according to which the transition from Abram to Abraham marks the divine promise that Abraham is to become "the father of a host of nations." The bestowal of a new name marks the beginning of a new moment in life, as when, for example, kings in the ancient Near East adopted throne names or titles upon their accession.

Abraham's place at the beginnings of Israel's faith is suggested in Exodus 3:6, 15, 16, where Yahweh reveals Himself to Moses as "the God of Abraham, the God of Isaac, and the God of Jacob" (cf. Mt 22:32; Mk 12:26).

In the New Testament, Abraham is portrayed as the faithful recipient of divine promises, one with whom God entered into a covenant from which his descendants benefit (cf. Lk 1:55). Abraham's fidelity is offered to Christians as a model of faithful conduct. In Galatians 3 and Romans 4, Paul presents Abraham as an example of justification by faith apart from the works of the law. He writes, citing Genesis 15:6, "Abraham believed God, and it was reckoned to him as righteousness" (Rom 4:3; Gal 3:6).

Those who approach John the Baptist to be baptized by him are warned against relying on the boast, "We have Abraham as our father," and are urged to "bear fruits that befit repentance" (Lk 3:8).

The connection between Abraham's faith and the faith of his descendants is brought to light in the controversy of John 8:31-59. Those who truly are Abraham's descendants are those who believe, thereby doing "what Abraham did" (Jn 8:39) by following his example of faith.

Hebrews 11:8-12 traces Abraham's faith from his journeying in obedience to God's call, to his sojourn in the promised land, to Abraham's trust that God would be true to His promise of an heir. Hebrews 11:17-19 speaks of Abraham's faith put to the test in the sacrifice of Isaac (cf. Gn 22:1-19). Elsewhere in Hebrews (7:1-10), the mysterious encounter between Abraham and Melchizedek (cf. Gn 14:18-20) serves as the foundation for presenting Melchizedek as a type of Christ.

For further reading: A. R. Millard, "Abraham," *Anchor Bible Dictionary*, 1:35-41.

Abraham's Bosom • The phrase occurs at Luke 16:19-31 in Jesus' parable about the rich man and Lazarus. Both men die on the same night; Lazarus is carried to the "bosom of Abraham," while the rich man finds himself in great suffering in Hades. Within Old Testament and other Jewish literature, the "just ones" are received by Abraham, Isaac and Jacob at their death, sometimes within the context of a heavenly banquet (cf. 2 Mc 1:2; Mt 8:11). During the New Testament period and generally throughout the ancient Near East, honored guests were invited to recline at the host's right side, the "bosom" side (cf. Jn 13:25). In Luke's text the phrase expresses God's judgment, justice and Lazarus's high place of honor and esteem in paradise, perhaps at the heavenly banquet with the greatest of patriarchs, Abraham.

Abram • As a reference to Abraham, this name occurs only in the Genesis narrative from 11:26 through 17:4 and in 1 Chronicles 1:27 and Nehemiah 9:7. The name is a composite of two Hebrew roots, *ab* (father) and *ram* (great, exalted). It may be a shortened form of "Abiram" ("My father is exalted").

Abrogation • In canon law, abrogation is the term applied to the revocation of ecclesiastical laws. But because legal systems are intended to promote stability, the abrogation of Church laws is not lightly accomplished. Canon 20 of the 1983 Code of Canon Law establishes the three methods by which ecclesiastical laws are considered repealed.

First, and most directly, the later law can expressly state that it is in abrogation of the earlier law. Second, the later law can be in direct opposition to the earlier law. The contrariness of the later law, however, must be clear in order to accomplish the abrogation of the former; mere inconsistency with the former is not sufficient. Indeed, Canon 21 cautions that in cases of doubt, the abrogation of the earlier law is not presumed, but that the later law is to be harmonized with the earlier. Frequently, the resulting canonical situation is one of abrogation of the former law. Finally, the later law can totally reorganize the subject matter of the earlier law in such a way that the former discipline cannot coexist with the newer.

It must be observed that universal laws, even if issued later in time, do not abrogate from particular or special laws, unless the universal law specifically states so. Canon 6 of the 1983 Code, identifies those types of ecclesiastical laws which were abrogated by the appearance of the 1983 Code. (Cf. Canon Law.)

Absolute • A philosophical term introduced into general use only at the end of the eighteenth century. It signifies what Scholastic philosophers described as perfect or complete being: i.e., the Divine Being, Whose very nature is to be, and Whose existence is therefore not dependent or contingent upon any other being. In modern philosophy, however, the term carries two implications that are not present in Scholasticism: (1) the Absolute is the sum of all being, and therefore, (2) no relations exist between itself and anything else. From the second implication, one must conclude that, since knowledge is a type of revelation, the Absolute is unknowable: hence, agnosticism. God, however, in Catholic philosophy, is the cause of all being, not the sum of all being. Because the divine mode of existence is utterly distinct from that of creatures (as their transcendent cause), there is already a relation between God and the world, upon which is founded the possibility of creatures knowing God. Only on the side of creatures, however, would the relation involve change, development or growth.

Absolute is commonly used to designate those truths that are the starting points of reason, such as the law of contradiction (something cannot both be and not be, at the same time and in the same way) or the first principle of morality (good is to be sought and evil avoided). Catholics believe that all the truths that are revealed by God — whether of faith or morality — are absolute by virtue of their divine source, even though our human understanding of these truths is far from perfect. As the starting points of reason are absolute because they cannot logically be denied, so the truths revealed by God are absolute because God is the Supreme Truth, Who can neither deceive nor be deceived.

Absolution • The forgiveness of any debt, especially the remission of sin. In Catholic theology, absolution is the forgiveness imparted to the penitent by the priest-confessor in Christ's name as the sacrament of Penance is celebrated. Absolution may also apply to the lifting of any ecclesiastical penalties or excommunications.

The ministry of Our Lord showed forgiveness to be an essential attribute of divine love. Examples from Sacred Scripture which can be cited include: the unnamed sinful woman (Lk 7:36-50), the woman caught in adultery (Jn 8:3-11), the healing of the paralytic (Mk 2:1-12) and, of course, the forgiveness of Christ from the cross (Lk 23:43). That Jesus had the power and authority to absolve sin and conferred this upon the Church, the Scriptures also attest. In Matthew 16:19, the Son of God

gave Peter the authority to "bind" and "loose." In Matthew 18:18, the power to absolve sin was extended to all the Apostles. And then, in John 20:22-23, the Risen Christ offered this same prerogative in a pneumatological context.

In the early Church, the bishop was the one who absolved a person from sin, following the performance of a public penance. During this time, however, a fixed formula for sacramental absolution did not yet exist. Later, as public penances and the *ordo paenitentiae* disappeared, deprecatory forms of absolution came into usage, that is, intercessory prayers said by the priest, who by now had replaced the bishop as the ordinary minister of the sacrament. Sometime during the Scholastic era, or the period of the Schoolmen, as it is frequently called, a declaratory formula for absolution emerged. At the Council of Trent (1545-1563), the declaratory formula of absolution ("I absolve you in the name of the Father, and of the Son, and of the Holy Spirit") was defined as the form of the sacrament.

When the Rite of Penance was revised following the Second Vatican Council (1962-1965), the declaratory formula of absolution remained unaltered, with the addition of an imprecatory formula. The revised Rite of Penance, however, did allow for absolution to be conferred both individually and communally.

The *General Instruction of the Revised Rite of Penance* states: "Through the sign of absolution God grants pardon to sinners who in sacramental confession manifest their change of heart to the Church's minister; this completes the Sacrament of Penance. For in God's design the humanity and loving kindness of our Savior have visibly appeared to us and so God uses visible signs to give salvation and to renew the broken covenant.

"In the Sacrament of Penance, the Father receives the repentant children who come back to Him, Christ places the lost sheep on His shoulders and brings them back to the sheepfold, and the Holy Spirit resanctifies those who are the temple of God or dwells more fully in them. The expression of all this is the sharing of the Lord's table, begun again or made more ardent; such a return of children from afar brings great rejoicing at the banquet of God's Church" (*Rite of Penance*, n. 6d).

Absolution of an Accomplice • The granting of sacramental absolution by a confessor to one who was an accomplice of his in a sexual sin. The accomplice can be either female or male. The absolution is invalid, except in danger of death (cf. Canon 977).

Abstinence, Penitential • Depriving oneself of meat or of foods prepared with meat (sauces, gravies, soups from meat stock) on days prescribed by the Church as "penitential." According to the 1983 Code of Canon Law (Canons 1249-1253), the universal Church designates as penitential days all Fridays of the year that are not solemnities, as well as Ash Wednesday and Good Friday. Each national conference of bishops, however, may adapt this universal law for particular regions. Accordingly, in 1966 the bishops of the United States determined that in their jurisdiction, abstinence would be obligatory only on the Fridays of Lent, Ash Wednesday and Good Friday. While strongly recommending that abstinence be observed on *all* Fridays of the year as the privileged and traditional way of commemorating the day of the Lord's Passion, the United States bishops permitted Catholics to substitute other works of charity and devotion on Fridays outside Lent. When issuing their pastoral letter on peace, the bishops recommended abstinence (and fasting, when possible) on all Fridays for the intention of world peace and as an act of

solidarity with the world's hungry.

Fasting is distinguished from abstinence as referring not to the *kind* of food but the *amount* of food taken (traditionally one full meal and two lighter meals not equaling the full meal, and nothing between meals). Fasting is mandatory only on Ash Wednesday and Good Friday. The Good Friday fast is known as the "paschal fast" and may be extended until the Easter Vigil as a fast of anticipation observed by the community in union with the catechumens preparing for Baptism. Fasting binds all adults until their sixtieth year. All who have completed their fourteenth year are bound by the law of abstinence.

It should be noted that, unlike some religious groups, the Catholic Church considers her tradition of fast and abstinence to be a positive discipline. The motivation is not to deny the goodness of creation or to "punish" the body, but to unite the believer through a discipline of self-sacrifice to the sacrificial love of Christ and to free the person from self-centeredness, in order to facilitate deeper prayer and more generous charity. It should be noted that the present canonical legislation presents the minimal requirements. Seeking the counsel of a spiritual director and avoiding all scrupulosity, the serious Catholic will want to make a conscientious decision about a personal program of fast and abstinence that goes beyond the minimal requirements and takes account of age, health, employment and family responsibilities. In an unusual "editorial" comment, the 1983 Code of Canon Law notes that "pastors and parents are to see to it that minors who are not bound by the law . . . are educated in an authentic sense of penance."

Abstinence, Sexual • To refrain from sexual intercourse completely (total abstinence) or at certain times for specific reasons (periodic abstinence or periodic continence).

Total abstinence is required in obedience to the sixth commandment of the Decalogue of all single persons and of those couples not united in a bond of marriage recognized as valid by the Catholic Church. Total abstinence is part of the gift of self freely chosen by those who embrace the evangelical counsel of chastity by making religious vows and by those in Holy Orders who commit themselves to lifelong celibacy at diaconal ordination (or at subdiaconate prior to the liturgical reform of the Second Vatican Council).

Periodic abstinence or *periodic continence* (as the encyclical *Humanae Vitae* refers to it) is observed by a married couple as a free and mutual decision (responsibly reached after mature deliberation) for the purpose of regulating conception according to natural methods approved by the Church or for ascetical motives. In his reflections on Pope Paul VI's teaching in *Humanae Vitae*, Pope John Paul II notes that "the virtue of continence . . . has an essential role in maintaining the interior balance between the two meanings, the unitive and the procreative, of the conjugal act (cf. HV, n. 12) in view of a truly responsible fatherhood and motherhood. . . . The correct way of intending and practicing periodic continence as a virtue (that is, according to *Humanae Vitae*, n. 21, the mastery of self) also essentially determines the naturalness of the method. . . : this is naturalness at the level of the person. Therefore, there can be no thought of a mechanical application of biological laws. The knowledge itself of the rhythms of fertility — even though indispensable — still does not create that interior freedom of the gift, which is by its nature explicitly spiritual and depends on man's interior maturity. This freedom presupposes such a capacity to direct the sensual and emotive reactions as to make possible the giving of self to the other 'I' on the grounds of the mature self-possession of one's own 'I' in its corporeal and emotive subjectivity" (general audience of November 7, 1984).

Abuse of Power • Abuse of power, or more precisely, abuse of ecclesiastical authority, was a canonical crime in the 1917 Code of Canon Law and has been retained in the revised Code of 1983 (Canon 1389). This canon can apply to anyone, cleric or lay, who is entrusted with some form of ecclesiastical power and abuses it. The Code treats of several specific abuses of ministerial power, such as violation of the seal of the confessional, trafficking in Mass stipends and solicitation in the confessional. It includes this general canon, without giving specific examples of abuse, to provide a means of imposing canonical penalties for other kinds of abuse not mentioned in the law (cf. Canons 1326, 1389).

Acacianism • A fifth-century branch of the Monophysite heresy, it was popularly attributed to Acacius, whose attractive personality and wide ecclesiastical experience led to his installation in the see of Constantinople. It seems likely, however, that Acacius was more the politician, with Daniel the Stylite serving as the intellectual father of the heresy that came to bear the patriarch's name. In any event, Acacianism held that the "Son was like the Father," an unacceptable variance from the doctrine of consubstantiality, and one which quickly saw a censure by Pope Simplicius. After some initial reluctance, Acacius threw his considerable prestige behind the movement and was excommunicated by Pope Felix III. Acacius, however, continued to grow in popularity throughout the East, and after his death in A.D. 489, the schism of which he was the chief author lingered for more than thirty years until a reconciliation was effected under Pope Hormisdas.

Academies, Pontifical • In the course of the centuries, several societies have been founded under the auspices of the Holy See to encourage studies in the sciences, the fine arts, music, archaeology, literature and diplomacy. By far the most significant of them is the Pontifical Academy of Sciences, founded in 1603. Its seventy members, nominated by the Sovereign Pontiff, are drawn from distinguished mathematicians and experimental scientists, regardless of creed. Also very significant is the Pontifical Ecclesiastical Academy, formerly the Academy of Noble Ecclesiastics, which is charged with the training of those chosen to serve in the diplomatic corps of the Holy See.

Acadians • The original Canadian region of Acadia was centered on Nova Scotia but included Prince Edward Island and the mainland coast from the Gulf of St. Lawrence, south into Maine. After the British attacked, and their subsequent mistrust and fear of the French-speaking Catholic inhabitants of the area, the British seized most of the Acadians in 1755 and deported them to the British colonies to the south, ranging from Maine to Georgia, with some even being sent to the West Indies and Europe. After 1767, with the political situation somewhat eased, many of the exiles returned to Canada, although others found refuge in other places. The best known of these areas is in southern Louisiana, where they are known as "Cajuns." There they maintain a separate culture which is reflective of their Catholic heritage.

Acathist Hymn • In the Eastern Liturgy, an Office of the Holy Virgin Mary recited in part from the Saturday morning of the first week of Lent until the morning of the fifth Saturday of Lent, when it is recited in its entirety.

Access • The term can carry several connotations in ecclesiastical parlance. It can refer to the preparatory prayers offered by the priest before celebrating Holy Mass. In canon law, the term was used at one time to describe certain ecclesiastical offices to which one had a claim upon the completion of certain requirements. Today, it can also refer to the right of a party to have one's case heard in an ecclesiastical tribunal.

Usually, however, one encounters the term access in regard to religious cloister. In virtue of Canon 667 of the 1983 Code of Canon Law, public access to the cloister is sharply limited, and sometimes actually forbidden, out of respect for the prayerful and contemplative vocation of the members of the institute.

Accident • Philosophers in the tradition of Aristotle make a distinction between beings that have existence in themselves (substances) and beings that exist only in another (accidents). An accident, therefore, is a quantity, quality or relation that could not exist by itself, but which does exist in, or is supported by the existence of, another. In other words, accidents modify substances. Thus, a man (substance) who weighs two hundred pounds (quantity) is happy (quality) because he has recently been married (relation). The weight, the quality of being and the marital status of the man are accidents, which could not be said to exist apart from the man without absurdity.

Although they cannot exist on their own, accidents are real and objective. Since accidents comprise all those aspects of a thing that are perceptible to the senses, to deny their reality or objectivity would be a radical form of idealism. The opposite extreme, radical materialism, results from denying the reality or objectivity of substances as distinct from their accidents. Modern philosophy has adopted both these extremes, as did the ancient pre-Socratic thinkers. Catholic philosophy, however, follows Aristotle and takes a mediating position between these two extremes: although the human mind cannot know substances except through their accidents, it cannot be claimed to know anything unless it penetrates through accidents to substances.

Acclamation • From the Latin *clamare*, to cry out. A response from the congregation giving strong assent to the words of the Lord and/or the actions of the celebrant. If sung with the joy intended, it brings emphasis to the most significant parts of the liturgy. During the Mass, there are five acclamations which should be sung: Alleluia; Holy, Holy, Holy; Memorial Acclamation; Great Amen; Doxology to the Lord's Prayer. The *General Instruction of the Roman Missal* states that "joining with the angels, the congregation sings or recites the *Sanctus*. This acclamation is an intrinsic part of the eucharistic prayer and all the people join with the priest in singing or reciting it." The Great Amen at the end of the Eucharistic Prayer complements "the praise of God expressed in the doxology to which the people's acclamation is an assent and a conclusion" (*General Instruction*, n. 55).

Accommodation of Scripture • Sometimes a passage from Scripture manifests a striking likeness to something completely unrelated to its specific text and context. For example, a politician might speak of his or her proposed plan for economic recovery for farm-based industry in terms of the "sower going out to sow seeds of economic prosperity." The language could be said to be from the parable of the sower in Matthew 13 but is applied to something completely unrelated to the intent of the author. This connection between Scripture and political strategies for economic recovery is more a matter of rhetoric than of substance and is called an accommodation of Scripture. Because the connection between Scripture and politics is a matter of rhetoric and because the gospel author did not intend any reference to politics, clearly the potential for the abuse of Scripture is great. Therefore, the following summary of principles should guide the use of accommodation of Scripture: (1) it does not express an authentic sense of Scripture intended by God or the human author; (2) it should have some analogous link with the text; (3) it should not contradict the text; (4) it cannot be used as a proof for a doctrinal position.

Acephalic or Acephalous • From the Greek, meaning "without a head." This term describes ecclesiastically any Christian group without a determinate leader in communion with a recognized hierarchy. This became the status of the ancient Eastern Church groups which became heretical and subsequently schismatic. The Nestorians, for example, after the Council of Ephesus (A.D. 431), did not accept the Council's teaching that Mary is truly the Mother of God. In the sixteenth century a major portion of the Assyrian (Nestorian) Church returned to communion with the See of Rome and today constitutes the Catholic Chaldean Patriarchate. The term is a derisive and unflattering designation and has become ecumenically insensitive. Its use is avoided in ecclesiastical parlance. (Cf. Autocephalous.)

Achiropoetos (Achiropoeta) • From the Greek for "not made by a (human) hand."

This term is used to designate the archetype of icon, Jesus Christ Himself, the Incarnate Son of God. The appearance of God-in-the-flesh is the underpinning for the justification of the use of sacred images. Since the Invisible now becomes Visible, we have the prototype Image. The Second Council of Nicaea (787) taught that the honor given to sacred images is referred to the originals they represent, so that by kissing, kneeling before or venerating them, we adore Christ and honor His saints, whose likeness they represent.

The term "icon-not-made-by-hands" more specifically refers to the scarf with which Veronica wiped the bloodied face of Our Lord on His walk to Calvary and upon which the image of His holy face became imprinted, according to tradition. Other "achiropoeta" include the painting of Christ in the sanctuary of the Lateran alleged to have been outlined by St. Luke and completed by angels; also, the painting of Our Lady of Guadalupe in Mexico, miraculously imprinted on the mantle of Juan Diego at the moment of the Blessed Mother's declaration to him in 1531.

Acolouthia • From the Greek for a sequence or ordering, acolouthia is the arrangement of all the Divine Praises, except for the Divine Liturgy itself, in the liturgical Offices of the Eastern Churches, particularly of the Byzantine Rite. The sequence begins with Vespers introducing the day to come (before sunset) and is followed by the Office of Compline at midnight, and Matins at dawn. Four "hours" are given over to a numerical sequence: First, early morning; Third, mid-morning (usually 9 A.M.); Sixth, early afternoon (usually 12 noon): and Ninth, midafternoon (usually 3 P.M.).

The Divine Praises are structured for public liturgical celebration and usually take place in a public context although, for reasons of personal piety, the Divine Praises may be privately read. The public celebration of the Divine Praises in Eastern Rite parochial life by and large has fallen into disuse yet many parishes, both Eastern Catholic and Orthodox, make use of Vespers and Matins. Among the Russian faithful, Vespers and Matins are usually combined and celebrated as an "All-Night Vigil." For the most part, Byzantine Rite monastic communities have retained the celebration of the Divine Praises as part of their monastic spiritual regimen.

Acolyte • This term, which comes from the Greek *akoloutheou* ("to follow"), denotes the office, ministry or order of clerics who assist at the altar and at other liturgical functions. The term "acolyte" originally applied to those ordained into the highest of the four minor orders which were suppressed by Pope Paul VI after the Second Vatican Council with the promulgation of *Ministeria Quaedam*. The term is still in use, however, to signify those men who are instituted into this ministry either in a permanent or in a transitory manner (as is the case with those studying for the priesthood) to assist the celebrant at Mass and to distribute Holy Communion as an extraordinary minister when necessity may dictate it and according to the laws of the Church.

While not technically correct, "Acolyte" is also commonly used to mean any layperson (female as well as male in dioceses where women are allowed to function as servers) who serves Mass and other liturgical and paraliturgical functions. The symbols of this order/ministry are candlesticks and candles and the cruets used for wine and water at Mass. The above-mentioned document of Paul VI also states that acolytes may also be called "subdeacons" according to the wishes of the regional or national episcopal conferences.

Since this was a ministry or order established by the Church to fill a particular need at a particular time, it has never been considered a sacrament. Rather, it was seen as a sharing, together with the subdeacon, in the ministry of the deacon. It has been and is still usually conferred as a stepping-stone to the priesthood, though today worthy and pious men may be instituted as acolytes to function in a more permanent way, especially where there is no full-time priest. This is especially useful and expedient in missionary lands.

Acquired Rights • An acquired right, also known as a vested right, is a right obtained through a completed legal transaction, either between two individuals (e.g., a contract or sale) or between a person and someone in authority (e.g., acceptance of an appointment to an office) (cf. Canon 6). While not inviolate in themselves, acquired ecclesiastical rights generally merit and receive heightened protection under Church law.

Acrostic Psalms: See **Alphabetic Psalms**

Acta Apostolicae Sedis • The *Acta Apostolicae Sedis* (Acts of the Apostolic See) is the official journal of record for the Holy See. It was formally instituted by Pope St. Pius X in the Apostolic Constitution *Promulgandi* (September 29, 1908) and was first published on January 1, 1909. The *AAS*, as it is frequently abbreviated, superseded the *Acta Sanctae Sedis* and contains the authoritative texts of Apostolic Constitutions, encyclical letters and allocutions, records of papal and curial audiences, as well as major decrees and other documents issued by various departments of the Roman Curia. One of the most important uses of the *AAS* is for the formal promulgation of canon law, as specified by Canon 8. The *AAS* is published monthly, or as necessity warrants, by

Libreria Editrice Vaticana and is available by subscription. It is also generally available in Catholic college and university libraries.

Acta Sanctae Sedis • The *Acta Sanctae Sedis* or Acts of the Holy See was a monthly publication, issued in Rome, that contained many important pronouncements and decrees of the Holy Father or Roman Congregations. Although it was not an official publication at first, it was accorded official status in 1904 until it was superseded by the *Acta Apostolicae Sedis* in 1909.

Action Française • A social and political movement founded in France by Charles Maurras in 1908 to promote antidemocratic, royalist and nationalistic ideals. Its platform was publicized through a daily newspaper of the same name and, because of its defense of the monarchy and the "old order," attracted some Catholics who opposed the anticlerical policies dominant in the French government. However, the movement tended to use the Church to advance its agenda, claiming that the Church was naturally allied to its nationalistic, reactionary goals. When it began to advocate an overthrow of the government and racial animosity, it was condemned in 1926 by Pope Pius XI, who insisted that all Catholic lay movements had to work in harmony with the bishops. In 1939, after its leaders expressed regret over past excesses, Pope Pius XII lifted the ban. Because of its involvement with the Petain government during World War II and its obstinate resistance to all democratic and social reform, it no longer is dominant on the French scene, although its influence is evident in the theories of Archbishop Marcel Lefebvre and Jacques Le Pin.

Act of God • A legal term referring to a happening in which the cause is beyond human foreknowledge or control; hence, the occurrence is attributed to God, the Author of nature. Natural disasters, such as earthquakes, are acts of God.

Act of Settlement • There are two very different legal events which are both referred to as the Act of Settlement. The first was enacted by the Irish Parliament in 1662 and sought to restore to both Protestants and Catholics certain properties which had been lost during the preceding religious strife. The second refers to an act passed by the English Parliament in 1701 which provided that if William III and Princess Anne should have no heirs, the succession should pass to Sophia of Hanover, who was the granddaughter of James I, and to her heirs, so long as they were Protestants. Among the other clauses of the Act was that all future sovereigns and their consorts must "join in Communion with the Church of England as by law established." Should a reigning monarch wish to convert, say, to Roman Catholicism, he or she would be legally required to abdicate the throne.

Act of Supremacy • In November 1534 the Act of Supremacy was passed, giving to King Henry VIII and his successors the title of "the only supreme head in earth of the Church of England, called *Anglicana Ecclesia.*" Although the Act was repealed by Mary Tudor, Elizabeth I passed a new Act of Supremacy in 1559 as the first act of her reign. This Act was somewhat revised from that of Henry VIII, and the monarch was declared to be "the only supreme governor of this realm, and of all other her highness's dominions and countries, as well in all spiritual or ecclesiastical things of causes as temporal," and all clergy and public officials were required to accept the Act of Supremacy by taking an oath. This title of Supreme Governor of the Church of England is maintained by the English monarch to the present day.

Act of Toleration • The Act of Toleration, not to be confused with the Edict of Toleration (cf. Edict of Milan), was passed by the English Parliament in 1689 for the purpose of uniting Protestants under William III against the deposed Catholic monarch James II. It granted freedom of worship to most dissenters, with certain conditions. It exempted them from several penalties, provided they took the Oaths of Allegiance and Supremacy, although dissenters continued to be forbidden from holding civil office until 1828. In order for dissenting ministers to be relieved from religious disabilities they were required not only to take the oaths, but also to sign the Thirty-nine Articles of the Book of Common Prayer (except for the two which require infant Baptism). Quakers were allowed to affirm, rather than take an oath, in accordance with the requirement of their belief; however, Catholics and those who denied the doctrine of the Trinity were given no benefits under this Act. It has since been supplanted by more generous legislation.

Acts, Canonical • The term "canonical acts" can have two very different meanings. First, it refers to the official record of any action or process which takes place according to canon law. The files of a tribunal process or beatification/ canonization, for instance, are referred to as the canonical acts of the case.

Secondly, the term can refer to any action that can have a legal effect in canon law. Some examples are: voting in an ecclesiastical election, issuing a judgment, imposing a penalty, establishing a parish.

Acts, Human • Actions are specifically human when they proceed from deliberation and issue in choice. Such actions are distinguished from the whole range of spontaneous, instinctual and biological processes and activities that are not deliberative and voluntary. In addition, human actions are distinguished from actions undertaken by agents without the use of reason or under compulsion. Strictly speaking, then, human actions are those over which the agent is master. Only properly human actions can be moral or immoral. Factors conditioning the knowledge (e.g., ignorance) and will (e.g., passion or violence) of the agent influence the moral character of his or her actions.

Acts of the Apostles • The sequel volume to the Gospel of Luke (cf. Acts 1:1). As an example of ancient literature, Acts resembles Hellenistic biographies of famous men such as Alexander the Great but is closer to Old Testament biblical histories such as the Books of Kings and Maccabees. Acts narrates the movement of God's saving action by the Holy Spirit in the early Church, beginning in Jerusalem and spreading by means of the Holy Spirit's intervention (e.g., cf. Acts 1:2, 5; 2:1-4, especially Chapter 10) throughout Judea, Samaria and indeed "to the end of the earth."

God's desire to save and to reconcile the world to Himself through His Son within the context of His Church will not be impeded by ethnic, linguistic or cultural barriers. Acts chronicles the universal mission of the Church.

Contents:
A. Introduction to the narrative: 1:1-3
B. Christianity in Jerusalem: 1:4-8:3
C. Outside Jerusalem: Judea and Samaria: 8:4-12:30
D. Paul's mission to the Gentiles: 13:1-21:16
E. Paul returns to Jerusalem: 21:17-22:30
F. Paul on trial: 23:1-26:32

G. Paul's final mission and his journey to Rome: 27:1-28:31

Major Themes: The Holy Spirit plays a decisive and prominent role throughout the work: The Church is empowered by the Holy Spirit (e.g., 5:12-16); the Holy Spirit guides the Church's missionary activity itself (e.g., 2:1-13; 8:26-40, especially vv. 29, 39). The inclusion of Gentiles into Christianity without first becoming full and legal members of Judaism was by divine intervention (Chapter 10) and the journeys and preaching outline why and how Christianity reached the Hellenistic world beyond Palestine (e.g., Acts 14:10-17; 17:1-15; 19:8-20). The continual rejection of Paul and his Gospel by some Jewish communities eventually led him to preach primarily to the Gentiles (Acts 13:46-47; 18:6; 28:28).

Authorship and Date: According to the consistent witness of early tradition and second- and third-century Fathers of the Church, both Luke and Acts are the work of a single author (cf. Lk 1-4; Acts 1:1-2), whom Irenaeus identifies simply as "Luke." Acts ends with an account of Paul's house arrest, c. A.D. 60-63, which presumably was just before his death; therefore, the earliest possible date for Acts would be 60 (the beginning of Paul's Roman house arrest) and the latest date probably after the fall of Jerusalem, perhaps as late as in the decade of 80.

For further reading: Richard J. Dillon, "Acts of the Apostles," *New Jerome Biblical Commentary*, 722-767; Luke Timothy Johnson, *The Acts of the Apostles*, Sacra Pagina 5 (Liturgical Press, 1992).

Acts of the Martyrs • The term "Acts of the Martyrs" actually applies to a large and disparate collection of writings in which are detailed the events surrounding the martyrdom of many of the Church's earliest saints. The great Bollandist Delahaye categorized these writings into several types, consisting especially of official court records of Christian trials, passions written or narrated by witnesses to the events and edited materials composed some time after the death of the saints. The earliest recognized parts of these collections are the accounts of the martyrdom of Justin Martyr and his six brethren in A.D. 164. The search for and study of these documents, so rich in Christian and social history, continues to this day.

Acts of Paul • An apocryphal writing, the Acts of Paul purports to provide information not given in the canonical writing of the Acts of the Apostles. Tertullian is the first to mention this work, but it was not until the twentieth century that the contents of the Acts of Paul could be determined. Contained within this writing is the story of Paul and Thecla, alleged correspondence of St. Paul with the Corinthians and a legendary description of the martyrdom of St. Paul. Although the Acts of Paul was never accepted as part of the canon of Sacred Scripture, this work has had considerable influence on Christian art and liturgy.

Acts of Pilate • A fifth-century work, containing some older material, the Acts of Pilate includes legendary accounts of Christ's trial, crucifixion and burial, as well as a description of the debates held by the Sanhedrin after the Resurrection, and an allegedly eyewitness account of the descent of Christ into hell.

Acts of the Saints • The Acts of the Saints (*Acta Sanctorum*) is an extensive and very well-known collection of saints' lives compiled by the Bollandists. The study, which marked a significant development in the critical studies of ancient Church literature, has itself been revised from time

to time, and is available (in part) in a variety of English sources. It has also sometimes been referred to as the "Golden Legend."

Actual Grace • Actual graces are those intrusions of supernatural assistance which God gives to human persons to enable them to perform actions conducive to their salvation. Actual graces are distinguished from habitual, or sanctifying, grace and the infused virtues in that they are transient, or temporary, interventions of divine activity, to aid the intellect and will of the human person in the performance of a particular action. Actual graces are also distinguished from the underlying divine causality, or concursus, which sustains all created activity in the natural order. Whether at the beginning of their conversion or during the course of their sanctification, human persons need actual graces so that their activities can be supernaturally efficacious. The divinely communicated, supernatural power is united to the human intellect and will as the one principle of the supernatural act. Thus, for example, actual grace accounts for the movement on the part of a sinner to seek forgiveness in the sacrament of Penance.

Although the term "actual grace" emerged only with late Scholasticism and became popular after the Council of Trent (though it was not employed by the Council), the teaching has a solid basis in the Scriptures. Our Lord Himself said that "apart from me you can do nothing" (John 15:5). The Church has understood our Lord's teaching to be echoed in many passages in St. Paul's letters. Two such passages are particularly striking: "Not that we are sufficient of ourselves to claim anything as coming from us; our sufficiency is from God" (2 Cor 3:5) and "for God is at work within you, both to will and to work for his good pleasure" (Phil 2:13).

Over the course of centuries, mainly in

response to heterodox teachings and especially with the help of St. Augustine and St. Thomas Aquinas, the Church's understanding of the complete meaning of these and similar passages deepened and became more explicit. Church teaching about grace has negotiated a middle course between naturalism, on the one hand, and an exaggerated supernaturalism on the other. Against Pelagianism, semi-Pelagianism, and modern forms of rationalism, the Church has consistently affirmed the necessity of actual grace to move the human person to faith, conversion, justification, salutary actions and final perseverance. Against Baianism and Jansenism, on the other hand, the Church has defended man's natural capacity to act in the moral and religious spheres without grace, while insisting that the natural law cannot be observed throughout the course of life without actual grace.

Actual Sin • The term "actual sin" can be understood only in the light of some traditional distinctions that have arisen in the Catholic theology of sin. *Personal* sin is distinguished from *original* sin, and, within personal sin, there is a further distinction between *actual* and *habitual* sin.

Sin is the deliberate transgression of the divine law. Since the divine law is given so that human persons can choose the ultimate good which is God Himself, sin in effect is a disordered choice. It involves a failure — in a particular thought, word or deed, or in a pattern of thoughts, words and deeds — to discern and choose the perfect good by which the agent, or acting person, is made good. Instead, in contravening the divine law, the sinner deliberately prefers some created good to the ultimate or perfect Good. Since this transgression must involve sufficient knowledge and free consent of the will, it is a personal action. Thus, in its most proper sense, sin is always *personal* sin.

For this reason, personal sin must be distinguished from *original* sin, which is the inherited weakness that affects human nature as a result of the *first personal sin* committed by our first parents. It is essential to note that original sin is not a tendency to evil, but rather the loss of original justice and thus a lack of facility in choosing the good. Personal sin is distinguished from original sin by the simple fact that it is a deliberately embraced action or pattern of action rather than an inherited privation of a weakened human nature.

Personal sins can be actual or habitual. Actual sin is the failure to choose the good in a particular thought, word or deed, while habitual sin is the failure to choose the good in a pattern of repeated and unrepented thoughts, words or deeds. In effect, then, the term "actual sin" is really synonymous with "sin" in its ordinary meaning.

Acus • The pins used by the Holy Father and all metropolitan archbishops to fasten the pallium to the chasuble are called *acus,* or plural, *aci*, which in Latin simply means "pin" or "needle." They are usually made of gold or gold-plated sterling silver and more often than not are adorned with precious or semiprecious stones and/or carvings of liturgical symbols (e.g., the Chi Rho or the cross).

Adam • In Genesis 2:4b-4:25, Yahweh forms "Adam" (Hebrew, *'adam*) from "earth" (Hebrew, *'adamah*). The term in Hebrew refers to the first man/human (Gn 4:1-25; 5:1-5; Tb 8:6) but also to human beings in general (Jb 14:1; 1 Kgs 8:46; Ps 105:14; Hos 11:4; Ps 94:11). Although the first three chapters of Genesis have various origins, the insights into the universality of sin and its power over all "Adam's sons and daughters" (echoed in Ps 51:7), and into the trustworthiness of God as Creator and Redeemer (echoed in Jer 1:5) are extraordinary compared to other literature of this period.

In the New Testament, St. Paul refers to Christ as the New Adam, comparing Him with the first Adam: "as in Adam all die, so in Christ shall all be made alive. . . . Thus it is written, 'The first man Adam became a living being'; the last Adam became a life-giving spirit. . . . Just as we have borne the image of the man of dust, we shall also bear the image of the man of heaven" (1 Cor 15:22, 45, 49). As the first Adam was a man of clay, whose fall into temptation unleashed an enormous rupture in his relationship to God and his spouse and which smashed the "image of God" from within, the New Adam, Christ the Lord (1 Cor 15:45-49; Rom 5:12-21), conquers sin, brings life, rejuvenates and restores our relationship to the Father and to one another.

For further reading: Howard N. Wallace, "Adam," *Anchor Bible Dictionary*, 1:62-64.

Adamites • The Adamites were a bizarre and obscure group which appeared at different periods of Church history. The first mention of them occurs in the second century when a Gnostic sect renounced marriage, shed their clothing and indulged in a variety of pagan and lustful practices. Clement of Alexandria, among others, not surprisingly denounced the situation. They reappeared nearly one thousand years later, claiming to be living only by the laws of nature, and were the object of considerable evangelical efforts on the part of St. Norbert. The last distinct appearance of the group seems to have occurred early in the fifteenth century when it is believed that a Frenchman by the name of Picard announced himself to be the reincarnation of Adam. This time ecclesiastical outreach to the group was supplanted by military force and the sect was obliterated by Jan Ziska in 1421.

Address, Papal • Broadly speaking, a papal address can be any formal or semiformal speech delivered by the Pope reflecting Catholic sensibilities on topics of the day. Recently, however, the term "papal address" has come to refer usually to exhortative or explanatory messages issued by the Holy Father on a more regular and continuing basis. A major example of this would be a series of papal addresses delivered over a period of several months by Pope John Paul II concerning the dangers of the contraceptive mentality to married life. Given the often impressive nature of papal addresses, it is not surprising that several Catholic publishing houses gather many of these speeches and publish them in quality vernacular translations. (Cf., for example, *The Pope Speaks*.)

Address, Terms of: See **Ecclesiastical Titles**

Ad Gentes • The Vatican Council II Decree on the Church's Missionary Activity, *Ad Gentes*, was promulgated on December 7, 1965. After a brief introductory section, the decree continues for six chapters to treat the doctrinal principles of the Church's missionary activity, the nature of missionary work, the importance of the new churches, a description of the role of missionaries, the structure of missionary planning and the deployment of the Church's resources in cooperative missionary activity. The decree as a whole offers a powerful reaffirmation of the fundamentally missionary character of the Church herself, based on the biblical notion of the People of God. The divine plan for humankind is that it should form a unified

People of God, of which the Church is the visible vanguard. The proclamation of this message to the whole world is an activity basic to the very identity of the Church. In *Ecclesia Sancta III* (August 6, 1966), Pope Paul VI promulgated norms for implementing this decree.

Ad Limina (Apostolorum) • Literally refers to a visit to the threshold or household of a particular person or persons. In this case, it refers to a visit to the threshold, a pilgrimage to the tombs, of the Apostles Peter and Paul in Rome. It stands, in short, for the visits to Rome and the Apostolic See which all ordinaries of dioceses are required to make.

At present, the discipline of the Church requires that this visit be made every five years. This is not only a time of spiritual renewal for the bishop making his *ad limina*, but also a chance for him to see and be seen by the Pope and the other curial officials. At the time of the visit, the bishop must make a detailed report on the diocese in his charge, as well as of all the institutions, persons and activities that take place therein. This tradition dates back at least to the time of Pope St. Leo III (d. 816). If for a serious reason the bishop cannot attend, he may send his coadjutor, if he has one, or another delegate from among his clergy to represent him.

The visit to the Apostles' tombs entails: (1) a personal visit to the tombs of Sts. Peter and Paul, recorded in writing; (2) a personal visit and interview with the Holy Father, during which the bishop renews his obedience and loyalty to the Vicar of Christ, receives his teaching in the form of an allocution and renders an oral report on the state of his diocese; and (3) a written report, or *relatio*, on the state of his diocese, which is presented to the Secretariat of State, the Congregation of Bishops and the other competent dicasteries of the Roman Curia.

Today this includes personal visits with the prefects and other officials of the diverse dicasteries (cf. Canon 400).

Adeste Fideles • A Latin Christmas carol whose text and music were composed by John Francis Wade (c. 1711-1786). The carol was translated into English with the title "O Come All Ye Faithful" by Frederick Oakley (1802-1880) and others.

Adjuration • An appeal or command to act in the name of God. The clearest case of this was in Matthew 26:63 where Jesus was commanded by the High Priest to declare if He was the Messiah or not. Such commands should only be given for very serious reasons, when the request is just and when the one asking the question sincerely seeks the truth.

Administration, Apostolic • A territorial division of the Church that is set up by the Holy See for the pastoral care of the people within its boundaries. It is not a diocese and therefore does not have a diocesan bishop as its head. Such entities are not constituted as dioceses because of particular difficulties such as Church-state problems, or the near impossibility of either financial support or sufficient clergy. An apostolic administration is under the pastoral care and direction of an apostolic administrator, who usually is not a bishop but who has many of the powers of a bishop, with the exception of those that can be exercised only by one with the episcopal dignity (cf. Canons 368, 371).

Administration of the Sacraments • The act of conferring one of the seven sacraments by an authorized minister, according to the appropriate liturgical, canonical and pastoral norms. Since the efficacy of the sacraments derives from the power of Christ, Who is their principal minister, the Church's designated minister acts in the place of Christ. The valid administration of the sacraments requires that the minister at least have the intention of doing that which the Church does. However, since the efficacy of the sacraments depends on the action of God, the validity of their administration cannot be affected by a lack of faith or a state of sin in the minister. One who administers a sacrament by virtue of his office in the Church is called the ordinary minister; one who does so by delegation or in case of necessity is called an extraordinary minister.

Administrative Act • A decree or precept issued by a person with the executive power of governance. There are numerous kinds of administrative acts, such as acts which inflict a penalty or restrict rights. If the administrative act refers to a matter in the external forum, it must be in writing or at least be delivered in the presence of two witnesses (cf. Canons 35-47).

Administrative Recourse • A special form of appeal to which a person is entitled if he or she feels that there has been harm or injustice done by means of an administrative decree of a superior. Administrative recourse is available for all administrative acts given in the external forum outside of a judicial trial, with the exception of those issued by the Roman Pontiff or an ecumenical council.

Before recourse itself may be had, the person who believes he or she is injured is first to ask the person who issued the decree either to revoke it or amend it. This request must be made in writing within ten days of the date the decree was received.

Within thirty days, the author of the decree is to respond with a confirmation of the original decree, revocation or amendment to it. If the person receiving the decree wishes to move to administrative

recourse, he has fifteen days to do so. The recourse is presented to the author of the decree, who must refer it to his or her lawful superior. For example, a local religious superior would refer it to the regional superior and a residential bishop would present the recourse to the Holy See. Ordinarily, the effects of the decree are suspended while recourse is pending (cf. Canons 1732-1739).

Administrator • A term that has several meanings in canon law, all of which involve some form of authority or responsibility for the management of Church property and temporal goods, a parish, diocese or other territorial entity in the Church.

A diocesan administrator is a priest or auxiliary bishop usually elected by the diocesan College of Consultors to govern a diocese when the see becomes vacant. The scope of his authority is outlined in the Code of Canon Law. He remains in place until the new bishop takes canonical possession of the diocese (cf. Canons 409, 413, 419).

A parochial administrator is a priest who is appointed by the bishop to administer a parish in the event that the pastor either dies or is unable to perform his duties for some reason. The appointment is temporary in nature. The parochial administrator has many of the same powers as a pastor, although he may not do anything that could prejudice the rights of the pastor or be detrimental to parish temporal goods (cf. Canons 539-541).

An apostolic administrator is a priest and sometimes a bishop who is appointed by the Holy See to direct an apostolic administration (cf. Canon 371).

Finally, the Code uses the term "administrator" for the person, cleric or lay, who has charge over the management of Church property or other temporal goods. The duties of the administrator in this sense are outlined in the Code of Canon Law (cf. Canons 1281-1289).

Admonitions, Canonical • Canon law requires that a person be issued a specific warning or admonition before a canonical censure or penalty is imposed by a duly authorized ecclesiastical superior. If the person refuses to cease his or her actions which resulted in the admonition, the process to apply the penalty can continue. The law requires only one admonition before proceeding.

The admonition is usually issued by the Ordinary or his delegate. The Ordinary also has the option of issuing an admonition to one who is in the proximate danger of committing an offense or who is suspected of having committed an offense as a result of a canonical investigation (cf. Canons 1339, 1348).

In the broader sense, admonitions can denote any delivery of prudent advice from an ecclesiastical superior.

Adonai • An Old Testament Hebrew term for God, best translated as "Lord" or "my Lord." About three centuries before Christ, the Jews, out of reverence for the revealed divine Name, *Yahweh* (Ex 3:13-15), ceased pronouncing it. Substituting for it most frequently were *Adonai* and *Elohim*.

For further reading: Julia M. O'Brien, "Adonai," *Anchor Bible Dictionary*, 1:74.

Adoption, Canonical • The relationship that arises from the legal adoption of a person can constitute an invalidating impediment to marriage. The impediment arises between those related through legal adoption in the direct line (parent and child) or in the second degree of the collateral line (siblings). In the second degree of the collateral line are included natural children of the adoptive parent, as well as adopted children.

The impediment arises only from a legally recognized adoptive relationship and does not include those who are never legally adopted (cf. Canon 1094).

Adoption, Supernatural • In the theological sense, the state of being a child of God in virtue of a redeemed kinship with Christ, the only true Son of the Father (cf. Phil 2:6-11). In the Bible, the contrast between "natural" and "adopted" progeny is exploited in order to indicate that, after the loss of original justice by our first parents, we are not "natural" children of God by virtue of our common humanity as descendants of Adam, but "adopted" children of God by virtue of our brotherhood with Christ, Who makes up for the sin of Adam and for all sin. Christ is the Son in the truest and fullest sense. The rest of us are sons and daughters of God, in grace, by virtue of our relationship with Christ, Who reconciles humankind to the Father.

Adoptionism • This heresy claimed that Jesus is the Son of God, not by nature, but by adoption. He was the natural Son of God, but as man He was only the adopted Son. In origin, it goes back to the Monarchian, Ebionite and Nestorian heresies.

In the eighth century, the Spanish Bishops Elipandus and Felix taught another form of "adoptionism." It was based on a radical distinction between the humanity and the divinity of Jesus, similar to that proposed by the earlier heresies. The Spanish "adoptionists" claimed that the human Jesus was the Son of God by adoption, but the divine Jesus was naturally the Son of God. These heresies were condemned primarily by the Second Council of Nicaea (787) and the Council of Frankfort (794).

Adoration • The external act of worship given to an individual or thing. The command to adore the one, true God was a command given to Moses (Ex 20:2-7), and Christians are morally obliged to worship God (Mt 4:10). The Eucharistic Sacrifice is the most perfect form of worship of God, but other forms (such as Eucharistic adoration) are also of great value. Both internal and external acts of adoration are of value in their own context and situation.

Adoration of the Cross • Showing reverence to the authenticated relics of the Holy Cross. Also, a ceremony in the Good Friday liturgy during which the congregation reverences a cross individually by genuflecting before it and/or kissing it, or communally by paying silent homage to it. It is sometimes referred to as Veneration of the Cross.

Adoro Te Devote • An adorational hymn to the Holy Eucharist written by St. Thomas Aquinas. Unlike his other Eucharistic hymns, St. Thomas did not originally compose it for the feast of Corpus Christi. Until the liturgical revisions after the Second Vatican Council, it was among the prayers in the Missal and Breviary which a priest may have recited after Mass. One popular version (among approximately twenty-five English translations) begins: "Lord and God, devoutly Thee I now adore; Hidden under symbols, bread and wine no more."

Adultery • Sexual intercourse between a married person and one who is not his or her spouse. Aside from the moral consequences of adultery, it also has legal and canonical consequences.

In many pre-Christian legal systems, adultery was punishable by death. The supreme penalty was not the result of the sinful nature of adultery but because it

constituted an offense against the proprietary rights of the husband. In some legal systems, only the wife and her accomplice were considered adulterers, a husband being allowed to have sexual intercourse with other women provided they were not married. Adultery was considered a severe offense against the institution of marriage in the Old Testament and, according to the Mosaic Code, was punishable by death.

In canon law, adultery is specifically mentioned as a cause for the separation of a husband and wife. If one spouse consented to or gave cause for the adultery of the other, that person too is considered an adulterer.

In the 1917 Code of Canon Law, adultery between two persons who had intended to marry each other was a diriment impediment (crime in the first degree). This was dropped in the revised Code.

Although adultery in itself is not sufficient to declare a marriage invalid, acts of adultery can indicate that a person had an intention to marital infidelity prior to the marriage and therefore exchanged invalid consent.

Advent • From the Latin term used in a secular context to denote the coming or arrival of the emperor, this four-week liturgical season inaugurates the entire liturgical year. The *General Norms for the Liturgical Year and Calendar*, issued by the Holy See in March 1969 as a result of the liturgical reform of the Second Vatican Council, offers this description of the season: "Advent has a twofold character: as a season to prepare us for Christmas when Christ's first coming to us is remembered; as a season when that remembrance directs the mind and heart to await Christ's Second Coming at the end of time. Advent is thus a period for devout and joyful expectation."

There is evidence from the mid-fourth

century on concerning some period of preparation for the Christmas-Epiphany celebration. Length and emphasis varied from place to place. Some regions kept a relatively long Advent (from St. Martin's feast in mid-November); others, a rather brief one. In Rome the season evolved to a four-week preparation whose focus was on the joyful celebration of the Lord's incarnation. In Gaul there was a longer, heavily penitential season emphasizing the Lord's glorious advent at the end of time as Lord of history and judge of the universe.

Roman practice from the twelfth century, codified by Trent and enhanced by the greatly enriched lectionary of Vatican Council II, combines these different emphases. The violet vestments (with rose as an option on the third or "Gaudete" Sunday) and the preaching of John the Baptist bespeak the penitential aspect which invites the people to reform. The First Sunday of Advent is clearly centered on the Lord's Second Coming, and the Preface used until December 16 emphasizes this theme. The Gloria is omitted, as during Lent, but for a somewhat different reason, as the official commentary on the revised Calendar notes: "So that on Christmas night the song of the angels may ring out anew in all its freshness." On the other hand, there is a clear note of joyful expectation: The *Alleluia* is retained before the Gospel and the *Te Deum* in the Liturgy of the Hours. There has been no mandatory Advent fast since the 1917 Code of Canon Law. During this first period of Advent, the readings from the prophet Isaiah continually speak of God's visitation, consolation and redemption of His people, while the corresponding Gospel selections portray Christ as the fulfillment of the prophetic promises.

From December 17 on, there is a notable shift in emphasis as the events immediately preceding the Lord's birth are presented in the Gospel readings (Mt 1 and Lk 1), while the first readings proclaim the more important messianic prophecies. At Evening Prayer throughout this second phase of Advent, the Great "O" Antiphons are sung: a skillful and poetic compilation of messianic themes set to melodies of incomparable beauty.

In addition to the prophet Isaiah, the liturgical "guides" for this season are John the Baptist (who makes his appearance in the lectionary midway through the Second Week of Advent) and, as one might expect, the Blessed Virgin Mary (who figures prominently in the final week of the season).

Advent always begins with Evening Prayer I of the Sunday which falls on or closest to November 30 (thus never earlier than November 27 or later than December 3). In the revised Calendar the Fourth Sunday of Advent must be celebrated, even when this falls on December 24. Advent ends with the celebration of Evening Prayer I of Christmas and the Christmas Vigil Mass (if one is celebrated). It should be noted that the Ambrosian Rite in use throughout the area around Milan, Italy, still observes a longer (six-week) Advent, while the Eastern Rites in general observe a shorter "pre-feast" period before Christmas.

Advent of Christ • Another way of referring to the *parousia*, a Greek term that originally referred to the arrival of the emperor on an official visit, the expression was adopted by Christians who used it to refer to the eagerly awaited glorious return of Christ. It is to this second coming in glory and for judgment that Christians look forward in hope during the liturgical season of Advent, a season that prepares for the celebration of Christ's birth as God's Word-become-flesh at Christmas. (Cf. Advent; Parousia).

Adventist • The term refers to a doctrinal position accepted by a number of small

Protestant groups that teach that Christ's Second Coming will be imminent and occur at "this" exact time and at "that" exact place. This doctrine is based on problematic interpretations of Sacred Scripture (e.g., Rom 13:12, 1 Pt 1:20 and Rv 20:3). The origins of the Adventist movement are clearest in the works of William Miller (1782-1849), who preached this and other doctrines around 1831 in Dresden, New York. The Mormons or Latter Day Saints are an example of an Adventist group; a lesser-known group would be the Seventh Day Adventists.

Advocate • A person who safeguards the rights of another in a legal process. Canon law requires that an advocate (lay or cleric) be appointed by the bishop and that he or she have a doctorate in canon law or otherwise be a proven expert in canon law. In order to act validly for a client, the advocate must have a mandate to do so from the person whom he or she represents.

An advocate is not required in marriage nullity cases, although in most tribunals, advocates are provided for petitioners and respondents, should they so desire. Canon law does, however, require that an advocate be provided for anyone who is accused of a canonical crime and who is being tried by an ecclesiastical court (cf. Canons 1481-1490).

The Church has specially trained advocates who practice before the Roman Rota and the Apostolic Signatura.

Advocates of the Roman Congregations

• Specially trained persons who are admitted to act as advocates before the Roman Congregations. They are lay persons (male or female) or clerics who have a doctorate in canon law and in addition receive special training at the Advocate School of the Roman Rota. They receive a fixed salary and represent persons who

have cases pending before the Roman Rota, the Apostolic Signatura or, in rare cases, before specially constituted Roman tribunals.

Advowson • The English term "advowson" is derived from the Latin root for "protector," and referred originally to those lay benefactors of the Church who, at least in theory, protected the rights of the Church, especially in matters of property. Usually these were persons who had at some point donated land to the Church and had in turn been granted the right to nominate the ecclesiastic who would fill the position supported by such property. As such, advowson was a major method for the provision of ecclesiastical office. Over the centuries, however, this practice came in for serious abuse, so that by the time of the 1917 Code of Canon Law, it was sharply curtailed. Today, the practice is for all practical purposes nonexistent and other more reliable methods of providing for certain material needs of the Church are in place.

Aeon • In Greek philosophy the term represents an element of cosmology which Gnostics later applied to divine beings. In Old Testament usage it generally refers to time, usually a long period of time, sometimes without end — "eternity." The authors of the New Testament continue the chronological referent to times "of old" (Lk 1:70), when the "world began" (Jn 9:32) or to the furthest point of the future without end (Jn 6:51, 58) or perpetuity (Rom 16:27; Heb 13:21). It can also refer to a so-called historical epoch or period (Mt 12:32; Lk 16:8), to material reality (Heb 1:2) or to powerful spiritual beings hostile to God (1 Tm 4:1; Eph 2:2; Col 2:15).

Aer • Large veil that covers both the chalice and the diskos in the Byzantine

Liturgy. *Aer* is the Greek word for "air," for this veil was often made of a very light material.

Aesthetics • Aesthetics is the study of the principles underlying the perception of beauty in nature and in the arts. Such conceptual truths can be applied in particular to critical judgments concerning landscapes, paintings, sculpture, architecture, literature, drama, dance, etc. St. Thomas Aquinas thought that the primary ingredients of beauty were: integrity of form, proportion or harmony, and radiance (brilliance, as of color).

The aesthetic value of beauty can also be applied to the nobility of moral attitudes and actions as well as to the supernatural beauty of God Himself.

Aeterni Patris • The encyclical of Pope Leo XIII, promulgated on August 4, 1874, that commended to the Church the study of philosophy, especially the work of St. Thomas Aquinas. This document laid the foundation for the revival of the study of the works of the great figures of Scholastic philosophy, which include not only St. Thomas, but also scholars such as St. Albertus Magnus, St. Bonaventure and Bl. John Duns Scotus. The influential neo-Scholastic and neo-Thomistic movements grew out of the issuance of this encyclical.

Aetianism • Aetius of Antioch was a fourth-century physician and grammarian whose intelligent mind often turned to theological questions. At a certain point in his life, Aetius fell into Arian errors, whereupon he tried to win over groups of young men preparing for the priesthood. Although he was unsuccessful in that effort, he moved about various Eastern territories where, despite his condemnation by the Third Synod of Sirmium, he was eventually consecrated a bishop by the Arians, in whose embrace he later died.

Affectio Maritalis • Meaning marital affection in English, it is an important element in the theology and law of marriage. It was first mentioned in Roman law and was considered to be the habitual attitude or continuous state of mind to be married. As long as the groom (and in later Roman law, the bride as well) had *affectio,* the marriage was considered to be in existence. Its meaning did not include any requirement of love or affection but merely the will to be married. When *affectio* was withdrawn or ceased on the part of either party, the marriage was considered terminated. No act of a civil authority was needed, since the spouses could divorce themselves.

The phrase is later found in the *Decree of Gratian* and in the *Decretals of Gregory IX.* Gratian uses the term in a number of canons in his treatment on marriage. Although he offered no clear definition, a reading of the canons indicates that in his mind, marital affection was a special attitude that accompanied consent, making the consent marital in nature. In short, it was the will to treat one's spouse as a spouse ought to be treated. In this regard, the Christian Tradition stood in marked contrast to both the Roman and other non-Christian understandings of marriage. For Gratian and other Christian theologians, marriage was a partnership or community and the spouses shared spiritual equality. The wife was not a possession or chattel of the husband, nor did she occupy a lower place than he. In this regard, marital affection is no longer the emotionally neutral term found in Roman law but takes on a radically different meaning.

The concept was further developed in the *Decretals of Gregory IX,* especially in a series attributed to Pope Alexander III

(1159-1181). Here, *affectio* was included in decrees enforcing clandestine marriages. (Cf. Clandestinity.) When suits were brought before Church courts concerning multiple marriages, the courts often determined who the first spouse of the man was and compelled him to take her back and treat her with marital affection. The most important decretal, however, is one that treats of marriages of lepers in general. After recalling the custom whereby lepers were separated from their spouses, the Pope stated that they ought not separate but remain together, with the healthy spouse caring for the afflicted spouse in the spirit of marital affection.

It is certain that the medieval canonists, including the Popes, did not understand the concept of *affectio* solely in terms of the right to marital intercourse. Rather, it was an essential ingredient to the marital community.

The concept of marital affection played little if any part in canonical jurisprudence from the close of the Middle Ages to the time of Vatican Council II. The Council, however, stated in its definition, as articulated in *Gaudium et Spes*, that the essence of marriage is conjugal love. In this definition the Fathers state: "The intimate partnership of life and the love which constitutes the married state has been established by the Creator and endowed by Him with its own proper laws" (GS 48). Referring directly to conjugal love, the document goes on to state: "Married love is an eminently human love because it is an affection between two persons rooted in the will and it embraces the good of the whole person" (GS 49). Thus the Vatican Council has not only clarified but given theological validity to the concept of marital affection, now known as conjugal love. Unfortunately, some misinterpreted the notion of married love to be the habit of love, believing that if the habit ceased, the marriage also ceased

to exist. In a 1970 decision of the Roman Rota, it was stated that conjugal love is the mutual gift of the spouses, one to the other. Consequently, it is equated with consent itself. This decision was appealed to a second panel of Rotal judges and although it was upheld, the second decision stated that love was not the efficient cause of marriage but rather a motivating cause. Jurisprudence since that time has further refined the legal impact of conjugal love to be an attitude of the will rather than an emotional feeling. It is more closely aligned with what St. Augustine referred to as *caritas conjugalis* or conjugal charity since charity, as a specific kind of love, is rooted in the will and amounts to a giving of oneself to the other on a habitual basis.

Affections • The term affections as used in spirituality refers to emotions and dispositions following from a response of love, desire and delight to what is perceived as good. Such responses of the heart also include revulsion in contact with evil and rejection of whatever is disordered and tainted with evil. For example, one may have a preference for what is pleasant, such as overeating, but through the asceticism of a reasonable diet, one can come to delight more in healthy food than in disordered eating. Someone may prefer watching television to going to Mass on Sunday, but through growth in appreciating God's gifts, he may come to love the Eucharist more than trivial amusements. Training the affections, or the heart, to respond in an ordered way to true values is a basic part of growth in virtue.

Affective Prayer • The lifting of the heart to God in words and silent longings expressive of loving devotion. It can be contrasted to prayer that may be motivated by a sense of duty but is not engaged in with the whole person. Some types of affective prayer can be heartfelt prayers such as, "Jesus, Mary, Joseph, save souls," the repetition, out of love, of holy words as in the "Jesus Prayer" or the Rosary; "praying in tongues" by means of this charismatic gift, or a simple quiet opening of the heart to God's presence. Such prayers lead to closer union with God and perfecting of the virtue of love. They can be a prelude to contemplative prayer.

Affinity • An impediment or barrier to a valid marriage. It arises between one spouse and all relatives in the direct line of the other spouse, that is, a husband and his wife's mother, grandmother or even daughter by another marriage. An attempt at marriage between persons related by affinity is invalid unless a dispensation is obtained from the bishop.

The impediment of affinity has a long and complex history. In the Middle Ages, the relationship of affinity extended not only to relatives in the direct line, but to relatives in many degrees in the indirect line (brothers, sisters, cousins, second cousins, etc.). At one time the relationship also existed between one person and the blood relatives of another person with whom he or she had extramarital sexual intercourse. By the time of the 1917 Code, affinity existed only between blood relatives in the direct line and those in the indirect line to the second degree (brothers and sisters, first cousins, nieces and nephews) (cf. Canon 1092).

Africa, Church in • The development of the Church in Africa has three distinct phases. In the first phase, two centers of Christian belief are of special importance: Alexandria in Egypt and Roman North Africa (an area bordering the Mediterranean in what is now Morocco, Algeria, Tunisia and Libya).

Alexandria, already a center of pagan and Jewish philosophical and religious thought, came into contact with Christianity in the first century and became the center of Coptic Christianity, with a distinctive liturgy and theology. Many theologians of the early Church (some heretical) were from Alexandria: Clement, Origen, Arius, Apollinaris, St. Cyril. Much of the Coptic Church went into schism after the condemnation of Monophysitism at the Council of Chalcedon (A.D. 451) and the Muslim invasion of Egypt in the seventh century practically eliminated Catholicism in Egypt.

Christianity came to Roman North Africa at an early date and regardless of persecutions and heresies (especially Arianism, Manichaeism and Donatism), it flourished, with hundreds of dioceses by the time of St. Augustine (d. 430). Tertullian (d. 220), despite the rigorism of the last part of his life, is rightly called the "Father of Latin Theology." The Vandal invasion and persecution weakened the Church and later domination by the Muslims almost totally destroyed Catholicism in this area.

The second period is the age of missionary activity, confined principally to sub-Saharan Africa. Early activity dates back to the fifteenth century, especially by the Portuguese. It was frequently hampered by the slave trade and by colonialism. The religious and political aims of colonial powers often inhibited missionary activity and frequently involved exploitation of lands and people. In this period, which lasted until the end of World War II, Catholicism was able to gain some foothold in almost all parts of Africa. Even Mediterranean Africa, so strongly Muslim, saw some missionary activity with the growth of Spanish, French and British influence in this area.

The third period (after World War II) was marked by the rapid development of the Church in most parts of sub-Saharan Africa. The first two bishops native of this area were ordained in 1939. By the 1950s, this was a common phenomenon; at present nearly all diocesan sees are occupied by native bishops. Despite the social and political unrest that sometimes accompanied the independence movement, the linking of the Church in the minds of some with the former colonial powers and some hindrance or even persecution of the Church, she flourished. In some countries the number of Catholics has doubled since World War II and in some countries about half the population is Catholic. In some places, formerly dominated by the Dutch or British (e.g., South Africa or Zimbabwe — formerly Rhodesia), the Catholic percentage is considerably lower. The Church in Mediterranean Africa, however, has not fared as well. With the end of the colonial era, most Catholics (Europeans and their sympathizers) left and the new governments frequently adopted a militantly Muslim stance.

Agape • Of the three most familiar Greek words for love (*eros*, *philia*, *agape*), it is *agape* which is most frequently used in the New Testament. In extra-biblical Hellenistic Greek, *eros* refers primarily to passionate attraction, though it can also include a mystical sense. The word *eros* does not appear at all in the New Testament. *Philia*, the most common word for love in extra-biblical Greek, has to do with the affection that results from interpersonal relationships, and can also involve concern and care for another person. The particular nuance of *agape* in extra-biblical Greek is elusive, since the word often occurs as a synonym of *philia*. It is perhaps due to the frequency of the verbal form *agapan* as the Septuagint's rendering of the Hebrew *aheb* that *agapan* and the noun *agape* entered the New Testament vocabulary as the terms of preference for describing love as a quality of describing human relationships and as a quality of the relationship between God and man.

The letters of St. Paul speak of the love of God for human beings, the love of human beings for God and the love of human beings for one another. Of the first, God's love for human beings, Paul writes that "hope does not disappoint, because the love of God has been poured out into our hearts through the Holy Spirit that has been given to us" (Rom 5:5). God's love is the basis for human hope. Further, God's love toward us is manifested in Christ's saving death: "God proves his love for us in that while we were still sinners, Christ died for us" (Rom 5:8). In Romans 8:35-39, Paul confidently writes that nothing can separate us from the love of Christ.

Similar confidence animates Paul's words about human love for God: "We know that all things work for good for those who love God, who are called according to his purpose" (Rom 8:1). With faith and hope, love is among the three things that last, and is the greatest of these (1 Cor 13:13). Without love, the exercise of the other spiritual gifts is empty. In Ephesians 5:2, believers are urged to "live in love, as Christ loved us and handed himself over for us as a sacrificial offering to God." The love of Christ for the Church is to be the model for domestic love (Eph 5:25-31).

In the Synoptic Gospels, love is the heart of the two Great Commandments, love of God and love of neighbor (Mt 22:34-40; Mk 12:28-34). Jesus extends the law of love to enemies as well (Mt 5:43-48; Lk 6:27-36).

The "disciple whom Jesus loved" was a central figure in the community from which the Fourth Gospel emerged (cf. Jn 13:23; 19:26; 20:2; 21:7, 20). In the Johannine literature, love characterizes the relationship between the Father and the Son. *Agape* describes the Father's love for the world and the love of the Son for those who are His own. The well-known text of John 3:16 tells us that "God so loved the world that he gave his only Son, so that everyone who believes in him might not perish, but might have eternal life." Even as

Jesus Himself "loved his own in the world and loved them to the end" (Jn 13:1), love is the "new commandment" Jesus gives to His disciples (Jn 13:34). By this love they will be recognized as Jesus' disciples (Jn 13:35), and will share in the love of the Father and the Son (Jn 14:21, 23).

The First Epistle of John proclaims, "God is love" (Jn 4:8, 16), insisting, "In this is love: not that we have loved God, but that he loved us and sent his Son as expiation for our sins" (1 Jn 4:10). From this follows the imperative, "Beloved, if God so loved us, we must also love one another" (1 Jn 4:11).

In the early Church, *agape* also designated the meal which Christians celebrated together as an expression of Christ's sacrificial love for them and their love for each other. St. Ignatius of Antioch uses *agape* in this secondary sense in his letter to the Romans (7:3), and in his letter to the Smyrnaeans he rules that "it is not permitted either to baptize or to celebrate the *agape* apart from the bishop" (Smyrnaeans 8:2). This suggests that *agape* may have been a way of referring to the Eucharistic meal. Yet, by the end of the second century, it appears that *agape* referred to a shared religious meal distinct from the Eucharist.

For further reading: Everett Ferguson, "Agape Meal," *Anchor Bible Dictionary*, 1:90-91.

Age, Canonical • Canon law computes the age of a person from the day of his or her birth. Persons who have not completed the seventh year of life are known as "infants" and are presumed not to have the use of reason. After the completion of the seventh year, a person acquires some canonical rights.

Those who have not completed their eighteenth year but who are beyond the seventh year are known as "minors." Those who have completed the eighteenth year are known as "adults" and have full use of canonical rights.

Canon law requires a minimum age for the reception of certain sacraments and for holding certain ecclesiastical offices. A man must have reached the age of twenty-five in order to be ordained a priest and must be thirty-five in order to be consecrated a bishop (cf. Canons 97-98, 378, 1031).

Age, Impediment of • Canon law requires that for a valid marriage, a male must have completed his sixteenth year and a female her fourteenth year. The same regulation was in force in the 1917 Code, but prior to that, the age requirements were fourteen and twelve, respectively. In spite of this canonical regulation, most states in the United States have higher age requirements.

The bishops' conferences of the various countries can establish a higher age requirement, but they cannot make it an invalidating impediment to marriage (cf. Canon 1083).

Age of Reason • In Church usage, the age at which a person attains a state of moral responsibility and also incurs the obligation to observe various legal and moral prescriptions (e.g., the obligation to fast and abstain).

In another sense of the term, "Age of Reason" sometimes designates eighteenth-century philosophical currents in which Encyclopedist, Deist and Rationalist thought was dominant, particularly in British and French philosophy.

Aggiornamento • This Italian word for "updating" was popularized by Pope John XXIII for the modernization, renewal and revitalization of the Roman Catholic Church by the Second Vatican Council. This word is used to indicate the attempt to present Roman Catholic teachings and practices so that people will better understand and accept them. It also means new approaches in ecumenical dialogue.

Aggressor, Unjust • An assailant who carries out an attack on an innocent person, with no provocation. It is morally permissible to use force against an unjust aggressor, even to the point of killing him, provided that the injury done does not exceed what is necessary for the defense of oneself, other innocent parties or of one's property.

Aglipay Schism • By the end of the nineteenth century the Philippines, long under Spanish rule, still had few native clergy. When revolution broke out there in 1896, many Spanish clergy left the islands and still more left when the United States took over the nation in 1898. In the resulting void, and probably with some backing from supporters in America, a Filipino priest named Gregorio Aglipay proclaimed himself head of the Church in the Philippines in 1902. At one point, over a million Filipino Catholics joined the schism, which bore the name of its leader and which carried off considerable Church property as well. In 1906 the Church's right to most of this property was restored in U.S. courts. Father Aglipay himself was reconciled with the Church and died in 1941, and since that time his schism has dwindled practically to insignificance.

Agnosticism • The philosophical theory which holds that it is impossible to know whether God exists or not since the human mind cannot reach that far. It arises from the denial that reason is capable of understanding anything beyond the laws governing physical happenings. Agnosticism denies that we can advance to a conceptual grasp of such truths as the immortality of the soul or the existence of God. In opposition to agnosticism, the Church teaches that the human mind is capable of understanding certain basic truths about reality, including the existence of God. (Cf. Atheism.)

Agnus Dei • (1) The liturgical chant which from ancient times has been sung at Mass at the time of the *fractio panis*, or the "Breaking of the Bread," which precedes the Communion Rite of both the priest and the people. The prayer reads as follows: *Agnus Dei, qui tollis peccata mundi, miserere nobis [bis] . . . dona nobis pacem*; or in the English: "Lamb of God, You take away the sins of the world, have mercy on us [twice] . . . grant us peace." The last invocation, which is usually the third (though in the revised liturgy the first is chanted until all of the Bread has been broken) was added in the tenth century. Up to this last revision, the invocation was changed at Requiem Masses to read: "grant them rest . . . grant them eternal rest." This has been dropped since the changes carried out by Pope Paul VI in 1969.

(2) The *Agnus Dei* refers also to a sacramental that consists of a small disc of wax upon which the seal of the Lamb of God is impressed, thus its name. The wax used is taken from candles blessed by the Supreme Pontiff on Candlemas Day or from the papal Easter Candle. It is often broken into smaller pieces and enclosed in leather or silk cases which are usually richly embroidered or painted and which may be worn about the neck. It is invoked as a protection against Satan, temptation, sickness, tempests, to aid a woman expecting a child and to ward against sudden death. It is also used as a spiritual aid and protection during travel. The use of the *Agnus Dei* in the Church dates back to the fourth century and therefore is backed by both a rich tradition and a sound theology of sacramentals.

Agony of Christ • The mental anguish and physical distress suffered by Christ when He prayed in the Garden of Gethsemane in the interval between the Last Supper and His arrest. In His prayer, Christ was both drawn by His determination to accomplish the divine will for our salvation and at the same time repelled by His anticipation of the suffering this would entail. The Agony in the Garden, as it is called, is the first Sorrowful Mystery of the Rosary.

Agrapha • A Greek word which literally translated means "unwritten things." The term seems to have been first used by J. G. Körner in the eighteenth century to designate sayings of Jesus not found in the four canonical Gospels. Some of the agrapha appear as glosses in various New Testament manuscripts, others in the writings of the Fathers and still others in the apocrypha. Perhaps the best known "agraphon" is the one found in Acts 20:35, "It is more blessed to give than to receive." It is not easy to ascertain which of all the sayings are genuine words of Jesus. Many of them are sound, edifying expressions, wholly compatible with the spirit and teaching of Jesus as known from the canonical writings. Indeed, a number of them are expansions, variations or suturings together of words found in the canonical Gospels.

For further reading: William D. Stroker, "Agrapha," *Anchor Bible Dictionary*, 1:92-95.

AID • "Artificial Insemination by a Donor" occurs when a man inseminates by artificial means a woman to whom he is not married. The action has been rejected as immoral by the Church in the teaching of Pope Pius XII in his "Address to the Fourth International Congress of Catholic Doctors" (September 29, 1949, AAS 41, 557-561). The moral malice of AID is seen in the fact that the parents of the child created are not married and the child is the product of an adulterous union.

Artificial insemination by the donor has become more common with the sexual revolution. This kind of action violates the right of the child to its father and to be reared in the presence of its natural parents.

AIDS • "Acquired Immune Deficiency Syndrome" develops in the presence of a virus that attacks the immune system of the individual, leaving the person prey to a wide variety of infectious diseases. Researchers are confident that this disease can only be transmitted through sexual intercourse, blood transfusions or by the use of intravenous injections. AIDS has reached epidemic proportions throughout the world.

AIDS is usually preceded by ARC, "AIDS Related Complex," and it can take years for the symptoms of AIDS to appear. It is exceedingly difficult to diagnose AIDS when it first appears, and the virus can remain latent for years. Death resulting from AIDS is often extremely long and painful, as the entire immune system breaks down. The best protection against the AIDS virus is sexual abstinence or fidelity to one uninfected sexual partner.

AIH • "Artificial Insemination by the Husband," a procedure in which a wife is impregnated by her husband through artificial and technological means. The Church has not objected to this procedure when it preserves the natural structure of the marital act. Generally this means that the couple must perform the marital act, and subsequent to that, cooperate with technological measures that can be taken to enhance fertility and aid conception. The Church has objected that other approaches violate the dignity of the child-to-be and immorally separates the unitive and procreative.

Aisle • In church buildings, the passageway between sections of pews or seats.

Aitesis • A long series of invocations to which the people answer: "Grant this, O Lord." There are two of them in the Divine Liturgy, one before and one after the Canon. The Aitesis is very similar to the Synapte and to the Ektene.

Akeldama • Aramaic for "field of blood" or, as some scholars suggest, "field of sleeping." The terrain bought by the Sanhedrin with the money that Judas had received in exchange for his betrayal of Jesus and which Judas returned to the Council. The field, which had previously been known as the "potter's field" (Mt 27:7), has traditionally been thought to lie outside the city walls of Jerusalem, south of the valley of Hinnom. The word *akeldama* occurs only once in the Scriptures — Acts 1:19.

For further reading: Robert W. Smith, "Akeldama," *Anchor Bible Dictionary*, 1:134-135.

Akolouthia • Greek for "sequence," this term may refer to any ceremony in the Byzantine Rite, but usually designates the recitation of the Liturgy of the Hours or Divine Office.

Alais, Treaty of • The uneasy peace between the Huguenots and the basically Catholic populace of France which followed the Edict of Nantes slowly disintegrated over the next generation. The famous Cardinal Richelieu, at the head of the royal army, finally laid siege to the Huguenot stronghold of La Rochelle, which fell in October of 1628. Following the capitulation of Alais a

few months later, Richelieu orchestrated the Treaty of Alais in June of 1629. Although affirming in principle the Edict of Nantes, it effectively removed the Huguenots as political rivals to the French throne and resulted in their civil disability until the advent of the Napoleonic Code.

Alamo • The site of a Franciscan mission, the Alamo was a fortress-like enclosure in San Antonio, Texas, which was defended against an army of Mexicans by a small group of Texans in a fierce battle on March 6, 1836. The Mission of San Antonio de Valero had been founded at San Pedro Springs in 1718, and moved to its present location in San Antonio in 1746. It consisted of a friary, church and hospital surrounded by a wall. The word is Spanish for "cottonwood."

Alb • This ecclesiastical vestment, which derives its name from the Latin word for "white," *albus*, is the white linen robe worn for all liturgical functions by ministers of the altar over their regular ecclesiastical garb. It is a development of the Graeco-Roman *tunica talaris* which was worn by Roman men and reached the ankles and the wrists. It was often decorated with colored bands or orphreys — a custom still in use today — in gold, silver or one of the liturgical colors, with the exception of black. Since the time of the Renaissance, with the proliferation of the lace industry, albs have often been decorated with lace reaching from the waist to the ankles and also the cuffs of the sleeves, which are often silk of the prelatical color of the wearer (sometimes even in a liturgical color). At the present time, the styles of decoration for albs are almost as varied as the wearers. The present *General Instruction of the Roman Missal* states that "the vestment common to ministers of every rank is the alb, tied at the waist with a cincture, unless it is made to fit without a cincture. An amice should be put on first if the alb does not completely cover the street clothing at the neck" (n. 298).

Albania, The Church in • Christianity in Albania dates from the fourth century. In 1054, the Albanian Church followed Byzantium into schism. After Albania became part of the Ottoman empire in the fifteenth century, many Christians were forced to convert to Islam. While over half of the population was Muslim, Catholicism prevailed in the northern part of the country. The Communist takeover in 1945 was calamitous for all religions in Albania, where persecution was so systematic and unrelenting that in 1967 the regime proclaimed Albania to be the first truly atheistic state in the world. With the worldwide collapse of Communism, the right to practice religion was restored in Albania in 1990, and in 1991 the Holy See revived diplomatic relations with the country. The effort to rebuild the Church in Albania is now getting underway.

Albigensianism • Of the many heretical sects that appeared around the eleventh century, Albigensianism was one of the most extreme. These neo-Manichaeans rejected the sacraments and Church authority, adopted vegetarianism and promiscuous behavior, and repudiated the right of the state to punish criminals.

Alb (Italy, 1600s)

Although present in Spain and Italy, the center of their power was in the French city of Albi, hence their name. Albigensians divided themselves into two branches, depending on their degree of commitment to the sect. Upon entry into the higher branch, Albigensians ran the distinct risk of being murdered by their friends, lest they fall into unforgivable sin. Others simply committed suicide. The offensiveness of such a sect was apparent to the state authorities as well as to the Church, and while the latter condemned their theories in numerous councils and synods, the former launched veritable crusades against Albigensian strongholds. By the fourteenth century, this bizarre sect was eradicated.

Alcantara, Knights of • A twelfth-century Spanish military order organized to combat the Moors, the Knights of Alcantara is today an honorary order of laymen.

Alcoholism and Related Drug Problems, National Catholic Council on • The agency, located in Washington, D.C., which promotes treatment for priests, religious and laity who experience a chemical addiction. The Council provides continuing education for those who work with the chemically dependent. Workshops and conferences are offered at regular intervals.

Aleph • The first letter of the Hebrew alphabet. In textual criticism, the letter aleph is used to designate a fourth-century biblical manuscript in Greek that is also known as the *Codex Sinaiticus* because it was discovered at St. Catherine's Monastery on Mount Sinai.

Alexandria, Church of • The city of Alexandria, located near the mouth of the Nile River in Egypt, has a glorious history in the ancient life of the Church. First evangelized by St. Mark, the city's location led not only to its importance in trade and culture, but, under the inspiration of such leaders as Clement, Athanasius and Cyril, gave rise to its crucial importance over the other Churches of the East. At the Council of Nicaea in 325, the preeminence of the Church at Alexandria was acknowledged when the patriarchate was ranked second only to Rome and even before Antioch. Unfortunately, Alexandria was also plagued by heresy for several hundred years, particularly Arianism and Monophysitism. This second-named heresy led the venerable Church of Alexandria to reject the Council of Chalcedon, by which act the Alexandrian Church was lost in schism for several centuries. The patriarchate gradually lost its influence, especially after the Muslim invasion of Egypt in 642. Today, however, following various reunifications with the West, the Coptic Catholic Church of Alexandria is recognized as one of the principal Patriarchates of the East. (Cf. Alexandria, School of.)

For further reading: Birger A. Pearson, "Alexandria," *Anchor Bible Dictionary*, 1:152-157.

Alexandria, School of • The history of the School of Alexandria closely tracks that of the Church of Alexandria. Already well-versed in Hellenic and Judaic studies, Christian thinkers including Cyril, Clement and Athanasius combined to place the ancient city at the center of Christian scholarship. The best-known work of its Jewish academicians doubtless was the Septuagint version of the Bible, so named because of a legendary explanation that a team of some seventy scholars had contributed to it.

Alexandrian Rite • The Liturgy of Alexandria is attributed to St. Mark and is the parent of all the Egyptian Liturgies. It was probably an adaptation of the Antiochene Rite (from Antioch), which was finalized by St. Cyril in the fifth century. The Liturgy of St. Mark is no longer celebrated, since it was used in Greek only by the Melchites, who later replaced it with the Byzantine Rite. It was adapted by the Copts and Ethiopians, who developed modified versions of it in their own languages (Coptic and Ge'ez). The present liturgy for the Catholic Patriarchate of Alexandria is that of the Coptic Rite.

Alexandrine Liturgy • In the patristic era, the Western liturgy had several major centers in addition to Rome. Among these was North Africa whose liturgy is often termed "Alexandrine." Various documents attest to the existence in the fifth century of collections of booklets with Mass prayers (called *libelli missarum*) and larger collections in sacramentaries. While the major parts of the Mass, Liturgy of the Word and Liturgy of the Eucharist were the same for all these non-Roman Western liturgies, the variations among them are of interest.

At the time of St. Augustine, it is most likely that the Alexandrine Liturgy was as follows: Entrance of clergy, Greeting, Epistle, Psalm, Gospel, Homily, Dismissal of Catechumens, Solemn Intercessions, Offering with Psalm sung, Preface dialogue, improvised Preface (without *Sanctus*), approved Eucharistic Prayer and Great

Amen, Breaking of bread, Lord's prayer, Communion distributed (with Psalm 33 sung), Final prayer, and Dismissal.

Alienation • The canonical term for the sale, gift or other form of transfer of ownership of ecclesiastical goods from the Church to another entity. Canon law contains special norms that govern the alienation of ecclesiastical goods. Depending on the value of the goods or their special nature as goods with proven historic value or as sacred objects, special permissions are needed for their alienation (cf. Canons 1290-1298).

Alimentation • An arcane term referring to those things necessary for the support of physical life, especially food and shelter. Its most common use today is found in discussions about artificial feeding. It was used in the past also to refer specifically to supplies and support offered to priests and religious in the course of their duties, but is only rarely encountered today.

Aliturgical Days • Days on which Mass may not be celebrated. In the Roman Rite, this happens only during the Triduum on Good Friday, when Communion is distributed after a service consisting of a Liturgy of the Word followed by Adoration of the Cross. In a way, it is also true of Holy Saturday because the Mass of the Easter Vigil, though celebrated Saturday evening, is properly considered the beginning of the Easter Sunday celebration.

In the early Church, the Eucharist was celebrated only on Sundays (although people received Communion daily in their homes from previously consecrated hosts as the *Apostolic Tradition* of Hippolytus attests). Gradually, celebration of martyrs' feast days and eventually other saints by means of the Mass filled up the calendar. In the Eastern Church, there are many aliturgical days, especially during Lent. Sometimes a communion service replaces the Divine Liturgy, or in some rites the people "fast" from the Eucharist altogether.

All Saints, Solemnity of • Feast honoring all the saints of the Church, celebrated on the first of November. There was a similar feast kept in the East from the fourth century, but it was expanded to include confessors of the Faith, virgins, holy bishops, etc.

In the West, the dedication of the Pantheon in Rome under the title of St. Mary and the Martyrs (c. 610) led to an annual commemoration on May 13. November first was the day that the Irish celebrated this feast; they often commemorated important feasts on the first day of each month. From Ireland, this date spread to England and the continent. Rome eventually adopted this date at least by the pontificate of Pope Gregory VII (d. 1085).

Allah • The basic tenet of Islam's profession of faith (the *shhadah*) proclaims that "there is no god but God [*Allah*]," an affirmation of the existence and of the oneness of God, to which is joined, "and Muhammad is the messenger of God." Islam's absolute monotheism is based on the teachings of the *Qur'an*. Grammatically, the Arabic word *Allah* is a contraction of the expression *al-ilah* which itself originates from the common Semitic root *el*. That term, *el*, is used in a number of Semitic languages as the designation of a deity, including its use in biblical Hebrew to designate the God of Israel.

For further reading: Louis Gardet, "God in Islam," *The Encyclopedia of Religion*, 6:26-35.

Allatae Sunt • The title, after its first two words (Latin for "they were carried away"), of Pope Benedict XIV's encyclical (1775) addressed to missionaries in Syria and Asia Minor. The encyclical provided guidelines for the missionaries' relations with the Eastern Churches and enunciated the principle that converts should be initiated, not into Latin Rite communities, but into Eastern Rite communities in union with Rome.

All Souls Day • The commemoration of all the Faithful Departed is observed on November 2. Solemn commemorations of the dead have been made from the seventh century on, but at different times. Odilo of Cluny is thought to have fixed the date at November 2.

From Cluny the observance of this date spread and was adopted by Rome in the fourteenth century. The Eastern Rites keep other days for these commemorations. In the Roman Rite, each priest may offer three Masses for the dead on All Souls Day, and for this purpose three different Mass formularies are given in the Missal of Pope Paul VI. This custom started at the Dominican Priory of Valencia and was extended to all priests by Pope Benedict XV in 1915, stating that one Mass must be offered for all the Faithful Departed and another for the Pope's intentions.

Allegorical Interpretation (Biblical) • A method of interpreting sacred literature in pre-New Testament Judaism, the New Testament Church and among Eastern and Western Fathers of the Church. The texts of Sacred Scripture are read at the literary and spiritual levels. Literary references to persons, places, events and things are interpreted as signifying other persons, places, events and things. For example, Moses led God's people out of Egypt through the parted sea to the land of promise (Exodus). They left a land of sin and oppression for the land of milk and honey. When we read this story and think about Baptism in Christ, we are reading the Book of Exodus from an allegorical point of view. The literary sense or meaning of the text is therefore only the beginning point of the sacred communication and as a "sign" points to something beyond itself, to the deeper spiritual realities it conveys. In the New Testament, Paul alone uses the term *allegory* (as a verb, Gal 4:24) and only once; even so, he often uses allegorical techniques to advance his arguments (1 Cor 5:6-8; 9:8-10; 10:1-11; Gal 4:21-31). A Gospel example of allegorical interpretation is Mark 12:1-12.

Allegory • A literary device found in Cynic and Stoic philosophical literature by which myths and religious values were communicated to successive generations. The device is used in Hellenistic Judaism to defend the authority of Jewish tradition. Initially, the device explained the origins of words and names of various mythological gods; eventually it developed into fully articulate narratives. Generally speaking, the figure or event in the past (the antitype) is linked to a current figure or event (the type) by means of comparison.

Alleluia • The word *halleluja* is directly from the Hebrew Bible, meaning "Yahweh be praised." It is used extensively in the Psalms (and elsewhere) as a doxology (e.g., Ps 104-106; 135). It appears in the New Testament and early Church liturgical texts.

Allocution • Coming from the Latin *ad loqui*, "to speak to," the term allocution or *allocutio* refers to a form of address made to a group of persons. In the terminology of the Legion of Mary, for instance, the spiritual director gives an allocution to the rest of the group during the weekly meeting. In a more solemn vein, the term also refers to a formal address made by the Pope from the throne to the College of Cardinals during a secret consistory.

Alma (Almah) • A Hebrew word meaning "virgin" or "maiden," it is used in the messianic prophecy of Isaiah 7:14: "Therefore the Lord himself will give you a sign. Behold, a young woman [Hebrew: 'almah] shall conceive and bear a son, and shall call his name Immanuel." In the Septuagint translation, *almah* is given greater specificity by being rendered *parthenos* (virgin).

Almanac, Our Sunday Visitor's Catholic • A comprehensive annual sourcebook of information on the Catholic Church, published by Our Sunday Visitor.

Almighty, The • This divine title is the English translation of the Hebrew term *Shaddai*, an expression which first appears in Genesis 17:1, where God introduces Himself to the patriarch Abraham saying, "I am God Almighty (*El Shaddai*); walk before me and be blameless." It is likely that this way of referring to God dates as far back as the Israelite patriarchs. The Hebrew term *Shaddai* was translated into Greek as *Pantokrator*, and that expression is among the divine attributes listed in the prayer found in 2 Maccabees 1:24-29, which invokes God as "Lord God, Creator of all things, who art awe-inspiring and strong and just and merciful, who alone art King and art kind, who alone art bountiful, who alone art just and almighty and eternal."

The Apocalypse of John uses the Greek form of this divine title, *Pantokrator*, more frequently than any other New Testament document. There it appears nine times. Among these occurrences is Revelation 4:8, "Holy, holy, holy is the Lord God Almighty," a declaration in which the four living creatures who attend God's throne cry out in words very close to those shouted by the seraphim in Isaiah 6:3, "Holy, holy, holy is the LORD of hosts." In the preface acclamation of the Mass, we sing, "Holy, holy, holy Lord, God of power and might" in a song that praises God's dynamic authority and saving strength (cf. Pantocrator).

For further reading: Betty Jane Lillie, "Almighty," *Anchor Bible Dictionary*, 1:160.

Almoner • This word, which comes from the Latin *eleemosynarius*, and before that the Greek verb *eleemosyne* ("to have pity"), designates an ecclesiastic at the court of a king or prince having charge of the distribution of alms to the poor. It is an ecclesiastic at the Papal Court or the curia of a diocesan bishop who is given charge of distributing alms to the poor. In the Vatican an archbishop is customarily the Pontifical Almoner. The office of the Pontifical Almoner has charge, among other things, of collecting the offerings for the poor who come to receive some assistance at the Vatican's doors. The Almoner also has the faculty to grant the Apostolic Blessing, which is attested to by the beautiful certificates hand-painted on parchment which are then sent to the faithful throughout the world who have requested them. These are commonly known as "papal blessings," though they are only the certificate verifying that the blessing has been bestowed by the Pope.

Alms • Financial offerings for the poor. Exhortation toward the practice of caring for the needy is found in every portion of the Old Testament. Provision for the needy is a theme found in the prophetic and other Old Testament literature which praises such practices (cf. Prv 3:27; 22:9; 28:27; Tb 4:6-11; Sir 3:30-4:10; 17:22; Dn 4:24). Giving all one has to the poor is a condition for following Christ as a disciple (Mt 6:24; 19:21; Mk 10:21; Lk 18:22). The early Church cared for the needy (Acts 4:32-37; 2 Cor 8—9), and believers will find ultimate satisfaction for their gifts of material and monetary goods from God (Mt 25:31-46).

Alms were understood to have sacrificial and sanctifying effects in later rabbinic literature; alms can express the combination of love of God with love of neighbor.

Almuce • A forerunner of the present-day mozzetta, it was an ecclesiastical garment which covered the shoulders and the head. Worn by canons during the chanting of the Divine Office, it was often lined with fur to ward off the extreme cold of many of the ancient churches. It was also worn by parish priests in some countries. With the coming of the biretta, the almuce assumed more the shape of the present-day mozzetta, which covers the shoulders and has a hood that is worn thrown back from the head. Even this decreased in size with time as it was not worn any longer. It is still part of the choir dress of prelates, as well as of canons of cathedral chapters. Remnants of this may still be found in the habits of the Orders of Canons Regular, such as the Premonstratensians (Norbertines) and the Augustinians.

Though its use was dropped for some time after the Second Vatican Council, it has been taken up again, especially with the encouragement of Pope John Paul II, who has required its use in all the canonries of Rome.

Alpha and Omega • The combination of the first (alpha) and the last (omega) letters of the Greek alphabet occurs in the New Testament only in the Book of Revelation (Rv 1:8; 21:6; 22:13).

In Revelation 1:8, God proclaims, "I am the Alpha and the Omega . . . who is and who was and who is to come, the Almighty." In Revelation 21:6, God repeats, "I am the Alpha and the Omega," and adds the parallel expression, "the beginning and the end." Revelation 1:8 and 21:5-8 are the only places in Revelation where the speaker is specifically identifiable as God Himself. In Revelation 22:13, it is Christ Who appropriates these terms, saying, "I am the Alpha and Omega, the first and the last, the beginning and the end." In Revelation 1:17-18, Christ identifies Himself as ". . . the first and the last, and the living one," and then in 2:8, "the first and the last" is the Christological title with which the letter to the Church in Smyrna begins.

The biblical background for the expression in Revelation can be located in texts such as Isaiah 41:4, "I, the LORD, the first, and with the last: I am He," Isaiah 43:10, ". . . Before me no god was formed, nor shall there be any after me," and Isaiah 48:12, "I am He, I am the first, and I am the last." In these phrases of Second Isaiah, God proclaims His cosmic dominion over time and space. God's self-description as Alpha and Omega in Revelation reiterates this biblical theme.

The fact that both God and Christ claim, "I am the Alpha and the Omega" proved difficult for some of the earliest commentators on Revelation. Although commentators struggled to explain how the same title could be applied both to God and to Christ, Revelation itself often says of each what can be said of the other, thus highlighting the intimacy of their relationship and the oneness of their nature.

For further reading: Mitchell G. Reddish, "Alpha and Omega," *Anchor Bible Dictionary*, 1:161-162.

Alphabetic Psalms • The alphabetic psalms are those in which the various parts of a single psalm begin consecutively with one of the twenty-two letters of the Hebrew alphabet. These parts may be verses, half-verses or strophes. Examples of this device are Psalms 9, 25, 34, 37, 111, 119 and 145. The form is also found in Sirach 51:13-30, Proverbs 31:11-31 and

Lamentations 1-4. This artificial device apparently was used simply as an aid to memory and had no theological meaning.

Altar • The Hebrew word for "altar" in the Bible comes from the word meaning "to slaughter" for sacrifice. The Eucharist in the early Church was celebrated on a table in homes. Even when churches were first built, altar tables were often wooden and moved in by deacons for the liturgy and then moved out after the liturgy. As the meal dimension of the Eucharist diminished (as the growing Christian communities made this inconvenient), the sacrificial dimension was highlighted in the fourth century. The decline of paganism and the demise of Temple Judaism made it possible to used fixed stone or metal altars without having pagan associations confuse the faithful; thus the danger no longer existed that the unique Sacrifice of Christ would be perceived as the same as the many animal sacrifices of the Temple in Jerusalem or those of the pagans. The altars were usually of marble and squarish in shape, usually large enough to hold the chalice and large paten, and later a book, when fledgling sacramentaries began to develop in the late patristic period.

The relics of the saints became associated with altars because the early Christians celebrated the Eucharist at the grave sites of the martyrs to honor them, but not on their tombs. Later in the fourth century, churches and altars were built over the tombs (Sts. Peter and Paul in Rome) and out of this association came much later the tomb-shaped altar (replacing the table shape) and the late medieval practice of hollowing a hole in the top of the altar, or *mensa*, for the placement of relics. The *General Instruction of the Roman Missal* of Pope Paul VI no longer requires relics as part of the altar, although it recommends the practice of enclosing them in the altar or under the altar (as was the ancient practice).

The liturgical tradition of the early Church was to have only one altar in each church, symbolizing the one Eucharist celebrated by the one bishop (cf. St. Ignatius of Antioch to the Philippians, 4:1). As altars became receptacles for relics, they were multiplied in the same church and this was further spread by monk-priests celebrating private Masses for special intentions at individual altars from the seventh century on in monastic churches (only one Mass a day on a given altar).

Orientation: In the early Church, the altar was free-standing and not against the wall of the apse. In Rome, the churches were built with the doors facing east, so that the celebrant (bishop) on his chair (*cathedra*) in the middle of the apse faced that direction as well. When he went to the altar, he faced the people. From the fifth century on, the Eastern custom of having the apse and its altar face east became popular in the West as well. The altar then tended to be built against the apse wall and the bishop's throne or the celebrant's chair to the side. Relics were often displayed on the altar or above, and churches without them would have paintings of saints on a vertical structure (the retable) behind the altar from the tenth century on. They grew higher and more elaborate with carved figures added in the later medieval period. The altar table often seemed to be only a base for the glorious screen of paintings of Christ and the saints. The Baroque era further complicated the altar structure by making it the usual place for a tabernacle for the reservation of the Blessed Sacrament (cf. Tabernacle), hitherto reserved in other ways. Gradines, or little shelves for flowers and candlesticks, were added, creating the elaborate high altars that were built throughout the nineteenth century and into our own time.

Today's altar is a return to that of the

early Church, both in its facing the people (as was the Roman basilical custom) and in being a table around which the clergy and people can gather. The *General Instruction* calls the altar the table of the Lord and sees it as the place where the Sacrifice of the Cross is made present under sacramental signs. The one table is seen as a symbol of the one Christ for one community, for it recommends that minor altars be few in number and placed in separate chapels in new churches so as not to conflict with the main altar. If altars are attached to the floor, and thus immovable, they are considered fixed and as such ought to have a stone (*mensa*) and a solid base and ought to be consecrated by the bishop. Movable altars (which no longer need an altar stone with relics enclosed) are simply blessed. The altar may be adorned with cross and candles, depending on the design of the altar or they may simply be placed around it. In any case, they ought not to block the view of the people.

Altar Bread • "I am the bread of life. . . . I am the living bread which came down from heaven; if any one eats of this bread he will live forever; and the bread which I shall give for the life of the world is my flesh" (Jn 6:48, 51). As here seen, the term "altar bread" has to do with the bread to be used in the Eucharistic Sacrifice of the Mass. As with all the sacraments, which require valid matter and form, so also is the case with the Eucharist. The form for the sacrament of the Eucharist is the formula of consecration, which must be pronounced by a man duly ordained to the priesthood or episcopacy. The matter for this sacrament of the altar is bread, just as Our Lord used bread at the Last Supper: "Now as they were eating Jesus took bread, and blessed, and broke it and gave it to the disciples and said, 'Take, eat; this is my body' " (Mt 26:26ff.). This the Church has continued to

do until this day and will do so until the end of time.

The altar bread which is licit and valid in the Latin Rite is unleavened bread made only with wheat and water. In the Eastern Rites it is the same but leavened. Thus we read in the *General Instruction of the Roman Missal*: "According to the tradition of the Church as a whole, wheat bread must be used for the Eucharistic celebration, unleavened according to the tradition of the Latin Church" (n. 282). Likewise, the valid matter for the consecration of the cup must be pure wine made from grapes: "The wine for the Eucharistic celebration must be made from grapes (Lk 22:18), natural and unadulterated — that is, not mixed with any foreign substance" (Ibid., n. 284).

Altar Cards • Memory aids introduced into the furnishing of the altar in the sixteenth century. There were normally three — one on the epistle side with the *lavabo* psalm for the washing of the hands, a large one in the middle with parts of the Ordinary, including the Gloria, the Credo, the Offertory and the Words of Institution, and one on the Gospel side with the Last Gospel (the Prologue of St. John). They were often highly decorative but are no longer needed in the present liturgy.

Altar Cloths • Since the early days of the Church the Eucharistic Sacrifice has been the central act of her life and worship, as well as the reason for her existence; thus the altar was always regarded with the highest respect, as a symbol of Christ and the place where the Sacrifice was re-presented. Among the marks of respect for both the Sacrificial Banquet in which Christ Our Lord is received and for the altar, the use of lighted lamps and eventually of candles as well as cloth coverings came into use very early. Thus with the passage of time, altar coverings made of precious materials such as damask and brocade, which were the ancestors of our *antependium*, were put over the altar and left there permanently. Over these were placed linen or hemp cloths, which at first were put on only for use during the Mass but by the seventh century were also left permanently on the altar. As such, until recently it was required for at least three linen cloths to be placed over the altar. The present legislation does not abrogate this custom but requires only one cloth. The material to be used may be linen or hemp, as has been used since antiquity — and which is still preferred for its beauty and durability — or other materials which are considered noble, durable and adapted for sacred use. The color of altar cloths has always been white, and this is still the case, although no mention of it is made in the actual legislation. The Oriental Churches also use altar cloths — a lower one of rich brocade or embroidery and a white linen cloth over it (cf. *Institutio Generalis Missalis Romani*, nn. 78, 268, 288; Joseph Jungmann, *The Mass of the Roman Rite*).

Altar, Consecration of an • When a permanent altar is installed in a new or renovated church, it can be consecrated by the bishop according to the elaborate rite provided for this in the pontifical ritual. Perhaps the most striking feature of this rite is the anointing of the *mensa*, or table, with consecrated oil, thus setting the altar apart for the celebration of the Holy Sacrifice of the Mass.

Altar, Gregorian • An altar to which the privilege enjoyed by the main altar of the Roman church of St. Gregory had been extended. According to this privilege, a plenary indulgence was granted to the soul of some faithful departed person upon the celebration of Mass at the altar.

Altar Linens • When used in distinction from altar cloths, the term refers to those that are used during the Eucharist itself, in particular the corporal, the purificator, and the finger towel. These cloths are treated with special reverence after Mass, since they may have come into contact with the Sacred Host or the Precious Blood.

Altar Societies • Parish organizations, usually women's, that maintain the altar and its accessories used in the liturgy. Sacred vessels, vestments and altar cloths are especially cared for to insure the fitting liturgical worship of God.

Altar Stone • The term can refer to two things: (1) By the words "altar stone" is meant first of all the permanent or immovable table of the altar which is made of one piece or slab of solid stone and is consecrated as one with the rest of the altar. Specifically, then, it is the *mensa altaris* upon which is celebrated the Mass. Since ancient times, in order for an altar to be consecrated (something usually done along with the church in which it was found), it must always be made of stone. This usually consists of three main parts. First is the so-called "altar stone," the *tabula* or *mensa*, one solid slab which at one time was only about three or four square feet but in later times became rectangular and even twelve or more feet in width. This rests and is cemented on the lower part or base of the altar, the *stipes*, *basis* or *titulus*, which is also fashioned out of stone. Finally there is the sepulchre, *sepulchrum*, wherein are kept the relics of two martyrs. All this makes up one whole and is consecrated as such by a bishop or someone to whom he has given the faculties. It must ever remain as a whole, lest the consecration be lost.

From ancient times the altar has been made of stone not only for its durability but also because of the symbolism involved, to illustrate the relationship between the altar and Christ, who is the cornerstone of the Church (Acts 4:11) and the rock foundation (1 Cor 10:4) upon which she is built. The burying of martyrs' relics inside the altar beneath the table of the altar goes back to the early Church when the persecuted Christians celebrated Mass on the *sarcophagi* and *arcosolia* of the catacombs which formed an underground honeycomb of mazes beneath the city of Rome. So, even when the Church was able to come out of hiding, the custom was maintained for the sacred mysteries of our Faith to be celebrated over the relics of the martyrs.

Already in the time of St. Ambrose and St. Augustine, this was deemed a most important part of an altar worthy of the Sacrifice renewed on it. St. Augustine thus wrote: "Rightly do the souls of the just rest beneath the altar, since on it the Body of the Lord is immolated. Quite properly by reason of a fellowship of suffering, so to speak, do the martyrs receive burial in the place where the death of the Lord is daily commemorated" (*Inter Serm. Suppositios*). Even in the Book of Revelation, St. John describes a vision of heaven in which he "saw under the altar the souls of those who had been slain for the word of God and for the witness they had borne" (Rv 6:9). Because of this, even though for a time after the Second Vatican Council the use of an altar stone was not strictly required, the new Code of Canon Law reiterates that this venerable tradition must be conserved. Only now relics of saints who are not martyrs may also be used (cf. Canon 1237.2). It is the duty of the pastors of the churches, that is, the bishops and the parish priests, to see to it that the furnishings of each church building conform to the nobility of the sacred actions which take place therein.

(2) The second meaning of "altar stone" is that to which most people refer when they use the term. This is the "movable" altar which is a solid slab of stone about eight by ten inches and large enough for the chalice and the paten to be placed on it. Like the above, the movable altar or altar stone is consecrated, though the altar table into which it is inserted is only blessed. There are five crosses carved onto the stone, one at each corner and one in the center. In the center of the lower portion of the altar stone there is a cavity into which the relics of martyrs (or now, of other saints) are placed and sealed. The altar stone may be mortised into the top portion of a larger altar table on which Mass is celebrated. This is placed in such a way that it is nearest to the spot where the priest stands to offer the Sacrifice, so that the chalice and paten rest on it. Because the altar stone is the altar itself, it is also referred to as a "movable altar."

Missionaries and military chaplains often use an altar stone when they have to celebrate Mass outside a sacred place. Another solution to this is the use of a Greek or Russian *antimensium* which is consecrated by an Oriental Rite bishop and contains relics of the martyrs. This type of "altar," however, is made out of cloth on which an icon of the deposition of Christ from the cross is depicted. The relics are sewn into a little pouch that lies between the two layers of the *antimensium*. It is usually shaped and folded like a corporal and is placed beneath the altar cloths, so that the chalice and paten lie over it. In former times special faculties were needed in order to use this. Now, however, the Congregation for Oriental Rites gives these to priests who request them and have legitimate use for a portable altar (cf. Canons 1235-1239; *Institutio Generalis Missalis Romani*, nn. 261-263, 265-266).

Altar, Stripping of the • In the Roman Rite before 1970, the altar was formally stripped by the priest and assistants on Holy Thursday, while part of Psalm 22 ("My God, my God, why hast thou forsaken me?") was chanted. In the old Dominican Rite, the altars were washed on the same day with water and a brush made of palms from Palm Sunday while appropriate responsories were chanted.

The Missal of Pope Paul VI directs that the altar be stripped without ceremony after the Mass of the Lord's Supper on Holy Thursday. A cloth is placed on the altar for Holy Communion on Good Friday, then removed immediately after the liturgical service.

Ambo • The *General Instruction of the Roman Missal* equates the ambo with the lectern from which the Scriptures are proclaimed. It states: "As a rule, the lectern or ambo should be stationary, not simply a movable stand. In keeping with the structure of each church, it must be so placed that the ministers may be easily seen and heard by the faithful. The readings, responsorial psalm, and the Easter Proclamation [*Exsultet*] are proclaimed from the lectern; it may also be used for the homily and general intercessions (prayer of the faithful)" (n. 272).

Ambrosian Chant • Simple chant in the iambic dimeter style. These melodies were composed by St. Ambrose or his followers for use in the Ambrosian or Milanese Rite. Over the centuries many of the rhythmic values of the chants have been lost. In recent years the syllabic form of these chants has been adapted to the vernacular with some success. The Ambrosian chants themselves were part of the development of Gregorian chant.

Ambrosian Hymnography (also Ambrosiani) • Hymns composed by St. Ambrose or one of his followers in a classical style yet readily accepted by the populace of his own day. The hymns presented Christian beliefs to those who were being evangelized by them. They also created a new school of hymnody.

Ambrosian Liturgy • The non-Roman Western liturgy celebrated from the time of St. Ambrose to the present in the diocese of Milan (and through many centuries in much of northern Italy). A major theological influence on this liturgical family was its anti-Arianism reflected in its carefully crafted prayers which are remarkably Christocentric. Among the particular characteristics of this liturgy was its own style and notation for chant (called "Ambrosian chant").

In the early Middle Ages the Mass celebrated in Milan would have been as follows: Entrance (no psalm), *Kyrie*, Prayer (*oratio super populum*), Reading from Prophets, Psalm, Epistle, Alleluia, Gospel, Homily, Dismissal of Catechumens, *Kyrie* and post-Gospel antiphon, *Oratio super sidonem*, Offertory procession, Proper Preface and *Sanctus*, Invariable Canon, Fraction and Mingling of consecrated bread and wine, Lord's prayer and embolism, Communion, *Oratio post communionem*, *Kyrie* and dismissal.

After the reform of the Liturgy of Vatican II, the diocese of Milan published its own Ambrosian Missal containing some differences from the Roman Rite, an example of which is the ceremony of lighting lamps at a "vigil Mass" for Sunday celebrated on Saturday evening, recalling the custom of lamp-lighting at Vespers. One contribution of the Ambrosian Liturgy to the present Roman Rite is the emphasis on Mary and Joseph on the Fourth (last) Sunday of Advent before Christmas.

Ambry: See **Aumbry**

Ambulatory • The extension of the aisles of the choir, or presbytery, of a church around the back of the high or main altar. It facilitates the path of some processions as well as the movement of servers from one side of the altar to another during liturgical ceremonies without being a distraction to the congregation. In ancient Christian architecture the side aisles or galleries of a basilica were also called ambulatories. This name may also be given to the covered galleries between buildings, usually Church buildings, as well as to the sides of a cloister.

Amen • A Hebrew word signifying assent and affirmation: "Certainly," "Truly," but also, "So be it," and even "I do believe."

In the Old Testament the Israelites used the word to express their willingness to accept and abide by the Commandments of God (cf. Dt 27:15-26), and as an emphasis in praise or worship (cf. Ps 72:19).

In the New Testament, the word is transliterated into the equivalent Greek characters. In the Gospels it is doubled ("Amen, amen, I say to you"), to signify the particular solemnity with which an assertion of Jesus is to be taken. In the epistles, "amen" appears as an affirmation of thanksgiving or praise (cf. 1 Cor 14:16). As an exclamatory affirmation of faith in the fulfillment of God's promises and the ultimate victory of Christ and His people, the word is used continually in the Book of Revelation (the Apocalypse); and, in Revelation 3:14, Christ Himself is called the "Amen."

In the Church's Liturgy, especially in the revised rites of the Second Vatican Council, "Amen" figures prominently as a response indicating the assembly's assent. Pope Benedict XIV had indicated it to be such when added to the text of a Creed, and as such it occurs throughout the Order of Mass of the Roman Rite. It is the people's conclusion to each of the principal prayers offered in their name by the celebrant: the

Opening Prayer, Prayer over the Gifts and the Prayer after Communion. One of the most important uses of "Amen" occurs at the conclusion of the Eucharistic Prayer, where the preferred form of the response is sung. In this instance, it is customarily sung several times and even referred to popularly as "the Great Amen." A second important occurrence of "Amen" in the Order of Mass is the affirmation of faith in the Real Presence of Christ under the Eucharistic Species. As the consecrated Host is presented with the statement "The Body of Christ," the communicant makes a Profession of Faith by responding, "Amen." The same invitation and response ("The Blood of Christ." "Amen.") is to take place when Communion is administered under both species.

For further reading: Bruce Chilton, "Amen," *Anchor Bible Dictionary*, 1:184-186.

Amendment, Purpose of • On the part of the penitent in the sacrament of Penance, the purpose of amendment is the firm resolution not to sin again. This resolution is required for the validity of the sacrament. Usually, it is implicit in the act of sincere contrition that is essential to a true confession, but it can be made explicit, particularly in regard to some specific sin that has been the subject of confession.

American Board of Catholic Missions • An official standing committee of the National Conference of Catholic Bishops which annually makes grants to dioceses; religious institutes; and national, regional and interdiocesan Catholic organizations in the United States and its dependencies. Funds are derived from two sources: forty percent of the receipts of the October Mission Sunday Collection and forty percent of the membership receipts of the Propagation of the Faith Society. The perpetual memberships go entirely to the Society for the Propagation of the Faith to be used for foreign missions. The purpose of the ABCM is to make the Church present where it is absent and to strengthen it where it is weak.

American Cassinese Congregation • A confederation of Benedictine abbeys in the United States and Canada, dating from the first Benedictine abbey — St. Vincent Archabbey in Latrobe, Pa., founded in the U.S. in 1846 by Father Boniface Wimmer, O.S.B., in order to serve the growing German immigrant population here. Among the congregation's more than twenty abbeys and priories, the best known are St. John's, Collegeville, Minnesota, founded in 1856, and St. Anselm's, Manchester, New Hampshire, founded in 1889.

American Protective Association • A society dedicated to the exclusion of Catholics from public office, the A.P.A. attained notoriety in the late nineteenth century when it tried and failed to block the nomination of William McKinley. It attacked Catholicism through tactics such as the circulation of bogus documents and other slanders.

Americanism • A movement within the Catholic Church in the United States in the late nineteenth century which posited a unique compatibility between Catholicism and American values and advances. Led by prelates such as Archbishop John Ireland of St. Paul, Bishop John Keane of Richmond and Monsignor Dennis O'Connell, the rector of the North American College in Rome, this school of thought held that the Catholic Church in the United States was in a providential position to

Amice

guide the Church universal into an accommodation with the modern age. Because it stressed an openness to contemporary social movements, and a defense of the separation of Church and state, it was considered a "liberal" cause.

In the zeal of the proponents to "Americanize" the Church, they upset more conservative-minded Catholics, especially in their de-emphasis of both parochial schools and ethnic consciousness. Their intellectual allies in Europe saw this Americanism as providing the model for renewal of the continental Church, especially in France, and for a time even Pope Leo XIII seemed to endorse some of their initiatives. When a biography of the founder of the Paulists, Father Isaac Hecker, which held him up as the "patron saint" of Americanism, caused controversy in France, Pope Leo XIII sent the American hierarchy a letter entitled *Testem Benevolentiae*, which condemned certain subjectivist inclinations noted in Hecker's spirituality. Although spokesmen such as Ireland, Keane, and even James Cardinal Gibbons of Baltimore insisted that such ideas popular in Europe were misinterpretations of their thinking, this apostolic letter removed Americanism as any coherent, organized force in the Catholic life of the United States.

Amice • A rectangular piece of linen cloth with long strips of linen attached at two corners, worn under the alb at liturgical functions by the priest and other ministers of the altar, in order to cover the other clerical garb underneath the sacred vestments.

At one time the amice was worn over the

alb and over the head as a cowl and then lowered before or during the Mass after the stole and chasuble were put on. By the eighth and ninth centuries its use was pretty much universalized as is testified by the Roman Ordines or liturgical books of the period. Though medieval writers gave it various and sundry meanings, the prayer which is used (optional today) when the minister dons it calls it "the helmet of salvation." Thus it became not only the scarf which protected the neck and head from the draft and cold of many ancient churches, but that which protected the wearer from the incursion of the Devil.

Other names for the amice which have been used at one time or another include *humerale, superhumerale, anaboladium* and *anabolagium.* During the Middle Ages and up to the early Renaissance, amices were also decorated with embroideries. Today all that remains of this is an occasional embroidery in the middle section of the amice, such as a cross or an image or liturgical symbol of Our Lord or Our Lady. The use of the amice is now optional if the alb is made in such a way that the minister's street clothing is concealed.

Amish • Followers of Jakob Ammann, who broke away from the Mennonites in Switzerland in the latter part of the seventeenth century. They shared fundamental Mennonite beliefs, but desired a more strict separation from the surrounding culture and a more uncompromising enforcement of "shunning" (avoidance of those excommunicated). In the eighteenth century, a large number of Amish migrated to America where they formed communities in Pennsylvania, Ohio, Indiana and elsewhere. The so-called "Pennsylvania Dutch" customs and language, which the Amish in Pennsylvania have retained, are a distinctive mark of their communities.

Ammonian Sections • Originally thought to be the work of Ammonius Saccas (d. A.D. 242) but now recognized to be more probably devised by Eusebius of Caesarea (d. 340), the Ammonian Sections are divisions of the texts of the four Gospels. These divisions are found in the margins of all Greek and Latin manuscripts and were designed to display the harmony of the Gospels.

Amos, Book of • The oldest book of the prophetical literature, the Book of Amos dates from the eighth century B.C. It bears a very special importance, being the first collection of prophetic preaching to find a place in the Old Testament as a separate book. There were prophets in Israel from the earliest time (e.g., Elijah, Nathan), but only bits and pieces of their utterances found their way into the Old Testament.

Amos was a shepherd and a trimmer of sycamore trees in the area of Tekoa, a village five miles south of Bethlehem. He appears to have been a layman without any special training for religious ministry. God abruptly took him from following the flock (7:15). He began his prophetic mission in the north, in Bethel and Samaria. From indications found at the beginning of the book (1:1), his activity could be dated roughly between 760 and 750 B.C.

It cannot be determined with certainty whether Amos himself put together written documents containing his oracles. However, the exceptionally good condition of the text invites the conclusion that either Amos himself or his secretary put his preaching into writing. Although Amos announces most insistently the judgment that awaits Israel for its unrepented sin, he does not foreclose all hope for a brighter future beyond the impending doom.

Specifically, Amos indicts the attitudes of those people in Israel who had grown affluent during a period marked by freedom from enemy attack. Wealth was being amassed by the leaders and a privileged few to the detriment of the poor. Amos would not let the consciences of the rich rest easy. He reminded the people that because of the covenant between God and Israel, God was more exacting in what He required of Israel than in what He demanded of other peoples: "You only have I known of all the families of the earth, therefore, I will punish you. . ." (3:2).

For further reading: Francis I. Anderson and David Noel Freedman, *Amos*, Anchor Bible Reference Library (Doubleday, 1989); Michael L. Barre, "Amos," *New Jerome Biblical Commentary*, 209-216; Bruce E. Willoughby, "Amos," *Anchor Bible Dictionary*, 1:203-212.

Amovability • Under the 1917 Code of Canon Law, the term amovability referred to the ability of the diocesan bishop to remove a person from an ecclesiastical office with a minimum of procedural delay (cf. 1917 Canon 192). It was tantamount to the modern concept of free removal from office as practiced under the 1983 Code. It did not imply that the bishop could behave arbitrarily in such matters, but clearly worked to give the bishop a freer hand in the governance of his diocese. It should be contrasted with the concept of Irremovability of Pastors, an institution which, notably, has been dropped from the 1983 Code.

Ampulla • Literally, a little vessel with a small neck and two handles (from the diminutive form of the Greek *ampho-phero*, "to carry by both"). In the *Ritus Servandus* (or "Rite to be Observed") in the Roman Missal promulgated by St. Pius V, *ampullae* generally referred to the wine and water cruets, *ampule* to the oil stocks. The Order of Mass revised after the Second Vatican Council speaks of the *urceolus*, or pitcher, seeming to indicate a preference for a somewhat larger vessel that will be more visible when presented by the faithful at the Preparation of the Gifts. In the singular, the word *ampulla* denotes any vessel used to store or carry holy oil or water blessed in honor of a saint or taken from a holy well or miraculous spring. In some contexts, the word was applied to phials containing the blood of a martyr.

Amula • In the early Church, a vessel for the Eucharistic wine that was presented by the people.

Amulet • A charm, carrying some inscription, that is worn in order to protect the wearer from evil or to aid in some endeavor. Anyone who seriously credits the power of amulets sins against the virtue of religion and the First Commandment (cf. *Catechism of the Catholic Church*, nn. 2110-2117).

Anabaptism • As its name suggests, Anabaptism is a heresy which rejects certain Church teaching on Baptism, particularly the appropriateness of infant Baptism. Although it is derived from Lutheranism, there is evidence that neither Luther (nor Calvin nor Zwingli) were at ease with all Anabaptist tenets. Since its appearance in Saxony in 1524, Anabaptism has also taught an absolute separation of Church and state and stressed an extremely simple style of life. The best-known example of Anabaptism in the United States is found among the Mennonites.

Anagni • An ancient city of central Italy where, in 1303, Pope Boniface VIII was held prisoner by the troops of Guillaume de Nogaret, who had been sent by Philip IV of France, in defiance of Boniface's claim to universal papal hegemony. Though the citizens of this city succeeded in freeing the Pope, the shock hastened his death and the humiliation caused by this "Crime of Anagni" has come to symbolize the decline in the power of the medieval papacy.

Anagnostes • From the Greek for "a reader." The term designates the individual who publicly reads or chants the lessons prescribed at liturgical services in the Byzantine Church. This function is usually fulfilled by the cantor. A reader may also receive ordination to this ministry. The lectorate, after tonsure, is the first step to the priesthood in the sequence of Holy Orders in the Byzantine Church.

Anagogical Sense • The adjective is from the Greek word *anago*, which means "I raise or lead up." It refers to that aspect of the spiritual sense in Scripture which foreshadows or in other ways anticipates what the Church will be/is now like in heaven. The anagogical sense is distinguishable from the allegorical sense.

Allegorical: When the subject matter of a scriptural text communicates truth at the level of Catholic belief, that truth is said to be allegorical *if* the Old Testament type prefigures the antitype found in the Church. For example, the exodus of God's people from Egypt and so their exodus from slavery and oppression is the type which prepares for our Exodus from sin and its oppression by means of sacramental Baptism. Here we read the Old Testament Book of Exodus allegorically and Christocentrically with reference to Baptism.

Anagogical: When a text from either the Old Testament or the New Testament communicates a truth about the Church triumphant, that is, in heaven, then we have the anagogical sense of Scripture. For example, at Galatians 4:26 Paul refers to the earthly city of Jerusalem as the heavenly city which is our mother. Here we have the anagogical anticipation of the heavenly reality.

Analecta • The Latin term for anthologies of selected texts drawn from other sources, such as the writings of Church Fathers. In its original sense, the term designated the servant who collected the crumbs left after a meal. In its common literary sense, it appears as the title of journals, serials or other collections.

Analogy • The term "analogy" has two important meanings in Catholic tradition. In the first place, Catholic theology speaks of the "analogy of faith" — and, more recently, of the "hierarchy of doctrines" — in order to make the important point that the meaning of an individual doctrine or passage of Scripture can be properly understood only within the total context of the Faith. A second sense of the term "analogy" refers to the Catholic understanding of the force of assertions about God, like "God is good" and "God is faithful."

In this second sense, "analogy" refers to a philosophical and theological account of the possibility that we can actually make true statements about God even though He surpasses our knowledge and experience. Because God completely transcends the sense perception and direct knowledge of created persons, our judgments that He is good, faithful, merciful and so on cannot encompass or comprehend what it means for God to be good, faithful and merciful. God does not possess attributes in the same way that creatures do. In God, goodness, faithfulness, mercy and so on are nothing other than God.

Since God so utterly surpasses human knowledge and discourse, some thinkers have argued that the most appropriate way for human beings to grasp His being is simply by remaining silent, or by denying imperfections in Him, or by employing metaphors. But, while this so-called "negative" or apophantic way certainly has its place, it has also been recognized as inadequate: we do, after all, have many true things to know and teach about God. And, while it is true that we often use metaphors in speaking about God, there are many occasions when we seem to be speaking literally about Him. We speak metaphorically when we say, for example, that God is a rock, but literally when we say that we mean by this that God is faithful.

There is a conviction in Catholic tradition that in our knowledge of God and discourse about Him we can avoid both the mistake of thinking that we can know nothing about God at all (agnosticism) and the mistake of thinking that we can know God as easily as we can know any object in our ordinary experience (rationalism). According to Catholic theology, one way of avoiding these two mistakes is to provide an account of how we can know God truly and yet never fully comprehend His mystery. "Analogy" is the name that has been given to this account.

Scripture itself furnishes the warrant for analogy: "All men who were ignorant of God were foolish by nature; and they were unable from the good things that are seen to know him who exists, nor did they recognize the craftsman while paying heed to his works" (Wis 13:1). In other words, we grasp something of the truth of God and express it in words because the basis of our knowledge and discourse are the very effects of God's causality that we see all around us. The goodness, faithfulness and mercy of which we have direct experience are caused by God and thus, in an imperfect but real way, reflect His very being. The created order is not opaque, but translucent: The perfections of the creaturely world direct the human heart and mind to the uncreated perfection which is God Himself. It is in this sense that all our talk about God is analogous. Without ever fully comprehending God's being, we nonetheless can speak truly about Him because the concepts we use in our discourse draw upon our experience of the world He created and sustains.

Anamnesis • This liturgical term comes directly from the Greek *anamnesis*, which means "remembrance," "commemoration" or "memorial." In the Latin Rite, this term applies to the section of the Eucharistic Prayer following the institution narrative and consecration. In the Roman Canon this text begins with the words *Unde et memores* ("Mindful then of. . ."). In the Latin Rite Liturgy this prayer has also been referred to as the *post pridie* or the *post secreta*.

The *General Instruction of the Roman Missal* states that the memorial section of the Eucharistic Prayer is preserved "in fulfillment of the command received from Christ through the apostles . . . [to keep Christ's] memorial by recalling especially His passion, resurrection and ascension" (n. 55).

In this prayer the Church recalls the death, resurrection and glorious ascension into heaven of Jesus. In other words, it is a memorial of the divine mysteries associated with the redemptive act of Christ which is mystically reenacted in the Divine Liturgy of the Eucharist. This is not done so much in a way of recalling or remembering something past but of actually rendering the said action present which takes place at every celebration of the Holy Eucharist.

Ananias • In the New Testament, the Acts of the Apostles identifies three persons by this name, which is a transliteration of the Hebrew name Hananiah (meaning "God is merciful"). The first is an Ananias married to a woman named Sapphira, who sold a piece of property and who, with his wife's knowledge, withheld some of the proceeds and contributed only a part of the proceeds to the Church. For this violation of the complete sharing of goods that characterized the earliest Christian community in Jerusalem, Peter rebuked him sternly, "Ananias, why has Satan filled your heart to lie to the Holy Spirit and to keep back part of the proceeds of the land?" (Acts 5:4). When Ananias heard these words, he fell down dead, and his death brought fear on those who heard of the incident.

The second figure in the Acts of the Apostles who bears the name Ananias is a Jewish Christian from Damascus, described in Acts 22:12 as "a devout man according to the law, well spoken of by all the Jews who lived there." It was to this Ananias that the Lord appeared in a vision, a vision in which he was commanded to "go to the street called Straight and inquire in the house of Judas for a man of Tarsus named Saul" (Acts 9:11), that is, Paul, who is to become the Apostle to the Gentiles. Obeying the command he received in the vision, Ananias went, found Paul and imposed hands on him. At that very moment Paul regained his sight, which he had lost during his experience of the risen Lord on the road to Damascus. Upon regaining his sight, Paul rose, received Baptism, took food and was strengthened (Acts 9:18-19). That sequence of events, which can be described as "enlightenment," mirrors the sequence of the sacraments of Christian initiation, the sacraments by which believers receive the light of Christ.

The third figure named Ananias in the Acts of the Apostles is the man who served as high priest during the reigns of the Roman emperors Claudius and Nero. St. Paul also crossed the path of this Ananias. After his arrest by the Roman authorities for causing a disturbance in the Temple, Paul was brought before Ananias for questioning. After being struck on the mouth by the attendants upon orders from Ananias, Paul insulted the high priest, threatening, "God shall strike you, you whitewashed wall!" (Acts 23:3). In Acts 24:1, the high priest Ananias was among those who proffered charges against Paul before Felix, the Roman governor. In addition to what is known about the high priest Ananias from the Acts of the Apostles, the Jewish historian Josephus provides further information about him. For example, in his *Jewish Antiquities* (20, 6, 2) Josephus reports that Quadratus, the Roman governor of Syria, sent Ananias to Rome in chains as a result of violence between Jews and Samaritans. Though he was subsequently released and returned to his position, he died at the hands of Zealots during the rebellion against Rome (*Jewish War* 2, 441-442).

For further reading: Robert F. O'Toole, "Ananias," *Anchor Bible Dictionary*, 1:224-225.

Anaphora • This term, which comes from the Byzantine or Oriental Rites, is the Greek and liturgical terminology for what is known in the West or Latin Rite as the Prayer of Offering or *oblatio*, which refers to the Canon of the Mass or Eucharistic Prayer, as it is called now in the revised Roman Missal of Pope Paul VI. At present in the Roman Rite in the United States, there are nine Eucharistic Prayers approved for use. The first is the Roman Canon; the next three were approved for universal use after Vatican II. Subsequently, three were introduced for Masses with children and two for Masses focused more specifically on reconciliation. Additional newly composed Eucharistic Prayers have been approved for use in various episcopal conferences, a chief example of which is often termed the "Swiss synod" prayer. It was composed for use initially in Switzerland and is now commonly used throughout Europe in the various vernacular languages. The constitutive elements of the anaphora as listed and described in the *General Instruction of the Roman Missal* (n. 55) are Thanksgiving, Acclamation, Epiclesis, Institution Narrative and Consecration, Anamnesis, Offering, Intercessions, Final Doxology.

Anastasis • The Greek word for "resurrection," this term was used interchangeably to refer to the Church of the Holy Sepulchre in Jerusalem, especially by Oriental Rite Catholics or Orthodox Christians.

Anathema • The excommunication of an individual for either apostasy, sin or heresy. St. Paul used this term for those who are separated from the Christian community for sins such as teaching a Gospel other than his or for not loving the Lord (cf. 1 Cor 5:5). In the post-Apostolic Church, it was used frequently against heretics. An anathema is different from excommunication for, according to Gratian, the latter excluded one only from the sacraments while anathema signified total separation from the Faith. Anathema was abolished after the Second Vatican Council. From the Greek *anatithenai*, meaning to set up, dedicate; a thing devoted to evil.

Anchor • A heavily weighted "bent arm" (Greek *agake*), at one time a stone, later a metal weight, which was attached to a cable and submerged into water to stabilize a vessel. In Paul's sea voyage to Rome (Acts 27:29-30, 40), his ship is said to have put down four anchors just off the coast of Malta. In Hebrews 6:19, the theological virtue of "hope" is said to be the "anchor of the soul."

Anchor-Cross • The anchor has always been a symbol or sign of safety, given its importance and function in navigation. The author of the Epistle to the Hebrews mentions the anchor in relation to the virtue of hope and its firmness and surety (cf. Heb 6:19-20). The early Christians combined the symbol of the anchor with that of the cross which, for a follower of Christ, is the hope of salvation, of all true safety. This symbol is to be found carved on the tombs of early Christians in the catacombs of Rome, especially those of Sts. Priscilla, Domitilla and Calixtus, from the second and third centuries. It was used to symbolize the hope that the deceased buried there had reached the port of eternal salvation or heaven.

Though its use disappeared for centuries, it came back into vogue during the Renaissance and Baroque periods. It is often associated with a patron saint of seamen, e.g., St. Nicholas. However, its principal significance is that of hope in eternal salvation.

Anchorhold • The cell or dwelling of an anchorite, who was enclosed within the anchorhold by the bishop. In the later Middle Ages this was sometimes attached to parish churches.

Anchorite • An anchorite or anchoress is a man or woman who practices a most severe withdrawal from the world in order to offer continuous prayer and sacrifice. Such persons were early precursors of the monastic life in the ancient Church, locating themselves particularly in the deserts of Egypt. Today, certain hermits in the Camaldolese or Carthusian orders may be considered their modern equivalents.

Ancient of Days • This divine title occurs in the Old Testament Book of Daniel. In the first of that book's apocalyptic visions, the seer Daniel describes a scene in which "thrones were placed and one that was ancient of days took his seat; his raiment was white as snow, and the hair of his head like pure wool; his throne was fiery flames, its wheels burning fire" (Dn 7:9). Daniel goes on to say that "with the clouds of heaven there came one like a son of man and he came to the Ancient of Days and was presented before him" (Dn 7:13).

The language of this theophany — a visual manifestation of God — draws on symbols and imagery common in ancient Israel and in the surrounding cultures, adapting them to serve as expressions of Israel's faith. For example, the epithet "father of years" was applied to the Canaanite god ʿEl. We find somewhat similar language in the Targum of Job found in Cave 11 at Qumran: "God is great, and his many days we do not know; the number of his years is endless."

For further reading: John J. Collins, *The Book of Daniel*, 274-302, Hermeneia (Fortress Press, 1993).

Andrew, St. • One of the Apostles, and the brother of St. Peter, with whom he is often associated in the Gospels. Although not one of the inner group of three, several incidents concerning him are recorded (e.g., Jn 1:35-42; Mt 4:18-20). According to tradition, he was crucified on an X-shaped cross. His feast is November 30, and since c. 750 he has been venerated as the patron saint of Scotland.

Angel • Purely spiritual or bodiless persons (Mt 22:30), some of whom behold the face of God and thus are in bliss (Mt 18:10). These spiritual beings comprise the celestial court and are called angels (from the Greek for "messenger") because, according to the Bible, they carry out missions at God's command. In order to complete these missions, they can at times assume bodily form. According to the Bible, their missions are sometimes of great importance — for example, the announcement of Christ's coming and birth (Lk 1:26; 2:9-14). Like us, the angels are the objects of God's grace and love. But because, unlike us, they are non-bodily creatures, their response to God's love did not require time and reflection to grow and mature. As soon as they were created and received grace, they had the opportunity to respond to God's love and thus be welcomed into bliss. While many did so, some did not.

Hence, there is also a group of purely spiritual beings — called fallen angels or demons — who, perhaps because of pride, did not return God's love. God did not destroy the fallen angels, but permits them a limited scope of activity. The condition of these two divisions of angels is permanent or fixed: No creature can turn away from the perfect good of the beatific vision once he has come to enjoy it, and no additional reflection could change the mind of a purely spiritual being who has turned away from God's love.

Perhaps the most significant continuing activity of the good angels is to be the agents of God's particular providence for humankind. Thus, the Church teaches that every human being possesses a guardian angel. On the basis of references to them in the Bible, angels are traditionally ranked in a so-called celestial hierarchy of nine orders: seraphim, cherubim, thrones, dominions, virtues, powers, principalities, archangels and angels.

Angel, Guardian: See **Guardian Angels**

Angels, Names of the • Michael, Raphael and Gabriel are the only angels mentioned by name in the Bible. Uriel and Jeremiel are the names of angels appearing in Jewish apocrypha. By tradition, Raphael and Gabriel are accorded the rank of archangel, along with Michael (Jude 9).

Angelic Salutation: See **Ave Maria**

Angel-Lights • In Church architecture, small sections of glass interspersed in the larger arch-patterns of church windows.

Angels, Evil: See **Devil and Evil Spirits**

Angels of the Churches • In the Book of Revelation, the risen Jesus orders John to write messages to the "angels" of each of the seven Churches: the angel of the Church of Ephesus (2:1), of Smyrna (2:8), of Pergamum (2:12), of Thyatira (2:18), of Sardis (3:1), of Philadelphia (3:7) and of Laodicea (3:14). These angels may be the supernatural guardians entrusted with the task of watching over each of the churches. The reference to the "angels of the churches" may also designate the human leaders of the individual churches, leaders who serve as authorized messengers who bring the word of Christ to the churches under their vigilant care.

For further reading: Duane F. Watson, "Angels of the Seven Churches," *Anchor Bible Dictionary*, 1:255.

Angelus • This term, which draws its name from the first word of the prayer in the Latin version, is used to denote the prayer which for centuries has been recited by the Church three times a day to commemorate the mystery of the Incarnation of the eternal Word in the womb of the Blessed Virgin Mary. Indeed, it is the custom to recite this prayer at six in the morning, at noon and at six in the evening.

The first recitation probably developed in the monasteries and surrounding areas when the bell for the morning office of Prime was rung. The noon recitation originated principally from the custom of ringing the church bells at noon on Fridays to commemorate the crucifixion of Our Lord as well as the ringing of the bells for the office of Sext, or Midday Prayer. This tolling of the bells in honor of Christ's passion was accompanied by three Hail Marys, to which were eventually added the responsories which are recited to this day (cf. below). This custom was extended to every day of the week by Pope Calixtus III in 1465, when he invited all Catholics to pray for victory against the threatening Turks. The evening *Angelus* goes back to the ringing of church bells in the evening, perhaps as a curfew.

Pope Gregory IX is said to have encouraged this prayer on behalf of the Crusades. The practice was widened by the spread of the Franciscans, who have always had a great devotion to the sacred Humanity of Christ. Already in 1318 the practice was indulged by Pope John XXII. By the sixteenth century the recitation of the prayer three times a day was unified and received great endorsements and indulgences from the Popes. In modern times it has been the custom for the Holy Father to come out and lead in the recitation of the *Angelus* from the window of his study in the apostolic palace on Sundays and other solemnities. This is usually accompanied by some exhortation or allocution beforehand on the part of the Pontiff and is followed by his apostolic blessing. It is always an occasion marked by great joy and festivity on the part of the faithful of Rome, as well as the thousands of pilgrims who also attend from all over the globe.

The ringing of the bells follows a certain order, for they are struck three times at each invocation and end with nine strokes for the recitation of the final prayer. The *Angelus* is usually recited while kneeling except for Sundays and holy days, when it is said standing with a genuflection at the third versicle. At Eastertime the Marian antiphon *Regina Caeli* is recited instead of the *Angelus*, always standing.

The prayer of the *Angelus* is as follows:

Leader: The Angel of the Lord announced unto Mary.

Response: And she conceived by the Holy Spirit.

Hail Mary. . .

Leader: Behold the handmaid of the Lord.

Response: Be it done unto me according to Thy word.

Hail Mary. . .

Leader: And the Word was made flesh.

Response: And dwelt among us.

Hail Mary. . .

Leader: Let us pray. Pour forth, we beg Thee, O Lord, Thy grace into our hearts: that we to whom the Incarnation of Christ Thy Son was made known by the message of an Angel, may by His Passion and Cross be brought to the glory of His Resurrection. Through the same Christ our Lord. Amen.

Anger • One of the seven capital sins. "Let every man be quick to hear, slow to speak, slow to anger, for the anger of man does not work the righteousness of God" (Jas 1:19-20). The contrary virtues to anger are peacefulness and meekness. Feeling angry at frustrations is perfectly normal and not sinful, nor is truly righteous anger at the sins of oneself and others. What makes anger sinful is when it is out of proportion to the cause, such as in cursing slow drivers or long, cold, resentful brooding; when it becomes uncontrolled, as in red rages; or harmful, as in battering.

For further reading: *Catechism of the Catholic Church*, nn. 1765, 1866, 2259, 2262, 2302.

Anglican, Anglicanism • The Anglican Church is not synonymous with "The Church of England" but is an organization of many member churches which form the worldwide Anglican Communion. In places where the British Empire once held sway, the Anglican Church was formerly the established church. The Anglican Church of Canada, the Anglican Church of Hong Kong and the Anglican Church of South Africa are examples. Today, the Anglican Church is still the state or government-supported Church in England and is popularly referred to as "The C of E" (The Church of England). The separation from the Roman Catholic Church began in the sixteenth century, when King Henry VIII declared himself head of the church and rejected papal claims to universal spiritual jurisdiction.

Anglican doctrine has always been comprehensive, for historical reasons. After the time of Henry VIII, doctrine swayed back and forth between Calvinistic positions and more moderate, even Catholic ones. The Book of Common Prayer, or Prayer Book, has always been a focus for Anglican worship and it underwent various revisions in the sixteenth century and in the twentieth century. Traditionalist Anglicans in the twentieth century prefer the 1928 version, opposing emendations brought in during the 1960s. This is perhaps more for the question of language than for the content. The official version for the United States was adopted in 1979.

The British monarch no longer has supreme authority as such in spiritual matters in the Anglican Church. The monarch and parliament have a legal relationship of governorship over the church in the United Kingdom. Supreme authority is to be found in the General Synod of the Church. The Archbishop of Canterbury is the nominal or symbolic head of the Anglican Churches, even though he has no power to enforce binding doctrine or moral practice.

After the American Revolution, the church became known as the Protestant Episcopal Church in the United States of America (PECUSA), later simplified by dropping the word "Protestant" (ECUSA). However, as late as 1990 the "President's church" in Washington, D.C., St. John's, continued to show the words "Protestant Episcopal" on its outdoor advertisement.

Symbolically, the Oxford Movement began July 14, 1833. This intellectual "renaissance" produced ferment in the Anglican Church. Some Anglicans, such as John Henry Newman, joined the Roman Catholic Church as a result. Others, notably Edward Pusey and John Keble, remained Anglicans and were content with the Branch Theory. This was an ecclesiology which held that there were equal sister churches — Roman, Greek and English — which could all be considered "Catholic." The divisions since 1054 were not regarded as touching the essence of catholicity. From the Oxford Movement's influence there finally crystallized three principal schools of thought within Anglicanism. They are still popularly known as the "high," the "low," and the "broad" churches. The high church was originally an emphasis on the authority of the bishop and the church as an institution; later, this group was identified with solemn ritual and pageantry. The low church was evangelical and its theological roots were Calvinistic. The broad church became a kind of vague description for Anglicans who were middle-of-the-road and considered themselves rather all-embracing and tolerant.

Perhaps the most famous Anglican apologist of our time was Clive Staples Lewis, who died November 22, 1963. His defense of Christianity continues to influence the English-speaking world. But the cultural climate which developed after his death proved devastating to Anglicanism in England and North America, especially in terms of moral erosion. Already in 1930 the Lambeth Conference of Anglican bishops had approved of artificial contraception within Christian marriage. Sixty years later, some Anglican clergy were openly espousing sterilization, abortion, divorce, euthanasia and homosexuality.

The ordination of women recently has been perhaps the most controversial issue in the Anglican Communion. In 1975, the first women were ordained to the Episcopal priestly ministry in the United States. Later, Barbara Harris was ordained the first Episcopal female bishop as suffragan to the bishop of Massachusetts. These ordinations have caused schisms of varying proportions and ecumenical friction with the Roman Catholics and Eastern Orthodox. The Continuing Anglican Movement was formed after 1975 and other groups have reorganized themselves to try to remain Anglican without approving of the actions of the main body. One such group, the Episcopal Synod of America, was formed when two thousand persons met in Fort Worth in June of 1989. This organization was concerned about the inroads made by radical feminism into the church's liturgy and theology. The leader of the Synod, Bishop Clarence Pope of Fort Worth, Texas, was received into the Catholic Church in February, 1995. Official sources admit that in the United States alone the Episcopal Church has lost at least a quarter of a million adherents in the second half of the twentieth century. It has also been indicated that more former Roman Catholics (clergy and laity) join the Anglican Communion than vice versa.

Vitality in the Anglican Church today is evidenced principally by two facts. The "low" or evangelical church, which at times resembles Fundamentalism, has a coherent morality and a clear doctrinal program. It is thriving in the First World, though remains relatively small alongside other evangelical or fundamentalist denominations. In the Third World, the Anglican churches in the developing nations of Asia and Africa, remnants of the colonial past, are alive and prospering. Observers have noted that today there are more non-white Anglican bishops than white ones, the most famous being Archbishop Desmond Tutu of Cape Town, South Africa.

Anglican Orders • The validity of Holy Orders in the Anglican Church was a disputed question among Catholics for centuries until it was settled by Pope Leo XIII in the papal pronouncement entitled *Apostolicae Curae* (September 13, 1896). With that decree, the Pope declared that Anglican Orders were considered invalid for two basic reasons: defect in the form of the Rite of Ordination and defect in the intention of the ordaining bishop. This pronouncement is still in force.

Anglo-Catholics • The Anglo-Catholics are a small minority of the worldwide Anglican Communion. After the Oxford Movement, this party was interested in the restoration of Catholic doctrinal and devotional practices. By the end of the twentieth century, the group finds itself increasingly frustrated, especially with the ordination of female clergy (of every rank) in various member churches of the Communion. Anglo-Catholics have generally favored corporate reunion with Rome and for this reason have continued their separate identity. But a number of them have converted to the Roman Church as individuals, especially after the Pastoral Provision was approved for the United States. According to this arrangement, married clergymen who convert may be ordained (if invalidly ordained) as Catholic priests.

Parishes may be set up, and the form of Mass and of the sacraments retains some elements of traditional Anglican usage found in the Prayer Book.

An organization known as S.S.C. or the Society of the Holy Cross is a group of Anglo-Catholic clergy who generally accept Catholic doctrine and moral practice, including *Humanae Vitae*, and who await the day of full communion with Rome. Some Anglo-Catholics joined the Continuing Anglican Movement after 1975, when the first female clergy were ordained in the United States. Others have gone in different directions, even joining the Eastern Orthodox Church, which accepts the Pope of Rome as "first among equals." This wing of Anglicanism — not to be confused with what is called the "High Church" — has produced such great scholars of the twentieth century as Eric Lionel Mascall.

Anima Christi • Prayer listed in the Missal of Paul VI as "Prayer to Our Redeemer," among those given for thanksgiving after Mass. Sometimes attributed to St. Ignatius Loyola, who recommended its use, it was already known in the fourteenth century. Authorship and exact date of this prayer are unknown. The text is as follows:

"Soul of Christ, sanctify me.
Body of Christ, save me.
Blood of Christ, inebriate me.
Water from the side of Christ, wash me.
Passion of Christ, strengthen me.
Good Jesus, hear me.
Within Thy wounds hide me.
Let me not be separated from Thee.
Guard me should the foe assail me.
Call me when my life shall fail me.
Bid me come to Thee above
With all Thy saints to sing thy love forever.
Amen" (Translation of John Henry Newman).

Animals in Church Art • The use of animals to symbolize persons, particular offices, states of being, virtues, specific roles and so on. Such symbolization dates from the earliest stages of Christian art and proliferates, especially in Byzantine and

Gothic art, architecture and ornamentation. Some of the best known of such symbols are the lamb and the pelican for Christ, the dove for the Holy Spirit, the lion for St. Mark, the ox for St. Luke and the eagle for St. John the Evangelist.

Anne de Beaupré, St., Shrine of: See **Canadian Shrines**

Anniversary • The annual remembrance in liturgical commemoration of some past event in the life of the Church (e.g., the installation of the Pope, ordination of a bishop or priest, consecration of a church, religious profession, marriage, etc.). Special Masses are found in the Missal (sacramentary) for these celebrations. More frequently, the term refers to requiem commemorations after the funeral. The Missal of Pope St. Pius V had special Masses for the third, seventh and thirtieth (Month's Mind) days after death. The present sacramentary omits these distinctions and has simply various Masses for anniversaries for different deceased persons.

Annuario Pontificio • The official directory, published each year, of all cardinals, bishops, prelates and major religious superiors throughout the Catholic Church, together with their vital statistics (e.g., date of birth, consecration, etc.), with addresses and telephone numbers as well. The *Annuario* concentrates on the membership of the staffs of the various offices of the Roman Curia and of the Papal Diplomatic Corps. Scrupulous attention is paid to accuracy, and while mistakes are bound to happen in a directory of over two thousand pages, a listing in the *Annuario* is tantamount to a statement of official status on the part of the Holy See. The practice of publishing an annual directory of ecclesiastical personnel was begun in 1716 and is presently carried out by the Central Office of Church Statistics in Vatican City.

Annulment • An annulment, or more properly, a declaration of nullity, is a decree issued by a competent Church authority or Church tribunal that an ecclesiastical act or a sacrament is invalid, thus having no canonical effects. The reasons for granting or issuing an annulment vary, depending on the act or sacrament in question.

Ordinarily most annulments pertain to marriage. A marriage can be declared invalid for a variety of reasons: lack of canonical form if one party is Catholic and thus required to be married in the presence of a priest, deacon or bishop; the existence of an undispensed impediment; the presence of an intention contrary to marriage at the time of the wedding; the presence of psychological factors that rendered one or both parties incapable of knowing what they were doing or of assuming the fundamental responsibilities of marriage. Annulments of marriage are only granted after a thorough investigation of all aspects of the marriage by a Church tribunal. Under very rare circumstances, the reception of Sacred Orders can be declared null. (Cf. Canons 1708-1712.)

Annunciation of Mary • The angel Gabriel greeted Mary with the words "Hail, full of grace" and announced to her that she would "conceive in her womb and bear a son" (cf. Lk 1:26-38). Because she was still a virgin, Mary was troubled by the angel's message. But Gabriel declared that the Holy Spirit would come upon Mary and that the child to be born would "be called holy, the Son of God" (Lk 1:35). Moved by grace and the Holy Spirit, Mary accepted this message with faith and love. "Behold, I am the handmaid of the Lord," she said. "Let it be to me according to your word" (Lk 1:36).

This event, which took place in Nazareth,

has always been recognized by the Church as a many-faceted mystery. It depicts the great truth that our salvation is a work of absolutely free grace on God's part. Mary herself is not ready for it on her own but is made ready by a divine grace. Only because she is "full of grace" — preserved from sin in her own Immaculate Conception and overshadowed by the Holy Spirit — can she respond with the complete acceptance expressed in her *fiat* (Latin for "let it be done"). The Annunciation teaches us that the salvation of the world and our own personal salvation do not depend upon a readiness that is humanly generated, but on the grace of God Who prepares the way for his Son.

This precious moment has been interpreted by countless painters through the centuries and is perhaps the single-most popular subject of religious iconography in the West. According to an ancient tradition, the Church celebrates the feast of the Annunciation of Mary on March 25, nine months before Christmas.

Anointing • A widespread custom across almost all ancient Near Eastern cultures which made sacred the person, place or thing anointed. Priests, the Ark of the Covenant, the tent of meeting and even its furniture (Ex 30:25ff.), the king of Israel (Saul, 1 Sm 10:1ff.; David, 1 Sm 16:13; Solomon, 1 Kgs 1:39, etc.) were all anointed. Anointing with oil and other materials is a sign of joy (Prv 27:9), occurs at festivals (Am 6:6) and is also a sign of honor (Ps 23:5; 92:10). Oil was used in anointing the sick (Is 1:6) and lepers (Lv 14:10-32) and in the expulsion of evil spirits (Mk 6:13). In New Testament occurrence, anointing refers to messianic joy (Heb 1:9), to honor (Lk 7:38-46; Mt 26:6-13; Jn 12:1-8), to the healing of the sick (Mk 6:13) and to the forgiveness of sins (Jas 5:14-15). Jesus is anointed with the Holy Spirit (Acts 10:38; Lk 4:18-21 [Is 61:1]) at the inauguration of His ministry. The followers of Christ receive an anointing (2 Cor 1:21; 1 Jn 2:20-27); anointing in baptismal and Confirmation rites is rooted in the above key texts.

Anointing of the Sick • The sacrament instituted by Christ and celebrated by the Church to offer the healing grace of God to the infirm and the aged, remit sin and make known the prayerful solicitude of the entire Body of Christ for those beset by illness or ailment.

The roots of this sacrament are indicated in two places in the New Testament. In Mark 6:13, the evangelist says of the Twelve who are given authority by Christ over unclean spirits: "They cast out many demons, and they anointed with oil many that were sick and healed them." And, in James 5:14-15, the sacred author writes: "Is any among you sick? Let him call for the elders of the church, and let them pray over him, anointing him with oil in the name of the Lord; and the prayer of faith will save the sick man, and the Lord will raise him up; and if he has committed sins, he will be forgiven." Careful not to say that the sacrament of the Anointing of the Sick is explicitly conferred in these pericopes, the Church nevertheless teaches that the matter, the form, the proper minister and the spiritual efficacy are indeed anticipated. The matter is the oil, the form is the prescribed formula, the proper minister is the presbyter and the spiritual efficacy is the restoration of the sick person's soul.

In the Old Testament, oil was used to fortify and make strong again. In the New Dispensation, oil continues to function as a symbol of fortification and strength. Only now, fortification and strength are found in the paschal mystery of Christ. Today, the oil placed on the forehead and palms of the sick person in the sacrament of the

Anointing of the Sick has usually already been blessed by the diocesan bishop on Holy Thursday. As he celebrates the sacrament, then the priest will trace the Sign of the Cross with the blessed oil on the forehead and palms of the sick person and use the Church's sacramental form. In the early Church, a uniform verbal formula did not exist for the anointing. In time, though, a prescribed formula was essential to the proper administration of the sacrament. The Rite of Anointing and Pastoral Care of the Sick indicates that the priest use these words: "Through this holy anointing, may the Lord in his love and mercy help you with the grace of the Holy Spirit. Amen. May the Lord who frees you from sin save you and raise you up. Amen." According to the clear testimony of the Letter of James and the definitive teaching of the Council of Trent (1545-63), the priest is the one to whom Christ through the Church has given the power to anoint. The spiritual effect of this sacrament is the pardon of sin and/or any of its remnants, the stirring up of faith in God's mercy and the strength to endure suffering of various kinds. By "spiritual effect," the Church does not intend to rule out the possibility of any physical cure for the sacrament's recipient. At the same time, the Church does not wish to imply either that a physical cure awaits one who has been healed spiritually.

For about the first thousand years of the Church's history, the sacrament of the Anointing of the Sick was just that: a sacrament for those who were sick. But, with the rise of the Scholastics in the twelfth century, a view that the sacrament was really for the dying emerged. This latter view, that it was a sacrament only for the dying, eventually gained ascendancy because of a misunderstanding of the effect of the sacrament. The misunderstanding revolved around the answer to this question: if sacraments always produce their effect in a recipient, how could one so seldom realized as recovery of health be a real effect? The Scholastics concluded that since the remission of sin was the principal effect of this sacrament, it could be held off until immediately before death because there were two other sacraments (Baptism and Penance) to remit sin. By delaying the anointing until near death, the sacrament could then be celebrated for the purpose of absolving the last vestiges of sin.

Reclaiming the original intent and the orthopraxis of this sacrament actually began as far back as the Council of Trent. At the Council of Trent, it was decreed that danger of death was *not* a condition for validity in the recipient of the sacrament. After Trent, there was a progressive yet organic understanding of the true meaning of the sacrament as a sacrament for the sick. This phenomenon eventually culminated in changing the name of the sacrament from Extreme Unction to the sacrament of the Anointing of the Sick at the Second Vatican Council.

Because it is a sacrament for the living, the Anointing of the Sick is celebrated in various places according to the ritual and the appropriate liturgical directives. For instance, a priest may celebrate the sacrament in a sick person's home, he may celebrate the sacrament with the sick whom he visits in the hospital and he may anoint infirm and aged Catholics during a Mass of the Anointing of the Sick. When a priest is called to minister to a Catholic who is dying, he will surely anoint this dying person for the purpose of readying him to meet the glorified Lord. Frequently, an anointing of this kind (near death) is preceded by a sacramental confession and followed by Viaticum, the reception of Holy Communion as spiritual food for the journey to the Lord.

When the sacrament of the Anointing of the Sick was restored, the Church obviously did not intend that the sacrament be celebrated indiscriminately or without a necessary pastoral prudence. For example, only those children who have attained the use of reason should be admitted to the sacrament. And the sacrament ought not be celebrated more than once during a time of crisis, unless of course the sick person's condition worsens. These and many other stipulations regarding this sacrament can be ascertained by consulting the revised rite.

The 1982 revision of the *Pastoral Care of the Sick: Rites of Anointing and Viaticum* provides rites for visits to the sick with readings from the Scripture and prayers, for visits when Scripture is read and Holy Communion is distributed, and for the varied rites of anointing already mentioned. The ritual presumes that priests, deacons and laypersons collaborate in visiting the sick of a local church community.

Anointing of the Sick, Rite for • The Liturgy Constitution of Vatican II decreed that the former rite of "extreme unction" may properly be considered the "anointing of the sick" which indicates that this sacrament is not reserved only for those near death. It specified further that the rites for the sick should be revised to combine Viaticum with the anointing rite and to accommodate some of the prayers of the anointing ritual to correspond to the varying conditions of the sick who receive this sacrament (nn. 73-75). Thus a new rite for this sacrament was published in Latin in 1972; the present English edition now used was published in 1983.

Of particular import is the fact that the title of this ritual is *Pastoral Care of the Sick: Rites of Anointing and Viaticum*, indicating that a large portion of this revision deals with visiting the sick (Chapters 1 and 2) and rites for communion of the sick at home and at the hospital (Chapter 3). When the rite of anointing itself is presented (Chapter 4), all three liturgies offered presume the participation of the faithful including the sick person, whether the sacrament takes place at home within the Mass, outside the Mass or in a hospital. For those who are near death, the ritual presents a wealth of texts for Viaticum (within or outside of Mass), as well as prayers for the dying. For emergencies, the revised ritual also includes continuous rites of Penance, Anointing and Viaticum. Thus, a major shift from the previous rite of extreme unction is the fact that liturgical participation of a community of the faithful is presumed for Viaticum and Anointing.

Anomoeans • Anomoeanism, or Eunomianism, was a radical Arian sect which broke off from that heresy late in the fourth century. This band, under Bishop Eunomius of Cyzicus, rejected any similarity between the Father and the Son. Eunomius died in A.D. 394, and virtually no Anomoean writings survived Emperor Arcadia's order that the literature be burned in 398.

Antediluvian • Meaning "before the deluge," the word refers to the period of time from Creation to the Great Flood. In contemporary language it usually carries a negative or derisive connotation, meaning antiquated or outdated, e.g., an antediluvian attitude. (The account of the Flood appears in Genesis 6:5—8:22.)

Antependium • A liturgical parament used in many churches throughout the world to decorate the front of the altar. As such, as its Latin root *ante pendere* (to hang before or in front) denotes, the antependium is a frontal hanging from the top edge of the altar table to the floor, thus covering the entire front of the altar. This may take a permanent form, as in wood covered with leather, silk or damask encrusted with precious or semiprecious stones or fine embroideries. It may take a more temporary removable form, consisting of a frame covered and decorated as above and which may be changed according to the particular liturgical season or feast. Some of these antependia — like those used on the papal altar in St. Peter's — are precious works of art.

Antependium (Germany, 1100s)

Anthem • An anglicized form of the term "antiphon," the anthem originally referred to a musical setting of a scriptural text sung by alternating choirs, and used within the liturgy. Modern usage of the word applies it to any choral piece of music with words which may be scriptural, generally religious or secular.

Anthropomorphism • Derived from the Greek word *anthropomorphos*, which means "of human form," the term "anthropomorphism" refers to any attribution of human-like traits or behaviors to non-human beings. In the religious realm, in particular, the term refers to depictions of God's being, thoughts, words, or actions in ways that suggest human traits or qualities, as when He is said to have eyes, a mouth, a heart, and the like. Because they seem to bring God down to the human level and thus to compromise His transcendence, anthropomorphic depictions are sometimes viewed with suspicion, as for example in Judaism and Islam. But the use of anthropomorphic expressions is well-warranted by the Bible itself. When properly employed and understood, such expressions provide an indispensable context for human descriptions of a fundamental element of divine revelation: the intense personal engagement of the Triune God with created persons.

Anti-Catholicism (in America) • Prejudice against the Catholic Church and her adherents is described by Arthur M. Schlesinger, Sr., professor of American history at Harvard University, as "...the deepest bias in the history of the American people." Its roots are obvious in the makeup of the first colonists from England, who detested the Church of Rome and who emigrated from a country which considered a loyal Catholic to be a traitor. In fact, many of the first colonists, the Puritans, felt that the penal sanctions against Catholics in England were too mild, and that the Church of England was still not sufficiently purified of odious "Romish" customs. Consequently, Catholics were proscribed in every colony except Pennsylvania — because of Quaker toleration — and early Maryland.

Anti-Catholic sentiment was so pervasive and potent in colonial America that furor over the Quebec Act — by which King George III granted Catholics freedom in Canada — is considered one of the major causes of the Revolutionary War. George Washington's exemplary respect for all religions and the exceptional loyalty of the tiny Catholic minority to the revolutionary cause somewhat mitigated anti-Catholicism. Still, John Carroll, as recognized leader of the Church in the United States, constantly had to counteract charges that Catholicism was contrary to democracy and that a sincere Catholic could never be a loyal citizen. A defense of Catholic rights and ringing affirmations of Catholic patriotism became consistent themes in the letters of the first generation of bishops in the new republic. Although anti-Catholicism waned a bit in the Federalist era, animosity toward the Church was always right below the surface, and it did not take much to activate it, inflamed by such respected Protestant clergy as Lyman Beecher and Horace Bushnell.

By the 1830s, the ingrained American bias against Catholicism was linked to a suspicion and prejudice against the immigrants — usually Catholic — called "Nativism." This led to a mob-attack and torching of the Ursuline convent in Charlestown, Massachusetts, in 1834, and a summer of destructive riots in Philadelphia in 1844, in which Catholics were killed and churches burned. Nativism became the guiding principle of the "Know-Nothing" political party in the 1850s, which was successful in implementing legislation burdening and controlling Catholic immigrants. Another political expression of anti-Catholicism, the American Protective Association, flourished in the 1880s and 1890s. Organized prejudice against Catholics in the twentieth century is obvious in the Ku Klux Klan and the "Protestants and Other Americans United for Separation of Church and State." Perhaps the last eruption of virulently overt anti-Catholicism occurred during the campaign of Alfred E. Smith for the presidency in 1928.

Although some commentators interpreted the election of a Catholic president in 1960 as evidence that bias against the Church was a thing of the past, subsequent developments demonstrate that anti-Catholicism is alive and well in the United States. Observers of the contemporary scene usually note two brands of prejudice against the Catholic Church: a religious animosity, prominent among biblical fundamentalists, who attack Catholicism as a perversion of true Christianity; and, secondly, a cultural hostility, popular among more liberal academics, social commentators and the media, who regard the Church as hopelessly backward and repressive. The latter group is so common that Yale Professor Peter Viereck has said that "anti-Catholicism is the anti-Semitism of the liberals." Recent instances of clear anti-Catholic prejudice in the media are mostly occasioned by the Church's opposition to abortion, with today's anti-Catholics positing that a Catholic's religious and moral convictions ought never to influence his or her social, cultural or political views.

For further reading: Michael Schwartz, *The Persistent Prejudice: Anti-Catholicism in America* (Our Sunday Visitor, 1984); Mark Hurley, *The Unholy Ghost: Anti-Catholicism in the American Experience* (Our Sunday Visitor, 1992).

Anticamera • The private anteroom adjoining the Pope's working office, and in which he meets those who have been scheduled for private audiences with him. From the Latin, *anti* (against) + *camera* (room).

Antichrist • The English term from the Greek *antichristos* meaning "against Christ" or "adversary of Christ." The term occurs only in 1 John 2:18, 22; 4:3; 2 John 7, but similar ideas are found elsewhere in the Old and New Testaments. Basically, the texts speak of a final war of cosmological proportions between the "antichrist" and God and/or Christ which will occur prior to the Second Coming of Christ and the final judgment of the world. The scenario of a final cosmological war between a saving-hero and his countertype is common for at least two centuries prior to the birth of Christ in both Judaism and other religious traditions. Collectively the New Testament authors express similar understandings related to the "antichrist" but in language drawn from a vast array of literary and popular sources. The Gospels speak of "false prophets," etc. (Mt 24:5, 23ff.; Mk 13:21ff.). Paul speaks of the "man of lawlessness" (2 Thes 2:3-12). A beast from the abyss is mentioned in Revelation 11:7ff., while at 13:1-10 a beast emerges from the sea, followed by yet another beast (13:11-18), etc. These varying images were chosen because they were part of the "language of the day" and because this language represented material especially suitable for what God wanted to communicate about His plans for the end times to the authors of the New Testament and subsequent generations.

Anticipate • This term refers to praying some part of the Liturgy of the Hours earlier than the time appointed. The *General Instruction of the Liturgy of the Hours* now gives greater flexibility for the precise time for recitation. Liturgically, it would seem appropriate that at least morning prayers should be said in the morning and evening prayers in the evening. The minor hours for non-monks are now reduced to one hour, with different prayers and readings, depending on whether it is read at midmorning, midday or midafternoon. Compline or night prayer should be said before retiring, even if that is after midnight (cf. *General Instruction*, n. 84).

It seems, therefore, that the only question of anticipation of Divine Office would be the Office of Readings, which still keeps its character as a "night office of praise" (*Sacrosanctum Concilium*, n. 89) and yet in a non-monastic setting may be celebrated or recited at any time of the day. It arose as a vigil office, anticipating the next day, based on the Jewish reckoning of the day from sunset to sunset, and so it would seem that after Vespers one could legitimately anticipate the Office of Readings of the next day, either in community or alone. On Sundays and holy days of obligation, the celebration begins with Vespers for the next day on Saturday, and so Mass may also be anticipated for the next day for the convenience of the faithful on Sundays and holy days.

Anticipated Mass • Prior to Vatican II, the obligation of assisting at the Sacrifice of the Mass on Sundays or holy days of obligation could be fulfilled only on the Sunday or holy day itself. Legislation was changed and later included in the revised Code, which allows the faithful to fulfill this obligation either on the day itself or on the evening before the day. An anticipated Mass is the proper Mass for the Sunday or the feast day, celebrated on the eve of the day (cf. Canon 1248.1). This change in practice can be understood in the light of ancient Hebrew liturgical tradition, wherein a Sabbath or feast-day observance began at sundown of the night before.

Anticlericalism • Appearing in many forms over many centuries in Church history, anticlericalism ranges from a coolness toward priests to the bitter persecution of the clergy of the Church. It has roots in personal envy, political expediency, religious or doctrinal differences or combinations of the above. It seemed to have entered a new phase in

France since 1830 and is still especially prominent in Mexico. In its broadest meaning, it connotes an opposition to any influence by the Church upon society.

Antidicomarianites • In Latin means "those who speak against Mary." The term refers to those members of a heretical sect found in ancient Arabia who held that Mary had other children after Christ's birth. They were doctrinal descendants of Apollinarius, who held, among other things, that Jesus had no human intelligence and that He brought His "flesh" or human nature with Him from heaven, thus not even having been conceived in the Virgin's womb. This had the ultimate effect of denying the hypostatic union and with it of denying both the divinity and the humanity of Christ while simultaneously affirming that it was God, the "man" Jesus, who died on the cross — something which is impossible for the divinity.

In this theological system Mary had little or no place, hence its name. St. Epiphanius wrote extensively against this heresy in his epistles (cf. *Heres* LXXVII, PG XLII). He also addressed another problem concerning those who went to the opposite extreme, the Collyridians. This was an heretical sect of women from Thrace and Scythia who offered cakes to Mary as to a deity and then ate them, perhaps as a sort of parallel Eucharistic service. (The Greek word for cakes, *kollyrides* — gave them their appellation.)

The Church, on the other hand, as expressed by St. Epiphanius, maintains that Mary indeed is to be honored by all who claim to be followers of Christ, her divine Son, but that she is a creature and only God is to be adored. This has been the Catholic principle regarding the honor to be paid the Mother of God by Christians since the very beginning of the Church's existence and thus remains today. (Cf. *Lumen*

Gentium, VIII; *Marialis Cultus* of Pope Paul VI; and *Redemptoris Mater* of Pope John Paul II.)

Antidoron • Literally, "that which replaces the gift," for it is given to those who have not received Holy Communion. Particles of bread distributed to the faithful after the celebration of the Divine Liturgy in the Byzantine Rite. These particles are taken from the unconsecrated portion of the bread of the offering.

Antigonish Movement • A social action and education movement originating in 1930 at St. Francis Xavier University in Antigonish, Nova Scotia. The movement organized trade unions, cooperative retail stores and credit unions worldwide.

Antilegomena • Eusebius of Caesarea (d. A.D. 340) gave this name to writings whose place in the New Testament canon of Scripture was disputed. Among this class of writings, Eusebius distinguished two subsets: those generally recognized to be part of the canon (e.g., James and 2 and 3 John) and those definitely excluded (e.g., the *Didache*).

Antimension • Literally, "that which replaces the table." A piece of linen, almost square in shape, and approximately twenty inches in size, upon which is imprinted the representation of the instruments of the passion and the scene of the burial of Christ. The relic of a saint is enclosed into it, usually with a waxen seal. Its original purpose in the Eastern Churches was to make an altar out of any unconsecrated table; it is now also used on a consecrated altar, and generally corresponds in its function to the altar stone of the Latin Rite.

Antinomians • In the early Church, this name was applied to those who followed the notion that Christians were exempt from following all the prescriptions of the Mosaic law or, in the extreme, even the Ten Commandments. They based their antagonism to the law, as their name means in Greek "against the law" (*antinomos*), upon an extreme interpretation of St. Paul's writings on justification and the law. This idea was found especially among Gnostic groups. During the Reformation, some Protestants who held that "justification by faith" reduced all acts, good or evil, to moral irrelevancy were also given this appellation. This notion, repudiated by Luther and condemned by the Council of Trent, resurfaced in seventeenth-century New England and, in an altered form, in Wesleyism.

Antioch • Antioch of Syria, the capital city of the ancient Roman province of Syria, located in the northwestern quartile of the province, on the river Orontes. It was the third largest city of the Roman Empire, a center of Greek culture ranked with Rome and Alexandria. It was an important center for earliest Christianity: (1) the city had a significant Jewish population, well established since its foundation in approximately 300 B.C. Many followers of Jesus fled Jerusalem after Stephen's martyrdom (Acts 7) and reached Antioch, at first carrying the Gospel of Christ's redemptive work only to the Jewish population of Antioch (Acts 11:19). (2) Gentiles were eventually evangelized and made up a significant portion of the Christian community of believers (Acts 11:20). The Church at Antioch becomes the major support for Paul's first missionary journey (Acts 13:2—14:28), which will lead to his mission to the Gentiles. (3) It is in Antioch that followers of Christ are first called "Christians" (Acts 11:26). (4) The episcopal see there is considered one of the original Apostolic Sees of the ancient Church (e.g., St. Ignatius of Antioch).

For further reading: Frederick W. Norris, "Antioch," *Anchor Bible Dictionary*, 1:264-269.

Antioch, Patriarchate of • In the fourth century, the patriarchate of Antioch ranked in importance only after those of Rome and Alexandria. Traditionally, St. Peter is regarded as the first bishop of Antioch. It receded in importance with the rise of Constantinople and, later, with the Nestorian and Monophysite controversies. At the time of the schism in the Church between East and West, Antioch sided with Constantinople. Today the Orthodox Patriarch of Antioch resides in Damascus. The Monophysite bishop also claims the title of patriarch of Antioch, as do the Catholic patriarchs of the Melkite, Syrian and Maronite Rites.

Antioch, School of • Antioch, a city in what is now Syria, was an important center in the early centuries of Christianity and was the See of St. Peter before he went to Rome. Christians at Antioch produced a distinctive school of theology, with a characteristic approach to the formulation of Christian Faith and to the interpretation of Scripture. Notable (and sometimes controversial) adherents to this school include Lucian of Antioch, St. John Chrysostom, Diodore of Tarsus, Theodore of Mopsuestia, Nestorius, Theodoret of Cyr.

Its importance is realized most fully in the fifth-century disputes about Christ. Each one of the disputes had values to offer; each involved limitations or dangers. Alexandria, Platonic in philosophy and allegorical in biblical interpretation, maintained the unity of Christ but in extreme formulations failed to affirm the human soul of Christ (Apollinarianism) or spoke of His humanity as "swallowed up" by divinity (Monophysitism). On the other hand,

Antioch (Aristotelian in philosophy and allegorical in biblical interpretation) asserted the reality and integrity of the humanity of Christ, although extreme formulations (e.g., Nestorianism) seemed to deny His substantial unity. At the Councils of Ephesus (A.D. 431) and Chalcedon (451), the Church took the truth from both positions and affirmed that Christ is one divine Person in two distinct natures, human and divine.

Antiochene biblical interpretation placed great emphasis on the careful study of the text itself and on literal exegesis.

Antiochene Rite: See **Rite, Antiochene**

Antiphon • From the Latin *antiphona* meaning sounding against, or singing opposite, or alternating.

An antiphon is a short verse from a psalm, or sentence from the Bible sung or recited before and after a psalm or between verses. It is usually a summation or the principal idea of the entire text. The book containing the antiphons with accompanying melodies is called the Antiphonary.

Antiphonal • A style of singing employed when the group is divided into two alternating sections. Both groups may sing the same melodic and rhythmic line, or a congregation might sing a simple refrain in response to a more elaborate cantor or choir section. The groups singing in antiphonal style might be: cantor/ congregation; cantor/choir; choir/ congregation; half congregation/half congregation.

Antiphonal Chants • In the Roman Liturgy of the Eucharist, certain chants have classically and customarily been used to accompany processions, such as at the entrance of the ministers and at Communion. These are called the *Introit* and the Communion antiphons. These short texts are taken directly from Scripture (most often a psalm verse) or are adapted from the Scriptures or relate to the feast of the day. These antiphons are first sung by the cantor or *schola cantorum* (or choir), are repeated by the whole assembly followed by verses of a psalm sung by cantor or *schola*, and conclude with everyone singing the antiphon at the end of the procession. The present *General Instruction of the Roman Missal* (nn. 25-26, 56i) describes these chants and their proper role in the Mass. These texts are a rich source for the theology of the Liturgy, season or feast being celebrated. In the *Appendix* to the *General Instruction on the Mass*, the American bishops retain this classical usage of the Roman Rite and also allow for other types of music to be sung at these parts of the Eucharist.

Antiphonary: See **Antiphon**

Antipopes • Since about the third century, the Church has been harassed by pretenders to the papal throne, although the term "antipope" was not used until the twelfth century. Some of the thirty-seven antipopes were merely cranks, while others garnered considerable ecclesiastical and/or political strength in their day. By the fifteenth century, however, the possibility of setting up an interloper in the See of Rome ceased to be a practical reality, and the antipopes since Felix V (who died in 1449) have been too trivial to notice. Today, of course, any attempt at inserting an antipope would be considered a grave usurpation of ecclesiastical office.

Anti-Semitism • A term of nineteenth-century origin, now it commonly means the psychological, social and behavioral antagonism and hostility toward Jewish people and their organizations and businesses. The expression, however, is technically imprecise, since Arabs are likewise Semitic peoples.

Persecution of the Jews started in the Persian Empire and continued in the Hellenistic period at Antioch in Syria and Alexandria in Egypt. Roman persecution became severe in the middle of the first century A.D. after the Jewish rebellion against the Roman occupation in the late-sixties. Under the Emperors Constantine, Theodosian and Justinian, religious and legal restrictions were imposed on Jews. In the Middle Ages more anti-Semitism provoked by the Crusades and bigoted preachers led to massacres and expulsions of Jews throughout Europe. With the rise of nationalism in the nineteenth century, new waves of anti-Semitism broke out in Europe, especially in Germany, because of Hegel's idea that Jews are a race apart and unable to be assimilated into society. This erroneous doctrine eventually led to Hitler's extermination of approximately six million Jews.

Anti-Semitism is completely opposed to Christian charity and biblical ideas (Jn 4:22; Mt 5:17; Rom 9:4, 11:1-2). Pope Pius XI stated clearly in *Divini Redemptoris* (1937) the Catholic teaching: "Anti-Semitism is incompatible with the sublime ideas and truths expressed in this text. We Christians can take no part in anti-Semitism. We acknowledge that everyone has the right to defend himself, in other words, to take necessary precautions for his protection against everything that threatens his legitimate interests, but anti-Semitism is inadmissible. We are spiritually Semites."

During the past generation, Jewish-Catholic relations have been addressed in several different ways by the Holy See. Beginning with *Nostra Aetate* (Declaration on the Relations of the Church to Non-Christian Religions) of the Second Vatican Council in 1965, a clearer direction began to emerge. Fundamental principles are established regarding the relationship of the Church to Judaism in the 1975 Vatican Guidelines. In 1985 *Notes on the Correct Way to Present the Jews and Judaism in Preaching and Catechesis in the Roman Catholic Church* made more explicit the teaching of Vatican II. Pope John Paul II stated in his talk at Mainz, Germany, in 1980: "If Christians are bound to see all humans beings as their brethren and treat them accordingly, how much more are they bound by their sacred obligations when face to face with members of the Jewish people."

Antistes • In liturgical use, it is found as a title of a bishop as the chief priest of a diocese, such as in the Roman Canon (First Eucharistic Prayer), ". . . *et Antistite nostro. . . .*" While it is used most often in a liturgical context, it appears in *Lumen Gentium*, the Dogmatic Constitution on the Church, n. 27, when speaking of the bishops as those who govern particular Churches which have been assigned to them.

Antitrinitarians • Antitrinitarianism, as its name implies, describes those heresies which, among other things, deny the reality of the Trinity. The earliest significant expression of antitrinitarianism was the Arian heresy, although the concept persists to this day, for example, among Unitarians.

Antitype • When a person, event or thing in the Old Testament foreshadows, prepares the way for, anticipates or "begins a path toward" a person, event or thing in the New Testament, the Old Testament subject is the "antitype" which corresponds to the New Testament subject, which is called the "type." This kind of interpretation uncovers the typological sense in texts of Scripture combining both Old Testament and New Testament passages so as to present the fullness of teaching. The uncovering of this fullness through the act of interpretation is a form of discovery of what God has made present in Scripture through inspiration.

Apocalypse: See **Revelation, Book of**

Apocalypticism • The English term derived from the Greek word meaning "revelation," *apokalypsis*, meaning "to uncover" or "to disclose." In particular, the subject matter of Revelation is God's intent for the immediate future. Apocalypticism was a widespread movement in Judaism between 600 B.C. and A.D. 200. The literature of this movement is our main source of information about it. Its roots are in Old Testament prophecy, an acute awareness of the power of sin and of a sinful world. Other themes include: treatment of Israel's national life, prophecies predicting impending catastrophic and cosmic war, a final and climactic conflict between God and evil in which God wins and the restoration is made to creation of its pristine pre-fallen state. The media for these revelations are either "seers" or visionaries who receive the revelations through visions, dreams, angelic beings or by interpreting historical events, numbers, etc. The message of this literature generally brings encouragement, hope and strength to those suffering for the Faith.

For further reading: Paul D. Hanson et al., "Apocalypses and Apocalypticism," *Anchor Bible Dictionary*, 1:279-292.

Apocalyptic Number • The number 666, also known as the Number of the Beast according to the text: "Let him who has understanding reckon the number of the beast, for it is a human number, its number is six hundred and sixty-six" (Rv 13:18). Commonly, this number is thought to refer

to the antichrist, in particular because each number represents one less than the perfect number seven. Hence, the so-called apocalyptic number has given rise to endless speculation — not to mention outright superstition — throughout Christian history. Since in Greek and Hebrew each alphabetical unit represents both a letter and a numeral and thus every name could be expressed by the "sum" of its letters, various identifications of the antichrist have been proposed (most commonly, Nero).

Apocatastasis • Also known as "universalism," this doctrine affirms the ultimate salvation of all rational creatures, including the fallen angels and unrepentant sinners. In short, the doctrine denies the reality and possibility of damnation. Origen (d. A.D. 254) is commonly thought to have held some version of this doctrine. It was among the propositions understood to constitute "Origenism" and condemned at a synod at Constantinople in 543 (a judgment confirmed by the Second Council of Constantinople in 553). Modern proponents of the doctrine have included among Christian sects, the Moravians and Anabaptists, and among Christian theologians, Friedrich Schleiermacher (1768-1834). Authentic Catholic teaching excludes the doctrine, since it implies that the good or evil conduct of life finally has no bearing on one's eternal destiny.

Apocrisarius • This term, from the Greek *apokrisis* ("answer"), was the name used for legates, nuncios, ambassadors or representatives from one prince to another, as they were usually sent to request an answer to some matter pertaining to the mutual business of the powers involved. The term is especially indicative of those representatives who were sent by the Roman Pontiff to conduct the business of the Holy See and the Church at the court of the various princes of Europe. This was especially so with regard to the court of the Byzantine emperor in Constantinople. As such, the apocrisarius was the earliest precursor of the vast and highly sophisticated diplomatic corps which the Holy See maintains throughout the world to this day.

Apocrypha — New Testament • The word is from the Greek, meaning "secret" or "hidden." The term applies to various types of literature which imitate and so resemble Old and New Testament books. These documents assert (falsely) divine inspiration by claiming to have been written by, for example, one of the patriarchs, or a great prophet or a great Apostle. The implication is that the literature passes on "true revelation" which clarifies what is found in canonical Scripture. Initially, the term referred to either late Jewish writings (after 550 B.C.) and early Christian literature (up to the fifth century) in which "secret teachings" from the Apostles were passed on; in this context the term was used by Christians in a pejorative sense. Old Testament apocryphal literature exists in various forms: historical, apocalyptic, didactic; New Testament apocryphal forms of literature include: Gospels, acts, epistles, apocalypses.

For further reading: Stephen J. Patterson, "Apocrypha," *Anchor Bible Dictionary*, 1:292-297.

Apodeipnon • From the Greek for "after the evening meal." This term is used to refer to the concluding office in the liturgical cycle for the day in the Byzantine Church, that is, the midnight (Compline) service.

Apodosis • From the Greek for "a giving-back." This liturgical term describes the conclusion of the period of time during which a feast is observed in the Byzantine Church. The Nativity of the Mother of God, for example, observed on September 8, has its conclusion (apodosis) on September 12, while the feast of the Universal Exaltation of the Holy Cross (September 14) concludes on September 21. Each feast also has a pre-festive observance which is marked on the day immediately preceding the feast.

Apollinarianism • A fourth-century heresy which taught that Jesus had a human body and a human soul but no human mind. It meant that Christ had one nature, not two natures. While Apollinarius attempted to safeguard the absolute divinity of Christ, he indirectly denied something of it. He actually accepted the Arian position minimizing the divine nature of Jesus, condemned by the First Council of Constantinople in A.D. 381.

Apologetics • The branch of theology concerned with providing a reasoned defense of the doctrines of the Faith in response to one or another set of objections posed to these doctrines either by non-believers or by heterodox believers. Depending on the circumstances, apologetical arguments may be directed either to the cultivation of tolerance for the Christian Faith where there is hostility or persecution (e.g., in Roman society in late antiquity, or in some Islamic countries in the present day), or to the evangelization and persuasion of persons who have not yet accepted the Faith or those who have fallen into error concerning some aspect of its contents.

St. Paul's sermon on the Areopagus (Acts 17:22-31) has provided a model for Christian apologists throughout the centuries in that he attempts to find a common ground with his disputants, using ideas and vocabulary familiar to them. Early Christians followed the lead of St.

Paul as they encountered the religiously diverse and philosophically cosmopolitan world of late antiquity. Many early Christian writers composed apologetical works; indeed, a group of these writers — Justin Martyr being the most famous — has actually come to be called "Apologists." Christian thinkers throughout the centuries have tried their hand at the genre and have produced a large body of literature. Among the best-known works of apologetics in Christian history are St. Augustine's *City of God* and St. Thomas Aquinas's *Summa contra gentiles*.

While all apologetical literature shares the common feature of striving to present a rational case for the Christian Faith, its actual content and approach depend on the particular kinds of objections and challenges which the author encounters in his or her milieu. Thus, for example, very different sorts of defense would be needed to address the objections that Marxists, or secular humanists, or Muslims, or Buddhists might pose to Christian belief and morals. For this reason, although it is possible to lay out some general principles in this branch of theology, the practice of apologetics always has an ad hoc quality about it, depending on the nature of the audience and the challenge it poses to Christianity.

St. Paul's lack of success with the Greeks at Athens adds a cautionary note to all apologetical endeavors. Faith is a gift from God, a grace that involves an interior transformation of the mind and heart that moves the person to accept revelation. For this reason, according to Catholic theology, no apologetical argument can demonstrate, on purely logical or scientific grounds, the essential truth of the Christian Faith. Such arguments can lead a non-believer to the point of faith by removing obstacles to belief or by disposing the understanding to the reasonableness of the Faith. But only God

can move the mind and will to believe in Him and in His word.

Apologist • The term derived from a Greek root implying explanation or defense. Originally, "apologist" was a title of honor bestowed on one well-versed in Christian doctrine and capable of defending it against attack. The term has passed into wider usage among Christians today, however, and denotes anyone who attempts, more or less effectively, to support and defend the teachings of the Church in the public arena. It should be noted, though, that for all practical purposes apologists speak on their own authority, even where their presentations conform to true doctrine.

Apology (or Apologia) • A Christian literary genre, characterized by the effort to defend or vindicate the Christian Faith against standard or specific objections. The earliest examples of such writings are the works of Christian writers, known as apologists (notably Justin Martyr), who defended Christianity against the pagan objectors of late antiquity.

Apolusia • From the Greek for "a washing." This liturgical term describes a ritual preceding Baptism in the Byzantine Church, performed eight days prior to its reception. This practice by and large has fallen into disuse. It symbolizes the eschaton, that is, the eighth day on which Christ arrives in glory to make all things new; hence, for the newly baptized, his or her life in Christ is the beginning of a new life of grace and a rebirth as a child of God and heir to His kingdom.

Apolysis • A dismissal prayer said by the priest at the conclusion of a liturgical ceremony in the Eastern Church.

Apolytikion • From the Greek for "dismissal." This liturgical term in the Byzantine Church describes the portion of a liturgical ceremony at which the congregation is dismissed and the ceremony concludes. More specifically, the apolytikion refers to the final prayer or hymn terminating a liturgical service. (Cf. Apolysis.).

Apostasy • The word refers to abandoning the Faith. In the Old Testament, Israel's unfaithfulness to God is an apostasy (Jer 2:19; Jos 22:22; 2 Chr 33:19). In the New Testament it refers to a baptized Christian's rejecting the life of faith and grace given at Baptism (Heb 6:1-8). The principal New Testament source for our current understanding is Acts 21:21 where the term is applied to Paul for allegedly having rejected Moses; at 2 Thessalonians 2:3, the term refers to a rebellion against God before the Second Coming. In Catholic teaching, following the New Testament, an apostate is one who completely repudiates the Faith of the Church and so commits a grievous sin because of the denial of truth about and from God and about and from the Church. Apostasy is defined in canon law as the total repudiation of the Christian Faith by one who had been baptized or received into the Catholic Church. An apostate from the Faith is automatically excommunicated. In the 1917 Code, apostasy was also used to describe a religious who left the religious life illegally without the intention of ever returning (cf. Canons 205, 751, 1364).

Apostle • From the Greek *apostolos,* meaning "one who is sent," the term Apostle appears in the New Testament to designate a specific group among Jesus' disciples whom He chose to serve as His emissaries and as authoritative witnesses to the Gospel.

In the Synoptic Gospels (Mt 10:1-4; Mk 3:13-19; Lk 6:12-16), we read that Jesus summoned twelve disciples and appointed them His Apostles. They were Simon Peter, his brother Andrew, James the son of Zebedee, his brother John, Philip, Bartholomew, Matthew (identified as a tax collector in Mt 10:3), James the son of Alphaeus, Simon (called the "Cananaean" in Mt 10:4 and Mk 3:18; called a Zealot in Lk 6:15), and Judas Iscariot. There is some slight variation in the lists. Thaddeus is mentioned in Matthew 10:3 and Mark 3:18, but not in Luke 6. Some New Testament manuscripts substitute "Lebbaeus, called Thaddeus." Luke 6:16 lists Judas the son of James, who does not appear in the Matthean or Marcan lists. Each of the lists begins with Simon Peter, who became the leader and spokesman of the Twelve, and each ends with a poignant reference to Judas Iscariot, who is identified as the one who betrayed Jesus.

In addition to the three Synoptic lists, a fourth list of the Twelve is found in Acts 1:13, where the Synoptic list is reduced to eleven. Acts 1:15-26 describes the selection of Matthias to round out the number of the Twelve after the death of Judas Iscariot.

In Mark 3:14-15, Jesus commissions the Twelve to be with Him, to preach and to drive out demons. Later (Mk 6:7-13), Jesus summons the Twelve and sends them out two by two, giving them authority over demons and instructing them for their mission. Mark 6:12-13 reports the activity of the Twelve during their first mission: "So they went out and preached that men should repent. And they cast out many demons, and anointed with oil many that were sick and healed them." Mark 6:30 then presents the Apostles' return to Jesus after the successful completion of their mission.

Unlike Mark 3, the Luke 6 version of the commissioning of the Twelve Apostles does

The Apostle St. Andrew

not include the bestowal of any particular authority. However, the Luke 9:1-6 parallel to the Mark 6:7-13 mission of the Twelve has them involved in exorcism, healing and preaching, an extension of Jesus' own ministry.

The Matthean version of the commissioning of the Twelve Apostles makes no mention of preaching, but includes conferral of authority to exorcise and to heal (Mt 10:1). Jesus' instructions to the Twelve immediately follow their commissioning in the missionary discourse of Matthew 10:5-42.

It is clear from Matthew 28:16-20 and from Acts 1:15-26 that the ministry of the Apostles did not end with the earthly ministry of Jesus. In Matthew 28:16-20, the risen Jesus appears to the remaining eleven, commanding them to "make disciples of all nations" (Mt 28:19), to baptize in the name of the Trinity, and to teach. The risen Lord assures them of His continuing presence.

Besides indicating that the Apostles' ministry continued after the death and resurrection of Jesus, Acts 1:15-26 suggests that others beyond the original twelve could become participants in what Acts 1:25 calls for the first time "this apostolic ministry." Acts 1:21 describes the apostolic ministry as a matter of bearing witness to Jesus' resurrection, for which task it was required that the candidate be "one of the men who have accompanied us during all time that the Lord Jesus went in and out among us, beginning from the baptism of John until the day when he was taken up from us."

The selection of Matthias to replace Judas highlights the biblical symbolism of the number twelve, which signifies the whole of Israel in its twelve tribes. Jesus says of the Twelve that they are to be enthroned to judge the twelve tribes of Israel (Mt 19:28; Lk 22:30). Thus, the Twelve symbolize Israel's eschatological renewal.

Acts refers to Barnabas and Paul as Apostles (Acts 14:4), extending the apostolic ministry beyond the circle of the Twelve while continuing to insist on the leadership role of the Twelve in the Jerusalem community (cf. Acts 2:37, 42-43; 4:33-37; 5:2, 12, 18-40; 6:6; 8:1, 14, 18; 9:27; 11:1; 14:4; 15:2-29; 16:4). Thus, in Acts the apostolic ministry takes two directions, the first focused on the leadership exercised by the Twelve, and the second focused on the missionary apostolic efforts of Paul and Barnabas.

St. Paul identifies himself as an Apostle (cf., for example, Rom 1:1; 1 Cor 1:1; 2 Cor 1:1), insisting that he received this ministry from God (Gal 1:1). He numbers himself among those who are witnesses to the Risen Christ (1 Cor 15:8), while calling himself "the least of the apostles" (1 Cor 15:9) and acknowledging the distinctiveness of his experience of the Risen Christ: "Last of all, as to one born abnormally, he appeared to me" (1 Cor 15:8).

Paul understood the apostolic ministry as

first among the ministries which serve to build up the body of Christ (1 Cor 12:28). He qualifies himself as an Apostle to the Gentiles (Rom 11:13), knowing that others were Apostles before him (Gal 1:17) and asserting, "the one who worked in Peter for an apostolate to the circumcised worked also in me for the Gentiles" (Gal 2:9). John's Gospel refers to the Twelve as a group in 6:67-70. There Jesus asks them, "Do you also want to leave?" as other disciples find the Bread of Life discourse too challenging and turn away from accompanying Jesus. As spokesman for the group, Simon Peter professes both faith and allegiance.

The only other reference to the Twelve in John's Gospel occurs in John 20:24, where Thomas is identified as one of the Twelve. Nowhere in the Fourth Gospel or in the Johannine Epistles are the Twelve called Apostles. In the Apocalypse, the "twelve names of the twelve apostles of the Lamb" are inscribed on the twelve courses of foundation stones of the new Jerusalem (Rv 21:14).

Christus Dominus, the Second Vatican Council's Decree on the Pastoral Office of the Bishops in the Church, describes the bishops as the successors of the Apostles in these terms: "The bishops also have been designated by the Holy Spirit to take the place of the Apostles as pastors of souls and, together with the Supreme Pontiff and subject to his authority, they are commissioned to perpetuate the work of Christ, the eternal Pastor" (CD 2). As successors of the Apostles in proclaiming the Gospel message and in shepherding the Church, the bishops carry on the work of Christ Himself.

During the rite of ordination of a bishop, the principal consecrator instructs those who are present in words which reflect on the continuing mission of the Apostles in the Church. Because the apostolic ministry "was to continue to the end of time, the apostles selected others to help them. By the laying on of hands which confers the sacrament of orders in its fullness, the apostles passed on the gift of the Holy Spirit which they themselves had received from Christ" (*Roman Pontifical*, Ordination of a Bishop, n. 18).

For further reading: Hans Dieter Betz, "Apostle," *Anchor Bible Dictionary*, 1:309-311.

Apostles' Creed • This formula of belief in twelve articles contains the fundamental doctrines of Christianity. Its authorship comes from being a summary of apostolic teachings, not from being written by the Apostles.

The Apostles' Creed reads:

"I believe in God the Father Almighty, Creator of heaven and earth; and in Jesus Christ, His only Son, our Lord: Who was conceived by the Holy Spirit, born of the Virgin Mary, suffered under Pontius Pilate, was crucified, died, and was buried. He descended into hell; the third day he arose again from the dead. He ascended into heaven and sits at the right hand of God the Father Almighty; from thence he shall come to judge the living and the dead. I believe in the Holy Spirit, the holy catholic Church, the communion of saints, the forgiveness of sins, the resurrection of the body, and life everlasting. Amen." (Cf. Nicene Creed.)

Apostles of Places and Peoples • These are similar to the patron saints of the various countries and are as follows:

Alps: St. Bernard of Menthon
Andalusia (Spain): St. John of Ávila
Antioch: St. Barnabas
Armenia: St. Gregory the Illuminator; St. Bartholomew
Austria: St. Severinus
Bavaria: St. Kilian
Brazil: Bl. José de Anchieta
California: Bl. Junípero Serra

Carinthia (Yugoslavia): St. Virgil

Colombia: St. Luís Bertrán

Corsica: St. Alexander Sauli

Crete: St. Titus

Cyprus: St. Barnabas

Denmark: St. Ansgar

England: St. Augustine of Canterbury; St. Gregory the Great; St. George

Ethiopia: St. Frumentius

Finland: St. Henry

Florence: St. Andrew Corsini

France: St. Remigius; St. Martin of Tours; St. Denis

Friesland (Germany): St. Swithbert; St. Willibrord

Gaul: St. Irenaeus

Gentiles: St. Paul

Georgia (Russia): St. Nino

Germany: St. Boniface; St. Peter Canisius

Gothland (Sweden): St. Sigfrid

Guelderland (Holland): St. Plechelm

Highlanders (Scotland): St. Columba

Hungarians (Magyars): St. Stephen, King; St. Gerard of Csanad; Bl. Astericus

India: St. Thomas, Apostle

Indies: St. Francis Xavier

Ireland: St. Patrick

Iroquois: François Picquit

Italy: St. Bernardine of Siena

Japan: St. Francis Xavier

Malta: St. Paul

Mexico: The twelve apostles of Mexico (Franciscans), headed by Fra Martín de Valencia

Negro Slaves: St. Peter Claver

Netherlands: St. Willibrord

Northumbria (Britain): St. Aidan

Norway: St. Olaf

Ottawa Indians: Father Claude Jean Allouez

Persia: St. Maruthas

Poland: St. Hyacinth

Portugal: St. Christian

Prussia (Slavs): St. Adalbert of Magdeburg; St. Bruno of Querfurt

Rome: St. Philip Neri

Rumania: St. Nicetas of Remesiana

Ruthenia: St. Bruno

Sardinia: St. Ephesus

Saxony: St. Willibald

Scandinavia (North): St. Ansgar

Scotland: St. Palladius; St. George

Slavs: Sts. Cyril and Methodius; St. Adalbert

Spain: St. James; Sts. Euphrasius and Felix

Sweden: St. Ansgar

Switzerland: St. Andeol

Tournai (Belgium): St. Eligius; St. Piaton

Apostleship of Prayer • A Catholic movement promoting devotion to the Sacred Heart and prayer for a specific monthly intention. It is associated with a pious association, the League of the Sacred Heart, founded in 1844 by the French Jesuit François Xavier Gautrelet. The monthly intention and devotional objectives of the apostleship are publicized by means of the *Messenger of the Sacred Heart* and the *Monthly Leaflet*.

Apostolate • A term derived from the New Testament word "apostle." As such, it draws an inspiration from the Twelve whom Christ called to Himself for the ultimate purpose of founding the Church. But, because St. Paul claimed to have an experience of the resurrected Christ and hence insisted on being called an Apostle too, the term cannot be interpreted too narrowly. In the widest sense of the term, then, an apostle is one who is sent on a mission.

Throughout the Church's history the term "apostolate" has consistently referred to work accomplished on the Lord's behalf, applied in a very specific sense to the work carried out by the non-ordained. In the decree *Apostolicam Actuositatem*, the Vatican Council II Fathers outlined the vocation of the layperson and identified the origins of this vocation in the sacrament of

Baptism. Through Baptism, the decree states, every Catholic is called to an active participation in the priestly, prophetic and royal office of Christ. The decree is quick to point out that the proper field of endeavor for the lay apostolate is the temporal order. In the temporal and nonecclesiastical sphere, that is, where people live, work and recreate, the layperson is called to witness to the light of Christ's truth and to become what the Gospel calls the salt of the earth.

The term "apostolate" may also be applied to the specific work done by members of a religious order or congregation. If so, an apostolate may be related to the founder or foundress of the order or congregation or the charism associated with the founder or foundress. For example, the apostolate of St. John Bosco (1815-1888), the founder of the Salesian Order, was the spiritual formation, education (general and technical) and career training of boys and young men. This work has been carried out by the Salesian priests and brothers since the death of their founder, who is frequently referred to as the patron saint of youth. In this sense, then, we can say that the Salesians have had an apostolate to and with the adolescent and young adult Catholic males of succeeding generations.

The post-synodal exhortation of Pope John Paul II entitled *Christifideles Laici* (1988) serves as an excellent treatise on the topic of the lay apostolate. Taking the seminal insights of Vatican II, combining them with the new urgency of the lay vocation and applying both of these elements to the contemporary scene, the Pope has offered the Church a timely yet perennially valid understanding of how the layperson witnesses to Christ and the Catholic Faith in the marketplace.

Apostolate of Lay People, Decree on the: See **Apostolicam Actuositatem**

Apostolate of Suffering • A pious association, founded in 1926 and dedicated to cultivating an awareness of the Christian value of suffering, especially among the terminally and chronically ill.

Apostolic Canons • A set of eighty-five canons concluding the seventh book of the fourth-century *Apostolic Constitutions*, whose author claimed apostolic authority for them. The canons referred primarily to the clerical state and conduct. Although their apostolic attribution cannot be sustained today, it remains true that the canons influenced Church law and institutions, both in the East (where they were accepted by the Trullan Synod in 692) and in the West (where the first fifty canons were translated into Latin in the sixth century by Dionysius Exiguus).

Apostolic Constitution • Usually abbreviated "ap. con.," an Apostolic Constitution is generally regarded as the highest form of ecclesiastical legislative document issued by the Pope himself. Historically, the term Papal Bull has often been used to describe those documents which today might be termed Apostolic Constitutions, although the continuity is not absolute.

Apostolic Constitutions treat of the most fundamental questions in Church life and practice, but they do not necessarily have a universal scope. A classic example of an Apostolic Constitution would be *Sacrae Disciplinae Leges* (January 25, 1983) which promulgated the 1983 Code of Canon Law. The official texts of Apostolic Constitutions appear in the *Acta Apostolicae Sedis* and translations (which can be either approved or unofficial) become available soon afterward.

Apostolic Datary • The date of institution of the Apostolic Datary is unknown but it was already functioning in the fifteenth century. This office was charged with granting requests for various favors, dispensations and benefices. The constitution *Regimini Ecclesiae* suppressed the Datary in 1967.

Apostolic Delegate • The official representative of the Holy Father to the Catholic Church in those countries that do not have diplomatic relations with the Holy See. An apostolic delegate is not the head of the Catholic Church in the country to which he is assigned. Rather, he represents the Holy Father to the country's bishops. Usually his duties include supervision of the process for presentation to the Holy See of candidates for the episcopate, as well as other matters that are within the mandate given him by the Holy See.

Although all apostolic delegates presently are archbishops, the revised Code of Canon Law does not require that the representative of the Pope have Holy Orders (cf. Canons 362-367).

Apostolic Fathers • Those select writers who either learned holy doctrine at the feet of the Apostles or, being at least very close to them in time, exhibited a profound respect for and understanding of their teachings. For some time, the writings of the Apostolic Fathers were held in quasi-canonical esteem and naturally merit continued study to this day. Among the lights of this group are Clement of Rome (Pope St. Clement I), Ignatius of Antioch, Polycarp of Smyrna and Hermas.

Apostolic Ministry • The comprehensive ministry exercised in the Church in the first place by the Apostles and in post-Apostolic times by their successors, the Pope and the bishops in communion with him. This ministry is comprehensive in the sense that it has primacy and oversight with respect to all other ministries in the Church. It is of the essence of the apostolic ministry to possess the responsibility for teaching and handing on the truth of the Gospel, for sanctifying the community through the liturgy and sacraments, and for guiding the Church's internal life and its relations with others.

Apostolic Prefecture: See **Prefecture, Apostolic**

Apostolic See • This title has been used when referring to Rome from the earliest centuries of the Church, because of its association with St. Peter and his successors. As the seat of the Vicar of Christ, it is the center of the Catholic Church, containing the papal *cathedra* and the offices of the various tribunals and congregations that assist the Pope in the government of the Church.

Although a less common use of the title refers to those ancient sees founded by the various Apostles, and which were seen as primary witnesses of the apostolic tradition, it is now used exclusively of Rome.

Apostolic Signatura • Dating back to the thirteenth century, this is the formal title for what amounts to the supreme administrative court of the Catholic Church. Unlike the U.S. Supreme Court, the Signatura deals mainly with questions involving the jurisdiction of lower courts over cases. It also has a section that deals with appeals of the clergy against decisions of their superiors.

The Signatura is composed of a body of Cardinals, but the day-to-day matters are handled by the cardinal prefect, who is its head, by the secretary (an archbishop) and a staff (cf. Canon 1445).

In more recent years, the Supreme Tribunal of the Apostolic Signatura, as it is more formally known, has been active in reviewing the appellate procedures of first- and second-instance courts in the United States and Europe.

Apostolic Succession • The relation of validly ordained bishops to the Apostles is designated by the term "apostolic succession." Christ entrusted the continuation of His ministry to the Apostles, who in turn became the founders and leaders of the first communities of Christ's followers. In dependence on the Apostles, and in recognition of their special bond with Christ, the new communities of Christians were authorized to conduct the ministries of teaching, sanctifying and guiding the Church. The prime responsibility for these ministries was vested in men designated by the Apostles and subsequently called bishops. These first bishops in turn selected other bishops, and so on.

The significance of this practice became evident in the second century in the course of disputes with Gnostic heretics who claimed to be in possession of a secret message whose transmission bypassed the successors of the Apostles. As a result of these disputes, the importance of the connection of the bishops with the Apostles — in many cases an actually traceable lineage — was articulated as the foundation for the authenticity and unity of the Faith proclaimed in the communities of the historic mainstream. The Christian doctrine affirming the church-forming significance of the connection of the bishops with the Apostles is referred to as the "apostolic succession." The bishops are those leaders to whom the Apostles entrusted the commission which they received from Christ Himself. In this way, the Church of post-Apostolic times maintains its continuity in faith with the community around Christ Himself. This continuity is not so much a matter of tracing the apostolic "pedigree" of every local Ordinary,

but consists in a relationship of incorporation into the college of bishops which, as a whole, possesses the apostolic commission.

Apostolic Union • Originating in the work of the Ven. Benedict Holzhauser in seventeenth-century Bavaria, an association of diocesan priests who live according to a rule fostering their spiritual life and their exercise of their pastoral ministry.

Apostolic Vicariate: See **Prefect, Apostolic;** also **Prefecture, Apostolic**

Apostolicae Curae • The title of a Papal Brief of Pope Leo XIII, issued in 1896. It declared that Anglican Orders were "absolutely null and utterly void" due to defect of form and defect of intention. In a letter to Cardinal Richard of Paris, dated November 5, 1896, Leo XIII declared that it was his intention "to deliver a final judgment and to settle the question completely."

Apostolicam Actuositatem • The Decree on the Apostolate of Lay People, *Apostolicam Actuositatem*, was issued by the Second Vatican Council on November 18, 1965, to define the mission of the Church to which the members of the laity are called, by virtue of their Baptism. "The Church was founded to spread the kingdom of Christ over all the earth for the glory of God the Father, to make all men partakers in redemption and salvation, and through them to establish the right relationship of the entire world to Christ" (AA 2). It is to this apostolate that every member of Christ's Mystical Body is called, and it is exercised by evangelizing and sanctifying those in the world, by working to influence all things with the Gospel, bearing witness to Christ and helping men to be saved. This decree emphasizes that the lay apostolate is carried out "in the midst of the world and of secular affairs. . ." (AA 2) and that "men, working in harmony, should renew the temporal order and make it increasingly more perfect: such is God's design for the world" (AA 7).

This decree also recognizes the right of the laity to establish, direct, and join associations for the carrying out of the lay apostolate, and it is the duty of the hierarchy to "furnish it with principles and spiritual assistance, direct the exercise of the apostolate to the common good of the Church, and see to it that doctrine and order are safeguarded" (AA 24).

The final exhortation of the decree appeals to the laity to "give a willing, noble and enthusiastic response to the voice of Christ" (AA 33), which calls each one to carry out the Church's apostolate, which is the work of the Lord Himself.

Apostolici • This term first came into use during the second, third and fourth centuries and was applied to various branches of the Gnostic heresies which preached, among other things, an extreme form of poverty in false imitation of the Apostles. The term reappeared in the thirteenth century and, in fact, is still used occasionally even today to describe those more eccentric groups which claim to be returning to what they believe were the pristine practices of the primitive Church.

Apostolicity • One of the Marks of the Church, apostolicity designates in the first place the fact that the Church is founded upon the Apostles. Thus, the Church shares in the mission entrusted by Christ to the Apostles, viz., to proclaim the Gospel to the whole world. The Church is also apostolic in that she preserves and teaches the Deposit of Faith which was Christ's gift to His disciples. Finally, apostolicity refers

to the succession of bishops — the historic episcopate — to whom the Apostles entrusted their own commission from Christ.

Apostolos • The Greek word meaning "apostle." In the Byzantine Rite, it is also the book containing the epistles, or the epistle itself.

Apparel (Paratura) • Comes from the French *appareiller* ("to make fit") and refers to a small oblong panel of embroidery on the cuffs and at the front bottom part of the alb, as well as along the top portion of the amice. Though the use of the apparel on the amice has fallen out of favor for several centuries, the custom of having the paratura along the bottom of the alb has returned, though not only on the front part of the alb, but all the way around it. This is especially so when lace is not used to decorate the alb. This has returned into vogue, especially in Europe. The apparel can be of gold or silver thread, as well as of the appropriate liturgical color for the day (except black). (Cf. Aurifrisium.)

Apparitions • The sense-perceptible vision or appearance of Christ, the Blessed Virgin, angels or saints. Many apparitions are recorded in the Scriptures (e.g., Tb 3:16-17; Gn 26:24; Lk 1:11, 26). The authenticity of apparitions is a matter for investigation and evaluation by the Church or an experienced spiritual director. Church approval is always required when a popular cultus arises in response to alleged apparitions.

Some of the most important approved apparitions center on visions of Our Lady: the Virgin of Guadalupe (1531); the Miraculous Medal (Paris, 1830); Our Lady of La Salette (1846); Immaculate Conception (Lourdes, 1858); Our Lady of Knock (1879); Our Lady of Fátima (1917). Since 1981 a group of teenagers in Medjugorje, Yugoslavia, have claimed to experience regular apparitions of Our Lady. The authenticity of these apparitions is still under evaluation by the Holy See.

Often, messages are entrusted to the persons who experience apparitions. Such messages are officially termed "private revelations," in order to signal their subordination to Revelation properly so-called, as conveyed in Scripture and Tradition and interpreted by the Magisterium. The interpretation of private revelations must take into account their expression in the thought-forms of doctrinally and theologically unlearned persons.

Appeal • As does every credible system, canon law provides a system for review and, if necessary, correction of the decisions of lower ecclesiastical courts.

In matters of judicial appeal against the decision of an ecclesiastical tribunal, the appeal court examines not only the procedures followed, but the substance of the case as well. It has the power to overturn the decision of the first court and retry the case itself. Every tribunal of every diocese is assigned an appeal court to which appeals are to be directed. If a further appeal against the decision of the appeal court is to be lodged, the court of appeal on this third level is the Roman Rota.

Every person who receives a decision from an ecclesiastical court has the right to appeal. Although this usually involves appealing to the court assigned as appeal court in what is called "second instance," this appeal may be made directly to the Roman Rota (cf. Canons 1628-1640).

Appellant Controversy • After the death of the illustrious Cardinal Allen, the founder of Douai College in Rome, where he was a special advisor to the Holy See on the state of the Anglican Schism, a dispute arose over who would be chosen as his successor. A group of some thirty English priests, known as the "Appellants," protested the process of selection, which was, however, resolved by papal decree in 1602. One year later, the various disputants were basically reconciled under the banner of a "Pledge of Allegiance."

Appellants • In common usage, an appellant in canon law is one filing an appeal against the judicial decision of an ecclesiastical tribunal (cf. Canons 1628-1640).

In Church history, however, "Appellants" was the term which designated a group of French clergy who in 1713, under the leadership of Cardinal de Noailles, appealed to an ecumenical council against a papal condemnation of certain Jansenistic materials. No such action was taken, of course, by a council, and indeed, in modern times, such an attempted appeal to a council would be considered delictual on the part of those so appealing (cf. Canon 1372).

Appetite • Appetite is the inclination or tendency that proceeds from what a thing is. Natural tendencies are universal in entities in the world: Everything tends to act in ways that flow from its nature and toward goals that will contribute to the good of that nature. These tendencies are called "natural appetites." One of the characteristics that distinguishes animals from plants and non-living entities is that animals have the power to apprehend the goal of their tendencies: to feel, and, in the case of human animals, to know what their tendencies are directed toward or away from. To capture this important distinction between animals and other beings in the world, philosophers distinguish natural from animal, or elicited, appetites. Animal appetites are described as elicited because they are aroused by the sense perception or intellectual knowledge of an object.

Because human beings possess both sense and intellectual knowledge, they possess both sense and intellectual appetites. Sense appetites or emotions that are directed toward a simple good are called concupiscible appetites (viz., love, desire, joy, hatred, aversion, and sadness), while those directed toward difficult or arduous goods are called irascible appetites (viz., hope, courage, despair, fear, and anger). Will is the name given to the intellectual appetite in human beings. Unlike other animals, human beings freely seek the goods that are apprehended by intellectual knowledge. Purely spiritual goods — like fellowship, justice, and immortality — are sought by the will, whereas spiritual evils — like deceit, chaos and death — are rejected by the will. A central aspect of the Christian moral life is the cultivation, enabled by divine grace, of those virtues that direct human appetites to embrace objects that are authentically good and that lead to the enjoyment of the ultimate good of communion with the Triune God.

Appropriation • The attribution to one of the Three Divine Persons of essential attributes or common activities which are in reality true of all Three Persons together. Thus, it is common practice in Christian Tradition to attribute wisdom (an essential attribute of the Triune God) to the Son or creation (a common activity of God) to the

Apse of Sant' Apollinare (circa 549)

Father. Appropriation is an important vehicle for Christians to express and worship the mystery of the Trinity.

Apse • This term designates the semicircular or polygonal eastern end of basilican-style churches, modeled on the Roman architectural design of official buildings. The altar is normally located in the center of the apse, with seats for the bishop and clergy located along the wall circling the altar.

Apsidole • A small apse. The term is used particularly in churches with more than one apse, in order to distinguish the smaller from the main apse.

Aquamanile • Medieval (twelfth or thirteenth century) bronze water pitchers for washing the celebrant's hands at Mass. Often shaped as lions, dragons, birds, etc., they were symbolic as well as functional.

Aquarians • An obscure heretical sect that held that the use of wine in the Holy Eucharist was sinful. This sect was strongest in the second century but quickly disappeared.

Aquileian Rite • The primitive rite used in the province of Aquileia, in northern Italy. It was also used in Verona, Trent and Pola. During the Carolingian period, it was superseded by a variant of the Roman Rite and was finally suppressed in 1597.

Aramaic • A term used to designate a cluster of Semitic languages. One of these, Galilean Aramaic, was the language spoken by Jesus. That it was appreciably different from the Aramaic spoken in Jerusalem can be discerned from Matthew 26:73, where Peter is recognized as a Galilean on the basis of his accent. Bits of the Old Testament have come down to us in Aramaic (e.g., Ezr 4:8—6:18; 7:12-26; Jer 10:11 and Dn 2:4b—7:28). In the New Testament one comes upon an array of words and phrases in Aramaic: *talitha koumi, ephphata, eloi, eloi, lama sabachthani, marana tha, Akeldama, Golgotha, Bethesda, Gethsemane*. A modern western form of Aramaic, much influenced in vocabulary and syntax by the Arabic spoken in the area, continues to be used as a household language in Ma'lula and a few other Christian villages of the Anti-Lebanon.

For further reading: Stephen A. Kaufmann, "Languages (Aramaic)," *Anchor Bible Dictionary*, 2:173-178.

Arca • The box or pyx in which the Eucharist was reserved by the early Christians in their homes and from which they daily received.

Arch • (1) A prefix joined to the title of a person or unit, signifying a preeminence over another, e.g., archbishop, archdiocese.
(2) In architecture, a term for a form which spans a space, giving support to the structure above it. Arches of various types (e.g., Norman, Gothic, Tudor), are fundamental features of much church architecture, and often define a particular style of building.

Archaeology, Christian • This area of archaeology studies Christian monuments to discover information about them, including the catacombs, cemeteries, churches, monasteries, sculptures, paintings, mosaics, frescoes, engravings, inscriptions, artifacts, pottery, weapons and historical records. Discoveries such as that of the Dead Sea Scrolls have given new insights into biblical, liturgical, catechetical, historical and ecclesiastical areas of Church life. (Cf. Dead Sea Scrolls.)

Archaeology, Commission of Sacred • On January 6, 1852, Pope Pius IX established the Commission of Sacred Archaeology. Its purpose is the study of ancient Christian monuments to ascertain the life and thought of early Christians. The objects investigated are monuments, catacombs, paintings, mosaics, sculptures and inscriptions. The commission is also responsible for the care of the Vatican State museums. Under its supervision, the most important excavations below St. Peter's Basilica between 1939 and 1949 led to the discovery of an entire early-Christian and pagan necropolis and the burial place of St. Peter.

Archangel • The term generally taken to mean "lead, chief or ruling angel" (Jude 9; 1

Thes 4:16). They are mentioned throughout Scripture. On a popular level the term refers to high-ranking angels, such as St. Michael the Archangel, who, within the hierarchy of the nine choirs of angels, is a princely Seraph. Just as guardian angels protect, so too the archangel has a unique role as God's messenger to people at critical times in the salvation process (Tb 12:6, 15; Jn 5:4; Rv 12:7-9).

Archbishop • Title of a bishop with jurisdiction over an archdiocese. Like every diocesan bishop, he is the authentic teacher of the Faith in his territory and is truly a successor of the Apostles. His pastoral authority comes from Christ Himself.

Archangel (Byzantine mural)

Some archbishops serve as metropolitans of an ecclesiastical province. In addition to his authority in his own see, the metropolitan archbishop has a certain supervisory jurisdiction over the other dioceses in his province. Such sees are called suffragan dioceses. Typically, in the United States, an ecclesiastical province may be equivalent to a state. The archbishop heads the principal see in a region, which may be composed of several smaller suffragan dioceses as well.

The symbol of a metropolitan archbishop is the pallium, a woolen vestment worn over the shoulders, with which he is invested by the Pope or a papal delegate. The Pope may also create an archbishop *ad personam*, which is a personal honor given to some who do not have authority over an archdiocese.

Archbishop, Titular • An archbishop not occupying a residential see, but one which is now extinct or defunct.

Archbishop-Elect • The proper title of a prelate in the interval of time between the date of the Holy See's announcement of his elevation to an archiepiscopal see and the day of his actual consecration and/or installation in that see.

Archconfraternity • A confederation of local chapters of confraternities or sodalities having the status of approved public associations in the Church. Such associations are distinct from religious or apostolic institutes of consecrated life. Such associations of clergy and laity are organized to promote a fuller Christian life for their members, to foster Christian teaching or other apostolic works, to cultivate piety and devotion or to advance the Christian cause in the public and social realms. Approval and erection are attained after the statutes of a public association are reviewed by the competent ecclesiastical authority. Examples of archconfraternities are the Holy Name Society and the Christian Mothers.

Archdeacon • This ecclesiastical office can be traced to the third century. It was held by one of the deacons whom the bishop selected to assist him in both liturgical and administrative tasks. On some occasions, the archdeacon was the delegate of the bishop for a particular area of the diocese. The powers of the office were ended by the Council of Trent. Today its functions are exercised by the vicar general and the vicars forane. The title is retained as an honorific of the cathedral chapters of some European cathedrals; it also exists in the Anglican Church.

Archdiocese • A territorial division of the Church that is governed by an archbishop. It differs from a diocese in that an archdiocese is the primary see of an ecclesiastical province consisting of one or more dioceses.

Archetype • The original pattern according to which something is modeled and produced. In Christian thought, the term is sometimes used for the so-called "divine ideas" in order to affirm that everything that exists is caused by God and therefore reflects His being and wisdom. The term has many other uses in philosophy and psychology. From the Greek *archetypon*, meaning "model."

Archiepiscopal Cross (Patriarchal Cross) • Probably of medieval origin, the archiepiscopal or patriarchal cross developed in imitation of the custom of bearing a cross before the Pope in solemn procession. In form, it is a simple crucifix mounted on a staff and borne with the corpus facing the prelate. Crosses with double and triple bars have for the most part only a heraldic existence. The contemporary Roman Liturgy does not recognize any distinctive archiepiscopal or patriarchal cross.

Archimandrite • Originally, the title of the head of a monastery in the Eastern Rites, but presently a title of honor conferred by a patriarch upon a deserving priest.

Architecture • The design and erection of Christian ecclesiastical buildings, in particular churches, chapels, monasteries, priories and convents. Distinctive Church architecture dates from around A.D. 313, when the Emperor Constantine granted toleration to the Christian communities and sponsored the erection of basilicas and other ecclesiastical buildings. Previously, Christian worship and ritual were carried out in structures adopting local house forms (*domus ecclesiae*). Then, and subsequently, Christians avoided adoption of pagan temple models, although they appropriated the style of Roman public buildings. A progression of styles has characterized ecclesiastical architecture over the centuries since the early basilican style: Byzantine, Romanesque, Gothic, Renaissance, Baroque and neo-Gothic. Contemporary architectural styles reflect the renewed emphasis on the church principally as the site of communal worship.

Archives • By Church law, the records of every diocese must be kept in a safe place. These records, which pertain to the spiritual and temporal affairs of the diocese, are called the archives. They are to be kept under lock and key, with only the bishop and the archivist having ready access. Their permission is needed for anyone else to enter the archives. Canonically, archives are under the administration of the chancellor, but many dioceses and archdioceses have full- or part-time archivists in their employ as well. Increasingly, albeit within the limits of confidentiality and usually sparse diocesan resources, diocesan archives are being recognized as important sources for secular history and family genealogies. The national Association of Catholic Diocesan Archivists exists to help individual archivists in their work.

In addition to the regular archives, canon law also dictates that every diocese have a secret archive that contains especially sensitive material, including the proceedings of any criminal trials that take place. Only the bishop has access to the secret archives (cf. Canons 486-491).

Archivist • Every diocese is required to have a person whose principal task is to gather, arrange and safeguard the written records of the diocesan curia or administration. Traditionally, the position of archivist has been that of the diocesan chancellor (cf. Canon 482).

Aside from the canonical position of archivist, the position is also held by persons whose responsibility it is to maintain records, especially those of historical interest, of any institution such as a religious community, hospital or college.

Archpriest • A title with several meanings: (1) From the fourth and fifth centuries, it designated a priest chosen to assist the bishop directly or to substitute for him in specific priestly functions. Today it applies to deans or vicars.

(2) During the sixteenth century in England, it denoted a superior over secular priests.

(3) By custom, another priest assists a newly ordained priest at his first Mass, in cassock and surplice at Low or Sung Mass, or in cope at Solemn Mass. Also, an ecclesiastical dignitary assists a greater prelate at Pontifical Mass in the same way, vested in cope. In either case, the proper term for such a priest is "assistant priest."

Arcosolium • Comes from the Latin for "seat of the arch" (*arcus* + *solium*) and refers to an arched niche with a flat bottom, which is very common in the Roman catacombs.

This flat slab was used primarily to seal the tomb, as well as to mark the place of the interred's grave. In the early days of the Church, when Christians were still being persecuted, Mass was celebrated on these *arcosolia*. Some traces of this still remain in Christian architecture where chapels and altars are so placed in an apse that they evoke the primitive arcosolium.

Arcula: See **Arca**

Areopagite • One who speaks at the Areopagus, a hill northwest of the Acropolis (the core of the ancient Greek city, walled and usually on a hill overlooking the districts of the larger city area) of Athens. At one time it was the meeting place of the two principal Athenian ruling bodies: the council and the court (c. 500 B.C.). By New Testament times it was primarily a gathering place for academic debate. The tone of St. Paul's preaching there (Acts 17:16-34) was in more philosophical terms rather than in his usual rhetorical style. His preaching led to the conversion of Dionysius and Damaris.

For further reading: Hubert M. Martin, Jr., "Areopagus," *Anchor Bible Dictionary*, 1:370-372.

Areopagus: See **Areopagite**

Arianism • A heresy of the fourth century which asserted that the Son of God was not truly divine but created; that He was not eternal but temporal. It is named from its principal proponent, Arius, a priest of Alexandria. He refused the command of his bishop, Alexander, not to advance these novel opinions and was excommunicated by a synod of Egyptian bishops around A.D. 319. Arius tried to gain popular support through his book, *Thalia*, and from influential bishops, especially Eusebius of Nicomedia.

Because of the unrest caused by this conflict Emperor Constantine called, with papal acquiescence, an ecumenical council in Nicaea in 325. The Council Fathers (about three hundred, mostly from the East) read from Arius's *Thalia* and declared it unacceptable. The formulation of a positive statement of belief which would reject Arian views was more difficult. The key word of the creed adopted, a forerunner of the Creed used at Mass, was *homoousios* (*consubstantialis*, one in being or nature). The creed explicitly anathematized those who denied the eternity of the Son or held Him to be of a different nature from the Father. Constantine enthusiastically accepted this statement, following the advice of his theological adviser, Bishop Hosius of Cordoba.

St. Athanasius, foe of Arianism (Venice mosaic)

The issue was doctrinally settled but continued to be the subject of fierce conflicts for about fifty years. Constantine wavered in his support of Nicaea and after his death (337) the Arian party waged a persistent campaign against the definition. They were supported by Constantius II, sole emperor after 350. St. Athanasius, present at Nicaea as a deacon with his bishop Alexander, succeeded Alexander, became the leader of the Catholic party, and for his efforts was exiled from his see of Alexandria for much of his life.

The various factions of Arians formed three major groups: the most extreme, *Anomoeans* (*anomoios*, dissimilar) asserted a difference in nature of Father and Son, with only a moral unity; *Homoians* (*homoios*, similar) avoided dogmatic precision; and the *Homoiousians* (*homoiousios*, similar in nature) or Semi-Arians wanted to stress both similarity and dissimilarity. After 379 the political situation improved and the theological contributions of the Cappadocians led to a new council at Constantinople (381), which reaffirmed Nicaea and taught the consubstantiality of the Holy Spirit.

Arianism is treated as a Trinitarian heresy, but its doctrine has Christological implications. The tendency of Alexandrian Christology was to speak of a union *in* nature rather than a union *of* natures (i.e., essential rather than personal union). With their neo-Platonic biases against matter, it is natural that they would question how a transcendent Logos can form one entity with matter. Thus Arianism is linked with the earlier subordinationism of Origen and some of the Apologists and with later Apollinarianism and Monophysitism.

Ariel • A Hebrew name meaning "the lion of God" or the "hearth of God." In Isaiah 29:1-2, 7, the term is used to designate the holy city of Jerusalem.

Ark • The word "ark" is used in four different ways in Scripture:

(1) The vessel in which Noah and his family escaped the flood (Gn 6-8). The ark had three decks and measured four hundred fifty feet in length, seventy-five feet in width and forty-five feet in height. Some biblical scholars think the biblical description was patterned after the ark of Utnapishtim of the Babylonian Flood.

(2) The ark, as a means of salvation through water, is a type of Baptism (1 Pt 3:20f.).

(3) A word used to describe a basket or chest in which Moses was placed in the Nile (Ex 2).

(4) The Ark of the Covenant (Ex 25:10ff.), a tabernacle God commanded Moses to build of acacia wood to hold the restored tables of the law.

For further reading: Isaac Kikawada and Lloyd R. Bailey, "Noah and the Ark," *Anchor Bible Dictionary*, 1:1122-1131; C. L. Seow, "Ark of the Covenant," *Anchor Bible Dictionary*, 1:386-393.

Arles, Councils of • Near Marseilles on the banks of the Rhone River, the town of Arles was the site of some fifteen councils. The first, in A.D. 314, was convoked by Constantine in order to address the Donatist schism in northern Africa. Among notable subsequent councils were one in 353 that favored Arianism, another in 1234 that sought to condemn Albigensianism and another in 1263 that repudiated the teachings of Joachim of Fiore. The last of this series of Councils of Arles was held in 1275.

Armageddon • This noun occurs only in Revelation 16:16, where it is said to be a Hebrew word. However, its Hebrew etymology is uncertain as is the location it represents because the term has various spellings in the Greek manuscripts. The term identifies the place of the final cosmic battle between God and Satan, where good triumphs over evil.

For further reading: Jon Paulien, "Armageddon," *Anchor Bible Dictionary*, 1:394-395.

Armagh, Book of • Now located in Trinity College, Dublin, the *Book of Armagh* (also known as the *Codex Dublinensis*) is an eighth- to ninth-century vellum codex, attributed to Ferdomnach of Armagh (d. 846) and comprising several important manuscripts. The most important of these are two lives of St. Patrick, a life of St. Martin of Tours by Sulpicius Severus and a Latin (but non-Vulgate) translation of the complete text of the New Testament.

Armenian Church • The Catholic Church, established by St. Gregory the Illuminator, flourished in Armenia (in northern Asia Minor) for several centuries, at least until the defeat of the Armenians by the Persians in the seventh century. Thereafter, it fell into various heresies and eventually went into schism. Armenians reject the sacrament of Anointing of the Sick and they permit divorce. They are also generally regarded as Monophysite. Several attempted reunions with Rome have failed, although over 160,000 Armenian Catholics (mostly in Germany and the United States) are presently in union with Rome under the spiritual leadership of their *Katholikos* in Cilicia. In 1981 an Armenian exarchate was established in New York.

Armenian Rite: See **Rite, Armenian**

Arms of Christ, The • The symbolic representation of the instruments used during the passion of Christ; viz., the nails, the scourge, the lance, the cross, and so on.

Art, Christian • The depiction of Christian subjects in a variety of artistic media, including mosaic, painting, sculpture, architecture, stained glass, calligraphy and illumination, metalwork, wood-carving and textile design. Christian art dates from the simple decorations on the walls of the catacombs and has flourished in almost all periods. Artists have been inspired to portray the great events and figures of salvation, as well as the central mysteries and ideas of the Christian Faith. The outpouring of creative energy has been immense. It arises from the conviction that the impact of the divine mysteries can be felt with greater force when expressed in visually impressive forms. The Church has consistently supported and preserved the work of artists. Indeed, many of the most creative initiatives in the history of art have been sustained and advanced through the active encouragement of Christian churchmen.

Art, Liturgical • The branch of Christian art that is concerned principally with the design of the objects and fabrics used in worship. This field includes the design and manufacture of sanctuary furniture, vestments, sacred vessels, candles, altar cloths, linens and hangings. Statues, church design and decoration may also fall within the competence of liturgical artists.

Art, Sacred • An umbrella term for the whole range of depictive, ornamental, decorative and sculptural arts which center on religious subjects and purposes. Sacred art is found not only in churches, but also in private homes, and even occasionally in public places. The earliest examples of specifically Christian art can be found in the Roman catacombs, and as the influence of the Church grew, so there was a corresponding opportunity for artists to employ their talents in art for sacred purposes, with the Church eventually becoming a major patron of the arts, providing the world with much of its finest and best-known works of art.

Artoklasia • From the Greek for "bread-breaking." This liturgical term of the Byzantine Church describes that portion of Vespers celebrated for a feast (e.g., Pentecost) at which five loaves of leavened bread, a container of wheat, of wine and of oil are blessed for distribution on the feast day. In practice, either on the feast itself or the Sunday following, the loaves are cut and the bread is distributed to the congregation, who are also anointed with the blessed oil. In times past, when an all-night vigil was observed for a feast, the congregation actually was sustained with the bread and washed with the oil. The ceremony is symbolic of the loaves and fishes blessed by Our Lord in the feeding of the five thousand.

Artos • In the Churches of the East, any bread used in a liturgical ceremony. The Hagios Artos, or Holy Bread, is the bread of the Offertory, also called Prosphora. It corresponds to the Host of the Western Liturgy. Also a term for the special bread of Pascha (Easter) shared on Thomas Sunday (the Sunday after Easter).

Arts, The Liberal • Usually, a term reserved for humanistic studies, as distinct from vocational or occupational fields of expertise. In this sense, the liberal arts include literature, history, languages, philosophy and science. In modern higher education, such studies are understood to cultivate general knowledge and culture, and to provide a broad background for subsequent specialization.

Ascension of Christ • Refers to the ascending of Jesus' risen and glorified body into heaven, such that His person exists in corporeal form with God the Father outside time and space. The New Testament witness to the Ascension can be organized under three headings: (1) Jesus' exaltation

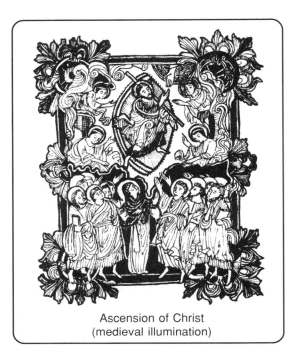

Ascension of Christ
(medieval illumination)

in heaven at the Father's right hand (Acts 7:55; Rom 8:34; Eph 1:20; 2:6; Col 3:1; 1 Pt 1:21: 1 Jn 2:1; Heb 1:3, 13; 10:12); (2) His ascension above, which fills all things and His being taken into glory as the great High Priest (Eph 4:10; 1 Tm 3:16; Heb 4:14; 6:19ff; 7:26; 8:1; 9:24); and (3) the historical witness to this event (Lk 24:50ff.; Acts 1:9ff.).

For further reading: Norman R. Gulley, "Ascension of Christ," *Anchor Bible Dictionary,* 1:472-474.

Ascetical Theology • The branch of theology that studies the dynamics of ordinary purification in the person who is beginning in the practice of virtue. In its subject matter, ascetical theology occupies a middle point between moral theology, on the one hand, and mystical theology, on the other. According to a distinction commonly drawn since the seventeenth century, moral theology is concerned with the absolute basics of Christian life, and mystical

theology is concerned with the higher states of prayer attained through the gifts of the Holy Spirit and the special graces conferred upon a person far advanced along the way of perfection. Although this system of classifying these branches of theology has some basis in the nature of the subject matter itself, it enshrines a certain artificiality and fragmentation that some contemporary theologians have sought to overcome by combining ascetical and mystical theology under the rubric of spiritual theology. But this expedient leaves in place a division in which moral theology is deprived of the indispensable context provided by the themes of divinization, grace and the call to union with God addressed to all the baptized. Pope John Paul II has encouraged initiatives in the continuing renewal of these branches of theology that may help to overcome their artificial and sometimes misleading disjunction.

Asceticism • A form or rule of life accepted by an individual as one struggles toward Christian perfection. The scriptural basis for ascetical practices is in the command to avoid the concupiscence of the flesh, of the eyes and of the pride of life (1 Jn 2:16). Asceticism is a disciplinary tool that puts order and harmony in the soul, expiates for sins and enables one to imitate the sacrificial life of Christ. It springs from God and seeks to overcome obstacles to union with God. Central to ascetical practices is the understanding that these practices and the negation of the self they bring about are necessary for growth in Christ.

There are two sides to ascetical theology, denying oneself and following Christ. The former calls for fasting, watchfulness, chastity and self-discipline; these are seen as the means of purifying the soul from its passions and are the necessary means of growing in love of God.

Asceticism was transformed in the Middle Ages and came to concern itself with sharing in the sufferings of the Redeemer. In the beginning of the modern era, there was a strong reaction against asceticism by the Reformers and Renaissance humanists. However, modern ascetics such as the Jesuits, Visitandines, some Puritans and some other modern Catholics adopted a more private and individual asceticism, and after Trent it was still widely practiced. Protestants such as the Puritans adopted a rigorous and negative asceticism, while Methodists have practiced a particularly modern form of asceticism. Asceticism has grown even further with the emergence of monastic communities in the Anglican and Lutheran Communions.

Aseity • An expression of the uniqueness of Divine Being, insofar as God does not receive His existence through any other being (Latin *a*, from; *se*, itself). God receives existence from Himself alone and not (like everything else except God) from another. It follows, then, that God is also His own reason for existing. If it were otherwise, creation might be thought of as somehow necessary to God, as providing the Creator with a reason for existing. However, precisely because God needs no reason but Himself to exist (because of His aseity), creation must be an act of pure love, pure self-giving, on His part. Similarly, the fullness of Divine Being precludes any becoming or development, any potentiality yet to be realized, in God. Indeed, it is only the fully realized state of God's existence that enables Him to be the "be-all and end-all" of the change and movement, the becoming, of each creature and of all together.

Ash Wednesday • The first day of Lent in the Roman Rite, on which ashes are blessed and used to mark the heads of the faithful as a sign of penance. In the fourth century, public penitents wearing sackcloth were sprinkled with ashes as a sign of penitence. As public penance was gradually discontinued, it became the custom for all the faithful to receive ashes (eleventh century) in beginning Lenten penance as preparation for Easter.

The choice of a Wednesday to begin Lent was originally not uniformly kept in the Church, since, from the fourth through the sixth centuries, the season lasted three, four, six or eight weeks — depending on local custom. The establishment of a season with six Sundays and an additional four days (from Ash Wednesday on) was determined when Lent was understood to be the Church's annual imitation of Christ's forty-day fast. Hence, calculating six fast days per week (Sunday excepted) times six weeks, adding up to thirty-six, required the addition of four days; thus, Ash Wednesday now begins Lent.

Ashes • In the Old Testament, to "gird on sackcloth" and "roll in the ashes" (cf. Jer 6:26) is an act symbolic of mourning, sorrow and repentance (cf. Est 4:1, 3; Jb 2:8; 42:6; Is 58:5; Jer 6:26; 25:34; Ez 27:30; Dn 9:3; Jon 3:6; 1 Mc 3:47). Sprinkling ashes on one's head as a token of repentance is found in 1 Maccabees 3:47 (with fasting and the wearing of sackcloth); 1 Maccabees 4:39 (along with wearing torn garments).

Because ashes themselves are what remain after a fire (Lv 4:12; 4:11-12), mourning and penitential practices involving ashes signify self-abasement and contrite self-humiliation.

In the New Testament, the phrase "sackcloth and ashes" appears in Jesus' reproach against the unrepentant towns of Chorazin and Bethsaida: "Woe to you, Chorazin! Woe to you, Bethsaida! for if the mighty works done in you had been done in

Tyre and Sidon, they would have repented long ago in sackcloth and ashes" (Mt 11:21 and Lk 10:13).

Ashes are placed on the foreheads of those who participate in the liturgy for Ash Wednesday, the beginning of Lent, as a sign of the penitential character of the Lenten season. These ashes, which come from the burning of palm branches used on Passion Sunday of the previous year, are blessed after the homily of the Mass. They are then imposed with either of two formulas: "Turn from sin and be faithful to the gospel" (cf. Mk 1:15) or "Remember, man, you are dust and to dust you will return" (cf. Gn 3:19). The blessing and imposition of ashes may also be done outside of Mass on Ash Wednesday, in which case the entire Liturgy of the Word precedes the rite, which is then followed by the General Intercessions.

Asperges • Derived from the Latin *aspergere* ("to sprinkle"), this is the ceremony which from ancient times has been performed just before the principal Sunday Mass wherein the priest sprinkles the congregation with holy water. At this time, the words of Psalm 51 are sung: "Purge me with hyssop and I shall be clean. . . ." In Latin this verse begins, *Asperges me, Domine, hyssopo*, thus giving the ceremony its name. During the Easter Season the antiphon *Vidi aquam*, "I saw water was issuing from the temple. . ." (cf. Ez 47:1-2, 9), is sung instead.

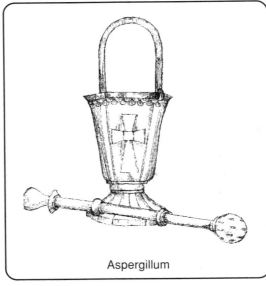
Aspergillum

Nowadays the *Asperges* ceremony has been replaced in the revised Mass rite by the Rite of Sprinkling, which may take the place of the Penitential Rite. Any suitable song or antiphon may be sung during this ceremony.

Aspergillum (Aspergill) • The liturgical instrument used to sprinkle people and objects with holy water in the Divine Liturgy and during blessings. The word comes from the Latin *aspergere*, "to sprinkle." It may consist of a silver, brass or wooden handle with a long brush or hollow multi-pierced orb through which the water is sprinkled. Sometimes the handle is also hollow when this latter form is used, in order to contain more water. (Cf. Asperges.)

Aspersion • A form of Baptism in which the candidate is sprinkled with water. The term carries the additional sense of sprinkling with holy water in blessings.

Aspersory (Aspersorium) • A bucket-like vessel for holding holy water used in blessings, along with an implement for sprinkling (cf. Aspergillum).

Aspirations • Short prayers expressing petitions, faith or charity. Such aspirations are: "*Marana tha!* Come, Lord Jesus"; "Jesus is Lord"; or "My Jesus, mercy," for example.

For further reading: *Catechism of the Catholic Church*, nn. 2671, 2700-2704.

Ass • The domesticated ass was employed as a work animal and for riding as early as the third millennium B.C. The animal figures frequently in the Bible. According to the prophets, the future king of Zion would come riding on an ass (rather than on horseback or in a chariot) to underscore the peaceableness of his reign (Zec 9:9) — a prophecy fulfilled in Christ's entry into Jerusalem amid the waving of palms.

Assessor • A canonical advisor who can assist a judge in an ecclesiastical trial or administrative process. Assessors need not be degreed in canon law, and can be either clerics or lay persons. Assessors are mandatory in the case of administrative penal processes. (Cf. Canons 1424, 1448, 1720.)

Assist at Mass • An expression used to describe active participation in the celebration of the Eucharist on the part of the faithful. Presence at Mass should never simply be a passive, non-involved attendance, but an active participation in which all join in — indeed, assist in — the offering of the Sacrifice by prayerful attention, singing and responding to the various prayers, as well as by the appropriate postures of standing, sitting and kneeling.

Assistant at the Pontifical Throne • Originally, those patriarchs, archbishops and bishops who were given a place of honor around the papal throne during liturgical ceremonies, but now the term is applied to those domestic prelates (episcopal members of the papal court) who have this honor.

Assistant Priest • A descriptive term rather than a technical title, this refers to any priest who aids another priest in carrying out his ecclesiastical duties. In particular, it is often used for parochial vicars assigned to parish ministry under the direction of a pastor. The 1983 Code of Canon Law has simplified the various types of assistant priests, and while it outlines proper subjection to those in authority, it also speaks of the spirit of cooperation among clergy, all of which contributes to the pastoral care of the faithful.

In the context of liturgical functions this term may be used for the chief clerical attendant of the bishop who presides. A newly ordained priest is permitted to have an assistant priest to give any necessary guidance in celebrating his first Mass.

Associate Pastor • The term commonly used for what the 1917 Code of Canon Law called a curate or assistant pastor and what the revised Code calls a parochial vicar. He must be a priest and is assigned to a parish to assist the pastor. The associate is to help with the overall ministry of the parish. He may be assigned by the pastor to specific duties for which he is responsible under the supervision of the pastor. Depending on the size and needs of the parish, more than one associate pastor may be assigned by the bishop (cf. Canons 545-548).

Associations of the Christian Faithful • In canon law, the term "Associations of the Christian Faithful" is a technical one referring to a wide variety of organizations to which the Catholic faithful may legitimately belong. Canon 298 of the 1983 Code of Canon Law outlines the major purposes served by these organizations: promotion of the more perfect life and public worship, evangelization and Christian education, works of piety and charity, and enhancement of a Christian social order. Members can be drawn from the laity, clergy or religious, although certain special norms govern clerical associations (cf. Canons 278, 302).

Although associations of the Christian faithful fall into two broad categories, namely, public and private, they both share certain canonical similarities.

Generally, under Canon 299 the faithful have the right to found any type of association, except that Canon 301 restricts the founding to ecclesiastical authority of those whose mission is dedicated to public worship or doctrine. Canon 299 also presumes that an association is canonically private unless Church authority explicitly determines otherwise. In practice, almost all associations are, in fact, private associations. Importantly, no association may use the term "Catholic" in its title without ecclesiastical permission (cf. Canon 300). This canon tries to protect the faithful-at-large, as well as society, from being deceived by organizations whose titles falsely seem to imply Catholic reliability.

Assumption of the Blessed Virgin Mary

• In the only declared exercise of papal infallibility in the twentieth century, Pope Pius XII, after consultation with all the bishops of the Catholic Church, on November 1, 1950, proclaimed the Assumption of the Blessed Virgin Mary a doctrine of the Faith. The dogma of the Assumption states that Mary was taken up body and soul into heaven, after the completion of her earthly life (in theological terminology, her dormition, or falling asleep in the Lord), since by reason of her Immaculate Conception she should not suffer the consequences of original sin.

While there is no direct biblical evidence for the Assumption, the Church has long held, on the basis of theological reasoning and Tradition, the implicit belief in Our Lord's taking His mother to Himself from the moment of her passage from this life, since she is declared "full of grace" or "highly favored daughter" of God the Father (Lk 1:28). The Archangel Gabriel further articulates Mary's relationship to the Trinity in this fashion: "The Holy Spirit will come upon you and the power of the Most High will overshadow you; therefore, the child to be born will be called holy, the Son of God" (Lk 1:35). It might be argued, then, as St. Francis de Sales suggests, that the Assumption is necessitated by the desire of the Trinity to behold for eternity Mary, who enjoys a unique relationship with each Person of the Trinity as daughter, mother and bride. In the Eastern tradition, the argument is advanced from the doctrine of the Incarnation that Christ took His mother into heaven so that He Who was perfectly human might gaze forever upon, at least, one other human being, glorified like Himself (cf. Glorified Body). The Second Vatican Council, in similar fashion, states: "Finally the Immaculate Virgin, preserved free from all stain of original sin, was taken up body and soul into heavenly glory, when her earthly life was over, and exalted by the Lord as Queen over all things, that she might be the more fully conformed to her Son, the Lord of lords (cf. Rv 19:16) and conqueror of sin and death" (LG 59).

As archetype of the Church, Mary exemplifies the very essence of the Church, and the dogma of the Assumption must have most significant consequences for all the faithful: "In the meantime the Mother of Jesus in the glory which she possesses in body and soul in heaven is the image and beginning of the Church as it is to be perfected in the world to come. Likewise she shines forth on earth, until the day of the Lord shall come (cf. 2 Pt 3:10), a sign of certain hope and comfort to the pilgrim People of God. . . .

"The entire body of the faithful pours forth urgent supplications to the Mother of God and of men that she, who aided the beginnings of the Church by her prayers, may now, exalted as she is above all the angels and saints, intercede before her Son in the fellowship of all the saints, until all families of people, whether they are honored with the title of Christian or whether they still do not know the Saviour, may be happily gathered together in peace and harmony into one People of God, for the glory of the Most Holy and Undivided Trinity" (LG 68-69).

The feast of the Assumption was celebrated by Christians as early as the seventh century. Today it is celebrated as a holy day of obligation in the United States on August 15.

Assumptionists • The Augustinians of the Assumption (A.A.), as they are officially known, were founded by Emmanuel d'Alzon in 1845 at Nimes, France. They engage in teaching (e.g., at Assumption College, Worcester, Massachusetts), parish ministry, mission work and other apostolic activities.

Asteriskos •
An implement used in the Byzantine Rite for the celebration of the Divine Liturgy, and composed of two strips of metal joined in the center and bent down to form a cupola. A small star is often suspended on a chain from the

Asteriskos

center. The Asteriskos represents the star of the Magi. It is placed on the paten, over the Holy Bread, and holds the veils away from it.

Astrology • The "science" which studies the alleged influence of the stars and other heavenly bodies on the fortunes of human beings. Chiefly on the basis of observation of the positions of the stars, astrology claims to be able to predict a person's fortunes over the course of a lifetime, or on an specific day, or under particular conditions. Astrology was popular in the late antiquity when it was widely thought that human beings were subject to fate and the caprice of the gods. But the critique of Christian thinkers — like St. Augustine in his *City of God* (V, 1-8) — eventually prevailed against the practice of astrology by exposing its extravagant inconsistencies, its offense against God Who alone knows the future, and its effective denial of the reality of human freedom and choice. Under the influence of Arab and Jewish scholars, interest in astrology resurfaced in the medieval period and peaked in the sixteenth century, only to decline again under the impact of eighteenth-century rationalism. In the late twentieth century, under the combined influence of the decline of faith and the growth of superstition, astrology is enjoying a revival. While it is not clear how seriously astrology is regarded by the people who consult its practitioners and their daily horoscopes, Catholics understand it to be a form of divination contrary to the virtue of religion when it seeks to predict with certainty future events dependent on free will. What the future will involve for any individual human being is determined by the infinite wisdom of divine providence and not by the position of the stars. That future depends on God's intention to bring all things to the Good, and on the exercise of each person's God-given freedom under grace to choose the Good in every circumstance and situation of life. The serious sin in the convinced practice of astrology lies in its denial of divine providence and human freedom.

Asylum, Right of • Also known as the right of sanctuary, the practice of according to criminals or combatants the refuge of a church or other ecclesiastical building or territory. It is understood that a person seeking such refuge cannot be forcibly removed from the place of sanctuary. Asylum often includes the right of safe passage to an agreed-upon place of exile. The custom dates from medieval times and is still widely respected.

Athanasian Creed: See **Creed, Athanasian**

Atheism • Until the emergence of the term "Agnosticism," this term referred to those who believed the existence of God was improbable.

Traditionally, there were three kinds of atheists: materialists, philosophical agnostics and pantheists. Philosophical agnostics consider the evidence invoked to justify belief in God insufficient to warrant affirming or denying the existence of God and they believe that any assertions about the existence of God are rash. Materialists are not strictly atheists because they do not believe that anything can exist outside the closed material system, but they are generally classified as atheists because their materialist presuppositions exclude spiritual realities. Logical positivists are most often material atheists, for they hold that assertions about God are meaningless and belief in God is not warranted. Much of contemporary atheism is a practical and not a speculative atheism, with the exception of dialectical materialism, which is explicitly atheistic.

Atheism can be culpable when a person deliberately rejects persuasive proofs for the existence of God, but the Second Vatican Council asserted that there were circumstances when atheism was not subjectively culpable because of the humanity of the Church which inhibited belief in the true God.

Atonement • The Christian doctrine that through Christ's passion, death and resurrection, infinite satisfaction is made to God for the sins of humankind. Through this satisfaction, we are reconciled to God. Christ's atonement consists, not primarily in the intensity of the suffering He endured, but in the perfectly obedient and loving acceptance of the Will of the Father which He displayed in embracing this suffering for our sake. Christ's perfect obedience atones for the disobedience of Adam and wins for us the grace of obedient discipleship and divinizing sanctification. Christ is the "Lamb of God who takes away the sin of the world" (Jn 1:29), the perfectly innocent Servant Who suffers in the place of the truly guilty (cf. Lk 22:37; Is 53).

The Epistle to the Hebrews expounds on the meaning of Christ's atonement by showing that it fulfilled and surpassed the sacrifices of the Old Law. The words of institution, employed in all celebrations of the Eucharist, speak of the cup of "the blood of the new and everlasting covenant" which "will be shed for you and for all so that sins may be forgiven." In the history of Christian doctrine, a variety of theological explanations have been developed to account for the mystery of the atonement. Theories that emphasize the love and obedience of Christ in suffering for our sake are preferable to those theories (either penal or substitutional) that center on the appeasement of divine wrath or the ransom paid to Satan.

Atonement, Day of • This phrase translates the Hebrew *Yom Kippur*, the highest of Jewish holy days which falls on the tenth day of the seventh month of the Jewish calendar. The ritual is for the reparation of sins and is described in

Leviticus 16:1ff. (cf. Lv 23:26ff.; Nm 29:7). In Acts 27:9, it is called the "autumn fast" because of when it occurred and the required fasting (a sabbatical day off was also required). This very important day was brought to a deeper and more permanent level with Christ's sacrifice on the cross. Christ is both the Priest and the Victim of the sacrifice. The New Testament witness does not put forth any theory of atonement but makes clear that Christ is the source of "at-one-ment" (Middle English for "atonement") with God (Mk 10:45; Rom 5:10; Eph 2:13, 18; 1 Pt 2:24; Heb 9:28; 2 Cor 5:19).

For further reading: David P. Wright, "Day of Atonement," *Anchor Bible Dictionary*, 2:72-76; Moshe David Herr et al., "Day of Atonement," *Encyclopedia Judaica*, 5:1376-1387.

Attention • In Christian usage, attention is that focusing of the mind on the substance of a particular activity (for example, the administration of a sacrament or praying) or the moral quality of some action. Thus, incomplete or confused attention could mitigate one's culpability for a moral failure. On the other hand, distractions in the course of administration of the sacraments, while possibly sinful, do not render the sacraments invalid.

Attributes of God: See **God, Attributes of**

Attrition • Sorrow for a sin that results from either a fear of punishment inflicted by God for sin or from the ugliness of sin. It is contrasted with contrition which is a sorrow for sin because it violates the love of God. Even though the motive of attrition is morally good it does not flow from a pure love of God and is therefore inferior to true contrition. Scholastic theologians such as Aquinas believed that attrition was sufficient to win forgiveness, but others such as Peter Lombard believed that contrition was necessary for absolution of sin. Martin Luther rejected the claim that attrition was sufficient for forgiveness and likened it to "gallows remorse."

This controversy is pointless, however, for true attrition requires authentic rejection of sin for religious motives. Contrition and attrition are different in the explicitness of their motives, but in the sacrament, attrition becomes contrition, for both stem from a real and actual revulsion of sin and bring the justifying grace of God.

Audience, Papal • Generally it means any reception given by the Pope to one person or to a group of people. Papal audiences are usually held in the Audience Hall, opened in 1971 on the south side of St. Peter's Basilica with accommodations for approximately 12,000 persons, or weather permitting, in St. Peter's Square. When the Pope is in residence at his vacation home, Castel Gandolfo, they are held in a small hall reserved for the receptions.

General papal audiences are scheduled weekly, normally on Wednesdays, and last approximately an hour to two hours. Arrangements are under the supervision of the prefecture of the apostolic household. Americans seeking admission tickets to general audiences may apply to the Casa Santa Maria, Via dell' Umiltà 30, 00187 Rome, Italy.

Semiprivate audiences are granted to small groups of people with a special purpose, enabling people to kiss the Pope's ring and exchange a few words with him.

Private audiences are granted almost exclusively to those who have the most urgent or important business with the Pope: bishops, heads of state, ambassadors, etc. They normally take place in the Pope's private library.

Auditor • An auditor is an official of an ecclesiastical court. He or she may be designated by a presiding judge from among the approved judges of the court or may be specially appointed by the bishop. Auditors may be either cleric or lay.

The function of the auditor is to gather evidence in the case. He or she has some discretionary power in deciding what evidence is to be collected and the manner in which it is to be collected (cf. Canon 1428).

Augsburg, Diet of • Augsburg, in Bavaria, was the center of important developments, disputes and settlements of the early Reformation. Lutheran influence in the city was strong as early as 1518; Zwinglian influence, after 1526. In 1530 it was the site of a significant Diet during which Emperor Charles V heard the petition of the Lutheran party that they be given equal standing with Catholics. This petition, the *Augsburg Confession*, had been drafted by Philipp Melanchthon, an early systematizer of Luther. Catholic theologians summoned to the Diet accepted nine of its articles without qualification and six others with reservations. The other thirteen articles were rejected. The Lutheran party attempted a partial defense of their position, but the emperor refused to accept it. A more elaborate defense (*Apologia*), published by Melanchthon in 1531, was more controversial in tone. The *Confession* and the *Apologia* became important confessional documents of Lutherans and a slightly modified version of the *Confession* influenced the Reform or Calvinistic Tradition.

Religious conflict continued in Augsburg, and Catholic worship was forbidden there in 1537. After the somewhat ambiguous results of two Schmalkaldic Wars, a settlement was formulated at a later Diet in 1555. This "Peace of Augsburg" accepted the Augsburg Confession and Catholic Faith as valid forms of religious understanding according to imperial law. The principle was accepted that determined the religion of an area by the religion of its ruler (*cuius regio, eius religio*).

Augsburg, Peace of • The political resolution of the competing religious claims of Lutheranism and Roman Catholicism within the German Empire, concluded at Augsburg on September 25, 1555, between the Electors and Ferdinand I. In effect, the settlement was a territorial one, following the rule that the religion of each land was to be determined by the ruling prince (a rule later expressed by the formula *cuius regio, eius religio*). The settlement affected Catholics and only those Protestants who had signed the Augsburg Confession (1530), the official standard of the Lutheran faith. Other Protestant groups, e.g., Calvinists, were not recognized. Those inhabitants unwilling to accept this arrangement were permitted to emigrate after disposing of their property. Only in the imperial cities were members of both communions permitted to coexist, if already in place.

Augustinian Fathers • A union of monasteries following the Rule of St. Augustine, approved by Pope Alexander IV in 1256, lies at the origins of the Order of St. Augustine (O.S.A.) as it exists today. Along with the Dominicans, Franciscans and Carmelites, the Augustinians were known as friars from medieval times. Education, parochial ministry and missionary work are the areas in which they focus their apostolic energies.

Augustinism • This term usually refers to the characteristic positions of St. Augustine of Hippo (A.D. 354-430) on the doctrines of the Fall and original sin, atonement, grace and predestination. Although St. Augustine addressed a wide range of topics in his prolific writings, his positions on the aforementioned doctrines are said to comprise "Augustinism." In fact, of course, much of St. Augustine's teaching on these topics represented an expression of fundamental Christian doctrine and was acknowledged as such when adopted as official Church teaching. Hence, it is perhaps misleading to label his teaching on these matters as "Augustinism" and thereby to marginalize a formulation of what is in fact widely recognized as authentic Catholic doctrine.

St. Augustine of Hippo

Aumbry (also Ambry) • A wall cupboard for the reservation of altar bread and wine, sacred vessels, liturgical books, holy oils, relics or the Eucharist itself. From the fourth century on, sacred objects were kept in the sacristy. After the decrees of Pope Innocent III, Eucharistic aumbries had locks and keys. As devotion to the Eucharist grew, aumbries were placed in more prominent places in the sanctuary. After the Council of Trent, tabernacles on the altar replaced aumbries for the reservation of the Blessed Sacrament, and aumbries were used for the holy oils — thus the *Olea Sancta* door in the sanctuary wall in many older churches.

Aureole • The gilt background completely surrounding figures of the Blessed Trinity, Christ or the Virgin Mary. In iconography it represents the glory attached to a particular person. It is mostly used to denote divinity and was extended in use to the Blessed Mother because of her exalted place in salvation history and in the life and mysteries of Christ. In early Byzantine art it appeared as an oval shape behind the person portrayed. Because of this, the Italian name for it, which has become regularly used in art, is *mandorla*, which means "almond" or "almond shaped." It should not be confused with the "nimbus" or halo that surrounds the head of Divine Persons or saints as portrayed artistically to denote their sanctity.

Auricular Confession • The Council of Trent held that all who have lapsed into sin must confess their sins according to number and species to regain grace (DS 1707).

Little is known of the form of confessional practice in the early Church, but it seems that auricular confession (confession to a priest) began in the Celtic Church at the beginning of the sixth century. This form of confession was a new system developed at the end of the patristic period, and by the end of the sixth century it was accepted by nearly all. Along with the auricular form, repeated reception of the sacrament became more common. Auricular confession seems to have also become widespread among the Syrian Monophysites around the eighth century as well.

The Second Vatican Council and the Church after the Council have insisted on the necessity of auricular confession of sins to a priest for absolution of sin, despite some efforts to grant absolution in the absence of this practice.

The *General Instruction of the Revised Rite of Penance* speaks about four principal parts of the sacrament: contrition, confession, act of penance and absolution. Regarding "confession," it states: "The Sacrament of Penance includes the confession of sins, which comes from true knowledge of self before God and from contrition for those sins. However, the inner examination of heart and the outward accusation must be made in the light of God's mercy. Confession requires, on the penitent's part, the will to open the heart to the minister of God and, on the minister's part, a spiritual judgment by which, acting in the person of Christ, he pronounces his decision of forgiveness or retention of sins in accord with the power of the keys" (n. 6b).

Auriesville • Near Amsterdam, New York, the site of the shrine of the North American Martyrs. In the seventeenth century, the Mohawk village of Ossernenon was located here. St. René Goupil was martyred here in 1642, and St. Isaac Jogues and others were held captive. It is the birthplace of Bl. Kateri Tekakwitha.

Aurifrisium (Apparel) • An embroidered stiff border used in medieval times to decorate the top part of the amice (before it came to be worn under the alb), used to make its appearance neater. Its use decreased during the Renaissance until it disappeared altogether (although some vestment makers today have revived the use of the apparelled amice). The term itself comes from the Latin for gold embroidery, since most border embroideries or orphreys were made of gold cloth or gold thread. However, the color of the aurifrisium varied and usually followed the liturgical color of the day.

Aurora, Mass of the • Of the three distinctive Masses provided to be celebrated on Christmas, the Mass of the Aurora is offered at dawn. These three Masses are said to symbolize the threefold birth of Christ: midnight being a reminder of the eternal birth of the Son from the bosom of the Father; at dawn, His birth from the womb of the Blessed Virgin Mary; and during the day, His mystical birth in the souls of the faithful.

Austerities • Self-imposed rigorous practices of discipline imposed to foster spiritual growth and perfection. Traditionally, austerities included such practices as fasts, deprivation of sleep and the wearing of a hairshirt. True repentance requires works of penance and deep sorrow for sin, and the austerities were means of manifesting that spirit of repentance. The austerities can manifest a proper spirit of penance that is necessary for spiritual growth, but these practices must be governed and regulated by a confessor. The austerities are a way of rejecting egoism and self-indulgence, and they should be undertaken in proportion to the dispositions and capabilities of the individual.

In our own time, these austerities may not be as necessary as they seemed before, but what is of necessity is the penitential spirit that fosters the austerities.

Australia, Christianity in • Late in the eighteenth century, British settlers, almost entirely Anglican, began to arrive in Australia in significant numbers. Since that day, the predominant religious affiliation of the Australians has been Anglicanism. In 1834 and 1841, however, the first Catholic dioceses were established, just in time to accommodate large numbers of Irish immigrants taking part in the Australian gold rush of 1851. Since that time Catholics have represented about one-fourth of the total population, with various Protestant sects now combining with Anglicanism to make up the majority.

Authenticity, Biblical • The concept refers to the reliability and trustworthiness of the manuscripts which form the basis of our Scriptures. Their "authentication" is in terms of their acceptance by ecclesiastical authorities, their exactness in expressing the words of their authors and their Christian use over the centuries. Apostolic authorship and widespread use in the early Church are crucial pieces of evidence regarding the authenticity of any scriptural manuscript.

Authority of Scripture • The Second Vatican Council's Dogmatic Constitution on Divine Revelation (*Dei Verbum*) states, "Sacred Tradition and sacred Scripture make up a single sacred deposit of the Word of God, which is entrusted to the Church. By adhering to it, the entire holy people, united to its pastors, remains always faithful to the teaching of the apostles, to the brotherhood, to the breaking of the bread and prayers (cf. Acts 2:42)" (n. 10). In this way, the Fathers of the Council outlined the authority of Scripture together with authority of Tradition, as authority that flows from its nature as divine revelation. Recognizing the unity of Scripture and Tradition as "a single sacred deposit of the Word of God," this statement counters the Protestant Reformation's principle, *sola Scriptura*, with a more balanced understanding of divine revelation and its transmission. In the previous paragraph, *Dei Verbum* specifies the particular authority of Scripture in terms of its origin: "Sacred Scripture is the speech of God as it is put down in writing under the breath of the Holy Spirit" (n. 9). In identifying Scripture as the Word of God,

the Council did not deny its human reality: the Council Fathers remind us that in Scripture God speaks in human fashion. From this it follows that "the interpreter of Scripture, if he is to ascertain what God has wished to communicate to us, should carefully search out the meaning which the sacred writers really had in mind" (DV 12).

The Council further specified that "the task of giving an authoritative interpretation of the Word of God, whether in its written form or in the form of Tradition, has been entrusted to the living teaching office of the Church alone" (DV 10). This work of the teaching office of the Church (Magisterium), *Dei Verbum* continues, "is exercised in the name of Jesus Christ. Yet this Magisterium is not superior to the Word of God, but is its servant" (n. 10).

Authorized Version • Strictly speaking, the expression "authorized version" designates any translation of the Bible into English authorized for use in the Church of England. In 1408, a provincial synod held at Oxford forbade translations of the Bible into English unless such translations had the previous authorization of the diocesan bishop or of the provincial council. The first such translation appears to have been the work of Miles Coverdale, whose edition was first published in Zurich in 1535 and then in England in 1537. The title page of the 1537 edition bore the words, "Set forth with the Kynges moost gracious license," indicating royal authorization. In 1540, the so-called "Great Bible" was the first to bear the indication, "This is the Byble apoynted to the vse of the churches," while two later editions indicated that this was the version "auctorised and apoynted by the comaundement of oure moost redoubted prynce and soueraygne Lorde, Kynge Henry the .viii," and that this version was "to be frquented and vsed in every church w'in this his sayd royal realm."

The King James Version, the plans for which were undertaken in 1604, on which work began in 1607, and which finally appeared in 1611, bore the legend, "Newly translated out of the originall tongues & with the former translations diligently compared and reuised by his Maiesties speciall comandement. Appointed to be read in Churches."

For further reading: F. F. Bruce, *History of the Bible in English*, 53-112, Third Edition (Oxford University Press, 1978); Jack P. Lewis, "Versions, English (Authorized)," *Anchor Bible Dictionary*, 6:830-834.

Autocephalous • From the Greek, meaning "self-heading." This term is used to describe the system of governance and authority a regional or national church has. Essentially, it means the national church can elect its own head (metropolitan, patriarch) without interference from any other patriarch or national church. Synonymous with "autonomous."

Auto-da-Fé • During the Spanish Inquisition the *auto-da-fé* (or personal edict of faith) was the name given to the public and eventually semireligious pronouncement of the tribunal against one accused of a crime. Its main parts included a condemnation of the guilty party followed by a reconciliation and sometimes also included pardons to those who had been previously adjudged guilty. It was, in any event, a proceeding separate from any action which might be administered later by the state in the case.

Autonomous Religious House • A community of religious that has no superior higher than the superior of the house, with due regard for the rights of the Holy See to intervene in serious circumstances. Strictly speaking, all monasteries are autonomous houses. Although several communities of men or women may join together in a federation of houses, each one retains its autonomy. Examples are the various Benedictine federations or the associations formed by the nuns in various monasteries that follow the same way of life.

Some autonomous communities of women are affiliated with religious institutes of men (Carmelites, Trappistines). They maintain their own order of life and governance according to their constitutions.

Autonomous monasteries with no other authority except their own superior are under the special vigilance of the diocesan bishop.

The permission of the bishop of the diocese is required for the erection of an autonomous religious house. If it is a question of a monastery of nuns, the permission of the Holy See is required as well. The suppression of an autonomous monastery of men religious pertains to the general chapter of the institute. The suppression of an autonomous community of nuns pertains to the Holy See (cf. Canons 613-616).

Autonomy • Most commonly associated with the philosophy of Immanuel Kant, autonomy suggests the independence of the moral agent. Actions done in full autonomy (or with full freedom, knowledge and consent, to use the older terminology), are those for which the moral agent is morally responsible. The promotion of autonomy has become a moral value in much contemporary ethics and moral thought because it is seen in this system as a prime ingredient of human happiness, fulfillment and flourishing. Kant held that only autonomous moral decisions were truly creditable and morality should seek to overcome the obstacles to autonomy.

In Catholic moral thought, autonomy serves growth in holiness and the spiritual life, but is not a moral value in itself. In much of contemporary American moral philosophy and ethics, autonomy is portrayed as trumping other moral values, but for Catholic ethics autonomy serves to promote the moral life, holiness and charity. Catholic moral thought has considered freedom and autonomy to be a subordinate value to other basic values, but is nonetheless one that should be promoted when possible.

Auxiliary Bishop • A bishop assigned by the Holy See to assist a resident bishop or archbishop in the pastoral care and administration of a diocese. Although an auxiliary has the fullness of Holy Orders, he does not have the same degree of jurisdiction or governing power as the residential bishop. The auxiliary must be appointed at least an episcopal vicar. He does not have the automatic right of succession when the residential bishop dies, is transferred or retires. Auxiliary bishops assist the residential bishop in the administration of the sacraments, especially Confirmation, and often represent him at various types of functions. In some dioceses, auxiliary bishops are given charge of either specific territories within the diocese or special areas of ministry, such as ministry to ethnic groups.

All auxiliary bishops are given what is called a "titular diocese." This is a diocese that once existed but has since been suppressed by the Holy See. Thus the auxiliary is bishop of a diocese in title only. The reason for this is that historically a bishop is supposed to be the head of a diocese. Yet the pastoral and administrative needs of many large dioceses are such that one bishop cannot adequately meet all of the demands. If assistance is needed in the form of one with the episcopal character, then auxiliary bishops are appointed (cf. Canons 403-411).

Avarice or Covetousness • A capital or principal sin. It is an extreme or unruly love of material goods in particular, but it also includes love of worldly honors. Avarice is ultimately a service of "Mammon" and abandonment of the heart to the perishable and fleeting. Avaricious individuals seek the acquisition of money and material goods over the good of the persons whom these objects are supposed to serve. Joy in material goods supersedes the happiness that we are supposed to create in others. Avariciousness leads to and fosters a craving for power that cannot be overcome, and it deters one from serving the legitimate needs of the poor, vulnerable and needy.

For further reading: *Catechism of the Catholic Church*, nn. 1856, 2536, 2541.

Ave Maria • This Latin expression refers to the Hail Mary, the Christian prayer that draws its origins from the greeting of the Archangel Gabriel to the Blessed Virgin Mary at the Annunciation, as recorded in Luke 1:28-30. It is sometimes called the Angelic Salutation. The first half of this prayer principally comprises the words of Gabriel to Mary, adding the words Elizabeth addressed to Mary by the inspiration of the Holy Spirit at the time of Mary's Visitation to her cousin. The latter part of this prayer grew out of the Church's traditional invocation of Mary as helper and intercessor both in life and at the moment of death in behalf of all her divine Son's adopted brothers and sisters whom she also claims as her children (cf. Lk 1:28, 42).

For further reading: *Catechism of the Catholic Church*, nn. 435, 2676-2678.

Avenir, L' (Future, The) • A newspaper published by the Catholic liberals of France beginning in 1831. The word itself means "the future," and its editorial policies reflected the thinking of Félicité de

Avignon papal palace (circa 1339)

Lamennais, Count Charles de Montalambert and Jean-Baptiste Lacordaire — namely, that the Church, if she were to prosper, should promote the legitimate ideas of the French Revolution, such as freedom of speech, democracy and separation of Church and state.

Aversion • The opposite of desire or attachment, aversion is a revulsion of what is truly good. Psychologically and spiritually, it is profoundly mysterious as to why we find aversion to what is truly good, and aversion exemplifies the mysteriousness of evil. Aversion is a sign of the effects of original sin and concupiscence. The disorderly character of our lives and desires without grace is manifested quite clearly in this psychological and moral phenomenon.

Avignon Papacy • Following the turbulent reign of Pope Boniface VIII, the College of Cardinals chose a compromise candidate in Pope Clement V, a man many believed could reconcile the Italian and French factions in the Western Church. Partly in response to the terrible feuds

between the Italian Guelfs and Ghibellines, the francophile Clement fled to the extraterritorial papal city of Avignon in southern France in 1309. For seven Popes and nearly seventy years thereafter, the Holy See was operated from this locale. Although the papacy was still, in France as in Italy, under the usual local pressures and interests, its succession was preserved intact. Indeed, especially in the matter of legal and administrative reforms, the Avignon papacy marked an improvement over past practices. At the urging of many, notably St. Catherine of Siena, several attempts were made through the decades to return the papacy to Rome (Pope Urban V being one of the more successful in this regard), but it was not until 1377 in the reign of Pope Gregory XI that the Holy See was finally transferred back to the Eternal City.

Azrael • Angel of death in Jewish and Islamic tradition.

Azyme • Taken from the Greek *azymos*, meaning bread that is unleavened. The custom of the Eastern Churches has been to use leavened bread for the Eucharist. In the West this custom ceded to the use of unleavened bread only. By the Schism of 1054, Western Christians were called "azymites" because they used unleavened bread for the Eucharist.

Azymites • A derogatory term which was commonly used by Oriental Christians after the Great Schism to refer to Latin Catholics, since they used azymes, or unleavened bread, for consecration in the Eucharist. Though it is still used sometimes in our own era, thanks to the great progress in the ecumenical movement spurred by Pope John XXIII and the Second Vatican Council, these slurs are mostly a thing of the past.

B.C. • The abbreviation for the English "Before Christ," it is used in the common system of dating by which years are marked as converging on the birth of Christ.

Baal • This Canaanite word literally means "lord" or "owner." It was used of men as well as gods and appears at times to denote locality as well as ownership. The name was applied especially to the Semitic gods of plant and animal fertility. From the second millennium B.C. onward, the word was used specifically of the Amorite god of winter, rain and storm, viz., the god Hadad. The prophets of Israel inveighed against the people's tendency to blend the cult of Yahweh with the local baals. Both Elijah and King Josiah moved to raze the "high places" where the worship of these deities was rooted. The pagan associations of the name prompted the Jews sometimes to substitute the word "bosheth" (shame) for "baal" when it occurred in the biblical text; so "Eshbaal" (1 Chr 9:39) and "Ishbosheth" (2 Sam 2:8) designate the same individual.

"Baal" was the proper name of the fourth son of Jeiel, one of Saul's ancestors from Gibeon (1 Chr 8:30-9:36); the father of Beerah, a chieftain of the tribe of Reuben was also named Baal (1 Chr 5:5).

For further reading: Marc Z. Brettler, "Baal (Person)," *Anchor Bible Dictionary*, 1:549-550; John Day, "Baal (Deity)," *Anchor Bible Dictionary*, 1:545-549.

Babel, Tower of • Etymologically, Babel means "gate of God." This structure is described in the story of the great tower erected in the land of Shinar and left unfinished because Yahweh confused the speech of the builders (Gn 11:1-9).

The Genesis account seems to refer to the ziggurat (temple-tower) of Babylon. The ancient Akkadian name of Babylon was Babilu, closely related to the Hebrew Babel. Due to the similarity of this name to the Hebrew word for "to confound," the Genesis writer may have related the ziggurat of Babel or Babylon with the confusion of tongues. Even if the identification of this particular structure with the biblical "tower of Babel" should prove not to be historically exact, it can at least give an idea of what the biblical account envisions.

The expression "confusion of tongues" may be understood to mean confusion due to construction arguments among the workers.

For further reading: Frank Anthony Spina, "Babel," *Anchor Bible Dictionary*, 1:561-563.

Babylon, The Patriarch of • The archbishop who has jurisdiction over Catholics of the Chaldean Rite; the Patriarch Katholikos of Babylon resides in al Mawsil, Iraq.

Babylonian Exile • The period during which the inhabitants of Judah and Jerusalem who had been forced to leave their native place for enforced residence in Babylonia. This exile is variously dated either from 598 B.C. (the first deportation) or from 587 B.C. (the second forced migration), to 538 B.C. when the Jews were permitted to return to their native homes by the decree of Cyrus. The inhabitants of the northern kingdom had earlier been carried off by Tiglath-pileser III to live in Assyria. In all, there were three deportations of Jews from Judah to Babylonia, viz., in 598 B.C., in 586 B.C., and finally in 582 B.C. Because of relatively benign Babylonian policies toward captives, in the end many Jews preferred not to return to Israel, even though Cyrus's decree gave them freedom to do so.

Bachelor • An unmarried or single man. According to the discipline of celibacy, only bachelors or widowers can be ordained to the priesthood in the Western Church, except those dispensed (e.g., under the "Anglican Use"). (Cf. Anglo-Catholics.)

Bad Faith • One who willfully acts contrary to the dictates of conscience is said to act in bad faith (particularly one who refrains from becoming Catholic even after becoming convinced that the full reality of the Church of Christ subsists in the Catholic Church).

Baha'i • Originating in the teachings of Mirza Ali Muhammad and founded as a religious community by Mirza Husayn Ali (known as Baha'u'llah, or "the glory of God"), Baha'i teaches the universal community of the human race and the unity of all religions. The worldwide headquarters of the religion are at Haifa, Israel, while the center for Baha'i in the U.S. is located in Wilmette, Illinois, the site of a large and distinctively designed temple. There are about twenty-five thousand local assemblies in the world. Baha'i religionists have been subjected to considerable persecution in Islamic countries.

Baianism • A system of unorthodox positions on grace and sin proposed by Michel Baius (1513-89) and condemned by Pope St. Pius V (1567) and Pope Gregory XIII (1579). Baius denied that, prior to original

sin, the state of original innocence enjoyed by our first parents was a supernatural gift, and thus in effect denied the possibility of a state of pure nature. Original sin itself, according to Baius, is identical with concupiscence and a moral evil, independent of its source in the human will. Baius asserted that all actions of men flow either from concupiscence or from charity. The sole purpose of redemption, in this view, is to substitute charity for concupiscence as the ground of human action. These themes were taken up later by Cornelius Jansen (1585-1638) and by Pasquier Quesnel (1634-1719), and were repeatedly condemned by the Holy See. (Cf. Jansenism.)

Baldacchino • (1) The canopy which provides a covering over the high altar. The baldacchino, also called "ciborium," "baldachin," or "baldaquin," is composed of metal, stone or wood and is generally dome-shaped. Chains or columns support the baldacchino, which is not as prevalent today due to the modern altar. Formerly, the materials used for the baldacchino came from Baghdad; hence, the Italian word *baldacco*. The famous artist Bernini (1598-1680) designed the baldacchino in St. Peter's Basilica for Pope Urban VIII, who reigned 1623-1644.
(2) The canopy, supported by poles, used in processions of the Blessed Sacrament, in order to protect the Host from dust.
(3) The canopy covering the *cathedra* or episcopal throne.

Balm (or Balsam) • Also called balsam for the type of conifer tree from which it is derived. In antiquity, the terebinth was the principal source of this thick, aromatic resin, prized for both its pleasant fragrance and assumed medicinal powers. Mixed with olive oil, balm is called chrism, used primarily for anointing kings and priests; it symbolizes their good and healing presence within the community.

Balm was a common export of Palestine (Sir 24:15-16), associated with Gilead as one common source (Jer 8:22, 46:11). It is one of the ingredients for chrism, used in the sacraments of Baptism, Confirmation and Holy Orders.

Baltimore • The first diocese in the United States, dating from the consecration in 1790 of John Carroll as the first bishop in this country. Three plenary councils were convened in Baltimore, in 1852, 1866 and 1884, which settled a number of administrative and disciplinary matters, and during the Second Plenary Council of 1866 certain warnings were issued against particular teachings which came to be known as "Americanism."

In 1791 the Sulpicians established the first seminary in the United States in this city, and it was an archbishop of Baltimore, James Gibbons, who was the first American to be named a cardinal.

Bishop John England,
Father of Baltimore Councils

Baltimore Catechism • A catechism is a valuable tool of religious education in which the essential teachings of the Faith are presented clearly, succinctly and cogently, usually in a question-and-answer format. The *Baltimore Catechism* was the one approved by the Archbishop of Baltimore, James Cardinal Gibbons, on April 6, 1885, as the official text recommended for the religious instruction of Catholic children in the United States. This catechism's association with Baltimore is due to the fact that the Third Plenary Council of bishops meeting in that city in 1884 had mandated a formal catechism and given the first bishop of Peoria, John Lancaster Spalding, the duty of composing one. To write it, Spalding delegated Monsignor Januarius de Concilio, a Jersey City pastor, who then submitted his draft to Cardinal Gibbons for the approbation previously noted.

The *Baltimore Catechism* thus became one of the most influential books in the history of Catholicism in the U.S., effectively imparting to generations of children a grasp of the fundamentals of their Faith. In the 1930s and 1940s, a committee of bishops, led by Bishop Edwin V. O'Hara of Kansas City, revised the work, making it more pedagogically attractive and useful, and dividing the presentation into three different volumes, each intended for progressive age groups.

During the 1960s some religious educators expressed discontent with the *Baltimore Catechism*, claiming that it was out of step with the postconciliar emphasis on Scripture, liturgy and social justice. However, in the 1980s, some catechists expressed the need for a return to a more content-centered religious education.

Baltimore, Councils of • The seven provincial (held when the entire country was one ecclesiastical province under the Archbishop of Baltimore) — 1829, 1833, 1837, 1840, 1843, l846, 1849 — and three plenary (including all the provinces in the United States) — 1852, 1866, 1884 — meetings of the hierarchy of the Catholic Church convoked to deal with the pastoral challenges faced by the Church. Although the archbishop of the premier see of Baltimore always presided, the real "father" of the Baltimore Councils was John England, the Bishop of Charleston (1820-1842), who insisted that only by regular meetings of a hierarchy adept at working in harmony could Catholic life in America be structured, defended and fostered.

Although each of the councils dealt with different topics, common concerns arose: the organization of dioceses, the recommendation of new sees, Catholic education, vocations, protection of family life, defense of moral values, vigilance against anti-Catholic bigotry, the problems of lay trusteeism, clerical discipline and Catholic literature. Probably the most influential of all was the Third Plenary Council of Baltimore, which mandated parochial schools, approved the idea of The Catholic University of America, and mandated the famous catechism which would bear the name of the first see.

Although that of 1884 was the last plenary council, the collegial tradition continued until World War I through the annual meeting of archbishops, then through the National Catholic Welfare Conference, and, since 1966, through the annual (sometimes biannual) meetings of the National Conference of Catholic Bishops.

Banner • A large, usually rectangular, piece of cloth depicting some religious figure or symbol. Banners can be affixed to the walls of churches or hung from pillars. They are also carried aloft in parades and religious processions.

Banneux, Apparitions of • The eight appearances of the Blessed Virgin Mary to Mariette Beco of Banneux, a tiny Flemish village near Liège, Belgium. The twelve-year-old girl received the apparitions in her family's garden between January 16 and March 2, 1933. Our Lady identified herself as the "Virgin of the Poor" and promised to relieve the sickness of the poor throughout the world. She appeared dressed in white with a blue sash and had a rosary draped over her right arm. In 1942, the Holy See approved public devotion to Our Lady of Banneux, while the Bishop of Liège gave final authorization in 1949 to the devotion to Mary as "Our Lady of the Poor, the Sick and the Indifferent."

Today, several million persons honor Our Lady of Banneux by belonging to the International Union of Prayer, by visiting the shrine near Liège and by attending any of the more than one hundred shrines dedicated to her under this title.

Banns • The public proclamation of an intended marriage. They are either issued verbally, as a form of announcement at Sunday Masses, or published in written form in a parish bulletin or some other public forum. The purpose of the banns is to determine whether or not any impediments exist or if there is any reason why the marriage should not take place. The persons in the congregation are asked to reveal to the pastor any reason why they think the marriage should be postponed or prohibited.

The custom of announcing banns of marriage probably started with Charlemagne (eighth century) as a means of determining if the prospective spouses were related in any way by blood. They became institutionalized with the Lateran Council of 1215. In the 1917 Code, the banns were to be proclaimed only if both parties to the marriage were Catholic. Furthermore, the publication was to take place in the parish churches of each party on three successive Sundays prior to the marriage. The bishop had the power to dispense from the publication of one or all of the banns.

In the revised Code, it is left to the bishops' conferences of each country to issue norms for the publication of the banns or some other manner of determining freedom to marry. Thus the general law no longer prescribes three successive publications, nor does it prohibit the publication in cases of mixed marriage.

The 1917 Code also prescribed the publication of banns before the ordination of candidates for Sacred Orders. The banns were to be announced in the candidate's parish church prior to his ordination to the three major orders of subdiaconate, diaconate and priesthood. This requirement has been dropped in the revised Code (cf. Canon 1067).

Baptism of Bells • Although the use of bells in Christian worship probably was not introduced until sometime in the fifth century, it became customary to summon the faithful to worship by the ringing of bells, and they are mentioned numerous times in the writings of St. Gregory of Tours (c. 585). Since the eighth century there has been a ritual for the blessing of church bells, in which the bishop uses holy water and chrism as part of the ceremony. Because both water and chrism are used in the administration of the sacrament of Baptism, this blessing popularly came to be called the "baptism of bells."

Baptism of Blood • A person (even an infant) who dies for the Faith before being baptized is said to have received the "Baptism of blood," that is, the removal of sin and the bestowal of sanctifying grace which are the effects of the sacrament of Baptism.

Baptism of the Dead • The Catholic Church forbids the administration of Baptism to persons who are known to be dead. Where a doubt exists, Baptism can be administered conditionally. Baptism of the dead is practiced by the Mormon Church in a ceremony in which a living person stands proxy for the dead.

Baptism, Lay • A Baptism administered in danger of death by an unordained (indeed, even a non-Christian) person when no priest or deacon is available. For validity, the person administering the sacrament must pour water while reciting the formula, "I baptize you in the name of the Father, and of the Son, and of the Holy Spirit," all the while intending what the Church intends. The full liturgical rites should be supplied if the person baptized survives.

Baptism, Sacrament of • The sacrament in which, by pouring water upon a person or immersing him in water, and using the words, "I baptize you in the name of the Father, and of the Son, and of the Holy Spirit," the one baptized is cleansed of original sin and (in the case of one who has reached the age of reason) of particular sin; he is incorporated into Christ and made a member of His Body the Church; he is infused with sanctifying grace and receives the theological virtues of faith, hope and charity, and the gifts of the Holy Spirit; and this enables him to receive the other sacraments effectively. The minister of Baptism is ordinarily a bishop, priest or deacon, but in an emergency anyone can baptize validly.

If it is impossible for an individual to receive the Baptism of water, the same benefits can be supplied by "Baptism of blood" (whereby martyrdom is suffered for the Catholic Faith or for some virtue) or by "Baptism of desire" (whereby a person has perfect contrition and at least the implicit intention of fulfilling God's will for man's salvation).

In conformity with the stated directives of the Liturgy Constitution of the Second Vatican Council (nn. 64-71), the rites for Baptism have been completely revised.

Under the general title of "Christian Initiation," the three revised rites are: Rite of Christian Initiation of Adults (including catechumenate), Rite of Baptism for Children and Rite of Confirmation.

Baptismal Font • A fixed pool or basin-like vessel used in Baptism. The person to be baptized is immersed, or bends into the water, or is held over it (while water is poured) for the act of water bathing and the statement of the bishop, priest or deacon, "I baptize you in the name of the Father, and of the Son, and of the Holy Spirit." The practice of immersion for Baptism, which was customary in the early centuries of the Church, has been revived in the present ritual. Hence, new fonts are often built to facilitate this practice.

The word "font" suggests living water, and new fonts often have flowing fountains incorporated into their design. The Order of Baptism mandates blessing fresh (or living) water for each Baptism except during the Easter Season, when what was blessed at the Easter Vigil is used. Early fonts were round, hexagonal, octagonal or cruciform and symbolized the death to sin. They were located in separated buildings (baptisteries) or near the door of the church to show

Baptism of Christ (illumination, circa 971)

Baptism as the "door to the Church." To focus more on the communal nature of the sacrament, Baptisms are often held during Sunday Mass and in or near the sanctuary. Some churches have visible fonts up front; where they are not, often makeshift and portable receptacles are used, a practice to be deplored.

Baptismal Name • There is evidence from the third century that adults changed their names in honor of the Apostles or Old Testament figures when they were baptized. Some parents gave their offspring names of martyrs or Christian virtues at Baptism, although a Christian name was not mandatory until the fourteenth century. The current Baptismal Rite no longer requires a saint's name, although it forbids any name obviously anti-Christian. (Cf. Name, Christian.)

Baptismal Robe • White garment once worn by the newly baptized from the Easter Vigil to Low Sunday (*Dominica in Albis*, or "Sunday to lay aside the white robes"), signifying their redemption by the Blood of the Lord applied in Baptism (cf. Rv 7:14). Infants are usually dressed in white robes to be christened — often heirlooms with lace, etc. In the U.S., frequently little liturgical garments, resembling bibs, are given at the Baptism.

Baptismal Vows or Promises • These are the promises to renounce Satan and serve God faithfully and are a part of the baptismal ritual. They were restored to the Easter Vigil in 1951 and are a part of all Masses on the day itself (replacing the Creed). After renouncing Satan, his pomps and works, the person to be baptized (or the parents speaking for the infant) then professes the Faith in a three-fold affirmation of the Creed in question-and-answer fashion, much as the actual Rite of Baptism was conferred in the early Church.

Baptismal Water: See Baptismal Font

Baptistery (also Baptistry) • Early Christian Baptism took place by immersion in lakes or rivers, but by the third century, separate buildings or rooms were built adjacent to the church in which the Eucharist was celebrated. Baptisteries were often polygonal and highly decorated with pools for immersion. Now the baptistery is often a space near the front of the church to stress the communal dimension of Baptism and the relation of this sacrament to the Eucharist. (Cf. Baptismal Font.)

Baptists • A family of independent evangelical Christian churches, broadly Calvinistic in doctrine, with more than thirty million members worldwide and an ancestry traceable to the seventeenth-century interaction of English dissenting Protestants with Mennonite Anabaptists. As founder of the first English Baptist church among the British exiles in Amsterdam in 1609, John Smyth (1554-1612) is generally regarded as the founder of the modern Baptist movement. In the United States, Baptist origins are traced to the 1639 foundation of a church in Providence, Rhode Island, by Roger Williams (1604-83).

The name "Baptist" derives from the movement's insistence on the baptism of conscious (as opposed to infant) believers and its widespread practice of Baptism by full immersion, as opposed to pouring or sprinkling with water. In addition, Baptist groups share a broad doctrinal consensus concerning the Lordship of Jesus Christ, the inspiration and sufficiency of Scripture, justification through faith and grace, the Church as a gathered community of regenerated believers baptized upon confession of faith, the independence of the local church and the fundamental freedom of individuals to approach God for themselves. Baptists have championed the separation of Church and state as crucial to the enjoyment of freedom of conscience and religion. Although broadly Calvinistic in doctrine, Baptists generally (though not without exception) follow the Arminian tradition in rejecting double predestination and insisting on the reality of human freedom and the universal scope of the atonement.

In order to foster fellowship among their churches — but without prejudice to local independence — Baptists join in national (e.g., the Southern Baptist Convention) and international (the Baptist World Alliance) associations whose roles are purely advisory.

Barefoot Friars • Barefoot (or discalced) friars are religious who, to enhance the simplicity and poverty of their lives, literally go without shoes and socks. In current practice, however, discalced usually designates the custom of wearing sandals without other foot covering, as in the case of the Discalced Carmelites and some Franciscans. Altered cultural patterns have diminished the religiously symbolic value of the practice.

Barnabas • The Aramaic meaning of the name is not certain. In Acts 4:36-37, the name was taken to mean "son of encouragement." He was a Levite from Cyprus named Joseph, who received the name "Barnabas" from the Apostles. He was the cousin of John Mark (Col 4:10) and a leader in the Jerusalem Church; he introduced Paul to the Apostles there (Acts 9:27), was their representative to the Church at Antioch (Syria; Acts 11:22ff.), and brought the recently converted Saul (Paul) there. Together they brought famine relief support to Jerusalem (Acts 11:29-30) and were both commissioned to preach the Gospel in regions not yet contacted by the early Church (Acts 13:1ff.). The mission team eventually separated, with Paul continuing with Silas, while Barnabas proceeded to Cyprus with John Mark (Acts 15:37ff.).

In post-New Testament Tradition the Epistle of Barnabas is attributed to him, and Tertullian believed Barnabas to be the author of Hebrews.

For further reading: Jon B. Daniels, "Barnabas," *Anchor Bible Dictionary*, 1:610-611.

Baroque Art and Architecture • A product of the sixteenth century, the Baroque style of art and architecture is chiefly characterized by the strong suggestion of movement and the resultant harmony between the environment and the building or the work of art. Typically, the Baroque artist employs picturesque, sweeping imagination, with a great sensitivity for the immensity of his subject. Baroque art embraces both sculpture and painting; gone is the earlier style that called for the orderly, clear and independent arrangement of figures; in the Baroque, the parts are assembled so that no part or figure stands alone; rather, all the figures constitute one sweeping panorama.

Baroque architecture is markedly flamboyant, with soaring, sweeping lines; cherubs, sunbursts and clouds are commonly employed as architectural details. Often the Baroque is criticized for its shameless showiness and its straining after effect merely for the sake of that belabored effect.

As art and architecture have frequently reflected the theology and intellectual climate of their age, so too the Baroque was a conscious representation of the Counter-Reformation in Catholic culture and enjoyed its greatest popularity in the openly Catholic countries, Italy, Austria, Bavaria and Bohemia. So strong was the Baroque influence in Rome that only Santa Maria sopra Minerva survives as an authentic representation of Gothic architecture in all the city. Certainly St. Peter's Basilica is the most famous example of Baroque art and architecture. In the United States, an outstanding example of the Baroque is the Cathedral of Saint Catherine of Siena in Allentown, Pennsylvania, consciously modeled on the Church of Santa Maria dei Pazzi in Rome; the overall Baroque effect has been completed with the outstanding Van Horn murals of the life of St. Catherine.

Bartholomew • The Greek term *bartholomaios* is from the Aramaic *bar talmai*, meaning "son of Talmai." He was one of the Twelve Apostles listed in Scripture (Mt 10:2-4; Mk 3:16-19; Lk 6:14-16; Acts 1:13). Bartholomew follows Philip in the above lists and so some speculate that Bartholomew may be the "Nathanael" whom Philip brought to Jesus (Jn 1:45-51). Eusebius records that Bartholomew brought the Gospel to India, and Jerome considered him an author of one of the apocryphal Gospels.

For further reading: Michael Wilkins, "Bartholomew," *Anchor Bible Dictionary*, 1:615.

Baruch, Book of • A book of a mere five chapters in length alleged to have been written by a son of Neraiah, a follower of the prophet Jeremiah. Today it is generally held to be the work of three separate authors which has been neatly bonded together by an editor into a consistent whole. At times the Letter of Jeremiah is added to the work as its sixth chapter.

The format of the book is tripartite. The first third is written in prose; the latter two sections are poetry. In great part, the text is an amalgam of texts drawn from the works of Jeremiah, Daniel, Deutero-Isaiah and from the Book of Job. It is directed to the Jews exiled in Babylon and was read to them before being sent on to Jerusalem, to be used in the liturgy there. The first segment derives from the ninth chapter of Daniel and contains a confession of sins followed by a plea for mercy and forgiveness. Borrowings from Isaiah, Deuteronomy, Leviticus and Jeremiah round out the section. The second part is a homily based on Job 28-29. The gist of the message is that Israel is languishing in an alien land because of having abandoned "the fountain of wisdom," i.e., the Torah. The final third of the book is in the form of a prayer for strength.

The present consensus is that the work was originally done in Hebrew. This would have to be inferred from its intended use in the liturgy. Since the book as a whole is now thought to have been translated into Greek around the middle of the second century B.C., it must have been composed before that time and not, as was once proposed, around A.D. 70.

For further reading: Aloysius Fitzgerald, F.S.C., "Baruch," *New Jerome Biblical Commentary*, 563-567; Jack R. Lundbom, "Baruch (Person)," *Anchor Bible Dictionary*, 1:617; Doron Mendels, "Baruch, Book of," *Anchor Bible Dictionary*, 1:618-620.

Basel, Council of • This Council is actually the first, and unhappiest, of the three councils that comprised the Council of Florence. The opening sessions were held in the Swiss city of Basel and were attended by about one hundred bishops. Also attending were several hundred theologians and canonists, many of whom, oddly enough, voted in at least some of the sessions. It was intended to enact reforms in the Church in the turbulent early years after the Western Schism, but instead it rather quickly degenerated into a debate on conciliarism. When Pope Eugenius IV attempted to curb this trend, he was greeted with a purported deposition by the Council, which then elected the antipope Felix V. It seems, however, that the Church was weary of antipopes, and little came of that latest attempt. In any event, numerous other disputes arose among the participants, and the Council dissolved itself without reaching any definite results. Eugenius transferred the site of the Council (twice), and most of its work was taken up by the Council of Florence.

Basic Teachings for Catholic Religious Education • A statement of the National Conference of Catholic Bishops in the United States that establishes the basic framework and context of religious education for Catholics.

Published in 1973, it preceded by four years a much larger volume entitled *The National Catechetical Directory*, which sought to provide standards and guidelines for the religious formation of Catholics in the United States. *Basic Teachings for Catholic Religious Education* contains those doctrines which the American bishops expect to be taught under the aegis of Catholic teaching. It is organized around three themes: the importance of prayer, participation in the liturgy and familiarity with Sacred Scripture. A listing of the topics covered in this work includes: God and salvation, the Trinity, the Church, the sacraments, sin, morality, the Blessed Virgin Mary and eternal destiny. Not unlike larger catechisms, *Basic Teachings* also offers readers a listing of the Ten Commandments, the Beatitudes and the Precepts of the Church. *Basic Teachings* should be seen in its proper relationship to the *General Catechetical Directory*, the universal Church's official compendium of all those items which have a place in communicating the Church's catechetical message.

Basil, Liturgy of • The basic structure of this Eucharistic liturgy is most likely the work of St. Basil the Great (c. 330-379), although it has undergone certain modifications from the date of the earliest manuscript (c. ninth century). Apart from some of the prayers, it is quite similar to the Liturgy of St. John Chrysostom. The Liturgy of St. Basil is used by some Eastern Orthodox churches, and by Catholics of the Byzantine Rite on certain appointed days of the liturgical year. Some scholarly opinion holds that this anaphora was actually the work of Pope St. Gregory the Great.

Basilian Fathers • The Congregation of Priests of St. Basil (C.S.B.) was founded in Annonay, France, in 1822. Members of the congregation serve in a variety of apostolates, with a concentration on education and evangelization. The Basilian Fathers are represented throughout the United States and Canada.

Basilian Rule • Beginning around A.D. 358, St. Basil (d. 379) composed what has come to be known as his Rule, in two forms — a longer and a shorter set of prescriptions. Because he insisted on the monks living together in community rather than as hermits, he became known as the founder of cenobitic monasticism. He is generally considered to be in the East what St. Benedict is to monasticism in the West.

Besides insisting on a cenobitic lifestyle, other prescriptions of Basil's Rule include poverty and chastity, fasting, a great emphasis on obedience and set times for community meditation and prayer. He also arranged for some type of social work to be added to the community's agenda. This often took the form of establishing schools for boys.

Basil's Rule was further developed by St. Theodore the Studite in the eighth century and was later adopted, in this form, by the monasteries of the Byzantine Empire. Today there are five branches of the Order of St. Basil the Great, as well as Basilian nuns who follow his Rule.

Basilica • This word comes from the Greek term for "royal hall," at first referring to the princely ruler, but with the conversion of the Roman Empire coming to refer to the King of Kings. Thus this term, originally applied to an official building in Roman times, built in a particular architectural style (adopted in the earliest basilica

Basilica of San Lorenzo, Rome (circa 330)

churches), now means a church of particular religious or historical importance, such as St. Peter's in Rome.

There are now two kinds of basilicas: the major, or patriarchal, basilicas, those great Roman churches one normally associates with the word; and the minor basilicas. Besides St. Peter's and the Lateran, the major basilicas are St. Mary Major, St. Paul Outside the Walls, Holy Cross in Jerusalem, St. Lawrence Outside the Walls and St. Sebastian.

Minor basilicas are other important churches in Rome and abroad which the Holy Father has honored with this title. Usually they have special privileges, such as certain indulgences, and their distinctive emblem is the "ombrellino," an umbrella striped in yellow and red to stand for the papal and senatorial colors. This "ombrellino" was formerly carried over the Pope when he would travel on horseback to make official visits. Other insignia of minor basilicas are a bell on a staff (formerly used to warn people of the Pope's approach) and the papal coat of arms in the sanctuary or above the front door.

There are thirty-one minor basilicas in the United States.

Basilidians • Followers of Basilides, an Alexandrian Gnostic of the second century who practiced rites of magic. Basilides, like all Gnostics, interpreted the Christian mysteries according to pagan symbolism. Their secret information and philosophic tenets were concealed from the uninitiated and taught to a small select group. Simon Magus, the magician mentioned in the Acts of the Apostles (8:9-24), may have been the founder of Gnosticism, according to some historians. From him the vice of simony, commercial traffic in sacred things, takes its name.

The School of Gnosticism was divided into two parts, commonly called the Syrian Cult and the Alexandrian Cult. These schools agreed in essentials, but the latter division was more inclined to be pantheistic, while the former was dualistic. While the Syrian Cult was largely Simonian, the Alexandrian School was the outgrowth of the clever Egyptian Christian Basilides, who claimed to have received his instructions from the Apostle Matthew.

Bay Psalm Book • First book published in the American colonies. The first edition (1640) contained only very poor translations of the texts of the one hundred fifty psalms. By the ninth edition (1698), some melodies were also included, and this number grew with each successive edition. By 1752, the book had had seventy editions. The original title was *The Whole Book of Psalms Faithfully Translated into English Metre*. Having been published in the Massachusetts Bay Colony, it soon became known as the *Bay Psalm Book*.

Beatific Vision • The clear, immediate, intuitive knowledge of God which results in heavenly bliss. By an act of the intellect, as defined by Pope Benedict XII in 1336, the blessed in heaven "see the divine essence by an intuitive vision and face to face, so that the divine essence is known immediately, showing itself plainly, clearly, and openly, and not mediately through any creature" (DS 1000-2). No longer do the blessed know God by reason and faith; in addition, the "knowledge" of God is greater than any other knowledge which was ever attained. Furthermore, the souls of the just see God as He truly is — Divine, One and Triune. The blessed "see" God because the intellect is enlightened by the "light of glory" which produces a corresponding delight in the will. The happy souls participate in the divine happiness by seeing and knowing God as He sees and loves Himself. Sacred Scripture (1 Cor 13:12-13; 1 Jn 3:2) affirms the reality of the beatific vision. Angels enjoy the beatific vision, as did Jesus in His human nature as He lived on earth.

Beatification • In the process for the canonization of a saint, this is the next to last step, the last being canonization itself. This act of beatification is performed by the Supreme Pontiff after a person's life, writings and teachings have been examined and found to contain nothing contrary to the teaching of the Church, nor to the demands of Christian perfection. At this stage, the person's heroic virtues are said to be recognized and the Holy Father, with the aid of consultors from the Congregation for the Causes of Saints and especially the Postulator of the person's cause, declares the person Venerable, that is, that the person may be venerated by the faithful.

At this point, all that remains are the miracles. In cases of martyrs, sometimes the necessity of a miracle is waived by the Pope, who in any case may do so *ad libitum* if he so chooses for any person whose cause has been introduced. However, the miracles are of great importance and must be of major proportions and proven to be an intervention of the supernatural order into the natural order whereby natural causes offer no plausible explanation. For beatification, one miracle is required and for canonization, two.

Once the required miracle has been performed through the intercession of the Venerable in question and recognized as such (that is, unexplainable by human science or causes), the way is made clear for this beatification, whereby the Pope grants the newly-elevated Blessed a Mass and Office of his or her own and a particular feast day to be celebrated in the places related to his or her life and in the religious order or diocese of origin. Sometimes the Blessed in question is of such a popularity or of such particular importance to the whole Church that he or she is honored with a universal cult. Unlike with canonization, the Pope does not exercise his infallible authority when beatifying. He simply grants permission for public acknowledgment. This act is also a declaration that the person involved did practice virtue to a heroic degree or suffered a true Christian martyrdom.

Among those Blessed held in honor native to the United States are Kateri Tekakwitha, Katharine Drexel and Junípero Serra.

Beatitude • (1) Among Eastern Rite Christians, the term "beatitude" is an honorific, similar to "excellency" or "eminence" and used to honor patriarchs.

(2) The Beatitudes (q.v.) are also the eight statements of Our Lord contained in the Gospel according to St. Matthew, delineating the qualities of one who aspires to blessedness.

Beatitude of Heaven • The perfect happiness possessed by the blessed in heaven, due to the attainment of God. Each soul in heaven, because of the light of glory, enjoys the unending vision of God; hence, the soul's desire is completely and perfectly realized. The beatitude of heaven consists not only in the vision of God but also in the possession of other things: i.e., freedom from illness, a glorified body, etc. What one attained on earth by nature and grace will not be destroyed; rather, those gifts will be preserved by the beatitude of heaven. Moreover, merit will determine the degree of beatitude, which will differ from person to person.

Beatitudes, The • Refers to the pronouncements of Jesus found in Matthew 5:3-12 and Luke 6:20-23. As a literary form, the "beatitude" is found throughout the Old Testament and Greek literatures in existence during Jesus' life. In Old

Testament literature "blessedness" is associated with the mighty and salvific deeds of God, prayer and wisdom sayings. A characteristic perception found in this literature is its hope in God in the midst of apparently overwhelming circumstances. The basic thrust of the Beatitudes is eschatological joy (i.e., blessedness) associated with the arrival of the kingdom of God and therefore the accomplishment of the salvation process. The paradoxical nature of the Beatitudes (the poor will inherit, the mourners will be comforted, etc.) forces the listener to redefine the suffering within the more global context of God's plan of salvation in Christ.

Beatus or Beata • Latin for "blessed one," the term refers to any holy person. Usually, it designates one who has been beatified.

Beauraing, Our Lady of • The title of the Blessed Virgin Mary referring to her apparitions at Beauraing, Belgium. Our Lady appeared thirty-three times to five children between the ages of nine and fifteen during the period from November 29, 1932, to January 1, 1933. The children were Andrée and Gilberte Degeimbre, and Albert, Fernande and Gilberte Voisin. They first saw Mary dressed in white with arms outstretched and wearing a crown of golden rays, with her golden heart exposed on her breast. Mary exhorted the children to pray and make sacrifices for sinners — much as she did at Fátima. After the apparitions ended, a ten-year investigation commenced, during which many cures were reported by those who visited the shrine. Consent was given for public devotion to "Our Lady of Beauraing" by the bishop of Namur on July 2, 1949.

Beautiful Gate • The gate called "beautiful" in Acts 3:2 is one of the entries of the Solomonic Temple as it was rebuilt in the time of King Herod, therefore contemporary with Our Lord and the Apostles. Although archaeologists are not convinced of its exact identification and location, it is generally taken to be the same as the Corinthian Gate spoken of by Josephus, who locates it on the east side of the Temple. Rabbinic tradition holds that the Messiah will enter Jerusalem in triumph through this gate; thus, it is of some significance that Christ did in fact enter the city on Palm Sunday from Bethany, east of Jerusalem and in all likelihood through the gate spoken of by Josephus. There is today on the east side of the Old City of Jerusalem a highly ornamented gate with Corinthian capitals which tradition holds to be the beautiful gate. For centuries Islamic authorities have kept it bricked up, lest it prove to be the gate through which the Jewish Messiah would enter and take control of the city; since the rabbis teach that the Messiah, according to Levitic practice, can have no contact with the dead, there is also an ancient Islamic cemetery which begins at this very gate.

For further reading: Jerry R. Pettengale, "Beautiful Gate," *Anchor Bible Dictionary*, 1:631-632.

Beelzebub • Called "the prince of demons" in Matthew 12:24, the name Beelzebub (or Beelzebul) appears in the New Testament in the context of the slanderous accusation that Jesus exorcises demons in collusion with a demon (cf. Mt 12:24, 27: Lk 11:15, 18-19) and the charge that Jesus Himself is Beelzebul (Mt 10:25) or is "possessed by Beelzebul" (Mk 3:22).

The meaning of Beelzebul is somewhat uncertain and several different spellings are attested: Beelzebul, Beezebul and Beelzebub. In the derisive form, meaning "lord of the flies," the name appears in 2 Kings 1:2 as Baalzebub, identified as the god of the Philistine city of Ekron. It is likely that the original designation would have been Baalzebul, meaning "lord of the dwelling" (Temple).

For further reading: Theodore J. Lewis, "Beelzebul," *Anchor Bible Dictionary*, 1:638-640.

Befana • In Italian folklore and culture, it is related that when the Three Wise Men (or Kings or Magi) were on their way to visit and pay homage to the Infant Jesus, they passed through the Italian peninsula. There they were in need of assistance and sought the hospitality of an old lady, "la befana." The latter, however, was not hospitable at all and thus God punished her, so that henceforth she would have to perform good deeds in memory of the Three Kings on the feast of the Epiphany and bring toys, candy and tasty morsels to all the children of Italy. To this day, Italian children expect a visit from the old witch-like hag, La Befana, on the sixth day of January and, without fail, she keeps her due appointment, to make up for her mistreatment of those who were on their way to worship the King of Kings and Prince of Peace.

Sometimes this term is used as a synonym for the feast of the Epiphany, also called "the feast of children."

Beguines and Beghards • These quasi-religious groups developed chiefly in the Low Countries during the blossoming of religious life in the Middle Ages. Although they did not take vows, they lived a common life and practiced the evangelical virtues. The male groups were called "beghards," the female, "beguines," and their residences "beguinages." They emphasized the development of personal spirituality linked with apostolic activities. Often confused with similar heretical groups, they were subject to occasional persecution. Several Belgian beguinages continue to maintain the

heritage of this form of medieval spirituality to the present day.

Being • Everything that exists has being. In Christian thought, God is understood as the Source of all being, and all created reality participates in the being that comes from God and depends on God's action to continue in existence. Metaphysics is the branch of philosophy that is chiefly concerned with the study of being.

Belfry • An architectural structure designed to house and protect bells, usually those of a church. When it stands in the center of the church roof, as is typical of churches built in the American colonial style, it is called a steeple. In churches built in the European style, one frequently sees two bell towers balancing the church facade. If there is only one, it usually stands to the side of the church; if freestanding, it is called a campanile.

In Catholic Tradition, one understands the pealing of the bells from the belfry to represent the voice of the Lord calling the faithful to prayer. Usually, this is done at the times of Masses, at the elevation of the Sacred Species during Mass and at the time of the recitation of the Angelus (6 A.M., 12 noon and 6 P.M.). These bells are also tolled in a mournful cadence at the beginning and end of funeral Masses.

Belial • In 2 Corinthians 6:15, a name given to the Devil. There St. Paul exclaims, "What accord has Christ with Belial? Or what has a believer in common with an unbeliever?" He does so in the context of advice he offers to the Corinthian Christians in the previous verse (v. 14), "Do not be mismated with unbelievers."

Though the word Belial is not used as a proper name in the Old Testament, it does appear in compound expressions that describe wrongdoers and wicked people. In

Proverbs 16:27, for instance, we read, "A worthless man (*ish beli'al*) plots evil, and his speech is like a scorching fire," and in Proverbs 19:28, "A worthless witness (*'ed beli'al*) mocks at justice, and the mouth of the wicked devours iniquity." In 1 Samuel 2:12, we read, "the sons of Eli were worthless men (*bene beli'al*)." The Hebrew phrase translated as "worthless men" can also be translated "sons of belial," and it was from this sort of usage that the term *beli'al* came to designate a wicked, demonic power in later literature.

Belial appears very frequently as a proper name in the Old Testament pseudepigrapha and in the writings found at Qumran, a proper name for a personal power opposed to God. For example, in the pseudepigraphical Book of Jubilees (second century B.C.), Moses prays, "O Lord, let your mercy be lifted up upon your people . . . and do not let the spirit of Beliar rule over them" (Jubilees 1:20). In the pseudepigraphical Testaments of the Twelve Patriarchs, it is said that God "will make war against Beliar . . . he shall take from Beliar the captives, the souls of the saints" (Testament of Dan 5:11). In the documents discovered in the caves at Qumran, the War Scroll describes the eschatalogical battle that will pit the Sons of Light against the Sons of Darkness. In that document Belial is often given as the name of the leader of the Sons of Darkness in their combat against the forces of God, the Sons of Light. The Sons of Darkness are spoken of as the "army of Belial." The War Scroll describes the blessing to be pronounced in the context of the eschatalogical battle, a blessing that clearly demarcates the two sides: "Blessed be the God of Israel for all his holy plan and for his unerring works. . . . But crushed be Belial for his invidious schemes, and damned be he for his guilty dominion" (13:1).

For further reading: Werner Foerster, "Beliar," *Theological Dictionary of the New Testament*, 1:607; Theodore J. Lewis, "Belial," *Anchor Bible Dictionary*, 1:654-656.

Belief • An act of the mind assenting to a truth; or, the truth to which assent is given can also be termed "belief." In theology the term refers especially to the act of faith by which the truths of revelation are accepted, and also to the particular truths themselves.

Bell, Book and Candle • In the Middle Ages, to signify that a major excommunication had been formalized, three symbolic actions were performed. The church bell was tolled as at a funeral, symbolic of the spiritual death of the excommunicated party. The Book of the Gospels was solemnly closed to signify that the heart and ears of the excommunicate were similarly closed to the message contained therein. As the Paschal Candle was lit at Baptism to symbolize the light of Christ burning brightly in the soul of the baptized, a candle was snuffed out to symbolize that the faith was now similarly extinguished.

Bells • Legend attributes the use of bells in Christian worship to St. Paulinus of Nola. By the sixth century they were in common use, especially among the Irish. The first bells were small, but from the eighth century they became larger and needed belfries and campaniles. The function of bells is to call the faithful to worship — important before clocks came into use — and to remind them of prayers to be said, e.g., the *Angelus* and *De Profundis*. They are also tolled at funerals as a reminder to pray for the dead, and they are rung at the consecration of the Mass to invite those not at Mass to join momentarily in worship. Bells were formerly blessed by a ritual resembling Baptism, and may still be — this refers to real bells and not electronic simulations.

Bema • Originally, a writing desk or raised platform in synagogues where the rabbi would discourse about the Scriptures and instruct the community about the Law. In the history of Christian liturgical architecture, the bema serves as the place where the Scriptures are proclaimed. In addition the term "bema" has come to be used to describe the sanctuary or elevated portion of an Eastern church, upon which are the Holy Table and, in cathedral churches, the Throne of the Bishop.

Benedicite • The *Benedicite* or "Canticle of the Three Children" (Dn 3:57-90) is that song of praise intoned by the three young men Shadrach, Mesach and Abednego (*Hananiah, Azariah* and *Mishael* in Hebrew) when they remained unharmed in the fiery furnace into which they had been thrown by order of King Nebuchadnezzar because they refused to adore him. The name comes from the Latin version of the canticle, which begins with the words, *Benedicite, omnia opera Domini, Domino,* "Bless the Lord, all works of the Lord." For centuries it has been chanted or recited in the Divine Liturgy at Lauds, or Morning Prayer, on Sundays and solemnities. Because of the liturgical revision resulting from the Second Vatican Council, it is not recited every Sunday, but on the first and third Sundays of the four-week division of the Psalter for the Liturgy of the Hours, and always on feasts and solemnities.

Benedict, The Holy Rule of • A rule for monasteries written by St. Benedict of Nursia (480-550), the Father of Western monasticism. Consisting of a prologue and seventy-three chapters, this text has been used from St. Benedict's time until now in the variety of settings and styles of monasticism indebted to him, i.e., whether cenobite ("in community") or solitary, whether Benedictines themselves or

Cistercians, Trappists, etc. Contemporary scholarship on the Rule ascribes Benedict's genius to his wise use of existing monastic documents, e.g., *The Rule of the Master* and the writings of John Cassian, St. Basil and Caesarius of Arles.

Noted for its tone of moderation, its concern to sustain monastic peace and its adaptability to the multiform ways that monasticism has been lived in the Church's history, the Rule concerns how the abbot should order all things in the monastery, spiritual and temporal, liturgical and economic. Of particular import are the section on the abbot, admission into the monastery, norms for communal living and the regulation of the Liturgy of the Hours. Among other types of consecrated witness in the Church, this Rule is notable for its stress on the monk's stability in one monastery for life and the virtue of *conversio morum* (ongoing conversion of life). Staples of the monk's spiritual practices besides the Liturgy include prescribed fasting and *lectio divina.*

Benedictines • This order includes both men and women religious, and follows the Rule of St. Benedict of Nursia, which was compiled in the first half of the sixth century, being based upon the earlier rules of St. Basil and St. Caesarius of Arles. The first monastery of Benedictines was founded in about 529 at Monte Cassino (approximately eighty miles south of Rome). Later, St. Benedict and his sister, St. Scholastica, established separate monasteries for nuns. The Benedictine Rule, with its emphasis upon obedience to superiors, the importance of the balance between liturgical prayer and manual labor, and the essential value of community life, became the foundation for all of Western monasticism.

St. Gregory the Great (d. 604), a Benedictine monk who became Pope, extended Benedictine ideals throughout the Church, and his *Dialogues* did much to make known the life and principles of St. Benedict. By the twelfth century St. Bernard of Clairvaux established the more austere form of Benedictine life as practiced by the Cistercian monks. Up until the Council of Trent monasticism continued to develop, sometimes relaxing its rules, and at other times undergoing reform. The Council of Trent took as part of its task that of passing decrees to regulate monastic life, and forming confederations of monasteries, so that it might have more of the unity envisaged by St. Benedict.

Benediction • (1) From the Latin word *benedicere*, benediction is the general term for any kind of blessing. Usually, a benediction is accompanied by extended hands and the sign of the cross over the one who is being blessed.

(2) More commonly, it refers to the action whereby the congregation is blessed with the monstrance in the context of Exposition of the Blessed Sacrament (cf. Benediction of the Blessed Sacrament).

Benediction of the Blessed Sacrament • The practice in which the Blessed Sacrament is put in a ciborium or a monstrance and placed on an altar lighted with candles — at least two for exposition in the ciborium, four or six for exposition in

St. Benedict
(after Fra Angelico painting)

the monstrance (*Ceremonial of Bishops*, nn. 1104, 1115) — after which it is incensed. There should be a time of silent prayer, while appropriate hymns and scriptural readings are recommended. Then after a prayer, the congregation is blessed by the celebrant (wearing the humeral veil) tracing the sign of the cross with the ciborium or the monstrance over the assembled congregation. Eucharistic hymns are sung, most often *O Salutaris Hostia* and *Tantum Ergo* in Latin or in the vernacular. After the benediction, the Divine Praises may be said or sung. The present ritual for benediction is found within the *Rite for Holy Communion and Worship of the Eucharist Outside Mass*. According to the General Instruction of this Rite, a major emphasis in the revised Rite theologically and liturgically is to show the intrinsic relationship between Eucharistic worship outside Mass and the Eucharistic celebration itself (nn. 1-4).

Benediction, Apostolic • A blessing imparted by the Pope or by one who has received the privilege of imparting such a blessing in his name.

Benediction with a Ciborium • For a small number of people, the Blessed Sacrament is exposed in a ciborium in the tabernacle or on the altar, incensed, and the people blessed with the Eucharist in this vessel.

Benedictional • A liturgical book containing a collection of blessings, especially those used in France, Spain and England in the early Middle Ages and inserted after the Our Father in the Mass. Many of these blessings were later published in the various rituals. The current *Ordo Benedictionum*, with blessings in a modified Jewish Berakah form and with optional Liturgies of the Word, has been published in the United States as the *Book of Blessings*.

Benedictus • In the Gospel of Luke, the *Benedictus* or "Canticle of Zechariah" is the song of praise Zechariah proclaimed as soon as his lips were loosed at the time of the circumcision of his son, St. John the Baptist (cf. Lk 1:68-79). Its first words in the Latin version used in the liturgy for many centuries are, *Benedictus Dominus Deus Israel*, "Blessed be the Lord God of Israel." It is the first word that gives this canticle its common traditional name. The Church uses this hymn at Morning Prayer of the Liturgy of the Hours each day.

For further reading: Frederick W. Danker, "Benedictus," *Anchor Bible Dictionary*, 1:669.

Benefice • Historically, a benefice was a grant of land for life in reward for certain services rendered. In the Church it came to mean an ecclesiastical office which carried certain obligations, as well as being a source of income for the office-holder. The benefice had to be permanently established by an ecclesiastical authority. At one time, secular authorities could present candidates for a benefice to the ecclesiastical authority for subsequent appointment. In time, all rights of presentation and inheritance, as well as the possibility of holding more than one benefice, were abolished.

The most common examples of benefices were parishes. Although some benefices still exist, the institution as such has been abolished by the revised Code and no new benefices are to be created.

Benefit of Clergy • A special form of the *privilegium fori*, whereby clerics accused of certain crimes are exempted from the jurisdiction of civil courts and instead are required to stand trial in an ecclesiastical court. The practice is of ancient origin and has been the subject, at times, of bitter disputes between Church and state. The Benefit is honored at least in some form by several nations under concordat today, although certain crimes (for example, treason) are usually omitted. The United States, however, refused to recognize the Benefit in 1790. Canon 120 of the 1917 Code of Canon Law contained rather extensive legislation on the Benefit. Most of these provisions, however, have not been carried over into the 1983 Code.

Occasionally one encounters the expression "benefit of clergy" when referring to the right of a person (frequently a prisoner) to have access to a priest or other minister.

Benemerenti Medal • An award given, as the name states, to "one who is well-deserving." This medal is given by the Pope in recognition of outstanding service to the Church and society. Traditionally, it has been intended for laity. Originally a reward for military merit, the Benemerenti Medal was first issued by Pope Pius VI (1775-1799). It has varied in appearance, but in 1891, Pope Leo XIII struck a Benemerenti Medal which served as a model for several succeeding Popes. It bore the likeness of the reigning Pope surrounded by a crown of laurels. The papal tiara and keys were above the medal, which was suspended by a ribbon in the papal colors of gold and white. Pope Paul VI changed it to depict the cross and a figure of Christ, the papal tiara on the left and the Pontiff's coat of arms on the right. On the back is the word "Benemerenti."

This award is granted at the request and endorsement of a diocesan bishop to the Vatican Secretariat of State, often done through the Apostolic Nunciature of the particular country.

Benjamin • The youngest of the Israelite patriarch Jacob's twelve sons, Benjamin was born to Rachel, as was Jacob's son Joseph. In Hebrew, the name Benjamin means "son of the right hand" or "son of the south," perhaps referring to the territory occupied by the tribe known by that name.

First mentioned in Genesis 35:25, Benjamin figures prominently in the story of Joseph in Egypt (Gn 37-50). Sold into slavery by his brothers who were jealous of their father's special affection for him "because he was the son of his old age" (Gn 37:3), Joseph rose to prominence in Egypt. Entering into the Pharaoh's service, Joseph "was governor over the land; he it was who sold to all the people of the land" (Gn 42:6). Charged with custody of the food supplies in Egypt, Joseph's careful planning saw the Egyptians through the seven years of famine he had foretold. During that famine, ten of Joseph's brothers (all but Benjamin) went to buy grain in Egypt. As they came before their brother, he recognized them without their discovering his identity.

Imprisoning them for three days on the false charge of espionage, Joseph threatened them, "you shall not go from this place unless your youngest brother comes here" (Gn 42:15). After three days, Joseph released his brothers, holding Simeon as hostage until the rest returned with Benjamin. Deeply troubled, Joseph's brothers interpreted this as punishment for their crime against him.

Returning to their father's house and informing Jacob of what had transpired, Jacob reluctantly allowed his sons to bring their youngest brother back to Egypt. Recognizing "his brother Benjamin, his mother's son" (Gn 43:29) Joseph controlled his emotions and then "made haste, for his heart yearned for his brother, and he sought a place to weep." Showing particular affection for his brother, Joseph gave Benjamin a portion of food from his own table, five times as large as the portion given to the other brothers.

As the brothers prepared to depart, Joseph had his steward place his own silver cup in Benjamin's sack, hiding it there so as to have an excuse to detain Benjamin by accusing him of theft. Even though the brothers insisted on sharing Benjamin's guilt once the planted cup was discovered, Joseph insisted, "Only the man in whose hand the cup was found shall be my slave" (Gn 44:17), allowing the others to return to their father, Jacob. Judah, the eldest brother, pleaded with Joseph to let Benjamin go free, saying, "For how can I go back to my father if the lad is not with me? I fear to see the evil that would come upon my father" (Gn 44:34). With these words, Joseph lost control of his emotions and revealed his true identity to his brothers.

In the so-called "blessing of Jacob" found in Genesis 49, where the dying patriarch Jacob announces to his sons, "what shall befall you in days to come" (v. 1), Jacob says of his youngest son, "Benjamin is a ravenous wolf, in the morning devouring the prey, and at even dividing the spoil" (Gn 49:27).

In the New Testament, St. Paul identifies himself as a member "of the people of Israel, of the tribe of Benjamin" (Phil 3:5).

For further reading: K. D. Schnuck, "Benjamin," *Anchor Bible Dictionary*, 1:671-673.

Berakoth • A Hebrew word, the plural of *berakah*, which means "blessing" or "benediction." *Berakoth* is also the title of the first tractate of the Talmud. The nine chapters of Tractate *Berakoth* discuss regulations for the recital of prayers and blessings, beginning with the *Schema* ("Hear, O Israel . . ." Dt 6:4-9; 11:13-21; Nm 15:37-41).

For further reading: A. Z. Ehrman, "Berakoth," *Encyclopedia Judaica*, 4:586-587.

Bestiaries • In the Middle Ages, bestiaries were popular didactic accounts of the activities of both real and imaginary animals, usually with an allegorical or moral value given to the animal. The medieval bestiary can trace its lineage to the classical models of Aristotle and Pliny and the patristic precedents of Ambrose's *Hexaemeron* and Isidore of Seville's *Etymologies*.

The bestiaries were often illustrated by way of illuminated capitals and marginal details depicting the animals discussed in the text; these, in turn, influenced the depiction of the animals in art and architecture, even into our own day, as seen in the gargoyles of the neo-Gothic style.

Perhaps one of the most popular subjects of medieval bestiaries was the unicorn. According to legend, the unicorn could be caught only when he rested his head in the lap of a virgin; his single horn, when removed, was reputed to have great medicinal power, even to the point of raising the dead. As such, the unicorn serves as an obvious symbol of Christ.

Bethel • A town approximately ten-and-a-half miles north of Jerusalem known today as Beitin, Bethel was the site of an important Israelite religious shrine during the biblical period. In the Book of Genesis, Bethel, which means "house of God" or "house of (the god named) El," is the place where the Israelite patriarch Jacob saw in a dream "a ladder set up on the earth, and the

top of it reached to heaven; and behold, the angels of God were ascending and descending on it." Upon waking from this dream, Jacob marked the sacredness of the place by setting up the stone on which he had been resting as a marker or sacred pillar (Gn 28:18).

Exclaiming, "How awesome is this place! This is none other than the house of God, and this is the gate of heaven," Jacob named the place Bethel, and the text explains that this was a change from Luz, its original name.

Another parallel etymological explanation of Bethel is found in Genesis 35:15. In that chapter God commands that Jacob travel to Bethel, dwell and build an altar there. While there is no mention of Jacob sleeping or dreaming in Genesis 35, it is in that text (vv. 10-11) that God changes Jacob's name to Israel and that God reveals Himself under the title "God Almighty" (in Hebrew, *El Shaddai*). The encounter between God and Jacob at Bethel is also recalled by the prophet Hosea (Hos 12:4).

According to 1 Kings 12:28-29, King Jeroboam (who reigned over the northern kingdom of Israel from approximately 922 to 901 B.C.) made two golden calves and set one in place in the shrine at Bethel and the other in the shrine at Dan. These sanctuaries represented, respectively, the southernmost and the northernmost boundaries of Israel. In 1 Kings 13, a prophet from the southern kingdom of Judah approached Jeroboam and condemned his king's religious innovations while the king himself stood at the altar at Bethel to offer incense at the inauguration of the festival he had just established there (1 Kgs 12:32-33).

Further indication of the importance of the sanctuary at Bethel can be found in the book of the eighth-century B.C. prophet Amos. In Amos 7:10, we read that Amaziah, priest of the sanctuary at Bethel, reported to

King Jeroboam that the prophet Amos was denouncing him in oracles he pronounced at Bethel. Amaziah expelled Amos from Bethel on account of his preaching, ordering, "O seer, go, flee away to the land of Judah, eat bread there, and prophesy there; but never again prophesy at Bethel, for it is the king's sanctuary, and it is a temple of the kingdom" (Am 7:12-13). In Amos 3:14, the prophet pronounced an oracle of judgment against Israel that threatened the sanctuary at Bethel warning that "on the day I punish Israel for his transgressions, I will punish the altars of Bethel, and the horns of the altar shall be cut off and fall to the ground."

For further reading: Harold Brodsky, "Bethel," *Anchor Bible Dictionary*, 1:710-712; James Leon Kelso, "Bethel," *The New Encyclopedia of Archaeological Excavations in the Holy Land*, 1:192-194.

Bethlehem • A town located some six miles southwest of Jerusalem. Although some Christians find it inviting to derive the name from two words meaning "house of bread," the fact is that this is only one of several suggested etymologies. In the Old Testament the importance of this town stems chiefly from its association with David. This was his home (1 Sm 17:12,15), and where he was anointed king by Samuel (1 Sm 16:1-13). In other ways as well, the place figures importantly in the story of David. Bethlehem is the setting for much of the Book of Ruth. But most of all, Bethlehem has prominence as the place where Jesus was born, according to three of the Gospels (Mt 2:1-16; Lk 2:4-15; Jn 7:42). Constantine built a basilica with a chapel above some caves that were believed to have been the site of Jesus' birth. This church was replaced by a larger edifice built by Justinian (527-65). Though some changes have been made in the structure in the course of time, the present building is essentially the one put up by Justinian. The town is sometimes referred to as Bethlehem in Judah (Jgs 17:7-9; Ru 1:1-2) to distinguish it from a lesser known town with the same name in the territory of Zelnon, the home of Ibzan, one of the judges (Jgs 12:8, 10).

For further reading: Moshe Stekelis, Michael Avi-Yonah and Vassilios Tzaferis, "Bethlehem," *The New Encyclopedia of Archaeological Excavations in the Holy Land*, 1:203-210; Henri Cazelles, "Bethlehem," *Anchor Bible Dictionary*, 1:712-715.

Betrothal • The betrothal or engagement is a formal mutual promise of a future valid marriage. The revised Code contains canonical provision for a formal Church betrothal: however, even if a couple goes through such a ceremony, there is no obligation on either part to go through with the marriage.

Although the betrothal or engagement is primarily a social affair in most contemporary societies, there are some cultures and groups wherein it still has social and even legal importance (cf. Canon 1062).

Historically, the betrothal, as a formal and legal act, predates Christianity. In most ancient societies, including the Roman Empire, a marriage came into being not by a single act (the exchange of vows), but by means of a process, usually officially begun with the betrothal. Sometimes the future spouses were betrothed at a very young age, with the actual marriage not beginning until years later. The legal action constituting the marriage was concluded by some form of religious or customary ceremony after which the parties were considered married.

In many legal systems, such as the Mosaic Code and in Roman law, the betrothal had force of law and was not easily dissolved. Often the law prescribed monetary compensation to one or the other party in the case of a broken engagement, usually because the betrothal was accompanied by a dowry.

Betting • A form of gambling in which someone lays down a sum of money or other valuable as a wager on an athletic contest, race or other event whose outcome cannot be predicted in advance. Like other forms of gambling, betting is not prohibited by Christian teaching, so long as it is done in moderation and does not jeopardize the livelihood and support of an individual or one's family.

Bible • The English word "bible" has its origins in the Greek word *biblia*, from *byblos* meaning papyrus (a form of "paper" common in antiquity). In the singular the term means a book, while the plural *biblia* means a collection of books.

Christians regard the Bible as Sacred Scripture, the Word of God. Catholics recognize that, together with Sacred Tradition, the Bible is the source of revelation about God's person and will. Scripture and Tradition together form the Rule of Faith.

Sacred Scripture has one author, God. Yet God made use of the authors of Scripture as true authors to communicate revelation by means of inspiration from the Holy Spirit. Therefore, this one book (Sacred Scripture) has one author (God); however, the one book is a collection of books written in diverse literary forms, each with its own individual human author.

This collection is "canonical" in that it contains the public expression of the mysteries of the Faith and measures or assesses the authenticity of new and vigorous expressions of the Church's Faith.

Sacred Scripture includes the Old Testament and the New Testament. The term "testament" is from the Latin *testamentum*, taken as an approximation of the Greek term *diatheke*, which is another approximation, but this time from the Hebrew *berith*, meaning "covenant." In Jesus' day there were two principal forms of the Old Testament, one in Hebrew, the other in Greek.

The Scriptures in Hebrew contain thirty-nine books. Portions of some of its books were written in Aramaic (Jer 10:11; Ezr 4:8—6:18; 7:26; Dn 2:4—7:8). The books can be subdivided into the following three groups: (1) The Law (Hebrew: *Torah*; Greek: *Pentateuch*): Genesis, Exodus, Leviticus, Numbers, Deuteronomy. (2) The Prophets (Hebrew: *nebi'im*), further divided into (a) Former Prophets: Joshua, Judges, (1 and 2) Samuel, (1 and 2) Kings. (b) Latter Prophets: Isaiah, Jeremiah, Ezekiel and the twelve prophets: Hosea, Joel, Amos, Obadiah, Jonah, Micah, Nahum, Habakkuk, Zephaniah, Haggai, Zechariah, Malachi. (3) The Writings: (Hebrew: *kethubim*): Psalms, Job, Proverbs, Ruth, Song of Solomon, Ecclesiastes, Lamentations, Esther, Daniel, Ezra, Nehemiah, (1 and 2) Chronicles.

The emergence of the Greek Old Testament was as follows. After the exile of 580 B.C., the common language of Judaism slowly ceased to be Hebrew and eventually became Aramaic. With the great military and cultural gains of Alexander the Great, Greek soon replaced Aramaic as the language of international diplomacy and commerce and in many regions became the common language as well. For Aramaic-speaking Jews, the Hebrew Scriptures were translated right after the Hebrew text was read in synagogue. These translations are collectively known as targumic literature. For Greek-speaking Jews, the Hebrew Scriptures were translated, giving a Greek Old Testament called the Septuagint or LXX (the Roman numeral equivalent of "70," which is the approximate number of scholars who did the translation into Greek). In addition to containing all of the books found in the Hebrew Scriptures (in slightly different arrangements), some of the LXX books were originally written in Greek (2 Maccabees; Wisdom; Daniel 13, 14), and some originally in Hebrew, for which only Greek translations have survived (Judith, Baruch, Sirach, 1 Maccabees).

The earliest New Testament manuscripts tell us that it was written entirely in Greek. The New Testament consists of four Gospels (Matthew, Mark, Luke, John) and Acts of the Apostles. Also included are Paul's Letters: Romans, 1 and 2 Corinthians; Galatians; Ephesians; Philippians; Colossians; 1 and 2 Thessalonians; 1 and 2 Timothy; Titus and Philemon. Other materials are: Hebrews; James; 1 and 2 Peter; 1, 2 and 3 John; Jude; Revelation.

In A.D. 90 the rabbinic school at Jamnia formalized the canon of the Hebrew Scriptures to include the thirty-nine books listed above. The Western and Eastern expressions of Christianity accepted the LXX, which in the West was eventually translated into the language of the Roman Empire (Latin), giving us the Vulgate Bible. During the Protestant Reformation only the thirty-nine books of the Hebrew Scriptures were accepted as normative (by the Protestants), while the Catholic and Orthodox Churches accepted the Greek canon of Scripture. Hence, the difference between Catholic/Orthodox and Protestant Old Testaments.

The formation of the New Testament canon of twenty-seven books is complex. The first list of all twenty-seven New Testament books does not appear until Marcion's second-century dispute with the Church's teaching on Gospel and Law, which led him to reject the Old Testament completely. During and subsequent to this dispute, incomplete lists of New Testament books were collected, and these indicated that the majority of the twenty-seven New Testament books were accepted in most of the lists. St. Jerome's full list of twenty-

seven New Testament books (late fourth century) led to the Latin Vulgate New Testament canon and influenced the Western Church, as did the councils held at Hippo (393) and Carthage (397). The Syrian Churches possessed a twenty-two-book canon by the fifth century. Eventually, on the basis of usage and common practice, all twenty-seven New Testament books were accepted by all sectors of the Church.

Bible, English Editions • Fragments of early translations of the Bible date from as early as the eighth century. But the first complete translation dates from 1382-1384 and is associated with the supporters of John Wycliffe (1330-1384). After the invention of printing, English translations and editions of the Bible proliferated among both Catholics and Protestants.

In line with the Council of Trent's teaching that the Latin Vulgate represented "the authentic edition for public reading, disputations, sermons and explanations," Catholic vernacular editions were based on the Vulgate, notably the Douay-Rheims (1582-1609), the Challoner Revision (1749-1763), the Confraternity Revision of the New Testament (1941), and the Knox Bible (1944-1950). Catholic versions translated from the original languages are: Westminster Version (1935-1949), the Kleist-Lilly New Testament (1950-1954), the New American Bible (1952-1970; 1972; 1987), and the English translation of the Jerusalem Bible (1966; 1985).

Important Protestant English editions prior to the King James version were: Tyndale's Bible (1525-1531), Coverdale's Bible (1535) and the Geneva Bible (1560). These were largely surpassed by the Authorized Version (King James, 1611) and by subsequent editions in this tradition, notably: the Revised Version (1881-1885) and the Revised Standard Version (1946-1952; 1990; published in 1966 with an imprimatur from Cardinal Cushing). The New Revised Standard Version appeared in 1989.

Other important English editions are the New English Bible (1961-1970), now the Revised English Bible (1989), Today's English Version (Good News Bible, 1966-1979), the New International Version (1973-1978) and the Living Bible (1962-1971).

For further reading: F. F. Bruce, *History of the Bible in English*, Third Edition (Oxford University Press, 1978).

Bible Reading • The spiritual exercise of reading the Scriptures as an aid to prayer and meditation. In monastic traditions, this meditative reading is called *lectio divina* and is regarded as especially beneficial for the development of a deep interior life. All Christians are encouraged to read from the Bible daily, in order to draw guidance and inspiration from the Word of God.

Bible Societies and Study Groups • Bible study groups have been fairly common from the time of *Divino Afflante Spiritu*, the encyclical of Pope Pius XII, which first encouraged Catholics to become informed regarding the Scriptures. This effort was further fostered by the Second Vatican Council in *Dei Verbum*. These groups generally meet informally for a discussion of the Scriptures and an attempt to relate their message to the daily lives of the participants. Since the Church is responsible for the interpretation of Sacred Scripture, these groups must be under the direction of a competent authority, ideally the parish priest or one with solid training in Catholic exegesis.

Bible Studies, Catholic • Bible reading and study by Catholics has grown in practice in recent years, especially since the end of the Second Vatican Council in the mid-1960s. This popular spiritual activity is in part the fruit of the biblical renewal which was encouraged by Pope Pius XII in his encyclical *Divino Afflante Spiritu* (1943). From that time until the end of the Council, biblical renewal and study remained largely on the academic level among professionally trained priests and scholars. Since the end of the Council, there has been an increase in Bible study at the popular, non-scholarly level, especially among laity not formally trained in Scripture and theology.

The movement toward Bible study among Catholics received strong endorsement in the Council's Dogmatic Constitution on Divine Revelation (1965): "The Christian faithful . . . [should] go gladly to the sacred text itself, whether in the sacred liturgy, which is full of the divine words, or in devout reading, or in such suitable exercises and various other helps which, with the approval and guidance of the pastors of the Church, are happily spreading everywhere. . . . Let them remember, however, that prayer should accompany the reading of Sacred Scripture, so that a dialogue takes place between God and man" (n. 25). The Council even recommended that "access to Sacred Scripture ought to be open wide to the Christian faithful" (n. 22). The Council Fathers taught that the reading and study of Scripture is vital for the life of the Church, for in Scripture, God "meets His children with great love and speaks with them." They further stated that "such is the force and power of the Word of God that it can serve the Church as her support and vigor, and the children of the Church as strength for their faith, food for the soul, and a pure and lasting fount of spiritual life" (n. 21). This was based on the teaching of Scripture itself: "The Word of God is living and active, sharper than any two-edged sword, piercing to the division of soul and spirit, of joints and marrow, and discerning the thoughts and intentions of the heart" (Heb 4:12).

The American bishops in recent years have also encouraged Bible study among Catholics, saying, "We need to educate — to re-educate — our people knowingly in the Bible. . ." and, "the current trend toward smaller faith-sharing and Bible-studying groups within a parish family is strongly to be encouraged" (*Pastoral Statement for Catholics on Biblical Fundamentalism*, 1987).

Bible Vigil • A paraliturgical service in which public readings from the Scriptures are combined with periods of prayer, singing and silence, and often involving a sermon or reflection on the themes of the readings. Such vigils are particularly appropriate on the eve of a feast.

Biblia Pauperum • Latin for "the Bible of the Poor." These were picture books that sought to illustrate Bible themes and situations, often with the intent of demonstrating the New Testament fulfillment of Old Testament prophecies. Few manuscript copies of these books have survived to the present. The *Biblia Pauperum* were among the first works to be duplicated by wood-block printing.

Biblical Chronology

The chief topics are: the chronology of Genesis, Exodus, the Jewish kings and Jesus Christ.

Chronology of Genesis: It is helpful to begin by presenting the chief data in Genesis. The accompanying table shows: the names of the twenty-three patriarchs; the age at which they begot their listed son; the number of years they lived after this event; their age at death; ordinal numerals for the vital dates of the beginning and end of their earthly lives.

A careful study of the biblical data will enable us to see the inner patterns used by the sacred writer. The absence of any such patterns should be taken as evidence that the figures have been garbled in transmission. The presence of such patterns should begin to convince us that the author had a symbolic intent and was not attempting to sketch the real chronology of all the patriarchs. This done, the more speculative adventure of translating these *Anno Adae* (post-Adamic) dates into B.C. dates will be attempted.

Adam	130 + 800 = 930	0001-1931
Seth	105 + 807 = 912	0131-1043
Enosh	090 + 815 = 905	0236-1141
Kenan	070 + 840 = 910	0326-1236
Mahalalel	065 + 830 = 895	0396-1291
Jared	162 + 800 = 962	0461-1423
Enoch	065 + 300 = 365	0623-0988
Methuselah	187 + 782 = 969	0688-1657
Lamech	182 + 595 = 777	0875-1652
Noah	500 + 450 = 950	1057-2007
Shem	102 + 500 = 602	1557-2159
Arpachshad	035 + 403 = 438	1659-2097
Shelah	030 + 403 = 433	1694-2127
Eber	034 + 430 = 464	1724-2188
Peleg	030 + 209 = 239	1758-1997

Reu	032 + 207 = 239	1788-2027
Serug	030 + 200 = 230	1820-2050
Nahor	029 + 119 = 148	1850-1998
Terah	070 + 135 = 205	1879-2084
Abraham	100 + 075 = 175	1949-2124
Isaac	060 + 120 = 180	2049-2256
Jacob	091 + 056 = 147	2109-2256
Joseph	— — 110	2200-2310

Jules Oppert, the famous pioneer in Assyriology, in the old *Jewish Encyclopedia*, showed that the interval between Adam and the Flood (1657 A.A.) was 1,656 years, the equivalent of seventy-two twenty-three-year solar cycles of 8,400 days. The total number of days was therefore 604,800, the same as the number of seconds in a week (60 x 60 x 24 x 7, or 3,600 x 168 or 7 x 86,400).

Thus Oppert showed the affinity between the "week of creation" and the whole antediluvian period, and so corroborated the now traditional theory that a "priestly author" contributed the arithmetical material in Genesis. He also unveiled the precise mind of the "priestly author," that he was not only a "day-counter" but also a "second-counter." He showed that writer as one seeking patterns in nature, the cycles governing the celestial movements by which we define time.

Without exhausting the topic, Oppert gave ample proof of the presence of the twenty-three-year cycle. He showed that: the total ages from Adam to Kenan came to 3657 (159 x 23); those from Mahalalel to Shem came to 5520 (240 x 23); and those from Arpachshad to Jacob amounted to 2898 (126 x 23). In so doing he demonstrated how accurately the figures had been transcribed.

Of three other clear uses of the twenty-three-year cycle, he noted only one, the 460-year interval (twenty such cycles) between the advent of Adam (0001 A.A.) and the birth of Jared (0461 A.A.). He did not observe that the same interval is found between the birth of Nahor (1850 A.A.) and

the death of Joseph (2310 A.A.) or that 230 years (ten such cycles) are given to Nahor's father, Serug.

Jewish priests, organized in twenty-four courses, served for one week at a time; thus they returned to duty every 168 days. They were fond of the Patriarchal Cycle of twenty-three years because it coincided nicely with their tours of duty (8,400 days = 50 x 168). Yet it is a very poor astronomical cycle, for it presumes a tropical year of 365.2174 days, farther from the true value of 365.2422 than the Dominical Cycle of 28 years, which has a value of 365.2500 days.

Had Oppert looked more carefully, he could have seen evidence of cycles much more accurate than the patriarchal. The Genesis chronologist thrice uses intervals of 800 years; this inclines us to believe that he knew the 400-year Gregorian Cycles we now use, which have a value of 365.2425 days. The life of Adam is equal to fifteen Prophetic Cycles of sixty-two years; this presumes the tropical year to be 365.2419 days long. The whole chronology of Genesis embraces 2310 years (not 2300), and in such a span there are seventy Christian Cycles of thirty-three years: this cycle presupposes a tropical year of 365.2424 days. We find 126 years, one Royal Cycle, between the birth of Terah and the death of Noah, which presupposes a mean tropical year only one second shorter than the true value. The life span of Seth (912 years) equals two Gregorian and four Royal Cycles.

In the past, naïve exegetes believed that Genesis offered an accurate chronology of mankind. This error has been thoroughly exposed by various sciences. This leaves us only the option of accepting the chronology as being symbolic, and the duty of showing what symbolism these events have in the Judeo-Christian Tradition. Actually, this seems to have been the view of the earliest Christian exegetes, who offered various Mundane Eras, some of which were meant to be applied to the Hebrew chronology of Adam, Eve or Seth, and others of which were best construed with the differing Greek tradition of the Septuagint.

Here a single Mundane Era will be offered for consideration, 3738 B.C., to indicate the advent of Adam. Coming as it does twenty-three years, one Patriarchal Cycle, after the Jewish Mundane Era of 3761 B.C. (still used by Jews), it has some initial legitimacy. The accompanying table shows, in greater detail, the resulting B.C. dates:

Adam	3738-2808	Shelah	2045-1612
?Eve	3732-2808	Eber	2015-1551
Seth	3608-2696	Peleg	1981-1742
Enosh	3503-2598	Reu	1951-1712
Kenan	3413-2503	Serug	1919-1689
Mahalalel	3343-2448	Nahor	1889-1741
Jared	3278-2316	Terah	1860-1655
Enoch	3116-2551	Abraham	1790-1615
Methuselah	3051-2082	Sarah	1780-1653
Lamech	2864-2087	?Melchizedek	1776-1641
Noah	2682-1732	Ishmael	1704-1567
Shem	2182-1580	Isaac	1690-1510
Arpachshad	2080-1642	Jacob	1630-1483
?Cainan	2061-1569	Joseph	1539-1429

Some interesting observations: (1) Adam's death is seven Gregorian Cycles (or one hundred Dominical Cycles) before the year to which St. Epiphanius assigns the birth of Jesus; (2) Seth's birth is one *sar* (3,600 years, the seconds in an hour), or nine Gregorian cycles, before the same date; (3) there are 2,310 years (seventy Christian Cycles) between the death of Adam and 498 B.C., a date which is seventy "weeks of years" before the birth of Jesus; (4) there are one hundred Patriarchal Cycles between the birth of Seth and the birth of Moses (eighty years before the Exodus of 1228 B.C.); (5) the birth of Isaac is 2,310 years, seventy Christian Cycles, after 4000 B.C.; (6) the death of Mahalalel is 2,480 years, forty Prophetic Cycles, before the death of Jesus (A.D. 33); (7) adding the date of Exodus (1228 B.C.) to that of Noah (1580) gives the death-date of Adam (2808 B.C.); (8) adding the date of Terah (1860, thirty Prophetic Cycles) to that of Adam (3738) gives the Grecian Mundane Era of 5598 B.C.; (9) taking the same date from 5592 B.C., the Mundane Era of Clement of Alexandria (*Stromata*, I, 20) gives the date of Eve.

Chronology of Exodus: There are two chronological schemes regarding the exodus of Hebrew slaves from Egypt: the earlier one — entirely symbolic — places this event in 1446 B.C.; and the later, more realistic, dates it to 1228 B.C. Like many other doublets in the Pentateuch, both seem to have the same author, at least the same principal author.

Just as the earlier Genesis dates began with 3738 B.C. (twenty-three years after the Jewish Mundane Era of 3761 B.C.), so the earlier date for the death of Moses (1406 B.C.) is twenty-three years after the previously given death-date of Joseph (1429 B.C.), which is admittedly one hundred eighty years too late.

The later and better date for the Exodus falls at the end of the reign of Rameses II, who seems best to qualify as the pharaoh of the oppression. If Moses was eighty at the time of the Exodus, he was born in 1308 B.C., one hundred Patriarchal Cycles after the birth of Seth (3608 B.C.). His chief companions on the journey were Miriam (born in 1320 B.C.), Aaron (1312 B.C.) and Joshua (1290 B.C.). (Just as Genesis ends some one hundred eighty years too late, so the Exodus chronology seems to begin forty years too soon: it is more reasonable to hold that Moses was forty at the time of the Exodus, and that he was born seventy-seven decades before 498 B.C., not seventy-seven decades before 538 B.C.)

That Moses had an elder sister is certain from the early narrative of his life; her identity with the sister who accompanied him into the desert is most probable. That she was twelve years older than he is conjectural, but the date (1320 B.C.) has the merit of being 460 years (twenty Patriarchal Cycles) after 1780 B.C., Sarah's birth-year. The same date is four Christian Cycles before the death of Moses (1188 B.C.), and forty Christian Cycles before the Christian Era. Her birth-year under the earlier unrealistic scheme would therefore be 1538 B.C., one hundred nine years before 1429 B.C., as 1320 B.C. is one hundred nine years after that same death-year for Joseph.

Joshua was born "seventy weeks of years" after Sarah (1780 B.C.), and Aaron was born seventy decades before the fall of Nineveh (612 B.C.).

The text indicates that Moses was one hundred twenty years old when he died, that Aaron was one hundred twenty-three, and that Joshua was one hundred ten. We may conjecture that Miriam, like Sarah, was one hundred twenty-seven when she died.

Consequently, the average for all four was one hundred twenty years, a norm which Moses exactly observed.

Counting from the too-early birth dates, this yields quite realistic death-dates of 1193 for Miriam, 1189 for Aaron, 1188 for Moses and 1180 for Joshua. Since 1184 B.C. is the traditional year for the fall of Troy, this suggested that Joshua's victory at Jericho — four years before his death — be identified with the colossal catastrophes (earthquake and fire) which had actually happened to Jericho four hundred or even eight hundred years earlier (in 1584 or 1984). We are aware of a Mundane Era beginning in 4138 B.C., which places the birth of Seth in 4008 B.C. (four thousand years before that of Jesus) and sets the death of Abraham in 2015 B.C., some four hundred years before its date under the era of 3738. There is another Mundane Era beginning in 4538 B.C., four thousand years before the liberation of the Jews from the Babylonian Captivity.

The biblical text gives various dates for the duration of Jewish subjugation to the Egyptians. The most realistic figure is three hundred eighty years, from 1608 to 1228 B.C.

The Monarchs of Judah: It is well known that the monarchy over the Jewish nation was established by Saul and continued over the whole nation by David and Solomon. After Solomon's death, the tribes in the north seceded and began the kingdom of Israel, which endured until the fall of Samaria in 721 B.C. The southern tribes continued to be ruled by twenty monarchs (nineteen kings and one queen) of Judah until the fall of Jerusalem in 587 B.C. Aside from these terminal dates (which sum to 1308, the later birth-year of Moses), there is little agreement about the chronology of these rulers. The following table exhibits a reasonable view of the correct dates for the rulers of Judah:

	This ruler	began to reign	and ruled for
01	Saul	Dec. 1, 1051 B.C.	2 < 40 years
02	David	Dec. 1, 1011 B.C.	40-1/2 years
03	Solomon	June 1, 970 B.C.	40 years
04	Rehoboam	June 1, 930 B.C.	17 > 16 years
05	Abijam	June 1, 914 B.C.	3 > 2 years
06	Asa	June 1, 912 B.C.	41 > 40 years
07	Jehoshaphat	June 1, 872 B.C.	25 > 24 years
08	Jehoram	June 1, 848 B.C.	8 > 7 years
09	Ahaziah	June 1, 841 B.C.	1 yr. > 4 mos.
10	Athaliah	Oct. 1, 841 B.C.	6 > 5 years
11	Jehoash	Oct. 1, 836 B.C.	40 > 28 years
12	Amaziah	Oct. 1, 808 B.C.	29 < 39 years
13	Azariah	Oct. 1, 769 B.C.	52 > 26 years
14	Jotham	Oct. 1, 743 B.C.	16 > 8 years
15	Ahaz	Oct. 1, 735 B.C.	16 > 8 years
16	Hezekiah	Oct. 1, 727 B.C.	29 years
17	Manasseh	Oct. 1, 698 B.C.	55 < 56 years
18	Amon	Oct. 1, 642 B.C.	2 years
19	Josiah	Oct. 1, 640 B.C.	31 years
20	Jehoahaz	Oct. 1, 609 B.C.	3 months
21	Jehoiakim	Jan. 1, 608 B.C.	11 years
22	Jehoiachin	Jan. 1, 597 B.C.	98 days
23	Zedekiah	Apr. 8, 597 B.C.	11 years

It is evident from the many reductions (<) or increases (>) that the biblical data (given first) have been subjected to extensive surgery.

(1) The first major change is the acceptance of the forty years allotted to Saul in Acts 13:21, instead of the two years given him in 1 Samuel 13:1. Surely Saul's career was so full that we cannot confine it to two years. No apology is needed to follow the New Testament instead of the obviously defective Old.

(2) Nine major changes involve the loss of eight years and eight months. Here are followed the great majority of exegetes who believe that for the rulers from Rehoboam to Amaziah, inclusively, the "accession-year" was counted as a full year, both for the monarch who had begun it and for his successor. This technique unduly bloats the chronology, and this can be compensated

for by dropping one year except for Ahaziah, who cannot be eliminated entirely, but is given four months.

(3) The figures for Jehoash and Amaziah may have been transposed. The biblical text gives the two of them sixty-nine years. They are here given sixty-seven (allowing for the accession year). This enables Amaziah to take the throne after the twenty-eight years of Jehoash, in 808 B.C., two thousand eight hundred years after Seth's birth (in 3608 B.C.).

(4) The second major change reduces the eighty-four years given to Azariah, Jotham and Ahaz (an average of twenty-eight years) to forty-two years. This enables the fall of Samaria to occur in the sixth year of Hezekiah, as is said in 2 Kings 18:10. It may be that these three monarchs observed two New Year's Days annually, the civil and the religious.

(5) A final minor change adds a year for Manasseh: He ruled for six years and a long jubilee (fifty years), not six years and a short jubilee (forty-nine years).

The net effect of these changes is to shorten the duration of the monarchy by eleven years and four months. Thirty-eight years have been added for Saul, and one year for Manasseh. Fifty years and eight months in all have been subtracted, forty-two years from the inflated trio (Azariah, Jotham and Ahaz), and eight years and eight months because of the accession-year. Were these changes not made, Saul's reign would have begun on August 1, 1062 B.C., eleven hundred twenty years (forty Dominical Cycles) after the birth of Shem in 2182 B.C., nine hundred ninety-nine years before the fall of Jerusalem to Pompey. After Saul's two years, David's rule would begin in 1060 and end in 1010; Solomon's Temple would have been begun in 1006. All authorities would recognize these dates as being entirely too early.

The table above shows the Judaean monarchy enduring for four hundred sixty-four years; this number is expressed by the three consonants in the name of David. It also shows the monarchy arising eleven hundred twenty years, forty Dominical Cycles, before the fall of Jerusalem in A.D. 70. When the one hundred twenty-one years of the united kingdom are deducted, there remain three hundred forty-three years for the divided kingdom. This is 7 x 7 x 7 years, or seven short jubilees of forty-nine years. One additional short jubilee would bring us to 538 B.C., that glorious year in Jewish history when Cyrus the Great liberated the Jewish people from the Babylonian Captivity. Nothing but the fact that it has not hitherto been detected prevents us from saying that the pattern is inescapable.

The Kings of Israel: We now turn our attention to the rulers of the northern kingdom. The chronological data given in the biblical text seem to be thirty-two years too long. In the following table of reigns, the eighty-four years credited to four of the kings of Israel are adjusted so as to total fifty-two years. Thus the entire monarchy lasted for ten Christian Cycles, the 330 years from 1051 to 721 B.C.

This king	became king	and reigned for
Saul	Dec. 1, 1051 B.C.	2 < 40 years
David	Dec. 1, 1011 B.C.	40-1/2 years
Solomon	June 1, 970 B.C.	40 years
Jeroboam	June 1, 930 B.C.	22 years
Nadab	June 1, 908 B.C.	2 years
Baasha	June 1, 906 B.C.	24 > 8 years
Elah	June 1, 898 B.C.	2 years
Zimri	June 1, 896 B.C.	7 days
Omri	June 8, 896 B.C.	12 < 20 years
Ahab I	June 8, 876 B.C.	14 years +
Ahaziah	June 8, 862 B.C.	2 years
Ahab II	June 8, 860 B.C.	8 years +
Jehoram	June 8, 852 B.C.	12 years
Jehu	June 8, 840 B.C.	28 > 20 years
Jehoahaz	June 8, 820 B.C.	17 years
Jehoash	June 8, 803 B.C.	16 years
Jeroboam II	June 8, 787 B.C.	41 years

Zechariah	June 8, 746 B.C.	6 > 3 months
Shallum	Sept. 8, 746 B.C.	1 month
Menahem	Oct. 8, 746 B.C.	10 years
Pekahiah	Oct. 8, 736 B.C.	2 years
Pekah	Oct. 8, 734 B.C.	20 > 4 years
Hoshea	Oct. 8, 730 B.C.	9 years

This table makes five needed changes. Baasha and Pekah have been reduced by sixteen years each. Omri gains eight years, and Jehu loses eight years. The twenty-two years attributed to Ahab are split between Ahab I (14) and Ahab II (8); they may or may not be the same person.

A preliminary critique should focus on the overall arrangement. All admit that Shalmaneser V besieged Samaria, capital of the northern kingdom, for three years, and that he died on 10 Tebet (December 17), 722 B.C. We also know (2 Kgs 17:6) that "the king of the Assyrians" took Samaria "in the ninth year of Hoshea." Assyrian records credit the destruction of the city both to Shalmaneser and to Sargon II, his successor, who usurped the throne on 12 Tebet (December 19), 722 B.C. The table above does not prejudice the question because it presents the ninth year of Hoshea as extending from October 8, 722 to October 7, 721 B.C.

The famous Jewish Mundane Era (which began October 7, 3761 B.C.) is exactly 3040 years (ten Hipparchian, or forty Callippic Cycles) before the end-day of Hoshea's reign. Thus, the year 721 B.C. terminates both ten Hipparchian Cycles and ten Christian Cycles (from 1051 B.C.).

So much for the *terminus ad quem*. The *terminus a quo* contained in the table is the same as that used for the monarchy in Judah, and the duration of Saul's reign is the same. If we had not eliminated thirty-two Julian years (eight Julian Cycles) from the given reigns of Baasha and Pekah, the schism would have begun in 962 B.C., a highly unrealistic date. Rejecting all three proposed reductions (coming to forty years)

would date the Temple's completion to 1000 B.C. (forty years before 960 B.C.), and the schism would be in 970 B.C., 330 years before Josiah of Judah.

We therefore seem to have here the same forty-year problem as we had with the birth-year of Moses. 1308 B.C. (eleven Dominical Cycles before 1000 B.C.) is a splendid symbolic date for that event, but 1268 B.C. (eleven Dominical Cycles before 960 B.C.) is surely more realistic.

On the other hand, failing to add eight years to Omri would destroy the needed synchronism between Jehu and Athaliah: both acceded to royal power in 841 B.C. (two Sothic Cycles after 3761 B.C.), but they have slightly differing dates for their first official year.

Ahab represents a peculiar problem and receives a peculiar solution. The table above shows his first regnal year to be 876 B.C. If sixteen years had not been deducted from Baasha, Ahab's first regnal year would be sixteen years later, 860 B.C. Curiously, the table adopts both dates, giving the first to Ahab I and the second to Ahab II. The biblical text is not wrong in giving a total of twenty-four years to Ahab and Ahaziah; the table does the same.

Zechariah is the first ruler to begin his reign after the chronological landmark of 753 B.C., the founding of the city of Rome. The minor change of Zechariah's reign (from six months to three months) may be the result of changing month-numbering from the Jewish Royal calendar (which began on December 1) to the old Roman system, in which March was the first month. Or perhaps, contrary to custom, at this point the biblical chronologist has counted from Zechariah's accession (March 8, 746?), rather than from the conventional date of June 8, in vogue since Omri.

The Chronology of Christ: Recent investigations lend credence to the view that Jesus was born in 8 B.C. and died in A.D. 33. This makes Him forty years old at the time of His crucifixion. A variety of factors (especially Lk 3:23) have conspired to persuade some to a minimum of 34 years, placing the birth in 5 B.C. and the death in A.D. 30. Still other exegetes adopt a policy of compromise between the two extreme views.

The birth-year: The infancy narratives require us to place the Holy Birth before the death of Herod, which came after a lingering illness in the early spring of A.D. 4. St. Luke requires us to place the birth of Jesus after Herod's census, taken when Saturninus and Cyrinus held high office in the Near East. It would seem that the Herodian regime followed the known Egyptian custom of taking a census every fourteen years, but in a cycle the year after the Egyptian. His first census would have been in 37 B.C. (the year he established his rule over the country), then in 23 and 9 B.C. Continuation of this cycle would coincide with the known census held in A.D. 6 (mentioned by St. Luke in Acts 5:37 and Josephus, *Ant.*, 18: 1 ss). Indeed, in the very year when St. Luke wrote his Gospel (A.D. 62?), such a census would have been due.

St. Matthew seems to indicate that two years intervened between the Nativity and the coming of the Magi, which motivated Herod's massacre of the innocents. At that time Herod appeared to be still vigorous, living in Jerusalem, not at all on his deathbed. The chronological indications in the Gospels, scanty though they be, incline us to accept the testimony of St. Epiphanius (*Haereses*, II, 50:10) that Jesus was born in the thirty-third year of Herod (8 B.C.), that the Magi came in the thirty-fifth year of

Herod (6 B.C.), who died in the thirty-seventh year of his reign (4 B.C.). The great historian Eusebius of Caesarea even places the birth in the thirty-second year of Herod, probably on the assumption that the birth and the census came in the same calendar-year.

The day of the Nativity: There is general agreement that Jesus was not born on December 25. What fragile evidence there is in the Gospels does favor the view that He was born at Passover, which, in the year 8 B.C., was on March 27, the eighty-sixth day of the Roman year. At that time, there were calendars used in the north of the Holy Land which began on October 1; by these calendars, December 25 was the eighty-sixth day of the year. In light of the fact that Mary had had a premarital pregnancy, when she and Joseph came back from Egypt and transferred their residence from Bethlehem to Nazareth, they may well have thought it wise to change the observance of Jesus' birth from Mar. 27 to Dec. 25. Such a step would have been more appealing if the visit of the Magi to Bethlehem was made at the time of the winter solstice, which at that time was on December 25, for this astronomical event marks the return of the longer days of sunlight.

In A.D. 30, December 25 and January 6 fell on the same day by the lunar calendar, the eleventh of Tebet. This fact may well explain the disaccord between the Eastern and the Western Church, for Oriental Christians generally observe Christ's birth on January 6. The choice may well have been made on the basis of authoritative information that in A.D. 30, Jesus' birthday came on the eleventh of Tebet.

The date of the crucifixion: Actually there are only two plausible opinions regarding the year and date of the death of Jesus: April 7, A.D. 30, and April 3, A.D. 33. No one doubts that Christ's death came on a Friday, at Passover time. The much-discussed conflict between the Synoptics (who seem to put Jesus' death on Passover — the fifteenth of Nisan) and St. John (who insists that it was on the fourteenth of Nisan, the day before Passover) may be resolved by the ambiguity of the word, which could denote the season (which began with the meal of Unleavened Bread, eaten from the start of the fourteenth of Nisan) or the day (which featured the eating of the Paschal Lamb, slaughtered on the fourteenth and eaten on the fifteenth of Nisan).

It is difficult to reconcile the earlier date with the "fifteenth year of Tiberius Caesar," in which St. Luke (3:1) places the Baptism of Jesus by John. All ancient authorities agree that this ended in the fall of A.D. 29. It is once again St. John who makes it impossible to confine the public ministry to a span of two years. Actually, the Catholic Church observed the nineteenth centennial of the crucifixion in 1933.

St. Luke seems to refer to an eclipse at the time of the crucifixion (23:44-45; Acts 2:20). Earlier astronomers realized that there was an eclipse of the moon on April 3, A.D. 33, but they thought this was not visible in the Holy Land.

Acceptance of the dates March 27, 8 B.C. (for the birth) and April 3, A.D. 33 (for the death) also has the advantage of placing the crucifixion on the anniversary of the circumcision. But their very proximity would incline early liturgists to separate the annual commemoration of the sorrowful and the joyful events.

Biblical Commission, Pontifical: See **Pontifical Biblical Commission**

Biblical Institute: See **Pontifical Biblical Institute**

Biblical Institute of Jerusalem: See **École Biblique**

Biblical Revival • The renewal of the study, reading and teaching of the Scriptures in the Catholic Church in the twentieth century and especially since the Second Vatican Council. The beginnings of this renewal are attributed to the French Dominican scholar Père M. J. Lagrange (1855-1938), who in 1890 founded a school for the study of the Bible in Jerusalem. Pope Pius XII confirmed and encouraged this renewal with his encyclical *Divino Afflante Spiritu*, issued in 1943. Today, Catholic biblical scholars are at the forefront of the fields of archaeology, Near Eastern languages, history and interpretation.

Bigamy • The attempt to contract a marriage while still bound to a living spouse in an undissolved marriage. Bigamy is forbidden by canon law, and in most countries by civil law.

Bigot • One who holds false or unreasonable religious and racial views, combined with prejudice and intolerance toward others who hold different views.

Bilocation • The simultaneous presence of the same substance in two distinct places. Bilocation does not imply the multiplication of a body's substance; rather, the person's bodily relations to other bodies are increased. The Body and Blood of Christ in the Holy Eucharist is an example of bilocation due to Christ's presence — not limited like material bodies to space — in tabernacles throughout the world. This phenomenon, reported in the lives of some saints, was said to exist in the life of the modern stigmatist Padre Pio (1887-1968).

Bination • Refers to the act of a priest celebrating two Masses on the same day. The word itself is derived from the Latin *bini* for "two" or "a pair." According to ancient Church law and custom, a priest may regularly celebrate only one Mass a day. For pastoral reasons, however, a priest is able to celebrate two, or at the most, three Masses in the same day. In the present Code of Canon Law, this is still prescribed, as Canon 905.1 sets down that, with exceptions such as Christmas or All Souls' Day (when three Masses may be celebrated) aside, the priest may licitly celebrate only one Mass a day. However, the second paragraph of the same canon, taking into consideration actual pastoral needs, states that where there is a lack of priests, two Masses may be celebrated on any day and three on Sundays and holy days of obligation if true necessity requires it.

Biretta • The square cap worn by clerics of the Latin Rite both within and outside liturgical functions. This evolved from diverse forms of head covering which were used by the clergy, particularly after the wearing of hoods and cowls fell out of use among the non-monastic clergy. At first, skullcaps were worn mainly to keep the wearer's head warm, especially important at a time when the clergy were rigorously required to wear the tonsure. This skullcap eventually evolved with the addition of a tuft, which made it easier to remove. Ridges along the corners later appeared for both practical and fashionable reasons. By the time of the Renaissance, the biretta was stiff, reinforced with a lining and taking on the appearance it still has to this day. Thus it is a square headdress with three ridges at the corners for most clerics and four ridges for those clerics who have attained a pontifical doctorate. (Four ridges are also usual for all clerics in France, Germany, Spain and Poland.)

Biretta

The color of the biretta varies with the ecclesiastical dignity or rank of the wearer. Normally it is completely black. (Until 1969, monsignori wore a purple tuft on the black biretta.) Bishops wear purple with matching tuft, while cardinals use scarlet with no tuft. The aforementioned doctoral biretta (not permitted for liturgical use) has, besides its four corners, piping and tuft of the color of the faculty, e.g., red for sacred theology, blue for philosophy. The Holy Father does not wear the biretta; for him, the camauro formerly took its place on certain occasions. A white biretta, however, is used as part of the habit of the Canons Regular of Premontré (the Norbertines or Premonstratensians).

Though the biretta is used for sacred functions, it is not strictly a liturgical parament. Also, even though the mortarboard used in academic dress today evolved from the clerical biretta, it is not strictly academic dress either. It is usually required for choir dress. The biretta has suffered from lack of popularity and has fallen into general disuse since the Second Vatican Council, but its use is still required of all the canons of the patriarchal basilicas in Rome.

Birth Control • A deliberately and directly intended action to prevent conception or birth from taking place. Birth control can include contraception, abortion and sterilization, for all of these aim at preventing birth. Methods of birth control include withdrawal before ejaculation or the use of devices such as condoms or contraceptive pills.

One of the most consistently held teachings of the Catholic Church has been that deliberately and directly interfering with the marital act in order to prevent conception or birth is a gravely evil action.

Contraception has been consistently and solemnly condemned throughout the history of the Church and this condemnation is one of the most important teachings of the Church. Pope Pius XI condemned it sharply in his encyclical *Casti connubii* in 1930 when he said that: ". . . any use of marriage, whatever, in the exercise of which the act is deprived through human industry of its natural power of procreating life, violates the law of God and of nature, and those who do anything of this nature are marked with the stain of grave sin."

Pope John XXIII established a commission in 1963 to study the morality of contraception, and in 1966 the majority of the commission recommended permitting some form of contraception, while a minority opposed this position. But on July 29, 1968, Pope Paul VI issued his encyclical *Humanae Vitae*, in which he condemned artificial contraception in clear and unequivocal terms. Because of the long time involved in the preparation of the encyclical, many thought he would change the teaching of the Church. It has been taught so frequently and with such gravity that some Catholic moral theologians now believe that it is part of the ordinary magisterial teachings of the Church.

Contraception is essentially wrong because it employs the sexual function in a manner to prohibit the natural purpose of that function, defeating the primary purpose of the marriage relation. Even if the motive is the expression of marital love rather than the releasing of drives due to sexual tension, the teaching of the Church is that the motive of love should not be separated from the sexual act's openness to new life.

Vatican II declared: "When it is a question of harmonizing married love with the responsible transmission of life, it is not enough to take only the good intention and the evaluation of motives into account; the objective criteria must be used, criteria drawn from the nature of the human person and human action, criteria which respect the total meaning of mutual self-giving and human procreation in the context of true love . . . sons of the Church, faithful to these principles, are forbidden to use methods [of regulating procreation] disapproved of by the teaching authority of the Church in its interpretation of the divine law" (GS 51).

Many Catholic couples think that overpopulation, the difficulties of raising children in urban environments and personal stress from physical, economic or emotional causes can make the use of some contraceptives correct. Catholic teaching urges couples who have *serious* reasons for limiting family size temporarily to make use of the now much-perfected techniques of natural family planning. It should also be a matter of serious concern that many contraceptives are inefficient, causes of critical health hazards for the mother and also abortifacient; that is, they cause the already joined sperm and egg to be flushed out of the woman's body, thereby constituting an early abortion, always a sin of utmost gravity. (Cf. Natural Family Planning.)

Birth Control Pill • One of a variety of anti-fertility drugs that suppress ovulation and thus prevent pregnancy. Birth control pills are a common form of artificial contraception, and morally unacceptable according to Catholic teaching. Furthermore, some of these are actually abortifacients.

Bisexual • One who can relate to individuals of both genders as sexual partners.

Bishop • From the Greek *episkopos* (overseer), the bishop is a successor of the

Apostles, in the highest order of the threefold ministry with the fullness of Christ's priesthood, having the power and authority to administer all the sacraments, including ordination.

Immediately before His ascension, Christ commissioned the Apostles to "make disciples of all nations" (Mt 28:19), and promised that He would be with them "until the close of the age [end of the world]" (Mt 28:20). As St. Peter and the other Apostles faced martyrdom, and with the growth of the Church, it became apparent to them that they must choose successors to carry out Christ's mandate. In approximately the year 96, in his *Epistle to the Corinthians*, St. Clement of Rome wrote that the Apostles "laid down a rule once for all to this effect: When these men die, other approved men shall succeed to their sacred ministry." These bishops, succeeding the Apostles, were recognized as shepherds who acted in the name of Christ, and loyalty to Christ was manifested by loyalty to the bishop. St. Ignatius of Antioch wrote in about A.D. 106 to the Church in Philadelphia, stating that it is "a source of everlasting joy, especially when the members are at one with the bishop and his assistants, the presbyters and deacons, that have been appointed in accordance with the wish of Jesus Christ, and whom He has, by His own will, through the operation of His Holy Spirit, confirmed in loyalty."

The Catholic Church is comprised of many "particular churches" (dioceses), each of which is under the care of an individual bishop, although he may have auxiliary bishops to assist him. He is the authentic

Bishop celebrating Mass
(German manuscript, 1300s)

teacher of the Faith in his diocese; he is the center of unity; and he is among the "stewards of the mysteries of God" (1 Cor 4:1) for the faithful under his care. The bishop carries out his ministry in cooperation with his priests and deacons, who have been made co-workers with him by ordination. However, no bishop is a shepherd in isolation. All the bishops, in union with the successor of St. Peter, constitute one college, and this collegiality has been evident from the earliest years of the Church, as the bishops have gathered together in councils to seek the guidance of the Holy Spirit in directing the Church (Acts 15:6ff.). (Cf. Christus Dominus; Ordination.)

Bishop, Auxiliary • An assistant bishop, appointed by the Pope to aid the bishop who is the Ordinary of a diocese. Large dioceses can have more than one auxiliary, who sometimes serve as territorial vicars. An auxiliary bishop does not have ordinary jurisdiction within a diocese, nor does he have the right of succession upon the death or resignation of the Ordinary. The term comes from the Latin *auxiliaris*, meaning "helpful."

Bishop, Coadjutor: See **Coadjutor Bishop**

Bishop, Suffragan • The residential bishop of a diocese within an ecclesiastical province wherein the primary bishop is known as the metropolitan archbishop. Auxiliary bishops are not suffragan bishops.

Bishop, Titular • A bishop who serves as an auxiliary, coadjutor, vicar apostolic or in the Roman Curia, and is not the Ordinary of a residential see, but who has been given the title to one of the ancient dioceses which is now extinct or defunct.

Bishop of Rome • The first Bishop of Rome was St. Peter, who founded the see in the year 42. It was to him that Christ had given the "keys of the kingdom of heaven" (Mt 16:19), and who was declared by Our Lord to be the rock on which He would build His Church (Mt 16:18). The divinely appointed primacy of St. Peter has been entrusted to each successor who has taken his place in the Roman See, and throughout history each Pope, as the Bishop of Rome, has been considered "another Peter" and, therefore, the head of the College of Bishops.

Indications of the primacy of the Roman See can be found in such examples as the first-century involvement of the Bishop of Rome with the Corinthian Church to heal a schism which was threatening their unity, and in the cases of many bishops such as St. Ignatius of Antioch (d. A.D. 107) who conformed to the instructions which came from Rome. Agreement with the judgment of the Bishop of Rome has been a test of orthodoxy from the earliest years of the Church, which is attested to by such writers as St. Irenaeus (d. 200).

Bishops, Collegiality of • The joint fellowship and authority enjoyed by all the bishops of the world in union with the Holy See. With the Pope at its head, the college of bishops, as successors to the Apostles, exercises supreme authority over the Church in teaching, sanctifying and leading. Vatican Council II gave renewed attention and emphasis to bishops' collegiality.

Bishops in the Church, Decree on the Pastoral Office of the: See **Christus Dominus**

Bishops' Committee on the Liturgy (BCL) • The BCL, as it is popularly known, is an appointed committee of experts whose responsibility is to assist the National Conference of Catholic Bishops and diocesan Ordinaries and liturgical commissions in fulfilling the directives of the Holy See in regard to the Sacred Liturgy. Information from the Congregation for Divine Worship at the Vatican is transmitted to the local level through the BCL, and requests for clarifications or adaptations of a liturgical nature are communicated to the Holy See on behalf of the bishops' conference through the BCL. In addition to supervising, on behalf of the national episcopate, the preparation and publication of official liturgical books, the BCL issues a periodic newsletter, provides expert consultation on liturgical matters and publishes an extensive array of educational resources regarding the liturgy.

Black • As a liturgical color, one of the three options (along with purple or white) permitted for Masses for the dead.

Black Fast • The so-called black fast refers to a day or days of penance on which only one meal is allowed, and that in the evening. The prescription of this type of fast not only forbids the partaking of meats but also of all dairy products, such as eggs, butter, cheese and milk. Wine and other alcoholic beverages are forbidden as well. In short, only bread, water and vegetables form part of the diet for one following such a fast. In former times the Latin Rite practiced this type of fast, but it has long since disappeared. It is still the general custom of the Orthodox Churches as well as some Eastern Rite Catholics. In the Latin Rite, some religious orders of strict observance have maintained such a fast.

Black Friars • The terminology used to describe members of the Dominican Order, or Order of Preachers, as is their official title. This was especially so in English-speaking countries, such as England and Ireland. The reason for this term stems from the Dominican habit, which comprises not only the white or off-white tunic, scapular and cowl, but also, when in choir or on the street (in countries where this is the custom), a black cape, "cappa" and cowl over that. As such, since most of what was seen of them as they walked on the roads was the black, they became known as the Black Friars.

Black Legend • An anti-Spanish legend describing the conquest and government of the New World in wholly malevolent terms and portraying the Spaniards as a universally rapacious, greedy and brutal people who were motivated by nothing more than the quest for adventure, power, territory and gold. While the historical truth of a certain amount of harm suffered by Native Americans at the hands of the conquistadors cannot be denied, the legend gives a completely one-sided account of these events, largely to exalt the rectitude and sobriety of English undertakings in the Americas. The legend ignores the civilizing and evangelizing accomplishments of the Spaniards. Ironically, Spanish colonization encouraged intermarriage with the Native American population, which still constitutes a major cultural and ethnic force in Latin American countries, whereas in countries settled by the English the Native Americans, after ferocious and unremitting warfare, were driven to the margins of society to a kind of internal exile.

Black Monks • A title given to Benedictine monks because of their black religious habit or garb. Similar designations were common for religious orders in the Middle Ages. Thus, for example, the Franciscans came to be known as Grey Friars because of their simple gray (or grey) habits, while the Dominicans came to be known as Black Friars and the Carmelites as White Friars because of the color of their outer cape or "cappa."

Black Pope • A sobriquet for the Master General of the Society of Jesus, indicating both the supposed power and influence of the Jesuits and the color of their religious garb.

Blaise, Blessing of St. • The traditional blessing of throats, conferred on the liturgical memorial of St. Blaise (February 3) who was said to have cured a young boy choking on a fish bone. Devotion to him as a healer of throats developed in the East by the sixth century. He became particularly popular in Germany and France during the Middle Ages. The blessing is conferred on the throats of the faithful by means of two crossed candles, invoking the intercession of St. Blaise, bishop and martyr, against ailments of the throat and every other disease.

Blasphemy • From the Greek *blasphemia* (verb, *blapto*), meaning abusive language damaging to someone's reputation. In Sacred Scripture it refers to abusive, contemptuous and irreverent language toward God. In the Old Testament it is punishable by stoning, and defiles the whole community (Lv 24:16); it need not be restricted to speech: adultery and murder are blasphemous (David: 2 Sm 12:14), as are stealing (Ps 10:3, 13) and unbelief (Nm 14:11, 23; 16:30; Is 1:4; 5:24). Jesus' claim to be the Messiah (Mt 26:64; Mk 14:61-62) and God's Son (Jn 8:49-59; 10:31-36) was taken as blasphemy. Jesus' power and authority over demons was attributed to the diabolical; such an attribution is considered a blasphemy "against the Holy Spirit" (Mt 12:31; Mk 3:28ff.; Lk 12:10).

Blasphemy is also mentioned in the earliest generations of the Church. Paul confesses the sin of blasphemy committed prior to his conversion (1 Tm 1:13). Later, he faced false accusations of blasphemy (Acts 13:45; 18:6). In the Book of Revelation, blasphemy will emerge from the mouth of the beast (Rv 13:1-6). Late New Testament teaching warns about blasphemy against God (2 Tm 3:2; 2 Pt 2:2, 10, 12; 1 Tm 1:20) and about the inevitable divine judgment (Rv 16:9, 11, 21).

In speaking of blasphemy, the *Catechism of the Catholic Church* (n. 2148) points out that it "is directly opposed to the second commandment. It consists in uttering against God — inwardly or outwardly — words of hatred, reproach, or defiance; in speaking ill of God; in failing in respect toward him in one's speech; in misusing God's name. . . . It is also blasphemous to make use of God's name to cover up criminal practices, to reduce peoples to servitude, to torture persons or put them to death. The misuse of God's name to commit a crime can provoke others to repudiate religion." It ends with, "Blasphemy is contrary to the respect due to God and his holy name. It is in itself a grave sin."

For further reading: *Catechism of the Catholic Church*, n. 1864.

Bless Oneself • To make the sign of the cross on oneself.

Blessed • Broadly speaking, any person graced by God is blessed, and somewhat more narrowly, one frequently encounters the term "blessed" in referring to the saints in heaven.

Usually, though, the official title "Blessed" is conferred upon a Servant of God after the completion of the beatification stage of the process of canonization. (Cf. Cause.) Upon designation as a "blessed," public veneration of the Servant is permitted, though usually on a rather smaller scale than that permitted to the saints.

For further reading: *Catechism of the Catholic Church*, nn. 1023-1029.

Blessing • Biblical blessings express God's generosity, favor and unshakable love for His children. It is as much *speech* as it is *goodness* (Greek, *eu-logia*; Latin, *bene-dictio*). In Hebrew, the substantive *beraka* ("blessing") is linked to expressions of reconciliation (1 Sm 25:14-27; 30:26-31; 2 Kgs 5:15; Gn 33:11); the most common use of the noun is in religious contexts, pointing back to God, Who is the source of all richness of life, fullness of health and well-being (Prv 10:6, 22; Sir 33:17). The verb *barak* ("to bless") is used as a greeting (2 Kgs 4:29), but more often is used to express fecundity and fertility (e.g., Gn 1:22, 28; 5:2); in addition, one's inheritance is rooted in paternal blessing (Gn 27:27-29). The Psalms are filled with phrases such as "Blessed be . . . for. . . ," usually referring to God and His wondrous deeds of salvation and should be understood as "praise be to . . ." or "thanks be to. . . ."

If blessing is one of the ways in which God communicates His life to us, then Mary is blessed in that God communicated an "immaculate" life to her by the grace of Jesus Christ; but she is doubly blessed, she received a second communication of divine life, namely, Jesus, the Son of the Living God. Jesus blesses the food He multiplies (Mt 14:19; Mk 6:41; 8:7; Lk 9:16) and the bread and wine which will become the food and drink of all who come to believe in His name (Mt 26:26; Mk 14:22).

For further reading: Kent Harold Richards, "Bless/Blessing," *Anchor Bible Dictionary*, 1:753-755.

Blessing, Apostolic • The benediction bestowed upon the faithful by the Pope. He gives the papal blessing at the conclusion of Mass and at various liturgical functions; in addition, he may bestow the blessing at the end of a papal audience, as he does on solemn occasions such as the event of his election and Christmas Day, when he grants the blessing *Urbi et Orbi* ("To the City and the World"). A plenary indulgence, under the usual conditions, is attached to the papal blessing and may be earned even by listening to the blessing over the radio or television. The blessing is delegated to bishops; a priest may give the apostolic blessing on the occasion of his first solemnly celebrated Mass and when he attends the sick at the moment of death.

Blessing, Last • (1) The apostolic blessing given to a dying person, after the administration of anointing, which bestows a plenary indulgence. The English text of the Last Blessing is, "By the power the Apostolic See has given me, I grant you a plenary indulgence and pardon for all your sins, in the name of the Father, and of the Son, and of the Holy Spirit." The indulgence which is granted is then gained at the moment of death.

(2) The final blessing at the conclusion of the celebration of the Eucharist, occurring just after the Postcommunion prayer and before the dismissal, is sometimes referred to as the Last Blessing.

Blessing of the Fire: See **Fire, Blessing of the**

Blessing of Throats: See **Blaise, Blessing of St.**

Blessings, Book of • The English translation of *De Benedictionibus*, the *editio typica* (i.e., the standard, official Latin edition) of that section of the Roman Ritual published by the Holy See in 1984, containing the blessing of persons, places and things in a revised format with many new formulas reflecting the liturgical principles promulgated by the Second Vatican Council. Distinctive features of the revised Rites of Blessings are: a proper greeting based on a scriptural text and related to the occasion for the blessing; a lectionary of scriptural readings (long and short forms) to be proclaimed before the prayer of blessing itself; a series of intercessions (similar to those found in the Liturgy of the Hours) for use with the longer rites of blessing; a concluding rite of blessing and dismissal which, like the greeting, incorporates scriptural themes and is related to the occasion.

Some rites are given in forms to be used within Mass and within a Liturgy of the Word; many are given in long and short forms, to be chosen according to pastoral circumstances. Provision is made for some blessings to be conferred by deacons or celebrated even by laity properly deputed by the bishop. Each national conference of bishops is to adapt the Latin table of contents, determining appropriate additions and modifications. The United States edition adds about forty blessings not found in the Latin original but designed to serve the pastoral needs of priests and laity in this country. In addition, a companion volume entitled *Catholic Household Blessings and Prayers* combines those blessings to be celebrated by laity in their homes with a treasury of traditional Catholic litanies and prayers.

Part I of the *Book of Blessings* contains blessings directly pertaining to people: families, married couples, the engaged, children, parents before childbirth or after a miscarriage, a blessing for adoptive parents and their child, birthday blessings and a blessing for the elderly. Blessings for the sick are provided, including prayers for those suffering from addiction and abuse, as well as victims of crime or violence. Prayer meetings and catechetical conferences, pilgrims and travelers are all provided for, as well as parish meetings and ecumenical gatherings. Part II contains blessings related to buildings and various forms of human activity. Especially noteworthy is the rich collection of meal blessings in new and traditional forms, including special formularies for various liturgical seasons and celebrations. Parts III and IV provide blessings for items used in public or private prayer. Parts V and VI are designed to be particularly helpful on the parish level, presenting a rich collection of blessings related to feasts and seasons, as well as the blessings for commissioning readers, altar boys, musicians, parish council and society members, and a rite for welcoming newly-arrived parishioners.

Blue Laws • Civil laws that seek to regulate public morality in regard to alcohol sale and consumption, sexual activity, gambling and Sunday observance.

Boat • (1) Often employed in literature and art as a symbol of the Church, most likely because of the common profession of the Apostles as fishermen. In particular, since Peter and his successors give the Church specific direction as would a helmsman, the Church is often called the boat or bark of Peter.

(2) Because of its shape, the small liturgical vessel used for containing incense is called a boat.

Boat Bearer • The server who carries the vessel, or "boat," containing the incense which will be placed in the thurible for burning at liturgical services in which there is incensation. If the thurifer carries both the boat and the thurible, there is no need for a boat bearer.

Bodily Defect • Some physical defect of a priest, such as blindness, the lack of a finger or hand, or being mute, which could prevent the proper celebration of the Eucharist, or which would interfere with the valid carrying out of any priestly function.

Body, Resurrection of the • In ancient Eastern religions, belief in some form of immortality of the soul or "life after death" was widespread. Many, if not all, of the belief systems were cyclically based on the rhythm of nature: the four seasons. The religious traditions offered narratives and rituals in which we find some deity to be lord of this or that aspect of nature and its corresponding life cycle. In many instances fertility, fecundity or long life were desired, but in terms of a stepping stone to eternal bliss under the patronage of a particular deity. The life of the deity was often reenacted by the initiated through one form of ritual or another, leading to eternal life.

In the Old Testament such is conspicuously not the case. The God of Israel, the One True God, is the Master of life and of death: the "resurrection" of nature in spring as well as its "death" are by His Word and Spirit, which hold and sustain them in reality (Gn 8:22; Ps 104:29ff.); it is a matter of understanding that nature expresses the Word of God. Hence, the cycles of life and death are at the command of God (1 Sm 2:6; Dt 32:39), Who even controls the "place of death," Sheol (Am 9:2; Ps 139:8). In the prophets and later, we see a belief in the corporate resurrection of God's people: God revives and raises up (Hos 6:1ff.), restores "dry bones" (Ez 37:1-14), raises up a dead Jerusalem (Is 51:17; 60:1) and His faithful friends who are "in the dust" (Is 26:19; Hos 13:14). Later Tradition attests to individual resurrection in the context of a final judgment (Dn 7:13-27; cf. 2:44) where life eternal with the Eternal One will be blissful or something less than this (Dn 12:2; 2 Mc 7:9-23; 14:46). This new life will differ radically from the current one (Dn 12:3). The Old Testament witness prepares for the fullness of revelation about the resurrection of the body, which occurs in the Person of Jesus Christ.

Jesus knew and spoke about His impending death and resurrection (Mt 16:21; 17:9; 17:23; 20:19; Mk 8:31; 9:9; 9:31; 10:34; Lk 9:22; 18:33; Jn 6:39-44, 54); even so, the many healings performed were themselves a language full of anticipation of His own resurrection: He restored to life Jairus's daughter (Mt 9:18-26; Mk 5:21-42), the son of the widow of Nain (Lk 7:11-17), and especially Lazarus (Jn 11:1-44). In the early Church the resurrection of Christ was a primary focus in the proclamation of the Apostles, be it in creedal form (Acts 7:37; Rom 10:9; 1 Cor 12:3), in hymns or prayers drawn from early Church liturgical practice (Eph 5:14; 1 Tm 3:16), or as found in apostolic preaching and catechesis (Acts 1:22; 2:24-28; 3:15, 26; 4:10, 33; 5:30ff.; 10:40-41ff.; 13:30-37; 17:3, 31; 26:22ff.).

It is helpful to distinguish between restoration to the same kind of life and resurrection of the body into a completely new sphere of existence (Mk 12:25; cf. Dn 12:3 and Col 1:18). Through the miracle of Baptism, the Church, as Christ's Body, over which He is Head (cf. Colossians and Ephesians), shares in and is an integral part of that new life which is His resurrection life.

Bollandists • A very small but distinguished group of Dutch Jesuits who, following the example of the Flemish Jesuit Heribert Rosweyde, were organized by the Rev. John Bolland and assumed the monumental task of discovering, sorting, editing and studying the voluminous records of the lives of the ancient saints. In 1635, Bolland, who had been working alone, was allowed the assignment of one of his most illustrious pupils, Godefroid Henschenius, and the scope of Bolland's project was greatly expanded and formally underway. Their first publication, which appeared in 1643, was highly acclaimed, as were subsequent volumes.

The death of John Bolland in 1665 was an irreplaceable loss, but the project continued to receive strong support from many Popes, including Alexander VII and Benedict XIV. The suppression of the Jesuits was perhaps the most serious blow to the enterprise, for during those years many carefully collected documents were lost. In 1840, however, the project was renewed and, now numbering scores of volumes, is continued to this day.

Bolshevism • This term was used loosely from the 1920s on to refer to the theory and practice of the communists who overthrew the provisional government of the Russian Empire in November of 1917. Vladimir Lenin led the Bolshevik Revolution against a fledgling republican government that was attempting to establish a constitution faithful to the democratic form. After dissolving an elected assembly called in Petrograd (Leningrad) to draft a constitution, Lenin's men established the Soviet government, waging war on all opponents of Bolshevik rule in a bloody civil war.

More exactly from a historical point of view, Bolshevik and Bolshevism referred to the majority wing of the Russian Social Democratic Labor Party (RSDLP). Bolshevism comes from the Russian word *bolshe*, meaning "greater" (or, "the majority"). Accordingly, the minority wing of the RSDLP, which split with the Bolsheviks over the party program in a London meeting in 1904, was called the Menshevik wing of the RSDLP. (*Menshe* means "lesser" or minority.) The Mensheviks were not really the minority faction in the fateful meeting but committed the tactical error of walking out, allowing the real minority, the Bolsheviks, to win the issue. The Mensheviks and Bolsheviks published their own newspapers from 1904 on, and Lenin waged a war against the Mensheviks, as he did against his other opponents, after the Bolshevik seizure of power in 1917.

The Mensheviks thought of themselves as more correct or orthodox followers of the German social theorist Karl Marx, particularly on the issue of not forcing Russia into a violent revolution before its economic and social conditions more nearly approximated European industrial societies. Led by Lenin, the Bolsheviks theorized that even a non-industrial society such as Russia was better off having an early communist revolution because world capitalism was finding ways to defuse revolutionary spirit and opportunity among the world's working classes. World capitalism delayed revolution through recruiting the workers to fight other capitalist societies for territory (imperialism) and through the use of the poorest classes to put down revolutionary movements (Bonapartism).

As a militantly materialist and atheistic form of revolution, Bolshevism was hostile to the practice of religion and to the freedoms needed for the practice of the smaller organizations so important to the Catholic social doctrine of subsidiarity. Moreover, Bolshevism had a rigid agenda of political uses for its puppet trade unions, erasing genuine worker independence in cooperating to earn a livelihood and define other workers' goals.

Bond of Marriage • The unique relationship between a man and a woman by which they are constituted husband and wife. It comes into existence at the time when consent is validly exchanged. It is not to be equated with the existential relationship or any quality of that relationship, for it continues to exist even if the spouses have physically separated. The bond of marriage, once constituted by means of the covenant between the partners, happens when they give and receive each other for the purpose of establishing the marital community.

For the first twelve centuries of the Church's existence, the bond was considered a strong moral obligation that held the spouses to complete fidelity. In the twelfth century, when the Church acquired direct authority over marriage, the notion of the bond shifted from one of strong moral obligation to that of an ontological reality that has a separate existence from the existential relationship of the spouses.

The bond of marriage comes into existence only from a valid marriage. Hence, if the consent is invalid because of an impediment or some other defect in consent, there is no bond.

The baptismal status of the parties determines the degree of dissolubility of the bond. If one or both parties are unbaptized, then the bond is referred to as a natural bond. Such a bond cannot be dissolved by the parties themselves, but it can be dissolved by the Roman Pontiff or by the Pauline Privilege.

If both parties are baptized, Catholic or not, the bond is known as a sacramental bond. A sacramental bond that has not been consummated by complete sexual intercourse subsequent to the exchange of consent can be dissolved by the Roman Pontiff, but a consummated sacramental bond can be dissolved by no power on earth (cf. Canon 1134).

Book of Common Prayer • The liturgical book of the Church of England and other churches of the Anglican Communion, e.g., the Episcopal Church in the United States. The first Prayer Book of Edward VI was imposed in England by the Act of Uniformity in 1549. This was the work of Archbishop Cranmer, who revised it in 1552; he translated many Roman prayers and Sarum texts into an English of incomparable poetry and beauty. This has undergone various revisions, including that for the United States in 1789, which was derived from the 1662 Prayer Book but with other influences, such as the Eucharistic Rite from the Scottish Episcopal Book of Common Prayer. (The 1662 version is still in use in England.) In our own century the 1928 American version was standard until 1980, when an Alternative Service Book was made official in England and a new American Book given for the U.S. in 1979. In each of these there is a first rite similar to the old rite. The Prayer Book contains the ritual and prayers for the Eucharist and the other sacraments, Morning and Evening Prayer and the Psalter.

Book of Hours: See Hours, Book of

Book of Life, The • The names of the saved are known by God and thus are written in the Book of Life, according to Revelation 20:15.

Books, Liturgical • The liturgical books are the officially approved sources for the liturgy of the Church. After the Council of Trent, a large number of preexisting liturgical sources were codified into the *Roman Missal* for Mass, the *Roman Breviary* for the Liturgy of the Hours and the *Roman Ritual* for the other sacraments and sacramentals.

Since Vatican II, all the Church's liturgical rites were revised and a new set of liturgical books was issued, first in Latin and then in vernacular translations by various episcopal conferences. The present liturgical books include, among others, the *Lectionary for Mass* containing the Scripture readings proclaimed at the Eucharist, the *Sacramentary for Mass* containing the prayers which the bishop or priest says at the Eucharist, a four-volume set of books, the *Liturgy of the Hours* for the Divine Office, the *Roman Pontifical* for rites reserved to the bishop, the *Ceremonial of Bishops* containing descriptions of episcopal liturgy and revised ritual books for all other sacramental and liturgical rites. Of particular importance is the introduction to each of the revised rites, called the "General Instruction(s)" which describe the rite at hand, theologically, liturgically and rubrically.

The procedure followed for revising liturgical books since Vatican II has been the publication in Latin of what is called the *editio typica* of the rite from which translations and adaptations approved by episcopal conferences are produced. The Holy See then reviews the proposed local rituals; if approved, they become normative for the liturgy of that episcopal conference.

Born Catholic • A popular term for a person who is born of Catholic parents and reared in the Faith from infancy. Sometimes such a person is also called a "cradle Catholic."

Bowing • A liturgical gesture in which either the head or the whole body from the waist is inclined to give reverence to a sacred object or to some person, such as a bishop or the principal celebrant of a liturgical service.

Boycott • The avoidance of business or other relations with some organization or institution in protest of its policies. Boycotting is a common form of moral and political protest.

Boys' Town • On December 10, 1917, Father Edward Flanagan founded an institution to care for abandoned, orphaned and underprivileged boys. At first named simply "Father Flanagan's Boys' Home," the venture was started by the priest with eighty-nine dollars and five boys. Now an incorporated self-sufficient city located ten miles west of Omaha, Nebraska, the institution has more than fifty-five buildings with complete educational and housing care for over a thousand boys from the fifth grade through high school. The education given by a fully professional staff of men and women stresses holistic formation, including religion, citizenship, academic studies, manual arts (such as mechanics, painting, electronics, baking, agriculture, computer skills), music, drama and athletics. The town is supported by voluntary offerings, and has also established a center at The Catholic University of America to promote the study of adolescent psychology. Since the late 1960s, girls have also been accepted.

Branch Theory • The opinion, proposed mainly by members of the Anglican Communion, that three distinct churches, the Anglican, Eastern Orthodox and Roman Catholic, comprise the one true church founded by Jesus Christ. Valid episcopal orders and priestly orders exist only within these churches, according to this theory's proponents. Differences between the three churches are recognized, however, the churches are united by virtue of their common essentials. This theory is opposed to "oneness" — a characteristic of the true Church. Moreover, Pope Leo XIII, in his decree *Apostolicae Curae* (September 13, 1896), stated that valid ordination is lacking in the Anglican Church.

Brasses • In ecclesiastical use brasses are the engraved sheets of brass used for funeral monuments or markers. Usually, they represent the person buried in life-size scale as he or she would appear beneath the marker; they also give the person's name and important dates from his or her life, at times with an epitaph or verse descriptive of the person's achievements. The brass may be placed flush with the floor or attached to the top of an above-ground sepulchre. Brass plates attached at the end of burial niches are also called brasses. Though most common in the medieval period, they remained in use through the eighteenth century and have a modern adaptation in brass plaques. Today the older and more detailed brasses are a popular source for brass rubbings which are obtained by rubbing a colored substance over paper placed on the incised surface; the ghostly image which emerges on the paper can then be taken away, leaving the brass intact and in place.

Brass rubbing of
Sir John Harpecon

Breach of Promise • After the making of a contract, the subsequent refusal of one party to fulfill his or her part of the contract. The term refers especially to the refusal to enter into Matrimony after a betrothal.

Bread • In several parts of Sacred Scripture, bread is considered a precious gift from God and a source of physical sustenance (Ps 104:14ff.). Ritual use of bread is common throughout the Old Testament: Passover and the Feast of Unleavened Bread (Ex 12:8, 14-20; 13:3-10); the bread of the presence (Ex 25:30; 40:22-23); cereal offerings (Ex 29:2, 23-25; Lv 2:4-16, 7:9; 1 Sm 10:3-8); the Lord's Supper (Mt 26:26-29; Mk 14:22-25; Lk 22:14-20; 1 Cor 11:23-26). God sustained Israel in the wilderness with bread from the heavens (Ex 16:14-30). It is not surprising to find that bread was often taken as a symbol of that which was essential (Am 4:6: Gn 28:20). In Exodus 25:23-30 bread is a symbol of communion between God and the faithful.

As a substance, bread exists in a kind of "transformed" state, in that it represents the combination of baser elements (water, flour, yeast, etc.) which have been refashioned into a union difficult if not impossible to reverse. Because of this status, bread provides an excellent image to speak of Eucharistic unity (1 Cor 10:17) and, more broadly speaking, is a common symbol of the age of Christ's salvation which holds at its center the assured hope of God's power to restore His creation to Himself. Within this context, bread is also a sign of the new creation. At His last paschal meal, Christ took the fruit of human work — bread — and raised it to a divine and higher dignity by offering to the world His very Body and Blood through it.

Bread, Blessed: See **Pain Bénit**

Bread, Eucharistic • The bread used for the consecration in the Eucharist. In the Western Church, unleavened wafers are used. Leavened bread is used in all the Orthodox and Eastern Rite Churches (except for the Catholic Malabar Rite, the Armenian Rite and the Maronite Rite).

Bread of Life • In the sixth chapter of John's Gospel, we learn that Jesus Himself is the "bread of life," which is from heaven and gives life to the world (Jn 6:33-35). In typically Johannine fashion, we are taken from the literal to the symbolic, from the material to the spiritual: Jesus feeds the crowd with loaves and fishes, which establishes His credentials as provider of sustenance (Jn 6:1-15). The dialogue on the need for signs, on belief and "true manna" or bread sent from God in heaven (Jn 6:22-40) leads to Jesus' Eucharistic discourse (Jn 6:41-58). The gift of Christ's Body and Blood at the Eucharistic meal draws the Church into the One Sacrifice and the One being sacrificed at Calvary. This liturgical act is focused on the bread and wine which become our spiritual food and drink. The "manna," which is Jesus, is the fullness Israel experiences of receiving daily bread from God (Ex 16), which in later Old Testament Tradition was understood as coming from God's mouth (Dt 8:3; Sir 24:3 [Ex 16]; Prv 9:1-6). In the Person of Christ Jesus, God does not simply *send* "bread from heaven"; He actually *is* the bread from heaven, which sustains all who partake of it.

Breaking of Bread • Although "breaking bread" is sometimes used today as a way of referring to an ordinary meal, in the early Church it is one of the ways in which Christians referred to the celebration of the Eucharist.

In Luke's Gospel, the disciples who encountered the risen Jesus on the road to Emmaus hurried back to Jerusalem and "told what had happened on the road, and how he [Jesus] was known to them in the breaking of the bread" (Lk 24:35). At the Last Supper, before His crucifixion and at the evening meal with these disciples after His resurrection, Jesus took bread, blessed it, broke it into several pieces and gave it to them. At the Last Supper, Jesus said of the bread, "This is my body," and of the cup of wine, "This is my blood."

In the Acts of the Apostles, we read of the life of the early Church: "They devoted themselves to the apostles' teaching and fellowship, to the breaking of bread and the prayers" (Acts 2:42). And: "On the first day of the week, when we were gathered together to break bread, Paul talked with them. . ." (Acts 20:7) (cf. Mt 26:26; Lk 22:19; 1 Cor 10:16 and 11:23-29).

Breath • Both in Hebrew and in Greek, the words for breath have several interrelated meanings. The Hebrew *ruach* and the Greek word *pneuma* can refer to breath and to wind, and, by extension to spirit — even to the Holy Spirit of God. In the book of the prophet Ezekiel, for example, God commands the prophet as Ezekiel stands in the midst of the valley full of dry bones, "Prophesy to the breath [*ruach*], prophesy, son of man, and say to the breath, 'Thus says the Lord God: Come from the four winds, O breath, and breathe upon these slain, that they may live' " (Ez 37:9). In this text, the word "breath" (the same word, *ruach*, is used throughout) can also be translated as "wind" or "spirit."

Real though invisible and intangible, essential to life, breath is used as a metaphor for life itself. Because God is the creator of all things and the source of all life, God is metaphorically said to breathe His spirit into creatures, thereby giving them 1121 ife. In the Book of Job, we read that if God "should take back his spirit to himself, and gather to himself his breath [*ruach*], all flesh would perish together, and man would return to dust" (Jb 34:14-15). In Psalm 104, a song of praise to God for the work of creation, the psalmist prays, "when thou takest away their breath [*ruach*], they die and return to their dust. When thou sendest forth thy Spirit [*ruach*], they are created; and

thou renewest the face of the earth" (vv. 29-30).

In the New Testament, the dialogue between Jesus and Nicodemus in John 3 provides an especially rich example of the significance of the word *pneuma*. Explaining to Nicodemus what it means to be born from above, to be born "of water and the Spirit [*pneuma*]," Jesus tells him, "The wind [*pneuma*] blows where it wills, but you do not know whence it comes or whither it goes; so it is with every one who is born of the Spirit [*pneuma*]" (Jn 3:8). Drawing on the distinction between flesh and spirit (*pneuma*), Jesus uses the double meaning of the word *pneuma*. He does so to overcome Nicodemus's misunderstanding about the meaning of the rebirth about which Jesus speaks in verse 3, "Truly, truly, I say to you, unless one is born anew, he cannot see the kingdom of God."

For further reading: Hermann Kleinknecht et al., "Pneuma," *Theological Dictionary of the New Testment*, 6:332-455.

Brethren of the Lord • The "brethren of the Lord" are mentioned a number of times in the Scriptures (Mt 12:46; 13:55ff.; Mk 3:31; 6:3; Lk 8:19; Jn 2:12; 7:3ff.; 20:17; Acts 1:14; 1 Cor 9:5 and Gal 1:19). Individual "brothers" are identified: James, Joses (another name for Joseph); Simon and Judas are found at Matthew 13:55 and Mark 6:3. The phrase is often misunderstood as referring to either Jesus' younger brothers and sisters who were conceived by Mary and Joseph or to Jesus' step-brothers sired by Joseph from a previous marriage. The linguistic evidence suggests otherwise: (1) the Greek word used for brother (*adelphos*) and sister (*adelphe*) meant "blood brother" or "sister" in Classical and Hellenistic Greek. (2) In the Greek Old Testament, the term is a translation of the Hebrew word "kinsman" (e.g., Gn 13:8; 29:12-15). The Old Testament linguistic phenomenon reflects a sociological system of the extended family — probably a holdover from nomadic usage where we also find the leader of a tribe being called "father" — which was in fact within the Semitic culture of Jesus' day. (3) Finally, the idea that a "brother" was in fact a relative and not a "blood brother" is commonly found in Greek papyri from the New Testament period.

It seems clear that reference to "cousin" is the more likely meaning of the Greek terms in the Gospel, given the Hebrew/Aramaic linguistic heritage of Jesus. Jerome has argued that James the brother of the Lord was an Apostle (Gal 1:19) who was identified with James the son of Alphaeus (Mk 3:18) and also with James the "younger" (Mk 15:40), the brother of Joses. The New Testament evidence supports Jerome's position: James and Joses are called "brothers" of Jesus (Mk 6:3); their mother is called Mary (Mt 27:56; Mk 15:40) who is Mary of Clopas, sister of Mary the mother of Jesus (Jn 19:25). Hence, James and Joses are cousins of Jesus.

Breviarium Romanum • At the direction of the bishops at the Council of Trent, in order to unify and correct a number of preexisting editions of the Liturgy of the Hours then in use, the first *Breviarium Romanum* for the use of the whole Church was published in 1568. The title "breviary" signifies the collecting into a single book of what had previously been found in several books: psalter, antiphonary, collectary, homilary, hymnal, etc. (One reason for this distillation is the awkwardness of trying to use so many books for those praying the Divine Office outside the choir.) This was the required book for the Office for the whole Church, except for those religious communities or dioceses which had been celebrating their own rituals for two hundred years or more. Thus, for example, the Dominicans and Benedictines retained their own usages, and the Roman Breviary became the required prayer book of the diocesan clergy.

Breviary • The term formerly (and often, still, popularly) used for the book containing the Divine Office, or fixed cycle of daily prayers now officially called (in its post-Vatican II revision) the Liturgy of the Hours. In its full form, as chanted in monasteries and cathedrals, the Divine Office required multiple books: The antiphonary, hymnary, lectionary, psalter and often the martyrology. For the convenience of the friars and secular clergy, the principal components of the Hours were compiled in a modified format and the book containing this was called *breviarium* (literally, "an abridgement").

Although the entire cycle of the Church's official public prayer was officially designated "the Divine Office," the books (in four volumes until 1961, in two volumes after the revisions of Pope John XXIII) were entitled *Breviarium Romanum*. The *editio typica* (or standard, official Latin edition) of the Vatican II revision is entitled *Liturgy of the Hours according to the Roman Rite*, though the heading still reads *The Divine Office revised by decree of the Second Vatican Ecumenical Council and published by authority of Pope Paul VI*. The four-volume English translation most common in the United States is entitled *Liturgy of the Hours* and its one-volume abridgement *Christian Prayer*. The hierarchies of England and Wales, Scotland and Ireland published their own translation in three volumes, entitled *The Divine Office*. (Cf. Liturgy of the Hours.)

Bribery • The offer and acceptance of a gift (usually, but not necessarily, monetary) in return for the performance of some favor by a person in a position of responsibility in some organization or institution. The presumption is that the individual offering the bribe would not otherwise obtain the desired favor without the influence or action of the person taking the bribe. Bribery is a sin against justice.

Bride of Christ • The understanding that the Church is the Bride of Christ is metaphorical or figurative at 2 Corinthians 11:2. The phrase occurs only here and nowhere else in the New Testament. However, the bridal character of the Church and the nuptial character of the Christ/Church relationship is a clear pattern in New Testament and early Church writings. In Christ we see the new humanity (Eph 2:15; Gal 6:15): He is the "New Adam" of the New Creation (1 Cor 15:22; Rom 5:12-14). Just as the first Eve was taken from the first Adam's rib, so also the New Eve, the Church, is taken from the side of the New Adam, at the cross (Eph 2:15). The unity of Christ and the Church is nuptial; it is as "one flesh" (Eph 5:31 citing Gn 2:24). It is no surprise that the Fathers of the Church teach that the New Eve was born from Christ's side during the death sleep in the tomb. The authors of Ephesians (2:15) and John (19:34ff.) see more in the cross than just death; they see a creative act which later Tradition clarifies in terms of sacramental life: the flow of blood and water from Christ's side are the sacramental signs of how He animates His Bride through the sacraments of Baptism and Eucharist.

Brief, Apostolic (also Breve) • A papal letter of less solemnity than a bull, a brief is authenticated with a stamped representation of the Seal of the Fisherman. Most often, the brief is signed by the Cardinal Secretary of State or his representative.

Brotherhood of Man • According to the Christian Faith, all men and women are created equal, in being, dignity and destiny,

and are called to true brotherhood in Christ as adopted sons and daughters of the Father. This spiritual and supernatural brotherhood has as its natural basis the identical biological species of all human beings of all races.

Brotherly Love • Christ commands us to love all other human beings as our brothers and sisters, precisely because in Him all are united in one family of God.

Brothers • Originally referring to members of a male religious community. Often, the term denotes the men of a community who are not ordained and who will not receive the sacrament of Holy Orders; however, it may also designate those men of a community or institute who are not yet ordained, but who are preparing for ordination.

Buddhism • The Western name given to a religious tradition that originated in India in the sixth century B.C., based upon the teaching of Gotama the Buddha. The doctrine preached by the Buddha is known as the Dharma. It presents an analysis of the human condition and the means by which suffering and mortality can be transcended. Central to the Dharma is the teaching of the Excellent Eightfold Path by which Nirvana, or "enlightenment," is to be attained. A monastic movement is central to the practice of Buddhism, but all forms of Buddhism incorporate some type of lay membership. The two principal forms of Buddhism are Mahayana and Hinayana (Theravada). The religion spread into all of southeast Asia and then into China and Japan, and today it shows signs of attracting a significant following in Western countries.

Bugia • A small, portable candle holder containing a candle which can be lit and held beside a bishop or other prelate during the celebration of certain liturgical functions. The name is the Latinized version of Bougie in Algeria, where candlewax was manufactured for export.

Bull, Apostolic • The common but not official name given to certain important decrees issued by the Holy Father. The name comes from the Latin *bulla* (seal), since a lead or waxen seal is affixed to the decrees.

Bulla Coenae • Beginning in the fourteenth century, it became the custom of the Roman Pontiffs to publish a comprehensive listing of the various excommunications then in force. The practice of having this list read in the presence of the Pope and cardinals on Holy Thursday led to the name by which these papal bulls are best remembered, the *Bulla Coenae*. In 1627 Pope Urban VIII gave the list its official form and the practice was continued until 1770, when Pope Clement XIV dropped the ceremonial reading of the offenses and their punishments. He did not abrogate the excommunications, however.

Through the centuries, the Popes requested that the *Bulla Coenae* be promulgated in various nations; but containing as they did censures against certain theo-political errors (cf. Febronianism), such requests were granted only sporadically. At the same time, however, such illustrious Church reformers as St. Charles Borromeo sought to have the *Bulla Coenae* posted in each confessional. The *Bulla Coenae* was finally abrogated in

Bulla of Pope Sixtus IV

1869 as part of the great penal reforms of Pope Pius IX.

Bulla Cruciata • The collection of papal documents meant to reward with privileges the citizens of Spain for their efforts against the Muslims during the Crusades. Initiated in 1063, the favors became permanent after Spain defeated the Muslims in 1492. The privileges were a dispensation from all fasting and abstinence, except for a few specified days and a plenary indulgence granted to all Spanish subjects while Spain was being reconquered. The Holy See has not revoked these privileges; hence, they apply to all persons, regardless of nationality or place of residence, on Spanish territory. The favor extends also to countries once under the domination of Spain.

Bullarium • As its name suggests, a bullarium is a collection of Papal Bulls, usually chronologically arranged. There are several major collections of Papal Bulls, totaling hundreds of volumes. Among the more widely-known collections are the *Bullarium Romanum*, the *Bullaria Romana*, the *Regesta Pontificum Romanorum* and the *Magnum Bullarium*. Several smaller collections, usually covering the reign of a single Pope, are also available. The greater collections tend, however, to be available only in larger Catholic university libraries, due to their increasing rarity.

Burial, Christian • The funeral rites of the Church, beginning with the prayers at the wake and concluding with the Mass of Christian Burial and interment in the consecrated ground of a Catholic cemetery (when possible). (Cf. Burial, Ecclesiastical.)

Burial, Ecclesiastical • The internment of a body after appropriate liturgical funeral rites have been conducted is known as ecclesiastical burial. The 1917 Code stipulated that deceased Catholics be buried in consecrated ground and forbade cremation. The revised Code strongly recommends but does not require that Catholics be buried in consecrated cemeteries, nor does it prohibit cremation.

Ecclesiastical burial can now be given to catechumens, unbaptized babies who died before their parents were able to have them baptized and to non-Catholic Christians (if there is good reason and with the permission of the bishop).

The law now states that ecclesiastical burial, as well as the funeral liturgy, can be denied to notorious apostates, heretics, schismatics and to public sinners for whom funeral rites cannot be conducted without scandal. If such a person gave some sign of repentance before death, an ecclesiastical burial with funeral rites may take place (cf. Canons 1176-1185).

Burse • (1) A stiff, cardboard pocket between nine and twelve inches square in which the folded corporal is placed. The burse is composed of two pieces of cardboard covered with silk that matches the Mass vestments. It is bound on three sides, thereby forming a "pouch" or "pocket." The burse often has a small cross on it and is lined with linen on the inside. The corporal is carried in the burse above the veiled chalice to and from the altar; however, the burse is used infrequently today. The burse is also known as the "bursary," "bursa" or "pera."

(2) The leather case in which the pyx containing the Blessed Sacrament is carried to the infirm or elderly. The burse, usually lined with silk, has a cord attached to it which allows the minister of the Holy Eucharist to wear the burse about his person.

(3) The fund which provides for the education of one or more seminarians. The faithful contribute to the burse, which may or may not have a fixed amount.

Burse, Financial • A financial burse is a special fund, usually endowed by a private benefactor and maintained by a diocese, religious institute or private foundation, often with the express purpose of educating candidates for the priesthood. They vary in size and availability, of course, but sometimes have been of crucial importance in providing for the expenses of priestly education. Depending on the ownership of the burse, generally it is regulated as a "non-autonomous pious foundation," that is, a special classification of temporal goods under Canons 1303-1310 of the 1983 Code of Canon Law.

Buskins • These are the ceremonial stockings worn by a bishop at Pontifical Mass. Although these were used primarily in the so-called "Tridentine" Mass, they are nevertheless still permitted. These are stockings reaching to the knees and worn over the ordinary purple stockings of the bishop (scarlet for cardinals, white for the Pope). They match the color of the vestments and are usually richly embroidered with gold thread.

Byzantine Art • That style of pictorial or architectural expression particular to the Byzantine Empire, formulated by the fourth century. Byzantine art is a blend of Greek culture and Christian ecclesiastical influences. Its most expressive medium is the mosaic. Byzantine art is rich in color, design and theme. The Byzantine Church, particularly through its monastic life, laid down detailed prescriptions to preserve the integrity of this art form in iconography. The classic example of Byzantine art was Justinian's temple of Hagia Sophia (Holy Wisdom of Christ), marked by thrust and counter-thrust, particularly in the setting of the massive dome. Byzantine sculpture is characterized by incision and the use of flat instead of curved surfaces. The painting of icons is always done on wood and the iconographer traditionally does not sign his work.

Byzantine Empire • The Eastern Part of the Roman Empire after its division into West and East became permanent in A.D. 395. Constantine had earlier made his capital at Byzantium in Asia Minor and renamed it Constantinople. With the fall of Rome in 476, the Byzantine emperors claimed power over the entire Roman world. Byzantine Christian culture reached its high point in the sixth and seventh centuries. The Byzantine Empire collapsed with the conquest of Constantinople by the Turks in 1453.

Byzantine Rite: See **Rite, Byzantine**

Byzantine painting of Holy Apostle Church

Caeremoniale Episcoporum • Latin for "Ceremonial of Bishops," this book published by the Holy See under the express command and authority of the Pope contains the rubrics and directives which govern the dress and ceremonies of the bishops of the Latin Rite of the Church throughout the world. This includes, for instance, the consecration of bishops, the blessing of abbots, their dress on different occasions and even the funeral of a bishop. The present Latin version or *editio typica* was published in 1984 under the auspices of Pope John Paul II, and published in English in 1989. This text contains important information on the theology of the liturgy celebrated by bishops in their dioceses. The various parts of the *Caeremoniale* concern general considerations about liturgy, the Mass (e.g., Stational Mass of the Diocesan Bishop), the Liturgy of the Hours, celebrations during the course of the Liturgical Year, sacraments, sacramentals and blessings, special days in the life of a bishop (e.g., election, ordination, funeral) and liturgies in connection with official acts pertaining to the government of a diocese.

Caeremoniarius • In ecclesiastical parlance, this is the Latin term for the master of ceremonies, usually a priest or seminarian, who guides the actions of the celebrant and others in the ceremonies of the Mass and other liturgical functions according to the norms prescribed by the Holy See. Every bishop should have a master of ceremonies to help direct him and all assisting him in the liturgical ceremonies at which he presides.

Caesaropapism • A recurring but pernicious theory which holds that the ruler of both Church and state should be one and the same individual. This same person invariably was primarily the civil ruler of a nation which usurped ecclesiastical authority. Its first and most pronounced period of attempted application was in the fourth-century Eastern Roman Empire, then centered in Constantinople. Under it, temporal leaders assumed ecclesiastical jurisdiction, called synods and councils, evaluated doctrine and so on. Although not every such exercise was marked by error or other spiritual danger (indeed, some such acts were later explicitly ratified by legitimate Church authority), the general trend of caesaropapism was toward a disruptive interference in Church affairs to the detriment of all concerned. It particularly helped to prepare the way for the Eastern Schism. (Cf. Anglican, Anglicanism; Gallicanism; Josephism.)

Calatrava, Order of • The oldest military order of Spain. Founded in 1158 by King Sancho III of Castile, it was placed under the Rule of St. Benedict and the Constitution of St. Bernard. The knights professed the religious vows of poverty, chastity and obedience. The Order's original purpose was the defense of the City of Calatrava, but this was expanded to the defense of the Faith and the kingdom of Spain against the Moors. It was approved by Pope Alexander

III in 1164 and by many subsequent Popes. As the reconquest progressed, the order became quite wealthy. Its assets were seized by Ferdinand and Isabella in 1489. Pope Adrian VI gave its grand mastership to King Charles I (V) of Spain in 1523. It became an honorary order of noblemen. An associated order of nuns of Calatrava was founded in 1219 and is still in existence.

Calefactory • Coming from the Latin meaning "to warm" (*calefacere*), this term can refer to one of two things: (1) in former times the calefactory was a heated room in the monastery where the monks could retire for a few minutes to warm themselves in the winter months during the chanting of the Divine Office, especially the nocturnal Hour of Matins (now Readings), which was then said at about one or two in the morning; and (2) a hollow globe made of either brass or silver, often gold-plated, which was filled with warm water and was used by the priest at Mass to warm his fingers during liturgical functions, especially before and after distributing Holy Communion to the faithful.

Even today in some ancient churches in Germany, France and northeastern European countries which do not have modern heating systems, types of calefactories are used. In Germany, for instance, the cruets for water and wine are placed on a little, stove-like contraption, which is either on the credence table or on the altar itself, to help keep them from freezing in winter. This could well fall within the definition of a calefactory.

Calendar • The early Christians followed the Roman calendar of Julius Caesar from 46 B.C. (hence called the Julian Calendar) and accepted a seven-day week and divisions into months from the Jews because the earliest converts to Christianity were Jews. They developed their own specifically Christian feasts, however,

somewhat parallel to Jewish feasts but set around the pivotal fact of the resurrection of Jesus Christ.

Jewish Christians celebrated Easter on the fourteenth day of the month of Nisan, at the full moon following the vernal (spring) equinox. Since this meant celebrating Easter on a different day each year, and since the Lord rose on the first day, Christians began celebrating it on the first Sunday after the first full moon after the spring equinox. This was sanctioned at the Council of Nicaea in A.D. 325. In the fourth century, Lent developed as a period of spiritual preparation for the great feast of Easter, with its reconciliation of penitents and baptizing of catechumens.

The second center of the liturgical year is the Christmas cycle, which began to be celebrated in the fourth century to offset the imperial feast of *Sol Invictus*, the Unconquered Sun. Epiphany was similarly developed in Egypt and was taken into the Christmas cycle of the West, while in the second half of the fifth century, Advent developed as a spiritual preparation for this season. The basic focal point for each week from earliest times has been Sunday, for we read in Acts 20:7 that apostolic Christians celebrated on the "first day of the week." This weekly celebration of the Eucharist at times had been overshadowed by saints' feasts, but various reforms (e.g., St. Pius X and Vatican II) have given Sunday its rightful prominence.

In Christmas and Easter, we have seen the two pivotal points of the liturgical year in its development. In the course of time, other feasts were celebrated as a part of those seasons, e.g., Pentecost and Ascension in Paschaltide. The various aspects of the paschal mystery of Christ (His birth, life, death, resurrection, ascension, etc.) in the course of time were spread throughout the whole liturgical year so that the faithful could enter more deeply into every aspect of the Mystery of Christ by means of the feasts celebrated. The Constitution on the Sacred Liturgy of Vatican II says this of the Church in relation to the liturgical year: "Thus recalling the mysteries of the redemption, she opens up to the faithful the riches of the Lord's powers and merits, so that these are in some way made present for all time; and the faithful lay hold of them and are filled with saving grace" (n. 102).

This is true not only of all aspects of the Mystery of Christ from His incarnation and birth to His death and resurrection and the outpouring of the Holy Spirit, but also the fruits of the redemption as realized in Our Lady, the martyrs (the first saints commemorated), the Apostles, virgins and other saints, whose feasts are interwoven throughout the observances and seasons of the Church.

Fra Junípero Serra

California Missions • After the expulsion of the Jesuits from Spanish territories in 1767, the Franciscans were asked to take on further mission responsibilities in Upper California (i.e., the area that eventually became part of the United States). The government of New Spain wanted a peaceful settlement of the region, partly as a buffer against possible Russian expansion in the area. These missions were therefore established under the authority of the king of Spain, with both religious and political motives. Bl. Junípero Serra (1713-1784), president of the missions in Lower California, was placed in charge, and under his energetic direction nine missions were founded, beginning with San Diego in 1769.

Of the twelve additional missions, nine were founded by Serra's successor, Fermín de Lasuén (1785-1803).

These missions were intended both to evangelize and to civilize the Indians who had been leading a seminomadic life. The process was much more difficult than was expected in the beginning. Conflicts sometimes arose between Indians and Spanish, between missionaries and royal officials. Overall, about 150 Franciscans were involved in the work of these missions in the six or seven decades of their existence.

In 1822 the territory came under the control of the newly independent Mexican government, which secularized the missions in 1833 and eventually sold the properties. Later, all the sites returned to Church ownership and are now used as parishes, shrines and schools.

These missions and the dates of their foundation are:

San Diego — July 16, 1769
San Carlos Borromeo — June 3, 1770
San Antonio — July 14, 1771
San Luís Obispo — September 1, 1771
San Juan Capistrano — November 1, 1776
Santa Clara — January 12, 1777
San Buenaventura — March 31, 1781
Santa Barbara — December 16, 1786
La Purísima Concepción — December 8, 1787
Santa Cruz — August 28, 1791
Nuestra Señora de la Soledad — October 9, 1791
San José — June 11, 1797
San Juan Bautista — June 24, 1797

San Miguel — July 25, 1797
San Fernando — September 8, 1797
San Luís Rey — June 13, 1798
Santa Inez — September 17, 1804
San Rafael Archangel — December 14, 1817
San Francisco Solano — July 4, 1823

Calling • A calling is a summons from God, Who communicates that the individual or the group called is chosen and commissioned for a particular work relative to God's plan of salvation. All of the key figures in the Old Testament were called by God (in many instances by personal name) with a specific mission, e.g., Abraham, land and descendants (Gn 12ff.); Moses, exit from Egypt to the promised land (Ex 3). The prophets also received calls from God with specific missions: Amos (Am 7); Isaiah (Is 6); Jeremiah (Jer 1) and Ezekiel (Ez 3), to name a few.

Jesus called forth the Twelve, by name (Mk 3:13); He called others who did not become His disciples (Mk 10:21; Lk 9:59-62); His call was to anyone as it is today (Mt 16:24; Jn 7:17). Paul was called to be an Apostle (Rom 1:1; 1 Cor 1:1, etc.) for the glory of God and the salvation of the Gentiles.

In the Protestant Reformation "call" became a technical theological term for ordained and non-ordained ministry (e.g., cf. the *Shorter Westminster Catechism of 1647*). Current Catholic use of the term reflects its biblical sense and is applied to both lay and ordained vocations.

Calumny • The uttering or publishing of statements or making claims about another that are not only unjust but are also false. Calumny is the most serious form of detraction because it does the most serious harm to the reputation and good name of others that one can do. Calumny is so serious and grave that it demands retraction and restoration of the good name of the person harmed by it; it sins against the virtues of charity, truthfulness and justice.

Calvary • The Aramaic *gulguta* ("skull"), transliterated into Greek, means "place of the skull." The Greek transliteration is sometimes in turn transliterated into English, resulting in "Golgotha." The Latin equivalent *calvaria* is the source for the English word Calvary. The term refers to Jesus' place of execution (Mt 27:33; Mk 15:22; Jn 19:17). Luke identifies this place simply as "Skull" (Lk 23:33; Greek, *kranion*). According to John 19:20 and from what is known of Jewish and Roman customs, this place was surely outside the city walls of Jerusalem. The Church of the Holy Sepulchre was constructed over what since the fourth century was thought to be the actual execution site. Eusebius identifies the site and tomb as being under what became a temple of Aphrodite in the Roman city of Aelia Capitolina, which Hadrian built upon the ruins of Jerusalem after the A.D. 132-135 Jewish Rebellion. Current scholarly opinion favors the site of the Church of the Holy Sepulchre.

For further reading: Virgilio C. Corbo, "Golgotha," *Anchor Bible Dictionary*, 2:1071-1072.

Calvinism • The form of Protestantism originating from the thought and activity of French Reformer John Calvin (1509-1564). Consistent with the major theme of the Protestant Reformation, Calvinism considers the Scriptures to be the only source of Divine Revelation. Calvin rejected the doctrine of a Catholic Church animated by the Holy Spirit as a supernatural instrument of salvation. Still, the Holy Spirit played a significant role according to the thought of Calvin, inspiring and empowering man to achieve some limited measure of truth, beauty or goodness. Like his contemporary,

Luther, Calvin taught that man is depraved and corrupt by himself and is capable of nothing good, except through divine grace. His will is not free.

A basic Calvinist tenet is that man cannot change his eternal destiny through his own merits. Regardless of man's own efforts, God has predestined him to either salvation or damnation. Man can resist neither sin nor grace. It is grace which saves, not good works. A man's faith and good works are merely signs that he is among the saved; his carelessness and sin would indicate the opposite.

Calvin acknowledged only two sacraments, Baptism and the Lord's Supper. In his major work, *Institutes of the Christian Religion*, he attacked the Catholic doctrine of the change of substance in the Eucharist, referring to the "superstitions" of traditional Eucharistic belief. Communion, he felt, does not bring about union with Jesus Christ. Instead, union with Christ is a result of faith and is the work of the Holy Spirit. Communion for him is a visible sign of this invisible union; it is not the Body and Blood of Christ per se. The bread and wine remind the recipient that intimacy with Jesus is available through the action of the Holy Spirit.

Concerning Baptism, Calvin saw this sacrament as a declaration that the justice of Christ is the believer's. The recipient's sins, past, present and future, are remitted. This is a result of the Blood of Christ, not the pouring of baptismal water. Calvin preferred immersion and sprinkling, and saw no difficulty with infant Baptism. He insisted that Baptism be conferred with no pomp or ceremony, but in its essentials only, as was done in the New Testament.

Like other denominations, Calvinism has had various manifestations and emphases over the centuries. The United Presbyterian Church and the United Church of Christ are among the followers of Calvin today.

Camauro • A red velvet cap, trimmed in ermine or other white fur, formerly worn by the Pope when he wore the mozzetta and rochet, thus taking the place of the biretta. (For Easter week, it was made of white brocaded satin, to match the Pope's Easter mozzetta.) Its original purpose, like that of the biretta, was to protect the tonsured head from the cold.

Although seen very commonly in papal portraits from the Middle Ages and the Renaissance, the camauro was mostly replaced by the white zucchetto from the time of Pope Pius VI (1775-1799) onward, being used primarily only to cover the head of the dead Pope lying in state in the Sistine Chapel, robed in mozzetta and rochet. Popes John XXIII and Paul VI occasionally used it for warmth in the bitter chill of the Vatican Palace, but the present Pope himself has not worn the camauro in public. The camauro is not used at liturgical functions.

Camera • Italian for "room"; it has similarly passed into ecclesiastical use with that meaning, though usually reserved for a division of the Roman Curia, specifically the Apostolic Chamber.

Camerlengo (also Camerarius) • The camerlengo of the Roman Church is an office always held by a cardinal. At one time the office carried with it wide responsibilities related to the management of the finances of the Holy See. Today the primary responsibility of the camerlengo is to direct the day-to-day administration of the Holy See during the period between the death of a Pope and the election of his successor. The camerlengo officially calls the conclave for the election of the new Pope.

Camisia • Derived from the Latin word which means "linen shirt," this is another name for the liturgical parament otherwise known as the alb. Indeed, in Italian to this day the common word in use is *camice*.

In ancient times, the Book of Gospels was enshrined in a gold or silver box-like covering during Solemn High Mass and was referred to as a *camisia*. This practice is returning today as a result of the emphasis the Second Vatican Council has recalled concerning the presence of Christ in His Word.

Campaign for Human Development • An effort of the United States Catholic Conference, begun in 1969, to fight poverty and injustice in America. This is done through educational programs for the general public intended to make people more aware of poverty and by funding self-help programs for the poor.

The first national collection was held in all American parishes in November 1970. Approximately seventy-seven percent of monies collected go to a national fund, with the remaining twenty-three percent used at the local level. A thirty-six-member National Advisory Committee, and a thirteen-member committee of bishops review requests for aid and the monies are issued accordingly.

Campanile • A free-standing bell tower is called a campanile. Although it is usually associated with Church architecture, it can also serve a totally secular purpose as a memorial bell tower. It is very typical of northern Italian Church architecture, with the leaning tower of Pisa as an obvious example. Although not entirely free-standing, the Knights of Columbus Tower is not integral to the symmetrical façade of the National Shrine of the Immaculate Conception, in Washington, D.C., and could be described as a campanile.

Cana • The Greek word *kana* is of uncertain meaning. Geographically, it refers to a village in Galilee where Jesus changed water into wine (Jn 2:1-11). Cana was the home of Nathanael (Jn 21:2) and is where the official's son was healed by Jesus, Who was in Capernaum when the healing took place (Jn 4:46-54). Ecclesiastical traditions identify the New Testament site of Cana with the modern Kefr Kenna (four miles northeast of Nazareth). Recent scholarly opinion favors an unexcavated hill at Khirbet Qana as the more likely site (nine miles north and northwest of Nazareth).

For further reading: James F. Strange, "Cana of Galilee," *Anchor Bible Dictionary*, 1:827.

Cana Conferences (also Pre-Cana) • These take their name from the wedding in John's Gospel to which Our Lord, His Blessed Mother and the disciples had been invited and at which Christ performed the first miracle of His public ministry by changing water into wine (Jn 2:1-11). Cana conferences are those sessions sponsored by the Church for engaged couples, in anticipation of their Church-approved weddings. While it is correct to say that marriage preparation in one form or another has always existed in the Church, today the expression "Cana conferences" is thought to mean formal and systematic presentations offered by priests, trained married couples and others qualified to lead engaged couples to a deeper and more profound appreciation of the sacrament of Holy Matrimony.

Among those topics considered essential in marriage preparation would be: communication in marriage, conscience formation, the Christian understanding of sexuality, the sacramentality of marriage, marital and family spirituality and the wedding liturgy itself. In the United States, successful completion of the Cana conferences (before the wedding ceremony) is required. In many cases, engaged couples may choose from among several options regarding how they will satisfy this requirement.

Canada, The Church in • Roman Catholicism was introduced to the region which now forms Canada by the French in the sixteenth century. Serious missionary work was undertaken by the Jesuits in New France in the seventeenth century, as their *Relations* record. At this time, the Church consisted of colonists and native peoples, notably Hurons. The Canadian Martyrs' Shrine at Midland, Ontario, today testifies to the spirit of the Church's early foundation. In the eighteenth century the territory fell under British rule, but the French-speaking Catholics were allowed to practice their Faith under somewhat careful supervision. The first bishop was consecrated in 1766, but was not permitted to use his title because of English law. The Quebec Act of 1774 somewhat ameliorated the conditions of Catholics in general, but it was not until 1844 that Archbishop Joseph Signay of Quebec was able to use the titles of archbishop and metropolitan fully and legally.

As in the United States to the south, the Church grew in Canada through immigration from Europe and other places. Large numbers of Irish and Scottish Highland Catholics settled in the Maritime Provinces and toward the end of the nineteenth century, great numbers of Ukrainian Catholics settled in the Prairie Provinces of Alberta, Manitoba and Saskatchewan. In 1899 the Holy See established the apostolic delegation and named Canada's first cardinal in the person of Archbishop Elzéar Taschereau of Quebec. In 1908 Canada was removed from the jurisdiction of the Congregation for the Propagation of the Faith and was no longer regarded as a mission territory.

A certain stage of maturity was achieved in 1959 when Georges Vanier became governor-general of Canada. He was the second Canadian and the first Catholic to hold this office. In 1950 Paul Émile Léger was made archbishop of Montreal and cardinal in 1953. At the end of Vatican II, he stunned the world by announcing his resignation in order to go to Africa to serve lepers and the poor. Somewhat later, he returned to Montreal, there to work for the missions and to live in retirement.

Immigration continued to help the Church to grow in Canada. After the Second World War, and over the next forty years, perhaps as many as half a million Italians immigrated to Toronto and other cities. Portuguese, East Europeans, Latin Americans, Vietnamese, Koreans, Filipinos and Caribbean Islanders all contributed members to the Church. Slovenian-born Aloysius M. Ambrozic was named archbishop of Toronto in 1989.

Today the Latin Church in Canada has sixteen metropolitan provinces and numerous suffragans, one archdiocese with no suffragans (Winnipeg) and the Military Ordinariate. The Ukrainian Catholic Church has an archeparchy of Winnipeg with four eparchates. Other Eastern Rites, such as the Slovak Greek-Catholic eparchy, are also represented.

Canadian Shrines • The devotion of the Catholic settlers in French Canada prompted the establishment of many shrines to saints of local significance or of importance to the settlers in their native regions. Except for the North American Martyrs' Shrine, near Midland, Ontario, all of the Catholic shrines in Canada are located in the province of Quebec: Ste. Anne de Beaupré, Quebec City; St. Joseph's Oratory, Montreal; Hermitage of St. Anthony, La Bouchette; Our Lady of the Holy Rosary, Cap de la Madeleine; Ste. Anne de Micmacs, Restigouche; Chapel of Atonement, Pointe aux Trembles; Our Lady of Lourdes, Rigaud; and St. Benoit du Lac, near Magog.

Cancelli • Low decorated walls in Roman basilicas that shielded the singers or *schola cantorum* from the view of the congregation and allowed them to see the altar facing the people. Good examples of these cancelli are found in the churches of Santa Sabina and San Clemente in Rome.

In the East, after the iconoclast controversy, the cancelli were hung with icons and become the iconostasis so essential to Byzantine Liturgy. In the West, they developed into rood screens separating the choir and sanctuary area from the people in the medieval church building. In the Baroque era, these were transformed into Communion rails at which Communion was received kneeling until Vatican II, when they were no longer required. Communion stations now are usually simply positions at the edge of the sanctuary where Holy Communion is distributed, although immediately after Vatican II, stone and wooden table-like structures were in vogue to mark the place.

Candle, Paschal • The special large Paschal Candle has its origins in the fourth century and is lit from the new fire at the Paschal Vigil, symbolizing the resurrection of Christ, Who is the Light scattering the darkness of sin and death. It is lighted in the sanctuary at Mass, and at Lauds and Vespers during the Easter Season until Pentecost. During the year, it should be kept

St. Simeon and the Child Jesus (Candlemas)

near the baptismal font unless it is brought out for special ceremonies (e.g., funerals).

Candlemas • Literally, the "Candle Mass." A popular name given to the liturgical celebration of February 2 (now officially "The Presentation of Our Lord" and formerly "The Purification of the Blessed Virgin Mary"), because of the blessing of candles and candlelight procession associated with the feast, both at Jerusalem (where the feast was called *Hypapante*, the "Meeting") and Rome (where this procession replaced a similar pagan practice). In the East, the celebration was known by the year 400 and took place on the fortieth day after Epiphany. In the West, mid-fifth-century sources designate the fortieth day after Christmas for the observance. Although Christmastide officially ends with the celebration of the Lord's Baptism after Epiphany, some liturgical commentators have referred to this feast as the formal ending of the Christmas season. The words of Simeon to Mary in the long form of the Gospel of the day ("a sign of contradiction") turn our reflections from the incarnation of Christ toward the paschal mystery established by His death and resurrection. (Cf. Purification of the Blessed Virgin Mary.)

Candles • From earliest times, Christians used candles for evening prayer (the Lucernarium), serving as the forerunner of the Paschal Candle. In the early Church, candles were lit before the tombs of the dead, especially those of the martyrs and later before the relics of the saints or their images. When the Church was recognized by Constantine, candles were used in great number around the altar to add splendor to the liturgy. Only in the eleventh century did candles appear on the altar itself. In the present Missal, at least two candles must be used for the celebration of Mass, and these may be placed on the altar, or near it, as was the custom of the early Church. Candles need not be blessed to be used at Mass.

Candlestick • (1) A special holder in which a candle is inserted and thereby able to stand upright on a table or shelf. The basic candlestick consists of a foot or base, a stem (which may vary in length), a knob about the middle of the stem, a bowl that receives any wax that drips down and either a pricket (a sharp point on which the candle is fixed to hold it in place) or a socket (a small cup-like container into which the candle is inserted). Most older types of candlesticks have prickets, while the newer ones usually have sockets to hold the candle straight in place. The size and length of the candlestick depends on the size of the candle, and in Church use, of the altar on which it is used. (For instance, the candles used at St. Peter's Basilica at the Altar of the Chair of Peter are about six feet tall. Likewise the candlesticks used are about six or seven feet tall.) Materials may vary. Gilt, silver-plated brass or bronze is most often used, but plain brass and even silvered or plain wood are also to be found.

(2) The candlestick, because of its use at the altar, is a symbol of the Holy Eucharist; thus, it is often depicted in art with a host above it. In former times, a candlestick with a candle was presented to those being ordained to the Minor Order of Acolyte.

(3) In the Church, candles have been in use since the early days of her history; there are documents that mention them already in use in the fifth century. Indeed, in the Book of Revelation (1:12), Christ, the Son of Man, is depicted in the midst of seven candlesticks which represent the seven Churches (dioceses) of Asia, to which the author addressed his book. Formerly, it was prescribed that there should be six candlesticks on the altar — three on each side. The present legislation states that the candlesticks may be kept either on the altar or near the altar. The number may vary — either two, four or six.

When a bishop pontificates, a seventh candlestick may be carried in the procession and placed on the altar, as was traditionally done *(Institutio Generalis Missalis Romani,* nn. 79, 269).

Canon • Directly derived from the Greek word for rule, *kanon,* this refers to a practical law, rule or standard. (1) The most commonly known use of this term regards the Church's body of laws, the canons of the Church, or canon law, by which the earthly society of the Church is governed. Most ecumenical councils, Vatican II being one exception, also issued a series of canons concerning faith or morals which bound all Catholics. (2) Another important use of this word refers to the canon of Sacred Scripture, that is, the books of the Old and New Testaments accepted as authentic and normative by the Church. (3) In the Mass, the oldest known Eucharistic Prayer used continuously in the Latin Rite of the Church is known as the Roman Canon, that is, the anaphora set for use by the Roman Rite. (4) The word "canonization," used to signify the elevation of a person to the honors of the altar, proclaiming him or her a saint of the Church, refers both to the authentic catalog or list of persons who may be venerated in this fashion, as well as to the fact that their names are now a part — even if only implicitly — of the Roman Canon (now also called "Eucharistic Prayer I"), where two separate symbolic lists, or litanies, of saints are enumerated. (5) A member of a canonically erected cathedral chapter, or other group or body of clerics — usually priests — set up to assist the diocesan bishop in ruling his flock and for solemnly celebrating the Liturgy of the Hours in public, is referred to as a canon. A member of such a chapter is endowed and addressed with the title "Canon," which is prefixed to his name. (6) Style of contrapuntal music where each voice enters at a different time, all imitating the first melody. This type of work may be used effectively to vary a simple melody sung by the congregation (e.g. "Amazing Grace"). Care must be taken that the hymn selected for this style may proceed without unresolved dissonance.

Canon Law • The name given to the official body of laws for the Catholic Church. The name is derived from the Greek word *kanon*, meaning a measure or rule.

The earliest Church laws were regulations, called canons, enacted by territorial synods or councils of bishops that met to discuss problems and other issues related to the Church, and to propose solutions. The earliest such gatherings date from the beginning of the fourth century. In time, the canons of the various synods and councils were gathered together in *Canonical Collections*. In addition to the legislation

Pope Gregory IX, reformer of canon law

enacted by local bishops' groups, the Pope also issued regulations. By the time of the Middle Ages, there were numerous collections of canon laws from around the Christian world, yet there had been no systematic collection of them. In 1140, a monk named Gratian published the *Concordance of Discordant Canons,* commonly known as the *Decree of Gratian*. It contained not only legal norms, but quotations from Scripture and from the Fathers of the Church. This was the first systematic arrangement of the canons as Gratian attempted to reconcile conflicting pieces of legislation. Although it is highly doubtful that the *Decree* was ever given official recognition, it nevertheless became the most important source of Church law.

In 1234 the Dominican canonist St. Raymond of Peñafort completed a systematic arrangement of papal decrees that was officially approved by Pope Gregory IX and became known as the *Decretals of Gregory IX*. This was the first official book of laws for the Catholic Church. By the end of the nineteenth century, the Church's laws were a confused and unorganized mass, consisting of *Gratian's Decree*, the *Decretals of Gregory IX*, legislation enacted by various Popes, and the canons enacted at the various ecumenical councils. St. Pius X recognized the need for a codification of Church law and assigned the task to Pietro Cardinal Gasparri. Gasparri and his associates labored for fourteen years, and in

1917 the first Code of Canon Law was promulgated. The Code is a book that contains the fundamental laws of the Roman Catholic Church. In addition to those laws contained in it, the body of canon law also includes the liturgical norms, contained in the liturgical books, as well as other laws enacted by the Popes but not contained in the Code.

When Pope John XXIII announced in 1959 that he would call an ecumenical council, he also announced the revision of the Code. The revision process actually started in 1965 and was completed in 1983 when Pope John Paul II promulgated the revised Code.

Only the Pope or an ecumenical council has the power to create legislation or interpret it officially for the entire Church. To assist him, there exists in the Vatican the Pontifical Commission for the Authentic Interpretation of the Code. This body studies inquiries sent to it and proposes official interpretations which are then approved by the Pope.

Gratian and others who have worked at the systematization and codification of Church law were influenced to a great degree by the Roman law system, which itself was a code system. This type of legal system differs from the common law system found in the United States and Great Britain, among other countries. The laws are contained in a Code and their interpretation and correct application are determined by the work of commentators or legal scholars, rather than by the judges, as is the case with common law. The legal system of the Catholic Church enjoys the reputation of being the oldest such system that has continued to function.

Canon Law, Eastern • For the first several centuries of Church history, there was no sharp distinction in canon law between Latin or Western canon law and Byzantine or Eastern canon law. If anything, canon law was predominantly Eastern in origin during those first centuries. But beginning around the seventh century, differences in spiritual and theological emphasis as well as considerable differences in political, economic and demographic conditions emerged, with the result that the Western Church experienced a tremendous development in canonical sciences, while the Eastern Church continued to rely on older legislation as supplemented by custom, the pastoral governance of the Eastern hierarchy, and certain pieces of papal legislation variously enacted, say, upon the return of some Orthodox Churches to union with Rome.

This situation remained throughout the Middle Ages and was reflected as recently as early this century in the opening canon of the 1917 Code of Canon Law, which declared that, for the most part, the 1917 Code dealt only with the Western Church and did not legislate for the Eastern Churches. It was not a particularly happy situation, however, for the same religious and political forces which argued for the twentieth-century codification of Western canon law were at work in the Eastern Churches as well, but without result.

Beginning, however, about ten years after the promulgation of the 1917 Code, the Holy See entertained a variety of proposals for the codification of Eastern canon law and in November 1929 appointed a pontifical commission to take charge of the project. On June 25, 1935, a redaction commission was appointed and formal work on an integrated Eastern Code was begun. Its progress was slow, due in part to the difficulty of gathering and analyzing many of the historical sources of Eastern law, as well as to ecumenical issues of special significance in Eastern Christianity.

Ironically, it was actually a political development which spurred the promulgation of the first section of Eastern law. A great many Eastern Catholics reside, of course, in the Middle East, a fact which placed them at the center of turmoil during the rise of the modern Arab states in the mid-twentieth century. These nations adopted Islamic law for much of their civil legislation, including their laws of marriage. Provision was made, however, for religious minorities (for example, Eastern Catholics) to use their own laws on marriage, but only if they could point to the formal existence of such laws as promulgated by their religious leaders. This, technically at least, Eastern Catholics could not do, leaving them subject to unfavorable Islamic law.

Although initial drafts of a comprehensive Eastern Code were ready for preliminary circulation by the mid-1940s, it was clear that Eastern Catholics needed a promulgated law on marriage far sooner than would be available if they had to wait for the entire Code to be reviewed, amended and published. Therefore the Holy See excerpted the canons on marriage and promulgated them separately in the apostolic letter *Crebrae Allatae* on February 22, 1949, which took effect the following May. This act set the pattern for a fragmented promulgation of Eastern law, with procedural law appearing in 1950, religious and temporal goods coming out in 1952, and the law on persons appearing in 1957. Shortly thereafter, when just under 1,600 canons had been promulgated (leaving many areas of Eastern law yet to be codified) the entire process was suspended by the news of the upcoming Second Vatican Council.

This Council, which had such great impact on the development of the 1983 Code, also carried significant implications for the proposed Eastern Code. On June 10, 1972, Pope Paul VI established the Pontifical Commission for the Revision of the Oriental Code of Canon Law, which has met regularly since that time. In 1975 the Commission launched its official publication *Nuntia*, to report on the progress of the codification of Eastern law.

By 1986, an integrated Code, intended to have effect throughout the Eastern Churches, was ready for final review. Large sections of this Code repeat canons from the 1983 Code, but other areas, naturally, reflect the unique traditions and legal institutions of Eastern Catholicism. Following a major review in 1989 it was promulgated in 1990 with only minor revisions.

Since 1969 a scholarly organization, The Society for the Law of the Eastern Churches, headquartered in Vienna, has been dedicated to the study of Eastern canon law and publishes a highly regarded journal, *Kanon*. (Cf. Canon Law, History of.)

Canon Law, History of • In a very real sense, the history of canon law dates back at least to the days of Our Lord as recorded in Sacred Scripture. Therein Christ — Who came to fulfill the law, not to destroy it — presents the fundamental norms for Christian behavior. Morality, sacraments, Church governance, relations with the world, all topics of vital canonical interest, are each treated in Holy Writ. To take but one concrete example, the basic framework of canonical penal procedure is well-contained in the Lord's admonition to confront an offender privately first, and then with only one or two witnesses, while reserving a final process before the community of the faithful as a last resort (cf. Mt 18:15 and Canon 1341).

During the first few centuries of Church history, canon law, such as it was, functioned almost exclusively as an adjunct of moral theology. Administrative matters, while even in those early years not entirely absent, were far from a major part of canon law. The norms outlined, for example, in the *Didache* or in the so-called Apostolic

Constitutions, stressed the distinctiveness of Christianity and were heavily concerned with establishing what was considered Christian behavior and belief and what was not. The sources of canon law, in fact, were entirely rooted in the synods and councils of the age, which, having debated and settled a given doctrinal point, set about enacting laws which would support the teaching so illuminated. Interestingly (especially given the later Latin predominance in legal thought), the great bulk of early Catholic legislation came from the Eastern Greek-speaking Churches and most of these canonical collections were simply arranged in the chronological order of their promulgation. (Cf. Canon Law, Eastern.)

Early in the fourth century, though, the development of canon law received an important boost when Christianity was granted legal recognition in the Roman Empire. By this time bishops were already assuming control of considerable properties donated by fervent faithful and their learning and prudence recommended them as arbitrators in secular as well as ecclesiastical disputes. In brief, the legal concerns of the Church jumped enormously during those years, and with them, her legal learning. But we must not exaggerate the impact of the recognition of Christianity on canon law. Several centuries would yet pass before canon law really emerged as a distinct science.

From roughly the fourth through tenth centuries, canon law remained, then, largely the province of the confessor who was increasingly being called upon to determine penances for post-baptismal sinners. These early attempts at arriving at "just" sentences led, especially among the Celtic monks, to the production of the famous penitentials, or handbooks for confessors which carefully listed a wide variety of offenses and the punishments to be meted out. Today these works are valuable sources of information on matters spiritual as well as on the daily life in society.

At the same time, the reestablishment of political order in Europe led to sometimes warm, but sometimes cool, relations between the emerging Church and states. Both situations, ironically, contributed to the growth of canon law: friendly monarchs, such as Charlemagne, supported the recovery of learning (legal and otherwise), while hostile ones gave cause for Church leaders to develop keen legal argumentation for protection against vastly superior civil forces. (Cf. Pseudo-Isidore.)

By the end of the first millennium, ecclesiastical administration had grown far beyond the days when the Apostles could choose seven deacons to handle food distribution. Canon law, spurred largely by the Gregorian reforms of the Papal Curia, began to be considered not merely as a handmaid to moral theology, but as an important mechanism for the smooth regulation of Church life and the protection of individuals against abuse both within and outside ecclesiastical circles. But as an independent science, canon law needed its own classifications and understandings. Its classifications were found growing out of the ninth- and tenth-century collections of canons, which were grouped, for the first time, under subject headings, instead of by mere chronology. Its first steps in self-understanding were reflected in the appearance of "glosses" or marginalia of the more important collections and which, in time, came to represent standard teaching on disputed points.

Then came two events which, although their precise interrelationship is not yet clear, combined with a momentous impact, forever changed the practice of canon law and secured its place as an independent and vital ecclesiastical science. Those two events were the publication of the *Decretum Gratiani* and the rediscovery of Roman law.

The rediscovery of Roman law (which, while never entirely lost, had been long practiced under greatly altered circumstances) gave canonists the legal categories and concepts necessary to administer a large and far-flung organization, such as the Church had become. These texts (some of which continue to be discovered to this day) burst upon the legal scene at the dawn of the High Middle Ages and changed the minds of advocates and scholars alike. Combined, then, with the colossal collection of Gratian of 1140 in which thousands of canons, decrees and interpretations were systematically gathered and expounded, there was no doubt that canon law had come into its own. (Cf. Decretalist.)

A century later, St. Raymond Peñafort compiled his classic *Liber Extra* which added the second stone in the edifice which in later centuries was to be called, after its Roman predecessor, the *Corpus Iuris Canonici.* St. Raymond's work, however, unlike Gratian's, was officially approved by the Holy See, a move which greatly enhanced the ability of canonists to command their field and effectively implement those policies deemed most conducive to the spread of the Gospel. In addition, the Roman Rota and the major dicasteries or departments of the Roman congregations all trace their roots to this period. Each made its own contribution to the burgeoning system of canon law and each borrowed concepts from other institutions. During this time, too, canon law exerted a healthy influence over the yet nascent common law system of England and was, and remains, intimately connected with the concepts of the civil law as practiced on the European continent.

The thirteenth, fourteenth and fifteenth centuries have been called by some the "Golden Age" of canon law, although such an appellation might unduly diminish its accomplishments and influences in other times. Nevertheless, those years saw the production of many of the classic canonical studies of Stephen of Tournai, Bazianus, John the Teuton, Henry of Susa, Guido de Baysio and Johannes Andreas. It might also be observed that these decades saw the last contributions of lay canonists for many centuries. The illustrious legacy of Johannes Andreas notwithstanding, it would be some four hundred years before the practical study of canon law was again entertained by laity.

The shattering of Christian unity in the West during the sixteenth century was, much like the emergence of Church and state some thousand years before, both a boon and a bane from the point of view of canon law. The loss of so many faithful (including many learned doctors and libraries) to heresy and schism was a severe blow. Yet the reforms enacted by the Council of Trent demanded careful implementation by those skilled in legal and pastoral procedures. This need combined with the new problems of a now transoceanic missionary effort to produce a sharp increase in ecclesiastical legislation and canonical interpretation.

The seventeenth and early eighteenth centuries were indisputably the zenith for the Roman Rota, which had been the object of many careful procedural reforms over the years, most notably by Pope Benedict XIV. The Rota, which had become the locus for the highest states of canonical erudition, handled cases from around the world on scores of subjects, not always purely ecclesiastical. The decisions handed down during those years are still not fully appreciated, perhaps the result of their sheer volume. The Roman congregations continued to function effectively as well.

It has been suggested with some evidence that in the eighteenth and nineteenth centuries, a decline in canon law began to set in. Some of this was clearly outside the ability of the Church to prevent: such as the damaging effects of the Italian Revolution on the Rota, which suspended operations from 1870 until 1909.

Of course, there was certainly nothing on the order of a serious rupture or collapse in canon law as a whole, for the Church, at whose service canon law always stood, continued to grow and required the services of canonists and canonistics. Yet it can also be said that a certain sterility or formalism appeared in many canonical commentaries. We are perhaps still too close in time to those events to recognize them and their causes accurately, but this much seems clear: canon law tended to move from a system which blended law and theology to one which relied too heavily on purely legal categories. Canon law, also, especially at the lower and intermediate levels of Church administration, took on a positivistic tone which made it appear to be more in the service of individual administrators than the general welfare of the Christian community. This was not a universal phenomenon, of course, and glittering exceptions to the trend abound. Indeed, the 1917 Code of Canon Law is in many ways free of these tendencies or at least free of the most exaggerated forms of it. Nevertheless, canon law increasingly came to be seen as the private reserve of bespectacled clerics and less the legal resource of an active and believing community.

Following the Second Vatican Council, which was called for by Pope John XXIII on the same day that he called for a reform of the Code of Canon Law, Pope Paul VI made his own famous observation that the interpretation of the forthcoming (1983) Code of Canon Law would require a *novus habitus mentis* — a new habit of mind. This, of course, is in reality a return of canon law to its theological and rational roots. Pope John Paul II, in turn, has repeatedly affirmed that the real sources of canon law are and must be Sacred Tradition, especially as reflected in the ecumenical councils, and Sacred Scripture, which, as previously suggested, has always been considered the taproot of canon law.

For further reading: R. Mortimer, "Western Canon Law" (University of California, 1953).

Canon Law, Interpretation of • According to the Apostolic Constitution *Sacrae Disciplinae Leges* (*Of the Sacred Discipline of Law*), with which the Code of Canon Law was promulgated on January 25, 1983, Pope John Paul II stated that the law "derives from one and the same intention, the renewal of Christian living . . . in constant fidelity to its divine founder." He further states that "canonical laws need to be observed because of their very nature," and so the proper interpretation of canon law is a matter of importance for all the faithful.

Canon 16 distinguishes between authentic and non-authentic interpretation, stating that authentic interpretation comes from the legislator, and has the same authority as the law itself.

Canon 17 states that the laws are to be understood in accord with the proper meaning of the words (both in text and in context), and where it is unclear, in the light of parallel passages and in accord with the mind of the legislator. As a practical matter, canon law is routinely interpreted in daily Church life by bishops, pastors and other church leaders.

Canon Penitentiary • A priest who is a member of a cathedral chapter and whose particular responsibility is the administration of the sacrament of Penance. Prior to the revision of the Code and the Order of Penance, canons penitentiary generally had broad faculties to absolve reserved sins and censures.

Canon Regular • As organized groups Canons Regular date from the eleventh century when certain communities of clergy adopted what was an essentially monastic regime. Most adopted the so-called Rule of St. Augustine. The largest of the medieval orders existing today is the Order of Premonstratensians, or Norbertines, with several houses in the United States.

Canon of the Mass • In the liturgy of the Eucharist, the Eucharistic Prayer is the section that was called the Canon of the Mass. It corresponds to the anaphora of the Eastern Rites, beginning with the Preface and concluding with the doxology. The central point of the Eucharistic Prayer is the Consecration: the changing of the species of bread and wine into the Body and Blood of Christ.

Presently there are nine for use in the United States: four regular Eucharistic Prayers: the first, also called the Roman Canon; the second, simple and brief, suited to small groups and ordinary weekdays; the third, somewhat longer, emphasizing the idea of sacrifice, appropriate for Sundays; the fourth, the longest, fitting for people devoted to Sacred Scripture: then three Eucharistic Prayers for children's liturgies and two for Masses of Reconciliation.

The Eucharistic Prayer is said by the celebrant only. The deacons and laity are expected to answer the introductory dialogue and join in the acclamations. (Cf. Liturgy.)

Canon of Muratori • Also known as the "Muratorian Fragment," this document of eighty-five lines was discovered by Lodovico A. Muratori (1672-1750) in an eighth-century manuscript. Dating from the second century, it is the oldest known list of the canonical books of the New Testament. Narrative portions at the beginning and end of the fragment are missing. However, it contains references to the four Gospels, Acts, the Pauline letters, the Apocalypse of John and the letters of John and Jude. (Cf. Canon of Scripture; Dead Sea Scrolls.)

For further reading: Gregory Allen Robbins, "Muratorian Fragment," *Anchor Bible Dictionary*, 4:928-929.

Canon of Scripture • Both the Greek *kanon* and the Hebrew *kaneh* mean "reed," in the sense of an instrument or standard of measurement. The term appears in the New Testament only four times. It can refer to a specific aspect of apostolic ministry (2 Cor 10:13-16 [referred to twice]) or to doctrinal statements in general (Gal 6:16; Phil 3:17).

In the post-New Testament Church the term eventually carried a double meaning. First, it referred to the "rule of faith" by which all movements of Church worship, liturgy, theology, morality and doctrine were "measured." Second, and perhaps in the earlier of the two definitions, it meant an authoritative list of Christian writings which would eventually become Sacred Scripture for Christianity. The *Hebrew Canon* refers to the Jewish Bible; the *Protestant Canon* includes an Old Testament (specifically, the exact same contents as the *Hebrew Canon*) and the New Testament; the *Catholic* and *Orthodox Canons* are the same — an Old Testament (specifically, the Greek [LXX] or Vulgate Old Testament) and the New Testament, for which there is complete agreement among the three major families of Christianity. (Cf. Bible.)

For further reading: James A. Sanders and Harry Y. Gamble, "Canon," *Anchor Bible Dictionary*, 1:837-861.

Canoness • From the fourth century, the term "canoness" (Latin, *canonica*) applied to a pious woman who performed some function in a church, in whose register (canon) she was inscribed. In the Middle

Ages it was often applied to women who lived a devout life without vows.

Most commonly, it came to designate women who lived a vowed religious life according to a rule similar to the Rule of St. Augustine followed by Canons Regular.

Canonical Hours • The canonical hours are the fixed parts of the Divine Office or the Liturgy of the Hours, which, according to ancient custom, are to be recited at various hours during the day in order to sanctify it and all that is done during the day for the glory of God. This applies mainly to communities of monks and nuns where fixed times of common prayer and the chanting of the Office make up a good portion of their contemplative vocation. As such, this is often referred to as the "work of God" or *opus Dei*. It also pertains to cathedral chapters and beneficiaries who are named to fulfill parts of the Office in public common prayer. Finally, it applies to priests and religious in active apostolates, but to a lesser degree, insofar as their active vocation permits.

Monastically, the canonical hours are: Matins, or Office of Readings, which is chanted in the middle of the night or very early in the morning before sunrise; Lauds, or Morning Prayer, at the beginning of the day; the "little hours" or "Midday Prayer," which are Terce, around nine in the morning, Sext at noon, and None about three in the afternoon; Vespers, or Evening Prayer, which takes place late in the afternoon or about sunset; and Compline, or Night Prayer, which is celebrated before retiring for the night. Vatican II encouraged the laity to participate in the praying of the canonical hours, especially Lauds and Vespers, which should be done in common in their parish churches or in private at home (cf. *Sacrosanctum Concilium*, nn. 84-85, 89; *General Instruction on the Liturgy of the Hours*, nn. 20-23).

Canonical Mission • The official conferring of an ecclesiastical office by a competent superior. In the revised Code, it sometimes refers to the official mandate required to teach in theological disciplines in institutes of higher studies. This mandate is conferred by competent authority, which certainly includes the Holy See and the local Ordinary. It is required of all who teach theology in Catholic colleges and universities (cf. Canon 812).

Canonical Possession • The official act whereby a person assumes an ecclesiastical office. This is not always the same as appointment to an office. For instance, canonical possession of the office of the papacy takes place from the moment the elected person accepts the election.

A bishop takes canonical possession of his diocese when he presents the Apostolic Letter of his appointment to the College of Consultors of the diocese in the presence of the chancellor and diocesan curia. It can happen that a priest takes canonical possession of a diocese even before he is consecrated a bishop. At the present time, however, it is common for a newly consecrated bishop to take canonical possession during the liturgical ceremony of consecration (cf. Canon 382).

Canonist • Broadly speaking, a canonist is any person with some expertise in canon law or one of its many subdivisions. A more precise definition would be any person with a graduate degree, i.e., a licentiate or doctorate in canon law earned from a pontifical faculty of canon law. There are just over twenty such pontifical faculties in the world, and presently the only one in the United States is located at The Catholic University of America in Washington, D.C.

The 1983 Code of Canon Law has, with very few exceptions, significantly restricted the practice of canon law to those possessing graduate degrees in the same, this for the better administration of justice within the Church and service to the faithful. There are approximately 2,500 canonists in the United States, the great majority of whom are bishops and priests, although religious men and women as well as laypersons are eligible to earn degrees in canon law. Many canonists also have graduate degrees in such fields as theology, civil law or other professional fields. It is estimated that approximately ninety percent of all canonists are involved in diocesan tribunal practice and specialize almost exclusively in matrimonial cases.

There are two national professional organizations for canonists represented in the United States: The Canon Law Society of America, and the Coetus on Canon Law of the Fellowship of Catholic Scholars. (Cf. Decretist.)

Canonization • The Church's official declaration that a person is already in heaven and worthy of public veneration and imitation. The process follows beatification and involves another investigation into a person's virtues, writings, reputation for holiness and miracles ascribed to the person's intercession since death. Miracles, however, are not required for martyrs. The Pope may dispense from some of the formalities usual in the canonization process, and he alone can make the formal declaration of canonization. St. Ulrich of Augsburg became the first formally canonized saint by Pope John XV in 993.

Canonization gives a sevenfold honor: (1) inscription of the name in the catalogue of saints and reception of public veneration; (2) invocation in the public prayers of the Church; (3) dedication of churches in the saint's honor; (4) celebration of Mass and Divine Office; (5) assignment of a day in the liturgical calendar; (6) pictorial

representations; (7) public veneration of relics. (Cf. Beatification; Martyrology.)

Canons, Chapter of • The chapter of canons is a collegiate body of priests whose duties include performing the more solemn liturgical functions at a cathedral or collegiate church. Included in these liturgical functions is the common recitation of the Divine Office in the cathedral. Canons are appointed by the bishop and ordinarily reside at the cathedral. Until the revised Code went into effect, the cathedral chapter of canons also exercised the duties of diocesan consultors, the office of consultor having been created for those dioceses which had no chapter of canons. The revised Code provides for a College of Consultors, even where there is a chapter of canons.

Historically, the chapter of canons seems to have arisen in the very early Middle Ages. They were groups of priests who lived at the bishop's residence and followed the "canonical rule," especially with regard to the common recitation of the Divine Office and performance of other sacred ceremonies.

There are chapters of canons in many European and South American dioceses but none in the United States (cf. Canons 503-510). In some European dioceses, the canons have the privilege of submitting candidates for the office of diocesan bishop to the Holy See.

Canons of the Apostles (also Apostolic Canons) • A collection of eighty-five documents dealing with Church order and discipline. Though attributed to the Apostles, they were actually compiled toward the end of the fourth century by an Arian or Apollinarian author. They are included in the larger collection of so-called Apostolic Constitutions. The canons are important for their list of acceptable books of the Bible, omitting Revelation, while adding the two letters of Clement of Rome and the very Apostolic Constitutions in which the canon itself is contained.

Canons Regular • The communities of clergy, dating from the eleventh century and often following the Rule of St. Augustine, which embraced a monastic form of life. The Order of Premonstratensians (Norbertines) is the largest such order existing today.

Canopy • This refers to an honorific covering of some type. In many churches, both old and new, a canopy is permanently built over the altar of sacrifice and/or the altar of repose in honor of the Divine Person there present and of the divine mysteries celebrated there as well. It can be of wood, gilt oftentimes, or of marble or other precious material. Often there is an image of the Holy Spirit, represented as a dove, in the center of the bottom part so that it is visible to those beneath. In former times, although this is still the case nowadays in some places, a canopy was always placed over the thrones of the Pope, cardinals, bishops and abbots.

Whenever the Blessed Sacrament is carried in procession (especially outdoors), a canopy is borne over the Blessed Sacrament and the celebrant. This consists of a rectangle of rich cloth carried on four to six poles (also of a suitable material and decoration).

The canopy was also used in former times over the Pope at the Papal Mass as he was carried on the *sedia gestatoria* in procession from the Vatican Palace to the altar of St. Peter's Basilica. Pope Paul VI discontinued this practice after Vatican II.

Canossa • A city in Tuscany where, in January of 1077, Emperor Henry IV made his famous submission to Pope St. Gregory VII. The Pontiff had excommunicated the emperor for his refusal to give up his right to appoint bishops, called "lay investiture."

Henry's act of public obedience came to symbolize the primacy of papal prerogatives, even over temporal rulers and thus "Canossa" has come to denote a zenith of papal prestige.

Canticle • From the Latin *canere*, meaning "to sing." A sacred song, other than a psalm, with text from Scripture and used as part of the official liturgy of the Church. The "evangelical canticles," all taken from the Gospel of St. Luke, are the *Magnificat*, the *Benedictus* and the *Nunc Dimittis*. These three are sung daily by those who pray the Liturgy of the Hours. Sections of the other canticles, taken from the Old or New Testaments, are sung during the Liturgy of the Hours on various days of the four-week Psalter.

Canticle of Canticles: See **Song of Songs**

Cantor (also Precentor) • The leader of plain (unaccompanied or non-choral) chant in the Eastern Churches. The cantor also regularly fulfills the ministry of reader at liturgical services. Either a male or female may serve in the capacity of a cantor who is not ordained; however, only a male may become an ordained cantor (reader).

In the West, any qualified person (male or female) may serve as a cantor, also known as leader of song. There is no ordination or formal institution into this office in the Latin Rite.

A cantor can be a singer of psalms and other texts not assigned to the choir or the congregation. The cantor may also lead the congregation at times as the Leader of Song. The cantor should be a properly trained musician, but more important, he or she must be a person of prayer, so that the people may be led in sung prayer and not just in song. This is especially true when the music presented is in antiphonal settings. The musical virtuosity of the cantor must be artistically veiled, so as to manifest the prayer aspect of the work rather than a performance aspect.

Cap-de-la-Madeleine, Shrine of • This shrine is also known as Our Lady of the Cape or Queen of the Most Holy Rosary. The first church was built in 1659 by Jesuit missionaries to honor the Blessed Virgin Mary.

In Three Rivers, Quebec, Canada, the present stone shrine was completed in 1714 and is considered the oldest stone church on the North American continent. On June 22, 1888, it was rededicated as a shrine of the Queen of the Most Holy Rosary. Eventually, the site became a pilgrimage and devotional center. In 1909, the First Plenary Council of Quebec declared the church a national shrine. In 1964, the church at the shrine was given the status and title of a minor basilica.

Capital Punishment • The taking of the life of a person convicted of a serious crime for which the community has determined death is the appropriate penalty. Capital punishment, often in barbaric and horrendous forms, existed in all of the ancient law codes, including that of the Old Testament Jews. With the coming of Christianity, the appropriateness of capital punishment was taken up by Christian leaders and teachers.

Tertullian, Lactantius and Popes Leo I (fifth century) and Nicholas I (ninth century) condemned the practice outright. St. Augustine, although he did not condemn it, called for mercy in dealing with accused criminals.

The Church has never officially condemned capital punishment. When asked for the Catholic opinion on the issue, reference is often made to St. Thomas Aquinas, who approved of capital punishment for the good of the community and upheld the right of legitimate

government to take the life of a criminal guilty of a serious crime.

Nevertheless, there has continued to be controversy over the morality of capital punishment. Various leaders of all denominations have regularly called for its abolition. In the United States, various individual bishops have done so, as have groups of bishops from either entire states or ecclesiastical provinces. In 1974 and 1976 the episcopal conference as a whole issued statements condemning the practice. Although many list capital punishment with murder, abortion and even the production of nuclear weapons, it is a radically different issue. The *Catechism of the Catholic Church* (cf. nn. 2266-2267) makes this point in a rather nuanced manner. Pope John Paul II, in *Evangelium Vitae*, seems to take it a step further by setting rather strict parameters for the moral exercise of capital punishment on the part of any state, even while not declaring its use to be immoral under all circumstances (cf. n. 56).

Capital Sins (also Capital Vices or Deadly Sins) • Sins that are sources or causes of other sins. Traditionally, the capital sins were counted as pride, envy, sloth, lust, greed, intemperance and anger.

Original sin is the first of all sins as it is the root of our alienation from God. The seven capital or deadly sins are perilous tendencies which threaten the life of charity and the grace of God within us. St. John terms the root of all sin to be ". . . the lust of the flesh and the lust of the eyes, and the pride of life" (1 Jn 2:16). The capital sins are disruptions of natural tendencies that are required for our human flourishing and happiness.

Pride is a sin by which a person unduly esteems himself or his accomplishments relative to the esteem that should be given to God. Envy is a tendency to begrudge the good of another because it is perceived as a threat to one's own excellence and glory. And the greater the good that is envied, the greater the malice of this sin.

Anger is a sin of excessively desiring to suppress what is hostile to us. Anger is morally good when used against true evils and is necessary for true love. However, when anger is imprudent and immoderate, it becomes sinful and destroys harmony and peace.

Avarice is an extreme or unruly love of material goods in particular, but it also includes love of worldly honors. Lust is a disorderly craving for sexual pleasure that is indulged in without discipline and without regard for the responsibilities of marriage and family.

Intemperance is a lack of restraint in our desire for food, drink, rest or recreation, and its malice lies in the disruption of our dignity that it causes. Intemperance in respect to food often has deep psychological roots. Intemperance in respect to alcohol or drugs is a grave sin because it degrades the person and opens the person to even greater evils. For those who are "addicted" to either drugs or alcohol, total abstinence is morally imperative. The sin of sloth, involving a lack of enthusiasm for spiritual growth and development, is the antithesis of love of God and leads to undue love of pleasure, discouragement and ultimately despair.

Lust of the flesh is a disruptive desire for pleasures. Lust of the eyes is an uncontrolled craving for possessions. And these two combine to create a spiritual laziness and apathy in relation to spiritual growth. The pride of life is a disruptive desire for honors and glory that leads to megalomania, envy and anger.

Capitulary • A body of laws particular to a chapter, that is, a society or community attached to a cathedral or other religious group. It is sometimes used to designate the collection of statutes or canons passed by a provincial council.

Cappa • (1) Comes from the Latin and Italian name for a cape, and is simply another name for the cope, the cape-like vestment used sometimes by the celebrant or others during the liturgy.

(2) The large mantle with shoulder cape worn by members of some religious orders in choir and out of doors. The Dominicans and Trinitarians, for instance, wear a black cappa as part of their religious habit. The Premonstratensians (otherwise called Norbertines, after their founder, St. Norbert) and the Carmelites include a white cappa in their habit.

Cappa Magna • A cloak with a long train and a hooded shoulder cape of ermine in winter and red silk in summer. It was formerly worn by the Pope (only for Christmas Matins, Tenebrae and Office of the Dead), cardinals and diocesan bishops when attending certain solemn liturgical services. The cappa magna was purple wool for bishops; for cardinals, it was scarlet watered silk (for Advent, Lent, Good Friday, and the conclave, purple wool; and rose watered silk for Gaudete and Laetare Sundays); and for the Pope, it was red velvet for Christmas Matins, red serge at other times.

Although the cappa magna was not abolished altogether, its use has been significantly limited since the revision of the norms for choir dress for prelates. At the present time, cardinals may wear it (with a silk hood year round) on solemn occasions, but outside of Rome. It is no longer restricted to diocesan bishops, but may be worn by any bishop on very solemn occasions. The Pope no longer uses a cappa magna.

Cappa Pluvialis (Pluviale) • Coming from the Latin for rain cape or cloak, this term refers to the cope, that liturgical vestment which may be worn when the chasuble is not demanded by the rubrics. This may be during processions, such as on Palm Sunday, Solemn Vespers, solemn blessings, Eucharistic processions, exposition or Benediction. It is usually the color of the day and always white for Eucharistic processions and the like. It consists of a cape reaching to the ankles all around and fastened at the neck or chest by a flap or clasp. There is usually a hood or triangular decoration on the back. In recent times the hood has returned in style as a result of monastic motifs in liturgical paraments. (Cf. Cope.)

Captivity Epistles • The phrase refers to the following four Pauline letters which, according to tradition, are thought to have been written by Paul near the end of his life while he was under house arrest in Rome (hence the term "captivity"): Philippians, Colossians, Ephesians and Philemon. Each letter mentions the imprisonment of its author (Phil 1:7; Col 4:18; Eph 4:1; Phlm 9).

Cardinal Legate • A cardinal who is named by the Pope to represent him in

French statue representing cardinal virtue of fortitude

person and perform a designated task of great importance or delicacy, as well as to perform some ceremony in his name. A cardinal legate is accorded the same privileges as if the Pope were present in person, and acts performed by him have the authority and backing of the Pope, for whom he acts and speaks. Nowadays the use of cardinal legates has become more restricted. The most common use the Supreme Pontiff makes of these special legates is in regard to national or international Eucharistic congresses which he cannot attend personally.

Cardinal Protector • In former days this designated a cardinal who was named by the Pope or one of the organs of the Roman Curia to assist and take under his care and protection a religious order, congregation or pious institute, as well as pious associations of lay persons (such as confraternities). He not only served them by his advice and counsel but also presented any business they had with the Vatican Curia or the Holy Father in their behalf. Since the advent of the national colleges in Rome during the Reformation and since the Council of Trent, these colleges were also given cardinal protectors. The practice of having an appointed cardinal protector is all but extinct now; however, most orders and other institutes have friends among the Curia to whom they have access in case of need.

Cardinal Vicar • A cardinal who is appointed by the Pope to serve as his vicar general for the Diocese of Rome. To him the Pope entrusts the day-to-day pastoral and administrative care of the main portion of his diocese. A distinct vicar general is appointed for the State of Vatican City.

Cardinal Virtues • Prudence, justice, temperance and fortitude are the cardinal virtues. They are the habits or powers developed by a person through practice which are the source of, and controlling influence over, all other virtues. All other virtues are specifications or modifications of these four virtues, which are the standard of right reason and of all moral action. The cardinal virtues set the outlines and structure of a full and complete human life. Development and promotion of them enable us not only to seek and obtain the good, but also to effect what is truly good in this life. The cardinal virtues enable human love to be perfect and complete.

Care of Souls • Properly speaking, "care of souls" is a canonical-theological term that describes the pastoral authority of the Pope, residential bishops and pastors. This authority includes the responsibility for seeing to the pastoral and spiritual needs of the faithful entrusted to them. It includes the authority to celebrate and administer the sacraments, to preach and to perform other actions necessary for the spiritual needs of the people.

Caritas Internationalis • The worldwide conglomerate of national Catholic charity-relief organizations which provide monies and material assistance for the destitute. Catholic Relief Services, located in New York, is the American arm of *Caritas Internationalis*. Persons in areas which have been damaged by drought, flood, earthquake or other natural disasters are helped as quickly as possible.

Carmel, Mount • A wedge-shaped promontory which juts out into the Mediterranean just above the port city of Haifa and divides the central plain of Israel into the Plain of Acco to the north and the Plain of Sharon to the south. From the earliest times it has played a role in the religious life of the people in the area. During the biblical period it was connected with the activities of both Elijah and Elisha (1 Kgs 18:19-46 and 2 Kgs 2:25; 4:25). It is also associated with the early devotion to Mary which surfaced within Christendom. The Carmelite Order venerates the spot as the site of its foundation.

Carnival (also Carnivale) • The time of celebration and merry-making before Lenten penance and fasting commence on Ash Wednesday, called Carnivale ("Goodbye to Meat") in Italy and Mardi Gras ("Fat Tuesday") in France and the U.S.

Carolingian Schools • During and following the reign of Charlemagne in the ninth century, a series of Church-sponsored, state-supported schools were opened, modeled after the educational reforms of Alcuin of York at the Palace School. The learning that took place there was little less than remarkable for the age. Among other things, it was credited with the development of the Vulgate Bible and revisions of the liturgy, and is, moreover, chiefly recognized as laying the intellectual foundations for the Renaissance a few centuries later.

Carthage, Councils of • A series of ecclesiastical synods held at Carthage between the third and sixth centuries. Synods held under St. Cyprian (A.D. 251, 252, 254, 255 and 256) focused first on the reconciliation of Christians who had wavered during the persecution of Decius (250), and then on the rebaptism of heretics, a matter in dispute with Rome. The earliest surviving canons from African synods are those of the Councils held at Carthage under Gratus (348) and Genethlius (390). Perhaps the two most famous of the Councils of Carthage occurred among a long series of synods held under Bishop Aurelius between 393 and 424; Pelagianism was condemned at the Council held in 412, and Rome's claim to exercise jurisdiction in Africa was challenged at the Council held in 419. The latter Council collected its own canons and those of earlier Councils in the *Codex Canonum Ecclesiae Africanae*. The final Councils in this group were those held under Boniface in 525 and 534.

Carthusians • This exclusively contemplative order was founded by St. Bruno (1032-1101) in 1084 at the Grand Chartreuse in Dauphiné. At first there was no special rule governing the Order beyond the stipulation that the Carthusian monks were expected to practice perfect mortification and renunciation of the world. Essentially hermits, they took a vow of silence, with conventual Mass. In 1133, Pope Innocent II approved a rule of life termed Carthusian Customs, and this form remains to this day fundamentally unchanged. The Carthusian rule is a hybrid of Benedictine monasticism and eremitical asceticism.

The Order also includes a number of monasteries of nuns who live under a similar rule, but they have separate cells instead of cottages and are under the direction of the Carthusian monks.

Cases of Conscience • Actual or hypothetical instances are developed in canon law or moral theology to examine canonical or moral principles. Initially, they were developed to aid confessors in determining what sorts of penances should be given to penitents. Widely criticized after the Second Vatican Council, cases of conscience have worked their way back into moral theology in contemporary medical ethical debates. For example, contemporary debates concerning the morality of such procedures as *in vitro* fertilization, fetal tissue transplantation and artificial hearts are, at root, cases of conscience. Furthermore, debates concerning the provision of artificially administered nutrition and fluids and the use or threat to use new nuclear weapons systems are also contemporary cases of conscience.

Cassock (also Soutane) • The close-fitting, ankle-length robe worn by the Catholic clergy as their official garb originated in the classical dress of antiquity. When newer, shorter garments became the style for men, the clergy continued the older way of dressing. There are different styles, such as the Roman with its many buttons, the Jesuit with fly front fastened with hooks, and the French with a wider pleated skirt and buttons on the cuffs. The latter two are always worn with a sash, while the Roman may be worn without one. Black is the usual color for the cassocks of diocesan priests, although white is favored in the tropics. The color for bishops and other prelates is purple, for cardinals scarlet, and white for the Supreme Pontiff. Cardinals, bishops and other prelates also have what is called a "house cassock," which is black with red or purple piping, buttons, buttonholes, and sash-loops; this is usually worn with a sash. Indeed, the complete ecclesiastical habit of a priest differs from the house cassock of a prelate only in the color of the piping, buttons and other trim, which must be black. Laymen serving a liturgical function often wear cassocks. In some countries the cassock has been virtually replaced by the clerical suit in general and the plain linen alb in the sanctuary.

Castel Gandolfo • Situated in the Alban Hills on the shores of Lake Albano, about eighteen miles southeast of Rome, this town is the site of the summer residence of the Holy Father. The present papal villa, the former Villa Barberini, was begun by Pope Urban VIII in 1629. According to the provisions of the Lateran Treaty of 1929, the papal villa enjoys extraterritorial status.

Casuistry • That aspect of moral theology which attempts to apply moral principles to specific cases. The term "casuistry" is derived from the Latin *casus*, meaning "case." The overall meaning of casuistry is to reduce any distance, morally speaking, between concrete action on the one hand and abstract norms on the other. Throughout its long history in the Church, casuistry has been used largely, but not exclusively, to assist seminarians studying moral theology and priests celebrating the sacrament of Penance.

Although its full-blown development came much later, the roots of casuistry are in the New Testament itself. For example, an incipient casuistry characterizes the question posed to Christ: "Teacher, we know that you speak and teach rightly, and show no partiality, but truly teach the way of God. Is it lawful for us to give tribute to Caesar, or not?" (Lk 20:21-22). In the Pauline corpus, examples of a proto-casuistry include the resolution of issues such as eating sacrificial food (1 Cor 8:7-13) and the charism of virginity (1 Cor 7:8-9; 25-28).

As Christianity spread throughout the world, requiring, as it would, Christian answers to the various problems of the day,

casuistry yielded many of these solutions. These were preserved in the writings of the Fathers of the Church, and, not unexpectedly, the topics were as diverse as military service and appropriate dress for the Christian. Following the Patristic era, and about the time that private auricular confession was taking a stronger hold in the spiritual lives of more and more Catholics, the Church's moral casuistry was written into the penitentials, books or manuals which priests could consult in their role as confessors.

The Church has relied on casuistry because of its essential role in clarifying the principles and, at the same time, making "real" their application to concrete circumstances. However, casuistry should not be considered by itself as a complete and thorough source of moral wisdom. For instance, it cannot replace the personal act of moral decision-making in one's own conscience and it cannot be separated from the virtue of prudence. Therefore, casuistry has limitations, and these limitations must be acknowledged by those who wish to benefit from its value as a moral tool.

Like the two dimensions of conscience, antecedent and consequent, which refer to when the appeal to conscience is made (either before or after moral decision-making), casuistry has its own temporal considerations. When referring to a moral act already performed, it is known as the merciful casuistry of the confessional. Here, this kind of casuistry serves the priest/confessor who must judge whether a penitent is culpable or not. In other cases, casuistry does not concern itself with actions already performed but with actions contemplated or hypothesized. Here, an effort is made to identify the morally correct course before engaging in any action. Hence, this can be thought of as the future orientation of casuistry.

Catacomb of St. Januarius, Naples

Generally speaking, casuistry has made a very positive contribution to the field of moral theology. Except for temporary historical lapses into various kinds of minimalism and laxism, casuistry has brought forth a rich harvest of clarity in the moral enterprise. Always emphasizing the concreteness of moral situations, casuistry insures that renewal in moral theology not be just an ethereal exercise.

Catacombs • Underground burial areas, usually consisting of a network of galleries and small chambers opening out of them. The word "catacomb" is derived from an early descriptive name of the cemetery of St. Sebastian in Rome, *ad catacumbas*. This Latin expression probably meant "near the hollows" and might well refer to a depression in the Appian Way near the spot where the cemetery is located. This nickname of an important cemetery was eventually adopted as a generic noun describing all underground cemeteries in use during the early Christian centuries.

The most characteristic feature of the catacombs, as distinguished from smaller underground burial chambers, were the networks of galleries whose walls offered ample room for creating niches in which to place the bodies of the dead. This

economical use of available space might have been initially developed by the Church to provide burial for its poorer members in a cemetery reserved exclusively for the use of the Christian community. Indeed, judging from catacombs that have survived, this type of burial area seems to have been used principally by Christians. An interesting group of catacombs belonging to the Jewish community of Rome has also survived.

An important prerequisite for the creation of these extensive underground passageways was a terrain whose geological substratum was soft enough to permit easy excavation. The abundant beds of tufa stone in Rome were ideal for this purpose, and by far the greatest number of catacombs which have survived were discovered there. Catacombs have also been preserved in Naples, Sicily and Malta.

It seems certain that some of the more affluent Christian families of Rome aided the Church by donating land for burials in the zone outside the city's walls. (Roman law forbade the burial of the dead within the city limits.) In some cases these properties already housed small underground chambers for the family's dead. In these cases the development of the community cemetery often consisted in the extension of the underground space by creating galleries leading off the original burial chambers.

The movement to create properly Christian cemeteries seems to date back to the early third century, and these burial areas served the Church's needs throughout the period of the persecutions. However, the idea that the catacombs were systematically used by Christians as hiding places during times of persecution is purely legendary. Their existence was well known to the imperial authorities, and around the middle of the third century they were even confiscated for a period of time. The greatest development of the catacombs actually occurred during the fourth century — after the establishment of peace between Church and Empire.

During the new era of peace, several of the catacombs gradually grew to considerable proportions, and the combined length of galleries in some cases reaches several miles, as in the case of the catacomb of Domatilla. During the course of this development, the original purpose of the catacombs as burial places for the Christian poor was extended to include Christians from all ranks of life, and in the process, the growing number of small chambers leading off the long galleries offered more ample and somewhat more elegant burial spaces for those who could afford them. The presence of the bodies of martyrs in certain catacombs led to extensive renovations, which sometimes involved the creation of underground sacred areas for veneration around the martyrs' tombs.

Catafalque • An elaborate stand on which the body of the deceased is placed for lying in state, as is customary for some dignitary. People of lesser rank are usually accorded a simple bier. For a memorial Mass or service when the body is not present, a mock coffin, covered with a pall, typically rests on a catafalque.

Catafalque is another name for the *castrumdoloris*, the middle coffin of the three in which a deceased Sovereign Pontiff is buried; it is that which is seen during his requiem Mass at St. Peter's. The word "catafalque" likely comes from the late Latin *catafalicum*, a word for a siege tower, not unlike a catapult; it is named for its physical resemblance, although the idea of the deceased besieging heaven from the catafalque is not totally absent from folk etymology.

Catechesis • The word "catechesis" is rooted in the Greek verb *katekhein*, to resound or echo. Luke in Acts uses the verb as instructing in the way of the Lord. In St. Paul, it refers to oral instruction, a handing on of all that has been received from Christ.

Today this oral instruction may also be accompanied by written, printed or visual aids. Catechesis is based on Scripture, Tradition and liturgy, as well as on the teaching authority and life of the Church. Its purpose is to develop a living, explicit and active Faith through the liturgical and sacramental life of the Church. The basic ideas are stated in the 1971 *General Catechetical Directory* and the 1979 U.S. *National Catechetical Directory, Sharing the Light of Faith*. Catechesis, then, is a lifelong process of conversion for the individual and the Christian community. (Cf. Preaching; Basic Teachings for Catholic Religious Education.)

Catechetics • The study of the history, nature, goals, principles and process of catechesis. Catechetics is interdisciplinary since it draws from other fields, such as theology, biblical studies and social sciences. Its main concern is a process of growth in the Faith. Therefore, the purpose of catechetics is to instruct the individual in the basic teaching of the Bible and the Tradition of the Church. The modern techniques of teaching and communication such as visual aids, television, video and audio cassettes, computers and instructional manuals are used in the catechetical process. (Cf. Catechesis.)

Catechism • A compendium of fundamental Christian truths, presented in a readily accessible and understandable form, sometimes in question-and-answer format and often structured around the Apostles' Creed, the seven sacraments, the Ten Commandments, and the Lord's Prayer. The style and contents of catechisms have varied, depending on the nature of their intended readership (bishops, parish priests, or the laity, as the case may be).

Although already in the Bible there are brief summaries of teaching, the first real catechism dates from the end of the first century. Important catechisms prior to the sixteenth century were those authored by St. Augustine, Alcuin and St. Thomas Aquinas. Both Luther and Calvin produced catechisms. The first catechism intended for the universal Church was commissioned by the Council of Trent; it is commonly known as the *Roman Catechism* and was issued by Pope St. Pius V in 1566. In late-nineteenth century America, an important national catechism, based on the *Roman Catechism* and known as the *Baltimore Catechism*, was published.

In response to the call of the Second Vatican Council for a fresh approach to catechesis, the Holy See issued a *General Catechetical Directory* in 1971. This was followed in the United States by the *National Catechetical Directory* in 1979. The process of catechetical renewal inspired by the Council culminated in the publication of the *Catechism of the Catholic Church*, commissioned by the Synod of 1985 and promulgated by Pope John Paul II in 1992.

Catechism of the Catholic Church • The *Catechism of the Catholic Church* was issued by Pope John Paul II on October 11, 1992 — the thirtieth anniversary of the opening of the Second Vatican Council. Upon the recommendation of the Extraordinary Synod of Bishops in 1985, Pope John Paul in 1986 appointed a commission of cardinals and bishops to launch the preparation of a catechism for the universal Church. By 1989, the commission was ready to circulate a draft text of the catechism for consultation among the bishops of the world. After reviewing many thousands of amendments received from the bishops, the commission submitted to the Holy Father in 1991 a final draft of the catechism for his official approval. This was granted in 1992, and the *Catechism of the Catholic Church* was promulgated by the Apostolic Constitution *Fidei Depositum*.

Structured in four parts or "pillars" (the Creed, the sacraments, the Ten Commandments, and the Our Father), the *Catechism* presents the fundamental content of Catholic Faith and morals in a complete way. While it does not supplant national catechetical works, the *Catechism* is intended to provide the point of reference in the preparation of national and diocesan catechisms. It is directed to the bishops, to all teachers of the Faith, to the Christian faithful and to all sincere inquirers.

The original French text of the *Catechism* has been translated into all the major languages. It has enjoyed phenomenal sales throughout the world. After its initial publication in the United States in the Spring of 1994, over two million copies of the *Catechism* were sold, making it the most successful English-language religious book, other than the Bible, since the invention of the printing press.

Catechist • In the Christian context, it is a clergyman, religious or layperson who instructs a person in the Catholic Faith. By word and example, the catechist shares his or her personal faith with other members of the community and/or with those who seek to join the Church. In a July 1981 talk, Pope John Paul II emphasized the significance of catechesis in families, parishes, schools and the mass media. He added that the catechist's Christian witness must match one's proficiency and skills in teaching doctrine. (Cf. Ministries.)

Catechumens • Literally, catechumens are people who are being given *catechesis* (Greek for instruction). The term has the specific, ecclesiastical meaning of someone who is receiving formal instruction in the Catholic Faith, with a view to reception into the Church and full participation in the sacramental life of the Church. The Rite of Christian Initiation of Adults created a new focus on the catechumenate, wherein the neophytes are gradually introduced both liturgically and catechetically into Church membership.

The Second Vatican Council is instructive in this regard: "Catechumens should be properly initiated into the mystery of salvation and the practice of the evangelical virtues and they should be introduced into the life of faith, liturgy and charity of the People of God by successive sacred rites" (AG 14). Elsewhere, the Council treats of catechumens: "Catechumens who, moved by the Holy Spirit, with an explicit intention to be incorporated into the Church, are by that very intention joined to her. With love and solicitude Mother Church already embraces them as her own" (LG 14).

The catechumenate has its origin in the early Church. When a pagan sought conversion to Christianity, he or she was given basic instruction as an inquirer into the Faith. Since the catechumens were allowed to attend only the first part of the Mass, what is today called the Liturgy of the Word was then called the Mass of the Catechumens. With Baptism, they entered into full union with the Mystical Body and could rightly participate in the Eucharist or Mass of the Faithful.

Categorical Imperative • The moral principle of Immanuel Kant (d. 1804) that the evaluation of any ethical duty must be consistent with a general and universalizable rule. The categorical imperative held that the moral agent must "act only on the maxim by which you can will that it, at the same time, should become a general law." In other words, the categorical imperative holds that if a rule imposes a strict moral duty, one must determine whether one can oblige all other moral agents to act in the same manner. It also holds that one is to treat all other moral agents as ends in themselves and not as means to other ends or objectives.

The categorical imperative is purely formal, and determining what precise material actions are required by it is a serious problem. This principle operates in conjunction with Kant's principle of universalizability, which holds that all human beings should be treated as ends rather than as means.

Cathari • A medieval sect of neo-Manichaeans who appeared in the East around the eleventh century and in the West about one hundred years later. Renouncing Baptism and marriage (or Matrimony) and preaching an extreme form of poverty, they attracted for a time a significant following in Italy. Papal rejections of their theories, combined with the healthy influence of genuine poverty as lived by the mendicant orders, eliminated the group's influence by the time of the Renaissance.

Cathedra • From the Greek and Latin for chair or throne; therefore, the church in which the bishop's chair or throne is placed is called the cathedral. In ancient times, the seat or chair was the sign of authority to teach, whence the early bishops usually preached while seated; medieval doctors of theology taught in the same posture. The doctoral chair of St. Thomas Aquinas is preserved in Naples.

When the Pope teaches formally, authoritatively and infallibly, he is said to speak *ex cathedra*, literally, "from the chair," thus denoting the teaching's official, solemn and binding nature on all the world's faithful.

In the Mass of Pope Paul VI, the emphasis on the celebrant's chair is derived from its symbolism of the celebrant's authority to preside at the celebration of the Eucharist.

Cathedral • From the Greek and Latin *cathedra* (chair), a cathedral is so called for the chair of the bishop who has jurisdiction over the diocese of which the cathedral is the central church and the bishop's official church. Ordinarily, the cathedral is the site of the principal liturgical activities of the bishop and his diocese. Here the bishop is consecrated and enthroned upon his *cathedra*, an ancient symbol of a someone's teaching authority; diocesan synods are usually held in the cathedral. In his cathedral, the bishop most properly ordains, confirms, blesses the sacred oils on Holy Thursday, celebrates the liturgy of the Sacred Triduum and presides at Pontifical Masses. Often bishops are interred in a cathedral crypt.

The cathedral must be located in the diocese, usually in the see city in which the bishop exercises his authority. Properly, only a cathedral named for the patron of the diocese can be called a cathedral; otherwise, it is termed a pro-cathedral.

Although St. Peter's Basilica is commonly identified with the Pope as Bishop of Rome, it is not his cathedral. The papal *cathedra* is at St. John Lateran, the actual cathedral of Rome and mother church for all Catholic churches.

The first cathedral established in the United States is the Basilica of the

Assumption, a masterpiece of the neo-Classic designed by Latrobe, also the architect of the U.S. Capitol. It was designated in 1790 as the cathedral of the primatial see of Baltimore; the Cathedral of Mary Our Queen now serves as Baltimore's

Cathedral of Aachen, built by Charlemagne

cathedral. Other historic cathedrals in the United States include St. Patrick's Cathedral, New York, a superb example of neo-Gothic architecture; St. Matthew's Cathedral, Washington, the site of President John F. Kennedy's requiem Mass, the annual Red Mass celebrated for the Supreme Court and others in the judiciary, and other religious events appropriate to the cathedral of our nation's capital; and the Basilica-Cathedral of Saints Peter and Paul, Philadelphia, completed by St. John Neumann, bishop of Philadelphia, and elevated to the rank of Basilica in 1976 by Pope Paul VI in recognition of its hosting the Eucharistic congress of that year.

Cathedraticum • Beginning in Spain and Italy around the sixth century, the practice developed of having parishes, lay organizations and other diocesan subdivisions pay annually a small financial tribute to the diocesan bishop known as the *cathedraticum* as a sign of their filial dependence on and subjection to the bishop. Sometimes this token was paid at the bishop's annual visitation; other times it was offered during the diocesan synod or at some other special event. Canon 1504 of the 1917 Code of Canon Law preserved this practice by directing that a moderate payment should be made to the bishop in accord with this tradition. The *cathedraticum* was not, however, to be considered a normal source of revenue for the diocese, and the Congregation of the Council warned French bishops, for example, that certain taxes they sought to impose ran afoul of the strictly honorary nature of the *cathedraticum*. Nevertheless, the misinformed practice of designating regular diocesan assessments as *cathedratica* did appear from time to time.

The 1983 Code has not maintained the *cathedraticum* (except perhaps by way of remote exception in Canon 1263). Should diocesan financial needs exceed freewill offerings and similar sources of revenue, procedures are provided for the assessment of ecclesiastical taxes in accord with the regular provisions on temporal goods.

Catholic • The word "Catholic" means general or universal, from the Greek word *katholikos*. It first occurs in Christian use in the letter of St. Ignatius of Antioch to the Smyrnaeans: "Wheresoever the bishop shall appear, there let the people be, even as where Jesus is, there is the Catholic Church" (*Smyr.* 8:20).

In Christian terminology, the word has been used in different ways: (1) as a description of the Church as a whole, as distinguished from local Christian churches or communities; (2) in application to the doctrine of the Church as a whole, as distinguished from unorthodox teachings; (3) of the Church before the split between Eastern and Western Christianity in 1054; (4) by the Anglican Church, Old Catholics and others who claim to possess a historical and continuous tradition of faith and doctrine; (5) individual Christians, insofar as they belong to the Catholic Church and are orthodox in their belief.

Today it applies to the Church membership, the creeds, churches, institutions, clergy and hierarchy who follow the same teachings of Christ as given to the Apostles. (Cf. Marks of the Church; Church.)

Catholic Action • This terminology has been a source of confusion, but its history can be accurately delineated.

Pope St. Pius X referred to it, but Pope Pius XI gave it a precise definition and relied on it to help the Church in the world. For Pius XI, Catholic Action was the cooperation of the laity in the task of the priest or, more generally, the hierarchy. For an organization to merit the name, it needed a mandate from the bishop; for the international level, from the Holy See itself.

Catholic Action flourished in Italy, Belgium, France and other parts of the world. In Belgium, it is associated with the name of Cardinal Cardijn, and in France with Cardinal Saliège. Its scope was often very broad, according to the needs of the civil society in which the Catholic laity labored.

In the United States many organizations of the laity fit the description of Catholic Action, especially in the first half of the twentieth century, even if they did not use the label of Pope Pius XI.

Pope Pius XII was very interested in this movement and continued the work of Pope Pius XI. Pope John XXIII was less interested in the juridical formulation, perhaps because in the 1950s the concept was becoming better understood simply as the "lay apostolate."

The Second Vatican Council makes reference to Catholic Action in *Apostolicam Actuositatem*, the Decree on the Apostolate of Lay People, n. 20, and again in *Christus Dominus*, the Decree on the Pastoral Office of the Bishops in the Church, n. 17. But it does not canonize the terminology as such, and leaves the way open for a broad interpretation of this movement and a flexible understanding of its use.

Since the Second Vatican Council was concerned about the laity and their role in the Church, we might see Catholic Action as forming a necessary historical buildup to the work of the Council on this theme. The international Synod of Bishops which met in Rome in 1987, and from whose work was published the Apostolic Exhortation *Christifideles Laici* in January 1989, no longer explicitly uses the terminology of "Catholic Action" but surely preserves its inspiration and develops it further, both pastorally and theologically.

Catholic Church • Universal in place, scope and time, the Catholic Church takes its name from the Greek term meaning universal, *katholikos*. The designation of "Catholic" was given to the Church by St.

Pope Pius XI,
Catholic Action supporter

Ignatius of Antioch (d. A.D. 107): "Wheresoever the bishop shall appear, there let the people be, even as where Jesus is, there is the Catholic Church" (*Smyr.* 8:2). The Catholic Church is no mere human invention, but the community called into being by Jesus Himself. As ancient as the first-century witness of St. Ignatius and as recent as the twentieth-century re-discovery of the Second Vatican Council of "The Church as the People of God" (cf. *Lumen Gentium*, Chapter II), and the statement of Pope Paul VI, at the beginning of the second session of the Council, "The mystery of the Church is not a mere object of theological knowledge; it is something to be lived. . . ," the Catholic Church has been understood in every period of her history as a living community, many members united by one Faith, professing one doctrine, sharing the same seven sacraments and governed by the Vicar of Christ on earth and the successors to the Apostles.

The Pope, as Bishop of Rome, exercises the particular authority given to St. Peter by Jesus Himself (Mt 16:13-20) to guide the Catholic Church in the ways of the Holy Spirit and to teach the faithful infallibly, with divine truth, in matters of dogma and the Christian life. Catholic bishops, in union with the Holy See, are entrusted with the mission of the Apostles to be the Church's shepherds, leaders and teachers. Priests and deacons, through the sacrament of Holy Orders, assist the bishops in their work of offering sacrifice, teaching and ministering to the People of God. Professed religious anticipate the *eschaton* in their vowed life of poverty, chastity and obedience. All the baptized, the majority of whom are the laity, benefit from these ministries and strive, especially in their faithful sacramental lives, to participate more fully in the Mystical Body of Christ and to present again to the Father His Beloved Son.

The Nicene Creed articulates what is implicit in Paul's Letter to the Ephesians as the four distinctive characteristics or marks of the Catholic Church: (1) One: though made up of many members, the Church, united to one Head, professes one Faith and shares one Baptism and one Communion with the Lord; (2) Holy: founded in God's grace, the Church subsists in Christ and through Him is made holy; (3) Catholic: the Church is universal, embracing all in the household of God, not tied to any one culture, nation or race; and (4) Apostolic: the Church's doctrine is that of Christ as He entrusted it to the Apostles.

Especially valuable in this regard is the observation from the *Apologia pro Vita Sua* of the Catholic apologist John Henry Cardinal Newman in describing his reasons for conversion to Catholicism: "In the Catholic Church . . . I recognized at once a reality which was quite a new thing with me. Then I was sensible that I was not making for myself a Church by an effort of thought; I needed not to make an act of faith in her; I had not painfully to force myself into a position, but my mind fell back upon itself in relaxation and in peace, and I gazed at her almost passively as a great objective fact. I looked at her — at her rites, her ceremonial and her precepts — and I said, 'This is a religion.' "

Catholic Communications Foundation • An organization founded in 1968 by the Catholic Fraternal Benefit Societies for the purpose of supporting and expanding the communications apostolate of the Church, most especially through radio and television broadcasting.

Catholic Epistles • Within this phrase the term "catholic" has its original Greek force — universal. Therefore, "catholic epistles" were written to the universal Church as a whole as distinct from a letter to a particular Church in a particular region (e.g., Paul's Letters to the Romans, Corinthians, Galatians, etc.). The following letters are commonly accepted as "catholic epistles": James; 1 and 2 Peter; 1, 2 and 3 John; Jude.

Catholic Foreign Mission Society of America • An American community of priests and brothers, more popularly known as Maryknoll. Organized in 1911 by Fathers James Walsh and Thomas Price and with episcopal approval, Maryknoll recruits, trains and sends missionaries overseas. As of this writing, there are 675 Maryknoll priests in the community, serving throughout the United States and around the world. Maryknoll also has priestly and lay associates who share in some of the society's missionary work, usually for a prescribed, temporary period.

In 1912 a community of sisters was founded in New York, called the Maryknoll Sisters of Saint Dominic. They number 875 and are also missioned around the world.

Catholic Household Blessings and Prayers • A companion volume to the ritual *Book of Blessings* (the English translation of the Latin *De Benedictionibus*). Whereas the official ritual is, by its nature, primarily for the use of priests and deacons (and lay leaders specifically designated by an Ordinary), *Catholic Household Blessings and Prayers* excerpts from that ritual material intended for use by families and individuals in the "domestic church" of the home.

Part I contains "Daily Blessings," prayers to be said upon rising, for the sanctification of the day's work, when returning home in the evening and at bedside. A rich selection of table prayers is presented, incorporating traditional texts, with graces specifically composed for the various liturgical seasons. Part II is arranged according to the liturgical year with blessings for the Advent Wreath, Nativity Scene, New Year, Lent, Easter and so forth. Specific "feasts and fasts" are presented along with "national days" (George Washington, Mother's Day, Father's Day, Thanksgiving, etc.). Part III is entitled, "Times in Life: Blessings of Family Members," tracing the full "life-cycle" of the average family from before conception, through childhood and adolescence, engagement and marriage, old age, sickness and death. Part IV contains blessings "for various times and places" (and objects). Part V is a treasury of prayers, with selections ranging from the psalms to the traditional litanies (Holy Name, Sacred Heart, Blessed Virgin Mary, St. Joseph), from Eucharistic and Marian devotions to a simplified form of the Liturgy of the Hours (Morning and Evening Prayer).

Catholic Household Blessings and Prayers was conceived by the bishops of the United States as a modern version of the famous *Manual of Prayers* published (along with an even more famous catechism) by the Third Plenary Council of Baltimore in 1888. The bishops of that time saw their *Manual* as providing a source of orthodox devotional prayer and making accessible, through vernacular translation, the too-often unknown or neglected liturgical texts of the Missal and Breviary. In their Foreword to *Catholic Household Blessings and Prayers,* today's bishops say that they "have sought ways in which our Church's liturgy can become a strong and constant source of the 'true Christian spirit' for clergy and laity alike. And so, this book is devoted to that

'bond of prayer' that joins the prayer of the Sunday assembly to the daily prayers of every Catholic, the bond between Roman Catholics of all descriptions and, in many ways, to Jews from whom we have learned so much of our prayer."

Catholic League for Religious and Civil Rights • Founded in 1973 by the late Jesuit priest Virgil Blum, the League was designed to protect the rights of Catholics in the exercise of their Faith and the discharge of their civic responsibilities. One could say that the need for such an organization has always existed in the United States, a nation where Catholics have always been a minority. But it was not until Father Blum, a professor of political science at Marquette University, galvanized Catholics around the country through a participation in local chapters to press their just claims when there was evidence that their rights had been violated that the task was formally undertaken.

This work has been carried out legally when civil attorneys for the League have argued cases in court to defend Catholic citizens against unfair and discriminatory labor practices, to uphold their freedom of conscience in moral and social matters and to enhance parental choice in education. On the educational side, members of the League, clergy and laity alike, have been instructed through conferences, workshops and other forums about claiming their rightful place in society, free of any insinuation that they somehow could not be both Catholic and American at the same time.

In 1990, the national headquarters of the Catholic League moved from Milwaukee to Philadelphia, then to New York two years later.

Catholic Press • The Catholic press, which includes all forms of the written word, is fostered by the Church for the purpose of forming and influencing individuals' opinions in accordance with Catholic principles and teaching. *Inter Mirifica*, the Decree on the Means of Social Communication, teaches that the Catholic press has as one of its purposes that of "bringing a knowledge of the Church to the world and a knowledge of the world to the Church" (IM 137).

While the Church encourages her members to read Catholic publications, *Inter Mirifica* cautions that "these must deserve the name of being Catholic" (n. 140). With the many events taking place which touch upon Christian principles, the Catholic press is charged "to interpret these in accordance with the Magisterium of the Church" (IM 141).

Catholic Press Association (CPA) • The association of Catholic newspapers, magazines and general publishers and their staff members in the United States and Canada. The CPA was founded in 1911 in Columbus, Ohio. Over 300 publication/publisher members, 180 of their staff personnel and 100 other members of various categories support a variety of services and programs determined by the board of directors of the association — at the service of CPA members and the Church at large — and carried out by the executive director and his staff. It is affiliated with the International Catholic Union of the Press which is recognized by the Holy See.

Catholic Truth Society • The organization founded in England in 1868 and reestablished in 1884 to promote the truths of the Catholic Faith. According to one of its pamphlets, the society has four objectives: to publish and disseminate low-priced devotional works; to assist all Catholics in obtaining a better knowledge of their religion; to spread among non-Catholics information about the Faith; to assist with the circulation of Catholic books.

Catholic University of America, The • The Catholic University of America was founded in 1889 by the bishops of the United States and is significantly subsidized by them to this day. It is located within the District of Columbia and adjoins the property of the National Shrine of the Immaculate Conception. The archbishop of Washington serves as its chancellor. It has a wide variety of civil undergraduate and graduate degree programs, and over the years it has also acquired the privilege of conferring pontifical or ecclesiastical degrees in philosophy, theology and canon law. Although a large number of its graduate students are priests and religious, all programs, both civil and ecclesiastical, are open to qualified applicants. A considerable number of religious houses and seminaries (both Latin and Byzantine) have been established near the university. The university also sponsors a number of academic journals and reviews, has its own book-publishing house and lends support to several scholarly and pastoral research institutes.

Catholic Worker Movement • A movement inspired by Peter Maurin (1877-1949) and Dorothy Day (1897-1980), founded in 1933 to raise the consciousness of Catholics regarding the situation of the poor and homeless and to minister to their needs. Day and Maurin sought to put the axiom "from each according to his abilities and to each according to his needs" into practice by promoting farming communes and by promoting greater awareness of the plight of the poor and destitute.

This movement has often been characterized as radical because of its opposition to the existing social order and its theoretical roots in Marxism, but it is at heart a lay-Catholic attempt to deal with pressing social and economic problems. It stressed the suffering of the poor and the inequalities brought about by the American economy and American racism and was not as politicized as many think. Day and Maurin propagated their ideas through weekly discussions and their paper *The Catholic Worker*, and believed Catholics should share in the lot of the poor as did they.

Neither Maurin nor Day pretended to be theologians, but their ideas were well expressed by Paul Hanley Furfey of The Catholic University of America. They rejected the traditional natural law approach to morality and social issues but invoked what they considered to be a scriptural and "supernatural" approach to resolving ethical problems, calling for a society based on grace and faith. They believed that their approach to poverty and the needs of the poor properly embodied this "pistic" (faith-based) society they espoused. During the Second World War, the Catholic Worker movement was strongly pacifist and lost much of its following, but since that time, Catholic Worker houses have sprung up all across America and have been a most effective witness by the Church to the poor.

Catholic Youth Organization • Its origins go back to 1930, when Cardinal Mundelein of Chicago directed Auxiliary Bishop Bernard J. Sheil to institute an organization under the auspices of the Church whereby the spiritual, mental and physical development of Catholic young people could be promoted. Since its creation more than sixty years ago in an urban and heavily Catholic area, the Catholic Youth Organization has expanded into socially and geographically diverse regions throughout the United States. Today, many dioceses in the United States have their own Catholic Youth Organization programs and their own

diocesan directors. In some cases, however, Catholic Youth Organization activities in a diocese come under the authority and supervision of a more general youth ministry.

Although the activities of the Catholic Youth Organization are not restricted to athletics, they are by and large athletic in nature. By offering Catholic young people the opportunity to compete against each other in various sports, the Catholic Youth Organization also affords them the opportunity to acquire and develop lifelong virtues and values such as strength of character, commitment to fair play and the acceptance of victory and defeat in life. Further, the Catholic Youth Organization shows that all of life, even leisure and recreation, has a spiritual and moral foundation from which an ultimate meaning can be derived.

Catholicos • The bishops of a number of major sees in nations on the eastern borders of the Roman Empire assumed this title in the early centuries of the Church. The title, meaning "universal" bishop, is used today by the heads of the ancient Oriental Churches of Armenia, Georgia and Assyria.

Catholics in Statuary Hall • There are thirteen Catholics honored with statues in the United States Capitol, Washington, D.C. Since each state may nominate two noteworthy people, these thirteen Catholics represent roughly half of the current Catholic percentage of the American population. Remarkable, however, is the large number of professed religious represented by statues, quite disproportionate to their presence both in the Church and in the country at large. There is one Catholic nun, Mother Joseph (1823-1902), representing Washington, a Sister of Charity of Providence, a missionary, educator and builder, honored in 1953 by the American Institute of Architects as "The First Architect of the Pacific Northwest."

There are four priests, all members of religious orders, honored with statues. The two Jesuits, Father Jacques Marquette (1637-1675), Wisconsin, and Father Eusebio Kino (1645-1711), Arizona, are honored for their efforts at exploring the Midwest and Southwest in their missionary endeavors. Similarly, the Franciscan Father Junípero Serra (1713-1784), California, is noted for his establishment of numerous California missions, among them San Diego and San Francisco, and for teaching the Indians means of self-sufficiency. Father Damien de Veuster (1840-1889), Hawaii, a priest of the Sacred Hearts Congregation, ministered to the lepers of Molokai; in time he himself succumbed to their disease.

The remaining Catholics honored in Statuary Hall distinguished themselves in the secular spheres of government, law and the military. Charles Carroll of Carrollton (1737-1832), Maryland, the brother of the first Catholic bishop in the United States, John Carroll, was a statesman and signer of the Declaration of Independence. Dr. John McLoughlin (1784-1857), Oregon, was a physician, who mastered the Indian languages and became a trader in the vast Northwest territories, where he was recognized as the chief authority prior to the establishment of the provisional government.

Brigadier General James Shields (1806-1879), Illinois, emigrated from Ireland, fought in the Mexican War and the Civil War, served briefly as governor of the Oregon Territory and was elected to the U.S. Senate as the only man ever to represent three different states, Illinois, Minnesota and Missouri. Edward Douglass White (1845-1921), Louisiana, was educated at Mount Saint Mary's College, Emmitsburg, Maryland; Jesuit College, New Orleans; and

Georgetown College, Washington, D.C.; he was appointed chief justice of the United States by President Taft in 1910. John E. Kenna (1848-1893), West Virginia, fought in the Confederate Army and later represented West Virginia in both the U.S. House of Representatives and the U.S. Senate.

John Burke (1859-1937), North Dakota, nicknamed "Honest John," as governor of North Dakota, rid the state of corrupt political control; he was appointed treasurer of the United States by President Wilson in 1913. Dennis Chavez (1888-1962), New Mexico, a graduate of Georgetown University Law School, when in Congress, supported the New Deal and championed the rights of Indians and Puerto Ricans. Patrick Anthony McCarran (1876-1954), Nevada, served as chief justice of the Nevada supreme court from 1917 to 1919; elected to the U.S. Senate in 1932, he was an early advocate of a separate U.S. Air Force and sponsored significant legislation in the 1950s.

Cause • Broadly, a cause (*causa*) is any trial conducted in an ecclesiastical court (cf. Canon 1400). More specifically, though, the term usually refers to the complex quasi-judicial process of investigation by which a Servant of God is proposed for canonization. These are conducted by the Congregation for the Causes of Saints. (Cf. Blessed; Saints.)

Causes, Four • A cause is that from which something else proceeds with a dependence in being. In trying to understand what it is that makes any entity or state of affairs to be the sort of thing it is, philosophers distinguish four factors that exercise a direct, or causal, influence upon it. Following Aristotle and Scholastic philosophers generally, these four causal factors have come to be called the "four causes" and are individually known as the material cause, the formal cause, the efficient or agent cause, and the final cause.

Since in common parlance we restrict our use of the word "cause" to refer to the agent or efficient cause, we find it difficult to grasp the important philosophical point at stake here: The agent is not the only factor upon which an entity depends for its being. To take a simple example, consider the causal factors that produced the statue of David. The name of Michelangelo immediately springs to mind when we think of the cause of the statue. But philosophers teach us that "Who made it?" is not the only question that can be asked about the constitutive elements in the being of an entity. Three other questions come to mind: What is this? What is it made of? What did the agent have in mind when he made this? Taken together with the efficient or agent cause, the answers to these questions — when they are available — provide a complete causal explanation of a particular entity.

With regard to the statue of David, the form, or formal cause, constitutes the statue to be the sort of thing it is, viz., a statue representing the youthful King David. The material chosen by Michelangelo for the final version of the statue was marble. As the material "cause," marble is crucial to making this statue to be what it is. A pencil drawing of the figure of David would be a very different sort of thing indeed. The final cause is that objective which Michelangelo intended in sculpting the statue, that which he had in mind in producing the statue and shaping it the way he did. The "why," or final cause, is the intention of the agent. Its realization is intrinsic to the being of the effect that is produced.

Causal explanation is fundamental in science and philosophy. It has also had many important uses in Catholic theology. Thus, for example, the unity of body and soul has been explained in terms of material and formal cause. In this way, creation is affirmed, but pantheism and cosmogenesis are ruled out. In addition, the theological account of the doctrine of creation has employed the four causes: God is the efficient and final cause, but not the formal and material cause, of the universe. Everything that exists depends upon God's agency and plan, but He does not enter into composition with anything created. Sacramental theology has also drawn upon causal explanation in order to explain how the sacraments give grace by effecting what they signify.

Cautiones • The *cautiones*, or promises, are the written or verbal guarantees required of Catholics who are seeking to enter a mixed marriage. They are required for either a dispensation from the impediment of disparity of cult or the permission for a mixed-religion marriage.

The Catholic must declare that he or she will remove all dangers to the practice of the Faith and must promise to do all in his or her power to see that any children born of the marriage will be baptized and raised as Catholics. These promises may be made in writing or verbally in the presence of witnesses. The *cautiones* are no longer required of the non-Catholic party (cf. Canon 1125).

Celebrant • The bishop, priest or deacon who presides at a liturgical function. Because the whole Christian community celebrates, each according to his or her own role or function, some prefer to call the presiding cleric the "president of the assembly" or even the "presider," neither of which titles reflects a uniquely sacral role.

Celebret • Latin for "let him celebrate," this term refers to a document carried by priests when outside their diocese to attest to the fact that they are authentic priests, duly ordained, in good standing and within the limits of ecclesiastical law. The origin of the celebret can be traced to commendatory letters for the clergy from at least the fourteenth century. This document is issued by the chancery of each diocese under the authority of the local bishop, or Ordinary. While in some places the celebret is an actual letter, in other places (e.g., Rome) it is a card bearing the priest's name and station and the signature of the curial official responsible for the clergy. It is like an ecclesiastical passport or I.D.

At one time, no one could celebrate Mass in private or in public without presenting his celebret. Presently, the Code of Canon Law still requires it, but the bearer can celebrate without it in private if it is morally certain that he is a priest. However, for a longer period of time or in the case of dispensing the sacraments to the faithful, the celebret must be presented to the proper superior of the place (cf. Canon 903).

At the present time, "celebret" also refers to the permission granted by Rome to priests who wish to celebrate the so-called Tridentine Mass or Mass of St. Pius V according to the 1962 Missal. In such cases, the Ordinary of the priest's diocese must be notified.

Celestial Hierarchy • The ranking of the angels in heaven according to perfection and duty. God alone is sovereign in heaven; however, the angels form nine choirs, with the lower grades being subject to the higher. The nine choirs of angels are: Seraphim, Cherubim, Thrones, Dominations, Powers, Virtues, Principalities, Archangels and Angels. (Cf. Angel.)

Celibacy • The practice of perfect continence by priests and bishops meant to foster single-minded devotion to God and service in the ministry. According to the long-standing discipline of the Latin Church, the rule of celibacy forbids marriage by priests and bishops, and it normally excludes married persons from ordination.

Married men may be ordained to the permanent diaconate, but they may not contract a second marriage after the death of their spouses; unmarried men may not marry after ordination to the diaconate. Under a recent pastoral provision for former Anglican clergy who have been approved for ordination in the Roman Catholic Church, those who are married prior to reception into the Church and ordination are permitted to remain married.

The practice and discipline are held to be warranted by Christ Himself (Mt 19:11-12) and encouraged by St. Paul (1 Cor 7:32). The earliest formulation of this discipline occurred at the Council of Elvira (A.D. 306), although evidence has recently been offered that suggests that the discipline may be of apostolic authority. Subsequent conciliar and papal enactments reinforced the discipline in the Western Church. The Eastern Church permits deacons and priests who are married before ordination to remain so; celibacy is required of bishops, and of unmarried deacons and priests after ordination.

Cell • The original meaning of cell in religious use comes from the Latin *cella*, meaning a small room; it was thus applied to the living quarters allotted to an individual monk, hermit or other religious. A small group of monks who live apart from their home monastery are also said to constitute a cell.

In the early Church, a small chapel erected over a tomb was likewise called a cell. Cardinals meeting in conclave to elect a new Pope are assigned small Vatican apartments called cells.

In the context of politics or sociology, a cell is a basic unit of an organization; usually, it refers to a small, effective group established for a specific purpose as, for example, a cell in Catholic Action may meet for the common goal of prayer, work or study.

Cellarer • The ancient monastic title of the monk responsible for all of the temporal goods and business transactions of the monastery. Today the term "procurator" is more commonly used.

Celtic Cross • The Celtic cross is distinguished by the circle at the intersection of the crossbar and upright shaft, usually with a continuous weaving line intertwined with the circle and cross arms; this serves as a double symbol of eternity and unity, both that of the Son with the Father and the Holy Spirit and of the believer with the Trinity, the common theme of St. Patrick's preaching. The Celtic cross comes from Ireland, where it is still commonly found; similarly, it is used to mark an object as having an association with Ireland.

Celtic Rite • This is not so much a single organized Western rite, like the Milanese, as much as a collection of rites and usages of the ancient Churches of Ireland, England and Wales. The *Bangor Antiphonary* (seventh century), the *Bobbio Missal* (seventh century) and the *Stowe Missal* (ninth century) are our principal sources of information, and they show a basically Gallican Liturgy with interesting variants.

The Celts had their own Easter date (which they gave up at the Synod of Whitby in 664) and their Mass, at which the gifts were prepared at the beginning of the rite. This feature is a Gallican characteristic found in the old Dominican Rite, probably borrowed from the East, which still has its Proskomide, or Preparation of the Gifts, before the Divine Liturgy proper.

The Mass of the Celtic Rite began with many *apologiae*, or prayers of unworthiness,

Celtic reliquary (eleventh century)

and then followed the Liturgy of the Word in the Roman pattern, except that between the Epistle and Gospel was a litany — another Eastern addition. The Offertory was elaborate and was followed by the reading of the diptychs (two panels containing the names of the living and the dead who should be prayed for at that liturgy). The Canon was the Roman Canon, with more than a hundred saints named, many Old Testament names and Irish saints as well.

Cemetery • A word deriving from the Greek *koimeterion* for "sleeping place" or "resting chamber." From earliest times, Christians have buried their dead underground (e.g., the catacombs), under churches or in the ground directly. Catholics are generally to be buried in "blessed ground," that is, in a Catholic cemetery. Where such a cemetery does not exist, the individual grave is to be blessed before burial.

Cenacle • From the Latin *cenaculum*, cenacle literally means "dining room." For Christians, it refers specifically to the Upper Room (Mt 26:17-19, Mk 14:12-16, Lk 22:7-

13) which the Apostles prepared for the Lord's celebration of His Last Supper. The cenacle was also the site of Christ's resurrection appearance to the Apostles (Jn 20:19) and the descent of the Holy Spirit upon the Apostles (Acts 1:13-14, 2:1-36).

Tradition places the cenacle in the southwest quarter of Jerusalem. Early reverence for the spot prompted the Emperor Hadrian to order its destruction and replacement with a pagan temple. This desecration helps the modern archaeologist in confirming its location; crusaders, using stone of the Herodian era, contemporary with the Upper Room's construction, built a chapel there. Today this chapel is a mosque, although the Islamic authorities allow the Patriarch of Jerusalem to celebrate Mass there once a year, on Holy Thursday.

Given its great significance at the inception of the Church, the cenacle has been called the first Christian church.

Cenobite • The term "cenobite" has the same meaning as our present-day understanding of "monk." As opposed to hermit or anchorite, the cenobite lives his or her religious life primarily in community. Benedictines, Cistercians and Eastern Rite monks are cenobites because they belong to a community. Other monastics such as the Carthusians, the Camaldolese and the Valambrosians can also be called cenobites because their life is a combination of the eremitic and the cenobitic. The term derives from that used to designate a group (*cenobium*) of monks who came to live together in the first centuries of the Church. (Cf. Monk; Monasticism; Benedictines.)

Censer • As its name implies, a censer is an instrument having to do with incense and, particularly in ecclesiastical parlance, its use in the Divine Liturgy. The shape and make of a censer is as varied as the purpose or culture for and in which it is used.

Among the chief purposes of incense, and thus of a censer, is that of sacred worship.

In the Judeo-Christian Tradition, incense has always played an important role (cf. Ex 30:1-8; 37:25-29). The liturgical censer or thurible, then, is a metal receptacle (usually bronze or brass, and sometimes silver- or gold-plated), in which burning charcoal or wood is placed and over which is poured the incense to be burned. To this receptacle are attached chains which enable the cover to be lifted from the bowl part of the censer and which also enable the thurifer and those others who use it to carry and swing it for the incensation of the Blessed Sacrament, the altar, the sacred ministers or the congregation (cf. Ex 27:3; Nm 16:6-7; Lk 1:9-11; Rv 8:3). (Cf. Thurible.)

Censor of Books • A person appointed by a local Ordinary or by an episcopal conference to read books that are submitted with a request for ecclesiastical permission for publication, and to give his opinion about them. He is to look at the teaching on faith and morals contained in the book and determine whether or not it is in accord with the Magisterium. He is to give his opinion in writing to the Ordinary, who then may choose to grant the required permission (cf. Canon 830).

Censure • One of the two broad categories of ecclesiastical penalties outlined in Canon 1312. Censures are medicinal penalties, which means that their primary purpose is the correction of the offender. They stand in basic contrast to expiatory penalties, whose primary purpose is the protection of justice and good order. Canons 1331-1335 establish that there are three types of censures in the Church: excommunication, interdict and suspension.

Most censures can be imposed through a *ferendae sententiae* process, while others (fewer, and generally more serious in nature) may be imposed *latae sententiae*. Canon 1347 specifies, however, that censures imposed differ from expiatory penalties in that they cannot be imposed validly unless the offender has been previously warned of the danger of incurring the penalty and has been given a suitable amount of time to withdraw from contumacy.

The fact that censures are directed to the reform of the individual results in another difference between them and expiatory penalties in the matter of their remission. Censures are not imposed for specific periods of time (because a predetermined period might or might not accomplish the reform of the individual). Rather, they are remitted when the offender has withdrawn from contumacy. This is considered done when the offender, for example, makes a sincere promise to repair the harm caused by his or her actions. Upon such withdrawal from contumacy, the offender has a right to the remission of the censure. Special rules apply, moreover, where the remission of censures is sought within the sacrament of Penance, especially when the remission of the censure was reserved to higher ecclesiastical authority. (Cf. Penalty, Ecclesiastical.)

Centesimus Annus • Latin for "the one-hundredth year," it is the title for the ninth encyclical letter of John Paul II's papacy. The document, dated May 1, 1991, commemorates the one-hundredth anniversary of Pope Leo XIII's encyclical *Rerum Novarum* (On Capital and Labor). In its effort to draw attention to the Church's social teachings, the papal letter addresses a variety of topics, including the necessary socioeconomic conditions for justice, the fundamental rights of workers, the rights to private property and ownership and the interrelationship between the free market and the welfare state, among others.

Cerecloth (Chrismale) • A linen cloth, waxed on one side, which formerly was required to be placed over the altar or altar stone to soak up any chrism left from the altar's consecration or blessing and to keep the Precious Blood, if spilled, from soaking into the stone of the altar. Because it is no longer required, the cerecloth is rarely used today.

Ceremonial of Bishops • The *editio typica* (official Latin edition), "revised by decree of the Second Vatican Ecumenical Council and promulgated by authority of Pope John Paul II," was published in Rome in 1985 and in English (Collegeville: The Liturgical Press) in 1989. The *Ceremonial* originates in the *Ordines Romani*, directives for papal liturgies in the late-seventh century. Pope Clement VIII's *Caeremoniale Episcoporum* (1600) codified and clarified the rubrics of liturgical books issued after the Council of Trent, and the last Tridentine *Caeremoniale* was issued under Pope Leo XIII (1886).

The new *Ceremonial of Bishops* is a concise presentation of rubrics for all of the revised rites promulgated according to the norms laid down in Vatican II's Constitution on the Sacred Liturgy (*Sacrosanctum Concilium*). Like its predecessors, it is not, strictly speaking, a liturgical book to be used in actual celebrations but is designed to be "helpful to bishops, to the several categories of ministers, and to masters of ceremonies" in planning and practicing for liturgies at which the bishop presides.

Though performing a function identical to that of the Tridentine *Caeremoniale*, the new edition is clearly a product of Vatican II. Not only does the *Ceremonial* faithfully present (and, where necessary, clarify) the rubrics of the revised rites, it also reflects the sobriety and simplicity which Vatican II rightly saw as the genius of the Roman Rite (cf. SC 34). Thus the new *Ceremonial's* principal goal is "a liturgy for bishops that is genuine, simple, clear, dignified, and pastorally effective" (decree of promulgation).

Part I of the *Ceremonial*, "General Considerations," begins with a number of important quotations from Vatican II's Decree on the Pastoral Office of the Bishops in the Church (*Christus Dominus*) and the Dogmatic Constitution on the Church (*Lumen Gentium*). In these foundational documents from the Council, Christ is seen as alive, present and continually active in His holy Catholic Church, and His holy Catholic Church is alive and present in each local (or "particular") diocesan Church. Rejecting secular models, the *Ceremonial* adopts the Council's vision of the Church: not simply a voluntary association of like-minded individuals or the smaller administrative unit of an international organization, but rather a gift from the Father brought to life by the Spirit, the Bride of Christ issuing from His pierced side and caring for her children as a mother. It is from this ecclesial perspective that the *Ceremonial* presents the importance of a liturgy at which the bishop presides. Of each particular Church the bishop is father and head, in communion with the Pope and under his authority. "In the person of the bishop, with the presbyters gathered round him, the Lord Jesus Christ, the High Priest, is present in the midst of the faithful" (n. 8). Far from being "a mere display of ceremony," liturgical celebrations led by the bishop are a *manifestation* of the Church. The bishop presides "not to give added outward solemnity to the rite, but to make the celebration a more striking sign of the mystery of the Church" (n. 18). Thus these celebrations should also be a *model* for the liturgical life of the diocese, "shining examples of active participation by the people. The whole gathered community should thus take part through song, dialogue, prayerful silence and attentiveness" (n. 12). The complementarity of the hierarchical priesthood and the priesthood of the baptized should be evident: "All those present have the right and the duty to carry out their parts in the different ways corresponding to their differences in order and office. . . . This way of celebration manifests the Church in its varieties of orders and ministries as a body whose individual members form a unity" (n. 19). Extolling the cathedral as "the express image of Christ's visible Church, praying, singing and worshiping on earth . . . the image of Christ's Mystical Body, whose members are joined together in an organism of charity" (n. 43), the *Ceremonial* offers detailed observations on chair, altar, tabernacle, sanctuary, ambo, baptistery, vesting room and sacristy. Diocesan officials are charged to care for the treasures of the past while insuring that newly commissioned or purchased articles meet the standards of "noble simplicity, refinement, gracefulness and artistic excellence" (n. 38) and that the liturgical books are "current editions . . . beautifully printed and bound" (n. 115).

Part II presents a detailed account of the "Stational Mass of the Diocesan Bishop." Formerly called "Pontifical Mass," the new title evokes the ancient custom of the Pope's presence among his people in the various Churches of Rome, especially during Lent. What, where, when, by whom: the *Ceremonial* examines almost every moment and movement of the Eucharistic celebration. The scope is quite comprehensive: signs of reverence in general, toward altar and Gospel, toward the bishop and other persons, incensation, sign of peace, hands raised and outstretched, hands outstretched over persons or objects, hands joined, use of holy water, the arrangement and ritual gestures of concelebrants (n. 153) and the reintroduction of festive ceremonial to surround the Eucharistic Prayer (n. 155).

In Part III, the *Ceremonial* echoes Vatican II's *Liturgy Constitution* by providing for prayer to enhance and extend the power of the Eucharistic Sacrifice. The Liturgy of the Hours in the cathedral church is "most highly recommended" especially during the Easter Triduum and at Christmas, and this form of prayer is to be encouraged in the parishes. Sunday Vespers as the completion of the Lord's Day observance, "Celebrations of the Word of God" and "Vigils" are encouraged as opportunities at which the bishop may exercise his teaching office by preaching to the people and offering sacramental catechesis.

Part IV presents the liturgical year as possessing a "distinct sacramental force and efficacy" because by means of its observance the faithful "lay hold of [the mysteries of redemption], enter into communion with them and live by them" (n. 232). Advent at the cathedral "should be marked by a moderation that reflects the character of the season but does not anticipate the full joy of Christmas itself" (n. 236). On Christmas Eve the bishop presides at an extended vigil (n. 238), on Epiphany the dates of the movable feasts are to be proclaimed (n. 240). There is to be a festive procession on Candlemas (n. 241), a penitential one on the First Sunday of Lent (n. 249) and a memorial one on November 2 (n. 233). Holy Week and the Triduum are set forth in great detail, and the Easter Vigil is marked not only by the sacraments of initiation, but by the bishop's threefold solemn intonation of the ancient Paschal Alleluia. To make the Fifty Days of Eastertide a truly festive experience, extensive suggestions are provided for various forms of liturgical celebration. All of this is to link the liturgy presided over by the bishop with the Christian life lived by the faithful "that what we celebrate and proclaim with lips we may inwardly believe, and what we inwardly believe we may bring

to bear on our personal and public lives" (n. 232).

The *Ceremonial*, in Part V, presents the bishop as "chief steward of the mysteries of God and the overseer of all liturgical life in the Church entrusted to his care" (n. 404). Beyond his obviously important role in the Christian Initiation of Adults, Confirmation and Holy Orders, the bishop is urged to celebrate the other sacraments for and among his people as well, for example, "occasional marriages . . . especially of the poor . . . mindful of the Lord's presence at Cana" (n. 598).

Part VI gives directions for the bishop's celebration of various sacramentals, Part VII surveys the principal celebrations in the bishop's life from appointment until death and Part VIII deals with important celebrations pertaining to the government of the diocese. Appendices provide notes on vesture and the ranking of liturgical days.

Although a similar *Ceremonial*, "for use in smaller churches," is presently in preparation, the *Ceremonial of Bishops* would be a helpful guide for anyone studying or planning the celebration of the rites as revised by Vatican II.

Ceremony • Refers to the complexus of signs, gestures, vesture, objects and movements that surround and embellish the liturgy of the Church. The essential sacramental signs may not be changed, but auxiliary signs in the ceremonies have changed from time to time through the ages.

Certitude • The adherence of the mind to any proposition without fear that this proposition is untrue. Canon law requires that judges in tribunal cases arrive at moral certitude in making their decisions. This is a specific kind of certitude that is based not on preponderance of evidence but on the belief, attained from the evidence presented, that the proposition is true beyond a reasonable doubt. Moral certitude means that there is the possibility but not the probability that the proposition is not true.

Metaphysical certitude is that certitude of a proposition whereby there is neither the possibility nor the probability that the opposite is true or that the proposition is false.

Chains of St. Peter • Chains preserved in Rome at San Pietro ai Vincoli that are said to be those that bound St. Peter prisoner, as recorded in Acts 12. As a feast, it was formerly celebrated on August 1.

Chair: See **Cathedra**

Chair of St. Peter • A throne known in the sixth century with parts that go back to the early years of Christianity. It was ensconced in Bernini's magnificent Altar of the Chair in St. Peter's Basilica in the seventeenth century. The feast celebrated on February 22 emphasized the primacy and authority of Peter, first at Antioch and later in Rome.

Chair of St. Peter, St. Peter's Basilica

Chalcedon, Council of • The fourth ecumenical council (A.D. 451) defined that Jesus Christ is one Son, one Person, with two complete and distinct natures: a divine nature consubstantial with the Father, a human nature consubstantial with us. This most significant Christological council brought to conclusion a quarter-century of fierce theological and ecclesiastical debate.

Nestorianism held that Christ was two Persons (human and divine) united in an intimate but accidental fashion, something like God dwelling in a human. The Council

of Ephesus, strongly influenced by the theology and terminology of St. Cyril of Alexandria, insisted on the unity of Christ but, to the dismay of Antiochene bishops, gave less attention to the reality and integrity of the humanity of Jesus.

Representatives of Cyril and the Antiochenes came to an agreement in the Formula (or Symbol) of Reunion in 433, a forerunner of the definition of Chalcedon. Extremists on both sides were unhappy with the formula.

After the death of Cyril (444), the aged and theologically inept Archimandrite Eutyches proposed an extreme Alexandrian position: That Christ was *from* two natures but merged *into* one nature. A more developed form of this Monophysitism held that the human nature of Jesus was transformed into His Divine Nature or was "swallowed up" by the Divine Nature.

Opposition to Eutyches led to his condemnation and deposition, but with the support of Dioscorus, patriarch of Alexandria, he persuaded Emperor Theodosius II to call a council at Ephesus in 449. Dioscorus manipulated the council, excluding opponents of Eutyches, refusing a hearing to the papal legates and intimidating antagonistic bishops by sending in soldiers, monks and a corps of stretcher bearers. The uproar caused Pope St. Leo to call it a *Latrocinium* or Robber Synod. It reinstated Eutyches, deposed and exiled Flavian, patriarch of Constantinople, and deposed other bishops opposed to Monophysitism.

Remonstrances of the Pope were unheeded, but in 450 the emperor died and was succeeded by his sister Pulcheria and her consort Marcian. A council was convened in a suburb of Constantinople, Chalcedon, with more than five hundred bishops, including two papal representatives. The doctrinal letter or *Tome* of Pope Leo to Flavian in 449 was accepted ("Peter has spoken through the mouth of Leo"), and a formula of belief was elaborated.

Rome refused to accept Canon 28 of this council, which gave to the See of Constantinople a patriarchal authority second only to Rome's.

Chaldean Rite • This form of Christian worship is the liturgy used by Catholics of the Chaldean Rite chiefly in Iraq. It is also called the East Syrian Rite, indicating its origin from the primitive liturgies of Jerusalem and Antioch and distinguishing it from the rite of the Jacobites and Syrian Catholics. It is also used by Nestorians; indeed, in the sixteenth century those who were reunited to Rome brought this rite with them into full Catholic unity.

The languages of this rite are Syriac and Aramaic, although contemporary vernaculars are also used. Although this rite is similar to the West Syrian Liturgy, a different calendar exists, as well as different gestures and prayers (these latter are primitive and simple, thus showing great antiquity), sometimes to the accompaniment of cymbals and triangles. There are three anaphoras or Eucharistic Prayers. That of Addai and Mari is used on most Sundays, while the other two are not often used. The Canon of Addai and Mari is a liturgical oddity, in that its primitive form had no Words of Institution, which fact had caused liturgists to speculate and propose various theories. The Preparation of the Gifts takes place at the beginning of the liturgy with the prayer, "To You, O Lord," and the incensation of the gifts and the whole church. The Liturgy of the Word opens with

the Trisagion ("Holy God, Holy Mighty One, Holy Immortal One," etc.), after which four readings are read, each followed by a litany led by the deacon. The Creed is said with the *Filioque*.

The Eucharistic Prayer has long intercessions before the Epiclesis. Before the Fraction, the hands of the celebrant are incensed. After Communion, the Mass quickly concludes.

Chalice • The English derivative of the Latin *calix*, this refers to the cup or goblet used for the consecration of the wine at Mass. Throughout the Church's history chalices have had various styles, shapes and sizes. When Communion under both species was common in the patristic era, chalices such as that from Ardagh were very large and had handles on both sides, presumably so that the faithful could communicate easily. With the passage to a time when Communion was administered only under one species, the size of chalices began to shrink, and they tended to become elongated so that they could be seen by all when the priest raised them after the consecration of the Mass. After the Council of Trent, they were commonly between eight and eleven inches high, with a base as wide or wider than the width of the cup portion to provide adequate support (otherwise, the chalice might be top-heavy, causing spills); a stem with a knob midway between the base and the cup connects these, and, of course, the cup, which may vary in size as well as in style. Most chalices are fashioned out of sterling silver (which may or may not be gold-plated), of gold or other precious or even more common metals, such as brass. Formerly, it was required by liturgical law that the inside of the cup be gold-plated if it was not of this material, no matter what the rest of the chalice was made of. There were some exceptions in some Renaissance chalices which had cups of coveted Murano crystal or rock crystal. Nevertheless these were highly ornamented chalices according to the style of the day — Baroque or the later Rococo.

The present legislation is that the chalice be made from solid materials considered noble in the particular country. The material used must not be easily broken or damaged; the cup portion of the chalice, which is to contain the Precious Blood of the Lord, must be fashioned out of a material which does not absorb liquids. Likewise, all the vessels which are to be used for the celebration of Mass must have been made for that purpose (cf. *Institutio Generalis Missalis Romani*, nn. 290, 291; John Paul II, "Instruction Concerning Worship of the Eucharistic Mystery" [*Inaestimabile Donum*], April 17, 1980, n. 16).

Chalice of Pope Pius IX

today refers to several officials of the Church.

(1) The Cardinal Chamberlain, or *Camerlengo*, of the Holy Roman Church assumes the responsibility for the temporal and governmental affairs of the Church while the Holy See is vacant.

(2) The Chamberlain of the College of Cardinals oversees the fiscal affairs of the Sacred College and records the business of consistories.

(3) The Chamberlains of the Sword and Cape were formerly laymen drawn from the nobility who attended the Pope during solemn ceremonies. This office was abolished by Pope Paul VI in 1968.

(4) Papal Chamberlain was an honorific bestowed upon priests, carrying with it the title of Very Reverend Monsignor. In 1969 it was replaced with the title of Chaplain of His Holiness and the title of Reverend Monsignor.

Chalice Veil (also Peplum and Sudarium) • The cloth used during Mass to cover the chalice before the Offertory and after the reception of Holy Communion. It is made of the same color and material as the chasuble of the Mass; however, the veil may "always be white in color" (*Eucharistiae Sacramentum* IV, 80). The veil is also referred to as the "peplum" or "sudarium."

Chamberlain • Originally a court official in the papal and most royal courts, this title

Chambre Ardente • French for "burning room," the *chambre ardente* was a commission created by the French Parliament in 1547, mainly for the purpose of trying heretics, especially the Protestant Huguenots, or followers of the Calvinist Hugues Besançon. The name was given perhaps because of the severity shown by this commission to those who were tried there. It is also possible that this name came from the fact that the room in which this commission tried cases was lighted by burning torches. Louis XIV also established a court to attempt to stamp out witchcraft and sorcery, which likewise received this appellation.

Chancel • That part of a church which includes the altar, space for clergy and sometimes space for the choir: the sanctuary area. Originally, the laity were not permitted in the chancel. Modern architecture and liturgical practice have generally made the distinction of chancel from the rest of the church less significant.

Chancellor • The chancellor of a diocese is the official appointed by the bishop whose primary obligation is the maintenance of the diocesan archives. Under present canon law, the chancellor need not be a priest, and in fact several bishops in the United States have appointed laypersons or religious as chancellors.

Although the chancellor's position was officially that of diocesan archivist, even in the 1917 Code it was required that it be filled by a priest. In this country and others, the chancellor was often given numerous delegated faculties to grant dispensations and to make other decisions on behalf of the bishop. Hence, the position unofficially became much more than that of a record keeper. With the promulgation of the revised Code and the possibility of appointing non-priests as chancellors, there is a trend to utilize the office more along the lines envisioned in the Code (cf. Canon 482).

Chancery • In the United States and certain other countries, "chancery" was the term commonly used to describe the administrative offices of a diocese or archdiocese. The term is not found in canon law and has been supplanted by the more accurate and official term "diocesan curia" in many places.

Properly speaking, chancery is a term from the Anglo-Saxon common law system. The chancery is the court of equity where certain types of cases are decided not by jury trial but by a kind of equitable decision of the judge.

Chancery, Papal (Apostolic) • An office of the Holy See created in the eleventh century and abolished in 1973, the Apostolic or Papal Chancery had responsibility for the issuance of certain documents, such as papal bulls, and had care of the Pope's leaden seal. Significant in the Middle Ages, the chancery was suppressed by Pope Paul VI in his restructuring of the Roman Curia. The work of the Apostolic Chancery is now done in the Secretariat of State.

Chant • A type of sacred singing. Rooted in ancient Jewish synagogue music and retaining intonation practices from there, Christian chants moved in various directions. Being plainsong or plainchant, it is always linear and correctly performed unaccompanied. Chant can be recitative-like with one note per syllable and having a short two to six tones for an accentus, or it can be more melodic in one of three styles: syllabic, neumatic or melismatic. Texts for the chants are taken largely from the Book of Psalms. Various versions of chants such as Ambrosian, Gallican, Gregorian and Mozarabic have been used throughout the Christian world over the centuries.

Chant, Ambrosian: See **Ambrosian Chant**

Chant, Gregorian: See **Gregorian Chant**

Chantry • (1) An endowment left for Masses for the dead; (2) a chapel where those Masses were said or chanted for the repose of the benefactor whose bequest built it and whose largesse supported the clergy who tended it or said Mass there. It may be a separate building or chapel in a larger church, especially a cathedral.

Chapel • The word is derived from the Latin word *cappa* or cape in the diminutive form *capella*. The cape of St. Martin of Tours was preserved by the Frankish kings in a special room which was named after the cape itself, a capella or chapel. Therefore, the cleric who cared for this shrine was called a "capellanus" or chaplain.

Often informal places of worship were erected where the relics of martyrs were enshrined or on estates of nobles far from the basilicas of the city, where the liturgy could be celebrated except on principal feasts. Today chapels are usually places for Mass in religious houses or institutions, or sometimes additions to larger churches. According to the current Code of Canon Law, chapels are called oratories when set aside by the bishop for divine worship for communities of the faithful, to which other members of the faithful may have access with the consent of the faithful. They are designated as private chapels when permitted by him for the use of one or more individuals according to his prescriptions.

Chapel of Ease • A more convenient or accessible place of worship in a large territorial parish which still falls under the jurisdiction of the local pastor of the mother parish church.

Chaplain • A canonical term that describes a priest to whom is entrusted the pastoral care of a special group of people, such as religious, military, immigrants, hospital patients, etc. Chaplains may be appointed by the bishop for the faithful in certain institutes, such as prisons or hospitals, or for all persons of a particular group or persons who have special needs, such as police, firemen, the handicapped, ethnic groups, etc.

Military chaplains are priests who provide pastoral care to members of the armed services and their families. In many countries such chaplains are also commissioned officers of the military service. While they remain priests affiliated with a religious order or diocese, military chaplains also fall under the primary jurisdiction of the military diocese of their country.

"Chaplain" is also the term used for priests and deacons who accompany or assist bishops who are attending but not actually celebrating liturgical functions.

Finally, a Chaplain of His Holiness is an honorary rank with the title of "Monsignor" that is bestowed by the Holy Father on certain secular priests at the request of their bishop (cf. Canons 564-572).

Chaplet • From the French word meaning wreath or crown, a set of beads strung together for counting prayers. This term is often used for the five-decade rosary (from *rosarium*, "rose-garden"), and is also applied to other devotions which use beads to count prayers or aspirations.

Chapter, Cathedral • During the Merovingian period, a movement developed which promoted a quasi-religious lifestyle among certain members of the diocesan priesthood. These priests, usually those assigned to duties in the diocesan cathedral, gathered on a regular basis for Scripture readings and other pious practices. Eventually these priests, known as canons, came to be highly accomplished liturgists and general advisors to bishops. Often they were specially trained and experienced in theological and moral questions.

By the time of the Council of Trent, the chapter of canons was a legally recognized entity with certain rights and duties peculiar to it in canon law. Their responsibilities in the governance of the diocese at times tended to approach that of the bishop, not always with happy results. They were, in any event, the subject of considerable legislation in the 1917 Code of Canon Law. The 1983 Code has significantly reduced the scope of authority of the chapter of canons, and consequently the amount of legislation devoted to them (cf. Canons 503-510).

Today, the chapter of canons, where it exists, functions primarily as a body of liturgical specialists, in accord with their long-standing talents. Beyond this, only the prescription of Canon 508, whereby a special priest (from the chapter of canons, or otherwise) is to be appointed in each diocese for the absolution of certain *latae sententiae* penalties, maintains any significance in this area.

The practice of establishing chapters of canons did not attract a wide following outside Europe. Indeed they were practically unheard of within the United States. (Cf. Collegiate Church.)

Chapter, Conventual • The membership of a house (*conventum*) of vowed religious gathered in assembly for the purposes of receiving instruction, confessing faults, electing superiors or deliberating about the affairs of the community. Conventual chapters are customarily regular elements of the monthly, weekly and sometimes even daily schedules of religious communities. Along with the common daily celebration of the Liturgy of the Hours and the Eucharist, conventual chapters constitute an important expression of the life, spirit and discipline of such communities. General chapters (representing the entire membership) or provincial chapters (representing the membership in a particular geographical region) are more solemn and less frequent assemblies of the community's membership. The term "chapter" is sometimes used to refer to the membership of a religious community as a corporate body, and also to bodies responsible for the supervision of ecclesiastical institutions of any kind.

Chapter House • Part of a cathedral or monastic complex, often a separate building, set aside for the meetings of the cathedral or conventual chapters. Their design is usually rectangular (though polygonal chapters exist), consisting of one large room with an ample open space in the center, a single row of benches along the walls and an elevated chair at the head for the bishop, abbot or prior.

Chapter of Faults • The chapter of faults is a spiritual exercise observed in certain religious communities. The members of the community gather together and, presided over by the superior, publicly confess faults committed and are given a penance. Sinful matter or sins are never confessed. Rather, the members acknowledge minor violations of the rule or constitutions of the community, such as breaking silence, being late for prayers, etc. The purpose of the chapter of faults is to instill or increase the virtue of humility.

Character • A term referring both to the aggregate of qualities which go together to constitute the distinctive identity of a person and to the permanent spiritual quality imprinted by the sacraments of Baptism, Confirmation and Holy Orders. Character in this second sense should not be thought of as a physical mark or a sense-perceptible quality. Rather, it is a spiritual power through which the recipients of these sacraments are deputed to the worship of God through the Christian Liturgy either for the reception (Baptism and Confirmation) or the transmission (Holy Orders) of the things pertaining to divine worship. This spiritual power is founded upon the believer's configuration to and participation in the priesthood of Christ.

Charismata (also Charisms) • Our English word "charism" is from the Greek *charisma(ta)*, which refers to a "free gift." The term has both a non-technical and a technical sense to it. At a non-technical level *charismata* refers to spiritual gifts in general (Rom 1:11; 5:15 ff.; 11:29; 1 Cor 12:1), eternal life (Rom 6:23) or answers to prayers (2 Cor 1:11). *Charismata* are special gifts which, as service directed to the Lord, manifest the work of God through the Holy Spirit — all for the common good of the body of believers, the Church. This "work of God" includes a myriad of behaviors and especially a knowledge of God, as the following four lists make clear: Romans 12:6-8; 1 Corinthians 12:8-10: 12:28; 12:29-30. The gifts always point to the giver; their authentic use in the Church is a fulfillment of God's work initiated in the Old Testament (e.g., prophetic discernment: 1 Kgs 22:28; gifts of the Spirit for the messianic age: Is 11:2; change of heart: Ez 36:26ff.).

Charismatic Renewal, Catholic • Those belonging to the Charismatic Renewal are sometimes called Catholic Pentecostals. The word "charismatic" has Greek roots and means "gifted." The personal experience that charismatics share is called the "baptism of the Holy Spirit," through which God's Spirit renews them and fills them with grace. Some claim special gifts, such as that of healing or the ability to speak in tongues (*glossolalia*). Charismatics often meet in small groups weekly to pray, sing, share the Spirit and testify about personal faith moments.

The Charismatic Renewal movement gained momentum through the efforts of the Chi-Rho Society of Duquesne University in 1967. In the 1970s international meetings were held at the University of Notre Dame. *New Covenant*, a magazine for Charismatics, is published by Our Sunday Visitor.

In 1976 the American bishops gave cautious support to the movement, and Popes Paul VI and John Paul II have also given the charismatics significant support. The bishops' caution is due to some historical problems of Protestant charismatics, who deny the authority of bishops and the value of sacraments, espousing biblical fundamentalism and group exclusiveness. In recent years the Catholic Charismatic Renewal has become characterized by a strong adherence to the Pope and a lively and biblically rooted devotion to the Eucharist and the Blessed Mother.

Charity • For the Christian, charity is a supernatural virtue that is infused by the grace of God. When charity is infused, the Christian loves God supremely and loves others with the love of God. Love of God is the highest virtue and the source of all other virtues (*Summa Theologiae* II, II, 184, n. 3). Charity flows from the nature of God, and it aims at an unrestricted love of both God and neighbor. It is different from other loves in that it is utterly selfless and seeks only the good of others. Supernatural charity aims at union with God, and it is the basis of love of neighbor, the emotions of good will, compassion and sympathy. Charity makes possible heroic works of self-sacrifice, in addition to the ordinary actions of self-giving.

Charity, Heroic Act of • An act by which one offers to God all the merits of a good deed performed during life, or all the suffrages and benefits gained after one's death for the souls in purgatory. The scriptural basis for such acts is John 14:23: "If a man loves me, he will keep my word, and my Father will love him and we will come to him and make our home with him." Entailed in such an offering is abandonment of all the spiritual graces and benefits one receives in this life to lessen one's punishments in purgatory. To undertake this sort of act, one would have to resolve firmly to live a life without sin here so as to avoid the punishments of purgatory.

Charity, Works of • Interpersonal and social in character and not merely sentiments, these are good works done for another without recompense to aid in situations of need. Works of charity include the corporal works of mercy and actions of social justice; they are deeds of self-giving for the sake of another, not done out of a desire for either compensation or profit, but simply to promote the well-being of another. Works of supernatural charity are deeds done to give honor, glory or praise to God. These sorts of action are ultimately actions of self-sacrifice as they are done not for profit or gain, but to show the love of Christ. For this reason, they represent the pinnacle of Christian action in the world.

Chartres, Cathedral of (Notre Dame de Chartres) • French High Gothic cathedral with magnificent sculptures and famous stained glass. The main doorway, the sculptured Royal Portal, is graced with restrained and yet vital statues which relate organically to the whole. The façade has two towers, one taller and more elaborate,

Cathedral of Chartres

completed in the sixteenth century, and the other more simple, completed in the twelfth century.

The interior is outstanding for its brilliant stained glass (particularly that of Our Lady); many consider that the rich reds and blues have never been equaled, although recent cleaning of them sparked a controversy as to whether this action destroyed their beauty. The church edifice, visible for miles around, figured prominently in French devotional life (especially in terms of pilgrimage) and still does. The most famous treasure of Chartres is Our Lady's veil, preserved in a beautiful Gothic reliquary.

Chartreuse, The Great • The title "The Great Chartreuse" was derived from Franco-Latin roots and meant simply "the great charterhouse." It was the name given to the original foundation of Carthusian monks established by St. Bruno near Grenoble, France, in 1084.

Chastity • The virtue which tempers, regulates and moderates our sexual desires, thoughts and actions. In marriage, chastity moderates desires for legitimate marital acts for the good of the family and of the union of the spouses; outside marriage, chastity restrains sexual desires, thoughts and actions *in toto*.

Chastity is primarily a natural virtue, related to charity and justice because it inhibits the individual from regarding others as sexual objects; it therefore promotes respect for the dignity of other persons. Chastity prevents the Christian from demeaning the dignity of others, enabling one to treat others as true sons and daughters of God.

Chasuble • The outer liturgical vestment worn by the celebrant at Mass. Originally the outer garment in the late-Greco-Roman world, more practical than the toga, it was a large cone-shaped cloth with a hole for the head, thus earning the name *casula* or little house, because it completely covered the person, serving as an outer cape or cloak covering the tunic. After the barbarian invasions, when shorter tunics and different capes became the fashion for men, the clergy continued to hold on to their older style of dress, and so the chasuble became associated with liturgical wear.

In a ninth-century *Roman Ordinal*, we have the first evidence of its presentation to newly ordained priests. Bands of decorative material called orphreys were used to cover the seams and they were often vertical stripes down the front and back and joined across the shoulders in a "Y" cross. Since medieval theology emphasized the Sacrifice of the Mass more and more, the Y-shaped crosses were often embellished with the image of the Crucified One.

Chasuble with orphrey cross

In the twelfth century, cloth was often cut away from the sides to facilitate arm movement (because richer and heavier fabrics were coming to be used) and by the sixteenth century, this tendency had so heightened as to leave the chasuble just two panels of rich brocades and frequently highly ornamented. These "fiddleback" vestments (so-called from their shape in front) caused antiquarians of the nineteenth century to attempt to revive earlier models to create the "Roman" chasuble, which was far less ample than the ancient *casula*. Rome forbade this development in 1863 and again in 1925, but relaxed the prohibition in 1957, perhaps in light of the fact that later revival attempts were more faithful to the ancient designs.

The chasuble may be made of any suitable cloth and an all-encompassing "chasuble-alb" is tolerated for traveling and for home Masses. The traditional symbolism of the chasuble is that it represents charity covering a multitude of sins, as this liturgical vestment covers the individuality of the priest with the priestly role of the High Priest, Jesus Christ.

Cherubikon • The hymn of the Cherubim chanted prior to the Offertory Entrance in the Byzantine Rite, taken from the hymn's opening words, "Let us who mystically represent the Cherubim and sing the thrice-holy hymn to the life-creating Trinity now lay aside all earthly cares. . . ."

Cherubim • In the Old Testament book of the prophet Ezekiel, cherubim are described as attendants around God's heavenly throne (Ez 9-10). As such they were closely linked with the manifestation of God's majesty. They were semi-human in overall appearance, with four wings and with the faces of a man, a lion, an eagle and an ox. They symbolized God's power over the entire universe. The New Testament Book of Revelation (Rv 4-5) alludes to these creatures, borrowing amply from the symbolism of the Book of Ezekiel. This biblical image is quite far from the popular connotation of the word cherub in English, according to which cherubs are plump, winged, child-like angels. The cherubim of Ezekiel's visions are awesome creatures, associated with the visible manifestation of the all-transcendent God.

Catholic Tradition describes cherubim as angels who have an intimate knowledge of God and who continually praise Him. In Christian angelology, cherubim rank after the seraphim and are the second highest of the nine hierarchies or choirs of angels.

(Cf. Angel.)

For further reading: Carol Meyers, "Cherubim," *Anchor Bible Dictionary*, 1:899-900.

Chevet • In many Romanesque and Gothic churches, the easternmost end developed into a structure known as the chevet. In some cases it consisted of a single apse surrounded by an ambulatory and radiating chapels; in others it became an elaborate termination consisting of multiple apses. The central chapel was usually dedicated to the Virgin Mary, known as the Lady Chapel.

Child of Mary • A person who belongs to a specific confraternity of the Blessed Virgin Mary. Bl. Peter de Honestis founded the oldest known Children of Mary sodality in Italy in the thirteenth century. The most famous of all Children of Mary sodalities is the one begun in 1847 by the Vincentian Fathers and the Daughters of Charity, in order to promote the Miraculous Medal. The manual of this sodality states the purpose of the organization: "The veneration of Our Blessed Lady in her Immaculate Conception, and with the personal sanctification of its numbers coupled with a true social apostolate."

Childermas • The medieval English name for the feast of Holy Innocents observed on December 28. This feast is often now celebrated in reparation for the crime of abortion of today's innocents.

Children, Duties of • The primary duties of children are to love and obey their parents and to love and obey God. The fourth commandment of the Decalogue held that children were bound to obey and honor their parents, and the Second Vatican Council taught that "it is . . . above all in the Christian family, inspired by the grace and the responsibility of the sacrament of matrimony, that children should be taught to know and worship God and to love their neighbor, in accordance with the faith which they have received in earliest infancy in the sacrament of Baptism" (GE 3). This commandment, of course, applies only to children who have reached the age of moral responsibility.

This commandment certainly applies to young children, as the disobedient child is seen in the Old Testament as a dishonor and disgrace to his or her parents. But it also applies to adult children, and it prohibits them from abusing, neglecting or killing their parents through euthanasia. This forgotten aspect of the fourth commandment needs to be recalled as secular propaganda for the social and legal endorsement of euthanasia grows. This perspective of the fourth commandment is probably more important than the emphasis on the obedience of the young child, for the neglect or hostility of an elder child can do greater harm to an elderly, feeble or incompetent parent than could that of the younger child.

Children, Mass for • In 1973 a special directory was prepared to adapt the Mass for the capacities of children, to help them to understand the liturgy and to participate in it. Greater freedom is allowed in this document for the actual place of the celebration, though the church building is recommended. Freedom is also encouraged in the celebrant's introductions to various parts of the Mass, texts that are to be sung, visual elements (e.g., pictures illustrating the homily) and even in the homily itself, for if the priest is not comfortable preaching to children or dialoguing with them, a competent layperson may instruct them at that time.

While the responses and the main lines of all liturgies should be the same, some of the introductory rites may be omitted, the readings may be reduced in number if it is thought necessary or other scriptural readings chosen if those in the lectionary seem unsuitable. New Eucharistic Prayers have been approved for children's liturgies. All should be done in such a way as to help the little ones participate in the Eucharistic mystery and not render it too childish even for them.

Educational psychologists are divided on the advisability of this type of introduction of children to "adult" activities.

Children's Communion • The practice, instituted by the decree of Pope St. Pius X, *Quam Singulari* (August 8, 1910), which allowed children who had reached the "age of reason" — declared to be the age of seven — to make their First Holy Communion.

Because of this act, Pope St. Pius has been dubbed "the Pope of the Eucharist."

Children's Crusade • Sometime after the Fourth Crusade to free the Holy Land from Muslim control, the idea spread that only the "pure of heart" could win the struggle. Eventually some 40,000 youths gathered from Germany and France, but most traveled only as far as Italy before the project collapsed. Thereupon, most were sent home, but some were betrayed, kidnaped and later sold as slaves.

Chiliasm • The term means "one thousand" (from the Greek *chilioi*) and is taken by some to be synonymous with "millennialism." In Revelation 20:1-5, we read that Satan will be bound for a thousand years, after which he will be freed, but only "for a while." During the time of Satan's imprisonment, those who were martyred for Christ will "come to life" and will reign with Christ (v. 4). This period is also called "the thousand-year reign." Because of the ambiguity of the text regarding the relationship of this time period to the Second Coming of Christ, there is some question as to the exact "place in history" for the thousand-year reign. Those who think that the sequence described above will be *preceded by* the Second Coming of Christ are called "premillennialists." Those who think the above sequence will be *followed by* the Second Coming of Christ are called "postmillennialists." The "amillennialists" do not hold to a literal thousand-year reign; instead, they take the period of a thousand years as symbolic of the period of history from Christ's life to the Second Coming (i.e., this "present age").

Chinese Rites: See **Rites, Chinese**

Chi-Rho • The term is a form of "Greek shorthand" for the title "Christ." "Chi" and "Rho" are the first two letters in the Greek word *Christos* or "Christ." In Greek capital letters they appear as "X" and "P" — many times with the "X" superimposed on the stem of the "P" (e.g., on liturgical vestments and appointments).

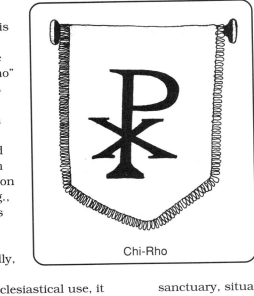

Chi-Rho

Chirograph • Literally, chirograph means written by hand. In ecclesiastical use, it refers specifically to a letter written by the Pope in his own hand to a dignitary of the Church or state concerning a significant concern of the Holy See.

Chirotony • From the Greek meaning "laying on of hands." This term in the Eastern Church designates the mystery or sacrament of Orders.

Chivalry • The body of customs and ideals which guided the actions of men during the Middle Ages. This set of principles dictated man's conduct whether during peace or war, in Church or civil society. Not only did chivalry advance the traditions of knighthood, but it also embraced such Christian virtues as charity in the face of hatred, fortitude in the midst of danger and modesty in the presence of women. The soldier endowed with this spirit, which blossomed in the ninth century in order to uphold Christianity, displayed loyalty to the Church's authority and defended the cause of Christ, even brandishing his sword if necessary.

Choir • (1) Architecturally, it is a term used to describe an area of a church building containing seats for the clergy. In the Roman basilica style of building, these seats were first placed in a semicircle around the apse behind the altar; later they were located in an area surrounded by rails in the nave. In other architectural styles, the choir was sometimes placed near the sanctuary, situated at a right angle to the altar, facing a central aisle leading to the sanctuary.

2. Musically, it is a group of singers which assists with the singing during liturgical services. The choir, at times, leads the congregation in singing, or it may sing alone. By the time of the fourth century choirs were in existence, being comprised of men in minor orders, and boys. By the time of St. Gregory the Great (d. 604), the *Schola Cantorum* was firmly established. The style and difficulty of the music sung by choirs became more elaborate throughout the centuries, until by the eighteenth century the singers in a choir were often highly skilled professionals. With the liturgical renewal taking place during this century, a greater emphasis has been placed upon the task of the choir in assisting the congregation to have a fuller participation in singing during the liturgy.

Chrism • A mixture of oil and balsam, or balm, used for liturgical anointings — Baptism, Confirmation, Holy Orders, the blessing of an altar and, in former days, the coronation of kings. Its symbolism is both royal and priestly, therefore fitting for both the royal priesthood of all Christians and the hierarchical priesthood of Orders. It is blessed on Holy Thursday at the Chrism Mass by the bishop, but this Mass may be celebrated at some other convenient time during Holy Week. Once the oil had to be olive, but now may be vegetable, seed or coconut oil if olive oil is too difficult to obtain or too expensive.

Chrismal (also Chrismatory) • The small cylindrical metal jar or container where the holy oils for the conferring of the sacraments — oil of catechumens, oil of the sick and holy chrism — are kept. In English these are also called "oil stocks." In former times, "chrismal" also designated several other things: (1) a cloth used to wrap around relics; (2) the pall or altar covering, consisting of a linen cloth saturated with wax, used over a newly consecrated altar not only out of respect for the sacred chrism still on it but also to protect the altar cloths over it; (3) a type of early pyx for the Blessed Sacrament; (4) the white-hooded robes of the newly baptized.

Another form for chrismal is "chrismatory."

Chrismarium • This term, which is derived from sacred chrism, may denote one of two things: (1) in former times, a place reserved in the church building for the conferral of the sacrament of Confirmation, during which the recipient is anointed on the forehead with sacred chrism; and (2) a jar used to store this and other holy oils.

Chrismation • The anointing with the holy oil of persons or things. It takes place in Baptism, Confirmation, Holy Orders, the Anointing of the Sick and in the blessing of things (e.g., altars). In the Eastern Church, it is the name for the sacrament of Confirmation.

Christ • The Greek *christos* is a translation of the Hebrew *meshiah* or "messiah," meaning "anointed one." In the Old Testament the term refers to the king (1 Sm 10:1; 2 Sm 2:4; 5:3; 1 Kgs 1:39) or to the priest (Ex 29:7; 30:22-33; 2 Mc 1:10). There are two essential elements within the Old Testament understanding of messiah: (1) that history (or time) is not cyclical but perhaps spiral-like, always moving toward a goal, an end point — the kingdom of YHWH (God); (2) that God's "anointed one" is the principal means by which God's kingdom is established. With Nathan's oracle (2 Sm 7:12-16), all messianic hope is on the royal line of David, from which each successive king will represent an incremental advance toward the kingdom of the God of Israel.

In the Person of Jesus we have the ultimate "anointed one," Who unites priestly, prophetic and monarchical strands of Old Testament expectations about God and the coming of His kingdom. Jesus brings the kingdom (Mk 1:15), is called Son of David (implying His messianic identity: Mt 12:23; 21:9) or Messiah (Jn 4:29; 7:40ff.). Jesus forbids others to call Him Messiah (e.g., demoniacs, Lk 4:41) but accepts the title in Peter's confession of faith (Mt 16:20). His hesitancy about accepting any straightforward application of the term to Him may be due to the fact that the Son of Man must suffer and die for the ransom of the many — the Anointed One is a king in the sense that in His humiliating death on the cross there is an ultimate victory of the king and His kingdom over the power of sin and death. His death is a service to all who enter into His rule — the king is servant, redeemer and obedient Son. The historical, religious and theological horizons of the term "Christ" are significantly reshaped in the Person of Jesus Christ.

Christ, Supreme Order of • This is the highest of the five pontifical orders of knighthood. Founded in 1318 under the name of the "Militia of Jesus Christ" by King Denis I and Queen St. Isabella of Portugal, its goal was the defense of Portugal against the Moors. The order was approved by Pope John XXII in 1319. The order retained a monastic character until the sixteenth century, when it was divided into two branches: one, essentially religious, under the Pope; the other, a distinct civil order, under the Portuguese sovereign. After falling into disuse, the order was restored and completely reorganized by Pope St. Pius X in 1905. In 1966 Pope Paul VI decreed that the Supreme Order of Christ would henceforth be awarded only to heads of state who profess the Christian Faith.

Christ of the Andes • The impressive statue of Jesus which commemorates the peaceful resolution of a boundary conflict between Chile and Argentina in the late nineteenth century. This memorial is perched atop a mountain 14,000 feet above sea level on the border between the two countries. The metal for the statue came from guns intended to be used by the two countries against each other. An inscription near the statue's base states in Spanish: "He is our peace Who hath made both one."

Christening: See **Baptism, Sacrament of**

Christian • The designation of believers in Christ. Christians themselves appear not to have used this term of themselves until the second century. Earlier they preferred to think and speak of themselves as "brothers," "disciples," "believers," etc. For the first two centuries, the forms "Christiani" and "Chrestiani" were used interchangeably. The word occurs in the New Testament only in Acts 11:26, Acts 26:28 and 1 Peter 4:16. Acts 11:26 tells us that "in Antioch the disciples were for the first time called Christians," but we are not told who coined the expression. In all likelihood, it was first used by non-Christians.

Christian Brothers • The Institute of Brothers of the Christian Schools (F.S.C.) was founded about 1690 by St. John Baptist de la Salle. Their apostolate is principally, though not exclusively, the Christian education of youth. The first Christian Brothers came to the United States in 1819. Their first permanent institution was Calvert Hall College, established in Baltimore, Maryland, in 1845. In the United States, they concentrate their efforts on secondary and college education.

The Irish Christian Brothers were founded in 1802 in Waterford, Ireland, by Edmund Ignatius Rice. They came to the United States in 1906. Today they staff schools in several dioceses, as well as Iona College in New Rochelle, New York.

Christian Democrats • A prominent political movement, dominant in Western Europe, which promotes human dignity, democratic participation in government, religious liberty, strengthening of the family unit, workers' rights and economic cooperation. While advocating governmental initiative in social welfare programs, it defends the right of private property and is generally viewed as a moderate center between the extremes of Communism and *laissez-faire* capitalism. After World War II, the Christian Democrats, led by dedicated Catholic laity, became the majority party in France, Belgium, Holland, Germany and Italy. During the 1960s, many criticized the Christian Democrats as clerically dominated and overly cautious on social reform. However, even today they are viewed as practical centrist leaders who enjoy the respect of the people.

Christian Doctrine • Those teachings that are considered applicable to all Christians for leading a Christian life. By Christian doctrine, the whole person, body, mind and soul, is developed according to the norms of reason and revelation with the help of God's grace, in order to prepare the Christian for a happy and useful life here and for eternal happiness in the life to come.

The Catholic Church understands Christian doctrine broadly as including the child's first learning of simple prayers, catechism, elementary religion courses and more advanced theology. More specifically, it comprises the early instructions given by the Apostles to the first generation of Christian believers.

Christian Doctrine, Confraternity of: See **Confraternity of Christian Doctrine**

Christian Education, Declaration on: See **Gravissimum Educationis**

Christian Family Movement • An outgrowth of the Catholic Action phenomenon, C.F.M. was formally organized in 1950. Its goal was the reformation of society and renewal of family life and values. Thus, C.F.M. entered the realm of social justice, not only of religious issues. Composed entirely of laity, and novel in its nonparochial approach, this movement became one of the first opportunities for large-scale lay leadership in the modern Church. After the first decade of its existence, membership in C.F.M. numbered 30,000 couples in the United States and several other countries. The rapid growth and popularity of the movement were at least partly the result of the large numbers of college-educated Catholics eager to exercise some form of leadership in the Church.

Christian Philosophy • This term has come to designate chiefly the practice of philosophy in the light of Christian Revelation, a practice that was championed especially in the works of the Catholic philosopher Étienne Gilson (1884-1978). In this sense, Christian philosophy is identical neither with pure philosophy (whose principles derive solely from reasoning about the structures of the world as these can be known by experience, generalization and analysis) nor with dogmatic theology (whose principles are derived from Revelation, but whose methodology involves the use of philosophical ideas).

Christian Science • A religious system of thought and therapy developed by Mary Baker Eddy (1821-1910), who claimed to know the principles which Jesus used to heal the sick and raise the dead. Her teachings are set out in *Science and Health*, a textbook which is the only official exposition of her religion. Originally appearing in 1875, *Science and Health* had gone through fifty-six editions in 1891. The mother church of Christian Science was opened in Boston in 1879.

Among the basic doctrines of Christian Science is the notion that the material world is unreal; man's true nature is spiritual. Experiences as we know them are imaginary. Physical objects and sin are unreal. Pain and sin are "mortal illusions" which disappear when confronted with spiritual truth. Illness is not cured by medicines but by knowledge, positive thought and "mental work," which is prayer. Prayer makes one's mind more like the mind of Christ. Cures of all kinds can take place when thought-patterns are corrected; thus, this religion has been referred to as a psychic art.

In 1881 Mrs. Eddy opened the Massachusetts Metaphysical College, where students paid three hundred dollars for a three-week course which led to their designation as "practitioners." A longer course produced "teachers" of Christian

Science. Practitioners treat patients by praying and affirming the truth in a kind of mental healing. Medical treatment is rejected.

There is no true liturgical life and no sacramental system in this religion. Baptism is not conferred. All churches of Christian Science follow a uniform cycle of readings and preaching topics, determined by a Boston-based committee. Church buildings consist of a "reading room" and often a Sunday school.

Today, about eighty-five percent of Christian Science practitioners and fifty percent of its teachers are women. Church by-laws forbid publication of membership statistics, so exact information is unknown. In 1908, a newspaper, *The Christian Science Monitor*, was founded by the Church. It strives to present news, especially positive news, without bias or sensationalism.

Christian Socialism • The movement of the nineteenth and twentieth centuries which sought to permeate modern society, politics and economics with Christian values. Christian socialism stresses harmony and cooperation among the various groups and corporations, not conflict and struggle as does Marx. Christian socialism holds that where there are common interests among the various vocational groups, there are "corporations." These natural vocational groupings and corporations that constitute society are an ordered unity. Pope Pius XI held that society was created for human convenience, so it provides the human person with the benefits that accrue to the division of labor.

Socialism sacrifices freedom to the community, but Christian socialism seeks justice for the individual by according a proper role to the individual in society. Christian socialism sought a middle road between socialism and free-market capitalism. It objected to socialism's

rejection of private property and argued that the person has a natural right to property. However, it held that this title to property was not absolute and that there was really a dual title to all property: that of society and that of the individual. Because of this dual title, society could preempt the individual's use of private property for the common good, but when this was not necessitated by the common good, the state had to respect the right of the individual over his or her property.

Christianity • Broadly understood, Christianity is the religion derived from the teachings of Jesus Christ as professed historically by Catholics, Orthodox and Protestants. Comprised of faith in the Person of Jesus as Messiah, the spiritual life He inspired and adherence to the moral dictates He advanced, Christianity has influenced the arts and sciences, government and society for nearly two thousand years. Christian humanism, in particular, looks to the mystery of Christ's incarnation and promotes the great dignity of the human person which the Second Person of the Trinity so values by His having shared our humanity in His earthly life and which He has now glorified in heaven. In the West, typically Christian values are joined to their historical antecedents in Judaism to produce what is called the Judeo-Christian ethic.

The Apostles continued, expanded and spread the teachings of Christ throughout the world; the hierarchical order was established, with the bishops as successors to the Apostles and the presbyterate for the continued administration of the seven sacraments instituted by Christ. With organization and growth, there followed the logical consequences of Christian thought, notably its effect on the family and society, especially the Christian condemnation of slavery, the dignity accorded the human person and the exercise of civil authority.

In this regard, the Second Vatican Council has stated: "In their pilgrimage to the heavenly city, Christians are to seek and relish the things that are above: this involves not a lesser, but rather a greater commitment to working with all men toward the establishment of a world that is more human" (GS 57).

Christifideles Laici • Pope John Paul II's apostolic exhortation on the laity was issued in January 1989. The chosen theme emanated from the world Synod of Bishops' gathering in 1987, where the "Vocation and Mission of the Laity in the Church and in the World 20 Years After the Second Vatican Council" was the principal subject of discussion. Billed as "a faithful and fruitful" by-product of the synod's sessions, the document explores various responsibilities of the laity within the Church and in the larger community, the distinctive roles of men and women, and the laity within parish life and administration.

Drawing upon Sacred Scripture, the Pope wrote: "It is no exaggeration to say that the entire existence of the lay faithful has as its purpose to lead a person to knowledge of the radical newness of Christian life that comes from Baptism. . . " Precisely the way and manner in which the laity accomplish this — in their dignity, in their participation in the Church as the Body of Christ and in their capacity as co-heirs to the Church's mission — are the objects of papal reflection in this seminal work. Following the lead of the Second Vatican Council, the Holy Father stresses that the primary focus of the lay apostolate is to be the transformation of secular society and culture, and not a preoccupation with internal ecclesiastical affairs.

Christmas • Our current English term can be traced back to at least 1123 and in one of the Old English spellings appears as *Cristes maesse*, which by 1568 clearly meant "Mass of Christ," that is, the celebration of His birth. By the sixth century the annual feast day was almost universally celebrated on the twenty-fifth of December (the exception still to this day being the Church of Armenia). Speculation about the correct birth date originates in the early third century when Clement of Alexandria suggested May 20. The date of December 25 is marked for Christmas in the Philocalian Calendar, which represents Roman practice in the year 336 (*natus Christus in Betleem Judeae*).

Scholars speculate that the selection of December 25 was aimed at replacing the pagan winter festival dedicated to the "Unconquered Sun" (*Natalis Solis Invicti*). In the Eastern part of the Church, the feast of the Epiphany, celebrating Christ's Baptism on January 6, was later connected to the Nativity (in the fourth century). By the sixth century most of the East had adopted the December 25 date.

Christology • The branch of theology which studies the person and nature of Jesus Christ, in particular the union of the divine and human natures in the one divine Person of the Son. Christology strives to articulate the clear confession of the New Testament that Jesus Christ is the Son of God.

The four Gospels provide the only accurate information available to us concerning the facts of Jesus' life, while the rest of the New Testament canon clearly affirms His full humanity and divinity. Reflection on the relation of the divine and human in Christ was stimulated primarily by a series of heresies which denied the fullness of His humanity (e.g., Docetism) or His divinity (e.g., Arianism), or exaggerated their distinctness (e.g., Nestorianism) or their unity (e.g., Monophysitism). These views came to be seen as at odds with the faith in Christ as held in the developing historic mainstream and expressed in a series of ecumenical councils.

The Council of Nicaea (325) affirmed the full divinity of Christ by adopting the term *homoousios* to express that the Son is of one substance with the Father. By affirming that Mary is truly the Mother of God (*Theotokos*), the Council of Ephesus (431) insisted on the unity of the divine and human natures in the one Person of the Son. The Council of Chalcedon (451) confessed the distinctness of the two natures in Christ, insisting that they do not coalesce to form a hybrid nature, thus maintaining the full humanity of Christ. Finally, the Third Council of Constantinople (680) affirmed the reality of the human and divine wills of Christ against Monothelitism. Throughout these controversies, certain Fathers of the Church played a prominent role in articulating authentic Christology, in particular, Irenaeus of Lyons, Athanasius, Cyril of Alexandria, Pope Leo the Great, and the Cappadocians.

Christophers • The name of the followers of the movement begun by Father James Keller, M.M., in 1946. The motto of the movement, "It's better to light one candle than to curse the darkness," is indicative of the organization's aim to promote "positive, constructive action." While the Christophers are loosely structured and have no regular meetings, millions of people have been reached by the television and radio programs sponsored by the Christophers. Furthermore, the *Christopher News Notes*, a small pamphlet proclaiming some aspect of the Christian Faith, and the newspaper columns published by the Christophers have inspired countless people of all faiths. "Christopher" is derived from the Greek

word *Christophoros*, meaning "Christ-bearer."

Christus Dominus • Issued on October 28, 1965, *Christus Dominus*, the Decree on the Pastoral Office of the Bishops in the Church, concentrates on the various roles of bishops in the universal Church, in their own dioceses and in their cooperation with one another. Because the Pope and those bishops in communion with him are the successors to St. Peter and the other Apostles, so they are to carry on the mandate which Christ gave, "to teach all peoples, to sanctify men in truth and to give them spiritual nourishment" (CD 2). This is accomplished through their sacramental consecration and place within the hierarchy of Christ's Church, and "together with their head, the Supreme Pontiff, and never apart from him, they have supreme and full authority over the universal Church" (LG 22).

A special emphasis of *Christus Dominus* is that of the necessary and proper collegiality of bishops, and to that end it encouraged the bishops to form episcopal conferences, "so that by sharing their wisdom and experience and exchanging views they may jointly formulate a program for the common good of the Church" (CD 37).

Chronicler • The author of 1 and 2 Chronicles. Little is known about him. It is frequently assumed he was a Levite. This view seems probable, considering the favorable treatment the Levites are invariably accorded in his work. W. F. Albright ventured the opinion that the Chronicler is to be identified with Ezra.

Chronicles, Books One and Two of • Originally a single work, it was first divided into two scrolls in the Septuagint. This became necessary because the Greek version required more space than the original Hebrew, which typically did not write in the vowels. The title of these books in Greek is *Paraleipomena* — "things left over" or "things omitted." It was Jerome who proposed the title "Chronicle of the Whole of Sacred History," whence the present English designation of the books as "Chronicles." These books present a narrative that runs from the creation to the return from the Exile under Cyrus. It parallels the account found in Genesis through 2 Kings. Chronicles reworks history in order to make a religious statement. The clear goal of the work is to foster regard for the Law and to assert the blessings that accrue from adherence to it.

For further reading: Ralph W. Klein, "Chronicles, Book of 1-2," *Anchor Bible Dictionary*, 1:992-1002.

Chronista • Latin for "narrator," *chronista* refers to the person (usually a priest or deacon, though in necessity also a layman) who chants or reads that portion of Christ's passion in the Liturgy of Passion (Palm) Sunday and Good Friday. There are three parts: the narrator, or *chronista*; the people, or *synagoga*; and Christ.

Chronology, Biblical: See **Biblical Chronology**

Church • Our English word is related to the Scots *kirk*, the German *kirche* and the Dutch *kerk*, all of which are derived from the late Greek *kyriakon*, meaning "the Lord's (house)." The classical Greek *ekklesia* meant "assembly of citizens" and implied a democratic equality among its members who met for legislative and other deliberations. In the Greek Old Testament (LXX), *ekklesia* represents the Hebrew *kahal*, meaning the religious assembly (Dt 23; 1 Kgs 8; Ps 22). In the New Testament the term *ekklesia* always refers to a group of people: (1) those Christians in a region or city (e.g., Acts 14:23ff.; 1 Cor 1:2; 2 Cor 1:1); (2) those gathered in a particular house (Rom 16:5; 1 Cor 16:19); (3) all Christians gathered in the Church (Mt 16:18; Eph 1:22).

The Church is a mystery which prior to Jesus was hidden in the people of Israel and, since Jesus is revealed, in successive generations of believers (Eph 1:9 ff.; Rom 16:25f.). The mystery is this: A sinful people possess an initial taste of salvation within a divine-human institution in which revelation from God, forgiveness and grace through the work of Christ at the cross and the Father at the Resurrection are like leaven working to transform what is broken and to free what is in bondage. The New Testament witness may be summarized thus: The Church is created by God, is the Body of Christ, Who is her Head (cf. Eph and Col), and is indwelt and empowered by the Holy Spirit (Eph 1:3, 22, especially 14; 2:22; 1 Cor 3:16). Jesus entrusted His teachings to the Apostles, chosen by means of the Holy Spirit (Acts 1:2), and to their successors (1 Tm 4:14; 2 Tm 1:6). The Holy Spirit guides the Church (Jn 16:13) and helps her guard the deposit of sound doctrine (2 Tm 1:13ff.) which includes her authentic role of teaching in the name of Christ. The Church's existence is drawn from the Person of Christ (Eph 2:16-18), is born of one Baptism (Eph 4:5), is fed with one Bread (1 Cor 10:17) and is a single people (Gal 3:28) for whom human division is anathema (Eph 2:14 ff.; 1 Cor 12:13; Col 3:11; Gal 3:28). The Church is a gathering of sinners who are somehow being made holy and perfect because of Christ's love for her (Eph 5:26-27). The Church's perfect model and witness to Christ's Gospel in terms of faith, hope and love is Mary, the Mother of God. She not only participated in the mysteries of salvation (e.g., Incarnation) and witnessed the Church's birth at Calvary (e.g., Jn 19:25) and Pentecost (Acts 1:14), she pondered and cherished these events and understood them (Lk 2:51).

At the Second Vatican Council the doctrine of the Church received much attention, particularly in *Lumen Gentium*. In this constitution, the Council affirmed that the Church is in the first place that assembly of people, united in Christ, that is called into existence by God Himself (n. 2). Stating a position with regard to some past and present controversies, the Council said: "The society furnished with hierarchical agencies and the Mystical Body of Christ are not to be considered as two realities, nor are the visible assembly and spiritual community, not the earthly Church and the Church enriched with heavenly things. Rather they form one interlocking reality which is comprised of a divine and a human element" (LG 8). An image of the Church much favored by the Council was that of "People of God," evoking a dynamic and communitarian understanding of the Church.

Church, Early • The first segment of time delineated by ecclesiastical historians in their attempt to analyze the nearly two millennia of the Church's existence. Scholars generally mark this period as beginning on Pentecost Sunday (c. A.D. 30) and concluding with the Edict of Milan (313). These three centuries are usually subdivided into two eras: The first is called the "Apostolic Age," from 30 to 180, and is of course dominated by the towering figures of the twelve Apostles, the disciples of Jesus and their immediate followers. Sometimes called the "primitive Church," this Apostolic Era was noted for the extraordinary missionary expansion of the Church, the development of the canon of Scripture, the formation of a rudimentary hierarchical structure, the articulation of the fundamentals of the Faith through creeds to counteract heresy, internal and external struggle, opposition and persecution, and the efforts of the Christian community to arrive at a *modus vivendi* with the Roman, Greek and Jewish cultures. The writings, worship and structure of the Church in this Apostolic Age show the effects of these three cultures upon evolving Christian thought and practice.

The second subdivision in the era known as the "early Church" is usually referred to as the "sub-apostolic Church," 180-313, which is characterized by numerical growth, geographical expansion, severe persecution, theological activity (especially in the cities of Antioch and Alexandria) and a growing attention to the problems presented by the world, especially the Roman Empire.

For further reading: Raymond E. Brown, S.S., Carolyn Osiek, R.S.C.J., and Pheme Perkins, "Early Church," *New Jerome Biblical Commentary*, 1338-1353.

Church, Dogmatic Constitution on the: See **Lumen Gentium**

Church History • The study of the development and growth of the institutional Church in space and time, in society and culture, from apostolic times to the present. The investigation of the Church's past is unique since, in her essence, the Church is spiritual and divine, thus defying classification and explanation. However, just as the Son of God took flesh and became man, so does His bride, the Church, become the outward sign, a sacrament, of this inner mystery. It is this outward sign, these external features of the Church, which provide the data for ecclesiastical historians. The first evidence of a work of Church history would actually be the inspired Acts of the Apostles by St. Luke, which records what happened in the years immediately after Pentecost. The patriarch of Church history is considered to be Eusebius of Caesarea (d. A.D. 339), whose *Ecclesiastical History* chronicles the reign of Constantine. Because the Church is the oldest continuing institution, scholars make various divisions of her almost two-thousand-year span, the simplest being tripartite: From apostolic times to Charlemagne (30-800); the Middle Ages through the Protestant Reformation (800-c. 1563); from the Counter-Reformation through the close of the Second Vatican Council (1563-1965).

Church Militant, Suffering, Triumphant: See **Communion of Saints**

Church Property: See **Temporal Goods**

Church and State • In antiquity, the Church was ambivalent about her relationship to the state and some Christians regarded the state as the instrument of Satan, while others regarded it as morally legitimate. In the Middle Ages, the Church sought to subordinate the state to herself because of the aim of incarnating Christian charity in the political and social order. In the modern era, the Church has come to see the state as an authoritative order charged with responsibility for preserving order and justice. The Church and state are not to be identified but must live side by side, for each was divinely created for specific ends.

Church-state relations must be considered in their historical context. The Church must recall that her normal lot in this world is persecution. In the New Testament, the Church recognized that the state came from God, but the state did not have the authority for complete domination of society. The New Testament called on Christians to pray for civil rulers even if they were not Christian.

The modern view of the state holds that the Church and state are autonomous, and while they pursue different ends, they are made up of the same members. While the Church has a higher objective than that of the state, in practice this makes no difference to the state which is concerned only with the promotion and protection of civil liberties, of which religious liberty is one. Only when civil law conflicts with the moral law can it be disobeyed. The neutrality of the state in respect to the Church makes it more difficult to promote the common good, but the Church encourages the state to promote this ideal.

At the present time, some states are independent of the Church, but they allow the Church the freedom to act publicly. Communist states are independent but generally do not allow this sort of freedom and public role for the Church. They have historically separated Church and state, but also the Church from the schools as well, which deprives the Church of significant influence over the young. Communist constitutional states may often proclaim freedom of conscience, but much is done to paralyze religion while offering atheistic propaganda considered to be scientific and worthy of support. Other states allow the old established Church relationship, which usually relegated to inferior status those who did not belong to the established Church, but this sort of relationship has generally passed.

After Vatican II, the Church in fact admitted the legitimacy of the secular state and affirmed that the state could be independent of the Church, so long as it fulfilled its basic moral requirements of protecting citizens and the common good. The Church after the Council saw that religion and policies could be regarded as supreme in their own sphere, but there were areas of overlap where they should cooperate and act in harmony. Neither the state nor the Church should interfere with each other unnecessarily nor deprive the other of those things necessary to carry out their responsibilities, and both should facilitate the attainment of each other's mission.

Church in the Modern World, Pastoral Constitution on the: See **Gaudium et Spes**

Churching of Women • The name for the rite which invokes God's blessing on a woman after childbirth, probably having its origin in Jewish purification rites (cf. Lv 12:1-8 and Lk 2:22-24). While Christians adopted this custom, it was not seen in the same way. Pope St. Gregory the Great (d. 604) protested the notion that any kind of defilement was incurred by childbirth. In the new rite found in the *Book of Blessings* (Latin edition, 1984), the emphasis is on the dignity of woman, who, like Our Lady, gives new life, so great a gift, to the world.

Churchyard • Literally, the churchyard is the property surrounding a church. The term is more common in rural communities, where the churchyard, which could be more expansive than in urban areas, would be used for the parish cemetery. The laity were buried in the position which they had taken at Mass while alive, facing the altar. Clerics were buried in the opposite direction, in the position they assumed when preaching. The term is almost obsolete today, except where such conditions still allow for the luxury of a churchyard. It can also be a significant concern where state laws exempt such land from real estate taxes.

Ciborium • Originally the term was the Greek *kiborion*, which meant a canopy resting on four pillars and placed over the altar as a sign of reverence. This custom spread to the West in the sixth century, and these canopies were often called civories or baldacchinos from the word *baldacco* (meaning Baghdad, because many rich fabrics from that city were used in the adornment of these canopies). In the Middle Ages, they were often suspended from the ceiling or projected from the wall to cover an altar or episcopal throne. Such canopies, whether pillared, suspended or protected, came to be required over the high altar and that on which the Blessed Sacrament was reserved, but the *General Instruction of the Roman Missal* of Pope Paul VI no longer requires this usage.

In the Middle Ages, the term "ciborium" was sometimes used to refer to the sacrament tower, where the Blessed Sacrament was reserved and from that to the actual vessel or pyx which contained the Sacred Species. A foot or base was added to the pyx to make it easier to handle and perhaps for greater dignity in exposition. In the Baroque era, when Communion was usually from pre-consecrated Hosts reserved in the tabernacle, the ciborium became larger and looked more like a chalice, to the displeasure of some contemporary liturgists who contend that it should look more like a dish for the consecrated Bread than a cup. Therefore, contemporary ciboria are sometimes more dish-like in appearance and now may be made of any worthy and durable material.

Cilicium: See **Hair Shirt**

Cincture • Also known as a girdle in some cultures, it is the cord, either white or the color of the day, used to gather the alb at the waist. It is not needed if the alb is made in such a way that this function is already accomplished.

Circumcillions • During the fourth century a schismatic church developed in the Roman provinces of Africa and Numidia (present-day Tunisia and eastern Algeria). Called the Donatist church after its founder, Bishop Donatus, this sect, which espoused a rigorist doctrine and enforced the rebaptism of lapsed Catholics, perdured into the fifth century. The Circumcillions (Latin, *circumcilliones*) were a fanatical movement on the fringe of the Donatist church. They considered themselves to be the true heirs of the early Christians and willingly sought martyrdom in the defense of their faith, against Catholics as well as pagans. Their fanatical enthusiasm was exploited by the leaders of the Donatist church, who used them to resist the imperial troops seeking to restore the Catholic bishops in the area. Some authors have tried to portray the Circumcillions as an agrarian reform movement, but the wealthy status of most of the Donatist leaders makes this thesis doubtful.

Circumcision • The practice of cutting the foreskin from the penis, an ancient and widespread practice not only in the ancient Near East but also in pre- and post-technological cultures. In Genesis 17, Abraham is circumcised and so carries the sign of the covenant with God. It is also a sign of identification with and membership in the people of Israel, without which a male cannot partake of the Passover (Ex 12:44-48). Circumcision of the heart is clearly present in the Old Testament; it is a sign of being supple to God's revelation and of God's favor (Lv 26:41: Dt 10:16; Jer 4:4; 9:25; Ez 44:7, 9).

Jesus' circumcision on the eighth day of His earthly life is a sign of His full membership in the people of Israel (Lk 2:21). In the early Church, Jewish Christians argued for the necessity of circumcision for all male Gentile converts to what was still a very Jewish form of Christianity (Acts 15:1ff.). However, the Council of Jerusalem (Acts 15:28ff.) decided against circumcision and merely prescribed dietary and ethical stipulations for Gentile converts.

In Paul's letters we see that circumcision is only a physical sign of a deeper reality of the covenant with God: faith. The foundation for circumcision is Abraham's faith in God; in light of Jesus Christ, faith is the ultimate element of the Abrahamic covenant with God (Gn 15-17; Rom 4:9-12). Since Christ's death and resurrection, membership within the People of God is not a physical matter of circumcision but a passing of the old creation into the death of Christ whereby the new creation linked to His resurrected Body emerges. True circumcision is spiritual (Rom 2:28ff.; Acts 15; 1 Cor 7:19; Gal 6:13), something hidden, emerging from faith, not done by the hands of men (Col 2:11) and for worship (Phil 3:3).

For further reading: Robert G. Hall, "Circumcision," *Anchor Bible Dictionary*, 1:1025-1031; Leonard V. Snowman, "Circumcision," *Encyclopedia Judaica*, 5:567-575.

Circumincession (Divine Perichoresis) • Circumincession or circuminsession (Greek: *perichoresis*) is the permanent mutual immanence, inexistence and compenetration of the Divine Persons of the Blessed Trinity. In speaking of His unity with the Father, Christ said: "I and the Father are one" (John 10:30), and "believe the works, that you may know and understand that the Father is in me and I am in the Father" (John 10:38). The Council of Florence (1441) expressed this mystery succinctly: "Because of [their] unity the Father is wholly in the Son and wholly in the Holy Spirit, the Son is wholly in the Father and wholly in the Holy Spirit, the Holy Spirit is wholly in the Father and wholly in the Son."

St. Gregory Nazianzen used the term *perichoresis* to describe the mutual compenetration of the human and divine natures in Christ against both Nestorians and Monophysites ("christological perichoresis"). St. John Damascene used it in this sense as well, but extended it to refer to the mutual compenetration of the three Divine Persons. The concept has an important role to play in Eastern trinitarian theology where it serves to underscore the unity in nature or consubstantiality of the three Divine Persons. In trinitarian theology generally, the concept of circumincession expresses the deep mystery of the intimate relation of the three Persons of the Trinity with one another. When they are distinguished, as they are by some theologians, "circumincession" refers to the active penetration of the three Persons and "circuminsession" to their passive coinherence.

Cistercians • A strict order of monks following the Rule of St. Benedict, founded in 1098 by St. Robert of Molesme (1024-1110) at Cîteaux, France. Its founding was defined by an austere Benedictinism, and its most famous member, often considered the Order's second founder, was St. Bernard of Clairvaux (1090-1153). Before the close of the 1100s, five hundred thirty Cistercian abbeys had been established and another one hundred fifty were constructed during the next century. The Cistercian way of life was to be one of silence, in a community devoted mainly to the celebration of the Mass and the Divine Office. Monasteries were built in isolated places, and churches and sacred vessels were simple in design. Strict rules of diet and rigorous schedules of manual labor were followed. Other medieval orders modeled themselves on the Cistercians' way of life. They declined in numbers and influence after the thirteenth century, but rose again in the seventeenth century, when La Trappe monastery was founded by Armand de Rance (1627-1700), from which arose yet another reform of a yet stricter observance, known familiarly as the Trappists.

Citation • In canon law, the citation is the formal and mandatory notification to a party that he is the subject of a proceeding in an ecclesiastical court (Canon 1507). The failure to cite all necessary parties in a case results in the invalidity of the proceedings.

Once a party has been cited, however, his failure to take part in the proceedings without an excuse can result in a declaration of absence, which means that the trial will proceed to judgment without him.

Citations are generally to be made in writing (an exception would be where the parties appear before the ecclesiastical judge on their own) and are usually sent through the mails, either first class or registered (Canon 1509). In canon law, the verifiable refusal to accept such a citation is considered proof of having been cited (Canon 1510). The citation must include such basic information as the name of the ecclesiastical court hearing the case, the nature of the case and the time and method directed for response.

City of God • Written by St. Augustine between A.D. 413 and 426, *De Civitate Dei libri XXII* offers a synthesis of his philosophical, political and theological teaching. Its writing was prompted by the renewal of pagan anti-Christian accusations after the sack of Rome in A.D. 410, answering the charge leveled against Christians that the sad fate of Rome had to do with their faith.

City of God is divided into two parts. The first (books 1-10) presents Augustine's refutation of paganism, while the second (books 11-22) is devoted to his presentation and defense of Christian doctrine. This portion of the work is further subdivided into three sections in which Augustine describes the origins, histories and ultimate destinies of the two cities — the city of God and the city of the world. While the city of the world is founded on love of self, the city of God is grounded in the love of God. In book 14, Augustine writes, "These two cities were made by two loves: the earthly city by the love of self unto the contempt of God, and the heavenly city by the love of God unto the contempt of self."

Civil Allegiance • The duty of all Christians to be loyal to their nation and society and to obey the laws. Citizens owe their nation allegiance in all instances, except when the demands imposed by a state are in violation of the requirements of morality or contrary to the liberty and autonomy of the Church. The requirements of civil allegiance include the duty to pay just taxes, support and defend the nation against unjust aggression, participate in legitimate governmental processes and show due respect for government officials. Showing civil allegiance is both an act of justice, because it returns to the state what is due it on account of the goods the state gives the individual, and also an act of charity because civil allegiance often calls for acts of supreme self-sacrifice.

Civil Law • The body of laws of secular governments: nations, states, cities, etc. Civil law is also a common name for the type of legal system used in many countries of the world. Civil law, from the French *Droit Civil*, refers to legal systems which are descended from Roman law and the Napoleonic Code, as opposed to the Anglo-Saxon common law system of the United States, Great Britain and other countries influenced by Great Britain. In the United States, the legal system of the state of Louisiana is partially patterned on the civil law system.

Civil Marriage • The union of a man and a woman which is officially witnessed by a secular official, such as a judge or justice of the peace. In most countries a marriage must be contracted before a civil official or another person recognized by the secular government as an official witness to marriages. In most Western countries, the secular governments recognize ministers of religion as such official witnesses, although in certain European and Latin American countries, couples are required to exchange vows at a civil ceremony as well as at a religious ceremony.

Ordinarily, Catholics are obliged to marry before a bishop, priest or deacon and two witnesses. In cases of mixed marriage, the bishop of the Catholic party can grant a dispensation from this law and allow the marriage to take place before a minister of another religion or before a civil official.

Civory • This term, which is an English derivative of the Latin *ciborium*, is another name for a permanent canopy or baldacchino set over the main altar of a church building. The style and materials used vary with time (i.e., architectural style) and place. In mystical liturgical symbolism, the civory is supposed to represent heaven and its special protection over the sacred actions taking place below and on the sacred ministers carrying them out. (Cf. Ciborium.)

Clandestinity • Refers to the exchange of marriage vows secretly or at least without the presence of an official witness. Clandestine marriages became somewhat common in the Middle Ages after Pope Alexander III, by a series of decrees, made it impossible for anyone to supply consent to marriage but the spouses themselves, following upon the abuse whereby parents or other guardians occasionally supplied marital consent for their children. Although it was recommended and even urged that Catholics marry in the presence of a priest, this was not required by law. Hence, clandestine marriage proliferated, often with a person having more than one spouse. The ecclesiastical tribunals in the Middle Ages were concerned primarily not with the annulment of marriages but with their enforcement. This happened when the court would be asked to decide which was the true spouse in cases when a man (rarely a woman) was accused by a spouse of having taken other vows subsequently. The court would decide which was the first marriage and order that the couple have the marriage solemnized in the presence of a Church official.

The abuse of clandestinity was ended in part at the Council of Trent, which decreed that Catholics were to marry in the presence of their parish priest and two witnesses in order to have a valid marriage. This decree was in force in only certain countries until 1909, when another decree was enacted imposing this requirement on Catholics throughout the world.

Clapper (also Clepper or Crotalum) • A wooden instrument designed to produce noise by means of wood striking against wood as a substitute for bells, which were to be silenced from Holy Thursday to Holy Saturday.

Clementine Instruction • The rubrics published by Pope Clement XII in 1731 for the Forty Hours Devotion. The Instruction for Benediction and Exposition of the Blessed Sacrament (1973) now supersedes this document.

Clergy • Canon law divides the Christian faithful into two classes: the clergy and the laity. All sacred ministers (deacons, priests and bishops) are members of the clergy. All others, including religious men and women who are not sacred ministers, are members of the laity. Only men may become members of the clergy. Permanent deacons, including those who are married, although often incorrectly called "lay deacons," are actually members of the clergy.

Prior to 1972, a man became a member of the clergy when he went through the Rite of

Tonsure, or the symbolic cutting of his hair. This rite originated in the fourth and fifth centuries as a custom by which young men, upon entering a monastery, had part of their heads shaved as a sign of their status. By the seventh century, it was common for men entering the secular clergy to go through such a ceremony at which a small portion of their hair, usually a small circle at the crown of the head, was shaved. However, entrance into the clergy or clerical state now takes place only after a man is ordained a deacon.

The secular clergy are sacred ministers who are canonically attached to a diocese and who are under the direct authority of the diocesan bishop. Religious clergy are deacons or priests who belong to a religious community.

Although Sacred Orders, once conferred, remain until death, a sacred minister must be a member of the clergy to exercise his orders (except in emergency situations or when a person is in danger of death). When a priest or deacon is returned to the lay state, he ceases to be a member of the clergy and becomes once again a layperson, losing the right and power to exercise his Sacred Orders (cf. Canons 265-293).

Clergy, Byzantine • Canonical legislation regarding clergy of the Byzantine Rite is found in the *motu proprio* of Pope Pius XII *Cleri sanctitati*, promulgated on June 11, 1957, which became effective on March 25, 1958. The *motu proprio* contains 558 canons and details the obligations, responsibilities and privileges of clerics. This has been amplified with the provisions of the Vatican II Decree on the Eastern Churches (*Orientalium Ecclesiarum*).

Particular legislation for the clergy of the Byzantine Rite in the United States was contained in a decree issued by Pope Pius XI on February 9, 1929, entitled *Cum Data Fuerit*. The decree was to be effective for ten years; however, it is now permanently binding. Among its provisions was the enforcement of celibacy on the clergy in the United States. In Europe, clergy of the Byzantine Rite still retain the option to marry. However, marriage must take place before ordination to the diaconate, and a married priest may not be ordained a bishop while his wife is still living. A married deacon or priest may not remarry after the death of his wife and remain functioning in the active ministry. The canonical practice of the Catholic Church for the Byzantine Rite clergy in the United States has not affected Orthodox clergy, who may choose to marry (but only before ordination to the diaconate).

Cleric • A man who is a member of the clergy. Since 1972, all clerics are either deacons, priests or bishops.

Clerical Dress: See Dress, Clerical

Clerical Obligations • Members of the clergy are bound by special obligations because of their state. First and foremost is their obligation to show obedience and reverence to the Supreme Pontiff and to their Ordinary (Canon 273). They are also bound by various spiritual obligations, such as pursuing holiness of life, fulfilling the duties of their ministry and devoting time to prayer. Priests and deacons preparing for the priesthood are obliged to say the Liturgy of the Hours daily (Canon 276.2.3). Clerics are to observe perfect continence and remain celibate (Canon 277.1). An exception to the obligation of celibacy is made for men who are ordained permanent deacons after having married.

Clerics are bound to continue their studies, especially in theology and Sacred Scripture (Canon 279). They are to wear suitable garb in accord with local legislation and custom (Canon 284). They are to refrain from any activities alien to the clerical state.

They may not assume public office, elected or otherwise, which entails the exercise of civil power, nor are they to act as secular administrators of temporal goods. Clerics are not to engage in secular business (Canons 285-286). Finally, clerics are not to volunteer for military service without the permission of their Ordinary. This last obligation does not refer to serving as a chaplain but to other forms of military service (Canon 289).

Clerical Privilege • At various times in Church history, clerics enjoyed certain privileges. They were not to be tried before secular courts, nor were they to serve in the military other than as chaplains. Since these privileges were found in Church law only, it was up to the secular authorities to respect them. In fact, many countries did not observe either canonical provision, and clerics were tried in secular courts for crimes committed, or required to perform military service the same as other males in the country.

Clerical privilege, as a canonical institution, has all but disappeared from canon law.

Clericalism • A pejorative term that refers to an excessively or obnoxiously professional attitude or conduct on the part of members of the clergy. It is often combined with the opinion that the clergy are somehow superior to the laity. Manifestations of clericalism can be found in an undue attachment to or use of clerical garb, other signs of the clerical state or other privileges. This term is sometimes used in a negative way by critics of the Church, who have as their aim the banishment of all religious influence from public life.

Clerks Regular • These are clerics (from the Old English clerks) who are engaged primarily in the active ministry of the

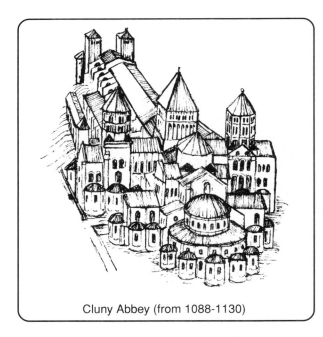

Cluny Abbey (from 1088-1130)

diocesan clergy, such as parish work or teaching, as distinct from the more restricted life of the monastic orders. They are called regular (from the Latin *regula* meaning rule) because they follow the rule of their founder or the rule established by a spiritual writer from within the Catholic Tradition. As examples of clerks regular, the Society of Jesus or Jesuits embrace the rule of their founder, St. Ignatius Loyola; similarly, the Redemptorists follow the rule of their founder, St. Alphonsus Liguori. Though founded by Don Bosco, the Salesians live the Directory of St. Francis de Sales, as do the Oblates of St. Francis de Sales, founded in the eighteenth century by Father Louis Brisson.

Clinical Baptism • An archaic term used to describe the Baptism given to an ill person. A close modern equivalent would be the circumstances of emergency Baptism, that is, urgent necessity, such as danger of death or religious persecution. Canon 850 specifies the requirements for valid Baptism, namely, the pouring of water with the

Trinitarian formula. In an emergency, anyone (Christian or not) may baptize, as long as the person has the intention to do what the Church does in the sacrament.

Cloister (also Close) • From the Latin *claustrum* (bar or bolt, from *claudere*, to close), cloister is the term for limited access to particular monastic communities who willingly embrace the contemplative life and thereby separate themselves from life in the world. A cloistered religious has limited opportunity to leave his or her cloister; similarly outsiders are restricted in entering the cloister. Frequently cloistered monasteries are surrounded with high walls to preserve the privacy of the enclosure and to keep outsiders at a distance. Cloister can also refer to this physical enclosure; in architecture, cloister is often restricted to the covered passageway around the open courtyard or quadrangle (technically called the garth) at the center of such an enclosed monastery.

Clothing • The name given to the formal reception into a religious order in which the novice receives the religious habit of the order. Current Church law allows this to be postponed until the taking of vows.

Cluny • A Benedictine abbey founded (910) in this Burgundian town in south-central France became a center of a renewal, not only of monasticism but of the wider Church. It was not founded in view of reform, but its prayerful monastic observance, a succession of dynamic and talented abbots, and freedom from secular interference gave it respect and influence on other monastic communities and in society. The abbey followed the Rule of St. Benedict of Nursia, with the particular observances of St. Benedict of Aniane (d. 821). Thus it put great emphasis on the dignity and beauty of liturgical life (at times extending these rites to great length) and preferred choral or scribal work to manual labor.

Many other religious houses — at times hundreds — were joined to Cluny, although their relationship varied considerably. Some were priories (even with large communities and frequently with dependent houses) that were directly dependent on the abbeys; others were abbeys that accepted the jurisdiction or at least the right of supervision of the Abbot of Cluny in a somewhat feudal style; still others were joined by a spiritual bond and common observances. Even those houses reformed under the authority of the Abbot of Cluny and which later gained their autonomy seemed to bear the Cluniac stamp. This influence was not confined to France. There were Cluniac houses also in Italy, Spain, Germany and England.

During the twelfth century the influence of Cluny began to wane. Abbots were chosen more frequently from the great noble families of France, and the concerns of these families sometimes swayed decisions. Cluniac houses then became limited to France. Economic conditions were less favorable; the centralization of power in one man, the abbot, for so many houses is effective only if the abbot is of extraordinary talent; some houses began to be held *in commendam* (in trust) by seculars. The new Order of Cîteaux and the newly revitalized Canons Regular offered alternative approaches to religious life. The abbey itself survived until 1790.

Coadjutor Bishop • A bishop assigned by the Holy See to a diocese to assist the residential bishop. Unlike an auxiliary bishop, a coadjutor is sometimes given special powers, with more authority than an auxiliary. Furthermore, a coadjutor has the right of succession when the residential bishop dies, retires or is transferred.

A coadjutor bishop is usually appointed in cases where the residential bishop is infirm or otherwise unable to assume all the responsibilities of governing the diocese (cf. Canons 403-411).

Coat-of-arms • A device based upon heraldic laws and traditions which represents an individual, a corporation, an institution or a political entity. In some European and Commonwealth countries the assumption and use of coats-of-arms are governed by civil law. There is no legislation regulating coats-of-arms in the United States.

Ecclesiastical coats-of-arms are governed by regulations issued by the Vatican Secretariat of State and amended from time to time. The coat-of-arms of the Holy See is a red shield ensigned with the papal tiara over crossed gold and silver keys. The coat-of-arms of a particular Pope includes the shield with his personal arms surmounted by the tiara and crossed keys. The arms of ecclesiastical personalities are distinguished by the color of the ecclesiastical hat (a low-crowned, flat, wide-brimmed hat worn in processions until 1870) and the color and number of tassels on both sides. A cardinal's hat is red with fifteen tassels on each side, a patriarch's is green with fifteen tassels, an archbishop's is green with ten tassels, a bishop's is green with six tassels. Behind the shield the processional cross is placed. A one-barred cross indicates a bishop, and a two-barred cross indicates an archbishop. Since 1969 it has been

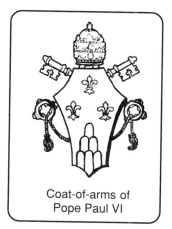

Coat-of-arms of
Pope Paul VI

prohibited to use miters or crosiers on coats-of-arms. The only knighthoods which may be indicated on ecclesiastical arms are those of Malta and the Holy Sepulcher. Prelates of the Eastern Churches often use different devices to indicate their rank. Hats of black and magenta with varying numbers and colors of tassels indicate ecclesiastics of lower rank.

Co-Consecrators • When a newly appointed bishop is to be ordained to the episcopacy, the rite (which is also called consecration) makes provision for at least two other consecrating bishops to assist the principal consecrator.

Code of Canon Law • The Code of Canon Law is the book containing the universal and fundamental laws of the Roman Catholic Church. The first Code was compiled between 1903 and 1917 and promulgated by the Pope in 1917. The Code was revised between 1965 and 1982, and the new Code was promulgated in 1983. The Code of Canon Law pertains only to the Churches of the Latin Rite. The Eastern or Oriental Rites of the Catholic Church have their own set of canon laws issued by the Pope. In some areas, they were subject to the Latin Rite Code. Eastern canon law has also been revised and a Code of these laws was promulgated in 1990.

The Code consists of 1,752 individual canons divided into seven books which deal with the various aspects of Church life and organization. The first book is entitled "General Norms." It contains canons dealing with the interpretation and application of law: dispensations, the power of governance, administrative and juridic acts and ecclesiastical offices. The second book, entitled "The People of God," treats the rights and duties of the faithful, the rights and duties of the various offices in the Church, groupings of particular churches

(such as provinces and dioceses), the internal ordering of dioceses and parishes and religious institutes. The third book, "The Teaching Office of the Church," deals with preaching, evangelization, missionary activity, Catholic educational institutions and the means of social communication.

The fourth book of the Code is perhaps the most important, for it contains the canons that pertain to the sacraments and other means of sanctification. Entitled, "The Office of Sanctifying in the Church," this book has a separate section for each sacrament. It also has canons that deal with sacramentals, sacred times and places, funeral rites, and sacred images and relics. The following book (Book Five) is entitled, "The Temporal Goods of the Church." Here are found the canons that relate to the acquisition, administration and transfer of Church property and other material goods.

The sixth book is entitled "Sanctions in the Church." It deals with ecclesiastical crimes and penalties. The final book is concerned with processes, and its title is just that. In this book are found the canons that outline the tribunal or court procedures used in Church trials, including marriage nullity trials, criminal trials and administrative actions.

Codex • The ancient prototype of our contemporary "book." Papyrus rolls (ancient forms of paper made of reeds) were cut into pages and stacked into piles. They were then folded one or more times to form a codex or book. Eventually parchment replaced papyrus, which made for easier folding and a more stable, less brittle book. Codices produced in the second century are almost entirely Christian biblical manuscripts which may suggest that the early Christians differentiated between Christian Scriptures (especially the Old Testament) and the Jewish scrolls of the synagogue. Our most famous parchment codices are biblical:

Codex Alexandrinus (a fifth-century manuscript of almost the complete Bible); Codex Vaticanus and Codex Sinaiticus (both fourth-century manuscripts); Codex Bezea (fifth-century bilingual manuscript of Gospels and Acts in Greek and Latin).

For further reading: Harry Y. Gamble et al., "Codex," *Anchor Bible Dictionary*, 1:1067-1075.

Codex, Canonical • In canon law, a codex is a technical term referring to a unified body of law known as a Code of Canon Law, and is to be distinguished from a mere collection of laws, variously ordered. There have been two codes in the Western Church, both issued this century: the *Codex Iuris Canonici* of 1917, and its replacement, the *Codex Iuris Canonici* of 1983. A *Codex Iuris Canonici Orientalis* (Eastern Code of Canon Law) was promulgated September of 1990. (Cf. Canon Law, Eastern; Canon Law, History of.)

Coelibatus Sacerdotalis • In his 1967 encyclical on priestly celibacy, Pope Paul VI explained the reasons for a celibate priestly class by drawing from a number of sources. First, while noting that the Second Vatican Council declared that priestly celibacy "is not . . . required by the nature of the priesthood itself," Paul VI argued that such a discipline exemplified the radical newness of the New Testament covenant.

On a strictly historical level, the Pope observed that the celibacy requirement accords with the life of Christ, Who remained celibate throughout His life of "total and exclusive dedication" to God and men. Indeed, Christ exhorted His Apostles to follow His example by leaving home, and in some cases family, to forge the kingdom of heaven.

On a deeper theological level, the Pope wrote that celibacy expresses the "fullness of love" to which Christ calls every man. It is

an unconditional love, spurring all to charity and capturing the uniqueness of man in his capacity for transcendence.

And finally, the consecrated celibacy of sacred ministers also carries a strong ecclesiological or communal significance, insofar as it renders manifest and concrete "the virginal love of Christ for His Church."

Coenobium • Derived from the Greek *koinon* (common), coenobium is the ecclesiastical term for a group of monks who live their religious life in community. The individual in such a community is called a coenobite or cenobite, a term used in the early Church for monks. While Isidore of Seville reflects a knowledge of the Greek etymology, he also relates this term to the Latin *cena* (meal), since the coenobites, as distinct from hermits and anchorites, would share their meals in common (Isid. Sev., *Etym.* VII:13, 2; XII:13, 2; XV:3, 7; 4, 6). St. Pachomius (d. 346), author of the earliest rule for coenobites, is honored as the "Founder of Monasticism."

Coenobium is also the Latin name for the monastery where the coenobites lived their community life; it can also be the specific name for the monastery church, as distinct from the other buildings.

Collateral • The word "collateral" refers to something "alongside." In canon law, collateral means blood relations outside the direct line of descent, such as brothers and sisters, nieces and nephews, cousins, etc. A collateral relationship is an impediment to marriage, except for the more distant degrees of kin, which are eligible for dispensation.

Collateral can, in a wider legal sense, also refer to properties put up as full or partial guarantees that debts will be paid or services will be performed. The canon law on temporal goods restricts the ability of Church leaders to use certain ecclesiastical property as collateral for loans (Canon 1295).

Collation • From the Latin *collatus* (from the infinitive *conferre*, to bring together), a collation is the light meal taken on a fast day in place of lunch or dinner. Its name likely derives from the *collationes*, selections from the Fathers of the Church usually read at mealtimes in monastic communities. In religious houses, a collation can also refer to light refreshments provided in the afternoon or evening, outside Lent or Advent.

In canon law, a collation is the act of appointment of a new person to an ecclesiastical office or benefice.

Collect • Now called the Opening Prayer in English, the Collect occurs at the conclusion of the Introductory Rites of the Mass, just before the Liturgy of the Word. It is usually addressed to the Father and is concluded (as is all Christian prayer) through the Son and in the Holy Spirit. In it, the celebrant "collects" the prayer of the assembly and officially offers it to God. Latin Collects often have a tightly constructed parallelism that is difficult to render in English, although Cranmer in his translations for the Book of Common Prayer did so incomparably.

Collection, Offertory: See **Offertory Collection**

Collection of Masses of the Blessed Virgin Mary • Promulgated in Latin on August 15, 1986, and appearing in English in 1988 (partial translation) and 1990 (complete), this compilation of over forty Mass formularies in honor of Our Lady fulfills in an admirable way Vatican II's desire to consider Mary in the context of the mystery of Christ and His Church (Dogmatic Constitution on the Church, *Lumen Gentium*) and to reorder popular devotion according to the norm of liturgical prayer (Constitution on the Sacred Liturgy, *Sacrosanctum Concilium*). The General Introduction to the Collection also makes mention of Pope Paul VI's *Marialis Cultus*, On the Right Ordering of Marian Devotion, as providing inspiration and guidance in preparing the Collection.

In preparing this *Collection*, the Congregation for Divine Worship drew on Marian Propers gathered from various dioceses and religious orders, frequently adapting the texts and adding a proper preface for each formulary. The Introduction to each Mass is a wealth of sound doctrinal, liturgical and spiritual orientation, providing ample study and homiletic material.

The Masses are designated according to Marian titles or mysteries and ordered so as to harmonize with the liturgical year. For instance, formularies for Advent include Masses to honor Our Lady "of the Annunciation," "of the Visitation." Lenten Masses are entitled "Mary at the Foot of the Cross," "the Virgin of Reconciliation." In Eastertide, one finds "Mary, Queen of the Apostles," and so forth. During Ordinary Time are numerous titles taken from the Litany of Our Lady (Loreto) or from popular devotion (e.g., Mother of Divine Providence).

Intended primarily for use at Marian shrines, and urging respect for the *cursus* (order of readings) of the lectionary especially during the privileged seasons, the General Introduction notes that the Collection will be helpful "to those ecclesial communities that wish to celebrate the Saturday memorial in honor of Our Lady according to the rubrics." The Collection commends itself to the universal Church as a successful attempt to bring from the Church's liturgical and devotional treasuries "the new and the old."

Collections, Canonical • The written accumulations of Church laws that provided the major source for the Church's legislation prior to the twelfth century. For the most part, the collections were compilations of the canons of local or territorial synods and councils that took place throughout the Church. There were also collections of the canons and decrees of the Church's general councils. Although often arranged by order of topic, these collections did not provide a systematic explanation of Church law. None were officially approved by the highest authority in the Church until 1234, when the *Decretals of Gregory IX* was promulgated as the first official law book for the Church.

Collectivism • Refers to an economic system in which property is owned and administered by the state. Under strict collectivism, private property and wealth are not allowed. The Soviet Union and Communist China are major countries where collectivism was practiced, although each of these regimes is now allowing some independent profit-making activity to alleviate shortages of agricultural goods.

The main focus of contemporary Marxist collectivism is the proletariat or working class. Under previous economic systems, such as feudalism and capitalism, the lords or capitalists, respectively, oppressed the propertyless workers. The goal of Marxist collectivism is to create a state in which the proletariat dominates its former class enemies, and in which the workers can enjoy the abundance of their collective efforts. In reality, however, economic motivation is poorer in countries founded on Marxist collectivism than in capitalist or mixed economies. The domination of society by a Communist party which does not have to submit itself to regular judgment by the people restricts the participation of persons in determining their own economic destiny.

Catholic social teaching, by contrast, affirms the person and not the economic class as the focus of social ethics. Persons need private property to carry out their natural obligations, such as providing for themselves and their families. Respect for the dignity of persons means respecting their autonomy. Persons who have no chance to participate in bargaining to determine the price the capitalist will pay for their labor are persons reduced to an undignified dependence. According to the National Conference of Catholic Bishops' pastoral letter, *Catholic Social Teaching and the U.S. Economy* (1985), persons also have a right to participate in the life of the community and in the decisions its institutions make regarding them. Thus a policy which permits the poor to participate is better than a well-designed solution to economic problems imposed on the poor.

Christian teaching about the common good of humankind, as it emerges from papal encyclicals and pastoral letters of bishops, has three major aspects. First, while the person is inviolable and never simply a member of a collective, the person is by nature social and realizes dignity in community with others. (Cf. Encyclicals, Social). Second, the wealth of the planet was given to humankind as a whole to use in stewardship in service of human dignity and well-being. The bishops support the freedom of "entrepreneurship, business, and finance," but believe that the well-off should pay to the community and its poor a percentage of the gains made possible by the resources of the earth. Third, in defending the rights of the worker to organize, papal encyclicals since Pope Leo XIII's *Rerum Novarum* maintain that laborers should be allowed to seek a collective agreement about wages with simply a contract between each isolated worker and his or her employer. Social institutions which prevent workers from organizing when they wish to do so are, therefore, unjust. Such anti-union laws interfere with the naturally social nature of persons, their participation and their bid for a share of God's gifts to the earth.

In this way, both Marxist collectivism and unrestricted market capitalism offend against the person. Collectivism undercuts the spontaneity of autonomous or independent groups in society as they seek realization of particular and personal goods. Unrestricted capitalism treats the human and inanimate resources needed for production as mere private property, while the Christian Tradition believes resources were given to humankind in common.

College • An organized group of persons having a common purpose. Canon law provides for several collegiate bodies or colleges in the structure of the Church. These include the College of Bishops, the College of Cardinals, the College of Consultors. The term "college" is used rather than "council" or a similar collective term because of the unique authority and responsibility connected with a college. The College of Bishops is the foremost such group in the Church for, together with the Pope, it is the highest authority in the Church. Other groupings, such as pastoral councils or finance councils, are sometimes erroneously referred to as collegial bodies; however, they lack both the authority and the responsibility for Church affairs that rest with a college.

The term "college" also refers to an institution of higher learning.

College of Cardinals • Has its origins in the clergy of the city of Rome and the bishops of the Roman Province, to which have been added specifically named Eastern patriarchs. The College is divided into three orders: bishops, who are titulars of the suburbicarian (suffragan) sees of Rome and Eastern patriarchs; priests, who are titulars of various presbyterial churches in the Diocese of Rome; and deacons, who are titulars of various diaconal churches in Rome. In 1961 Pope John XXIII decreed that all cardinals be invested with episcopal dignity. Until that time it was possible for an individual to become a cardinal without even priestly ordination. The last cardinal who was not an ordained priest was Giacomo Antonelli (1806-1876), the Secretary of State of Pope Pius IX, who was ordained to the diaconate.

The cardinals serve as the chief counselors and collaborators of the Holy Father in the government of the Church and have the most important task of electing a Pope when the office falls vacant.

College of Consultors • A stable body involved in the governance of a diocese. It is composed of between six and twelve priests and is presided over by the diocesan bishop. Members are chosen by the bishop from among the members of the presbyterial council. The bishop is required by law to consult with the College on certain matters and to obtain their consent on certain other matters about which he must make a decision (Canon 502).

The College of Consultors is given specific duties by the general law. These include the election of a diocesan administrator when the see falls vacant (Canon 421.1), specific decisions while a see is vacant (Canons 272, 413, 419, 422, 501) and certain financial duties such as advice regarding the hiring and firing of the finance officer (Canon 494), consent for certain acts of extraordinary administration (Canon 1277) and for the alienation of certain types of ecclesiastical property (Canon 1292.1) are also proper to the consultors.

Under the 1917 Code, the consultors constituted a board and were not referred to as a college. Furthermore, they were appointed only in those dioceses that did not have a chapter of canons. Under the revised Code every diocese must have a

College of Consultors, even those having a chapter of canons, unless particular law has transferred the duties of the consultors over to the chapter of canons.

Collegiality • A broad term that describes the exercise of authority in the Church. The fundamental teaching and governing authority, ordered to the building up of the Body of Christ and ultimately the salvation of the members of the Church, has been handed down from the Apostles. The Apostles did not act in isolation as they continued the mission of Christ, but rather as one body, even though they might have been geographically separated. They formed one college with St. Peter as their head. In the most fundamental sense, collegiality means the working together to promote the mission of the Church. It does not mean that all have equal authority with regard to ecclesiastical offices held.

In the strict sense, collegiality describes the manner in which the body of bishops in communion with the Church, together with the Pope, exercises its power. It does so solemnly when the bishops gather in ecumenical council acting in union with the successor of Peter (cf. LG 23, 25). The bishops also act in a collegial manner when they exercise their responsibilities while dispersed throughout the world. The concept of collegiality means that the bishops do not function as vicars or representatives of the Pope. Rather, they act as representatives of Christ in their dioceses. Because the Lord named Peter to be the head of the Church, the bishops act collegially only when doing so together with the successor of Peter.

Collegiate Church • A collegiate or collegial church is any church staffed and served by specially designated (arch)diocesan priests known as canons and united in a group called the chapter of canons. If the church happens to be the cathedral, as is often the case, the chapter of canons is known as the cathedral chapter. The 1983 Code of Canon Law has generally reduced the role of chapters of canons to care for the more important liturgical celebrations in that church (Canon 503). Formerly, many such chapters also had considerable administrative responsibilities. The practice of establishing churches as collegial is in decline and is quite rare in the United States.

A collegial church, finally, should not be confused with a "college church" which is an unofficial title sometimes bestowed on churches serving colleges and universities.

Collegiate Tribunal • A panel of three or five (for more difficult or serious cases) judges assigned to hear a case in an ecclesiastical court. The law requires that certain types of cases be tried before a collegiate tribunal: contentious cases concerning the bond of marriage and the bond of ordination; penal cases concerning possible dismissal from the clerical state or imposition of excommunication.

In deciding a case, each judge prepares a *votum*, or opinion, stating his decision. They meet at a time set by the presiding judge, and the decisions are read. The judges then have the opportunity to discuss the case and change their votes, if necessary. A majority is needed for a decision. Once the decision has been made, the judge appointed to be the *ponens*, or recording judge, composes the definitive sentence from the elements found in the three written opinions (Canons 1425-1426, 1609).

Although a collegiate tribunal is the rule for the types of cases mentioned above, if sufficient judges are not available, the bishop, with the approval of the episcopal conference, can entrust certain cases to a single judge. This is regularly done with marriage nullity cases.

Collegium Cultorum Martyrum • In 1897 the Collegium Cultorum Martyrum was founded to spread devotion to the saints by arranging for remembrances and special addresses on their various feast days. It was also intended to further the archaeological efforts of the Church, in particular, the excavation work then being conducted beneath the City of Rome, the burial place of so many of the ancient martyrs. (Cf. Dulia.)

Colors, Liturgical • The classic listing of the liturgical colors of white, red, violet, green and black is found in the *De Sacro Altaris Mysterio* of Pope Innocent III (1198-1216). Before this codified development, the practice of the West was doubtless that of the East, which still uses darker, more somber vestments during penitential seasons and brighter, more glorious ones for great feasts.

The color sequence used in the Roman Rite is: white for feasts of Our Lord (except of His passion) and Our Lady, for the seasons of Christmas and Easter, for the angels and for saints who were not martyrs; red for Palm Sunday, Good Friday, feasts of Apostles and evangelists (except John) and for martyrs; purple for Lent and Advent, except for Laetare Sunday in Lent and Gaudete Sunday in Advent, when old-rose (*not* pink) vestments are permitted. Green is the color for Ordinary Time and black may still be used for Masses of the Dead, although purple and white are also permitted, and white has become the most popular color in many countries.

Blue was permitted by indult in Spain for feasts of Our Lady, and some are trying to revive it for Advent today to give a Marian cast to the season and to distinguish this season from Lent. The American Bishops' Committee on the Liturgy notes, however, that this has no official standing. Some have defended its use as supposedly being simply another shade of violet, originally produced in northern Europe from berries yielding a bluer violet dye than that from the mollusks in the South, which rendered a redder violet.

Colossians, Epistle to the • Colossae was a city in the northwest region of Asia Minor called Phrygia, whose other principal cities were Laodicea and Hierapolis. Paul brought the Gospel to the first two cities on his second (Acts 16:6) and third (Acts 18:23) missionary journeys. The Church in Colossae may have been founded by Epaphras (Col 1:7), who was a native (Col 4:12).

Major Themes: There were faulty teachings about the direct effect which spiritual beings known as "principalities and powers" (Col 2:15) were thought to have on the destiny of humans. In addition, Jewish and non-Jewish cultic practices were being "combined" (syncretism) (Col 2:16, 21). Given the cultural context of the Church's Gentile and Jewish population, it is highly likely that belief in the principalities and widespread use of unacceptable cultic and liturgical rituals were combined with the biblical traditions about angelic mediation of divine revelation (e.g., Dn 10:21; 12:1). The author of Colossians addresses these problems, which ensued from such a combination.

Contents:
A. Introduction: 1:1-12
   1. Greetings: 1:1-2
   2. Thanksgiving: 1:3-8
   3. Prayer: 1:9-12
B. Doctrinal Section: 1:13—2:3
   1. Christ, supreme redeemer and reconciler: 1:13-23
   2. Paul's proclamation of Christ's primacy: 1:24—2:3
C. Polemical Section: 2:4-23
   1. Persevere against "false teachers": 2:4-8
   2. Christ is authentic life and true freedom: 2:9-15

3. Abandon practices which enslave: 2:16-23
D. Ethical/Moral Exhortations: 3:1—4:1
  1. Resurrection foundation: 3:1-4
  2. The virtues and relationships: 3:12-17
  3. The family household: 3:18-21
  4. Continued prayer, relating to non-Christians: 4:2-6
E. Conclusions: 4:7-18
  1. Paul's representatives: 4:7-9
  2. Salutations: 4:10-17
  3. Signature: 4:18

Authorship and Date: Long-standing tradition accepts the Pauline authorship of the epistle. Current opinion is divided on this question for the following reasons. Some of the vocabulary in Colossians is not found in any of the uncontested Pauline writings (e.g., eighty-six words found in Colossians are not in Paul's undisputed letters, thirty-four of which are nowhere else in the New Testament). The differences in style between, on the one hand, Romans, 1 and 2 Corinthians and Galatians and, on the other hand, Colossians, as well as the highly developed theological view of the universal Church in Colossians, have led some scholars to question Pauline authorship. Objections to Pauline authorship are intriguing but unconvincing, given the quantitative lack of historical data currently available. Pauline authenticity should not be rejected. Traditional dates should be followed, placing the time of writing sometime during Paul's Roman house arrest, c. A.D. 62-63.

For further reading: Victor Paul Furnish, "Colossians, Epistle to the," *Anchor Bible Dictionary,* 1:1090-1096; Maurya P. Horgan, "The Letter to the Colossians," *New Jerome Biblical Commentary,* 876-882.

Commandments of the Church • The Commandments of the Church emerged during the Middle Ages in association with confessional practice. They were described by Cardinal Gasparri as being "of very great significance for the general spiritual life of the faithful." In their most widespread form, they are derived from St. Peter Canisius (1555), and they required: (1) observance of particular feast days; (2) reverent attendance at Mass on Sundays and holy days of obligation; (3) observance of obligatory days of fasting and abstinence; (4) annual confession; and (5) reception of Holy Communion at Easter. Under the influence of St. Robert Bellarmine, the commandment requiring support for the Church was added, and others regarding "forbidden times" and obligations to give Catholic education were promulgated. Yet, despite their long-standing acceptance by the Church, the commandments were never officially approved by the Church.

They have as their immediate goal the preservation of public order in the Church. Obedience is to be demanded to the extent required by the common good of the Church and the well-being of the faithful. Ecclesiastical legislation may legitimately seek to assure and promote the development of the spiritual life of the faithful, for this is not detrimental to the free working of the Holy Spirit. The Commandments of the Church foster a sense of personal responsibility by reminding the faithful of their minimal responsibilities toward the Church. Their observance instills a sense of discipline that fosters a sense of responsibility. The Commandments of the Church must be linked to pastoral education which promotes this sense of responsibility and encourages personal initiative in the spiritual life.

Commandments of God • The Decalogue, the "Ten Words" given by God to Moses on Mt. Sinai, are considered to be the divinely instituted ordinances concerning the requirements of true worship and morality.

The Commandments of God articulate what is required for the attainment of human fulfillment and union with God. They are constituted by the covenant, giving material content to the covenantal demand for human fidelity and worship.

The Decalogue also articulates the *minimal* requirements of true worship and fidelity to divine love, while the Commandments of God in the New Covenant (the Great Commandment of Love) articulate the *fullness* of the covenant. The New Covenant requires all that is demanded by the Decalogue as well as the Great Commandment. (Cf. *Catechism of the Catholic Church*, n. 2080.)

For further reading: *Catechism of the Catholic Church*, nn. 2056-2082; Raymond F. Collins, "Commandment," *Anchor Bible Dictionary*, 1:1097-1099.

Commemoration • The former practice of adding Collects to the collect proper to the feast being celebrated, thereby "commemorating" the other feast not kept. The current liturgy now observes the ancient Roman practice of having only one Collect in a given Mass. If several optional memorials fall on the same day, then only one may be selected and celebrated.

Commemoration of the Living and the Dead • Traditionally in the Roman Liturgy special commemorations to pray for the living and the dead have been included in the Eucharistic Prayer. In the early Church names were listed on two tablets called *diptychs*, which lists were read by the deacon or priest. In all the present Eucharistic Prayers, the tradition of prayer for the living and dead continues. In the Roman Canon the priest and people may silently call to mind those for whom they wish to pray.

Commendation of the Soul • The Lord died praying the verse from Psalm 31, "Into thy hands, I commit my spirit," as did St. Stephen (cf. Lk 23:46; Acts 7:59), and the Church has always surrounded the moment of dying with prayer. Special prayers for this time had developed by the seventh century and included psalms (later the penitential psalms) and antiphons, the *Subvenite* and *Chorus Angelorum* and a litany. The present practice of the Church is found in the Rite for the Pastoral Care of the Sick published in 1972.

Commentaries, Biblical • Books or series of books written in an attempt to explain the Scriptures. Jewish tradition includes biblical commentary among the rabbinical writings such as *haggadah*, *halakah* and *midrash*. In Christian biblical commentary, distinctions are made among the patristic (such as Origen, Jerome, Augustine, Ambrose and Theodoret of Cyr), the medieval (Rabanus Maurus, Bernard of Clairvaux and Peter Comestor) and the modern (the first of which must be the Jesuit Cornelius Lapide). Among commentaries in use today, certainly the *New Jerome Biblical Commentary* is the premier work in the field; other Catholic commentaries include the *Collegeville Bible Commentary*, and the *Old Testament Message* and *New Testament Message* series.

Commissary • A person who has delegated jurisdiction. Generally, there are four kinds of commissaries:

(1) An apostolic commissary is one who, having been designated by the Holy Father, either serves as an administrator or pronounces judgment in a particular case.

(2) The commissary of the Holy Land is a Franciscan priest who collects monies for the maintenance of the Holy Places of Palestine.

(3) A provincial commissary serves as the superior of a province of Franciscan Conventuals and Franciscan Friars Minor where there is an inadequate number of religious to form an independent province. Therefore, this group of few members is dependent upon another province.

(4) A simple commissary is a priest who possesses jurisdiction from a bishop.

Commissions, Ecclesiastical • Broadly speaking, any distinct body to which is entrusted a specific, even if broad, task or duty. Commissions are found at every level of the Church (universal, diocesan or parish) and can also serve such intermediate structures as episcopal conferences. Commissions are usually established for the purpose of gathering information on special problems or issues and therefore tend to serve in a consultative capacity. Following the curial reforms of *Pastor Bonus* under Pope John Paul II, the number and status of papal commissions were somewhat modified. Two commissions remain of particular importance, however, namely the International Theological Commission and the International Biblical Commission (instituted in 1902); both commissions are auxiliary to the Congregation for the Doctrine of the Faith.

Commixture, Liturgical • The dropping of a piece of the consecrated Bread into the chalice after having broken the Host while the prayer *Haec commixtio* ("May this mingling of the Body and Blood," etc.) is said. The origins of this rite are to be found in the *fermentum*, during which a piece of the consecrated Bread was broken off and sent to be part of another Eucharistic celebration to show the essential unity of the Church in the Eucharistic Sacrifice. When this was no longer done, the piece was dropped into the chalice and medieval allegorical explanations were developed to explain the practice.

Common Life • Phrase describing religious life as sharing a common ideal and apostolic goal, as well as a common table, dwelling and fund. Those religious so living submit to a common rule and superior.

Common Prayer, Book of: See **Book of Common Prayer**

Common of the Saints • The body of prayer formularies and texts in the sacramentary and Liturgy of the Hours in which can be found the Masses and Offices for saints not having their own prescribed texts. They are divided into various classes: pastors, martyrs, virgins, etc.

Common Teaching of Theologians • A classical theological note used in dogmatic theology to characterize certain opinions. This certitude was traditionally lower than a theological conclusion in the strict sense, but in contemporary theology this note is rarely cited, because of the welter of conflicting opinions.

Communicatio Idiomatum • The term *communicatio idiomatum* ("communication of properties") is the Latin tag for a linguistic rule for predications about Christ, according to which divine and human attributes may be interchangeably ascribed to the divine or human natures in Him by reason of their unity in the one Divine Person. Church Fathers, for example, Cyril of Alexandria (d. A.D. 444), propounded the rule in order to counter the sharp disjunction between the two natures in Christ characteristic of the Nestorian heresy. The rule found its way into normative Christian tradition by its inclusion in Pope St. Leo's *Tome* (449). Since there is one hypostasis or Person possessing both natures, properties of either nature refer to that one hypostasis. Thus, it is proper to say both that "Jesus Christ is God" and "Jesus Christ is man." Although it is inappropriate, according to this rule, to distinguish things predicated of Christ, still we do distinguish the basis upon which they are predicated: What belongs to the Divine Nature is predicated of Christ in His Divine Nature, and what belongs to the human nature is predicated of Christ in His human nature.

Communicatio in Sacris • *Communicatio in sacris* means the reception of the sacraments of the Church by persons who are not members of the Church. Under the 1917 Code, even worship in common was strictly forbidden.

The revised Code has made dramatic changes in the regulation on sharing the sacraments. In certain cases, baptized non-Catholics can receive the sacraments of Penance, Anointing of the Sick and, of course, Matrimony. It is also possible for Catholics to receive the sacraments of Penance, Anointing of the Sick and the Eucharist in non-Catholic denominations.

Whenever necessity requires, or if a genuine spiritual advantage suggests it, if a Catholic cannot approach a Catholic sacred minister, he or she may receive the sacraments of Penance, Anointing or the Eucharist from non-Catholic clergy in whose Churches these sacraments are valid. For all practical purposes, this applies only to priests of the Eastern Orthodox Churches. This canon would apply to Catholics who find themselves in areas where there are few if any Catholic churches or ministers or where it is morally or physically impossible to approach a Catholic minister (Canon 844.2).

Catholic ministers may administer the same three sacraments to members of the Eastern Orthodox Churches or other churches with valid sacraments when they approach a Catholic minister, are properly disposed and ask for the sacrament on their own. Catholic ministers are not to invite such persons to receive the sacraments (Canon 844.3).

Finally, in certain instances these same sacraments may be administered to other Christians, e.g., Protestants. Certain special conditions apply in such cases. First, there is to be a danger of death or other grave necessity. Second, the approval of the diocesan bishop is required. Third, the person requesting the sacrament must be properly disposed, manifest a Catholic belief in the nature of the sacrament and be unable to approach a minister of his own denomination (Canon 844.4).

Communication, Decree on the Means of Social: See **Inter Mirifica**

Communications Foundation, Catholic: See **Catholic Communications Foundation**

Communion, Holy • The Body and Blood, Soul and Divinity of Jesus Christ, which can be received by any baptized Catholic at any Mass as long as he or she is free of mortal sin and therefore in the state of grace. A fast from food and drink (water is not considered drink for fasting purposes) at least an hour before the reception of Communion is required, except for those ill or advanced in age. In the Western Church, children before the age of reason (usually thought to be about seven years of age) are excluded.

In the Roman Rite, Communion is given under the form of unleavened bread. According to the guidelines of the Church and the local bishops' conference, Communion may be received under both species, by intinction or directly from the chalice. Catholics of the Byzantine Rite receive the Host (under the appearance of cubed, leavened bread) soaked in the

Precious Blood from a little spoon used by the priest.

In the Roman Rite when the Host is offered to the communicant, he or she replies "Amen," and the same is true should the chalice be offered. Hymns may be sung at this time by the people or the choir. This was the time when the Latin-chant piece the "*Communio*" was sung in the old rite and it may still be used in the current rite. Silence after Communion is recommended in the present *Ordo Missae.*

Those who are not able to receive Communion, because they have not fasted or are in a state of serious sin (e.g., irregular marital situation) or are not Catholic, are encouraged to make a "spiritual Communion," whereby one expresses one's desire to receive by acts of love and thanksgiving to God which prepare the person to receive grace.

Communion of the Mass • The Order of the Mass is structured around three principal parts: the Introductory Rites, the Liturgy of the Word and the Eucharistic Liturgy. The Communion of the Mass comprises that section of the Eucharistic Liturgy beginning with the recitation of the Our Father, moving through the sign of peace, the fraction of the Bread, the Communion of the celebrant and then the Communion of the faithful. The Communion of the Mass is in a real sense the organic culmination of the whole celebration and the climax of the participation of the faithful. It is at this very moment that the intimate bond between Christ and His community is confirmed by their reception of His Body and Blood. This Communion is itself the basis of the union of Christ with us, and of our unity with each other in Him, and thus a foretaste of the eternal fellowship of heaven.

Communion of Saints • Affirmed by the Second Council of Nicaea, the Council of Florence and the Council of Trent, the ninth article of the Apostles' Creed states that a spiritual union exists among the saints in heaven, the souls in purgatory and the faithful living on earth; this communion of the saints is described as "the living communion which exists between us and our brothers who are in the glory of heaven or who are yet being purified after their death. . ." (LG 51).

The Second Vatican Council further declared: ". . . our community with the saints joins us to Christ, from whom as from its fountain and head issues all grace and the life of the People of God itself. It is most fitting, therefore, that we love those friends and co-heirs of Jesus Christ who are also our brothers and outstanding benefactors, and that we give due thanks to God for them, humbly invoking them, and having recourse to their prayers. . ." (LG 50).

Communism • The doctrine that promotes the common sharing of goods, while simultaneously denying the right to own private property. Karl Marx (1818-1883) was a primary force behind this radical kind of socialism. Communism exalts matter over spirit; hence this philosophy, known as "dialectical materialism," jettisons any notion of and need for God. In addition, economics is believed to be the foundation of civilization; thus all other ideas — religious, social, political, etc. — depend upon the prevailing economy. The state is supreme in Communism and applies a totalitarian grip to the masses, thereby attempting to indoctrinate the people while suppressing any ideas contrary to Communism. The Church has opposed Communism since its beginning. In his 1937 encyclical *Divini Redemptoris*, Pope Pius XI condemned Communism and urged Catholics not to collaborate with Communists in political or social endeavors.

Community • This term has several important meanings in Catholic usage. In the first place, it refers to that unity or communion in which all the followers of Christ participate by virtue of being joined to Him through justifying and sanctifying grace. Just as the people of Israel were "no people" until God had called them out of Egypt, so the diverse gathering of believers in Christ is constituted a community, precisely in virtue of His reconciling grace. By this grace, we are joined with one another by being joined to Him. This gathered community of the faithful is the vanguard and promise of the union of all human beings as children of God which will be revealed in the *eschaton* when all things will be one in Christ. The bond which unites this community is none other than the bond of charity that unites us to the indwelling Trinity.

In this light, the ultimate ground of the community of persons united in Christ is the uncreated community of the Three Persons who are God. For Catholics, all other senses of the term "community" depend on this fundamental meaning. Particularly important expressions of the community of those gathered in Christ are the local communities constituted by each diocese and parish, and each religious order and its houses. The sense of the wider community gathered in Christ is fostered in the concrete by the experience of the community of persons that forms the ordinary circle of our daily faith and practice. Each Christian is in an important sense formed in faith by this local community, by service to it and, with it, by service to others in the name of Christ.

Comparative Religion • The comparative study of the fundamental doctrines of the world's religions, both major (e.g., Hinduism, Buddhism, Judaism, Christianity, and Islam) and local or traditional (previously termed "primitive," e.g., Amerindian and African) by historical and social scientific methods. Comparative religion dates from the nineteenth century when the universality of religious ideas and the recurrence of certain patterns of religious belief and practice came under intense study. The interest of Western intellectuals was aroused at least in part as a result of their wider and deeper awareness of the diversity of the religious beliefs and practices encountered through colonization, travel and reading. Philosophical interest in the anthropological basis of religious experience was also a stimulus to the comparative study of religion. Given the Christian background and (sometimes) convictions of many early practitioners of this study, comparative religion often centered on the analysis of parallels and contrasts between Christianity and non-Christian religions, or at least between Western and non-Western religious ideas. A century of energetic work by comparatists has generated an impressive body of editorial, descriptive and analytical literature on the world's religions. Central elements of religious belief and practice have been particular foci of attention: ideas of a supreme being, salvation, sin, evil, suffering, incarnation, sacred times and places, ritual and worship, and ethical systems. In the modern academy, the comparative study of religions has become a highly diversified and internally specialized set of disciplines under the general rubric of "religious studies." Fundamental to the discipline's self-understanding is a scientific neutrality as to the validity of the religious ideas studied. Issues of truth are commonly thought to be the competence of philosophers and theologians rather than comparatists.

Competence • The ability of an ecclesiastical court or judge to hear and make a decision about a case. Competence, or jurisdiction over a case, is based on a number of possible factors.

First, the cases of certain juridic and physical persons are reserved to certain persons or courts for judgment. No one is competent to judge the Holy See or the Roman Pontiff (Canon 1404.1). Only the Roman Pontiff can judge the cases of cardinals, the heads of state, apostolic legates, the penal cases of bishops, or any other case the Pope chooses to reserve to himself. Certain cases are reserved to the Roman Rota: contentious cases of bishops, all cases involving abbots primate, abbots of monastic congregations, supreme moderators of religious institutes of pontifical right and dioceses or other juridic or physical persons who do not have a superior below the Roman Pontiff (Canon 1405.3). In all the above cases, if anyone other than the person or court mentioned judges a case, the process and decision are invalid.

Competence can also depend on the place where the disputed actions took place. This includes such things as the place of marriage if it is a marriage nullity case, the place where an ecclesiastical crime took place, or the place where an object actually is, if it is a suit over property ownership. In all such cases, by "place" is meant within the territory of the diocese (cf. Canons 1410-1412).

Competence in some cases depends on the residence of one or both parties to a dispute. Ordinarily, a person can be brought before the tribunal of the diocese wherein he or she has either a domicile or a quasi-domicile (Canon 1408). A wanderer can be brought before the tribunal of the diocese wherein he or she is actually staying at the time.

There are special rules for marriage nullity cases. Always competent are the tribunals of the dioceses where the marriage took place or where the respondent has a domicile or quasi-domicile (Canon 1673.1.2). The petitioner can ask that the tribunal of his or her diocese declare itself competent, but to do so it is required that the judicial vicar of this diocese seek permission of the judicial vicar of the diocese of the respondent. The respondent must be asked if he or she has any objections, but this does not mean that actual permission is required (Canon 1673). Finally, a case can be tried in the tribunal of the place where, in fact, most of the proofs are to be gathered, provided the judicial vicar of the tribunal of the respondent consults the respondent and then gives his permission (Canon 1673.4). In all cases, with the exception of those reserved to the Holy See or to the Roman Rota, if a suit is heard and decided by a judge who is not competent, the process and decision remain valid but are considered illicit (Canon 1407).

Complaint of Nullity • A canonical act whereby a person charges that a sentence in a case suffers from a substantial defect. In some instances, the defect can render the decision itself invalid, which means that the case must be tried again. This is called "irremediable nullity." In other instances, the error is remediable, which means that it is automatically corrected if no complaint against it is lodged within three months; in other cases, the sentence can be rectified by simply healing or correcting the error. Nullity of a sentence is the result of some procedural error of a greater or lesser magnitude.

The law specifies that a sentence is irremediably null in the following cases: the judge had no jurisdiction because the case was reserved to the Holy See or the Roman Rota; the judge lacked the power of judging in the tribunal where the case was settled; the judge passed the sentence under grave fear or duress; the trial began without a petition or had no respondent; neither party to the trial had standing in the court; the right of defense was denied the respondent; a procurator acted in the name of another without a mandate to do so; or the sentence failed to address the controversy (Canon 1620).

A sentence is remediably null and can be corrected without repeating the entire judicial process in the following cases: fewer than the required number of judges passed the sentence; the sentence does not contain the reasons or motives for the decision; the sentence lacks the signatures required by law (those of the judges and a notary); the date of the decision is omitted in the sentence; the sentence was based on a non-corrected judicial act; the sentence was passed before the respondent, who was cited but legitimately absent, could offer proofs (Canon 1622).

The possibility of entering a complaint of nullity serves to protect the rights of the parties involved in the case. The rights protected in this area include the right to due process.

Compline (Complin) •
Derived from the Latin *completorium* for the completion of the day, Compline is the night prayer that completes the *cursus* (course) of the Liturgy of the Hours that is prayed during the day. Now it is usually called Night Prayer. As its name implies, it is said at the end of the day not long before retiring for the night. In it the Church thanks God for the blessings

received that day and begs His protection for her children during the night.

Compostela, Pilgrimage of • Santiago de Compostela in Spain is the site of the medieval shrine of St. James the Greater, to which pilgrims have traveled from as early as the eighth century. Typically, the pilgrims to this shrine, which have included Pope John Paul II, identify themselves with a seashell or some portrayal of one; often the shell may hang from their pilgrim's staffs or it may be worn on their clothing, especially on the front of their hats, as in the typical portrayal of the saint himself.

Compostela entrance

Comunione e Liberazione • A movement of lay people, particularly the young, founded in 1958 by Monsignor Luigi Giussani, a professor of philosophy at the Catholic University of Milan, in order to help its members restore Catholic values to secular society. This fast-growing organization, whose name is translated "Communion and Liberation," stresses fidelity to Christ and the Church, recognizing that Christ's presence is most evident in the solidarity of believers, and that a true relationship with Christ entails three essentials: Scripture, the sacraments and the teaching authority of the Church. Since, according to Monsignor Giussani, contemporary society ignores God and religion, the followers of *Comunione e Liberazione* are encouraged to bring their Christian convictions to the workplace, school, home and politics, thus functioning as the leaven of the Gospel. While some members live together in community, others are free to continue a life of work, home and family. The movement has enjoyed the backing of Pope John Paul II, and is also known for its popular publication *Trenta Giorni (30 Days)*.

Concelebration • The verb "to concelebrate" in the early Church had a somewhat different meaning from the present, more technical understanding. In Christian antiquity, all Christians "concelebrated" according to their role or liturgical order in the Church. The bishop presided at the Eucharist, assisted by priests who at first just stood there, later extending hands and pronouncing the words of consecration. The deacons assisted in their role, as did the readers, the choir and the ordinary members of the congregation — all celebrating together but in different roles.

In the Middle Ages, this term came to mean exclusively the celebration by bishops and priests together (or just priests) of one Mass, and that is how this term is technically used today. After the medieval period, the growth of private Mass as among the clergy reduced the times of concelebration to the ordination of priests and the consecration of bishops in the West, although the Eastern Churches preserved the practice.

Vatican II's Constitution on the Sacred Liturgy extended the occasions for concelebration, and the new rite mandated by that Council was influenced less by the ritual of the early Church than by the medieval emphasis on the common recitation of the Words of Institution. Although there were many theological opinions as to what was necessary to have valid concelebration, the present rite has the concelebrants appropriately vested in the sanctuary and reciting together the core prayers of the Canon, including the words of Consecration. This practice is especially recommended to show forth the unity of the priesthood.

Conciliar Theory (also Conciliar Movement) • Conciliarism is a condemned but recurring theory holding that the Pope is subject to an ecumenical council. Debates on conciliarism were especially heated in the fifteenth century, for example, in the Council of Constance, and they reached near-crisis proportions in the Council of Basel convoked by Pope Martin V. The theory was firmly put down, however, at the Council of Florence in that same century, and was finally repudiated by the First Vatican Council. Today, the 1983 Code of Canon Law makes punishable by censure any attempt to have recourse against the Pope before an ecumenical council (Canon 1372).

Conclave • From the Latin *con* (with) + *clavis* (key), which refers to the enclosed meeting of the cardinals for the purpose of electing a Pope. The practice of having the election take place behind locked doors was initiated by Pope Gregory X in 1274 for the purposes of eliminating any outside interference and also to hasten the process, since a vacancy in the papacy had existed for nearly three years before his own election.

The method of electing a Pope was one that developed throughout the centuries, including the early practice of having the clergy and laity of Rome take part. In 1059 Pope Nicholas II decreed that the cardinal bishops would be the electors of the Pope, and this was modified further by the Lateran Council in 1179, which ordered that an election would require a two-thirds majority vote of the cardinals. After the development of the actual "conclave" by Pope Gregory X the process remained essentially the same until 1975, when Pope Paul VI instituted several changes in the rules governing papal elections. These changes include limiting the number of electors to one hundred twenty, excluding those cardinals over the age of eighty and outlining the particular forms of election which are acceptable. Strict rules must be followed by the conclave, which dictate those who can be present, assure freedom from any undue influence or interference, and demand absolute secrecy from all those involved.

Conclaves traditionally take place in the Vatican's Sistine Chapel, and one of the best-known customs is that of burning the ballots, producing the white smoke which indicates that a Supreme Pontiff has been elected. If the newly-elected is not a bishop, he must be ordained to the episcopacy before he is proclaimed Pope; if he is already a bishop he becomes Pope immediately upon his acceptance, and when he has given the name by which he will be known the cardinals pledge their obedience to him, after which his election is proclaimed to the world.

Concomitance • The state in which one object is associated with and simultaneously present to another object. The doctrine of concomitance is used to explain why the entire Christ — Body, Blood, Soul and Divinity — is present under each Eucharistic Species of bread and wine. When a validly ordained priest, using valid matter with the proper intention, during Mass says, "This is My Body," the Body of Christ is substantially present, while His Blood, Soul and Divinity become present by concomitance, precisely because His Body cannot be separated from His Blood, Soul and Divinity. Christ cannot be divided. When a validly ordained priest, using valid matter with the proper intention, during Mass says, "This is My Blood," the Blood of Christ is substantially present, while His Body, Soul and Divinity become present by concomitance.

Concord, Formula of • Drafted in 1577 by a number of Lutheran theologians, notably, Martin Chemnitz (1522-86) and Jakob Andreas (1528-90), this formula gave definitive expression to classical Lutheran orthodoxy. On the chief issues of doctrinal controversy with Catholics on the one hand and Calvinists on the other (mainly, sin, justification, human freedom and divine foreknowledge, predestination and the sacraments), the formula sought to clarify the fundamentals of Lutheran doctrine with the precision characteristic of confessional pronouncements.

In 1580 it was joined both with classical formulae and with previous Lutheran confessional documents (including notably the Apostles', Nicene and Athanasian Creeds, the Augsburg Confession, the Schmalkaldic Articles and Martin Luther's two Catechisms) to constitute the Book of Concord. This document sought to articulate the Lutheran consensus in a way that would match the formulations of the Council of Trent on the Catholic side. But the Book of Concord did not gain universal acceptance and never acquired the authority of the more widely influential Augsburg Confession (1530) among Lutheran churches outside Germany.

Concordance • From the Latin *concordans* (putting things in harmony), a concordance is a research tool that lists in alphabetical order the principal words of an author or of an individual book; it gives the word in its immediate context and the exact location of the word. For classical authors and books of the Bible, this is done by citing the source by book, chapter and verse. By example, in a concordance of Virgil, one might look up *arma* and find the context: *arma virumque cano*, and the location: Aeneid I:l. Similarly, in a biblical concordance, for "beginning," one finds the context: "In the beginning God created . . ." with the location: Genesis 1:1.

As translations of the Bible differ one from the other, so do biblical concordances, and an individual concordance is useful only insofar as it lists the words of a particular translation or text. Concordances exist for many translations of the Bible into modern languages, as well as for the Vulgate, the Septuagint and the original Hebrew, Aramaic and Greek texts. Many concordances are now available on computer disks.

Concordat • A treaty or agreement drawn up between the Holy See and a secular government. The purpose of such an agreement is the protection or enhancement of the spiritual welfare and even the temporal goods of the Church in the country with whom the Holy See signs the concordat.

Concordat of Worms • This agreement, also called the *Pactum Callixtinum*, was negotiated intensely for several weeks and followed a long dispute between the Holy See and the Holy Roman emperors over the right to appoint bishops in certain territories. In September 1122, the Concordat of Worms was reached between Pope Callistus II and Henry V, whereby the Pope's right to appoint bishops without interference from the state was recognized in most cases, while the election of German bishops was thenceforth to take place in Henry's presence. Clear rules for investing the bishops with their spiritual and temporal signs of authority were also set forth. The Concordat is generally believed to have served its purposes well.

Concupiscence • More broadly, it refers to a general tendency, inclination or attraction to evil, but more specifically, it refers to desires and inclinations toward bodily and fleshly pleasures. Passion or concupiscence is not evil in itself, except when unethical acts done under its impulse are chosen and given free consent. Concupiscence radically disrupts our emotional life and can be the cause of severe emotional disturbance.

Concursus • (1) The activity of God by which He, as the First Cause, relates to finite (secondary or created) causes, in order to preserve His creation. Without concursus, the activity of all creation would cease. All creatures depend upon God for their very existence and subsequent activity. Concursus is also called "divine cooperation."

(2) The examination in which a candidate competes with others for an ecclesiastical office.

Condign Merit • A grace or favor bestowed by God upon a person who has done a morally good action. In effect, condign merit is the right in justice that a person has to receive a supernatural benefit from God, due to the execution of a supernatural act. God rewards the person who performed the act; the benefit is not transferable to another person. In order to merit condignly, the living person must be in the state of grace while freely performing a morally good action directed to God. The reward for a good action is in keeping with God's revealed will and is equal or proportionate to the act. When a person merits a grace, he is cooperating with the meritorious act of our redemption wrought by Christ.

Conditional Administration of the Sacraments • Since the sacraments of Baptism, Confirmation and Holy Orders imprint a permanent character, they cannot be conferred more than once. But, for various reasons (Was the proper form employed? Was the minister duly authorized?), doubts may arise as to whether one of these sacraments has been truly and validly conferred in the first place. If investigation cannot resolve such doubts, then these sacraments can be conferred "conditionally," i.e., on the condition that the sacraments were not conferred on the occasion concerning which a legitimate doubt exists.

Conferences, Clergy • Occasional gatherings of diocesan and/or religious priests, often for the purposes of ongoing education, reflection or consultation. In a related vein, councils of clergy, called presbyterial councils, representative of the presbyterate, are mandated in each diocese "to aid the bishop in the governance of the diocese according to the norm of law, in order that the pastoral welfare of the portion of the People of God entrusted to him may be promoted as effectively as possible" (Canon 495).

Conferences, Episcopal • A grouping of all the bishops of a given territory, whereby they jointly exercise certain pastoral functions for all the Catholics within the territory. For the most part, episcopal conferences are made up of the bishops of a particular nation or country, although the law provides for the creation of conferences that are either larger or smaller than a given country.

Although many countries had groupings of their bishops prior to Vatican II, it was only with the Council that such entities received official approbation from the Holy See. Each conference is made up of all the bishops (residential, coadjutors, auxiliaries and retired bishops) within the territory. It can also include the bishops of the Oriental Rites.

Episcopal conferences are to draw up their own statutes, which need the approval of the Holy See. By law, the episcopal conference is primarily a pastoral body with only very limited legislative power accorded it. When the revised Code of Canon Law was promulgated, it contained several matters that were left to the conferences of bishops to decide, such as a higher age for marriage than that of the Code. The episcopal conferences are not the corporate headquarters of the Catholic Church in each country, nor is the elected president of each conference the supreme authority figure in the country. Each bishop is independent in his own diocese and answers directly to the Pope.

An episcopal conference can issue pastoral letters and similar documents, but it lacks the teaching authority that resides in the College of Bishops (cf. Canons 447-459).

Confession • The act of admitting or telling something not previously known. In Catholic theology, confession refers to the act of admitting personal sin to a priest and receiving sacramental pardon upon expressing contrition for it. While confession, properly speaking, only refers to the act of telling one's sins to a priest, it is also used to refer to the entire celebration of the sacrament of Penance.

By Church law (Fourth Lateran Council, 1215), Catholics are required to go to confession annually, so that they might fulfill their Easter duty. All mortal sins that Catholics are aware of must be confessed. The Council of Trent (1545-63) decreed that Catholics must confess their sins according to kind and number. Regarding the confession of children, Pope St. Pius X (1903-14) declared that the young may be admitted to the sacrament when they have reached the age of reason, determined to be at or about the seventh year. Furthermore, it is normative that children celebrate their

First Confession before receiving their First Holy Communion (*Quam Singulari*, 1910).

Catholics are urged to confess their sins to a priest in the sacrament of Penance frequently as a way of growing in holiness and virtue. Even if penitents are conscious of only venial sin, they should still have recourse to the sacrament of Penance, because it is the ordinary means of obtaining God's merciful forgiveness for any sins committed after Baptism. The surpassing spiritual benefit of confession is the subject of *Reconciliatio et Paenitentia* (1984), the post-synodal Apostolic Exhortation of Pope John Paul II.

Confession of a Martyr (also Confessio) • The Latin *confessio* has three meanings (cf. Augustine's *Confessions*, I:l): the admission of sin, the proclamation of praise and the Profession of Faith. Originally, the tomb of a martyr, particularly one in the catacombs, was called the confession of a martyr since it was in these precious relics that one saw a witness to God's glory and a witness to the Faith in a death suffered for the Lord. Today it refers to the crypt where the remains of a martyr are kept beneath the main altar of a church. In the style of the basilicas and many of the major churches in Rome, the crypt is entered from above by a grand staircase, at the top of which is a low railing with a gate in the middle. Since the crypt is not always accessible, there is usually a *prie-dieu* with the Nicene Creed attached (as is, for example, the case at St. Peter's Basilica in Rome); thus the modern pilgrim is provided the opportunity of realizing again the ancient act of the *confessio*, whereby he makes a Profession of Faith and proclaims the glory of the Lord present in the Eucharist immediately above the crypt or *confessio*.

Confessional • The place designated for the celebration of the sacrament of Penance.

For most of the history of the Church, there was no special place for the hearing of confessions. In the Middle Ages, confessions were heard in front of the altar. The need for secrecy and the felt need for anonymity occasioned the providing of screens for the penitents. After Trent, St. Charles Borromeo's design of the confessor's chair boxed in with screens for the privacy of the penitents' confessions became standard. The new Rite of Penance or Reconciliation allows both the confessional and face-to-face confession. This has given rise to reconciliation rooms, where the penitent has a choice of confessing his or her sins through a screen or facing the confessor directly. The option for anonymity must always be present, and it is the penitent's option.

Confessor • (1) From the Latin *confiteri*, to declare openly or to confess one's faith. The martyrs did this by shedding their blood. Those who had been imprisoned for the Faith but were not executed were called confessors in the early Church and eventually the term was used for male, non-martyr saints.

(2) A priest with faculties to hear confessions. In the Code of Canon Law, if he has these faculties in his own diocese, he can exercise that office everywhere, as long as he is a priest in good standing (Canon 967.2). The Code also states he is bound to the sacramental seal (Canon 983.1); i.e., he must keep secret all sins confessed, may ask only those questions pertinent (Canon 979), is to remember that he is "both judge and healer . . . constituted by God as a minister of both justice and mercy" (Canon 978) and is to impose "salutary and appropriate penances" (Canon 981).

Some people go to the same confessor for the purposes of spiritual growth from the ongoing advice of the confessor. In such cases, the confessor is one's regular confessor. The term is also used for the confessor who regularly comes to a religious house; one who comes on occasion for the freedom of conscience of the religious is called an extraordinary confessor.

Confirmation, Sacrament of • A sacrament instituted by Christ in promising to send the Holy Spirit (Jn 14:15-21). We find this fulfilled in the Pentecost event, and after Peter proclaims the basic gospel message, the people moved by it ask, "What shall we do?" Peter responds, "Repent and be baptized every one of you in the name of Jesus Christ for the forgiveness of your sins; and you shall receive the gift of the Holy Spirit" (Acts 2:37-38).

This suggests a twofold aspect of Christian Initiation — Baptism for the forgiveness of sins and the Spirit given in Confirmation. In Acts 8 and 19, we have scriptural witness to a rite after Baptism, the laying on of hands, which gives the Holy Spirit. In the early Church, it was difficult to distinguish between the sacraments of Initiation (Baptism, Confirmation and the Eucharist) because they were administered by the bishop as a continuous rite on Holy Saturday to adult catechumens.

At first, in the East and later in the West, the laying on of hands ceded to anointing and this was heightened by the Fathers' describing this action as the "sealing" with the Spirit. As infant Baptism became more and more the practice (fourth and fifth centuries onward), the East kept the three sacraments together and had the priest administer them, whereas in the West the local priest began the sacramental initiation of infants with Baptism and had the bishop confirm them as older children or adolescents later on when he was able to make a pastoral visit.

This Western separation of initiation caused speculation on what specifically Confirmation did over and above Baptism.

Western theologians emphasized the patristic teaching that the seven gifts of the Holy Spirit were given then (cf. Is 11:2-3). This listing of the gifts of the Spirit placed a special emphasis on fortitude from medieval theologians. The Holy Spirit was seen as giving a particular strength to fight for the Christian Faith and life. This emphasis even found its way into the medieval ritual, which had the bishop administer a light tap or slap on the cheek of the one being confirmed, to show him that he must be ready to lay down his life for the Faith, must defend it and be a soldier for Christ — an emphasis that accorded with the Catholic Action movement of the 1930s and 1940s. (Actually, this "blow" was a remnant of the sign of peace formerly given to the newly confirmed, as evidenced by the accompanying words of the bishop, *Pax tecum* — "Peace be with you.")

Contemporary theology sees Confirmation as a completion of Baptism, a sealing with the Spirit to enable the Christian to witness to his Faith in a mature way. Pope Paul VI, in the *Apostolic Constitution on the Sacrament of Confirmation*, still sees this sacrament as endowing the recipients "with special strength" and obliging them "to spread and defend the Faith both by word and by deed as true witnesses of Christ." Normally, in the West young people in adolescence are confirmed rather than in infancy, as is the Eastern custom. The usual minister is the bishop, though priests may help for large groups and in certain cases (e.g., reception of converts at the Easter Vigil) confirm by themselves. Vatican II decreed a reform of the rite, and a new form was provided: "N., be sealed with the gift of the Holy Spirit," which is really an ancient Byzantine formulary said by the minister while anointing with holy chrism, the royal and priestly oil.

Confirmation Name • Name chosen by one to be confirmed, properly that of a patron saint on which to model one's life. This name is no longer required; in fact, it is no longer mentioned in the Apostolic Constitution of 1971. (Cf. Confirmation, Sacrament of.)

Confiteor • In Latin, "I confess," one of the forms of the Penitential Rite at Mass. This form grew out of medieval *apologiae*, or prayers of unworthiness said by the clergy during the procession to the altar as their devotional preparation. Although the *Confiteor* had long been optionally recited as part of the priest's preparation for Mass, St. Pius V mandated it in the 1570 Roman Missal as one of the prayers to be said at the foot of the altar at the beginning of Mass.

The present form is:

"I confess to Almighty God, and to you, my brothers and sisters, that I have sinned through my own fault, in my thoughts and in my words, in what I have done and in what I have failed to do; and I ask blessed Mary ever virgin, all the angels and saints, and you, my brothers and sisters, to pray for me to the Lord our God."

To which the celebrant responds:

"May Almighty God have mercy on us, forgive us our sins, and bring us to everlasting life."

This is not considered a form of absolution. It is not the sacrament of Penance, nor is it to be celebrated as communal absolution, although in the light of the patristic teaching and that of St. Thomas on the power of the Eucharist to forgive sin, Roguet maintains that we can see this rite as forgiving venial sins. This prayer is also a good preparation for confession.

Confraternity • A voluntary association of clergy or laity established under Church authority. The revised Code uses the generic term "association of the faithful," rather than "confraternity," although this term is still used by many groups.

Confraternity of Christian Doctrine (CCD) • One of the numerous societies that appeared about the time of the Council of Trent (1545-1563). Its purpose was to provide religious education for children and adults in Milan who had never undergone formal catechesis in a Church-sponsored program. The decrees of the Council, and Pope St. Pius V's approval of a catechism in 1566, gave impetus to the movement. The CCD remained a purely lay organization, consisting of trained men and women who voluntarily taught the catechism on Sundays and holy days. Saints such as Charles Borromeo, Robert Bellarmine, Francis de Sales and Peter Canisius embraced the aims of the Confraternity, and it enjoyed the support of the Popes through the centuries.

It was Pope St. Pius X (1903-1914) who renewed and extended the confraternity, issuing twenty-one documents on the topic of catechetics during his pontificate. The most forceful of the teachings, the virtual *magna carta* of the CCD, was the encyclical *Acerbo Nimis* (April 15, 1905), in which he expressed the purpose of the CCD as follows: "Let religion classes be founded to instruct . . . the young people who frequent the public schools. . . ." The Pontiff also mandated the establishment of the CCD in every parish. In the United States, the most aggressive promoter of the CCD was Edwin V. O'Hara, who died in 1956 as Bishop of Kansas City-St. Joseph. In the 1920s, while organizing the National Catholic Rural Life Conference, O'Hara had come to appreciate the value of the CCD in isolated country parishes that were without Catholic schools. Through the 1930s and 1940s, as chairman of the episcopal committee of the CCD, O'Hara established the national center at The Catholic University of America in 1935, and vigorously pressed for its establishment in every parish.

Although the CCD is mostly considered as providing religious instruction for Catholics unable to attend parochial elementary schools, it is actually a network of "cradle-to-grave" catechesis, involving religious vacation schools, correspondence courses, high school and college sessions, and adult theological education.

Congregation • As a general term, "congregation" refers to a grouping of persons. In Church law, it has several distinct meanings.

First, a congregation may refer to all the people joined together in a parish or to the people assembled at a liturgy.

A religious congregation is a commonly used but unofficial term for a group of men and women who are joined as a religious community, live a common life and take only simple but perpetual vows. Such a description is more aptly suited to the 1917 Code of Canon Law than to the revised Code. In the revised Code, the entity comparable to a religious congregation is known as a society of apostolic life.

A congregation of the Roman Curia is an administrative department of the Holy See that has delegated authority over a particular area of Church affairs. Of the various types of administrative organisms of the Holy See, the congregation is the most important and most authoritative. At present, there are ten Roman congregations: the Congregation for the Doctrine of the Faith, the Congregation for the Oriental Churches, the Congregation for Bishops, the Congregation for the Evangelization of Peoples, the Congregation for the Clergy, the Congregation for the Sacraments, the Congregation for Divine Worship, the Congregation for Catholic Education, the Congregation for Religious and Secular Institutes, and the Congregation for the

Causes of the Saints. Each congregation is headed by a Cardinal Prefect, who is assisted by a secretary, usually a titular archbishop. The congregation itself is made up of several members of the College of Cardinals and, in some cases, archbishops. Certain cardinals serve on more than one congregation. The members come together several times a year for plenary meetings. In some congregations, the members residing in Rome meet on a regular basis, sometimes weekly. In addition to the prefect, secretary and members, each congregation also has a staff of clergy, religious and laity to assist in the day-to-day affairs.

The congregations act not on their own authority but on delegated authority of the Pope. The heads of each meet with the Pope on a regular basis to apprise him of their activities and to seek his approval for their more important decisions.

Congregational Singing: See **Singing, Congregational**

Congregationalism • The name given to a form of church government which holds that the individual congregation is the only visible expression of the Church of Christ. Each congregation is sovereign and autonomous in matters of church policy and government.

Developing in England in the sixteenth and seventeenth centuries, its adherents were originally called "Independents." They hold that the only head of the church is Christ and the Bible is the sole rule of faith. They are typical of "gathered" churches, in which membership is determined by the individuals acknowledging the Lordship of Christ in their lives and accepting the covenant of a particular congregation. Thus each church is independent, only federating with others for practical purposes.

In the United States, the main denominations representative of this approach are the Congregationalists, the Baptists and the Disciples of Christ. The Presbyterians, similar in many ways, recognize that there is a greater church than the individual congregation.

One of Congregationalism's early writers, Robert Browne, declared (1583): "The church is a company or number of Christians or believers, which by a willing covenant made with their God are under the governance of God and Christ, and keep His laws in one Holy Communion."

Congresses, Eucharistic • Assemblies of the Catholic faithful intended to show and foster greater devotion to the Lord in the Eucharist. Devotion is shown by the public celebration of the Mass, reception of Holy Communion by the properly disposed Catholics in attendance and periods of exposition with Benediction of the Blessed Sacrament. Devotion is promoted by way of lectures and discussions conducted during the congress.

Since the first formal Eucharistic congress held at Lille, France, in 1881, there have been over forty international congresses, two in the United States, at Chicago in 1926 and at Philadelphia in 1976. As Archbishop of Kracow, Karol Cardinal Wojtyla, now Pope John Paul II, attended the 1976 Philadelphia congress.

Congruism • Propounded by Luís de Molina, S.J. (1535-1600), and developed by Francisco de Suárez, S.J. (1548-1617), "congruism" refers to a theory of grace according to which God is said to bestow grace upon a person with the foreknowledge of the favorable circumstances in which it will be received and be effective. The efficacious grace is thus said to fit the foreseen situation of the person receiving it (*gratia de congruo*). The theory posits a "middle knowledge" (*scientia media*) in God, between His knowledge of simple intelligence (His knowledge of all that is possible) and the knowledge of vision (His knowledge of all that is). The objects of the divine middle knowledge are the future contingent actions of free agents. The theory is thus an attempt to reconcile human freedom with divine causality. Many theologians have objected that the theory in effect makes the bestowal of grace contingent upon a foreseen human worthiness, and thus compromises the absolute gratuity of grace. In addition, congruism seems to conceive of the relationship between divine causality and human agency as if these were parallel, whereas in fact the divine causality — as a strictly uncreated universal causality — at once absolutely transcends and sustains all created agency.

Consanguinity • A blood relationship between persons. This relationship is divided into persons in the direct line and the indirect or collateral line. The direct line refers to persons who are directly descended one from the other, such as grandparents, parents and children. In the indirect line, it refers to persons who have a common ancestor, such as brothers and sisters, first cousins, second cousins, etc.

Consanguinity is an impediment to marriage in certain instances. Persons related in the direct line may never validly marry each other. Persons related in the second degree of the indirect line, that is, brothers and sisters, likewise may never validly marry. Persons related in the third (aunt-nephew, uncle-niece) and fourth (first cousin) degrees of the indirect line are also prohibited from marriage, although in these cases the bishop has the power to dispense from the impediment and permit a marriage. Dispensations from the impediment in the direct line or second degree of the indirect line are never granted, for they are contrary to natural law (cf. Canons 108, 1078).

Conscience • In the New Testament the word *synedesis* appears twenty-five times in Pauline writings. For Paul, it is the awareness of the difference between good and evil, deriving from Stoic thought which considers *synedesis* or *conscientia* to be the ultimate and autonomous judge of human actions. For Paul, the Christian has a strong conscience which identifies what is truly good and truly evil, but others have a "weak" conscience by which they cannot tell the difference. A pure conscience brings forth pure love and genuine faith. False apostles have seared and insensitive consciences. For Paul, to the pure of conscience all things are pure, but those of bad conscience see all things in a twisted fashion. And for him, Christ purifies the conscience, which the law is unable to do.

For Aquinas, conscience is the judgment of practical reason reached by human intelligence seeking to know what is the morally permissible and commended form of action in a given practical situation. The primary function of conscience is to associate the private judgment of the person with objective moral norms and to guide individual actions by this conjunction. For Aquinas, conscience is based on *synderesis*, which is a natural inclination or openness to the moral good. Modern understandings of conscience have tendencies to absolutize conscience and to make it totally autonomous and unrestricted, but these tendencies are opposed by both Aquinas and the Church. The Second Vatican Council resisted this tendency, holding that authentic conscience had to be formed in accord with the dictates of "right reason" and the authentic moral teachings of the Church.

Consecration • The setting aside of a person or an object exclusively for God and His service. Many such prayers over people or objects that were called "consecrations" formerly are now called blessings in the new rites (e.g., altars and churches), although virgins are still consecrated.

The term is also used for the Words of Institution, "Take and eat," etc., by which the bread and wine at Mass are transubstantiated into the Body and Blood of Christ. In both Sts. Hippolytus and Ambrose, we find an emphasis on the power of the Word, Christ, acting through the *words*, but the Christian East put more emphasis on the power of the Holy Spirit as seen in the prayer of the Epiclesis. Perhaps this is why the Chaldean Canon of Addai and Mari has no Words of Institution, although some scholars think they were considered too holy to write down but were nonetheless recited at the proper time in the liturgy.

The word "consecration" is also used in a derived sense to refer to giving oneself to the Blessed Virgin in the fashion described by St. Louis Grignon de Montfort, or to her Immaculate Heart as requested by Our Lady herself at Fátima. Perhaps because the word strictly used refers to God alone, Pope John Paul II in his prayers of consecration of the world to Our Lady uses the term "entrustment."

Consecration Cross • When a church is formally consecrated by a bishop, chrism is used to sign the form of a cross on the inside walls of the church in twelve places, symbolic of both the twelve tribes and the Twelve Apostles, since the Church is the New Israel and is apostolic in her origin and life. A consecration cross is painted, sculpted or attached at each of the places where the bishop anoints the walls. Church law forbids the removal of these crosses; it is traditional on the anniversary of the church's consecration that a lighted candle be burnt before each of the twelve crosses.

Consent, Marital • The action whereby a man and a woman give themselves to each other for the purpose of establishing marriage. Canon law defines consent thus: ". . . an act of the will by which a man and a woman, through an irrevocable covenant, mutually give and accept each other in order to establish marriage" (Canon 1057.2).

This definition of consent is substantially different from that of the 1917 Code, which defined consent as an act of the will whereby a man and a woman exchanged the right over each other's bodies for heterosexual, reproductive acts. The object of consent was the right to these acts and not the acts themselves. In the revised Code, the object of marital consent is the right to the marital community itself.

The revised law also uses the term "covenant" in reference to the kind of agreement brought about by marital consent. Although the older law referred to this agreement as a unique kind of contract, "covenant" best captures the theological nature of the marital relationship. Traditionally, in ancient Judaic usage, a covenant was a relationship between persons that could not be broken, similar to a blood relationship in its perpetuity and firmness. Since the marriage relationship is a mirror of the relationship of Christ to His Church, it should reflect the same degree of totality as Christ's marriage to His Church.

Furthermore, by their giving of consent to each other, a man and a woman become "one body." This biblical saying, which comes from the Genesis account of creation, does not refer to the physical joining through sexual intercourse but to the total joining of a man and a woman. Thus the revised law describes consent as a "giving and accepting" of the persons themselves.

To be valid, marital consent must be manifested in a legitimate manner, that is, before a sacred minister and two witnesses. Furthermore, there must be no impediments to the marriage. Consent must be sufficiently free and its meaning adequately understood by both spouses. If consent is feigned, that is, if one or the other party actually does not intend to fulfill the marriage obligations, consent is invalid. Finally, to exchange consent validly, the parties must be psychologically and mentally aware of what they are doing and also capable of fulfilling the essential marital obligations.

Consequentialism • The moral theory that the plan, action or choice which brings about the best consequences, effects or state of affairs is the morally preferable action. Consequentialism is of the utilitarian and proportionalist family of moral theories, and it holds that the moral malice of actions is *ultimately* determined by the effects or consequences of actions, rather than by the intrinsic nature of the actions. Consequentialism does not straightforwardly claim that the end justifies the means, but only that the outcomes of actions must be taken into serious consideration whenever the moral quality of actions is assessed.

Consequentialism is flawed by its inadequate understanding of intentionality and also by its understanding of the relation of the intention of the agent to the action. In consequentialist analyses, it is not clear if the intentionality of the agent has a bearing on the morality of the action or not, but if the intentionality of the agent is excluded, this would be a serious flaw in the consequentialist theory. While Abélard would hold that intentionality determines morality, consequentialism would hold that morality is constituted independent of intentionality.

Consequentialism also creates the serious problem of denying, for example, a beneficial surgical procedure to a person because better consequences would come to the community from so doing. Consequentialism removes the person from the action by demanding unswerving fidelity to the principle that good consequences are to be promoted and espoused.

Like utilitarianism, consequentialism allows agents to act in behalf of many different systems of goods or values. For example, good consequences can be not only pleasure but also knowledge, love, peace and truth. Because there are a variety of ultimate unifying values for the consequentialist, virtually any kind or type of action could be morally justified consequentially as promoting a given value or system of values or goods.

In modern debates, consequentialism has been opposed to deontology, which holds that actions are moral or immoral irrespective of their circumstances. However, classical moral theory held that the circumstances or effects of an action could in some instances alter the nature of an action and make a morally good action morally bad. Giving a gift to a woman for the purpose of seducing her would be such a circumstance. But it held that the moral malice of an action is determined by its intrinsic moral character, which was determined not only by the consequences of the act, but also by the motive and intention of the agent. The truth of the matter seems to lie between these two extremes, for the moral malice of actions is determined by their intrinsic character, but the intrinsic nature of actions is often partly determined by the unique conditions surrounding an action.

Consistent Life Ethic • Sometimes referred to as "the seamless garment" ethic, this principle, first enunciated and popularized in the 1980s by Joseph Cardinal Bernardin of Chicago, acknowledges the sanctity of human life in all its developmental stages and conditions, from conception to natural death. It condemns, among others, the acts of abortion, euthanasia, infanticide, unjust war and capital punishment as grave sins against God and man, while wading yet deeper into issues of social and economic policy of a clearly more ambiguous and disputed character. As a consequence, the consistent life ethic has drawn some criticism from those within the Church who believe its intentions and underlying motivations, while admirable, have projected an equivalency of evil among acts of decidedly varying degrees of moral seriousness and public urgency. They note, for instance, that this approach has advanced a sense of moral equivalency between the destruction of innocent preborn human life and the state-countenanced execution of condemned criminals, for Catholic morality views deliberate abortion as always reprehensible, while traditional teaching permits capital punishment under certain conditions.

Consistory • Traditionally, "consistory" was a legal term that referred to a chamber in the imperial palace in Rome where the emperor administered justice. Later on, Church courts, particularly in England, were called "consistory courts."

In the Catholic Church a consistory is a particular kind of assembly of the College of Cardinals, convoked by the Pope and conducted in his presence. Consistories are either public, at which the Pope and cardinals gather in the presence of others for some important purpose, or private, at which only the Pope and cardinals are present. An example of a public consistory is the assembly at which the Pope raises new members to the College of Cardinals. Private consistories are held to discuss the most important of Church matters.

Consortium Perfectae Caritatis • This association was formed in 1971 to assist women religious in developing the religious life in accordance with those principles which were set forth by the Second Vatican Council in *Perfectae Caritatis*, the Decree on the Up-to-Date Renewal of Religious Life, and other related documents. One of its fundamental beliefs is that the true renewal of religious life comes from faithful obedience to the teaching of the Church, which is the mind of Christ.

Constance, Council of • The sixteenth ecumenical council was held at Constance (near modern-day Baden) in Germany between 1414 and 1417. Situated in one of Europe's largest dioceses, the Council of Constance surely ranks as one of the most impressive councils ever convoked. Nearly three hundred fifty archbishops and bishops, thirty cardinals, a hundred abbots, hundreds of theologians and canonists, and even a dozen secular princes attended its forty-five sessions. The council is best known for its final resolution of the Western Schism by the election of Pope Martin V in November 1417. It also enacted reform legislation on a variety of disciplinary matters and rejected the doctrinal errors of Wycliffe and Huss.

Constancy • The virtue by which one learns to endure suffering, trials, failure, misunderstanding and persecution for the sake of the Gospel without falling into indolence, discouragement or apathy. Constancy is best promoted by prayer for

Pope Martin V
(Council of Constance)

the gifts of patience and fortitude, and also by participation in the sacraments. Constancy is a hallmark of the spiritually and psychologically mature, and it signifies progress in the Christian life of justice and charity.

Constantine, Donation of • This document (*Constitutum Constantini*) was probably written not long after the middle of the eighth century. It became widely known through its incorporation in the Pseudo-Isidorian Decretals (c. 847-853). Parts of it were included in most of the medieval collections of canon law, including Gratian's *Decretum*. It claims to reproduce a legal text in which the Emperor Constantine the Great recognizes the superior dignity of the Pope of Rome in the spiritual order and also confers upon him certain privileges in the temporal realm. This remarkable document was almost universally accepted as genuine from the ninth to the fifteenth century. It has been called the most famous forgery in European history. The Italian humanist Lorenzo Valla is generally credited with the proof of its falsity.

Constantinople, Councils of • As political and social forces of the fourth and fifth centuries forced Rome into eclipse, Constantinople (now called Istanbul), the "Rome of the East," began to be considered the *caput mundi*, "head of the world." Thus from A.D. 381 to 869 four ecumenical councils were convoked in this city on the Bosphorus, the capital of the Byzantine Empire: the first (381), which was the second ecumenical council after Nicaea, condemned the Arian heresy and reaffirmed the teaching of its predecessor; the second (553) condemned the Nestorian heresy; the third (681) reasserted the Christological clarifications of the Council of Chalcedon; the fourth (869) condemned Photius and his followers.

Constantinople, Patriarch of •

"Patriarch" is a title of honor rendered to a bishop of a see with special dignity, usually due to its historic connection to one of the Apostles. The traditional patriarchates were listed by the Council of Nicaea (A.D. 325) as Rome, Alexandria and Antioch, with the Council of Chalcedon (451) adding Jerusalem and Constantinople. This last one was so honored because of its claim to be the "new Rome," established by Constantine I in 330 at Byzantium on the Bosphorus. Because of this prominence, the bishop, or patriarch, of Constantinople began to assume prerogatives similar to those traditionally reserved to the bishop, or patriarch, of Rome, the Pope, thus leading to tension.

To indicate that his spiritual authority was parallel to the temporal power of the emperor, who resided in Constantinople, the bishop of that city began to use the title "Ecumenical Patriarch" around the beginning of the sixth century. As the Church in the East began to accent its differences from the Church in the West, eventually leading to schism, the patriarch of Constantinople began to emerge as the major spokesman for the East and exercised a primacy of honor, though not one of jurisdiction. The split between East and West is the most tragic of all divisions, since both agree in doctrinal and devotional areas, but differ in their understanding of the position of leadership and authority given to the successor of St. Peter, the Bishop of Rome.

Recent Pontiffs have indicated a healing of this rift to be high on their agenda, and Pope Paul VI's touching visit to the patriarch of Constantinople in 1965 dramatically portrayed this desire for unity.

Constantinople, Rite of: See **Rite of Constantinople**

Constitutional Clergy •

In 1790, at the height of the French Revolution, the National Assembly of France mandated that every Catholic priest had to take an oath professing allegiance to the aims of the revolution and pledging to obey the regime in all matters. The oath split the clergy of France into "juring," or "constitutional" clergy — those who took the oath — and "nonjuring" clergy — those who refused. The latter were harassed and persecuted, although many fled France to serve the Church elsewhere, e.g., the Sulpicians who came to Baltimore in 1791 to open St. Mary's Seminary. Pope Pius VI condemned the oath, and it was revoked by the concordat of 1801.

Constitutions •

Within the Church, a constitution has two distinct meanings. First, it is the highest and most authoritative form of papal pronouncement. Similarly, a conciliar constitution, issued by an ecumenical council and signed by the Pope, is the most authoritative kind of statement issued by a council.

More commonly, a constitution is a set of organizational rules for a body within the Church. Religious communities are governed by constitutions that they draw up and submit to the Holy See for its approval. Other Church bodies also have constitutions that may or may not be required by canon law.

Consubstantial •

The term, propagated by the Council of Nicaea in A.D. 325, referring to the belief that the Three Persons of the Blessed Trinity — while distinct and separate — are of one and the same substance. The Father, the Son and the Holy Spirit share exactly the same nature.

Consubstantiation • Also known as "impanation," this theory asserts the coexistence of the substance of bread and wine with the Body and Blood of Christ in the Eucharist. Espoused by the followers of Luther during the Reformation, consubstantiation was rejected by the Church at the Council of Trent when it defined the Catholic doctrine of transubstantiation.

Consultors • Specialists or experts in some field who assist someone in authority. The various congregations and other entities of the Roman Curia all have consultors who assist them in studying problems and proposing solutions. So do many national episcopal conferences as well as diocesan and archdiocesan bishops.

"Consultor" is also a specific term in canon law. The law stipulates that each bishop is to choose from his council of priests between six and twelve members who constitute the College of Consultors. The bishop must meet with the consultors to seek their advice and/or consent on certain matters defined in the law or on other issues that he chooses.

When a diocese falls vacant because of the death, retirement or transfer of a bishop, the College of Consultors (if there is no auxiliary bishop) governs it until an interim administrator is either appointed or elected. Shortly after the see has become vacant, the consultors are obliged to meet for the purpose of electing a diocesan administrator, unless the Holy See has already appointed an Apostolic Administrator. The administrator governs

the diocese until the new bishop takes possession (cf. Canon 502).

Consummation • The act of sexual intercourse which takes place between a man and a woman after marital consent has been exchanged. If the marriage is between two baptized persons, the act of consummation adds the quality of absolute indissolubility to their marriage bond.

The present law states that consummation must take place in "a human manner." This refers to sexual intercourse which is not forced, is not unnatural, and is a free and loving act between the parties. Church law and theology use the term "consummation" to describe this initial act of marital intercourse because by means of it, the complete union of the man and woman in marriage is both symbolized and completed.

In the Middle Ages a lengthy debate went on between theologians as to what actually brought a marriage into being — the consent of the parties or sexual consummation. The debate was settled by Pope Alexander III, who decreed, in a succession of marriage cases presented to him, that consent brought a marriage into existence but that consummation made consent absolutely indissoluble.

Contemplative Life • The term referring to a way of existence which focuses on communion with God through prayer and self-denial. In the "active" life, a person commits himself to doing works of charity (e.g., feeding the poor, caring for the sick, etc.). However, in the "contemplative" life, one spends his time in prayer and sacrifice for the salvation of his soul and the world. The contemplative life — in the context of "vowed" religious life — offers a higher degree of perfection than the active life. Vatican II's *Perfectae Caritatis*, the Decree on the Up-to-Date Renewal of Religious Life, mentions the necessity of the contemplative life: "These [communities] will always have an honored place in the Mystical Body of Christ, in which 'all the members do not have the same function' (Rom 12:4), no matter how pressing may be the needs of the active ministry" (PC 7).

Contentious Trials • The two types of trials provided for in the procedural law of the Church are penal and contentious trials. A contentious trial has as its object the vindication of the rights of physical or juridic persons or the declaration of juridic facts. Most of the canons on the manner of conducting trials refer specifically to contentious trials. The Code contains special provision for penal cases and certain types of contentious trials, such as nullity of marriage or Sacred Orders. In all trials, the general rules for the contentious trial are followed unless exception is made in these special sections.

Unlike the trials of the common law system, a contentious trial does not rely on the decision of a jury. Rather, the matter is decided by the judge or judges to whom the case has been entrusted. The course of the trial is directed or instructed by the presiding judge. Unlike common-law trial judges, the judge takes a very active part in the process. It is he who gathers the proofs and examines the parties and the witnesses.

The contentious trial begins with the submission of petition and its acceptance or rejection by the presiding judge. If the petition is accepted, the judge issues a decree of acceptance and at the same time calls the other party to the suit into court. This is known as the citation, and it is necessary for the very validity of the trial. Even though the other party, known as the respondent, refuses to take part in the trial or completely ignores the citation, the judge can proceed. Then follows the "joinder of the issues," which is a session at which the judge examines the petition and the response of the respondent, if there is one, and determines the grounds or terms of the controversy before the court. Once the parties have been notified of this, the gathering of proofs begins. Possible proofs include the declarations of the parties, authentic documents, testimony of witnesses and of experts.

When the judge is satisfied that all proofs have been collected, he issues a decree publishing the acts; that is, allowing the parties to submit additional proofs and to inspect the acts of the case at the tribunal. If the judge believes that serious dangers could result from full inspection of the acts by both parties, he can declare that certain acts in the case be closed to inspection.

If the parties declare they have nothing more to add or if the time limit for inspection set by the judge expires, he decrees that the case is concluded or closed to further evidence-gathering. Then comes the discussion of the case, during which the defender of the bond or promoter of justice and the petitioner's advocate prepare their briefs in defense of their position in the case. The respondent's advocate does likewise. These are presented in writing to one another, and the opportunity for rebuttal is given. This having been completed, the entire case together with the defense briefs goes to the judges. The presiding judge sets a time for the oral discussion of the case between himself and the other two judges (if it is a collegiate tribunal). The judges vote on the issue and must arrive at a majority decision. The decision or sentence is composed and communicated to the parties in the case. Either party can appeal the decision before the judge who issued the sentence within fifteen available days. In marriage nullity cases, the defender of the bond is obliged by law to appeal every affirmative decision.

The appeal process is similar to the ordinary contentious process. However, the appeal judge can move from the joinder of the issues directly to the discussion of the case and issuing of the sentence, unless additional proofs are to be submitted. If the decision of the first court is reversed on appeal, the parties can appeal to the court of third instance or they can drop the issue. In order for a decision to have legal effect, it must, if appealed, have two sentences that agree with each other. Thus the third court becomes pivotal, since whatever it decides will determine the eventual outcome of the suit. The appeal court notifies the original judge of its decision, and he in turn notifies the parties to the case (cf. Canons 1400, 1501-1670).

Continence • Broadly speaking, continence refers to various degrees of restraint exercised in the area of sexual pleasure. Properly speaking, continence is the virtue that resists the strong impulses of lust. In this sense, continence is less complete in its control than the virtue of temperance in which the passions are perfectly subordinated to intelligence. The term continence is also used to refer to complete abstention from sexual pleasure. Attention to the context will help determine the sense in which the term is meant.

Contract • In every culture and legal system, contracts play an immense and crucial role. Basically, a contract is an agreement between persons regarding certain actions, but a contract differs from a mere agreement in that a contract carries certain legal (whether civil or canonical) implications. These implications, which usually concern the ability of the parties to secure performance of the contract, can be serious. Indeed, it is an ancient maxim that *pacta sunt servanda*; that is, "contracts are meant to be fulfilled."

Contracts are grouped according to various attributes, but perhaps the most common division of contracts focuses on how many parties there are to the contract. In this manner, contracts are considered: (1) unilateral (where "A" contracts to do something for "B," but "B" has no return obligation); (2) bilateral (where "A" contracts to do something for "B," and "B" in return contracts to do something for "A"); or (3) multilateral (where several persons contract to perform various actions for one another). (Cf. Canon 1062 for some examples of this type of terminology.) Most of the contracts encountered in daily life, of course, are of the bilateral type.

For simplicity's sake, Canons 22 and 1290 of the 1983 Code of Canon Law establish the general rule that canon law will accept the conclusions of civil law in the regulation of contracts, unless such regulations are contrary to divine or canon law. Thus, for example, a parish that wished to purchase an automobile would be required to show proof of insurance where that is required by the laws of the state, for such a contractual requirement is not contrary to divine or canon law. On the other hand, a civil law which forbade a bishop from contracting to sell diocesan property to a certain religious order would almost certainly run afoul of the canonical rights of the bishop over his diocese and thus would not bind the bishop. It is possible, furthermore, to envision contracts which are not only canonically void but objectively sinful, such as simony in the provision of ecclesiastical office. The place of execution of a contract, or the place where it is to be fulfilled, can give the ecclesiastical tribunal of that place jurisdiction over the parties in order to resolve disputes that might have arisen under a contract (Canon 1411).

In ecclesiastical circles, of course, one of the most common uses of the term "contract" occurs in connection with the sacrament of Matrimony. Canon 1012 of the 1917 Code, for example, used the actual term "contract" in declaring that "Christ the Lord has raised the matrimonial contract to the dignity of a sacrament for the baptized." The understanding of marriage as a contract was very useful for stressing the fact that both parties shared rights and responsibilities in the marriage, and these rights and duties were meant to be seriously honored. The notion of contract as applied to marriage also provided a workable method for assessing the ability, or "capacity," of the parties to enter into such a relationship. (Cf. Annulment.)

At the same time, some deficiencies in contract terminology were noted when it was applied to Christian marriage. The idea of the sacredness of Holy Matrimony was obscured by cold-sounding legal terminology, and the centrality of the indissolubility of marriage was often overlooked when people reasoned that no other mere contract was really meant to last a lifetime. It came as no surprise, then, that the 1983 Code, while retaining contract terminology in much of its regulation of Catholic marriage, recast the basic description of marriage contained in Canon 1055 and now spoke in more descriptive terms of the "matrimonial covenant."

Contrition • The Council of Trent held that contrition was "sorrow of heart and detestation for sin committed with the resolution not to sin again" (DS 1676, 1705). Contrition is not just a resolution to live a good life; it must be linked to trust in divine mercy, and it must be a voluntary and explicit rejection of the previous life. In the larger context, contrition signifies true conversion, metanoia and change of heart. The dynamics of true conversion have been the subject of debate for centuries. Contrition derives from God's initiative, and it causes justification by receiving it from God.

There are two degrees of contrition — perfect and imperfect. Perfect contrition is sorrow born of proper motivation, a sign of which is the desire to be charitable. It hates sin because God is good, and sin offends Him. Imperfect contrition is less complete, lamenting evil for some secondary reason, such as fear of God's wrath.

Contrition and the purpose of amendment are necessary if the person is ever to know the supernatural peace of sacramental absolution. An "act of contrition" is a prayer that expresses to God the sorrow one feels and the willingness to avoid sin in the future. It may be memorized or spontaneous and is prayed regularly in a healthy Catholic spirituality.

Contumacy • Generally speaking, contumacy is the deliberate disregard for legitimate authority. In canon law, contumacy is discussed in two matters.

First, a party to an ecclesiastical case or controversy, though usually the respondent, who willfully and without reason refuses to appear before an ecclesiastical court, or who otherwise withholds necessary cooperation from the court, can be declared absent, that is, contumacious, and thereupon forfeits all or some of his or her rights before the tribunal (Canons 1592-1595). In this sense contumacy closely parallels civil law notions.

The second and rather more common use of contumacy occurs in the matter of ecclesiastical penalties. In this sense, one who, after a warning, refuses to desist from delictual behavior is considered contumacious, and thereby renders oneself liable to censure (Canon 1347). Indeed, prolonged contumacy can result in the increase of the penalty (Canons 1326, 1364). Contumacy is said to cease, however, when the offender sincerely repents of the offense and either makes a suitable reparation or at least seriously promises to do so. Upon withdrawal from contumacy, one has a canonical right to remission of a censure (Canon 1358) although not a right, strictly speaking, to remission of an expiatory penalty.

Contumely • Unjustly ridiculing and mocking another through the use of insults and gestures, it is contrary to both charity and justice. Contumely is contrary to justice and charity because it deliberately and willfully causes suffering to a person for no good and because it is unjust. Contumely fosters contempt in others and is contrary to charity and benevolence, but the proper response to contumely is silence and patience (Rom 12:19).

Convalidation • A valid marriage comes into being with the exchange of the consent by the spouses. If at least one of the spouses is Catholic, consent must be exchanged according to canonical form. If canonical form is not observed, if an undispensed impediment is present or if consent was deficient for a canonically recognized reason, the marriage is invalid.

If consent is invalid and yet the spouses continue to share a common life, the law provides a remedy for making consent valid. This is known as convalidation, which is the legal means by which consent, originally invalid, can be made valid. The term "convalidation" is preferred to "validation," because it connotes the making valid of an act which had some appearance of validity the first time it was performed.

The most common manner of convalidation is the renewal of consent according to canonical form, commonly but incorrectly referred to as the "blessing of a marriage." Convalidation always presupposes that the original consent of the parties, though canonically invalid, continues to exist. At the time of convalidation, the parties are asked to express a new act of consent, at which time the marriage covenant comes into existence and with it all the obligations of marriage (Canon 1157).

Convalidation by means of renewal of consent according to canonical form, which amounts to a wedding ceremony, is obligatory for any marital invalidity due to lack of canonical form or some defect in canonical form. The Catholic party must understand that the attempted marriage is null and must supply new consent. If the other party is not a Catholic, he or she is not required to acknowledge that the prior consent was invalid but must express to the sacred minister acting as official witness that the prior consent perdures (Canon 1160).

If the marriage is invalid because of a public impediment — that is, one that is provable in the external forum but not necessarily publicly known — the impediment must have ceased or been dispensed and convalidation must take place according to canonical form (Canon 1158.1). If it is a case of an occult impediment — that is, one that cannot be proven in the external forum — it is sufficient that consent be renewed privately and in secret by the party who was aware of the impediment. In the case of impediments, it is possible that only one party could be aware of both the impediment and consequent invalidity of the marriage. If it is a public impediment, this fact must be made known to the other party before the convalidation takes place.

If the consent is invalid through a defect such as simulation, condition, force and fear or fraud, it may be renewed privately, provided the defect has been removed. If the defect can be proven or has been proven in the external forum (e.g., a couple who have received a declaration of nullity based on the defect), the convalidation must take place according to canonical form (Canon 1159).

Cope from Spain, made in 1430

Convalidation according to canonical form is to be accompanied by all the canonical formalities of an ordinary wedding. The investigation into the parties' freedom to marry takes place and pastoral preparation for marriage, if warranted, is to be offered. The marriage is duly registered as such in the parish marriage book, and notification is sent to the churches of baptism. If the original marriage is still recognized by civil law, the civil formalities, such as a marriage license, are not required.

Convent • Etymologically, it comes from a Latin word meaning "an assembly or gathering of people." It means a building or buildings in which a community of religious live. In the United States, it is generally applied to the residence of female religious. Occasionally, it can refer to a corporate monastic community of sisters or nuns.

Conventual Mass • The title given to the daily Mass offered publicly either in churches where professed religious live in community or in churches of religious who daily celebrate the Liturgy of the Hours publicly. The term "conventual" refers to all aspects of monastic or religious life and distinguishes community living from solitary living.

Conversion • Turning toward something or someone and away from someone or something else. In the Old Testament and New Testaments, conversion generally means turning from the ways of sin and toward the ways and life of God. In the New Testament, Christ preaches conversion as a preparation for the coming of the kingdom. The theme of conversion is at the center of the preaching of the prophets, John the Baptist and Jesus. Conversion is brought about as a result of preaching and from hearing the word of God. Aquinas held that conversion consists in preparation, merit and glory, and there are special graces correlative to each of these. In the Church it refers to turning toward God through the Church.

Convert • (1) Generally, it means a person whose ideas, convictions, beliefs and values have changed from one position to another.
(2) Religiously, it can denote a person who turns away from a life of sin to a life of moral goodness and integrity. The Greek word *metanoia* expresses this idea of an interior change of mind and heart.
(3) Denominationally, it refers to one who accepts a new religious affiliation, implying a renunciation of former loyalties.

Cope • The vestment, resembling a cloak, worn by clergy at various rites, including Benediction, processions and solemn Liturgy of the Hours. Worn around the shoulders, the cope extends to the floor and is fastened at the breast by either a flap or a metal clasp. Exquisite embroidery often adorns the vestment. A conventionalized hood, usually in the shape of a shield, is on the back. The secular origin of the cope is found in the Roman *pluviale* (raincoat).

Copt • A term used to designate an Egyptian Orthodox or Catholic Christian. After the Monophysite heresy in the fifth century and the Orthodox split in the eleventh century, some Copts returned to Catholic unity in 1741. Copts live in Egypt and the Near East; their liturgical languages are Coptic, Greek and Arabic.

The Orthodox Coptic Christians are under the jurisdiction of their patriarch in Alexandria, Egypt. They deny the supremacy of the Pope, but their Orders and sacraments are valid. The Catholic Copts are governed by their own patriarch, who also resides in Alexandria.

Coptic Rite • Properly part of the Alexandrian Rite, the Coptic members of this rite resumed communion with the Roman Catholic Church in 1741, under the jurisdiction of the patriarchate of Alexandria. Their liturgy incorporates elements of the Byzantine Rite of St. Basil and the Liturgies of St. Mark, St. Cyril and St. Gregory of Nazianzus, or Nazianzen. The days and seasons of the Church year are marked by using the designated liturgies of those saints, in Coptic translation; i.e., St. Basil's is used on Sundays, weekdays and for the departed; St. Gregory's is used on some particular feast days, and St. Cyril's is used during Lent and on the eve of the feast of the Nativity of Our Lord. The Alexandrian Rite is known also as the Liturgy of St. Mark.

Cor Unum • A Latin expression, meaning literally "one heart." It is the name given to an organization set up by Pope Paul VI in

Coptic illumination (ninth century)

1971 for the purpose of disseminating information and coordinating the various relief efforts under Catholic auspices all over the world.

Coram Cardinale (Episcopo) • Latin for "before, or in the presence of, a cardinal or bishop." These terms are usually used to describe liturgical ceremonies performed in the presence of a prelate. Since bishops are the primary teachers and, in union with the Pope, preach in the name of Christ, to worship God *coram episcopo* is considered an honor and a privilege.

Corinthians, First Epistle to the • What is now called "1 Corinthians" is the first of two surviving letters written to the Church Paul founded on his second missionary journey and his first visit to Corinth (Acts 18:1-18) about A.D. 50-51. He lived with Aquila and Priscilla for about eighteen months before eventually continuing on his missionary journey. He wrote 1 Corinthians from Ephesus (16:8), accompanied by Sosthenes (1 Cor 1:1) and three representatives of the Corinthian Church (Stephanus, Fortunatus and Achaicus, 16:17-18).

Major Themes: In 1 Corinthians, Paul addresses several problems which arose since his departure: "Chloe's people" informed him that factions existed (1:11-12), as did the practice of a type of incest (5:1-13). In a letter written to Paul prior to 1 Corinthians, other problems were outlined, to which Paul responded beginning at 7:1: sexual intercourse in marriage "in Christ" (7:1 ff.), eating meat ritually sacrificed to idols (8-10), community worship and the spiritual gifts (11-14), the resurrection of the dead in light of Christ's resurrection (15), and the collection for the Church in Jerusalem (16).

For Paul, "faith" is the unshakable confidence and complete trust in God's intent to rescue humanity from the power of sin and death, specifically through the manifest power of Christ's cross, which is the power of God (2:5) expressed in apparent human weakness (1:18-25). The cross expresses in concrete terms God's intent to rescue and free the whole of humanity from sin and death; hence, it is wisdom which opens up the believer to the mystery of salvation. The work of the cross includes the new creation, which is comprehensive and requires constant movement toward freedom in the Lord (7:23-24, 35). The quest to build others up in Christ is somehow related to Christ's work on the cross (8:11-12). The gifts of the Spirit and the freedom they bring should be grounded in love (13). Freedom gained should contribute to the holiness and growth of others in salvation (10:31-33). "Power" means that dynamism which frees from the force and effect exerted by sin on the person; "power" propels the believer onward in works of the Lord and in the Lord's work of salvation (15:1-11, 58).

Contents:

A. Opening: 1:1-9
  1. Address and Blessing: 1:1-3
  2. Thanksgiving: 1:4-9
B. Body of Letter: 1:10—16:4
  1. Recent Problems Addressed: 1:10—6:20
    a. True wisdom and the Cross of Christ: 1:10—4:21
    b. Incest and immorality: 5:1—6:20
  2. Paul Answers Some Questions: 7:1—16:4
    a. Intercourse, marriage, divorce: 7:1-40
    b. Food offered to idols: 8:1—11:1
    c. Gifts of the Spirit and public worship: 11:2—14:40
    d. Resurrection of believers: 15:1-58
    e. Financial obligations: 16:1-4
C. Closing: 16:5-24
  1. Future Itinerary: 16:5-24
  2. Closing Admonitions: 16:13-18
  3. Closing Greetings: 16:19-20
  4. Signature and Blessing: 16:21-24

Authorship and Date: This letter is universally accepted as from Paul. It was written approximately A.D. 54.

For further reading: Hans Dieter Betz and Margaret M. Mitchell, "Corinthians, First Epistle to the," *Anchor Bible Dictionary,* 1:1139-1148; Jerome Murphy-O'Connor, O.P., "The First Letter to the Corinthians," *New Jerome Biblical Commentary,* 798-815.

Corinthians, Second Epistle to the • In the past two centuries scholars have noted the contrasts in tone and subject matter between 2 Corinthians 1-9 and 10-13; these and other considerations have led scholars to suggest that these two sections were once individual letters, which were later combined into their current canonical form.

That is the form which will be considered, for the sake of conciseness.

Major Themes: In 2 Corinthians 1-9, Paul encourages the Corinthians from his heart and in love to continue their repentance from various maladies which have recently infected the community; in doing so, he also defends his apostolic authority over them and his care for them (1:12—7:16). He exhorts them to be generous in their donations to the Church at Jerusalem (8-9). In Chapters 10-13, Paul rejects charges against his apostolic authority and pastoral integrity, counter-challenging his adversaries (10-11). His personal integrity is grounded in his suffering for the Gospel (11:21—12:13). Put in the form of a question, the central issue both Paul and the Corinthians were struggling with is, "What is an Apostle?" Paul's authentication of his ministry is in terms of service to the Gospel of God's great reconciling love through Christ (5:11-19). The "credential" of an Apostle is ultimately an act of God. The mystery of Christ's death and resurrection must be present and witnessed to in that apostolic ministry (4:10-12).

Contents:

A. Opening: 1:1-11
1. Address: 1:1-2
2. Thanksgiving: 1:3-11
B. Body of letter: 1:12—13:10
1. Paul's encouragements and self-defense: 1:12—7:16
2. The collection for Jerusalem: 8:1-15
3. Paul's representatives: 8:16—9:15
4. Paul's adversaries are rejected: 10:1—11:21
5. Apostleship, renunciation and sufferings: 11:21—13:10
C. Closing: 13:11-13
1. Final admonitions and greetings: 13:11-12
2. Apostolic blessing: 13:13

Authorship and Date: As with 1 Corinthians, scholars of all persuasions accept 2 Corinthians as from Paul. If we date 1 Corinthians around A.D. 54, then the earliest we can date 2 Corinthians would be sometime after this, perhaps during the summer or fall of 55.

For further reading: Hans Dieter Betz, "Corinthians, Second Epistle to the," *Anchor Bible Dictionary,* 1:1148-1154; Jerome Murphy-O'Connor, O.P., "The Second Letter to the Corinthians," *New Jerome Biblical Commentary,* 816-829.

Cornette • The massive, spreading white linen headgear originating in fourteenth-century France and worn by both men and women in some religious orders. The Daughters of Charity of St. Vincent de Paul wore the cornette until recently; only a few congregations maintain this headdress.

Corona • (1) The band of hair left after shaving the crown of the head of a male religious for monastic tonsure. This is rarely worn today; (2) a circlet of candles hung over the altar in the early Church; (3) the Franciscan Crown. (Cf. Crown, Franciscan.)

Coronation of the Blessed Virgin Mary • (1) The fifth glorious mystery of the Rosary; (2) any image or painting of Our Lady surrounded by the saints and angels as she is crowned by Christ the King as Queen of Heaven and Earth. A particularly fine representation of this was painted by Beato Angelico and hangs in the Uffizi in Florence.

Coronation of the Pope • Once the Pope was elected, he was (until 1978) crowned with the papal tiara after celebrating his first Papal Mass in St. Peter's. This crown with its three coronets represents the fullness of spiritual and temporal power and jurisdiction.

Pope Paul VI, however, had his tiara sold, with the money from the sale given to the poor. (It is now in the Shrine of the

Immaculate Conception in Washington, D.C.) Pope John Paul I, who reigned only for a month, declined the coronation rite, regarding it as a feudal and secular ceremony, not showing the spiritual jurisdiction and role of the Pope as the successor of Peter. Instead, during his "installation" (as he termed it) as Bishop of Rome, he emphasized the ancient rite of receiving the pallium, the sign of spiritual jurisdiction, and the sign of the unity of all other metropolitan archbishops with the See of Peter. Pope John Paul II has also refused to use the papal tiara.

Corporal • This term, coming from the Latin for "body" (*corpus*), refers to the square piece of linen cloth, about twenty inches square, used during the Sacrifice of the Mass and other liturgical ceremonies involving the Blessed Sacrament, the Body (*Corpus*) of Christ. The chalice, paten and host are placed on it, from the

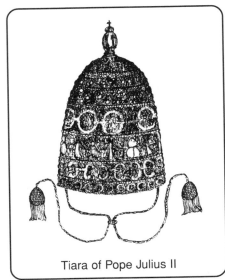

Tiara of Pope Julius II

Offertory or Preparation of the Gifts to the Communion ablutions. In the former order of the Roman Mass (so-called "Tridentine"), the host was placed directly on the corporal, hence its name. A corporal should also be placed on the "floor" of the tabernacle beneath any vessel (pyx, ciborium) containing the Blessed Sacrament. It is also placed beneath the monstrance for Eucharistic adoration or Benediction. It is usually heavily starched so that it is stiff and smooth, especially on the upper surface. It is folded into nine smaller squares and handled with great care, lest any particles which may have fallen upon it be lost through carelessness.

Corporal Works of Mercy • Traditionally, these are defined as: feeding the hungry, giving drink to the thirsty, clothing the naked, sheltering the homeless, visiting the sick, visiting the imprisoned and burying the dead. Of these, six are found in Matthew's account of the Judgment (Mt 25:34-40). The only one of this list not found in Matthew's Judgment scene is the last one — burying the dead. Presumably, burying the dead was included in deference to the body's being the "temple of the Holy Spirit" (1 Cor 3:16). The seven corporal works of mercy are usually distinguished from the spiritual works of mercy, of which there are also seven.

Corpus Christi • The feast of the Body and Blood of the Lord, also called *Corpus Domini* (or *Fête-Dieu* in France). This feast to honor the Real Presence of Christ, especially after the controversies generated by Berengar (who made the presence of Christ in the Eucharist more symbolic than real), was promoted by the visions of Juliana of Liège, an Augustinian nun who understood from them that God wanted a feast to honor the Blessed Sacrament.

Cardinal Hugh of St. Cher, Dominican legate of the Pope to the Lowlands, imposed the feast in the countries over which he had jurisdiction. Pope John XXII confirmed this feast by law and Pope Urban IV extended it to the Church universal. At that time, a new

Office was demanded for the feast and the tradition is that the task fell to St. Thomas Aquinas. Although his authorship of the Office is not confirmed, there is good evidence for at least his re-editing and reworking the texts and sources previously in use and adding new compositions.

At a time of infrequent Communion, many felt the need to see the Host at Mass, and so the elevation of the Host and chalice after the Consecration at Mass came into vogue, as well as placing the Host in a monstrance to be exposed on the altar, or in a transparent Sacrament-tower, or carried in procession. This last aspect became an important feature of the feast of Corpus Christi: a procession either in the church, or more likely through the streets (often carpeted with flowers and the buildings decorated with hangings) with three or four Benedictions of the Blessed Sacrament.

The procession is still encouraged, and the number of Benedictions is no longer specified. This feast is celebrated on the first Thursday after Trinity Sunday, or it may be (as it often is) transferred to the following Sunday. The present calendar has suppressed the former feast of the Precious Blood (July 1), to have both the Body and Blood commemorated at the same feast, now classed as a solemnity.

Corpus Iuris Canonici • The term *Corpus Iuris Canonici*, or Body of Canon Law, is obviously analogous to the term *Corpus Iuris Civilis*, or Body of Civil (Roman) law, which is used to denote the main collections of Roman legal sources. In Church history, the term *Corpus Iuris Canonici* has been used in somewhat varying senses, but since 1580 at least, the expression applies unambiguously to a composite of five extremely influential canonical collections. Pope Gregory XIII in the Apostolic Constitution *Cum Pro Munere* established those five sources to be as follows:

First, the seminal *Decretum Gratiani*, published in 1140, would serve as the foundation; second, the five books comprising the *Decretals of Gregory IX*, or the *Liber Extra* of 1234, as it was called, because it contained documents "outside" Gratian; third, the *Liber Sextus* of the canonist Pope Boniface VIII, issued in 1298, deriving its name from the fact that it was the "sixth book" in supplement to Gregory's five; fourth, the *Clementinae* authored by the first Avignon Pope, Clement V, and promulgated originally in 1314 but reissued in 1317 purged of scribal errors; and fifth, the *Extravagantes*, actually made up of two different sets, both dating from the early fifteenth century, and imaginatively so-named because they consisted of materials "wandering outside" these preceding collections. Upon these five collections of canonical materials, then, turned the practice of canon law until the promulgation of the 1917 Code of Canon Law.

Not all the collections are of equal value to contemporary scholars, however, just as not all the sets were of equal value to canonists in their day. Gratian's *Concordance* dwarfs the others in size and scope, while the *Decretals of Gregory*, compiled by St. Raymond of Peñafort, represent a milestone in legal and historical accuracy. Indeed, Gregory's *Decretals*, along with Boniface's *Liber Sextus* and the albeit flawed *Clementinae* were pontifically vested with official character, that is, they were considered authoritative and binding, in some matters even until this century. On the other hand, Gratian's *Concordance* and the *Extravagantes* (also not free of errors) were never granted such authority, and technically remained the work of private, if influential, individuals. In any case, the immense contribution of the *Corpus Iuris Canonici* to modern canon law and Church discipline can be seen by a mere glance at the footnotes to the 1917 Code of Canon

Law upon which, although not relisted, the 1983 Code clearly draws.

Cosmology • The Greek term literally means "the science of the world." As a designation for an area of philosophy, it is modern (used by the German philosopher Christian Wolff in 1730) and somewhat ambiguous. The term was adopted by modern Scholastics to refer to the philosophical study of inorganic nature. They applied the principles of metaphysics to the current understanding of the world in the physical sciences. They explain such concepts as space, time, motion, matter, energy and discuss the creation and organization of the universe. It became a common designation in Scholastic manuals, and courses were taught under the title "Cosmology." The issues carry on the tradition of Aristotle's *Physics*. The more common term today is "philosophy of nature."

As an area of astronomy, cosmology is the study of the structure and evolution of the universe.

Costume, Clerical • Clerical costume has changed greatly through the centuries and has adapted to different cultures. The cassock or soutane was the normal street dress for the diocesan cleric before the French Revolution. Its color denoted the rank or office of the individual. In the United States today the normal public dress of the Catholic priest is a black suit and Roman collar. The cassock is often worn on church

Cotta

grounds. The cassock may be worn for liturgical ceremonies, but it is not obligatory.

Cotta • This Italian word is simply another name for the liturgical parament known as a surplice in English. (The latter comes from the French *surplis*, and more remotely from the Latin *superpelliceum*, signifying something worn "over the fur," once worn by clerics to keep warm in the very chilly ancient churches.) The Italian term, which refers to something cut or abbreviated, also denotes the fact that the surplice was originally a shortened version of the alb. As such, "cotta" is sometimes used to signify a surplice which is very short in length and whose sleeves are also very short.

Council • A formal meeting of Church leaders, convoked by the appropriate bishop, to deliberate, clarify, study and enact decrees pertaining to the life and belief of the Church. There are various levels: a *diocesan council* is referred to as a *synod*, and is a meeting of a bishop, representative clergy, religious and laity, in which matters of diocesan Church discipline and procedure are discussed. A *provincial council* is an assembly of the metropolitan archbishop with his suffragan bishops, while a *plenary council* summons all the bishops of a given nation. The highest convocation of all is an ecumenical council, in which all the bishops of the world meet in union with the Bishop of Rome.

Councils, Ecumenical • The most solemn and official assembly of all the bishops of the world (thus "ecumenical," or universal), which, when summoned by the Bishop of Rome, constitutes the highest teaching authority in the Church. These meetings are usually convoked at pivotal, critical moments in the life of the Church, and are charged with discussing and then articulating formal statements on doctrine or discipline. At times throughout Church history, secular rulers, theologians, superiors of religious orders and, most recently, representatives of other creeds have also been invited to attend. Catholics recognize twenty-one ecumenical councils, listed as follows, with the Orthodox Churches accepting the first seven:

1. Nicaea I, A.D. 325, condemned Arianism and declared the Son consubstantial with the Father.

2. Constantinople I, 381, condemned Macedonians and declared the Holy Spirit consubstantial with Father and Son.

3. Ephesus, 431, condemned Nestorians and Pelagians and formally approved the use of the title "Mother of God" for the Blessed Virgin Mary.

4. Chalcedon, 451, condemned Monophysitism.

5. Constantinople II, 553, condemned the Three Chapters.

6. Constantinople III, 680, condemned Monothelitism and censured Honorius.

7. Nicaea II, 787, condemned Iconoclasm.

8. Constantinople IV, 869, ended the Greek schism and deposed Photius.

9. Lateran I, 1123, issued decrees on simony, celibacy, lay investiture and confirmed the Concordat of Worms.

10. Lateran II, 1139, ended the papal schism and enacted reforms.

11. Lateran III, 1179, condemned Albigenses and Waldenses and regulated papal elections.

12. Lateran IV, 1215, planned a crusade, issued decrees on annual Communion, repeated the condemnation of Albigenses and enacted reforms.

13. Lyons I, 1245, deposed Frederick II and planned a crusade.

14. Lyons II, 1274, reunited the Church with the Greeks and enacted disciplinary reforms.

15. Vienne, 1311-1312, abolished the Knights Templars and enacted reforms.

16. Constance, 1414-1418, ended the Great Schism and condemned Huss.

17. Basle, Ferrara, Florence, 1431-1445, effected union of Greeks and enacted reforms.

18. Lateran V, 1512-1517, treated of the Neo-Aristotelians and enacted reforms.

19. Trent, 1545-1563, condemned Protestantism and enacted reforms.

20. Vatican I, 1869-1870, condemned errors and defined papal infallibility.

21. Vatican II, opened by Pope John XXIII, October 11, 1962, until the close of the first session on December 8, 1962. After Pope John's death it was reconvened by Pope Paul VI in three additional sessions: September 29 to December 4, 1963; September 14 to November 21, 1964; September 14 to its solemn closing on December 8, 1965. It promulgated sixteen documents.

Counseling, Pastoral • A process of human interaction normally done by a priest or other Christian to help individuals deal with difficult situations or personal problems. Pastoral counseling embraces the totality of human life. It gives serious consideration to the spiritual dimension of man, including God's revelation and the reality of divine judgment. The competent pastoral counselor offers sound spiritual advice to the questioning, confused or troubled person. Prayer for guidance and peace of soul are important and distinctive dimensions of this form of counseling.

Pastoral counseling need not take a formal, therapeutic form; it may be the everyday healthy guidance which most Catholics expect from priests. Its results should include a more mature faith and a deeper longing for holiness on the part of the recipient.

Counter-Reformation • Movements for Church renewal emphasizing deeper personal holiness, works of the apostolate and exercise of charity were developing in a number of places prior to the Reformation; they took on a new urgency because of the challenge to Catholicism. These intensified movements are usually called the Counter-Reformation.

Five dimensions of this movement are worthy of special consideration:

(1) New vitality in religious life. One aspect of this is the formation of new religious communities; e.g., Theatines, Barnabites, Ursuline Nuns and especially the Jesuits. Older orders were renewed, sometimes leading to new branches of a religious family, e.g., Capuchins, Discalced Carmelites.

(2) Work of the Council of Trent (1545-1563). The teaching of the Church was proposed authoritatively in doctrinal decrees on the role of Sacred Scripture, original sin, justification and sacraments. Reform decrees aided the renewal of Church life. Of special importance was the decree establishing the seminary system.

(3) Development of the spiritual life. A true vitality of Catholicism involves a deep interior union with Christ. The Church was strengthened by the lives of heroic men and women who were later canonized, e.g., Teresa of Ávila, John of the Cross, Catherine de Ricci, Ignatius Loyola. Confraternities encouraged more frequent reception of the sacraments. The Rosary and other forms of popular devotion developed.

(4) Flourishing of theology. Especially in Spain and Italy, theology, both scholastic and positive, developed and prepared trained Church leaders.

(5) Growth of missionary spirit. There was a new interest in missionary activity in the New World, Africa and Asia, as well as in the areas previously Catholic but now dominated by Protestants.

This movement, characteristic of the century or so after the beginning of the Reformation, had a significant effect in later centuries.

Courts, Ecclesiastical • Usually called a tribunal, an ecclesiastical court is a canonical entity that administers justice according to canon law. Each diocese, unless dispensed by the Holy See, is obliged to have a diocesan tribunal. This is called the court or tribunal of first instance. Courts of second instance or appeal courts receive decisions appealed from the courts of first instance and decide on their validity. In many countries, the court of the metropolitan archdiocese serves as the appeal court for all of the other dioceses in the province. In some countries a separate appeal court is set up for groupings of dioceses and/or archdioceses.

There are also two courts of the Holy See. The Roman Rota, made up of judges from around the world, acts as the court of third instance for all lower courts. It can also act as a court of second instance for any appeal legitimately brought before it. The Rota acts as the court of first instance for cases involving bishops, the heads of religious institutes, and physical or juridic persons who have no superior below the Pope.

The Tribunal of the Apostolic Signatura is the other Roman court. (Cf. Apostolic Signatura.)

The diocesan courts are headed by a judicial vicar, formerly called the *officialis*, who is appointed by the bishop. The bishop also appoints associate judges and other officials, such as defenders of the bond, notaries, and the promoter of justice.

Although Church courts are empowered to handle most types of cases involving canon law, for the most part they deal with marriage cases, wherein one party petitions the court for a declaration of nullity of marriage.

The process to be followed by Church courts is outlined in the Code of Canon Law. In many ways it is similar to the judicial processes used in countries governed by a code system of law, such as France, Holland or Belgium. Cases are not tried before juries but by panels of either three or five judges. A single judge can decide certain types of cases. There are two kinds of judicial procedures: criminal trials, dealing with accusations of canonical crimes; and contentious trials, which deal with other matters, such as the nullity of marriage. In all cases, the aggrieved persons have the right to present evidence, the right to an advocate and the right to appeal.

Competence is the canonical term used for the jurisdiction or right of a court to hear a case. Ordinarily, a person is to submit a case before the court of his own diocese or before the court of the diocese where the act or crime in question took place. There are exceptions, however. In marriage nullity cases, a petition for court action is ordinarily submitted by the petitioner either to the court of the diocese where the marriage took place or to the court of the diocese wherein the other party resides. Under certain circumstances defined by the law, such a petition can be submitted to the petitioner's own court or to the court of the diocese wherein most of the proofs are to be collected.

The rules of competence also apply to certain types of persons. The law states that the Roman Pontiff alone is capable of hearing the cases of cardinals, heads of state, apostolic legates and bishops in penal cases. When a case is presented to the Pope, he usually assigns it to a specially constituted panel of judges who act on his delegated authority.

The court system of the Church has its origins in the Middle Ages. At first, the bishops administered justice, but in time the number of cases presented increased to the point that bishops appointed priests learned in the law to represent them. By the twelfth century, the court system was in place throughout most of the Church (cf. Canons 1400-1445).

Covenant • A solemn promise, fortified by an oath, concerning future action. The oath might be expressed in words or in a symbolic action. In the rhetoric of the Near East, covenants were spoken of as oaths and stipulations. Diverse situations of secular life were regulated by covenants, e.g., international relations. In the Old Testament the usual (but not the only) word for covenant is *b'rith*. The religious covenants spoken of in the Old Testament may be divided into two classes, those in which God makes a promise, as for example, the covenant struck by Abraham (Gn 15), and secondly, covenants in which Israel is bound (e.g., Jos 24). In the New Testament, the notion of covenant surfaces preeminently in the account of the Last Supper (Mk 14:24), where the meaning of Christ's sacrifice is defined as the "new covenant." Both the Sinai covenant and the covenant in Christ's blood brought into being a People of God and called for complete surrender to God in response to His love.

For further reading: George E. Mendenhall and Gary A. Herion, "Covenant," *Anchor Bible Dictionary*, 1:1179-1202.

Cowl • From the Latin *cucullus*, cowl refers either to the hood worn by monks and other religious or to the large robe worn for choir by monastic men and women, such as the Benedictines, Cistercians and others.

Creation • God's free activity by which He brings all things into existence. Since there is no preexistent material upon which God has to act, it is said that creation is *ex nihilo* (or "out of nothing"). The doctrine of creation thus rules out dualism (the notion that the created order is the outcome of a primordial competition between or a juxtaposition of coeval forces). The doctrine of creation also rules out emanationism (the notion that things develop automatically out of the divine substance), since God causes things to exist by a personal determination and not out of necessity.

Only God Himself is sheer existence. Everything else, visible and invisible, is radically distinguished from Him in being just derivatively and dependently existent. This rules out pantheism (the notion that the divine substance is continuous with and indistinguishable from the world). Although God is distinct from the world, He is still present to it: The continuance, or conservation, of all things in existence depends on God's activity. Since God is their cause, things in the created order reflect Him, though in a limited fashion. Whatever goodness or perfection we can observe or experience in the world is the faintest reflection of the goodness and perfection of God. Moreover, just as all things have a beginning, they also have an "end." Built into all that God has made — individually and globally — is the tendency toward goodness and flourishing that can ultimately come to rest only in God Himself.

In Catholic Tradition, the doctrine of creation and scientific knowledge about the world are completely compatible. According to the *Catechism of the Catholic Church*, "The question about the origins of the world and of man has been the object of many scientific studies which have splendidly enriched our knowledge of the age and dimensions of the cosmos, the development of life-forms and the appearance of man. These discoveries invite us to even greater admiration for the greatness of the Creator, prompting us to give him thanks for all his works and for the understanding and wisdom he gives to scholars and researchers" (n. 283).

For further reading: *Catechism of the Catholic Church*, nn. 279-327.

Creationism • Has both a wide and a narrower meaning. In the wide meaning it refers to any belief that the world is created by God. The very reality of the world comes from God's freely bestowed love for us. Though human science can explain many features of the world (for example, the biological theory of evolution by natural selection can explain the number of species of living things and their relations), the reality of the world and its ultimate purpose, because of its creation and conservation in being by God, cannot be adequately explained by science. The Catholic belief that God is the Maker of heaven and earth is the creationist view in this wider meaning.

A narrower meaning of creationism has become popular, especially among conservative Protestants, in opposition to the widespread secular assumption that the biological theory of evolution makes God's creative deed meaningless. Creationism in the narrower meaning agrees with Catholic Faith in denying that the theory of evolution is a whole or adequate explanation of our world. But this narrower creationism goes further by rejecting the theory of evolution or any such account, even as an explanation of some of the secondary or instrumental causes through which God providentially guides His created world and develops bodily life apt for His direct infusion of a human soul. Thus creationist leaders often seek to have their creationist view of the origin of species supplant or at least be included alongside the theory of evolution in the science classes of government schools.

Catholic Faith in God as our Creator does not reject the instrumental causality of beings in the world — which can be studied scientifically — since such instrumental causality is itself derived from God's primary creative causality.

For further reading: *Catechism of the Catholic Church*, nn. 279-327.

Creator • The title referring to God alone as Maker of all things from nothing. By an act of His will, He sustains and directs the universe. The Apostles' Creed speaks of God as "the Creator of heaven and earth," while the Nicene Creed, in the current vernacular translation used in the Mass, refers to God as "the Maker of heaven and earth."

Crèche • From the Old French for manger, the term crèche is used more specifically for the manger in which Christ was born in Bethlehem. Tradition holds that this very manger is today preserved as a relic at the Basilica of St. Mary Major, in Rome, although the authenticity of that crèche cannot be proven. Crèche is also used for any representation of the Nativity, with figures of the significant participants: Jesus, Mary and Joseph, the ox and the donkey, and the shepherds with their sheep. On the Epiphany, the figures of the three kings and their camels are added. Over it all is usually an angel with a scroll proclaiming, "*Gloria in Excelsis Deo*." Often this angel is further elevated to the top of the Christmas tree, with the crèche placed beneath the tree.

Credence • Part of the sanctuary furnishings and also known as the "credence table," this small side table is usually covered with a white cloth and holds the chalice, paten with hosts, cruets for the wine and water, small lavabo dish, purificators and anything else needed for the celebration of the Eucharist. Originally, the term designated a buffet sideboard upon which food was placed before serving at the table. That the term "credence" (or "credenza"), which derives from the Latin *credentia* ("security"), came to be used in this sense suggests that in its earliest meaning it referred to the tasting of food by servants — prior to its being served to the master of the house — to be sure that it contained no poison.

Creed • A creed is a concise statement of Christian belief (from the Latin *credo*, "I believe"). The creeds commonly in use in the Church today developed from simple Trinitarian baptismal formulae employed by early Christians. The act of initiation by which one became a member of the Christian community was seen to entail an affirmation of the community's faith. For this reason, creedal formularies have always had an important place in the celebration of the sacrament of Baptism, as well as in furnishing a guide for instruction and study in the initial and ongoing formation of the new Christian. Most of the brief New Testament formulae and the other ancient creeds, especially the Apostles' Creed, served this baptismal-catechetical function. The baptismal interrogation of St. Hippolytus (c. A.D. 217) is similar to the Roman Creed, which may have been formulated in the reign of Pope St. Victor (189-199) and to the Apostles' Creed, which dates from roughly the same period and which the Fathers of the Church regarded as a rule of faith handed down by the Apostles.

The creedal function of providing a rule of faith is apparent in the more elaborate creeds produced by ecumenical councils, like the Nicene Creed, which is recited every Sunday throughout the Christian world. Such creeds provide a normative standard by which to measure the orthodoxy of teaching on specific but fundamental elements of Christian Faith. When disputed points of doctrine were settled by the great councils, their resolutions or determinations were often expressed in creedal formularies. Such formularies were intended not so much as elementary professions of faith, but as guides to inquiry and reflection concerning the doctrines of the Trinity, Christology and grace. The most widely known and influential formulary of this kind is the Nicene-Constantinopolitan Creed, which was composed at the Council of Nicaea (325) and amplified at the Councils of Constantinople (381) and Chalcedon (451).

In addition to these properly catechetical and doctrinal functions, the creeds have a significant doxological role, signaled by their incorporation into the Eucharistic liturgy. Since they recount the wondrous deeds of the Triune God — the work of salvation that brings Christians into the very life of the Trinity — the creeds are appropriately employed in praise and worship. The Nicene Creed, for example, has been set to music both by Latin chant composers and by classical composers. With one voice, the community of faith sings of the ultimate communion it enjoys by grace with the Father, Son and Holy Spirit.

Creed, Athanasian • One of the approved statements of the truths of the Faith, dating back to the fourth or fifth century. It was not written by St. Athanasius, but its expressions and ideas reflect his influence. Some scholars think it may have been written or revised by St. Ambrose.

The Athanasian Creed gives a summary of the Church's teachings on the Trinity and the Incarnation, with passing reference to other dogmas. Unlike other creeds, it deals almost exclusively with these two dogmas, which it states and restates in various ways. It also emphatically states the penalties to be incurred by those who refuse to accept the articles of the Creed.

Cremation • The disposal of a dead body by burning it and reducing it to ashes. Cremation was the normal custom in the ancient civilized world, except in Egypt, Judaea and China. It was repugnant to the early Christians because of the belief in the resurrection of the body. By the fifth century, cremation had been largely abandoned in the Roman Empire because of Christian influence.

For centuries it was forbidden for Catholics to be cremated because it was believed that to do so was a sign of disbelief in the immortality of the soul, as well as an act of disrespect for the body. This prohibition was lifted in 1963; in the revised Code of Canon Law, cremation is permitted, provided it is not done for reasons contrary to Christian Faith (cf. Canon 1176.3).

Crib: See **Crèche**

Crimen • Crimen or crime is an impediment to marriage. In the revised Code it arises when a spouse brings about the death of another's spouse or his or her own spouse, in order to marry the other person. It also arises if they cooperate in the death of the spouse of one, but not necessarily for the express purpose of marrying each other. The impediment exists if the spouses or one of them actually commits the murder, or if they hire or otherwise obtain the services of someone else to do it (Canon 1090).

This impediment is ordinarily dispensed only by the Holy See. In danger of death, it may be dispensed by a local Ordinary, or by the priest or deacon involved with the marriage if the local Ordinary cannot be reached.

Under the 1917 Code, however, the impediment of crimen had three, somewhat wider, senses. The first was mutual adultery between two people, with an intention of marrying each other. The second was adultery and murder of a spouse, with intent to marry. The third was murder of a spouse by conspiracy between the parties, with intent to marry, but not necessarily with adultery between them.

Criticism, Biblical • The scholarly evaluation of the human elements contained in Sacred Scripture. Both Pope Leo XIII (*Providentissimus Deus*, 1893) and Pope Pius XII (*Divino Afflante Spiritu*, 1943), stressed the importance of biblical criticism. The Church insists that Scripture is inspired by God; hence, the Holy Books must not be treated as merely human works. Because the Church, due to the inspiration of the Holy Spirit, is the guarantor and interpreter of the Bible, she alone can decide the meaning of a specific passage. Catholic exegetes who have at their disposal various tools in discerning the literary and historical contexts of Scripture enjoy freedom in their research within the parameters determined by the Magisterium.

For further reading: William Baird, "Biblical Criticism," *Anchor Bible Dictionary*, 1:725-726.

Crosier (fourteenth century)

Crosier (also Crozier) • A pastoral staff conferred on bishops and abbots at their installation. In the West, the top of the staff is curved to remind the bishop of the shepherd's crook and of his pastoral care of the people entrusted to him. The earliest known liturgical reference to the crosier is in the seventh century. From the twelfth century up to the time of Paul VI, the Popes did not use a crosier, but now they use one in the form of a crucifix mounted on a long staff. Present day crosiers tend to be of simple design and material.

Cross • As the instrument of Christ's sacrifice on our behalf, the cross is the principal symbol of the Christian Faith. The Roman use of the cross for the execution of criminals (normally slaves or non-citizens) was borrowed from Carthaginian practice. The cross used for the crucifixion of Christ was probably tau-shaped (the transverse beam flush with the top of the upright beam) or t-shaped (the transverse beam fit into the upper half of the upright beam just below the top). Christian depiction of the cross almost always adopts the latter form. Given what is known about Roman practice, it is likely that Christ carried the transverse beam through Jerusalem to Calvary. Especially after the finding of the remains of the True Cross during the time of Constantine (probably by St. Helena), depiction of the cross became an important feature of Christian symbolism and iconography. It appears in many forms and settings, prominently displayed atop Christian churches and central to the internal arrangement of the church sanctuary. Crosses are worn by prelates, by religious and by many of the faithful. The sign of the cross is the typical religious gesture that expresses the Christian Faith and invokes divine protection and grace.

Cross, Relics of the True • These are authenticated relics, and while there is some cynicism about how many relics there are, in the nineteenth century Rohault de Fleury catalogued all known relics of the cross and estimated that they constituted less than one-third of the cross thought to have been used in the Crucifixion. (Cf. Cross, Veneration of the.)

Cross, Veneration of the • The True Cross on which Jesus died was said to be discovered by St. Helena about A.D. 325, but historical evidence does not seem to support this claim. Yet there is solid evidence that it was found before 350 and was venerated by pilgrims in Jerusalem. St. Cyril clearly attests to this. In fact, Egeria, the Spanish nun pilgrim, describes veneration of the True Cross on Good Friday, which became a very popular rite brought back to the West by pilgrims to the Holy Land. At home they venerated other crosses, rather than the True Cross, indeed as is done today.

At Christian beginnings, the followers of Christ considered the crucifix a symbol of execution and while they revered the redemption, they depicted it through Old Testament symbolism, e.g., Jonah in the whale or Daniel in the

Cross given Vatican by Emperor Justinian II

lion's den. They did not depict the cross, nor the near-nude Christ on the cross, until the fourth and fifth centuries. The carving of Christ and the two thieves on the doors of Santa Sabina is one of the earliest representations of the crucifixion, although there are no crosses in the picture. When crosses and crucifixes began to be used, they were crosses of victory — the *Crux Gemmata* — from the sixth century to the early Middle Ages. In the medieval period, devotion to the suffering Christ caused the fashioning of crucifixes emphasizing the passion more than victory; this continued even into the Baroque era, when crucifixes became extremely realistic.

Crown, Episcopal • The miter of Eastern bishops, but more like a solid royal crown surmounted by a cross. It resembles a jeweled turban of the Persians, from whom the Byzantines probably borrowed it.

Crown, Franciscan • In the Franciscan tradition, there is a legend that the Blessed Virgin appeared to a Franciscan novice and taught him to say the crown, a Rosary of seven decades on which one meditates on the seven joys of Mary: the Annunciation, the Visitation, the Birth of the Lord, the Adoration of the Magi, the Finding in the Temple, the Resurrection and (as one mystery) the Assumption and Coronation.

Crown of Thorns • In Matthew 27:29, Mark 15:17 and John 19:2, we read that Jesus was given a "crown of thorns" as part of the humiliation suffered at the hands of His jailers. "Thorns" (Greek, *akanthai*) means "briers" and is used in a consistently negative light throughout Jesus' teachings (e.g., Mt 7:16; Mk 4:7, 18; cf. Heb 6:8).

A crown of thorns was fashioned either in the form of a ringlet and placed on the skull, or in the form of a helmet covering most of the upper half of the skull. The plant is thought to have been plentiful in the region surrounding Jerusalem, had a very slender thorn, and was often used for firewood. The crown's alleged survival as a relic is noted first in the fifth century; in the sixth century Cassiodorus may have seen it in Jerusalem on its way (eventually) to Constantinople. Other traditions indicate that it was actually broken into smaller pieces and later distributed as relics.

Crucifix from Pisa (twelfth century)

Crucifix • A cross upon which is placed a reproduction of Christ's crucified body. This version is popular in the Western Church in both private and public (Good Friday) devotion. The Eastern Church values the crucifix in a different design — a flat likeness of the Christ in the form of an icon. Most in the Protestant movement replaced the crucifix with the cross. Exceptions to this revision are found in various Lutheran congregations and within the High Church element of the Anglican Communion (especially during the reign of Elizabeth I).

Crucifixion • An ancient form of execution or capital punishment for treason, sedition or rebellion. The ancient Persians appear to have the distinction of initiating this method of execution; the Greeks made little use of it, in contrast to both the Carthaginians and the Romans, who utilized it extensively.

The key ingredient to crucifixion was public shame to discourage rebellion, sedition and runaway slaves. Shame was brought about by forcing the condemned to carry the horizontal beam through public roads and areas. The execution site was usually close to a public place (if not actually at one); the horizontal beam was connected to the vertical one and the prisoner was crucified, but only after being scourged and stripped naked. Death was normally very painful: The naked person was not able to care for bodily needs and the crowd was often close enough to realize this and make derisive comments, further adding to the humiliation and further robbing the person of human dignity. The hands and feet were either nailed or roped to the appropriate beam with the middle section tied to the vertical beam, so as to prevent the condemned from wriggling free. Muscle fatigue, exhaustion from physical and psychological stress, lack of food and drink, and exposure to the elements over a period of days usually led to heart failure, asphyxiation or other forms of death. The first-century A.D. Jewish historian Josephus called it the "most wretched of deaths." Jesus' crucifixion was the result of applying the Roman law against the crime of treason (or rebellion), with which a few Jewish leaders of Jerusalem charged Him before Pilate (Lk 23:2-5; Jn 19:12). Jesus' crucifixion is recorded in Scripture (Mt 27; Mk 15; Lk 23; Jn 19).

The "cross" is a kind of symbol naturally charged with potential meanings. Its association with the historical death of Jesus elevates, shapes and links the ultimate meaning and reality of the cross with Christ's selfless act of filial and obedient sacrificial love for the Father and all who would accept this irrevocable gesture of friendship. The "cross" becomes a way of life for Jesus' followers who dare to love unconditionally and by so doing "gain" a life never before imagined (Mt 10:38, 16:24; Mk 8:34; Lk 9:23, 14:27). In the letters of Paul, the cross is the power of God to save, to create the "new *anthropos*" (new inner man) (Rom 6:6; Gal 2:20, 5:24). The cross or "tree" of death and humiliation (of the curse) becomes the "tree of life" from which the New Adam brings about the new creation (Eph 2:14-18). In the Person of Jesus, this grotesque and awful symbol of death becomes a pathway to God through resurrection life in Christ.

For further reading: Gerald G. O'Collins, "Crucifixion," *Anchor Bible Dictionary*, 1:1207-1210.

Cruet • The vessel used to hold the wine or water for the celebration of the Mass. Though cruets are usually made of glass or crystal with a matching tray on which they sit, it is permissible for them to be fashioned out of any worthy material capable of holding liquids. In addition to crystal and glass, cruets can be made of brass, pewter, silver, gold, and even less expensive materials such as well-sealed ceramics. They usually have handles and are covered with matching stoppers, and are of many styles and sizes. Another name for cruet is "ampulla." Traditionally, the cruets were engraved with the initials "V" and "A," for the Latin *vinum* and *aqua*, wine and water, in order that no mistake be made in pouring the wrong substance into the chalice. This is commendable but not obligatory, however.

Crusade, Children's: See **Children's Crusade**

Crusades • Those expansive military expeditions which Western Europe undertook between 1096 and 1270 for the purpose of driving the Muslims ("the Infidel") from, or keeping them out of, Palestine, the Holy Land. The name comes from the cross embroidered on the garments worn and pennants carried by the participants. These initiatives lasted almost two centuries, and, since proclaimed by the Pope and commissioned to rescue the holiest shrines of

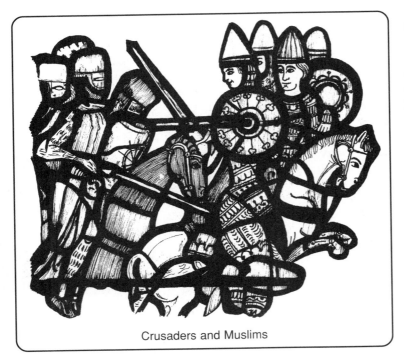

Crusaders and Muslims

Christendom, were looked upon as holy causes. However, although many of the participants were indeed inspired by such a lofty motive, others entered for more political, economic, adventuresome or selfish motives.

Because they lasted so long, and involved hundreds of thousands of people from every country and background, the Crusades, while ultimately failing to make Palestine a Christian kingdom, did have profound cultural effects on both Europe and the Middle East. Commerce and travel were encouraged, religious zeal was promoted now that the papacy was the center of a stable Europe, eastern views and products entered the western scene, and a sense of freedom prevailed in the continent. Negative effects, such as a widening of the cleavage between East and West, and the scandal caused by the excesses of these ventures, cannot be overlooked.

Although somewhat difficult to number since many of them overlap, scholars generally list eight major crusades. The First Crusade (1095-1101), proclaimed by Pope Urban II, ended with the Christian forces entering Jerusalem. Pope Eugene III commissioned St. Bernard to preach the Second Crusade (1145-1148), calling for the recapture of Edessa from Islam, but it ended in failure. The Third Crusade (1188-1192), sparked by Pope Gregory VIII, ended when the Emperor Frederick Barbarossa, Philip Augustus of France, and Richard the Lion-Hearted agreed upon a truce with Saladin. Pope Innocent III ended up excommunicating the leaders of the Fourth Crusade (1207-1214) when they abandoned the drive. Sometimes the fifth one (1217-1221) is called the "Children's Crusade," in which perhaps 40,000 children, mostly from France and Germany, boarded ships in the hopes of arriving in the Holy Land to help the cause, and ended up in Muslim slave markets. This Fifth Crusade also included a military scheme to recapture Jerusalem, not by way of Syria, but through Egypt, which failed. Jerusalem was open to Christians as a result of the Sixth Crusade (1228-1229), led by Frederick II, who signed a treaty with the Sultan. St. Louis of France led both the Seventh Crusade (1248-1254), which had been commissioned by Pope Innocent IV, and, along with Charles Anjou, the Eighth Crusade (1267-1270), which both ended disastrously with the loss of the last Christian bastions.

Crypt • Etymologically, it comes from a Latin word, meaning a vault or hidden cave. Normally it refers to a subterranean chamber or vault, especially one beneath the main floor of a church for a burial place. In the early Church, it was used for divine services, meeting places and burial places for martyrs. (Cf. Confession of a Martyr.)

Cubiculum • In the Roman catacombs one may see these burial chambers, or *cubicula*, which are hewn out of the tufa rock, a middle stratum of rock not used for other buildings and in which the catacombs are generally found. These *cubicula* are found on both sides of the galleries of a catacomb. The word in Latin means "bedroom," or simply a small room. Since this was the place where the bodies of the deceased would lie in the sleep of death, the transfer of the meaning of the word to these "cubicles" in the catacombs is obvious. Along their walls are to be found the *loculi*, or "small places," where individuals were buried. The more imposing of these *loculi*, which were arched, with the sarcophagus resting on the bottom shelf, were called *arcosolium* (plural, *arcosolia*).

Culpability • *Culpa* is the Latin term for fault or blame. In canon law, *culpa* refers specifically to negligent or otherwise blameworthy conduct which is considered serious enough for ecclesiastical penalties to be applied. As such, *culpa* is distinguished from *dolus* or malice, whereby one commits an offense knowingly and deliberately. Generally, delicts committed with *culpa* are punished rather less severely than are those committed with *dolus* (cf. Canons 1321-1326). (Cf. Penal Process.)

Cult (also Cultus) • In ecclesiastical parlance, the term "cult" broadly refers to that devotion or honor afforded to a person or persons. This devotion is itself divided into various categories, differing both in their degree of intensity and, consequently, in the level of approbation given the cult by ecclesiastical authority. Not surprisingly, this devotion can also, under certain circumstances, be manifested within Sacred Liturgy, likewise subject to ecclesiastical regulation.

In recent years, however, societal speech has, regrettably, co-opted the innocuous term "cult" and used it to describe any number of aberrant or bizarre organizations that impose inhumane restrictions on their members. This usage, not to mention the underlying practices, is alien to sound Catholic thought. (Cf. Dulia, Hyperdulia; Latria.)

Cult, Disparity of • An impediment to marriage, arising between a baptized Catholic and an unbaptized person. This impediment is commonly dispensed by the bishop of the Catholic party or the bishop of the diocese wherein the marriage will take place. In order to obtain the dispensation, the Catholic party must make a declaration that there will be no dangers to his practice of the Faith and that he will do all possible to have any children born of the union baptized and raised as Catholics. A marriage entered into with a dispensation from this impediment is not a sacramental marriage because both parties are not baptized (cf. Canons 1086, 1125-1126).

Curate • A commonly used term in some English-speaking countries that refers to a priest who is an associate pastor or parochial vicar of a parish. The term is more widely used in Canada and England than in the United States.

Curator • A curator or guardian is a person appointed by an ecclesiastical judge to represent or stand for another. A curator is appointed if the person before the court is a minor or lacks the use of reason. The role of the curator is to see that the rights of the person represented are protected. These rights are also to be protected by the judge.

Curators are most often used in marriage nullity trials when one of the parties is incapable, because of a mental or psychological illness, of participating in the trial. The judge has the discretionary power to decide when such a person is incapable (cf. Canon 1478).

Curia, Diocesan • A collective term for the institutions, offices, bodies and individuals who assist a bishop in the pastoral and administrative governance of the diocese. Certain members of the curia are mandatory according to canon law: the vicar general, chancellor and notary. Also, there are certain entities which must be included in the curia: the archives, secret archives and the finance council.

Other officials and offices, not mentioned in the Code, may also be established to serve the particular needs of the diocese.

Strictly speaking, the diocesan court or tribunal is not part of the curia but a separate entity. In practice, the diocesan courts are often situated in the same building as the diocesan curia, with some members of the curia holding tribunal positions as well as their administrative positions (cf. Canons 469-494).

Curia, Roman • The entire body of officially established agencies which assists the Pope in the governance of the universal Church.

The most important and authoritative agencies of the Curia are the ten congregations, each directed by a cardinal prefect. Similar to a congregation because of their high levels of authority are the Secretariat of State and the Council for the Public Affairs of the Church.

Other types of agencies are the offices of the Curia. These attend to special administrative needs and include the Apostolic Camera, the Prefecture for the Economic Affairs of the Holy See, the Administration of the Patrimony of the Holy See, the Prefecture of the Papal Household and the General Statistics Office of the Church.

The Pontifical Councils handle affairs related to certain non-Catholic groups, as well as specific Catholic groups. These councils include the Pontifical Councils for the Laity, Christian Unity, the Family, Justice and Peace, the Pastoral Care of Migrants and Itinerants, the Interpretation of the Code of Canon Law, Interreligious Dialogue, Dialogue with Nonbelievers, Culture and Social Communications and, finally, the Pontifical Council *Cor Unum.*

There are also several commissions and committees that serve as agencies of the Roman Curia. These are: the Commission of the Roman Curia, the Council of Cardinals for the Study of Organizational and Economic Problems of the Holy See, the International Theological Commission, the Commission of Cardinals for the Pontifical Shrines of Pompeii, Loreto and Bari, the Pontifical Biblical Commission, the Pontifical Committee for the International Eucharistic Congresses, the Pontifical Commission for the Revision and Emendation of the Vulgate, the Pontifical Commission for the Vatican City State, the Pontifical Commission for Sacred Archaeology, the Pontifical Commission for History and the Pontifical Commission for the Ecclesiastical Archives of Italy.

In addition to the above, there are three tribunals, including the Roman Rota, the Apostolic Signatura and the Apostolic Penitentiary (cf. Canons 360-361).

Cursillo • The term, literally meaning "little course," referring to the renewal movement which seeks to restore the world to Christ. This method of renewal began with a group of laymen who met at the San Honorato Monastery on the island of Majorca, Spain, on January 7, 1949. Bishop Hervas y Benet gave his assistance to the group's endeavors.

The program is divided into three sections of three days each: preparation (pre-*cursillo*), the course itself (*cursillo*), and the follow-up (post-*cursillo*). Those who take part are called *cursillistas*, while those who meet after the *cursillo* in small-group gatherings called *ultreyas*. The key to the movement is first to change one's own mind according to the mind of Christ and, then, to gather with and support others who have committed themselves to Christ, in order that the world might be transformed.

Cursing • The calling down of some form of evil on another. It is a sin against charity and love of neighbor, and if done in front of some such as children, it can be scandalous as well.

It is difficult for modern Westerners to imagine the frequency and intensity of cursing among Orientals in the Old Testament and New Testament era. It was quite common and very bitter in the Old Testament, and it was often done according to a ritual that was almost magical and appeared akin to sorcery. In the ancient Orient, cursing was a very solemn and ritualized action. It was not simply the result of explosive tempers but was seen as a means of protecting oneself against the malice of an enemy.

In the New Testament, there is little mention of cursing. Jesus tells His Apostles to return a curse with a blessing, for cursing was regarded as a violation of the command to love one's enemy (Lk 6:28). Paul curses those who preach another Gospel (Gal 1:8) and anyone who does not love the Lord. St. Paul said that Christ has removed a curse from humanity by becoming Himself a curse.

For further reading: Douglas Stuart, "Curse," *Anchor Bible Dictionary*, 1:1218-1219.

Cursing Psalms: See Imprecatory Psalms

Custom • A manner of doing something that has its roots not in a legislative act but in human behavior itself. In the Church, custom plays an important role in shaping the way individuals relate to the community. It can also be found in certain liturgical practices, particularly those which come out of ethnic groups. In canon law, custom is a norm of action that arises out of accumulated human wisdom and is approved by the appropriate Church authority.

The Church will not allow a custom to attain the force of law if it is contrary to natural or Divine law or if it is contrary to or apart from canon law. Furthermore, a custom must have been observed for at least thirty years to attain the force of law. It must be observed, if it is intended to attain the force of law, by a community that is capable of receiving a law, i.e., a diocese, episcopal conference or parish (cf. Canons 23-28; J. McIntyre, "Customary Law in the Corpus Iuris Canonici," *Studies in Canon*

Law No. 527, Catholic University of America, 1989).

Custos • From the Latin for "custodian," a *custos* is a minor official entrusted with rather limited duties. Outside Franciscan circles, however, and those areas with cathedral chapters, the term is rarely encountered today.

Cycle: See Calendar

Cycle of Readings • In the *Lectionary for Mass* revised after Vatican II, the Scripture readings are assigned according to two principles: harmony and semicontinuous reading of a scriptural book. The principle of harmony determines the Scriptures designated for feasts and some parts of the weekday readings for seasons such as Advent and Lent and arranges them around a given theme. The precise term "cycle of readings" refers to the way a semicontinuous reading of a given scriptural book is established for proclamation in the Lectionary on Sundays and weekdays. At present, on Sundays one of the Synoptic gospels is read semicontinuously for Ordinary Time in a given liturgical year, i.e., St. Matthew in what is termed "Cycle A," St. Mark in "Cycle B," and St. Luke in "Cycle C." For these Sundays, the Old Testament reading is selected to correspond to the Gospel; the New Testament text is normally from the semicontinuous reading of an Epistle. On weekdays in Ordinary Time, it is the first reading which is on a "cycle" in that two readings are offered to be read prior to the Gospel, the first read in "cycle 1" and the second in "cycle 2." On the Sundays of Advent, Lent and Easter, the principle of assigning readings according to a "cycle" is also operative (A, B, C), but during these seasons the Gospels are chosen to reflect specific themes of the season.

Dalmatic • This vestment which draws its name from its place of origin, Dalmatia, is today the proper liturgical vestment of the deacon at Mass, though it is not solely worn by him. It is worn over all the other vestments, that is, the amice, alb, cincture and stole. As was the case with most vestments, the dalmatic was originally a garment used in secular society that gradually fell out of use and was retained and became proper to the clergy.

In its primitive form, it was a loose, gown-like tunic reaching the ankles and having loose sleeves. It was ornamented with two vertical stripes of red or purple running from the bottom hem to the shoulders, front and back. There was usually an opening at the sides reaching from the bottom to the waist (or even the shoulders in some later styles of the dalmatic). It is believed to have been worn only by the Roman Pontiff at first and then extended to the Roman deacons as a privilege and then to others as time elapsed. It was also worn under the chasuble by the bishop during Pontifical Masses.

According to the latest edition of the *Caeremoniale Episcoporum* promulgated in 1984 by Pope John Paul II, the dalmatic still should be worn by the bishop under the chasuble and over the pectoral cross during his consecration, as well as during Pontifical Masses (cf. nn. 56, 61, 657; and of deacons, n. 511). The color of the dalmatic is that of the day, that is, the same as the color of the chasuble worn by the celebrant and concelebrants at the Mass at which the deacon assists.

As with chasubles, there are many styles of dalmatics — from those adhering to the primitive model described above and much in vogue today, to those developed in the High Middle Ages and Renaissance which at times reach only to the knees or slightly below them and with shorter sleeves, some short to the point of appearing ridiculous to the modern eye and no longer in use.

Spanish dalmatic (sixteenth century)

Dance, Liturgical • The practice of dancing during the liturgy arose during the years after the general liturgical reform of Vatican II. Although it has occurred in various dioceses in the United States and no doubt in other countries as well, it has never been approved by the Holy See. In fact, on several occasions the Holy See, when made aware of instances of liturgical dance, has asked that the practice be discontinued.

Daniel • This Hebrew name means "God is my judge." In the Old Testament, Daniel is the name of the main character of the book that bears his name. In the Book of Daniel, we are told that he was exiled to Babylon during the sixth century B.C. There God gave him great wisdom and the ability to interpret dreams because of Daniel's unyielding fidelity to the commandments of the Torah. Upon falling into disfavor with the king, Daniel was thrown into the lions' den, from which he was saved by God's intervention. (Cf. Daniel, Book of.)

Daniel, Book of • This Old Testament book presents the wisdom, virtue and fortitude of Daniel as an example to believers. The work falls into two parts: the first (Chapters 1-6) consists of five stories relating to Daniel and one which concerns his three friends, Shadrach, Meshach and Abednego. The second segment of the book tells of four visions granted to Daniel. The work has come down to the present partly in Hebrew (1-2:4a and 8-12) and partly in Aramaic (2:4b—7:28). The date of composition is set by some as c. 166-165 B.C. The message conveyed to the book's contemporaries and beyond is that God will deliver those who, as Daniel did, remain loyal to the Faith and exhibit courage in professing it.

The imagery and apocalyptic perspective of the Book of Daniel influenced the New Testament Book of Revelation.

For further reading: John J. Collins, "Daniel," *Anchor Bible Dictionary*, 2:29-37; Louis F. Hartmann, C.Ss.R., and Alexander A. DiLella, O.F.M., "Daniel," *New Jerome Biblical Commentary*, 406-420.

Dark Ages • A somewhat inaccurate term used in the past by some historians to describe the centuries following the collapse of the Roman Empire, usually given as from the middle of the fifth century to the eleventh century. Although the social and political upheaval brought on by the advances of the barbarians and the destruction of the stability of the Roman Empire did indeed cause some intellectual and cultural stagnation, the heritage of Western civilization was guarded and fostered by the monasteries and some towering figures, e.g., Pope St. Gregory the Great. The flourishing of art and education in the Middle Ages was only possible because of the protection of learning — under the most adverse of circumstances — characteristic of these so-called "Dark Ages."

Dark Night of the Senses • The initial stage of perfection in which God draws the person from the practice of meditation to the higher form of prayer known as contemplation. God uses this period to lead souls to Christian perfection. The senses are of no benefit to the person who seeks God by faith alone. Prayer may seem repulsive; the person may also experience scruples (temptations against faith) or even illness. According to St. John of the Cross (1542-1591), ". . . God introduces a person into this night to purge his senses, and accommodate, subject, and unite the lower part of his soul to the spiritual part by darkening it and causing a cessation of discursive meditation. . ." (*The Dark Night*, Book I, Chapter XI, Article III).

Dark Night of the Soul • The term which describes the purification by which God draws a person to Himself and, therefore, to a higher level of holiness. Before a person can enjoy "mystical union" with God, he must be purged of all self-love. During this period, a person feels abandoned by God; in addition, this "night" immerses the soul in a "darkness" through which he cannot see God as he normally did in his previous spiritual condition. Hence, the soul is deprived of the usual light of faith by which

King David (Tissot painting)

he knows God. The Dark Night happens only to those who have attained contemplation; furthermore, this stage is transitory but may return again. Purgatory and the Dark Night are similar in that both are stages of purification before being united to God: purgatory, before seeing God in heaven; the Dark Night, before being united to God in the mystical embrace. St. John of the Cross, in his work *The Dark Night,* writes that a soul feels pain during this period because of the soul's inadequacies and weakness; hence, "the soul has to suffer when the divine light shines upon it" (Book II, Chapter IX, Article XI).

David • David (1000-961 B.C.) is called the greatest of Israel's kings. It is possible that the name means "beloved one." His ancestry places him as an Ephrathite of Bethlehem in Judah, the youngest son of Jesse (cf. 1 Sm 16:20—30:31; 2 Sm; 1 Kgs 1:1—2:11). Because of his bravery and strong leadership, Jews and Christians consider him as the ideal ruler of the Hebrew people.

Among his noted accomplishments were the unification of the twelve tribes of Israel into one nation; the establishment of Jerusalem as the capital; the conquest of the Philistines, Edomites, Moabites and Ammonites; the preliminary building plans for the Great Temple (cf. 2 Sm 8-12). His human failures are recorded as well: his adultery with Bathsheba, his murder of her husband Uriah, his rebuke by the prophet Nathan, and the rebellion of his son Absalom (cf. 2 Sm 9-20). Despite these failures, he was considered a deeply religious man, a shrewd politician, a mighty soldier, a poet, a musician and a great king. The New Testament notes that Jesus is a descendant or Son of David, indeed the promised Davidic Messiah. (Cf. Psalms, Book of.)

For further reading: David M. Howard, Jr., "David," *Anchor Bible Dictionary,* 2:41-49.

Day of Atonement: See **Atonement, Day of**

Day Hours • In liturgical usage the word "Hour" refers to any section of the daily cycle of prayer, known in its totality, officially since Vatican II, as the Liturgy of the Hours, and formerly as the Divine Office. (It should be noted that the title page of the Liturgy of the Hours still refers to the whole cycle of prayer as "the Divine Office, restored by decree of the Second Vatican Ecumenical Council and published by authority of Pope Paul VI." Monastic usage frequently continues the practice of referring to the Liturgy of the Hours as the Divine Office or, as in the Rule of St. Benedict, *Opus Dei:* "the Work of God." Technically, the term "day hours" is best suited to what is now called Daytime Prayer, which may (but need not) be celebrated in three sections: midmorning (officially, Terce or the "third" hour, about 9 A.M.), midday (Sext, the "sixth" hour, noon), and midafternoon (None, the "ninth" hour, about 3 P.M.). Only one of these "Hours" is obligatory for clergy and religious working in an active apostolate. Contemplatives are expected to keep the traditional sequence. Prior to Vatican II, there was also a "first" hour, Prime, celebrated after the prayer at dawn, Lauds, and before beginning the day's work. In actual practice, books issued before Vatican II under the Latin title *Diurnale* or in English *Day Hours of the Roman Breviary* (the Benedictine version was called *Monastic Diurnal*) generally included all the "Hours" of the Divine Office except Matins (in monastic usage "Vigils"), with its lengthy psalms and readings. The equivalent volume today would be any one-volume edition of the Liturgy of the Hours. In some Latin countries this is still called a *Diurnal*, but in the United States and Canada *Christian Prayer* and in other English-speaking countries *Daily Prayer*. Pocket-sized abridgements have recently been published as well: *Shorter Morning and Evening Prayer*, *Shorter Christian Prayer* and, outside the United States, *Shorter Daytime Prayer*. All of these are modern equivalents of books formerly entitled *Day Hours*.

Day of Indiction • The title of that day, September 1, when the liturgical year begins in the Byzantine Rite. While the Roman Rite begins each new year on the First Sunday of Advent, the Byzantine Calendar commemorates the beginning of Advent on December 10.

Day of the Lord • As an Old Testament expression which may have its origins in the language of ancient Israelite holy war, the "Day of Yahweh" was understood to be the occasion on which Yahweh would defeat His enemies in combat. This is the case in texts such as Ezekiel 30:4, where the Day of the

Lord is the day when "a sword shall come upon Egypt." It followed that because Yahweh's enemies were also Israel's enemies among the nations, their defeat should be an occasion for Israel to rejoice.

The expression "Day of Yahweh" first appears in the book of the eighth-century B.C. prophet Amos. The prophet warns, "Woe to you who desire the day of the LORD! Why would you have the day of the LORD? It is darkness, and not light!" (Am 5:18). The woe is addressed to complacent Israel, which believed that the Day of the Lord would mean punishment only for Israel's enemies. Instead, for idolatrous and unjust Israel the Day of the Lord would be "gloom with no brightness in it" (Am 5:20). Accustomed to being Yahweh's chosen instrument, the agent by which Yahweh's victory was gained, and accustomed to enjoying the spoils of victory, Israel could instead expect to be the object of Yahweh's punitive judgment.

In other Old Testament texts, the Day of the Lord is spoken of as a past event, so that it would be more appropriate to speak of days of the Lord, moments of divine vengeance and vindication. Ezekiel 13 speaks out against the prophets of peace, who have not "built up a wall for the house of Israel, that it might stand in battle on the day of the LORD" (Ez 13:5), referring to the fall of Jerusalem in 587 B.C. Lamentations 2:22 speaks of this time as the day of the Lord's blazing wrath.

The Day of the Lord is the dominant theme of the book of the prophet Zephaniah, from which the hymn *Dies Irae* draws its inspiration: "A day of wrath is that day, a day of distress and anguish, a day of ruin and devastation, a day of darkness and gloom, a day of clouds and thick darkness, a day of trumpet blast and battle cry" (Zep 1:15-16). That day will be "the day of the wrath of the LORD" (Zep 1:18), a manifestation of Yahweh's punitive judgment against corrupt Jerusalem.

In postexilic prophecy, the Day of the Lord acquired an apocalyptic tone, as in Malachi 3:23, which promises the return of the prophet Elijah "before the great and terrible day of the LORD comes." There, as well as in the book of the prophet Joel, the Day of the Lord is the day of God's definitive judgment against the wicked and on behalf of the faithful, who are urged to prepare themselves by penance (cf. Jl 2).

The apocalyptic tone of the expression "Day of the Lord" in postexilic Old Testament prophecy was transformed when the expression entered the New Testament vocabulary as the "Day of the Lord Jesus Christ." In the letters of Paul, the "Day of Christ" is the *parousia*, the glorious eschatological return of Christ. The Day of the Lord will come unexpectedly (cf. 1 Thes 5:1-11) so that believers must ready themselves by remaining vigilant, faithful, pure and blameless (cf. Phil 1:10), prepared for the advent of the eschatological judge and savior.

In the Apocalypse of John, the seer's inaugural vision takes place "on the Lord's Day." This is the *kyriake*, the day on which Christians gathered for worship. This combines the Christian liturgical meaning of the Lord's Day as the occasion when believers gather for the Eucharistic celebration with the Old Testament prophetic sense of the Day of the Lord as the moment of God's eschatological advent as righteous Judge.

For further reading: K. J. Cathcart, "Day of Yahweh," *Anchor Bible Dictionary*, 2:84-85; Richard H. Hiers, "Day of the Lord," *Anchor Bible Dictionary*, 2:82-83.

Days of Prayer • At these times, once called rogation days and Ember days, the Church continues the custom of publicly thanking the Lord and prays to Him for the needs of all, especially for the productivity of the earth and for human labor. The general norms for the Calendar of the Liturgical Year promulgated in 1969 leave the time and manner of the celebration of these days to national episcopal conferences. The American Conference of Bishops in 1971 left the determination of such days to the local bishops, and since then they seem to have fallen into disuse.

De Condigno • The Latin term meaning "from worthiness," referring to the merit a person gains when the reward is equal to his action. The reward is "in justice" because it was promised in exchange for the specific action. (Cf. Grace.)

De Congruo • The Latin term meaning "from suitability," which refers to the merit a person gains when no reward was promised but, nevertheless, is appropriate for the action performed. Hence, the reward is "in charity" because it is due to the beneficence of the giver and not because of strict justice (cf. Grace).

De Profundis • The opening Latin words of Psalm 130, by which that psalm is sometimes known. It falls into two categories, viz., the gradual psalms and the penitential psalms. The tone and content of the psalm have traditionally been thought to be suitable as a prayer for the faithful departed. It is a call for rescue from the toils of sin and an expression of hope and trust.

Deacon, Permanent • In 1967 the Holy See restored to practice the permanent diaconate. Henceforth, with the approval of the episcopal conference, bishops could ordain single and married men to the permanent order of deacon. The Vatican regulations stipulated that unmarried candidates observe clerical celibacy. Married men who are ordained are prohibited from remarrying if their wives die.

Permanent deacons are clerics who can perform all of the functions associated with their order. These include proclaiming the Gospel, preaching the homily, assisting the priest at Mass, administering solemn Baptism, distributing Communion, presiding over funeral and burial services (but not celebrating the funeral Mass), acting as the official witness at weddings and exercising certain ecclesiastical offices.

Permanent deacons receive training in theology, canon law and pastoral ministry over a period that can last several years. In preparation for their ordination, they receive the ministries of lector and acolyte. Once ordained, they are in the clerical state; however, certain exceptions are made in regard to the obligations of clerics. Permanent deacons are not obliged to wear clerical dress. Rather, they are to follow the norms in place for their country or diocese. Although they are urged to recite the Liturgy of the Hours, they are not obliged to as are deacons preparing for the priesthood.

Permanent deacons perform a variety of pastoral services in various settings. In addition to general assistance in parishes, some function as directors of parishes without a permanent pastor.

Deacon, Transitional • One who will ultimately be called to the priesthood. At his diaconal ordination he commits himself to a celibate life and the daily recitation of the Divine Office. As a deacon, he may baptize solemnly, distribute Holy Communion, preach during the liturgy and witness marriages.

His sign of office is the stole, which hangs from his left shoulder and across his chest; on solemn occasions he also wears the dalmatic.

Deaconess • It is beyond doubt that from the beginning women were welcomed not only as members of the Church but also as helpers in the work of the Church. Some were officially recognized as such by being called "deaconesses." Widows, who had no other means of livelihood and no families of their own to care for, were especially drawn to this role.

What is unclear is their relationship to that of the liturgical offices and the ordained ministry. Given the loose terminology and informal atmosphere of the early Church, it was not and is not always clear what services they were authorized to perform and by what ceremony, if any, they were authorized to perform them. The word *diakonos* is not basically a religious term; indeed, the first deacons were chosen as stewards, not of a service of worship, but of a charitable ministry which the Church had assumed.

As time passes, deaconesses appear more often and their role is more clearly described. Early documents indicate that only a widow could become a deaconess, and only at the age of sixty (later reduced to forty). Some deaconesses were in charge of the widows and were installed by a liturgical rite, but with no evidence of the imposition of hands, used in ordination properly so called.

The scope of the assistance of some of these women might have varied from place to place, depending on the priest's need of it. Deaconesses had an understandable part in the Baptism of women converts, especially when it was done by immersion; they restrained disorderly women at the Eucharist; they lit the candles and adorned the sanctuary; they read the Scriptures to the assembled congregation; they presided at prayer groups for women; and they distributed the Eucharist to other deaconesses when a priest was unavailable.

As doors were opened, the question of limits arose. There was a parallel tendency of male deacons to aggrandize their role in the Eucharist, leading some to assume the very consecration of it. The first ecumenical council of the Church (Nicaea), in its nineteenth canon, declared that deaconesses are to be accounted laypersons and that they do not receive ordination truly so called. While other local councils adopted similar negative stances, the legislation was often and widely disregarded until medieval times.

The feminist movement has given the topic current interest. The ordination of lectors and acolytes, long an empty formality, has been all but abandoned, and yet at the same time unordained people of both sexes have been permitted to perform some of these liturgical ministries, with clarification yet needed and expected.

Deacons, First Seven • Seven members of the Jerusalem Christian community who were chosen and ordained to help the Twelve in distributing provisions to the widows of Greek-speaking Jews (Acts 6:1-6). This was the upshot of a quarrel in the Christian community between the Jewish Christians and Gentile or Diaspora Jewish Christians. The latter alleged that their widows were being neglected in the daily charitable distribution of funds. This instance as narrated in Acts is generally looked upon as the institution of the Order of deacon. It may be noted that Acts does not employ the term "deacon" to define these men but rather uses the verb *diakonein* to define their function of "serving."

Dead Sea Scrolls • Manuscripts and fragments of manuscripts written chiefly in Hebrew and Aramaic, found in the vicinity of Khirbet Qumran (some seven or eight miles south of Jericho) near the Dead Sea from 1947 onward. These works are thought to be the remains of an extensive library of a community of Essenes living in this area from c. 125 B.C. to about A.D. 66-70 (with an interruption of about thirty or forty years).

The script of these manuscripts has been identified as typical of the first century B.C. and the first century A.D. This dating of the works is supported as well by archaeological data.

The manuscripts were enclosed in jars, as manuscripts in ancient times were often stored. Nearly every book of the Old Testament is represented in the finds at Qumran. A variety of other works as well has been found, including commentaries on a number of biblical books and documents pertaining to the particular beliefs of the Essenes, including *The War of the Sons of Light Against the Sons of Darkness, The Manual of Discipline*, a document detailing the government of the group, the scrutiny and admission of candidates, rules of conduct, and various ritual regulations. The correspondence between the Qumran community (as revealed in the scrolls) and Christianity is interesting but does not postulate a contact between the two. For that matter, the differences between the two ought not to be minimized.

For further reading: John J. Collins, "Dead Sea Scrolls," *Anchor Bible Dictionary*, 2:85-101.

Dean • Apart from its meaning as an academic post, a dean is also a canonical position. He is a priest, appointed by the bishop, with limited authority over the common pastoral activities of a specific area of the diocese. The canons state that the dean is to perform a supportive role to the other clerics in his territory, to see that the liturgy is properly celebrated and to assist clerics when they are ill.

Traditionally, the dean represented the bishop in rural or outlying areas of the diocese and is also known as the vicar forane. More recently, deans have been appointed to urban or metropolitan districts of dioceses or archdioceses (cf. Canons 553-555).

Deanery

• An optional, but very common, grouping of parishes within a diocese or archdiocese, typically established because neighboring parishes face common pastoral

Dance of Death (illustration, 1480)

issues and would benefit from combined resources and approaches. Each parish in a deanery retains its canonical identity and integrity. Pastoral leadership in a deanery, under the bishop, is coordinated by a dean (cf. Canon 374.2).

Death • A natural and a personal event: the end of vitality, the end of personal existence and history, and the separation of soul and body. In death, the spiritual principle of the human person assumes a different relation to the person's body. At the personal level, death is the end of free personal self-realization. In death the soul draws closer to God than before, and death is the beginning of eternity.

In the Old Testament, it was not consistent or clear that death resulted from sin, but this view and perspective came to be adopted more widely and authoritatively as time progressed. Hebrew thought considered the person to be an incarnate spirit, and when that spirit departed, death occurred. Reflection on the nature of death reveals that it contains the mystery of the human person, for the death of Jesus Christ

was the most important event in human history.

The New Testament affirms that death is a consequence of sin (Rom 5:12ff). "Then desire when it has conceived gives birth to sin; and sin when it is full-grown brings forth death" (Jas 1:15). The human race was created immortal, but that life comes through Christ (1 Cor 15:22). Death is the last adversary confronted by Christ (1 Cor 15:25ff.), and it has been rendered powerless by Him (Heb 2:14). By sharing in the death of Christ, the Christian overcomes death (Rom 6:5). Living according to the Spirit gives us life (Rom 8:13). Partaking of the Eucharist assures us that one overcomes death (Jn 6:50ff.). Nonetheless, all men are subject to the law of death, and Christians reject the notion of transmigration of souls because death is the end of personal history.

Deborah, Song of • The Song (or Canticle) of Deborah constitutes the entirety of the fifth chapter of the Book of Judges. It celebrates the victory inspired by Deborah (c. 1125 B.C.), a *nebiah* (prophetess) and wife of Lappidoth, who accompanied Barak and the Israelites in battle with the Canaanites under Sisera and their King Jabin. It is likely the oldest extant Hebrew literary composition, going back to the period of the Judges, though probably not the work of

Deborah herself. Because of her noble work on behalf of the nation, Deborah is called the "Mother of Israel" (Jgs 5:7): "The peasantry ceased in Israel, they ceased until you arose, Deborah, arose as a mother in Israel."

Decade • In Roman Catholic usage, a section of the Rosary of Our Lady, consisting of one Our Father, ten Hail Marys, and one Glory Be. These prayers are recited while meditating upon the "Mystery" assigned to that decade. Although the particular subjects for meditation have varied over the centuries, the most common schema traditionally in use consists of fifteen decades and corresponding mysteries for the complete Rosary (five joyful, five sorrowful, five glorious mysteries), while the more commonly seen and used Rosary consists of five decades and is sometimes referred to as a "chaplet." The rosaries and chaplets of some religious orders and those recited in honor of various saints may vary in the number or decades prescribed or may change the number of prayers to more or less than a decade.

Decalogue • Etymologically, a Greek word meaning "ten sayings." Normally, it refers to the Ten Commandments given to Moses by God at Mt. Sinai (cf. Ex 20), inscribed on two tablets of stone (cf. Dt 4:13). In the New Testament, Jesus accepted them as the basis of His teaching and promised to carry them to completion (cf. Mt 5:18). (Cf. Commandments of God.)

For further reading: *Catechism of the Catholic Church*, nn. 2056-2082.

Declaration • Any kind of statement of fact. The Holy Father, agencies of the Holy See and other Church authorities frequently issue declarations about a variety of topics. A declaration, in the strict sense, is not a law. Rather, it is an expositive

pronouncement about some matter important to Catholics.

Decorations, Pontifical • Honors given by the Holy See to laypersons by virtue of their exemplary service to the Church or society. The award is presented either in the recipient's home diocese by the local bishop or in Rome by a representative of the Holy See. Papal decorations include titles of nobility (baron, knight, prince), crosses (*Pro Ecclesia et Pontifice*) and medals (*Benemerenti*, Medal of the Holy Land).

Decree • A decree is a generic term for an official pronouncement announcing some decision of an authority, clarification of an issue or judgment of a court. Examples of the ecclesiastical use of the term would be a decree of nullity, a decree of excommunication, a decree on the use of *mustum* (fresh grape juice) in place of wine at Mass, etc.

Decretalist • The title given to a commentator on selected works in canon law. A decretalist, to be distinguished from a decretist, was a specialist in at least one of three sets of canonical documents which figured prominently in the history of canon law. These were, in chronological order, the Five Compilations, the Decretals of Pope Gregory IX, and, variously, the Liber Sextus, Clementinae, or Extravagantes. The best recognized name among these many learned doctors is easily that of the Cardinal Henry of Susa. The decretals commented upon were part of the *Corpus Iuris Canonici* and were of such fundamental importance that they and the commentaries written on them perdured in significance until the advent of the 1917 Code of Canon Law. (Cf. Glossator.)

Decretals • A historic term for papal letters which are issued in response to a question. Various collections of decretals have been published; some, such as the Decretals of Gregory IX, the Decretals of Boniface VIII and the Decretals of Clement V, were given the force of law.

Many collections of decretals, both official and unofficial, are still used in the study of canon law.

Decretals, False • The celebrated canonist and one-time apostolic delegate to the United States Amleto Cicognani has described the False Decretals as "a forgery altogether unique, a bold and successful fraud." The appearance, use and eventual decline and repudiation of this canonical collection is one of the most unusual episodes in the history of canon law.

The False Decretals, or, as they are sometimes called, Pseudo-Isidore, were composed around A.D. 850 in northern France during the latter days of the Carolingian reforms. Building upon four earlier collections of canonical legislation (the best of which were themselves already spuriously attributed to St. Isidore because of his fame), unknown composers compiled a large collection of canons made up of authentic papal and conciliar decrees and liberally interspersed with false, forged decrees touching upon the same topics. This collection they then attributed to St. Isidore. The skill with which the false decrees were drafted, coupled with only crude methods for verifying the authenticity of documents in that day, resulted in the widespread acceptance of the collection throughout Europe.

The motives behind the production of the False Decretals are complex. Two seem chief among them: first, the great majority of the false documents lend themselves to a genuine and necessary reform in ecclesiastical discipline in the regions of the Gaul of that day; second, many of the forgeries served as effective deterrents to the growing encroachment of ecclesiastical

rights by civil authorities. Both goals, curiously, were served by the same basic method. The collection, it was claimed, was simply rediscovering ancient (read: pristine) Church practice and thus was a light to the modern needs of ecclesiastical reform. Moreover, by claiming to show that certain rights and privileges were of centuries-old status, civil authorities (who were using the same types of arguments) could interfere less with the operation of ecclesiastical affairs.

Although internal evidence excludes the possibility that the collection was produced in Rome or at its behest, the majority of canons point the way to a greater centralization of the Holy See's authority. Nevertheless, at no time, interestingly, did the Roman See recognize or grant authenticity to the Pseudo-Isidorian collection. Furthermore, many prerogatives purported to have been Rome's (such as the necessity of the Pope's consent to convoke a provincial synod) were never exercised by the Supreme Pontiff.

The great influence of the collection notwithstanding, it was beset by growing doubts about its authenticity from the very outset. Stephen of Tournai (d. 1203), Marsilius of Padua (d. 1324), Nicholas of Cusa in 1450 and the learned Cardinal Bellarmine were among the many ecclesiastics doubting the veracity of at least parts of the collection. Several Protestant apologists also attacked the collection, some admittedly with not the noblest of intentions. In 1628, however, the Calvinist scholar Blondel demolished the few remaining arguments favoring the authenticity of the collection and thus closed a remarkable chapter of canonical history.

Decretist • A scholar in canon law who studied the Decree of Gratian and composed a commentary on it, offering scholarly opinions on the meaning of various parts. The work of the decretists remains an important source in the study of the history of canon law.

Decretum Gratiani • The *Decretum Gratiani* or Decree of Gratian is the commonly used name of the *Concordantia Discordantium Canonum* or Concordance of Discordant Canons. This is the first systematic collection of the laws of the Catholic Church. It contains patristic texts, conciliar decrees, papal pronouncements and the canons and decrees of local synods and councils. Unlike other canonical collections that preceded it, the *Decretum* reconciles contradictory texts and contains Gratian's comments on the meaning of various source-texts.

The work was composed by a monk named Gratian, who lived in the twelfth century and about whom almost nothing is known. It gradually became the most respected work of canon law and received recognition when it was included as the first part of the *Corpus Iuris Canonici* or Body of Canon Law. The *Decretum* contains entries or information on nearly every aspect of Church life: the duties of the various grades of clerics, the sacraments, religious life, church property, and crimes and penalties. Many of the canons of the 1917 and 1983 Codes of Canon Law trace their origins to pertinent sections of the *Decretum*.

Dedication of a Church • The term formerly denoted a simple blessing of a church as opposed to the more solemn "consecration," but the revised Vatican II rite makes no such distinction.

The prayers of the Mass of Dedication celebrate the church building as an image of the universal Church built of the living stones of God's baptized people, and so it is not surprising that the liturgical rite dedicating the building evokes in many ways

the rite for baptizing Christians. The church is also, of course, the place of intercessory prayer, proclamation of the living Word and celebration of the Eucharistic Sacrifice, the very dwelling-place of God among His people, and the rite manifests these realities as well.

Ideally the Entrance Rite takes the form of a procession to (or at least a gathering at) the locked door of the new church. Here representatives involved in the planning or building "present" the new church to the bishop, who in turn asks the pastor to open the door. Then the bishop leads the assembly into the building while all sing an appropriate psalm. The Entrance Rite concludes with the Blessing of Water which is then sprinkled on the people, as well as on the walls and altar of the new church.

The Liturgy of the Word begins with the bishop formally presenting the lectionary to the people with a prayer that God's Word ever resound in the new church.

After the homily, the rites of dedication proper begin:

(1) the Litany of the Saints is sung and, optionally, the relics of the martyrs or saints are deposited in the altar; (2) the bishop offers the Prayer of Dedication; (3) first, the altar is anointed and then the walls of the church where four or twelve crosses have been placed; (4) incense is burned in a brazier on the altar and the walls and people are then incensed; (5) the altar is "vested" in a white cloth; (6) then the deacon receives a lighted candle from the bishop and proceeds to light the altar candles as well as candles placed at the crosses where the walls were anointed; (7) after Communion, the tabernacle for reservation of the Blessed Sacrament is inaugurated and then the final blessing given.

The liturgical book for the Dedication of a Church provides auxiliary rites for the blessing and laying of a cornerstone, the dedication of a church already in use, the blessing of a new altar, and a simple blessing for a place that is going to be used for worship only temporarily.

Defect, Irregularity of • An irregularity is a perpetual impediment established by ecclesiastical law forbidding either the reception of Holy Orders or the exercise of orders. An irregularity differs from a simple impediment to orders in that it is perpetual, while an impediment can cease to exist in the course of time.

The 1917 Code distinguished between irregularities by defect and irregularities by delict or crime. An irregularity by defect arises from lack of quality in the person which is required either for the reception of Orders or for their proper exercise. Ordinarily, they do not imply culpability.

The 1917 Code listed the following as irregularities by defect: illegitimacy, physical defects, mental defects, canonical bigamy, infamy, having been a judge who imposed the death sentence, having been a public executioner or his assistant. These irregularities were dispensed only by the Roman Pontiff.

The 1983 Code did not retain the distinction between the two kinds of irregularities, although it does retain irregularities. Comparable to irregularities by defect are the following: mental or psychological infirmity and self-mutilation or attempted suicide. The other irregularities included in the revised Code are: the canonical offenses of heresy, apostasy or schism; attempted marriage while prohibited from doing so by an existing marriage bond, sacred order or public vow; attempted marriage with a woman already validly married or under public vows; willful homicide or abortion, or having positively cooperated in either; falsely exercising an act of the order of priesthood or episcopacy while either not possessing the order or

being barred from exercising an order held (cf. Canons 1041-1049).

Defect of Form • Refers to a marriage of at least one Catholic that is not celebrated in the presence of a priest or deacon. It includes only marriages for which the Catholic did not receive a dispensation from canonical form.

Properly speaking, marriages celebrated without a dispensation before someone other than a Catholic minister are referred to as invalid due to lack of form, since there is no form at all. A marriage invalid for defect of canonical form is one in which the Catholic minister acting as official witness lacked jurisdiction to do so, or in which he failed to ask for and receive the vows. Defect of form also applies to marriages celebrated with only one of the two required witnesses or when one or both of the witnesses lacked the ability to know what was happening at the time of consent.

Defender of the Bond • An official of an ecclesiastical court, appointed by the bishop. His duties include the defense of the marriage bond in cases where the nullity or dissolution of a marriage is being considered. The defender participates in the processing of the case and has the right to be present and to intervene when the parties to a case are being examined by the judge. After the evidence has been gathered, and before the case goes to judgment, the defender is to study the acts of the case and present his observations in writing. He may make reasonable objections concerning the weight of the evidence or the use of the processes. On the other hand, he may state that he has no objections to a decision for nullity or dissolution.

The office of defender of the bond was constituted by Pope Benedict XIV in 1741, in order to prevent collusion between parties seeking a decree of nullity. In time, the defender intervened not only in marriage cases but in cases where the nullity of Sacred Orders was being considered.

At times, the defenders of the bond were expected to argue for the validity of marriage at all costs, often creating artificial defenses. Pope Pius XII warned against such abuses in an address to the Roman Rota in 1944.

Traditionally, the role of defender of the bond could only be held by a priest. The revised Code, however, opens this office up to non-clerics as well, providing they have a doctorate or licentiate in canon law (cf. Canons 1430-1437).

Defender of the Faith • Prior to his split from Rome, Henry VIII of England turned his not insignificant intellect and his growing political popularity to a consideration of certain theological questions of the day. His compact and neatly-done book, *An Assertion of the Seven Sacraments*, was written in response to some of the Lutheran challenges to Catholic doctrine and won for Henry the title of "Defender of the Faith" from a grateful Pope Leo X. Despite what followed (cf. Anglican, Anglicanism), Henry and his successors have retained the title to this day.

James V of Scotland was similarly honored by Pope Paul III. The third recipient of such a title (actually, Defender of the Catholic Faith), as bestowed by Pope Pius XI in 1936, was the famous convert G. K. Chesterton, also an Englishman, in recognition of his outstanding contribution to Catholic literature.

Defensor Ecclesiae • The person charged in former times with handling the Church's temporal affairs. This "defender of the Church" was appointed by the ruler of the territory.

Definition, Papal • The determination concerning a matter of faith or morals given by a Pope in virtue of his office as Vicar of Christ, which admits of no error or possibility of change. Papal definitions articulate the explicit or implicit content of divine revelation as contained in Scripture and Tradition. They may be pronounced by the Pope himself as universal teacher, or by an ecumenical council of bishops convened and confirmed by him. The First Vatican Council declared: "The Roman Pontiff, when he speaks *ex cathedra* — that is, when in discharge of the office of Pastor and Teacher of all Christians, by virtue of his supreme apostolic authority, he defines a doctrine regarding faith or morals to be held by the universal Church — by divine assistance promised to him in the blessed Peter, is possessed of that infallibility with which the Divine Redeemer willed that His Church should be endowed in defining doctrine regarding faith or morals; and therefore such definitions of the Roman Pontiff are irreformable of themselves, and not in virtue of the consent of the Church."

Definitors • Designated members of the general or provincial governing councils of some religious orders. Normally, definitors exercise an authority equal to and in conjunction with that exercised by the major superior, at least for the duration of the general or provincial chapters at which they have been elected or appointed. During the interval between chapters — which usually constitutes their term in office — the definitors join with other elected councilors and with the major superior to form the governing council at the general or provincial level. The office of definitor does not play a role in the governance of local communities (i.e., in the conventual council).

Defrocking • A common but incorrect term that often refers to the reduction of a cleric to the lay state. More precisely, it refers to the permanent deprivation of the right to wear clerical dress. This was a penalty that could be imposed on a cleric for the commission of an ecclesiastical crime under the 1917 Code. Imposition of this penalty also entailed the loss of the right to clerical privileges. The revised Code does not provide for this penalty. However, a cleric who is reduced to the lay state is no longer entitled to wear clerical dress.

Degradation • The term formerly used to describe the process whereby a cleric was reduced to the lay state against his will. Prior to the 1983 Code, degradation was the most severe penalty that could be imposed on a cleric. It could be imposed administratively by the Holy Father or by sentence of an ecclesiastical court following a penal trial. The old Roman Pontifical even contained ceremonies for formally degrading a cleric.

In the revised Code, "degradation" has been replaced by the terms "dismissal" and "loss of the clerical state." A cleric can be involuntarily dismissed from the clerical state by penal process or by decree of the Holy Father. In either case, dismissal does not automatically carry with it the dispensation from the obligation of celibacy if it had been assumed by the cleric (cf. Canons 290-293).

Dei Verbum • The Dogmatic Constitution on Divine Revelation, *Dei Verbum*, was promulgated by Vatican Council II on November 18, 1965. This succinct document of twenty-six paragraphs was initially intended to complement the Dogmatic Constitution on Catholic Faith of Vatican Council I, *Dei Filius*. The new statement carefully incorporates a number of scholarly agreements on the nature of Divine Revelation and its transmission which had developed since *Dei Filius* was issued in 1870.

The fundamental revelation was of God Himself and of the mystery of His will (n. 2). It is composed of deeds and words, which are intimately bound up with one another, and have to do with mankind's access to the Father, through Christ, the Word made Flesh, in the Holy Spirit. God's revelation in Christ is not the first time He revealed Himself to His people, but it is "the new and definitive covenant [which] will never pass away and no new public revelation is to be expected before the glorious manifestation of Our Lord, Jesus Christ" (n. 4).

This definitive revelation was faithfully transmitted by Christ to the Apostles, and by them to others either by their preaching or in written form. Thus there were born the twin sources of revelation, Sacred Scripture and Sacred Tradition (n. 7). To them is added a third component, the Magisterium, "at the divine command and with the help of the Holy Spirit" (n. 10). "It is clear therefore that in the supremely wise arrangement of God, Sacred Scripture, Sacred Tradition and the Magisterium of the Church are so connected and associated that one of them cannot stand without the others" (n. 10).

In its discussion of inspiration, *Dei Verbum* sums up the previous doctrine of Trent and Vatican I (n. 11). It then adds an important clarification: ". . . we must acknowledge that the books of Scripture, firmly, faithfully and without error, teach that truth (*veritatem*) which God, for the sake of our salvation, wished to see confided to the sacred Scriptures" (n. 11).

Dei Verbum acknowledges the fact that God made use of human means of communication when He inspired human authors, as well as of literary forms: "Due attention must be paid to the customary and characteristic patterns of perception, speech and narrative which prevailed at the age of the sacred writer" (n. 12).

Regarding the Old Testament, *Dei Verbum* affirms that it was designed to "prepare for and declare in prophecy the coming of Christ. . ." (n. 15).

Addressing the question of the authorship of the New Testament, *Dei Verbum* accepts the consensus of contemporary New Testament scholars which speaks of a three-part development of the composition: the New Testament faithfully hands on "what Jesus . . . really did and taught. . . . The sacred authors . . . selected certain of the many elements which had been handed on, either orally or already in written form . . . always in such a fashion that they have preserved for us the honest truth about Jesus" (n. 19).

Finally, *Dei Verbum* strongly encourages ongoing study of the Sacred Scriptures, especially by priests, whose responsibility, together with the bishops, is to preach the Word.

Deification • A major theological theme of the Eastern Churches regarding salvation. By uniting God to mankind in Himself, Jesus, God the Son Incarnate, made it possible for all humanity to be redeemed from enslavement to sin and death, and to be raised up to share in God's eternal life and glory. Literally, we become partakers of the Divine Nature (2 Pt 1:4) by living the life in Christ through prayer, meditation, fasting, good works, the sacraments and God's grace acting in us. Also called "Theosis."

Deipara • This Latin translation (from *Deus*, God, and *parire*, to bring forth, to bear) of the Greek *Theotokos* (literally, God-bearing) was conferred as a title on Mary, the Mother of Jesus, at the Council of Ephesus in A.D. 431.

Deisis • From the Greek for "prayer" or "entreaty." This term describes prayers of petition in the liturgy of the Byzantine Rite.

Also, in Byzantine art, the depiction of Christ as Judge, together with Mary, His Mother and St. John the Baptist.

Deism • A philosophy popular especially during the Enlightenment and exemplified by thinkers such as Voltaire, John Toland and Matthew Tindal. The general Deist view is that God does exist and did, in the beginning, create the world and determine the laws according to which the world works. God's activity of creation is like the activity of one who winds a watch which he has made. But just as one winds a watch only to let the watch run according to its own laws without further bother, so God created the world and humankind to operate according to their own laws without divine interferences. Indeed, according to the Deist understanding of creation, a need for miracles or revelation from God within history would suggest that God failed in the work of creation. With such a philosophy, Deists often disputed the credibility of the events recounted in the Bible. Likewise, they attacked the authoritative position in society of Church leaders and argued for legal impartiality regarding religious opinions.

Though not many twentieth-century thinkers would identify themselves as Deists, the philosophy of Deism has not totally lost its appeal. It still serves as a rationale for repudiating all the definite religious obligations involved in the revealed religions of Judaism or Christianity, without appearing to surrender belief in a personal God and general ethical obligations.

According to Catholic Faith, God's creative deed of bringing us into being out of nothing is by no means merely a past event. Rather, God conserves us in being at every moment of our existence. Furthermore, the order of creation is not intended to be complete in itself but is the "stage" on which God reveals Himself and offers salvation to us, ultimately in Christ. Thus miracles and the Incarnation are not arbitrary interventions showing any failure in God's creative work as Deism would have it. Rather, they are the means by which God fulfills the intention contained in creation from the beginning (cf. Col 1:15-22).

Delator • The accuser; the person appointed by the pagan rulers who denounced anyone suspected of being a Christian in the early Church. As a result, the believer was captured by the authorities and often martyred.

Delegation • Canonical act whereby a person with ordinary power of governance in the Church shares the power to perform certain acts with another person who is capable, in law, of exercising delegated power. Delegated power may be granted for a specific act, or for all acts of a certain kind. Delegated power ceases upon completion of the mandate, if one was given, upon expiration of the time allotted, or upon completion of the number of cases for which it was granted. It also ceases if revoked by the one granting the delegation or upon the retirement of the person holding the delegated power.

A person with ordinary executive power — that is, power proper to his office — can delegate power to another for all cases. One who has such delegated power may in turn subdelegate it, but only for individual cases. Subdelegated power cannot be again subdelegated unless this was specifically allowed by the one with ordinary power.

Of the three kinds of powers of governance (legislative, executive and judicial), executive power is most commonly delegated. Legislative power can only be delegated by the Pope, the supreme legislator in the Church. Lower authorities or authoritative bodies with legislative power cannot delegate it unless the law specifically provides for this. Judicial power, which resides in duly appointed judges, cannot be delegated except for acts in preparation of a decree or judgment, but the power to judge itself cannot be delegated.

Common examples of delegated power include the power to grant dispensations and the power to witness marriages (cf. Canons 135, 137-138, 140-142).

Delict • An ecclesiastical crime. In canon law, a crime is any external and canonically imputable violation of a divine or ecclesiastical law, to which is attached at least an indeterminate penalty. The specific forms of delicts are divided into six categories and enumerated in Canons 1364-1398.

Under the basic understanding of delict, it can be observed that the Church does not punish as a crime any internal deed (such as hatred of one's neighbor or contempt of Church doctrine), but only those acts which are externally recognizable. Moreover, external acts must be considered imputable; that is, one must be considered canonically culpable for the offense before one is subject to punishment. Finally, not every violation of ecclesiastical law is a crime, but only the violation of those to which a penalty is attached. For example, if one discards the Sacred Species, that person is liable to excommunication. Such an act is an ecclesiastical crime. On the other hand, one who, for example, baptizes an infant outside a church or oratory without necessity has violated Canon 857, but has not thereby committed a delict.

Delicts are classified into a wide variety of types and are usually rooted either in the Code of Canon Law or in the particular precepts of an ecclesiastical superior. To continue an example from above, a bishop may issue a precept in his diocese (or even to a specific offending priest) forbidding baptisms outside churches or oratories, the violation of which precept could carry a penalty. Such a violation would then be considered a delict.

An important qualification on the above comments is contained in Canon 1399. By this canon, any external violation of divine or ecclesiastical law can be met with an ecclesiastical penalty (and thereby classified as a delict) if the "particular seriousness of the situation demands it and there is urgent necessity to prevent or repair scandal." The invocation of the Church's penal power under Canon 1399 is, of course, very rare. (Cf. Penal Process; Censure; Interdict; Suspension; Contumacy.)

Deluge • The Great Flood of Genesis 6:5—9:17, from which Noah and his family were preserved in the ark. The story of the deluge represents God's judgment against human wickedness and God's decision to save Noah, "a good man and blameless in that age, for he walked with God" (Gn 6:9b-10a).

The deluge and ark (painting, 1100)

As found in Genesis, the deluge actually interweaves two flood narratives from distinct traditions, namely, the Yahwistic (J) and Priestly (P) sources of the Pentateuch. (The J account comprises Genesis 6:5-8; 7:1-5, 7-10, 12, 16b, 17b, 22-23; 8:2b-3a, 6, 8-12, 13b, 20-22; while the P account includes 6:9-22; 7:6, 11, 13-16a, 17a, 18-19; 9:1-17.)

A number of significant differences exist between the two accounts. For example, in the J version Noah is to bring seven pairs of each clean animal and one pair of each unclean animal aboard the ark (Gn 7:2-3); while in the P version only one pair of each animal species, whether clean or unclean, is to be brought aboard (Gn 6:19-20; 7:15-16). For J, the flood is a deluge of rain lasting forty days (Gn 7:12), while for P, the subterranean waters are unleashed and the floodgates of heaven are opened (7:11), thus restoring the chaos that existed before God established order in creation (cf. Gn 1:6-10). While P offers a careful chronology of the deluge (Gn 7:11; 8:3b-4), the chronology of the J version is sketched only briefly (Gn 7:4). Besides these points of disagreement between the J and P versions, we also find duplication and repetition. For example, God's decision to wipe out mankind is described twice (6:5-7 [J] and 6:11-13 [P]). So too is the command to enter the ark (7:1-3 [J]: 6:18-21 [P]); the onset of the deluge (7:10 [J]: 7:11 [P]); the death of all living creatures (7:22-23 [J]; 7:20-21 [P]); the end of the deluge (8:2b, 3a [J]; 8:3b-5 [P]); and the promise never again to unleash such a flood (8:21b-22 [J]; 9:15 [P]).

Catastrophic deluge stories can also be found outside the Old Testament, and there are noteworthy analogies between these stories in the epic literature of the ancient Near East and what is found in Genesis.

In Tablet 11 of the Mesopotamian epic of Gilgamesh, the hero Gilgamesh listens to the deluge survivor Utnapishtim tell the story of the great flood. Utnapishtim tells of being warned about the gods' decision to send a great flood (cf. Gn 6:13, 17). The informer is the god Ea who instructs Utnapishtim to build a ship (cf. Gn 6:14-16) in which to survive the flood and to bring aboard "the seed of all living things" (cf. Gn

6:20; 7:2-3). After seven days, the storm subsides and Utnapishtim's ship comes to rest atop Mount Nisir (cf. Gn 8:4). Three times he sends out birds to seek out dry land (cf. Gn 8:7-12). When the third fails to return, Utnapishtim disembarks and offers sacrifice which produces a fragrance pleasing to the gods (cf. Gn 8:20-21).

Another flood narrative is found in the Babylonian Atrahasis epic. While the Gilgamesh epic does not explain the gods' reason for sending the flood, Atrahasis dwells on this point. There, the head of the pantheon, the god Enlil, complains to the great gods, "Oppressive has become the clamor of mankind. By this clamor they prevent sleep." For this reason, the gods send the flood.

Despite the analogies, the biblical account also differs in important ways from the deluge of extra-biblical ancient Near Eastern epics. The polytheistic perspective of these epics contrasts sharply with the monotheistic perspective of the biblical deluge, which might even be said to represent an effort at demythologizing. Further, while in Atrahasis the flood is a matter of divine punishment, in Genesis it is a matter of divine judgment against human wickedness.

In the New Testament, 1 Peter 3:20-21 taps the biblical story of the Great Flood as a source of baptismal symbolism, and this is reechoed in the blessing of baptismal water at the Easter Vigil: "The waters of the great flood you made a sign of the waters of baptism, that make an end of sin and a new beginning of goodness."

Demiurge • The term is from the Greek *demiurgos* which can mean "craftsman," "maker," "fashioner." In the fourth century B.C., the philosopher Plato used this term in his treatise on the beginning and nature of the world, called the *Timaeus*. In his cosmology (i.e., "how the world was created as an explanation of why it is the way it is"), Plato affixed the term "demiurge" to a Divine Being who created or fashioned the visible/material universe. This term was applied to the God of the Old Testament by various Greek-speaking Jewish communities before and after the birth of Christ. It appears only once in the New Testament at Hebrews 11:10, where it refers to God the Creator. Second-century Gnostic Christianity made much use of the term, applying it to the God of the Old Testament because this Divine Being was the Creator of the material universe (e.g., Gn 1). The Gnostics devalued material reality, viewing it as *intrinsically* evil; any force or power which creates material existence (e.g., the God of the Old Testament, women giving birth, etc.) must be intrinsically inferior or of a status less than the Supreme Being. This unfortunate understanding of God and creation can lead to anti-Semitism and other forms of fear and hate. After a number of heated exchanges between various orthodox and Gnostic theologians, the universal Church rejected this teaching about God and creation.

Demon • The English term is from the Greek *daimon*, which in classical Greek culture referred to the existence of spiritual beings of an order lower than gods and goddesses. By the sixth century B.C., it was widely believed that demons held influence over spheres of ancient Near Eastern politics, economy, religious rituals and other practices. This conviction led to the understanding that many of these beings were in collaboration with the forces of evil. In the Old Testament, such a belief, if not widespread, is found with modifications necessary for a theocentric point of view (Gn 6:1-4; Lv 16:6-10; Is 34:14; Jb 6:4; Ps 91:5).

The New Testament perpetuates and assumes the Old Testament view and clarifies that these beings are antagonistic toward believers and indeed toward all human life (Mt 8:31; Mk 5:12; Rv 18:2). The New Testament witness is that the demonic kingdom is hierarchical, led by "principalities" (*archai*) followed by "authorities" (*exousiai*), evil angels (Rom 8:38), and the "powers" (*dynamis*). According to the New Testament, their powers are not limited to the spiritual realm; and it is as spiritual forces that they can cause mental illness, physical disease, blindness, epileptic-like illness, etc. Perhaps John's Gospel is the clearest on this point: Satan, the prince of this world, the father of lies who was a murderer from the beginning (Jn 8:44), leads this massive rebellion of spiritual beings against God, His love, Son and plan for creation (e.g., Jn 13:27ff.).

Exorcisms performed by Jesus (Mt 8:28-34; Mk 5:1-20; Lk 8:26-39; Mt 12:22-32; Mk 3:22-27; Lk 11:14-26) demonstrate the power of God's kingdom over Satan at several levels of reality. First and foremost, the exorcisms express God's compassionate mercy, love and irrevocable commitment to those oppressed at the deepest level of existence (i.e., spiritual) where only God can reach. Second, when physical healing is involved, they demonstrate that the kingdom of God is indeed more powerful than the kingdom of evil. Third, the kingdom of God is the specific "power sphere" through which God reconciles all of creation back to Himself. All these powerful beings hostile to God have been defeated in Christ (1 Pt 3:22; Col 2:15).

For further reading: Joanne K. Kummerlin-McLean and David George Reese, "Demons," *Anchor Bible Dictionary*, 2:138-142.

Demoniac • The English word "demoniac" is from the Greek participle *daimonizomenos*, which means "one-who-is-demonized" or someone "possessed" by a demon. Such a belief is consistent with pre-technological cultures which make very little distinction between nature and the supernatural. Demonic possession does not seem to be widespread within the pre-Christian Jewish tradition. The Greek term occurs only once in the Jewish historian Josephus (*Antiquities* VIII.ii.5), and there is no formal corresponding term in rabbinic literature. It occurs only thirteen times in the New Testament (Mt 4:24; 8:16, 28, 33; 9:32; 12:22; 15:22; Mk 1:32; 5:15-16, 18; Lk 8:35, 36; Jn 10:21). Possession by a demon apparently caused mental illness (Mk 5:15; Lk 8:35) and physical illnesses (Mt 4:24; 8:16; Mk 1:32), such as dumbness and blindness (Mt 9:32; 12:22).

In popular understanding the term "demoniac" is usually associated with that part of the Gospel narrative known as the "Gerasene Demoniac" (Mt 8:28-34; Mk 5:1-20); that story makes dramatically clear that the kingdom of God is present in the Person of Jesus and that such a presence has complete power over the kingdom of Satan, of darkness and of death, personified in the possessed man (in a graveyard, no less). Jesus does come to destroy the kingdom of darkness once and for all at the cross. The exorcism He performs by the word of His mouth is simply a foretaste of the effects which His work on the cross and the Father's work in the Resurrection will have on all who become God's friends. In short, God's kingdom liberates mankind from the clutches of the demonic and frees people to become what they were intended to be: children of God as brothers and sisters of Jesus.

For further reading: Joanne K. Kummerlin-McLean and David George Reese, "Demons," *Anchor Bible Dictionary*, 2:138-142.

Denunciation • The reporting to an ecclesiastical authority the fact that a priest solicited a person in the confessional for purposes of committing a sexual crime. It also refers to the accusation of some other offense which is addressed to an ecclesiastical superior. The term is used in the Code in reference to the crime of false denunciation.

One who falsely denounces a priest of the offense of solicitation is not to be absolved until the denunciation has been withdrawn and proper restitution made. Furthermore, such a person incurs the automatic penalty of interdict and, if he is a cleric, of suspension.

One who calumniously denounces an offense to a superior, or otherwise injures the good name of another, can be punished with appropriate penalties, which can include censure (cf. Canons 982, 1390-1391).

Deontological Ethics • The term comes from the Greek word *deon* meaning "duty" or "binding." The central theme of deontological ethics is that some duties and obligations are incumbent on an individual, irrespective of the effects, circumstances or consequences of the action. Deontological ethics finds support in many religious doctrines whose moral precepts are often exceptionless, but particularly in the ethical system of Immanuel Kant. Catholic moral theology objects to deontological ethics because it does not give an adequate place to prudence and to the necessity of fulfilling our moral obligations in such a way that true goods are actually brought into existence through our actions.

Deposing Power, Papal • In virtue of his divine mandate, the Supreme Pontiff has the right to declare the subjects of a temporal ruler no longer bound in allegiance to that ruler. This power, to be exercised only in the gravest of cases, has been used very sparingly since the Middle Ages and is a logical extension of the Church's right and duty to make pronouncements upon the moral aspects of the temporal order. (Cf. Church and State; Unam Sanctam.)

Deposit of Faith • The Deposit of Faith is the body of saving truth entrusted by Christ to the Apostles and handed on by them to the Church to be preserved and proclaimed. In this sense, the term is very nearly coextensive with "objective revelation," in that it embraces the whole of Christ's teaching as embodied in Revelation and Tradition. But the metaphor of "deposit" highlights particular features of the apostolic teaching. It suggests that this teaching is like an inexhaustible treasure, one that consistently rewards reflection and study with new insights and deeper penetration into the mystery of the divine economy of salvation. Although our understanding of this teaching can develop, it can never be augmented in its substance. Thus, the teaching is a divine trust, something not to be tampered with, altered or, as it were, "devalued." This feature of the apostolic teaching has also been expressed in the traditional conviction that Revelation, properly so-called, was complete with the death of the last Apostle. The treasure of saving truth — in itself nothing other than Christ Himself — contains the definitive revelation of God's inner life and of His intentions in our regard. There can be no more complete revelation than that imparted by the very Word of God, the Son Who is the perfect image of the Father and Who sends the illuminating Spirit into the Church. The position of the Church with respect to the Deposit of Faith is thus something similar to that of a trustee: charged to preserve a living tradition with fidelity, she must nonetheless proclaim it in new historical circumstances in such a way that its efficacy and richness are undiminished. Although the term "Deposit of Faith" entered official Catholic teaching only with the Council of Trent, its substance is well-attested in the Scriptures and the Fathers.

Deposition • A written statement of evidence or testimony that is submitted to an ecclesiastical court or competent superior. Ordinarily, a deposition is to be signed by the person giving it, dated and notarized (cf. Canon 1528).

Deposition, Bull of • In February 1570, Pope St. Pius V issued a Bull of Deposition, *Regnans in Excelsis*, excommunicating Queen Elizabeth I and absolving English Catholics of their allegiance to her. The bull was issued on the heels of a doomed Catholic uprising in the northern counties, which was itself in response to the latest series of anti-Catholic measures then being taken by the Queen. It would appear, however, that the only practical effect of the papal deposition was to serve as the rationale for further penal laws against English Catholics. (Cf. Anglican, Anglicanism.)

Desecration of a Church • The new *Ceremonial of Bishops* notes that "crimes committed in a church affect and do injury to the entire Christian community, which the church building in a sense symbolizes and represents" (n. 1070). Without specifying particular acts, the *Ceremonial* refers to crimes that do grave dishonor to sacred mysteries (especially to the Eucharistic Species), crimes that are committed to show contempt for the Church, or crimes that are "serious offenses against the dignity of the person or of society" (n. 1070).

The diocesan bishop is to decide if such a crime has taken place, and he himself, if possible, is to preside at the "rite of penitential reparation" before any Mass or other sacramental rite (except Penance) may be celebrated.

The altar is stripped bare "and all customary signs of joy and gladness should be put away. . . ." In violet vesture the bishop and clergy go in procession to the church chanting the Litany of the Saints (a form for simple entrance is also provided), water is blessed and sprinkled on the people and walls. Before the Liturgy of the Eucharist, the altar is adorned and reverenced by the bishop. If the desecration involved profanation of the Eucharistic Species, the liturgy ends with Exposition and Benediction.

Desire, Baptism of • The act of perfect contrition for one's sins and the concomitant desire for Baptism. Baptism of desire is the equivalent of Baptism of water; however, the former does not impart the indelible character as does the latter. When one receives Baptism of desire, he receives a sufficient amount of God's grace for salvation. The person is still obliged to receive Baptism of water, when possible. As *Lumen Gentium*, the Dogmatic Constitution on the Church, teaches: "Those who, through no fault of their own, do not know the Gospel of Christ or His Church, but who nevertheless seek God with a sincere heart and, moved by grace, try in their actions to do His will as they know it through the dictates of their conscience — those too may achieve eternal salvation" (LG 16).

Despair • The deliberate and willful abandonment of hope in God and rejection of trust in His power, mercy and love, it is the most serious sin possible against the theological virtue of hope. But not only is it contrary to hope, it is also contrary to faith and charity. One in despair implicitly denies that the realities promised by Christ exist, an attitude which displays profound mistrust.

The sin of despair is also contrary to charity because one in despair abandons love of God as well as love of neighbor. Despair is not only abandonment of God, but also abandonment of His creation and His plan of salvation, and is ultimately a form of atheism. The despairing person refuses to perform actions in support of a neighbor because such action is seen as ultimately futile and ineffectual. Hope is the ultimate driving engine of human accomplishment and progress, and hope impels us to cooperate with God's saving initiatives, but despair renounces all of this. The despairing person denies that there can be anything truly new in creation, and he or she implicitly affirms that God has not intervened in the created order.

Despair is not to be confused with anxiety, fear or doubts which lack the deliberateness, willfulness and consent that are often involved in despair. Some people who manifest what looks like despair are subject to highly disturbed emotional states or have suffered a severe trauma which compromise their responsibility for any actions they might perform, and they are not fully responsible for what they say or do in their state of despair.

Detachment • The virtue which frees man from any inordinate or excessive attachment to another person, thing or state of mind. Detachment should rightly be seen within the overall context of the universal call to holiness. As the Christian grows in holiness, he is less subject to those things which do not bring one to attain the end of our creation. In the classical spiritual tradition, detachment is sometimes referred to as "the perfection of indifference."

Detachment ought to be carefully distinguished from any willful spirit of disregard for ourselves, others and the world in which Christians live. True detachment is not any pervasive lack of care but a correct ordering of what can and cannot bring us to God. As far as the interior life is concerned, the Christian ought to seek a detachment from any and all desires, passions and false securities which prevent him from being genuinely dependent on God. As far as material goods are concerned, the Christian should detach himself from any objects which can serve as idols or substitutes for his heart's true contentment. And, finally, the Christian wills not to enter into or remain in any relationship which precludes an authentic communion with God and/or the true good of the person.

A spirit of detachment has characterized the lives of all the canonized saints of the Church. A few of them, most notably St. Teresa of Ávila and St. Francis de Sales, have written eloquently and movingly of how detachment has prepared them to have an intimate and profound relationship with God. Detachment is a virtue which can be practiced regardless of one's state in life and is surely not restricted to cloistered or contemplative vocations. Rather, detachment is a virtue to be exercised in the midst of the world because it bears strong witness here and now to the ultimate aim of our existence: attachment to God alone in eternity.

Detraction • An unjust verbal attack or injury to another, it is the revelation of truths about another, either for the purpose of injuring another or for some other purpose. Detraction differs from calumny, which reveals false material about another for the purpose of defaming the other person. Detraction is wrong even if it does not spring from malicious intent. It is malicious because it destroys what can be irreplaceable: a person's good reputation.

Detraction can come about either by spoken word or by actions which disparage the good done by another. Innuendos are often more damaging than explicit statements of fact. Detraction often arises from a motive of envy or jealousy, and it is a violation of justice. It is unethical knowingly to listen to detraction, and restoring the good name of a person who suffers from detraction is morally required.

Despite the fact that detraction is immoral, the revelation of the faults of others can be necessary in some cases to preserve the community from grave harm or to prevent future grave harm. This is permissible because the right of an evildoer to a good name is only conditional. But where such conditions do not prevail, detraction remains a serious violation of charity and justice.

Deuterocanonical Books • Those books which are found in the Septuagint, an early Greek version of the Old Testament, but are not included in the Hebrew Old Testament. They are 1 and 2 Maccabees, Tobit, Judith, Sirach, Wisdom, Baruch and additional parts of Daniel and Esther.

Although it is sometimes asserted that there was a definition of the Jewish canon of Scripture at the synod of Jamnia (c. A.D. 100), which definitively excluded the deuterocanonicals from the roster of inspired books, too little is known of the activities of this gathering to say with certainty. In the third century, Origen defended the right of Christians to use the deuterocanonical books, even though these were disapproved of by the Jews. The Reformers seemed loath to put these books on a par with the rest of Scripture, but the Council of Trent on April 8, 1546, listed all the books of the Old Testament, including the deuterocanonicals, and declared that they were being accepted by the Council Fathers "with equal devotion and reverence."

The reformed bodies refer to the deuterocanonicals as "apocrypha." There is some sentiment among Protestants today for conceding the spiritual value of these books. The expression "deuterocanonical" derives from Sixtus of Siena (1528-1569), who used the word to designate those books of Scripture whose placement in the canon of Scripture was at some time challenged.

Deuteronomy, Book of • The fifth book of the Old Testament, it is cast in the form of a farewell address given by Moses. Its content is a mixed bag of materials: a tally of events from the time the Hebrews left Sinai until their arrival in the area east of the Jordan, followed by an exhortation to observe commands and statutes, then a throwback to the Sinai period as the message received by Moses at that time is now communicated to the people (5:29—6:3). There follows a call for loyalty, obedience and thanksgiving as the people are about to set foot in Canaan. Next comes a rundown of individual legal regulations — rules for worship, the Year of Release, the indenture of debtors, feasts, the responsibilities of king, priests and prophets. The appointment of Joshua as leader is given, and the book concludes with an account of Moses' demise on Mount Nebo (Chapter 34).

It is quite possible that many of the texts of Deuteronomy are in fact what they appear to be, liturgical and legal treatises intended to be read to large groupings of people in Israel.

Deuteronomy (as a literary source) is one of the four widely accepted sources of the Pentateuch. It is to be found exclusively in this book. Traces of the other three sources (Yahwist, Elohist and Priestly) as found in this book are insignificant.

In the original Hebrew no name is given to the book. It was referred to with the words of the opening clause. The term "Deuteronomy" stems from the Septuagint, the early Greek translation, with the word ("second copy of the law") occurring in Deuteronomy 17:18 of that version.

Perhaps the strongest impact the book had was on the centralization of the cult of Israel at the place determined by God.

For further reading: Joseph Blenkinsopp, "Deuteronomy," *New Jerome Biblical Commentary*, 94-109; Moshe Weinfeld, "Deuteronomy," *Anchor Bible Dictionary*, 2:168-183.

Development of Doctrine • The notion that the Church's understanding of divinely revealed truths grows and evolves throughout the centuries. The substance of the Truth always remains the same; however, the grasp of the Truth — due to the gradual unfolding of the divine mysteries — changes. Nothing has been added to or subtracted from the Deposit of Faith since the death of the last Apostle. However, the mysteries revealed by Christ to His Apostles are clearer now than they were in the first centuries, through the penetration of these truths by the early Fathers and Doctors of the Church. It is God's desire that the faithful assent and understand the truth as best they are able. At times, a mystery which seemed implicit in the Scriptures was made explicit by a papal definition (e.g., the Immaculate Conception). According to John A. Hardon, S.J., the progressive realization and understanding of the Church's doctrines is due to "the prayerful reflection of the faithful, notably of the Church's saints and mystics; the study and research by scholars and theologians; the practical experience of living the Faith among the faithful; and the collective wisdom and teaching of the Church's hierarchy under the Bishop of Rome" (*Modern Catholic Dictionary*, p. 155).

Development of Peoples • The concept that society must meet the needs of the people if all are to reach true fulfillment — spiritually, individually, economically, socially — which God intends. All individuals are guaranteed certain human rights which are to be respected. In addition, the poor must be aided in their plight.

Authentic peace and justice must be sought by civil and religious leaders if the society is to develop correctly. The Church has constantly proclaimed the dignity of man and the necessity of maintaining a society where, individually and collectively, man could realize true fulfillment. Seven papal encyclicals have championed this theme: *Rerum Novarum* (1891); *Quadragesimo Anno* (1931); *Mater et Magistra* (1961); *Pacem in Terris* (1963); *Populorum Progressio* (1967); *Laborem Exercens* (1981); *Sollicitudo Rei Socialis* (1987). The Second Vatican Council, in *Gaudium et Spes*, the Pastoral Constitution on the Church in the Modern World, also emphasized the importance of the development of peoples: ". . . the Council asks individuals and governments . . . according to their ability to share and dispose of their goods to help others, above all by giving them aid which will enable them to help and develop themselves" (GS 69).

Devil • In the Old Testament, the term is always used with an article "*the* satan." The LXX (Septuagint) renders the word *diabolos*, which means accuser or a military adversary.

In Jewish apocrypha, the concept of Satan is more definite, and he inflicts evils out of hatred for man. Satan is the prince of evil spirits, and he works to bring death. He tempts Adam and Eve and speaks through the serpent, disguising himself as an angel of God. The reason for his hatred is that he was expelled from heaven by Michael because he refused to adore man, the image of God. Satan flees those who are righteous and disappears in the millennium, either because he is restrained or destroyed. In Job (1:6ff.) the Devil is not an evil spirit, but an accuser whose function is to test the authenticity of human virtue and fidelity to God. To achieve this, he can inflict evils on human beings, for virtue is not genuine unless tested.

In the New Testament, there is no distinction drawn between *diabolos* and *satanas*. Satan is the strong one (Mt 12:29), the evil one (Mt 13:19) and the prince of the world (Jn 12:31). He takes the seed of the Word of God and of life from the mouth of those who receive it (Mt 13:19), and he seeks to sift the disciples like wheat (Lk 22:31). He tempts with designs (1 Cor 7:5) and deceit (Eph 6:11). He disguises himself as an angel of light (2 Cor 11:14) and seduces some of the faithful (1 Tm 5:15). All the kingdoms of the world are under his power (Lk 4:6), and his power is frustrated until his time (Lk 4:13). The Antichrist comes with the active power of Satan (2 Thes 2:9), is bound at the millennium in the pit (Rv 20:2), and is released to work for destruction until the end of the world (Rv 20:7f.). He is identified with the serpent of the creation story and is associated with the great dragon of ancient mythology. Satan remains subject to the power of God and is ultimately overcome by Jesus. The sons of the Devil are those who do not love the brothers and do not act in righteousness. Heresy refers to "the deep things of Satan" (Rv 2:24).

The Devil is not just a personification of evil, and the existence of the Devil must not be denied. The doctrine of the Devil points to the calamitous situation faced by humanity, which is not entirely man's doing and can only be remedied by God. The doctrine of the Devil affirms that there is an evil domain into which humanity has been plunged and is redeemed from that only by God and human freedom contributes to this situation.

Dogmatic theology and the Second Vatican Council are reserved about the power of the Devil over human actions. Despite his power, he is a finite creature, and his power is circumscribed by the power of God. The Devil remains a created essence whose nature is good even though he employs this nature for evil purposes. The reality of the Devil is to be seen in the sinister suprahuman power of evil in human history, a power which cannot be trivialized. But it should also be recalled that because these created powers have a nature that is good they serve a positive function in the created order.

For further reading: Duane F. Watson, "Devil," *Anchor Bible Dictionary*, 2:183-184.

Devil and Evil Spirits • Evil spirits are fallen angels, among whom one — called the Devil or Satan — is traditionally held to exercise leadership. The fallen angels are those purely spiritual beings who, after being created by God and endowed with grace, failed to respond to God's love and turned away from Him (2 Pt 2:4; cf. Mt 25:41; Jude 6). According to Christian Tradition, their sin was one of pride: They preferred to usurp or claim as their own a likeness to God that could only be received as a gift. As purely spiritual beings who do not require time and reflection to come to knowledge and decision, their refusal of God's love was irrevocable. Their situation is thus comparable to the post-mortem state of unrepentant human sinners.

Although they have lost supernatural grace, the fallen angels retain the powers of purely spiritual beings. They deploy these powers in a variety of ways to obstruct the fulfillment of God's plan and to block the progress of human beings toward bliss. They do this not simply by tempting people to sin, but chiefly by fostering despair and unrepentance (or impenitence) in sinners who otherwise might turn with confidence to the sure mercy of God.

According to the Scriptures, the Devil and the fallen angels were active in bringing about the passion and death of Christ, and in general in striving to thwart His saving mission in the world. As great as their powers are, however, they are now under the dominion of Christ, Who has imparted to His Church the power to forgive sins and to drive out demons. While Divine Providence permits them a limited scope of activity, they are powerless to block in any decisive way the consummation of the economy of salvation, the movement of all things toward God.

Devil's Advocate • A term used to describe an official of the Congregation for the Causes of Saints, the dicastery concerned with the beatification and canonization process. The name came from the fact that he is required to raise objections to a person's alleged sanctity or reputation for having worked miracles. The office is first mentioned during the papacy of Leo X (1515-1521). (Cf. Canonization.)

Devolution • The term devolution has two distinct meanings in canon law. The first appears in regard to certain types of provisions for canonical office. Sometimes an individual or group of persons is allowed to appoint or at least to nominate someone for ecclesiastical office. If that person or group delays unacceptably in the selection, however, the right to make provision for the office is said to devolve upon higher authority. There was considerable legislation on this matter in the 1917 Code of Canon Law, but under the 1983 Code the subject has been simplified to a few canons. For example under Canon 421, if, during the vacancy of a diocesan see, the College of Consultors fails to elect a diocesan administrator within the prescribed time, the selection of the diocesan administrator devolves to the metropolitan archbishop of the province.

The other sense in which the term devolution appears is in the matter of appeals of and recourse against ecclesiastical judicial sentences and administrative decisions, respectively. An appeal or recourse in devolution basically means that the sentence or decision being contested stands unless overturned by higher authority. Devolution, then, is in contrast to appeals or recourse in suspension, which means that the effect or implementation of the contested sentence or decision is suspended until and unless confirmed by higher authority. As a practical matter, most appeals or recourse are in devolution, thus lending stability to the legal system. An exception, however, is found in Canon 1353, which states that appeal of or recourse against the imposition of an ecclesiastical penalty is always in suspension of that penalty, this obviously for the zealous safeguarding of individual rights in the penal process.

Devotion • Readiness and willingness to dedicate oneself to the service of God. Devotion, essential to inner devotion, is abandonment to God in prayer and openness to His call. Devotion is the very heart and vitality of religion and promoting it is the aim of liturgy, morality and preaching. The life of prayer also aims at promoting devotion, and devout prayer is worthy prayer, for it honors God and makes the one who prays a friend of God. Related to devotion is piety, which is a filial affection for God.

Diabolical Possession • Occurs when an evil spirit is said to possess and control the personality and body of a person. A number of instances of this are recorded in the four Gospels and Acts (e.g., Mt 8:16; Mk 1:34; Lk 7:21; Acts 5:16). These and other accounts in Sacred Scripture show the power which both the demonic and sin have on the human condition. The reign of evil overcomes human freedom at the psychological, physical and social levels. The witness of Sacred Scripture that human shortcomings are indeed connected to sin and in some cases to demonic activity only serves to heighten one's awareness of the need for a savior, a deliverer, a redeemer. The Son of God's mission to redeem includes "set[ting] at liberty those who are captive." This theme from Isaiah, on which Jesus draws to describe His own commission from God, is key to understanding that the kingdom of God has the power to overcome diabolical possession.

Unlike illustrations in popular films such as *The Exorcist*, God's power over demonic forces is not relative but absolute, not a struggle but a *fait accompli* in Christ's death and resurrection. The Church provides for exorcisms but only after specific conditions have been met and only under competent ecclesiastical authorities (i.e., under the supervision of the local bishop).

Diakonikon • The place, usually a table, in or near the sanctuary in Byzantine churches, attended to by the deacon on which may be placed vestments, sacred vessels, books or other items utilized in the celebration of liturgical services. Architecturally, the diakonikon often is balanced with the Proskomide or Table of Preparation on the opposite side of the sanctuary. It is not essential to the sanctuary appointments and thus may even be absent in some churches.

Dialogue Mass • The revised Roman Missal, promulgated in 1970, fulfilled the mandate of Vatican II's Constitution on the Sacred Liturgy (*Sacrosanctum Concilium*) that the faithful's participation in the liturgy was to be "full, active and conscious." This participation was to manifest itself particularly by the people singing or saying (whether in Latin or the vernacular) those parts of the liturgy pertaining to them, and responding to the greetings, invitations,

invocations and verses pronounced by priest, deacon, lector or cantor.

In Masses celebrated according to the former rite ("Tridentine"), however, it was sufficient for the server to make the responses in the name of the people and common practice for the choir alone to sing the chants that were really meant to be sung by all. From Pope St. Pius X (1903-1914) on, numerous instructions from the Holy See urged "congregational participation" in the Mass. Those Masses at which this request was fulfilled were called "dialogue Masses," a term obviously rendered obsolete by the normative Mass promulgated after Vatican II.

Diaspora • Greek for "exile," this is the name given, first to the Jews, and then to any nation or large national group which is dispersed throughout foreign lands. In the case of the Jews in biblical times, they were divided into two classes. Those who lived in the eastern lands of Babylonia, Persia, etc., were referred to as the Aramaic Diaspora or Dispersion. Those who lived in the lands surrounding the Mediterranean, such as Egypt, Greece and its islands, Italy or Asia Minor, were called the Diaspora of the Greeks (cf. 2 Mc 1:1; Jn 7:35).

Diatesseron • A harmony of the Gospels drawn up by Tatian c. A.D. 170. There are no extant complete manuscripts of the *Diatesseron*, save for a single fragment in Greek (fourteen lines that give an account of Joseph of Arimathea's request for the body of Jesus). All the other witnesses are secondary or tertiary. Still under discussion is the question of the language in which the *Diatesseron* was originally written and the question of its place of origin. Some scholars have judged that the work was originally drawn up in Greek and subsequently put into Syriac. Others seem to feel that it was composed by Tatian in his native tongue,

Syriac. There is also the opinion of F. C. Burkitt, according to which the *Diatesseron* began as a Gospel harmony compiled in Latin at Rome, a Greek copy of which came to the attention of Tatian, who forthwith put it into Syriac.

The *Diatesseron* enjoyed a wide circulation in the Syriac-speaking Churches. Until the fifth century it served as the standard Gospel text in those Churches.

For further reading: William F. Peterson, "Diatessaron," *Anchor Bible Dictionary*, 2:189-190.

Dicastery • A department or agency of the Holy See. The several dicasteries together constitute the Roman Curia, whose duties are spelled out in Canons 330-367 and elaborated in the Apostolic Constitution *Pastor Bonus* of Pope John Paul II, promulgated on June 28, 1988.

Didache, The • A short but important early Christian work by an unknown author, written probably in Syria around A.D. 60, presenting in sixteen chapters a summary of Christian moral teaching framed in terms of the two ways of life and death (Chapters 1-6), instructions concerning liturgical practice (Chapters 7-10) and a set of disciplinary norms (Chapters 11-15). The final chapter contains a prophecy of the approaching end of the world and mentions the Antichrist. Perhaps the chief interest of the work lies in the picture it presents of the life of the early Christian community, for example: Baptism by immersion, station fasts on Wednesday and Friday, thrice daily recitation of the Lord's Prayer and confession of sins before prayer in church. Two primitive Eucharistic Prayers are also included. The disciplinary instructions reflect a still developing Church order in which prophets continue to play an important role; bishops and deacons, though not the presbyterate, are mentioned

as well. Although the *Didache* was known to the Fathers of the Church and exercised considerable influence on early Church orders (such as the *Didascalia* and the *Apostolic Constitutions*), modern acquaintance with the complete text dates only from 1873 when a manuscript (from 1056) was discovered in a monastery in Constantinople.

Didascalia Apostolorum • "The Teaching of the Apostles." Attributed to the Apostles, yet it seems to have been written in the first part of the third century, probably by a convert from Judaism who also from the text seems to have been a physician. The work is modeled on the *Didache*, but the format is unmethodical.

Christian living and government are first treated, with a section on penitents which is more lenient than other ancient documents on readmitting sinners back to communion. The liturgy is described as hierarchical and eastward in orientation, of great importance and therefore not to be neglected for work or amusements. Fasting is enjoined on Wednesdays and Fridays, as well as for a week before Easter. The duties and roles of husbands and wives, widows, deacons, deaconesses, presbyters and bishops are spelled out as members of the local Church, as well as a concern for catechumens, the persecuted and the imprisoned.

Dies Irae • Sequence of the Requiem Mass. This piece is no longer in use at liturgical functions, except as a hymn for the Divine Office during the 34th Week of Ordinary Time. It is a fifty-seven-line poem divided into nineteen three-line stanzas. Authorship of the *Dies Irae* has been the search of historians over the centuries. It has been translated into almost every language and has been set to music by some of the greatest composers of all time. The Gregorian chant melody of it has also been used as a primary or secondary theme of master composers throughout the ages.

Diet of Augsburg: See **Augsburg, Diet of**

Diffinitor: See **Definitors**

Dignitatis Humanae • The Fathers of Vatican II recognized the need for a statement on religious liberty for two basic reasons: The Catholic Church could not be silent in the face of repressive totalitarian states that were depriving half the human race of religious freedom; and in the religiously pluralistic societies of modern times, the Church felt obliged to lead the way toward justice and peace, especially in the field of conscience.

Reading "the signs of the times," the Fathers were aware of the 1948 Universal Declaration of Human Rights of the United Nations which included freedom of conscience and religion in both public and private observance (Article 18). Furthermore, during the Council itself, in 1963, Pope John XXIII's *Pacem in Terris* pointed in the same direction: the Church must speak out.

The Nature of the Right to Religious Liberty: Following traditional teaching dating back to Tertullian in A.D. 212, the Council had no problem in agreeing that the act of faith must be free and conscience untrammeled. But there was a difference of opinion on the nature of this right.

A minority held that religious freedom is a civil right to be incorporated into laws protected by the state for all its citizens. A majority opinion, which in the end prevailed, saw it as a fundamental human right quite antecedent to civil law. The state must recognize this human right as already inherent in the human person, which is to be reaffirmed as a civil right protected by the state.

Historical Note: On November 19, 1965, the Decree on Religious Liberty was passed with 1,997 affirmative votes and 224 negative votes. The document was signed by Pope Paul VI and the Council Fathers, and promulgated December 7, 1965, the final vote being 2,308 to 70. The document was immediately seen to be of historic importance, not only for the Church herself but for the whole human race.

The debate had been sharp and extensive. Arguing for the minority position, Cardinal Bueno of Seville, Spain, spoke in favor of a declaration as "politically prudent." Just as all rights have clear limitations, so too religious liberty because the state must see to it that "orderly and peaceful existence can be preserved for everyone." Religious freedom should not jeopardize public morality.

The majority position was led by the American bishops; an American Jesuit, John Courtney Murray, was its chief architect, closely assisted by Monsignor Pietro Pavan of the Lateran University of Rome.

Cardinal Cushing of Boston said it was a historical imperative that the Church, which has always insisted on religious liberty for herself, now become the champion for other churches and indeed for all human beings. Bishop Primeau of Manchester, New Hampshire, explained the difference between an entitlement to liberty, i.e., the moral ability to act according to conscience, and an immunity which meant freedom from unjust coercion.

The distinction was typically American, stemming from the American Constitution which prescribes limitations on government, specifically in the free exercise of religion. The Council was not saying that a person had a right, i.e., an entitlement, to be wrong but rather that a person in error in religious and conscience matters enjoyed an immunity, sanctioned in law, from unjust coercion.

Denying that a certain pragmatism justifies the Declaration and affirming that the United States was not the perfect model of religious liberty, Bishop Wright of Pittsburgh affirmed that "religious liberty is often more complete in other countries than it is in America," citing the denial of equal rights in education as an example.

Looking at a deeper issue, Cardinal Garronne of Toulouse, France, saw the Declaration as a true development of doctrine, "an evolution of social matters and because of reflections on the person in society." The Church, even in light of her history, was not making an about-face; liberalism and indifferentism were condemned (in the nineteenth century) and remain condemned.

Contents of the Declaration: "This Vatican Council declares that the human person has a right to religious freedom. Freedom of this kind means that all men should be immune from coercion on the part of individuals, social groups and every human power, so that, within due limits, nobody is forced to act against his convictions in religious matters in public or in private, alone or in association with others" (n. 2).

This right is based on the dignity of the human person both as an individual and as simultaneously a social being, as revealed by the Word of God and by reason itself. Thus there is the right to select one's own minister, to profess faith publicly, to propound a religious message in public, in literature, in liturgy and in schools.

Conscious of the rights of the family, the Declaration affirms the right of parents to choose schools they wish for their children "with genuine freedom" without subjection "directly or indirectly to unjust burdens" for making their choice (n. 4). Furthermore, states which force children to attend schools under a single compulsory system of education from which all religious instruction is excluded violate "the rights of the parents" (n. 5).

The Church recognizes, as does civilized society, that there are certain limitations on freedom in the interest of public order, public peace and public morality. Abuses in the civic order make possible restrictions in the name of religious liberty, abuses from which it cannot protect itself. The Council advises: "Freedom should be given the possible fullest recognition and should not be curtailed, except and insofar as is necessary" (n. 7).

In a final comment, the Declaration noted that constitutions around the world include religious freedom in its rights, as do international documents, such as the International Bill of Human Rights (1948) and *Pacem in Terris* (1963), but some countries' governments deny the right to religious liberty. The Council "gladly welcomes the first of these two facts as a happy sign of the times. In sorrow, however, it denounces the second as something deplorable" (n. 15).

"The disciple has a grave obligation . . . to grow daily in his knowledge of the truth . . . to be faithful in announcing it and vigorous in defending it without having recourse to methods which are contrary to the spirit of the Gospel" (n. 14).

Dimissorials • Dimissorials, or dimissorial letters, are required official letters which the proper bishop or religious superior of a candidate for the priesthood or diaconate presents to the bishop who will ordain the candidate. If, however, the ordaining bishop is the proper bishop of the candidate, these letters are not required.

The dimissorial letters attest to the fact that all the canonical requirements for ordination have been fulfilled.

If the candidate belongs to a religious community, his major superior is the proper authority to grant the dimissorial letters. If a candidate is ready for ordination to the diocesan ministry and the see is vacant, the apostolic administrator or the diocesan administrator is empowered to grant dimissorial letters to the ordaining bishop (cf. Canons 1015, 1017-1023).

Diocesan Administrator • A priest elected by the College of Consultors to govern a diocese while the see is vacant, to be elected within eight days of notification of the vacancy. The diocesan administrator need not be a vicar general or an auxiliary bishop but may be any priest who has reached his thirty-fifth year and has not already been appointed, presented or elected for the same see. He may not be the financial administrator of the diocese.

The diocesan administrator attains his power upon election. He has the same governing powers as a diocesan bishop but can make no innovations, such as erecting or closing parishes or making permanent personnel assignments that had not already been agreed upon by the previous bishop. He may not do anything in the diocese that might in any way prejudice the rights of the diocese or the new bishop, and he can be removed by the Holy See. His appointment ceases when the new bishop takes possession of his office (cf. Canons 421-430).

Diocesan Clergy • Diocesan clergy, or secular clergy as they are sometimes called, are priests or deacons attached to a diocese with the diocesan bishop as their proper superior or Ordinary. Generally, diocesan clergy serve in their own diocese unless they have been given permission to serve elsewhere. Clergy who are members of religious communities may, in fact, work in diocesan parishes or in other diocesan positions, but they are not called diocesan clergy (cf. Canon 265).

Diocesan Pastoral Council (also Archdiocesan Pastoral Council) • A body of the faithful that is established in a diocese to assist the bishop in the pastoral matters of the diocese. The pastoral council lacks any legislative or governing power and functions solely as a consultative body. It is established under the authority of the bishop and, although strongly urged by canon law, is not a mandatory organism of the diocese.

Membership on a pastoral council is open to lay men and women, religious and clerics. All must be practicing Catholics. The common law states that membership is determined in a manner established by the bishop (cf. Canons 511-515).

Diocesan Right • Refers to the type of authority exercised over a religious institute. Unlike institutes of pontifical right, those of diocesan right are under the authority of the bishop of the diocese wherein the institute has its principal headquarters. A bishop has the right to erect, by decree, religious institutes in his own diocese, provided the Holy See has been consulted. The bishop then has the authority to approve the constitutions of the institute and to grant dispensations from the constitutions when they are required. The bishop of the principal seat of a diocesan institute also presides over the election of the supreme moderator (Canons 579, 589, 594-595).

Diocese • Utilizing the terminology and ecclesiology of Vatican II, the law now defines a diocese as a "particular Church, in which and from which the one and only Catholic Church exists." A diocese is composed of all the Catholics usually within the boundaries of a specific geographic territory. A diocese is always under the authority of a bishop. Dioceses are established by the Holy See when it is clear that the pastoral needs of the faithful in a given territory will be better served by a new diocese.

In certain cases, a diocese may be personal rather than territorial. This means that it is created for all the people of a certain class. Most such dioceses are for the faithful of the Oriental Rites. While these dioceses have geographical limits, they are often much larger in territorial expanse than the dioceses of the Latin Rite.

A unique type of diocese is the military diocese. These are established by the Holy See to serve the pastoral needs of the military personnel and their families for a specific country. Since such personnel often are stationed worldwide, military dioceses are personal, serving the military and their families wherever they may be, and territorial, having jurisdiction over the geographic territory of military installations (cf. Canons 368-369).

Diptychs • A set of tablets, hinged in the center, containing the names of the living and the dead, read by the deacon during the canon of the Divine Liturgy. At the present time, any memorial listing.

Direct Line • A phrase used to describe one kind of blood relationship between persons. Such persons who are descendants one from another are related in the direct line, such as grandparents, parents and children (cf. Canon 1091).

Directorium: See **Ordo**

Diriment Impediment: See **Impediment, Diriment**

Discalced • The term, meaning "unshod" or "barefoot," is applied to those religious congregations of men and women whose rule requires sandals rather than shoes. This discipline was begun in the West by St. Clare and St. Francis of Assisi. Some

discalced communities are the Augustinians, the Clerks of the Holy Cross and the Discalced Carmelites.

Discernment of Spirits • In 1 Corinthians 12:10, Paul lists one of the gifts of the Holy Spirit — "the ability to distinguish between spirits" (Greek, *diakrisis pneumaton*). The English term "discernment" is from the Latin *discernere* (to "distinguish between," to "resolve" [as in a conflict], to "decide") which parallels the New Testament term *diakrisis*, meaning to "distinguish," "differentiate" or "see through" to the source, which inspired either an interior movement or a specific behavior. Discernment includes making a judgment aided by the Holy Spirit, so that it is a grace-filled human judgment. The goal of discernment is to "see through" a given behavior or movement in one's interior life to its source and inspiration: God (or angels), our own "heart," or evil spirits/the Tempter. The New Testament gives ample witness to the necessity of this gift (e.g., Mk 2:17; Lk 5:22; Mt 22:18; Mk 10:21; Lk 20:23; 1 Cor 11:29; 12:3; 14:32; 2 Cor 13:5; Gal 4:6; 5:19-23; 1 Jn 4:1-6).

Why do we need to discern the spirits? God's promise to reconcile the world to Himself involves a plan which neither the human heart nor the most brilliant human intellect can conceive. Both Genesis 3:15 and the Incarnation show that salvation is an act or work of God which uncovers and manifests God's absolute goodness, friendship and express will for salvation, to which humans respond with the help of grace. Discernment of spirits is necessary for the sake of the People of God, so that they may recognize and participate in the act/work of God in their midst as this relates to the unfolding of His great plan of salvation; in effect, it is God's gift of "spiritual sight" which helps identify the critical path of our pilgrimage to God.

There are two basic means of verifying what is discerned. First, at the theological level, any movement of the interior life or behavioral pattern which claims to be from God affirms the basic gospel message (e.g., Christ's death, resurrection and *parousia*, etc.), is verified throughout Sacred Scripture, is echoed in the Sacred Liturgy, and is consistent with the lives of the saints. Second, on the pastoral and practical level, one always judges an authentic prophecy (e.g., as with Old Testament prophetic traditions, cf. Jer 28:8-9; Dt 18:21-22) the same way one judges whether or not an attractive tree is not full of sickness instead of being full of life — by the fruit produced (Mt 7:17; Rom 8:9); such "fruit" would normally include a deepening love for God, others and even one's enemies, etc. (Gal 5:22-23; 1 Cor 13; Jas 3:17-18).

Disciple • From the Latin *discipulus* (student), disciple is the general term for any student or follower of a particular teacher. In the New Testament, the disciples are understood more specifically as the seventy-two who received instruction from Jesus (Lk 10:1-24). They, in turn, were to share this privileged knowledge with others as teachers of the Faith; so important was this knowledge of the Lord that the heresy of Gnosticism arose as the Gnostics claimed to have received a special revelation directly from the disciples.

The disciples are the object of the Lucan Beatitude (Lk 10:23-24): "Blest are the eyes which see what you see! For I tell you that many prophets and kings desired to see what you see, and did not see it, and to hear what you hear, and did not hear it." Tradition identifies St. John as the "Beloved Disciple" singled out in John 13:23 as the disciple "whom Jesus loved."

After Our Lord's ascension, the Apostles added to the number of disciples, with one hundred twenty gathered at Jerusalem in Acts 1:15. Consistent with the etymology of their names, the Apostles were distinguished in the early Church from the disciples; each Apostle had a singular mission, while the disciples were to go out only in pairs with the specific charge of preparing for the coming of Christ (Mk 6:7). These two ranks of Apostles and disciples are often compared to the Old Testament offices of priests and levites and to the New Testament bishops and presbyters.

Since the Middle Ages, the number of seventy-two disciples determined the limit to membership in the College of Cardinals; however, Pope Paul VI, with a view to Acts 1:15, expanded membership to allow for one hundred twenty active cardinals. In modern usage, the term disciple is generally applied to all the baptized.

For further reading: Hans Weder, "Disciple, Discipleship," *Anchor Bible Dictionary*, 2:207-210.

Disciplina Arcani • "Discipline of the Secret." This was the practice of the early Christians in an era of persecution of not discussing their beliefs freely and openly, but only revealing them gradually to catechumens as they were prepared by instruction for the sacraments of Christian initiation. This would hold especially for the most sacred of mysteries, the Eucharist. Whether some influence of the mystery religions of the time is seen in this practice is disputed by scholars. Allusions to the practice are seen in many of the Fathers, both Eastern and Western. By the sixth century this custom had disappeared with the widespread Christianization of many areas and the collapse of the Roman Empire.

Discipline • A small whip with which some ascetics in antiquity and the Middle Ages lashed themselves to discipline, mortify and punish themselves for their sins. Its use was referred to as "taking the discipline," but the practice has all but vanished in the contemporary era and is no longer recommended or even permitted by most spiritual directors.

It can also mean an instruction, system of teaching or of law, given under the authority of the Church. Discipline, in this sense, can be changed with the approval of proper authority, as opposed to doctrine, which is unchangeable.

Discrimination • The act of making distinctions in favor of one person or thing over another. This process is essentially necessary in human development, for example, when choosing to avoid a life of drug abuse or to embrace higher education.

In common usage the word "discrimination" is often linked with bias and prejudice against people on the basis of race, religion, sex, etc. The Church recognizes such discrimination as a sinful violation of the command of Christ to love one another. The Second Vatican Council's Pastoral Constitution on the Church in the Modern World stated clearly: "Forms of social or cultural discrimination in basic personal rights on the grounds of sex, race, color, social conditions, language, or religion must be curbed and eradicated as incompatible with God's design. It is regrettable that these basic personal rights are not yet being respected everywhere, as is the case with women who are denied the chance freely to choose a husband, or a state of life, or to have access to the same educational and cultural benefits as are available to men" (GS 29).

Diskos • A rimmed and circular tray with a stand or foot, used in the Eastern Liturgy like the paten in the West.

Dismissal • A canonical process whereby a cleric is dismissed from the clerical state, or a religious from an institute of consecrated life. Dismissal is always a canonical penalty imposed because of the commission of a canonical crime. It can be incurred automatically, imposed by an administrative act or imposed at the conclusion of a canonical trial.

Dismissal from the clerical state can be imposed by an administrative decree only by the Holy See (although there are no known examples of this since the promulgation of the new Code in 1983). On the diocesan level, it can be imposed by a diocesan tribunal. It is mentioned as a possible penalty in cases of heresy, apostasy and schism (Canon 1364.2), desecration of the Holy Eucharist (Canon 1367), laying violent hands on the Roman Pontiff (Canon 1370.1), in more serious cases of solicitation in the confessional (Canon 1387), attempted marriage (Canon 1395.1), certain other sexual crimes, including relations with a minor below the age of sixteen (Canon 1395.2).

A dismissed cleric loses all rights, privileges and ecclesiastical offices he might have had. He is prohibited from exercising Sacred Orders, except in danger of death; however, he is not, by the fact of his dismissal dispensed from the obligation of celibacy.

A member of an institute of consecrated life is considered automatically dismissed if he or she has notoriously defected from the Catholic Faith or has attempted marriage. A member may be dismissed for a number of canonical offenses and a variety of other very serious matters. In such cases, the superiors are obligated to follow the process of dismissal outlined in the Code (Canons 694-704). When a religious is dismissed, all vows, rights and obligations cease. If the member was a cleric, he is forbidden to exercise the ministry unless he finds a bishop who will accept him.

Disparity of Worship: See **Cult, Disparity of**

Dispensation • According to Canon 85, a dispensation is the relaxation of a merely ecclesiastical law in a particular case granted by one with the proper authority. There are five major elements to be considered in the assessment of a dispensation.

First, in practice, the Church admits of dispensation only from those laws of which she is the author. For example, it is "merely ecclesiastical" law which requires candidates for priestly ordination to be twenty-five years old (Canon 1031). As such, this age can, under certain circumstances, be dispensed with. But it is of divine law that candidates for priestly ordination be baptized (Canon 1024), and thus such a requirement is beyond the reach of dispensation. But determining that a law is "merely ecclesiastical" does not entirely settle this first issue. A major category of laws which, notwithstanding their "merely ecclesiastical" nature, cannot be dispensed from are those which essentially constitute a juridic institute or act (Canon 86). For example, the vow of obedience is constitutive of religious profession. As such, a prospective religious could not be dispensed from vowing obedience to his or her lawful superior. Similarly, procedural laws (because they are instituted to protect rights and aid in the discovery of truth) and penal laws (because they are designed to protect the community) are not subject to dispensation (Canon 87.1).

The second question to be considered regarding dispensations is precisely who is empowered to grant them. The 1917 Code limited the power of dispensation to the legislator and his properly designated subordinates (cf. Delegation) in keeping with the notion that the advisability of relating ecclesiastical laws is best determined by the one who drafted the law in question. In contrast, the 1983 Code has established that, as a rule, dispensation is more of an executive act which should normally be determined by those entrusted with executive power within the limits of their authority. Additionally, Canon 85 recognizes that the Code itself, under certain circumstances grants, or restricts, the authority to dispense. Canon 1245, for example, grants a pastor qualified authority to dispense from the obligation to observe a feast day or day of penance. Canon 1078, on the other hand, restricts the ability of a local Ordinary to dispense from certain matrimonial impediments. The particular form of restriction found in this canon, and also the most common, is known as "reservation." This means that although a dispensation is possible, the ability to grant it has been reserved to a higher ecclesiastical authority. As a rule, the reservation of a dispensation is indicative of the greater importance attached to the law in question. In grave circumstances, however, an Ordinary may dispense even from certain laws reserved to the Holy See (Canon 87.2).

The third and fourth elements in assessing dispensation are determining the reasons for granting a particular dispensation and the exact scope of a dispensation so granted. Dispensations, because they are exceptions to laws which presumably were drafted for the good of the faithful in the first place, are not to be lightly issued. Canons 85 and 87 state that dispensations are to be granted only to the extent that they contribute to the spiritual good of the faithful. Moreover, Canon 90 directs that dispensations may be granted only after determining the existence of a just and reasonable cause for the dispensation. Disregarding these provisions can result in a dispensation which is illicit and in some situations even invalid. Dispensations are also subject to "strict interpretation" in canon law, which means that they extend only so far as is necessary to serve the underlying purpose of the dispensation in question. For example, if a dispensation is granted in order that a young man might be ordained to the diaconate at age twenty-two (instead of age twenty-three), that would not imply a dispensation for that same man to be ordained to the priesthood at twenty-four (instead of age twenty-five).

The final matter to be considered in the area of dispensations is that of who may benefit from a given dispensation. According to Canon 91, one who has the power to issue a dispensation may do so on behalf of his subjects wherever they may happen to be, as well as for those who actually happen to be present within his territory at the time of the dispensation. Finally, that person may issue such a dispensation in his own behalf, providing of course that all the requirements outlined above have been met.

Dissidio • The Italian word for "division" which has come to designate the rift between the Holy See and the government of Italy from 1870 to 1929. The Popes had exercised temporal sovereignty over central Italy, with Rome as their capital since the eighth century, although such a rule was frequently challenged and modified due to military and economic developments. The last, and most successful, challenge came from the forces of Italian unification called the *Risorgimento* which led to the establishment of the kingdom of Italy in 1870. With that development, Pope Pius IX (1846-1878) became a self-maintained "prisoner of the Vatican" with the Italian government allowing him, through the "Law of Guarantees" of 1871, possession of the 108-acre area within the Leonine Wall called "Vatican City." However, Pius IX warned the loyal Catholics of Italy not to cooperate with their new government, thus creating the

dissidio. Subsequent Popes reaffirmed the *non expedit*, which prohibited Italian Catholics from any participation in Italian politics, but gradually they came to realize that a return of the Papal States was impossible, and that their loss was actually a blessing. Not only that, but the *dissidio* left the Church powerless to influence the development of the country. It was Pope St. Pius X who began to encourage Italian Catholics to resume their civic duties. The *dissidio* was finally formally healed with the Lateran Agreement and Concordat of 1929.

Dissolution of Marriage • An act whereby a valid, even sacramental marriage, is dissolved and declared to exist no longer. A dissolution presumes that a true marriage had been present but, for a reason founded in divine or canon law, is dissolved.

Dissolution is not the same as a declaration of nullity, for this latter presumes that no marriage, in spite of the appearance of marriage, ever existed.

The Church permits the dissolution of a marriage in three specific cases. A sacramental marriage that has not been consummated by sexual intercourse may be dissolved by the Holy Father. Similarly, a marriage between a baptized Christian (not only Catholic) and a non-baptized person may be dissolved by the Holy Father in favor of the faith of a Catholic affected by the marriage. Finally, the marriage of two non-baptized persons is automatically dissolved when one of the parties accepts Christian Baptism and is subsequently married. In this latter case, it is the second marriage itself which dissolves the first. This is known as the Pauline Privilege (cf. Canons 1141-1150).

Dives in Misericordia • This reflection on the mercy of God, the English title of which is "Rich in Mercy," was offered by Pope John Paul II in November 1980. In it, the Pope probes the complex nature of divine mercy through a largely Christological study, getting at the true nature of God the Father by an examination of the life of Christ His Son. In Jesus, the Pope contends, we have the fullest revelation of God's mercy, just as in his prior encyclical, *Redemptor Hominis*, John Paul argues that in the Incarnate Word is found the clearest revelation of the truth about man.

Through several examples, the Pontiff seeks to illustrate the continuity of divine mercy, as it manifests itself in the words and actions of Jesus Christ in the New Testament as well as in God's mercy generously shown to the Israelites in the Old Testament.

John Paul also explores in depth the mercy of God as it is displayed in the passion, death and resurrection of Jesus; for the cross, the Pontiff notes, is God's strongest link to man, and shows God to be a loving Father instead of a merely impersonal Creator.

As a model for Christians, Mary is, among humanity and in the grand sweep of salvation history, the "Mother of Mercy," and as such enjoys "the deepest knowledge of the mystery of God's mercy." The Pope concludes that it is the Church's mission to proclaim that mercy — and a spirit of conversion — to a world gripped by an "uneasiness" and unfulfilled longing.

Dante, *Divine Comedy* author (fifteenth-century fresco)

Divination • Practices or uses of materials to learn either of the future or of other realities not given by ordinary means of human knowing. Divination includes palmistry, reading of crystal balls, tarot cards or ouija boards. Divination also includes spiritualistic methods of gaining occult knowledge, such as seances with the dead, reading of horoscopes or zodiac reading. Divination, like spiritism and other attempts to gain occult knowledge, should be resisted as an implicit challenge to the omniscience, love and power of God.

For further reading: *Catechism of the Catholic Church*, nn. 2115-2117.

Divine Comedy • The title of an allegory written in 1321 by Dante Alighieri (1265-1321). This masterpiece, originally written in Italian with the hope of calling the world back to Christ, is recognized as one of the greatest Christian literary works. Written in verse form and exquisite language, it can be divided into three parts: *Inferno* (Hell), *Purgatorio* (Purgatory) and *Paradiso* (Heaven). The *Divine Comedy* was first printed in Italy in 1472 and is based on the writings of Aristotle, St. Augustine, St. Bernard, St. Thomas Aquinas and the early Fathers of the Church.

Divine Office • The former name for the official, public (although often recited privately), daily liturgical prayer by which the Church sanctifies the hours of the day. Hence the Vatican II revision of this prayer is entitled *The Liturgy of the Hours*, although the title page of the official books still bears the designation: "The Divine Office: revised by decree of the Second Vatican Ecumenical Council. . . ." *Officium* was the common Latin word for public services of prayer, and indeed "office" is still more or less commonly used among the Churches of the Reformation to describe their non-Eucharistic worship services. (Cf. Liturgy of the Hours; Breviary.)

Divine Praises • Acclamations which traditionally conclude Benediction. Although the present official rite makes their use optional during the reposition of the sacrament, the Divine Praises are still generally recited or sung immediately following the blessing with the Host. The recitation sometimes takes the form of a litany, recited by the priest and repeated by the people, or priest and people recite the Praises together.

Attributed in their original form to the eighteenth-century Jesuit Luigi Felici, who promoted them as a reparation for public blasphemy, they have been added to over the years and indulgenced by the Holy See until assuming their present form:

Blessed be God.
Blessed be His holy Name.
Blessed be Jesus Christ, true God and true Man.
Blessed be the name of Jesus.
Blessed be His most Sacred Heart.
Blessed be His most Precious Blood.
Blessed be Jesus in the Most Holy Sacrament of the Altar.
Blessed be the Holy Spirit, the Paraclete.
Blessed be the great Mother of God, Mary most holy.
Blessed be her holy and Immaculate Conception.
Blessed be her glorious Assumption.

Blessed be the Name of Mary, Virgin and Mother.
Blessed be St. Joseph, her most chaste Spouse.
Blessed be God in His Angels and in His Saints.

Divine Revelation, Dogmatic Constitution on: See **Dei Verbum**

Divine Worship, Congregation for: See **Rites, Sacred Congregation of**

Divinity of Christ • The witness of Sacred Scripture is clear about the divinity of Christ and is polyphonic in nature. The pages of Sacred Scripture both assume and proclaim the divinity of Christ. Where there is no explicit reference, His divinity is either assumed or implied (e.g., Mk 3:1-6). From the perspective of Christ's preexistence, we see that He was with God from the beginning and was God (Jn 1:1). Jesus' use of "I AM" (Jn 8:58) is normally taken as a direct reference to God's words to Moses (Ex 3:14), thus implying His divinity; Christ is supreme above all things and prior to all things (in this instance, priority implying superiority: Jn 1; Col 1:16-17).

In Christ's relationship to the Father we see His divinity with ease and certainty — at His Baptism a voice from heaven (God) called Him "Son," thus indicating Jesus' divine status (Mt 3:17; Mk 1:11; Lk 3:22); Jesus is the Father's only begotten Son (Jn 1:14), not by adoption but by nature (Heb 1:1); Jesus was with the Father from the beginning (Jn 1:1), reveals the Father (Jn 1:18), is in the Father as the Father is in Him (Jn 14:11), in unity (Jn 10:30).

The Church's faith in Christ expresses a clear conviction about Christ's divinity — from Peter's confession at Caesarea Philippi (Mt 16) including the centurion's confession at Jesus' death, preserved and proclaimed in the Gospel (Mk 15:39) to the post-resurrection confession of Thomas (Jn 20:28), to name only a few. In a special way Jesus' authority to forgive sins, which in Judaism was restricted to God alone, shows not only His divinity but also something about divinity — it is the compassionate and loving King of kings, Whose kingdom arrives in force and power for the reconciliation and re-creation of a world scarred by the forces of sin and death.

Divino Afflante Spiritu • On September 30, 1943, Pope Pius XII issued an encyclical which draws its title from the first three words of the document, *Divino Afflante Spiritu* (DAS). This document was to provide guidance to Catholic biblical scholars for whom the use and abuse, the advantages, and limits of historical and linguistic methods in biblical research had become a pressing issue. The atmosphere into which this document was inserted was less stressful than that of fifty years earlier, when Pope Leo XIII issued the encyclical *Providentissimus Deus*, also intended as guidance for Catholic scholars and professors of Sacred Scripture who were using scientific (e.g., history, archaeology, ethnography, etc.) and linguistic approaches to the analysis of Sacred Scripture.

Divino Afflante Spiritu encourages the careful study of the original languages in which Sacred Scripture was written, in order to study and determine (called "lower criticism" or "textual criticism") which of the surviving manuscripts of Sacred Scripture are closest to the "autographs" which did not survive. One cannot study the manuscripts without competent knowledge of the language in which they are written.

In addition, *Divino Afflante Spiritu* warned against excessive application of the sciences mentioned above, especially when the rash application of these methods led to questioning and, in some instances, outright rejection of essential elements of the Faith.

Much of the teaching found in *Divino Afflante Spiritu* is reaffirmed in *Dei Verbum* (Dogmatic Constitution on Divine Revelation), issued at the Second Vatican Council. The Catholic scholar must master the technical details of Sacred Scripture and also test the yield of that research against the witness of the whole of Sacred Scripture, the teachings of the Fathers, the Councils, the liturgies (East and West) and the lives of the saints.

For further reading: Raymond E. Brown, S.S., and Thomas Aquinas Collins, O.P., "Church Pronouncements," *New Jerome Biblical Commentary*, 1166-1174.

Divorce • A legal act severing the bond of marriage between two people. Civil divorce exists in most countries and is regulated to a greater or lesser degree by civil law. Many Christian denominations accept a civil divorce as the sign that the marriage is terminated and thus permit subsequent marriage.

The Catholic Church does not recognize a civil divorce as proof that a marriage bond no longer exists. If persons wish to enter a subsequent marriage that will be recognized by the Catholic Church (persons who receive a divorce) they must obtain either an ecclesiastical dissolution of the prior marriage or a declaration of nullity.

Although it has been commonly assumed that the Catholic Church does not allow or condone divorce, this is not actually the case. For many years, the Church required the faithful wanting to divorce to obtain permission from Church authorities. What the Church has always taught, however, is that a civil divorce does not render the marriage bond nonexistent.

As to the condoning of divorce, while the Church has never approved of it and certainly has never encouraged it, the attitude toward divorce and divorced persons has gradually evolved. All of the canonical penalties related to civil divorce have been dropped. Rather than expect an attitude of condemnation or accusation, divorced persons now can go to their parishes for support, encouragement and help in working through the trauma that goes with the breakdown of a marriage and family.

Divorce From Bed and Board • The term used in the 1917 Code to describe the separation of spouses with permission of Church authorities. It did not constitute a civil divorce nor a decree of nullity or dissolution of the marriage. The spouses remained bound to the obligation of fidelity to each other.

The revised Code provides legislation to deal with the separation of spouses on grounds of adultery or other grave reasons (cf. Canons 1151-1155).

Docetism • Derived from the Greek word *dokeo*, "to seem," the term is used to refer to the heretical view that the humanity and sufferings of Christ are apparent rather than real. What is denied by Docetism is the real, hypostatic union of the divine and human natures in the Incarnation. Thus, Christ is said merely to assume the appearance of a human body — rather like a costume or a temporary disguise — and hence only seems to suffer and die. This view did not take the form of an articulated doctrine until the time of the second-century Gnostics, although signs of its existence can already be seen in

such New Testament texts as 2 John 7, which complains of "deceivers . . . who will not acknowledge the coming of Jesus Christ in the flesh" (cf. 1 Jn 4:1-3).

Doctor • The term "doctor" is derived from the Latin *docere*, meaning to teach; historically, then, a doctor was an accomplished teacher. In modern times, a doctor is one who has attained the highest academic degree in a given field.

St. Gregory Nazianzen, a Doctor of the Church

In ecclesiastical usage, "Doctor of the Church" is the title ascribed to a select few writers whose tremendous erudition and insight have been of fundamental importance in the development of Church learning. The title does not imply, however, that the entirety of their writing is free of errors. Doctors commonly recognized as such before the eighth century include Sts. Ambrose of Milan, Jerome (the Father of biblical science), Augustine (the Doctor of grace), Pope Gregory the Great, Athanasius (the Father of orthodoxy), Basil the Great (the Father of Eastern monasticism), Gregory Nazianzen (the Christian Demosthenes), and John Chrysostom ("the Golden-Tongued").

Doctors formally proclaimed as such by Church authorities are: Thomas Aquinas (the Angelic Doctor, in 1568); Bonaventure (the Seraphic Doctor, in 1588), Anselm of Canterbury (the Father of Scholasticism, in 1720); Isidore of Seville, the most learned man of his age (1722); Peter Chrysologus, archbishop of Ravenna (1729); Pope Leo the Great, who saved Rome from Attila in 452 (1754); Peter Damian, the Benedictine cardinal (1828); Bernard of Clairvaux (the Mellifluous Doctor, in 1830); Hilary of Poitiers (the Athanasius of the West, 1851); Alphonsus Liguori, perhaps the greatest moralist (1871); Francis de Sales, expert on the devotional life (1877); Cyril of Alexandria, who presided over the fifth-century Council of Ephesus, and Cyril of Jerusalem, the great bishop-catechist (both in 1882); John Damascene, the monk (1890); Bede the Venerable, the Father of English history (1899); Ephraem of Syria (the Harp of the Holy Spirit, 1920); Peter Canisius, a Dutch Jesuit leader of the Counter-Reformation, in 1925; John of the Cross (the Doctor of mystical theology, 1926); Robert Bellarmine, reformer and canonist (1931); Albert the Great (the universal Doctor, 1931); Anthony of Padua (the evangelical Doctor, 1946); Lawrence of Brindisi, the Capuchin (1959); Teresa of Ávila, the mystical Carmelite, and Catherine of Siena, who promoted the end of the Avignon Papacy, both proclaimed in 1970.

Doctor Angelicus • The "Angelic Doctor" is a title given to one of the greatest theologians of the Church, St. Thomas Aquinas (1224/25-1274). St. Thomas, a Dominican friar, is the author of the landmark scholastic work the *Summa Theologiae*.

Doctor Communis • This title, which means in Latin "the Common Doctor," has been conferred upon St. Thomas Aquinas (1225-1274) by the generations and denotes the universality and timeless character of his teaching, which is of such great scope and for all times, places and peoples, in short, for all those seeking to know and appreciate the Truth. Aquinas is the only theologian whose work has ever been recommended by an ecumenical council. Vatican II urges all students of theology, in particular those studying for the priesthood, to "learn to examine more deeply, with the help of speculation and with St. Thomas as teacher, all aspects of these mysteries (of salvation), and to perceive their interconnection" (cf. OT 16).

Doctor Gratiae • The title of "Doctor of Grace" has been traditionally conferred on St. Augustine of Hippo (A.D. 354-430) because of the importance of his work in the field of the theology of grace which mainly took place in the context of his refutation of the Pelagian and Semi-Pelagian heresies of the fourth and fifth centuries.

Doctor Marianus • St. Anselm of Canterbury (1033-1109) earned this appellation because of his writings concerning the role and privileges of the Blessed Virgin Mary in the history of salvation, which can be found in his works on the Incarnation and the perpetual virginity of Mary, *Cur Deus Homo?* and *De Conceptu Virginali*. Among some of his other works of great renown are the *Proslogium*, the *Monologium*, *De Veritate*, and *De Fide Trinitatis*. St. Anselm is considered to be the Father of Scholasticism.

Doctor Mellifluus • The title of "the Mellifluous [or 'Honeysweet'] Doctor" has been given to St. Bernard of Clairvaux (1090-1153), a Cistercian abbot, considered the second founder of the Cistercians and one of the greatest minds of his age, having been consultor to Popes and kings during his life. Not only was he famous for his wisdom and knowledge, but he was a most powerful and influential preacher, which perhaps gave rise to this title. He is renowned for his mystical works, his teaching on and devotion to the Infant Jesus and the Virgin Mary, his commentary and sermons on the Song of Songs, as well as his sermons, of which over three hundred are extant. His writings are among the most beautiful in Christian literature, well earning him this title. The Mellifluous Doctor is, moreover, considered to be the last Father of the Church.

Doctor Seraphicus • St. Bonaventure (1231-1374) is referred to as the Seraphic Doctor. A great Scholastic theologian, he is noted in particular for his writings about the hypostatic union and the humanity of God-made-man, Our Lord Jesus Christ. As a Scholastic, however, he touched on all the major areas of the Faith as was the case with other Scholastics, such as St. Albert the Great and St. Thomas Aquinas. The term "Seraphic" refers to the fact that St. Bonaventure was a Franciscan (at one time elected Minister General of the Order). St. Francis had received the stigmata in connection with a vision he had near the end of his earthly life in which the crucified Christ was borne aloft by Seraphim. As such, he himself is known in Franciscan circles as the Seraphic Father and things Franciscan are often referred to since then as "Seraphic." Thus on St. Bonaventure, who was a great theologian, teacher and Doctor of the Church, has been conferred this title of "Seraphic Doctor."

Doctor Subtilis • John Duns Scotus (1270-1308), one of the great Scholastic theologians of the Church, is referred to by this title of "Subtle Doctor" by Franciscans mainly because of the subtlety and exquisite detail of his work, mainly to be found in his "Commentary on the Sentences" of Peter Lombard. He is said to personify therein the genuine spirit of Scholasticism. It is to Duns Scotus, a Franciscan friar (as was St. Bonaventure), that is credited the solution to the theological problem which concerned scholars with regard to the Immaculate

Conception of the Virgin Mary and thus paved the way for its definition centuries later by Pope Pius IX in 1854.

Doctor Universalis • It is to St. Albert the Great (1206-1280) that this title of "Universal Doctor" has been given. St. Albert, a Dominican theologian credited with being the teacher and mentor of St. Thomas Aquinas, is known by this title because of the extent and scope of his knowledge and theological and philosophical work. He was also archbishop of Cologne in Germany at the time of his death.

Doctrine of the Catholic Church • Broadly taken, the doctrine of the Catholic Church comprises all those teachings in faith and morals entrusted to the Church by Christ through the Apostles and given for the sake of our salvation. In this broad sense, the term "doctrine" is coterminous with the whole of revelation or the Deposit of the Faith. It may also refer to any particular teaching drawn from this body of doctrines. A narrow sense of the term refers to specific formulations of doctrines in the creeds (e.g., the doctrine of the Trinity), conciliar definitions confirmed by papal authority (e.g., the doctrine of infallibility), papal definitions (e.g., the doctrine of the Immaculate Conception), or other magisterial pronouncements. These doctrines are "defined" and thus unoptional and authentic teachings of the Church. They are also said to be *de fide* — as belonging to the very substance of the Faith — and thus calling for the assent of all Catholics. Normally, such definitions are formulated in response to heterodox challenges to a particular doctrine, or to give suitable expression to a universally held doctrine. In recent usage, the definition of doctrine in this narrower sense is said to represent an exercise of the "extraordinary Magisterium," while the main substance of Catholic doctrine — which has not been the subject of explicit dogmatic formulation — is taught by the Church in her "ordinary Magisterium."

Documentary Process • A judicial process whereby the nullity of a marriage can be declared based on proof from certain and authentic documents. The documentary process can be used only for cases of nullity based on the presence of an undispensed impediment or a defect of canonical form. In such a process, the parties are cited and the defender of the bond is present, but all the other formalities of the judicial trial are omitted. There is a right to appeal but, unlike formal nullity trials, an affirmative sentence is not automatically appealed.

An impediment is proven to be present if an authentic document shows that the basis for the impediment existed at the time of the marriage. If the parish and diocesan records where the marriage took place do not contain evidence of a dispensation, it is presumed that one was not granted.

By "defect of canonical form" is meant that the marriage was performed according to form but that for some reason there was an invalidating defect, such as lack of jurisdiction, on the part of the officiating witness (Canons 1686-1688).

Dogma • A teaching of the Church revealed implicitly or explicitly by Sacred Scripture or Sacred Tradition, to be believed by the faithful by virtue of solemn definition or the Church's ordinary Magisterium. For a teaching to be a "dogma," the specific truth must have been formally revealed and taught as such by the Church; in addition, the dogma must be proposed as binding on the faithful. Hence, the dogma's acceptance is necessary for salvation.

Dogmatic Theology • The systematic study of the truths of revelation as formulated and presented by the doctrines of the Church. Although since the seventeenth century dogmatic theology has been regarded as the branch of theology concerned with matters of belief, in a true sense it is coextensive with the whole of theology as a science of faith whose object is God and His activity. Today dogmatic theology is commonly distinguished from moral theology and focuses chiefly on the study of the doctrines of the existence and nature or God, the Blessed Trinity, creation, anthropology and grace, incarnation, redemption, Mariology, the Church and the sacraments and the last things. In this study, dogmatic theology has both a historical and a speculative interest: it is concerned both to establish the sources and contents of Christian doctrines and to penetrate the inner intelligibility of these doctrines individually and in their interconnections. As a science of faith, dogmatic theology seeks to understand and exhibit, insofar as this is possible for the human mind, the contents and inner coherence of truths that articulate the never fully comprehensible or expressible Truth of God Himself.

Dogmatic theology is sometimes called "systematic theology" in order to signal these speculative or scientific elements in its work.

Dom • From the Latin *dominus* (master, ruler), a title prefixed to the names of monks belonging to some monasteries of Benedictines, Carthusians, etc.

Domestic Prelate • An honorary title conferred by the Holy Father upon a priest, usually at the request of his bishop. In some cases the title is conferred directly by the Holy See because of a position held in the Vatican. A domestic prelate has the right to the title of "Monsignor." Once this title is conferred, it is retained for life.

In 1968 the title "Domestic Prelate" was changed to "Honorary Prelate of His Holiness." In addition, the dress worn by such prelates was changed the following year. Presently the prescribed costumes are the black cassock with red trim for everyday and the purple cassock for liturgical ceremonies, both worn with a purple sash. The mantelletta, ferraiolone, patent shoes with silver buckles and the purple tuft on the biretta have been abolished.

Domicile • Generally, ecclesiastical laws are presumed to be "territorial" rather than "personal." That is, they bind only those persons within certain geographical areas. Our mobile age has made the need to determine precisely who is bound by an ecclesiastical territorial law more complex. These determinations are governed primarily by the canonical concept of domicile.

According to Canon 102, there are two ways to acquire domicile in a given ecclesial territory: either one can be physically present in the territory (for example, a diocese) *and* have the intention of remaining there at least indefinitely, or one can simply be physically present in the territory for at least five years. If either of these conditions is met, one is considered to have acquired domicile in that territory, and is generally bound by ecclesiastical laws having force within that territory.

In addition to these methods, certain classes of persons can acquire domicile in other ways. For example, children generally have the domicile of their parents as long as they are under their care (Canons 101, 105), spouses usually have a common domicile, and members of religious institutes and societies of apostolic life have a domicile in the place of the house to which they are attached (Canon 103).

Upon acquiring domicile, one is known as a "permanent resident" (*incola*) and can lose that domicile only by leaving the territory with the intention of not returning (Canon 106). Merely traveling outside of one's domicile is not sufficient (Canon 100). It is possible to have more than one domicile (the most common example being domicile in a parish and domicile in a diocese; cf. Canons 102, 107), although it is more likely that one actually has one or more quasi-domiciles.

Dominations • The name of the first order within the second hierarchy of the nine choirs of angels. The Dominations control the Powers and the Virtues, the second and third orders of the intermediate hierarchy, and direct them as they perform their appointed duties.

Dominic, St. • Founder of the Order of Preachers (Dominicans). Born in Calaroga, Spain, in 1170, Dominic de Guzmán graduated from the University of Palencia in 1194. He was ordained to the priesthood and resided at the cathedral as a canon regular of St. Augustine. Dominic led a very contemplative life until called by his bishop to fight against the Albigensian heresy. Gathering a group of preachers, he set out to repel the error of the heresy and also established a convent of nuns to receive converts from the heresy. By 1214, his group was in the process of becoming a religious community. In 1216 and 1217, it was accepted as the Order of Preachers by Pope Honorius III. The order follows the Rule of St. Augustine and is a synthesis of contemplative life and apostolic ministry. The order is known for study and boasts of some of the greatest minds of all time, St. Thomas Aquinas and St. Albert the Great. St. Dominic died in Bologna, Italy, on August 6, 1221. He is commemorated in the liturgy on August 8. (Cf. Dominicans.)

Dominicans (also Order of Preachers) • The Dominican Order, officially known as the Order of Preachers, is a mendicant order founded by St. Dominic de Guzmán, a canon of the cathedral of Osma, Spain, in 1215. The original purpose for the foundation of the order was to teach and preach against heresies rampant at the time. From its inception, the order stressed the study of the Scriptures and theology and in time included among its members some of the Church's foremost theologians, such as St. Albert the Great, St. Thomas Aquinas and Melchior Cano.

The order was founded as a mendicant community, thus allowing its members the ability to travel about in order to exercise their ministry of preaching and teaching. Within the first century of its existence, chapels and churches were entrusted to the Dominicans where they preached and taught. Today Dominicans teach at universities and colleges, work in campus and parochial ministry and continue to exercise the preaching apostolate.

The order is highly democratic in structure. All superiors, including the Master of the Order, provincials and priors, are elected. The chapter is the primary legislative organ of the order and is held on an international, territorial and local level on a regular basis.

Part of the Dominican family are the Second Order of Dominican cloistered nuns and the Third Order of laity. There are also numerous congregations of Dominican Third Order sisters.

Dominum et Vivificantem • Released on the occasion of the solemnity of Pentecost in May 1986, the fifth encyclical of Pope John Paul II, "The Holy Spirit in the Church and the World" assailed the twin cultures of materialism and death prominent in the contemporary world. Proclaiming the Holy Spirit "the life which is stronger than death," the Pope delineated the many "signs and symptoms of death" prevailing in various sectors of modern society, including the dialectical and historical materialism at the heart of Marxism. Initiating a larger discussion of good and evil, the Pontiff singled out abortion, terrorism, genocide and torture as particularly violative of the dignity and integrity of the human person, asserting conversion from such an antilife ethos is only possible through the transforming power of the Holy Spirit at work in the conscience of man.

Donation of Constantine: See **Constantine, Donation of**

Donatism • A North African rigorist movement that takes its name from Donatus, who in A.D. 313 succeeded Majorinus as second schismatic bishop of Carthage and then became principal leader of the sect. Majorinus himself had been elected bishop of Carthage in 312 by a group of Numidian bishops who opposed the earlier election of Caecilian. They challenged the legitimacy of Caecilian's consecration by Felix of Aptunga, who, they alleged, had lapsed during the persecution of Diocletian and thus could no longer validly administer the sacraments. Despite unsuccessful appeals to the Pope (313), to the Synod of Arles (314), and to the emperor (316), the movement continued to spread. It appealed in part to the rigorist bent of African Christianity and to local dissatisfaction with Roman involvement in the religious, social and economic life of the reign. Political violence by roving bands associated with the Donatists (*circumcelliones*) provoked imperial intervention in 347.

After becoming bishop of Hippo in 397, St. Augustine for fifteen years devoted his formidable theological skills to the refutation of Donatism. But when an imperially sponsored conference at Carthage in 411 — attended by nearly four hundred bishops from each side — failed to achieve a doctrinal resolution, persecution of

Church of the Dormition,
Daphni, Greece (circa 1080)

reunited, soul and body, to enjoy eternal happiness.

From the fifth century on, legend told of Our Lady's death surrounded by the Apostles, when her soul was taken into heaven, only to be followed by their keeping vigil at the grave and witnessing the Assumption of her body as well. The fanciful aspects of these legends notwithstanding, they bear witness to the truth of early belief by the faithful in Our Lady's being taken to heaven, soul and body. This feast was observed in the East as early as the sixth century and spread throughout the whole of the East. It was adopted in Rome during the seventh century, when Pope Sergius I (687-701) ordered a solemn procession for the feast. The Western emphasis has always been on the glorification of Our Lady rather than on her dormition or her death, although when Pope Pius XII solemnly defined her Assumption, he left open the question as to whether she died or was taken bodily into heaven alive.

Dossal (also Dorsal) • The suspended drapery behind the altar, extending the length of the altar, which serves as the backdrop for the crucifix hanging above the altar. Also called the "dorsal," the dossal generally is made of tapestry or an expensive cloth such as velvet. Today, banners which are used as a background in the liturgy often replace the dossal.

Douai Bible (also Douay or Doway Bible) • An English Catholic translation of the Scriptures done by members of the English College at Douai, Belgium, founded in 1568 by William Allen. The translation was begun at Douai, but when the college was transferred to Rheims in 1578, work on the New Testament was brought to completion and published there in 1582. The Old Testament was completed back in Douai, to which the college had meantime returned.

Donatism resulted. Chiefly in the form of economic sanctions against the Donatists (fines, confiscation of property, etc.), this persecution greatly weakened the movement.

Remnants of Donatism survived until the seventh-century Arab invasion of Africa. The movement possessed a perduring doctrinal significance. It challenged the Church to articulate a profound truth about the sacraments: their efficacy depends not on the worthiness of their ministers but on the power of Christ, Who, as St. Augustine vigorously maintained, is their true minister.

Doorkeeper: See **Porter**

Dormition of the Blessed Virgin Mary • The falling asleep of Our Lady, a feast celebrated in the East on August 15 (when the West celebrates her Assumption) and considered one of the twelve great feasts of the East. Originally all Christians spoke of death as falling asleep (cf. 1 Thes 4:14) until the general resurrection when all would be

This translation was published in 1609. The language of this version, to a certain degree, influenced the language of the Authorized Version. A revision of the Douai-Rheims Bible was undertaken in 1749-1750 by Richard Challoner, a convert, in his early years, from Presbyterianism.

For further reading: Jack P. Lewis, "Douay Version," *Anchor Bible Dictionary*, 2:227-228.

Double • The name formerly given in the Missal for the highest rank of feasts in the liturgical calendar. There were ordinary doubles, major doubles, doubles of the second and first class, in ascending importance. The new terminology is simplified to memorials, feasts and solemnities.

Doubt of Law, of Fact • A doubt of law is an objective uncertainty about the meaning of a law. In such cases, the law does not bind. Doubt of law arises when the text of a law is so obscure or so confusing that it cannot be understood. The canon which refers to doubt of law speaks of objective doubt, arising from the text itself, and not subjective doubt, which refers to the inability of a person to understand a law.

A doubt of fact is an uncertainty about the facts of a particular case to which a law applies. That is, it is objectively uncertain whether some relevant facts can be known or whether the facts, as they stand, coincide with the obligation or action of the law. In cases of doubt of fact, the Ordinary can grant a dispensation. For example, if there is a doubt about the perpetuity or absolute nature of physical impotence, the law prohibiting a marriage of a such a person can be dispensed (cf. Canon 14).

Dove • "Doves" in the Bible are birds of the Columbidae family, popularly known as the pigeon family. The dove is mentioned in the Old Testament in varying contexts, most frequently in connection with the offering for purification from ritual uncleanness by the poor (e.g., Lv 5:7, 11; 12:6, 8; 14:22). The dove's sacrificial function extended into the New Testament period (Mk 11:15; Jn 2:14; Lk 2:24).

At Matthew 3:16; Mark 1:10; Luke 3:22 and John 1:32 the Holy Spirit descends in the form of a dove on Jesus immediately after His Baptism in the Jordan. The source of this depiction is not clear — to date no biblical or extra-biblical parallels have been discovered. Some suggest that the New Testament connection between the Holy Spirit and the dove reflects the development of a tradition which may have begun within Jewish meditations on the role of the Spirit of God hovering over the primordial waters (Gn 1:2). In addition, Jewish proverbs about the dove (attested to in Mt 10:16) clearly witness to its gentleness, whereas the Greek Jewish philosopher Philo understood the dove as a symbol of virtue and reasoning (cf. his *Question and Answer on Genesis* II.39-44; III.3); the Talmud records Rabbi Jose making a connection between the cooing of the dove and the divine voice (Ber. 3a [Talmud abbreviation]). All of these instances are at best merely suggestive of possible connections. (Cf. also *Catechism of the Catholic Church*, n. 701.)

Doxology • Our English term is from the Greek *doxologia*, which is made up of the two nouns *doxa* ("glory") and *logos* ("word" or "utterance" or "saying" or "speech"). In Sacred Liturgy our habit of giving praise to God for Who and what God is, and, for what God has done and will do, is rooted in some of the oldest literary strata in Sacred Scripture.

God is always called "blessed" for His great deeds (Hebrew, *baruch*; Greek Old Testament [LXX], *eulogetos*; Gn 24:27; Ex 18:10). Ancient Jewish liturgies and prayers are filled with the phrase, "Blessed are you, our God, King of the universe." Many biblical hymns begin by praising God (1 Chr 29:10; Dan 2:20; Lk 1:68; Eph 1:3; 1 Pt 1:3) or conclude with a shower of praises to God (1 Chr 16:36; Ps 41:14; 72:18; 89:53; 106:48). Paul saw that giving praise to God had great benefits (Rom 1:25; 2 Cor 11:31). In the Old Testament, God is the object of the doxology or "words of glory/blessing," as in some New Testament passages (Lk 2:14; Rom 9:5). In the New Testament, Christ is praised in language equal in substance to what God receives throughout Old Testament doxologies (e.g., 2 Pt 3:18; Rom 11:36); even God praises Christ (Rv 5:12).

In early Christian liturgical practice we see strong parallels between the praise of Christ and the praise of God in the Old Testament (e.g., Rom 16:27; 1 Pt 4:11). The doxology is the climactic point of prayer, the highest moment of verbal expression and liturgical gesture of the gathered faith community. Tradition indicates three types of doxology. (1) *The Greater Doxology*: What we find at Mass in the "Gloria" (Latin, *Gloria in excelsis Deo*, "Glory to God in the highest"). (2) *The Lesser Doxology*: What we find in the prayer "Glory be to the Father. . . ." (3) *The Metrical Forms*: This pre-Vatican II term refers to those doxologies which refer to a particular mystery of Christ or a particular season of the Church in which a salvific event or some other aspect of salvation history is remembered and inspires praises to God.

Dreams • As products of subconscious activity during sleep, dreams are the object of intense study in current physiological and psychological sciences. In Christian thought and practice, dreams figure prominently in the scriptural accounts of God's dealings with individuals, particularly in order to indicate to them a course of action to be undertaken or to reveal knowledge of His purposes or of some future event (Gn 37:1-11; Dn 2:19; Mt 1:20). Generally, however,

Christians are cautious about according analysis of dreams too wide a scope. As a therapeutic practice, Freudian analysis of dreams can aid in the healing of persons with psychological disorders or more simply in helping people to understand their anxieties. But the use of dreams for the purposes of divination, or predicting the future, is regarded as a superstitious practice and excluded by the virtue of religion.

For further reading: Janet Meyer Everts, "Dreams in the New Testament and Greco-Roman Literature," *Anchor Bible Dictionary*, 2:231-232.

Dress, Clerical • Traditionally, Church law has held that clerics should dress in a distinctive and appropriate manner. The present law states that "clerics are to wear suitable ecclesiastical garb in accord with the norms issued by the conference of bishops and in accord with legitimate local custom" (Canon 284).

The manner with which legislation has been observed throughout history has varied from country to country. The Councils of Baltimore II and III issued legislation applicable to the United States. Clerics were to wear cassocks or religious habits in the church and rectory and a black suit with a Roman collar outside. Clerics were forbidden to wear beards and elaborate hairstyles.

The 1917 Code contained the provision about wearing suitable and distinctive garb. It also prohibited the wearing of rings, except when allowed by law (bishops, abbots, vicars apostolic and those with doctorates in theology or canon law from pontifical universities). There were several penalties set for laying aside clerical dress.

After Vatican II, there were significant changes in the norms for clerical dress. In those countries where the wearing of the cassock and religious habit on the streets was the norm, clerics were allowed for the first time to wear black or gray suits with the Roman collar.

The appropriate garb for permanent deacons is another matter. The general law leaves this matter up to the episcopal conferences. In the United States permanent deacons have been encouraged to wear lay dress, although no specific prohibition has been made from their wearing clerical garb.

Drug Education, Catholic Office of •
Begun in 1972, this agency is a part of the United States Catholic Conference, the administrative arm of the National Conference of Catholic Bishops (NCCB). This office oversees the development of educational material and appropriate resources for community involvement in the fight against substance use and abuse. It is located in Washington, D.C.

Dualism • The term dualism has two distinct but related applications. First, it denotes theories according to which human nature is composed of two principles, material and spiritual. In the history of philosophy, there has been considerable controversy about how to conceive of the relation of these components of the human person. In the context of the history of these debates, the term dualism has come to be applied more narrowly to views that conceive of the link between the material and spiritual as fairly loose (e.g., Cartesianism) in contrast to those that conceive of the material and spiritual as substantially unified in the human person (e.g., Thomism). Secondly, dualism refers to philosophical or religious systems that conceive of good and evil as metaphysically distinct causal (and sometimes personified) principles. It is typical of dualistic systems to ascribe empirical good and evil to the eternally conflicted causation of these transcendent principles. In such systems, human beings are seen to be caught in a cosmic struggle whose outcome they are relatively powerless to affect.

Sometimes dualism in this metaphysical sense encompasses views of the composition of the human person (dualism in the first sense) when the spiritual (or good) is seen as being entrapped in the material (or evil). Sharply dualistic conceptions of human nature, and dualistic explanations of the problem of evil are contrary to the Christian Faith in the goodness of God, the goodness of His creation, human freedom and moral responsibility, and the essential unity of human bodily and spiritual being, attested to by faith in the resurrection of the body.

Due Process • In the broad sense, due process is the service of the law which is established to protect the rights of individuals. Legal process itself is ordered to the discovery of truth and the protection of the rights of both individuals involved in a controversy and the rights of the community. Individuals have a right to the safeguards set forth in the law, hence these are "due" them.

Due process includes conciliation, arbitration, administrative recourse and judicial recourse. If a matter ends up in the judicial forum, the persons involved have a number of procedural rights: the right to counsel, the right to present evidence, the right to know the identity of their accusers, the right to examine the facts of the case and the right to appeal.

Duel • A fight, usually with weapons such as swords, lances or guns, between two individuals at an agreed-upon time and place that aims at either maiming or death. Duels have usually been fought either to maintain one's "honor" or one's position of power or to win the hand of a woman.

Dueling has been consistently condemned by the Church, but this condemnation was resisted on a widespread basis up until this century. The condemnation of dueling by the Church bears many similarities to the Church's teachings on other topics which were consistently and emphatically taught but disregarded by most people throughout the centuries. Only with the demise of gunfighters in the American West in the twentieth century did dueling come to an end. Despite claims by its proponents, dueling is simply murder and is the use of an evil means for a (usually) good end.

Dulia • Derived from a Greek root meaning "slavery" or, more broadly, "respect." Dulia, in ecclesiastical speech, denotes the kind and degree of honor given to the angels and saints. Dulia rendered to publicly proclaimed angels and saints is governed by ecclesiastical authority. It is to be distinguished, moreover, from hyperdulia and latria.

Duties • There are many duties and responsibilities imposed by the Church on her members. The most important are those emanating from the Decalogue and the Great Commandment. In addition to these religious and moral duties, the Church also requires that the faithful receive Communion during the Easter season and confess their sins annually. The Church has the right to impose duties, precisely to foster the growth of the spiritual lives of the faithful. These duties mark the minimal requirements of authentic Christian life, and the failure to fulfill these duties generally indicates a failure of commitment to Christ.

Duties of Parents • The duties of parents in matters that regard the welfare of their children can be considered from many different perspectives, for these duties are rooted and reflected in the natural law, ecclesiastical laws and the laws of the state. The duties fall to parents based on the intimate and unique relationship they as adults have to their children. For parents, not the state and not even the Church, are, with God, the co-creators of their children.

As infants, children are totally dependent on their parents for even the most basic biological needs; and for these needs children will remain dependent, albeit in a gradually decreasing manner, for many years. As the child's intellect begins to awaken, moreover, parents are bound to educate and instruct the child with the manifold information necessary to function as an active member of the family and society. Likewise, as the child develops in moral responsibility, parents, before all others, are required to instruct, by word and example, in the behavior and attitudes proper to civilized society.

These educational and instructional duties, it should be stressed, bind the parents in matters religious and spiritual no less than secular. Indeed, these duties extend to every facet of their child's life. Canon 1136 of the 1983 Code of Canon Law puts it most succinctly: "Parents are bound by the most serious duty and enjoy the primary right of providing with the very best of their ability the upbringing of their children, including their physical care, social and cultural preparation, and their moral and religious training as well." It goes without saying, of course, that in matters of doctrine, for example, parents must see to it that their instruction (or that of those to whom they might have entrusted their children) is in harmony with the teaching of the Church. Nor should Christian parents shrink from such duties as being beyond their abilities amid the pressing concerns of modern society. Indeed, Canon 1134 observes that "the sacrament of Christian marriage strengthens and consecrates the parents for the duties and the dignity of their state."

No less importantly must parents recognize and foster the gradual independence of their children with the passing years, so that by the time their children reach adulthood, they are adequately equipped to face the demands of life as responsible citizens and believers. For it is true that in many areas of parental rights, parents are in fact acting as stewards of their children's rights until they have sufficient wisdom and prudence to fend for themselves.

The admittedly heavy burdens on parents must, of necessity, be actively supported by the rest of society. Parents must be free to call upon Church and state for assistance with their duties, assistance which when rendered does not usurp the primacy of parental responsibility, but rather helps the parents fulfill it to the best of their ability.

This assistance from the Church comes most especially through the availability of Catholic schools, which the Church should provide and which the faithful have an obligation to use and support.

Finally, lest the duties of parents be cast in an overly-legal form, we might recall the observation that the duties of parents are no less their honors and their privileges. Parents can call to mind that the infant in their arms, child on their knee, the son or daughter at their side is just as much a child of God as they themselves are, and that their offspring was equally ransomed by the same Blood of Christ which was shed for them. Just as parents know well enough that their duties can be fraught with trials, they can rest assured that those duties are nevertheless designations of trust granted by God.

Dying, Prayers for the • The prayers for the dying or the commendation of the soul (not the Last Rites or Extreme Unction, as the sacrament of Anointing of the Sick used to be called) consisted in the Asperges, the Litany of the Saints, prayers, the Kyrie and various aspirations, as well as the apostolic blessing. In the current rite much of the same material has been retained but is greatly enriched with psalms and other biblical selections and with more as optional. The apostolic blessing for the dying is not mentioned in the new rite.

E

Early Church: See **Church, Early**

Easter • The feast of the resurrection of Christ derives its name from Eastre, the goddess of Spring, according to St. Bede the Venerable, but others think that the term comes from a misunderstanding of *Hebdomada Alba* when *alba* ("white") was mistranslated into the High German word for dawn, when the Risen Lord was seen by the holy women. In any event, this festival is the high point of the Christian year, as it celebrates the central mystery of Christ, His triumph over death and the cross in His resurrection, which in the Synoptic Gospels is associated with the Jewish Passover.

The Hebrew commemoration of *pesach* ("passover") forms the theological and liturgical background for the Church's Easter celebration. The important terms *pascha* (Greek) and *passio* (Latin) describe the theology of Easter as a feast of Christ's victory over sin and death accomplished through His suffering, death and rising to new life.

In celebrating the Pasch, the early Christians no longer focused so much on the exodus from Egypt, but on the new exodus from the slavery of sin into new life in the Risen Lord wrought by Christ. This new focus was central to each Sunday's celebration of the Eucharist, but the natural tendency was to historicize it by celebrating it yearly on the first Sunday after the fourteenth of Nisan (the date of the Jewish Passover). Not all accepted this way of computing the Easter date, but eventually the Council of Nicaea furthered uniformity by fixing it on the Sunday following the full moon after the vernal equinox. There are still difficulties between those who follow the Gregorian (Western) and Julian (Russian Orthodox) calendars.

The feast itself was considered the time to welcome new catechumens into the Church by Baptism at the Great Vigil, where the whole of salvation history was read. After Baptism, the catechumens were sealed by Confirmation and then made their First Communion at the Easter Eucharist. They had a long catechumenate with special preparation forty days before; and as all Christians began to see the need for preparation for the Easter feast, Lent developed. The vigil itself was kept in the night in the East, but in the West in the tenth century it was moved to the afternoon, and in the fourteenth century to the morning. Pope Pius XII permitted the Vigil Mass to be celebrated as such in the evening as an option in 1951 and made this practice obligatory in 1956. At this time, he restored all the Holy Week rites, especially those of the Triduum, which were further revised after Vatican II.

The spirit of the feast of Easter begins with the vigil and its festival of lights, symbolizing the Light of the Resurrection seen in the new fire, the Easter Candle, and the Exsultet. The Liturgy of the Word commences with the whole of the history of salvation commemorated in the readings from the Old and New Testaments. The Liturgy of Baptism takes place for those to be initiated, and the faithful renew their baptismal promises. All of this leads to the celebration of the Easter Eucharist in the middle of the night, which makes this night different from all other nights and the "mother of all vigils," in the words of St. Augustine. The next day at festive Easter Masses the baptismal promises are renewed by all the faithful who did not attend the vigil. The Easter Season lasts until Pentecost, with the Paschal Candle lit at Mass, Lauds and Vespers until then.

Easter Controversy • The Easter Controversy was a series of three distinct disputes over the date for the observance of Easter.

The first dispute was in the second century between Rome and a group of Christians in Asia Minor known as the Quartodecimans, who celebrated Easter on the day of the Jewish Passover. Rome maintained that Easter should be celebrated on the Sunday following Passover, and Pope Victor I attempted unsuccessfully to impose this custom on the Quartodecimans. Their practice continued until the group waned in the third century and finally disappeared in the fifth century.

The second controversy was engendered by difficulties in reconciling the lunar and solar calendars. The date of Passover, the fourteenth day of Nisan, was determined by the lunar calendar, but by the third century, most Christians were using the Julian solar calendar. Various competing schemes of multi-year cycles were proposed in Rome and Alexandria and at the Councils of Arles (A.D. 314) and Nicaea (325). It was apparently Nicaea which approved observing Easter on the first Sunday after the first full moon following the vernal equinox. This scheme was then gradually joined to the multi-year cycle of the Roman monk Dionysius, and by the eighth century, most of the Church observed the same date for Easter.

The final conflict arose in England between the Irish monks, who used the Celtic calendar, and St. Augustine of Canterbury, who used the Roman calendar. The Roman usage gradually prevailed throughout the British Isles, and by the ninth century, the observance of Easter was uniform in the Western Church.

Easter Duty • The obligation, established at the Fourth Lateran Council (1215), that the faithful were obliged to confess their sins and receive Holy Communion at least once a year during the Easter season. This precept is still binding (cf. Canon 920), with the common understanding that the period in question lasts from the First Sunday of Lent through Trinity Sunday.

Easter Season • "The fifty days from Easter Sunday to Pentecost are celebrated in joyful exultation as one feast day, or better as one 'great Sunday' (St. Athanasius)" (*Ceremonial of Bishops*, n. 371).

Prior to Pope Pius XII's reform of Holy Week (1956), the Holy Saturday morning "anticipated" celebration of the Easter Vigil led to the popular reckoning that "Lent ends at noon on Holy Saturday." The Calendar issued after the Second Vatican Council makes the ordering of this sacred time clearer still. Lent ends quietly during the afternoon of Holy Thursday, and the Easter Triduum begins with that evening's Mass of the Lord's Supper. On Good Friday the *paschal fast* (not the disciplinary fast of Lent but an anticipatory fast in preparation for Easter) is observed, prolonged whenever possible through Holy Saturday as well. The Triduum culminates in the Easter Vigil and closes (ideally) with the Easter Vespers (repeated instructions from the Holy See urge the restoration of "baptismal vespers," at which the psalms are sung in procession to the baptismal font, a procession in which the neophytes take part in their white robes as honored participants). Fifty days of Easter joy ensue.

According to the *Ceremonial*, "these above all others are the days for the singing of the Alleluia" (n. 371). The first eight days (Octave) are celebrated as solemnities of the Lord (the highest rank possible), and the double Alleluia with its ancient and beautiful chant closes every liturgy. The Easter Candle is lighted for Mass, Morning and Evening Prayer, and "all the more solemn liturgical celebrations of this season" (n. 372). The water blessed at the Easter Vigil is used for Baptism throughout the Easter Season. This is the time for the neophytes to receive "mystagogical catechesis," a deepening understanding of the paschal mystery and an ever greater assimilation of it in daily life through meditation, participation in the Eucharist and the practice of charity. The daily Scripture readings always include a passage from the Acts of the Apostles (as the Church relives her early history and shares it with the newly-baptized) and from *the* "Paschal Gospel," that of St. John.

On the fortieth day of the Easter Season, the ascension of the Lord is celebrated, and the nine days from Ascension to the Vigil of Pentecost (the original "novena") are an intensive preparation for the coming of the Holy Spirit. New texts were provided by the Holy See in 1988 for an extended Pentecost Vigil (in the form of an Office or Mass). The *Ceremonial* notes: "This sacred season of fifty days comes to an end on Pentecost Sunday, which commemorates the giving of the Holy Spirit to the apostles, the beginnings of the Church and its mission to every tongue and people and nation. On Pentecost the bishop as a rule celebrates a stational Mass and presides over the Liturgy of the Hours, especially Morning and Evening Prayer" (n. 376).

Easter Water • The holy water blessed during the celebration of the Easter Vigil is used for Christian Initiation on that night, for the renewal of baptismal promises at the Masses of Easter Day, and for Baptism throughout the Easter Season. The restoration of the elaborate blessing prayer for this water is most significant theologically and liturgically. It is important theologically because of the rich biblical images and traditions reflected in it. It is important liturgically because this same blessing prayer is used at baptisms celebrated at other times of the liturgical year. The revised *Book of Blessings* encourages pastors to continue the practice of blessing homes during this season as well, and the Easter Water with its powerful reminder of the baptismal covenant and ecclesial communion is most fittingly used for this blessing as well. By popular custom among many ethnic groups, and worthy of revival or introduction throughout the Church, is the practice of taking the Easter Water home from the Vigil celebration to be used for personal prayer and devotion in the setting of "the domestic church" of the household.

Eastern Churches • That division or group of four Churches tracing their origin to the original four patriarchates of Jerusalem, Antioch, Alexandria and Constantinople (Byzantium), and distinct from the Western Church of Rome, the fifth original patriarchate. To the Antiochene Church belong the West Syrians, Maronites and Malankarese, as well as the Chaldeans (Iraqi and Malabarese) and Armenians. To the Alexandrian Church belong Coptic and Ge'ez Ethiopians. The largest of the Eastern Churches is the Byzantine, among whom are Greeks, Bulgarians, Georgians, Italo-Albanians, Syrians (Melkite and Arab), Russians, Ruthenians, Ukrainians, Rumanians, Croatians, Yugoslavs,

Estonians, Hungarians and Serbians. All of the Eastern Churches, Orthodox and Catholic, have communities and jurisdictions permanently established in the United States.

The Eastern Schism in 1054 separated Constantinople from Rome and marked a major break in Christian unity that persists to our own time. Earlier schisms involving the Nestorians, Armenians, Coptics and Syrian Jacobite Churches have also contributed to the scandal of Christian disunity. There have been major reunions of Eastern Orthodox Churches with the Church of Rome in centuries past, chief of these being the Union of Brest Litovsk in 1596 among the Ukrainians and the Union of Uzhorod in 1646 among the Ruthenians. These and other reunions have earned in the eyes of Orthodox the pejorative term "Uniates" for Eastern Catholics. The Orthodox view the reunions as a submission or surrender to Latinism, a sacrifice of one's patrimony and native religious heritage for an artificial unity. Nonetheless, Eastern Catholics and Orthodox share a common tradition which includes for Roman Rite Catholics as well a valid sacramental system, orthodox moral teachings, a deep devotion to the Mother of God and the indelible stamp of the genius of the Eastern Fathers of the Church: Ignatius, Ephrem, Athanasius, Cyril of Jerusalem, Cyril of Alexandria, Gregory of Nyssa, Basil, Gregory of Nazianzus, John Chrysostom and John Damascene. Christian theology and monasticism began in the East before being adopted and modified in the West. For nine hundred years every ecumenical council took place in the East. Prayers borrowed from the Eastern Liturgies — the Kyrie, the Gloria, the Nicene Creed and others — are still in use today in the Roman Liturgy.

The Eastern Churches are rich in symbolism, mysticism and a deep sense of the transcendence of God. The Eastern Churches are organized under a system of collegiality. Local autonomy is emphasized, with the role of the local bishop stressed. The Church is seen as a theophany, that is, the manifestation of the eternal in time, an unfolding of the divine life through the deifying transformation of humanity in worship and sacrament. Life in the Eastern Churches is spoken of in terms of glory, light, vision, union and transfiguration.

The decree of the Second Vatican Council on the Eastern Churches emphasizes their equality with the Church of the West and enjoins Eastern Catholics to know and preserve their unique heritage while urging Westerners to become familiar with and to respect the rites, discipline, doctrine, history and characteristics of Easterners.

Eastern Churches, Decree on the Catholic: See **Orientalium Ecclesiarum**

Eastern Monasticism • Christian monasticism originated in the East, in particular in early third-century Egypt. St. Anthony (A.D. 251-356) sold all his possessions and went into the desert in order to follow Christ more perfectly. When his disciplined life of prayer and asceticism attracted followers to his place of retreat, he emerged from solitude for a time, in about 305, in order to organize them as a community of hermits under a rule of life. This formulation of a way of Christian life — given particular definition shortly thereafter in the Rule of St. Pachomius — marked the beginning of monasticism. The Eastern models were soon imitated in the West, notably by John Cassian and St. Martin of Tours. While Western monasticism came to be shaped decisively by St. Benedict's transformation of the Eastern models (his Rule dates from around 540), in the East it was the Rule of St. Basil the Great (dating from 358-364) that came to have the widest influence. In contrast to Western developments — where distinctive religious vocations and orders emerged — Eastern monasticism evolved essentially as two variants of the single tradition stretching back to St. Basil and beyond him to the Desert Fathers: in one form, the large community living under one roof (cenobitical); and in another form, a group of individuals living in separate quarters but coming together for common prayer and meals (idiorrhythmic). Monasticism flourished throughout the Byzantine Empire, spreading from Greece to Russia and the Slavic countries. The monastery at Mt. Athos in Greece occupies a position of particular eminence in the East and attracts monks from every branch of the Orthodox Church. Throughout the Communist period monasticism remained a powerful force — despite intense persecution — and has now emerged as an important source of Christian renewal in Eastern Europe.

Eastern Studies, Pontifical Institute of • This house of studies, situated near the Basilica of St. Mary Major in Rome, specializes in areas particular to the discipline of the Eastern Churches, both Catholic and Orthodox, under the direction of the Society of Jesus and affiliated with the Gregorian University. The Institute was founded in 1917 by Pope Benedict XV.

Ebionites • Jewish converts to Christianity who held that Christians were still bound by the Torah. They went on to deny the divinity of Christ, although they accepted Him as the Messiah. This title, they reasoned, was Jesus' in virtue of His Baptism by John and His perfection in the law. St. Paul, meanwhile, they branded an apostate. The Ebionites, as their Hebrew name implies, practiced extreme poverty and were vegetarians as well. By the fourth century, the last of the Ebionites were

absorbed into various Gnostic sects. (Cf. Jerusalem, Council of.)

For further reading: Stephen Goranson, "Ebionites," *Anchor Bible Dictionary*, 2:260-261; William L. Petersen, "Ebionites, Gospel of the," *Anchor Bible Dictionary*, 2:261-262.

Ecce Homo • This Latin phrase translates into English as "behold [here is] the man" and is taken from John 19:5 (Greek, *idou ho anthropos*), the words Pilate used to present a disfigured Jesus crowned with thorns to the chief priests and their attendants. The Gospel scenario just described is often depicted throughout the history of Western art as the beginning of Christ's passion.

The phrase has two other meanings. First, it also refers to renditions of Christ's resurrected body associated with either the Last Supper or other Eucharistic themes and as such is called "Eucharistic *Ecce Homo*." Second, in English-language literature the term *Ecce Homo* refers to an 1865 rendition of the life of Christ written (originally anonymously) by Sir John Seely in which Christ is depicted much less as the Divine Son of God and much more as the moral reformer. Even though the chief inspiration for the work was not the biblical witness, the publication flourished for a brief period of time. The credibility of the work was successfully challenged by many notables of the day, not the least of whom was John Henry Cardinal Newman.

Ecclesia • The term is a Latin transliteration from the Greek *ekklesia*, which has three semantic values in the New Testament.

First, at Acts 19:39 the term refers to an assembly of citizens gathered (the key concept) for political purposes.

Second, the use of the Greek term in the Old Testament (LXX) does express the notion of "gathering"; the term is a translation of the Hebrew word *kahal*, which refers to the assembly or gathering of God's people for a specific purpose: the worship of God (Dt 23; 1 Kgs 8; Ps 22:26). The choice of *ekklesia* as a translation for the Hebrew *kahal* is most appropriate, given that *ekklesia* comes from the verb *ekkaleo* meaning "I call from, I convoke." In the person of Abraham, Israel was called into the journey of salvation history and so was called into existence by God.

Third, the word refers to the Church of Christ; in particular, it can mean local meetings of the Church (1 Cor 11:18; 14:4ff.; 3 Jn 6); it can apply to a Christian community living in a specific region or location (Mt 18:17; Acts 5:11; Rom 16:1, 5; 1 Cor 1:2; Gal 1:22; 1 Thes 1:1); yet it can also refer to the universal Church (Mt 16:18; Acts 9:31; 1 Cor 12:28; Eph 1:22; 3:10; 1 Cor 10:32).

Ecclesiam Suam • Issued on August 6, 1964, *Ecclesiam Suam* (His Church) was the first encyclical letter to be written by Pope Paul VI. Published while the Second Vatican Council was still meeting, this encyclical refers to itself as a "conversational letter" which is not intended to interfere in any way with the proceedings of the Council; rather, its purpose is to share with the bishops "three thoughts" about the Church at the time when it was seeking both to renew itself internally and to prepare itself for its continuing apostolic efforts externally. The first thought is that the Church "should deepen its consciousness of itself," in considering its origin, its nature, its mission and its destiny. In doing this, the Church should strive to make the image which it projects to the world to be closer to the "ideal image of the Church just as Christ sees it, wills it,

Ecce Homo (Renaissance painting)

and loves it as His holy and immaculate Spouse. . . ."

The second thought is that, because it is "so clearly incumbent on the Church, of correcting the defects of its own members and of leading them to greater perfection," so a way must be found to accomplish this, and the encyclical calls upon the bishops to be courageous in undertaking the necessary reforms, and to advise and assist the Pope in implementing them.

The third thought is concerned with "the problem of the dialogue between the Church and the modern world." Because the world seems to have "come to the point of separating and detaching itself from the Christian foundations of its culture" so the Church must seek to present the Gospel in new and more effective ways. A major theme throughout the encyclical is that of dialogue, both within the Church and with those outside her circle, and it calls upon the bishops meeting in the Council to cooperate in that work.

Ecclesiastes, Book of • This wisdom book of the Old Testament appears under this Greek name, a translation of the Hebrew *Qoheleth*. The name, meaning "a member of the [religious] assembly," is broad enough to hide the identity of the author, as does the appellation "son of David." The son of David famous for wisdom was, of course, Solomon, and the book begins by claiming his authority, but modern scholars are sure that this book was written in the third century B.C.; both Jews and Christians accept the book as canonical.

The book emphasizes the vanity of merely human desires and achievements. Its outlook is pessimistic in the extreme and may be justified only when viewed in the context of a needed rebuke to arrogant and overconfident people. The traditional maxims on which such may rely are quoted and subjected to repeated rebuttals.

Like the Calvinism of a later age, Jewish theology rightly tended to emphasize the worth of hard work and virtuous living, as well as the earthly rewards they bring. It was just such a philosophy that raised the Jews from the abject misery with which their history began; after centuries of demoralizing slavery, they needed such motivation. However, the hard experience of

life does not always confirm such an outlook. The evil do prosper, and natural forces can frustrate the best-laid human plans. Qoheleth was wise enough to realize that much human unhappiness is caused by the conflicting efforts of people with unlimited ambitions. Unlike his superficial predecessors, he is insightful enough to realize that no single proverb encompasses all wisdom. At root, wisdom is knowing which proverb to recall at which time.

For all Qoheleth's pessimism, Ecclesiastes is not cynical. Rather, it preaches a sobering realism and counsels a moderate pursuit of this world's good things. One begins to see a new virtue emerging, the Christian virtue of detachment, along with the larger context of virtue and reward which includes the vision of a life to come which sets things right. In this way, Ecclesiastes needed to be supplemented, not by Job, but by Wisdom.

For further reading: James L. Crenshaw, "Ecclesiastes, Book of," *Anchor Bible Dictionary*, 2:271-280; Addison G. Wright, "Ecclesiastes (Qoheleth)," *New Jerome Biblical Commentary*, 489-495.

Ecclesiastic • A man who has been admitted to the clerical state. This is an informal term used to designate a member of the clergy.

Ecclesiastical • In a narrow sense, canon law uses the term ecclesiastical to describe certain types of Church property, the administration of which, because they belong to public juridic persons, is governed by the norms of the 1983 Code of Canon Law (Canon 1257).

In a wider sense, however, the term ecclesiastical may be used to describe those aspects of Church life which have developed in response to the needs of the times. It is contrasted, then, with the term ecclesial, which tends to denote those aspects of

Church life which perdure through the ages. Examples may be helpful.

That every diocese is to be headed by a bishop is an ecclesial facet of Church life because the Lord intended bishops to oversee His particular Churches, always and everywhere. But that bishops should be at least thirty-five years of age is an aspect of ecclesiastical life, because this age was determined by legitimate Church authority in the exercise of its governing responsibility. Other periods of time have seen different ages for bishops, but all ages have seen the office of bishop itself.

The above was an example of ecclesial institution, the episcopacy, being regulated in this century by an ecclesiastical provision, a minimum age. At other times, a whole institution might be ecclesiastical in origin, for example, a diocesan chancellor or conference of bishops, or the requirement of having a degree in canon law before assuming certain duties in a diocesan tribunal.

The distinction between the ecclesial and the ecclesiastical is not always easy to draw, nor, adding to the confusion, is the distinction always honored in speech or written word. It must be stressed, however, that the mutability of ecclesiastical provisions does not render them optional in the lives of the faithful, for such provisions partake ultimately in the authority of Christ expressed through His Holy Church. But keeping clear the useful distinctions between the ecclesial and the ecclesiastical is an aid to the ongoing process of reform and refinement in the life of the Church and her faithful. (Cf. Office, Ecclesiastical; Penalty, Ecclesiastical.)

Ecclesiastical Law • A law that has been enacted by competent ecclesiastical authority. An ecclesiastical law is not a repetition in Church law of a divine or natural law. Ecclesiastical laws include disciplinary laws, liturgical laws, procedural laws and penal laws. Most ecclesiastical laws of a disciplinary nature can be dispensed by local Ordinaries unless such dispensation has been reserved to the Holy See.

Ecclesiastical Regions • A grouping of neighboring ecclesiastical provinces that fosters cooperation and common pastoral action in the region. Ecclesiastical regions are created by the Holy See, often in large countries with a number of ecclesiastical provinces, such as the United States, or in areas where the ecclesiastical provinces of a number of small countries with some sort of common identity render regions advantageous.

Unlike the ecclesiastical province, the region has no preeminent see, nor do the combined bishops of the region have any special powers for the dioceses within the region. The region is not comparable to an episcopal conference (Canons 433-434).

Ecclesiastical Titles • The following titles are the standard forms for referring to ecclesiastical persons in the English language.

The Pope: His Holiness Pope N. (with number)

Cardinals: His Eminence N. Cardinal N.

Bishops and Archbishops: His Excellency N.N.

(In writing, one uses in the address: "The Most Reverend N.N., [Arch-]Bishop of N.")

Abbots: The Right Reverend Abbot N.N. (Speaking to: "Father Abbot.")

Monsignori: The Reverend Monsignor N.N. (Speaking to: "Monsignor.")

Priests: The Reverend [Father] N.N. (Speaking to: "Father.")

Abbess or Superior of Religious Women: [Reverend] Mother.

Ecclesiasticus: See **Sirach, Book of**

Ecclesiology • The study of the Church in all her dimensions, with emphasis on her nature, mission and structure. Scholars have pointed out that ecclesiology is essentially a synthesis of other branches of theology, since it is dependent on correct Trinitarian, Christological, patristic and even Mariological thought.

Valid ecclesiology begins with the Church's self-understanding as revealed in apostolic writings, conciliar documents and the like. It acknowledges that God has revealed and continues to reveal His will for the definition and direction of the Church.

Among the essential elements of Catholic ecclesiology are the doctrines that the Church is the Body of Christ, the People of God, founded on the Apostle Peter and under the pastoral care and universal episcopate of his successors. The Church is one, holy, catholic and apostolic, and carries out Christ's work for the redemption of mankind.

These basic teachings have been taught from the Apostolic Age and were reaffirmed vigorously in *Lumen Gentium*, the Dogmatic Constitution on the Church, issued at the Second Vatican Council. The same document admitted weakness within the Church. The Lord "came to call sinners." Thus, the Church, "clasping sinners to her bosom, at once holy and always in need of purification, follows constantly the path of penance and renewal" (LG 8).

École Biblique • An institution for higher study in the biblical sciences conducted by French Dominicans in Jerusalem. The school opened on November 15, 1890, under the direction of Père Marie-Joseph Lagrange, O.P. Its location in the city of Jerusalem is on the Nablus Road, in the vicinity of the Damascus Gate. Among the scholarly achievements of the École Biblique are the quarterly publication of the *Revue biblique* and the *Bible de Jérusalem* (1946 onward).

Economic Affairs, Prefecture of • This prefecture was established in 1967 by Pope Paul VI. Consisting of a commission of five or more cardinals, it oversees the administration of the finances, investments and properties of the Holy See.

Economics • The branch of the social sciences which seeks to understand the dynamics of human commercial relations, the exchange of goods and services, and the material advances of societies. It attempts to articulate the laws, patterns and dynamics that govern these activities. The Church holds that all these relations and activities are to be guided by the moral requirements that govern all other human activities. She further holds that economics is to aim at the material advancement of peoples and to seek to learn more fully the laws, economic patterns and dynamics that enhance the material prosperity of peoples.

Economics has become an increasingly important field of study because many of the greatest of the world's ills are economic. The contemporary global problem of feeding the world's hungry is more a problem of economics than food production, and many of the uprisings and revolutionary movements originate more from economic than from political causes. The Church urges greater efforts to understand economic forces and problems and the development of new economic theories, in the hope that these will operate to alleviate many of the crushing burdens of poverty throughout the world.

For further reading: John Paul II, *Sollicitudo Rei Socialis*; John Paul II, *Centesimus Annus*.

Economy, Divine • The orderly dispensation of God's plan of salvation, which existed fully developed in the divine mind from all eternity, but was revealed only with the coming of Christ: His incarnation, redemptive death and resurrection, and ascension. This divine plan embraces all creation, which in the "fullness of time" is to be "set forth in Christ" (Eph 1:9-10). Before the coming of Christ, it was not known, except obscurely through the prophets, but since the ascension of Christ, it is the substance of the apostolic preaching. Included in the divine plan, as a guarantee of its final fulfillment, is the gift of the Spirit, Who directs the apostolic preaching, protects its integrity through succeeding generations in the Church and applies the fruits of Christ's redemption to human beings by means of the sacraments.

In the theological tradition of the Eastern Churches, the word economy has a technical meaning as the branch of theology which studies the restoration of friendship between God and man in Christ. In the same tradition, it has a secondary meaning as the merciful application of the Church's canonical power to particular cases.

Ecstasy • The state of "standing outside oneself," or the elevation of the soul above the senses, which is the effect of the Holy Spirit giving a person in prayer an experience of union with God. In Sacred Scripture, ecstasy accompanies the communication of God's Word to the prophets, and in the New Testament, both St. Peter and St. Paul are said to have gone into ecstasy while praying (Acts 10:10; 22:17).

In Christian mysticism, ecstasy is a temporary state which accompanies contemplative prayer: it is an intense, though passing, awareness of the soul's union with God, which may be either pleasant (as when sensory awareness is gently suspended) or painful (as when the soul is suddenly "seized away" from its senses). A person in ecstasy is usually radiant in the face and unaware of anything around him (including things touching him).

Ecstasy is a by-product of prayer, whose object is not to produce an experience but to progress in the love of God. Deliberate attempts to produce ecstasy (as in Transcendental Meditation) are not consistent with Christian prayer and may be both psychologically and spiritually dangerous.

For further reading: Helmer Ringgren, "Ecstasy," *Anchor Bible Dictionary*, 2:280-281.

Ecthesis • The formula — drafted by Sergius, patriarch of Constantinople, imposed by Emperor Heraclius and accepted by councils convoked at Constantinople in A.D. 638 and 639 — in which it was asserted that the divine and human natures in Christ are united in one will (hence, "Monothelitism"). Heraclius later repudiated the formula, and Popes Severinus (638-640) and John IV (640-642) condemned it as heretical. Since will is a capacity that forms part of the very nature of a rational being, Monothelitism in effect represented a reversion to Monophysitism in denying Christ's fully human and fully divine natures, united but unconfused in the one Person.

Ecumenical Councils: See **Councils, Ecumenical**

Ecumenical Theology • This term can refer to a variety of ecumenically conceived approaches to theology and to the relations among the Christian confessions. Two important approaches to ecumenically conceived theology can be distinguished here: thematic and procedural.

A thematic approach to ecumenical theology involves the study of the doctrinal disagreements which have divided the various ecclesial communities, and the analysis of the results of the bilateral and multilateral dialogues launched in recent years to overcome the divisions they have spawned. In thematic ecumenical theology, the confessional and ecclesial identities of the various Christian traditions remain matters of central concern. In addition, theology can be procedurally ecumenical when it reflects an acquaintance with sources and thinkers representing a diversity of Christian confessional traditions. Ecumenical theology in this sense may also be transconfessional in its methods, themes and conclusions.

Ideally, in present circumstances, ecumenical theology will combine both thematic and procedural approaches. In recent times, however, procedurally ecumenical theology has manifested a decreasing sense of the importance of ecumenical and confessional identities, and thus of the need to pursue the sort of dialogue that will foster institutional unity. It remains to be seen whether theology practiced ecumenically can combine the strengths of both thematic and procedural approaches to the diversity of affirmation represented by the distinctive traditions and confessions of worldwide Christianity.

Ecumenism, Decree on: See **Unitatis Redintegratio**

Eden, Garden of • The word Eden means "prairie" or "steppe." In the Old Testament, it refers to a place of happiness and immortality (cf. Gn 2:8); Adam and Eve enjoyed God's garden (cf. Gn 13:10); they were banished from it (cf. Gn 3:23). Scripture sets the Garden of Eden "in the east," where God planted a garden by the river and placed man whom He created (cf. Gn 1:26-29). Eden is described as fertile and with beautiful trees; from it came four rivers: Pishon, Gihon, Tigris and Euphrates (cf. Gn 1-2). Later Scripture writers mention Eden as an illustration of a delightful place (cf. Is 51:3; Ez 28:13; Jl 2:3).

For further reading: Howard N. Wallace, "Eden, Garden of," *Anchor Bible Dictionary,* 2:281-283.

Edict of Milan • More of an agreement between the Roman co-emperors, Constantine I and Licinius, reached in February A.D. 313, in the city of Milan. It allowed Christianity to exist as one of the sects tolerated within the empire, thus theoretically ending the era of persecution.

Edict of Nantes • Following seven separate military campaigns between the French Calvinist Huguenots and the basically pro-Catholic French monarchy was King Henry IV's attempt to forge a peace between the contending factions. The 1598 agreement restored the rights of the Catholic clergy and granted freedom of worship to the Huguenots, along with control of some hundred cities, most in southwestern France. After some reinforcement by the Treaty of Alais, King Louis XIV, seeking alleged political advantages, revoked the Edict of Nantes and launched a persecution of the Huguenots, which in turn led to the emigration of nearly 300,000 adherents of the system. The subsequent disapproval of this action by the Holy Father Bl. Innocent XI contributed to a serious rift between the Papacy and the Church in France, lasting several years.

Edict of Restitution • A decree issued by Ferdinand II, the Holy Roman Emperor, in 1629, hoping to restore Catholic supremacy and further Hapsburg dominance. It was issued by the emperor after a string of victories by imperial forces during the Thirty Years' War, without consultation of the Diet. Among its provisions were the restitution of all Church property, the outlawing of all Protestants except Lutherans of the Augsburg Confession, and the reinstatement of the principle *Cuius regio eius religio,* whereby religion became a regional matter. Reacting against the enforcement of this edict, Gustavus II Adolphus intervened on the Protestant side.

Edification, Christian • From the Latin *aedificare* (literally, to build a house or temple; more specifically in a religious sense, to give instruction, especially of a spiritual nature), edification within the Christian community begins with the recognition by the individual members of the need to build up one another into the Temple of the Holy Spirit (1 Cor 14:5), especially as the edifice of living stones which make up the Church (Eph 4:1-6, 25-32). The concept of Christian edification finds particular expression in the Pauline letters (cf. Rom 14:17-18; 2 Cor 10:8), where St. Paul elaborates on the need for edification by the witness of good example for the upbuilding of the Mystical Body of Christ.

Christian edification is further developed by Cardinal Newman in his *Pastoral Sermon IV, 170*: "This then is the special glory of the Christian Church, that its members do not depend merely on what is visible, they are not mere stones of a building, piled one on another, and bound together from without, but they are one and all the births and manifestations of one and the same unseen spiritual principle or power, 'living stones,' internally connected, as branches from a tree, not as the parts of a heap. They are members of the Body of Christ. That divine and adorable form, which the Apostles saw and handled, after ascending into heaven became a principle of life, a secret origin of existence to all who believe, through the gracious ministration of the Holy Ghost. . . . So that in a true sense it may be said that from the day of Pentecost to this hour there has been in the Church but one Holy One, the King of kings, and Lord of lords Himself, Who is in all believers, and through Whom

they are what they are; their separate persons being but as separate developments, vessels, instruments, and works of Him Who is invisible."

For Cardinal Newman, like St. Paul before him, the Christian community by its mutual edification, in fact, builds up the very Mystical Body of Christ, members and Head in total union.

Editio Typica • "Official version," *editio typica*, is the original, authoritative and legally binding text of an ecclesiastical document. Only the *editio typica* of a document carries the weight of law, and all translations of the same (where they are permitted) must be in conformity with the original text and receive the prior approval of the author of the document.

Education, Declaration on Christian: See Gravissimum Educationis

Efficacious Grace • The aspect of actual grace in which free consent is given, so that it produces the desired effect. Báñez and the Dominicans held that the efficacy of such grace depended on the grace itself, while the Jesuits and Molina contended that it is given in situations congruous to the dispositions of the recipient. Both agreed that the act of the will was not necessary and that it would achieve its results without the volitional act.

Eileton • In the Byzantine Rite, a piece of linen spread out on a consecrated altar beneath the chalice and the paten. It is now generally replaced by the Antimension, but its name is retained by the outer wrapping of the Antimension.

Ejaculation • A short prayer, usually a phrase or brief sentence, prayed frequently from memory. When the psalter became less known by laypersons, prayers such as the

Our Father, Hail Mary and ejaculations took their place as the staple of the way to fulfill the injunction to "pray always." Early examples include: "Have mercy on me, God; Forgive me my sins, Lord," "My Lord and my God," "My Jesus, mercy." The revised edition of the *Enchiridion* (Handbook) *of Indulgences* (June 29, 1968; English translation, 1969), which replaced the *Raccolta*, contains many examples of ejaculations.

Ekphonese • In the Churches of the East, the elevation of the voice of the priest at the end of certain prayers, or the parts of the prayers that are said aloud.

Ektene • A litany. There are two Ektenes recited during the celebration of the Divine Liturgy in the Byzantine Rite.

Elect • The elect are God's people chosen by Him to live with Him in love for all eternity. Their purpose on earth includes their participation in God's saving action of reconciling all things to Himself. The existence of the "elect" is grounded in a deliberate and sovereign act of God, Who, in the language of the Old Testament, "sets His heart" on a people, Israel (Dt 4:37ff.; 7:6ff.). The language of "election" in the Old Testament (Hebrew, *bhr* and cognates) and New Testament (Greek, *eklegomai* and cognates) are without true synonyms.

This linguistic peculiarity strongly suggests that this biblical language expresses a precise and technical meaning not found in other terminology. One aspect of this language is that it reveals a characteristic of God — He is the One Who elects, chooses and makes a people. Even prior to choosing Abraham ("I took your father Abraham," Jos 24:3; cf. also Jos 24:15; Ex 34:9; 19:5), God made choices, manifesting preferences in accord with His plan to reconcile the cosmos back to Himself (e.g., Cain: Gn 4:4-5; Enoch: Gn 5:24; Noah:

Gn 7:1; etc.). His call to the patriarchs and prophets participates in the forming of a people for His purposes (e.g., Isaac: Gn 18:19), namely, to be a blessing not for themselves alone but for the whole earth (Gn 12:3; 22:18; 26:4; 28:14). Just as the rejection of God and His choice brings special consequences for the elect (Jer 31:11; Hos 11:8; Ez 20:32), so also does God reassure His beloved of His desire to pursue and reclaim His people even after infidelity on the part of the elect (Zec 1:17; 2:16; 3:8; Is 14:1; 6:13).

In short, God continually pursues the elect (Is 41:8; 43:10, 20; 45:4; 65:9, 15, 22). Why? The elect are to be a holy people (Dt 14:2), a consecrated nation who above all nations gives honor and glory to God, Who is creator of all (Dt 26:19). In the New Testament, Jesus is God's Chosen One (i.e., Messiah), God's Elect (Mk 13:20-27; Mt 22:14; Ti 1:1; 1 Pt 1:2; 2:4-6, 9-10). The reference to Jesus as "my elect one" at Luke 9:35 and 23:35 echoes the "words of God" in the language of Psalm 89:4 and that of Isaiah 42:1. In Revelation 17:14, those connected with the Lamb are called the "chosen." In this instance we have a clear shift in the application of language — the language of election once applied to Israel in the Old Testament is, now in the New Testament, applied to the Church (Acts 13:17; Is 45:4), who are God's elect (Ti 1:1). The Church is the royal priesthood, the holy nation, God's own people (1 Pt 2:9; Is 43:20; Ex 19:4-6). In Ephesians 1:4, we learn most clearly about God's choice for a Church holy and blameless — a choice made before the cosmos was ever formed (cf. 1 Pt 1:2, 15, 16, alluding to Lv 11:44, 45).

In summary, the elect were chosen by God to live with Him in holiness and blamelessness before the creation of the cosmos. The elect's identity begins in the person of Abraham and reaches its fullest manifestation in the Person of Christ and in the Church, the gathered "elect."

For further reading: Dale Patrick and Richard E. DeMaris, "Election," *Anchor Bible Dictionary*, 2:434-445.

Election, Canonical • Election is one of the oldest means of provision for ecclesiastical offices. Canon law determines which offices are eligible for provision by election. As a practical matter, most elections for ecclesiastical office occur in the context of religious institutes, but this is by no means an absolute rule. Canons 164 to 179 of the 1983 Code of Canon Law contain the general norms on the conduct of ecclesiastical elections. It should be noted, however, that particular law might vary from some of these norms.

Elections are not to be needlessly delayed; three months is the general time allotted to fill an office (Canon 165). All those eligible to vote must be notified of the election. If at least one of those eligible (but fewer than one-third of the total number) is overlooked, that one has the right to have an election rescinded, provided he or she makes recourse against the election within three days of receiving notice of it (Canon 166). If more than one-third of those eligible are not properly notified, however, the election is automatically invalid. Notably, politicking is strongly discouraged by Canon 626.

Voters must cast their ballots in person, and may cast only one ballot, even if they hold several offices (Canons 167-168) to which a voting right is attached. Naturally, only those eligible to vote may do so, and the voting must be free, certain and unconditional (Canons 169-172). Generally, Canons 119 and 176 require that an absolute majority be gained for one to be considered elected. Special provisions are made for a larger group to choose a smaller subgroup to effect an election by "compromise" (Canons 174-175). Canon 349

indicates that special rules govern the election of the Roman Pontiff.

Election, Papal • The normal manner of selecting a Pope. The election is governed by the Code of Canon Law and any subsequent norms established by the Pope. All cardinals who have not reached the age of eighty are eligible to vote. The cardinals are locked in conclave and the vote is by secret ballot. A candidate must receive two-thirds plus one of the votes cast and accept election to be declared elected.

Eleemosynary Office • This is an office within the Vatican City State which assists in the coordination of the smaller projects of charity carried on by the Holy See. It is an extremely old office within the Curia (dating back at least to the time of Pope Gregory X) and concentrates on the corporal works of mercy.

As an aside, if one looks carefully at the certificates representing the special papal matrimonial blessings which are a common gift at Catholic weddings, one will note that many are granted under the signature of the Archbishop Eleemosynary, who uses the donations which accompany the requests for such certificates to further the charitable outreach of the Holy See.

Elevation at Mass • The first documented reference to the elevation of the Host at Mass is in a manual written for priests by Peter of Roissy (d. c. 1213). This text refers to an elevation connected with words describing Jesus' actions at the Last Supper ("He took bread in His holy and venerable hands"), not with the words of consecration which follow. At the elevation, it was customary for the people to prostrate "with their hands joined and raised to heaven." Between 1205 and 1208, a synod was held at Paris to deal with a number of questions regarding the Eucharist, among them: the controversy about the moment of consecration, the already popular form of elevation in its early form (with the danger of encouraging material idolatry if the people adored the Host before it was actually consecrated), and questions about unintentional mishaps in the celebration of Mass. The synod insisted on a consecratory elevation, by stating that priests "are to hold [the Host] just in front of their chest until they have said the words, 'This is my body.' At that point, they elevate the Host, so that all may see It." The elevation of the chalice, as well as a genuflection after the consecration of the bread and another after the consecration of the wine, appeared in the fourteenth century. These practices gained universal acceptance with the Missal of Pius V (the so-called "Tridentine Missal") in 1570.

An additional elevation (sometimes called the "little elevation") of the Eucharistic bread and chalice together occurs at the end of the Eucharistic Prayer just before and accompanying the words "Through him, with him, in him. . . ." This gesture is actually more ancient than that used at the institution narrative, and it coincides with the earliest known acclamation of the people at Mass, the Great Amen. It has also been commented upon in terms that bring out some of the sacrificial aspects of the Eucharist.

The present Order of Mass states that at the beginning of the institution narrative, the priest takes the bread, "raising it a little above the altar," and that after the words "This is my body which will be given up for you" he "shows the consecrated host to the people, places It on the paten, and genuflects in adoration." He does the same with the chalice. Before the doxology at the end of the Eucharistic prayer the priest "takes the chalice and the paten with the host and, lifting them up, sings or says, 'Through him, with him, in him. . . .' " The

1975 revised edition of the *General Instruction of the Roman Missal* states that "depending on local custom [the server] also rings the bell at the showing of both the host and the chalice" (n. 109). In addition, the 1975 *General Instruction* states that one of the places when incense may be used is "at the showing of the Eucharistic Bread and chalice after the consecration" (n. 235).

Elizabethan Settlement • The term refers to the series of legislative provisions enacted by Queen Elizabeth of England during the sixteenth century which cemented the Anglican Schism launched by Henry VIII three decades earlier. By 1560, the English monarchy was, according to these laws, vested with final authority in matters of religion. The anti-Catholic nature of the "settlement" waxed and waned with the decades, but perdured basically intact for centuries. (Cf. Church and State; Josephism; Caesaropapism.)

Elkesaites • A second-century heretical group of Jewish Christians whose name derives from the Book of Elkesai, sacred writings alleged to have been revealed to Elkesai. Similar to other heretical forms of Jewish Christianity (e.g., the Nazarenes and Ebionites), the Elkesaites regarded Jesus as one of the prophets, but otherwise as a man like other men. Possibly deriving from sectarian Judaism, they appear to have had a strong ascetical bent. Frequent purification by water baths and washings seems to have been a central feature of their religious practice.

Elne, Council of • The "Truce of God" was proclaimed by a canon of this council held southwest of Marseilles in 1027. It prohibited hostile engagements between Saturday night and Monday morning. This enactment was an important early step in the sustained effort on the part of the

Church to cultivate peace among the warring feudal lords throughout medieval times by ordering the temporary suspension of hostilities at least on designated days and during certain times of the year.

Elvira, Council of • The Council of Elvira (near modern Granada) was the earliest Spanish council of which records have survived. Convened about A.D. 300 and attended by nineteen bishops, the council enacted over eighty canons on a variety of disciplinary, non-doctrinal matters. The tone of the canons is strongly penitential and includes early affirmation of the value of clerical celibacy, among other things. Some fourteen of the canons enacted at Elvira were deemed useful enough to be carried into the Council of Nicaea.

Ember Days • These are the Wednesdays, Fridays and Saturdays of four weeks of the year on which fast and abstinence were required for the universal Church in preconciliar custom and liturgical legislation. Their origins are difficult to define precisely. Controverted matters include whether there were three or four originally and whether they originally corresponded to the four seasons of the calendar.

Pope Leo the Great repeatedly reminded his listeners of the nature of the days: that they ought to fast on Wednesday and Friday and keep vigil (like the Easter Vigil) on Saturday, whose Eucharistic Liturgy contained a number of lessons (usually six or twelve) with accompanying collects. The Roman tradition associated Ember Days with agrarian concerns, including sowing and reaping festivals. In addition, there has been a close connection between these days of prayer and fasting with ordination. The notion of a preceding vigil of prayer made Ember Saturdays an obvious choice for ordinations, a custom exemplified as early as the era of Pope Gelasius (d. 494).

The 1969 *General Norms for the Liturgical Year and the Calendar* describes Ember Days as days on which "the practice of the Church is to offer prayers to the Lord for the needs of all people, especially for the productivity of the earth and for human labor, and to give him public thanks" (n. 45). The local conference of bishops is to determine the "time and plan of their celebration" (n. 46). "On each day of these celebrations the Mass should be one of the votive Masses for various needs and occasions that is best suited to the intentions of the petitioners" (n. 47). (Cf. Days of Prayer.)

Emblems of Saints • Since few pictures of the early saints exist and certainly none survive from their lifetime, the Church has employed a system of symbols or signs associated with particular saints to signify by these emblems what saint is depicted or intended by the artist. As the frescoes of the catacombs attest, early Christian artists were surely capable of skilled representations of the human form, but possibly they still felt the Old Testament restrictions against depicting the divine in human form and extended that prohibition to those close to God, the saints, and for that reason preferred only the emblematic or symbolic representation of the saints. In parallel fashion, the depiction of Christ in human form upon the cross is seen for the first time only in the third century.

Even when the saints were eventually represented as they were known or remembered in their physical form, emblems still remained popular as a way of distinguishing similar saints from one another and also as an aid in identifying saints from a distance, as was required for those depictions of saints in mosaics, typical of the domes of Byzantine churches, and in stained glass, popular in the Gothic style from the twelfth century on.

The halo, nimbus or aureole, representative of the divine presence emanating from the head of the saint, is the symbol of sanctity for all the saints. When a saintly person was depicted during his lifetime, a square halo was used, though such recognition was quite rare. The halo behind the head of Christ has a cross inside it.

Symbols of Christ include the devices of His passion (cross, nails, crown of thorns, lance, sponge, whip) and the banner of His victory over death. The fish is a symbol of Christ, since the Greek *ichthys* (fish) contains the first letters of the Greek phrase for "Jesus Christ, Son of God, Savior." A common symbol for Christ is the Latin representation of the first three letters of the name of Jesus in Greek: IHS. Iconography commonly shows Christ as the Teacher, Judge or Good Shepherd.

Of all the saints, Mary and Joseph are the most frequently depicted in Christian art. In Catholic churches, it is usual to have two altars or shrines dedicated to the Mother of God and to Christ's foster father. St. Joseph's foremost symbol is the lily, often flowering at the end of his staff; he is

Dragon, emblem of
St. Margaret of Antioch

recognized by his carpenter's tools, apron, saw, hammer, square and plane. He is usually shown with the Christ Child at his side. Generally, he wears a brown cloak to signify the earth and so to symbolize Christ's human nature. The Blessed Virgin Mary is always shown in a blue mantle to signify the heavens and to call to mind her Son's Divine Nature. Often she carries the Infant Jesus in her arms. She has the largest number of symbols associated with any one saint. The lily (especially in the form of the *fleur-de-lis*) is the most common symbol of her virginity; it is the flower of the Annunciation. Other symbols of her virginity, with special allusion to Songs 4:12, are the enclosed garden, a closed well, a fountain and a closed gate. The mythic unicorn is a popular medieval symbol of the Blessed Virgin, since the unicorn could be captured only once it rested in the lap of a virgin; so Christ could only be born from the womb of the Virgin.

In representations of the Immaculate Conception, Mary stands on a crescent moon (cf. Sg 6:10 and Rv 12:1) and has a halo consisting of twelve stars representing the twelve tribes of Israel, the twelve patriarchs of the Old Testament, and the

Twelve Apostles of the New Testament. A single star represents Mary's virginity and is also her attribute as the Star of the Sea (*Stella Maris*) and as Star of Jacob (Nm 24:17). Either the sun or the moon alone represents Mary as the woman from the Apocalypse (Rv 12:1).

Since Gabriel's *Ave* literally reversed *Eva* and the consequences of Eve's sin, Mary is understood as the "new Eve" and is often shown with objects that refer to Eve, such as the apple and the serpent, the head of which Mary or her Offspring crushes underfoot. Other symbols of Mary include: a mirror, referring to Mary's nature as a reflection of God; a tower, for she is the Tower of David (cf. Sg 4:4); a rose, as the Mystical Rose, the rose without thorns; an olive or palm branch, symbolic of Mary's triumph over death; a cedar, equating Mary's beauty, strength and dignity with that of the cedar of Lebanon. A book, when closed or sealed, refers to Mary's chastity; an open book signifies her wisdom.

Mary's mother, St. Anne, is usually shown with her daughter by her side; her father, St. Joachim, is recognized by the turtledoves in a cage, which he carries for Mary's Presentation in the Temple.

The four Evangelists are known by the symbols or their Gospels: St. Matthew, by a winged man, since he stressed Christ's humanity; St. Mark, by a winged lion, for he presented Christ as the Lion of Judah; St. Luke, by an ox, because he was meticulous in presenting the most mundane matters; St. John, by an eagle, since his Gospel is thought of as taking flight on the wings of an eagle. St. Luke is also shown with a paintbrush and palette, symbolic of the tradition that he was an artist.

St. Peter is usually shown with the keys of the kingdom entrusted to him (Mt 16:19); a boat symbolizes that he guides the barque of Christ; the cock refers to his triple denial of Christ (Mt 26:69-75; Mk 14:66-72; Lk 22:55-62; Jn 18:17-27). St. Peter is often represented alongside St. Paul (as they appear in front of St. Peter's Basilica in Rome), who usually holds a book or scroll and a sword, representing his martyrdom. Similarly, all of the Apostles are symbolized by the instruments of their martyrdom, some with other details from their lives:

St. Andrew: Saltire (bent) cross, fish

St. Bartholomew: Curved knife, flayed skin

St. James the Greater: Sword, pilgrim's staff, shell, key

St. James the Less: Halberd, fuller's club, square rule

St. John the Evangelist: Chalice with poison (from the unsuccessful attempt to martyr him)

St. Jude: Sword, club

St. Matthew: Lance, purse

St. Matthias: Ax, open Bible

St. Peter: Inverted cross

St. Philip: Column, serpent, three loaves of bread

St. Simon: Saw, book with a fish

St. Thomas: Lance, ax, carpenter's square

The Apostles are thus depicted as a group at the Basilica of St. John Lateran in Rome. Judas Iscariot, not a saint, is symbolized by a rope or money bag.

Common symbols of the saints include the following:

Ax, lance or club: instruments of martyrdom

Book or pen: scholarship

Crown or other royal emblem: royalty, or victory over sin and death

Crucifix or cross: exceptional sanctity

Flag or banner: military service

Lily and rose: virgin-martyr

Lion: hermits

Mitre or crosier: bishops, abbots or abbesses

Palm, olive branch, or sword: martyrs

Triple tiara: Popes

Wolf, bear or other wild beast: ability to convert the savage pagans

Sometimes a saint is shown holding a building; often it is a miniature of the church or monastery in which the image of the saint is located. As such, this depiction is meant to invoke the aid of the saint in protecting the building under his patronage.

Saints not discussed elsewhere in this entry, with the emblems commonly associated with them, are listed below:

St. Agatha: tongs, veil

St. Agnes: lamb

St. Ambrose: bees, dove, ox, pen

St. Angela Merici: ladder, cloak

St. Anthony, Hermit: bell, hog

St. Apollonia: tooth

St. Augustine of Hippo: heart, dove, shell, child

St. Barbara: cannon, chalice, palm, tower

St. Barnabas: ax, lance, stones

St. Benedict: bell, broken cup, bush, crozier, raven

St. Bernard of Clairvaux: pen, bees, instruments of Christ's passion

St. Blaise: iron comb, two crossed candles

St. Bonaventure: cardinal's hat, ciborium

St. Boniface: ax, book, fox, fountain, oak, raven, scourge, sword

St. Bridget of Kildare: Cross, candle, flame over her head

St. Bridget of Sweden: book, pilgrim's staff

St. Bruno: chalice

St. Catherine of Alexandria: lamb, sword, wheel

St. Catherine de' Ricci: crown, crucifix, ring

St. Catherine of Siena: cross, lily, ring, stigmata

St. Cecilia: organ

St. Christopher: Christ Child, giant, torrent, tree

St. Clare: monstrance

St. Colette: birds, lamb

Sts. Cosmas and Damian: box of ointment, vial

St. Cyril of Alexandria: Blessed Virgin holding the Child Jesus, pen

St. Cyril of Jerusalem: book, purse

St. Dominic: rosary, star

St. Dorothy: flowers, fruit

St. Edmund: arrow, sword

St. Elizabeth of Hungary: bread, flowers, pitcher

St. Eustace: Roman soldier, stag with crucifix between his antlers, oven

St. Francis of Assisi: birds, deer, fish, skull, stigmata, wolf

St. Francis Xavier: bell, crucifix, ship, flame, lily

St. Genevieve: bread, candle, herd, keys

St. George: dragon

St. Gertrude: crown, lily, taper

Sts. Gervase and Protase: club, scourge, sword

St. Giles: crozier, hermitage, hind

St. Gregory the Great: crosier, dove, tiara

St. Helena: cross

St. Hilary: child, pen, stick

St. Hubert: stag with the crucifix

St. Isidore: bees, pen

St. Jerome: lion, skull, raven, cardinal's hat

St. Joan of Arc: armor, banner of France, fleur-de-lis

St. John the Baptist: head on platter, lamb, skin of animal

St. John Berchmans: Rule of St. Ignatius, cross, rosary

St. John Chrysostom: bees, dove, pen

St. John Climacus: ladder

St. John of God: alms, crown of thorns, heart

St. Josaphat: chalice, crown, winged deacon

St. Justin Martyr: ax, sword

St. Lawrence: book of Gospels, cross, gridiron, dalmatic, coins

St. Leander: pen

St. Liborius: pebbles, peacock

St. Longinus: lance

St. Louis: crown of thorns, nails, crusader's cross

St. Lucy: cord, eyes, lantern

St. Margaret: dragon, pearl

St. Martha: dragon, holy water jar

St. Martin of Tours: cloak shared with beggar, goose

St. Mary Magdalene: alabaster box of ointment

St. Matilda: alms, purse

St. Maurus: crutch, scales, spade

St. Meinrad: two ravens

St. Michael Archangel: banner, dragon, scales, sword

St. Monica: girdle, tears

St. Nicholas: anchor, three boys in boat, three purses or balls

St. Patrick: shamrock, baptismal font, cross, harp, serpent

St. Rita: crucifix, rose, thorn

St. Roch (Rocco): angel, bread, dog

St. Rose of Lima: anchor, city, crown of thorns

St. Scholastica: lily, crucifix, dove at her feet

St. Sebastian: arrows, crown

Sts. Sergius and Bacchus: military uniform, palm

St. Simon Stock: scapular

St. Stephen: dalmatic, stones

St. Teresa of Ávila: arrow, book, heart

St. Thomas Becket: altar and long swords

St. Ursula: arrow, clock, ship, white banner with red cross

St. Veronica: veil with imprint of Christ's face and the crown of thorns

St. Vincent: boat and gridiron

St. Vincent de Paul: children

St. Vincent Ferrer: captives, cardinal's hat, pulpit, trumpet

While some of the more recent saints are recognized from their physical features, other devices, such as their episcopal coats of arms and mottoes, make them more readily identifiable. St. Charles Borromeo, who is usually shown in his cardinal's choir dress and holding the Host, is thus distinguished by his coat of arms with the motto "Humilitas" from his episcopal contemporaries — St. Philip Neri, who is usually represented standing in a chasuble before the altar and holding a vial, and St. Francis de Sales, who is usually dressed in a manner similar to that of St. Charles and St. Philip but is always shown with a pen and a copy of *Philothea*, *The Introduction to the Devout Life*, or his *Treatise on the Love of God*. St. Ignatius of Loyola is usually shown in Mass vestments and a shield with the letters IHS, symbolic of the Society of Jesus of which he was the founder; St. Bernardine of Siena is also depicted with a tablet or sun inscribed with IHS, but his Franciscan habit distinguishes him from St. Ignatius; similarly, St. Anthony of Padua is always depicted in the Franciscan habit, but is distinguished from other Franciscan saints by his emblems of the lily and bread and by his depiction as holding the Christ Child above an open book.

St. Thomas Aquinas, whose girth alone distinguishes him from most other Dominican saints, is also identifiable by the sun emblazoned on the front of his habit. He is also recognizable from the typical depiction of him composing the *Summa Theologiae*, while the Lord addresses him from the cross: "You have spoken well of Me, Thomas." In a similar fashion, St. Margaret Mary is always recognized from her depiction as receiving the message of the Sacred Heart; her habit of the Visitation Sisters is seen again in representations of St. Jane Frances de Chantal, who is usually shown holding a heart inscribed with the words "Vive Jésus," in recognition of her extreme ascetic action of carving those words on her own breast.

Modern saints are seldom associated with emblems, since they are immediately identifiable from their portraits or photographs. Thus, St. Elizabeth Ann Seton, Bl. Katharine Drexel, and Bl. Kateri Tekakwitha are easily recognized, and the distinctive habits of the Sisters of Charity and of the Most Blessed Sacrament and the typical garb of the Mohawks aid in their identification. Likewise, St. Maximilian Kolbe is more readily recognized from the uniform he wore to his martyr's death in a Nazi concentration camp; St. John Neumann is easily identified from the combination of his episcopal dress and Redemptorist habit. St. Thérèse of Lisieux, the Little Flower, is identified with the roses entwining the crucifix.

Embolism • At the celebration of the Eucharist, the rites introducing the reception of Communion include the recitation of the Lord's Prayer, the embolism, the doxology, the sign of peace and the Lamb of God. The nature of the embolism is that it derives from and offers a fuller development of some part of the Our Father. An important Roman example of the embolism, the *Libera* of the Tridentine Mass, may well date from the time of St. Gregory the Great. In the *Libera*, the Apostles Andrew, Peter and Paul are asked to intercede for the present congregation, along with "the blessed and glorious ever-virgin Mary, Mother of God," so that the faithful may enjoy peace as they come to share in the Eucharist. Many Eastern Rites add similar extensions of the Lord's Prayer. Liturgical tradition attests to the use of a variety of texts at this point.

The present *General Instruction of the Roman Missal* notes that the embolism beginning with "Deliver us . . ." is said by the priest with the congregation participating in the concluding doxology, "For the kingdom, the power, and the glory are yours . . . ." "The embolism, developing the last petition of the Lord's Prayer, begs on behalf of the entire community of the faithful deliverance from the power of evil" (n. 56a).

Eminence • "Your Eminence" ("His Eminence," "Most Reverend Eminence") is the proper form of address given to cardinals of the Holy Roman Church. The only exception to this is the Grand Master of the Knights of St. John of Jerusalem who is also addressed as "Eminence." This title was first bestowed on cardinals by Pope Urban VIII in a decree of 1630. At one time it had also been the form of address of German ecclesiastical prince-electors.

Emmanuel (also Immanuel) • Hebrew for "God [is] with us" or "[May] God [be] with us." The word occurs in Isaiah 7:14 and 8:8. In the New Testament it is found in Matthew 1:23. The traditional view of the text in Matthew construes it as a prediction of the virgin birth of Jesus. The first occurrence of the word in Isaiah has been subjected to a welter of conflicting opinions. Perhaps the understanding of the word that offers the least difficulty — but is not altogether certain — is to see it as referring to the son of King Ahaz, viz., Hezekiah. The use of the word in Isaiah 8:8 is not as a personal name but perhaps as an ejaculation, a concise prayer.

Empire, Holy Roman • When, on Christmas Day, 800, Pope St. Leo III crowned Charlemagne as he knelt in St. Peter's Basilica, the crowd chanted "Emperor of the Romans," and people celebrated the reestablishment of the Roman Empire. The term "Holy Roman Empire" did not actually appear until 1254. Although Leo's action certainly elevated Charlemagne's prestige as the major temporal power in Europe, it also insured that subsequent Popes would be viewed as having the authority to impose and depose emperors. Leo also hoped to formalize the role of the King of the Franks as the protector of the Papacy, a duty that soon faded, although it was restored by Otto I in 962. For the regions involved in the Holy Roman Empire — chiefly the Germany and

Italy of today — the system allowed for political cohesion under the emperor, an understanding — albeit often tense — of the authority of Church and state, and an extension of the feudal system. Increasing power in the hands of the emperor, especially through lay investiture, caused constant conflict with the Pope. Rising nationalism and the disruption of the Reformation shook the empire, but it formally lasted until 1806, when Napoleon defeated the Hapsburg Emperor Francis II.

Enchiridion • Derived from the Greek word *encheiridion* ("in hand, close at hand"), this pertains to a reference manual which makes handy a number of pertinent facts according to the subject matter. There are several important enchiridia of note:

(1) The *Enchiridion Indulgentiarum* or "Enchiridion of Indulgences" is by far the best known and most important of the enchiridia. In this volume the Church lists all the indulgences which are granted to the faithful for certain prayers, devotions, pious practices or charitable works and the conditions which must be met. The last edition of this was published under the authority of Pope Paul VI in 1968 as a result of his previous Apostolic Constitution on the Revision of Indulgences, *Indulgentiarum Doctrina*, of January 1, 1967. This volume is readily available in its English translation from any dealer in Catholic books.

(2) The second most important enchiridion refers to just such a manual which has gained tremendous importance over the years to theologians and students of theology, the *Enchiridion Symbolorum, Definitionum, Declarationum de Rebus Fidei et Morum*, the "Enchiridion of Symbols, Definitions, and Declarations Concerning Faith and Morals." First compiled by a noted German theologian, Henricus Denzinger, in 1854, it has since undergone about fifty reprintings. It is often simply referred to as the "Denzinger" even in scholarly works. As can be seen from its title, it is a list of the symbols of Faith, the "creeds," of all dogmatic definitions and officially binding declarations of Popes and councils and of the Holy See which concern faith and morals since the inception of the Church's history. The most recent editions were amplified and reedited by Father Adolphus Schönmetzer, so that it is often cited as Denzinger-Schönmetzer. It has always been printed in the original languages in which the declarations were first issued, i.e., Greek and Latin, with Latin translations for the Greek documents.

(3) Another famous enchiridion which pertains to the scholarly world is the *Enchiridion Patristicum*. First compiled by the French theologian Rouet de Journel, it is a manual of the most important sayings (*loci*, or places, as it terms them) in the writings of the Fathers of the Church. Though it is arranged chronologically, as is Denzinger's, a very thorough index by subject matter is also found, to guide the reader in his research. Since it first appeared in 1911, there have been over twenty-four editions printed.

(4) Though not the best known, one of the oldest such enchiridia of which we know and have possession is that compiled by St. Augustine, one of the greatest Fathers of the Church. In response to the request of a Roman friend, Laurentius, St. Augustine wrote a manual on the Christian life, the "Enchiridion on Faith, Hope, and Charity" in A.D. 421. In it he tried to provide answers to questions on the Faith and what it entailed in practical daily life for the troubled Laurentius and other Roman Christians who formed part of the cultural circles of Rome. In his own words St. Augustine describes this work: "I have in this enchiridion adequately covered how God is to be worshiped, a worship which Divine

Scripture defines as man's true wisdom" (Migne, *Patrologia Latina*, XXXII).

Enclosure (also Cloister) • Also known as "cloister," enclosure is the practice of reserving a part of a religious house for the sole use of its residents, in order to ensure their privacy for prayer and study (Canon 667). The section of the religious house so reserved is also known as "the enclosure." All religious have enclosure of one degree or another. Its purpose is not to lock them in, but to protect their way of life.

There are several types of enclosure, depending upon the character of the religious institute. The strictest type of enclosure is for monasteries of contemplative nuns: papal enclosure, which follows the norms prescribed in the postconciliar document *Venite Seorsum* (August 15, 1969). The purpose of this type of enclosure "is to be regarded as an ascetical regulation particularly consistent with the special vocation of nuns, in that it is the sign, the safeguard and the characteristic form of their withdrawal from the world" (*motu proprio, Ecclesiae Sanctae*, II, D. 48, n. 30). The enclosure of each house may vary slightly in accordance with these norms, and commonly nuns are permitted to go out of the cloister in cases of necessity, e.g., for medical treatment, to exercise civil rights. There is also a less strict form of enclosure for nuns known as "constitutional enclosure."

Encratism (or Encratites) • A movement of early Christian groups who carried their ascetical doctrines to extremes. Apparently they rejected taking wine or flesh meat, and some even refused marriage. The name was generally and imprecisely applied by Irenaeus and Clement of Alexandria to many Gnostic, Ebionite and Docetic sects. They were generally responsible for the writing of the Apocryphal Gospels and Acts, and many of them taught the evil of the material world.

Encyclical • A letter written by the Pope and usually addressed to all Ordinaries in the world, although sometimes encyclicals are addressed to all the faithful, or to the Church in specific regions. Technically, there are two types of encyclicals, namely encyclical letters and encyclical epistles, of which encyclical letters are the more frequent and formal. The distinction, however, is of minor importance.

Encyclicals express the mind of the Holy See on matters of greater importance. Pope Pius XII observed that encyclicals, while not the usual way for infallible pronouncements, do reflect the ordinary Magisterium of the Church and merit that respect from the faithful. The title of the encyclical is taken from the first few words of the *editio typica* of the document; for example, Pope Paul VI's 1968 encyclical on the immorality of contraception was titled *Humanae Vitae*, or "Of Human Life." The original texts are published (though sometimes after a delay) in the *Acta Apostolicae Sedis* and English translations are available from a variety of Catholic publishing houses or in journals, such as *The Pope Speaks*.

Encyclical Epistle: See **Encyclical**

Encyclicals, Social • The encyclicals of the Popes issued since Leo XIII, originating from a concern about mounting problems of poverty, inequality, discrimination, political violence, labor-management relations and peace. Initially spurred by the terrible plight of industrial workers in the nineteenth century, these encyclicals outlined Catholic teachings on private property, the obligations of society toward workers, families and employers. The aim of these encyclicals was to insure justice in the social order, protect the vulnerable and needy, foster international peace and deepen harmony in society.

The social encyclicals have had a profound impact on the relation of the Church to the modern state and society. Rather than showing herself to be implacably hostile to modern life, these encyclicals have shown that the Church seeks to aid contemporary society in achieving her goals and objectives. The encyclicals injected new vitality into the Church, a vitality which to this day has made the Church a strong force in the progress of society not only in the developed, but also in today's developing nations.

Encyclopedists • A group of about sixty French intellectuals of the second half of the eighteenth century who contributed to the *Encyclopedie, ou Dictionnaire raisonné des sciences, des arts, et des métiers* (*The Encyclopedia or Explanatory Dictionary of the Sciences, Arts, and Occupations*). This was, in its completed form (1777), a thirty-three-volume work intended to be a compendium of all human knowledge to date, suitable for either schools or private reading. With a subscription list of about 4,000, and

Pope Leo XIII, first encyclical writer

contributors including such famous names as Diderot (the general editor), Rousseau and Voltaire, the *Encyclopédie* was to a great extent a propaganda organ for the contributors' own political, philosophical or religious points of view. The views expressed (belonging generally to "the Enlightenment") tended to challenge the authority of the Church and the monarchy, and the success of the French Revolution (1789) may be attributed partly to the Encyclopedists' influence. Although their ideas no longer seem radical (compared to those of their nineteenth-century successors), the Encyclopedists inaugurated the secularization of European Christian culture.

End • In philosophy and theology, the term "end" has the twofold sense of objective and purpose. It is defined as that for the sake of which something exists or is done, or that for which an agent acts or action occurs. The intrinsic end (or objective) of an action is that which the action achieves: e.g., practicing enough to attain facility and virtuosity in playing the piano. An action may also have an extrinsic end (sometimes called purpose): e.g., gaining virtuosity in the piano in order to earn a livelihood or win the applause of an appreciative audience. Thus the intrinsic end is the full development or completion of an action or substance, while the extrinsic end is something gained in addition to this. Ends are usually ordered, so that some are more intermediate than others, while some are more ultimate than others. The ultimate end of a thing or action is the final good which it is meant to achieve, a state to which all other ends are understood to be intermediate. The ultimate end thus subordinates rather than excludes intermediate ends that do not conflict with its attainment.

End of Man • The direct vision of God, the deliverance from sin and evil, and the attainment of full and personal union with God. The end (or purpose) of man is an encounter with the infinitely loving, intelligent Persons of the Trinity, and it aims at establishing a new relationship with the Divine Three: one of eternal unity with God and participation in the life of the Divine Three.

In the Catholic perspective, the end of man is achieved through repentance, faith and discipleship. Catholicism is unique in positing this personal end for man, but it is in harmony with its understanding of salvation. This end is not simply present at the end of time, but is proleptically present here and now through grace and the Church. The end of man is to enter into eternity and the resurrected flesh of Christ, which is also the objective of the conferral of grace aiming at the restoration of union between God and humanity. Through the revelation and grace of God, when one achieves his or her end with God, the divine *colloquium* begins, and the end of man is to bring that "conversation" with the Divine Three to its completion.

The human person is created *imago Dei* (as the "image of God") with a spiritual nature, intelligence, freedom, the capacity for morality and dominion over creation. The end of man must consist in the full and free exercise of these powers. The end of man is to share in the new creation, the cosmos perfected by the definitive revelation of God's grace and freed from the cosmic powers of death, the law, dominions, powers and thrones. Recent trends in eschatology have argued that considerations of the end of man should give greater consideration to the human existential condition, historicity and human psychological dynamics. The end of man is to share in the triumphant end of grace.

End of the World • In theology, the word "end" has the sense both of termination and of culmination. Both senses are embodied in Catholic teaching about the end of the world. Christian Faith affirms a hope in a final consummation at the end of time that will involve both an end to the world as we know it and a transformation in which the world will realize its divinely willed finality. Hence, Christian Faith speaks both of the end of the world, and of a new heaven and a new earth. The Second Vatican Council declared: "We know neither the moment of the consummation of the earth and of man, nor the way in which the universe will be transformed. The form of this world, distorted by sin, is passing away, and we are taught that God is preparing a new dwelling and a new earth in which righteousness dwells, in which happiness will fill and surpass all the desires of peace arising in the hearts of men" (GS 39).

Employing the characteristic apocalyptic style of the Old Testament, Christ foretold the end of the world (cf. Mt 24:25; 28:20). The theme of a fiery end to the world appears throughout the New Testament (cf. Mt 3:10; Lk 17:29-30; 2 Pt 3:7, 10, 12). The

Book of Revelation speaks of the end of the world in striking terms, but these images are commonly held to be symbolic rather that literal descriptions of the end of the world.

Speculation about the events that will comprise the end of the world is understandable, but Christ Himself cautioned against it. Despite the rich biblical imagery in which these events have been foretold, the time and nature of the end of the world are neither known by science nor disclosed by revelation (Mk 13:32). Faith is certain only of the truth that there will be a final judgment and a consummation that will be both an end and a new beginning for the created order in its totality.

Endowment • In ecclesiastical circles, an endowment is any gift of property. Though usually it is cash or securities, it is sometimes productive land, which is donated to a Church institution with the understanding that, at least for a certain time, the institution in question will have access only to the income derived from the donated property and not to the property itself. Endowments are generally regulated by the canons on temporal goods. They have been for centuries and remain a great service to the Church by alleviating for her some of the demands of providing for such necessities as the training of priests and the retirement of elderly religious. (Cf. Burse.)

Ends of the Mass • In the patristic era a constantly reiterated theme about the value of the celebration of the Eucharist was that it was for the unity and peace of the Church. A particularly forceful proponent of the ecclesial nature of all liturgical celebrations was St. Augustine. This same theology marked St. Thomas Aquinas's theology of the Eucharist which held that the ultimate aim of the Mass was the building up of the Church. That the Church as the Body of Christ is built up by the Eucharistic Body of Christ was a convenient way that this theology was summarized.

As the Church's reflection on the Eucharist progressed, she came to appreciate that each Mass is offered by the Church — regardless of the specific intention — with four general intentions: adoration, thanksgiving, contrition and petition. God is adored as Creator of all things, thanked as the generous Father Who abundantly blesses His children, pleaded with as the merciful Lord Who forgives sin, and entreated as the kind Master Who alone can fulfill humanity's needs.

Energumen • One who is possessed by evil spirits, a demoniac.

English Martyrs • About four hundred martyrs of England and Wales who gave their lives rather than deny their Faith during the reigns of Henry VIII (1509-1547), Elizabeth I (1558-1603), James I (1603-1625), Charles I (1625-1649) and Charles II (1660-1685). Most were executed for treason (hanged, drawn and quartered), but some died as a result of imprisonment. In general, these martyrs refused to accept the English Reformation, with its conferral of headship of the Church on the British monarch and proscription of the celebration of the Mass. Among those who have been canonized are St. John Fisher and St. Thomas More. Groups of martyrs were beatified by Popes Leo XIII (in 1886 and 1895), Pius XI (in 1929) and John Paul II (in 1987). Some of the beatified are under consideration for canonization. The other English martyrs are either venerables or *dilati* (i.e., those whose cause has been postponed until further evidence of their martyrdom is forthcoming).

Enkolpion • From the Greek for "on the breast." This liturgical vesture in the

Byzantine Rite is proper to a bishop. It is equivalent to the pectoral cross in the Roman Rite. The enkolpion is a medallion suspended on a chain around the neck, having on it an icon of the Mother of God or an icon of Christ.

Enlightenment, The Age of • The title given the broad intellectual movement, begun in the eighteenth century, which held that the most reliable guide to knowledge was, not faith or authority, but human reason. Learning, freedom and science were all emphasized at the expense of faith. Since the Church has traditionally held that faith and reason should act in concert, it might seem that the Church and the leaders of the Enlightenment would act in harmony, but the opposite proved true. Many proponents of the Enlightenment felt that the Church and the light of faith were outmoded, serving only as constraints on the power of human reason, while some in the Church felt threatened by an intellectual movement which seemed to downgrade authority and revelation. Before the Enlightenment, knowledge was viewed as coming from faith, the Church, authority and Tradition, all of which aided human reason, while Immanuel Kant would describe the Enlightenment as ". . . man's release from his self-incurred tutelage . . . [his] inability to make use of his understanding without direction from another."

The advance of the Enlightenment is especially dramatic in five intellectual areas, all of which challenged the Church: Cosmology, wherein astronomers were questioning the medieval belief that the earth was the center of the universe, leading to the condemnation of Galileo in 1633; Rationalism, where philosophers such as Descartes placed reason over faith; religious freedom, with thinkers such as Diderot holding that religious assent cannot be coerced; history, which was seen as always improving and exalting man as always progressing, by writers such as Rousseau; and Deism, a movement positing a detached God, with people such as Voltaire questioning whether revealed religion was even possible. Much of Church history after the eighteenth century can be interpreted as the Church reacting to this Age of Reason.

Entelechy • A term transliterated from the Greek, meaning literally "to have in completion." It is often translated as "actuality," "perfection" or "state of fulfillment." Aristotle uses the term to describe the soul: the soul is the first entelechy of a naturally organized body having life potentially. In line with his teaching that all material things are composed of form and matter, he sees the soul as the form of the body. Thus the soul as form refers to the organization of matter that brings about its state of fulfillment as a living body. St. Thomas adapts this understanding of Aristotle to emphasize that the human person is both body and soul and not just a soul using a body, as Plato had taught.

The term was modified by later philosophers to describe special situations; e.g., G. W. Leibniz says that his monads are entelechies.

Enthronement of the Sacred Heart • A devotional ceremony, accompanied by prayers and hymns, in which a picture or image of the Sacred Heart of Jesus is installed in a prominent place in the home. The devotion, originated in the work of a nineteenth-century Chilean priest named Mateo Crawley-Boevey, was approved by Pope Pius X in 1907 and introduced into the United States in 1913.

Enthusiasm, Catholic • A broad term used to refer to a wide variety of movements in Christian history that have in common a stress on the felt experience of the Holy Spirit and the manifestation of this experience in a heightened sense of fidelity and authenticity among those sharing it. Such movements have often been the source and impetus of renewal for the wider Church, particularly when their charismatic vision has been submitted to the assessment of ecclesiastical authorities and thus channeled into the mainstream community. But enthusiastic movements have inevitably involved separatist or sectarian tendencies, arising both from their self-ascribed authenticity and from the reaction of their co-religionists. Ironically, their appeal to the restoration of primitive Christian traditions has often been construed as innovation and heterodoxy. Crucial to a truly "catholic" enthusiasm is the recognition that the Holy Spirit is manifest not only in the charismatic but also in the institutional elements of the life of the Church, and that, while one manifestation may give rise to reform and renewal in the community, the other guarantees its unity, stability and perseverance in the Faith.

Entrance Antiphon/Song • Formerly known simply as the "Introit," this chant is restored by the Vatican II Missal to its more ancient title and form. Now called the *antiphona ad introitum* (entrance antiphon or song), it is clearly seen as a refrain to the psalm which accompanies the entrance of the celebrant and his ministers. In the Missal (sacramentary) and people's participation booklets, only the antiphon (or refrain) itself is given, the complete psalm being found in a separate publication for the cantor called the *Roman Gradual* or its abridgement the *Simple Gradual.*

The Foreword to the United States edition of the Roman Missal notes several ways in which this chant may be sung: the antiphon with psalm verses taken from the two

sources noted above, songs from other approved collections of psalms and antiphons, or other sacred songs chosen in accord with the season or feast. Only in the absence of song is the antiphon to be recited. The United States edition further notes the difficulty of communal recitation of such a brief text and therefore suggests its recitation by priest, deacon, reader or other minister, or its incorporation into the brief introductory remarks which may follow the greeting. It may be observed that this latter suggestion is more difficult to accomplish in a satisfactory way than communal recitation, which generally presents no problem at all. These antiphons, most of them carried over from the former Missal and of great antiquity, are a minor but nonetheless important part of the liturgical heritage of the Roman Rite. The seasonal and sanctoral antiphons especially set the tone for the celebration in a concise and scriptural way. In the Roman liturgical tradition, the singing of hymns was generally reserved to the Offices, while antiphonal singing prevailed at the Eucharist. It is unfortunate that common practice, in the United States at least, omits the antiphons altogether or replaces them with metrical hymns of a generally inferior quality. These remarks could apply equally to the Communion antiphon which remains in the present Missal and to the offertory antiphon which the present Missal omits, but which may still be found in the *Graduals.*

Envy • A capital sin, it is the misery, grief, sadness of loss or pain that one feels when another experiences success or prosperity. The sadness of envy is experienced because the successes of others are seen as detracting from one's happiness, success or prosperity. Envy is against charity, which holds that the other is to be loved and esteemed without qualification. The sin of envy is also contrary to justice because the envious person begrudges the other what is rightfully and justifiably one's own. The envious person is unjust and uncharitable because the person of accomplishment deserves honor, deference and respect, rather than the detraction or sadness that the envious person often manifests.

Eparch • In the Byzantine Rite a bishop enjoying canonical jurisdiction is called an eparch (diocesan bishop); his area of jurisdiction is called an eparchy (diocese).

Eparchy • This Byzantine term describes the portion of jurisdiction or territory over which a bishop or episcopal substitute has charge. The equivalent term in the Roman Rite is "diocese." The resident bishop is called an eparch.

Ephesians, Epistle to the • In earlier and more reliable manuscripts, the mention of the recipients of the letter ("at Ephesus" at Eph 1:1) is completely absent. The earliest source which identifies this epistle "in Ephesus" is from the late second century — Irenaeus (c. A.D. 180). Marcion, a generation earlier, refers to this letter as being "to the Laodicians." These peculiar facts suggest that this letter was probably a general or circular letter from Paul to many Churches in Asia Minor. Its purpose is to encourage a continuing knowledge of God's great plan of salvation, to unite all things under Christ (3:10-11). If this letter has been correctly described as a masterful summary pinnacle of Paul's teachings, scholars are not agreed as to the precise literary form in which it is expressed. Is it an early form of theological treatise, a meditation on Christ, the Church and God's eternal plan, a baptismal homily, an introduction and summary of Paul's teachings? Each suggestion has merit. The continued reception of divine revelation, the knowing with all spiritual knowledge (1:8-9)

leads to an awareness of being children of the Light (5:8) and to specific ways of relating to other believers within the Body of Christ (Chapters 4-6). The emphasis on the unity of the universal Church and on the reconciling effect of Christ's death on the cross both suggest that Ephesians may have been written to remedy the malady of schism, fragmentation, alienation and perhaps cultural forms of bigotry either against Jewish Christians or against Gentile Christians.

Major Themes: The divine plan that all be reconciled to the Father in Christ (1:10), which existed in the mind of God prior to creation (1:4), has now been revealed to the Apostles and prophets (3:5) and has been accomplished through Christ's death and resurrection. Christ's Lordship over all the metaphysical beings and cosmic powers is a *fait accompli* (1:20-23). Chapters 1-3 provide the doctrinal and theological outline of the Father's plan, its unraveling in Christ, and the believer's status relative to this plan and its unfolding. Chapters 4-6 flow from the doctrine and theology to point out the moral and practical considerations implied in the revelation outlined in those first three chapters.

Contents:
A. Address: 1:1-2
B. The Church, Family of the Redeemed: 1:3—3:21
C. The Church, Unity, Gifts, New Life: 4:1-24
D. Believers, in the World and at Home: 4:25—6:20
E. Conclusions: 6:21-24

Authorship and Date: Until the mid- to late-1700s, Paul was universally accepted as the author of Ephesians. Since that time, studies in stylistic matters (e.g., 1:3-14 is one sentence, unusual for Paul), use of vocabulary ("head" and "body" are not used in Ephesians and Colossians as they are elsewhere in the Pauline Corpus) and other matters have convinced some that Ephesians is not from Paul. If it is not, it was written by a disciple or someone otherwise quite close to his teachings, for this epistle is a masterful summary and fruitful penetration of the deepest truths which Paul taught about Christ crucified. If the letter is from Paul, it should be dated late in his life, perhaps in the early A.D. 60s. If the missive is from a disciple it can be dated any time from after the mid-60s to as late as 110.

For further reading: Victor Paul Furnish, "Ephesians, Epistle to the," *Anchor Bible Dictionary*, 2:535-542; Paul J. Kobelski, "The Letter to the Ephesians," *New Jerome Biblical Commentary*, 883-890.

Ephesus, Council of • In response to the heresies of Nestorianism and Pelagianism the Emperor Theodosius II convened what became the third Ecumenical Council at Ephesus in A.D. 431. Pope Celestine I delegated St. Cyril of Alexandria to be his official representative among the some two hundred bishops there assembled. In the course of seven sessions, the Council Fathers condemned the above-named dangers to doctrine and, most notably, defined the hypostatic union of the two natures in the one Person of Christ and also recognized the beautiful Marian title of *Theotokos* (or Bearer of God).

Ephesus, Robber Council of • In A.D. 451, the Emperor Theodosius II, with the approval of the Holy See, decided to convene a council for the general purposes of ecclesiastical discipline. The time granted for the council, however, was so short that the Pope was unable to supply a representative and indeed, few Western bishops attended at all, although some one hundred fifty Eastern bishops were present. In the resulting void, the heretical bishop Dioscorus of Alexandria seized control of the council and forced through several Nestorian decrees, repudiated the Marian title of *Theotokos* and generally trampled the established rights of the Roman Pontiff. This robber council, also known as *Latrocinium*, was, in any event, repudiated by the Council of Chalcedon that same year, and Dioscorus was deposed.

Epiclesis (also Epiklesis) • The calling down of the Holy Spirit upon the Holy Gifts after the Consecration in the Eastern Liturgy and before the Consecration in the Roman Rite.

Epigonation • In the Eastern Church, a diamond-shaped board covered with cloth and adorned with a cross, worn by ecclesiastics as a sign of dignity. The epigonation is worn by pastors and priests of higher rank. It symbolizes the sword of power.

Epimanikia • In the Eastern Church, a pair of stiff embroidered cuffs, laced on one side, worn by the priest over the sleeves of the sticharion.

Epiphany • The term is from the Greek *epiphaneia*, meaning "manifestation." In the liturgical calendar of the Roman Rite of the Catholic Church the solemnity of the Epiphany occurs on January 6, which commemorates the "manifestation" of God through Christ to the whole "world" symbolized by the Three Magi from the East (Mt 2:1-12). The feast day originated sometime in the third century in the Eastern Church, where originally and currently it refers to the "manifestation" of God to the world through the Baptism of Christ (cf. Clement of Alexandria's *Stromata* i.21). By the fourth century, the feast ranked in importance with Easter and Pentecost. When introduced into the Western Church in the fourth century, the focus of the feast shifted from Christ's Baptism to His birth. In St. Leo's homilies, reference to Christ's birth is with the noun *theophania*, illustrating the link between the "manifestation" of God and the birth of Christ.

In the United States, the Epiphany is celebrated on the Sunday nearest January 6.

Episcopacy • The episcopacy is another term for the office of bishop. It is derived from the Greek word *episkopos*, meaning bishop or overseer.

Episcopal Vicar • An episcopal vicar is a priest who is appointed by the bishop to exercise authority over a specific territory of a diocese or over a certain group of persons for a particular task. An episcopal vicar has the same powers as a vicar general, except that he can only exercise them within the limits of his area of competence. (Cf. Canons 475-481; J. Penna, "The Episcopal Vicar," *Studies in Canon Law* No. 475, Catholic University of America, 1971.)

Episcopalians • The members of the Episcopal Church in the United States (formerly the Protestant Episcopal Church). The name indicates the form of government of the Church (episcopal), which distinguishes it from many other Protestant communities. It is one of fourteen churches which make up the Anglican Communion. The Church of England, the Mother Church of the Anglican Communion, separated from the Holy See during the reign of Henry VIII (1509-1547), and the separation was made definitive during the reign of Elizabeth I (1558-1603).

Anglicans arrived in America with the English explorers of the sixteenth century. The first Anglican Eucharist was celebrated in 1607 in Jamestown, Virginia. The Anglican Church became the established church in many of the southern colonies, but was banned for many years in New England. After the American Revolution, the church sought independence from the jurisdiction of the Church of England. Its first bishop, Samuel Seabury, was consecrated in Scotland to avoid taking the oath of allegiance to the king, required in England. He was recognized a bishop by a General Convention assembled in Philadelphia, in 1789. This convention also formally established the Protestant Episcopal Church of the United States. It adopted a constitution for the church and issued a specifically American version of the Book of Common Prayer.

The Episcopal Church holds to the Apostles' and Nicene Creeds as symbols of the faith and a modified version of the Thirty-Nine Articles as a general statement of doctrine. There exists a wide latitude of expression ranging from "high church" to "low church" and "broad church." The high church movement, which originated in the nineteenth-century Oxford Movement, is characterized by formal liturgy quite similar to the Roman Rite. In most cases, it takes a traditional approach to doctrine. Low church exemplifies the evangelical strand in Anglicanism and is manifest in a simple liturgical style and often a rather broad interpretation of doctrine.

The Episcopal Church is governed by the General Convention which meets every three years and consists of the House of Bishops and the House of Deputies, the latter composed of priests and laity. The General Convention elects the chief officer of the Episcopal Church, the Presiding Bishop. The diocesan bishop is the head of the local diocese and is elected by the clergy and laity of the diocese, subject to the approval of a majority of the standing committees of the dioceses and a majority of the diocesan bishops. Each diocese has an annual convention, composed of clergy and laity, which sets diocesan policy within the framework of the national canons of the Church. The parish is governed by the lay vestry which calls the rector, subject to the approval of the bishop.

In recent years the Episcopal Church has revised its order of worship and revised the Book of Common Prayer. It has also opened to women its orders of clergy: bishops, priests and deacons.

Episcopalism • An ecclesiological theory which holds that supreme authority within the Church resides with the body of bishops independent of the Holy See. This opinion has taken form in various movements through the centuries. It was expressed in the Middle Ages as conciliarism, which stated that the Pope was subject to a general council, as well as in Gallicanism, a nationalist movement in seventeenth-century France. It should not be confused with the doctrine of episcopal collegiality expressed at the Second Vatican Council. Vatican II states that the College of Bishops exercises authority as a group, but only when acting in union with the Pope as head of the episcopal college.

Epistle • A written communication. It has become common to distinguish between "epistle" and "letter." An epistle is a kind of essay directed to the general public. The letter format (e.g., the greeting) serves in the epistle only as a literary device. The epistle treats of broad topics which are of interest or concern to a general readership. It is not a private or confidential communication. The letter, on the other hand, is a person-to-person communication. It could on occasion be an exchange between a person and a specific group of people. The letter envisions a definite, clear-cut situation. It is personal and assumes a certain mutual knowledge, and such is the theoretical distinction between epistle and letter.

When it comes to the Pauline correspondence, this distinction cannot be too rigidly imposed. Although Paul's writings have been classified as letters, the fact is that in several places Paul has spun a doctrinal treatise not particularly tied to any local situation, in other words, material of epistolary quality.

Epitaphion • A representation of the tomb of Christ, richly decorated and covered with flowers, solemnly venerated on Friday and Saturday of Holy Week in the Churches of the East.

Epitrachelion (also Epitakhelion) • In the Byzantine Rite, a stole sewn down along the middle with an opening on top for the head. The epitrachelion is part of the holy vestments of the priest, corresponding to the priestly stole of the Roman Rite. Normally, it is decorated with seven crosses, three on each side of the double band and one at the back of the neck, to symbolize the seven sacraments. The priest is required to wear the epitrachelion when administering any sacrament. It is the distinguishing vestment of a priest.

Equality • By reason of creation, there is a fundamental equality among all human persons because they are made in the image and likeness of God. Their spiritual, intelligent and free natures give them a dignity that commands respect. Fundamental equality before the civil law is espoused by the Catholic Faith, as was seen in the documents of the Second Vatican Council: "Civil authority must see to it that the equality of the citizens before the law, which is itself an element of the common good of society, is never violated either openly or covertly for religious reasons and that there is no discrimination among citizens" (DH 6).

All Christians share a fundamental equality before God because they share equally in the victory of Christ, the gifts of the Holy Spirit and divine forgiveness. Catholics are not to discriminate because all have equal access to the grace and forgiveness of God, and all can grow equally in holiness. However, this does not mean that everyone proceeds to Christ by the same path, for some are called to serve Christ and His Church in different ways.

If the Church has denied some people certain positions within the Church, it has been to protect qualities that the Church deemed necessary or to promote the good order of the Church. Reserving higher orders to males was clearly and expressly desired by Christ, for He had the opportunity to include women in the apostolic community, but did not do so. Doing this would have jeopardized their particularly feminine qualities of charity and mercy. In Greek and Roman society women acquired honor by adopting distinctively masculine qualities, such as aggressiveness and strength, but the Christians extolled the feminine ones and placed them under male protection.

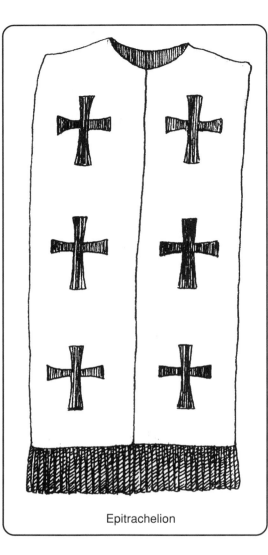

Epitrachelion

Furthermore, there is a complementarity of roles in the ecclesial community, with men as images of Christ and women as images of the Church — equal dignity in different roles.

In the ancient Church, women showed exceptional courage, but it was in the form of gentleness and femininity. One of the primary reasons why Christianity grew so rapidly in antiquity was that it did provide such exceptional protection to women. Some claimed that Christianity was a religion only for women, but that points to the fact that it sought to protect the distinctively feminine. This suggests that women are equal but different from men and have their own distinctive role and position in the Church.

For further reading: John Paul II, *Mulieris Dignitatem.*

Erastianism • The term applied to a specific but none-too-original sixteenth-century heresy which held the state to be the lawful superior of the Church, even in ecclesiastical affairs.

Developed by a Swiss Zwinglian physician, Thomas Erastus (whose real name was

Thomas Lieber), it was in fact never the main interest of its own author, who was much more concerned in his writings with what he termed "excommunication," which was actually closer to the Catholic concept of interdict and which, in either case, he claimed was forbidden by Sacred Scripture.

The theo-political elements of Erastianism did gain some following in Germany, and for various reasons found no little support in Great Britain for a time, but like its many cousins, Erastianism was repudiated by the definition of papal supremacy in the First Vatican Council.

Error and Marriage • Error about a person one intends to marry can possibly make the marriage invalid. First, if one person makes an error about the person of the intended spouse and actually marries someone who is not in fact the person he or she intended to marry, then the marriage is invalid.

Error can also refer to a quality about the other spouse. A quality is some aspect of the person that contributes to the shaping of the overall personality. Qualities can be moral, spiritual, religious or legal. Marital consent is exchanged with a person, however, and not a quality of a person. If, however, a person intends to marry a person principally and directly because of a specific quality of that person, and later discovers that he or she was wrong about the existence of the quality, the marriage is invalid. Actually, there would be no community of life in the true sense, because this community depends upon the exchange of the persons and not a person with a quality (Canon 1097).

Finally, error about the unity (one man and one woman), indissolubility or sacramental dignity of marriage does not invalidate unless this error influences the will of the person in error. This means that if a person deeply believed that marriage is dissoluble or that fidelity is not an absolute requirement, and exchanged consent fully believing that these qualities were not part of marriage, then it can be said that the error influenced the will to choose a type of marriage that is contrary to what Christian marriage actually is all about. In such cases, the person chose not true marriage but an erroneous form of marriage he or she believed to be true (Canon 1099).

Error, Common • Common error is the false belief which is prevalent among an identifiable community or group that a person lacking the executive power of governance or faculties exercised an act of jurisdiction validly. It is the belief that such a person had faculties when, in fact, he did not. In such cases, the law itself supplies the faculties and the acts exercised are valid. In some cases, a cleric may think he has faculties when, in fact, he does not (e.g., if they ran out or if he had lost them through resignation); in other cases, a priest may exercise an act of jurisdiction knowing that he lacked the power to do so. In either event, the Church supplies the faculties for the good of the community, rather than the good of the cleric.

The most usual type of common error is when a community thinks that a priest has faculties to hear confessions when, in fact, he lacks them. The confessions heard are valid (Canon 144).

Eschatology • The origins of this term stem from its use as a technical theological term by nineteenth-century theologians who studied the doctrines concerning the "end times." The English term is derived from the Greek adjective *eschatos* and refers to the "teachings about the last things" (or "end times"). The subject matter of the "teachings" includes death, Christ's resurrection, the status of the dead prior to Christ's Second Coming (*parousia*), the general resurrection of the dead, heaven, hell, judgment, justice, etc.

The phrase "last things" refers to a final period of world history when God's majestic plan of salvation is realized as all creation is finally reconciled to Him, reaching the beginning of its fullest possible realization. After this, both history (i.e., time) and this world as we know it will cease to exist, being replaced with something else (e.g., the City of God). This final period of world history begins with the birth of Christ, includes the pilgrim journey of the Church, and will be consummated with the Second Coming of Christ. Four basic points (three theological and one pastoral) about this period of salvation history should be kept in mind.

First, there is the initial phase which includes all that has happened, beginning with the birth of Christ, commonly referred to as the "already" of salvation history (Heb 1:2; 1 Pt 1:20). For example, the outpouring of the Holy Spirit upon Jew and Gentile is itself a sign of the "final age of salvation," of the "messianic age" (cf. Acts 2:17), which is therefore already upon us and continues to be upon us through the historic and sacramental life of the Church. The biblical witness indicates the final period of history has already begun.

Second, there is that phase of salvation history which is yet to come and which is commonly called the "not yet" of salvation history. For example, believers still await Christ's return, His Second Coming (Parousia), and the "day of judgment" at some future point within this final period of history, something which has not yet happened (other examples: the eschatological plagues have not yet happened [Rv 15:1; 21:8]; the resurrection of the dead, the last judgment and final salvation have not yet happened [Jn 6:37-44, 54; 11:24; 12:48; 1 Pt 1:5]; the final tribulations are not yet fully realized [2 Tm 3:1; Jas 5:3; 1 Jn 2:18; Jude 18; 2 Pt 3:3]).

Third, there is a relationship between what we expect in the future and what we experience in daily Christian life. Thus, even though believers have already been raised with Christ in the heavenly places (Eph 2:1, 5, especially 6) and are the new creation in Christ (2 Cor 5:17; 1 Cor 10:11), the full realization of resurrection life is not yet fully mature, hence the need for teaching and encouragement in the ways of life as pleasing to God, as are "sweet-smelling sacrifices" (Eph 4-6), all of which are empowered by the Holy Spirit (Eph 5:18).

Fourth, the pastoral perspective: Jesus' preaching about the kingdom of God, the Son of Man and the final judgment all illustrate the inaugural moments of the "end times" (Mt 4:17; 16:27-29; Mk 1:15; 8:38-9:1; Lk 9:26-27) which form the context of specific pastoral practices. For instance, the preaching of repentance (Mt 10:5-23; Lk 10:1-12) and the exorcisms performed show the deep and powerful force of God's kingdom, with obvious practical considerations (Mt 12:25-29; Mk 3:22-27; Lk 11:17-22; Lk 10:17-20).

In summary, for those who have become friends of God, the hope of living eternally in love with God is already realized in the baptismal relationship with God in and through Christ, just as the hope for final union with God is not yet fully realized.

Espousal (also Betrothal) • A promise of marriage more popularly termed engagement. In times past, such a promise to marry was the equivalent of a binding contract to marry. The promise to marry, however, does not carry with it the exercise of any rights of marriage, such as sexual intercourse.

The use of the rights of marriage is gained only subsequent to the actual sacramental celebration of the contract of marriage.

Espousals of the Blessed Virgin: See Spouses of the Blessed Virgin Mary

Essence • In philosophy, a distinction is made between the existence of a being and its essence. For example, if in a dark room someone says, "I know that there is something there, but I don't know what it is," it could be said that it is known that something exists in the room, but it is not clear of what essence, or nature, that something is. Classification of the different kinds of things by their essence or nature leads to such distinctions as genus and species. For example, among all the existing animals, of some the essence is of mammals, whereas others have the nature of insects.

Essenes • The term is thought to be derived from Aramaic, with the probable meaning, "the pious ones." The name refers to an ascetic Jewish religious group. Our knowledge of the group stems from their writings uncovered at Qumran, the Dead Sea Scrolls. Prior to this discovery, there was only information about them provided by Philo and Josephus, along with scattered references in Pliny and some Church Fathers.

The Essenes are believed to have originated in the second century B.C. and to have continued until the second century A.D. Their mode of life was highly structured. The group was divided into a priestly class and laity. The sacerdotal group was invested with legislative and judicial competence. There was also an assembly of "the Many" (apparently all those who enjoyed full membership in the community). Members had to undergo a two-year probation (Josephus asserts that it was a three-year period). After the first year, the novice was admitted to a limited number of community functions. After two years he achieved full standing. All property was held in common.

The community was believed to be the true Israel. Great emphasis was laid on the sinfulness of man (as evidenced by the Essene stress on ritual baths), but at the same time much was made of the mercy of God and His forgiveness.

For further reading: John J. Collins, "Essenes," *Anchor Bible Dictionary*, 2:619-626.

Established Church • A church recognized by law and supported by civil government as the official church of a nation is called an established church. It usually implies some form of financial support. The Church of England is such for the English part of the United Kingdom, the Presbyterian Church for Scotland, the Lutheran Church for much of Scandinavia, Judaism for Israel, and Islam for much of the Islamic world. In pluralistic societies such establishment is becoming rarer.

Esther, Book of • This book has its setting in Persia, in the fifth century B.C., when thousands of Jews were still in captivity. Named after its Jewish heroine, the Book of Esther extols the patriotism of this woman who saved her people from destruction at the hands of the Persians. The Greek version is longer than the Hebrew and has a more religious tone. The book has the purpose of explaining the origin of the Jewish feast of Purim (14 and 15 of Adar).

Set in the time of Xerxes (called Ahasuerus), King of Persia from 485 to 465 B.C., the story tells how the plotting of an official hostile to the Jews (Haman) was foiled. Hadassah (Esther), a beautiful Jewish girl, was taken into the harem and ultimately made queen. When Haman succeeded in having the king decree the extermination of the Jews (on a day to be chosen by lot), Esther prevailed upon him to nullify the decree by permitting the Jews to kill all those known to be their enemies. As a consequence, Haman, with his ten sons and 75,000 others were put to death.

For further reading: Carey A. Moore, "Esther, Book of," *Anchor Bible Dictionary*, 2:633-643; Irene Nowell, O.S.B., Toni Craven and Demetrius Dumm, O.S.B., "Tobit, Judith, Esther," *New Jerome Biblical Commentary*, 576-579.

Eternity • The definition of eternity that has attained classical status in Catholic theology is that given by Boethius (c. A.D. 480-524): "Eternity is the perfect and simultaneous total possession of interminable life." Eternity in this strict sense is true only of God. Only the uncreated possesses divine being without beginning or end, and without succession in a permanent and undivided now. Scripture attests to this truth in many passages, notably Psalm 90: "Before the mountains were brought forth, or ever thou hadst formed the world, from everlasting to everlasting thou art God" (v. 2). Catholic theology has understood the divine eternity in connection with the doctrine that God is completely without potentiality: He is all in all. Since God is uncreated, He is without beginning or end. Furthermore, there can be no development in God, no progression from the imperfect to the more perfect, no change from the potential to the actual, and therefore no temporal succession. Creatures can participate in God's eternity, but they cannot be eternal in this strict sense. For this reason, Catholic theology has distinguished between eternity strictly speaking and the "aevum" or "aeviternity" which is enjoyed by spiritual substances (angels and human souls) whose life has a beginning but no end. It is in this sense that creaturely persons are said to enjoy the eternal life of heaven.

Ethics • The systematic analysis of the constituents of human goodness and rightness and of the conditions of human fulfillment and morally good action which is regulated and governed by the requirements of reason. Ethics articulates the ends of human existence and action, defines the means of attaining those ends, and justifies these judgments. Ethics defines those qualities of persons that determine a fulfilled, completed and perfected person and provides a rational defense of these judgments.

As each person must take charge of his or her life, give it meaning, order and purpose, so ethics is the field of systematic thought in which the person sets the limits and outlines of his or her life. Ethics is unique to persons because the person is not imprisoned by natural determinations, but possesses freedom and self-determination and can choose between a variety of real possibilities. For, through deliberate and conscious choices which involve the entirety of the person, the choice and action endorsed constitutes the person, and the chosen reality is integrated into the person.

Mores or customs are the first attempts to do this, but they do not derive from the rigorous and systematic reflection and logic of ethics, and only after they develop this rigor do mores acquire an ethical character. Ethical analysis develops in historical, cultural, economic, social and political situations, and its concrete expression is historical, but its governing principles are not historical.

Ethics preserves the freedom, dignity and integrity of the person by preventing capitulation to the various tyrannies we encounter in our life. Ethics creates a structure and framework which enables the person to enhance freedom, creativity and life itself. It bridges the gap between what the person is already and what the person should be.

Ethics, Situation • A method of moral analysis which only considers concrete, historical circumstances as relevant factors in moral decision-making and does not acknowledge either the existence, applicability or binding nature of universal norms.

In this century, Pope Pius XII condemned situation ethics in a 1952 speech delivered to the Fédération Mondiale des Jeunesses Feminines Catholiques.

The case for situation ethics usually proceeds something like this: Every moral situation is unique and unrepeatable, and the person making a decision is said to encounter God immediately in his own conscience. As long as the moral agent is sincere and believes himself to be acting in good faith, the action which he takes or does not take is judged immaterial.

There are multiple flaws in situation ethics.

First, situation ethics denies the absoluteness of moral norms. That is, by taking individual circumstances as the lone axis upon which moral decisions turn, situation ethics refuses to admit that there are certain moral principles which transcend particularities like time and place and are thereby permanently valid.

Second, situation ethics fails to take into account the inherent nature of objects. Not understanding that certain things by their very nature (*de natura*) are morally good or evil, situation ethics offers its adherents a sophistry which cannot reliably and authoritatively pronounce moral judgment.

Third, situation ethics averts positive moral obligation. Because the Christian ethic binds in conscience, it requires that moral agents act in a certain way. Situation ethics does not recognize there to be a powerful enough authority to assert that human beings act in accordance with the dictates of a properly formed conscience.

Fourth, by declaring the intention of the moral agent to be the exclusive determinant of morality, situation ethics erroneously makes the self the frame of reference for all moral analysis. Good intentions are important, but they do not of themselves bring about morally correct behavior. Neither do good intentions wholly vindicate moral agents from responsibility. For these reasons, then, situation ethics is totally incompatible with Catholic moral theology.

Although situation ethics can never be considered a legitimate aspect of Catholic moral theology, it has a great many proponents and champions outside the Church. Among the most important of these has been the American Joseph Fletcher.

Ethiopian Church • One of the ancient Oriental Churches, the Ethiopian Church was evangelized from the See of Alexandria, from which it received much of its liturgy and doctrine. The Ethiopian Church, like Alexandria, did not accept the Council of Chalcedon or any subsequent ecumenical councils. After the Islamic expansion into Northern Africa in the seventh century, this Church was effectively cut off from much of the world for almost a millennium. It retained contact with the patriarchate of Alexandria, from which it received confirmation of its bishops. Together with the see of Alexandria, it was considered part of the Coptic or Egyptian Church, even though its liturgical language is Ge'ez, not Coptic, the ancient tongue of Egypt. In 1959 it severed all official dependence on Alexandria and elected its own patriarch.

Because of missionary efforts in the nineteenth and twentieth centuries, a large number of Ethiopians entered into union with the Holy See. The head of the Ethiopian Catholic Church is the archbishop of Addis Ababa.

Euangelion • The Greek word meaning "Gospel." In liturgical use it refers to the proclamation of the "good news" at the divine liturgy.

Eucharist, Celebration of the • The action of the Church which makes present the supreme sacrifice of Christ on the cross. The celebration of the Eucharist is popularly known by various names, including "the Holy Sacrifice of the Mass" and "the Eucharistic Liturgy." Yet, the Mass and the Eucharist are distinct. The former is the sacrifice offered in conjunction with Christ's self-offering on the cross, whereas the latter is the permanent gift of the Body and Blood of Christ under the appearances of bread and wine which nourishes and fortifies those on pilgrimage to God. A validly ordained priest, with the proper intention and using valid matter and correct form, offers the same sacrifice which Jesus offered to the Father on Good Friday. The priest uses Jesus' words pronounced at the Last Supper: "This is my body. . . . This . . . is . . . my blood. . . . Do this in remembrance of me" (Lk 22:19-20). (Cf. Sacrifice of the Mass.)

Eucharist, The • The Eucharist (from the Greek *eucharistia*, "thanksgiving") is the sacrament of the Body and Blood of Jesus Christ, in which He is present under the forms of bread and wine offering Himself in the Sacrifice of the Mass and giving Himself as spiritual food to the faithful. The two principal parts of the Mass are the Liturgy of the Word and the Liturgy of the Eucharist. In the Liturgy of the Word, Sacred Scripture is proclaimed from the texts assigned in the *Lectionary for Mass*. These are responded to by the assembly through the responsorial psalm, gospel acclamation and the short spoken responses to each text ("Thanks be to God.") At the beginning of the Liturgy of the Eucharist, bread (unleavened is prescribed in the West; leavened bread is generally used in the East) and grape wine are placed on the altar to be transformed into the Body and Blood of Christ in the Eucharistic prayer. The Roman Catholic doctrine on the Eucharist calls this transformation "transubstantiation."

The Eucharist was instituted at the Last Supper by Christ Himself (cf. Mt 26:26-28; Mk 14:22-24; Lk 22:17-20; 1 Cor 11:23-25) "in order to perpetuate the sacrifice of the Cross throughout the ages until he should come again, and so to entrust to his beloved Spouse, the Church, a memorial of his death and resurrection: a sacrament of love, a sign of unity, a bond of charity, a paschal banquet in which Christ is consumed, the mind is filled with grace, and a pledge of future glory is given to us" (SC 47).

The celebration of the Eucharist is the action both of Christ and His Church. "For in it Christ perpetuates in an unbloody manner the sacrifice offered on the cross, offering himself to the Father for the world's salvation through the ministry of priests. The Church, the spouse and minister of Christ, performs together with him the role of priest and victim, offers him to the Father and at the same time makes a total offering of herself together with him" (*Eucharisticum Mysterium, Instruction on the Worship of the Eucharistic Mystery*).

Because of the importance and holiness invested in it by Christ Himself, the Eucharist is the chief act of worship in the Catholic Church, and the Consecrated Species of the Eucharist are to be adored by the faithful with the same worship due to God, because of Christ's substantial presence.

Eucharistic Devotions • The postconciliar ritual and instruction regarding *Holy Communion and Worship of the Eucharist Outside Mass* (1973) appropriately places Eucharistic devotions in the context of instructions about the relationship between Eucharistic worship outside Mass and the celebration of the Eucharist, the purposes of Eucharistic reservation (the administration of Viaticum and adoration) and the forms of worship of the Eucharist. It asserts that "the Eucharistic Sacrifice is the source and culmination of the whole Christian life" and that the cult of Eucharistic devotion "should be in harmony with the sacred liturgy in some sense, take their origin from the liturgy, and lead people back to the liturgy" (n. 79). Four forms of Eucharistic devotions derive from reserving the sacrament: exposition, Benediction, processions and congresses.

In the Middle Ages processions with relics, images of the cross or the Eucharist were very popular. Among the latter were processions for Viaticum. On Holy Thursday some solemnity accompanied the procession of the Eucharist from the place of liturgical celebration to a place of reservation until the liturgy of Good Friday. The establishment of the feast of Corpus Christi by the bull *Transiturus* of Urban V in 1264 for the entire Church saw the quick adoption of Eucharistic processions throughout the Church (although these were already in place in some areas of Austria and Italy, for example). Reliquaries were used for the reserved sacrament and thus became models for the first monstrances. In the new ritual, the determination of whether to hold such processions is left to the local Ordinary (n. 101). It is desirable that such a procession "begin after the Mass in which the host to be carried in procession has been consecrated" or after "a lengthy period of public adoration" (n. 103). The service ends with Benediction (nn. 107-108).

The first Eucharistic congress, held in Lille in 1881, was followed by several local, national and international congresses, which custom continues to the present. The international congress at Munich in 1960 marked the merging of this devotion with the liturgical movement; since then the celebration of the Eucharist has been the center of these congresses. The 1973 ritual indicated that the Eucharistic celebration should be prolonged by celebrations of the Word, catechetical meetings, communal prayer, private adoration and processions with the Blessed Sacrament (n. 112). This same ritual states that preparation for such a congress should include catechesis about the Eucharist "as the mystery of Christ living and working in the Church," about the importance of active participation in the liturgy, "in order to encourage a reverent hearing of the Word of God and the spirit of mutual love and community," and "research into the means and pursuit of social action for human development and the just distribution of goods, including the temporal," since "the goal is that every Eucharistic table may be a center from which the leaven of the Gospel spreads as a force in the growth of contemporary society and as the pledge of the future kingdom" (n. 111).

The 1973 Rite for Exposition (n. 82) describes the custom of taking the Eucharist from the tabernacle and placing it in the vessel in which it is ordinarily kept (in the ciborium, *in pyxide*) or in a vessel that enables the consecrated Bread to be seen, e.g., in a monstrance or ostensorium. The celebration of the Eucharist does not occur while the sacrament is exposed (n. 83). Normally, exposition lasts as long as there are faithful present to pray in silence or to join in prayers, songs or readings. The ritual encourages a lengthy period of exposition annually in churches. Exposition ends with Benediction, a blessing with the Blessed Sacrament. This is always preceded by a suitable (Eucharistic) song and prayer; it is followed by replacing the Eucharist in the tabernacle (nn. 94-100). A shorter period for Benediction is possible, provided that there is suitable time for adoration and prayer; however, "exposition merely for the purpose of giving Benediction is prohibited" (n. 89). The ordinary ministers of exposition are priests and deacons (n. 91); in their absence an acolyte, an extraordinary minister of Communion or, "upon appointment by the local ordinary, a member of a religious community or of a pious association . . . which is devoted to Eucharistic adoration" (n. 91) may expose and repose the sacrament. "It is not lawful, however, for them to give the blessing with the Sacrament" (n. 91).

Eucharistic Prayers • The term "Eucharistic prayer" derives from the Greek term *anaphora* (literally, "elevation, lifting up") and the Latin terms *oratio oblationis* (prayer of offering), *illatio* (contribution or sacrifice), *canon* (rule or norm), *prex* (prayer) and *canon actionis* (rule of action). Earliest evidence of the outline of the Eucharistic prayer (not the text itself) comes from the apostolic tradition of Hippolytus (d. A.D. 215). The fourth and fifth centuries saw important developments in both East and West toward establishing these texts which formed the center of the Eucharistic celebration, during which bread and wine are changed into the Body and Blood of Christ. The Eastern anaphoras of St. Basil, of the Apostles, of St. John Chrysostom, St. James, St. Mark, Addai and Mari, Nestorius, Theodore of Mopsuestia, from the Apostolic Constitutions, and from the *Testament of Our Lord* attest to the richness of this prayer's content, theology and style. In the West the comparatively sober and direct language of the Roman Canon is attested to in the writings of St. Ambrose, St. Leo the Great and Gelasius; the canon reached its definitive form sometime after Gregory the Great.

In the West the single Eucharistic prayer text, the Roman Canon, was preceded by variable prefaces and variable prayers throughout the canon itself, customs attested to in writings of Pope Vigilius (c. A.D. 538), where he states that he uses "the same text in consecrating the gifts offered to God," but that when celebrating feasts such as Easter, Ascension and Epiphany, "we add special paragraphs proper to the day" (Vigilius, *Epistle 2*, 5, P.L. 69:18).

Contemporary research into the Jewish origins of this prayer indicate reliance on the *berakah* (acknowledgment, blessing and praise) and *todah* (thanksgiving) forms of prayer for the theology and style of Eucharistic prayers. The limitation of the use of the single Roman Canon, coupled with consideration of its stylistic and theological adequacy in light of the proliferation of themes that are found in the wealth of anaphoras derived from liturgical tradition, led to the development of additional Eucharistic prayers for the Roman Rite as part of the contemporary liturgical reform. For the universal Church these include three additional Eucharistic prayers (promulgated by the decree *Prece Eucharistica* in 1968), three for Masses with children and two for reconciliation (promulgated by the decree *Postquam de Precibus* in 1974). Additional Eucharistic prayers have been approved since Vatican II for use in local churches, an example of which is the Eucharistic prayer composed for the Swiss Synod (Switzerland), a prayer that has been adopted by other episcopal conferences (e.g., the Italian bishops in the second edition of the revised Roman Missal, 1984).

The *General Instruction of the Roman Missal* states that "the Eucharistic prayer, a prayer of thanksgiving and sanctification, is the center and high point of the entire celebration" (n. 54). It begins with an introductory dialogue of three parts, which dialogue itself sets the prayer apart from the other parts of the Mass to indicate its centrality. The dialogue begins with "The Lord be with you. . ." and the response, "And also with you." The second part of the dialogue, "Lift up your hearts / We lift them up to the Lord" is from Lamentations 3:41. The third part, "Let us give thanks to the Lord our God," is likely from the Jewish invitation to blessing over the cup of wine, which invitation is followed by the Greek-inspired statement of agreement, "It is right to give him thanks and praise." The congregation is both to "listen to the Eucharistic prayer in silent reverence and share in it by making the acclamations" (n. 55).

The structure of the new prayers is noted in the *General Instruction* as follows (n. 55): thanksgiving, acclamation [Sanctus], epiclesis, narrative of the institution and consecration, anamnesis, offering, intercessions, final doxology. The thanksgiving is most fully expressed in the preface where "in the name of the entire people of God, the priest praises the Father and gives him thanks for the work of salvation [most commonly acknowledged as accomplished by Christ] or for some special aspect of it in keeping with the day, feast or season" (n. 55a). This text ends with an invitation to the *Sanctus* most often by referring to the "choirs of [arch]angels," "the whole company of heaven," or "the angels and the saints." This reference draws out the eschatological theme as constitutive of the Eucharistic prayer.

The first Eucharistic acclamation ("Holy, holy, holy Lord") is taken from a combination of Isaiah 6:2-3 (used at the morning synagogue prayer) and Matthew 21:9, the acclamation at Christ's triumphal entrance into Jerusalem. This combination of texts derives from the sixth century in Gaul, and in Rome by the seventh century. By the Middle Ages this acclamation of the congregation was assumed by the choir with complex melodies to accompany it. This acclamation eventually separated into two parts (*Sanctus* and *Benedictus*) because of such melodies. Part of the liturgical revival in the 1950s reunited these and made them acclamations of the people once more.

The thanksgiving theme continues after the acclamation to the explicit invocation that God the Father would send the Holy Spirit (the epiclesis) on the gifts and/or the community. The *General Instruction of the Roman Missal* states that in the epiclesis "the Church calls on God's power and asks that the gifts offered . . . may be consecrated, that is, become the body and blood of Christ, and that the victim may become a source of salvation for those who are to share in communion" (n. 55). In the present Eucharistic prayer structure, the epiclesis before the institution narrative is called "consecratory," the one after the anamnesis is called "communion."

The institution narrative follows. A review of the more than eighty versions of the anaphora in liturgical tradition shows no striving for exact uniformity in this text. However, it is characteristic of the Roman Canon that it included the phrases "into his holy and venerable hands" and "the mystery of faith." The use of the Matthean version with the text (unique to Matthew) "for the forgiveness of sins" marks most anaphoras and perdures in the present Roman Rite. The two sections of the institution narrative are followed by the elevation of the consecrated Bread and then the consecrated Wine.

The addition of a memorial acclamation after the institution narrative (or after the *anamnesis* ["memorial" prayer] in the Eucharistic prayers for children) in 1969 is new to Western usage on Eucharistic prayers. The phrase "mystery of faith" is transferred from its former position in the institution narrative and now forms the invitation to the acclamation: "Let us proclaim the mystery of faith." The acclamation itself focuses on the central mystery commemorated through the Eucharist, Christ's dying and rising. The use of four English texts here derives from three texts offered in the Latin original, two of which contain explicit eschatological references.

The *anamnesis* ("memorial") section of the prayer now follows. The *General Instruction* (n. 55e) states that "in fulfillment of the command received from Christ through the Apostles, the Church keeps his memorial by recalling his passion, resurrection, and ascension." The origins of this prayer reach back to the Jewish Passover, a memorial feast whereby succeeding generations of God's people would share in the same salvation experienced by those whom God saved at the first Passover. The notion of memorial has come to describe the whole Eucharistic action as the means through which present believers share in the paschal mystery in an intimate and unique way. The present Eucharistic prayers draw explicit attention here to Christ's death, descent among the dead, resurrection, ascension and coming in glory. Most often this prayer is linked with a statement that the Church is offering the Eucharistic bread and cup (or some equivalent). The Roman Canon makes this statement in a number of ways, including "this holy and perfect sacrifice: the bread of life and the cup of eternal salvation." The Second Eucharistic Prayer (derived from the *Apostolic Tradition* of Hippolytus) speaks about "this life-giving bread, this saving cup." The Third Eucharistic Prayer refers to "this holy and living sacrifice," while the Fourth Eucharistic Prayer speaks of offering Christ's "body and blood." The *General Instruction* states that in the offering, the Church "offers the victim to the Father in the Holy Spirit" and that the Church's intention is "that the faithful not only offer the spotless victim but also learn to offer

themselves daily to be drawn into ever more perfect union" through Christ with the Father and one another (n. 55f).

The precedent of intercessions as part of prayers of thanksgiving also derives from Jewish origins. Liturgical tradition attests to their being placed at various places in the anaphora: at the end of the prayer (Antioch), before the institution narrative (Alexandria), and both before and after the institution narrative (Roman Canon). The present structuring of the Eucharistic prayer in the Roman Rite establishes their place after the second epiclesis, before the final doxology. The nature of these prayers is that they draw the particular congregation beyond its own needs to those of a more universal nature, albeit in prayers that are restrained and which pray for the Church (along with special mention of the Pope and local bishop), the immediate community and for the dead. As the *General Instruction* states, the intercessions "make it clear that the Eucharist is celebrated in communion with the whole Church of heaven and earth, and that the offering is made for the Church and all its members, living and dead. . ." (n. 55g).

The final doxology of the Eucharistic prayer is attested to as early as the mid-second century, in the *First Apology* of Justin the Martyr, who states that "all present give their assent with an Amen [which means 'so be it']." This solemn ratification of the anaphora prayer is customarily Trinitarian, mentioning Father, Son and Spirit; its doxological nature derives from Jewish blessings and acclamations. This is accompanied by the elevation of Host and chalice, a custom which derives from the ancient liturgy. In the Middle Ages this gesture diminished in emphasis, and from the fourteenth century the priest would place Host and chalice on the altar before inviting the response "Amen" to his prayer *Per omnia saecula saeculorum*. The *General Instruction* states that "the praise of God is expressed in the doxology which is confirmed and concluded by the acclamation of the people" (n. 55h).

Euchites • Also known as Messalians or men of prayer, a fourth-century mendicant movement dedicated to literal application of the Sermon on the Mount. The sect, which originated in Mesopotamia and spread to other parts of the Church, won the notice and opposition of such writers as St. Epiphanius and St. Basil the Great, and was condemned by the Council of Ephesus (A.D. 431).

Euchologion • The liturgical book of the Eastern Church containing the text and rubrics of the Liturgies of Sts. John Chrysostom and Basil the Great, and that of the Presanctified (used during Lent). It also has the invariable parts of the Office, as well as all the formularies for the celebration of the sacraments.

Eulogia • The unconsecrated bread given to those who could not communicate in the early Church. This custom lasted into the nineteenth century, for St. Thérèse of Lisieux speaks of asking for "blessed bread" after Mass when she was still too young to receive. The Byzantine Rite has never given up the practice.

Eunomianism • A radical form of Arianism formulated in the middle of the fourth century by Eunomius, a clever dialectician, it restated the Christian doctrine of the Trinity in Neoplatonic terms, asserting — against the Nicene definition — that there was no generation in God and, since the Trinity was three mutually exclusive substances, the Son was not strictly God.

In A.D. 399 the emperor ordered Eunomius's writing to be burned. Therefore, we know most of his works only through the writings and refutations of St. Basil, St. Gregory of Nyssa and Apollinaris.

It is also called Anomoeism (*anomoios* meaning unlike), since it taught that the Son is unlike the Father.

Eusebians • People who take their name from Eusebius of Nicomedia (d. A.D. 342), who converted them from paganism to Arian Christianity. Although Eusebius accepted the anti-Arian creed of the Council of Nicaea (325), he refused to recognize the council's excommunication of Arius, who had appealed personally to Eusebius for help. That same year, the Emperor Constantine deposed and banished Eusebius, presumably for his support of Arius. Within two years, however, the two were reconciled, and Eusebius became the emperor's primary ecclesiastical adviser. In fact, it was Eusebius who administered Constantine's deathbed Baptism. Constantine's heir, Constantius II, appointed Eusebius as bishop of Constantinople.

Euthanasia, Active • The deliberate killing of a disabled, dying or chronically ill person by positive means to enable the person to escape from suffering. Active euthanasia (which is to end suffering) is different from murder in its motive. Because of this, some believe it is not true murder, and it should not be punished as a crime, and in fact they believe it should be considered as a morally good and justifiable act.

However, active mercy killing remains the deliberate, direct and positive killing of the sick, dying, chronically ill and disabled, precisely because they suffer from these conditions. Were these people not in this condition, they would not be candidates for killing. Mercy killing is morally wrong because it is the deliberate and direct killing of these people, and for that reason it should be legally and morally prohibited. But it should also be prohibited because it is uncontrollable in principle. There is nothing in the principle that one can kill another to end suffering that could limit the killing. For who is to say that the suffering of the dying is greater than the suffering of the lovelorn? Euthanasia exploits and is discriminatory against the sick, disabled, incompetent and despairing, and it kills them precisely because they are in this condition. Legal and moral permission for active mercy killing puts the entire class of the disabled and dying in danger of being made the victims of sentimental murder. Prohibitions against euthanasia are designed to protect these people not only from themselves but also from others as well, for euthanasia is not a threat to the healthy, happy and prosperous, but only to those who are sick, dying, despairing and disabled.

Euthanasia, Passive • The deliberate killing of another by passive means to enable the person to escape suffering. One's obligations to provide life-sustaining measures are determined by the nature of the measures to be taken. If they involve successful, inexpensive and non-risky measures, they are obligatory; and if not, they can be refused or denied.

Culpable passive mercy killing is refusing to take a lifesaving measure that involves little risk or expense and that is expected to achieve its therapeutic effect. The most commonly practiced form of passive euthanasia is the denial of food and water to the medically stable who are in bad medical condition. Successful provision of food and water by readily available methods should be provided for all patients. In our society, euthanasia is being transformed into a duty and an obligation under the nebulous and ill-defined category of "death with dignity."

Euthanasia is also immoral because it is the deliberate killing of an innocent person by omission and because it cuts off

communication with the dying, disabled or despairing person in the time of greatest need. It changes the health care provider or physician from a healer and life-giver into a killer and destroys the meaning by making him or her a death-dealer. In many instances active or passive euthanasia is doubtfully voluntary, and it is usually quite difficult to determine if the suffering that is being alleviated is that of the patient or of onlookers and associates of the patient. Active and passive involuntary euthanasia are usually requested by family members, and this calls into question their right to make decisions concerning the provision of life-sustaining measures. Strangely, it is often from family members that the medically vulnerable need the most protection by the law.

Eutychianism • Eutychianism closely tracks a much larger heresy, Monophysitism, and although not identical to it, is often lumped together with it. It is usually attributed to a monk from Constantinople named Eutyches, but considering that this monk was not a man of letters, it is more likely that his honorable reputation was usurped, at least in part, for purposes of spreading the errors which bore his name.

Eutychianism arose in response to another heresy, Nestorianism, but like Monophysitism, erred in the opposite direction by holding that Christ had but one nature. By implication, it denied the title of Our Lady as *Theotokos*. The extreme position taken by some Eutychians, especially in Armenia, on this and other matters seemed to alarm even the Monophysites, who began to use the term "Eutychian" with opprobrium. Both heresies were, in any event, finally condemned by the Council of Chalcedon.

Evangeliarum • Gospel book containing the four Gospels in their complete form, or a book with the Gospel pericopes for Mass for each day of the year. The 1969 *Ordo Missae*, Order of Mass, envisions the use of two ceremonial books at the Eucharist, one for the first and second readings (a lectionary) and the other for the Gospels (the Gospel Book), the latter receiving the honor of being carried in procession by the deacon, placed on the altar at the entrance rite, and carried in procession with candles and incense to the lectern for proclamation.

Evangelica Testificatio • A 1971 apostolic exhortation of Pope Paul VI on religious life. The principal and most authoritative statement on the subject in the postconciliar Church, it recognized the threats and challenges to religious life posed by the modern world. The document's chief aim was to urge a renewal of commitment among the world's religious to the particular charism of their respective founders, as well as a rededication to the centrality of the Eucharist in the life of the Church and her servants.

Evangelical Counsels • The evangelical counsels are gifts given by God to the Church whereby individual members, by dedicating themselves to a life following the counsels, build up the Church in a special way. The three evangelical counsels are poverty, chastity and obedience. Members of religious institutes take public vows to follow the counsels. Members of societies of apostolic life and secular institutes profess the evangelical counsels by other sacred bonds such as promises.

Religious, clergy and lay persons are all able to profess the evangelical counsels; however, members of each group live out their commitment according to their state in life. The counsel of poverty means a renunciation of the use or radical ownership of material goods for religious and some form of moderation and self-denial for others. The counsel of chastity means perfect continence for religious and celibate clerics and absolute fidelity to one's spouse for married lay persons. The counsel of obedience means obedience to one's superiors, in addition to obedience to other Church authorities for religious. For clergy who are not religious and lay persons, obedience means accepting and following the will of Church authority as closely as is possible (Canons 573-577).

Evangelical United Brethren • Broadly Methodist in doctrine, discipline and polity, the Evangelical United Brethren Church in 1968 merged with the Methodist Church to form a single denomination as the United Methodist Church. The Evangelical United Brethren Church was itself the outcome of a merger in 1946 joining two closely related groups, the United Brethren in Christ and the Evangelical Church.

The United Brethren in Christ had its origins in 1800 in the preaching activities of William Otterbein (1726-1813) and Martin Boehm (1725-1812) among the Germans in Pennsylvania, Maryland, and Virginia, while the Evangelical Church similarly grew in 1807 from the preaching of the formerly Lutheran Jacob Albright (1759-1808) among Germans in Pennsylvania. The Church of the United Brethren in Christ broke from this group because it opposed the constitutional changes of 1889 and continued as an independent denomination with nearly 20,000 members. Some congregations of the Evangelical United Brethren Church rejected the merger that created the United Methodist Church in 1968 and established the Evangelical Church in North America. But at that time 750,000 Evangelical United Brethren swelled the ranks of the new United Methodist Church to make it, with about ten million members, the largest Methodist body in America.

Evangelii Nuntiandi • Pope Paul VI's apostolic exhortation, "On Evangelization in the Modern World," released December 8, 1975.

Recalling the statements on evangelization at the Third General Assembly of the Synod of Bishops during the preceding year, Paul VI sought to illustrate the "profound" and "inseparable" link between Christ, the Church and the important work of evangelization, the core message of which is salvation in Jesus Christ through a conversion of the human heart. This message, the Pope noted, is spread through a variety of means: preaching, particularly when done as part of the Liturgy of the Word, catechetics, a sophisticated use of the mass media, celebration of the sacraments and the practice of popular piety.

Addressed also is the more fundamental question of why evangelization is important. Who reaps in the vineyard of evangelization, and who sows? That is, who are the beneficiaries of such activity, and who are its workers?

In an increasingly "de-christianized world," Christians and non-Christians, believers as well as non-believers, constitute the fertile soil in which global missionary work is to be done. And in line with its truly global nature, the work of evangelization, the document concluded, is the obligation of the universal Church as well as that of her constituent parts. All the Church's workers of evangelization — bishops, priests, religious and laity — are called to carry out "diversified ministries," thereby effectively spreading the Gospel message of truth and love with all "the fervor of the saints."

Evangelion: See **Euangelion**

Evangelist • The Greek *euangelistos* means "one who announces good news." Originally, the term referred to those who proclaimed the Gospel in apostolic days. St. Paul called Timothy an evangelist (2 Tm 4:5) and Luke refers to Philip as one (Acts 21:8). In Ephesians 4:11-12, the office of evangelist is listed after Apostles and prophets, as "building up the body of Christ."

More popularly, the term refers to the four men whose names are associated with the four Gospels: Matthew, Mark, Luke and John.

In Protestant usage especially, one finds the word used to describe a preacher who seeks to introduce (or reintroduce) people to the Gospel, usually in a rousing manner.

Evangelium • The Good News, or the Gospel of Jesus Christ. In more common usage, it frequently means the New Testament exclusively, as distinct from the Old Testament.

Evangelium Vitae • The eleventh encyclical of Pope John Paul II, *Evangelium Vitae*, or *The Gospel of Life*, condemns a culture of death which has given rise to widespread abortion and euthanasia, "crimes which no human law can claim to legitimize."

John Paul writes: "To claim the right to abortion, infanticide and euthanasia, and to recognize that right in law, means to attribute to human freedom a perverse and evil significance: that of an absolute power over others and against others." Catholics have "a clear obligation" to resist such laws.

While little new ground is broken in the 194-page encyclical — the document, for example, restates long-standing Church teaching against the use of artificial means of contraception as well as most embryo research and prenatal diagnostic testing intended to justify "eugenic abortion" —

Evangelium Vitae marks the first time abortion and euthanasia have been made the focus and given the weight of an encyclical. In another important development, the document also sets severely circumscribed parameters within which a state may legitimately carry out capital punishment, namely in only those "very rare" cases when society can be protected in no other way.

John Paul does countenance political efforts aimed at merely limiting access to abortion in those circumstances in which a complete curtailment is neither likely nor possible. "In a case . . . when it is not possible to overturn or completely abrogate a pro-abortion law, an elected official, whose absolute personal opposition to a procured abortion was well-known, could licitly support proposals aimed at limiting the harm done by such a law and at lessening its negative consequences at the level of general opinion and public morality," the Pontiff writes.

Still the message of the *Gospel of Life* is clear: "No circumstance, no purpose, no law whatsoever, can ever make licit an act which is intrinsically illicit, since it is contrary to the Law of God which is written in every human heart, knowable by reason itself, and proclaimed by the Church."

Evangelization • An all-inclusive term used to describe the entire range of activities by which the Church proclaims and communicates to the world the saving message of Christ. The literal sense of the word — deriving from *euangelion* ("Good News" or Gospel) — remains fundamental to its broader meaning, since the saving message of Christ is contained in its fullness in the Gospel accounts of His words and deeds. Evangelization takes many forms and employs many media of communication: the preaching of the Gospel in the setting of the Eucharistic and sacramental celebrations;

missionary ventures in foreign lands; personal witness in one's circle of friends and co-workers; television and radio preaching; books, newspapers and magazines devoted to the spread of knowledge of Christ; and so on. It is understood that, with the sacraments of Baptism and Confirmation, every Christian receives the commission to bear witness to the message and work of Christ, so that others may believe in Him. Thus, the inspiration of evangelization is love — for Christ, who enjoins us to make Him known, and for our neighbors, whose destiny is to be joined to Him forever.

Evangelization of Peoples, Congregation for the • Still popularly known by its original name, the Congregation for the Propagation of the Faith, this congregation was established by Pope Gregory XV in 1622. Its responsibility is to coordinate and direct all missionary activity in the world, except in those areas which are within the competence of the congregation for the Eastern Churches. In addition, it has direct jurisdiction over the Church in parts of southeastern Europe, parts of the Americas, almost all of Africa, the Far East, New Zealand and the Pacific Islands, excepting Australia. All missionaries and missionary institutes are responsible to this congregation. Dependent upon this congregation are the Missionary Union of the Clergy, the Society for the Propagation of the Faith, the Society of St. Peter the Apostle for Native Clergy, the Society of the Holy Childhood and the Fides news agency.

In 1967 its official name became the Congregation for the Evangelization of Peoples, or *de Propaganda Fide*.

Eve • The name given to the first woman by Adam, the first man (Gn 3:20).

According to the biblical narrative, Eve is the mother of Cain and Abel. As mother of these two sons, she is referred to as "the mother of all the living."

Through her primordial disobedience, Eve suffered sin and loss along with her husband Adam. Eve's disobedience, though, was supplanted by the New Testament obedience of Mary, the Virgin of Nazareth. Citing several patristic sources, the Second Vatican Council, quoting St. Irenaeus, puts it this way: "The knot of Eve's disobedience was untied by Mary's obedience: what the virgin Eve bound through her unbelief, Mary loosened by her faith" (LG 56). From a spiritual perspective, Eve is really the antitype of the Blessed Mother.

For further reading: Howard N. Wallace, "Eve," *Anchor Bible Dictionary*, 2:676-677.

Evil • Evil is not something, but it is real. Strictly speaking, evil is the absence or lack of a quality or state that should be present in some entity or situation. For this reason, though evil is real enough, there is no such thing as pure evil or personified evil. Evil occurs in entities (in themselves good) or actions (in themselves aimed at real or apparent goods) because of some defect in them. But not any kind of negation is an evil. In order to indicate this, evil is described as a form of privation — the lack of something that should be present. Thus, blindness is an evil for a sparrow but not for a stone. Similarly, that human beings cannot fly is not an evil (but simply a limitation arising from their nature), though that they sometimes act badly is (a failure to seek the genuinely good).

Creaturely limitations are sometimes described as "metaphysical evils," but this way of speaking is imprecise. Evil is commonly divided into two kinds: bad things that happen (physical evils), and bad things that are done (moral evils). There are many forms of physical evil in the natural run of things. In itself, an earthquake, for example, is the sudden movement of tectonic plates along a geological fault; but this natural process produces vast destruction for the inhabitants of the affected areas. According to traditional Catholic teaching, moral evils are of two kinds: guilt arising from bad deeds and habits (*malum culpae*) and the punishment incurred by these (*malum poenae*).

The "problem of evil" refers to the issue of God's role in the causation of evil. Since God is perfectly good, He cannot be the direct cause of any evil. He permits physical evils that occur as a matter of course in the universe. He sometimes does not prevent bad deeds (not interfering with the exercise of freedom), but He permits the purification of repentant sinners and the punishment of the incorrigibly wicked. (Cf. Devil; Devil and Evil Spirits.)

Evolution • The process by which existing organisms have developed from earlier forms through transformations of characteristics in successive generations. The most widely accepted theory explaining this process is that originally advanced by Charles Darwin and Alfred Russell Wallace in 1858, and subsequently amplified by the work of other scientists. According to this theory, evolution occurs by natural selection in combination with hereditary adaptations. Natural selection is seen as a process favoring the emergence of transformations in a population of organisms that enable it to survive and flourish in a particular environment over the course of several generations. These adaptations involve transmissible alterations (mutations or recombinations of genes) in the genetic code and thus the emergence of new species. In the present state of knowledge, the theory of evolution by natural selection has been the most successful (although by no means completely so) in explaining the available data.

Whatever theory is advanced to explain evolution, that such a process underlies the emergence of existing species and organisms presents no challenge to the Catholic understanding of the doctrine of creation. The doctrine of creation affirms that God brought all things into existence. Since at least the time of St. Augustine, the Genesis account of the process of creation has been recognized to be largely symbolic. There is no reason why God could not have employed some natural evolutionary process in the forming of species, even if this process appears to scientific observation to be largely random in its activity. Christians can also accept the view that the material conditions for the emergence of the human species may have developed by evolution, as long as the immediate creation of each human soul by God is affirmed.

Ex Cathedra • Literally "from the throne," this Latin expression is used to designate papal pronouncements of the greatest solemnity and authority. Teachings pronounced *ex cathedra* are understood to be infallible. The expression highlights the four conditions under which, according to Vatican Council I, infallible definitions of Church dogma can be taught by the Pope: he must speak (1) not as a private theologian, but as the supreme pastor and teacher of all Christians; (2) in virtue of his apostolic authority as the successor of Peter; (3) in matters of faith or morals; (4) proposing something to be held by the universal Church.

Ex Corde Ecclesiae • An Apostolic Constitution on Catholic universities issued by Pope John Paul II in 1990. *Ex Corde Ecclesiae* proposes principles and guidelines for securing and promoting the Catholic identity and mission of institutions of higher learning conducted under Catholic auspices. It calls upon the bishops to take an active role in fostering the identity and mission of Catholic universities by cultivating a pastoral relationship with their chief administrators. Each episcopal conference is directed to undertake the local implementation of *Ex Corde Ecclesiae*. In response to this directive, the National Conference of Catholic Bishops in 1991 established a Committee for the Implementation of *Ex Corde Ecclesiae*. This committee of bishops and college presidents produced a proposed set of norms in 1993. After consultation and discussion, it was agreed that an additional period of dialogue is needed in order to foster the general understanding and climate necessary for the effective implementation of the constitution.

Ex Opere Operantis • Term in sacramental theology ("by the work of the doer"), meaning that the effectiveness of sacraments depends on the moral rectitude of minister or participant. When it first evolved in the thirteenth century, this term was applied to rites of the Old Testament in contrast with those of the New Testament.

Ex Opere Operato • Term in sacramental theology ("by the work done"), meaning that sacraments are effective by means of the sacramental rite itself, and not because of the worthiness of the minister or participant.

Exaltation of the Cross • The liturgical festival of the Exaltation (now translated as the "triumph") of the Holy Cross on September 14 can be traced to two historical occurrences in the city of Jerusalem. The first was the dedication of the Constantinian Basilica of the Holy Sepulchre on this date in the fourth century. The other event was the recovery of the True Cross from the Persians in the seventh century, which event prompted the declaration of this special feast.

In the present revision of the Roman Calendar this day ranks as a feast, that is, second in prominence in the ordering of liturgical days and seasons. The liturgical observance thus begins with Evening Prayer I and extends to Evening Prayer II on the day itself. The lectionary readings for the feast are from Numbers 21:4-9, Philippians 2:6-11 and John 3:13-17. A special Preface is assigned to the feast in the present sacramentary containing the important central text: "You decreed that man should be saved through the wood of the cross. The tree of man's defeat became his tree of victory; where life was lost, there life has been restored through Christ our Lord."

Examen • An examination of conscience made on a daily basis for the purpose of eliminating faults, failings and imperfections, to root out one's sins and to practice the ways of Christian holiness and virtue. The *examen* is an important aspect of our spiritual life, because through it we confront the common and everyday evils of our life and root them out. The *examen* fulfills the command to "pray always." It is the measure we employ to determine our growth in the spiritual life. In the *examen*, we respond to the call to conversion and metanoia, for it points out to us the area(s) in our lives in which we need repentance and conversion. True growth in the spiritual life cannot be accomplished without this, and we cannot grow in the likeness of Christ without this spiritual discipline.

Examination of Bishops • As part of the Rite of the Ordination of a Bishop, an examination is made in which the bishop-elect is required to answer certain questions. These questions elicit his promise that he resolves to: discharge the office of bishop to the end of his life; be faithful and constant in proclaiming the Gospel of Christ; maintain the Deposit of Faith in its entirety

as it has been handed down by the Apostles and professed by the Church; build up the Church as the Body of Christ, and remain united to it within the order of bishops under the authority of the Pope; be faithful in obedience to the successor of Peter; sustain the People of God and guide them in the way of salvation in cooperation with the priests and deacons who will share his ministry; show kindness and compassion to the poor, to strangers and to all who are in need; be a good shepherd in seeking out those who stray, gathering them into Christ's fold; and pray for the People of God constantly, carrying out the duties of one who has the fullness of the priesthood, giving no reason for reproach.

The examination is made by the principal consecrating bishop, in the presence of the faithful.

Examination of Conscience • The conscious and deliberate act of evaluating one's actions, attitudes, thoughts and words for the purpose of distinguishing good from evil, right from wrong, and grace from sin. As such, an examination of conscience will require, of one who undertakes it, a spirit of correct discernment, sound judgment, honesty, integrity and utter veracity. An examination of conscience may be undertaken by anyone at any time, but is generally done as a spiritual exercise or preparation for the sacrament of Penance.

In some religious orders and congregations, members are required to make an examination of conscience each day as prescribed either by the founder of the order or congregation or its constitution. Apart from the members of orders and congregations, many other Catholics examine their consciences as a way of growing in holiness and faith. When used as preparation for celebrating the sacrament of Penance, the Catholic would consider a specific period of time for the evaluation of the moral and spiritual content of his life. Usually, this means the period of time which has elapsed since his last confession.

An examination of conscience may be described as general or particular. A general one probes the various aspects of a person's life: relationship with God, relationship with others, the vast array of virtues associated with the Christian life, etc. Customary areas of inquiry for a general examination of conscience are likely to include but are definitely not restricted to: the Ten Commandments, the Beatitudes and the Precepts of the Church. A particular one focuses on a predominant fault, an unacquired virtue, or a duty connected with a specific vocation.

The examination of conscience has been a part of the Christian life since the earliest times and should always have a preeminent place in every Catholic's interior life. In the New Testament, St. Paul urged that there be an examination of conscience before receiving the Eucharist (1 Cor 11:28). So important was the examination of conscience to St. Ignatius Loyola (1491-1556), the founder of the Society of Jesus, that he made it a key element in his *Spiritual Exercises*. And, to show its importance in the life of the diocesan priest, the documents of the Holy See on priestly formation and the Program of Priestly Formation of the American Bishops call attention to the regular examination of conscience as a way of making and marking progress in the Christian life.

Examiners, Synodal • The 1917 Code prescribed that priests be appointed during the diocesan synod to serve as special examiners for the bishop. They were to conduct examinations of candidates for pastor and candidates for Holy Orders. They were also to conduct examinations of applicants for faculties to hear confessions or to preach. Finally, the synodal examiners were to act as advisors to the bishop during procedures for the removal or transfer of pastors.

Although the revised Code dropped the office of synodal examiners, the bishop is free to appoint persons to fulfill these duties (cf. Canon 469).

Exarch • From the Greek for "a guide." In the ancient Byzantine Empire, an exarch was the governor of an outlying province. In the Byzantine Church, this term came to be applied to the patriarch, and later to an archbishop or bishop or other clergyman serving in the place of a bishop but without the power to ordain priests. Today this title is given to a priest who is not a bishop but who heads a Church area. The area of an exarch's jurisdiction is termed an exarchate.

Excardination • The canonical action whereby a cleric is separated from the particular church or institute of consecrated life to which he had been attached. This can be accomplished in two ways. The first is when the cleric's Ordinary gives him a letter of excardination, allowing him to become attached or incardinated to another particular church. The Ordinary of the church to which he wishes to become attached must also sign a letter of incardination.

Secondly, after a cleric has lawfully moved from his own particular church, after five years he is automatically incardinated into the particular church to which he has moved. It is necessary that he have declared his intention to be so incardinated in writing to both Ordinaries and also necessary that neither Ordinary indicate opposition in writing within four months of receiving the cleric's request.

Clerics are not to seek excardination except for just reasons. The law mentions two areas: the advantage to the Church or the good of the cleric. An Ordinary is not to refuse a cleric's request to excardinate if the cleric is prepared to move, is in good standing and wishes to exercise his ministry in regions with serious shortages of clergy (cf. Canons 268-270).

Excellency • "Your Excellency" ("His Excellency," "Most Reverend Excellency") is the proper form of address in the Roman Church for bishops and archbishops. This title is also given to ambassadors from other countries to and accredited by the Holy See. In some countries, e.g., Great Britain and Ireland, bishops are often addressed as "Your Lordship," though this is less common today. Archbishops may be also addressed as "Your Grace."

Exclaustration • The permission given by a competent authority to a member of a religious community whereby the member leaves the community and lives apart from it. While living apart, religious are dispensed from those obligations that are incompatible with their new condition in life. Practically speaking, this means that they are not bound by the obligations of the vow of poverty as well as certain of the day-to-day obligations arising from the vow of obedience. They remain bound by the vow of chastity, however. They may or may not be able to wear the religious habit, depending upon the terms of the superior's decision.

The supreme moderator, with the consent of his or her council, can grant a decree of exclaustration to a religious for a period of up to three years. To extend the period beyond this or to grant an original decree of longer than three years is a permission only the Holy See can give for religious who are members of pontifical-right institutes or diocesan bishops for members of diocesan-right institutes (cf. Canons 686-687).

Excommunication • As its name implies, excommunication is the penal exclusion of one of the faithful from the community of the faithful. Tracing its biblical roots to the curse, excommunication has varied widely in scope over the centuries. The primary canonical effects of excommunication, nevertheless, have always been sacramental and governmental. The spiritual and eschatological effects, contrary to public perception, were and are rather limited. The social effects vary in severity with culture, historical period and the station of the offender. By any measure, though, excommunication is one of the most ancient, serious and controversial censures imposed by the Church. Canon 1331 of the 1983 Code of Canon Law represents the present discipline of the Church in this matter.

Excommunication can be incurred in either of two ways. According to the norms of the penal process, excommunication, like other ecclesiastical penalties, is usually to be imposed *ferendae sententiae*, that is, only after a formal proceeding. Canon 1425 generally restricts the imposition of *ferendae sententiae* excommunications to a judicial trial consisting of at least three judges. The pretended celebration of the Eucharist or of sacramental confession (Canon 1378) and violation of the seal of confession by an interpreter (Canon 1388) are delicts punishable by *ferendae sententiae* excommunication.

Certain other offenses, on the other hand, are considered so seriously disruptive of ecclesial life that they may be met with excommunications imposed automatically, or *latae sententiae*. Although there were some thirty such offenses listed in the 1917 Code, these have been reduced to seven in the 1983 Code: apostasy, heresy or schism (Canon 1364), violation of the Sacred Species (Canon 1367), laying violent hands on the Pope (Canon 1370), absolution of an accomplice (Canon 1378), episcopal consecration without authorization from the Holy See (Canon 1382), violation of the seal of confession by a confessor (Canon 1388) and procuring abortion (Canon 1398).

In regard to the effects of excommunication, every excommunicate is forbidden to have any share in the Eucharist or other acts of public worship or to celebrate or receive the sacraments or sacramentals. An excommunicate is therefore clearly deprived of sacramental grace. From the point of view of Church governance, those under excommunication are forbidden to place any acts associated with ecclesiastical office or other ecclesiastical functions. This prohibition, however, only affects the liceity of such acts, unless the excommunication has been imposed *ferendae sententiae*. If this is the case, any attempts at placing ecclesiastical acts by an excommunicate are invalid. Moreover, should one excommunicated *ferendae sententiae* attempt to participate in liturgical actions, such actions are to cease until the excommunicate is removed. The former distinction between so-called "forbidden excommunicates" and "tolerated excommunicates," however, has been dropped from the 1983 Code, and the faithful are under no canonical restriction in regard to associating with excommunicates, although prudence and Christian concern for an excommunicate might well indicate a special response in a given situation.

Absolution from an excommunication has ever been a complex matter because each case inevitably involves the legal sanction of excommunication and the underlying moral offense which led to the excommunication. Briefly, however, an excommunicate has the right to remission of the canonical effects of excommunication upon withdrawal from contumacy, although the formal act of absolving from the penalty of excommunication might be reserved to a higher ecclesiastical authority. Canon 1357, moreover, provides the basic guide for sacramental absolution in cases of excommunication. This canon evidences the Church's keen concern for the spiritual welfare by offering generous means for the absolution of excommunicates. It cannot be stressed enough that, as a medicinal penalty, excommunication is intended principally to bring about the reform of the offender.

Exegesis • A Greek word that means "to bring out," more specifically, the process for bringing out the meaning of a text. Exegesis proceeds under the rules of the science of hermeneutics. At times exegesis has been distinguished from exposition; the latter being the process of determining the meaning of a text for today, exegesis being the steps taken to ascertain the original meaning. Exegesis is indicated any time the text is not self-evident. The need for biblical exegesis is immediately understood when one realizes that the Bible derives from a rather different cultural, ethnic and socioeconomic milieu. Because of the obscurities in the text of Scripture, exegesis has been practiced from the earliest times (cf. DV 12).

For further reading: Douglas Stuart, "Exegesis," *Anchor Bible Dictionary*, 2:682-688.

Exegete • A practitioner of exegesis or one who interprets Sacred Scripture. (Cf. Exegesis.)

Exemption • A privilege held by religious institutes whereby they are removed from the authority of the local bishop and placed directly under the authority of the Holy See or some other agency determined by the Holy See. In the 1917 Code, and in the revised Code as well, exemption from the authority of the diocesan bishop applies only to the internal affairs of the religious community. It does not apply to the exercise of the apostolate, which is always under the authority of the bishop. This means that for any exercise of the apostolate or any ministry to the faithful of a diocese, the religious community must subject itself to the approval and ongoing authority of the bishop. This applies particularly to liturgical celebrations to which the faithful have access, to schools, hospitals and other organized apostolates for the faithful. If the bishop hears of abuses and a warning to the religious superior is not heeded, he has the right, by law, to intervene. Historically, the first instance of exemption seems to have been that granted to the Benedictine monastery of Bobbio in A.D. 628. It has served to protect religious communities from illegitimate interference and has been particularly helpful to the centralized apostolates of the mendicant religious communities (cf. Canon 591).

Exequatur: See **Exsequatur**

Exercises, Spiritual • A treatise of spiritual theology and practice composed by St. Ignatius Loyola (1491-1556), in order to guide souls in deepening the Christian life. Normally, one undertakes to practice the exercises over a period of thirty days of spiritual retreat under the guidance of a director. The four sets of exercises presented by St. Ignatius can then be distributed over a four-week period: consideration, first, of sin and its consequences (*deformata reformare*); second, the reign of Christ (*reformata conformare*); then, consideration of the "Two Standards," the Passion of Christ (*conformata confirmare*) and the Risen Christ (*confirmata transformare*).

The mainstay of these exercises is the practice of meditation, keyed to these moments of spiritual development, and the recommendation of various ascetical rules for life. The first draft of this treatise dated from shortly after St. Ignatius' conversion, but he revised and amplified the text throughout his life. This work of mature and distilled practical wisdom has won a wide readership and the status of a spiritual classic.

Existence • Essence and existence are the fundamental principles of every actual existing being. Metaphysics points out that, with respect to any actually existing entity, it is possible to ask what it is (*quod*) and by what does it exist (*quo*). Essence is the quiddity or whatness of an actually existing entity, while existence is the act by which a thing is present in nature or in mind. The significance of this distinction for theology is that it helps to specify the difference between creatures and God. God's essence is identical with His existence, because it is fully subsistent actuality. Creatures, on the other, receive existence from God.

Existence of God: See **God**

Existentialism • A philosophy of the nineteenth and twentieth centuries, emphasizing concrete experience of human existence, especially in its crisis moments, over more abstract speculations about the whole of reality.

There are many types of existentialism. Atheistic or agnostic existentialism, such as can be found in the writings of Jean-Paul Sartre and Martin Heidegger, focuses on the plight of human existence shorn of all certain relationship to a Creator-God. Religious existentialisms, such as those of Søren Kierkegaard, Martin Buber or Gabriel Marcel, are interested in highlighting the reality of God in the face of the desperate human need for an alternative to debasing conformity.

Rejection of existentialism as a philosophy is often based on the claim that this philosophy, while rich in its analyses of human experience, has other, more important deficiencies. Particularly, existentialism is lacking in the proofs of God's existence and of the immateriality and immortality of the soul, on which a classical metaphysics bases rational hope.

Exodus, Book of • The second book of the Old Testament is so named because it centers around the departure of the Jewish slaves from their captivity in Egypt. It tells the story of how the Jews came to be a nation and happened, after forty nomadic years, to occupy the territory, promised long before to Abraham, which they still claim as their own. The great hero of the book is Moses, whose life-story is told in such great detail as to contrast sharply with the brevity of the narrative about the many centuries the Jews suffered in servitude in Egypt.

Moses is traditionally regarded as the author of the book, and there can be no doubt that oral traditions from him and about him influenced the written narrative which we have. The book and the wisdom which it embodies had great political importance for the Jews. It kept alive as a unifying force the story of their oppression at the hands of the Egyptians; it nourished their conviction that they were God's Chosen People, and that God had supported them both by sending plagues upon their enemies and by providentially feeding and guiding them in the desert. From the religious point of view, Exodus explained the origin of the great feast of Passover, the importance of monotheism and the folly of the idolatrous and licentious religious practices of their pagan neighbors.

The giving of the Ten Commandments in the desert has made a lasting impact on the moral education of many nations in the world. The Sabbath law both showed economic wisdom in its insistence on six days of labor and revealed a humane spirit in equally insisting on a strict day of rest. Other penal legislation, which may seem to us overly severe, was no doubt necessary for a people recently emancipated from slavery.

From the covenant given after the Exodus, grew the notion that a people is wisely governed when it recognizes its responsibility to the higher Power Who made the universe. A covenant (pact or treaty) had been made between God and Abraham, progenitor of the Jewish people. Its external sign was the rite of circumcision; its promised blessing was the multiplication of his offspring. It was broadened to include all the Jewish people through the revelation made to Moses: The external sign of God's special favor to them was the annual immolation of the paschal lamb at Passover; the promised blessing was the earthly prosperity of Israel. Christianity introduced the notion that people of all nationalities and races are beloved of God; all are offered a new covenant, for Christ established a theocracy embracing all men and women, and promised to all who observed it the transcendental reward of everlasting life and happiness.

For further reading: Richard J. Clifford, S.J., "Exodus," *New Jerome Biblical Commentary*, 44-60; K. A. Kitchen, "Exodus, The," *Anchor Bible Dictionary*, 2:700-708; Nahum M. Sarna, "Exodus, Book of," *Anchor Bible Dictionary*, 2:689-700.

Exorcism • The term refers to the practice (sometimes by ritual) in which demons or evil spirits are expelled from persons or things. This practice was widespread in Mesopotamia and Egypt by the third century B.C. It was rare in classical Greece but at the core of Hellenistic magical practices and was widespread in Greco-Roman religions of all kinds.

The practice was well known in Jewish literature written during the three centuries prior to Christ's birth. During this period of Judaism, there developed a strong conviction that God would finally conquer

Satan and all forms of evil and that this victory would mean the utter and complete defeat of the kingdom of darkness, lies and death. The Messiah, it was believed, would be God's great champion of spiritual and material power and might.

It is in the ministry of Jesus of Nazareth and of the Church that we find this great Jewish eschatological expectation fulfilled with force (Mk 1:21-28; Mt 8:28-34; Lk 4:31-37). With Jesus' ministry Satan's kingdom is coming to an end (Mk 3:26-27). The world, once completely and utterly in bondage to evil forces hostile to God and human life, is being reclaimed by God's Son. The witness throughout later portions of Sacred Scripture is that exorcisms are a manifestation of God's sovereign reign and power to conquer all strangleholds which sin, illness, evil and ultimately Satan have on a humanity originally created in His image, created with the goal of living with God forever in love. It is to this biblical witness that we point when we say in the Lord's Prayer the following words: "And deliver us from (the) evil (one)."

Exorcist • Formerly one of the traditional Minor Orders suppressed in 1972 with the revision of the sacrament of Orders, it conferred the power to drive out demons through prayer and the imposition of hands. In current discipline, the bishop grants to certain priests in his diocese the power to perform exorcisms. According to the Code of Canon Law (Canon 1172): "No one can legitimately perform exorcisms over the possessed unless he has obtained special and express permission from the local ordinary." The exorcist must be a priest "endowed with piety, knowledge, prudence and integrity of life."

Experts • Experts, or expert witnesses as they are also called, are persons with a particular knowledge in some field or science. They may be called as witnesses in canonical trials if the judge ascertains that their knowledge is required to establish some fact or to clarify the truth in some matter.

Unlike ordinary witnesses in trials, who generally are asked only to present factual knowledge about the issue at hand, the expert is asked to consider the facts presented and to offer his opinion on some matter.

Expert witnesses are regularly used in the course of matrimonial trials. Generally, they are psychiatrists or psychologists who are asked to give an opinion on the psychological state of the party or parties to the marriage, with a view to their capacity to contract marriage or to fulfill its responsibilities (cf. Canons 1574-1581).

Expiatory Penalty • A type of penalty that can be imposed for the commission of certain canonical crimes. They differ from censures in that there is more of an effort at remedying the social values done to the community than at remedying the offender. Expiatory penalties were also called vindictive penalties in the 1917 Code, while censures were referred to as medicinal penalties.

They also differ from censures in that they can be imposed forever, for an indefinite period of time or for a definite period of time. A censure cannot be imposed forever and ceases when the offender has reformed. In a sense, the expiatory penalty looks more at the punishment of the offender than at his reform.

Examples of expiatory penalties are the following: prohibition from living in a certain place; deprivation of power, office, function, right, privilege, faculty, favor, title or insignia; prohibition against exercising but not deprivation of power, function, right, etc.; penal transfer to another office; dismissal from the clerical state.

In imposing an expiatory penalty, the competent authority must of course have the facts of the case before him, but he need not extend the warning to the offender to cease and desist that is required with the imposition of a censure. Furthermore, the offender must be clearly informed that the penalty imposed on him is an expiatory penalty and not a censure.

Exposition of the Blessed Sacrament • The ceremony in which a priest or deacon removes the Sacred Host from the tabernacle and places It on the altar for adoration by the faithful. It is private when the Eucharist remains in the ciborium and the door of the tabernacle stays open. Solemn (public) exposition takes place when a large Host in the lunette of the monstrance is positioned for all adorers to see.

Private or solemn adoration ceremonies have Scripture readings, hymns, prayers and some time for silent adoration, followed by the blessing with the monstrance. Its purpose is to highlight the presence of Christ in the Eucharist.

The ceremony was introduced in the Middle Ages through the influence of the feast of Corpus Christi in the thirteenth century. Some religious monasteries, convents and other pious groups practice Eucharistic adoration for various periods of time.

The Sacred Congregation of Rites in its *Instruction on Eucharistic Worship* (May 25, 1967) declares that Eucharistic exposition is a valuable devotion which "stimulates the faithful to an awareness of the marvelous presence of Christ and is an invitation to spiritual communion with Him" (n. 60). The *Instruction* also insists that Exposition be seen in relation to the Mass and that Mass not be celebrated before the Blessed Sacrament exposed (n. 61). (Cf. Eucharistic Devotions; Divine Praises.)

Exsequatur (also Exequatur) • From the Latin for "let him act," the term is closely linked to the term *regium placet* ("royal approval") and is used to describe a claimed right on the part of civil authorities to approve ecclesiastical decrees before such documents are allowed to have force in their territories. In technical usage, the *exsequatur* was claimed in response to episcopal decrees, while the *regium placet* was invoked for pontifical decrees.

Although obviously similar to certain condemned notions of Church-state relations and while patently open to abuse by civil powers, the claim of *exsequatur* was not without a modicum of historical foundation in right. During the Western Schism, Pope Urban VI granted certain civil leaders the right to demand proof of the authenticity of papal decrees, lest those leaders be duped by the false decrees of rival claimants to the papal throne. With the passing of the Schism, however, Pope Martin V withdrew the concession, although certain leaders were reluctant to relinquish it. Several individuals and groups, notably Luther and then the Jansenists, found the *exsequatur* or *regium placet* to be useful in fending off attempts at papal control, and the institution passed irregularly from nation to nation until about the middle of the nineteenth century, despite frequent papal condemnations in the annual *Bulla Coenae*. Over the last century, the technical forms of *exsequatur* and *regium placet* have fallen into disuse, and the few related issues which still remain are now controlled by concordat.

External Forum • The external or public ordering of the Church as a society. It is distinct from the internal forum, which is the area of conscience. Acts or actions which take place in the external forum can be verified by an official and public record. The ecclesiastical power of governance is usually exercised in the external forum. Although some acts of this power are confidential in nature, they still may be verified by official document. In certain cases, the power of governance can be exercised in the internal forum, such as the remission of a reserved censure or penalty by a confessor under certain circumstances (cf. Canons 130, 1357).

Extraordinary Form • Although Catholics are obliged by law to marry according to canonical form for validity, the law recognizes certain circumstances when the presence of a sacred minister is neither possible nor feasible. Since the spouses themselves are the ministers of the sacrament of Matrimony, the requirement of a sacred minister is not absolutely necessary. Under certain circumstances a couple may exchange vows in the presence of two witnesses only.

The circumstances are these: in danger of death (not necessarily imminent death), if it is foreseen that a sacred minister is not readily available; when a sacred minister will not be available for a period of one month.

Those who marry according to the extraordinary form must be free to marry and must be capable of fulfilling the marital responsibilities. Furthermore, they must not be bound by any undispensed canonical impediment. Extraordinary form may not be invoked for persons who would otherwise be barred from marrying according to the ordinary canonical form of marriage (cf. Canon 1116).

Extraordinary Medical Treatments • Life-sustaining forms of care administered by a physician that are either: (1) radically painful; (2) excessively expensive; (3) doubtfully able to accomplish their designated therapeutic objective; or (4) radically expensive or burdensome

financially or in other such ways for those responsible for the patient.

In making evaluations of the obligatoriness of medical treatments, one must judge the treatments themselves and not the "quality of life" that they effect for the patient because such quality-of-life judgments are discriminatory against disabled, terminally ill or dying patients. By focusing on what the treatments do for the patient, one can make an objective assessment of the burden of the treatments. In addition, when assessing these burdens, one must evaluate them relative to the benefits they bring to the patient.

The Catholic tradition in medical ethics has held that extraordinary medical treatments are elective, and one does not violate one's duties to preserve, promote and protect life by declining to accept them. However, extraordinary medical treatments can be made mandatory for the sake of the common good, and thus, for example, a society can force its leader to receive an extraordinary treatment if so doing would significantly benefit the common good. And a society could legally require that some extraordinary treatments be received by patients if not dying so would increase the risk of euthanasia and place the medically vulnerable in greater jeopardy.

Extreme Unction, Sacrament of: See **Pastoral Care of the Sick**

Ezekiel • This prophet, whose name means "May God strengthen [this person]," began his ministry during the fifth year of the exile of King Jehoiachin, that is 593 B.C. At the beginning of the prophetic book that bears his name, we read that "the word of the LORD came to Ezekiel the priest, the son of Buzi, in the land of the Chaldeans by the river Chebar; and the hand of the LORD was upon him there" (Ez 1:3). This indicates that the prophet exercised his prophetic ministry among his fellow Judahites who were exiled in Babylon during the first deportation, prior to the final fall of Jerusalem in the year 587 B.C. He continued prophesying until approximately 571 B.C.

The Book of Ezekiel is very clearly organized into three main sections: (I) Judgment Oracles against Israel (1-24); (II) Judgment Oracles against Foreign Nations (25-32); and (III) Salvation and Restoration Oracles for Israel (33-48).

In all likelihood, the present form of the book is the result of extensive editing by redactors subsequent to the life and ministry of Ezekiel himself.

The chapters describing Ezekiel's own prophetic vocation (Ez 1-3) is a vivid visionary narrative in which he is granted a theophany, that is, a manifestation of God, seated on a heavenly throne and surrounded by four fantastic living creatures. God addresses Ezekiel, saying, "Son of man, I send you to the people of Israel, to a nation of rebels, who have rebelled against me" (Ez 2:3). God warns him that "the house of Israel will not listen to you; for they are not willing to listen to me" (Ez 3:7). The people's rebellion against God and their disobedience is the reason why God's glory departs from the Temple in Jerusalem (Ez 8-11), the reason why the city and Temple are devastated.

Ezekiel's vision of the restoration of the Temple focuses on the return of the glory of the Lord to a new and purified sanctuary, free from the corruption and idolatry of the original sanctuary. Chapters 40-48 describe in detail the plans for the new Temple, in language that is taken up in the New Testament description of the heavenly Jerusalem found in the Apocalypse of John.

The renewal promised by God and announced by Ezekiel is not only a matter of the rebuilding of the Temple and the observance of ritual regulations. All this is to be the external manifestation of an inner renewal brought about by God. God promises Israel, "I will sprinkle clean water upon you, and you shall be clean from all your uncleannesses, and from all your idols I will cleanse you. A new heart I will give you, and a new spirit I will put within you; and I will take out of your flesh the heart of stone and give you a heart of flesh" (Ez 36:25-26). It is God Himself Who will enable Israel to maintain itself faithful in the obedience of the commandments.

Scholars have often drawn attention to the frequency of Ezekiel's ecstatic experiences. On numerous occasions, the prophet is taken up by the Spirit of God to the settings where his visions occur. This is reminiscent of the action of the Spirit in the preclassical prophets, including Elijah and his disciple Elisha. Preaching not only in words, but also in symbolic gestures, Ezekiel often acted out his oracles in what amounted to prophetic "street theater." For example, in Chapter 4 he acts out the siege of Jerusalem. A number of scholars of this book have also pointed out the ways in which Ezekiel's own priestly sensibilities can be perceived both in his careful attention to the requirements of proper worship and in his revulsion at the idolatry that was taking place even within the Temple precincts.

For further reading: Lawrence Boadt, C.S.P., "Ezekiel," *Anchor Bible Dictionary*, 2:711-722; Lawrence Boadt, C.S.P., "Ezekiel," *New Jerome Biblical Commentary*, 305-328.

Ezra • The Vulgate contains two biblical books under the name of Ezra, but modern authorities list the second of these under the name of Nehemiah. Both men returned from the exile after the first return of the sixth century, Ezra in 458 B.C. (or 428 or 398) and Nehemiah in 445 B.C. Nehemiah was a civil governor; Ezra, a priest and scribe. To follow the history, it is wise to read Ezra 1-6 before Nehemiah 1-13 and Ezra 7-10 after.

The Jews were certainly grateful to have been liberated from their slavery and to be permitted to return to their homeland, but this was made into a province of the Persian empire. Prophets such as Ezekiel had convinced the repatriates that God had punished the infidelity of their forefathers; thus they were ready for reform. The Temple had been rebuilt toward the end of the preceding century, and priests such as Ezra were filled with zeal. Ezra was insistent that the religious renewal was to begin with devout Jewish families: Non-Jewish wives were expelled, and further mixed marriages were strongly disapproved. The survivors in Samaria had profited from the downfall of Jerusalem, resenting the returnees; this explains the hostility shown by Ezra toward the Samaritans.

No attempt was made to restore the monarchy, but the priests grew more and more influential, so that they even became political authorities.

For further reading: Ralph W. Klein, "Ezra-Nehemiah, Books of," *Anchor Bible Dictionary*, 2:731-742; Robert North, S.J., "The Chronicler: 1-2 Chronicles, Ezra, Nehemiah," *New Jerome Biblical Commentary*, 362-398; Robert North, S.J., "Ezra," *Anchor Bible Dictionary*, 2:726-728.

Fabric (also Fabbrica) • This term can refer to several things. In the first place, the *fabbrica* of a particular institution or church is the building itself, as well as its material possessions (as a juridic person). Thus, by consequence, that term is also applied to the specific sector or department of said institution which oversees the maintenance and restoration of the building's assets, especially the works of art found therein. St. Peter's Basilica in the Vatican has had a *fabbrica* since the time of Pope Julius II (1503-1513).

In his Constitution *Pastor Bonus* of June 1988, Pope John Paul II states that: "The Fabbrica of St. Peter, according to its own laws, will continue to occupy itself with everything that regards the Basilica of the Prince of the Apostles, be it for the preservation of the decorum of the building, be it for the internal discipline of the custodians, as well as the pilgrims who come to visit the temple." To oversee this task, a cardinal is named as President of the Fabric of St. Peter, assisted by a delegate invested with the dignity of archbishop.

The *Duomo* or Cathedral of Milan is another instance of a church which has its own fabric for the upkeep and restoration of the holy temple.

The term "fabric" may also refer to a particular fund or endowment for the upkeep of a particular church edifice. (Cf. Annuario Pontificio.)

Faculties • The term "faculties" commonly refers to the permission required of a sacred minister to exercise a specific power of Sacred Orders. For instance, a priest needs faculties or permission from his Ordinary to hear confessions. Faculties are also needed to witness marriages and to preach.

Faculties, Canonical • The term "canonical faculties" can have two distinct meanings. It can refer to an educational institution or a department of an educational institution that has been officially erected or recognized by the Holy See. Such entities are subject to the authority of the Holy See and may grant degrees in the name of the Holy See.

Canonical faculties can also refer to the power granted to a person to perform certain ecclesiastical acts, such as witnessing marriages, preaching, hearing confessions or judging a case. Faculties are granted by an ecclesiastical superior or, in some cases, by the law itself.

Faculties, Ecclesiastical • Ecclesiastical faculties are educational entities that either stand alone or are part of a larger educational institution, such as a college or university. Also known as canonical faculties, they are erected and supervised by the Holy See through the Congregation for Catholic Education. Ecclesiastical faculties exist in several countries of the world. In some instances, the department of philosophy or theology of a university has the character of an ecclesiastical faculty. In others, a seminary may be erected as an ecclesiastical faculty. Most ecclesiastical faculties are erected to teach philosophy, theology, canon law or missiology.

Ecclesiastical faculties may have accreditation from the Holy See to grant certain degrees. These degrees include the baccalaureate, licentiate and doctorate (cf. Canons 815-821).

Faculty, Pontifical • A pontifical faculty is an institution of higher learning officially established by the Holy See and governed by the specific regulations of the Holy See for pontifical faculties. An already existing college can petition to be erected as a pontifical faculty, provided it has met the requirements set forth by the Holy See through the Congregation for Catholic Education. Also one or more departments of a college or university can petition to be erected as a pontifical faculty while remaining part of the civil structure of the institution. Pontifical faculties are empowered to grant pontifical degrees. Most pontifical faculties are erected for the teaching of philosophy, theology or canon law.

Faith • The term "faith" has an objective and a subjective sense: (1) it refers to the body of saving truth, contained in the Scriptures, Creeds, conciliar definitions, teachings of the Magisterium and the writings of the doctors and saints of the Church (*fides quae creditur*); (2) it refers to the subjective acts and disposition by which these doctrines are believed (*fides qua creditur*).

In this second sense, faith is one of the three infused theological virtues. Together with hope and love, faith constitutes the operative side of the life of sanctifying grace in the human person. Just as the entire nature of the person is transformed by the gift of grace, so also are his particular spiritual capacities by faith, hope and love. The life of grace does not introduce additional faculties of intellect and will so that they can function at an entirely new

level in knowing and loving God. Thus, the infused theological virtue of faith makes it possible to know God and all that He has revealed.

Properly speaking, therefore, the disposition and acts of faith have God Himself as their primary object, and secondarily the various truths about Him that are taught in the Church. It is for this reason that Tradition has taught that we believe in revelation on the strength of God Himself revealing. Nothing less than the First Truth itself — revealed and revealing — is the proper object of faith. Although primarily a disposition of the intellect, faith nevertheless involves an act of the will. For faith is not like the adoption of a conclusion on the basis of sufficiently compelling evidence and argument: the grace of God is active in moving the will to believe. For this reason, faith is never only intellectual, but also fiducial: One's whole being responds to the revealing God in obedience and trust.

Faith, Mysteries of • Many truths of the Christian Faith are known only because God has revealed them to us. Discovery of such truths and full comprehension of their depths surpass the capacity of the human mind. Taken together, such truths comprise the mystery that is the hidden wisdom of God by which our salvation is accomplished. Thus, in the first place, the term "mystery" refers to the entire plan of our salvation in Christ. By extension, the term also refers to particular aspects of this plan, to particular truths about God's nature, His intentions in our regard, and the actions He has undertaken in order to bring about the consummation of these intentions.

Thus, Christians have come to speak of the "mysteries" of the Faith. In this properly Christian sense, the term means far more than is suggested by its ordinary sense of an intellectual puzzle that needs to be solved or a strange event that needs explanation. In referring to the unsearchable wisdom of God, the term "mystery" suggests that revelation involves such depths of truth and intelligibility as to merit continual reflection, inquiry and contemplation. Mystery occurs in the Christian Faith, not because God's ways are opaque and irrational, but because the human mind does not have the power to discern or comprehend them. At the edges of what we can understand of the mystery lies not darkness but the blinding light of divine wisdom itself. Finally, as St. Bernard once said, the mysteries of the Faith invite worship, not scrutiny.

Faith Healing • Sometimes called "divine healing" or "healing" or "faith cure," the phenomenon called "faith healing" is relatively recent within the history of Christianity and began as various healing movements. The phrase refers to two elements: a group of believers and a particular kind of praying. Those believers who hold that all disease and illness can be cured by God's intervention in connection with prayers of deep faith form part of the healing movement. The "prayer of faith" includes taking authority over whatever illness is present, casting it out or addressing it, invoking the name of Jesus Christ or His Blood (or His stripes or His cross) and claiming the act of faith and healing process to be under God's sovereign rule. Depending on what period of Church history one examines, miraculous healings occurred either in mainstream or fringe movements of the Church. Such occurrences certainly have their basis in the life and ministry of Jesus and the earliest experiences of the Church (Acts 5:15-16).

Recent increased interest in faith healing among Protestant and Catholic groups can be traced back to the middle of the nineteenth century. During this time there arose healing movements with their own leaders, doctrines (about sin, sickness,

salvation, regeneration, holiness, etc.) and followers — in short, an emerging subculture, discovering God's power to heal. An example of a precursor to the healing movement as it occurred within various congregations would be the mid-seventeenth-century leader of the Society of Friends (Quakers) George Fox, who, although remembered for his preaching, actually had a greater reputation for his healing ministry. Interest in the ministry of faith healing also sprang up in sectarian cults which emerged on the East Coast in the nineteenth century — at times with less than desirable results. The Holiness Movement contributed theological depth to the healing movement by providing specific doctrinal positions regarding the nature of sin, sickness, healing, holiness, and the necessity of personal renewal. Many of the pioneering ministers saw mixed reactions from their churches and the public — everything from public humiliation to deep respect for work done with the poor, homeless, uneducated, alcoholic residents of slums in industrialized cities. The movement has grown and touched all of the major Christian denominations.

Faithful (Christifideles) • Canonically, those who, inasmuch as they have been incorporated in Christ through Baptism, have been constituted as the People of God in the Catholic Church (Canon 204) and have not been excluded by declaration or by their own acts. By becoming sharers in Christ's priestly, prophetic and royal office in their own manner, the faithful are called to exercise the mission which God has entrusted to the Church to fulfill in the world, namely, the salvation of souls.

In a broader sense, then, "the faithful" are all the baptized; but, in a more narrow sense, the term pertains to baptized Catholics in full communion with the See of Rome, whether they belong to the Latin Rite or to one of the Eastern Rites. Protestants and Orthodox and other baptized non-Catholics are not in full communion because they lack one or more of the three essential elements of unity: the Profession of Faith, all the sacraments and ecclesiastical governance.

Among the rights and obligations of all the faithful (clergy, religious and laity alike) are: equality in dignity and action by their rebirth in Christ; freedom to make their needs known to ecclesiastical authorities, especially spiritual needs; the right to make known their opinion to Church authorities about those things which pertain to the good of the Church; the right to receive through those Church authorities assistance from the spiritual goods of the Church, especially the Word of God and the sacraments; the right to participate in the worship of God according to their own rite approved by legitimate ecclesiastical authorities; the right to follow their own form of spirituality, provided it is consonant with Church doctrine; the right to Christian education; and the right to vindicate and defend their ecclesial rights in the competent ecclesiastical forum according to the norm of law.

Among the obligations of the faithful are: to observe communion with the Church, even in their external actions; to use their energies to lead a holy life and to promote the growth of the Church and her continuous sanctification; to work for the ever-increasing spread of the divine message to all peoples of all times in every part of the world; to follow in Christian obedience whatever Church authorities, as representatives of Christ, declare as teachers of the Faith or decree as leaders of the Church; to provide for the needs of the Church, in order to make available those things which are necessary for divine worship, for the works of charity and for the support of the Church's ministers; and to promote social justice, mindful of the command of the Lord to support the poor from one's own resources.

Faithful, Prayer of the: See **Prayer of the Faithful**

Falda • Italian for "train," this term refers to a white silk train formerly worn by the Pope over his rochet on certain solemn occasions, such as when he sang Papal Pontifical Mass or when he presided at a function in mantum and mitre. It was so long that two monsignori had to hold it up in front and two in back whenever the Pope walked in it. It is first mentioned in the diaries of Johann Burckard, papal master of ceremonies under Pope Alexander VI (1492-1503). Although the falda has fallen into disuse, some are still kept in the sacristy of the Sistine Chapel, along with other unused papal insignia, such as the fanon.

Faldstool • In the preconciliar liturgy the *faldistorium* was a backless stool used instead of a throne by a bishop who was not the Ordinary of a diocese, or by the Ordinary himself in the presence of a prelate of higher rank. It consisted of a frame of gilt metal or wood, shaped like the letter "X," with a seat of leather or cloth stretched across its upper extremities. When used as a seat, the faldstool had a covering and cushion of the proper liturgical color, normally with silk material for a cardinal and wool for a bishop. According to the revised *Ceremoniale Episcoporum* (1983), "mention is no longer made of the faldstool" (n. 30).

Fall of Man • The Judeo-Christian account of the origin of human death, evil and suffering. Genesis 3 asserts that the first man and first woman disobeyed an explicit command of God, and as a result they lost their immortality and their intimate, friendly relationship with God was changed to estrangement, alienation and fear. Their fall radically disordered not only their own spiritual and interior life by weakening their will and reason and radically disrupted their emotions and passions; it also created chaos in physical nature itself. These consequences were communicated to the entire human race and are counted as the cause of human suffering.

According to the *Catechism of the Catholic Church*, "The account of the fall in *Genesis* 3 uses figurative language, but affirms a primeval event, a deed that took place *at the beginning of the history of man*. Revelation gives us the certainty of faith that the whole of human history is marked by the original fault freely committed by our first parents" (n. 390; emphases in original). This "original sin" is reckoned as the ultimate cause and source of all personal sins committed by individuals. The doctrine of the fall accounts for the cause of human suffering, evil and death without making God their cause.

For further reading: Richard J. Clifford, S.J., and Roland E. Murphy, O.Carm., "Genesis," *New Jerome Biblical Commentary*, 8-13; S. J. DeVries, "Fall," *Interpreter's Dictionary of the Bible*, 2:235-237.

Familiar • In monastic communities, laypersons who live and work in the monastery but who take no religious vows are called familiars. They share in the spiritual benefits of the prayer and good works of the monks.

Familiaris Consortio • An apostolic exhortation by Pope John Paul II which took as its theme "The Role of the Christian Family in the Modern World." Released in November 1981, the papal document begins with a discussion of the current state of the family, both the "bright spots and the shadows," and continues with an exploration of the divine dimension to marriage and the love between a man and a woman fully expressed in the divine gift of children.

The Pope restates Church teaching on the moral impermissibility of artificial birth control, as reflected both in the Magisterium's pronouncements and repronouncements down through the ages and in the more definitive statement, *Humanae Vitae* (*On Human Life*), promulgated by Pope Paul VI in 1968. John Paul's letter also considers the issue of parental responsibility in the sexual education of children, the related subject of the family household as the domestic sanctuary from which evangelization in the wider world is made possible, and the more specific, and increasingly relevant, questions centering on mixed unions, divorce and remarriage.

Families, Rights of • The family is an institution of parents and children, a unit that is autonomous from the state and society. The family is the basic institution of society and the state because it is primarily responsible for instilling moral values necessary for them: The spouses help each other to holiness in their married life and by the rearing and education of their children (cf. 1 Cor 7).

Catholic social encyclicals have repeatedly called for respect for the rights of families. Families have rights against society and the state not to have their unity and life disrupted purely to serve social and political ends, and they have rights to dwell in peace. Families have rights to laws and social institutions to promote and protect their unity and integrity. The basis of these rights is the fact that families are the first "school" of children, and families have obligations to train, rear and educate children. If they are not protected so that they can fulfill these responsibilities, children are deprived of what they need to cope with the demands of life in society, and society itself suffers.

Fanon • The fanon, or *fanone* in Italian, is part of the sacred vesture of the Roman Pontiff. It is a type of shoulder cape of white silk striped in gold, with a narrow stripe of red bordering each gold stripe. Consisting of two pieces of silk sewn together, it is nearly circular in shape with a hole in the middle for the head. Worn over the chasuble and under the pallium, this parament can be traced back to the first millennium of the Church's history and is a descendant of the ancient *anabolagium* which was used by all ecclesiastics. Since this was an early ancestor of the present-day amice, it stands to reason that originally it developed in order to keep the vestments underneath clean and the wearer warm in winter. Since in Late Latin the word *fano* was used for a type of small napkin, further credibility is lent to this explanation of its origins. By the twelfth century, it had become exclusively reserved to the Pope and took its present general form. Its present appearance dates back at least four or five hundred years. Though with the use of Gothic-style chasubles the ancient practice of wearing the fanon has almost disappeared, on occasion Pope John Paul II wears it when he wears Roman-style vestments.

Fascism • One of the most quoted descriptions of this political ideology comes from one of its most vociferous opponents, Pope Pius XI, who stated in his encyclical of June, 1931, *Non abbiamo bisogno*, that Fascism sought ". . . to monopolize completely the young, from their tenderest years up to manhood and womanhood, for the exclusive advantage of a party and a regime based on the ideology which clearly resolves itself into a true, pagan worship of the state — the 'Statolatry' which is no less in contrast with the natural rights of the

family than it is in contradiction with the supernatural rights of the Church."

Thus, Fascism is that governmental system in which one person, or small group of people, holds dictatorial power, forcibly suppressing all opposition, controlling all industry, trade and business, and emphasizing an aggressive nationalism. Fascism often exhibits overtones of racial superiority, as occurred most notoriously in the brand of Fascism called Nazism, which gripped Germany under Adolf Hitler's rule (1933-1945). The word is most commonly associated with the style of Benito Mussolini, who governed Italy 1922-1943.

Fast • In Sacred Scripture, a fast is not eating or drinking (or not engaging in conjugal relations) for a given period of time, normally within a twenty-four-hour period (e.g., from sunset to sunset). It is important to be clear that in Sacred Scripture the prime reason for fasting is not to initiate an ascetical adventure, nor is it a technique for acquiring "altered states of consciousness" or inducing euphoric psychological "experiences." Stated positively, the many motivations for fasting all proceed from a basic assumption about the human's need for and dependency on God. It is by means of the fast that one stops what is *auto*matic (i.e., self-controlled) and waits upon God — the hunger pains acting like constant reminders to listen for the voice of God in personal and liturgical prayer, through conversations and events of the day, and in reading Sacred Scripture. When food is understood in its ultimate meaning as a gift from God (Dt 8:3; Mt 6:11; Lk 11:3), then to fast is to be willing to open up to and face one's own weakness, frailty and need for not only the provision but also for the Provider; fasting is like a living parable or an "embodied language" which makes visible or externalizes an interior need for God's provident care. Some concrete examples of need for God are: after a disastrous military defeat (Jgs 20); in the midst of a crisis of national proportions (Est 4); seeking forgiveness (1 Kgs 21:27); as part of the atonement process (Lv 16:29-31); seeking God's mercy in healing (2 Sam 12:16, 22); in mourning (Jdt 8:6; Lk 2:37); for relief from ongoing anguish (Jl 2:12-17; Jdt 4:9-13); in seeking divine light (Dn 10:12); for assistance in choices and plans (Acts 13:2; 14:23).

The key in each instance is dependency on a loving God who is faithful and promises action. Jesus' life expressed the epitome of dependency on God. His forty-day fast, understood in light of that of Moses (Ex 34:28) and Elijah (1 Kgs 19:8), expresses the inauguration of His messianic mission which begins with a complete surrender to the loving Father. Jesus' will and mission are those of the Father; Jesus' mission to announce and bring the kingdom of God begins with a complete and total self-gift to the Father, in love, through fasting. Our concrete needs, bodily and spiritual, are living parables of our deeper need to live in God's kingdom. Fasting is not only a bodily expression of our need for God; the practice itself is a pathway which can lead us to the reality of God's kingdom.

For further reading: *Catechism of the Catholic Church*, nn. 538-540, 1434, 1438; John Muddiman, "Fast, Fasting," *Anchor Bible Dictionary*, 2:773-776.

Fast, Eucharistic • A means of disciplining and preparing oneself to receive Christ in the Eucharist. Prior to the Second Vatican Council, abstaining from all food and drink (with the exception of water) from midnight until reception of the Eucharist was mandatory and then substantially mitigated at the end of the pontificate of Pope Pius XII. Since the Council, this fast was reduced to one hour before the reception of Holy Communion. However, even this fast may be reduced to even fifteen minutes for those who are sick or who must eat before receiving the Eucharist for some important reason.

Fasting • Limiting the intake of food and drink for a religious purpose. Full participation in the saving mysteries of Christ not only demands that Christians share in the Christ Who is resurrected and glorified, but also in the suffering Christ. Fasting has traditionally been one of the foremost ways in which we express our desire to share in His suffering.

Fasting is legitimately undertaken to discipline our passions and desires and to express our commitment and devotion to God. Customarily, fasting required that a person take only one meal a day, but current Church discipline permits one to take a main meal and two lesser meals which together do not equal the main meal. Mandatory fast days now are Ash Wednesday and Good Friday, on which days one must abstain from meat and eat only one main meal. Fridays in Lent are days of abstinence, and meat may not be taken on those days; and on the other Fridays of the year, individuals may either fast, abstain or practice other forms of mortification.

Fatalia Legis • The Latin term which refers to the time limits set by the law for certain procedural acts. The purpose of time limits is to ensure that a process not be overly prolonged.

The judge may set certain time limits according to his own discretion in some instances. In others, time limits are set by the law itself. All judicial time limits refer to useful or available time.

Time limits set by the law itself include: ten days for a party to appeal the rejection of a petition by a judge (Canon 1505.4); ten years to enter a complaint of irremediable nullity of a sentence (Canon 1621); three

St. Basil the Great, a Father of the Church

months to enter a complaint of remediable nullity against a sentence (Canon 1623); fifteen days to file an appeal in a contentious case (Canon 1630); one month to process an appeal (Canon 1633); one month to appeal in a case of status of persons that has received two concordant decisions (Canon 1644); one month for the judge to respond to the aforesaid appeal (Canon 1644); three months to petition for a reinstatement (Canon 1646). There are also special time limits for marriage cases: The respondent has fifteen days to challenge the petition following receipt of the citation (Canon 1677); twenty days for the judge to send an affirmative sentence to the appeal court (Canon 1682).

Father • In the early Church those who gave special witness to the Faith were called Fathers, and this title was extended to all bishops because of the spiritual authority and care which they exercise over the faithful as "fathers in God." St. Jerome (A.D. 342-420) writes that by the fourth century the monks in Palestine and Egypt were addressing one another as "father," and it came to be used for confessors, who were called "ghostly fathers" in medieval England. During the last century the title came to be used for all priests in English-speaking countries, a custom which originated in Ireland and traveled to other places as Irish priests immigrated with their people. It was particularly encouraged by Cardinal Manning (1808-1892) of Westminster, and has become a common form of addressing priests.

Catholics call their priests Father because they are the ordinary ministers of Baptism, through which the faithful receive the new birth of supernatural grace (Jn 3:5), and because of the pastoral care which is given by priests; thus, they are "spiritual fathers" not only through their sacramental ministry (which begets and sustains the children of God), but also through their ministry of counseling and guiding the faithful in the Christian life.

There has been some objection to the use of this title, by an erroneous interpretation of Matthew 23:9, in which Our Lord says, "And call no man your father on earth, for you have one Father, who is in heaven." When this passage is considered within its context, it is apparent that Christ was not finding fault with the use of the term "father," but rather that He was rebuking the Pharisees for their pridefulness, and reminding them that God alone, Who is the Father of all, is the source of all authority. St. Paul himself says that he is the spiritual father of those whom he had converted (1 Cor 4:15), and so adds scriptural support to that of tradition in the use of this title.

Fathers of the Church (also Apostolic Fathers) • Those towering intellects of the early centuries of the Church, whose writings, sermons and holy lives influenced dramatically the definition, defense and propagation of the Faith. As a precise group in Church history, they are noted for their antiquity (the last of the Western Fathers being Gregory the Great, who died in A.D. 604, and the last in the East considered John Damascene, who died in 749), erudition, orthodoxy and personal sanctity. Most scholars delineate the following groupings: the Apostolic Fathers, such as Pope St. Clement I (d. 97), who lived with or in the shadow of the Apostles (to the last half of the second century); those of the second and third centuries as Apologists, such as Justin Martyr, who presented the doctrines of the Faith with cogency and clarity; and the "golden age" of the fourth and fifth centuries, with the presence of men such as Basil (d. 379), Gregory Nazianzen (d. 390), John Chrysostom (d. 407), Athanasius (d. 373), all from the Greek Church; and Ambrose (d. 397), Jerome (d. 420) and Augustine (d. 430) of the Latin Church.

The study of the Fathers, perennially urged by the Church, is called Patristics or Patrology.

Fátima, Apparitions of • Fátima, north of Lisbon, Portugal, is one of the most famous modern shrines of the Blessed Virgin Mary. She appeared to three children (Lucia dos Santos and her cousins Francisco and Jacinta) six times between May 13 and October 13, 1917. On October 13, "the lady" revealed that she was Our Lady of the Rosary. She requested frequent recitation of the Rosary, penance, increased devotion to her Immaculate Heart, prayers for the conversion of Russia and a church building in her honor. On October 13, as she had promised, a miracle (the spinning sun) was seen by 50,000 people. Pope Pius XI in 1930 authorized devotion to Our Lady of Fátima. Pope Pius XII in 1952 implemented the request to pray for the conversion of Russia. Pope John Paul II in 1982 visited the shrine to give thanks for having survived the attempt on his life on May 13, 1981.

Reportedly, a "secret" was given during the Fátima apparitions. While there have been many reports and speculations about what the secret might be, it has never been revealed.

Favor of the Law • A canonical phrase that indicates that a certain juridic or canonical act is presumed to be valid unless the contrary is proven. For instance, the law clearly says that a marriage celebrated according to the norms of law enjoys the favor of the law (cf. Canon 1060). This means that after a celebration of marriage, it is presumed to be a valid union unless this presumption is subsequently overturned by an ecclesiastical court.

Fear • The trepidation of the mind because of the threat of great evil. A person can perform an action because of fear when he or she would otherwise not do so. The action is performed because the primary intention is to escape the cause of the fear.

Grave fear can affect the validity of canonical acts. A marriage entered into because of grave fear on the part of one or the other party is invalid (Canon 1103). Similarly, an ordination is invalid if the man being ordained was compelled to do so by grave fear (Canon 1026). Public vows are invalid if the person professed them out of grave fear (Canon 1191). A canonical election is invalid if the electors voted for someone compelled by grave fear that to do otherwise would result in serious harm from a danger from without (Canons 170-172).

Grave fear can also remove or diminish the culpability for the commission of a canonical crime (Canons 1323.4-1324.5).

Fear of God • The biblical phrase occurs with a number of themes, each corresponding to the range of Hebrew and Greek terms which the English phrase approximates. In general, "fear of God" is not flight from threat, not pure terror, nor simply alarm or fright.

Rather, it is that experience and knowledge of God as utterly holy, totally other, incomprehensible, absolute, almighty, all-powerful, all-knowing and absolutely majestic. This experience leads to a detestation of sin, principally due to a deeper awareness of how offensive sin is to God's perfect love, justice and care for us. The experience also leads to a deep consolation and love for God and "neighbor," resulting in deep praise, worship and adoration of God which themselves become grace-filled moments of joyful life with God here on earth. In other words, "fear of God" is both an action (i.e., worship) and a knowledge about God (*mysterium tremendum*). Two biblical illustrations: (1) Exodus 19:16: peals of thunder, lightning flashes, dense clouds, the whole environment exudes the presence of God which is overwhelming; (2) 1 Kings 19:9-13: a mighty wind, an earthquake, fire — God is not *in* these elements; His is a gentle voice which is also overwhelming (v. 13). In general, the witness of Sacred Scripture indicates that thunderstorms often accompany God's self-disclosure (Ps 18:7; 29:3; 77:16-17; 97:2; etc.).

Perhaps a contemporary analogy (and certainly imperfect) to the biblical witness about knowing God and His ways through "fear of God" is the experience of hearing and seeing millions of cubic gallons of water rushing over the Horseshoe Falls in Niagara Falls; or witnessing a violent and earth-shaking clap of thunder; or surviving the overwhelming and imposing winds of a hurricane; or seeing majestic mountains for the first time. In each case an unrelenting and imposing force overtakes the senses, leading one to a spontaneous consciousness about one's own insignificance in the presence of an extraordinary force or power qualitatively different from oneself.

The difference between these experiences in nature and the biblical revelation is that in Sacred Scripture a genuine knowledge of God emerges, leading to worship, to profound gratitude or to an inaugural prophetic mission. This kind of "fear" is found throughout Sacred Scripture: In Gideon's response to fire (Jgs 6:11-24); in Isaiah's response to God's call (Is 6:1-8); in the disciples' response to Christ walking on the water (Mt 14:22-33); in Simon's response to Christ after a massive catch of fish (Lk 5:1-11). Usually the divine agent (God; an angel of the Lord; Christ, etc.) reassures the person ("Fear not, God has sent me / You are favored / It is I"), and a new step in God's majestic plan of salvation unfolds. Because the "fear of God" is connected to salvation history, and in light of the clear, consistent and panoramic witness to "fear" in Old Testament wisdom literature, a way of life or a sociology of holiness based on revelation from God is connected with the phrase "the fear of God." Such a knowledge of God and His will for a way of life (usually called the way of wisdom, of peace, etc.) is, in the early Church, connected with the Holy Spirit; in Acts 9:31, the "fear of the Lord" is connected with receiving consolation from the Holy Spirit; in Ephesians 5:17-21, being filled with the Holy Spirit (vv. 17-18) is intimately connected with mutual subordination in the "reverence for Christ" (v. 21).

For further reading: S. Terrien, "Fear," *Interpreter's Dictionary of the Bible*, 2:256-260.

Feasts of the Church • Technically, one category of liturgical day, namely, of lesser rank than a "solemnity," and of higher rank than a "memorial." In popular usage, however, "feast" is applied indiscriminately by the faithful to all liturgical days on which the Church commemorates a mystery of the

Lord or Our Lady, or keeps the memory of a saint.

Febronianism • In 1763 Bishop John von Hontheim, writing under the name of "Justinius Febronius," published a work attacking the power of the Pope over ecclesiastical matters and asserting that Scripture would have the state serve as the arbiter of Church discipline, albeit subject to an ecumenical council. This latest resurrection of various heresies was immediately condemned in 1764 by Pope Clement XIII. The condemnation applied not to the author, however, but only to the book, which had by then been translated into several languages.

Following continued agitation by the bishop, who had submitted only a vague and unsatisfactory retraction, Pope Pius VI specifically condemned Febronius in 1778. The movement went into decline thereafter, but not before attracting the attention of Joseph II of Austria, with unfortunate results for all (cf. Josephism). The notion of Febronianism, along with many others of its stamp, was firmly repudiated in the First Vatican Council. (Cf. Conciliar Theory; Gallicanism.)

Federation of Diocesan Liturgical Commissions (FDLC) • The FDLC, as it is known in liturgical circles, was formed in 1971 to provide a forum in which representatives of diocesan liturgical commissions could discuss matters of mutual concern, exchange ideas on the state and development of liturgy, provide educational materials to assist the work of dioceses and parishes, and present to the hierarchy (through the official Bishops' Committee on the Liturgy) the fruit of pastoral experience to assist the bishops in their decisions regarding implementation or adaptation of official rites. The FDLC is based in Washington and carries out its work through a national newsletter, regional meetings and an annual convention.

Feminism, Christian • In the most general sense, feminism can be understood as a movement protesting the oppression of women. As a theoretical construct, it advances the claim that women have been oppressed, discriminated against or patronized because they have been relegated by men to a secondary status in societies of all times.

Christian feminism, in general, protests against the position of women in the Church. As a philosophy, it usually, but not always, holds that such discrimination is based on patriarchal male attitudes which are said to infuse scriptural language and traditional attitudes and practices.

Distinctions should be made among moderate, radical and pro-life feminists. Whereas all feminists, non-religious and religious, call for an end to male attitudes of brutality, exploitation and ridicule, there is a great difference between different types of feminists when it comes to what societal realities are regarded as oppressive and what means are suggested to eliminate injustices.

For example, most moderate and radical non-Christian feminists regard abortion as a reproductive right. Pro-life feminists, however, would consider abortion to be a violation of feminine dignity and the abortion industry to be a prime example of male exploitation of women. Availability of abortion is considered by pro-life feminists as reinforcing the non-responsibility of the male for his sexual behavior and making profit for preponderantly male doctors and administrators.

Among Christian feminists, here are some of the issues most often debated:

Is there such a thing as an intrinsically feminine type of human nature based on God's creation, or are all but physical female characteristics only the result of cultural programming?

Is it valid to use language that implies that God is a masculine Father and/or to employ the word "man" or "brother" to include women and sisters, or would it be better to make use of more feminine imagery in the translation of Scripture, in liturgical language, in the lyrics of songs and in Christian conversation?

Is it imperative that there be women priests in order to overcome male domination of Church structures, or should the priesthood reflect Tradition seen as fidelity to the will of Christ?

Should a new Christian ethics be developed that would give more emphasis to a feminine evaluation of sexual morality in the direction of greater "freedom of conscience" concerning birth control, abortion, remarriage after divorce, etc.?

The Apostolic Letter of Pope John Paul II *Mulieris Dignitatem* (*On the Dignity and Vocation of Women*) suggests the possibility of a Christian feminism which would ground the dignity of women in their creation by God the Father. Part of the personal love for each woman by Christ as expressed in the Gospels is His rejection of oppressive male characteristics forbidden to men who would be His followers. Faithfulness to the Catholic Tradition in its unchangeable ethical teachings and liturgical norms for the community is viewed not as impeding women in service to the Church but as providing a path to holiness within their different states of life.

Ferendae Sententiae • A Latin term found in the Code of Canon Law in the section on crimes and penalties. It means that the penalty for a canonical crime must be applied or imposed by a judge or other ecclesiastical authority capable of doing so, rather than being applied automatically by the very fact that a canonical crime is committed.

Most of the crimes mentioned in the revised Code are to be punished by the imposition of a penalty. This is done either by means of a judicial process or by an administrative act (cf. Canon 1356).

Feria • Originally, the Latin word for feast, but in ecclesiastical usage it has come to mean a day with no proper feast. The former usage was to repeat Sunday's Mass readings on such a day, but since the introduction of the 1969 lectionary, there are readings for every day of the year.

The current nomenclature for feria is simply "weekday."

Ferraiolone

Ferraiolone • A large silken cloak, worn over the house cassock or the choir dress by ecclesiastics as a formal wrap on solemn extraliturgical occasions. That of a cardinal is scarlet watered silk; for a bishop or protonotary, purple silk; for all others, black (simple priests should wear black cloth, however, not silk). It was formerly obligatory to wear the ferraiolone to a papal audience, but Pope Paul VI made its use optional.

Festival of Lights: See **Hanukkah**

Fetishism • An irrational and either conscious or unconscious attraction to a person or object, one that gives the object almost magical qualities.

Fetishism is common in voodoo where the practice of placing pins in fetishes is supposed to bring harm, pain or evil to other persons. These fetishes are unethical because their object is simply to bring harm to one's enemies. Rather than loving and seeking the good of one's enemies, the fetishist seeks evil and harm for him.

Fetishes can be psychological and sexual in nature when the object is a person, clothing or other objects. Sexual fetishes are immoral because they denigrate the person to an object to be employed for sexual gratification.

Feudalism • A social, economic and political system which flourished in Europe during the Middle Ages. At its core was the organization of society with the landed aristocracy at the top, with lesser lords beneath, both served by the great mass of people with definite duties such as farming, crafts and the military. This clear system of responsibility held that the lord provided protection and sustenance for his serfs, while the serfs owed their nobles work, respect and obedience. This system permeated Church structure as well, with bishops viewed as lords, free to award benefices to lesser clergy. Abuses — such as buying and selling of offices, and lay investiture, wherein the temporal ruler could appoint bishops — at times abounded. With nationalism, urbanization and a freer economy, the feudal system disintegrated.

Fides • A news agency of the Congregation for the Evangelization of Peoples, a dicastery of the Holy See. Its chief purpose is to provide press releases, background data and official commentary on the Church's missionary efforts throughout the world,

especially in developing countries. It is headquartered in Rome.

Filioque • The Council of Toledo (A.D. 589) added the Latin phrase *filioque* ("and the Son") to the article on the Holy Spirit in the Nicene-Constantinopolitan Creed so that it would read: "the Holy Spirit . . . who proceeds from the Father and the Son." Since the ninth century, this addition has been a bone of contention between the Catholic Church and the Orthodox churches of the East. The Orthodox object to the interpolation on disciplinary and doctrinal grounds: (1) Since the Councils of Ephesus and Chalcedon forbade additions to the Nicene Creed, the action of the Council of Toledo was unauthorized and should have been repudiated by the Roman Church. (2) Since the Father is the source of both the procession of the Son and the procession of the Holy Spirit, Eastern theology prefers to speak of the procession of the Holy Spirit as being from the Father through the Son.

The history of the *filioque* after Toledo is complex. The interpolation was defended by Paulinus of Aquileia at the Synod of Friuli in 796, and after 800 became common in the chanting of the Nicene Creed throughout the Frankish Empire. In 847, the chanting of the Creed with this addition by the Frankish monks of the monastery on the Mount of Olives in Jerusalem aroused the strong opposition of the Greek monks of St. Sabas. The effort of Pope Leo III to suppress the addition without opposing the doctrine was unsuccessful; by 1000 it had been adopted in Rome. Since the time of the Patriarch Photius (810-895), the offending phrase has been one of the chief grounds for Orthodox objection to Rome. At the Councils of Lyons (1274) and Florence (1439), acceptance of the doctrine of the double procession of the Holy Spirit, though not the formula, was imposed on the East as a condition for reunion settlements that generally turned out to be quite short-lived.

The *filioque* remains an emotionally and doctrinally charged issue in Orthodox-Catholic dialogue to this day. The Western theological tradition, as it has been influenced by St. Thomas Aquinas, tends to regard both formulas ("and the Son" and "through the Son") as acceptable from a doctrinal point of view. At least from the Roman side, a compromise will likely be sought in which two versions of the Nicene Creed (one containing and the other omitting the *filioque*) would be authorized in the Church. Since the Western formula seems to compromise the monarchy of the Father — the doctrine that all being in the Trinity flows from the First Person — it remains unclear at this time whether the Orthodox would accept such a compromise.

Final Perseverance • The Catholic spiritual Tradition has long recognized that the moment of death is especially trying, and in many instances is the moment when the life of grace is most sorely tested. As part of God's providential love and care, a special grace is given whereby one is preserved in the state of sanctifying grace during this time of trial until death; this grace is known as the grace of final perseverance. It comes from God alone, and it implies that sufficient grace will be given to aid one seeking salvation.

This grace works against despair, a sin to which the sick and dying are particularly vulnerable, and against *acedia*, or sloth, in the face of the trials presented at the end of life. Final perseverance is given to those who show a profound love of God and who are not attached to the world; it is a grace for which Christians seeking fidelity should pray and seek, as they do not know what the circumstances surrounding their deaths might be.

Finance Council • Like the diocesan finance council, the parish finance council is required by the common law of the Church for every parish. It must be composed of at least three members of the faithful who are laypersons. Its purpose is to assist the pastor in the management of the temporal affairs of the parish. The finance council does not have authority but is consultative. The pastor remains the official agent and administrator of the parish goods (cf. Canons 492-493, 537).

Finance Officer • Canon 494 of the 1983 Code of Canon Law requires the diocesan bishop to appoint a diocesan finance officer whose task is to administer the financial affairs of the diocese under the authority of the bishop. This is one of the more important innovations of the 1983 Code and is reflective of the concern of the Church for more efficient administration and improved accountability. The concept of having a financial administrator apart from the diocesan bishop, however, was not entirely unheard of under the 1917 Code.

The position of finance officer is open to any Catholic skilled in financial matters and distinguished for honesty. The bishop is required to consult with the diocesan finance council and with the college of consultors in the selection of the finance officer, and must appoint the finance officer to a five-year term. Appointment as finance officer entails membership in the diocesan curia and with it all the professional and canonical obligations of confidentiality and integrity (Canon 469). This appointment is renewable, and the finance officer cannot otherwise be removed from office except for grave cause. During the vacancy of the See, the diocesan administrator cannot hold that position and that of diocesan finance officer (Canon 423).

Although local law can elaborate on the duties of the finance officer, they must include the regular administration of financial assets and liabilities in accord with the directions of the budget determined by the finance council. The finance officer is also required to produce an annual accounting of the diocesan financial condition. Thus they function in a manner very similar to that of a treasurer. It is advisable that the canonical norms on the finance officer outlined in the 1983 Code be reflected in any civilly enforceable contracts affecting the duties or powers of the officer.

Religious institutes and the major subdivisions of the same are also strongly urged to establish finance officers within their organizations, although the specifications on such positions are considerably less developed than those affecting the diocesan finance officer (Canons 636-638).

Finding of the Cross • Tradition holds that in A.D. 326, St. Helena, mother of the Emperor Constantine, found the actual cross of Christ at the site in Jerusalem long revered as Calvary (cf. Cross, Relics of the True). Here Constantine would build the Church of the Holy Sepulchre.

It is said that, upon finding three crosses, Helena brought in a blind man, who was miraculously cured when he reverenced the third cross, which was then taken to be the

St. Helena: Finder of Christ's cross

cross on which Christ was crucified. The remains of this cross, together with the veil of Veronica and the lance of the Centurion Longinus, constitute the three major relics of St. Peter's Basilica.

The finding of the cross is celebrated in the liturgy on September 14 as the Triumph (or Exaltation) of the Cross. (Cf. Holy Places.)

Fire, Blessing of the • The opening rite of the Easter Vigil. The rite prior to Vatican II specified the lighting of "a new fire, struck from flint," but the Vatican II rite simply calls for the blessing of a fire (outdoors if possible, since the Latin term actually indicates a rather sizeable fire) that may already have been kindled before the arrival of the celebrant and ministers. The celebrant begins by reminding the assembly that "this is the passover of the Lord," observed by the Church throughout the world, as on this night she calls her children together "in vigil and in prayer." The fire is blessed, and then from it the Easter Candle is lighted, and from this in turn, eventually, the candles of the people and the altar tapers as well.

Without denying the practical character of the rite (light being needed, obviously, for the readings of a nocturnal vigil), the obvious symbolism, Christ the Light of the world, appears to have been present from the beginnings of the liturgical celebration of

Easter. Both the Jerusalem Church and the Spanish Church began the Easter Vigil with a candle-lighting more solemn than that which usually marked the beginning of Vespers or Vigils. In a custom attributed to St. Patrick, the Celtic Church began with the lighting of an outdoor fire, "baptizing" the practice of local pagan priests, the warmth of the fire no doubt evoking the sense of the "quickening to life" accomplished definitively for the Christian by the resurrection of Christ. This practice spread to Gaul in the eighth century, being combined with the vesperal candle-lighting in Rome during the twelfth century, so that our present rite would seem to be a combination of both traditions and symbolisms: candle-lighting and fire, light and life. Christ is the light which "darkness has not overcome" (Jn 1:5), in Whose light Christians are called to walk (Eph 5) and the life-source of the Church and of the individual Christian who is baptized into His death and resurrection (cf. Rom 6).

In the Eastern Church primarily (though not exclusively), it was the custom to bring the "new light" home for the lighting of the lamps and, in some places, for the rekindling of the home or "hearth" fire that would have been essential for warmth and nourishment.

First Friday Devotions • Deriving from revelations made by Christ to St. Margaret Mary Alacoque (1647-1690), the practice of receiving Holy Communion on nine consecutive First Fridays in reparation to "the Heart that has loved men so and is loved so little in return" (Christ to Margaret Mary). Among the graces Christ is said to have promised to those who are faithful to this devotion: final perseverance in the Catholic Faith, reception of the last sacraments and death in the state of grace, the consolation of the love of Christ's Sacred Heart at the time of death.

At a time when frequent Communion was not common but rather discouraged by the prevailing Jansenism of the age and culture, the message of Christ's enduring love which came to the faithful through St. Margaret Mary brought an outpouring of devotion and commitment from the ordinary faithful among whom the Sacred Heart devotion became very popular. Although the devotion remains popular to this day, it must be acknowledged that fidelity to it in generations past involved no small amount of sacrifice in light of the formerly quite severe Communion fast, early morning Mass and Friday abstinence, all in the context of a longer and usually more strenuous workday for most of the faithful.

The Apostleship of Prayer, specially committed to spreading this and other devotion to the Sacred Heart, also promotes the practice of a First Friday Holy Hour, including exposition of the Blessed Sacrament, the Litany of the Sacred Heart, the Act of Consecration of the Human Race ("Most sweet Jesus, Redeemer of the human race, look down upon us humbly prostrate before Thine altar . . ."), and Benediction. Because the solemnity of the Most Sacred Heart of Jesus occurs on the Friday following the Second Sunday after Pentecost (Corpus Christi, or the Body and Blood of Christ in countries where this is not a holy day), and therefore always in June, the month of June is traditionally designated as the "Month of the Sacred Heart."

First Fruits • As sacred to Yahweh, the first fruits of man, animals, fleece, trees, grain, wine, oil and "whatsoever was sown in the field" were by the law of Moses to be offered to the Lord (Ex 23:19, 34:26; cf. Lv 19:24, 23:9-11, Nm 18:12, Dt 26:1-4). In Ezekiel 44:30, it is further specified that the first fruits are the proper domain of the priests; those Old Testament regulations are taken as the biblical basis of the Precept of the Church that requires the physical support of the Church and of priests.

The first fruits of Yahweh is a metaphor for Israel (Jer 2:3); similarly, the Church, as the New Israel, is described as the first fruits of God (Jas 1:18, Rv 14:4), while other Christians are called first fruits because they were the first to be converted (Rom 16:5, 1 Cor 16:15), and all Christians are said to possess the first fruits of the Holy Spirit (Rom 8:23). As the first to rise to new life, Christ is described by St. Paul as the first fruits of the dead (1 Cor 15:20). (Cf. Tithe; Stewardship; Stipend.)

For further reading: Richard O. Rigsby, "First Fruits," *Anchor Bible Dictionary*, 2:796-797.

First Holy Communion • The act of receiving Holy Communion for the first time. Usually it is the culmination of instruction and catechesis concerning the doctrine, nature and reality of the Eucharist.

Pope St. Pius X (1903-1914) strongly encouraged Catholics to receive Holy Communion frequently — weekly, or even daily, if they could. It was he who also determined the age at which young Catholics could receive their First Holy Communion. According to St. Pius, Catholics who had reached the age of reason (generally regarded as the age of seven) could be admitted to the Holy Eucharist. By the age of reason, it is judged that the recipient of Holy Communion can know and believe that a consecrated Host is really and truly the Body of Christ.

In the decree *Quam singulari* (1910), in which St. Pius X ordered that children be admitted to the Eucharist when they have reached the age of discretion, it is also taught that children should celebrate the sacrament of Penance before receiving the Eucharist. The Church's *General Catechetical Directory* holds that sacramental confession must precede the reception of First Holy Communion. Further, Canon 914 of the 1983 Code of Canon Law stipulates that those admitted to First Holy Communion have recourse to the sacrament of Reconciliation first.

First Saturday Devotion • Those who practice this devotion are to receive Holy Communion on five consecutive first Saturdays, receive the sacrament of Penance within an octave before or after this reception, recite five decades of the Rosary and make a fifteen-minute meditation on one of these mysteries.

Closely affiliated in style and substance with the Sacred Heart Devotion, the origins of this practice may be traced to St. John Eudes (1601-1680), the "apostle of devotion to the Hearts of Jesus and Mary," and to Venerable John J. Olier (1608-1657), founder of the Sulpicians. But it was after the apparitions at Fátima in 1917 that this devotion gained momentum, since Our Lady was said to have recommended it specifically, promising her intercession for final perseverance at the hour of death to all who would be faithful to it.

As in devotion to the Sacred Heart, the dominant theme of this devotion is reparation offered to Christ, in this context "to the Divine Son through the Immaculate Heart of His Mother." In the revision of the Calendar following the Second Vatican Council, the memorial of the Immaculate Heart of Mary was transferred to the day after (that is, Saturday) the solemnity of the Sacred Heart of Jesus.

Firstborn • In Genesis 49:3, the patriarch Jacob addresses his son Reuben as ". . . my first-born, my might and the first fruit of my strength, preeminent in pride and preeminent in power!" This reveals the privileged status which the firstborn male child enjoyed in ancient Israel. In Genesis 25, Jacob himself usurps the birthright which properly pertained to his brother Esau as Isaac's firstborn son, and in Genesis 27 Jacob tricks Isaac into bestowing on him the paternal blessing promised to Esau.

The legislation of Deuteronomy 21:15-17 protects the birthright of the firstborn son, defining it as a double share of the father's property and preventing a father from denying this inheritance to his firstborn son, even if the firstborn is the son of a wife whom the father dislikes.

Psalm 89:28 speaks of the Davidic king as God's firstborn, the recipient of divine protection and divine promise according to the covenant.

In Exodus 4:22, God lays claim to Israel as His firstborn, commanding Moses to address the Egyptian Pharaoh: "Israel is my first-born son and I say to you: Let my son go, that he may serve me. If you refuse to let him go, behold, I will slay your first-born son." God carries out this threat in the tenth plague against Egypt (Ex 11-12), in which "at midnight the LORD smote all the first-born in the land of Egypt, from the first-born of Pharaoh who sat on his throne to the first-born of the captive who was in the dungeon and all the first-born of the cattle" (Ex 12:29).

Israel is spared from the plague against the firstborn through the observance of the Passover sacrifice, which continues to be celebrated in memory of this event (Ex 12:24-26). As the event through which Israel gained freedom from bondage in Egypt, the plague against the Egyptian firstborn is celebrated in Psalms 78:51; 105:36; 135:8; 136:10 (cf. 11:28).

Israel's liberation from Egypt as a result of the plague against the firstborn is also the reason behind the legislation found in Exodus 13:1-16, the consecration to God of Israel's firstborn. "All the males who first open the womb" (Ex 13:15) must be sacrificed to the Lord. To avoid the abhorrent practice of human sacrifice (cf. Ez 20:26), the firstborn son had to be spared from such sacrificial consecration by the presentation of a substitute offering. Such substitution could also be applied for the firstborn of an ass, for which a sheep could instead be sacrificed (Ex 13:13).

In Numbers 3, the cultic service of the tribe of Levi is explained in terms of the consecration of Israel's firstborn to the Lord: "The LORD said to Moses, 'Behold, I have taken the Levites from the people of Israel instead of every first-born that opens the womb among the people of Israel' " (Nm 3:11-12). In Numbers 3:40-51, a census is taken of all the Israelite firstborn, and a ransom of five shekels is paid as a substitute offering for each of them.

In the New Testament, Jesus is the firstborn in a preeminent way. In the Lucan infancy narrative, He is identified as Mary's firstborn son (Lk 2:7). In Luke 2:22-24, the presentation of Jesus in the Temple takes place in accord with the law concerning the consecration of the firstborn, cited in Luke 2:23.

Paul writes in Romans 8:29 that God predestined those whom He foreknew to be conformed to the image of Jesus His Son, ". . . in order that he might be the first-born among brethren." Colossians 1:15 calls Jesus "the first-born of all creation," and, by calling Him "the first-born from the dead," Colossians 1:18 proclaims that by His resurrection Jesus is the firstborn of the new creation. Revelation 1:5 highlights the exalted status of Christ by calling Him "the first-born of the dead, and the ruler of kings on earth."

As firstborn, Jesus is the Son in a preeminent way, sharing a unique relationship with the Father. Through the Spirit, believers are children of God and brothers and sisters of Christ, "heirs of God and joint heirs with Christ" (Rom 8:17).

For further reading: V. H. Kooy, "First-Born," *Interpreter's Dictionary of the Bible*, 2:270-272; J. Milgrom, "First-Born," *Interpreter's Dictionary of the Bible*, Supplementary Volume 337-338.

Fiscal Procurator • Although not a proper canonical term, it can refer to the official appointed by an ecclesiastical superior to oversee the financial matters of a Catholic institution. In many religious communities, the member charged with overseeing the management of funds or even the physical upkeep of the buildings is called a procurator.

Fish • Classified as aquatic, gilled creatures, fish are found all over the world. They are mentioned in biblical references to the Mediterranean Sea and the Sea of Galilee. Sacred Scripture makes no distinction between fresh- and salt-water fish. According to archaeological finds, both types of fish were regularly eaten in first-century Palestine. According to Leviticus 11:9-12, fish with fins and scales were considered clean and therefore acceptable as food, whereas all others were not. The New Testament data conforms to the broader Mediterranean dietary custom which used fish as a common source of protein (Mt 7:10; 14:17; 15:36; Mk 6:41; Lk 9:16; 11:11; 24:42; Jn 21:9-13). In the Old Testament, "fish" symbolized death from plagues (Ex 7:21), death from drought (Is 50:2), untimely death (Eccl 9:12). Early in Christian Tradition, the Greek word for fish, *ichthus*, became an acrostic for a proclamation about Jesus, representing the first letters of the five Greek words: "Jesus [*iesous*] Christ [*christos*], God's [*theou*] Son [(h)*uios*] (and/is) Savior [*soter*]." In Luke 5:10, the Apostles are characterized as "fishers of men." In later Christian iconographical art, the fish became and remains a popular public

symbol of one's relationship with God through Christ.

For further reading: F. S. Bodenheimer and W. S. McCullough, "Fish," *Interpreter's Dictionary of the Bible*, 272-273.

Fisherman's Ring • The signet ring of the Pope is called the Fisherman's Ring because of the engraving upon it which depicts St. Peter in a boat fishing, recalling the words of Our Lord to him, "Henceforth you will be catching men" (Lk 5:10). The name of the Pope, as the successor of Peter, encircles the central engraving. The earliest reference to the Fisherman's Ring is in a letter of Pope Clement IV in 1265. Although it is placed upon the finger of a new Pope by the cardinal camerlengo, it is not subsequently worn. Since the fifteenth century it has been used to seal Papal Briefs. Upon the death of a Pope the ring is ceremonially broken, and a document is drawn up testifying to its destruction, so that it cannot be used for any false purposes.

Fistula • A liturgical "straw" or tube for drinking the Precious Blood, in use during the Middle Ages. Its usage continued into modern times only at the solemn Papal Mass. Even with the reintroduction of Communion under both species after Vatican II, it was one of the methods recommended which seems never to have caught on.

Five Wounds • The penetrations of Our Lord's Body (His two hands and two feet), so that He could be nailed to the cross, and the gash in His side, the result of a soldier thrusting a lance there. Devotion to Our Savior's five wounds started in the Middle Ages as a way of vividly and graphically recalling the passion.

A rendering of the five wounds is to be found in the Portuguese coat of arms. At various times, too, a facsimile of the five wounds has been grafted onto shields in battle or have been sewn into banners carried in pilgrimage.

Flabellum • The flabella (as they are known in the plural) are the long-handled fans which up to recent times were used in the liturgy to keep away insects from the Sacred Species. They were formerly part of the solemn procession of the Pope at Papal Masses. They were made of leather upholstered in red velvet with gold embroidery and had white ostrich feathers. In the Oriental Rites, fans (*rhiphidia*), fashioned out of brass and sometimes gilt, are used for the same purpose. The word *flabellum* means "fan" in Latin.

Flagellation • Taken from the Latin *flagellum* (whip). In imitation of the scourging of Jesus (Mt 27:26, Mk 15:15, Jn 19:1), some ascetics have willingly subjected themselves to a similar beating, usually self-imposed, but also inflicted by others with the individual's consent. Flagellation is considered an extreme form of ascetical piety and is generally discouraged by spiritual writers and Church authority. Where there have been movements such as the Brotherhood of Flagellants, they have consistently met with papal prohibition. In the fourteenth century, the Flagellants organized religious ceremonies and set forth their own heretical doctrines, which were condemned by Pope Clement VI in 1349.

Flat Hat • The flat hat or "cappello Romano" (Roman hat) is the proper hat to be worn by ecclesiastics when the cassock is used out of doors. Its use was obligatory until 1966. It has a round crown with a brim about three inches wide. It is usually made of beaver but may be of felt. The Pope's hat is red with an elaborate red and gold band, and small gold strings hold up the brim. Cardinals have a black hat with

red and gold cord around the crown, and bishops have a green and gold cord. Simple priests have a black hat with a black cord.

Flectamus Genua • The spoken invitation ("Let us kneel"), usually offered by the deacon or an assistant minister. In response to the invitation, the whole congregation kneels for a few moments in silence; at the invitation *Levate* ("Let us rise"), they stand again. Among the earliest evidence of this is the custom in Egyptian monasteries during the recitation of twelve psalms at the major hours of the Divine Office. At the end of the solo recitation of a psalm, a monk would invite the community to stand in silent prayer with arms outstretched: the invitation *Flectamus genua* would follow, as would their rising and listening to a concluding prayer. This action accompanied each of the twelve psalms.

During the solemn intercessions of the celebration of the Lord's passion on Good Friday, this invitation is sung or spoken by the deacon after he introduces each intention.

Flock • It is no surprise to see the image of "flock" used as a description of the Church. The culture within which Christianity was born and toward which it directed its missionary effort was very familiar with the shepherd, sheep and goats, and the flock. In the early Church the image of Christ as the Good Shepherd (Jn 10) suggests that the Church is the Good Shepherd's flock. Although the term "flock" does not occur often, throughout the New Testament that image is certainly implied, whenever sheep are mentioned as symbols of people: at Matthew 10:6 (cf. Is 53:6), Jesus compares Israel to "lost sheep" without a shepherd (Mt 9:36). The image of "flock" is implied in the parables about sheep (Mt 12:11-12; 18:12; 25:32-33). The theme of the Good Shepherd giving His life for His sheep (Jn 10:11) did not begin in the New Testament but is actually a development of Old Testament imagery scattered in many texts (e.g., Ex 20:24; Ps 23:1; Heb 13:20).

Florence, Council of • The Council of Florence was the seventeenth ecumenical council and began as a continuation of the Council of Basel. It opened in Ferrara, but for safety and political reasons it was moved to Florence. Although it operated against the backdrop of conciliarism, the Council of Florence is by far best remembered for its near-accomplishment of the reunion of the Orthodox Churches with the See of Rome. Through more than two dozen public and private sessions, the Council Fathers hammered away at doctrinal and disciplinary matters then separating the Churches. A decree of reunion was approved in 1439, whereupon the Eastern prelates returned home, while the Latin Fathers remained until 1445 in an attempt at similar resolutions for some of the other smaller schismatic churches in the East.

When the decree of reunion was presented to the other Greek Churches, however, it was greeted with lack of interest or suspicion. In particular, one Mark Eugenicus, then metropolitan of Ephesus and a participant at the Council, railed against the decree. His words, combined with the advent of Muslim military power in the region, sufficed to doom any hopes for a major reunion of the Eastern and Western Churches in his day. (Cf. Filioque.)

Florida Pascua • Spanish for flowery or blooming Easter, for since this great feast falls during springtime, there are usually many flowers in bloom. The Spanish explorers under Juan Ponce de León discovered what they thought was an island on April of 1513, and gave it the name Florida since it was found during the Easter season. It turned out to be a peninsula, which after changing hands several times became part of the United States. To this day it has retained the name given to it by the Spanish conquistador.

Focolare Movement • This movement was begun in Trent, Italy, in 1943 by Chiara Lubich. It is an association of men and women which is officially approved by the Church. The purpose of this association is one of making a contribution to Jesus' last prayer: "That they may all be one" (Jn 17:21). The spirituality of unity proper to the Focolare has proven to be a powerful means of introducing the Gospel into modern life, bringing a greater unity to society. Centers of the movement have been established in sixty countries throughout the world. U.S. centers are located in New York City, Chicago, Boston, Los Angeles, San Antonio, Washington, D.C. and Columbus, Ohio; a center for spirituality is located in Hyde Park, New York.

Fontes • The *Fontes* or sources are the background documents upon which each of the canons in the Code of Canon Law are based. The *Fontes* appear as footnotes in some editions of the official Latin text of the Code.

The *Fontes* of the 1917 Code included citations of papal statements of various kinds, canons from the *Decree of Gratian*, official statements from the various Roman congregations and decretals from the *Decretals of Gregory IX*. A more complete understanding of the history and context of each canon is obtained from a study of the *Fontes*. The sources themselves are found in the nine-volume work entitled *Codicis Iuris Canonici Fontes* (Sources of the Code of Canon Law), edited by Pietro Cardinal Gasparri and published in Rome in 1926.

The *Fontes* of the revised Code do not include all of those from the 1917 Code.

Rather, when pertinent, there is a reference to the similar canon from this Code. Other sources include documents from Vatican Council II, papal statements, documents from the various Roman congregations issued since the Council and citations from the liturgical books.

Form • In classical and Scholastic philosophy, form is the intelligible structure of a being as distinct from any material component that may be included in its nature. For example, rationality is part of the form, the essential structure of a human being.

Substantial form is further distinguished from accidental form. Having a particular skin color would be accidental, while being a rational person would be substantial.

The proclamation "all men are created equal" would refer to the form of humanity, not to accidental differences, such as I.Q., race, sex or class.

In relation to the sacraments, form is used in theology to designate the words and signs that accompany the sacrament. These cannot be substantially changed for a sacrament to be valid. For example, it would not be valid to substitute, "I baptize you in the name of the Creator, the Redeemer and the Spirit," for "I baptize you in the name of the Father, the Son and the Holy Spirit."

Form, Canonical • Canonical form refers to the external formalities which accompany the exchange of marital consent. While traditionally couples with due capacity and expressing proper consent were able to marry, beginning about the sixteenth century the added requirement of satisfying canonical form was introduced in Church law. At first, the requirement of form was supported by the need to reduce various abuses then plaguing marriage, such as spousal abandonment in cases where secret marriages had been celebrated. Over the centuries, however, canonical form has also served as a practical means for pointing couples toward marriage preparation programs and for protecting the solemnity of the ceremony. By the requirement of canonical form, the Church holds that certain formalities must be present when the exchange of consent takes place.

Basically, canonical form involves the exchange of consent in the presence of the Ordinary of the place, the pastor of one of the parties or a priest or deacon delegated by one of them. It is also required that two witnesses be present.

The sacred minister is also known as the official witness. He is not merely present but must ask for and receive the consent of the spouses in the name of the Church. The two witnesses must have the use of reason and must be capable of knowing what is going on and attesting to it. They need not be Catholic, nor must they be one male and one female.

All those baptized or received into the Catholic Church who have not left it by a formal act are bound to marry according to canonical form. By "formal act" is meant some external sign that a person has left the Catholic Church, such as adherence to another Christian denomination or sect or even a formal declaration that one has left the Church.

The sacred minister or official witness must have jurisdiction, either ordinary or delegated, over at least one of the parties. Thus, at least one of them must be a member of the Latin Rite if it is a mixed-rite marriage.

Marriages should be celebrated in the church where either party has a domicile or quasi-domicile but not necessarily the parish church of the bride. A marriage can be performed in another church, provided the permission of the local Ordinary or pastor of the parties is obtained.

Although canonical form is required for validity for the marriages of Catholics, when the marriage is a mixed marriage, the Ordinary of the Catholic party can dispense from the obligation of form. The Catholic party is thus permitted to enter into a valid marriage witnessed by a minister of another denomination or a civil official (Canons 1108-1123).

Form Criticism • This method of analysis focuses on small literary units within, for example, a Gospel or one of Paul's letters. It assumes that the small units of material have their own unique existence and, therefore, history prior to their inclusion into the Gospels or letters. Thus, the overall goal is to establish the history of the unit under scrutiny from its earliest existence to its final version or form as it exists in the Gospel narratives we possess. The principal means of doing this are twofold: tradition-history and literary criticism. In tradition-history the goal is to trace the history of the literary unit from its oral stages (i.e., the preaching of Jesus and His followers) to its written stage, to its Gospel stage. This tracing is done primarily by means of literary criticism. The unit is examined, and any literary elements, such as words or phrases (or structures), which seem clearly to be from the hand of, for example, the author of Matthew's Gospel, would be deleted. The assumption is that what would emerge is the rough shape or the literary unit prior to its inclusion within the canonical Gospel. Knowledge derived from the literary shape or form offers a major clue to how the material was understood at various stages of the transmission or journey to its final resting spot in the Gospel, so to speak. Form criticism thus can help reconstruct the history of a literary or oral unit: literary peculiarities, grammatical relationships, vocabulary items within the unit, all provide a window to the attitudes of the people who shaped the material prior to its inclusion in the canonical Scriptures.

For further reading: John Barton, "Form Criticism (Old Testament)," *Anchor Bible Dictionary*, 2:838-841; Vernon K. Robbins, "Form Criticism (New Testament)," *Anchor Bible Dictionary*, 2:841-844.

Fortitude • A cardinal virtue and gift of the Holy Spirit. Fortitude is a disposition to achieve good even when this demands suffering, pain or great effort. This virtue gives the Christian the will and strength to overcome whatever obstacles are encountered in the course of following the way of the Gospel. Under the impulse of the Holy Spirit, it prevents succumbing to temptations, and in so doing it facilitates and promotes Christian life in general.

Fortune-Telling • The practice of predicting or determining another's fate or fortune by using such means as crystal balls, cards or palm-reading. Fortune-telling is contrary to the First Commandment because only God truly knows our fate, and fortune-tellers attribute to themselves powers properly possessed only by God. Consulting fortune-tellers is irreligious consulting of false prophets and is a counterfeit prophecy. Those who practice fortune-telling are guilty of superstition and also of perpetrating a hoax on those who credulously believe them. To practice this merely for the sake of a joke is not sinful, however.

Forty Hours Devotion • A time of forty (semi-)continuous hours adoration of the Eucharist in a monstrance, customarily held annually in each parish or oratory. The origins of this devotion are hard to trace exactly. There is some consensus that it originated in the sixteenth century, probably in Milan. Both St. Anthony Zaccaria and St. Philip Neri championed the devotion, the latter having introduced it to the Churches in Rome around 1550. St. Charles Borromeo (Milan) was also influential in its spread; he even referred to it as though it were an ancient custom. Pope Paul III approved a petition soliciting indulgences for those who participated in the devotion, and in 1560 Pope Paul IV issued a Papal Bull of approbation entitled *Divina disponente clementia*. By the end of that century, Pope Clement VIII published the bull *Graves et Diuturnae*, which granted a plenary indulgence to those who participated in the Forty Hours.

The 1973 *Instruction on Holy Communion and Worship of the Eucharist Outside Mass* does not specify forty hours; however, it states that in churches where the Eucharist is reserved, "it is recommended that solemn exposition of the Blessed Sacrament for an extended period of time should take place once a year, even though this period is not strictly continuous" (n. 86).

Forum • Originally, the Latin word *forum* meant a marketplace and, later, a court of justice. In canonical usage, it has come to mean the place where either a judgment is made or some other ecclesiastical act takes place. A distinction exists between the internal forum and the external forum.

"Competent forum" refers to the court or the judge who has the authority to try a case.

Foundation Masses • A popular term referring to the laudable practice of donating a specific sum of money to be used for the support of the clergy or works of religion, in return for which the beneficiaries of the donation agree to offer a specific number of Masses for the intention of the donor over a set period of time. In earlier days it was not uncommon for a sum to be donated in trust to a parish, the interest from which would support the financial activities of that parish

for many years. Over the decades, however, the actual value of the income fell, sometimes precipitously, so that a large number of Mass obligations would burden the parish for what became trifling sums. To protect donors and recipients, then, most ecclesiastical institutions have placed a general limit on the number of Masses which will be offered or on the period of time for which the obligation will be honored under such arrangements. Generally, Canons 1299-1310 of the 1983 Code of Canon Law regulate this practice, although local laws may supplement these rules.

Four Causes: See **Causes, Four**

Fraction • The rite of fraction is also called the rite of "breaking the bread" of the Eucharist for its distribution. The *General Instruction of the Roman Missal* (1975) notes that "in apostolic times this gesture of Christ at the Last Supper [breaking of bread] gave the entire Eucharistic action its name" (n. 56c). Strong ecclesiological understandings are attached to this rite, as derived from the injunction of St. Paul in 1 Corinthians 10:16b-17, "The bread which we break, is it not a participation in the body of Christ? Because there is one bread, we who are many are one body, for we all partake of the one bread."

This rite was a necessary preparation for the reception of the Eucharist and took some time when the number of communicants was large. In *Ordo Romanus Primus* (the first of the Roman ordos describing various papal ceremonies), this rite is carried out by bishops and priests with a certain solemnity. In the seventh century Pope Sergius I introduced the singing of the chant *Agnus Dei* ("Lamb of God") to accompany the fraction, which chant contains strong sacrificial overtones of the Eucharist as a means of the forgiveness of sins. The *General Instruction of the Roman*

Missal states that the *Agnus Dei* is sung or said aloud during the breaking of the bread and the commingling. "This invocation may be repeated as often as necessary to accompany the breaking of the bread. The final reprise concludes with the words *grant us peace*" (n. 56e).

The rite of commingling consists of placing a small particle of the consecrated Bread into the chalice. This custom derives from the *fermentum* practice (literally "leaven"). The *fermentum* was originally a part of the Eucharistic Bread consecrated by the Pope in Rome (as attested in the letter of Pope St. Innocent I in A.D. 416 to Bishop Decentius of Gubbio) and then sent to the various *tituli* (parish churches) in the city to denote the unity of the one Christian community despite their having to celebrate separate Eucharists.

Franciscan Controversy • A dispute among Franciscans of the thirteenth and fourteenth centuries concerning the authentic observance of the vow of poverty by the Order. Divergent interpretations of the rule against both personal and corporate possessions (already discernible before the death of St. Francis and becoming more pronounced in the altered circumstances of the order's rapid expansion) engendered, especially after 1245, bitter conflict between the "Spiritual" Franciscans who opposed corporate ownership of property, and the more numerous moderates who considered it necessary for carrying out the order's ministries.

A split in the order was averted through the wise leadership of St. Bonaventure, who was Minister General for nearly twenty years (1257-1274). He held the view that corporate property really belonged to the Church and was entrusted to the stewardship and use (rather than ownership) of the order. But the disagreement remained a source of contention into the next century, when the issue was debated before Pope Clement V (1310-1312). Finally, John XXII declared the Spiritual party to be in heresy and permitted the order corporate ownership in the bulls *Sancta Romana* (1317) and *Gloriosam Ecclesiam* (1318).

This measure provoked the opposition of the Spirituals, whom the Pope then excommunicated (and four of whom he had burned at the stake). The Spirituals subsequently won the support and protection of Louis of Bavaria, while the Franciscan theologian William of Ockham (1285-1347) took up their defense. But John XXII reiterated his condemnation of their doctrine, insisting that Christian perfection did not require complete renunciation (*Ad Conditorem Canonum*, 1322). In the end, persecution sapped the Spirituals' cause. But the movement later gave rise to a reformed Franciscan group — the "Observants" — which won Church approval in 1415.

Franciscans • Those men and women who follow the Rule of St. Francis of Assisi (d. 1226) as professed religious. This renowned rule stressed a communal life of gospel simplicity, with special attention to the first of the three evangelical counsels of poverty, chastity and obedience. Today, three separate groups attempt to follow this rule: men religious, women religious and laity. Among professed men who adhere to the Franciscan tradition are three orders: Friars Minor, Friars Minor Conventuals and Friars Minor Capuchins. Although there are hundreds of congregations of religious women dedicated to St. Francis, the "Second Order" refers particularly to the Poor Clares. Lay people can adapt the Franciscan charism to their life as "tertiaries" or members of the Third Order, now called Secular Franciscans.

Frankfort, Council of • In 794, Charlemagne, with the approval of the Holy See, convened a local council in Frankfort which was attended by representatives of the Pope. The main task of the council was to enact reforms in general ecclesiastical discipline, which it did in the form of fifty-six canons. It also drafted two documents rejecting the heresy of Adoptionism. The council is, ironically, best remembered, though, for its repudiation of certain "errors" of the Council of Nicaea. Because of faulty translations, the Frankfort Fathers had mistakenly been led to believe that the Nicene Council had approved the adoration of images, which of course the latter had never done. The Council of Frankfort nevertheless promoted true discipline on the matter, however, as it turned out, superfluously.

Frankincense • This gum-like substance carries a sweet fragrance and is produced in yellow-brown, tear-like drops from the Boswellia family of trees which grow in South Arabia, Ethiopia, Somaliland and India. It was used as a perfume (Sg 3:6; 4:6, 14), but more frequently in a religious context, in rituals (Ex 30:34-38), for offerings at the temple (Is 43:23; 66:3; Jer 17:26; 41:5); it was placed beside the bread of presence (Lv 24:7). Frankincense was offered to the Christ Child by the Wise Men from the East (Mt 2:11) as an acknowledgment of Christ's future priestly role; the gold mentioned signifies His kingly role; and the myrrh (which was normally used to prepare a corpse for burial) probably anticipates Christ's death on the cross.

Fraternal Correction • The practice of correcting the faults of another for the purpose of promoting the growth in charity

Charlemagne: Convened Frankfort council

and love of God in the other. Fraternal correction is not malicious in intent, and it only aims at increasing the holiness and love of the person corrected. Fraternal correction intends to motivate the other to more perfect charity and practice of the virtues, and thus it is imperative that this correction be done with prudence and discretion. Indiscreet or imprudent fraternal correction can readily engender animosity, resentment and hostility, thus defeating its primary purpose; but charitable, prudent and thoughtful fraternal correction is of great help in one's spiritual life.

Fraud in Marriage • Fraud or deceit is a deliberate act of deception by which one person hides a significant fact about another to achieve a given end. In this case, one party to the marriage deliberately deceives the other about the presence or absence of a certain quality about himself or herself. The quality is of such significance that the discovery of its presence or absence could destroy the marriage.

For fraud to invalidate a marriage, canonists generally point to certain elements which must be proved: the fraud must be deliberately perpetrated in order to obtain consent; the quality must be real, grave and present at the time of marital consent; the discovery of the fraud must be directly instrumental in the termination of the marriage. Obviously, if the fraud is discovered and has only a minimal effect on the marriage, then it is difficult to presume that the quality involved was of such importance that its presence or absence could seriously harm the relationship. Some examples: lying about one's religious affiliation, sexual orientation, nationality, marital status or criminal record (Canon 1098).

Freedom • The capacity to determine for oneself and one's actions, independent of extrinsic causes. There are various kinds of freedom.

First, there is transcendental freedom, which is the fundamental property of human persons to declare that they are "over and above" other entities and are able to judge and evaluate other entities from that vantage point. Second, there is a freedom from things, such as the freedom from poverty and ignorance. And third, there is a freedom to develop potentialities in their various forms.

Catholicism has consistently defended the radical freedom of man, a freedom so extensive and profound that it is able to reject even the gifts of divine grace and forgiveness. As a result of this profound respect for freedom, Catholic Faith has come to espouse political, social and economic freedom as moral values of great significance.

The Catholic understanding of freedom is different because it regards it as an ordered freedom, espoused as a means of promoting the well-being and good order of the community. Catholic Faith also gives freedom a religious dimension, for it becomes the condition under which we respond to the divine initiatives. In the modern era, this profound respect for freedom has been concretely manifested, for Catholicism has become a major champion of human freedom and liberty by challenging the tyrannies of Marxism and capitalism in the Third World.

Freedom, Religious: See **Liberty, Religious;** also **Dignitatis Humanae**

Freemasonry • The set of principles, rites and usages upheld by a federation of fraternal organizations whose remote origins lie in the medieval guilds of stone builders or freemasons. Modern Freemasonry dates from the establishment of the Grand Lodge in England in 1717, gaining wide acceptance among the upper classes after 1721 and spreading to continental Europe throughout the eighteenth century.

Essentially, Masonic lodges are organized to provide occasions for fellowship and benevolent social activities. But Freemasonry's religious tone has brought it into conflict with almost all the main branches of Christianity. Fellowship and philanthropy are embedded in a quasi-religious structure with special initiation procedures, a complex hierarchical organization and elaborate ritual. In addition, British Freemasonry was broadly deistic and naturalistic in religious belief, while European Freemasonry had a markedly anticlerical and anti-Christian bent.

As early as 1738, Pope Clement XII condemned Freemasonry and forbade Catholics to join Masonic lodges. Similar condemnations were promulgated by Benedict XIV, Pius VII, Pius IX and Leo XIII, culminating in the proscription of Freemasonry by the 1917 Code of Canon Law (Canon 2335). There is no mention of Freemasonry as such in the new Code and no censure of excommunication for Catholics who join Masonic lodges. But there is a provision for such a sanction in cases, to be identified locally, where an organization works against the Faith or the Church (Canon 1374). A note from the Congregation for the Doctrine of the Faith in 1983 referred to Masonic membership as a "grave sin."

There are about six million Freemasons in the world, with U.S. membership passing the four million mark.

Friar • Usually, a member of one of the mendicant orders founded during the Middle Ages. The term arose to distinguish the itinerant apostolic character of the new orders from the various monastic orders then in existence. Although most friars follow many of the religious observances associated with monasticism, their religious profession does not tie them to allegiance to one monastery as in the case of monks, but binds them rather to a worldwide fellowship under the leadership of a superior general. The most important orders of friars are the Dominicans, the Franciscans, the Carmelites and the Augustinians. Other orders of friars still extant are the Trinitarians, Mercedarians, Minims, Servites, the Brothers of St. John of God and the Order of Penance. The term "friar" derives from the Latin word for "brother" — *frater* — by way of the Old French and Middle English words "frere" and "fryer."

Friary • In theory, this term could refer to the residence of any order of friars, but in practice it usually designates a house of one of the branches of the Franciscans. Other orders of friars, such as the Dominicans and the Carmelites, use the word "priory" for their houses.

Friends of God • A fourteenth-century group of religious and laity, originating in Basle (Basel), Switzerland (1339-1343), and spreading through the Rhine Valley to Strasbourg and the Netherlands. (The Friends of God are not to be confused with the Religious Society of Friends, known also as the Quakers.) The movement drew its inspiration from such passages as John 15:14: "I have called you friends, for all that I heard from my Father I have made known to you." In reaction to the externalism and political turmoil they observed in fourteenth-century Christianity, movements like the Friends of God (*Gottesfreunde*) emerged, in order to provide centers of spiritual fellowship. Influenced by the Dominican Rhineland mystics (Meister Eckhart, Johannes Tauler and Henry Suso), they sought to cultivate a personal union with God and a strong devotional life. A Strasbourg mystic named Rulman Merswin emerged as the central figure of the movement with his apocalyptic work *The Book of Nine Rocks*. Historians generally regard the Friends of God and related movements as precursors of the Reformation.

Friendship • Words commonly associated with friendship are closeness, esteem, intimacy, companionship, helpfulness, unity of purpose.

In calling His disciples friends, for whom He will lay down His life (cf. Jn 15:13-17), Christ elevated friendship in Him from a matter of mere pleasant association to an essential part of Christian life. Our response to the friendship of the Lord for each of us overflows in generous love toward our brothers and sisters in the Christian community, and to all those with whom we come in contact, in the form of respect for their value as loved by God.

More specifically, Catholic Tradition affirms friendships based not only on universal Christian charity, but also on the gift of a special rapport. Although there can be dangers in exclusive attachment to particular friends, there is also a need to overcome unhealthy self-enclosure. Vatican II's *Apostolicam Actuositatem* states that "by affording mutual spiritual aid by friendship and the exchange of personal experiences, they [the laity] get the courage to surmount the difficulties of too isolated a life and activity and can increase the yield of their apostolate" (n. 17).

Such holy friendships as those between Sts. Mary and Joseph, Augustine and Monica, Bernard and his brother, Francis and Clare, Teresa of Ávila and John of the Cross provide inspiration for Catholics concerning how fruitful friendship in Christ can prove to be.

Fruits of the Holy Spirit • The phrase appears only at Galatians 5:22-23, which lists nine fruits: love, joy, peace, patience, kindness, goodness, faith, gentleness, self-control (cf. the *Catechism of the Catholic Church*, nn. 733-736). These fruits are mentioned in the context of contrasting Christian freedom in Christ (5:1, 13) to slavery (5:1), which occurs by accepting circumcision as a means of reconciliation with God (5:2-3, 11) or in contrast to a life lived under the power of the "flesh" (our fallen nature: 5:13, 16-17, 19-21). The fruits of the Spirit are in direct contrast and quite antagonistic to a life in the flesh (Gal 5:17).

These "fruits" are the result of two fundamental steps in the process of salvation. First, the "fallen nature" or, in Paul's language, "flesh" must be crucified, that is, it must undergo a death which is linked to Christ's death on the cross (Rom 6:5); it must cease to have power over the mind, the will and the whole personality. Second, with the death of the "flesh," God and Christ fashion a new creation (2 Cor 5:17; Eph 2:15; 4:24), which means that one has entered into the reality of resurrected life at an initial stage (Gal 6:15). The "fruits" are the net effects of living this life in the Spirit or resurrected life within relationships. In the language of classical theology, when infused graces transform the person's heart, mind, soul and will, one can expect to find an ample yield of fruits of the Spirit.

Fruits of the Mass • The fruits of the Mass are those effects which result from the Mass for the human beings who participate in its celebration (i.e., reception of grace, propitiation for the sins of the world and the satisfaction for the punishment due to sin) in contrast with those effects which are directed to God Himself (i.e., worship and thanksgiving). Although the Sacrifice of the Mass is of intrinsically infinite worth, its fruits are limited by the dispositions of the one who offers the Mass and of the persons receiving them. The fruits of the Mass are traditionally distinguished with reference to the persons whom they benefit: (1) the general fruits benefit the entire Church, living and deceased; (2) the special fruits are enjoyed by those who participate in the celebration; (3) the personal fruits are received by the celebrant; (4) the ministerial fruits benefit those for whose intention the Mass is offered.

Fundamental Articles • A set of doctrinal statements that originated within conservative Protestant circles in early twentieth-century America and expressed the fundamental beliefs of the Christian

Faith. The movement that produced these articles sought to preserve and reaffirm Reformation orthodoxy in reaction to the modernism and liberalism in the ascendancy in some mainline Protestant denominations throughout the nineteenth century.

In 1909 a widely influential series of twelve pamphlets, written by an assortment of American Protestant theologians and ministers, were published under the title "The Fundamentals," with the financial support of the California financiers Lyman and Milton Stewart. Christian communities and persons espousing "The Fundamentals" came to be called "Fundamentalists." It is characteristic of the movement to issue creedal statements — fundamental articles — defining the basic content of the Christian Faith. Typically, such lists run to nine articles.

Since the first article affirms the verbal inspiration of the Old and New Testaments and the inerrancy of the Bible, "fundamentalism" is popularly but inaccurately thought to consist chiefly in advocacy of these beliefs about Scripture. However, the movement intends to affirm not only these beliefs but also the full content of the Christian Faith against the inroads of modernity and the accommodationist strategies of some mainline Protestant denominations. Thus, the remaining articles express traditional faith as it is commonly confessed among all Christian communities (though the seventh article is distinctive in affirming the premillennial return and reign of Jesus Christ).

The reaffirmation of Protestant orthodoxy in fundamentalist movements was paralleled by antimodernism in the Roman Catholic Church during the same period and remains an enduring force in American Protestantism to this day.

Fundamental Option • The basic orientation of the life of the human person in relation to God, either toward obedience and fidelity to God or to selfishness and disobedience. The more moderate view of the fundamental option holds that this basic orientation can be altered by one free, knowledgeable and consented action, such as by killing an innocent person or apostasy. However, a more radical view contends that this basic orientation cannot be changed by one single action unless that action flows from the "center" of the person and meets the above-mentioned conditions.

The more moderate view is more solidly grounded in Catholic Tradition, and the more radical view reduces human actions to peripheral phenomena. This more radical view implies that actions are not mortally, but only gravely sinful, because they do not touch the core of the person. The radical view holds that our fundamental option can only be altered if a grave moral act also touches the "core" of the person.

Fundamental Theology • Theological subfield that considers two distinct but related topics: the sources (Where did we get the things we believe and the practices we follow?) and warrants (Why is it reasonable to have our lives shaped by these teachings?) of the Christian Faith.

The first topic encompasses the following issues: revelation as divine communication; its chief vehicles, Scripture and Tradition; Christ as unsurpassable Teacher; the Apostles and their successors as transmitters and interpreters of the original revelation; the confirmatory character of the miracles recounted in the Scriptures; the role of divine inspiration in the authorship of the Scriptures; the formation of the canon; the Church as divinely designated bearer and teacher of revelation.

Secondly, when considered in the light of their warrants, the whole range of Christian doctrines comes up for discussion in fundamental theology. The theological subfields of fundamental theology and apologetics thus tend to overlap, although apologetics is distinguished by the more defined objective of defending the Christian Faith against particular challenges. The kinship between the two subfields is understandable.

Fundamental theology emerged as a distinctive subfield in the aftermath of the Enlightenment when, for various reasons, controversy about the sources and warrants of Christian Faith came to occupy center stage in academic and intellectual circles in Western Europe. Focused attention on these issues is a distinguishing feature of modern theology in comparison with both classical and medieval theology, where discussion of the sources and warrants of Christian Faith tends to be more unsystematic and *ad hoc*.

Funeral Mass • In the *Order of Christian Funerals*, the official name for the second and principal service associated with the death of a Catholic. First the Vigil (or Wake) Service is celebrated, usually in a funeral home; then, after the body has been placed in front of the altar in church, the Holy Sacrifice of the Mass; and finally, the Rite of Committal at graveside. Formerly this, and all Masses for the dead, bore the designation "Requiem Mass," from the first word of the Latin chant that opened the Mass ("*Requiem aeternam dona eis, Domine* . . . Eternal rest grant unto them, O Lord"). In more recent times, with the emphasis on the dead Christian's share in Christ's resurrection, this Mass was (mistakenly) designated by some as the "Mass of Resurrection." The *Order of Christian Funerals* promulgated in 1989 makes official the designation of this as a Funeral Mass.

The Funeral Mass begins with the greeting of the body and mourners at the door, and the sprinkling of the casket with holy water as a reminder of the dead Christian's baptismal incorporation into Christ's death and resurrection. A white pall, recalling the white robe of Baptism and the Christian's dignity, may be placed on the casket in silence, then the procession goes forward and Mass continues with the Liturgy of the Word (for which an extensive selection of scriptural passages is provided) and the Liturgy of the Eucharist.

At the conclusion of Mass, after a moment of silent prayer, the Song of Farewell is sung by the community as the body is honored with (holy water and) incense. The Prayer of Commendation and invitation to join the procession to the grave brings the Funeral Mass to a close.

G

Gabbatha • The Greek term occurs only at John 19:13 and is a transliteration of the Aramaic *gabbetha*, a term of unknown meaning. The Greek word used here is *lithostratos*, which means "pavement" or "pathway" or "flagstone pavement." It refers to that place where Jesus' trial was conducted by Pontius Pilate. Historians do not agree as to the exact location of this place. In the Gospel of John, we learn that it was just outside the Praetorium, barracks for Pontius Pilate's official guard and where

Pilate often found accommodations when in Jerusalem. The first-century Jewish historian Josephus (cf. *Wars* 2.14) writes about a paved yard next to Herod's palace; scholars have yet to discover such a place. Many speculate that a probable site might be near the citadel adjacent to the Gate of Jaffa. Another reasonable proposal is the lower structure of the Convent of Notre Dame de Sion in Jerusalem, under which archaeologists have discovered a paved court with double arches, a guardroom and a stairway leading to a terrace — all of which could house soldiers and also be official rooms for legal matters. The paved court is generally accepted as the site for the fortress of Antonia which Herod built. It is not clear, however, whether or not the particular paved court now there is from this period (i.e., prior to the destruction of Jerusalem in A.D. 70) or after it, perhaps having been built during the period of the city Aelia Capitolina, which Hadrian built after he crushed the rebellions during 132-135.

For further reading: John McRay, "Gabbatha," *Anchor Bible Dictionary*, 2:862.

Gabriel • Meaning literally, "God is my hero" or "God is my warrior," Gabriel is among the three named angels in the Old Testament (Dn 8:16; 9:21). The others are Michael

St. Gabriel the Archangel (medieval fresco)

(Dn 10:13; 12:1) and Raphael (Tb 5, 3:17).

In the New Testament, Gabriel appears in the Lucan infancy narrative, announcing the birth of John the Baptist to Zechariah (Lk 1:19) and the birth of Jesus to Mary (Lk 1:26). The appearance at these crucial moments of an angelic figure whose only previous biblical appearances are in the apocalyptic visions of Daniel suggests a tone of eschatological fulfillment in the birth announcement which Gabriel pronounces.

For further reading: Carol A. Newsom, "Gabriel," *Anchor Bible Dictionary*, 2:863.

Galatians, Epistle to the • Paul preached in Galatia during his missionary journeys and founded communities or churches in Galatia (Acts 13:4—14:28; 16:6; cf. 1 Cor 16:1; Gal 1:2). Paul wrote to the Galatians after he learned that other preachers had come and taught that converts to Christianity could become "true" or "authentic" followers of Christ by first becoming full and legal Jews (i.e., accepting circumcision, the practice of Judaism in the fullest). Paul exhorts the Galatians not to follow this counterfeit version of the Gospel. The letter to the Galatians is one of Paul's sharpest retorts to his "Judaizer" opponents.

It is difficult to identify both those churches he founded and the identity of his opponents. To whom did he refer when he wrote at Galatians 1:2: "the churches of Galatia"? Scholars disagree as to the exact geographical region referred to as "Galatia" (cf. 1 Pt 1:1; 2 Tm 4:10). Option 1: The New Testament term could refer to a region in north central Asia Minor, a plateau bordered by Bithynia, Phrygia, Pisidia, Cilicia and Cappadocia, settled sometime around 279 B.C. by Gauls (1 Mc 8:2; cf. 2 Mc 8:20), who established a kingdom in Anatolia. This option is commonly referred to as the "North Galatian Hypothesis." Option 2: In 64 B.C., "Galatia" became a vassal state under the Roman Empire which was expanding its sphere of power eastward. When Galatia's last king died (Amyntas, 24 B.C.), the kingdom was absorbed into the southern Roman province, Galatia (which included Pisidia, Pamphylia and parts of Lycaonia). This reference to "Galatia" (i.e., the Roman Province in the south) is known as the "South Galatian Hypothesis." The question is: To what do Acts 16:6 and 18:23 refer, the north or the south? The debate continues.

Major Themes: Paul wrote this letter to correct the teaching circulated by his opponents, the so-called Judaizers. The position of Paul's opponents can be reduced to two propositions. First, because Christ Himself was a faithful Jew, the Jewish Messiah, every believer in Christ must first become a full Jew according to the demands of the law and sacred cult; second, therefore Paul's preaching about the law, circumcision and that freedom which comes from Baptism in Christ is wrong — a false gospel preached by a false or pseudo-Apostle. Paul counters this argument with reminders to his flock that when they heard the Gospel he preached (3:2-5), they received the Holy Spirit (3:3-4, 14; 4:6) and became sons and daughters of God, the true offspring of Abraham in faith (3:26-28). Thus as with Abraham, it is justification from God, now linked to faith in Christ and the work of His cross, and not one's own efforts at fulfillment of the Jewish Law, which brings one into a right relationship with God (1:4; 2:15-16). It is in the gift of faith and the reception of the Holy Spirit — and not the "works of the law" — that the Galatians can have confidence in their rightful inheritance of the kingdom of God (3:29; 5:5; 6:8, 16-18).

Contents:

A. Opening of prescript 1:1-5
   1. Author to sender 1:1
   2. Associates of author 1:2
   3. Salutation 1:3-5
B. Introduction 1:6-10

1. A different gospel? 1:6-10
2. No other gospel is acceptable 1:8-9
C. In defense of his Apostleship 1:11—2:21
  1. His call 1:11-17
  2. His preaching 1:18-24
  3. His acceptance in Jerusalem 2:1-10
  4. His defense of the gospel before Peter 2:11-21
D. The validation of Paul's teaching/ preaching 3:1—4:31
  1. The Galatians did experience the Spirit 3:1-5
  2. His preaching linked to God's promise to Abraham 3:6-14
  3. Analogy from common law 3:15-18
  4. The role of Torah (Jewish Law) 3:19-25
  5. The reality of new life in Christ 3:26—4:11
  6. Paul's relationship to the churches 4:12-20
  7. Allegory of Sarah and Hagar 4:21-31
E. Final Exhortations 5:1—6:10
  1. Christ is Freedom; Torah is slavery 5:1-12
  2. Walk in the Spirit, not in the enslaved self 5:13-26
  3. Specific ethical injunctions 6:1-10

Authorship and Date: It is universally accepted that Paul wrote Galatians (1:1; 6:11-18) and most likely in the form we now possess. The letter was written at least fourteen years after Paul's conversion (2:1); and, if Acts 15 and Galatians 2 refer to the same date (the so-called Council of Jerusalem), and, if the referent for "Galatia" is in the north, then Galatians 4:13 could refer to his second visit to Galatia (mentioned in Acts 18:23) on his way to Ephesus, and therefore Galatians could have been written sometime around A.D. 55.

For further reading: Hans Dieter Betz, "Galatians, Epistle to the," *Anchor Bible Dictionary*, 2:872-875; Joseph A. Fitzmyer, S.J., "The Letter to the Galatians," *New Jerome Biblical Commentary*, 780-790;

Frank J. Matera, *Galatians*, Sacra Pagina 9 (Liturgical Press, 1992).

Galilee • The word in Hebrew means "ring," "circle," "district." In Isaiah 8:23 is first found the expression "Galilee of the nations," that is, "the region of the Gentiles." This would be a reference to the ethnic and cultural mix that characterized the region. Its situation as a crossroads of trade routes explains its mixed population. In New Testament times the word designated an area that was bounded by the Mediterranean on the west, the Jordan River and the Sea of Galilee on the east, on the north by the present-day Nahr el-Qasimiyeh, and on the south by the Plain of Esdraelon. Lower or Southern Galilee is rolling hill country interspersed with lush plains. Upper or Northern Galilee is the continuation of the Lebanon range of lofty mountains. Galilee is not the setting for much of the action in the Old Testament. In the New Testament it is, for the most part, the focal point of Jesus' life and ministry.

For further reading: Sean Freyne, "Galilee," *Anchor Bible Dictionary*, 2:879-899; Avraham Ronen et al., "Galilee," *The New Encyclopedia of Archaeological Excavations in the Holy Land*, 2:449-458.

Galileo Affair • The infallibility of the Church's Magisterium is often attacked for a supposed official teaching against the heliocentric (sun-centered) theory of the universe developed by the Polish clergyman Copernicus and defended in the early seventeenth century by the Italian scientist Galileo Galilei. The trials of Galileo in ecclesiastical courts are also pointed to as evidence that the Church is antagonistic to free scientific thought and thereby obstructs the advance of learning. But a review of the events and the issues at stake in them shows the reasonableness of the Church officials in the Galileo affair and the lack of any ground for impugning the Church's claim regarding the infallibility of the ordinary Magisterium.

In 1616 theological experts working for the Holy Office responded to a court of the Inquisition concerning the orthodoxy of views supported by Galileo. The views in question were first that the sun, as the supposed center of the universe, was immobile, and second, that the earth was mobile. The opinion of the theological experts was that both views were dangerous, the assertion of the immobility of the sun more so, and it was judged to be formally heretical. A sense for what was at stake may be gained by recalling that asserting the immobility of the sun is at least apparently inconsistent with scriptural references to the motion of the sun; for example, see Joshua 10:12-13, in which the usual motion of the sun is presumed. Until Galileo's hypothesis could be harmonized with the Scriptures, it would remain suspect in faith. In any case, in light of the in-house opinion of the consulting theologians, the Pope simply directed Cardinal Bellarmine to have Galileo agree to cease holding the opinion and supporting it.

In 1632 Galileo was brought to the Inquisition court again by several private enemies for various personal faults and for breaking his earlier agreement by publishing *Dialogue on the Two Great World Systems.* He was cleared of the charges concerning personal faults, but was found guilty of the same errors he repudiated years before. He renounced those errors as ordered, and the sale of his book was stopped. In the 1632 court records, the 1616 opinion of the theological consultants was mentioned, the first public mention of the view that the heliocentric assertion of the sun's immobility was regarded as heretical by the consultants. Such hardly qualifies as a public announcement of what the Church considered the good news to the nations.

Since neither the Pope nor any official promulgated the theological opinion as if it were official Church teaching, the credibility of the infallibility of the ordinary Magisterium cannot be undermined.

The Church's censoring of Galileo has passed into the mythology of anti-Catholic circles and secular humanism as the preeminent example not only of mistaken Church teaching but also of a purported opposition between adherence to the Church's faith and approval of rational scientific progress. Such interpretations of the Galileo affair manifest a failure to understand the intellectual and religious situation of the time, the limits of Galileo's own accomplishments and the limited character of experimental science.

In the early seventeenth century, modern scientific method was in its infancy, and the distinctive and limited mathematical character of its conclusions were not grasped as clearly as they are in twentieth-century philosophy of science. Early scientists such as Galileo often mixed in mistaken philosophical assumptions (the distinction between what came to be called mathematical or objective primary qualities and merely subjective secondary qualities) and even theological assumptions along with what we appreciate as their enduring and strictly scientific thought (for that matter, would contemporary scientists agree with Galileo that the sun is immobile?).

Church officials rightly focused criticism on the implications which Galileo's publications actually had regarding matters of faith, for his writings did not even attempt to show how the heliocentric astronomy could be harmonized with the Scriptures and the Church's faith. Church officials would have been negligent if they had failed to defend central truths of life from relatively peripheral opinions which, in their historical situation, were reasonably thought to cast doubt on God's truthfulness. From a scientific point of view, it is interesting to observe that today Galileo is known to have been in error since he equated the universe with what is only our solar system.

Christians in the twentieth century can easily recognize that, for purposes of greater simplicity of mathematical calculations, the sun (or a point very near the sun) can be treated as the gravitational center of the solar system, while, for the far more important purpose of openness to salvation and to consummated worship of God, Christ must be recognized as the ultimate center of creation. Profession of Catholic Faith is thoroughly compatible with and even supportive of authentically scientific progress, when scientific results are appreciated as scientific and not mistaken as an integral understanding of reality.

Gallican Liturgies • Unlike other ecclesiastical centers in the West (e.g., Rome and Milan) which spawned distinctive Western liturgical rites, what have come to be termed the "Gallican liturgies" actually had no organizing center. Thus to speak of Gallican liturgies is to speak in a general way about rites emanating from and in use in Gaul between approximately the fifth and eighth centuries. Indirect references to local Gallican liturgical practices are found in the sermons of Cesarius of Arles (d. A.D. 542), the writings of Gregory of Tours (d. 594) and in the Merovingian Councils. The seventh-century *Explanation of the Gallican Liturgy* by Pseudo-Germanus of Paris attests to a strong Eastern influence on Gallican liturgy and contains the first example in the West of an allegorical interpretation of the liturgy. Another locale which spawned what has been termed a Gallican liturgy is Ireland, where in all likelihood an old Gallican rite was mixed with Celtic customs. It is generally asserted that forms of private prayer, devotions, the cult of the saints and

the confession of sins point at least indirectly to Celtic influence.

Stylistically the prayers of the Gallican liturgy are more expressive than those of the Roman Rite; theologically, the prayers reflect a strong reaction to Arianism. Along with a number of prayers, prefaces and blessings, some of the more expressive ceremonies from the Gallican liturgy have found their way into the Roman Rite, e.g., the procession with palms on Passion (Palm) Sunday and the rite for the dedication of a church (and altar). Sources for the Gallican liturgies are the *Missale Gallicanum Vetus*, the *Missale Gothicum*, the *Lectionary of Luxeuil*, the *Bobbio Missal*, the *Missale Francorum*, the *Antiphonal of Bangor*, and the *Stowe Missal*.

Gallican Psalter • Although it represents a revision of the Vulgate Psalter, done by St. Jerome in A.D. 346, the Gallican Psalter is so called because it was introduced into Church use primarily in Gaul (modern France) by St. Gregory of Tours in the sixth century. In the ninth century, it was established as the official Psalter of the Church by the Emperor Charlemagne.

Gallicanism • A complex amalgamation of theological and political theories more or less associated with the peculiar situation of the Church in France. At root, Gallicanism held for the autonomy of the French Church against the authority of the Roman Pontiff. As such, it was arrayed against ultramontanism. The roots of Gallicanism are generally traced to the period of the Western Schism when, in 1398, the king of France announced his "rediscovery" of certain allegedly ancient rights and privileges to be accorded the French Church.

After the resolution of the Schism, however, Gallicanism survived but waxed and waned with the times, and received a notable boost with the work of Pithou in 1594. In 1683, however, matters reached a peak with the publication of a manifesto by the Association of French Clergy asserting extensive Gallican prerogatives. In 1690, Pope Alexander VIII condemned the declaration, and the movement went into a general decline, abetted by changing social conditions and internal bickering among the Gallicans themselves, who by this time were also infected with Jansenism. The final repudiation of Gallicanism came in the declaration of papal supremacy by the First Vatican Council. (Cf. Conciliar Theory; Josephism; Exsequatur.)

Gambling • A game in which a risk of losing a present finite good is accepted in the hope of obtaining a future greater good. Not condemned by the moral or Divine law, it is the sort of action which is open to great abuses. Because it is so prone to abuse, it is prudent and morally legitimate in many circumstances to place legal limits on gambling to protect the common welfare and public order. Gambling is to be conducted under proper restraint and should be pursued purely for recreational purposes.

Garden of Eden: See **Eden, Garden of**

Gaudete Sunday • In the preconciliar delineation of the liturgical year, this term referred to the Third Sunday of Advent, a day which was regarded as a day of particular joy with Advent half over and Christmas soon to follow. The custom of wearing rose vesture, as opposed to violet as during the rest of Advent, was the most dramatic demonstration of the uniqueness of this Advent Sunday. The term *Gaudete* refers to the first word of the Introit for this day (both past and present), taken from Philippians 4:4-5. In the present *General Norms for the Liturgical Year and the Calendar*, the term "Gaudete Sunday" is

absent; the Sundays of Advent are listed as the First, Second, Third and Fourth. However, *General Instruction of the Roman Missal* states (n. 308f.) that rose-colored vesture may be used on *Gaudete* Sunday and on *Laetare* Sunday (Fourth Sunday of Lent). The second reading in the present lectionary for this Sunday "C" cycle is Philippians 4:4-7, the traditional text for this Sunday in the Roman Rite, from which the term *Gaudete* derives.

Gaudium et Spes • The pastoral constitution is so named from the first words of its official Latin text, and is subtitled "On the Church in the Modern World." It was the last of the sixteen documents promulgated by the Second Vatican Council and was doubtless designed to complement *Lumen Gentium*, the more heavily theological Dogmatic Constitution on the Church. *Gaudium et Spes* thus forms a kind of final exhortation of the Council to the faithful and to humanity as a whole regarding the Council's hopes and true intentions, and can be profitably read as the least technical but most summary of the Council's acts.

Important for background to *Gaudium et Spes* is the almost century-long body of what have been called the social encyclicals, beginning in 1890 with *Rerum Novarum* of Pope Leo XIII. The contents of the document, while explicitly based on revelation and the Church's teaching, include reasoned analyses of the present social situation and the application of Christian principles to that situation in order to bring about progress. Likewise present, but on a secondary level of importance, are precautions against moral infractions and imprudent applications of principles. Fairly frequently, invitations are made for further study. All of these factors combine to produce a very optimistic tone and approach.

Gaudium et Spes is evenly divided into two parts. The first is the Council's effort to describe the conditions of contemporary humanity (nn. 11-45), while the second includes a host of various concrete issues and applications of the insights developed in Part One (nn. 47-90).

The universalist perspective which characterizes this document is established in its first sentences: "The joy and hope, the grief and anguish of the men of our time . . . are the joy and hope, the grief and anguish of the followers of Christ as well. Nothing that is genuinely human fails to find an echo in their hearts." Despite the cautious negativity in elements such as "grief and anguish," *Gaudium et Spes* has come to be interpreted as an essentially positive and innovative statement of the Council. Likewise, its undeniable focus on humanity has constituted a basis for a new Christian and Catholic secularism which did not typify the preconciliar period: "Believers and unbelievers agree almost unanimously that all things on earth should be ordained to man as to their center and summit" (n. 12). The pastoral nature of the document is clear, however: "The Church is keenly sensitive. . . . Enlightened by divine revelation she can offer a solution to [these difficulties] by which the true state of man may be outlined, his weakness explained, in such a way that at the same time his dignity and his vocation may be perceived in their true light" (n. 12).

To the extent that *Gaudium et Spes* presents man as created in the image of God (n. 12), guilty of sin (n. 13), composed as a unity of body and soul (n. 14), and possessed of the dignity of an intellect (n. 15) and a moral conscience (n. 16), despite his physical mortality (n. 17), *Gaudium et Spes* presents a summary of the most traditional biblical and magisterial pronouncements on the Christian understanding of anthropology.

Really new ground is broken, however, not only in its frank treatment of atheism, but also in its candid admission that in some cases atheism may have been caused paradoxically through the fault of believers themselves (n. 19): "To the extent that they are careless about their instruction in the faith, or present its teaching falsely, or even fail in their religious, moral, or social life, [believers] must be said to conceal rather than reveal the true nature of God and of religion."

The emphasis of *Gaudium et Spes* on the communal nature of humanity is again unmistakable (nn. 23-31), but the opening that such insights provides toward secular and scientific human endeavors is new at least in the tone of welcoming optimism: ". . . Methodical research in all branches of knowledge, provided it is carried out in a truly scientific manner and does not override moral laws, can never conflict with the faith, because the things of this world and the things of faith derive from the same God" (n. 36).

The ecumenical perspective is not absent from *Gaudium et Spes*: "The Catholic Church gladly values what other Christian Churches and ecclesial communities have contributed and are contributing. . ." (n. 40), but its universal perspective is remarkable: "Similarly it [the Catholic Church] is convinced that there is a considerable and varied help that it can receive from the world in preparing the ground for the Gospel. . ." (n. 40).

In the Second Part, subtitled "Some More Urgent Problems," *Gaudium et Spes* undertakes to apply the affirmations of Part One in a specific and concrete way.

Emphatically first in the Council's mind are the problems encountered in the modern world by the family. The constant doctrine of the Church on the holiness of marriage and the family (n. 48), the nature of married love (n. 49) and the intended fruitfulness of the marital contract are repeated: ". . . it must be said that true married love and the whole structure of family life which results from it is directed to disposing the spouses to cooperate valiantly with the love of the Creator and Savior, who through them will increase and enrich his family. . ." (n. 50). The perennial issue of the ends of marriage is authoritatively addressed: "But marriage is not merely for the procreation of children: its nature as an indissoluble compact between two people and the good of children demand that the mutual love of the partners be shown, that it should grow and mature . . . marriage still retains its character of being a whole manner and communion of life. . ." (n. 50).

This context is a prelude for *Gaudium et Spes*'s important lessons on contraception: ". . . it is not enough to take the good intention and the evaluation of motives into account; the objective criteria must be used, criteria drawn from the nature of the human person . . ." (n. 51). The Council's concern regarding the dignity of human life is unmistakable: "Life must be protected with the utmost care from the moment of conception; abortion and infanticide are abominable crimes" (n. 51).

The next section places important stress on the importance of culture, "the cultivation of the goods and values of nature" (n. 53). This section forms an important preface and establishes a context for *Gaudium et Spes*'s later treatment of economics, politics and world peace. As the creation of man (n. 55), culture and civilization are also his responsibility. As regards the Church, *Gaudium et Spes* proposes a new direction: ". . . to seek and relish the things that are above . . . involves not a lesser but a greater commitment to working with all men toward the establishment of a world that is more human" (n. 57).

Logically, *Gaudium et Spes* identifies education as a practical means to promote everyone's right to culture (n. 61), and even speaks of the possibilities of a new and universal culture. It distinguishes between the "deposit and the truths of the faith" and "the manner of expressing them" as two quite different things (n. 62), and so declares that ". . . the faithful, both clerical and lay, should be accorded a lawful freedom of inquiry, of thought, and of expression. . . ."

In the following section (nn. 63-72), *Gaudium et Spes* avoids a Marxist reduction of everything to economy, but courageously underscores the importance of economy in human and social progress. On one hand, "every man has the right to possess a sufficient amount of the earth's goods," but men are also "bound to come to the aid of the poor and to do so not merely out of their superfluous goods" (n. 69).

In a significant reversal of policy for the Holy See, *Gaudium et Spes* declares, "the Church by reason of her role and competence, is not identified with any political community nor bound by ties to any political system" (n. 76). In a practical summary of the Council's doctrine of politics, it states: "The political community and the Church are autonomous and independent of each other in their own fields. . . . Nevertheless, there are close links between the things of earth and those things in man's condition which transcend the world, and the Church utilizes temporal realities as her mission requires it" (n. 76).

Reflecting the concerns and the signs of the times in which it was written, *Gaudium et Spes* contains clear and eloquent doctrines regarding peace and war. "Every act of war directed to the indiscriminate destruction of whole cities . . . is a crime against God and man, which merits firm and unequivocal condemnation" (n. 80). "The arms race is one of the greatest curses on the human race" (n. 81). "It is our clear duty to spare no effort in order to work for the moment when all war will be completely outlawed by international agreement" (n. 82).

Finally, the Council Fathers urge: "Let there be unity in what is necessary, freedom in what is doubtful and charity in everything" (n. 92). An essential component for interpretation of *Gaudium et Spes* comes from the massive, postconciliar documentation published by the Holy See, in particular, *Populorum Progressio* (1968), *Octogesima Adveniens* (1971), *Evangelii Nuntiandi* (1976), and *Christifideles Laici* (1988).

Ge'ez (also Gheez) • The liturgical language of the Ethiopian Rite, whose books were translated from Greek, Coptic or Arabic into the Semitic language of Ge'ez, once the vernacular of the Ethiopian race, but now a dead language.

Gehenna • From the Hebrew *ge-hinnom* through the Aramaic *ge-hinnam*, "valley of the son of Hinnom." This is conjectured to be the name of the original Jebusite owner of that property. It is a valley to the south-southwest of Jerusalem that eventually joins the Kedron Valley, which runs along the east side of the city. In the later Old Testament writings, the valley bore an ominous air about it for having been the location of Tophet, a pagan shrine where human sacrifice was practiced (cf. 2 Kgs 23:10). The word is used seven times in the New Testament. It is part of the apocalyptic imagery used in the New Testament to speak of judgment and punishment for sin. The frequently occurring description of the Valley of Hinnom as a garbage dump with its accompanying smoldering refuse appears to be without any archaeological basis. This notion is traceable to Qimhi, writing in

1200, but there is apparently no earlier reference to this.

For further reading: Duane F. Watson, "Gehenna," *Anchor Bible Dictionary*, 2:926-928.

Genealogy of Christ • In the ancient Near East, the genealogy represents the principal way of recording lineages of persons, families, tribes or nations. The Old Testament contains approximately two dozen lists, each varying in historical value. Genealogies secured personal rights and privileges in the clan or tribe and represented (often the only) written record of membership. Genealogies are an important source of historical information because they contain historical data not found in other sources (e.g., inscriptions, ancient monuments, manuscripts, etc.).

Given the above, it is important to note that genealogies do more than record genetic and social/economic pedigree — they also contain "stories" about families, tribes, clans or nations with the assumptions, underlying beliefs and values of the recorder and his social setting which can be detected by noting what materials (names of people or of places, specific events recalled, etc.) were used to tell the story or connect the generations. After the Babylonian exile (587 B.C.), genealogies rose in importance within Judaism because they provided a proof for priestly descent and so helped to determine inclusion in the priesthood and exclusion from it.

The two genealogies of Jesus at Matthew 1:1-17 and Luke 3:23-38 should be viewed in light of the literary, social and especially religious intent the Gospel writers had in mind. The two lists represent two very different ways of communicating not only Jesus' lineage but the revelation of His Divine Person and the role He has relative to God's self-disclosure for the coming of His kingdom and His plan of salvation for the world. Comparing similarities and differences helps detect what the authors intended to communicate. Similarities: In both Gospels Jesus' lineage is traced on Joseph's side, the legal father upon whom Jewish Law conferred complete legal paternity and all the rights of natural paternity. Both genealogies make clear Jesus' Davidic descent (Mt 1:1, 6, 17; Lk 3:31); Matthew begins the list of ancestors from Abraham (Mt 1:1—2:17) while Luke traces Jesus' ancestors back to "Adam, the Son of God" (Lk 3:38). Differences: Matthew lists forty-two names divided or organized into three units of fourteen names, omits names from David's royal line between Joram and Uzziah and counts Jechoniah twice (Mt 1:11-12). Luke lists fifty-six names for the period corresponding to Matthew and an additional twenty for the period of Adam. Why the differences? Matthew's interest in addressing the Gospel to a Jewish Christian listener/reader helps explain the significance of Abraham, the Father of Israel and the first to receive the promises of God in the form of the covenant which was "signed" by circumcision. Another way of putting it might be: "In the person of Jesus we find fulfilled all of the Old Testament hopes, anticipations and prophecies about God's promises of friendship, love and salvation to Abraham (the Father of Israel) and David (the great king of Israel)." The birth of Jesus at the conclusion of three groups of fourteen generations might suggest that God's sovereign plan of salvation is both carefully planned and indeed sovereign (Mt 1:18-25). With Luke, the emphasis is on the universal scope of God's plan of salvation through the Gospel which Jesus brings in Himself, His teachings and actions. In both instances there are aspects of salvation history central to the history of Judaism which reach their fullest possible expression in the life,

teaching and person of Jesus and the Church which embodies His message.

For further reading: Raymond E. Brown, S.S., "The Genealogy of Jesus," *The Birth of the Messiah*, 57-95, Anchor Bible Reference Library (Doubleday, 1993); Robert R. Wilson, "Genealogy, Genealogies," *Anchor Bible Dictionary*, 2:929-932.

General • The term "general," short for superior general, is the common term denoting the highest leader of a religious institute under the Roman Pontiff. A general is usually chosen by canonical election and may serve for a specific term or, as is the case with the Jesuits, for life. The powers of the general are spelled out in the particular law of the institute, but the trend has been to give the superior general rather wide discretion and authority in the direction of the institute.

General Absolution • The practice of giving sacramental absolution to a number of penitents without their previous individual confession in extreme cases, such as danger of death and grave need. The postconciliar revision of the rites for the sacrament of Penance offers a "Rite for Reconciliation of Several Penitents with General Confession and Absolution" (Chapter Three, nn. 50-66), containing additions to the "Rite of Reconciliation of Several Penitents with Individual Absolution" (Chapter Two, nn. 48-59). The rite for General Confession and Absolution provides two formulas for sacramental absolution, the one rather expanded form proper to this rite and the other taken from the other rites (i.e., for individuals). Some indications as to what constitutes "grave necessity" for the use of general absolution are given in the Rite of Penance itself (nn. 31-34), in the Code of Canon Law (Canons 961-963) and the decree from the Congregation for the Doctrine of the Faith,

Normae pastorales circa absolutionem sacramentalem generali modo impertiendam of June 16, 1972 (AAS 64 [1972], 510-514).

General Chapter • The primary legislative body of a religious institute. Canon law accords the general chapter the supreme authority in the institute according to the institute's own constitutions.

Membership in a general chapter consists of *ex officio* and elected delegates representing the entire institute. The number of delegates, means of electing or selecting them and the frequency of chapters is determined by the constitutions of the institute. The general chapter usually deals with issues that concern the entire institute, such as governance, common life, formation, finances, apostolate and the obligations of various officials of the institute. An important task of the general chapter is the election of the supreme moderator or superior general of the institute.

In most institutes, the acts of a general chapter are sent to the Holy See, either for its approval or for observation. Similarly, the elected supreme moderator is presented to the Holy See for confirmation, unless the institute has a privilege whereby this confirmation is not required (cf. Canons 631-633).

General Confession • The repetition of some or all of the previous confessions of one's life. The reasons why a general confession is suitable vary. Such a confession would be strictly necessary when it is morally certain that some previous confessions were in fact invalid (for whatever reason). Beyond such cases, general confession may be spiritually salutary to summon the penitent to renewed sorrow for sin and confidence in the mercy and forgiveness of God. Sometimes people seek to make a general confession in preparation for some significant milestone in life, perhaps the reception of Matrimony or Holy Orders, or the pronouncement of religious vows. It is important to seek the advice of a prudent confessor or spiritual director before making a general confession, particularly in order to avoid the danger of scrupulosity.

General Instruction of the Roman Missal: See **Roman Missal, General Instruction of the**

General Intercessions: See **Prayer of the Faithful**

Genesis • This first book of the Old Testament sketches the Jewish view of the origin of the world, of mankind and of the Jewish people. Traditionally thought to be the work of Moses, it is today considered to be a compilation made by a redactor who formed a patchwork of four different sources, all of whom lived some centuries after Moses.

Of the fifty chapters, the first eleven are devoted to what is called primeval history. In Chapter 1, the creation of the world is artistically presented as having been done on the six working days of the Jewish week. Light is created on the first day, the sky on the second, the dry land and the plants on the third. On the fourth day, the sun, moon and stars are made, on the fifth the animals in the sea and the sky, and on the sixth day the earth is commanded to bring forth the animals which inhabit it, and God makes man in His own image.

Chapter 2 presents a more detailed description of the making of man and woman, their primitive happy state. It was their disobedience which brought the origin of evil and the fall of our first parents, depicted in Chapter 3.

Adam is shown (Chapters 4-5) to have ten generations of offspring before the Flood, eight of them in his own lifetime: Only Noah and Shem (who survived the Flood) were born after Adam died. This flood is shown to have covered the entire land and to have exterminated all life, except that saved by Noah in the ark. After the Flood, there are eight generations leading to Abraham, from whom the Jewish nation took its origin.

Chapters 11-25 cover the life of Abraham. Born in southern Mesopotamia, he is called by God with the promise that he will be the founder of a great nation in which all the nations of the earth will be blessed. His was a seminomadic life, taking him north from Ur to Haran, then southward through the Holy Land to Egypt and back to Hebron. In Chapter 14, we find him in Jerusalem, in significant contact with the mysterious priest Melchizedek. In Chapter 17, the promise is repeated, and the rite of circumcision is mandated. Since his wife Sarah was barren, Abraham's first son was by her maid, Hagar. But when Isaac was born (Chapter 21), Sarah's jealousy brought the expulsion of Hagar and her son Ishmael. The great testing of Abraham's faith came when God asked him (Chapter 22) to sacrifice Isaac, but then mercifully accepted a substitution.

The significant events in the life of Isaac and his son Jacob are told in Chapters 24-36. Isaac is a mild, even bland, figure, who returned to Mesopotamia to take a wife, Rebekah, by whom he had the twin sons Esau and Jacob. When Isaac was old, by a ruse (Chapter 27) Jacob obtained the blessing intended for the firstborn. As his father had done, Jacob also went back to Mesopotamia to take a bride (Chapter 29), but was first deceived into taking Leah, the elder sister of his intended, Rachel. God renewed the great promise to Jacob and it was he, renamed Israel, who fathered the men who were the ancestors of the twelve tribes of Israel: Reuben, Simeon, Levi, Judah, Dan, Naphtali, Gad, Asher, Issachar, Zebulun, Joseph and Benjamin.

The final fourteen chapters (37-50) focus on Joseph. Envied and sold by his brothers, he yet attained high position in Egypt. When a famine came, Jacob and his remaining sons had to go to Egypt for food. There Joseph magnanimously welcomed them, and during his lifetime they prospered. It was in Egypt that they multiplied into clans and tribes, and although they became slaves of the Egyptians for many centuries, the children of Abraham did indeed become a great nation.

For further reading: Richard J. Clifford, S.J., and Roland E. Murphy, O.Carm., "Genesis," *New Jerome Biblical Commentary*, 8-43; Ronald S. Hendel, "Genesis, Book of," *Anchor Bible Dictionary*, 2:933-941.

Genocide • The planned, indiscriminate slaughter of entire groups of innocent persons to achieve a political objective. Genocide includes not only the killing of racial groups, but also nations, tribes or simply great numbers of innocent persons as well. The Second Vatican Council condemned genocide in no uncertain terms when it declared: ". . . all offenses against life itself, such as murder, genocide, abortion, euthanasia and willful suicide; all violations of the integrity of the human person . . . all offenses against human dignity . . . all these and the like are criminal" (GS 27). And even more specifically, the Council held that "the most infamous among these actions [against universal principles] are those designed for the reasoned and methodical extermination of an entire race, nation, or ethnic minority. These must be condemned as frightful crimes" (GS 79).

Gentile • In the Old Testament books of later composition, the word *goy* (plural, *goyim*) refers to people other than the

Israelites. Originally, it appears to have been used interchangeably with *am* to mean "people." After the exile, the Jews seem to have developed a deeper self-awareness and to have pressed the distinction between themselves and all other people (Gentiles). The Vulgate translated *goy* as *gentilis*, whence the English "gentile." Curiously, though the early Christian communities soon became preponderantly Gentile, that is, non-Jewish, they employed the same term, viz., "Gentile," to mark the distinction between themselves and non-Christians. From the usage, it may be inferred that the Christians viewed themselves as the true Israel, vis-à-vis all other peoples.

Genuflection (also Genuflexion) • This act of bending the right knee to the floor and rising up again has had a number of meanings associated with it, from an act of penitence and supplication (e.g., before one's master), to an act of veneration in front of a person of prominence (e.g., emperor or bishop) or a holy object (e.g., altar, relics, especially those of the True Cross), to an act of reverence before the exposed or reserved Sacrament in church. Evidence of the liturgical use of the genuflection goes back as far as John Cassian and the custom in Egyptian monasticism of reciting twelve psalms for the major hours. Eleven of these were recited solo by a monk, after which all would stand, pray in silence with arms outstretched, kneel for a moment, then stand for a concluding oration prayed by the monk leader.

When the act of elevating the consecrated Bread and Wine came into the Roman Liturgy, the prescribed gesture for the faithful was an act of genuflection (before and after); later the gesture became prolonged into the act of kneeling from the *Sanctus* through the Great Amen. In the Baroque era, when Mass was frequently celebrated *coram Sanctissimo* (in the presence of the Blessed Sacrament on the main altar), the number of genuflections for the priest increased to show reverence as he passed before the tabernacle.

The postconciliar liturgical books indicate that "three genuflections are made during Mass: after showing of the Eucharistic Bread, after the showing of the chalice, and before Communion" (*General Instruction of the Roman Missal*, n. 233) and that "genuflection in the presence of the Blessed Sacrament, whether reserved in the tabernacle or exposed for public adoration, is on one knee" (*General Instruction on Holy Communion and the Worship of the Eucharist outside Mass*, n. 84).

Georgian Byzantine Rite • The Church of Georgia (an area between Russia and Turkey) was founded in the fourth century by the preaching of St. Nina to the royal family of the realm, which adopted the Christian religion for their land. The Georgian Church avoided Monophysitism and flourished particularly in the eleventh through the thirteenth centuries, although it ended up in schism from the Church, as did the Orthodox Churches. In the nineteenth century, it was absorbed by the Russian Orthodox Church, although at the same time some of its members were attracted to Catholicism, returning to full communion with Rome. Some of these adopted the Latin Rite, and others the Byzantine.

Gethsemane • The Greek term is from either Aramaic or Hebrew and means "oil press." It refers to the place on the Mount of Olives where Jesus prayed after the Last Supper and where He was handed over to the temple guard (Mt 26:36; Mk 14:32). Matthew and Mark refer to a "place" called Gethsemane, the name implying a location somewhere on the Mount of Olives. Luke does not mention Gethsemane but does record "Mount of Olives" (22:39). The Gospel of John records that Jesus went to a "garden" on the Mount of Olives (probably on its western slopes across from the Kidron Valley). The current location of Gethsemane contains very few olive trees (by some counts, no more than eight, none of which are older than nine hundred years) and is in an enclosed grove. It is one of several sites which various traditions claim to be authentic. None of the traditions can be traced back beyond the fourth century. The current location, if not the correct one, is undoubtedly very near the original.

Ghibellines: See **Guelfs and Ghibellines**

Gifts of the Holy Spirit, The Seven • Of the promised "shoot" that "shall come forth . . . from the stump of Jesse," Isaiah 11:2 says that "the spirit of the LORD shall rest upon him, the spirit of wisdom and understanding, a spirit of counsel and might, a spirit of knowledge and the fear of the LORD, and his delight shall be the fear of the LORD." In the Septuagint and then in the Vulgate, "piety" is substituted for the first instance of "fear of the LORD," and this yields the traditional seven gifts of the Holy Spirit: wisdom, understanding, counsel, strength (fortitude), knowledge, piety and fear of the Lord.

Although the New Testament makes no reference to Isaiah 11:2 with regard to the gifts (plural) of the Holy Spirit, it does speak of the gift of the Spirit bestowed on Jesus' disciples (cf. Jn 14:16-17, 26; 16:7, 13; 20:22; Acts 2:1-4) and of the fruit which the Spirit bears in the lives of believers (cf. Gal 5:22).

In Chapter 87 of the *Dialogue with Trypho*, Justin Martyr identifies the seven "spirits" of Isaiah 11:2 as gifts of the Holy Spirit which were bestowed on Christ in their fullness and which are again given "by Him, from the place of His Spirit's powers, to all His believers according to their merits."

The sevenfold gifts of the Spirit were objects of active theological reflection throughout the patristic period and during the Middle Ages, with efforts made by some to correlate the seven gifts with the petitions of the Lord's Prayer (cf., for example, Augustine, *De sermone Domini in monte*, I, 4, 11; I, 11, 38 [PL 1234, 1236]), along with efforts to rank the seven gifts according to the order of their relative importance.

It was St. Thomas Aquinas who articulated the most fully developed theology of the gifts of the Holy Spirit. Aquinas distinguished the gifts of the Holy Spirit from the theological and moral virtues, identifying them as abiding dispositions which perfect human beings so that we may readily follow the Holy Spirit's own promptings (cf. the *Commentary on the Sentences*, III, d. 34-35 and the *Summa Theologiae*, Ia IIae, q. 68-70).

The hymn *Veni Creator Spiritus* invokes the Holy Spirit as *septiformis munere*, sevenfold gift; and the sequence for Pentecost, *Veni Sancte Spiritus*, asks, "Give your seven holy gifts to your faithful, for their trust is in you." In the Rite of Confirmation, the prayer over the candidates asks God to "give them the spirit of wisdom and understanding, the spirit of right judgment and courage, the spirit of knowledge and reverence. Fill them with the spirit of wonder and awe in your presence." During the ordination of deacons, the bishop prays over the one being ordained, "Lord, send forth upon him the Holy Spirit, that he may be strengthened by the gift of your sevenfold grace to carry out faithfully the work of the ministry."

Gifts, Preternatural • Gifts bestowed upon Adam and Eve by God that are above and beyond the need and powers of human nature. The preternatural gifts included immortality, freedom from suffering, superior knowledge and proper ordering of the passions and emotions to the mind and will. These gifts were lost with the First Sin, but the dignity and value of the human person were not diminished by their loss. Despite their loss, man remains the *imago Dei* (image of God), spiritual and free in nature, and the preternatural gifts were restored by the redemptive actions of Christ.

Gifts, Supernatural • Spiritual endowments superior to those possessed by the human person that are unmerited and gratuitously bestowed by God. The supernatural gifts include faith, hope and charity and the gifts of the Holy Spirit; when they are infused, they enable the person to accept the self-communication of God in grace.

Gift of Tongues • The phrase refers to "glossolalia" or "speaking in tongues." It is one of the *pneumatika* or gifts of the Holy Spirit (1 Cor 14:1). Scholars count thirty-five references to this gift principally in Acts and 1 Corinthians, less so in Mark. The term refers to speaking in a language which is incomprehensible to the speaker or hearers. Paul encourages the Corinthians to seek the spiritual gifts (1 Cor 14:1), above all which is the gift of love. One of the gifts he lists is tongues (14:1-8; cf. 12:31).

The New Testament points to three functions for this "word-gift." (1) A heavenly language: its principal role is to assist in the praise and worship of God (1 Cor 14:2, 14-15, 28), perhaps when the intellect and its companion, human language, are neither capable nor adequate for expressing what the Spirit reveals or when language is no longer adequate for the level of prayer being experienced (e.g., Rom 8:26). Luke understands the powerful experience of the Holy Spirit as a fulfillment of Scripture (Acts 2:4, 18; 19:6). Because the strength of a

person's reaction to the Holy Spirit can often appear pathological to the uninformed observer (Mk 3:21; Acts 2:13; 26:24), two points should be noted: first, ecstasy and emotion are *not the conditions* for authentic "tongues" but rather can be a result of a strong movement of the Holy Spirit; second, as with the gift of prophecy, authentic promptings to pray with the gift of tongues are always subject to the free will of the one praying.

(2) As a human language: it is inspired by the Spirit but for purposes of communicating the "mind of God," so to speak; (i) a gift of being able to speak in a language which the speaker may not know but which is recognizable by the hearer of the communication (e.g., Acts 2); (ii) as a prophetic utterance which then needs to be "interpreted" (1 Cor 12:3; 13:1ff.; 14:32). It is critical to understand that the gifts of the Spirit are subordinate to love (1 Cor 14:1) and are for the building up of the Church (14:5b). The gift of tongues is mentioned in many early Church documents after the New Testament period, which indicates that with the other gifts of the Spirit it is not to be taken as a dispensation of grace restricted to the apostolic period (e.g., Mk 16:17; Iren. Her. V.vi.l; Ter. Marcion V.viii; Origen *Contra Celsum* VII.ix).

For further reading: Luke Timothy Johnson, "Tongues, Gift of," *Anchor Bible Dictionary*, 6:596-600.

Glagolithic Alphabet • The ancient Slavonic alphabet devised by St. Cyril in the ninth century and still used by the Roman Rite in Dalmatia (part of present-day Bosnia and Serbia). It is a version of the Cyrillic alphabet but has round or flowing letters, rather than the block letters employed by the latter.

Gloria in Excelsis Deo • The first words of the Latin version of the hymn *Glory to God* *in the highest*, presently used at Masses on Sundays outside of Advent and Lent, on solemnities and feasts (*General Instruction of the Roman Missal* n. 31). These first words of the hymn derive from the angels' song at the birth of Jesus (Lk 2:14). The text is highly Christological, but also addresses God the Father and the Holy Spirit. In early Christian literature this hymn is described as among the "non-biblical psalms" (*psalmoi idiotikoi*) used in liturgy (*Phos hilaron* is another), modelled after New Testament hymns.

It was used originally in the Liturgy of the Hours in the East and was assigned to Morning Prayer in the West, probably by St. Hilary (d. A.D. 367); St. Cesarius of Arles (d. 542) notes its use at Morning Prayer. It was moved to the Eucharist in the sixth century, when it was first used at the Papal Mass of Christmas Day. It was later extended to Masses for Sundays and feasts of martyrs, but at first this occurred only when a bishop presided at these Masses. According to *Ordo Romanus II* (a seventh-century Roman Ordo), a priest could sing it, but at first only at Easter.

Gloria Patri • The doxology "Glory be to the Father and to the Son and to the Holy Spirit, as it was in the beginning, is now and ever shall be, world without end" is

Angel of the Gloria (Byzantine mural)

customarily added to the end of the psalms at the Liturgy of the Hours and to the entrance and Communion verses at Mass. The original text of the doxology was "Glory be to the Father, through the Son, in the Holy Spirit"; however, this text was changed at the height of the Arian controversy, lest it appear to diminish Christ's divinity. (Such was not the case, however, for the ending to the collects retained the important mediatorial role "we ask this through Christ. . . .") Important ecclesiological connotations derive from the doxology worded "in the Holy Spirit," since this referred both to the Third Person of the Trinity and to the Church assembled to voice their praise in that same Spirit.

The *General Instruction of the Liturgy of the Hours* (1971) states that "this is a fitting conclusion endorsed by Tradition, and it gives to Old Testament prayer [specifically the Psalms] a note of praise and a Christological and Trinitarian sense" (n. 123). The directives to the present *Graduale Romanum* (*Simple Gradual*, 1967) for Mass state that the verses for the entrance and Communion antiphons conclude with the *Gloria Patri* and the *Sicut erat* (n. 15).

Glorified Body • The Risen Christ calls humanity to the glory of His resurrection, a theological premise which presupposes that, like Christ, all of His brothers and sisters will be transformed physically, to the state of the glorified body which will be man's definitive state in eternity. The ascension of Christ, "now raised from the dead, the first fruits of those who have fallen asleep" (1 Cor 15:20), demands similar corporal fulfillment for His brothers and sisters: "For as by a man came death, by a man also has come the resurrection of the dead. For as in Adam all die, so also in Christ shall all be made alive. But each in his own order: Christ the first fruits, then at his coming all those who belong to Christ" (1 Cor 15:21-23; cf. First Fruits).

It is humanly unknowable how the physical body will be glorified or spiritualized; this is the mystery of which St. Paul writes: ". . . we shall all be changed — in a moment, in the twinkling of an eye, at the last trumpet. For the trumpet will sound, and the dead will be raised imperishable, and we shall be changed. For this perishable nature must put on the imperishable, and this mortal nature must put on immortality" (1 Cor 15:51-53). St. Paul also writes: "So it is with the resurrection of the dead. What is sown is perishable, what is raised is imperishable. It is sown in dishonor, it is raised in glory. It is sown in weakness, it is raised in power. It is sown a physical body, it is raised a spiritual body. If there is a physical body, there is also a spiritual body" (1 Cor 15:42-44).

It is Catholic doctrine that resurrected bodies will have four essential qualities: (1) impassibility, freedom from all pain, suffering or other physical defects; (2) clarity, the brightness of glory and splendor that overflows from the beatific vision and transforms all bodies; (3) subtlety, the true nature of the body, docile in a spiritual manner; and (4) agility, that quality of the body, as a perfect instrument of the soul, whereby the glorified body will exist in harmony with and have access to the wonders of creation.

Glory • The English word "glory" is the usual translation of the Hebrew word *kabod* and the Greek word *doxa*, concepts present in both the Old and New Testaments.

The primary meaning of *kabod* is weightiness or impressiveness, and the Hebrews adapted this meaning in the Old Testament to express the unutterable awesomeness of Yahweh. The glory of the Lord, which is usually described as fire and light, went before Israel at the Exodus and settled on the mountaintop as a consuming fire (Ex 24:15-17). The glory of the Lord is also conceived of as God's abiding presence in the Ark of the Covenant and as the fiery presence of God in heaven, such as in Isaiah's vision (Is 6:1-5). The glory of the Lord is an important theme in Ezekiel (Ez 1:26-28) and Daniel (Dn 7:13-14), and in many of the psalms (Ps 19, 29, 66, 96).

In the New Testament, Jesus Christ is the locus of God's glory, thus demonstrating His divinity. Several times the Synoptic Gospels explicitly declare Jesus' glory: (1) at His birth (Lk 2:9); (2) at His transfiguration (Lk 9:31-36); and (3) at the predictions of His Second Coming (Mt 16:27, 24:30, 25:31; Mk 8:38, 13:26). In the Gospel of John, however, the glory of Christ is not restricted to extraordinary events; the glory is always present and available to those with faith (Jn 2:11; 11:40). And yet, like St. Paul, St. John realizes that in His life on earth, Christ had laid aside the fullness of the glory He possessed before the Incarnation and would possess again after the Resurrection (Jn 17:5; Phil 2:6-11). St. Paul, who was temporarily blinded by the glory of the Risen Christ (Acts 9:3-8), refers to the effects of glory on the face (cf. Ex 34:27-35) and conceives of Christians as sharing in the glory of the Lord (Rom 5:2, 8:17-18; 2 Cor 3:18; 4:6).

For further reading: G. Henton Davies, "Glory," *Interpreter's Dictionary of the Bible*, 2:401-403.

Glossator • A scholar in theology or canon law, who studied the most famous or important texts and wrote notes of explanation or clarification in the margins of the texts. In time, the *glossae* or works of the glossators took on great importance for the historical study of the sacred sciences, particularly canon law.

Gloves, Episcopal • Normal preconciliar episcopal liturgical vesture for Pontifical Mass and at certain Low Masses included the wearing of gloves, either white or the liturgical color of the day. During a Pontifical Mass, except for the Requiem, gloves were worn from the beginning of Mass to the Offertory. The 1968 Instruction *Pontificalis ritus* ("On the

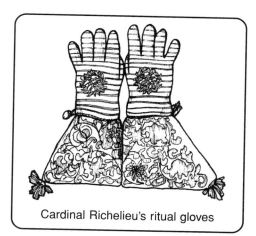

Cardinal Richelieu's ritual gloves

simplification of pontifical rites and insignia"), states that the use of gloves ("which may be white on all occasions") is left to the bishop's discretion (n. 15).

Gluttony • A sin against temperance, it is either the excessive and uncontrolled desire for food or drink, or the extreme and excessive use of food or drink. Gluttony also includes the excessive liking for exquisite food and drink and fastidiousness about food and drink. Excessive drinking is venially sinful if it causes partial loss of reason, and it is mortally sinful if it causes complete loss of reason.

Gnosis • The Greek term (*gnosis*) translates "knowledge." In the New Testament *gnosis* can refer to "knowledge" which is an attribute of God (Rom 11:33) or of humans (1 Cor 8:1, 7, 11) or that which is embodied in the law (Rom 2:20). The term also refers to a class of knowledge about and from God which is specific to Christianity; we might call it "revelation" which we cannot know or come to know by reason alone. This is especially the case in terms of knowledge about the nature and character of God and how such knowledge directly affects and strengthens one's life (e.g., Wis 2:13; 14:22; 2 Cor 6:6; 10:5; 2 Pt 1:5). This kind of knowledge enlightens the intellect and originates from God (not the human: 2 Cor 4:6; 11:6; 1 Cor 1:5). Divine "enlightenment" of the intellect enables it to grasp the profound depths of the Faith, God's wisdom, God's will and intent for the unfolding of His majestic plan of salvation in Christ (Eph 1:9, 18). Hence, this type of "gnosis" is "charismatic," in that it is a gift guided by the Holy Spirit and is grounded in love; as such, it illuminates the knower with a light which radically alters the believer's interior life and self-awareness by means of a more intimate knowledge of God.

In Christian Tradition after the New Testament period, various sectarian movements (e.g., Valentinians, Manicheans, Mandeans) developed heterodox interpretations of "revelation," "illumination" and "gnosis." Differences among these groups notwithstanding, they shared specific assumptions and orientations which collectively are called Gnosticism. The characteristic features of Gnostic thought are: (1) Cosmological Dualism: wherein body and matter are diametrically opposed to each other. Spirit is in essence morally good, while matter (i.e., our bodies, creation, etc.) is in essence morally evil (as distinct from being essentially good but under the domination of sin and death). (2) Secret Gnosis: the written words of Jesus in the New Testament are for the commoners and virtually worthless for "true salvation." The words and teachings of Jesus were transmitted orally, in secret and only to the Twelve Apostles (Jesus' inner circle of "true disciples"). This "secret teaching" was in turn transmitted orally through a line of the spiritually gifted. (3) This "gnosis" liberates the soul. Salvation occurs by or through enlightenment, and not by means of God's action.

For further reading: Kurt Rudolph, "Gnosticism," *Anchor Bible Dictionary,* 2:1033-1040.

Gnosticism: See **Gnosis**

God • The word "God" in the twentieth century encompasses several different meanings. Some mean by "god" anything loved with devotion, as in, "She obeys him like a god" or "He's made a god of his utopian political ideology." When some people say they believe in God, they mean no more than a sense of some all-pervasive spiritual something at the foundation of the universe or the laws of nature.

The Catholic believes in God as the absolute perfect Being, Creator of heaven and earth, personal and loving. The conviction that God exists is based on both faith and reason.

The God of Scripture is a living being, infinite, all-knowing, omnipresent, Who intervenes in history in the creation and guidance of all lower beings.

Proofs based on reason show that what we know about the beings we observe every day presupposes the existence of such an absolute Being, God, as cause and foundation.

The best formulation of such proofs of God's existence can be found in the *Summa Theologiae* of St. Thomas Aquinas (1, Q.2, A.3). For example, since every being we see around us must have a cause, it can be understood that the universe itself must have a cause. Only a perfect absolute Being, God, would not need itself to be caused.

Or, since everything we have around us can be destroyed, there is no reason it should always have been here. In an infinite amount of time, there would have been a time when there was nothing at all. But if there was once nothing, then there would be nothing now, since nothing cannot be a source of anything else. Therefore, there must have always been some absolute necessary Being, God, at the foundation of all mere possibilities.

Among other reasons why philosophers, theologians and many thinking people are convinced that there is a God, one that stands out is the wonderful design of the elements of the universe which point to an intelligent Creator. Many contemporary scientists think that the probability of a universe such as ours coming about by sheer chance is as unlikely as all the letters in a Scrabble game simply falling out in the form of a sonnet by Shakespeare.

Even if many Christians think it is reasonable to believe in God on the basis of informal or formal considerations about the nature of the world around them, personal knowledge of God is based less on reason than on faith and experience. "Blessed are the pure of heart, for they shall see God" (Mt 5:8). Knowledge of God comes primarily because God loves us and sends His Son to reveal that love in person.

God, Attributes of • Essential characteristics or various aspects under which God is viewed in His perfection. God does not have *separate* attributes because God is one, but our finite minds are not capable of grasping God in His unity. Therefore, we can think of Him in terms of various attributes such as simplicity, immutability, infinity, eternity, omnipotence, omniscience, etc. (cf. Analogy). Catholic teaching concerning the attributes distinguishes itself from the view of some that God is so transcendent that we cannot speak of Him at all.

God, Presence of • God's presence to the created order can be understood in three ways: causal, personal and hypostatic. In the first place, God is present to everything that exists as uncaused cause. Nothing would exist or continue in existence without this sustaining causality of God (termed by theologians, "divine conservation"). Secondly, through grace God allows Himself to be known and loved by created persons in His very identity as the three-personed God. Finally, the most intimate presence of God to the created order is also a personal presence. But it surpasses in nature and degree every other presence of God to the world, in that it involves the freely embraced hypostatic union in which the Second Person of the Blessed Trinity unites to Himself a human nature. In sum, God's presence to His creatures is by reason of divine conservation, by reason of divine indwelling, and by reason of the hypostatic union. The higher degrees of presence represented by the divine indwelling and the hypostatic union involve, not a change in God, but a change in the creaturely order. God cannot become more present to the created order than He already is. In grace, a transformation of the created person allows for a more intimate presence to God than the purely causal presence He maintains as the source of the existence of all that is. In the incarnation, the assumption of human nature now united with the divine nature in the Person of the Son entails a transformation of human nature.

Godparents • Persons who act as sponsors for persons who are to be baptized. Historically, the sponsors were baptized Catholics who assisted adult converts during their preparation period and attested to their preparedness when they were presented for Baptism. When infant Baptism became the norm, the sponsors, together with the parents, presented the child for Baptism. Traditionally, it has been the responsibility of the sponsors, or godparents, to assist the parents in the Catholic education of the child, or if the parents were negligent in this regard, to see to this education themselves.

Sponsors are called for at Baptism and Confirmation. The law requires that there be one sponsor of each sex. They must be practicing Catholics, chosen for Baptism by the candidate or by his or her parents, be at least sixteen years of age, not bound by any canonical penalty and not the parent of the one baptized. In the revised law, provision is made for non-Catholic Christians who may, together with a sponsor, act as a witness at the Baptism. Non-Catholics, however, may not be godparents as such.

The revised Code suggests but does not mandate that the sponsors at Confirmation be the same as those who were sponsors at the Baptism of a person. The reason for this is to emphasize the continuity between Baptism and Confirmation, both being integral steps in the overall Rite of Initiation. The requirements for the sponsors at Confirmation are the same as those for Baptism (cf. Canons 872-874, 892-893).

God-spell • As a translation of the Greek *euangelion*, meaning good news, the Anglo-

Saxon *godspel*, literally "good tidings," is the origin of the modern English "gospel."

The musical play *Godspell* was so named for its attempt to present anew and in a popular fashion the abiding message of the Gospels.

Gold • This precious metal was known from antiquity in Israel, as it was imported mainly from southern Arabia and used for coinage. Representing what was beautiful, rich and honorific, gold was offered to the Infant Jesus on Epiphany by the Magi as an acknowledgment of His future kingly role. It is also one of the substances traditionally and properly used for the sacred vessels employed in the Church's worship.

Golden Bull • A bull is a variety of papal document so-called from the lead seal (Latin, *bulla*) attached to it. For documents of great importance and solemnity, a bull of precious metal would substitute for the leaden one. The bull of Leo X granting Henry VIII the title *Fidei Defensor* was such a bull.

The term specifically refers to the "Golden Bull" of 1356 which regulated the elections of the kings of Germany and the Holy Roman emperors. This bull remained in force until the dissolution of the Holy Roman Empire in 1806.

Golden Legend • The Golden Legend, written by Jacobus de Voragine, O.P. (c. 1228-1298), archbishop of Genoa, is a collection of lives of the saints and accounts of events in the lives of Jesus and Mary. Extremely popular in the Middle Ages, it was a source of much medieval iconography. It fell into disuse as historical criticism discounted the authenticity of much of its contents.

Golden Rose • Traditionally blessed by the Pope on the Fourth Sunday of Lent (Laetare Sunday, also known as Rose Sunday), this ornament made of gold and gems, fashioned into the form of a spray of roses, is presented as a token of special favor to a chosen individual, institution or community in appreciation for some special service or particular fidelity to the Holy See. Included in the center of the principal rose is a container of musk and balsam. The origin of the custom of presenting the Golden Rose is obscure, but as early as 1049 Pope St. Leo IX referred to it as an ancient practice.

Golgotha • From the Aramaic *gulgulta*, meaning "skull," this was the site of Christ's crucifixion, otherwise known as Calvary (Luke 23). The place of state executions was so called because it resembled a head or skull. Just outside Jerusalem, Golgotha was the place set aside by the Romans for the execution of criminals.

Good Faith Solution • The so-called "Good Faith Solution," also known as the "internal forum solution," was an unofficial process used in some dioceses of the United States and more recently in Germany as a means of reconciling divorced and remarried Catholics to the Church when it was difficult or impossible for them to obtain a declaration of nullity.

The use of this process depended on the probability that the marriage or marriages in question were invalid, yet the invalidity could not be proved in the external forum. The parties involved were asked to participate in a program of spiritual direction whereby they would be led to the possibility of making the decision to return to Holy Communion. The process did not amount to a priest giving permission for the parties, otherwise prohibited, to receive the Eucharist.

The practice first received national attention in 1971, when the late bishop of Baton Rouge, Louisiana, established a quasi-judicial process whereby persons who could not obtain an annulment were allowed to receive the sacraments. The Holy See directed that the process be halted. In 1973 the American bishops received a letter from the Congregation for the Doctrine of the Faith counseling them to see that abuses were avoided and advising them that persons in irregular unions could be reconciled using "the approved practice of the Church." Since this phrase was unclear, the president of the NCCB wrote to the Congregation asking for further clarification. The response, from the same Congregation, stated that the phrase was to be understood within the context of traditional moral theology. Couples could be allowed to receive the sacraments on two conditions: that they try and live according to the demands of Christian moral principles and that they receive the sacraments in churches where they are not known, in order to avoid giving scandal. The Holy See, as recently as 1994, has continually criticized so-called good faith solutions on the grounds that they fail to address the real problems in troubled marriages, are prone to abuse and self-justification, and that admittedly difficult cases are too quickly written off as unprovable, thereby failing one of the solution's own requirements.

Good Friday • From the fourth century, this day preceding Holy Saturday and the Easter Vigil was regarded as an intrinsic part of the liturgical observance of the Easter Triduum. In addition, there is clear evidence from this century that a full-day fast on Good Friday was linked to the full-day fast on Saturday as preparatory for the solemn night Vigil of Easter. At Jerusalem in the late fourth century there were many liturgical observances from Thursday night through Easter which included readings and prayers assigned to Good Friday.

Before sunrise on Good Friday the narrative of Jesus' trial before Pilate was read at the Sanctuary of the Cross; this was followed by a gathering for prayer at the column where Jesus was scourged. Later that morning, the people would assemble again at the Sanctuary of the Cross to venerate a casket containing a relic of the True Cross. From noon until three o'clock, they would remain in the open courtyard of the Sanctuary for the reading of lessons about Jesus' passion and to offer prayers between readings. The service ended with the reading of the Johannine account of Jesus' death. That evening the account of Jesus' burial was read at the Anastasis (the Sanctuary of the Resurrection), and a vigil of prayer was maintained there throughout the night.

The present afternoon liturgy on Good Friday is entitled the "Celebration of the Lord's Passion," which term derives from the early Christian understanding that the liturgy this day was *in passione Domini* ("the passion of the Lord"), with the understanding that *passio* included both suffering and redemptive death. The antiquity of the present Good Friday liturgy is seen in the absence of any rites before the opening prayer (without "Let us pray"), the lack of any greeting before the proclamation of the passion according to John and the use of the solemn form of intercessions (which form is proper to the Roman Liturgy, but which is customarily used only on this day). The Good Friday liturgy contains three parts: Liturgy of the Word, Veneration of the Cross and Holy Communion.

The readings are Isaiah 52:13—53:12 (fourth Suffering Servant song), Hebrews 4:14-16; 5:7-9 (Christ as High Priest, the source of eternal salvation) and John 18:1—19:42 (the Johannine passion account, preceded by the gospel acclamation, "Christ became obedient for us even to death. . . ." from Phil 2:8-9). A series of ten General

Intercessions follow for the Church, the Pope, the clergy and laity of the Church, those preparing for Baptism, the unity of Christians, the Jewish people, those who do not believe in Christ, those who do not believe in God, all in public office and those in special need.

The Veneration of the Cross includes the showing of the uncovered cross (veiled before the liturgy) to the sung acclamation *Ecce lignum crucis* ("This is the wood of the cross, on which hung the Savior of the world" and the response "Come, let us worship") and the Veneration of the Cross itself (either collectively or individually).

The rite for Holy Communion is relatively simple. It includes the invitation to and the communal praying of the Lord's Prayer, the invitation to Communion ("This is the Lamb of God who takes away the sins of the world. . ."), the distribution itself, period of silence, concluding prayer and prayer over the people. Significantly, the theology of these latter prayers reiterates the triumphant Johannine theology of Christ assuming the cross triumphantly and willingly to accomplish our redemption. The Prayer after Communion states: "You have restored us to life by the triumphant death and resurrection of Christ." The Prayer over the People states: "Lord, send down your abundant blessing upon your people who have devoutly recalled the death of your Son in the sure hope of the resurrection."

The preconciliar custom of praying a form of the Liturgy of the Hours called *Tenebrae* ("darkness") on Thursday, Friday and Saturday of Holy Week has been changed to include only Friday and Saturday mornings (since the Triduum begins with the Evening Mass of the Lord's Supper on Holy Thursday evening). The rather elaborate ceremonies surrounding the extinguishing of several candles on a high candle stand (after each psalm was sung) and the singing of several texts from the Lamentations of Jeremiah have been adjusted in favor of a much simplified form of Office of Readings and Morning Prayer combined. By custom, however, some places continue some of the *Tenebrae* practices, including the singing of the famous chant text, *Christus factus est pro nobis* (from Phil 2:8-9), as the response to the Scripture reading at Morning Prayer, which text in the Gregorian chant melody placed great emphasis on the word *obediens*, indicating the importance of Christ's obedient acceptance of His Father's will. The psalms at the Office of Readings for Good Friday are Psalm 2, 22:2-23 and 38. At Morning Prayer, they are Psalm 51, Hebrews 3:2-4, 13a, 15-19 and Psalm 147:12-20. Instead of a series of Lamentations, the present Liturgy of the Hours assigns the reading of Hebrews 9:11-18 (about Christ the High Priest, Who entered the heavenly sanctuary once for all) and the reading from the Catecheses of St. John Chrysostom (subtitled "the power of Christ's blood").

Good Shepherd • The New Testament image of Christ as the "Good Shepherd" is consistent with the Old Testament depiction of God as shepherd (Ez 34). The notion that God is like a shepherd is especially clear in the liturgical worship of Israel (Ps 23), and this image occurs in scattered fashion throughout the New Testament (e.g., Mt 2:6; 9:36; Mk 6:34; Rom 8:36; Heb 13:20; 1 Pt 5:4). These various biblical strands find their deepest penetration into the mystery of God in John 10.

Jesus identifies Himself as the Good Shepherd in John 10:11-18, specifying in verse 11 that "a Good Shepherd lays down his life for the sheep," adding in verse 14 that as the Good Shepherd "I know mine and mine know me." The Good Shepherd metaphor in John 10:11-18 is but part of the pastoral imagery presented in John 10. The chapter begins with the parable of the

The Good Shepherd (circa fourth century)

sheepfold (10:1-6), where Jesus distinguishes between the true shepherd, who enters the sheepfold through the gate to lead out the sheep he knows by name, and the thieves and robbers who climb into the sheepfold by another way and are not recognized by the sheep. Explaining the imagery, Jesus first identifies Himself as the gate through which the sheep are safely led to pasture (10:7-10), and then by identifying Himself as the Good Shepherd. The imagery of John 10 has its background in the pastoral imagery of the Old Testament. In a society where the care and feeding of sheep and other domesticated animals was a matter of everyday economic importance involving a significant portion of the population, metaphors involving sheep and shepherding were immediately accessible and easily understandable. The Old Testament often refers to human leaders as shepherds, and the prophets employed this image to criticize leaders who were ineffective and unfaithful (cf. Jer 23:1-4).

Because a shepherd is one who carefully tends and protects the flock under his care, the Scriptures refer to God as the shepherd of His people (cf. Gn 49:24; Ps 23:1-4; Ps 80:1). In Ezekiel 34 God speaks through the prophet to denounce the "shepherds" who are Israel's leaders, to decree their punishment and to announce that God Himself will take charge of shepherding His own flock. The contrast between the ruthless shepherds who "pastured themselves and did not pasture my sheep" (Ez 34:8) and God as the vigilant and provident shepherd provides a background for John 10.

In John 10 it is Jesus Who assumes the role of the Good Shepherd, while the "thieves and marauders" are the Pharisees of John 9. The description of the Good Shepherd as One Who knows His sheep and Who is known by them is connected in John 10:14-15 to the mutual knowledge which exits between Jesus and the Father. That communion of knowledge underlies the mutual knowledge of the sheep and the Good Shepherd, for it stems from Jesus' loving fulfillment of the Father's command (10:17-18). Thus the Good Shepherd is the One Who willingly lays down His life for the sheep.

There is strong emphasis on a personal relationship from within the context of mutual knowledge; the Good Shepherd knows His sheep and so calls them by name (v. 3); the sheep know and recognize the Good Shepherd's voice (v. 4; contrast with v. 5). The mutual knowledge between Shepherd and sheep (vv. 11, 14, 16) parallels the Shepherd's knowledge of the Father and the Father's knowledge of the Shepherd; this mutuality implies that to hear the voice of the Good Shepherd is to hear the Father. Second, the Good Shepherd's love for the sheep is sacrificial (in its radical sense: it makes holy) and salvific, irrevocable and complete, not stopping at death (vv. 3, 9, 10-11, 15b, 18). The Good Shepherd's sacrificial and salvific death is linked to the Father's saving action in and through the Good Shepherd, and the unity of the sheepfold (v. 16) is linked to the Good Shepherd's death.

In conclusion, first, in the Old Testament the image of the shepherd is connected to God's saving care and guidance. Second, the application of this imagery to Jesus' life and mission in John 10:1-21 suggests that God the Father continues His mighty and wondrous work of salvation in a definitive way through the one Mediator, the doorway for the sheep (v. 7), the Good Shepherd Who shows forth to the world the Father's great love.

For further reading: Jack W. Vancil, "Sheep, Shepherd," *Anchor Bible Dictionary*, 5:1187-1190.

Goodness • The word "goodness" can be used in a moral sense as connoting positive thoughts, feelings, words and deeds. It can also signify something fundamental about being in the ontological sense, i.e., that all being is good because it is created by God (cf. Gn 1:31).

God is perfect goodness in both senses of the word, for God is absolute Being without limitation or defect. Evil always involves some kind of limitation. A human being or an angel might choose a lesser good over a higher one because of ignorance or willful perversion. For example, Satan, an angel of light, chose his own autonomy over loving obedience to God because his pride led him to consider such independence as a higher good. Many human beings choose the lesser good of pleasures of the table over the higher good of the physical health that would come from more moderate eating habits.

That all being has goodness because of its creation by God is a truth that stands in great contrast to some contemporary philosophies which would make the value of a human being, for instance, strictly dependent on his chances for success in this world. Considering life itself to be an evil or only neutral, such thinkers believe that it must be shown that a given human being will have a "quality" lifestyle before protection would be given to him by the rest of the community. Thus abortion and euthanasia seem to be justified once the idea is rejected that all being is good, simply as created by God.

Love or moral goodness is an essential ingredient in the life of Christian holiness, to which all Catholics are called. We become good not just by avoiding clearly defined moral evils, but also by the growth in love of God and neighbor that comes from participation in the Christ-life in the sacraments and praying for the gifts and fruits of the Holy Spirit.

Goods, Temporal: See **Temporal Goods**

Goods of Marriage • The goods of marriage are three "good things" or aspects of Christian marriage. St. Augustine first enumerated them in one of his works on marriage. Traditionally, the goods of marriage are children, fidelity and permanence. By the good of children is meant an openness to God's will that a couple share with Him in the work of creation through the procreation and Christian nurture of children. The good of fidelity means that a couple are able, with God's grace, to remain totally faithful to each other for life. By fidelity is meant not just sexual fidelity but total fidelity of one person to another. The good of permanence means that a couple, because of their lifelong fidelity, are permanently bound to each other in the Christian marital community.

The three goods of marriage are intimately connected in such a way that they are not only necessary for but flow from a true Christian marriage. Permanence depends on absolute fidelity. The good of children is realized not simply by procreative sexual intercourse, but by the faithful and permanent union of the spouses which is essential for their marital relationship. This relationship, in turn, is the primary source for the Christian and human nurture of children.

Traditionally, Church law has been concerned with violations of the obligations which flow from the three goods, or with the denial of the right to any or all of them.

The theology of marriage provided by Vatican II, as well as canonical jurisprudence which has developed around this theology, has given rise to what might be called a fourth good of marriage, namely, the mutual good of the spouses, which both theology and law say is an essential element of marriage. By this good is meant that in giving themselves to each other in marriage, the spouses oblige themselves to promoting the general spiritual and human welfare of each other.

Gospel • The English term, derived from the Old English (Anglo-Saxon) word *godspel* ("good spell"), means "good news" and is a translation of the Greek word *euangelion*. The use of the term within Greco-Roman culture and within Judaism prior to Christianity clearly prepares the way for the New Testament use of the term. Greco-Roman use of the term *euangelion* indicates a clear development in meaning; at one point it referred to the regard which the messenger received for bringing good news, as in the announcement of victory at battle (one of the earliest examples of this use is in Homer's *Odyssey*, 14, 152ff. and 166ff.). In later writings (e.g., Cicero and others) the term became equivalent to the announcement itself. In Aristophanes's *Knights* 656, "gospel" takes on a religious meaning by virtue of its use within the context of a sacrificial liturgy. By 9 B.C., it refers to an announcement about the birth of the emperor, the savior (Greek, *soter*) of the Empire and protector of peace, as is clear from an inscription issued by proconsul Paulus Falsius Maximus, who honored the Emperor Caesar Augustus by proclaiming the emperor's birthday as the beginning of a new year. The inscription reads:

"The birthday of the god was for the world, the beginning of joyful tidings which have been *pronounced on his account* [Greek, *ton di'auton euangelion*]."

Thus in Greco-Roman culture prior to Christ the word *euangelion* referred to a reward for announcing good news; it also contained a religious meaning and was connected to the birth of a savior figure, the emperor. Within the late Old Testament period and Judaism, the Hebrew terms *bissar* and *besorah* manifest a decidedly religious meaning. For example, in passages such as Isaiah 40:9; 41:27; 61:1 and 52, "gospel" is connected to God's mighty acts of salvation. In Isaiah 52:7-10, the announcement of "good tidings" or "good news" is that God has *already acted* and has *already begun* to save Israel from the political and religious oppression after their deportation into exile in Babylon (begun in 587 B.C. with the destruction of the Temple in Jerusalem). In this instance, "gospel" introduces a level of reconciliation between God and Israel that surpasses the original Exodus — here we have a "new Exodus." Israel's song of joy (Is 52:8) is based on God's saving action (v. 7), marking the beginning of the time of salvation.

During the New Testament period, the term "gospel" refers to the fulfillment of Old Testament expectations about God's sovereign salvific actions in history, actions in which the people of Israel longed to see victory over the enemy (2 Sm 18:19), to see deliverance from oppression (Na 2:1), for pardon from sin and for consolation (Is 40). In the person of Jesus Christ, these expectations are "now fulfilled" and "at hand" (Mk 1:15; Mt 12:28). God is *already* working His great plan of salvation in a definitive way through Jesus Christ; the good news simply announces this marvelous fact. Thus, as with later Greco-Roman use of the term "gospel," the Christian use also refers to a savior figure, but in this case Christ's royalty far surpasses that of a mere emperor and the scope of his actions is cosmic. The New Testament announcement or "good news" of what God has done in and through Christ and the cross is seen as the authentic fulfillment of those Old Testament expectations.

At the end of the New Testament period, the term "gospel" became associated not only with the *content* of a message but also with the *communication* of the message and so became associated with *written* accounts of God's saving actions in Christ (*Didache*

8.2; 11.3; 15.3-4). These accounts were sometimes called "memoirs of the Apostles" (Justin Martyr, *Apology* I, 66). Thus in Christian use, "gospel" refers to both the content of the message of salvation, as well as to the literature which contains that message.

For further reading: O. A. Piper, "Gospel," *Interpreter's Dictionary of the Bible*, 2:442-448; William S. Vorster, "Gospel Genre," *Anchor Bible Dictionary*, 2:1077-1079.

Gospel, The Fifth • P. T. Forsyth, in *The Church, the Gospel and Society* (1962), called St. Paul "the Fifth Evangelist"; his letters, then, are rightly understood as constituting the Fifth Gospel. Chronologically, his letters antedate the written composition of the Synoptics and John; as such, the Pauline letters might more correctly be termed the first or archetypal Gospel.

Gino Concetti, in the March 21, 1974, edition of *l'Osservatore Romano*, applied the title of Fifth Gospel to the Holy Land, where the stones themselves are said to speak of Christ and salvation history, and the inhabitants constitute the "living stones" of the Lord's Church: "The geographical and historical setting of Palestine bears a quite special witness to Christ. It has been said that the Holy Land is itself a gospel, the fifth gospel. The judgment is not an exaggerated one. Everything in Palestine speaks of Christ, His announcement by the prophets, His birth, His life, His miracles, His passion, His death and His resurrection."

Gospel, The Last • This refers to the Prologue of St. John's Gospel (1:1-18), which, being a summary of the entire Gospel and of the mystery of the Incarnation, has from earliest times been regarded with great respect and love. St. Augustine repeats the saying of a contemporary of his who had remarked that this pericope of the Gospel of

St. John should be written in gold letters and placed in a prominent place in every church. Indeed, this was often copied by the faithful and carried about on their person as a sacramental. Just as blessings were and are imparted through the use of some sacramental or other — a cross, a relic, an icon — so blessings were imparted using the words of the Prologue. The Dominican Rite was among the first to prescribe it for the priest privately after Mass (in their Ordinarium of 1256), and eventually the custom arose here and there of reciting it right after Mass. In 1558 the Jesuits voted at their general chapter to use in their Missal either this text or that of Luke 11:27: "Blessed is the womb that bore Thee! . . ." By the time the Missal of Pope St. Pius V was published after the Council of Trent in 1570, it had become a regular appendage at Low Mass. Again, this pericope was regarded as a form of blessing.

Around the time of the Second Vatican Council its use was discontinued; however, because of its special place in the Gospel writings, it should be used by good Christians everywhere in order to ponder the great things God has done for us and for their own spiritual growth and edification (cf. J. Jungmann, *The Mass of the Roman Rite*).

Grace • The term "grace" refers generally to any divine assistance given to persons (human or angelic), in order to advance them toward their supernatural destiny of fellowship with God. In its most proper sense, grace transforms a person's nature so that it can function at an entirely new interpersonal level, where the object of knowledge and love is none other than God Himself and where other persons are known and loved in God. This new level of existence and activity is properly supernatural: It involves the transformation and elevation of the natural states and capacities of the creaturely person. Grace in this sense is traditionally termed habitual or sanctifying grace. This grace involves both the transformation of the whole nature and the infusion of dispositions (the theological virtues and the gifts of the Holy Spirit) that permit real engagement with the indwelling Triune God. As a quality transforming the soul in this way, grace is something created. But because the term "grace" refers also to the very indwelling of God, there is an important sense in which grace is uncreated, identical with God Himself.

Furthermore, insofar as grace repairs the effects of original and personal sin in the soul, it is called healing. Insofar as grace is frequently experienced as a special divine aid given for particular occasions of need, it is called actual. Insofar as actual grace is necessary at the very outset, before the reception of the sacraments, to launch the human being on the road to salvation, it is called prevenient. The doctrine of the necessity of grace for salvation was formulated with great clarity by St. Augustine against the Pelagian view that human beings can take the initial steps toward salvation and perform good actions by their own efforts.

Grace, Actual: See **Actual Grace**

Grace, Efficacious: See **Efficacious Grace**

Grace, Habitual: See **Habitual Grace**

Grace, Sanctifying: See **Sanctifying Grace**

Grace at Meals • The custom of offering a prayer of thanksgiving and blessing before and after food and drink are taken at meals. This custom is frequently emphasized as an important family ritual to carry over the spirit of the day's liturgical prayer, especially at morning and evening, as well as to acknowledge God in a prayer of blessing for His providence in offering sustenance for His creatures. This derives largely from the important Jewish domestic ritual custom of offering special prayers at meals, especially the weekly sabbath meal and the annual seder. To offer a "blessing" is to acknowledge God as the source of all blessings. Attitudes of praise, glory and thanksgiving are denoted in the Hebrew word *berakah* ("to bless").

Often monastic rules and books of customs emphasize the sharing of a meal as an extension of the fraternity and fellowship upon which cenobitic monasticism is based. Sometimes these blessing prayers derive from the psalms (especially Ps 104:27-28) or are paraphrases of gospel passages which speak of Jesus' table fellowship and hospitality. Such themes are reminders that the taking of a meal together is to share in a relationship and bond of intimacy with those with whom one shares the meal.

Gradine • A ledge or shelf above and behind the altar proper (when affixed to the wall) for cross, candles, flowers, etc. In former liturgical legislation and theory, it was stressed that gradines were not part of the altar, nor necessary, but with the possibility of altars facing the people, they have all but disappeared.

Gradual • A term denoting the psalmody sung (most often responsorially) between readings at the celebration of the Eucharist, derived from the Latin *gradus* (literally "step"), indicating that the reader would sing this chant from the step of the ambo. St. Augustine refers to "the psalm which we have just heard sung and to which we responded in song" (*Enarr. in ps. 119*); often he made it the subject of his homily. At times the chant was sung by a deacon, a practice which St. Gregory the Great ended

because it led to the abuse of selecting deacons only for the quality of their voices. Its later evolution often saw it reduced to a few verses of the psalm with very elaborate musical notation sung by a soloist. In this case, the congregation was unable to participate in singing and could only reflect on what it heard sung.

In the present *Ordo Missae* the preferred usage for the psalm that follows the First Reading at Mass is the Responsorial Psalm. However, the terms *Graduale Simplex* ("Simple Gradual") and *Graduale Romanum* ("Roman Gradual") are used as the titles of the books containing the Gregorian chant settings for the texts of the Mass Propers of the revised liturgy.

Gradual Psalms • From the Latin *gradus* (step), gradual psalms are those psalms sung or recited by Jewish pilgrims as they made their way (or went step by step) to Jerusalem to celebrate the major festivals. Also called pilgrimage psalms, they include Psalms 119 through 133.

Graduale Romanum • The liturgical book containing Gregorian chant notation and Latin text of the proper chants sung at Mass (e.g., Introit, Responsorial Psalm, Alleluia, etc.). The book is distinguished from the *Liber Usualis*, which contained all the chants at Mass, plus the musical notation and texts for much of the Divine Office.

The postconciliar *Graduale Romanum* is an adaptation of its predecessor in accord with the directives of *Sacrosanctum Concilium*, the Constitution on the Sacred Liturgy, n. 114. It eliminates Mass propers no longer in use (e.g., the season of Septuagesima, octave of Pentecost), transfers the texts or those saints whose feast days were changed and adds new chants for new Mass propers. A shortened version "for use in smaller churches" has been published in accord with *Sacrosanctum*

Concilium, n. 117, under the title *Graduale Simplex.*

Graffito • Broadly speaking, a graffito (plural, graffiti, from the Greek *graphein*, to write) is simply an inscription done by hand. In archaeology, it usually refers to a crude inscription or picture scratched on a stone or other hard surface. Quite often these inscriptions are useful in determining the identification and the dating of a specific archaeological site. Even when erroneous, they may indicate a believer's devotion and appreciation for a particular place. Numerous graffiti are found in the catacombs of Rome. A particularly significant graffito was found during the mid-twentieth-century excavations under the main altar of St. Peter's Basilica. The inscription appears to be *Petros eni*, that is, "Peter is here," and indicates the belief of early pilgrims that the tomb of St. Peter was located near that spot.

Grail, The Holy • The search for the cup or grail used by Our Lord at the Last Supper has been an inspiration for legends for over a millennium. The story of the Holy Grail dates from the twelfth-century romance *Perceval,* or *Le Conte de Graal,* by Chrétien de Troyes. The story had several national variations, including *Parzifal* and *Perlesvaus.* It entered the English language through Mallory's fifteenth-century *Morte D'Arthur.*

Grail Movement, The • Founded in the Netherlands in 1921 by the Jesuit Jacques van Ginneken, the Grail is an international movement of Catholic laywomen dedicated to the deepening of the Christian life in the spread of Christian values throughout society. Its members are both single and married, represented throughout the professions and on all continents. Grail teams are active in religious education, apostolic formation, community development and social action, medical services and wide-ranging cultural programs. Personal commitment to Christ through prayer and worship are hallmarks of the movement. Members' participation varies with their single or married status. The center of the movement in the U.S. is located in Grailville, near Loveland, Ohio, while the international movement is headquartered in Paris.

Gravissimum Educationis • The original plans of the Second Vatican Council envisioned the completion of sixty-four documents. Shortly after the Council opened, it was seen clearly that the preliminary judgment projected too much; the result was that the sixty-four were pared down to just sixteen. Almost lost in this reduction process was the document on education, *Gravissimum Educationis,* which survived only because of the strong lobbying and effective interventions of the bishop-members of the Conciliar Commission on Education.

No one doubted the critical importance of the schools and of Christian education. Some argued, however, that the matter was so vast and complex that it would be better left to postconciliar action, such as papal encyclicals and Vatican decrees. However, with so much of the Church Universal's investment in schools and education, in hundreds of thousands of teachers and millions of students, it was evident that silence by the Council would be unconscionable.

The Need for a Statement: Before the Council opened, the Preparatory Commission's statement accented the rights of the family and the Church in education, the right to state support, the value of national and international cooperation (especially among universities), with Rome as central coordinator. It also stressed the role of the student himself and the active role of the teacher in the education process, points which were all but lost in the final draft.

Bishops from developing nations asked for a defense of missionary schools, particularly noting that many of these schools had non-Catholics in majority numbers. European bishops described the Catholic school as an authentic apostolate, especially the universities, and called for an affirmation of the right to liberty in scientific research. Bishops from the Americas wished the Council to take note of the pluralistic societies of the twentieth century and the place not only of the school but of education in and out of the institutions.

Still fearful that a document could not possibly do justice to such a fundamental subject, the bishops called for a post-conciliar commission and the various national episcopal conferences to implement and apply locally the principles in the document.

The Council Debate: November 17-19, 1964: In the brief time allotted, there were twenty-one oral interventions and thirty-seven written submissions, many calling for a missionary, apostolic, pastoral, ecumenical spirit, but not a proselytizing one.

Some treated the philosophy of education, calling for a crucial distinction to be made between society ("we the people") and the state or government, a confusion which has bedeviled Church-state relationships for decades, especially in the field of education. A coalition of one hundred sixty-eight bishops asked for a strong statement on financial aid for Catholic schools along the lines of Cardinal Spellman's call for equal justice for parents in their choice of schools.

The Cardinal-Archbishop of New York pleaded for equal treatment by all states, adding: "Moreover, if these schools serve the public purpose of popular education, the fact that they are religious in their orientation should not exclude them from a right measure of public support."

Montreal's Cardinal Leger moved the debate into the field of higher education, calling for greater coordination among Catholic universities of the world, and a clear vindication of the right of liberty of research not only for the universities, but equally for the scientists themselves. Cardinal Staffa of the Roman Curia successfully argued that the name of St. Thomas Aquinas be included in the text as exemplar of scholarly research.

One year later, on October 28, 1965, Pope Paul VI signed and promulgated the text, approved by a vote of 2,290-35.

Content of the Declaration: The Church vindicates the inalienable right of every human being, particularly the young, to a suitable education, and of the Christian to a Christian education. There must be true freedom for parents to choose the schools they wish for their children, free from unjust coercion, whether through direct or indirect burdens because of their choice. There must be true liberty externally, i.e., vis-à-vis the state, and internally within schools themselves in the freedom and spirit of the Gospel.

Education is broader than just schools. The Council expressed its support for all special education for the handicapped, the mentally retarded and others. Likewise, it supported the university as well, as a true apostolate. The teaching of religion must be extended to those outside Catholic schools, especially to students in state and other schools and universities and to the non-Catholics in them.

The Council praises all teachers at every level as bearers of culture and civilization who are doing "God's work." The sacred sciences have a place in true moral education in universities where there must be liberty of research in these as well as in the natural sciences.

The service of all mankind is the sworn duty of the Church; therefore, the Council praises the acceptance of non-Catholics into her schools, especially in missionary countries. There must be a reapportionment of resources in personnel and material resources but not to the detriment of the Catholic schools. Universities in particular must be noted for their excellence rather than numbers.

In two places the declaration took up the question of sex education. Teachers are enjoined that "They should, together with parents, make full allowance for the difference of sex and for the particular role which providence has appointed to each sex in the family and in society" (n. 8); in a word, God created male and female.

The Council resisted all attempts to condemn coeducation *per se*: rather early in the text (n. 1), it said simply that children "should receive a positive and prudent education in matters related to sex" (n. 1). Pope Pius XI's encyclical on education (1929) condemned coeducation based on naturalism, warned against early exposure to the occasions of sin and the denial of original sin. The Pope stated that "all things considered," those with a commission to teach could impart such education. The Council agreed with all these points but decided that "all things considered," modern youth was being inundated with false education in matters of sex, and therefore called for "positive and prudent" sexual education. In sum, where the Pope had said such education *might* be indicated, the bishops and the Pope affirmed that it was *in fact* indicated.

Finally, the Council affirmed true freedom in education, with each subject seen to have its own principles, methods and liberty of scientific inquiry. It was support for scientific research, including theology,

philosophy and Sacred Scripture, for "God is the Lord of sciences," as Vatican I stated, so that "there may be a deeper realization of the harmony of faith and science," as Vatican II stated.

The Future of Catholic Education: The debate indicated certain directions for Catholic education, both by what it said and what it did not say. Four areas were projected: (1) There must be a reappraisal and consequent reassessment of Church resources in education. (2) There must be a very special reassessment in higher education. (3) Intensive research must continue to evolve a more viable philosophy of education, particularly in respect to Church-state problems over the whole world. (4) A postconciliar commission must compose a *Directorium* (practical conclusions from the conciliar text); make relevant legislation for the projected new Code of Canon Law; and update Pius XI's great encyclical of 1929.

In the post-conciliar period, many documents have been issued by the Congregation for Catholic Education on various aspects of Catholic education. Papal documents, especially on higher education, have also been promulgated, most notably, *Sapientia Christiana* and *Ex Corde Ecclesiae*.

Greater Double • In preconciliar liturgical legislation this was one of the terms used to designate the priority of a given liturgical feast. Feasts were graded (in descending order): doubles of the first class, doubles of the second class, greater doubles, doubles and simples. Sometimes feasts of the greater double or higher rank were known as "red letter days" because their titles were printed in red in the Calendar. Examples of greater doubles were: Commemoration of the Baptism of Our Lord (January 13; now celebrated as a feast on the Sunday, or day, following Epiphany when celebrated on Sunday); St. Peter's Chair at Rome (January

18, now celebrated as a feast on February 22); Conversion of St. Paul (January 25, now celebrated as a feast on the same day), the Commemoration of St. Paul (June 30, now eliminated) and St. Ignatius Loyola (July 31, commemorated as a memorial on the same day).

Greca • This Italian word, which means "Greek," refers to the modern overcoat worn since the nineteenth century, particularly, but not solely, by the Roman clergy. It is a double-breasted woolen coat which is worn over the cassock and reaches to the ankles. The Pope often wears a white *Greca*, while all others wear black. The reason it is called *Greca*, or "Greek," is that in the minds of some of those who first saw it worn, it resembled the Greek or Byzantine *rason* which is also an overcoat worn over the "cassock."

Greek Church • Properly speaking, this term refers to the Orthodox Church of Greece. The rite of the Greek Church is the Byzantine Rite, which it shares with many other churches of eastern Europe and the eastern Mediterranean. Because of this, many people erroneously refer to other churches of the Byzantine Rite as "Greek." Sometimes the error is compounded, and the term is extended to include all Eastern Churches.

Greek Church, United • This term is often used to describe all Catholics of the Byzantine Rite, since the original liturgical language of that rite was Greek, having its origins in the eastern half of the Roman Empire where Greek was used. In reality, the term is a misnomer since only some Catholics of the Byzantine Rite are actually Greeks by ethnic origin; to apply a particular designation to a much wider ranging concept is a false generalization and to be avoided because of the ensuing inaccuracy or confusion. Catholics of the Byzantine Rite in full communion with the See of Rome are more accurately termed Eastern Catholics. (Cf. Eastern Churches; Uniate Churches.)

Greek Corporal • A modification of the usual square of white linen material placed on the altar for Mass, on which are placed the chalice and paten. The Greek corporal contains the relics of a saint and in the preconciliar liturgy supplied for the relics placed in the altar stone. Hence, Mass could be celebrated in a place other than a church and not on an altar, provided that a Greek corporal was used.

Greek Fathers • The term "Greek Fathers" is used in contrast to "Western" or "Latin" Fathers, and denotes those giants of early Christian thought who wrote primarily in Greek. Sts. Basil the Great, Gregory of Nyssa and John Chrysostom lead this impressive list. Their thought, like that of the Western Fathers, continues to be studied, refined and treasured by the whole Church to this day.

Gregorian Calendar • By the late fifteenth century, the Julian calendar (so-named for its promulgator, Julius Caesar, in 46 B.C.) was ten days out of step with the seasons. In response, then, to growing agricultural and navigational turmoil, Pope Sixtus IV contracted with the astronomer Johann Müller to reform the calendar, but shortly later Müller was murdered. Efforts at calendar reform shifted then to the secular arena for the next century, but the obstacles of nationalism quashed any hope of concerted efforts there.

Finally, Pope Gregory XIII was able to assemble a team of scholars under the supervision of Lilius. When Lilius died, before completion of the calculations, the renowned Jesuit mathematician Clavius took over and finished the task. In February 1582, the Supreme Pontiff issued a brief which corrected the system of reckoning days within the calendar and, to erase the ten-day error, decreed that October 5, 1582, would be October 15, 1582. Lingering suspicions of Rome's motives notwithstanding, most of Europe quickly adopted the Gregorian calendar, although for a brief period during the French Revolution, it was discarded in favor of a decimal-based week.

The Orthodox Churches notably have not adopted the Gregorian calendar, and their Julian calendar is now thirteen days off. The Gregorian calendar is considered accurate to within one day in 20,000 years.

Gregorian Chant • A plain chant with more individuality and characteristic expression than other early chants (e.g., Ambrosian). These chants appear to have been compiled and arranged by Pope St. Gregory the Great (540-604), thus the name Gregorian. After Vatican Council II and the introduction of the vernacular into the liturgy, Gregorian chant was put aside by most Church musicians. In 1974, however, a publication, "Letter to Bishops on the Minimum Repertoire of Plain Chant," was sent to all bishops and heads of religious congregations throughout the world, at the express direction of Pope Paul VI. This letter spoke of the booklet *Jubilate Deo* which contains basic chants that should be taught to all the faithful, a copy of which was also sent to the bishops and religious leaders.

Pope St. Gregory the Great

Gregorian Masses • A set of thirty Masses, said on thirty consecutive days for the deceased. Because of the difficulties of doing this in a parish with the many requests for Requiem Masses, Gregorian Masses are often taken by a monastery or a house of religious priests. Pious belief attributes a special efficacy to this series of Masses, named after Pope St. Gregory the Great, who began the custom.

Gregorian Modes • Musical "scales" used for Gregorian chant. The eight modes were divided into related authentic and plagal groups. In the authentic modes the cadential figure (final) appears at the lower portion of the range, while in plagal modes it is in the middle. Within the modes, there is only one accidental possible and that is the halftone lowering of the seventh note of the scale (Bb).

Gregorian Reform • An eleventh-century reform movement aimed at correcting moral abuses within the Church and against those elements, connected with feudal society, that weakened her independence. It was named from its most significant leader, Pope St. Gregory VII (Hildebrand), although it took definite shape earlier, at least from the election of Pope St. Leo IX (1049-1054).

The earlier reformer Popes concentrated on two persistent problems: simony (paying for spiritual favors, including election to ecclesiastical office) and the neglect of clerical celibacy. Another serious problem was the interference of secular rulers in the elections of bishops and Popes, and the investiture of clerics by laymen. Often those chosen in this way were unworthy. Nicholas II, in a synod of 1059, took a significant step toward achieving freedom in papal elections. This led to the twelfth-century practice of election of Popes by the cardinals.

The most resolute reformer, Gregory VII (1073-1085), moved strongly against simony and clerical incontinence, but the fiercest battle involved investiture in the prolonged conflict with Emperor Henry IV. Gregory's reign was marked by a number of dramatic incidents: defiance of papal rights by Henry, leading to his suspension from office and excommunication; the emperor's dramatic appeal for forgiveness at Canossa and his subsequent interference with Church life; his second excommunication; naming of an Antipope (Clement III); attacks on Rome; defense of the Pope by the Normans, whose subsequent sacking of the city turned the populace against Gregory. Although he died in exile in Salerno, Gregory laid the foundation of ecclesiastical freedom and affected the role of the papacy for future centuries.

Gregorian Sacramentary • The sacramentary was the book containing the prayers and texts which priests and bishops needed to celebrate different liturgical rites (e.g., the Mass and other sacraments); it did not contain the Scripture readings or chants. The Gregorian is one of three (Leonine, Gelasian, Gregorian) which figure prominently in the development of the Roman Liturgy through the Carolingian era. The Gregorian is known from a copy sent by Pope Hadrian I to Charlemagne around A.D.

788. Known as the *Hadrianum*, this text was likely compiled at Rome around 630; it contains approximately eighty prayers that have been attributed to St. Gregory the Great himself (590-604). To the *Hadrianum* was added a supplement (termed *Hucusque* because of its first word) attributed to St. Benedict of Anianne (formerly ascribed to Alcuin) that completed what was lacking in the original text to make it serviceable for the whole Church year. A second type of Gregorian sacramentary is entitled *Paduensis*, a papal sacramentary that was adapted for use by priests; it is dated between 670-680. A third type is entitled the *Tridentinum*, the central part of which closely paralleled the *Hadrianum*, and is dated before the reign of Pope Sergius I (687-701).

•

Gremial (also Gremiale) • An episcopal liturgical veil (or "apron") made of silk in the variety of liturgical colors formerly used at Pontifical Masses to cover the bishop's knees while he was seated. The rubrics called for the placing of the miter on the bishop's head after the gremial was put in place.

Grille • This term refers to: (1) the wooden or metal grating prescribed by canon law (Canon 964.2) that must be permanently fixed in the confessional between the penitent and the confessor when confession is not made face to face but anonymously. This latter has been and remains an important right of the penitent when confessing his sins to a priest. This is emphasized by the above-mentioned canon, which makes it a precept that a traditional confessional with a grille separating the confessor and the penitent be found in every church or oratory where confessions are heard. (2) The so-called grille, usually constructed of wrought iron or bronze, is also to be found in monasteries of religious women, or nuns, of strictly enclosed orders, referred to as papal enclosures or cloisters. It is usually found in the parlors of these monasteries where the families of the nuns and other guests may visit them. It usually takes the place of a wall and goes from the ceiling to about three or four feet from the floor. A grille is also to be found in the chapel between the sanctuary and the nuns' choir.

Guadalupe, Our Lady of • On December 12, 1531, the Blessed Virgin appeared at Tepeyac, Mexico, to Juan Diego and requested that a church building be erected there. Juan Diego presented himself to the local bishop, carrying a cloak on which an image of the Virgin had been inexplicably imprinted. Two years later, a church was erected there and in 1555 a feast was established in honor of the church's patroness, Our Lady of Guadalupe. By 1746 the Virgin of Guadalupe was the patroness of New Spain. In 1910 she was declared the patroness of Latin America and in 1946 Pope Pius XII declared her to be the patroness of all the Americas. In 1988 the liturgical celebration of Our Lady of Guadalupe on December 12 was raised to the status of a feast in all dioceses in the United States.

Guardian • In canon law, a guardian is one who is authorized to watch over the rights of another. For the most part, canon law will accept the designation of guardians made by civil law, except where those designations might be in conflict with canon law, or unless the diocesan bishop determines that another guardian is more suitable (Canon 98). The assumption of the duties of guardianship is not to be done lightly.

Guardians can act on behalf of their charge in a wide variety of matters, but must keep in mind that they act for their charge, and not for themselves. Negligent guardians can be held liable for any damages they cause to their charge (cf., for example, Canon 1521). Generally, guardians of minors enjoy all of the rights and duties which would have been recognized in the parents of the minor (cf., for example, Canon 914, but also cf. Canon 1478). Although there is no explicit prohibition of clerics or religious serving as guardians, Canons 285 and 672 would seem to discourage the practice.

Guardian Angels • A heavenly spirit assigned by God to watch over each individual during life. The doctrine of angels is part of the Church's constant Tradition, based on Sacred Scripture and the teaching of the Fathers of the Church. Their existence is mentioned in Paul's letters (Rom 8:38; Eph 3:10; 6:12; Col 1:16; 2:15) and in Acts (12:15). The role of the Guardian Angel is both to guide the person to good thoughts, works and words, and to preserve him from evil. Since the seventeenth century, a feast honoring the Guardian Angels has been celebrated in October throughout the universal Church. Since the calendar revision, the feast is celebrated on October 2.

Guelfs and Ghibellines • These words refer to rival medieval factions or houses that represented papal and imperial concerns. The German word *Welf* refers to the Saxons who allied themselves with the papacy; the Italian form of their name is *Guelfo*. The Hohenstaufens of Swabia had a rallying cry (*Weibelungen*) after a castle at Weibelung, and the Italian form came to be *Ghibellino*.

Welf VI joined an alliance with the papacy in 1162, but the emergence of two distinct parties belongs more fully to the reign of Frederick II (1218-1250). The imperial or Ghibelline cause under the grandson of

Frederick Barbarossa ignited a furious struggle with the papal or Guelf allies, with Italy torn apart by this feud. By the year 1300, however, the Guelf allies had largely won. At that point, Ghibelline and Guelf represented only lingering local and familial frictions.

Guilds • In Europe during the Middle Ages, associations or societies organized for the promotion of individual initiative, special skills, social standing and religious life of their members. The merchant guilds were composed of town merchants, who established a monopoly on the town's commerce. They set standards of quality for goods and set a price which was considered to be fair to both consumer and producer. Craft guilds were established to supervise the production of goods and services by specific crafts, such as weaving or carpentry. These craft guilds also supervised the training of their workers (artisans), who were divided into three classifications: (1) master craftsman, (2) journeyman, (3) apprentices.

All medieval guilds had a religious dimension, normally adopting a patron saint and keeping the saint's feast day. Universities arose from guilds of scholars who regulated their profession and set requirements for entry into it. Guilds sometimes came under criticism from Church authorities because of drinking brawls, unorthodox beliefs and price-fixing.

The Protestant Reformation was generally hostile to guilds, which gradually declined in the eighteenth and nineteenth centuries. In a sense, they were the forerunners of labor unions and religious social-action groups.

Guilt • Objectively, the liability to punishment incurred by the transgression of a law. Thus, a court of law pronounces a defendant guilty when a particular violation is established beyond reasonable doubt. In Christian life, guilt has this primary objective sense. It refers to the obligation to undergo punishment that is the necessary consequence of sin. Guilt also has a subjective, psychological sense when it refers to the remorse for sin that is felt by the sinner. It should be noted that a sinner can be objectively guilty even though he does not feel guilt. At the same time, feelings of guilt may perdure even after a particular sin is forgiven and the penance accepted and performed. A healthy Christian moral life requires that the objective and subjective kinds of guilt be understood as distinct.

Gyrovagi • Wandering monks who are either not attached to a monastic community or never reside in one. This style of life has always been regarded as an abuse in the Church (St. Benedict himself was critical of such monks), and reform efforts have often included the proscription of the practice.

Habakkuk, Book of (also Habacuc) • Not long before Nebuchadnezzar attacked Jerusalem (598 B.C.), his plans to conquer Judah and the likely success of that plan became clear to this seventh-century minor prophet.

His short (three chapters) book is a monument to his own questioning (and that of his people) about God's justice in allowing the Chosen People to suffer, and particularly to suffer at the hand of another.

This is the same problem, raised to a national level, which confronted Job. As Job entered a lengthy dialogue with three of his friends, so Habbakuk enters into dialogue with God, registering his complaint. The Lord replies that He has chosen this instrument to punish the people, but they should not lose faith in Him. God's justice is not instantaneously revealed; His people must learn patience. Babylon itself will eventually fall, and the promised Messiah will surely come. The third chapter is a magnificent canticle of faith, wrung from an anguished heart.

For further reading: Marvin A. Sweeney, "Habakkuk, Book of," *Anchor Bible Dictionary*, 3:1-6; Thomas P. Wahl, O.S.B., Irene Nowell, O.S.B., Anthony R. Ceresko, O.S.F.S., "Zephaniah, Nahum, Habakkuk," *New Jerome Biblical Commentary*, 255-264.

Habit • A habit (from the Latin *habitus*) is a stable disposition of a human capacity to facilitate a specific pattern of activity. This philosophical (and theologically useful) notion of habit must be distinguished from the idea of purely rote or repetitive behavior.

Human capacities need the dispositive influence of habits for activity to be directed and successful. Thus, for example, the human mind needs the discipline of sciences in order to pursue ordered inquiry in particular fields. The musically talented individual must cultivate a disciplined coordination of intellectual, emotional and physical powers in order to play difficult works on a piano or cello. Such examples can be multiplied. Philosophers owe to Aristotle the recognition of this important level of development between basic human capacities or powers and the successful performance of a wide range of activities. It was Aristotle who first identified and described in a systematic way the dispositive influence of habits on human action. Far from being merely routine or mechanical in its influence on human action, as the common understanding of habits suggests, a habit is a perfection or actualization of a human capacity that enters intrinsically into the performance of an activity.

The philosophical analysis of habits has had many uses in Catholic theology, particularly in providing the basis for the systematic discussion of character in moral theology, and of grace and the infused virtues in dogmatic theology. Virtues and vices can be understood as good or bad habits. A virtue is a stable disposition of human capacities that directs them to the ready performance of specifically good actions, while a vice represents the failure to develop good habits of action. Virtues can be acquired or infused: acquired through a pattern of repeated good actions, or infused by divine grace.

In the theology of grace, the distinction between entitative habits and operative habits has been applied to understanding the transformation of human nature and capacities by sanctifying grace. As the term suggests, an entitative habit is a disposition of the component parts of a whole being (entity). Health and beauty are classic examples of entitative dispositions that affect the whole nature of a particular being. Operative habits, as we have seen, are dispositions of the powers (sources of activity or operation) of an entity. On this account, then, sanctifying grace is an infused entitative disposition that transforms the very being of the one who receives it. Sanctifying, or habitual, grace is a kind of second nature, enabling the human person in grace to live a "supernatural" life of participation in the divine life itself. Activity at this new level of life is made possible by infused operative habits: The infused theological (faith, hope and charity) and moral virtues (prudence, justice, fortitude and temperance) are grace-given transformations of the human powers of knowing and loving, and of the human emotions, that form the basis for a divinized or theological life.

Habit, Religious • The distinctive garb worn by members of religious institutes and societies of apostolic life. The purpose of the habit is twofold. It is a sign of the religious life and a testimony to poverty. The law requires that members of religious institutes wear a distinctive religious habit (Canon 669). Members of societies of apostolic life wear a habit if their constitutions require it, but they are not bound to do so by universal law.

Habitual Grace • Also called "sanctifying grace," habitual grace is an infused gift of the Holy Spirit into the soul of the person. Habitual grace gives the individual the constant capability of acting in accord with the demands of faith, hope and charity. This grace is the constant possession of the person until and unless an actual sin is committed. Habitual grace instills the habits of faith, charity and hope, and it facilitates performance of these actions. The aim of the moral life is the development of the ability to perform acts commanded by the moral law and the new Law of Love with great facility and ease; the infusion of habitual grace makes this possible.

Haceldama: See **Akeldama**

Haggai, Book of (also Aggai or Aggaeus) • The Book of Haggai (also Aggai or Aggaeus) takes its name from the purported author, the minor prophet Haggai, whose name is derived from the Hebrew *hag*, meaning "feast." Post-exilic, probably written c. 520 B.C., the book is unusual in the prophetic corpus in that it is written in the third person. It contains five oracular utterances, concerned primarily with the building of the Second Temple and the survival of the promise of the messianic dynasty in the person of Zerubbabel (2:20-23).

For further reading: Aelred Cody, O.S.B., "Haggai, Zechariah, Malachi," *New Jerome Biblical Commentary*, 349-361; Carol Meyers and Eric M. Meyers, "Haggai, Book of," *Anchor Bible Dictionary*, 3:20-23.

Hagia • The name of the Consecrated Species in the Byzantine Liturgy, from the Greek for "holy things."

Hagiography • A term derived from two Greek words (*hagios* meaning "holy," and *graphein* meaning "to write"), signifying the writing of the lives of the saints or books about the saints. Sources for investigation include martyrologies, liturgical texts, calendars, legends and biographies. From the seventeenth century, the Bollandists have been responsible for this investigation.

Hail Mary • This popular prayer of Christian devotion is composed of two texts from the Scriptures: the angelic greeting to Mary in Luke 1:28, "The Lord is with you. Blessed are you among women," her cousin Elizabeth's greeting to her in Luke 1:42, "Blessed are you among women and blessed is the fruit of your womb," and a section composed in light of the growing popular devotion to Mary as the *Theotokos*, "Holy Mary, Mother of God, pray for us sinners, now and at the hour of our death." This second section received official recognition when Pope Pius V included it in the Roman Breviary of 1568.

St. Peter Damian (d. 1072) is the first to testify that the Hail Mary had become a favorite prayer of the people. From the Synod Statutes of Paris around 1210, episcopal directives express the desire that the faithful should learn the Hail Mary in addition to the Lord's Prayer and the Creed.

For further reading: *Catechism of the Catholic Church*, nn. 2676-2679.

Hair Shirt • A coarse undergarment worn by Christian ascetics as a means of mortification and discipline. In modern times the hair shirt has been abandoned by and large as a means of discipline and mortification and has been replaced by other forms of self-discipline because of changing values, lifestyles and understandings of Christian spirituality.

Halo: See **Aureole**

Hampton Court Conference • In 1604, representatives of the two main branches of English Protestantism met in Hampton Court Palace near London. Their goal was to settle differences between the established Anglican Church and the stricter Puritan faction. King James I presided over the conference and eventually rejected the Puritan proposals, uttering his famous dictum: "One doctrine and one discipline; one religion in substance and ceremony." The conflicts which the conference intended to resolve were, in fact, somewhat worsened by the outcome and resulted in a long-lasting rift between the Puritans and the English Crown. The conference did, however, approve a resolution calling for a team of scholars to produce over the next several years an English translation of the Bible, which came to be known as the King James Version.

Hanukkah • Hebrew for "dedication," a feast celebrated by Jews to recall the rededication of the Temple by Judas Maccabeus in 166 B.C. In accordance with 1 Maccabees 4:52-59, the festival is celebrated for eight days. The celebration centers around the lighting of the menorah (the eight-branched candelabrum), and it is also called the "Feast of Lights." According to rabbinical legend (*Tosefta Shabbat* 21b), one small container of oil was able to fuel the Temple lamp for eight days until more oil could be obtained.

For further reading: Moshe David Herr, "Hannukah," *Encyclopedia Judaica*, 7:1279-1287; James C. Vanderkam, "Dedication, Feast of," *Anchor Bible Dictionary*, 2123-2125.

Happiness • The attainment of comprehensive human fulfillment. For Christians, happiness is only attained through union with God, which is the consequence of grace. In the Christian perspective, the fullness of happiness is not possible without faith in God, for ultimate happiness consists in the beatific vision, or full human participation in the life of the Trinity.

In the Catholic perspective, happiness is attained through discipleship of Jesus Christ, possession of the life and gifts of the Spirit and full union with Christ. Unlike with many other religions, happiness does not consist in the possession of such impersonal qualities as power or unending existence. Rather, it consists in an eternal *colloquium* with the infinite, perfect, all-powerful and perfectly loving Trinity. For Catholic belief, happiness consists in an encounter with the perfect Persons of the Divine Three, and because this understanding of human happiness emphasizes the love, intelligence and personal character of happiness with God, it possesses some distinct advantages to the teachings of other religions and philosophical systems.

Harmony, Biblical • A biblical harmony attempts to integrate the four Gospels in such a way that a single narrative is produced, with the verses of all four Gospels arranged in chronological order. In recognition of the distinctive theological perspectives and characteristics peculiar to each of the evangelists, most biblicists today reject the attempt at a biblical harmony which otherwise imposes an artificial reordering of the biblical texts at odds with the original intentions of the inspired writers.

For further reading: Stephen J. Patterson, "Harmony of Gospels," *Anchor Bible Dictionary*, 3:61.

Hasmoneans • The name is from the Hebrew word *Hashmon* and means "descendants of Hashmon," a Jewish family which eventually produced the lineage of the high priesthood and of the monarchs which ruled in the century prior to the birth of Jesus. The family can be traced back as far as c. 135 B.C., beginning with the

Maccabeans (the immediate ancestors of the high priests and monarchs of Jesus' day).

According to Josephus, a first-century Jewish historian, Asamonaeus (Hebrew, *Hashmon*) was the father of Mattathias, who in 168 B.C. led a revolt against the religious and political oppression of Antiochus IV (cf. 1 Mc 2:1-70). The victories they earned came to an end around 68 B.C., when Pompey focused the great military might of the Roman Empire on Jerusalem and conquered it and surrounding regions.

For further reading: Teresa Rajak, "Hasmonean Dynasty," *Anchor Bible Dictionary*, 3:67-76.

Hatred • "Hate the sin; love the sinner" was St. Augustine's wonderful way to distinguish rightful hatred out of love for justice and for the victims of evil, from corrosive, evil hatred out of envy, pride or vindictiveness.

It is not a Christian virtue to be mild, even in the face of injustice, for such an attitude can be based on apathy or self-serving non-involvement. The prime example of righteous anger on the part of Jesus in the Gospels is the scourging of the money-changers in the temple (cf. Mt 21:12).

On the other hand, cherishing hatred, even toward personal enemies, in the form of wishing them ill, is always wrong. It is not in our power to avoid all feelings of hatred when we have been treated badly, but as Christians, we must always ask for the grace to forgive and to hope for the greatest blessings, including the grace of repentance, for those who have hurt us or those we love.

"Forgive us our trespasses as we forgive those who trespass against us" is part of the prayer that Jesus wants all of us to make our own (cf. Mt 6:9-15).

Hearse • This term comes to us from the Latin *hirpex* via the French *herse*, both meaning "harrow," and can refer to various things:

(1) A hearse can be a metal or wooden framework placed over the bier or coffin at funeral services. Since numerous prickets were placed throughout it to hold burning tapers and this bore a resemblance to the spikes of a harrow, the name "hearse" was given to the whole structure.

(2) This led to the extension of the word to mean any receptacle in which the coffin was placed for transportation, as in our modern understanding of the word, whether a carriage as originally used and sometimes still used in some cultures, or the modern motorized vehicle.

(3) In Church parlance, however, the word "hearse" has another meaning. It is peculiar to the type of candelabrum used since the seventh century for the Holy Week service of Tenebrae, during which the candles are extinguished ceremonially, one by one. This hearse is a triangular candlestick on which, historically, there have been from seven to twenty-four candles of unbleached wax. The usual number nowadays, where Tenebrae has been revived (as it fell into disuse after the Second Vatican Council), is fifteen. The Tenebrae hearse is laden with symbolic meaning. The triangle itself represents the Blessed Trinity. The highest candle (sometimes, incorrectly, bleached) represents Christ. The rest of the candles represent the eleven Apostles and the three Marys.

Heart of Mary, Immaculate • Both Pope Leo XIII and Pope St. Pius X called St. John Eudes (d. 1680) the "father, teacher and first apostle" of devotion to the hearts of Jesus and Mary. By 1643, there was a public celebration in honor of the Immaculate Heart of Mary in the diocese of Autun; Pope Pius VII extended the celebration to any diocese requesting it. The liturgical text to be used was slightly modified from that of

Our Lady of the Snows (August 5). The Missal of 1914 assigned the Mass to an appendix, but Pope Pius XII raised it to the rank of double in 1942 (the year he had consecrated to the Immaculate Heart of Mary) and assigned it to the last day of the octave of the Assumption, August 22. The 1969 reform of the Calendar changed the status of the celebration to an optional memorial to be celebrated on the day following the feast of the Sacred Heart, the Saturday after the Second Sunday after Pentecost. In *Marialis Cultus*, the Apostolic Exhortation on devotion to Mary, Pope Paul VI cited devotion to the Immaculate Heart of Mary as one example of contemporary devotions to Mary (n. 8). Pope John Paul II develops the theme of the unity of Mary's heart with her Son's in *Redemptor Hominis*, the *Redeemer of Man*, n. 22.

Heaven • In Sacred Scripture "heaven" (Hebrew, *shamayim*; Greek, *ouranios*) refers to both the material cosmos — what we call "sky" — as well as to a religious and spiritual dimension, namely, the "abode" of God. The visible sky is a natural symbol for the invisible spiritual reality of heaven: to the eye, the sky appears to be without limits or walls or any kind of barrier; and yet it appears to "contain" countless stars, unlimited wind, endless rain and clouds — in effect, the sky is almost without end or apparently infinite. It is because of its natural power to communicate the idea of "endlessness" or "infinity" that the sky can be thought of as God's abode (1 Kgs 8:30) and yet, paradoxically, Sacred Scripture proclaims that nothing in the world can contain God (1 Kgs 8:27).

(1) Physical Universe: The witness of Sacred Scripture contains several descriptions of the three-layered cosmos of heaven, earth and the abyss of water under the earth (e.g., Ex 20:4); or heaven, earth and Sheol (Ps 115:16); heaven separates the

earth from the waters above it (Dt 5:8) and so is said to be substantial, having pillars (Jb 26:11) and foundations to support it (2 Sm 22:8). When its windows are opened, it rains (Gn 7:11-12); it stores snow and hail (Jb 38:22) and wind (Jb 37:9). This hemispherical vault called heaven is said to stretch out like a tent (Is 40:22; 45:12; Ps 104:2). The Apostle Paul was "taken up" to the third heaven (2 Cor 12:2).

(2) Spiritual Reality: In Sacred Scripture the religious reality we call heaven is not known through direct experience or natural knowledge. Thus this concept represents a symbolic locus by which we can understand what is not in our direct experience (i.e., death, afterlife, infinity, etc.). Quite often poetic language serves to penetrate the deepest mysteries about God's sovereign majesty over the universe which is saturated with signs of His existence. This sacred view of the cosmos leads to the understanding that indeed "the heavens" are the abode of God, where God is surely enthroned (Is 66:1; Ex 24:9-11), the locus of God's heavenly court and palace (Ps 104:2ff.; 1 Kgs 22:19-23), from where He manifests Himself (Mt 3:16 and parallels; Jn 1:32).

The physical and spiritual are united in an absolute fashion for the first time in New Testament texts about the resurrection and ascension of Jesus (Acts 1:9, 11), Who sits at the right hand of the Father (Mt 26:64; Mk 14:62; Lk 22:69: Acts 7:55; Rom 8:34; Eph 1:20). Jesus will return from heaven at some future date (*parousia*) (Mt 24:27; 26:64; Mk 14:62; 1 Thes 1:10). Christians are citizens of heaven (Phil 3:20), a home built by God for the believer (2 Cor 5:1-5), a veritable host of mansions (Jn 14:1-3). Heaven represents the believer's inheritance (1 Pt 1:4), reward (Mt 5:12) and treasure (Mt 6:20; Col 1:4-5), that final state of perfect happiness with God.

For further reading: Mitchell G. Reddish, "Heaven," *Anchor Bible Dictionary*, 3:90-91.

Hebdomadarius • Title derived from the Greek (*ebdomas*, "week"), generally given to the member of a religious community bound to the common celebration of the hours (e.g., monastery, canonry, convent) who leads the prayers at the community's celebration of the hours. The leader changes weekly (hence the name) in rotation with others in the community. The *General Norms of the Liturgy of the Hours* states that "in the absence of a priest or deacon, the one who presides at the office is only one among equals and does not enter the sanctuary or greet or bless the people" (n. 258).

Hebrew-Catholic • A Hebrew-Catholic is a person of Jewish heritage who is a part of the Catholic Faith community. This category includes not only those who convert to the Catholic Church by their own choice, but also those of Jewish descent who are baptized as children by virtue of the Catholic Faith of one or both parents.

"Hebrew-Catholic" is viewed by some as being a more accurate name than "Jewish convert" for such members of the Church. This is because many Hebrews who are now Catholics previously had no relationship to rabbinic Judaism as a religion. As well, to many Jews, the term "Jewish convert" can mean one who converted *to* Judaism from some other religion.

Hebrew Feasts • The Jewish calendar is a lunar calendar, that is, it is based on the revolution of the moon about the earth. Since Jewish feasts must be kept in their proper season, the calendar is adjusted every few years to the cycle of the sun. The Bible records only four original Hebrew names of the months. The Hebrew names were dropped, however, and all twelve months now have names of Babylonian origin, established after the Babylonian Exile.

Rosh Hashanah (literally, "Head of the Year") takes place during the first two days of the month of Tishri (September-October). Frequently it is called the Feast of the New Year. It emphasizes spirituality, morality and holiness and is not tied to national historic events (cf. Nm 29:1). Yom Kippur (Day of Atonement) takes place at the end of the ten days of repentance which Rosh Hashanah inaugurates. The entire day is given to fasting, prayer and contemplation (cf. Nm 29:7), emphasizing the same things as Rosh Hashanah. Sukkot (Feast of Tabernacles) is celebrated on the fifteenth of the month of Tishri and lasts for seven days. As is true with Passover and Shavuot, it is associated with both agriculture and history (cf. Ex 23:16; Lv 23:34; Dt 16). Hanukkah (Feast of Dedication or Lights) is celebrated for eight days in the month of Kislev (November-December). It commemorates the victory of Judas Maccabeus and his men over the Seleucids during the second century before Christ. Though not biblical in origin, it is a historical feast.

Purim (Feast of Lots), falling on the fourteenth day of Adar (March), is a biblical festival based on the story in the Book of Esther. Jews of Persia were saved from being destroyed by Haman through the efforts of Mordecai and Queen Esther. Passover (Pesach) is celebrated in the month of Nisan (March-April) and is one of the three pilgrimage festivals named in the Bible (the other two being Shavuot and Sukkot). It is the celebration of the Jewish people's deliverance from Egyptian slavery through the intervention of God (cf. Lv 23:5-8). Shavuot (Feast of Pentecost) comes in the May-June months and commemorates God's giving of the Torah (Ten Commandments) to Moses on Mt. Sinai.

Hebrew Language • A member, along with Aramaic, of the Northwest Semitic language family. It is the language in which the bulk of the Old Testament was written, with the exception of some chapters in Daniel and Ezra. Hebrew was spoken in Palestine up until about the fourth century B.C., at which time it gave way to Aramaic as the common language of the place.

The language is characterized in part by its triliteral roots which enshrine the essential meaning of its words. Modifications of a word's meaning are signified by prefixes, vowel changes or affixes to the basic three-letter roots. Originally, only the consonants were written. As time went on, the need was felt to preserve what was thought to be the traditional pronunciation. Accordingly, rabbinical scholars (the Massoretes) in the first millennium A.D. devised a system of points and marks which were placed above or below the consonants to express these vowels.

For further reading: Gene M. Schramm, "Languages (Hebrew)," *Anchor Bible Dictionary*, 4:203-214.

Hebrew Poetry: See **Psalms, Book of**

Hebrews, Epistle to the • The letter "to the Hebrews" is "a word of exhortation" (13:22), most likely addressed to Christian converts from Judaism. The recipients of the letter are not recent converts (5:12) and have undergone some persecution (10:32-39), which has not ceased (12:3-13; 13:3). Scholars do not agree as to the exact purpose of the letter. The believers are encouraged and exhorted to hold fast to their confession of faith (4:14-16), not to "drift away" from the message of salvation (2:1), and not to avoid community worship (10:25). They are urged to push on and not lose their enthusiasm for the Faith (10:23-25, 32-39). Much of the teaching illustrates how superior and potent is the work of salvation effected by Christ, the High Priest, which is contrasted to what was revealed in the past.

Major Themes: Jesus, the exalted One (1:3), is the culmination of God's prophetic Word to man (1:1ff.). Christ, Son of God and High Priest (3:1), has passed into heaven (4:14) and is far superior to the angels and even the greatest high priest of old — Melchizedek (7:3). He, therefore, is supreme ruler of the House of God (3:6), the Author of salvation (2:10), the Great Shepherd (13:20). Christ proclaims and brings salvation (2:3) and is the cause of salvation for those who obey Him (5:9), which salvation He will dispense at His Second Coming (9.28). He saves from sins by cleansing (10:3) and bringing about the remission of sins (8:12; 9:14; 10:18), which renews and sanctifies the soul (2:11).

Contents:

A. Introduction: 1:1-4

B. Christ, Exalted and Incarnate: 1:5—2:18

C. Faith and the Compassionate High Priest: 3:1—5:10

D. Exhortation, Encouragement, Christ as High Priest: 5:11—10:25

E. Call to Faith and Endurance: 10:26—11:40

F. Christ's Perfection, Endurance to the End, Worship: 12:1—13:17

G. Conclusion: 13:18-21, 22-25

Authorship and Date: The authorship of Hebrews is unknown. The document itself gives no indication of who its author may be, and it does not conform to the epistolary format followed by the letters of Paul.

Among the external witnesses, from the second century onward the Church in Alexandria held that Hebrews was an authentic letter from Paul. Origen and a few others had serious doubts about its Pauline origins. In the Latin West, Tertullian and others doubted its Pauline authorship from the beginning. By the fourth century through to the Reformation, both East and West accepted the letter as being from Paul. Names which have been proposed as alternatives include: Apollos, Barnabas, Prisca, Aquila, Silas and Jude. The latest date for the letter is c. A.D. 95, the traditional dating of 1 Clement, which mentions Hebrews in Chapter 36.

For further reading: Harold W. Attridge, "Hebrews, Epistle to the," *Anchor Bible Dictionary*, 3:97-105; Harold W. Attridge, *Hebrews*, Hermeneia (Fortress Press, 1988); Myles M. Bourke, "The Epistle to the Hebrews," *New Jerome Biblical Commentary*, 920-941.

Hedge Schools • The manner of providing Catholic education for Irish children during the early eighteenth century. In 1695, the Irish parliament under King William III decreed that it was illegal to use buildings and private homes to teach the Catholic Faith. Therefore, qualified teachers and their students would gather under the hedges near the road to continue the educative process. Not all parents could afford the exorbitant fees for the hedge schools. The schools moved back to buildings when the laws were relaxed in 1760.

Hedonism • The ethical view which holds that human fulfillment is found by the pursuit and possession of material and physical pleasures. Radical hedonism holds that all physical pleasures should be pursued, but a more moderate hedonism contends that the pursuit of pleasures should be moderated because that enhances their enjoyment. Hedonism is actually no moral system at all because it does not demand any moral virtues, and it is not clear that pleasure is a "moral" or "ethical" quality or virtue. Catholic belief opposes hedonism because it implicitly undermines the spiritual values of charity, faith, justice, self-sacrifice and the moral virtues.

Hegoumenos • In the Eastern Churches, the title given to the superior of a monastery. It is equivalent to that of "abbot" in the West, although their prerogatives differ. A hegoumenos rules for life, assisted by a council.

Hell • The place, state or condition prepared for Satan, his subjects and the unrepentant for all eternity. The term derives from the Teutonic mythological place for the dead and corresponds to the Old Testament Sheol or dwelling of the dead. Theologians generally agree that hell is a place of pain and suffering that is derived from alienation from God and from an outside source and is also a place of punishment. The suffering of those in hell is proportionate to the gravity of their sins, and it is without end.

There is a pain of loss of vision of God and a sensible pain that derives from punishment. This punishment should not be conceived of as a purely psychological pain, for there is an objective aspect and content to it. Just as heaven involves an objective relationship to God and an objective pleasure, so also hell involves an objective condition and an objective punishment and suffering. The eternity of hell can be explained by the obduracy and hardheartedness of sinners. It is conceivable that some sinners are so frozen in their sinful attitudes that they cannot repent even in the face of the punishments and sufferings of hell.

The New Testament relates fire with hell, but darkness is also associated with it, and the New Testament repeatedly identifies hell with exclusion from the kingdom of heaven. While there is no explicit doctrine of hell in the words of Christ, there is clear mention of pain at the loss of the kingdom of heaven. The Church has defined hell and the eternity of hell against Origen and other ancient writers who held that all would be ultimately reconciled to God.

Hellenism • The term used to describe a wide variety of predominant Greek influences which helped shape the identity and activity of the ancient Church. Greek language, sciences, history and philosophy were major cultural influences in the world during the Apostolic Age, and it is not surprising that the Church devoted considerable attention to evangelizing that culture and in turn borrowing ideas from it for her own development. Greek thought was particularly influential in theology (cf. Alexandria, School of), and in the study of Sacred Scripture.

For further reading: Hans Dieter Betz, "Hellenism," *Anchor Bible Dictionary*, 3:127-135.

Henotikon • A formulary of Trinitarian and Christological doctrine issued by the Emperor Zeno in A.D. 482, intended as a concession to the Monophysites. The document represents a stage in doctrinal controversy between the Council of Chalcedon (451) and the Second Council of Constantinople (553). The Henotikon accepted as a statement of orthodoxy only the Nicene Creed as interpreted by the Councils of Constantinople (381) and of Ephesus (431), but not by the Council of Chalcedon. The positions of both Nestorius and Eutyches were condemned, but in a way that disapproved of Chalcedon as well. This concession did not mollify the Monophysite party and provoked opposition from Rome.

Heortology • Technical term referring to the study of the history, development and theology of the feasts and seasons of the liturgical year.

Heptateuch • Greek for "seven books." A term for designating the first seven books of the Old Testament, that is, the Pentateuch plus the books of Joshua and Judges. Some scholars in the past, who felt there was an underlying unity to these books, devised this category. The term is employed by St. Ambrose, but not in the sense of the later critics.

Heresy • The word comes from the Greek *hairesis*, which originally referred to a sect, party or school of thought. In Christian usage, a heretic is someone who deviates from the accepted norm of faith.

In contemporary usage, a formal heretic is a baptized person who knowingly, willingly and culpably refuses to accept the Church's divine teaching authority. A material heretic is one who does not recognize this authority and consequently denies its ruling. According to the *Code of Canon Law* (c. 751), "Heresy is the obstinate post-baptismal denial of some truth which must be believed with divine and catholic faith, or it is likewise an obstinate doubt concerning the same." (Cf. Apostasy.)

For further reading: *Catechism of the Catholic Church*, n. 2089.

Heretic • A baptized and professed person who is pertinacious, that is, one who knowingly, willingly and culpably refuses to accept the Church's divine teaching authority. Such a person is considered a formal heretic. A material heretic is one who does not recognize this authority and consequently denies its ruling. (Cf. Apostasy.)

Hermeneutics • From the Greek word *hermeneuein*, meaning "to interpret," hermeneutics is the science and methodology of interpretation. More specifically, hermeneutics refers to the theory of biblical interpretation. In the past, hermeneutics was distinguished from exegesis: exegesis was understood as a matter of putting into practice the rules of interpretation formulated by hermeneutics. Today, hermeneutics is often understood more broadly as methodical reflection on the production of meaning in texts, sacred and secular — whether written, spoken or transmitted through other media.

For further reading: Bernard C. Lategan, "Hermeneutics," *Anchor Bible Dictionary*, 149-154; Anthony C. Thiselton, *New Horizons in Hermeneutics: The Theory and Practice of Transforming Biblical Reading* (Zondervan, 1992).

Hermesianism • The theological and philosophical teachings of the theologian Georg Hermes (1775-1831), who attempted to accommodate Catholic thought to Enlightenment philosophy. He held important professorships at Munster and Bonn, but after his death many of his characteristic positions were condemned by Pope Gregory XVI (*Dum acerbissimas*, 1835). Hermes accepted the Kantian view of knowledge, but against Kant held that the existence of God could be proven by theoretical reason. His position on the relation of faith and reason was semi-rationalist, in that it accorded to reason a decisive role in assessing and acquiring knowledge of supernatural truth. Along with other cognate positions of nineteenth-century Catholic theologians (viz., those of Anton Gunther and Jakob Frohschammer), Hermesianism was again condemned at Vatican Council I.

Hermit • A title given to a religious ascetic who lives alone to contemplate God through solitude, silence, penance and prayer. The eremitical life developed in the early centuries of the Church following the persecutions of the third and fourth centuries. Because of the hermit's deep spirituality, he was visited by individuals for advice. Hermits were the pioneer monks and gave rise to the religious life. Gradually, hermits were joined by others, and a transition was made from a solitary form of monastic existence to a modified community existence, often coming together for the celebration of the Eucharist. As the solitary life of hermits gradually evolved into a monastic community life, the great monastic leaders differed in their evaluation of the hermit's life. Basil stressed community life, while Benedict favored self-discipline. By the eleventh century, semi-eremitical orders such as the Carthusians and Cistercians flourished. This spiritual style of life has always succeeded more in the East. Today there is an awakening interest in the West.

Hermitages of Syria (medieval fresco)

Heroic Virtue • The exemplary practice of the four cardinal virtues (prudence, justice, temperance and fortitude) and the three theological virtues (faith, hope and charity) over an extended period of time out of just and worthy service. Proof of the practice of heroic virtue on the part of a Servant of God is considered a crucial part of the canonization process. (Cf. Cause; Blessed.)

Hesperinos • A Greek term meaning "pertaining to the evening." Hence, the liturgical office of Vespers in the Byzantine Church.

Hesychasm • Derived from the Greek term for tranquillity, silence or condition of rest, hesychasm is a method of interior prayer of the spirit characterized by a conscious and constant attitude and awareness of the Presence of God, a style of uninterrupted prayer as regular as the beating of the heart or breathing. This method of prayer is a part of the patrimony of the Eastern Church and is of great antiquity. It was transmitted by Eastern monks from master to disciple by word of mouth, by example and by spiritual direction, and was only committed to paper at the beginning of the eleventh century in a treatise attributed to Symeon the New Theologian. Some Western writers have fixed their attention on the external technique of this prayer, and some have criticized it as a form of spiritual yoga or rationalist asceticism with no correlation to contemplation in its authentic sense.

There is a certain physical aspect involved: procedures in the control of breathing, bodily posture and the rhythm of prayer. However, this external discipline is only an aid to concentration. The whole of one's attention must be given to the text of the short prayer, "O Lord Jesus Christ, Son of God" (as the person breathes in deeply), "have mercy on me, a sinner" (as the person exhales). This prayer, continually repeated at each drawing of breath, becomes to the practitioner, as it were, second nature. Far from rendering the interior life mechanical, it has the opposite effect, of freeing it and turning it toward contemplation by constantly driving away from the region of the heart all contagion of sin and every external thought or image; and this by the power of the Most Holy Name of Jesus. Thus this particular style of spiritual prayer makes the heart ready for the indwelling of grace by constantly guarding its interior disposition. This constant remembrance and perpetual prayer in the Name of Jesus is meant to produce in the practitioner the habit of loving God perfectly and without hindrance.

Hesychasts • Practitioners of hesychasm, usually applied to monks of the Eastern Church who lead a life of contemplation.

Hexaemeron (also Hexahemeron) • From the Greek, *hexaemeron* (or *hexhaemeron*) means literally six days; more specifically, it is the term for the narrative of the six days of creation recorded in the first chapter of Genesis. It is also the title of a poetic account of creation by St. Ambrose.

Hexapla • Greek for "sixfold." The designation given to an edition of the Old Testament worked up by Origen. It is thought to have been begun by Origen before he left Alexandria and was completed at Caesarea sometime around A.D. 245. It consisted of the Old Testament in Hebrew characters, a transliteration of the Hebrew into Greek, plus four Greek translations, those of Aquila, Symmachus, the Septuagint and Theodotion. These versions were arranged in parallel columns. In spite of the name — sixfold — part of the Old Testament is given in seven Greek versions, the four noted above and an added three. Because of the magnitude of this work, it is generally believed to have never been reproduced in its entirety. Parts of the work did circulate and manuscripts of various parts of it have survived to the present.

For further reading: D. C. Parker, "Hexapla of Origen, The," *Anchor Bible Dictionary,* 3:188-189.

Hexapteryga • In the Byzantine Rite, a fan representing a six-winged cherub, used after the Consecration to ventilate the Holy Body and Blood. Also called Ripidion.

Hexateuch • From the Greek for "six books." A term devised by biblical scholar Julius Wellhausen to designate the first six books of the Old Testament, from Genesis up to and including Joshua. This grouping sprang from the belief that all six books, like the Pentateuch, derive from the same array of literary sources. Modern scholarship tends to feel otherwise and prefers to distance Joshua from the first five books, preferring to link it with "Deuteronomic history."

Hierarch • Any member of the hierarchy may be called a "hierarch." In practice, though, while the term can apply to curial officials in the Latin Church, it usually refers to leaders of the Eastern Churches possessing episcopal status. (Cf. Canon Law, Eastern.)

Hierarchy • From the Greek *hierarchia* (holy rule), this word has been used since the early centuries of the Church to describe the ordered body of clergy which gives spiritual care to the faithful, governs the Church and guides the Church's mission in the world. The *hierarchy of order* consists of the Pope, bishops, priests and deacons. Through the sacrament of Holy Orders, their purpose is to carry out the sacramental, teaching and pastoral ministry of the Church. The *hierarchy of jurisdiction* consists of the Pope and the bishops by the divine institution of Our Lord Himself, for the pastoral governance of the faithful. This jurisdiction may be delegated by ecclesiastical mandate.

The hierarchy of the Church has a scriptural basis, which is apparent from the accounts of Our Lord choosing the Apostles (Mt 10:1-42; Mk 3:13-19; Lk 6:13-16), thus making them into a college, and he appointed St. Peter, one of their number, to be at the head (Jn 21:15-17). He commissioned them to make all people His disciples, and gave the Apostles authority to sanctify, teach and govern them (Mt 28:16-20; Mk 16:15; Lk 24:45-48; Jn 20:21-23). They were given a special outpouring of the Holy Spirit (Jn 20:22-23; Acts 1:8; 2:4); they transmitted this to others through the imposition of hands (1 Tm 4:14; 2 Tm 1:6-7), and this gift has been passed down through the ages to our own day.

Hieratikon • The prayer book of a priest in the Byzantine Rite. It contains the texts of the usual liturgical services, except for the Divine Liturgy (Mass) itself, which is found in a book called the *Leitourgikon.*

Hierodeacon • In the Byzantine Church, the title of a monk who has been ordained a deacon.

Hieromonk • A monk invested with the priesthood in the Eastern Church.

Hierurgia • A term derived from the Greek, meaning to act as priest or to perform some holy service. It is a kind of umbrella designation and may include the administration of the sacraments, the celebration of Mass or the imparting of a simple blessing.

High Priest • Although Exodus 28 has an account of the institution and garb of the high priest and Aaron is spoken of in that account as the first high priest, the office and person of the high priest emerge from the mists of antiquity into clear focus only in the post-exilic period. During this period, the high priest presided over the Great Council, the Sanhedrin and oversaw the formal worship at the Temple. Among his special prerogatives was the sole right to officiate at the liturgy of the Day of Atonement. On that day he alone could set foot in the Holy of Holies. It was the high priest, too, who represented the interests of the people before the foreign rulers who controlled Palestine at the time. The high priest was unquestionably the preeminent person in Palestinian Jewry in those years. In the latter years (from 37 B.C. onward) under the rule of the Romans and of the Herods, the high priesthood became a largely political office, manipulated by the civil authorities.

For further reading: Merlin D. Rehm, "Levites and Priests," *Anchor Bible Dictionary,* 4:297-310.

Hirmos • In the Byzantine Rite, an ancient Troparion which has become the model from which others have derived their rhythm and melody. The opposite of the Idiomelon. (Cf. Canon.)

History, Church • Ecclesiastical history is the theological discipline which studies "the growth in time and space of the Church founded by Christ" (Hubert Jedin). This study applies all the methods of secular historical scholarship, but in such a way as to subordinate these tools to the light of faith. For in this light, the Church is confessed to be a divine-human reality, an extension of the Incarnation itself, a mystery of the communion of human beings in Christ across time and culture.

As a visible society with a past and a history, the Church is naturally subject to historical study. But the Church is also a visible, social, historical institution that is also the mystical Body of Christ. In the light of faith, the Church's history is the history of the realization of salvation, the fulfillment of the divine plan from Pentecost to the *parousia*. As a visible institution, the Church is subject to historical observation. Historical explanations can be offered for development, for her engagement in the events of world and religious history and for the role of her leaders and membership.

Nonetheless, such observation and explanation are understood not to be exhaustive. The presence of the Holy Spirit directing the Church on her way through time can never be the object of complete historical observation and explanation. In a sense, the first exercise in ecclesiastical history occurs within the canon of Scripture in the Acts of the Apostles. But Eusebius of Caesarea (c. A.D. 260-c. 340) is generally regarded as the father of Church history. His *Ecclesiastical History* is the chief source of knowledge of Church history from apostolic times to his own day. Church history has continued to be the object of vigorous scholarship and investigation, particularly since the sixteenth century.

Hogan Schism • The Hogan Schism was a short-lived but intense episode in the history of the Church in America, particularly for the Church of Philadelphia. Father William Hogan, an Irish priest who apparently had been in conflict with his ecclesiastical superiors there, arrived in New York in 1819 but, without authorization, moved to Philadelphia (the see being then vacant) and ingratiated himself with the lay trustees of St. Mary's Cathedral.

Hogan's manner, at least at first, was winning, but his behavior was highly suspect. He came into conflict almost immediately with the newly-arrived but aged bishop of Philadelphia, Henry Conwell. Amid mounting evidence of immoral behavior on the part of Hogan, Conwell warned, then suspended Hogan. At this point, the trustees of St. Mary's, who still supported him, proposed Hogan as the new bishop of the city, an idea that was promptly rejected by Roman authorities. Hogan then intensified his attacks on the bishop and began finally to agitate for a separate (i.e., schismatic) Church in America. All this received wide play in the secular press of the day.

During the final phases of the conflict, the beleaguered Bishop Conwell (an unfortunate man already slipping into senility) made some rather minor concessions to the trustees of St. Mary's, only exacerbating the situation. These concessions, the subject of still more civil litigation, were repudiated by Rome and won for Conwell the invitation to spend his last years in retirement in the Eternal City.

At this point, however, Hogan's private life began to catch up with him, and he was suddenly forced to resign his position at St. Mary's. He dropped out of any active ministry and twice attempted marriage. He faded from the scene and became a proponent of anti-Catholic nativism, especially ironic considering his own foreign birth. After a brief appointment in the State Department, Hogan died in 1848, apparently unreconciled. Bishop Conwell, meanwhile, returned from Rome in even poorer health and was for all practical purposes replaced by his coadjutor bishop, Francis Patrick Kenrick, who was left to resolve the remaining problems.

Holiness • Principally an attribute of God. According to 1 Samuel 2:2, "There is none holy like the Lord," and according to the cry of the seraphim in Isaiah 6:3, "Holy, holy, holy is the Lord of hosts; the whole earth is full of his glory." Holiness refers to the complete separation of God from the sphere of the profane, the complete transcendence of God.

Individual human beings and groups of people can be holy by dedicating themselves fully to the holy God and by demonstrating the sincerity of that commitment by faithful observance of the commandments. Deuteronomy 7:6 explains that "you are a people holy to the LORD your God; the LORD your God has chosen you to be a people for his own possession, out of all the peoples that are on the face of the earth." Israel's holiness, the result of God's election of the Chosen People, demands that Israel's conduct reflect the grace of that election.

In the New Testament, St. Paul begins his letter to the Christians in Rome with the words, "To all God's beloved in Rome, who are called to be saints." "The saints," or "the holy ones," was the designation by which the earliest Christians often referred to each other. The First Letter of Peter underlines the reason for that designation, with the exhortation that "as he [God] who called you is holy, be holy yourselves in all your conduct; since it is written, 'You shall be holy, as I am holy' " (1:15-16). Peter quotes Leviticus 11:44-45 here, "I am the LORD your God; consecrate yourselves therefore, and be holy, for I am holy."

The *Catechism of the Catholic Church* underlines the universal vocation to holiness, stating: "All are called to holiness" (n. 2013). Citing Jesus' challenging words in Matthew 5:48, "Be perfect, as your heavenly Father is perfect," the *Catechism* explains these words with a quotation from the Second Vatican Council's Dogmatic Constitution on the Church (*Lumen Gentium*): "In order to reach this perfection the faithful should use the strength dealt out to them by Christ's gift, so that . . . doing the will of God in everything, they may wholeheartedly devote themselves to the glory of God and to the service of their neighbor. Thus the holiness of the People of God will grow in fruitful abundance, as is clearly shown in the history of the Church through the lives of so many saints" (n. 40).

For further reading: David P. Wright, "Holiness, (Old Testament)," *Anchor Bible Dictionary*, 3:237-249; Robert Hodgson, Jr., "Holiness (New Testament)," *Anchor Bible Dictionary*, 3:249-254.

Holiness Churches • A group of loosely related sects emerging from the late-nineteenth-century southern Appalachian Holiness revivals that preached the restoration of the pure "Church of God" against the encroaching modernism perceived in mainline Methodist, Baptist and Presbyterian churches and the secularism of the surrounding culture.

Accommodation to modernity is countered by a strict adherence to the Bible as infallible and a reaffirmation of broadly Protestant doctrines construed in the light of biblical notions, such as "entire sanctification," "baptism in the Spirit" and "speaking in tongues." Purity and authenticity are maintained by a sectarian withdrawal and isolation.

Representative groups of Holiness churches emerged from the preaching activities of A. J. Tomlinson (d. 1943) and his sons Homer and Milton of Cleveland, Tennessee. Chief among these are the Church of God (Cleveland), the Original Church of God, the Church of God of Prophecy and the Church of God (Huntsville, Alabama). Within the black community, the Holiness revival gave rise to the various Churches of God in Christ, and in Arkansas and Missouri, the Assemblies of God. Most, though not all, of these churches, are "pentecostal" (i.e., permitting speaking in tongues).

Holiness, Mark of the Church • With oneness, catholicity and apostolicity, holiness is confessed in the Apostles' and Nicene Creeds as one of the four marks or properties of the Church. The holiness of the Church arises formally from her constitution as a communion of faithful members under the headship of Christ Himself. In its theological essence, the Church is the vital communion of Christ and His members, thus constituted as the People of God. The institutional forms of the Church are themselves drawn into this holiness. Their purpose is to foster the sanctification of the Church's members. Although there is no disagreement about the essential holiness of the Church, reformation communities — in affirming the priesthood of all believers and rejecting the hierarchical constitution of the Church — generally reject the notion that she mediates holiness for her members. In addition, in contrast to Catholic doctrine, reformation communities affirm that the Church is the gathering of the elect. In the Catholic view, the Church comprises all those who are called to holiness, not only those who are predestined to it. It is the work of the Holy Spirit to sanctify the Church as a whole and her members.

Holocaust • One of the several types of sacrifice described in the Old Testament, the holocaust sacrifice was burned entirely on the altar. The English word "holocaust" derives from the Hebrew term *'olah*, which refers to an ascending offering. By burning the offering on the altar, the scent of the offering rose heavenward. Regulations for these burnt offerings are found in Leviticus 1. For example, verse 13 says of the offering of sheep or goats that "the priest shall offer the whole, and burn it on the altar; it is a burnt offering, an offering by fire, a pleasing odor to the LORD."

In modern times, the word "holocaust" has been used to describe the genocidal massacre of the Jews by the Nazis.

For further reading: Gary A. Anderson, "Sacrifice and Sacrificial Offerings," *Anchor Bible Dictionary*, 5:870-886.

Holy Alliance • The Holy Alliance was a remarkable treaty signed by Catholic Austria, Orthodox Russia and Protestant Prussia in 1815, which declared the intention of the signatory nations to settle future disputes in a spirit of Christian fraternity. After centuries of Machiavellian utilitarianism, the Holy Alliance, although only minimally effective, was a veritable breath of fresh air in the political history of Europe. In later years, several other nations became co-signers, but it may be noted that, due to a certain religious indifferentism (which was unnecessarily introduced into the document), the Papal States under Pope Pius VII were not signatories. History has looked rather favorably on this ultimately unsuccessful but laudable attempt to rediscover the fruits of religiously inspired peace and national cooperation.

Holy Communion • The sacrament of the Holy Eucharist, the Body and Blood of Jesus Christ received by the faithful, usually during Mass. The word "communion" indicates the union into which its recipients are drawn with God and with one another. They share the one Faith and the one salvation.

Holy Communion may be received under different species, that is, in the form of the consecrated Host alone, the Precious Blood alone or both. The Councils of the Church have stressed the doctrine that Christ is present, whole and entire, risen and alive, under the appearance of bread and also under the appearance of wine. No greater intimacy with Christ is possible in this life than that which comes from the worthy reception of Holy Communion.

The normal conditions under which one may legitimately or worthily receive Holy Communion are that one be a believing Catholic in a state of grace, and have the proper disposition toward the sacrament and the spiritual life. A fast from food of one

The Holy Family (from a Benin design)

hour's duration is also required as a sign of repentance, reverence and respect. To receive the Sacred Species unworthily is "profaning the body and blood of the Lord." Whoever does so "eats and drinks judgment upon himself" (1 Cor 11:27-29).

Finally, at the hour of death, Jesus in this sacrament becomes our "Viaticum," our Companion on our way to the next world. Thus the reception of Communion as death approaches is a great spiritual consolation and grace. (Cf. Eucharist, The.)

Holy Days • Also called days of precept, holy days are feasts of such importance in the liturgical calendar that attendance at Mass is required. The Code of Canon Law (Canons 1246-1248) discusses these, rightly beginning with Sunday, describing it as "the day on which the paschal mystery is celebrated in light of the apostolic tradition and is to be observed as the foremost day of obligation in the universal Church" (Canon 1246). It then lists the following to be observed: Christmas, Epiphany, Ascension, Corpus Christi, Mary Mother of God, Immaculate Conception, Assumption, St. Joseph, Sts. Peter and Paul, and All Saints. This list is the same as that given in the

1917 Code, with the feast of the Circumcision eliminated in favor of the restored title for January 1 — Mary, Mother of God. The present Code then states that "the conference of bishops can abolish certain holy days of obligation or transfer them to a Sunday with the prior approval of the Holy See" (Canon 1246). The United States bishops decided not to make the feasts of St. Joseph and Sts. Peter and Paul days of precept and transferred the solemnities of the Epiphany and Corpus Christi to Sundays.

Holy or Royal Doors • The double door in the center of the Ikonostasis. It only opens for a bishop, a priest or the deacon during the most solemn part of the celebration of the Divine Liturgy.

Holy Family • By this name is known the grouping of the sublime community comprised of Our Lord Jesus Christ, the Blessed Mother and her chaste spouse, St. Joseph. It is often referred to as the Holy Family of Nazareth as well. Since the individuals involved in this happy consortium were of such dignity and holiness, the Holy Family has always been regarded by the Church as the exemplar and model for all Catholic families and, by extension, as the exemplar of all persons living in community, whether active or contemplative: the loving faith, obedience and providence of the hard-working Joseph; the faith, love, obedience and strength of the Blessed Mother; the perfection of the Son of God made Man, Who submitted Himself in obedience to a human mother and foster father. Thus in the earthly trinity of Jesus, Mary and Joseph can be found a perfect model of all virtues, both personal and social. But not only were they holy, saintly and virtuous, they also lived a human life like ours which makes it possible for us to seek to imitate them and their virtues.

The feast of the Holy Family is celebrated on the Sunday which falls within the Octave of Christmas or, if no Sunday falls within the Octave, on December 30 (*Universales de Anno Liturgico et de Calendario*, n. 35, a).

Holy Father • This title of the Pope is the commonly shortened translation of the Latin title *Beatissimus Pater* (The Most Holy Father), and refers to his position as the spiritual father of all the Christian faithful. It came into English usage, when speaking of the Pope, in the latter part of the fourteenth century. (Cf. Father.)

Holy of Holies, The • The innermost compartment of the Temple building. At the entrance to the Temple stood an area called the *ulam* (vestibule, portico, porch). This led into the Temple proper, often referred to as the *hekhal*. It was at times spoken of as the "holy place," the "main room," the "nave." From this room, two double doors opened into the "holy of holies," a cube-shaped area which housed the Ark of the Covenant. Apparently it was kept in total darkness. Entry to it was barred to the faithful: only the high priest could set foot into it and then only seldom.

For further reading: Carol Meyers, "Temple, Jerusalem," *Anchor Bible Dictionary*, 6:350-369.

Holy Hour • An uninterrupted hour of prayer and meditation in the presence of the Blessed Sacrament, which may be exposed on the altar or reposed in the tabernacle. The inspiration for the Holy Hour is the comment of Jesus to His Apostle Peter in Jesus' Gethsemane agony: "So, could you not watch with me one hour?" (Mt 26:40). Thus the content of reflection in a Holy Hour is usually directed toward the Lord's passion.

A Holy Hour is an expression of faith in the Real Presence of Christ in the Holy Eucharist. Hence, Catholic parishes are obliged to offer regularly exposition of the Blessed Sacrament for adoration by the faithful. The quality of Eucharistic faith and devotion is the truest measure of a parish's overall spiritual health.

Holy Name of Jesus • This refers specifically to a feast in the Roman Rite which used to fall on the first Sunday after the Octave of Christmas, that is, between January 1 and the feast of the Epiphany on January 6. If there was no Sunday in between these two dates, the feast was observed on the second of January. First celebrated in the northern European nations of Germany, Belgium, England and Scotland, this feast in honor of the Holy Name of Our Lord was extended to the universal calendar of the Church by Pope Innocent XIII (1721-1741). It was suppressed by Pope Paul VI when he revised the Roman Calendar after Vatican II. The idea behind the feast remains, however, since to anyone who loves and respects the Name of Jesus, it is only natural to pay honor and homage to it, for the Name of Jesus ". . . is above every other name . . . that at the name of Jesus every knee should bow, in heaven and on earth and under the earth, and every tongue confess that Jesus Christ is Lord, to the glory of God the Father" (Phil 2:10-11).

Holy Office, Congregation of the • The Holy Office was the pre-Vatican II name for what is now known as the Congregation for the Doctrine of the Faith. Prior to being called the Holy Office, it was known as the Holy Roman and Universal Inquisition.

This congregation is charged with vigilance over matters of faith and morals. It studies theological issues and examines books and other theological writings for correctness. For a time, it also handled certain types of marriage cases, particularly Privilege of the Faith cases, as well as the process of laicization of priests. These duties have now been transferred to other Roman congregations.

Holy Oils • As one of the consecratory prayers for the oil of holy chrism recalls, oil is frequently mentioned in the Old Testament in connection with the commissioning of priests, prophets and kings. It is celebrated in the psalms as a sign of joy and gladness, and even the olive branch brought back by Noah's dove in Genesis as a sign of the Deluge's end was seen by the early Fathers of the Church as a sign of the peace and new life that sacramental anointing would bring in the sacraments of the New Covenant. Likewise, the descent of the Spirit upon Christ after His Baptism by John in the Jordan was taken to be the fulfillment of the promise that the Messiah would be anointed "with the oil of gladness above your fellows" (Ps 45:8). Christ sent His Apostles to anoint the sick (Mk 6:13), and the Apostle James tells the sick to have the presbyters of the Church do the same (Jas 5:14-15).

Accordingly, from the earliest days of the Church, oil has been used in the sacramental rites. For centuries the custom, retained in the present liturgical legislation, prescribes the consecration of holy chrism and the blessing of the oils of the catechumens and of the sick to take place at the Chrism Mass concelebrated by the bishop of his diocese with his presbyterate on the morning of Holy Thursday (or now on another day near Holy Thursday if necessary, for instance, because of distance and the approaching Triduum).

Holy Chrism is, traditionally, pure olive oil (though more recent legislation permits the use of oil from other plants, if necessary), mixed with balsam or perfume. Holy chrism is used to anoint the newly-baptized, to seal the candidates for Confirmation and to anoint the hands of presbyters and the heads of bishops at their ordination, as well as in the rites of anointing pertaining to the dedication of churches and altars.

The *Oil of Catechumens*, is used with candidates for Baptism in the ceremonies of prayer and exorcism prior to Christian Initiation and is optional at the end of the prayer of exorcism which precedes infant Baptism.

The *Oil of the Sick*, which a priest may bless in cases of necessity, is used, as its name indicates, to bring comfort and support to the infirm in the sacrament of the Anointing of the Sick.

According to the ancient tradition of the Latin Rite, the blessing of the Oil of the Sick takes place toward the end of the Eucharistic prayer, while the blessing of the Oil of Catechumens and the consecration of holy chrism occur after Communion. The Vatican II revision of the rite permits the entire rite of blessing and consecration to take place after the Liturgy of the Word.

The holy oils are kept in vessels called "stocks" or *ampullae* and are stored in an "aumbry," which is sometimes made in the form of a sanctuary "wall safe" or small sacristy "tabernacle." Beginning in 1990 in the dioceses of the United States, the Bishops' Committee on the Liturgy authorized a new Rite for the Reception of Holy Oils to be celebrated in parishes on Holy Thursday at the evening Mass of the Lord's Supper. The oils are carried in procession, placed on the altar and incensed together with the altar during the entrance rite. After the greeting, the celebrant mentions the oils and a brief formula explains the significance of each and the link which these oils provide sacramentally with the diocesan Church and its bishop. Then the oils are carried reverently to the place of reservation. Parish priests

Basilica of the Nativity, Bethlehem

contained within the Church of the Holy Sepulchre. Across from the city, on the Mount of Olives, are the Church of *Dominus Flevit*, where Our Lord was said to have wept over the city of Jerusalem, Gethsemane (the Church of All Nations) and the Sanctuary of the Ascension, where it is also thought Christ taught the Our Father. Included among the Holy Places are the site of the Temple, the Church of the Dormition of Our Lady and the Sanctuary of her Assumption.

The Crusades, of course, were waged largely to regain control of these Holy Places from the infidels. Since the thirteenth century, care of the Holy Places has been entrusted to the Order of Friars Minor, Franciscans, who also provide in the United States an opportunity of viewing a representation of the Holy Places at their Holy Land Shrine in Washington, D.C.

traditionally "carry the oils," meaning the Oil of the Sick, in a small, pocket-size "stock," a metal vessel with a screw-cap to which is often affixed a ring for ease in holding during emergency administrations of the sacrament.

Holy Places • Those sites in the Holy Land, modern Israel, associated with the life and ministry of Our Lord. In many cases, we must rely on tradition for the location of these places, which are so important for the faith and reverence of Christian believers, but for the most part biblical archaeology has confirmed the reliability of these traditions. Typically, the Holy Places would include the Basilica of the Annunciation in Nazareth and the Basilica of the Nativity in Bethlehem. In Jerusalem the most important holy places are the Cenacle (Upper Room), the Basilica of the *Ecce Homo* (once thought to be the site of Pilate's Praetorium), the *Via Dolorosa* (the original Way of the Cross to Calvary) and Calvary itself, together with the tomb of Jesus, both

Holy Roman Empire • Some date the beginning of this political entity to Christmas, A.D. 800, when Pope Leo III crowned Charlemagne as "Emperor ruling the Roman Empire," thus restoring the imperial dignity to the West. More properly the "Roman Empire" may be said to have been effectively established by Otto I (ruled 936-973). It was not called "Holy" until the reign of Frederick I Barbarossa (ruled 1152-1190). Never a unitary state in the modern sense, it was a federation of kingdoms, duchies, principalities and free cities, over which the emperor exercised loose authority. The office of emperor was, in theory, elective, but from the thirteenth century until the end of the empire, it was held by the Hapsburgs of Austria, with one exception. After the sixteenth century, the title of emperor was largely honorific. At its greatest extent the Holy Roman Empire included modern Germany, Austria, Switzerland, the Low Countries and parts of Italy, France, Czechoslovakia, Yugoslavia and Poland.

The existence of the empire continued to remind Europe of the dream of political unity which had been lost with the collapse of the Roman Empire. In the eighteenth century, the French philosopher Voltaire remarked that it was "neither Holy, nor Roman, nor an Empire." In 1806 Napoleon I abolished the empire. The Hapsburg emperors of Austria continued to regard themselves as the heirs of the Holy Roman Emperors until the collapse of that monarchy in 1918.

Holy Saturday • The Saturday of Holy Week. The Roman Missal notes that according to a most ancient tradition, the sacraments are not celebrated on this day (with the exception of Penance and emergency ministrations of Anointing or Viaticum). The Church keeps vigil at the tomb of the Lord, reflecting on His saving death and looking forward to His life-giving resurrection.

This does not mean, however, that the Church does not gather for prayer on this day. In the cathedral certainly, and in parish churches most fittingly, the Office of Readings and Morning Prayer are celebrated (perhaps at the time usually reserved for the celebration of the Eucharist from which the Church fasts on this day "when her Bridegroom is taken away from her"). Midday Prayer and Vespers are also celebrated, since the Easter Vigil cannot begin until after sundown. In preparation for Christian Initiation at the vigil, preparatory rites may be celebrated with the catechumens. Wherever possible the paschal fast (not the disciplinary fast of Lent, which ends on Holy Thursday, but the anticipatory fast which is observed universally on Good Friday) is prolonged until the vigil.

Holy See • The moral and spiritual authority, jurisdiction and sovereignty exercised by the successor of St. Peter, the Pope, through the central government of the Catholic Church. While localized in and near Vatican City, the Holy See is not synonymous with Vatican City State, the latter serving as the international guarantee of the independence essential to the Holy See's mission. The word "see" comes from the Latin word *sedes*, "chair," the ancient symbol of authority, and, as such, refers to the locus of every bishop's pastoral government over his diocese. The modifier "Holy," or sometimes "Apostolic," is added to denote the prominence traditionally rendered St. Peter and his successors in their universal jurisdiction over the entire Church.

The organs used by the Supreme Pontiff in his pastorate of the Church universal are the Secretariat of State, the Congregations, Tribunals and Pontifical Councils, all sometimes called "dicasteries," and all sometimes grouped under the title "Roman Curia," whose duties are outlined in Canons 330-367, and elaborated in the Apostolic Constitution *Pastor Bonus* of Pope John Paul II on June 28, 1988. An integral element of the Holy See is also the system of representation to the Catholic Church of a given nation, as well as to that nation's government, through apostolic nuncios and delegates. As such, the Holy See is the oldest diplomatic sovereignty active in international affairs, contributing the moral voice without which true diplomacy becomes ineffective. Over one hundred sixty nations have formal diplomatic relations with the Holy See, including the United States and Canada.

Holy Sepulcher in Jerusalem, The •
"Accordingly, on the very site which witnessed the Savior's sufferings, a new Jerusalem was constructed, over against the one so celebrated of old. . . . It was opposite this city that the emperor now began to rear a monument to the Savior's victory over death, with rich and lavish magnificence. And it may be that this was that second and new Jerusalem spoken of in the predictions of the prophets. . ." (Eusebius, *Vita Constantini*, 3.33).

Eusebius here described the intention and work of the Emperor Constantine who initiated and completed the first Church of the Holy Sepulcher in Jerusalem, dedicated in A.D. 335.

The site, originally used for earlier Jewish burials, had been covered over by Hadrian's temple of Venus, built during the imperial construction of the pagan Jerusalem, Aelia Capitolina (A.D. 135). The temple was destroyed by the Emperor Constantine in 326, which revealed the Tomb of Christ, along with the True Cross and other relics of the death of the Lord. Immediately, Constantine instructed Bishop Macarius of Jerusalem to erect a magnificent structure to enshrine the sites of the Lord's death and resurrection.

In his *Vita Constantini*, Eusebius gives us a detailed image of the Constantinian Basilica and the various structures within. The entire building was a massive rectangle, which housed the major edifices and shrines: two open courtyards, or atria, the basilica proper, the Rock of Calvary and the shrine of the Sepulcher, known as the Anastasis.

From the colonnaded main market road, the pilgrim entered by the eastern façade, passing through a large, rectangular atrium, "open to the pure air of heaven." Passing further westward through the main portico, one entered the basilica proper, called the Martyrium, or place of witness. The basilica was a typical Roman affair, rectangular, with central and four side aisles, terminating at the west with a semicircular apse. The walls and floors of the church were adorned with marble, while the beamed ceiling was coffered and sculpted, overlaid with gold, which "caused the entire building to glitter as if it were with rays of light."

The pilgrim was drawn westward by the procession of marble columns to the sanctuary, housed in the apse or "Hemisphere," as Eusebius termed it. Here was placed the altar, enshrined by the apse, and the Rock of Calvary, surrounded by a metal grille and rising approximately twelve feet from the ground. On the far western side of the second atrium was the Anastasis, a large, round and domed structure housing the Sepulcher of Christ.

The present-day structure is the product of centuries of destruction and rebuilding. The entire monument was set ablaze in 614 during the Persian invasion under Chosroes II. In 935 a mosque was built on the site of the eastern atrium, and in 1010 the edifice was destroyed, this time by Muslim forces under Caliph Hakim. By 1048, various smaller churches had been created in place of the original structure to house the holy places once contained within Constantine's building. These remained until 1149, when a new Romanesque church was built by the Christian crusaders, incorporating into the larger edifice the Calvary Rock and the interior atrium of the Constantinian monument. Another fire destroyed much of that basilica in 1808, causing the rotunda to collapse in upon the Tomb itself. A new monument above the actual Tomb was constructed in 1810, when the present church was built by the Greeks and Armenians, to replace the one destroyed by fire. The present dome and rotunda date from 1868, with the construction financed by Turkey, France and Russia.

Today, the Holy Sepulcher is housed within the small shrine built in 1810, under the rotunda of the main church. This shrine measures only twenty-six feet long by eighteen feet wide, having a slightly rounded apse at its west end, capped by a small dome. The monument is built of Palestine breccia of red and yellow hues. The severity of the exterior walls is enlivened only by an array of pilasters, while the eastern entrance is relieved by three religious pictures.

One gains access through the one small door in the eastern façade. The first chamber, known as the Chapel of the Angel, is revered as the place where the angel rested while awaiting the arrival of the holy women and the Apostles at the tomb following the Resurrection. Stooping, one passes through a low entranceway into the Tomb itself. It is a tiny room, measuring seven feet in length, six feet in width, and seven and one-half in height. The rock of the Tomb itself has been sheathed in white marble, lest the faithful carve it to pieces and cart it away. Icons, hanging lamps, candles and offerings of flowers enliven this otherwise stark and unpretentious interior of the original Sanctuary of the Resurrection.

The entire structure of the Basilica of the Holy Sepulcher is a hodge-podge of architectural styles, fragments from previous monuments, buildings and shrines, much of which is under constant restoration and reconstruction. The architectural disharmony is echoed by that of the various Christian Churches which control sections of the Church. The Sepulcher is divided among various Christian Churches, primarily the Latins, Greeks, Armenians, Copts and Syrian Jacobites.

Another site, known as Gordon's Calvary, was declared to be the true location of the Lord's crucifixion by Otto Thenius in 1849. It is today a popular tourist site, offering a recently constructed rendering of an artist's imagined Sepulcher. Various Protestant communions hold this to be the true Calvary, even though there is no archaeological evidence at all to support this view.

For further reading: Oliver Nicholson, "Holy Sepulcher, Church of the," *Anchor Bible Dictionary*, 3:258-260.

Holy Sepulcher, Knights of • The origin of the Equestrian Order of the Most Holy Sepulcher of Jerusalem can be traced back to the First Crusade in 1099. The foundation received the approval of Pope Callistus II in 1122. The aim of the Knights was to defend the Church universal, defend the city of Jerusalem, guard the Basilica of the Holy Sepulcher, watch over pilgrims and fight the Muslims. After the Knights were driven out of Jerusalem in 1244, the order went through several transformations. They were reestablished in 1847 by Pope Pius IX, and their most recent constitutions were approved by Pope Paul VI in 1977. The order comprises five grades, all of which may be awarded to women. The grand master is a cardinal, and he is named by the Pope.

Holy Souls: See Purgatory

Holy Spirit • The third Person of the Holy Trinity, distinct from, but consubstantial, coequal and coeternal with the Father and the Son. The Holy Spirit is God in the fullest sense and therefore is not generated, but proceeds from the Father and the Son by a single spiration (Latin, *spirare*, to breathe).

The doctrine of the Spirit gradually unfolds in the Old Testament as an instrument of divine action in the created order. The Spirit of God is operative at the creation (Gn 1:2), and is seen as being present in the activities of such warriors as Joshua (Dt 34:9) and the prophets (cf. Is 61:1). In the New Testament, teaching about the Holy Spirit is further developed. It was by the "overshadowing" of the Spirit that the Blessed Virgin conceived Our Lord (Lk 1:35). The Spirit descended upon Christ at His Baptism (Mk 1:10), and strengthened Him against Satan in the wilderness (Mk 1:12). St. John's Gospel (14:26; 15:26) describes Him as the "Counselor" or "Paraclete" (advocate), and it is revealed that the Spirit's fullest mission will take place after the glorification of Jesus. It was after the Resurrection that the Apostles received the Holy Spirit from Our Lord, with the power to forgive sins (Jn 20:22-23). At Pentecost the Holy Spirit descended fully upon the Church (Acts 2:1-13), and the Apostles were conscious of the Spirit's direct operation in their activities (Acts 11:12; 16:6). The Holy Spirit took part in the Apostles' deliberations (Acts 15:28), and was conveyed to others by the imposition of the Apostles' hands (Acts 8:17; 19:6). The Spirit has an important place in the theology of St. Paul, with his frequent contrasting between life in the Spirit and life in the flesh, and his description of the many gifts of the Spirit (cf. 1 Cor 12:4ff.).

The Holy Spirit is the expression of God's boundless love, with the essential work of making the faithful more holy. This begins at Baptism, when the Spirit endows the soul with sanctifying grace. It continues throughout the life of the believer as he grows in faith and love, and exhibits the "gifts of the Holy Spirit," which are wisdom, understanding, counsel, fortitude, knowledge, piety and fear of the Lord (Is 11:2-3).

Holy Spirit, Sins Against the • Among these sins are: (1) despair concerning the possibility of salvation; (2) presumption of God's mercy and forgiveness; (3) denial of the truths of faith; and (4) final impenitence and refusal to turn to God. Sins against the Holy Spirit are most grave because they reject the dignity of the One sent by the Father to sanctify us and restore us to full union with Him. While other sins might be against one's neighbor, sins against the Holy Spirit are immediately and proximately against God; because of this, sins against the Holy Spirit undermine the entirety of Christian life, for neither faith, hope nor charity are possible when God is directly and immediately rejected through these sins.

Ultimately, sins against the Holy Spirit are sins against faith, and prayer for the gift of faith is the best means of avoiding them.

Holy Thursday • Thursday of Holy Week. In the morning the Chrism Mass is celebrated at the diocesan cathedral (unless pastoral necessity requires that it be moved to another day or place). This Mass is concelebrated by the bishop and his presbyterate as a sign of their unity in the priestly service of God's people, to which service they renew their ordination commitment after the Liturgy of the Word.

All Masses without a congregation are forbidden on this day, and ideally the only Mass celebrated in parish churches is the Evening Mass of the Lord's Supper. The new *Ceremonial of Bishops* describes this Mass as "first of all, the memorial of the institution of the Eucharist, that is, of the memorial of the Lord's Passover, by which under sacramental signs He perpetuated among us the sacrifice of the New Law. The Mass of the Lord's Supper is also the memorial of the institution of the priesthood, by which Christ's mission and sacrifice are perpetuated in the world. In addition this Mass is the memorial of that love by which the Lord loved us even to death" (n. 297), this last dimension being manifested in a dramatic way by the foot washing which follows (optionally) the Liturgy of the Word.

The Evening Mass of the Lord's Supper may begin with the solemn reception in the parish church of the holy oils blessed previously by the bishop at the cathedral. The homily expounds the three above-mentioned themes as noted in the *Ceremonial*. The foot washing may follow. Enough Hosts are consecrated at this Mass to provide for the people's Communion on Good Friday, and at the end of the Mass the Blessed Sacrament is borne in solemn procession to the place of repose, where solemn adoration follows for a suitable period of time up until midnight.

Holy Water • This term refers to water originally blessed at the Easter Vigil for the Baptism of catechumens and infants that night. This blessed "Easter water" is kept throughout the Easter season and is used at the Rite of Blessing and sprinkling with holy water at Sunday Mass or for baptisms celebrated during this season. In the former rites for Baptism, this blessed water was kept in the baptistery for any baptisms that took place from Easter to the following Holy Week. For symbolic and hygienic reasons, in the present Rite of Baptism (outside the Easter Season), water is blessed each time Baptism is celebrated. The important symbolism in using water for Baptism is brought out in a striking way in the blessing prayers in the baptismal ritual. The hygienic reason behind the change is that the former rite required the pouring of oils into the water and these components often led to water that appeared rancid or stale, as opposed to fresh and life-giving.

Holy Water Font • Receptacle at the entrance to churches containing holy water so that upon entering, the faithful can dip their fingers into the font and bless themselves by making the sign of the cross. This symbolic gesture signifies the renewal of one's baptismal commitment. Another way of doing this is to bless oneself at the Mass's introductory Rite of Blessing and

sprinkling with holy water (formerly called *Asperges*). In some contemporary churches the holy water font in the church vestibule is actually the church's baptistery.

Holy Week, Liturgy of: See **Triduum, Paschal**

Holy Year • Customarily declared every twenty-five years by the reigning Pontiff. In 1974 Pope Paul VI issued the bull *Apostolorum limina*, announcing the Holy Year of 1975 as a year of "renewal and reconciliation." In accord with established Catholic custom for holy years, the Pope granted a plenary indulgence to those who made a pilgrimage to one of the patriarchal basilicas of Rome. Additional indulgences are specified in accord with the special faculties granted from the Apostolic Penitentiary. On the occasion of this particular holy year, two Eucharistic prayers for Reconciliation were added to the Missal, as was a Mass formula for the Mass of Reconciliation.

At certain other times the Pope can decree the observance of another holy year. For example, Pope John Paul II decreed that the "year" beginning with the solemnity of the Annunciation in 1983 and ending with the solemnity of Easter in 1984 should be a special holy year in commemoration of the redemption. He decreed that one of the themes of the year was sacramental reconciliation because this theme was taken up in the Synod of 1983.

Home-Schooling • The education of children is one of the most basic duties of parents. Home-schooling is the process by which parents choose not to delegate that responsibility to an organized school system, but rather assume direct control over their children's education themselves. Estimates on the breadth of this movement in the United States vary, but range from 500,000 to over one million students now being educated in all subjects at home. The majority of children are in grades Kindergarten through nine.

What is today called home-schooling is actually the way education was achieved for many centuries. Compulsory mass education of children did not gain acceptance in the United States until late in the nineteenth century, when it was utilized as a method for assimilating large numbers of poorly educated immigrants into American society. The impressive parochial school system established by the Church in the United States served a similar interest, but with the additional goal of forming young Catholics in the Faith. It has been suggested, however, that the size and admitted success of both the public and private school systems during those years led, over time, to a lessening of the recognition by parents (and society) that the education of children was first and foremost the responsibility of parents.

Several factors over the last quarter of a century have led to a major resurgence in home-schooling. Deteriorating academic performance in many public school systems, combined with often severe disciplinary problems in those schools, have no doubt contributed to the search for educational alternatives. This seems to have been an especially important element in the return to home-education among American Protestants. Likewise, the rising cost of private education, despite generous if burdensome subsidies from Church leaders, along with a marked reduction in the visible presence of religious personnel within those schools, has worked to reduce their original attractiveness in many instances.

On the other hand, recent developments in educational techniques and greatly improved technological aids have made home-centered education considerably more manageable than was the case not many years ago. Many Catholic parents also cite an enhanced, postconciliar appreciation of their roles as Christian parents as a factor which motivated their decision to educate their children at home. The rise of professional organizations promoting home-schooling and the appearance of many social support groups has also eased the apprehensiveness of many parents initiating home-education.

The speed with which home-schooling has spread, even among Catholics, has of course taken some civil and ecclesiastical authorities by surprise, in a few cases leading to disputes and even to litigation. It seems clear, however, that almost without exception, these matters are resolved in favor of the parental choice to home-educate, provided that accurate records are kept for civil purposes along with standard evaluations of the academic progress of the child, and provided that, for religious purposes, parents see to the regular sacramental education of their children in accord with the teachings of the Church.

Homiletics • That sacred science which provides the principles for effective preaching of the Word of God.

Homily • The homily is the most important form of preaching. It is the address or sermon given after the Gospel during the celebration of Mass. A homily is recommended at all Masses and is required at Masses celebrated on Sundays and holy days of obligation. It is forbidden for anyone but a bishop, priest or deacon to give the homily, and it is strongly recommended that the celebrant of the liturgy also give the homily, rather than another sacred minister.

Since the revised Code made provision for those other than sacred ministers to preach on certain occasions, it was hoped by some that this would include preaching the homily. An authentic reply from the Code

Commission indicated that this could not be done (cf. Canon 767).

Homoousios and Homoiousios • *Homoousios* (Greek for consubstantial) is the term accepted at the Council of Nicaea (A.D. 325) and incorporated into the Nicene Creed to affirm the full divinity of the Son, as He shares the divine substance of His Father. By the 360s, *homoousios* was also applied to the Holy Spirit. In contrast, Cyril of Alexandria taught that the Son was merely like, *homoiousios*, the Father. As Harnack remarked, never has so much rested on the presence or absence of a single iota, the Greek letter that distinguishes the two words; hence, the English expression: "not an iota of difference."

Hood • A conical, flexible and brimless headdress which, when worn, covers the entire head, except for the face. It is either a separate garment (as in the Franciscan habit) or is part of a cloak. The latter may be short, like a shoulder cape (as in the Dominican habit). At other times, the hood may be attached to a long cape, as in the case of the liturgical cope and the cappa of certain religious orders. In this day and age, the hood is usually associated with orders made up of contemplatives, monks as well as nuns, and of mendicant orders.

Hope • The virtue infused by sanctifying grace that gives assurance of salvation, moves the individual to place one's faith in God and brings one to perform morally good actions.

For Christians, Jesus Christ is the focus of hope and His resurrection is the sign that Christian hope is not futile or empty. Traditionally, hope was individualistic and oriented toward future life, but in recent decades, a more communal and practical approach has been given to Christian hope. Hope is seen as the ultimate source of faith and charity. It causes Christians to show charity to the poor because they are the most esteemed by the One Who conquered death. Christ gives hope in our struggle against hatred, sin and evil because He was victorious by His fidelity and obedience to the Father. Christian hope is thus a more profound hope than is that of other world-views. It challenges atheism, secularism and rationalism to provide hope in our struggle against hatred, evil and death. Catholicism does not explain away the domain of evil which holds sway in our world, but it provides hope for overcoming and escaping it through the grace and saving actions of Jesus Christ.

Horologion • A term derived from the Greek meaning, "book of hours." It closely parallels the Roman Breviary and contains the ordinary portions of the Church year.

Hosanna • A Hebrew imperative meaning, "Grant your salvation!" (cf. Ps 118:25); in time, the term came to be used as a form of exultant greeting and acclaim, as in Our Lord's triumphal entry into Jerusalem on Palm Sunday (Mt 21:9, Mk 11:9-10, Jn 12:13). Isidore of Seville explains its liturgical use as having the understood object of "your people" or "the whole world" (Isidore of Seville, *Etymologiae*. VI:19, 2223). It is used in this sense in the *Sanctus* at Mass (both in Latin and in the vernacular) and in the traditional Palm Sunday hymn, *Pueri Hebraeorum*.

For further reading: Marvin H. Pope, "Hosanna," *Anchor Bible Dictionary*, 3:290-291.

Hosea, Book of • His prophetic activity was a continuation of the work of Amos and is directed to the people of the northern kingdom. It extends over a long period in the eighth century, probably ending before the fall of Samaria in 721 B.C.

Israel enjoyed prosperity in the eighth century B.C., but much of its wealth was gained by social injustice and was spent on frivolous pleasures. True religion was forgotten, with many of the Jews embracing the licentious worship of Baal. Many of the priests had become corrupt, negligent and avaricious. The external rites were carried on, but with no inner spirit of love.

Hosea himself was a married man, and he envisions Yahweh as the husband of Israel. Since his own wife had been unfaithful to him, he found it easy to empathize with Yahweh, forsaken by His Chosen People, and much of his writing employs this comparison. Hosea makes it clear that God does expect fidelity of His people, that He is grievously offended by their sins, but that He is ever ready to forgive them and receive them back.

For further reading: Dennis J. McCarthy, S.J., and Roland E. Murphy, O.Carm., "Hosea," *New Jerome Biblical Commentary*, 217-228; C. L. Seow, "Hosea, Book of," *Anchor Bible Dictionary*, 3:291-297.

Host • Originally referring to any victim (Latin, *hostia*) used in sacrifice to a divinity (in pagan lands, to their gods), but more specifically to God. As such, Christ the perfect Sacrifice is also the perfect and spotless Victim, or Host. By extension and intrinsic association — as designated by Christ Himself — the bread that is used at the Eucharistic Sacrifice of the Mass, the unbloody reenactment of the bloody Sacrifice of the Cross on Calvary, is also signified by this term. Strictly speaking, then, this bread which will receive consecration is not yet a "host" and becomes this only after the Consecration and in view of its consummation at Holy Communion.

Hosts: See Sabaoth

Hours, Book of • To be distinguished from the Liturgy of the Hours, these were devotional books used by lay people who could not participate in the celebration of the Liturgy of the Hours (because the liturgy was in Latin or because they lived far from a church or oratory where the hours were observed). Such books were popularized during the thirteenth century and were frequently commissioned by rather wealthy people. The resulting books contained prayers of popular devotion to be recited at the seven canonical hours of the day; they were also most usually works of fine calligraphy and artistic illumination. Chief among the persons revered in these prayers and in the art work of these books is the Blessed Virgin Mary. Books of Hours played a significant role in late medieval popular piety, as well as in the fabric of medieval social life.

Hours, Little • The little hours, also known as the minor hours, were the four lesser sections of the Divine Office. Originally, they were chanted or recited at the portions of the day from which they received their names. Later it became common for the little hours to be recited or chanted either together or at two separate times. The little hours were Prime (first), Terce (third), Sext (sixth) and None (ninth). They consisted of a hymn, three psalms, a brief Scripture passage and the prayer of the day. When the Divine Office was revised, the little hours were dropped and replaced by a section now referred to as Midday Prayer.

Huguenots • The French Calvinists of the sixteenth and seventeenth centuries were called by this name, though the origins of the name itself are disputed and unclear.

From the time of Calvin onward, the Huguenots grew in number and strength in France and soon assumed political dimensions. Their members were drawn from all strata of society, including the nobility. The Huguenots were generally persecuted by the French monarchy, with both religious and political motives intertwined.

The most famous massacre occurred on August 23-24, 1572, St. Bartholomew's Day, when perhaps three or four thousand men in Paris alone are said to have died. The event was actually a conspiracy on the part of Catherine de' Medici to protect herself from being exposed as the perpetrator of a plot to kill Admiral Gaspard Coligny. Even so, the Protestants considered it a Catholic move against them.

For the monarchy, religious unity was regarded as necessary for the survival of the kingdom, and the Huguenot-fortified towns with garrisons were feared as "states within the state." After a series of struggles and concessions, King Henry IV, himself recently converted to Catholicism, granted toleration to the Huguenots in the famous Edict of Nantes (1598), which was to continue until its revocation in 1685 by Louis XIV.

At the time the Edict of Nantes was proclaimed, the Huguenot minority numbered about 1.2 million adherents, or a good twelfth of the total population of France. As early as the time of Calvin himself, the Reformed were advised to emigrate rather than practice their religion in secret. After the revocation of the Edict (which Pope Innocent XI, knowing the motives of the king, did not celebrate with the usual *Te Deum* until a full year later), emigration became widespread, and perhaps two to three hundred thousand left France after 1685. They settled in North America, South Africa, Holland and England. Their absence from France upset the economy, since they took their wealth with them. Forced conversions prepared the way for religious relativism and indifferentism in the eighteenth century. Painful and dangerous, the condition of the Protestants remained a constant source of unrest for the remainder of the *ancien régime*. Even the king had to admit the revocation was a failure, and large pockets of Huguenot resistance remained in France. The revocation, furthermore, was beyond doubt one of the causes of the French Revolution. Some of the Huguenot rights were restored in 1787, but full equality under the law was not granted until the Napoleonic Code.

Human Acts • Actions done with deliberation, free consent and knowledge. Human acts are distinguished from acts done without knowledge, freedom or consent.

Nonhuman acts are those over which the person has no control or which are purely spontaneous. But human acts are those over which the person has control, and they derive from uniquely human principles; because of that, they are expressions of the very nature of the person. In a human act, the person reaches out either to a good or to what is perceived to be a good, and the sort of good that is sought by the person who performs a human act defines the moral character of the person. In a human act, the agent implicitly affirms the norm of morality by volitionally moving toward a good and away from an evil; it is through the performance of morally good human acts that we perfect and fulfill ourselves *qua* persons. Conscious, free, deliberate and knowledgeable acts make us better or worse, and when one performs a morally good human act, one follows the call and summons to goodness. As creation serves the human person, human acts oriented to what is inherently good focus creation on the good, and bring material creation to participate in what is truly good.

Human Dignity • The value or worth of the human that is unique and distinctive. Classical Christian thought asserted that the human person was the highest of all created beings because created in the image of God. Of all the material creatures, the human person alone possesses a spiritual nature that was free, intellectual and capable of free and knowledgeable moral action. Because of this spiritual nature, the human person is a "microcosm," a miniature universe, possessing all of the basic elements of the cosmos: inanimate matter, vegetative and animal natures and a spiritual nature. The intelligent and free spiritual nature of the person gives the person dominion and superiority over all material creation.

More modern understandings of the worth and dignity of the human person have not denied these previous assertions, but have stressed the role of human freedom in establishing our unique human worth and dignity. Unlike other beings that are burdened with their various determinations, the human person is not bound by prior objective restraints and has a unique capacity for indefinite self-determination. Contemporary articulations of the nature of human worth and dignity have stressed the human person's capacity for self-determination and ability to hear the Word of God spoken and to respond to that Word.

The Second Vatican Council affirmed the human dignity on the basis of the person's possession of a conscience and on the ability to respond to it: "Deep within his conscience man discovers a law which he has not laid upon himself but which he must obey. Its voice, ever calling him to love and to do what is good and to avoid evil, tells him inwardly at the right moment: do this, shun that. For man has in his heart a law inscribed by God. His dignity lies in observing this law, and by it he will be judged" (GS 16). Contemporary Catholic understandings of man have also emphasized that the human person, alone among all material creatures, is immortal in nature.

Human Life International • Founded by Father Paul Marx, O.S.B., in 1981, Human Life International has four purposes: to protect the unborn, the elderly and the handicapped; to strengthen family life; to encourage chastity; and to promote the practice of natural family planning. Its apostolate includes research, education and service programs, and it seeks to give Catholic clarification to those issues which have an impact upon human life.

Humanae Vitae • The encyclical issued by Pope Paul VI on July 29, 1968, which condemned the use of artificial measures to prevent births. The encyclical is not only in harmony with the teachings of the Second Vatican Council, but also with the long-standing teachings of the Church concerning the intrinsic immorality of artificial means of contraception.

This encyclical created extraordinary controversy. Large numbers of theologians openly protested it, and it became the primary source of division in the Church after the Second Vatican Council. Many rejected the total ban on contraceptive practices and held that dissent was morally legitimate. A virtual schism has resulted from this encyclical, but this has not deterred the Church from continuing this teaching. The encyclical held that the moral malice of contraceptive acts lies in the deliberate turning against human life and the intention to bring to doom a being on an immediate trajectory toward human life.

However, the final verdict on this encyclical and its judgment against contraception may not have been reached yet, for over the years many who were previously critical of it have come to see the truthfulness of its assertions and have come to support it. The primary cause of this change of attitude seems to have been the sexual revolution which contraception made possible. This moral revolution has proven to be a nightmare for many persons and families and a serious problem for our society. In the wake of this revolution, widespread marital breakup and epidemics of sexually transmitted diseases have erupted in recent decades. Such widespread epidemics had been previously unknown, and it seems that these are in large part attributable to the promiscuity permitted by the new contraceptives.

Pope Pius XII, author of *Humani Generis*

Opinion about contraceptives also appears to be changing because of the increasing evidence that they are exceedingly dangerous to women. An encyclical which seemed to be foolishness at the time of its promulgation is now being increasingly viewed as a statement of wisdom and insight.

Humani Generis • An encyclical issued by Pope Pius XII in 1950 and bearing the full title, *Warnings against Attempts to Distort Catholic Truth.* Reflecting a mid-century assessment of twentieth-century Catholic theology, the encyclical is perceptive in its delineation of the challenge posed for Christian theology by the appropriation of the thought-forms of modernity. The encyclical insists on the necessity of revelation for our knowledge of God's intentions for us. While applauding the results of modern exegesis, the encyclical stresses the importance of interpreting the Scriptures within the context of the Catholic doctrinal and theological tradition. The encyclical accepts the plausibility of evolutionary theory as an account of biological development, but rejects relativistic evolutionism in philosophy. Overall, the encyclical insists on the integrity of Catholic doctrine and cautions against "accommodationism" in appropriating the results of modern thought.

Humanism • A historical movement among nobility of the fourteenth and fifteenth centuries to justify the Renaissance. This movement generated a scholarly and religiously neutral approach to ancient culture, an approach that was independent of Scholasticism. Petrarch, its founder, sought to "humanize" the virtues of the ancient Romans. These humanist views came to dominate the private culture of the aristocratic and ecclesiastical courts in the fifteenth century, and by the time of Erasmus it dominated European culture.

Humanism revived the controversy of the relationship between pagan culture and Christian culture based on Revelation. Erasmus sought to develop a Christian philosophy by going back to Scholastic predecessors, as is seen in his attempt to uncover the original texts of the Bible, and this effort paved the way for the Reformation. The Reformers were absolutely confident of having been grasped by the Word of God and stood in contrast to the humanists. The Reformers ended independent humanism, for they permitted no religiously neutral forces.

Humanism reemerged in another form in post-Jansenist France, seeking to reconcile the claims of independent self-understanding under the rubric of reason with revelation. Humanism often rationalized theology against religion, but Lessing and Kant advanced the controversy significantly by their study of the movement of the human spirit as an aspect of religion. However, it was eighteenth-century aesthetic theory and history of philosophy reacting against the rationalism of the Enlightenment that gave a new standard for autonomous self-understanding: the "humanism" of the Greeks. This new approach, which gave much more emphasis to the aesthetic aspects of ancient culture, came to dominate middle-class culture up to the twentieth century.

Humanism was united to politics and economics through the work of Marx and Lenin, and the state was given the task of eliminating "dehumanizing" alienation from society and culture. Contemporary "existentialist" philosophy also sees itself as humanistic but envisions itself as a reaction against Marxist humanism. Sartre releases human freedom from any extrinsic norms, and this independent freedom tests all moral norms. This counteracts the arbitrariness of Marxism, but it spurred the Heideggerian egocentric approach to humanism. Individual selfhood is integrated into the authentic self of being for him, which is in marked contrast to classical humanism.

Christian humanism asserts that true human existence involves the eschatological transformation of humanity by God. It does not see Christianity itself as an alien force imposed on humanity, and it regards its own development as the authentic development of humanity. Many Christian humanists have sought to reconcile Christian salvation history with evolution and Christian eschatology and Marxism. Christianity confronts atheistic humanism with the claim that humanity has never been able to achieve its destiny because it has denied the historical and interpersonal character of our human striving and because it has denied the role of religion in human development. Recognizing this historical and interpersonal character of humanity, Christian humanism regards Jesus Christ as essential for full human flourishing because of His historical and interpersonal character.

Humanitarianism • The ethical and social philosophy focused on promotion of human happiness. While human happiness has often been promoted by Christian faith and love, nonetheless traditional humanitarians would have grave reservations about Christianity, since Christian love of neighbor is ultimately undertaken from the motive of love of God in Christ, rather than solely for love of human beings. Humanitarianism treats human happiness as its own final end without reference to any further end such as loving and serving God. Since Christian faith acknowledges the duty to love the neighbor for the sake of the love of God, the humanitarian sees Christianity as ultimately unfaithful to human happiness.

Several Catholic thinkers (for example, Jacques Maritain in *Integral Humanism*, Henri de Lubac in *The Drama of Atheist Humanism*) and Popes (especially Pope John Paul II in his encyclical *Redemptor Hominis, The Redeemer of Man*) have attempted to show that humanitarianism undermines human happiness by cutting men off from the only possible source of human happiness, God, whereas God's love for us in Christ authentically promotes human happiness.

Humeral Veil • The humeral veil, or shoulder veil as its Latin roots denote, is a scarf-like liturgical parament about eight or nine feet in length and two to three feet in width, worn over the shoulders for certain liturgical functions. Since it is most often used in conjunction with the cope, the material and style usually match the latter. Already in use in the seventh century, the humeral veil is worn out of reverence when certain sacred objects, such as relics, are carried in procession or when the faithful are blessed with them. It is also used to hold the monstrance at Benediction or processions of the Blessed Sacrament. The minister covers his hands with the ends of the veil so that it, not his hands, touches the monstrance. Thus when he lifts the Sacrament to bless the faithful, it further accentuates that it is Christ, not the particular priest, Who blesses them. It is always white, silver or gold when worn for Eucharistic adoration, Benediction or processions. Another term for the humeral veil, rarely used today, is "sindon."

Humeral veil

Humiliati • Founded in the twelfth century and following the Rule of St. Benedict, the Humiliati were an order of penitents dedicated to an austere life of mortification and care for the poor. By the sixteenth century, a marked decline in discipline and a ferocious resistance to reform led to the order's suppression in 1571. An indication of the low state of the order at this time is that some of its members were involved in a plot on the life of St. Charles Borromeo. They nearly succeeded. St. Charles was injured in 1569 in an assassination attempt by a Humiliati priest named Jerome Donati Farina.

Humility • The supernatural virtue by which a Christian gains a proportionate and fitting understanding of his or her relationship to God. This virtue brings recognition that all good is ultimately from God, is the result of His grace and cannot be attributed to human agency. Humility is the basis of authentic love of others, and it draws us into closer conformity with Christ as it harmonizes us with His humility. It recognizes that the humility of Christ enabled Him to bring humanity the gifts of salvation by enabling Him to enter our mortal and sinful condition.

Christian humility is unique because it descends from above and does not spring from below. It recognizes the difference between Greek *eros* where the human tends upwardly toward the Divine and Christian *agape* where the Divine stoops down toward us. Humility governs our entire relationship to God and neighbor, and is not counted among the four cardinal virtues. The Incarnation struck at the impoverished condition and the presumptuous pride of our humanity in allowing the God-Man to suffer exile, persecution and death to alleviate that poverty. Even though Christ was utterly sinless, He showed on Calvary how the humility of sinners should be manifested. Although He was not a creature as we are, He submitted to the will of the Father in everything and became the model of humility for us. Humility opens us to the grace of God, and thus the humble one can better resist temptations than can those without this virtue. Humility is at the very foundation of prayer and the spiritual life, for discipleship and the imitation of Christ is not possible without humility. Humility in the Syro-Phoenician woman was rewarded by Christ.

Humility is also the natural virtue which opposes pride, arrogance and vanity, which are the roots of all evil. Humility is the basis of all good action, for it acknowledges our obligations to serve and to be lovingly obedient to God. Humility recognizes the worth and value of the neighbor and does not demean his or her accomplishments or virtues. Humility promotes the well-being of conscience, leading to prudence, astuteness and thoughtfulness.

Hylics • One of the many subsects of Gnosticism, this group (also known as Materials) held for the superiority of matter over spirit. Although dualistic in their thinking, they were distinguished in weighting the material realm in this manner.

Hymn • A song of praise or petition to God or the saints. Age-old discussions continue as to the thin line separating sacred and secular hymns and within the sacred realm, those in the liturgical group as opposed to those in the non-liturgical group. The document "Music in Catholic Worship" aids in the clarification of music suitable for liturgical use by its threefold judgment. (Cf. Judgment, Pastoral; Judgment, Musical; Judgment, Liturgical.)

Hymnal • Book of hymn texts, usually with music. Many hymnals include recommendations for liturgical or paraliturgical use, metrical index, hymn sources and/or other aids for use of the hymns.

Hymnody • Religious lyric poetry. Hymnody may be either liturgical or non-liturgical, depending on how it should be used.

Hymnology • Historical study of the origins and development of various hymn styles.

Hyperdulia • As its Greek roots suggest, hyperdulia is above and beyond the *dulia*, or respect, which is rendered to most of the angels and saints. Hyperdulia, or extended praise, is reserved to Our Lady alone because of her unique place among creatures in salvation history. Although the Blessed Mother ranks first among the blessed ones, the respect accorded her is on an altogether different plane from that reserved for God alone, otherwise known as *latria*.

Hypostasis • A Greek philosophical term used, somewhat confusingly, to designate both the substantial reality or nature of something, and an individual instance of such a nature. In the course of third- and fourth-century Trinitarian and Christological controversies, the latter meaning gained ascendancy and the term came to designate an individual instance of a complete — usually intelligent — nature. In this way, the term acquired a sense roughly synonymous with the Latin term *persona*. After the Council of Constantinople (A.D. 381), Trinitarian orthodoxy was measured by adherence to the formula "Three *Hypostaseis* in one *Ousia* (substance)."

At the Council of Chalcedon (451), the term figured in the affirmation of the substantial union of the divine and human natures in the One Person (Hypostasis) of Jesus Christ.

Hypostatic Union • The substantial union of the divine and human natures in the One Person (hypostasis) of Jesus Christ. The expression signals Christological orthodoxy against views that deny the substantial unity of the divine and human natures in

Christ (Nestorianism) and views that deny their perduring distinction in the Incarnation (Monophysitism). The divine and human natures remain distinct in Christ (they are not dissolved into some *tertium quid*), yet they are united in the Person of the eternal Word of God. The doctrine of the hypostatic union was developed by St. Cyril of Alexandria (d. A.D. 444) and proclaimed at the Council of Chalcedon (451).

Hyssop • A caper plant indigenous to the Near East, hyssop was used by the elders of Israel, at Moses' command, for sprinkling the blood of the Passover lamb on the lintels of Hebrew households (Ex 12:22). Its sprigs bound into a bunch were used by the ancient Hebrews for other rituals of purificatory sprinkling. Since its pungent leaves have a medicinal property, hyssop was considered symbolic of healing.

I

Icon (also Ikon) • A representation of Our Lord, the Virgin Mary or a saint, painted on a wall, a partition or a wooden panel. The icons of Eastern Churches take the place of the statues of the West.

Iconoclastic Controversy • Controversies about the veneration of images occurred in the Eastern Church in two phases from A.D. 726 to 842, in both cases inspired by imperial enactments. The term "iconoclastic" derives from the Greek for "image-breaking" and identifies a position of opposition to the use of images first adopted officially in the East by Emperor Leo III in 726.

Believing that icons fostered idolatry and prevented the conversion of Muslims and Jews, Leo ordered their destruction and thus inaugurated the first phase of the iconoclastic controversy. The imperial edict met with bitter opposition, especially from the monks. In response to Leo, St. John Damascene composed a famous defense of the veneration of icons and Pope Gregory III condemned iconoclasm (731). Leo's successor, Constantine V, continued his father's policy, going so far as to convene the Synod of Hieria (753) to secure the condemnation of images.

After the death of Constantine's successor, Leo IV (who had not pressed the issue), his wife, the Empress Irene, reversed the iconoclastic policies of the previous emperors. Along with Pope Hadrian I, she was instrumental in the convocation of the seventh ecumenical council at Nicaea (787), which condemned the Synod of Hieria. This Second Council of Nicaea articulated the principle that the veneration accorded to an image passes to that which it represents.

Christ the Savior
(thirteenth-century icon)

Iconoclasm had a resurgence in the East in 814, when Leo V ordered the destruction of icons and the persecution of those who opposed him. Many monks suffered martyrdom during this outbreak of iconoclasm, and St. Theodore of Studios was exiled for his defense of images. Leo's successors continued his policies until Empress Theodora restored the veneration of images in 842 with a great feast in their honor, kept now in the Eastern Church as the feast of Orthodoxy.

Iconostasis (also Ikonostasis) • Properly speaking, any support for an icon (or ikon).

Generally, the screen, covered with icons, separating the sanctuary from the rest of the church in the Eastern Church.

Ideology • Late in the eighteenth century, French thinkers coined the word "ideology" to mean a system of ideas focusing on sensation and shunning religion. In the nineteenth century, British thinkers likewise used "ideology" to refer to a system of ideas comprising a philosophy of mind. Napoleon Bonaparte was perhaps the first to use the word "ideology" in a derogatory way when the original French ideologues fell out of favor with him. Since the term has taken on unflattering meanings, thoughtful people seldom use "ideology" to refer to their own views about society.

Karl Marx launched the field of "ideology criticism" in the 1840s. In contrast to the Christian position affirming the role of human choice in adopting ideals, Marx held that the economic life of man and the struggle of classes for economic dominance are the real factors driving human history, and that the realm of ideas is merely "ideology":

"The phantoms formed in the human brain are also, necessarily, sublimates of their material life-process, which is empirically verifiable and bound to material premises. Morality, religion, metaphysics, all the rest of ideology and their corresponding forms of consciousness, thus no longer retain the semblance of independence" (Marx, *The German Ideology*, in Robert C. Tucker, *The Marx-Engels Reader*, Second Ed. [New York: W. W. Norton & Company, 1978]).

A definition of ideology by Dr. Johannes Messner reflects current usage: "Ideologies, in the sociological sense, are views of the nature and purpose of man and society which influence the form and functioning of the social order" (Messner, *Social Ethics: Natural Law in the Western World*, Rev. ed.,

Trans. J. J. Doherty [St. Louis: B. Herder Book Co., 1965]).

Many contemporary ideologies are hostile to the Christian view of the world on account of their emphasis on the material and secular. Ideologies which do not regard the adoption of ideas as a matter of accountable choice, or which pretend to guide humankind toward its complete fulfillment, are incompatible with Christianity. The selection of the goals embodied in any dominant system of social thought is important to Christians. If the goals of an ideology depart "from the essential ends of human nature, such a system is bound to fail to realize the common good and so to make possible the 'good life' of all members of the community" (Messner, p. 360).

Idiomelon • In the Eastern Liturgy, a troparion which is sung on a melody that belongs to it alone. The opposite of the Hirmos.

Idioms, Communication of: See **Communicatio Idiomatum**

Idol • In the broadest sense, an idol is anything which is accorded a supreme worth in life, a value to be ascribed to God alone. Strictly speaking, an idol is an object — usually an animal figure or the representation of a deity — which is venerated or worshiped in place of the true God. The Bible is forceful in its condemnation of idols (cf., for example, Is 40:18-26 and Rom 1:18-32).

For further reading: Edward M. Curtis, "Idol, Idolatry," *Anchor Bible Dictionary*, 3:376-381.

Idolatry • Giving to another person or object the worship, respect and veneration due to God alone. Idolatry is a most serious sin because it implicitly degrades God to the rank of a creature and denies His status as Creator and Master of the universe. Idolatry is a most serious sin, for it implicitly denies the role of grace and the self-communication of God. It violates not only the love of God which we owe Him, but also the duties we have to God to pay Him the honor and reverence He deserves as Creator.

According to the *Catechism of the Catholic Church*, "Idolatry not only refers to false pagan worship. It remains a constant temptation to faith. Idolatry consists in divinizing what is not God. Man commits idolatry whenever he honors and reveres a creature in place of God, whether this be gods or demons (for example, satanism), power, pleasure, race, ancestors, the state, money, etc. . . . Idolatry rejects the unique Lordship of God; it is therefore incompatible with communion with God" (n. 2113).

For further reading: Edward M. Curtis, "Idol, Idolatry," *Anchor Bible Dictionary*, 3:376-381.

Ignorance • The absence of knowledge about a subject on the part of one in whom such knowledge could be presumed. Ignorance is said to be invincible if it cannot be removed, and vincible if it is assumed or affected by one who wills not to learn anything. Ignorance can affect the validity of an act or the imputability of one accused of a crime.

Ignorance is mentioned in several places in the revised Code. Ignorance about an invalidating law does not prevent that law from having an effect. Ignorance about a law, penalty or fact is not presumed unless express provision for the contrary is stated in a law (Canon 15). Ignorance of the fact that marriage is a partnership ordered to the procreation of children through some form of sexual cooperation can render a marriage invalid (Canon 1096). One who, through no fault of his own, was ignorant of the

violation of a law cannot be punished for the violation (Canon 1321).

IHS • A monogram for the name of Jesus, using the first three letters of the word written in Greek. In the Middle Ages, it was erroneously thought that IHS stood for *Iesus Hominum Salvator* (Jesus, Savior of Men) or *In Hoc Signo [Vinces]* (In this sign [you shall conquer]), or even popularly in English, "I have suffered." As a sign for the Holy Name, it was popular with the Dominicans and Franciscans, as well as with the Jesuits.

Illegitimacy • A legal and canonical category which refers to the status of children born out of wedlock. A child born of a man and woman not actually married is presumed illegitimate. It has no moral or spiritual effects. In civil law it may mean, according to the legal system in effect, that an illegitimate child is not entitled to a share of his or her father's inheritance.

Today, canon law defines illegitimacy as the status of a child born of a man or woman not married or of a man and woman whose marriage is certainly invalid, with both aware of the invalidity. Illegitimacy is cured by the subsequent marriage of the couple or by a rescript of the Holy See. It should be noted that an annulment does not render any children born of that union illegitimate (cf. Canon 1137).

In the present Code there are no canonical effects of illegitimacy. In the 1917 Code, illegitimacy was an impediment for entrance into the seminary, nomination to the episcopate or cardinalate, or appointment as a prelate or abbot nullius.

Illuminative Way • The intermediate stage of the mystical life between the purgative way, in which one gains a facility for virtue by the practice of mortification and meditation, and the unitive way in which one achieves union with God, passive contemplation and habitual practice of the virtues, often to a heroic degree. In the illuminative way, one aims at perceiving Christ through the infused gifts of the Holy Spirit and following Him. Achievement of this level of mystical union comes about through the ordinary movements of grace, and most mystics have been able to express their experience in rather ordinary terms.

Image of God (also Imago Dei) • The human person is created possessing a spiritual nature that is free, spiritual and moral, and which therefore mirrors the Divine Nature. This image remains within the human person, even after original sin, and the personal sins of individuals cannot abolish it. Because this image remains intact, it was possible for God to become Incarnate.

The image of God in the human person means that there is a certain proportionality or similarity between God and the human person, and this similarity of nature made the Incarnation possible, for through this image, God was able to take on human flesh. The image of God in man was not destroyed by original sin, even though our "likeness" to God was abolished by it. Through the imparting of the gifts of the Holy Spirit, this likeness to God was restored. Thus, the redemptive work of Christ is in a sense a "new creation" because it restored what was lost by Adam. However, it is not an entirely new work, as it restored what was already present but deformed.

The image of God in the human person spurs the Christian to faith and hope. It induces faith, because only through God's grace is it possible to restore the fullness of our humanness. Only through the infusion of the gifts of the Holy Spirit, which reconstruct the likeness of God destroyed by original sin, is it possible to regain human fullness. The image of God in the human person also induces hope because it is only

through the gratuitous love that God confers on the person is restoration of the image brought about. Hope is not to be placed in anything human but only in God.

Images • The representation in art of Christ, the Blessed Virgin, angels, saints or other sacred subjects for the purposes of veneration, instruction or decoration. Despite the Mosaic prohibition of images to counter idolatry (Ex 20:4), the Christian community early in its existence saw the benefits of representations of sacred subjects. The first examples of such representations occur in the catacombs and date from the second century. Clearly, the Christian understanding of the meaning of the Incarnation played an important role in this development.

In Christ, the perfect Image of the Father, the invisible God is made visible. The aptness of the artistic depiction and then the veneration of images may be seen as an extension of the Christian understanding of the Incarnation. Holy images draw the mind and heart to the worship of the invisible realities which they represent. Appealing to this principle, doctrinal and theological support for the veneration of images has been consistent. Among theologians, Basil, John Damascene and Thomas Aquinas are notable defenders of this principle. Opposition to the use of images in the eighth and ninth centuries during the iconoclastic controversies in the Eastern Churches led to the first formal teaching on the subject (Second Council of Nicaea, A.D. 787). Again in the sixteenth century — in response to the Protestant Reformers (especially Zwingli and Calvin) — the Council of Trent sought to correct abuses in popular practice but insisted on the appropriateness of the veneration of images, invoking the traditional principle that the reverence accorded to sacred images passes to that which they represent. Throughout Christian history, recognition of the importance of this principle has sparked an immense outpouring of creative energy in all the representational arts.

Imitation of Christ • A famous work in spiritual and moral theology which instructed Christians to find spiritual perfection by imitating the life and actions of Christ. The book is a collection of ordered maxims and aphorisms written in such a way that the reader believes he or she is being instructed by Christ Himself. The work is divided into four parts; the first two contain general prescriptions for the spiritual life, while the last two deal with the inner disposition of the soul and the Eucharist. The work is a spiritual classic and has had a profound impact on Christian spirituality ever since its publication.

The tradition that it was written by Thomas à Kempis (c. 1380-1471) around 1418 remains intact because a manuscript with his signature still exists in Brussels. Attempts made to assign it to an earlier period and to Pope Innocent III have failed. Born Thomas Hemerken of poor parents, Thomas à Kempis was educated at Deventer at the school of the Brethren of the Common Life; in 1399, he entered the house of canons regular of Agnietenbert near Zwolle. His brother John was co-founder and prior of the community, and he spent almost all his life there preaching, teaching and writing.

Immaculate Conception • The doctrine of the Immaculate Conception affirms that "the Blessed Virgin Mary was preserved, in the first instant of her conception, by a singular grace and privilege of God omnipotent and because of the merits of Jesus Christ the Savior of the human race, free from all stain of original sin" (from the declaration of the dogma by Pope Pius IX, December 8, 1854).

The perfect sinlessness of Mary had been taught by the Fathers of the Church, appealing especially to such texts as Genesis 3:15 and Luke 1:28. A feast commemorating the conception of Our Lady was known in the East as early as the seventh century and in the West by the ninth century. The doctrine that Mary's sinlessness began from the first moment of her conception was opposed by some medieval doctors of the Church (e.g., St. Albert, St. Bonaventure and St. Thomas Aquinas) on the grounds that it detracted from the truth of her natural conception: original sin is transmitted in every human conception. Others (especially Duns Scotus) defended it, and by the sixteenth century — when the Council of Trent excluded Mary from original sin in its decree on that topic — the doctrine had become the common teaching of all theologians.

According to this doctrine, Mary was conceived in the state of perfect justice, free from original sin, and all its consequences and penalties, in virtue of the redemption won by Christ on the cross. In this sense, the privilege of the Immaculate Conception was the anticipated fruit of Christ's saving passion, death and resurrection. It was fitting that she who was to bear the Savior of the world should herself be preserved by Him from sin and its consequences and thus be the first to benefit from what He would win for the whole human race.

Immaculate Conception, Basilica of the National Shrine of the • The bishops of the United States in 1847 petitioned Pope Pius IX that the Blessed Mother be declared the patroness of the United States under the title of her Immaculate Conception. With the approval of the Holy See, plans were then made to erect a monumental church, to be called the National Shrine of the Immaculate Conception, in the nation's capital, Washington, D.C., at the intersection of

Fourth Street and Michigan Avenue, on the campus of the Catholic University of America.

Covering 77,500 square feet, it is the largest Catholic church in the United States, the second largest Christian church in the U.S. after the Episcopal Cathedral of St. John the Divine in New York, and the fifth largest religious edifice in the world. Given its size, many assume that it is the cathedral of the Archdiocese of Washington; it is not, St. Matthew's Cathedral serves that purpose. The National Shrine has, nevertheless, hosted many significant events. The wedding of President Lyndon Johnson's daughter, Lucy Baines, to Patrick Nugent was celebrated there. During his pastoral visit to the U.S. in 1979, Pope John Paul II addressed women religious during a service there. Regularly, the National Conference of Catholic Bishops uses the shrine for Mass during their annual meeting in Washington. The Archdiocese of the Military Services regularly uses the shrine in place of a cathedral of its own.

The cornerstone was laid in 1920; with the completion of the external structure, the National Shrine was formally dedicated on November 20, 1959, although some interior work still remains to be completed. The shrine is built in an eclectic fashion, combining elements of both neo-Byzantine and Romanesque design.

The National Shrine has many outstanding features: the Knights' Tower, the bell tower named for the Knights of Columbus who donated it; the elaborate mosaics of the exterior dome, which can be seen from many parts of Washington and the Maryland suburbs; the various shrines dedicated to Our Lady as she is venerated in different cultures; the crypt church with its exquisitely carved altar; the mammoth marble pillars in the upper church that support the baldacchino; the seven-foot statue of Mary Immaculate by sculptor George Snowden, which surmounts the baldacchino; and the forbidding mosaic of "Christ in Majesty," designed by John Rosen. The papal tiara of Pope Paul VI and the stole worn by Pope John XXIII at the opening of the Second Vatican Council are reverently displayed in the crypt.

The gift of the American Catholic people, the National Shrine of the Immaculate Conception is a place of devotion and pilgrimage for the hundreds of thousands who come to the National Shrine for daily Mass or to receive this unique catechesis in stone. On December 8, 1990, Pope John Paul II designated the shrine a basilica. It is the 34th basilica in the United States.

Immanence • From the Latin *immanere*, it means literally to remain within. It is the opposite of transcendence, which means to go beyond. Immanence and transcendence are key notions in describing the relationship between man and the world and man and God.

Immanence can describe an aspect of many things, including life, being and God. In all these descriptions there is also the complementary aspect of transcendence. Life is something immanent to the organism and sustained by such activity as nourishment. Human thinking always includes immanence, the interior act of the mind building up its knowledge, and transcendence, as it goes outside itself in order to know the object. Finite being has the aspect of immanence insofar as it exists with some independence. Yet, since it is not cause of itself, it witnesses to the need for a transcendent Creator.

God alone is perfectly immanent, never needing to go beyond Himself. Nor does He leave Himself when He comes to us. Teachers of the Faith use the term "immanence" to describe how God is closer to us than we are to ourselves. By grace, God is in us, and we are in God. This is not the immanence of pantheism where God is limited to be the world-soul and therefore not transcendent.

Immanuel: See **Emmanuel**

Immensae Caritatis • Instruction of the Sacred Congregation for the Discipline of the Sacraments of January 29, 1973, which provided for the creation of extraordinary ministers of Holy Communion without requiring Ordinaries to apply for special indults. The Instruction notes three circumstances which must be present for such ministers to be designated (for a given period of time or permanently): the absence of a priest, deacon or acolyte; the inability or inconvenience of priests, deacons or acolytes to distribute Communion because of illness or engagement in other pastoral ministry; and the presence of so many communicants that without such ministers the Mass would be unduly prolonged. According to Canon 230, acolytes and extraordinary ministers of Holy Communion may distribute Communion when needed both during Mass or outside of Mass. They may distribute either the Eucharistic Bread or the Precious Blood.

Immersion, Baptism by • A way of administering Baptism whereby the person's whole body is immersed in water three times during the pronouncement of the Trinitarian formula for Baptism ("I baptize you in the name of the Father and of the Son and of the Holy Spirit"). In the present rites for adult and infant Baptism, immersion is cited first as the proper way to administer Baptism, followed by infusion. Normally, immersion takes place in a pool or water that a candidate walks down steps to enter, the water in the pool being no higher than the person's waist. Many significant patristic catecheses on initiation speak of the importance of immersion for baptismal symbolism and theology. Among the more common images of immersion in such commentaries concerns the baptismal font as both a "tomb" and a "womb," where "tomb" refers to the Tomb in which Jesus was placed after the crucifixion and "womb" refers to Mother Church giving new birth to the candidate through water — Baptism. Often the candidate had to descend three steps to enter the baptismal water, recalling the three days Jesus lay entombed before the Resurrection.

Immortality of the Soul • Generally, this signifies eternal life and freedom from death. Belief in eternal life has been affirmed in many religions throughout the history of the world, as is seen in the burial books, gifts to the dead, and other artifacts and teachings. In general, most religions throughout history have considered the life of the dead to be similar to that of the living, and the rank of the dead was generally in proportion to the moral qualities of the person.

Plato established the basic Western tradition on this topic by defining the soul as the spiritual part of the human person which survived death. "Man is nothing else but his soul" (*Alcibiades*, 129e, 130c). He claimed that the separated soul possessed the characteristics previously possessed in its preexistence. The soul is immortal because it is the principle of life, because of its simplicity (which means it cannot be reduced further to more simple substances), and because of its ability to grasp the eternal forms (which means that it must be similar to the forms which are eternal). In contrast to Plato, however, Aristotle affirmed a closer unity of body and soul than did Plato, but that made its immortality more difficult to affirm.

In the Old Testament, the human soul survives in Sheol, but this survival is in no way comparable to the earthly life of the person. The soul is distinguished from the flesh of the person, and deliverance of the soul from Sheol is often prayed for in the Old Testament. The soul is sometimes not used in a sense that is identical to life, but this is often the case.

In the New Testament, the Greek term *psyche* is used to refer to the immortal soul, but Greek thought had little influence on New Testament thought concerning the soul. The soul in the New Testament is the seat of supernatural life and the object of supernatural salvation, and it is subject to temptation. In the New Testament, immortality of the soul is presumed by the teachings about the kingdom of God which Christ has initiated. The body can be killed, but not the soul, and one is to "hate" (that is, to prefer the greater to the lesser) this life in order to save it for the next life.

The Magisterium has spoken on the body-soul relationship, but it does not explain the immortality of the soul. St. Augustine affirmed the immortality of the soul by noting its power to apprehend the truth. It was affirmed by the Scholastics who affirmed the theological and ethical capabilities of the person. During the Renaissance, its immortality was debated by the Platonists, and Leibniz considered it to be one of the central doctrines of the Enlightenment in Germany. Elsewhere, it was regarded with skepticism, and Kant rejected rational proofs for the immortality of the soul, but argued for its existence because of the nature of the moral duties imposed on the person. Hegel was ambivalent about the immortality of the soul, and his followers were sharply split on the issue. Protestant thought has not given theological consideration to the question of the immortality of the soul, but has affirmed its paradoxical character.

Immovability of Pastors • The 1917 Code dealt with the stability of pastors by dividing them into immovable, movable and religious. Immovable pastors were those assigned to fully established diocesan parishes. They could not be removed against their will without the permission of the Holy See. Immovable pastors could, however, be removed or transferred if the bishop had reason to believe that their ministry was inefficacious, but a definite procedure was required. Immovable pastors could also be removed through voluntary retirement or by their own request.

Although the revised Code does not speak of immovable pastors as such, it does recommend that since pastors should have stability for the proper exercise of their ministry their appointment should be for an indefinite period of time. This is not mandatory, however, and in many dioceses, especially in the United States, pastors are appointed for fixed terms. The Code still retains a procedure for the removal or transfer of pastors who do not wish to be removed or transferred (cf. Canons 522, 1740-1747).

Immovable Feasts • Liturgical observances which are assigned to a specific date (month and day) which do not change annually, e.g., January 1, Solemnity of Mary, Mother of God; February 2, feast of the Presentation of Our Lord; March 19, solemnity of St. Joseph; November 30, feast of St. Andrew Apostle.

Immunity • An exemption from some form of responsibility or from certain laws. Immunity, not to be confused with exemption, does not exist under the revised Code of Canon Law.

Immutability • The truth that God's pure actuality and absolute perfection exclude all possibility of change in Him. The doctrine of Scripture on this point has been confirmed by philosophical and theological reflection. The truth, as expressed in the Letter of

James (1:17), that in God "there is no change nor shadow of alteration," has been consistently affirmed by the Fathers and Doctors of the Church. Mutability presupposes the possibility and need that an entity will continually progress, or change, from potential states to new actualizations of its being. But in God there can be no lack of actuality. Since He is sheerly existent and actual, it follows that He is immutable. In order to avoid a common misunderstanding according to which God's immutability is said to signify a lack of engagement with His creatures, it is important to see that the theological truth of the divine immutability does not exclude, but rather presupposes, an intensely active causality on God's part in preserving the human race in existence and in redeeming us through the death of His only begotten Son.

Impeccability • Not merely the absence of sins committed by a person, but also the impossibility of sinning. In theology this quality is applied to Jesus. He was sinless in fact and impeccable in theory. The Church Fathers and theologians unanimously teach the impeccability of Christ. His freedom from original sin was declared by the Council of Florence and from personal sin by the Council of Chalcedon. The Second Council of Constantinople condemned the theory that Christ became completely impeccable only after the Resurrection.

The Blessed Virgin Mary also possesses this special quality. She was free from original and personal sin (Immaculate Conception) because of the divine grace of God in choosing her to be the mother of His Son. The blessed in heaven are also impeccable, since they are eternally realizing the purpose of their lives. They possess the beatific vision of God, which renders sin impossible.

Impediment • A barrier that prevents the reception of the sacrament of Matrimony or that of Sacred Orders. Impediments arise out of some condition of the individual or out of something he or she has done or out of the relationship itself.

The impediments to marriage render a marriage invalid unless a dispensation from the impediment has been obtained. The impediments to Orders are known as simple impediments and prohibit the reception of Orders but do not render the ordination invalid. The following are impeded from receiving Orders: a man who has a wife unless he is destined for the permanent diaconate or is a member of one of the Oriental Churches where a married priesthood is allowed; one who exercises an office or administration forbidden to clerics and neophytes (cf. Canon 1042).

Impediment, Diriment • A diriment impediment is a barrier to a valid marriage. It arises from a condition of the person, from something he or she has done or from some circumstance which arises out of the relationship itself.

Impediments exist because of the Church's concern for the welfare of the individuals proposing marriage, the institution of marriage itself, or the effect of a marriage on the community. They are based on the fact that although persons have the right to marry, this is not an absolute right and depends, for its exercise, on the capacity to fulfill the marital obligations and responsibilities.

Some impediments have their origin in divine law itself and are based on marriage as a natural law institution. They affect all persons, baptized or not. Commentators on canon law generally agree that the divine law impediments include prior marriage bond, impotence and consanguinity in the direct line and in the indirect line, second degree. The remaining impediments are of ecclesiastical law origin because they refer to marriage as a sacramental institution and affect only Catholics. The Holy See alone is competent either to establish or abrogate an impediment.

Certain of the impediments may be dispensed. The local Ordinary can dispense his own subjects and those staying in his territory from the impediments of age, impotence if there is a doubt about its perpetuity, disparity of cult, affinity, consanguinity in the third and fourth degrees of the indirect line, abduction, public propriety and legal relationship. Only the Holy See can dispense from the impediments arising from Sacred Orders or public vows and from the impediment of crime.

In danger of death, the law allows the local Ordinary or the priest or deacon assisting at the marriage to dispense from each impediment of ecclesiastical law origin with the exception of the impediment arising from the Order of priesthood.

In the 1917 Code there were two kinds of impediments: diriment impediments, which rendered a marriage invalid, and impedient impediments, which did not invalidate a marriage but rendered it illicit. The impedient impediments were either dropped (private vows), located in a separate section of the Code (marriages of mixed Christian confessions, undesirable marriages), or joined with a diriment impediment (simple vows, legal or adoptive relationship). The only impediments in the revised law are lack of age, impotence, prior marriage bond, Sacred Orders, public vows, abduction, public propriety, consanguinity, affinity and crime (cf. Canons 1073-1082).

Impediments, Hindering • The hindering impediments were the impediments to marriage found in the 1917 Code of Canon Law. These impediments rendered a marriage illicit but not invalid. They consisted of simple vows which included: the public vows of chastity; private vows of virginity, not to marry, to receive Holy Orders or to embrace religious life; legal adoption in those countries where an adoptive relationship made a marriage illicit but not invalid in civil law; mixed religion, that is, marriages between a Catholic and a baptized non-Catholic; undesirable marriages, that is, marriages between a Catholic and one who has either notoriously abandoned the Faith or one who is a notorious public sinner.

The hindering impediments as such were dropped from the revised Code. Private vows no longer have any effect on the liceity or validity of marriage. The public vow of chastity, even though a simple vow, invalidates a marriage. Mixed-religion marriages have been given a special section of the Code and require the permission of the bishop to take place. The undesirable marriage has been included in a category of special marriages that require the bishop's permission.

Imperfections • Deficiencies or flaws in the moral character of the person not considered to be grave or serious. Despite the fact that they are not serious, they are impediments to growth in morality, charity and the spiritual life. Rather than approaching the sacrament of Penance for these faults and flaws, fraternal correction, penance and prayer are considered as adequate means for eliminating them, although sacramental confession (and the grace flowing from it) is certainly helpful in overcoming imperfections.

Imposition of Hands • A ritual gesture used in such varied contexts as sacrifice, healing, blessing, Baptism, commissioning and ordination, the imposition of hands is found in the Old Testament and in the New

Testament, as well as in subsequent Christian practice.

According to the Old Testament, someone offering an animal in sacrifice to God would impose one hand or both hands on the animal's head. For example, in Exodus 29:15 God commands, ". . . you shall take one of the rams, and Aaron and his sons shall lay their hands upon the head of the ram," and then the ram is to be slaughtered and burned in sacrifice on the altar. Among the interpretations that have been suggested for the imposition of hands on a sacrificial victim is the suggestion that some characteristic of the person offering the sacrifice would be transferred to the sacrificial animal by virtue of the contact.

In Leviticus 16:21, the imposition of hands has a different meaning. There the ritual for the Day of Atonement is described in which "Aaron shall lay both his hands upon the head of the live goat, and confess over him all the iniquities of the people of Israel, and all their transgressions, all their sins; . . . and send him away into the wilderness." The so-called "scapegoat" on which hands are imposed is not a sacrificial animal. It serves instead to bear symbolically the sins of the people, carrying them off into the wilderness.

In the New Testament, the imposition of hands does not appear in either of these two contexts. The imposition of hands was occasionally employed by Jesus to cure the sick (Mk 6:5, Lk 4:40), and the New Testament also indicates that followers of Jesus healed by the imposition of hands (e.g., Acts 9:12, 17; 28:8). In addition to healing, the imposition of hands was a gesture used to confer blessings. In Mark 10:16, Jesus welcomed children, "And he took them in his arms and blessed them, laying his hands upon them."

In the Acts of the Apostles, the imposition of hands is a gesture associated with the conferral of the Holy Spirit and with the sacrament of Baptism. For example, Acts 19:5-6 describes what happened during St. Paul's encounter with some disciples at Ephesus who had received Baptism from John the Baptist. After their Baptism in the name of Jesus, "when Paul laid his hands upon them, the Holy Spirit came on them." The imposition of hands continues to be a gesture used in the administration of the sacrament of Baptism.

The Apostles imposed hands to confer authority and power, and, coupled with the invocation of the Holy Spirit, this action very soon came to be recognized as the normal means of ordination to Church office. The text of Jeremiah 1:9, in which the Lord reaches out to touch Jeremiah's mouth, thereby commissioning him for a prophetic vocation, furnishes part of the background for the imposition of hands in this context. Thus, Holy Orders are conferred by the ordaining bishop as he lays his hands on the head of the ordinand (deacon, priest or bishop). The New Testament urges, "Do not be hasty in the laying on of hands" (1 Tm 5:22); for it is gravely serious, since its effects are permanent. The New Testament also exhorts one who has been ordained to "rekindle the gift of God that is within you through the laying on of my hands" (2 Tm 1:6).

With its significance as a gesture of blessing, of healing, and of invocation of the Holy Spirit, the imposition of hands is a key element in the celebration of the sacraments of Penance and of the Anointing of the Sick. As a gesture by which the Holy Spirit's power is invoked and by which that power is granted to the Church, the imposition of hands is used at Baptism, at Confirmation and in the conferral of Holy Orders. During the Eucharistic prayer of the Mass, the priest extends his hands over the offerings of bread and wine that are to become the Body and Blood of Christ.

Catholic liturgical rites regularly include the laying on of hands, e.g., in the Anointing of the Sick, or the extension of the hands, in granting absolution from sin, or invoking the Holy Spirit over the gifts to be consecrated at Mass.

For further reading: David P. Wright and Robert F. O'Toole, "Hands, Laying on of," *Anchor Bible Dictionary*, 3:47-49.

Impotence • The incapacity or inability of a man or a woman to have normal sexual intercourse. It gives rise to an impediment that renders a marriage invalid if the impotence is both antecedent and perpetual. If, however, there is a doubt as to whether the impotence is either antecedent or perpetual, a dispensation can be obtained.

Potency consists of the ability on the part of the man to have an erection, penetrate the vagina and ejaculate. On the part of the woman, it is necessary to have a vagina that is capable of receiving the male organ.

Impotence may be organic, that·is, caused by a physical injury or serious malformation of an organ necessary for intercourse. It may also be functional, that is, caused by a psychological or nervous disorder which renders the person incapable of sexual intercourse even though all organs are intact (cf. Canon 1084).

Imprecatory Psalms • Sometimes called the "Cursing Psalms." These are psalms that give expression to a wild vindictiveness. In their extravagant way they speak of the retribution that is exacted for evil that is done. A certain amount of poetic license should be invoked in interpreting these. Though five psalms (7, 35, 69, 109, 137) are generally designated as imprecatory, there are recurring instances — stray verses — of these sentiments strewn about the rest of the Psalter, e.g., 2:9 and 59:10-13.

Imprimatur • Literally, "let it be printed," the *imprimatur* is required for the publication of certain religious or scriptural texts. The law requires that all books of the Sacred Scriptures, including translations, be published with the permission of the Holy See or the episcopal conference. The publication of liturgical books also requires the permission of the Holy See.

Publication of catechisms, prayer books, and books about morals, Scripture, theology, Church history or canon law that will be used as textbooks are to receive the approval of the bishop or other competent ecclesiastical authority before being published.

The law no longer requires that any book about a religious subject receive the *imprimatur*. It does urge, however, that books about religious subjects that are not to be used as textbooks be submitted for approval (cf. Canons 824-832).

For further reading: James A. Coriden, Thomas J. Green and Donald E. Heintschel, eds., *The Code of Canon Law: A Text and Commentary*, 580-585; translation and commentary on Canons 824-832 (Paulist Press, 1985).

Improperia (or Reproaches) • A series of reproofs addressed by the Lord from the cross to His ungrateful people. These were chanted on Good Friday during the solemn service of the Veneration of the Cross from the seventh century on and are still in the current rite, although optional. They seemed to be discouraged for a while as anti-Semitic, but were generally understood by most Catholics as addressed to them for their hardness of heart and need for repentance.

Impurity • A condition of physical or moral contamination or corruption. The *Catechism of the Catholic Church* treats the struggle against moral impurity in the light of the sixth beatitude, "Blessed are the pure in heart, for they shall see God" (Mt 5:8). According to the *Catechism*, " 'Pure in heart' refers to those who have attuned their intellects and wills to the demands of God's holiness, chiefly in three areas: charity; chastity or sexual rectitude; love of truth and orthodoxy of faith. There is a connection between purity of heart, of body, and of faith" (n. 2518; cf. also nn. 2519-2533).

The biblical foundation of which the Church's teaching on purity and impurity has to do with the absolute holiness of God. According to Psalm 24:3-4, "Who shall ascend the hill of the LORD? And who shall stand in his holy place? He who has clean hands and a pure heart, who does not lift up his soul to what is false, and does not swear deceitfully." Merely external cleanliness is secondary to purity of heart; true holiness and purity are not merely matters of external propriety. When the prophet Isaiah saw the Lord enthroned and heard the seraphim call out, "Holy, holy, holy is the LORD of hosts," he cried out, "Woe is me! For I am lost; for I am a man of unclean lips, . . . for my eyes have seen the King, the LORD of hosts!" (Is 6:3, 5). Isaiah's unworthiness to stand in the presence of the all-holy God is remedied by the seraph who touches a burning coal to the prophet's lips, symbolically purifying him from sin.

In the Gospels, the Pharisees criticized the followers of Jesus for failing to observe the purity regulations regarding food, regulations by which pious Jews sought to conform their external behavior to the purity of heart that genuine faithfulness to the commandments demanded. Mark's Gospel (7:3-4) explains that "the Pharisees, and all the Jews, do not eat unless they wash their hands, observing the tradition of the elders; and when they come from the market place, they do not eat unless they purify themselves." While these may strike us as ordinary practices of normal hygiene, they had a much deeper religious significance. They served to remind those who observed them that as members of the Chosen People of Israel, they were held to a higher standard of conduct, standards of moral and physical purity befitting the Chosen People of the Holy One. The Pharisees were puzzled that the disciples seemed to have no regard for these commandments.

Setting purity and impurity in proper perspective, Jesus taught that "there is nothing outside a man which by going into him can defile him; but the things which come out of a man are what defile him" (Mk 7:15). He went on to specify the sorts of things that come from within people which are sins against purity: "from within, out of the heart of man, come evil thoughts, fornication, theft, murder, adultery, coveting, wickedness, deceit, licentiousness, envy, slander, pride, foolishness. All these evil things come from within, and they defile a man" (Mk 7:21-23).

For further reading: Hans Hubner, "Unclean and Clean (New Testament)," *Anchor Bible Dictionary*, 6:741-745; David P. Wright, "Clean and Unclean (Old Testament)," *Anchor Bible Dictionary*, 6:729-741.

Imputability • The character of a moral act which is attributable to a person is known in canon law as imputability. Essentially, it means that the person is morally responsible for the act performed. The term is used in reference to canonical crimes.

No one can be punished for a canonical crime unless that person is proven to be imputable or morally responsible, by reason of malice or culpability (Canon 1321).

The imputability of a person is removed — that is, he or she is considered not morally responsible and therefore incapable of receiving a penalty — if any one of seven separate factors is present at the time of the commission of the act: one who has not completed the sixteenth year of age; one who, without fault, was unaware of violating a law; one who acted because of physical force or because of an accident that could neither be foreseen nor prevented; one who acted out of grave fear, out of necessity, or out of serious inconvenience, unless the act was intrinsically evil or verges on harm to souls; one who acted out of self-defense with due moderation; one who lacked the use of reason; one who, without fault, believed he was acting out of grave fear or in self-defense (Canon 1323).

Other factors diminish but do not remove imputability. This means that the accused cannot be punished with the penalty set by law but can receive a lesser penalty. It also means that the accused cannot incur an automatic penalty. The factors that reduce imputability are: imperfect use of reason; culpable drunkenness or mental disturbance that did not remove all culpability; serious heat of passion which did not precede and impede all deliberation of the mind and which was not deliberately stirred up; commission by a minor between the ages of sixteen and eighteen; force or grave fear to perform an act which is intrinsically evil; self-defense without due moderation; action against one unjustly and gravely provoking a person; lacking awareness that a penalty was attached to the crime; one who acted without full imputability (Canon 1325).

In Articulo Mortis • Term referring to the time when a person is in the emergency situation of "danger of death." Most frequently employed as a technical term when discussing emergency situations concerning the administration of the sacraments, both in the rite of the particular sacrament and in canon law. Examples where "danger of death" clauses are included in the present canon law or sacramental rites are: sacramental absolution, Anointing, Baptism, celibacy dispensations, censures and remissions, Confirmation, powers of dispensation, reception of the Eucharist, laicization, marriage, religious profession, suspension of penalty, Viaticum and the power of penalized clerics in such situations.

Incardination • The canonical act whereby a cleric is attached to a diocese or religious community and subjected to the authority of its Ordinary. Every cleric, without exception, must be incardinated to a particular church or to a religious community before he can be ordained to the priesthood. After ordination, every cleric must similarly be incardinated somewhere, since the law prohibits wandering clergy.

A man becomes incardinated into his diocese or religious order when he is ordained to the diaconate, even if his own bishop is not the ordaining prelate. A member of a religious institute or society of apostolic life must have taken perpetual vows (or their equivalent) to be ordained a deacon and thus incardinated into the institute or society. Permanent deacons also are incardinated to the diocese for which they have been ordained. After ordination, a cleric can be incardinated into another diocese if he receives a letter of excardination from the bishop of the diocese he is leaving and a letter of incardination from the bishop of the diocese he is entering.

If a diocesan cleric lawfully leaves his diocese and resides in another diocese, he may petition both bishops for permission to incardinate after having been in the host diocese for five years. If neither bishop objects within four months of receiving the request, the cleric is automatically incardinated into the new diocese.

If a member of a religious institute seeks to be incardinated into a diocese, he must first receive an indult to leave the institute, which carries with it the automatic dispensation from vows. He receives this indult when he has found a bishop who will incardinate him or receive him on probation. If he is received on probation, he is automatically incardinated after five years unless the bishop rejects him.

A diocesan cleric who seeks incardination into a religious community must first be allowed to do so by his bishop. He remains incardinated in his diocese until he makes perpetual profession in the religious institute, which is the act whereby he becomes incardinated into it (cf. Canons 265-272).

Incarnation, The • According to the Christian doctrine of the Incarnation, the eternal Son of God assumed a complete human nature and was born of the Virgin Mary by the power of the Holy Spirit. While the Incarnation itself is a work of the Blessed Trinity acting together, only the Second Person of the Trinity is united with a human nature. The resulting union is a substantial one, traditionally designated as "hypostatic," in which the divine and human natures are joined in the one Person (*hypostasis*) of Jesus Christ.

The doctrine of the Incarnation received formal expression at the Council of Chalcedon (A.D. 451) after two centuries of controversy. The Chalcedonian definition stated that Christ is "perfect in divinity and perfect in humanity, the same truly God and truly man composed of rational soul and body, the same one in being (*homoousios*) with the Father as to divinity and one in being with us as to the humanity, like unto us in all things but sin." The definition sought to exclude views that denied the substantial unity of the divine and human

The Incarnation (medieval painting)

natures in Christ (Nestorianism) and views that denied their distinction in the Incarnation (Monophysitism).

The Christian understanding of this mystery rules out the notion that the Incarnation is a merely transitory theophany: The union of the divine and human natures in Christ is a permanent and abiding one. In addition, a fundamental soteriological conviction is at stake in the doctrine: Whatever is not assumed is not saved. According to the Scriptures, the Incarnation has a salvific purpose that embraces both the restoration of the image of God in us through the cross of Christ and the foretaste of the perfect union with God that is our destiny in Christ.

Incense • Granulated or powdered aromatic resin, obtained from various plants and trees in Eastern or tropical countries. When sprinkled on glowing coals in a vessel called a censer (also known as a thurible), the incense becomes a fragrant cloud of smoke and so is used to symbolize prayer rising to God (Ps 141:2, Rv 8:3-5) and to honor sacred persons and things in the context of liturgical worship. In the Eastern Church, more so than in the Latin Church (where the symbolism is largely taken over by holy water), incense is seen also as an agent of ritual purification of persons and places.

The use of incense comes into the Church both from pagan worship (hence the Church's apparent misgivings concerning it during the first centuries) and, as abundant references to incense in the Old Testament would seem to indicate, from Judaism as well.

While the use of incense is normative for all celebrations of the Eucharist in the Eastern Church, and for the daily Offices as well, its use in the Latin Church is associated with celebrations of greater solemnity. In fact, the pre-Vatican II (Tridentine) rite restricted the use of incense to High Mass and surrounded its use with many prayer formulae which served to explain its symbolism.

The Vatican II rite eliminates the prayer formulae, preferring to let the symbolism speak for itself, but extends the use of incense to any Mass. The *General Instruction of the Roman Missal* lists a number of occasions during the Mass when the use of incense is appropriate:

✧ during the entrance procession and upon arrival in the sanctuary to honor the altar after kissing it and before greeting the assembly;

✧ during the Gospel procession and to honor the Book of Gospels after greeting the people and announcing the evangelist;

✧ at the Preparation of the Gifts, to honor the altar, the gifts, the ministers and the assembly;

✧ at the elevations which follow the consecration, to honor the Body and Blood of Christ now present;

✧ and, finally, to add solemnity to the recessional if another ceremony follows.

Incense may also be used during the celebration of Morning and Evening Prayer during the chanting of the Gospel Canticles (the *Benedictus* or Canticle of Zechariah at Morning Prayer, and the Magnificat or Canticle of Mary at Evening Prayer). The altar, ministers and assembly are incensed at these times. Some modern adaptations of Evening Prayer imitate the medieval "cathedral"-style celebrations and Eastern usage by fixing the "incense psalm" (Ps 141) at the beginning of the evening psalmody, during which incense is burned in a censer or even in a stationary brazier placed before the altar.

The Latin Church also uses incense (again, more sparingly than the Eastern Church) in some of her other liturgical rites. The Rite for the Dedication of a Church, for instance, specifies that incense is to be burned in a brazier placed on the altar after the anointing with chrism, and from this brazier, coal is placed in a censer for the incensation of the church building, walls and assembly.

Incense is likewise prescribed for use at the rite of commendation and farewell which concludes the Funeral Mass. Usually during the chanting of the "song of farewell," the celebrant honors the remains of the deceased (the body which had been the temple of the Holy Spirit during life) with fragrant incense.

Incense is also commonly used during processions. Indeed, the *Ceremonial of Bishops* always places the thurifer (censer-bearer) with smoking incense at the head of the procession just before the processional cross, unless the Blessed Sacrament is being borne in procession, in which case the thurifer (or two thurifers) would be directly before the Blessed Sacrament. Finally, incense is used whenever exposition with Benediction of the Blessed Sacrament takes place.

Indefectibility • The condition of the Church according to which it is assured that she will perpetually be the Church that Our Lord founded, despite the defection and weakness of her members. Confidence in the indefectibility of the Church rests on the promise of Christ Himself, Who said that "the powers of death shall not prevail against it" (Mt 16:18).

Index of Forbidden Books • An official list of books and writings that members of the Catholic Church were forbidden to read or possess. In order to read a book on the Index, permission of the Holy See, obtained through the Holy Office, had to be secured. Those who wrote, published, read or kept forbidden books were subject to automatic excommunication.

The Index was first issued by the Congregation of the Inquisition under Pope Paul IV in 1557. In 1571, Pope St. Pius V established a special Congregation of the Index, which had charge over the Index and revised it as needed. This Congregation survived until 1917, when its duties were transferred to the Holy Office. On June 14, 1966, the Index and all excommunications related to it were abolished.

Indifferentism • This doctrine can refer to one of two religious realities. On the one hand, it can refer to the refusal to give worship to God because of sloth or a refusal to recognize one's obligation to worship and obey God. Catholic Faith holds that one has an obligation to worship, obey and follow

Christ, and it condemns this form of religious indifferentism.

But it can also refer to the belief that one need not practice a given faith because all religions are "relatively" true and of equal value. The Second Vatican Council protested against this sort of indifferentism and argued that while there is truth to be found in all religions, the fullness of truth is found only in the faith expressed by the Catholic Church.

The secular doctrine of religious freedom, which is based on this latter form of indifferentism and holds that one can choose any religion one desires, is based on the principle of religious indifferentism. But the Council's doctrine of religious liberty is based on the position that one has an obligation to follow the judgments of one's conscience about which religion is to be pursued. Because one has an obligation to seek the truth, one has a general obligation to move to Catholicism and the fullness of truth, but this obligation can be overridden by a belief that the Catholic Church is not the true Church because of perceived scandals in the Church or because of a sincerely held conviction that the Catholic Church is in error.

Indissolubility • The quality of the marriage bond which means that it may not be dissolved. Historically, there have been different degrees of indissolubility. In some ancient legal systems, all marriages were intrinsically dissoluble, meaning that the spouses themselves could dissolve the marriage simply by a declaration of the fact by one, the other, or both (depending on the legal system) that it had ceased to exist.

In most cultures today, marriage is intrinsically indissoluble but extrinsically dissoluble. This means that the spouses cannot legally dissolve their own marriage, but that an external authority can dissolve it, usually a judge or magistrate.

In Church law all marriages are considered intrinsically indissoluble. Only non-sacramental or non-consummated marriages are extrinsically dissoluble by Church authorities. A consummated, sacramental marriage is considered to be absolutely indissoluble by any human power.

Individualism • A philosophical attitude emphasizing the importance of individual rights over communal values. Many consider the United States to be a country founded on respect for the individual and his rights as higher than any considerations of the good of the community.

Some examples of individualistic attitudes that are compatible with Catholic philosophy would be the protection of religious freedom and the right to life of the unborn and elderly. On the other hand, many times individualism is advanced as a justification of actions contrary to God's Law, as in the insistence that active homosexuals should have a right to teach children about their lifestyle or that a person's right to create and sell pornography is an absolute. Inconsistently, some pro-abortion advocates believe that the individual rights of the mother are more important than the rights of the father or of the unborn child.

In religious philosophy, the rights of the individual must always be understood in the context of creation by God and the obligation of following God's plan, even when involving the sacrifice of an individual's own plans.

Indulgences • Remission of the temporal punishments for sins, and therefore the giving of satisfaction owed God for one's sin. Indulgences are granted either after the sacrament of Penance or by perfect contrition. Indulgences are either plenary (when all punishments are remitted) or partial (when only part of that punishment

is remitted). Plenary indulgences demand that one be free of all venial sin, but partial indulgences do not require this.

Partial indulgences remit the amount of temporal punishment that would be remitted in the ancient Church by performances of penances for the designated period of time. Indulgences can only be gained for oneself or for those in purgatory, but not for other living human beings. Indulgences are derived from the treasure of merits of the saints, from Christ Himself or from His Mother.

Indult • A special permission given by the Holy See for a person to deviate from a Church law. Permissions by indult can include dispensations, privileges, permissions or faculties. Although not true by definition, indults tend to have applicability over a wider group of faithful than do privileges. For example, the recent rule allowing Catholics in certain western states not to observe Ascension Thursday was granted by indult.

Indwelling of the Holy Spirit • The presence of the Triune God in the hearts of those who love Him is ascribed in a special way to the Holy Spirit. As the union of the Father and the Son, the Spirit's personal presence in grace makes us sharers in the Trinitarian life itself. Our Lord Himself promised this indwelling of the Trinity when He said: "If a man loves me, he will keep my word, and my Father will love him, and we will come to him and make our home with him" (Jn 14:23). Since the Holy Spirit is the love whereby the Father loves the Son and also the love whereby He loves the creature, it makes sense that the loving presence of the Triune God should be attributed to the Spirit. To speak of this indwelling is really to speak of the perfection of charity: uncreated love enabling and reaching out to created love. Here, the causal presence of God — the power that sustains all things in existence — becomes a truly personal presence. In love, omnipresence becomes indwelling.

Inerrancy • Although this term has the broad meaning of complete freedom from error in any field, its normal theological force is to ascribe this attribute to Sacred Scripture. In traditional Catholic teaching, inerrancy is an effect of inspiration. The Scripture's freedom from error is implicit in its divine authorship. It has always been recognized that the Scripture could contain errors of fact in some area — biology or history — and yet be inerrant in the required sense that it teaches "firmly, faithfully and without error . . . that truth which God, for the sake of our salvation, wished to see confided to the sacred Scriptures" (DV 11). Christian teaching insists that, in inspiring the human author, God makes use of his talents and limitations in insuring that revelation will be communicated through these writings. The grace of inspiration leaves the human instrument intact. Hence, the human author's lack of knowledge or proneness to error in certain areas does not undermine the inerrancy of the Scripture's communication of Divine Revelation.

Infallibilists • The term used to describe those bishops — in the majority — who wanted the First Vatican Council (1869-1870) to proclaim solemnly that the Pope, when he taught *ex cathedra* on matters of faith and morals, was infallible due to the special grace of his office as successor of St. Peter. These bishops, who were especially devoted to Pope Pius IX (1846-1878), were led by the Archbishop of Westminster, Henry Edward Cardinal Manning, and eventually saw their position promulgated by the Council in the decree *Pastor Aeternus*, July 18, 1870.

Infallibility • The double negative has the precise meaning, "the inability to err." It is not conceptually equivalent to "being correct." One could be simply correct without being necessarily so. Infallibility in the absolute sense is predicable of God alone, but in the sense meant here, it is the result of the divine assistance. In Catholic theology and teaching, it refers to three subjects: the Church, the Pope and the Episcopal College.

Vatican II taught that the Church herself is infallible insofar as she preserves and propounds the deposit of revelation entrusted to her by Christ (*Lumen Gentium*, n. 25).

In *Pastor Aeternus* (n. 4), Vatican I taught that the Roman Pontiff is infallible under three conditions: that he exercise his office as Pastor and Doctor of all Christians, that he speak of faith or morals and that he indicate that the doctrine must be held by the universal Church.

It was also taught by Vatican II in *Lumen Gentium*, n. 25, that the bishops of the Church are infallible as well, either as a college or as a council. As a college, they are infallible if they are in communion with the Pope, speak of faith or morals and agree that a doctrine must be held by the universal Church. The same conditions apply to conciliar teachings, which, however, must be promulgated by the Pope.

This acknowledgment of an infallible but ordinary Magisterium was one of the principal doctrinal contributions of the Second Vatican Council. It effectively prevents the simplistic equation between infallible and solemn or extraordinary (papal or conciliar) teaching.

Infamy • A canonical penalty contained in the 1917 Code, but dropped in the revised Code. There were two kinds of infamy: infamy of law and infamy of fact.

Infamy of law was a penalty that was incurred upon the commission of a very serious ecclesiastical crime. In all but one of the crimes involved, infamy of law was incurred together with excommunication. The cases that included excommunication were: profanation of the Holy Eucharist; violation of graves; laying violent hands on the Pope, a cardinal or a legate of the Pope; dueling; and bigamy. Lay persons who engaged in sexual relations with minors under the age of sixteen were *ipso facto* infamous and subject to other indeterminate penalties.

There were severe consequences of infamy of law. The person was incapable of holding any ecclesiastical office or dignity and of exercising any ecclesiastical right, act or function, and finally, was prevented from taking any part in the exercise of any ecclesiastical function.

Infamy of fact was contracted when a person, in the judgment of the Ordinary, had either committed a crime or was of such corrupt morals that his good reputation had been lost. Such a person was to be held up from receiving Orders, if a cleric, and similarly prevented from holding any ecclesiastical office or dignity and from exercising all ecclesiastical acts, including the sacred ministry.

Infamy of law ceased only by dispensation of the Holy See, and infamy of fact by means of a reversal of the judgment by the Ordinary who had made it.

Infidel • In its broadest sense, this term refers to anyone who has not embraced the Christian Faith. According to traditional Christian usage, an infidel is a person who maintains a positive disbelief in Christian Faith in any form (as distinguished from heretics and agnostics). Current English-speaking ecclesiastical usage, however, tends to distinguish between non-Christians (persons who are the adherents of other religious traditions) and non-believers (persons without religious affiliations or beliefs of any kind). The preference for these terms over the more pejorative "infidel" reflects the Church's stated commitment to engage in dialogue with persons and communities holding to alternative religious views or to none at all. Traditional Catholic teaching affirms, nonetheless, that the divine offer of grace is universal in its scope and thus allows for the possibility that non-Christian persons, in ways known only to God, can be saved by their response to that grace and through morally upright lives.

Infinite • Negation of limitation; not limited. Infinite is applied most basically to God (His being) and all His attributes (for example, unity, truth, goodness, beauty). These characteristics are also found in the created things we know, but only to a limited degree. Thus the truth, being or goodness that characterizes any creature does not exhaust all possible truth, being or goodness itself but merely shares in them.

Historians of ideas have pointed out that infinity has a pejorative meaning for most of the great Greek pre-Christian thinkers; it connoted indefiniteness or imperfection and was characteristic of matter, rather than the divine. But as Christianity influenced the course of philosophy, the non-pejorative meaning of infinity as unlimited perfection itself was distinguished from infinity as indefiniteness. Thus the Christian acknowledgment of God as infinite (especially as clarified by Gregory of Nyssa and Thomas Aquinas) means that God's existence, truth and goodness, etc., are incomprehensible and inexhaustible to us without thereby being indefinite or meaningless.

Infinity can also be used to signify a lack of limit within some reality which is itself limited. Thus, though the human intellect is quite limited in its accomplishments (we do not actually know everything), its range can be characterized as infinite, since there is nothing which is in principle impossible for us to know. Infinite in this sense is derived from the absolute sense of infinite as attributed to God.

Infused Virtues • Associated with sanctifying grace are supernatural gifts that transform human capacities to enable them to function within a theological life: the theological virtues of faith, hope and love; the moral virtues; the gifts of the Holy Spirit.

The theological virtues transform the human powers of knowing and loving, so that they can be engaged in supernatural activities that have the Triune God as their object. Through the infusion of sanctifying grace and the theological virtues of faith, hope and love, the Triune God permits Himself to be the personal object of creaturely knowing and loving. Created persons do not require new powers in order to know, love and hope in God, but rather the supernatural empowerment of their creaturely powers by the infusion (as distinct from the acquisition) of "theological" dispositions that fit them for a divinized life.

Sanctifying grace brings with it a transformation of the moral virtues as well, the divinely aided transformation of the active disposition by which our efforts make possible the acquisition and development of the virtues.

Finally, the gifts of the Holy Spirit are supernatural, permanent dispositions of the powers of the soul by which human persons are enabled to respond easily and joyfully to the promptings of the Holy Spirit. The gifts are really distinct from the infused virtues in that the virtues arise from the supernaturally transformed powers of the soul while the gifts respond to the Holy Spirit directly. While the virtues empower us to perform the ordinary actions of the Christian life, the gifts impel us to

extraordinary or heroic activities. The theology of the infused virtues and gifts is crucial to understanding that grace is a gift that, far from suppressing natural human capacities, involves their empowerment for activity on the supernatural level in a divinized form of life.

Infusion: See **Baptism, Sacrament of**

Inopportunists • The term used to describe those bishops — in the minority — who felt it would be untimely for the First Vatican Council (1869-1870) to proclaim solemnly the infallibility of the Pope. This group was thus at odds with the dominant party of Council Fathers, the "infallibilists," and generally looked to Georges Darboy, the archbishop of Paris, and Wilhelm Emmanuel von Ketteler, the bishop of Mainz, for leadership. When it became clear that the Council would indeed promulgate the decree *Pastor Aeternus*, thus officially articulating papal infallibility, many of the "inopportunists" left the Council rather than vote against the majority. After the Council, all of the minority bishops submitted and accepted the decree.

Inquisition • In 1233, Pope Gregory IX set up this special court to help curb the influence of the Waldensian and Albigensian heresies. Technically, the term "inquisition" means a judicial procedure to ascertain the orthodoxy of one accused of heresy, and as such was in use before this date. Usually, this tribunal was an internal ecclesiastical affair, with the penalties being spiritual, the most severe being excommunication. In the twelfth and thirteenth centuries, however, Church officials began to count on civil authorities to levy fines, imprisonment, confiscation of property and even torture to cure heretics, maintaining that crimes against religious unity upset all of society. The local bishop was the technical officer of the court, but it also functioned as an arm of the papacy in France, Germany and Italy, ordinarily staffed by Dominicans and Franciscans. It faded from practice by the early fourteenth century.

It should be noted, however, that the Roman congregation charged with preserving doctrinal integrity was known as the Inquisition from 1542 to 1908. Its contemporary name is the Congregation for the Doctrine of the Faith.

Inquisition, Spanish • The tribunal established by Pope Sixtus IV in 1478 at the request of Ferdinand and Isabella of Spain in order to preserve religious unity and doctrinal orthodoxy within their realm. It initially considered as its special subjects Jews and Muslims who had submitted to Baptism in order to remain in Spain, but later broadened its aim to include anyone suspected of heresy. The monarchs organized a "Supreme Council of the Inquisition" under the Dominican Tomás de Torquemada, who served as Inquisitor until 1498. This court became an agency of both Church and kingdom to protect Spain from outside threats. Although its excesses have been exaggerated, it was indeed guilty of brutality and injustice, especially against Jews, and Pope Sixtus IV himself warned the Inquisition against such excesses less than six years after its inception. It was also functional in Spain's New World colonies.

I.N.R.I. • These letters, to be found inscribed above the head of the figure of the crucified Christ, the "corpus," on most crucifixes, are the initials for the inscription which Pontius Pilate had placed on the cross of Our Lord, as the charge for which the Lord was crucified. The Gospels give accounts of this inscription, stating that Pilate put "Jesus of Nazareth (literally, the Nazarene), King of the Jews." The Gospels tell us that this was inscribed in Hebrew, Latin and Greek (cf. Mt 27:37; Mk 15:26; Lk 23:38; Jn 19:19-22). "I.N.R.I." stands for the initials of the Latin inscription *Iesus Nazarenus, Rex Iudaeorum.*

Inspiration of Scripture • Scripture is inspired because it is authored by God. The texts of 2 Timothy 3:16-17; 2 Peter 1:19-21; 3:15-16; and John 20:31 are the classical sources for understanding the witness of Sacred Scripture. These texts affirm what we read at 2 Timothy 3:16: "All scripture is inspired by God" ("inspired": Greek, *theopneustos* meaning, "God-breathed"; Latin Vulgate, *inspirare*, meaning "to breathe into"). Language which is "inspired" is prophetic because it communicates the mind of God, as it were. The Old Testament is the initial witness for the inspiration of Scripture (e.g., 2 Sm 23:2; Dt 31:19; Mal 4:4).

Jewish thought before and after the birth of Christ expressed varying views on the exact nature of inspiration: The Babylonian Talmud (TB Sam. 93a) viewed the Pentateuch as "*the* Word from God." The first-century A.D. Hellenistic Jewish philosopher and theologian Philo of Alexandria (*Q. div. rer. her.* 249-258) understood inspiration in terms of a "god-indwelt possession and madness." Similar is the view of Theophilus (of Antioch, third century) who viewed the authors of the Sacred Scriptures (which he called: "the holy writings" [Greek, *hai hagiai graphai*]) as "manifestors/bearers of the Spirit" (Greek, *pneumatophoroi*). Thus, the ancients considered human authorship an activity derived from ecstatic experiences; those authors thought to have been possessed by the Holy Spirit were actually considered as prophets and as having been instructed by God. Justin Martyr suggested (*Apol.* 1.36) that the preexistent Christ prompted and instructed the prophets.

In sum, from the time before and during the Old Testament period through to the Protestant Reformation and the Catholic Counter-Reformation (especially up to the Council of Trent), the dominant view of divine inspiration derived from the prophetic mode of communication. Two conclusions can be drawn: (1) The sacred writings are first and foremost the Word of God; (2) because of their divine origins, they have an authority which surpasses even the most sublime and profound teachings of even the holiest and most brilliant of theologians. The second-century apologist Athenagoras anticipated the classical Scholastic teaching of instrumental causality when he wrote that the sacred authors inscribed what the Spirit inspired them to communicate, just as the divine flutist blows into the flute (cf. *Legatio* 9).

Vatican II's *Dei Verbum* sums up Catholic teaching from Augustine (*De genesi ad litteram* 2.9.20; *Ep.* 82.3), to Aquinas (*De Veritate* 1.12, a.2), to Trent (Session IV, *Scriptural Canons*), to the key encyclicals of Leo XIII (*Providentissimus Deus*), to Pius XII (*Divino Afflante Spiritu*) to the First Vatican Council (Dogmatic Constitution on the Catholic Faith, Ch. 2, "On Revelation"). The text of *Dei Verbum* makes clear that the human authors were true authors, in full command of their rational faculties and literary skills, yet at the same time instruments of God. They wrote everything and only those things which God wanted to communicate. Thus, the Scriptures, "firmly, faithfully and without error, teach that truth which God, for the sake of our salvation, wished to see confided to the sacred Scriptures" (DV 11).

Installation • The popular term used to describe broadly the provision of an ecclesiastical office by the competent authority, and more specifically, the formal assumption of that office by the designated individual(s).

Strictly speaking, installation is that form of provision which takes place when an individual or group has the right to nominate a person or persons for ecclesiastical office, and the competent authority selects one of them in the post (Canons 147, 158-163). It is becoming, however, an ever rarer practice in the Church.

In common usage, moreover, installation usually refers to the assumption of duties by a local Ordinary, generally the diocesan bishop. The technical assumption of duties by the bishop-designate basically occurs when he presents his apostolic letter of appointment to the diocesan College of Consultors. One frequently sees, however, and with ample appropriateness, a more ceremonial and public liturgical celebration of that ecclesial event in the form of an "Installation Mass," which opens the pastoral administration of the new bishop.

Institute, Religious • A type of institute of consecrated life, in which its members take public vows of poverty, chastity and obedience, and live the common life.

"Religious institute" is the term used by Vatican II and the revised Code to describe any religious order, society or congregation in which the members take public vows.

A religious institute is distinguished from a society of apostolic life because in the latter, the members do not take public vows. Rather, they are bound to the institute by some other form of sacred bond (cf. Canon 607).

Institute on Religious Life • In 1974, in Chicago, the Institute on Religious Life was founded to assist in the promotion of vocations to the religious life and the priesthood in accordance with the teachings of the Church. Its principles also include helping all the members of Christ's Body to attain holiness in their various states in life.

Institute, Secular • An institute of consecrated life made up of lay persons and/or clerics, who live in the world and strive for the perfection of charity and the sanctification of the world. Members of secular institutes profess the evangelical counsels of poverty, chastity and obedience, not by means of public vows but by some other bond determined by the institute's own law. Lay members retain their marital or single status and their occupation in life. In short, they are organizations of people who consecrate their lives in a special way to God through the life and work of the institute.

Members are required to fulfill a period of probation before making temporary profession into the institute. When the period of temporary profession is completed, they may make permanent profession or incorporation into the institute. An indult from the Holy See is required to leave the institute.

Although secular institutes have existed in the Church since the sixteenth century, they were only officially recognized by the Holy See in 1947. Although no provision was made for secular institutes in the 1917 Code of Canon Law, they were nevertheless covered by the Apostolic Constitution *Provida Mater Ecclesiae*, issued by Pope Pius XII. Legislation on secular institutes has been included in the revised Code (cf. Canons 710-730).

Instruction, Canonical • The term instruction has two basic meanings in canon law, both of which are distinct from instruction in the catechetical sense.

Canon 34 of the 1983 Code of Canon Law defines an instruction as a clarification and elaboration of the methods to be used in implementing a law. Thus they differ from general decrees, in that instructions are primarily intended for the use of ecclesiastical officials whose task it is to bring about compliance with laws (and, one may suggest, general decrees). In other respects, instructions closely track general executory decrees. They are subsidiary to the laws which they foster, and if they are in any way inconsistent with those laws, they lack force in that matter. Instructions are issued by those with executive authority in the Church.

Instruction also has a second meaning within canon law, this time one associated with the administration of justice in the Church. Broadly speaking, the instruction of a case refers to the process of gathering evidence and other information relevant to the adjudication of an ecclesiastical case or controversy. The task of instructing a case falls naturally to the judge of the case, or with the approval of the bishop, to an individual known as an "auditor," who works under the direction of the judge.

Intellect • The power possessed by persons by which they can know beings in their essence. Intellectual knowledge is distinguished from sensation and imagination, the powers by which sentient beings know material beings in their particularity. Three types of intellect should be distinguished: human rational intellect, angelic intuitive intellect and divine intellect, the actuality of knowing itself. Human intellect is a potency for knowledge, that rational knowledge achieved only in conjunction with the senses and imagination and in the course of laborious development. Angelic intellect is in no need of development and does not depend on sensation; it is, however, still received from God. God's intellect is identical with His infinite actuality in being and is infinite knowing as such. Primarily, God's knowing is of His own essence and, secondarily, is of all things other than Himself.

Aristotle and Aquinas clarified the character of human intellectual knowledge. By knowing something, the intellectual knower becomes identical in form to the known object. The form of the being to be known is abstracted from conditions of materiality by the human being's active or agent intellect. By abstracting the form from the materiality in which it naturally exists, the intellect does not set aside part of the reality of that which is to be known. Rather, the thing's form or essence is actualized at a level of actuality — the intentional level — beyond that of its natural existence. Such intellectual actuality may be said to benefit both those material things which we can know directly, as well as human beings ourselves. We are benefited, in that, by knowing we become that which by nature we are not; our intellect is our capacity to become everything, in the intentional order. And we may say that material things are benefited by being known by us, in that thereby they gain intentional existence and can contribute to the worship of God given voice in our mouths.

The Church has affirmed that by the nature we are given in creation, our intellects include the ability to learn of "God's eternal power and divinity" from "the things he has made" (Rom 1:20). The limits of the human intellect are many and perfect knowledge of God, though naturally desired, is impossible by our natural powers (cf. Thomas Aquinas, *Compendium of Theology*, nn. 104-105). In spite of the limits of the human intellect, its range as intellectual is infinite; thus our intellect can be elevated by God's grace to faith's sharing in the infallible truth of God's own inner life. The ultimate end of our intellect will be fully realized only after the resurrection in the sharing in God's truth of realized glory.

Intention • The aim, purpose or objective for which a knowledgeable, free and deliberate human act is willed or chosen by a moral agent. The concept of intentionality is one of the most complex and difficult in all of moral philosophy, for distinguishing the intention from the motive, end and circumstance of an action is exceedingly difficult.

Sacramentally, the intention is the disposition and purpose necessary for both the administration and reception of the sacrament. The one who administers the sacrament must have an actual intention to administer the sacrament, and the aim must be to administer it to the actual person receiving it. And the person receiving the sacrament must have at least a habitual intention to receive it. For ordination to the priesthood, an explicit intention to receive the sacrament is necessary. For marriage, a virtual intention (an intention consciously posited prior to the act, even if one is distracted at the moment of the act) is permitted.

Intention may also refer to the special object for which a prayer or sacrifice is made; thus, the intention of a Mass is the particular end for which the celebrant prays that the fruits of the sacrifice might be applied by God, e.g., for the repose of the soul of one departed.

Intercession • Prayer of petition offered on behalf of other persons and their needs. Such prayer is an expression of the bond of charity that unites the entire Church — on earth, in purgatory and in heaven — in Christ, Who is the first and chief mediator. Thus, in virtue of this bond in Christ, anyone in the Church can and should make intercession for others. After Christ Himself, the chief intercessor is Our Lady, who continually prays for those whom Christ has made her children. The saints are involved throughout the Church as intercessors, offering their prayers to God on our behalf.

In addition, intercessory prayer is a basic form of prayer, both liturgical and private, for every Christian. The communal celebration of the Eucharist, as well as of the other sacraments, normally includes explicit formularies for intercessions, usually after the proclamation of the Scriptures and the homily. Each of the Eucharistic prayers (or Canons) contains sections for intercessions in behalf of the Pope, the bishops and clergy, and the people of God — both living and deceased. In short, intercession is a fundamental form of prayer in the Church, whether it be expressed in definite petitions or simply by commending others in silent meditation.

Besides petitionary prayer, another important form of intercession is the offering of good actions to God for the intentions and benefit of other persons. All these forms of intercession, by prayer and deed, participate in the one loving act of mediation by which Christ continually pleads our cause before the Father.

Intercommunion • A term to express a relationship between churches in which each accepts members of the other for Holy Communion. It also refers to permission granted one's own members to receive Communion from another Christian body.

For non-Catholics to receive Holy Communion within the Catholic Church, certain criteria have been established in two documents: (1) Pope Paul VI's "Instruction on the Admission of Other Christians to the Eucharist," issued on July 8, 1972; (2) Vatican II's Decree on Ecumenism with its "Directory of Ecumenism" of the Secretariat for Promoting Christian Unity, issued in 1967.

Non-Catholic Christians may receive Communion in the Catholic Church under the following circumstances: (1) a serious spiritual need (e.g., danger of death, persecution); (2) inability to have recourse to their own minister for a prolonged period of time; (3) the same fundamental belief in the Catholic understanding of the Eucharist; (4) living a genuine Christian life; (5) permission from their own ecclesial community to receive Communion in another.

Intercommunion among Catholic and Orthodox Christians is allowed by Vatican II, provided no church of one's own tradition is available. This procedure is permitted because both have the same Mass and priesthood by apostolic succession. However, this is frowned upon by the Orthodox since full unity does not exist. Catholics are forbidden to receive Communion in other denominations (cf. Canon 844.2).

In the ecumenical movement, intercommunion is regarded in two ways: (1) it is a means of expressing unity, despite differences; (2) it should be practiced only when the goal of unity has been achieved.

Interdict • An ecclesiastical penalty incurred for the commission of certain ecclesiastical crimes. In the 1917 Code, an interdict was a prohibition against using sacred things. It applied either to groups of persons or to places. A personal interdict was a censure imposed on all the people of a territory, diocese or parish, preventing them from attending liturgical services, receiving certain sacraments and receiving Christian burial. A local interdict prohibited the celebration of liturgical services in certain places, especially churches, shrines and chapels of a given territory.

Only the Holy See could impose either type of interdict on an entire territory or diocese, but a bishop could impose either type on a parish within his diocese. By reason of an interdict, the faithful were not excommunicated.

In the revised Code, the meaning of an interdict has been changed and significantly simplified. Interdict now applies to individuals and not groups of persons or places. An interdicted person is prevented from participating in any ceremonies of public worship, including the celebration of the Eucharist, and is forbidden to receive any of the sacraments or sacramentals. If the penalty has been formally imposed or publicly declared, the interdicted person is to be removed from liturgical celebrations if he attends in defiance of the prohibition. If he cannot be removed, the liturgical action is to be suspended.

An interdict is automatically incurred for the commission of the following acts: a physical attack upon a bishop, pretended celebration of the Eucharist or of the sacramental absolution of sins by one not a priest, false accusation of a confessor of solicitation in the confessional, and attempted marriage by a non-clerical religious in perpetual vows. An interdict is to be imposed but is not incurred automatically for stirring up opposition to the Holy See or to an Ordinary, promoting or governing a forbidden society contrary to the Church, and receiving a sacrament through simony. All these penalties may be lifted by a competent Church authority and none are reserved to the Holy See for absolution (cf. Canons 1332, 1370.2, 1373, 1374, 1378.2, 1380, 1390.1, 1394).

Inter Mirifica • The Decree on the Means of Social Communication, *Inter Mirifica*, was issued by the Second Vatican Council on December 4, 1963, to define the nature, use and proper content of communications media. Because all of the various media are the fruits of man's God-given intelligence, the Church claims the right to use them for pastoral formation and care. To that end, those who are responsible for the media must "know the principles of the moral order and apply them faithfully in this domain" (IM 4). The Council gave express direction in this decree that there should be published "a pastoral instruction, with the help of experts from various countries, to ensure that all the principles and rules of the Council on the means of social communication be put into effect" (IM 32), and this resulted in the publication of *Communio et Progressio*, the *Pastoral Instruction on the Means of Social Communication*, on January 29, 1971. In these two documents are outlined the great opportunities and responsibilities presented to the Church in the use of the media for the propagation of the Gospel.

Internal Forum • The place of judging or dispensing that remains completely confidential. Confession of sins in sacramental confession is a matter of the internal forum. Furthermore, any bishop can remove a canonical penalty that has not been reserved to the Holy See in the course of sacramental confession which is, of course, in the internal forum. A confessor can similarly remit non-reserved penalties which have not been imposed or formally declared if it is truly difficult for the person to remain under penalty (cf. Canons 130, 1355, 1357). As Pope John Paul II has repeatedly observed, it is always necessary that conflicts between the requirements of the external forum and the integrity of the internal forum be reduced as much as possible.

International Committee (or Commission) on English in the Liturgy, Inc. (ICEL) • Commonly known as ICEL, with its Secretariat based in Washington, D.C., this commission came into existence at the end of the Second Vatican Council as the English-language nations' response to the Holy See's desire for a single translation of liturgical texts in each of the major modern languages. Translations prepared by ICEL are submitted for critique and approval to the national conferences of bishops of all countries where English is spoken. Then individual conferences must submit their approved texts to the Holy See for confirmation.

Initially concerned almost exclusively with translating the newly-revised Vatican II rites, ICEL's scope of activity has broadened in recent years to include more suitable arrangements of ritual texts, the composition of original prayer-texts in English, sponsorship of scholarly articles relating to liturgical language, new translations of critical editions of classic euchological texts, and an ecumenical effort to prepare English translations of prayers common to the liturgical worship of both the Catholic and Protestant communities.

ICEL's agenda for the future also includes a wide-scale revisions project to prepare fresh translations of already published ritual books.

International Theological Commission (ITC) • At the first postconciliar Synod of Bishops in 1967, the idea was first suggested that an international theological commission be established. After provisional establishment in 1969, Pope John Paul II gave definite status to the commission (ITC) by the *motu proprio Tredici Anni* on August 6, 1982.

The primary purpose of the ITC is to study doctrinal problems of great importance and to offer the results of its study to the Magisterium, especially to the Congregation for the Doctrine of the Faith, to which it is attached and whose prefect is *ex officio* the president of ITC. The thirty members are appointed for terms of five years by the Pope, who receives recommendations for appointments from the various episcopal conferences. Those appointed are to be eminent in scholarship, prudence and

fidelity to the Magisterium. The commission meets once a year in Rome, usually in the autumn. The names of the ITC members are listed in the *Annuario Pontificio*.

Internuncio • A special legate of the Pope with lesser authority and prestige than a nuncio. Internuncios were sent as temporary representatives to certain governments, to foster better relations with the Holy See, or to transact dealings of a more personal nature. This term is no longer used.

Interpretation, Scriptural • In current theological language "Interpretation of Scripture" is called "hermeneutics." Current approaches include: (1) Speech which interprets its referent; for example, words we use to communicate our thoughts. In biblical terms, the understanding of divine realities (for example, God's "mind," "will" and "person") communicated in human language. (2) The translation or transference of meaning as it exists in one cultural context (e.g., first-century A.D. Jewish Palestine) into another culture (e.g., North American Catholicism). (3) A commentary and explanation of a passage, which can include number two above.

There are different senses of Sacred Scripture (neomantics) which are discovered and verified by specific methods (heuristics); rules for commenting (prophoristics) on each of these levels within a passage are then applied to that passage. Whether one examines the spiritual sense of a passage or some other aspect of a pericope, "meaning" or "interpretation" must in some way accord with the factual features of the text. Any meaning of a particular theme within a given passage of Sacred Scripture must be viewed in light of the whole of Sacred Scripture, the use of the passage in the Sacred Liturgy, Magisterial pronouncements, the Fathers and Doctors of the Church, and the lives of the saints.

Interpretation of Law • The Code of Canon Law contains several canons dealing with how laws are to be interpreted. An authentic interpretation is that given by the legislator in a case where the law is objectively unclear or imprecise. An authentic interpretation must be communicated or promulgated in the same way as a law is promulgated. In effect, it is treated as if it were a new law (Canon 16).

Ordinary interpretation is that which is done by people who have the responsibility of applying the law to specific cases. Ecclesiastical laws are to be interpreted or understood with the proper meaning of their words considered in the text and in the context of the law. If the meaning remains doubtful or obscure, the person is directed to look at parallel passages or to the mind of the legislator. The mind of the legislator may be determined by non-legal or even legal statements concerning the matter about which the law is concerned. Another source which may be used in the understanding of the meaning of a law is the commentaries of the law written by canonical scholars. If there is consistency among the scholars about the meaning of a law, this is a good indication of its meaning and the mind of the legislator.

In canon law, unlike common law, a series of judgments about a matter do not constitute its legal meaning. Nevertheless the consistent decisions of the Church's highest courts (the Signatura and the Rota) are an indication of the meaning of a law (Canons 17-19). Furthermore, at the time of the promulgation of the new law, the Pontifical Council for the Interpretation of the Code was also established, precisely to offer authentic interpretations when questions were raised about a particular canon's meaning. As in any legal system, it should also be recognized that the application of canon law by those charged with its administration also represents a means of interpreting the law and can serve as one indicator of what works in the practical and pastoral order and what does not.

Interregnum • The period between the death of a sovereign and the assumption of rule by his successor is known as the interregnum, from the Latin meaning "between reign(s)." The period between the death of a Pope and the election of his successor is a period of interregnum but is more commonly known as the period of *sede vacante*, also Latin meaning, "While the See is vacant." During this period the exercise of the functions of the papal office is governed by the norms set forth in the Code of Canon Law and the relevant Apostolic Constitutions.

Interstices • The periods of time that must elapse between the reception of ministries or Orders leading to ordination to the priesthood. The Code of Canon Law specifies an interval of six months between the transitional diaconate and the priesthood (Canon 1031.1). Additionally, a candidate for the priesthood must be deemed sufficiently mature and may not be ordained before he has completed the age of twenty-five. A man destined for the priesthood may not be admitted to the order of deacon until he has completed the age of twenty-three.

Canon law also stipulates that before a man may be advanced to either the permanent or transitional diaconate, he is required to receive the ministries of lector and acolyte and to have exercised them for a suitable period of time. Between the conferral of acolyte and diaconate, there is to be an interval of at least six months as well (Canon 1035).

The purpose of these requirements is to give the candidates the opportunity to experience and exercise a particular ministry or order, as well as to become better acquainted and more comfortable with service at the altar. It also provides the Church herself an opportunity to judge the performance of her candidates in the exercise of their respective orders.

Intinction • One of the ways of distributing the Eucharist under both species. The *General Instruction of the Roman Missal* describes the rite by stating that the minister of distribution dips a particle of Eucharistic Bread (or a small Host designed for individual communicants) "into the chalice, and showing it, says: *The body and blood of Christ.* The communicants respond: *Amen*, receive communion . . . and return to their place" (n. 247b). The 1970 Instruction *Sacramentali Communione* of the Sacred Congregation of Divine Worship, extending the practice of Communion under both kinds, gives preference to drinking from the chalice if Communion is received under both forms. However, it then goes on to say that among the ways of communicating under both species, the choice of intinction "is more likely to obviate the practical difficulties and to ensure the reverence due the sacrament more effectively. Intinction makes access to Communion under both kinds easier and safer for the faithful of all ages and conditions; at the same time it preserves the truth present in a more complete sign" (as opposed to the Eucharistic Bread only).

Introduction, Biblical • In contemporary Catholic universities, colleges, professional schools of religion and seminaries, courses abound which introduce the student to each book of Sacred Scripture under the following categories: time and place of composition, content and structure, purpose for writing

the book, its authenticity (whether it is a unified or composite document), its recipients; its overall literary form and individual literary forms, its literary sources, its manuscript tradition, etc. Mainstream academic practice of the past couple of centuries was known neither in Christian antiquity nor in the Middle Ages — it is a phenomenon born of eighteenth-century theological and philosophical currents.

The Oratorian Richard Simon was the Catholic originator of the "Introduction" method. The ancient "Introduction" pattern from which eighteenth-century "Introduction" models developed is arguably the Muratorian Canon (late second century), which not only enumerates the canonical books but also provides basic information about the author, content, authenticity and occasion for writing for each book. The ancient Church asked slightly different "Introduction" questions than did their eighteenth-century counterparts. Around A.D. 450, the Greek Adriano wrote an Introduction (*Eisagoge*) to the Divine Scriptures. He focused more on hermeneutical issues such as how meaning can be gotten from the sacred text (others followed in his footsteps: Cassiodorus, d. 570; Tyconius the Donatist, d. 380; St. Augustine, d. 430; Eucherius of Lyons, d. 450; Junilius Africanus, d. 550).

For various historical reasons, the term "Introduction" can be divided into two categories. First, "Special Introduction" refers to scientific study of the circumstances in which each book was composed (authorship, unity, purpose, recipients, time and location of composition, literary form, sources, etc.) — that is, literary and historical data of a given book of Sacred Scripture. Second, "General Introduction" refers to a scientific study of the history of the canon and belongs under the heading of the History of Dogma. In addition, the question of the transmission of the texts, called textual criticism, for each book of Scripture also belongs in this second category. Thus the current mode of thinking referred to by "Introduction" is historical and literary, not necessarily theological, religious or philosophical.

Introit • In the pre-Vatican II rite, the Introit consisted of an antiphon, psalm verse, Glory Be, and the antiphon repeated, all of which was sung by a schola, choir or soloist at High Mass and recited by the celebrant at all Masses after he finished the prayers at the foot of the altar. In the Missal published after Vatican II, the chant is restored to its more ancient title and form: called *antiphona ad introitum* (entrance antiphon or song); only the antiphon itself is given in the Missal, the full psalm being provided in a separate book for the cantor called the *Roman Gradual*. (Cf. Entrance Antiphon/Song.)

Investiture • Broadly speaking, investiture was the regular legal (and sometimes colorful) process by which a superior turned over control of real property to a subordinate, especially during the eleventh and twelfth centuries. The problem with investiture arose, however, as certain bishops and abbots assumed their sacred offices, sometimes involving the administration of enormous tracts of land. Often this temporal aspect of their office was in the control of lay overlords. With time, these lay overlords also claimed the right to nominate and appoint the religious holder of the office attached to the land, with the unhappy result that religious offices often went not so much to the spiritually qualified, but to family and friends of lay landholders.

Various methods were proposed to protect the rights of the Church in the appointment of her chief leaders while at the same time satisfying the demands of lay landholders

and rulers. While such agreements were reached in England and France, much of what later became modern Germany persisted, sometimes violently, to claim the right of lay investiture for many spiritual offices. The matter there was not really resolved until the Concordat of Worms. (Cf. Iuspatronatus; Advowson.)

Invincible Ignorance • A lack of knowledge for which a person is not morally accountable. From the Latin *in* ("not") plus *vincibilis* ("easily overcome"), this state may be due to the difficulty of subject matter, insufficiency of evidence, or lack of opportunity and cognitive skill on the part of an individual.

Invitatory (also Invitatorium) • The verse or psalm which begins the Liturgy of the Hours for a given day. The *General Instruction of the Liturgy of the Hours* states that "the whole Office is normally begun with an invitatory" (n. 34). This consists of the verse, *Domine, labia mea aperies: Et os meum annuntiabit laudem tuam* ("Lord, open my lips. And my mouth shall proclaim your praise"), and Psalm 95 (94). Sometimes another verse is added as a response to Psalm 95, for example, during the first days of Advent: "Come let us worship the Lord, the King who is to come." Other psalms that may be used instead of Psalm 95 are Psalms 100 (99), 66 or 23. The *Instruction* states, "The invitatory should begin the whole sequence of daily prayer; thus it begins Lauds or the Office of Readings depending on which of these liturgical actions begins the day" (n. 35).

"In Vitro" Fertilization • The process by which human conception is accomplished by uniting sperm and ovum "in glass," or artificially and through technological means. This process has been condemned by the Church because it separates the unitive and procreative ends of marriage. The child has a right to be united to its parents not only through the course of its minority, but also in its conception. In the process of *in vitro* fertilization, the child is "manufactured" by the technologist and is not the immediate product of the love-act of the parents, but of the skill and expertise of the technologist.

In vitro fertilization dehumanizes the child-to-be because it makes the child-to-be the product of the skill, craft or technology of another and not the immediate fruit of the love of the child's mother and father. This process injects another person in between the parents and the child and makes that extrafamilial individual the primary causal agent of the child's coming into being. The moral malice of *in vitro* fertilization is that it alienates the child from its parents at the precise moment of the conception of the child.

At a time when there is great concern for the protection of children against adults who would exploit them for their own advantage, *in vitro* fertilization alienates children from the love that is due them by making them products of manipulation, science and technology.

For further reading: Congregation for the Doctrine of the Faith, *Donum Vitae.*

Ipso Facto • Latin for "by the very fact" or "in the very nature of the thing," the term is applicable in ecclesiastical law when referring to excommunications taking effect the very moment a person commits a particular crime or denies a particular essential dogma of the Faith publicly. The phrase may at times also pertain to the rights and prerogatives attached to an office or rank.

Ipsum Esse • Latin for "existence itself," it is used to describe God as a subsistent Being, i.e., the Being Whose essence is existence and Who is unable not to exist, unlike human beings or lower creatures.

Irenicism • The determination to pursue a course of conciliation rather than polemics in the midst of doctrinal or factional disputes, where peace and harmony are sought by reducing denominational partisanship and fostering mutual understanding. Irenic theology is distinguished from polemical theology in seeking to discover the areas of convergence and agreement that promote Christian unity, and in downplaying the doctrinal disagreements that foster division. To describe its connection with the cognate term "ecumenism," it could be said that while all irenic theology is ecumenical, not all ecumenical theology is irenic. Ecumenical theology can countenance a forthright recognition of the differences that divide Christians, although it cultivates attitudes of tolerance, respect and charity. Irenicism bespeaks a more active pursuit of the resolution of such differences.

Irregularity, Canonical • An irregularity is a condition which, as long as it perdures, prevents a man from receiving Sacred Orders or, if he has already received orders, from exercising them. The following are the irregularities that prevent a man from receiving orders: (1) insanity or mental instability that would prevent a man from fulfilling the ministry; (2) apostasy, heresy or schism; (3) having attempted marriage, even a civil marriage, while bound by an existing marriage bond, Sacred Orders or perpetual and public vow of chastity, or having attempted marriage with a woman so bound by existing bond or vow; (4) willful homicide or actual procurement of an abortion or direct cooperation in the same; (5) gravely and maliciously mutilating oneself or another or attempting suicide; (6) carrying out an act of a Sacred Order which one does not in fact have or which one has been barred from carrying out because of an ecclesiastical penalty.

One who has already received orders is irregular for the exercise of any function of Sacred Orders if: (1) he has unlawfully received orders while bound by an irregularity; (2) one, after ordination, has publicly committed the offense of apostasy, heresy or schism; (3) one has committed any of the offenses mentioned in numbers three through six above.

If the fact of an irregularity has been brought to the judicial forum, then the irregularity may be dispensed only by the Holy See. Also reserved to the Holy See are the irregularities arising out of public apostasy, heresy, schism or attempted marriage, as well as homicide or abortion, whether public or not. All other irregularities may be dispensed by the bishop.

The irregularities for exercising orders that are reserved to the Holy See for dispensation are public cases of attempted marriage and all cases of homicide or abortion (cf. Canons 1041, 1044-1048).

Irremovability of Pastors • Under the 1917 Code of Canon Law, and indeed for some time prior to it, certain parish pastors were canonically designated as "irremovable." This status was tied to the concept of benefice, and meant in actuality not that such a pastor was absolutely irremovable from office, but rather that very strict procedures had to be followed in the event that the diocesan bishop wished to remove him from that parish.

This process was increasingly felt to be an obstacle to the bishop in the exercise of his duty to see to the overall welfare of his diocese. With the demise, then, of the benefice in the wake of the Second Vatican Council, it came as no surprise that the status of irremovable pastor was dropped from the 1983 Code, although careful provisions were retained for the just protection of the rights of pastors generally (Canons 1732-1752). (Cf. Office, Ecclesiastical.)

Isaac • Hebrew name meaning "he laughs." The word is believed to be a shortened form of a word meaning "God laughs." In Genesis (17:17f. and 18:11-15), the name is explained in terms of Sarah and Abraham's laughter at the promise of a son to be born of them in their old age. Isaac is the half-brother of Ishmael (Gn 16), the husband of Rebekah (Gn 24), and the father of Esau and Jacob (Gn 25:19-26). In Genesis, Isaac remains a hazy figure who never comes into the forefront of the patriarchal stories. In the New Testament, Isaac surfaces in Paul's Epistle to the Romans (9:7; cf. Gal 4:28-31), where he is spoken of as a type of the Gentile Christian community in the sense that he was a son born to Abraham, not just in a carnal way but by a promise. St. Paul asserts that all who share Abraham's faith in God's promise are genuine sons of Abraham and are heirs of the promise.

For further reading: Robert Martin-Achard, "Isaac," *Anchor Bible Dictionary*, 3:462-470.

Isaiah • This Old Testament prophetic book takes its name from Isaiah of Jerusalem, a prophet active in Judah from approximately 742 until 701 B.C. Chapters 1-39 belong to the time of Isaiah himself (with the possible exception of Chapters 24-27, the so-called Isaian apocalypse), while Chapters 40-66 belong to a later period. Chapters 40-55 are generally considered the work of a prophet who was active just before the fall of Babylon to the Persians (539 B.C.), and scholars generally refer to this anonymous prophetic writer as Second Isaiah (also called Deutero-Isaiah). Chapters 56-66 are usually considered to be the work of yet another anonymous prophet, designated as Third Isaiah (also called Trito-Isaiah).

Isaiah of Jerusalem was active during the reigns of Uzziah, Jotham, Ahaz and Hezekiah as kings of Judah. He received his prophetic vocation "in the year King Uzziah died" (Is 6:1), that is, 742 B.C. Very little is known of the prophet's personal life, except that we know he was married to a woman who is called a prophetess (Is 8:1), and that his two sons were given symbolic names (7:3: Shearjashub, "a remnant will return"; 8:3: Mahershalalhashbaz, "speedy spoil, quick plunder").

The power and the holiness of God are key themes of the prophetic message of Isaiah of Jerusalem. The power of God is supreme over the destinies of all nations, not only Israel, and Israel's fate is linked to its faithful obedience to God's will. During the prophetic career of Isaiah, Assyria and Egypt were the major powers on the international scene, and Judah was often caught in the tension between these two great nations. For Isaiah, pride was the greatest sin, and foolhardy self-reliance — by individuals or by entire nations — was the worst manifestation of this attitude, an attitude which implied reliance on merely human strength and not the power of God.

Isaiah's prophetic activity often included giving advice to the king himself in God's name. For example, in Chapters 7 and 8, he counsels King Ahaz during the period of the Syro-Ephraimite War (734-733 B.C.), warning the king against seeking assistance from Assyria against the military threat that Syria and the northern kingdom of Israel posed against Judah.

Isaiah (twelfth-century statue)

The message of the anonymous exilic prophet who is known to us through the oracles of Isaiah 40-55 is a message of hope and consolation. Second Isaiah, as the author of these chapters is designated, describes his prophetic commissioning in Chapter 40. God commands him, "Comfort, comfort my people, says your God. Speak tenderly to Jerusalem, and cry to her that her warfare is ended, that her iniquity is pardoned, that she has received from the LORD's hand double for all her sins" (Is 40:1-2). The Babylonian exile, understood as punishment for Israel's sins, was soon to come to its end, and the Persian victories over the neo-Babylonian empire made that a very proximate hope. Writing from Babylon, the land of exile, Second Isaiah exhorted those with him that the time had come for them to return to Jerusalem. That return would be a new Exodus, in which God would prepare a path for His people to return to their land.

Second Isaiah describes God's work as a new creation, in which God defeats all opponents as a manifestation of His holiness. It is Second Isaiah who speaks of the "Servant of the Lord" in four poems (Is 42:1-7; 49:1-7; 50:4-11; 52:13—53:12) that Christians later read and applied to the perfectly obedient Servant of the Lord, Jesus, Who "was wounded for our transgressions" (Is 53:5).

Third Isaiah is the way in which scholars refer to the last twelve chapters (56-66) of the Book of Isaiah and to the anonymous prophet who was their author. These chapters are somewhat more difficult to date than Second Isaiah (Chapters 40-55), but there is widespread agreement that this material is later than the work of Second Isaiah. It is distinguished from the material that precedes it by its setting, for Third Isaiah presumes a Palestinian (and therefore postexilic) setting and not the Babylonian setting that Second Isaiah presumes. Third Isaiah presents a renewed focus on the Temple and on Jerusalem itself. The well-developed eschatology of Third Isaiah anticipates the still more elaborate eschatology of later apocalyptic literature.

For further reading: Richard J. Clifford, "Isaiah, Book of (Second Isaiah)," *Anchor Bible Dictionary*, 3:490-501; Joseph Jensen, O.S.B., and William H. Irwin, C.S.B., "Isaiah 1-39," *New Jerome Biblical Commentary*, 229-248; William R. Millar, "Isaiah, Book of," *Anchor Bible Dictionary*, 3:472-490; Christopher R. Seitz, "Isaiah, Book of," *Anchor Bible Dictionary*, 3:501-507; Carroll Stuhlmueller, C.P., "Deutero-Isaiah and Trito-Isaiah," *New Jerome Biblical Commentary*, 329-348.

Islam • The word in Arabic means "submission to the will of God." Islam is the religion of the Muslims, and was founded by Muhammad in A.D. 622. Thus it is the most recent of the world's major religions and is enjoying rapid growth in many parts of the world. As of 1990, there were 881 million Muslims in the world (over seventeen percent of the world's population). This ranks second only to all Christian denominations combined (1.7 billion).

Muslims consider Muhammad to be the greatest of the prophets, whose role was to bring the Koran, God's final revelation, to the people. Included in the same category of prophets are Noah, Abraham, Moses, and Jesus, who is considered human only, not divine. God is known as Allah. The Koran is the book of Allah's revelations to man, delivered to Muhammad by the angel Gabriel.

Islam teaches that the righteous will live in eternal bliss, while evildoers are tormented in hell. The "Five Pillars" of the Muslim faith, as taught by the Koran are: (1) belief in Allah and his prophet Muhammad; (2) prayer to be offered at dawn, noon, afternoon, sunset and after nightfall, facing in the direction of the Muslim holy city, Mecca; (3) alms to be given often; (4) fasting to take place, since it inclines one to Allah; (5) all Muslims to go to Mecca on pilgrimage.

The Islamic religion does not have a formal clergy. Prayers are led by an imam.

Israel • The name given to Jacob, according to Genesis 32:22-32. The word came to apply as well to the descendants of Jacob, the Hebrew nation. (Cf. Jacob.) The meaning and derivation of the word remain obscure. The family of Jacob is variously referred to as "sons of Jacob" and "sons of Israel." It may be noted that the expression "sons of (a particular man)" embraced more than the lineal descendants of the man named. The word appears to designate not only the immediate family of Jacob but his more remote descendants also.

Up to the split of the kingdom after Solomon's reign (Israel in the north, Judah in the south) and again after the fall of Samaria, the word in the Old Testament embraces all the descendants of Jacob. In the interim (between the division of the kingdom and the destruction of Samaria),

"Israel" generally refers to the Ten Tribes of the Northern Kingdom as distinguished from Judah in the south. After the Exile, the word at times identifies the Jewish laity, vis-à-vis the clergy (cf. Neh 11:3).

In the Synoptic Gospels, Israel denotes the religion and the people. Paul makes a distinction between the physical descendants of Jacob, "Israel according to the flesh" and the Christians, "the Israel of God" (Gal 6:16).

In recent times, this is the name for the modern Jewish state which came into existence on May 15, 1948, following upon the United Nations partition of Palestine. The State of Israel borders on the Mediterranean to the west, Lebanon to the north, Syria to the northeast, Jordan to the east and southeast, and Egypt to the southwest.

For further reading: Niels Peter Lemeche et al., "Israel, History of," *Anchor Bible Dictionary*, 3:526-576; Addison G. Wright, S.S., Roland E. Murphy, O.Carm., and Joseph A. Fitzmyer, S.J., "A History of Israel," *New Jerome Biblical Commentary*, 1219-1252.

Itala Vetus • A term used to identify an old Latin translation of the Bible which predated the Vulgate translation. The term (*Itala*) appears to originate in St. Augustine's work on Christian doctrine. In that setting, it has been construed by different scholars as designating a variety of early Latin texts.

For further reading: Kurt Aland and Barbara Aland, *The Text of the New Testament*, 187-190 (William B. Eerdmans, 1989).

Iuspatronatus • The "right of making appointment," *iuspatronatus*, was the technical term for the institution of advowson as it governed the practice in what turned out to be its final days, for under Canons 1450-1451 the creation of any new *iuspatronatus* was prohibited.

By the Code of Canon Law of 1917, only ecclesiastical authority could grant the *iuspatronatus* to the founder of a benefice, and that founder had to be Catholic. The *ius* was differentiated into whether it was "real" or "personal," depending on where the rights were vested, and into "ecclesiastical," "laical" or "mixed," depending upon the status of the person(s) possessing the *ius*. The *ius* could be passed by last will, but numerous restrictions were placed on other attempts to transfer the *ius*. During the time of the *ius*, Canon 1469 required the patron to make necessary repairs on the church or to supplement the revenues of the parish if the same were deficient.

In addition to having the right to present the candidates for a benefice, the patron also had a limited claim on the excess income of the benefice in the case of the patron's own property, and certain ceremonial privileges in liturgical celebrations held within the church. It was up to the local Ordinary, however, to make a final determination on the suitability of a proffered candidate. Finally, the *ius* could be lost through the negligence of the patron, through suppression of the church or benefice, by prescription or by the commission of one of several delicts.

J

Jacob • The name is believed by some to be a shortened form of the Hebrew *Jacobel*, "let God protect," or *Jacobhar*, "let the God of the mountain protect." Genesis 25:26 gives a popular etymology of the name, viz., "he will trip by the heel."

Jacob was the son of Rebecca and Isaac. He was the younger twin of Esau, from whom he purchased the rights of the firstborn. On the occasion of his epic struggle with the "divine stranger," his name was changed to "Israel." The twelve tribes of Israel are said in Scripture to take their origin from his twelve sons. (Cf. Israel.)

For further reading: Stanley E. Porter, "Jacob," *Anchor Bible Dictionary*, 3:599; Stanley D. Walters, "Jacob Narrative," *Anchor Bible Dictionary*, 3:599-608.

Jacob and the angel
(medieval illumination)

Jacobins • A name originally given to the Dominicans in France because their first house in northern France was founded in Paris in 1218 on the Rue St.-Jacques. During the French Revolution in 1789, this house was acquired by the radical Club Breton. Consequently, they came to be called Jacobins. The term is now applied to all holding revolutionary views.

Jacobite Church • The Syrian Monophysite Church, which did not accept the teaching of the Council of Chalcedon (A.D. 451) on the two natures united in One Divine Person of Christ. They took their name from Jacob Baradaeus, who formed them into the national Church of Syria in the sixth century. During the Muslim invasions in the mid-seventh century, the Jacobites suffered great losses but have survived into the twentieth century. Interestingly, one of their distinctive customs is to make the Sign of the Cross with one finger to express their belief that Christ has one nature, not two.

Since 1959 the Jacobite patriarch resides in Damascus, ruling over eleven dioceses: four in Syria, two in Iraq, two in Turkey, one in Lebanon, one in Jerusalem and one in Hackensack, New Jersey.

James, Epistle of • This letter is the first of the Catholic Epistles (1-2 Pt, 1-3 Jn and Jude) and is classified as such because in the West these letters were *accepted* by *all* the Churches ("canonical"); in the East they were taken as *addressed* to *all* the Churches — hence their universal acceptance. The fact that this epistle is written in elegant Greek style, coupled with the letter's distinctive emphasis on an authentic faith of single-mindedness and humble devotion to God through action (e.g., 1:22-25; 2:15-16; 5:3-6), suggests that the author was familiar with Hellenistic Judaism. The author draws from practical biblical wisdom, as well as from teachings of Jesus (Jas 1:2/ Mt 5:12; Jas 1:5/Mt 7:7; Jas 1:22, 2:14/Mt 7:26; Jas 4:11/Mt 7:1), to encourage and exhort Greek-speaking Jewish Christians who suffered under various trying circumstances. The letter teaches in general rather than in specific terms, applying wisdom rooted in an active faith in the living God to problems arising from persecution.

Major Themes: Trials and persecutions originated from within the faith community (1:1-4, 12; 5:7-11, 13). The threat of deception is serious (1:13-16, 22; 3:1-2; 4:1, 8; 5:19). The rich appear to exploit the poor (2:6; 5:1-6). The need for divine wisdom (1:5-8) to guide the community through its difficulties cannot be oversimplified. Knowledge of the human condition (e.g., 3:1ff.; 4:1ff.; 5:1ff.) calls for patience (5:7) and endurance rooted in that divine wisdom from above (3:17-18). All of the wisdom and exhortation can be summed up: Be hearers and doers of the Word, and your faith will be manifest.

Contents:
A. Opening Formula: 1:1
B. Initial Exhortations: 1:2-18
C. Doers of the Word and Authentic Faith: 1:19-27
D. Favoritism is not of God: 2:1-13
E. Faith is connected to works: 2:14-26
F. Moral Exhortations and True Wisdom: 3:1-18

G. Specific Problems Addressed: 4:1—5:6
H. Conclusions: 5:7-20

Authorship and Date: Who is James? The tone of authority throughout the epistle, the reference to "servant" (1:1), and the address to "the twelve tribes in the Diaspora" suggest someone of authority, perhaps James "the brother of the Lord" (Gal 1:19; Mt 13:55; Mk 6:3) and leader of the early Church in Jerusalem (Acts 12:17; 15:13; 1 Cor 15:7; Gal 2:9, 12), who was later known as James the Just (Eusebius, *Ecclesiastical History* 2.23, 4). There is very little evidence in the letter which helps us fix a date with certainty. If the date is prior to A.D. 70, then the letter could have originated in Jerusalem; if the date is after that, then it could have originated in Antioch or Alexandria.

For further reading: Sophie Laws, "James, Epistle of," *Anchor Bible Dictionary,* 3:621-628; Thomas W. Leahy, S.J., "The Epistle of James," *New Jerome Biblical Commentary,* 909-916.

James the Greater, St. • James and his brother John, sons of Zebedee, were called by Jesus from their livelihood as fishermen to become "fishers of men" as Apostles. By reason of their impetuous temper, James and John are identified in Mark 3:17 as the Sons of Thunder (*Boanerges*). In keeping with their personality traits, James and John are shown guilty of blind ambition in seeking prominence in the Lord's kingdom (Mt 20:20-28, Mk 10:35-45). With John and Peter, James was a privileged witness to the raising of the daughter of Jairus (Mk 5:35-43, Lk 8:41-56), Our Lord's Transfiguration (Mt 17:1-13, Mk 9:2-13, Lk 9:28-36) and the agony in the garden at Gethsemane (Mt

St. James
(fourteenth-century art)

26:36-46, Mk 14:32-42). Herod Agrippa ordered his beheading in A.D. 44.

He is called "the greater" not by reason of any ecclesiastical prominence but merely to distinguish him from the other Apostle of the same name, who was likely smaller or younger.

For further reading: Ron Cameron, "James," *Anchor Bible Dictionary*, 3:617-620; Florence Morton Gillman, "James, Brother of Jesus," *Anchor Bible Dictionary*, 3:620-621.

James, Liturgy of St. • The liturgy of the city of Jerusalem, whose texts bear great resemblance to the *Catecheses* attributed to St. Cyril of Jerusalem. Its anaphora appears to be the result of a fusion of the older Jerusalem rite with an early edition of the anaphora of St. Basil. It was then influenced by the Byzantine version of the anaphora of St. Basil and the Egyptian version of St. Mark. A Syriac version was available shortly after the Council of Calcedon (A.D. 451). The Greek version commonly used today is a later recension. The Liturgy of St. James was widely used outside Jerusalem until it was suppressed in the twelfth century. It contains the Prothesis (three prayers), Enarxis (four prayers), Little Entrance (*Monogenes* and prayer), Prayer, Synapte (Litany), and Trisagion, a Psalm, the Epistle, Alleluia, prayers and Litany, Gospel, Litany for the Catechumens, Great Entrance, Cherubic Hymn, Five Prayers, Creed, Peace (with prayer), Catholic Synapte, Prayers (of the Faithful, of the Offertory, of the Veil), the anaphora (quite elaborate and effusive in style and theology), Lord's Prayer, Prayer of Inclination, Prayer of Elevation and Fraction, Communion, Incense-Prayers, Prayer of Inclination, Thanksgiving for Communion, Dismissal and Prayer (in sacristy).

Jansenism • A particularly dangerous heresy which appeared first in Belgium, then throughout much of French-speaking Europe in the mid-seventeenth century. Its primary proponent was the bishop of Ypres, Cornelius Jansen, whose central tenets were published in 1640 in his book *Augustinus*, which appeared two years after Jansen's death. Jansen's work grew out of an ultimately unsuccessful attempt to rediscover the thought of St. Augustine, particularly his ideas on grace. Jansen's rigoristic misinterpretations of Augustine, however, were many. They included the tenets that free choice was lost and that temptation was irresistible, that Christ did not die for all, that only the most worthy should even receive Holy Communion. Jansen also held that Christ's humanity was overemphasized, leading him to scorn devotion to the Sacred Heart. These beliefs also led Jansenists to engage in extreme forms of penance and to foment scrupulosity among the faithful.

Over the decades, Jansenism became as much a political faction as a religious movement, and opportunely joined forces with various theo-political movements in France, for example, Gallicanism. At the same time Jansenism, through its most articulate spokesman Blaise Pascal, engaged in lengthy and sometimes bitter disputes with, among others, the Jesuits. At length, the French monarchy responded to the political entanglements of the Jansenists by forcibly destroying their center at the convent of Port-Royal. This action led to the emigration of many Jansenists to Holland and elsewhere. Elements of the sect known today as the Old Catholic Church derive in part from these émigrés.

In 1654 Pope Innocent X issued the first formal condemnation of Jansenism, and his pronouncement was followed by those of Clement XI and Pius VI. By the late eighteenth century, organized Jansenism was defunct in France. Many of it sentiments, however, survived in a form known as "moral Jansenism." This puritanical moral rigorism was transmitted beyond the borders of France in part through the seminary system. For example, Irish clergy, then predominantly trained in France, carried it back to Ireland. The result was that what started as a set of theological premises was transformed into a political movement and concluded as a cultural inheritance. Moral Jansenism has lingered rather widely, although attempts have been made to oppose it. Pope St. Pius X, for example, advocated early and frequent participation in the Eucharist, in part as an antidote to moral Jansenism. Today the term "Jansenism" is often used, though not accurately, to describe any type of strictness or rigor in moral matters. (Cf. Pistoia, Synod of.)

Januarius, Miracle of St. • A vial of dried blood, said to be that of the martyr St. Januarius, is kept in the Cathedral of Naples. On several feast days during the year, this blood liquifies during the public exposition of the relic. If the liquefaction does not take place, it is considered to portend ominous events. The liquefaction has been the subject of investigation, and there is photographic evidence of the event. The Church has never given official confirmation of the "miracle."

Jehovah • In time (c. the third century B.C.), out of reverence and in part out of fear, the Jews refrained from enunciating God's proper name, Yahweh. Instead, they read and said "Adonai" (my Lord). As a prompter to this usage, they pointed the consonants of the word "Yahweh" with the vowels of the word "Adonai." Hence, the hybrid word found in earlier English versions and elsewhere, viz., "Jehovah," grew out of a

St. Januarius (silver bust)

combination of the consonants YHWH with the vowels of "Adonai", i.e., a-o-a. The first "a" was modified to "e," since it was to be pronounced with the first consonant "y," which is not a guttural.

For further reading: Henry O. Thompson, "Yahweh," *Anchor Bible Dictionary*, 6:1011-1012.

Jehovah's Witnesses • A religious movement which was formally established at Columbus, Ohio, in 1931. The name "Jehovah" is a variation of the Hebrew name for God, Yahweh. Jehovah's Witnesses are an outgrowth of a fundamentalist movement led by Charles T. Russell, known as the "Millennial Dawn Bible Students," which began in 1879 with the publication known as *Watch Tower*. Upon Russell's death in 1916, J. R. Rutherford rose to power in the Bible Student movement, which was enjoying growth and affiliation with various Protestant religious groups.

Because of the Bible Students' pacifist stand and anti-government rhetoric, Rutherford was jailed for a time in Atlanta on charges of sedition. Rutherford's writings began to replace those of Russell, as did his theological views. Disciples were to sell and distribute *Watch Tower* literature and Rutherford's books. Profits went to the purchase of "kingdom halls" across the country.

Jehovah's Witnesses are Unitarian in belief; they deny the Holy Trinity and the divinity of Jesus. Among their other doctrines is the idea that by the year 1914, 144,000 people were sealed or chosen to be saints in heaven. The end of the world was expected to have taken place around 1975. Those who became saved after 1914 were not to go to heaven, but were to live forever on earth. Determined to "save the lost," Jehovah's Witnesses ardently dispute with Christians in an effort to convert them.

Traditionally, Jehovah's Witnesses are political pacifists, though not politically active. They refuse blood transfusions and will not salute the flag. Devout Witnesses have no contact with non-Witnesses, except in their efforts to convert them.

Jeremiah, Book of • The prophet Jeremiah, whose prophetic ministry is described in the book that bears his name, was active in the land of Judah from approximately 640 to 587 B.C. He survived the destruction of Jerusalem by the Babylonians in 587 B.C. and lived out the rest of his life in Egypt, where he was brought by refugees escaping the devastation that resulted from the Babylonian conquest of the land of Judah.

Born during the reign of Manasseh (the king who undid the religious reforms brought about by Hezekiah), Jeremiah was the son of Hilkiah, a member of a priestly family in Anathoth, a village located a few miles north of Jerusalem. Jeremiah's prophetic call came in the year 627 B.C., the thirteenth year of the reign of Josiah, the great religious reformer during whose reign the scroll containing at least a portion of the Book of Deuteronomy was discovered in the Temple. The book's account of Jeremiah's prophetic call emphasizes his youth at the time of his vocation. The prophet exclaims, "Ah, LORD God! Behold, I do not know how to speak, for I am only a youth" (Jer 1:6). God reassures Jeremiah that he will be duly equipped for the challenges that face him and commands the prophet, "See, I have set you this day over nations and over kingdoms, to pluck up and to break down, to destroy and to overthrow, to build and to plant" (Jer 1:10). This twofold presentation of Jeremiah's ministry as both negative and positive, a matter both of pronouncing judgment and of offering hope, provides an accurate summary of the substance of this prophet's preaching.

The Book of Jeremiah is a lengthy and complex composite work. Its present form follows a basic outline that includes:

I. Oracles of Judgment Against Judah and Jerusalem (1-25)
II. Oracles of Restoration (26-35)
III. The Martyrdom of Jeremiah (36-45)
IV. Oracles Against Foreign Nations (46-51)
V. Historical Appendix (52)

Jeremiah's words of judgment against his own people focuses on their infidelity to the covenant between God and His own Chosen People. Pronouncing oracles in God's name, Jeremiah accuses them, "I solemnly warned your fathers when I brought them up out of the land of Egypt, warning them persistently, even to this day, saying, Obey my voice. Yet they did not obey or incline their ear, but every one walked in the stubbornness of his evil heart. Therefore I brought upon them all the words of this covenant, which I commanded them to do, but they did not" (11:7-8). Jeremiah warned that the destruction of Judah and Jerusalem would be the consequence of the people's disobedience of the commandments of the covenant.

Once that promised destruction had taken place, Jeremiah turned from the oracles of judgment to oracles of hope, offering words of consolation and encouragement, offering the promise of a new covenant between God and His people. In Chapter 31, Jeremiah announces in God's name, "Behold, the days are coming, . . . when I will make a new covenant with the house of Israel and the house of Judah, . . . I will put my law within them, and I will write it upon their hearts; . . . I will forgive their iniquity, and I will remember their sin no more" (31:31-34).

There are considerable differences between the Hebrew text of the Book of Jeremiah and the Greek version found in the Septuagint. For example, the Septuagint version places the oracles against foreign nations after Chapter 25. The Hebrew text that underlies the Septuagint version represents a different (and probably older)

tradition than the Masoretic text of Jeremiah.

For further reading: Guy P. Couturier, "Jeremiah," *New Jerome Biblical Commentary*, 265-297; William L. Holladay, *Jeremiah 1*, Hermeneia (Fortress Press, 1986); William L. Holladay, *Jeremiah 2*, Hermeneia (Fortress Press, 1989); Jack R. Lundbom, "Jeremiah," *Anchor Bible Dictionary*, 3:684-698 and 3:706-721.

Christ entering Jerusalem (icon)

Jerusalem • An ancient city mentioned as far back as c. 1900 B.C. in the Egyptian execration texts. It stands on a plateau, some 2,400 feet above sea level. It is separated from Mt. Olivet to the east by the Kidron Valley; to the south and west, it is girded by the Valley of Gehinnom. Within the confines of the city originally ran a central valley, called by Josephus the "Tyropoeon" or "cheese-makers' valley." With the passage of time, this depression has become more shallow with the deposit of rubble. The modern city is not coextensive with the ancient one, lying farther to the north and somewhat to the west of the ancient city.

Jerusalem was inhabited by a Canaanite clan, the Jebusites, at the time of the Israelite occupation of Canaan. It stood in neutral territory between the lands of Benjamin and Judah. David captured the city and made it his capital. Because it lacked association with any one tribe in

Israel, it would have been more acceptable to all the tribes as a capital. With time, Jerusalem took on a theological symbolism stemming from the fact that the Temple stood within its confines. Hence, it became known as the Holy City.

For further reading: Philip J. King, "Jerusalem," *Anchor Bible Dictionary*, 3:747-766; Benjamin Mazar et al., "Jerusalem," *The New Encyclopedia of Archaeological Excavations in the Holy Land*, 2:698-804.

Jerusalem, Council of • In the first century, Jewish Christians moving north from Jerusalem to Antioch began preaching to Gentiles and winning their conversion. The question soon arose as to how many Jewish traditions needed to be adopted by these non-Jewish converts to Christianity. That question arose when, according to Acts 15:1, "some men came down from Judea and were teaching the brethren, 'Unless you are circumcised according to the custom of Moses, you cannot be saved.' "

Paul, Barnabas and Titus were appointed to present the question to the Apostles in Jerusalem (Peter and James), arriving there about the year 50. During this meeting, which has since come to be known as the Council of Jerusalem, it was decided (following an invocation of the Holy Spirit) that Jewish traditions, notably circumcision and certain dietary rules, should not bind Gentile converts to the Christian Faith. The leaders of the Church in Jerusalem did impose some minimal requirements on new Gentile converts, telling them that they should "abstain from what has been sacrificed to idols and from blood and from what is strangled and from unchastity" (Acts 15:29). These restrictions may have been imposed so as to prevent even the vestiges of idolatry from surviving among the new Christians.

For further reading: Charles B. Cousar, "Jerusalem, Council of," *Anchor Bible Dictionary*, 3:766-768.

Jerusalem, Patriarchate of • The original sees which received the title of patriarchate because of their apostolic foundation and civil importance were Rome, Antioch and Alexandria. When Constantinople became the capital of the empire, it was raised to this rank. The Council of Chalcedon in A.D. 451 raised Jerusalem to patriarchal rank because of the sacred nature of the city. Today it is the seat of several patriarchs of Eastern Catholic, Eastern Orthodox and Ancient Oriental Churches. It is also the seat of a Latin patriarch. The Latin Patriarchate was established during the Crusades in 1099, lapsed into a titular see, and was restored as a residential see in 1847.

Jesse-Window • A stained-glass window depicting Christ's human genealogy. Jesus is shown at the top of a multibranched tree, while His best-known ancestors occupy the lower branches. The window's name is derived from Jesse, the father of King David, who is shown as the root of the tree, in accord with the identification of him as the "root" of the family line in Sacred Scripture (1 Sm 16:18-22; Is 11:1).

Jesuit Reductions • Some sixty years after the opening of the Jesuit missionary efforts in South America, many Jesuit priests became involved as leaders in certain semiautonomous settlements of local Indians. These hundred or so "reductions" consisted of a few thousand Indians forming a nearly self-sufficient community, largely free of the dangers of exploitation by less scrupulous explorers. Although the reductions did not originate with the Jesuits, theirs were by far the most successful both economically and religiously, especially in Paraguay and Uruguay. In the century and a half following their establishment in the early 1600s, nearly 750,000 converts to the Faith were made. The reductions were largely apolitical, but the proximity of many of them to national borders was used as a pretext by civil authorities for expelling the Jesuits and suppressing the communities around them.

Jesuit Relations, The • A large collection of letters and reports written by Jesuit missionaries to their superiors in France about conditions and progress primarily in the North American territories. The bulk of these reports, written in Latin or French, were compiled between 1632 and 1672, although some later ones were included in subsequent editions of the *Relations*. They include vital information on such topics as native culture, natural resources, geography, weather conditions and the like. Such evident usefulness saw to it that the *Relations* were circulated far beyond the confines of Jesuit mission offices. Although complete collections of the *Relations* are rare, an English translation was done by the Wisconsin State Historical Society in 1896 and reprinted in 1957.

Jesuits • The Society of Jesus, founded by St. Ignatius of Loyola on August 15, 1534, is, by any measure, one of the most illustrious religious orders in the history of the Church. There is scarcely a field of ecclesiastical inquiry or effort which has not been the recipient of the invaluable contribution of "Jesuits," as they are more commonly known.

The constitution of the Society was substantially approved by Pope Paul III on September 17, 1540. By its terms, the Society was dedicated to the salvation of its individual members and to that of the whole world. The life of the Society rested upon the monumental spiritual insights of St.

St. Ignatius Loyola, founder of the Jesuits

Ignatius, chiefly represented in his *Spiritual Exercises*. Their rule called for the intensive education, both profane and religious, of its members, and in particular, excellence in the virtue of obedience. The Rule of the Society was streamlined in many ways (for example, Jesuits are permitted to recite the Divine Office in private), in order to obtain the greatest flexibility for its operations. Precision and efficiency were, indisputably, hallmarks of the order for many centuries.

Even a bare listing of the accomplishments of the Jesuits is impossible here, but at least two aspects of their work must be noted. First, the Jesuits were especially devoted to the education apostolate and founded (and in some cases still administer) some of the world's finest universities and secondary schools. Second, the Jesuit devotion to missionary work has led them to every corner of the world. They have brought with them not just the Good News, but often profound cultural, scientific and historical information as well. The famous "fourth vow" of the Jesuits, in fact, is one of special obedience to the Holy Father in the matter of accepting missions. The Jesuits also won early acclaim as leaders of the post-Tridentine reforms of the sixteenth century.

The rapid growth of the Jesuits, their obvious success in education and mission work, their entry into the highest positions of trust in civil and religious society, their steadfast dedication to the doctrine of the Church and their other accomplishments led over time to conflicts with certain civil powers and, it must be admitted, to some jealousy even within ecclesiastical circles. (Cf., for example, Jansenists.) By the 1750s, the Jesuits were experiencing the pain of expulsion from several nations and, within twenty years or so, had been shut out of nearly half the territories in which they formerly labored.

But the enemies of the Jesuits were not yet satisfied. The conclave which elected Pope Clement XIV was racked with debate over the future of the Society. Although Clement held out for four years against calls to abolish the Society, he finally ordered its suppression in 1773.

The decree of suppression, interestingly, called for the suppression of the Society only on the grounds of prudence and the peace of the Church. It certainly involved no rejection of the Jesuit apostolate or spirituality. Moreover, Clement's decree included a clause which subjected the suppression to local promulgation. Because at least two governments (namely, Russia and Poland) did not promulgate the decree, the Jesuits remained continuous, although sharply curtailed, in those two areas until the Society was finally rehabilitated by Pope Pius VII in 1814. In the following decades it regained much of its former stature and did notably well on the North American continent.

The Society is governed for all practical purposes by a Father General, sometimes nicknamed the "Black Pope." He is elected for life, although technically a General Congregation could remove him under certain circumstances. Administration is divided among numerous provinces under which there are houses, the larger ones being headed by a rector.

The Society of Jesus, like most other religious institutes, has suffered its share of turmoil and decline in recent years, although it remains the largest single institute in the Church. On October 5, 1981 the Holy See appointed a special pontifical delegate to the Society due to the incapacitation of the Father General and in response to concerns that the Society was moving away from its original charism. (Cf. Patrimony, Spiritual.) In 1983, the Thirty-Third General Congregation responded: "In the light, therefore, of requests coming from the whole Society, the needs of the world, and the Church's teaching, the Thirty-third General Congregation readily receives the calls which the Pope has made to the Society, and commits itself to a full and prompt response."

Jesus Seminar • A regular gathering of biblical scholars begun by Robert W. Funk, a former Protestant minister and, at this writing, the head of the Westar Institute. A forum for the radical fringes of the New Testament criticism, the seminar's participants meet to debate the authenticity of the people, events and words of the Bible.

In the last several years, the Jesus Seminar has considered the words of Christ as recorded by the four evangelists, and most of the scholars in attendance have agreed that they were, in large measure, never spoken. The overwhelming majority of these exegetes have concluded that the Virgin Birth and the Resurrection, the central tenet of the Christian Faith, are also fictitious.

Jewish Canon of Scriptures • The Hebrew Canon of the Old Testament (Masoretic Text) was settled by the rabbis around A.D. 100 at the Council of Jamnia. It contains twenty-four books and is divided into three categories: (1) the Law (Torah), the five books of Moses (Genesis, Exodus, Leviticus, Numbers, Deuteronomy); (2) the Prophets: Joshua, Judges, 1 and 2 Samuel, 1 and 2 Kings, Isaiah, Jeremiah, Ezekiel, Hosea, Joel, Amos, Obadiah, Jonah, Micah, Nahum, Habakkuk, Zephaniah, Haggai, Zechariah, and Malachi; (3) The Writings: 1 and 2 Chronicles, Ezra, Nehemiah, Job, Psalms, Proverbs, Ecclesiastes, Song of Songs, Ruth, Esther, Daniel.

The Protestant Canon of the Old Testament, which is arranged in thirty-nine separate books, is the same as the Hebrew Canon. The difference in number is due to the Protestant consideration of the minor prophets as twelve books and Samuel, Kings, Chronicles, and Ezra-Nehemiah as two each.

The Catholic Canon of the Old Testament, identical with the Septuagint used by the Early Church, was finalized by the Council of Trent (1546) and includes the books contained in the Alexandrian Canon. The Hebrew Canon rejected these books and accepted only those books in the Palestinian Canon. Therefore, the Catholic Old Testament Canon includes more books than the Jewish Old Testament Canon. These are the books of Tobit, Judith, Wisdom, Sirach (Ecclesiasticus), 1 and 2 Maccabees, Baruch, Daniel (Chapter 3:24-90; Chapters 13-14), and parts of Esther.

Today Protestants generally do not put these books into their Bibles, or if they do, they put them at the end of the Bible under the name "Apocrypha." Eastern Orthodoxy uses the same canon as does Catholicism. (Cf. Bible.)

For further reading: James A. Sanders, "Canon," *Anchor Bible Dictionary*, 1:837-852.

Jews • Historically, the word "Jew" is the name of the people descended from the Tribe of Judah or the word used to designate those who profess the religion of Judaism. That Jesus, His Mother and Apostles, and most of the early followers of Christ were Jewish is something sometimes forgotten by anti-Semites, i.e., those, including some who call themselves Christians, who detest all Jews.

Presently those calling themselves Jews include people who consider themselves part of the Jewish people by ancestry but not by religion, such as atheistic, agnostic and non-practicing Jews, as well as Jews who have converted to Christianity or other religions.

Jews who practice the Jewish religion broadly divide themselves into orthodox, conservative and reformed Jews. These divisions are based on the degree of practice of rabbinic laws concerning such matters as diet, keeping of the Sabbath, dress, rites, contact with non-Jews, and attitudes toward modernity in general.

Present-day interfaith dialogue between Jews and Catholics involves a building up of friendship and understanding to overcome prejudices based on ignorance and also to repent for unjustifiable, sometimes horrendous, victimization based not on Church teaching but on hatred and greed. Such evils have unfortunately sometimes sought rationalization in misinterpretation of Scripture. For example, many pogroms and killings took place on Good Friday on the basis of vengeance to contemporary Jews for the acts of some of the Jewish leadership related to the crucifixion of Christ.

Although Christians express their love for Jewish people by including them in the general call to evangelize all, that they may experience the love of their Savior, such effort must never be construed as implying that the Jewish people as such are not loved by God as they are. Vatican II states that the Jewish people are "most dear for the sake of the fathers, for the gifts of God are without repentance" (LG 16).

For further reading: Bruce Chilton, "Jews in the New Testament," *Anchor Bible Dictionary*, 3:845-849.

Jews for Jesus • One of a number of so-called "messianic Jewish" groups in the United States founded in the 1960s and '70s, "Jews for Jesus" is an evangelical Protestant movement founded in 1973 by Martin Meyer Rosen. Its members are former Jews who claim that they can be Jewish and Christian at the same time. This causes confusion for Jews and Christians alike because "Jews for Jesus" combines Christian proselytizing recruitment with their continued use of some Jewish religious practices (use of prayer shawls, singing and praying in Hebrew, militant support of Israel and — prior to the breakup of the Soviet Union — support for Soviet Jews).

It is important to distinguish the twentieth-century "Jews for Jesus" from the Jewish-Christians at the beginnings of Christianity. Jesus Himself and His followers were Jews, and the Christian Faith made strong inroads among Gentiles (non-Jews) only later, as a result of the preaching of the Apostles.

The "Jews for Jesus" movement is also to be distinguished from Catholics of Jewish heritage living in the State of Israel. With the renewal of the Catholic Liturgy after the Second Vatican Council and the allowance for the vernacular languages in the celebration of Catholic ritual, modern Hebrew naturally became the vernacular for Catholics in Israel, many of whom are of Jewish heritage. These Israeli Catholics celebrate the liturgy of the Latin Rite, but in the Hebrew language.

Job, Book of • Suffering in the world, especially the suffering of the innocent, has been a classic religious problem. In this sapiential book, the problem is presented, not abstractly, but in a very concrete and intensified form.

The book should not be classified as history; it is rather a philosophical discussion offered in a personalized and novelized form. Job is presented as being a very just and holy man, having all the earthly blessings Jews were led to expect from the faithful observance of their covenant with God. In a trice, he lost all these and was reduced to the most miserable state imaginable. Naturally, he wondered why, and so began his dialogue with his few remaining friends.

Religious people have always seen moral guilt as being at the base of human misery. Often the accusatory finger is pointed at the suffering individual himself; this was the reaction of Job's friends. Sometimes, when this fails, the source is sought in the sins of the parents, in the corrupt structures of society or in evil spirits. Irreligious people, on the other hand, find in these misfortunes the best proof that there is no God; they conclude that the forces ruling the universe are fundamentally amoral or impotent.

The Book of Job touches all these explanations. The initial narrative establishes the role of the evil spirit: Satan is shown as being permitted by God to afflict Job. Job's friends belabor the supposed factor of his own guilt. When Job steadfastly continues to protest his innocence, they accuse him of pride and self-righteousness.

The high point of the book is Job's dialogue with God. God does not explain things to Job's satisfaction, but He does bring Job to realize his own intellectual limitations. He is led to perceive that at this stage of religious development he must not expect a satisfying answer. When, in humility, he accepts this, his former blessings are restored to him many times over; the author, living on that theological plateau, could conceive of no happier ending.

Like most dramatic treatments of the topic, the question is more effectively presented than the answer. It is not until the New Testament presents the problem in its most excruciating form, with the crucifixion of Jesus, that we have a more satisfying reply. Human history is not meant to end here on earth, but it embraces an infinitely larger perspective. It is the consoling message of the Beatitudes that God's justice is displayed very imperfectly in time, but perfectly in eternity. We may and should strive to bring about God's dominion here and now, but we should not expect perfect success in that endeavor.

For further reading: R.A.F. MacKenzie, S.J. and Roland E. Murphy, O.Carm., "Job," *New Jerome Biblical Commentary*, 466-488; James L. Crenshaw, "Job, Book of," *Anchor Bible Dictionary*, 3:858-868.

Jocists • The popular name for a Catholic movement of factory and industrial workers known officially as the *Jeunesse Ouvrière Chrétienne* (J.O.C.) and founded by Joseph (later Cardinal) Cardijn (1882-1967) in Brussels after World War I. The inspiration for the movement came from the Church's social teaching, especially the encyclical *Rerum Novarum* of Pope Leo XIII. The movement spread to France in 1926 and later took the form of corresponding associations for students, sailors and agricultural workers. In the English-speaking world, such groups are known as the Young Christian Workers and the Young Christian Students. Regular local and regional meetings are held, with the structure of discussion, reflection and proposed action developed in the writings of Cardijn. The movement belongs to a broad series of twentieth-century initiatives directed to the Christian formation of an active and socially aware laity within the Church.

Joel • A Hebrew name meaning "Yahweh is God." The best-known of the several men in the Old Testament who bore this name is the prophet whose book is found among the works of the minor prophets. The only source of information about Joel, viz., the book he wrote, makes no note of his dates, place of origin or social status. Since his words were directed to Judah and Jerusalem, it is conjectured that he was a Judean.

For further reading: Steven L. McKenzie, "Joel," *Anchor Bible Dictionary*, 3:872-873.

Joel, Book of • We know nothing of the life of this prophet. Scholars rely on scanty evidence to place its composition in the postexilic period, perhaps during the fourth century B.C. (The book mentions that the cities of Tyre and Sidon were still in existence, and these cities were destroyed in 332 and 343 B.C., respectively.)

The book falls into two parts, the first of which describes a plague of locusts (1:1—2:17), and the second of which provides an interpretation of this disaster (2:18—4:21). The plague is presented as a manifestation of divine judgment against the people and as a call for profound and genuine repentance on their part. God invites, " 'Yet even now,' says the LORD, 'return to me with all your heart, with fasting, with weeping, and with mourning; and rend your hearts and not your garments' " (2:12). At the heart of the book is an expression of God's change of heart toward His people. After the description of the plague's devastation and of the people's laments, Joel tells us: "Then the LORD became jealous for his land, and had pity on his people" (2:18).

For further reading: Theodore Hiebert, "Joel, Book of," *Anchor Bible Dictionary*, 3:873-880; Elias D. Mallon, "Joel, Obadiah," *New Jerome Biblical Commentary*, 399-405.

John, First, Second and Third Epistles of • All three letters serve a single purpose: To open us up to the concrete struggles within the Johannine Church of the late first century. According to 1 John 2:19, it appears that there was a schism in the Church which John had founded. This first letter is written to believers who stayed in the main Church ("the faithful") and encourages them not to follow the error of those who have left. In 1 John 4:2, we learn of the necessity of confessing, not just that Jesus is God, but that He is God come *in the flesh*. The opponents appear to have denied Christ's humanity, perhaps because of an overly-spiritualized view of His divinity. Such a view could have easily been rooted in Platonic philosophy or other Hellenistic influences which viewed the body as necessarily unspiritual or morally evil. When read in reverse order, 3 John seems to be a cover letter for a messenger bringing either written or oral communication from the Elder to the community in question. The point of the letter is to encourage hospitality and a warm reception. In 2 John, we infer that the original problems were not rectified, thus the need to encourage positive relationships. This letter was probably a cover letter for 1 John, which is not in the traditional form of an ancient letter. In 1 John, we read about the substantial doctrinal matters at the heart of the problems. This letter is a remarkable expression of the intricate and inseparable links between orthodoxy and orthopraxis in the early Church. That is, it not only teaches the Truth but also how to live it.

Contents:
A. 1 John
   1. Prologue: 1:1-4 (cf. Prologue in Jn 1:1-18)
   2. Walk in the Light, not in sin: 1:5—2:29
   3. We are the Father's children in love: 3:1-24
   4. Reject falsehood; love and believe: 4:1—5:12
B. 2 John
   1. Opening of Letter: 1-3
   2. Be faithful, avoid the dissidents: 4-11
   3. Conclusion: 12-13
C. 3 John
   1. Opening greeting: 1-2
   2. Missionaries: 3-8
   3. Diotrephes's refusal: 9-10
   4. Hospitality: 11-12
   5. Conclusions: 13-15

Authorship and Date: Tradition attributes authorship of 1, 2 and 3 John to "John," the author of the Fourth Gospel. Current scholarly opinion supports the proposition that First John was written as an interpretive guide for the Fourth Gospel by the same author who "finalized" its narrative. Second and Third John were clearly written by the same person; it is not certain whether or not their author was that of First John. It would be prudent to follow Tradition. If the Gospel was written around A.D. 90, then the epistles are sometime after that, perhaps between 92 and 100, or later.

For further reading: Raymond E. Brown, S.S. *The Epistles of John*, Anchor Bible 30 (Doubleday, 1982); Pheme Perkins, "The Johannine Epistles," *New Jerome Biblical Commentary*, 986-995; Rudolf Schnackenburg, *The Johannine Epistles: A Commentary* (Crossroad, 1992).

John, The Gospel of • Traditionally known as "the Fourth Gospel" because of its place in the Canon, this Gospel is distinct from the other three Gospels because of its overall structure and thematic expression. When set against either the texts of the Old Testament or their first-century A.D. interpretations within Judaism, many of Jesus' discourses, as well as their accompanying circumstances, convey deep religious, theological and spiritual meaning. The use of such key images as "light," "darkness," "truth," "lies," "love," "hate," "from above," "from below," "sign," and "glory" unlock the worldview of the human author, while expressing the deeper meaning of salvation from the Divine Author. The Gospel is written to lead the believer to a deeper and fuller knowledge of the Father's plan of salvation revealed through Jesus Christ.

St. John (ninth-century illumination)

Major Themes: The narrative begins with hymn-like material focusing on Jesus as the Word or Logos Who became flesh. As the Logos, Jesus is active in creating the world (Jn 1:1-4; cf. Gn 1-2 and Prv 8:22-30; 9:1-9 for the background to this text). But Jesus is also the "language of God," in that both His words and His life communicate God's message of salvation. His words and deeds reveal the Person and mind of the Father above. Jesus' mission is to descend, reveal the Father, die and enter His own glory, return to heaven (14:25-31), and send the Paraclete (e.g., 15:26-27; 16:4-24). Jesus' death is *the* moment of glory, at which point love reigns supreme over all evil, now defeated. Those who witness Jesus' words, works and signs either come into belief (become children of God; cf. 2:11; 3:2; 4:54; 6:2, 14, 26, etc.) or remain in unbelief. Other key themes include: rebirth from above (1:13; 3:3, 5, etc.), belief that Jesus is the Christ, the Son of God, and is the only source of eternal life (6:35; 7:38; 11:25-26; 12:44; 14:1, 12, etc.). The use of double meanings (e.g., the Greek word *pneuma*, breath or spirit), irony, symbolism and the narrator's asides all suggest that the Gospel was intended for those Churches which came to faith through the oral preaching and teaching which preceded this Gospel.

Contents:

A. Prologue: 1:1-18
B. Book of Signs: 1:9—12:50
    1. Disciples: 1:19—4:54
    2. Is Jesus from God? 5:1—10:42
    3. Jesus is the Resurrection and the Life: 11:1—12:50
C. Book of Glory: 13:1—20:31
    1. Last Supper and Farewell Discourses: 13:1—17:26
    2. The Passion and Death of Jesus: 18:1—19:42
    3. Empty Tomb and Resurrection: 20:1-31
D. Conclusion and Epilogue: 21:1-25

Authorship and Date: St. Irenaeus, the second-century bishop of Lyons, wrote that "John, the disciple of the Lord, who leaned on his breast, also published the gospel while living at Ephesus in Asia" (*Adversus Haereses* 3, 1, 2). According to Clement of Alexandria (c. 150-215 A.D.), as quoted in Eusebius's *Church History* (4, 14, 7), "Last of all John, perceiving that the bodily facts had been made plain in the gospel, being urged by his friends and inspired by the Spirit, composed a spiritual Gospel." By ascribing the authorship of the Fourth Gospel to John the Apostle, St. Irenaeus rescued this Gospel from the erroneous interpretations to which Gnostics were subjecting it, and secured its place as an authoritative document that had apostolic authenticity. Clement of Alexandria sought to explain the real differences between the perspective of the Gospels of Matthew, Mark and Luke and the perspective of the Fourth Gospel. This strategy served to defend the Fourth Gospel against charges of historical inaccuracy, by insisting on the inspiration of the Gospel and on its particular purpose.

While these early Christian witnesses point to John as the author of the Fourth Gospel, that Gospel itself gives evidence of its authority on the basis of the eyewitness testimony of the figure who is identified in John's Gospel as "the disciple whom Jesus loved." Even though this figure is never named in the Fourth Gospel, there is no reason whatsoever to doubt his historicity. (Note that the name of Jesus' mother, Mary, is not given in John's Gospel, either. She is identified by her relationship to her divine Son. Cf. Jn 19:25-27.) "The disciple whom Jesus loved" appears at crucial junctures in John's Gospel. The mention of his presence at the Last Supper (13:23-26), at the foot of the cross (19:25-27), at the empty tomb (20:2-10) and among those to whom Jesus appears after the Resurrection (21) is clear evidence of the quality of his testimony as an eyewitness.

In John 21:24, we are told of the "disciple whom Jesus loved" that "it is this disciple who is bearing witness to these things, and who has written these things; and we know that his testimony is true."

In all likelihood, the Gospel of John was the last of the New Testament Gospels to have been written, probably completed between A.D. 90 and 125. It is unlikely that the evangelist made use of the Synoptic Gospels (Matthew, Mark, Luke) in his own work.

For further reading: Raymond E. Brown, S.S., *The Gospel According to John I-XII*, Anchor Bible 29 (Doubleday, 1966); Raymond E. Brown, S.S., *The Gospel According to John XIII-XXI*, Anchor Bible 29A (Doubleday, 1970); Rudolf Schnackenburg, *The Gospel According to St. John*, 3 vols. (Crossroad, 1980-1982).

John the Baptist • Son of Elizabeth and the priest Zechariah. An account of his annunciation and birth is given in Luke 1. John conducted a ministry of preaching and

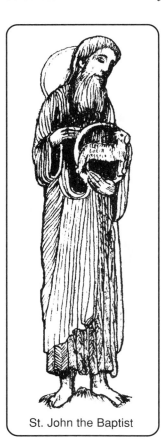

St. John the Baptist

baptizing in the Judaean desert and in the Jordan valley (cf. Mt 3:1-10; Mk 1:4-6; Lk 3:1-9). John's manner of dress and style of life call to mind Elijah's style of life (Mt). The Gospel of John details John the Baptist's forthright testimony to Jesus as "Messiah" and "Lamb of God." Because of his censure of Herod Antipas the tetrarch, he was imprisoned and subsequently executed (Mt 4:12; Mk 1:14; Lk 3:19f.).

Since the discovery of the Dead Sea Scrolls, the parallels between John and Qumran have been duly noted. It would seem that he may well have had some contact with Qumran, but it is unwarranted to assume that he was himself an Essene. Besides the Bible, John is also referred to in Josephus (*Antiq.* XVIII, v. 2). Sometime during the late fourth century, the feast of his birth was set on June 24 in the West (June 23 in the East), the time from which the days begin to grow shorter. This is contrasted with the celebration of Christ's birth on December 25, the time after which the days become longer. This was inspired by John's statement as given in John 3:30: "He must grow greater, I must grow smaller." The name "John" is from the Hebrew *Yehohanon*, "Yahweh is gracious."

For further reading: Paul W. Hollenbach, "John the Baptist," *Anchor Bible Dictionary*, 3:887-899.

Joinder of Issues • Referred to in Latin as the *contestatio litis*, this is a procedural act or step in a canonical trial at which the terms of the question to be decided are defined by the judge. The canonical judicial process is introduced when a person, known as the petitioner, submits a petition asking the court to decide an issue. The judge then sends a citation or official notice to the other party to the issue. When the other party, commonly called the respondent, answers the citation, the judge studies both the petition and the response to the petition and determines the canonical nature of the issue. This is also known as setting the grounds of the case. In marriage cases, the most common type of case presented to canonical courts, the grounds for alleged nullity that must be proven by the petitioner are determined at the joinder of the issues.

After the joinder of the issues takes place, the parties to the suit are given the opportunity to furnish proofs (Canons 1513-1516).

Jonah, Book of • Modern exegetes regard this book, not as a historical narrative, but as a didactic short story about a reluctant prophet of the same name. The author is anonymous and does not appear in the story.

Once upon a time, Jonah was called to take up a prophetic role in Nineveh, the capital of Judah's fierce enemy, Assyria. He ran away, taking a ship to escape so hopeless a task. Thrown overboard by his shipmates, he was swallowed by a whale, but after praying to God for three days and three nights he was disgorged. He went to Nineveh, preached his message of repentance and divine justice, and the entire city was speedily converted.

The book no doubt has its religious value: one should not shrink from an apostolic task, even when there seem to be insuperable difficulties. Older commentators and preachers assumed the historicity of the story, partly because it was divinely inspired and partly because Jesus used Jonah in the whale as a type of His own resurrection from the grave. On second thought, neither premise justifies the conclusion drawn therefrom. An inspired parable can be a fictional vehicle for conveying a truth, and fictional characters can serve as very striking types or antitypes.

Jonah, Sign of • In Mark 8:11-12, the Pharisees' demand that Jesus give a sign from heaven to lend credibility to His claims is met with Jesus' reply that "no sign shall be given to this generation." In Matthew 12:38-42, 16:1-4 and Luke 11:29-32, Jesus responds to the demand for a sign by declaring that no sign will be given "except the sign of Jonah." The sign of Jonah

567

episode is found both in Matthew and in Luke. Although the "men of Nineveh" and the "queen of the south" are mentioned in different order in Matthew 12:41-42 and Luke 11:31-32, the wording of the sign of Jonah episode in Matthew and Luke is virtually identical. Three principal differences between the Matthean and Lucan versions lie in the additional material found in Matthew 12:40: "For as Jonah was three days and three nights in the belly of the whale, so will the Son of man be three days and three nights in the heart of the earth."

For Luke, the meaning of the sign of Jonah is found in Luke 11:32 (parallel to Mt 12:41): "The men of Nineveh will arise at the judgment with this generation and condemn it; for they repented at the preaching of Jonah, and behold, something greater than Jonah is here." The sign of Jonah, the prophet who came to pagan Nineveh from afar, was his preaching, which led the Ninevites to repentance and conversion. The sign of Jesus, the "one greater than Jonah," is Jesus' own preaching, a sign which "this generation" failed to recognize. To the material found in Q, Matthew adds an allegorization of Jonah 2:1 to indicate that

Jesus' death and resurrection, together with His preaching, constitutes the "sign of Jonah." This is true even though the preaching of the biblical Jonah makes no reference to that prophet's sojourn in the belly of the fish. Jonah's announcement is quite brief: "Forty days more and Nineveh shall be destroyed" (Jon 3:4).

St. Joseph being visited by an angel

Joseph, St. •
The name "Joseph" is from the Hebrew *yosep* and can be translated as "let God add/gather." The New Testament figure appears in Matthew 1-2 and Luke 1-2, is the spouse of Mary and the adoptive father of Jesus. A "just man" (Mt 1:19) from the House of David (Mt 1:1ff.; Lk 2:4ff.), he appears to have been a carpenter (Greek, *tekton*) (Mt 13:55), as was Jesus (Mk 6:3). If Luke's infancy Gospel is narrated from Mary's experience and point of view, Matthew's Gospel narrates the major events from a distinctly Josephine perspective. It is Joseph who received revelation from an angel concerning the virgin birth of Jesus (Mt 1:20-25) and concerning the escape to and return from Egypt (Mt 2:13-15, 19-23). Joseph witnessed the birth of Jesus (Lk 2:16), His circumcision (Lk 2:21-22) and, along with Mary, experienced the stress of

searching for Jesus while He was in the temple (2:41-52). Aside from the infancy narratives, Joseph is mentioned at Luke 4:22, Matthew 13:55 and Mark 6:3. Joseph assumes varying degrees of importance under different aspects of Christian life. In the non-canonical *Protoevangelium of James*, he is described as being very old when he married Mary — and thus becomes the model of holiness and asceticism during the years after the persecutions, which coincided with the rise of monasticism and the development and ascendancy of the ascetical way of life.

During the fourth through the seventh centuries, in Eastern Christianity, the apocryphal document, *History of Joseph the Carpenter*, was very popular and either stimulated or grew out of a strong veneration of Joseph. In the Western Church, St. Bernardine of Siena and John Gerson (fifteenth century) reflected on the theological implications for Joseph's role as foster-father of Jesus. This theological development found its way into the liturgical tradition with the introduction of St. Joseph's feast day on March 19, 1479, in the Roman Calendar.

After this point, St. Joseph's importance in the devotional life of the Church developed even further, the highlights of which follow. Formal liturgical devotion to St. Joseph became popularized through the work of St. Thérèse and St. Francis de Sales. Pope Clement XI created a special Office of the Hours for St. Joseph's feast day (in 1714); Benedict XIII established St. Joseph's name in the Litany of the Saints; St. Joseph was declared patron of the universal Church in 1870 by Pius IX. Between 1914 and 1955 his feast day was the third Wednesday after Easter. In 1955 the feast day of St. Joseph (the Worker) was transferred to the first of May, which ceased to be obligatory in 1969. Pope Leo XIII wrote an encyclical (*Quamquam pluries*, 1889), in which St.

Joseph's preeminent sanctity was proclaimed. At the conclusion of the first session of the Second Vatican Council, Pope John XXIII decreed the addition of Joseph's name to the Roman Canon.

For further reading: Stanley E. Porter, "Joseph, Husband of Mary," *Anchor Bible Dictionary*, 3:974-975.

Josephism (also Josephinism) • A variant of several other aberrations of Church-state relations holding that the state is the legitimate superior of the Church, even in ecclesiastical affairs. This particular manifestation arose under Austro-Hungarian Emperor Joseph II in the late eighteenth century, although he borrowed many of his ideas from his mother Maria Theresa, who in turn was influenced by Erastianism and Gallicanism. Using a starkly utilitarian measure, Joseph II was especially harsh on the religious life, closing over seven hundred monasteries as "useless." He instituted limits on the number of religious who could reside within Austrian borders and closed many Catholic schools, replacing them with state-controlled centers. In 1781 a euphemistically-named Act of Toleration was enacted which actually served to exacerbate the situation through its tacit condoning of Freemasonry.

After a brief relaxation in the anti-Catholic spirit of Josephism under Leopold II, the movement was reinvigorated by Francis II and was not finally repudiated until the 1850s under Francis Joseph I. The air of mistrust for the state which was created by Josephism, however, lingered on for many decades.

Joshua, Book of • Among the several Old Testament figures who bear this name, the most prominent is the successor of Moses, the Joshua who directed the Israelite conquest of the land of Canaan and oversaw the allotment of lands to the tribes of Israel. At the beginning of the Book of Joshua, we find God's command to Joshua, entrusting him with responsibility for the people's progress: "Moses my servant is dead; now therefore arise, go over this Jordan, you and all this people, into the land which I am giving to them, to the people of Israel" (Jos 1:2).

The Book of Joshua tells of the conquest of Canaan (1-12) and of the division of the occupied territory (13-21). Like the books of the Pentateuch, it seems to be a composite derived from several different sources, but scholars have not yet come to agreement about their identity. The historical accuracy of the account of the conquest of Canaan contained in the Book of Joshua is not certain. Extensive archaeological research has caused scholars to reexamine the biblical data in the light of the material evidence pertaining to the Israelite settlement in Canaan between the thirteenth and eleventh centuries B.C.

For further reading: Robert G. Boling, "Joshua, Book of," *Anchor Bible Dictionary*, 3:1002-1015; William G. Dever, "Israel, History of (Archaeology and the 'Conquest')," *Anchor Bible Dictionary*, 3:545-558; Michael David Coogan, "Joshua," *New Jerome Biblical Commentary*, 110-131; George W. Ramsey et al., "Joshua," *Anchor Bible Dictionary*, 3:999-1002.

Joy • The pleasure, satisfaction, contentment, rest and happiness experienced as a result of the possession of a basic human good. Christ is seen as the cause of all authentic Christian joy because He fulfills the Old Testament promises, brings forgiveness, grace, truth and divine love. Joy for the Christian is the result of charitable actions, forgiveness for sin and life under the promise of redemption and salvation. Essentially, Christian joy is a sharing in the joy of Christ at the accomplishment of the works of divine salvation. Joy is the completion of happiness, the aim of human life and the completion of human action and existence.

The Augustinian tradition asserted that only God could provide the fullness of human joy as only He could meet all of our human needs and fulfill all of our human longings. The Christian conception of joy is significantly different from that of the Marxist, materialist or agnostic concepts because it affirms that God provides it perfectly. Agnostics or materialists would be skeptical of this, for they would contend that joy is ultimately materialist in its nature and content. Christian Faith affirms that the spiritual joy of union with discipleship of Christ made possible by faith and grace is of a different order from that which others can imagine or ask.

Joys of the Blessed Virgin Mary • The ancient popular devotion which commemorates the principal joys of the Virgin Mary. At first, there were only five, but later the number grew to seven to match that of the Seven Dolors or Sorrows. This devotion was especially popular in England from the Middle Ages to the time of Henry VIII's breaking away from the Church. Forming a part of the Franciscan Crown or Rosary, the Seven Joys were propagated widely by the members of this religious order. The joys are: the Annunciation, the Visitation, the Nativity of Christ, the Adoration of the Magi, the Finding in the Temple, the Resurrection and the Assumption of the Blessed Mother.

Jubilee • Deriving from the reference in Leviticus 25:8-55 to a "jubilee year," the Old Testament attests to a year of jubilee occurring every fiftieth year (Lv 25:10) or to coincide with every seventh sabbatical. This day was a special year of remission of guilt and sin, of emancipation and the return of lands to their original owners. The year began on the Day of Atonement, the tenth day of Tishri.

The Catholic Church has more recently observed years of jubilee (or "holy years") every twenty-five years, as times of effecting reconciliation with God and of receiving favor and blessing from Him. This term is also used of extraordinary years of jubilee declared by the Pope. One example is Pope Paul VI's Apostolic Constitution *Mirificus eventus*, declaring and promulgating an extraordinary jubilee from January 1 to May 29, 1966, throughout the Catholic world (in celebration of the end of the Second Vatican Council). He asserts that the year is a "special period of heavenly salvation and . . . [of] opening the fonts of heavenly graces. . . ." In this Catholic application of the jubilee, the local cathedral and the bishop become major focal points for the desired year of celebration.

When the observance of a jubilee year is centered in Rome, the so-called "holy doors" of the four major basilicas (St. John Lateran, St. Mary Major, St. Paul Outside the Walls, St. Peter), which are customarily bricked closed, are opened for the specified duration of the jubilee, in order that pilgrims might walk through this door and receive special jubilee graces.

For further reading: Christopher J. H. Wright, "Jubilee, Year of," *Anchor Bible Dictionary*, 3:1025-1030.

Judaism • Generally, it refers to the religious, political, ethnic, social and historical background of the Jewish people. Historically, Judaism goes back to the beginnings of the twelve tribes in Canaan, which developed through the Persian period (539-333 B.C.) and evolved through the Greek (333-63 B.C.), Roman (63 B.C.-A.D. 70), Rabbinical (A.D. 70-400), Medieval (East, seventh to twelfth centuries; West, twelfth to sixteenth centuries) and Modern (eighteenth to twentieth centuries) periods.

Judaism is a religion revealed by God and originated with the Mosaic covenant and identified with the land of Canaan (Israel today), expressing belief in one God Who reveals Himself through the law, the prophets and the events of history. The faithful Jew is one who lives according to the covenant ("I am your God, and you are my people"). Therefore, a Jew follows the law and worships God by prayer, reflection upon the sacred writings and the observance of Sabbath and other festivals.

According to Vatican II, there is a relationship between the Church and the Jewish people, "that people to which the covenants and promises were made, and from which Christ was born according to the flesh: in view of the divine choice, they are a people most dear for the sake of the fathers, for the gifts of God are without repentance. . ." (LG 16). (Cf. Hebrew Feasts; Anti-Semitism.)

For further reading: J. Andrew Overman et al., "Judaism," *Anchor Bible Dictionary*, 3:1037-1089.

Judaizers • These first-century Jewish Christians held that in order to become fully Jewish one had to observe all the commandments of the Torah, including circumcision. This question prompted the first Church Council, the so-called Council of Jerusalem, c. A.D. 50, a summary account of which can be found in Acts 15. The Church's final decision included reference to restricted dietary practices and the inclusion of a general moral code based on the traditional teachings from the Torah.

There is further evidence concerning the Judaizers in Paul's letter to the Galatians. In Galatians 2:14, we read the term *ioudaidzein*, which occurs only there in the New Testament and which literally means "to Judaize." In this context, Paul rebukes

Peter for his "double mindedness" concerning his relationship with Gentile and Jewish-Christians on dietary and other purity laws. It is clear from the use of this term in the Greek Old Testament (LXX) that it refers to those non-Jews who live as the Jews live (e.g., Est 8:19; but cf. also Plutarch's *Cicero* 7:6; Josephus's *Jewish Wars* II.xvii.1O; xviii.2).

For further reading: James W. Aageson, "Judaizing," *Anchor Bible Dictionary*, 3:1089.

Jude, Epistle of • The letter is designated as a "catholic" epistle because it is addressed not to an individual or local Church but to the universal (i.e., "catholic") Church (1-2). The author challenges the authenticity of certain teachers who held the position that living in Christ meant that no law, Jewish or other, was binding on the Christian, least of all moral law. By identifying himself with the Jerusalem Church, and as one of the "brethren [cousins] of the Lord," Jude is claiming apostolic authority for teachings used to challenge the dissenters from orthodoxy. He appeals to the Deposit of the Faith (3) and to the Apostles (17).

Major Themes: The appeal to the Faith (3, 20-23) is critical for Jude's argument, as is reference to the fulfillment of judgment against those who reject God's commands.

Contents:

A. Address and Greetings: 1-2

B. Reason for the Letter: 3-4

C. Fulfillment of Prophecies of Judgment:
   1. Examples from the Old Testament: 5-12
   2. Examples from Judaism: 14-16
   3. Examples from the Apostles: 17-19

D. Final Appeal: 20-23

E. Doxology: 24-25

Authorship and Date: The author identifies himself as "Jude, a servant of Jesus Christ and brother of James" (1). Tradition identifies this person with Judas, one of the

St. Jude
(fourteenth-century painting)

"brethren" of Jesus (Mt 13:55; Mk 6:3). Scholarly opinion holds that "Jude" is a pseudonym for a later first-century author who is familiar with the Jerusalem Church and its teachings. The debate on the pseudonymous nature of the document is not closed. There is no internal evidence which helps determine an exact date for its composition. The letter is quoted in 2 Peter, which most would concede is dependent on Jude. If 2 Peter is dated c. A.D. 100, then Jude would have been written at least before then. Most scholars estimate the date of composition to be c. A.D. 90.

For further reading: Richard Bauckham, "Jude, Epistle of," *Anchor Bible Dictionary*, 3:1098-1103; Jerome H. Neyrey, S.J., "The Epistle of Jude," *New Jerome Biblical Commentary*, 917-919; Jerome H. Neyrey, S.J., *2 Peter, Jude*, Anchor Bible 37C (Doubleday, 1993).

Judges • Canon law requires that every diocese have a tribunal. The bishop is to appoint a judge or judges to decide cases presented to the tribunal. The bishop is the first judge of all cases not excepted by the law from his jurisdiction. He can exercise this power personally or through others. Usually, the bishop does not act as judge but refers cases to the diocesan judges.

In general, judges are to be clerics, either diocesan or religious, and must possess a doctorate or at least a licentiate in canon law. If the episcopal conference deems it necessary, individual bishops can appoint qualified lay persons to the office of judge. As such, lay judges can sit on a panel of judges but cannot hear and decide a case acting as sole judge (cf. Canons 1419-1427).

Judges, Book of • This Old Testament book follows the Book of Joshua and continues its description of Israel's history up to the establishment of the monarchy by Saul (1051 B.C.).

Throughout this book the Israelites are settled in villages, united only in a religious way, worshiping the one God. They were not troubled by the great powers to the east (Mesopotamia) or to the west (Egypt). There were, however, intermittent periods of oppression by neighboring tribes; when these came, God sent brave and talented leaders to vindicate the just claims of His people. From this judicial function (which they enforced militarily), the "judges" are so called. The judges are: Othniel, Ehud, Deborah and Barak, Gideon, Abimelech, Jephthah, Samson, Shamgar, Tola, Jair, Ibzan, Elon and Abdon.

For didactic moral purposes (later imitated by the prophets), Israel's setbacks are uniformly ascribed to their sin in abandoning Yahweh and following Canaanite gods. But after their repentance, the judge appears and his victory restores peace and happiness.

For further reading: Robert G. Boling, "Judges, Book of," *Anchor Bible Dictionary*, 3:1107-1117; M. O'Connor, "Judges," *New Jerome Biblical Commentary*, 132-144.

Judges, Synodal • Synodal judges were judges of the diocesan tribunal appointed by the bishop during the course of a diocesan synod. Those judges appointed outside the synod were known as prosynodal judges. The jurisdiction and power of both types were the same.

The revised Code does not speak of either prosynodal or synodal judges, leaving their appointment to the discretion of the bishop.

Under the 1917 Code, neither synodal nor prosynodal judges needed to have canonical degrees, unlike judges appointed under the 1983 Code. For approximately ten years following the appearance of the 1983 Code, these non-degreed judges were permitted to continue in their office in virtue of their acquired rights, but in more recent years, bishops have been required by the Holy See to appoint only degreed judges to their tribunals or to request specific dispensations for non-degreed judges. The Holy See, citing the need for more academically qualified judicial officers, has generally not granted such requests.

For further reading: G. Graham, "Synodal and Pro-synodal Judges," *Studies in Canon Law*, No. 452 (Catholic University of America, 1967).

Judgment, General • The judgment rendered by God at the end of time. This judgment will occur after Christ's Second Coming (the *parousia*), and Christian Tradition holds that at this judgment the bodies of the dead will be raised and united to their souls.

Christ will judge all according to their holiness, faith and love for Him, and for their charity toward others. The Christian is charged with proclaiming the Good News of

Christ, and shouldering this awesome burden is made possible by the joy which Christians experience knowing that awaiting them at the end of that journey is the full and perfect joy of union with Christ. With the General Judgment, the eschatological era and the reign of God will come about in their fullness, and all the saved will experience the eternal joy of union with Christ.

Those who have been saved at the particular judgment will have their bodies united with their souls to experience the beatific vision. Those who have been damned will have their bodies united with their souls to experience eternal torment. And those who remain in purgatory will have their bodies united to their souls and will be given the gift of the beatific vision.

According to the *Catechism of the Catholic Church*: "On Judgment Day at the end of the world, Christ will come in glory to achieve the definitive triumph of good over evil which, like the wheat and the tares, have grown up together in the course of history" (n. 681).

The *Catechism* goes on to say, "When he comes at the end of time to judge the living and the dead, the glorious Christ will reveal the secret disposition of hearts and will render to each man according to his works and according to his acceptance or refusal of grace" (n. 682).

Judgment, Liturgical • To help with the implementation of the then "new" Liturgy, in 1972 the (American) Bishops' Committee on the Liturgy issued the document *Music in Catholic Worship*. In that document three basic "judgments" are to be made of the music that is to be used in the celebration of the Liturgy: liturgical, musical and pastoral. The liturgical judgment is multifaceted and includes a determination which must be made regarding structural and textural requirements, role differentiation and the parts to be played by various individuals or groups such as congregation, cantor, choir and instrumentalists. This judgment must be made by a competent liturgist and may not be based on personal preferences but on legitimate liturgical regulations.

Judgment, Musical • In the 1972 document from the NCCB Committee on the Liturgy, *Music in Catholic Worship*, there are three judgments to be made of music to be used in the celebration of the Liturgy: liturgical, musical and pastoral. The musical judgment must be made by a competent musician and be based on musical values, not style. Never used alone, it is always linked with the liturgical and pastoral judgments. Music may not be admitted into the liturgy if it does not successfully pass all three judgments.

Judgment, Particular • The judgment made at the moment of the person's death. At this judgment, the soul will either be condemned to hell, be rewarded with the blessings of heaven or be given a time of purgation. At the General Judgment the bodies of those judged at this particular judgment will be joined to their souls for eternal bliss or eternal salvation. However, this is not a mere intermediary step to the General Judgment, but a fulfillment of hope in its own right.

Judgment, Pastoral • In the 1972 document from the NCCB Committee on the Liturgy, *Music in Catholic Worship*, there are three judgments to be made of music to be used in the celebration of the Liturgy: liturgical, musical and pastoral. The pastoral judgment is made for a particular group of worshipers, in a particular place, age and culture. This judgment presupposes a sensitivity to liturgy and a pastoral concern for the group gathered for prayer. A musical composition that is deemed acceptable in the pastoral judgment must then be judged as to appropriateness by virtue of the liturgical and musical judgments. These must be made by individuals with competency in those fields. Only after the selection has approval in each area is it to be used in the liturgy.

Judgment, Triple • The threefold judgment used to determine the appropriateness of any musical piece for a liturgical celebration. It includes the musical, liturgical and pastoral judgments. The triple judgment was introduced in the 1972 document of the Bishops' Committee on the Liturgy, "Music in Catholic Worship." (Cf. Music in Catholic Worship; Judgment, Musical; Judgment, Liturgical; Judgment, Pastoral.)

Judica Psalm • Psalm 43 in the Hebrew counting and 42 in the Vulgate enumeration often used by the Church. This psalm, with its versicle, "I will go to the altar of God," is recited at the beginning of the so-called "Tridentine Mass" or the Mass of St. Pius V. It served as the opening line for the "Prayers at the Foot of the Altar," replaced by the penitential rite in the Missal of Pope Paul VI.

Judith, Book of • A legendary Jewish heroine, of uncertain date, whose name seems derived from "Judah." Her chief claim to fame was her assassination of Holofernes, the cruel Assyrian general and hated enemy of the Chosen People.

The story of Judith seems to have been composed of bits and pieces of Jewish history. Nebuchadnezzar, king of Babylon from 605 B.C., is here presented as king of Assyria, which actually fell to Nabopolassar, Nebuchadnezzar's father, in 612 B.C. Nebuchadnezzar is presented as reigning after the completion of the Second Temple (515 B.C.), when many Jews had already been restored to the Holy Land. Such details

incline modern scholars to classify the book as religious fiction, and to assign its origin to Maccabean times.

Tyrannicide and political assassinations were defended even by Christian theologians of the Scholastic period, and some will still defend them as involving the lesser evil. If one can abstract from the bloody deed she had in mind, Judith's prayer (9:2-14) is an inspiring cry of faith and hope, and it is still used for that purpose in the liturgy, mercifully out of context. The book is of a piece with Jewish morality at that time, as seen in Judges.

For further reading: Carey A. Moore, "Judith, Book of," *Anchor Bible Dictionary*, 3:1117-1125; Irene Nowell, O.S.B., Toni Craven, Demetrius Dumm, O.S.B., "Tobit, Judith, Esther," *New Jerome Biblical Commentary*, 568-579.

Juridic Person • An aggregate or group of persons or things that is treated by the law as if it were a person, that is, it is recognized by the law as a duly constituted aggregate and given specific rights and duties. Some examples of juridic persons that are groups of people are religious communities, dioceses, parishes or public associations in the Church. Juridic persons that are aggregates of things are colleges, hospitals, seminaries, etc.

To be a juridic person, the group of persons or things must be officially constituted as such by a competent Church authority. A juridic person is by its nature perpetual, but it may be extinguished by competent Church authority. For instance, a religious community or parish that is a juridic person remains as a juridic person even when all the people that made it up have departed. Goods held in the name of the juridic person do not belong to the sum of the members but to the juridic person and are disposed of according to law (Canons 113-123).

Jurisdiction • In general, the term "jurisdiction" is synonymous with the power of governance in the Church. Ordinarily, only those in Sacred Orders are capable of exercising jurisdiction; however, the law makes certain exceptions to this rule, particularly in the exercise of judicial power.

The power of jurisdiction is divided into legislative, executive and judicial. Ordinary power of jurisdiction is that which is attached to an ecclesiastical office, such as the office of the papacy, the office of ordinary, or the office of judge. Ordinary jurisdiction is either proper (if it is possessed by an individual who exercises it in his own name, e.g., a diocesan bishop) or vicarious (if it is attached to an office exercised in the name of someone else, e.g., vicar general or episcopal vicar). Jurisdiction is delegated if it is exercised by someone not by reason of an office held but by one who has received it from another who has ordinary jurisdiction.

Only the Pope has the fullness of jurisdiction over the entire Church. Diocesan bishops have jurisdiction over their subjects and those temporarily staying within their territory.

Legislative jurisdiction is the power to make or authentically interpret laws. General legislative jurisdiction is possessed only by the Pope or those to whom he delegates this power. The diocesan bishop has legislative jurisdiction within his own diocese and can enact laws only in cases allowed by the general law. The chapters of religious communities have legislative jurisdiction according to the norms of both canon law and their own constitutions. Ecumenical councils, particular councils, synods and episcopal conferences have legislative jurisdiction, but only for those matters allowed by the general law of the Church.

Executive jurisdiction involves the power to dispense from non-reserved ecclesiastical laws of the Church, the power to impose penalties, to issue precepts and to perform other official ecclesiastical acts. Executive jurisdiction may be delegated.

Judicial jurisdiction is the power to judge cases brought before ecclesiastical courts. This jurisdiction is held by the Pope, diocesan bishops and judges appointed by competent Church authorities. They exercise this jurisdiction according to the norms of law. It may be limited to certain kinds of cases, those of certain persons or those presented in a certain territory. A diocesan judge, for example, may not exercise jurisdiction outside his diocese. Judicial jurisdiction cannot be delegated, except for the execution of certain minor judicial acts which are in preparation for the final decision.

Jurisdiction in general is usually carried out in the external forum; however, in certain instances it can be carried out in the internal sacramental or non-sacramental forum, such as in cases of confessional absolution or remission of certain ecclesiastical penalties (cf. Canons 129-144).

Jurisprudence • In the proper sense of the word, jurisprudence is the science of the law. Its function is to ascertain the principles upon which legal rules are based, the relationship of laws one to another, and the application of the law to specific cases. Simply put, jurisprudence is the science whereby the law, which is general and abstract, is applied to a case, which is concrete and specific.

In the Anglo-American common law system, jurisprudence plays the primary role in determining the meaning of a law. In deciding cases, judges and lawyers look to decisions in similar cases and to the jurisprudence of the higher courts, especially the Supreme Court of the United

States. This is known as the principle of *stare decisis*, to abide by decided cases.

In canon law the role of jurisprudence is different. The meaning of a law is determined by the legislator. In specific cases, however, the judge determines whether or not a law is applicable and indicates the reasons for the applicability. This jurisprudence, when it fits into a pattern of similar decisions in similar cases, does not determine the meaning of the law but is a strong indicator of the means for interpreting and applying the law.

In formulating jurisprudence, judges look to decisions in similar cases, official interpretive statements from the legislator and the works of the respected commentators on the canons.

Jus Patronatus: See **Iuspatronatus**

Just War Theory • Any of the ethical theories which attempt to explain why certain types of war and acts of war may be ethically just, in spite of the presumption against intentional homicide. Just as there are different basic ethical theories, so there are different basic approaches to analyzing the justice of war and acts of war. Catholic ethical thought is predominantly in the tradition of natural-law ethics, which studies whether actions are in accordance with their own nature and end.

Natural-law ethicians identify those types of activity which are inherently against their own rationally identifiable nature as ethically wrong, sinful offenses against both God and man. In the context of natural-law ethics, Catholic discussion of warring has focused upon identifying the nature and end of warring. That end provides the criterion for evaluating particular acts and particular wars. Emphasis, especially since the pontificate of Pope Pius XII and the advent of nuclear weaponry, has been on the defensive end of war: The rationally

distinctive and discernible end of a nation's use of destructive force against another is solely to defend those whose rights are being violated. Given such an understanding of the nature of warring, a war may be justly entered by a nation (or its allies) whose rights are under attack, as long as the war is legitimately undertaken solely to thwart the unjust invasion. Furthermore, in the conduct of the war, only those acts of war may justly be committed whose whole direct intent is the defense of the unjustly attacked people, and which would not entail side-effect evils so great as to outweigh the good of defending the endangered rights.

Serious questions have arisen whether the use of nuclear weaponry can ever be justified on the strictly defensive criteria of Catholic just war theory. Bishops' conferences in several nations whose armed forces include nuclear weapons have issued pastoral letters (cf. U.S. bishops' *The Challenge of Peace*) calling the attention of Catholics and others to the challenging ethical issues involved.

Justice • Giving to another what is due, either strictly or proportionately. Justice is a universal concern, and it is loyalty in one's debts to others.

In recent years, the Church has recovered more of a biblical notion of justice. In the Old Testament, it is primarily a style of action in relation to another person. To be just means to be free of faults that would harm one's relations with others. The just man of the Book of Wisdom is so prudent in his dealings with all that the poor who place their hope in him ultimately profit from their dealings with him, and because of this, the just ones are rewarded with true happiness and the blessings of God. In the psalms, the just ones have a correct relationship to God and take joy in God and His commands. Later writings questioned whether Israel could be just before God, but it was never doubted that Yahweh was fully and entirely just.

The New Testament concept of justice incorporated elements of Old Testament writings. Matthew and Paul give justice primary importance, and they note that justice will be demanded in the judgment to come, a justice only achieved by accepting the Gospel of Jesus. Becoming a disciple of Jesus removes one from the company of the unjust, and fulfillment of the commands of justice is an expression of the justice of God. Jesus is the teacher of justice for His community, and for Matthew, justice means being free of sin. Luke identifies justice with fear of God, and in Matthew, justice is obtained through Baptism, but in Mark's Gospel, little mention of justice is made because of the unique objectives and purposes he had in composing his Gospel.

For Paul, justice is a gift from God to humanity, and being in Christ means being in the justice of God (2 Cor 5:21ff.). God opens a cosmic sphere where justice dwells. Justice is a gift from God, and for Paul it is the faithful execution of His promises to the patriarchs. The justice of God is revealed not through the law, but by the sort of faith shown by Abraham, for faith is the means by which justice is obtained. One is tempted to follow not the justice of God, but one's own justice. In the apocalyptic tradition, the just ones endure persecution in fidelity to the Lamb.

Concepts of justice in the modern world have changed. As a result of the rise of capitalism, economic concepts of justice have come to dominate thought, and this has stripped Judeo-Christian notions of justice of their transcendental and metaphysical connotations. The idea of justice being an entire outlook on life has been lost, and justice has been reduced to commutative justice, which only obeys the requirements of contracts. The classical concept of justice as a gratuitous gift from God and a comprehensive virtue (general justice) that permeates one's life has been in large part lost and is in need of recovery. This general, or legal, justice is a justice that exercises all of the virtues to the extent that they bear upon the common good of the community. Recovering this might require reasserting the view of the Fathers that the human person belongs to God and must give back to God what is due. Justice is ultimately surrendering oneself to God and not asserting oneself, one's power or one's possessions absolutely.

In moral theology, justice is the cardinal virtue by which one gives to another what is due. There are two standards for determining this: an arithmetical and a geometric standard. The arithmetical standard requires that the debtor give exactly the same amount to the other, while the geometrical standard requires only a proportional compensation for what was received. Commutative justice regulates actions between individuals, while distributive justice regulates relations between groups and individuals. Social justice refers to the rights and obligations of society and individuals to one another. Original justice refers to the condition of Adam and Eve before original sin, in which they possessed what was *due* to them from God.

Justification • The process by which a sinner is made righteous, pure and holy before God. St. Paul condemned claims that salvation came about through the "works" of the law. However, the New Testament concept of "good works" which merit eternal life are different from those condemned by Paul, for the term is ambivalent.

Justification in the Catholic Tradition comes about by means of faith in Christ, and in a life of good works lived in response to God's invitation to believe. Against classical Lutheran doctrine, Catholic Faith holds that faith without good works is not sufficient to merit justification, for good works show one's willingness to cooperate with the initiatives of grace. Catholic doctrine rejects any notion that justification comes about through an "inwardness" or merely a disposition, but it also objects to the mere performance of a physical act (*actus externus*) without an inward disposition of faith, hope and charity. What is necessary for salvation is a faith that represents itself both externally through acts and internally through faith.

Given the fact that the person exists concretely in the universe, it is necessary for the salvation which occurred objectively and historically, that the person respond historically and objectively to that gift of salvation. As the human person is an embodied spirit, there is a dialogical relationship between the person and the world. Works are necessary for faith simply because they posit an act, accepting the gift of salvation, that is necessary to be redeemed.

That works are clearly required in the New Testament for union with Christ is seen in the many parables such as the Good Samaritan, Lazarus and Dives, and others. The true disciple of Jesus is one who labors in the vineyard, who tills the soil, who proclaims the Good News.

Kanon: See **Canon**

Kantism (also Kantianism) • The philosophy of Immanuel Kant (d. 1804) and later thinkers who adhere to the main tenets of his philosophy. Kant's philosophy was developed as an alternative to both the skepticism of David Hume's empiricist philosophy and the rationalism of Descartes and popular German philosophers. Kant appreciated Hume's attack on the rationalist attempt to attain necessary truth about topics beyond experience — such as the character of the soul or the existence and character of God — solely on the basis of rational analysis of supposed innate ideas. Hume argued that the mere analysis of ideas yields no knowledge of reality. Knowledge of reality is gained only in sensory experiences, by which all ideas must be tested for what is, at best, a merely contingent, nonabsolute truth. Thus Hume offers skepticism as the best theoretical philosophy.

Kant disliked Hume's skepticism and yet accepted the claim that knowledge was bound within experience; Kant wished to defend the possibility of absolute knowledge within physical experience and concerning ethics. He tried to move beyond Hume's skepticism by treating the innate ideas insisted upon by the rationalists as *a priori* functions by which we construe sense data. The mind's innate functions do not, according to Kant, give knowledge by themselves; rather, they are the ways in which we connect and objectify the otherwise unconnected sensory data. Hume's focus on the sensory materials or contents of knowledge failed to clarify how those contents are received and formed as knowledge. Kant's breakthrough was to point out the mind's *a priori* active formative powers.

Kant's active role for intellect bears some resemblance to the active or agent intellect mentioned by Aristotle or St. Thomas. But the role of Kant's "pure concepts of the understanding" and "ideas of reason" is not to free the forms of things from the restrictions of a merely material existence by actualizing them in the intentional order. Rather, the role of Kant's active intellectual powers is merely to connect purportedly discrete atoms of sensory data into organized fields of consciousness.

Kant's approach to the activity of intellect leaves an unbridgeable gulf between the mind and the things themselves which somehow cause the sensory data. We cannot know the reality of anything in itself; we know only reality as it appears to us and as we succeed in objectifying its appearances. Kant attempts to show that assertions of the immortality of the soul in itself or of the existence of God in Himself exceed what can be objectively or meaningfully known by human beings.

Likewise, Kant insists that ethics cannot be built on insight into the nature of human life or on the natural end of any act, since we cannot know what reality in itself is or is for. But the impossibility of knowledge of our nature does not relativize all moral duties. Kant holds that philosophy cannot do justice to the absoluteness of duty by focusing on the changeable ends pursued in action. The categorical character of duty follows from the inevitably formative role or reason in its practical exercise, by which our actions are distinct from merely instinctual events in brute animals. One acts dutifully by acting in accord with practical reason's harmonious self-imposed (autonomously) laws, rather than guiding one's actions by one's idiosyncratic inclinations for pleasure or happiness.

Practical reason categorically demands that one treat oneself no differently from how one would treat others in similar situations. Thus it is an absolute demand that respect be shown for the freedom of all persons, oneself and all others. One must never treat a person as a mere means to extrinsic ends. It is quite difficult to see how Kant's purely formal notion of absolute duty could yield specific norms (e.g., about sex, war, etc.) and thus be practically useful.

Contemporary thinkers may be identified as Kantian when they insist that humans can attain objective knowledge — "facts" — but only within experience and only of things as they appear, and furthermore that there is an ethical absolute but only in a purely formal sense which excludes recognizing inviolable meaning in any concrete area of life, such as sexuality.

Kantian philosophy, whatever its merits vis-à-vis its rationalist and empiricist philosophic predecessors, is generally recognized to have serious philosophical as well as theological problems. Vatican I insisted that knowledge of God's existence is not impossible through right natural reason. And the Church's ordinary Magisterium, of course, witnesses to many ethical norms in concrete areas of life which Kantians would regard as infringements on human ethical autonomy.

Catholic philosophers in the twentieth century have tended to argue either, with Étienne Gilson, that Kant's starting point (his attempt critically to analyze the mind) is mistaken or, with Bernard Lonergan, that his way of characterizing the mind's activity was itself uncritical and self-defeating and that an adequate critical philosophy harmonizes with St. Thomas's realistic philosophy.

Kathisma • The division or separation into twenty sections for the Book of Psalms, as it is used in the Byzantine Rite. Each kathisma is divided into three segments called "Glories" because each segment concludes with the Glory Be. Psalm 119, because of its length (176 verses), however, forms one single kathisma; the other nineteen contain as few as six or as many as fifteen psalms, according to their length.

Katholikon • A term derived from the Greek language to designate the principal church of a Byzantine Rite bishop or monastic community; its approximate equivalent in the Western Church is the designation "cathedral."

Katholikos • A Greek term meaning literally "universal." It is applied in some Eastern Churches to mean "patriarch" in reference to the wide or "universal" sphere of jurisdiction the patriarch encompasses.

Kenosis • The term is from the Greek verb *kenoun*, which occurs in the early Christian hymn which St. Paul quotes from Philippians 2:6-11. In Philippians 2:7, we learn that Christ "emptied himself" (Greek, *heaton ekenosen*), taking the form of a slave, born in the likeness of man. Christ's emptying of Himself or His humbled state is expressed in verses 6-8, and His exaltation is in verses 9-11. The passive voice of the verb at verse 7 suggests Christ's being rendered powerless, ineffective, just like any slave. The point here is that Christ's free choice to live as a slave, assuming the condition of a slave when in reality He was the King, expresses the great love God the Father has placed in His mission to draw back to Him all of His creation through the forgiveness of sins by the work of the cross. Christ's self-emptying consisted of His free renunciation (expressed in the fact of the Incarnation), by which He renounced His being God ("in the form of God"), which meant renouncing the Divine Majesty and Dominion, and therefore taking on existence as God in "the form of a servant." Exactly what one makes of "taking the form [of a servant]" is still highly contestable. Suffice it to say that it included a full and real humanity, totally integrated with His divinity.

Kerygma • The English noun is a transliteration of the Greek *kerygma*, which means "preaching" or "proclaiming," as distinct from teaching or instruction (Greek, *didache*). In Christianity the term refers to more than just the mode of communication (i.e., preaching, proclamation); it refers to a specific content, namely, the Good News of what God has done and is doing in the Person of Jesus Christ. Because there exists an inner unity between the words in Sacred Scripture and the events to which they point and which they proclaim, the language of the kerygma about God's salvific acts of power in and through Jesus Christ is a veritable epiphany or divine self-expression. The linguistic icon of God called "kerygma" is *the* Word of salvation about God's rule, His kingdom which is here and now (Mt 4:23; Lk 9:6), which includes deliverance (Acts 8:5; 9:20), reconciliation (2 Cor 5:19), truth (Col 1:5; Eph 1:13) and grace (Acts 20:32).

King James Version • An English Protestant translation of the Scriptures first published in 1611. The King James Version resulted from a suggestion made at the Hampton Court Conference, called by King James I in 1604. Fifty-four outstanding scholars, including the professors of Greek and Hebrew at both Oxford and Cambridge, were recruited for the task. The translators worked in teams, each team addressing a particular segment of the biblical text. Each team circulated its work to the other groups for critique. The work was in course from 1607 to 1610. The preface asserts that the KJ is not so much a new translation as a revision. The version is generally spoken of as "The King James Bible"; in England, it is more commonly referred to as "The Authorized Version."

Because of its beauty of expression and its influence on English literature, many find it hard to admit the existence of inadequacies; thus, efforts at revision have not always met with approval.

For further reading: F. F. Bruce, *History of the Bible in English*, Third Edition, 96-112 (Oxford University Press, 1978); Jack P. Lewis, "Versions, English (King James)," *Anchor Bible Dictionary*, 6:832-834.

Kingdom of Christ • The phrase refers to an eschatological event (i.e., an event to happen at the end of history) which is outside history and which concludes history at one and the same time (Mt 16:28). There are several references to Christ's kingdom throughout the New Testament. For example, at Matthew 13:26-43, there is an implied reference (v. 41), when the Son of Man sends angels to gather sin and evil out of His kingdom. This parable about the kingdom of God refers to the end of the world as we now understand it, when the righteous will shine like the sun in their Father's kingdom. Thus the notion of kingdom has more to do with the justice and mercy of God's full reign than it does with any geo-political reference to a specific realm *per se*. Consistent with this notion of end-time consummation of God's majestic plan which will see all things reconciled to Him (e.g., 1 Cor 15:28) is the Son's dominion or kingdom (Mt 13:41), which is linked to the Father (Mt 13:43). Here "kingdom" signifies the authoritative might of God to bring ultimate justice and mercy in truth for both the righteous and unrighteous.

In Luke 23:32-43, Jesus is crucified with two criminals, one on the left and the other on the right side of Jesus. In verses 40-42, the repentant criminal asks to be remembered when Jesus enters into His kingdom. Jesus assures him of his eternal destination, Paradise. From this text it might be concluded that Christ's kingly rule is fully manifest at the King's dying on the cross, where forgiveness of sins occurs (Jn 18:28—19:30), in rather dramatic fashion, one might add. This kingdom or sphere of rule over sin and forgiveness, this capacity to grant eternal happiness with God, is given to Christ from God and includes the enjoyment of the great eschatological banquet (Lk 22:29-30).

In 2 Peter 1:3-11, the author encourages believers to understand that faith must be complemented with virtue and knowledge of God. Such matters are essential ingredients for entrance into God's eternal kingdom. The explicit reference to Christ's kingdom reflects the common understanding that it is Christ Who receives believers in Baptism and at the end of their pilgrimage on earth. In summary, Christ's kingdom represents His rule, reign and dominion, which includes the granting of salvation and occurs both within time and space and outside of history, at the end of all history.

Kingdom of God • This phrase is best understood in terms of a sphere of authority and power, of God's sovereign Lordship or rule over the destiny of world history, leading to the eternal goal of living with God in love for all who live their lives and finally die in friendship with God. Based on the "Our Father," it might be said that the kingdom of God is where God's will is done.

The Old Testament abounds with references to God as King (e.g., Dt 33:5; Jgs 8:23; Is 43:15; Ps 24:9; 47:3, 7-8; Ps 93; Ps 96-99). However, these and other Old Testament texts are not the critical

Christ the King (from the Godescale Gospels)

antecedents for the New Testament use of this phrase. Regardless of which aspect it expresses, the "kingdom of God" has a double-time referent to the here-and-now, as well as to that which is out of history, on the other side of history's last day. John the Baptist announced the coming of God's sovereign reign (Mt 4:23; 9:35; Lk 4:43, etc.). That kingdom indeed has arrived (Mt 3:2; 4:17; 10:7; 12:28; Mk 1:15; 11:10; Lk 10:9, 11), and is experienced as righteousness, peace and joy in the Holy Spirit (Rom 14:17) through acceptance of a subordination to God's rule.

This "here-and-now" aspect includes the invitation issued through Jesus' teachings in the Sermon on the Mount, for example. And yet this kingdom does not originate in this world — it is other-worldly and cannot be controlled by human will. It is everlasting (Lk 1:33) and eternal (2 Pt 1:11), heavenly (2 Tm 4:18) and manifests Jesus (2 Tm 4:1); it includes the messianic banquet (Mt 8:11ff.; 22:1-10; 26:29; Mk 14:25; Lk 13:29f., etc.). Both the present and future aspects are detectable in the kingdom parables (Mt 13; 18:23-25; 20:1-16; 25:1-13; Mk 4; Lk 8:4-18; 13:18-21). The sphere of power which issues from God's reign/kingdom is for the benefit of all who would be free from decay, death, sin, alienation, for those who wish to taste the fruit of all of God's fulfilled promises to the People of God.

For further reading: Dennis C. Duling, "Kingdom of God, Kingdom of Heaven," *Anchor Bible Dictionary*, 4:49-69.

Kings, First and Second Books of • In translations from the Vulgate (such as the Douai-Reims, also spelled Douay-Rheims), there are four books about the Jewish kings. The first two of these are now called, as they always were in the Hebrew Bible, 1 and 2 Samuel, and the latter two are 1 and 2 Kings.

The First Book of Kings (1-2) begins by finishing the history of David. The history of Solomon occupies Chapters 3-11, and the remaining eleven chapters tell of the monarchs of Judah and Israel up to Ahab. The Second Book of Kings (1-17) covers both kingdoms to the fall of Samaria (721 B.C.), while the last eight chapters focus on Judah to the fall of its capital city, Jerusalem (587 B.C.).

After Saul, David and Solomon, the kings of the northern kingdom (Israel) were: Jeroboam I, Nadab, Baasha, Elah, Zimri, Omri, Ahab, Ahaziah, Jehoram, Jehu, Jehoash, Jeroboam II, Zechariah, Shallum, Menahem, Pekahiah, Pekah and Hoshea. The rulers of the southern kingdom (Judah) were: Rehoboam, Abijam, Asa, Jehoshaphat, Jehoram, Ahaziah, Athaliah, Jehoash, Amaziah, Azariah, Jotham, Ahaz, Hezekiah, Manasseh, Amon, Josiah, Jehoahaz, Jehoiakim, Jehoiachin and Zedekiah.

There is a stereotyped pattern to the narrative for each of the kings, giving the impression of a catalogue source. Curiously, the date (up to the last in Samaria) for the first year of each ruler is given in the regnal year of the other monarch. The length of each reign is also given, but the sum of these does not generally coincide with the other chronology.

The books refer to more complete sources: the chronicles of Judah, those of Israel. But inasmuch as the references are given in a questioning way, and these chronicles have not survived, even in fragmentary form, one may wonder whether such sources ever existed.

A moral evaluation is given for each of the rulers; generally, this is made on the basis of the fidelity of the people to the law and the efforts of the ruler to extirpate the licentious pagan shrines. Of all the rulers, only Hezekiah and Josiah are highly praised. Every king of Israel is condemned for maintaining separate worship-centers at

Dan and Bethel. The ultimate author of the narrative material seems quite clearly to be a partisan of the southern kingdom.

It is this moral analysis which is, in the author's opinion, the key to understanding the history of the kingdoms. He remains faithful to the idea, universal in the prophets, that the political disasters which befell the Jews were the result of their failings in religion and morality. It is not until the time of Ecclesiastes that we hear the counterpoint that godly behavior does not always bring forth blessings in this life.

For further reading: Steven W. Holloway, "Kings, Book of 1-2" *Anchor Bible Dictionary*, 4:69-83; Jerome T. Walsh and Christopher T. Begg, "1-2 Kings," *New Jerome Biblical Commentary*, 160-185.

Kingship of Christ • In the Gospel according to John, Pontius Pilate asks Jesus, "Are you the King of the Jews?" To this Jesus replies, "My kingship is not of this world; if my kingship were of this world, my servants would fight, that I might not be handed over to the Jews; but my kingship is not from the world" (Jn 18:33, 36). John's Gospel goes on to tell us that Pilate wrote out a title which he ordered to be affixed to the cross of Jesus. That title, written in Hebrew, Latin and Greek, read "Jesus of Nazareth, the King of the Jews" (Jn 19:19).

The kingship of Christ, which became such a prominent part of the charges leveled against Him at His trial, is also found at the very beginning of Jesus' life. Matthew's Gospel tells of magi from the east who came to seek the newborn King Who had been born in Bethlehem (Mt 2:2). The scholars convened by King Herod to ascertain the newborn King's birthplace cite the text of Micah 5:2, "But you, O Bethlehem Ephrathah, who are little to be among the clans of Judah, from you shall come forth for me one who is to be ruler in Israel." Bethlehem was the birthplace of King David,

and the Gospels of Matthew and Luke make it clear that Jesus Himself was a descendant of David. As such, Jesus fulfilled the messianic promises of the prophets, who looked forward to the coming of an anointed king of David's dynasty, a king who would rule justly in accord with the law of God, and whose reign would restore peace and prosperity.

As the Gospels indicate, Jesus the Messiah is not a king in the earthly sense of that word, not a political or a military hero. He is instead, in the words of the messianic prophecy of Isaiah 9, the Prince of Peace. Isaiah declares of the promised Messiah that "of the increase of his government and of peace there will be no end, upon the throne of David, and over his kingdom, to establish it, and to uphold it with justice and with righteousness from this time forth and for evermore" (Is 9:7).

During His earthly ministry, Jesus proclaimed the coming of the kingdom of God, and He embodied the coming of that reign of justice, love and peace in His own words and deeds. Sadly, His own disciples themselves misunderstood the nature of His kingship, not fully recognizing the whole truth about their Lord until they received the gift of the Holy Spirit after Christ's resurrection and ascension. In the Acts of the Apostles, Luke tells us that just before the Ascension, the Apostles asked Jesus, "Lord, will you at this time restore the kingdom to Israel?" (Acts 1:6). In Peter's Pentecost sermon the Apostle expresses the new understanding given under the inspiration of the Holy Spirit, an understanding of the cross and resurrection of Christ as the Lord's enthronement as heavenly king: "Let all the house of Israel therefore know assuredly that God has made him both Lord and Christ, this Jesus whom you crucified" (Acts 2:36).

Kinonikon • In the Byzantine Rite, the Troparion of the Communion of the Priest. There is a proper Kinonikon for each of several major feasts.

Kiss, Liturgical Use of • Liturgical tradition attests to two usages: a reverential gesture as prescribed in the rubrics (toward objects such as the Gospel Book and altar) and as one way of exchanging the sign of peace before Communion. In the 1964 Instruction *Inter Oecumenici*, on the orderly carrying out of the Liturgy Constitution, the Sacred Congregation of Rites states that in the interest of simplifying the rites (in accord with *Sacrosanctum Concilium*, the Constitution on the Sacred Liturgy, n. 34) the kissing of the hand or of objects (such as the cruets at the presentation of the gifts) shall be omitted (n. 36d) and that the celebrant kisses the altar only at the beginning of Mass and at the end of Mass. The 1967 instruction *Tres abhinc annos* of the same Congregation (the second instruction "on the orderly carrying out of the Liturgy Constitution") states that the celebrant kisses the altar only at the beginning and at the end of Mass (n. 8). The 1975 *General Instruction of the Roman Missal* directs the celebrant (n. 85) and deacon (n. 129) to kiss the altar at the beginning and at the end of Mass (nn. 125, 141). It also directs the deacon (or whoever else proclaims the Gospel, the celebrant or an assisting or concelebrating priest) to kiss the Gospel Book at the end of the proclamation of the Gospel, saying the words (inaudibly), "May the words of the gospel wipe away our sins" (n. 131). The 1984 *Caeremoniale Episcoporum*, the *Ceremonial for Bishops*, states that at the conclusion of the Gospel's proclamation, the deacon "carries the *Book of the Gospels* to the bishop to kiss, or he may kiss it himself" (n. 52). The *General Instruction of the Roman Missal* also states that "according to traditional liturgical practice, the Altar and the Book of the Gospels are kissed as a sign of veneration. But if the sign of reverence is not in harmony with the traditions or the culture of the region, the conference of bishops may substitute some other sign, after informing the Apostolic See" (n. 232).

The present order for the celebration of Mass contains no explicit reference to the way the gesture of peace is to be shared prior to Communion. It states that after speaking the words, "The peace of the Lord be with you always," and the people's response ("And with your spirit"), "then the priest may add: 'Let us offer each other the sign of peace [Latin, *Offerte vobis pacem*].' All exchange some sign of peace and love according to local custom" (n. 112).

Knights of Columbus • The leading Catholic laymen's organization in the world. The society was founded in 1882 in New Haven, Connecticut, by Father Michael J. McGivney. It has councils in many countries besides the United States.

It is a fraternal organization organized under a Supreme Knight, with the goal of uniting Catholic laymen for useful religious and civic activities. Their particular aim is to be of generous service to the Church in the various fields of the social apostolate in complete harmony with Church leaders.

Among its many activities are the welfare of members and survivors of members, the promotion of education, the support of historical studies and a wide range of charities. The society has been generous in providing financial assistance to the Holy See in many ways.

Knights of Malta (Hospitallers) • The sovereign Military Hospitaller Order of St. John of Jerusalem, of Rhodes and of Malta is the most ancient religious order of chivalry. The order began in Jerusalem during the First Crusade in 1070, as a hospice-infirmary for pilgrims from Amalfi. In 1113 the institution was approved by Pope Paschal II. The Knights are a religious order made up of lay brothers and chaplains, whose original purpose was the protection and nursing of pilgrims in the Holy Land. Forced to leave by the Muslim invasions, they went first to Cyprus, then Rhodes and finally Malta. They were the temporal rulers of Malta until the invasion of 1798 by Napoleon Bonaparte.

Not only a religious order approved by the Holy See, the Knights are also recognized in international law as a sovereign entity. Originally, membership was restricted to the nobility, but a new category of Knights and Dames of Grace and Devotion is open to meritorious persons who are not of the nobility. A National Association of Knights and Dames of Malta exists in the United States.

Knights, Orders of • In the Middle Ages the term "knight" was used to designate a man raised to an honorable military rank by the king or other qualified person. The knight was usually a person who had served an apprenticeship as a page or a squire to the profession of arms. Eventually, sovereigns organized various orders of knights, to which only the most worthy were admitted. Among the oldest still existing orders are Britain's Order of the Garter, Spain's Order of the Golden Fleece and Denmark's Order of the Dannebrog. Some orders were composed of knights who took religious vows, such as the Knights Hospitallers of St. John of Jerusalem.

Knights, Papal • The Pontifical Orders of Knighthood presently existing are, in their order of precedence: The Supreme Order of Christ, The Order of the Golden Spur, The Order of Pius IX, The Order of St. Gregory the Great and The Order of Pope St. Sylvester. The first two of these orders are

granted by the Sovereign Pontiff on his own initiative. The latter three may also be so granted but are usually granted on the basis of presentation of worthy candidates to the Secretariat of State by the diocesan bishop of the candidate.

Other papal awards are also conferred as a reward for services rendered to the Church and society, especially in the direct exercise of the apostolate. The main awards are the Golden Rose, the Cross Pro Ecclesia et Pontifice (for the Church and the Pontiff) and the Medal Benemerenti (for a well-deserving person).

Religious but not pontifical orders of knighthood recognized by the Holy See are the Sovereign Military Order of St. John of Jerusalem, of Rhodes and of Malta, and the Equestrian Order of the Holy Sepulchre of Jerusalem. The Holy See also recognizes other legitimate orders of knighthood granted by states and sovereigns.

Knock, Our Lady of • On August 21, 1879, an apparition of the Blessed Virgin Mary, St. Joseph, the Lamb of God and St. John the Evangelist occurred in Knock in County Mayo, Ireland. The four figures appeared on the wall of the parish church but did not speak. Twice in 1880 the apparition was repeated, but the light was too intense to recognize anyone but Mary. Because of many miracles, Knock became a popular pilgrimage place. In 1976 a large church dedicated to Our Lady, Queen of Knock, was erected. Pope John Paul II visited the shrine on September 30, 1979, to mark the centennial of the apparition. Over 300,000 pilgrims visit the shrine annually.

Knowledge • Acquired through the act of the mind which assimilates external information and experience, knowledge then represents it internally. There is "objective knowledge" which implies a relationship between the knower and the thing known, and there is "existential knowledge" in which the thing known becomes a factor whereby the self-consciousness of the knower is affected in a particular way.

Knowledge is an essential part of the practice of the Christian Faith, since it is used to make judgments which can bring the individual closer to God, and the Christian is admonished by St. Paul to "put on the new nature, which is being renewed in knowledge after the image of its creator" (Col 3:10).

Knowledge which has been gained in this life, and which is edifying, is carried with the individual into heaven, and knowledge will be gained there, resulting from that perfection which has been promised by God.

Know-Nothingism • From the 1830s through the 1850s, immigration to the United States waned from the predominantly Protestant regions of Europe, but increased from the more Catholic areas of the Continent. This demographic change was perceived as a threat by certain American-born Protestants who, in the 1850s, revived a moribund Nativist party into a considerable political machine known as "Know-Nothingism." Sworn to secrecy (hence the name "know-nothing"), these extremists pushed a Nativist agenda which far exceeded a nation's right to police its borders. The Know-Nothings included such measures as a minimum twenty-one-year residency prior to citizenship and a permanent ban on any foreign-born persons from holding any political office. They made no secret of the fact that the primary objects of their scorn were the Catholic immigrants arriving in America.

The Know-Nothings seized upon the increasing political unrest which foreshadowed the War Between the States and by 1864 were significantly represented in several Eastern state assemblies, administrations and congressional delegations. At one point, over thirty states had Know-Nothings in various political offices, where they managed to enact several pieces of legislation disabling to Catholic rights and interests. In 1855, however, Abraham Lincoln penned his widely-circulated letter to Joshua Speed, in which he observed that "if the Know-Nothings get control, [the Declaration of Independence] will read 'All men are created equal except negroes, foreigners, and Catholics.' "

As the country began to face the impending war, the Know-Nothings faded in popularity. Their last bastions of political influence were in the strife-torn border states and when these too turned away from Know-Nothingism, its few remaining adherents were absorbed, perhaps rather ironically, into the Constitutional Union Party and Mr. Lincoln's Republicans. The legislative gains of the Know-Nothings were repealed and the movement disappeared, although many of its ideas are consistent with the contemporary Ku Klux Klan.

Knox Version of the Bible • At the request of the Catholic hierarchy of England and Wales, Monsignor Ronald Knox, a distinguished biblical scholar and linguist, undertook in 1939 a translation of the Bible from Jerome's Vulgate. His stated aim was to express the Bible "in timeless English" in a style that was "accurate, intelligible, idiomatic, readable." With the *imprimatur* of Cardinal Griffin, the Knox Version of the Bible was published in 1949.

At times too free in style and given to personal idiosyncrasy, the Knox Version has never been especially popular as an English translation; its great importance, however, lies still in the impetus it gave to later translations, such as the Revised Standard Version and the Jerusalem Bible.

For further reading: F. F. Bruce, *History of the Bible in English*, Third Edition, 206-212 (Oxford University Press, 1978).

Koimesis • A Greek term meaning "a falling-asleep." In the Byzantine Church this is applied to death in general; in particular, *koimesis* refers to the holy dormition (assumption) of the Mother of God, observed on August 15. July 25 marks the *koimesis* of St. Anne, the mother of Mary.

Koinonia • The Greek *koinonia* in its widest usage meant anything from an association, communion (social), fellowship and sometimes close relationships, to solidarity or generosity, to the more abstract notion of a verbal sign of fellowship or proof of brotherly unity, to the explicit concept of participation and sharing in or of something.

The New Testament carries several of the above meanings. The term can refer to communion or fellowship with God (1 Jn 1:3, 6), the Son (1 Cor 1:9) and the Holy Spirit (2 Cor 13:13; Phil 2:1). The emphasis Luke places on the word at Acts 2:42-47 concerns the deeply committed relationships of the Church in Jerusalem. Consistent with the very nature of the Trinity's communal life, the collectivity of believers called the Church shared their lives not just within her own confines but with the poor (Rom 15:26), and resisted fellowship with darkness (2 Cor 6:14). Such outward movements of divinely inspired life undoubtedly were rooted in the community's intimate relationship with the Gospel (Phil 1:5). This idea of being "associated with" translates easily to participation and sharing in, as in our participation in the Faith (Phlm 6), in Christ's sufferings (Phil 3:10), in the Holy Spirit (2 Cor 13:13), in the Body and Blood of Christ (1 Cor 10:16).

Kontakion • A troparion containing a summary of the subject of a feast. There is a proper kontakion for every feast in the Byzantine Rite.

Koran • The sacred book of Islam is called the Koran, a word derived from the Arabic word *qur'an*, meaning "read." It is composed of the revelations and commands delivered to the prophet Muhammad by the angel Gabriel. The first verse was said to be the command of the angel, declaring: "Read! read in the name of your Lord who created man."

Thus the word Koran was applied to each of the revelations announced by Muhammad and then to the entire book, including those verses believed by some scholars to have been compiled after his death by his secretary, Zaid Ibn Thabit, at the command of the Caliph Abu Bekr. In the entire Koran there are 114 chapters, called *suras*, metrical in style and arranged by length, rather than logically or chronologically. The Koran urges submission to the one God, Allah. It shows a progression of revelation from Moses and Christ to the final prophet, Muhammad himself. Its aim is the guidance of the pious who believe in the mysteries of the faith, say their prayers, give alms and, of course, accept the Koran as the eternal word of God. Because it is classic in language, it has become the standard of Arabic literature. For much of Islamic society it is the last word in science, philosophy, law, morality and all worldly dealings.

Ku Klux Klan • A secret society in the United States, the Ku Klux Klan began in the South as a response to the post-Civil War reconstruction of the Southern states. Formed in 1866 in Pulaski, Tennessee, it derived its name from the Greek word *kyklos*, meaning "circle." Its masked membership and bizarre ritual led by a grand or imperial wizard was designed to terrorize the newly freed slaves and to prevent them from exercising their legitimate rights. When fright did not succeed, the Klan practiced cross burnings, lynching, whipping and other forms of terrorism. At its height, from 1868 to 1871, the Klan had about 500,000 members. The original Klan disappeared by 1877.

A second Klan was founded in Georgia in 1915. By 1924 it enrolled 5,000,000 members. It blamed any and all social and economic problems on blacks, Jews and Catholics. It unleashed a reign of terror particularly in the rural South, chiefly against blacks. Discredited by internal scandals and newspaper revelations of its behavior, its membership dropped to about 30,000 in 1930 and dissolved in 1944.

A third Klan was revived in 1946, and was placed on the U.S. Department of Justice's subversive list that same year. Revived somewhat by the U.S. Supreme Court's desegregation order in the landmark Brown v. Board of Education case of 1954, the Klan fought actively against the presidential candidacy of John F. Kennedy in 1960. It occasionally surfaces to wage campaigns of bigotry against African-Americans and Jews.

Membership in the Klan is considered incompatible with the practice of the Catholic Faith.

Kulturkampf • The German word for "culture struggle," it refers to what was perhaps the first systematic persecution of the Church by the modern state. Otto von Bismarck of Prussia, a genius of bureaucratic organization, embarked on a program of national unification which, in his mind, meant the replacement of "foreign" Catholicism with German Protestantism. Beginning in 1872, the Prussian State systematically set about undermining the ecclesiastical authority of Rome over her churches and expelling the members of religious orders. In the first year of the persecution alone, over five hundred Jesuits were expelled, to be followed by the Redemptorists and others the next year. Under the pretext of "inspections" mandated by the May Law of 1873, moreover, Catholic

schools and religious houses were closed and priests or bishops who refused to cooperate in the same were severely fined and later imprisoned.

Such actions, while they did spread into certain other Germanic regions, naturally galvanized Catholic resistance in those areas, most notably in Bavaria and in ethnically Polish territories. This so-called Central Party grew in strength, and when Pope Pius IX refused Bismarck's demand to dissociate himself from the Central Party (actually, Pius responded by annulling the May Law in 1875), Bismarck was forced to reconsider his plans. By 1887, Bismarck and the Holy See reached an accord, although the net result of the persecution was renewed animosity between Protestants and Catholics in the region for many years.

Kyriale • Book of some Gregorian chants. The music found in this book is predominantly from the Ordinary of the Mass and not the Proper of the Mass. It predates Vatican II and is not in use today. Some of its chants can now be found in *Jubilate Deo*.

Kyrie Eleison • This is the single remaining vestige of the use of Greek in the Order of Mass of the Latin Rite. The translation, "Lord, have mercy," is literally correct yet deficient in that it does not render the praise and acclamatory sense of the original. To state, "Lord, you are ever merciful" or "Lord, you are the merciful one" would be more precise. Eastern liturgical usage attests to a much more frequent use of *Kyrie eleison* in the liturgy than occurs in the West. Western liturgical tradition attests to two main uses for this phrase: as a response to a litany of intercessions (such as at the prayer of the faithful) and as part of the Introductory Rites at Mass. It is still unclear as to when this was introduced into the Mass, but *Ordo Romanus I* (seventh-century papal book of ceremonies) attests that the number of acclamations is left to the discretion of the celebrant; by the eighth century there were three *Kyrie* acclamations and three *Christe eleison* acclamations in customary usage. In the present Order of Mass, *Kyrie eleison* may be used as part of the third form of the penitential rite where it follows a trope addressed to Christ (e.g., "You were sent to heal the contrite. Lord, have mercy") and forms the congregation's response "Lord, have mercy." If it is not used as part of the act of penance, then the *Kyrie* itself follows in pairs, "Lord, have mercy," "Christ, have mercy" and "Lord, have mercy." In all these places the Latin *Missale Romanum* uses the Greek *Kyrie*. In the present English-language sacramentary the responses to the tropes are in English; the *Kyrie* invocations themselves are both in English and Greek. In both the present Latin and English sacramentaries *Kyrie eleison* is offered as one of the options as a response to the "Sample Formulas for the General Intercessions"; most fittingly, it is supplied in both texts for the sample intercessions for Advent.

Labarum • The military standard of the Christian Roman emperors, first used by Constantine. Eusebius, in his celebrated *Vita Constantini*, describes it as "a long spear, overlaid with gold, with a crossbar giving it a cruciform shape." On the top of the whole was affixed a wreath of gold and precious stones, and within this the symbol of the Savior's Name, two letters indicating the name of Christ by means of initial letters, the letter "X" intersecting "P" at the center. Hanging from the crossbar was a purple banner inscribed with the Latin for, "In this sign conquer," an allusion to Constantine's vision before the battle of the Milvian Bridge.

Labor • The activity by which human beings secure the means for their physical existence and develop their natural gifts and talents. Of all the creatures, only the human person has the natural endowments to apply reason, imagination and creativity to the development of natural, human and spiritual resources to better our human condition through the enterprise of labor.

In the New Testament era, the Church demanded respect, justice and fair treatment for those who labored. She did not seek to restructure labor relationships radically, but only to permeate them with Christian justice, charity and truth. Thus, Paul did not demand that Philemon liberate Onesimus but only that he treat him with Christian justice and love. In Christian antiquity, Christians sought to restructure labor relationships by freeing slaves, and in the Middle Ages, the Church sought to

provide greater security for laborers through the guild system, despite the fact that this system radically undermined the development of technology and production.

Throughout all of human history, work and labor were viewed as essential, and it was only in the capitalist and post-capitalist era that the question of the rights of laborers truly came to the fore. During this era, workers were left totally unprotected by governments and societies, and labor was considered as a "soulless" commodity that was to be purchased and traded like any other.

In the capitalist era, laborers were terribly exploited, and with the issuing of the great social justice encyclicals, the Church came to their defense. These encyclicals argued forcefully that laborers have natural human rights that must be respected by employers and society. They have a right to strike for a just cause, but laborers also have an obligation to provide a just return for their wages. Laborers are to be given adequate housing, medical attention and opportunities for education. The basic right of laborers is to receive a just compensation for their work and for the products of their labor, and the Church has taught that they have a right to a family wage, that is, a wage sufficient to support a family. In addition, just as an artist, composer or scholar has a right to claim that the products of one's efforts are truly his own, so also does the laborer have the right to claim that the products of his efforts are truly his; the Church has also taught that the possession of private property is legitimate, even if not an absolute right.

The encyclicals taught that the relationship between managers and laborers is not to be one of competition and conflict, but of harmony, trust and cooperation. Managers are to provide security for laborers, and laborers are to strive to improve production, efficiency and the design of their products. (Cf. Rerum Novarum; Laborem Exercens.)

Laborem Exercens • The encyclical letter, *On Human Work,* issued by Pope John Paul II in 1981, in which the Church's teaching regarding economic ethics is organized in a new fashion around the theme of the meaning of human work. The Pope sets his reflections in the context of biblical references to work and to the recent tradition of papal social encyclicals. He stresses the need to distinguish between the *objective* meaning of work and its sense as a *subjective* or *personal* reality.

The objective meaning of work is its measurable contribution to society's overall production; the objective meaning of work abstracts from the person performing the work and from the work as part of that person's own life. The personal or subjective meaning of work is the role of work in God's plan for creation as a whole (by working, human beings co-create the world) and especially for each particular human worker. When considered as a personal reality, work is no mere unavoidable human drudgery necessary solely to earn a living. Rather, work is one essential way in which human persons realize their own imaging of God as Lord of the world.

Awareness of the essential personal meaning of human labor leads us to notice the many ways in which our economic organizations, customs and laws degrade persons by treating their work merely objectively and thus as devoid of inherent worth, regardless of its great or small objective worth. The historical roots of the world's present economic organization are found in the tendency of both individualist/ capitalist and Marxist policies to fail to do justice to the subjective or personal meaning of work; the dignity of labor is made subordinate more or less directly to the merely derivative worth of capital.

Economies based solely on the objective dimension of work inevitably demean the persons involved. The solution to our problems is impossible without the discovery and implementation of policies which respect the essential meaning of work — both menial work and the more objectively useful forms, both the work of mothers and of fathers — as the personal act of the worker in solidarity with fellows (both equals and subordinates). Change which overcomes demeaning status quo conditions and which develops respect for the personal sense of work is called socialization (this is not socialism). The forms in which socialization or personalization can be achieved will vary, depending upon the circumstances found in each particular society. In Marxist economies, the government should play a smaller role so that true socialization (respect for the personal and social meaning of work) can be fostered. In non-Marxist economies, governmental policies should either be developed or changed so that the same personal purpose can be achieved in the different circumstances.

Lady Chapel • A chapel dedicated to the Blessed Mother has been traditionally referred to by this name, especially in England and France. In medieval times it was often attached to the choir of a church and at times was the central, hence the crowning, chapel of the several chapels which were found in the perimeter of the apse. In French architecture this arrangement of an apse with radiating chapels, which always was in the easternmost part of the church building, was called the *chevet*. Sometimes the Lady Chapel was actually a separate, small building joined to the church by a covered passage.

Lady Day • This is another name for the solemnity of the Annunciation, which commemorates the visit of the archangel Gabriel to the Blessed Virgin Mary and her assent to become the Virgin Mother of God and the Incarnation of the eternal Word in her womb (cf. Lk 1:26-38). In the Latin Rite this feast is celebrated each year on March 25.

Laetare Medal • The award given by the University of Notre Dame on Laetare Sunday (Fourth Sunday of Lent) to an American who has served Church and country in an outstanding manner. This gold medal is conferred with a citation explaining the origins of the honor and the achievements of the individual. The medal was founded in 1883 at the suggestion of Father Edward Sorin, C.S.C., founder of the University.

Laetare Sunday: See Gaudete Sunday

Laic Laws • A series of laws enacted in France between 1875 and 1907, flowing from the declared anticlericalism of the ruling Republicans. With the goal of complete separation of — if not animosity between — Church and state, these decrees

Lady Chapel in Salisbury Cathedral

were termed "laic," in that they were supposed to wrest power from the clergy and restore it to the people. They were passed in the decades following the establishment of the Third Republic (1870) and resulted in the secularization of the educational and charitable initiatives traditionally undertaken by the Church in France. The Republicans justified these laws by pointing to the antidemocratic sentiments of some more-conservative Catholics, and by claiming that the Church had never fully accepted the results of the revolution, and thus had to be controlled.

Pope Leo XIII (d. 1903) realistically encouraged the French hierarchy and faithful to cooperate with their government in a policy called *ralliement*, elucidated in his encyclical *Nobilissima Gallorum Gens* (1884). Although the subsequent harmony resulted in some temporary mitigation of the laws, they were even strengthened after the turn of the century, under the leadership of Justin Combes, culminating in the Law of Separation in 1905. Pope St. Pius X (d. 1914) then reversed the policy of Leo, severing relations between the Holy See and France, a rift which would continue until the early 1920s. The Law of Separation, the most extreme of the Laic Laws, stopped all governmental assistance to religion, declared that every religious group could exist only with the permission of the state and furthered the secularization of French life, the results of which challenge the

Catholics in this "eldest daughter of the Church" to this day.

Laicism • An idea prominent in the nineteenth century which held that the role of the hierarchy and clergy should be de-emphasized, both in ecclesiastical and civil affairs, and that all temporal and almost every spiritual matter should be the responsibility of the laity. In its exaggerated form, it came close to anticlericalism and secularism, as it was militantly opposed to any influence by the Church upon political or cultural matters. Thus, it was listed among those theories condemned in 1864 by Pope Pius IX in the *Syllabus of Errors*.

Laicism should not be confused with the legitimate movement encouraging lay Catholics to accept the duties, rights and obligations proper to them through the sacraments of Baptism, Confirmation and Matrimony.

Laicization • The common term for the process whereby a cleric is officially returned to the lay state. When this happens the cleric, although he retains the Sacred Orders received, cannot exercise any of the powers of those orders. An exception is made by the law to allow laicized priests or bishops to minister to those in danger of death.

A laicized cleric is prohibited from holding ecclesiastical offices, exercising the power of jurisdiction and wearing clerical dress.

Laicization can come about in three ways. The most common is when a cleric petitions the Holy See to be returned to the lay state. The Holy See, acting through the Congregation for the Clergy, prepares the request, which is presented to the Holy Father for decision. The return to the lay state in this manner is usually, but not always, accompanied by a dispensation from clerical celibacy, with the consequent right to marry.

A cleric can also be returned to the lay state if he is dismissed from the clerical state by a judicial penal process. In this case, laicization is a penalty imposed for a crime committed. The penalty of dismissal does not carry with it the dispensation from clerical celibacy. Such trials have been extremely rare in recent times.

Finally, a cleric can be involuntarily laicized by an administrative process and decree of the Holy See (although no instances of this have come to light since the new Code). This is usually done at the request of his bishop or religious superior. It usually involves a cleric who is manifestly unsuited to ministry for most serious reasons. Dispensation from celibacy is an option that depends on the Holy See.

A cleric who has been returned to the lay state either voluntarily or by dismissal can be reinstated in the clerical state, with the right to exercise ministry, by a decree of the Holy See.

Large numbers of priests requested and received laicization in the years immediately following Vatican II, but more recently Roman practice has become stricter. Generally, requests for laicization from priests under age forty are not considered because modern young men not uncommonly try to change their life's direction more than once and, if a laicization request is granted too hastily, the obstacles to reentering ministry in later life are greatly increased. On the other hand, petitions from priests who have been away from the ministry for many years, or who have civilly married and started families, as well as requests based on the traditional hardship reasons (e.g., personal or family health problems) are considered in due course.

Most voluntary laicizations are investigated at the diocesan level by a priest-instructor appointed by the local bishop. When petitions and testimony are forwarded to Rome, they are divided into two types, "petitions in justice" (in which the appropriateness of having ordained the priest in the first place is studied) and "petitions in charity" (in which the hardship of the priest's remaining in the clerical state is the focus of inquiry). Both types of petitions require extensive testimony from the petitioner and qualified witnesses, as well as supporting statements from the superior of the priest in question. Generally, the laicization process used by priests is the same as that used for deacons.

There never has been an instance when a bishop has been voluntarily laicized and given permission to marry (cf. Canons 290-293).

Laity • All those baptized faithful who are not in Holy Orders, or in some religious state of life approved by the Church, are properly termed laity (cf. AA 31). *Lumen Gentium*, the Dogmatic Constitution on the Church, teaches that "the faithful who by Baptism are incorporated into Christ, are placed in the People of God, and in their own way share the priestly, prophetic and kingly office of Christ, and to the best of their ability carry on the mission of the whole Christian people in the Church and in the world" (LG 31). The role of the laity is *priestly*, through the offering of themselves and their own daily lives to be united with Christ and His sacrifice; the role of the laity is *prophetic*, through their acceptance of the Gospel and their willingness to proclaim it to the world; the role of the laity is *kingly*, because they belong to Christ the King, and have been called by Him to spread His kingdom.

God issues a vocation to holiness to each member of the laity, which is to be manifested in daily work and activity. In seeking to fulfill this vocation, the laity help to bring about the sanctification of the world and assist in its evangelization. "The characteristic of the lay state being a life led in the midst of the world and of secular affairs, laymen are called by God to make of their apostolate, through the vigor of their Christian spirit, a leaven in the world" (AA 2).

In 1987 at the assembly of the Synod of Bishops, the theme which was discussed was "The Vocation and Mission of the Laity in the Church and the World Twenty Years after the Second Vatican Council." The document which resulted from that synod was the Apostolic Exhortation issued on January 30, 1989, *Christifideles Laici*. In it Pope John Paul II brings together the teaching of the Second Vatican Council on the character and mission of the lay apostolate in relation to those developments which have taken place in the years following the Council. *Christifideles Laici* encourages the laity "to overcome in themselves the separation of the Gospel from life, to again take up in their daily activities in family, work and society, an integrated approach to life that is fully brought about by the inspiration and strength of the Gospel."

Laity, Institutions of • Any attempt to chronicle briefly the flowering of lay-run or lay-oriented institutions in the Church which have appeared (especially after the Second Vatican Council) would be doomed to terrible incompleteness. What follows, then, are only high points in this development.

Shortly after the promulgation of the Second Vatican Council's Decree on the Apostolate of Lay People, *Apostolicam Actuositatem*, it was proposed to institute within the Roman Curia an office dedicated primarily to the needs of lay Catholics. This Pope Paul VI did in January 1967. Just under ten years later, this same Pontiff granted the Pontifical Council on the Laity permanent status within the Curia and established its primary concern as the study and facilitation of the apostolate of the laity. This council is headed by a cardinal and, following the recent curial reorganizations of Pope John Paul II, ranks first in precedence among the pontifical councils. Its members are mostly laity from around the world. The Council on the Laity maintains an especially close relationship with the Pontifical Council on the Laity.

In the United States, as in many other nations, at both the diocesan level, at least in many cases, and within the support staff of the episcopal conference, there are offices concerned chiefly with the particular needs and interests of lay Catholics. These are frequently listed, though, under a wide variety of titles, depending upon the particular matter under consideration. There are, finally, scores of private organizations serving particular groups of laity or the special concerns of those groups. Some of these seek to further devotional practices suitable to the lay state, others to promote the various missions of the Church, and still others are concerned with providing a Catholic response to secular or civil needs. (Cf. Associations of the Christian Faithful.)

Lamb (Eucharist) • In the Byzantine Rite, the name given to the larger portion of the Bread of Offering detached by the priest for Consecration. The Lamb is inscribed with the Greek lettering "IC," "XC," "NI," "KA" (Jesus Christ conquers).

Lamb of God • "Behold the Lamb of God, who takes away the sins of the world. Happy are those who are called to his supper." Saying these words, the priest shows the consecrated host to the faithful immediately before Communion. Moments earlier, the congregation sings or says the litany, "Lamb of God, you take away the sins of the world, have mercy on us . . . grant us peace." These liturgical prayers have deep roots in Sacred Scripture. In the Old Testament, Jeremiah

described his experience of persecution as a lamb which one leads to the slaughter (Jer 11:19). The idea of a slaughtered lamb provides the impetus for Isaiah to describe the suffering servant of God whose death pays for the sins of God's people — "like a lamb that is led to the slaughter, and like a sheep that before its shearers is dumb, so he opened not his mouth" (Is 53:7). Philip explains to the eunuch of the Ethiopian queen how this passage from Isaiah is fulfilled in the action and Person of Jesus Christ (Acts 8:31-35). Reference to this Old Testament suffering servant tradition, which Christ's mission on earth fulfills and perfects, may be at least implied at John 1:29.

The Old Testament background for the Lamb of God obtains its fundamental importance in God's command to offer a lamb in preparation for the exodus from Egypt (Ex 12:5). In biblical and pre-Christian rabbinic tradition (Pirqe R. Eliezar 29; Mekhelta, Ex 12) note the stated belief that it was because of the paschal lamb's blood that the Hebrews were freed from slavery in Egypt, leading to their becoming a kingdom of priests (Ex 19:6). Jesus is the Lamb (1 Pt 1:19; Jn 1:29; Rv 5:6) without blemish (Ex 12:5) or sin (Jn 8:46; 1 Jn 3:5; Heb 9:14), Who delivers by His Blood (1 Pt 1:18ff.; Rv 5:9ff.; Heb 9:12-15). Thus the Paschal Lamb delivers from "earth" (Rv 14:3), builds up the redeemed by helping them to avoid sin (1 Pt 1:15ff.; Jn 1:29; 1 Jn 3:5-9), forming a new royal priesthood and consecrated nation (1 Pt 2:9; Rv 5:9ff.). The contrast between the immolated Lamb and the exalted Lamb lies in the exalted Lamb's power, situated on the throne (Heb 12:1-3), receiving adoration (Rv 5:8-13; 7:10), executing God's judgments (Rv 6:1) and finally being consecrated King of Kings and Lord of Lords (Rv 17:14; 19:16). The Lamb is also the Shepherd, leading the faithful to living water and heavenly blessedness (Rv 7:17; 14:4).

For further reading: John R. Miles, "Lamb," *Anchor Bible Dictionary*, 4:132-134.

Lambeth Conference • The gatherings of bishops of the worldwide Anglican Communion, first convoked in 1865, are held at Lambeth Palace, the London residence of the Archbishop of Canterbury, who convenes and presides over them. The conferences are usually, though not always, held at ten-year intervals. They symbolize the unity of the churches of the Anglican Communion and are an important occasion for consultation, discussion and decision. The conferences discuss topics of internal interest to the communion, as well as various interchurch and interreligious matters. The conferences normally issue letters and declarations at the end of their deliberations. The decisions of the conference are not binding on the churches of the communion, which must adopt them by synodal or other constitutional means. However, the fact that all the diocesan bishops of the communion are invited gives the decisions and declarations of the conference great weight.

Lamentations, Book of • Personal grief was often expressed in the Near East in literary forms such as the dirge. After the fall of Jerusalem, the city so dear to devoted Jews, it was natural that those who grieved over the city should express this deep emotion in this way.

The five chapters of this short book are the relic of such compositions. They have often been ascribed to Jeremiah — indeed, in the Greek and Latin versions they are an appendix to his prophecy — but they are more likely the work of his disciples.

The first four have an alphabetical structure, with two or three successive verses beginning with the same letter of the alphabet. The last Lamentation does not follow this pattern, but it does have twenty-two verses, as there are twenty-two letters in Hebrew.

Their teaching is an answer of believing Jews to the complaints of those whose faith was faltering after the disaster. They declare that God has not abandoned us or His covenant with us; it is because we have been unfaithful to His covenant that He has punished us.

The Catholic Liturgy has made use of these poems during Holy Week to express the mourning of Christians over the sufferings and death of the Messiah.

For further reading: Michael D. Guinan, O.F.M., "Lamentations," *New Jerome Biblical Commentary*, 558-562; Delbert R. Hillers, "Lamentations," *Anchor Bible Dictionary*, 4:137-141.

Lamp-Lighting • The ceremony of lamp-lighting at Vespers derives from the Jewish ritual of lighting lamps at the beginning of the Sabbath. This tradition carried over into the Church's celebration of evening prayer, particularly in the cathedral (otherwise termed the "ecclesiastical" or "parish") tradition of the Hours, as well as at the Easter Vigil with the lighting of the Paschal Candle, a procession with it into the body of the church and the singing of the *Exsultet*. This represents an elaboration on the Western liturgical tradition, attested as early as the *Apostolic Tradition* of Hippolytus of Rome (c. A.D. 215), of lighting lamps at the beginning of Vespers. This ceremony was often accompanied by the singing of the *Phos Hilaron* (originally in Greek, third century) which exclaims: "Joyous light of glory of the immortal Father: heavenly, holy, blessed Jesus Christ. We have come to the setting of the sun, and we look to the evening light."

In her fourth-century diary reflecting liturgical practice in Jerusalem, Egeria states that Vespers was prayed toward the end of the afternoon (the service itself entitled *lucernarium*) and that lights were kindled from the lamp that always burned in the grotto of the Anastasis (the Sanctuary of the Resurrection). The custom of the *lucernarium*, with accompanying *Phos Hilaron* and Vesper psalmody, prayers, readings and canticles, has been revived in some contemporary ritual and prayer books of Christian churches by way of offering a contemporary adaptation of this cathedral usage (e.g., 1978 *Lutheran Book of Worship* in America).

The theme of light that runs through many Vesper antiphons, psalms and prayers derives from this liturgical tradition.

Lamps • (1) The symbol used for God's Holy Word. Often, a lamp is shown representing knowledge, one of the seven gifts of the Holy Spirit. The psalmist used the lamp imagery: "Thy word is a lamp to my feet. . ." (Ps 119:105).

(2) The object which honors the Real Presence of Christ in the Holy Eucharist. According to Church law: "A special lamp to indicate and honor the presence of Christ is to burn at all times before the tabernacle in which the Most Holy Eucharist is reserved" (Canon 940). The advent of the sanctuary lamp dates from the thirteenth century. Prior to that, lamps were placed even near reliquaries and used as a practical means of providing light during the liturgy.

Lance, Holy • A liturgical knife, double-edged like the tip of a spear, recalling the lance of the crucifixion. It is used by the priest to detach the Lamb or Seal from the Bread of Offering in the Eastern Churches.

Languages, Biblical • The original languages of Sacred Scripture are: Hebrew-Aramaic for the Hebrew text of the Old Testament and Greek for the Greek text of the Old Testament; Greek for the text of the New Testament.

(1) *Hebrew* is a dialect of Northwest Semitic, within the Canaanite family of languages. It is called a "Semitic" language (initially by J. G. Eichhorn) because this language was spoken by those descendants of Noah's eldest son, Shem (cf. Gn 9:18, 26ff.; 10:21-31). The Old Testament refers to its own language as the "language of Canaan" (Is 9:18) or the "language of Judah" (2 Kgs 18:26). The New Testament reference to "Hebrew" may refer to Classical (i.e., Biblical) Hebrew (Rv 9:11; 16:16) or to Aramaic (Jn 5:2; 19:13, 17). Other dialects from the first millennium include Phoenician, Moabite, perhaps Edomite and Ammonite, more certainly Ugaritic, Aramaic and Amorite. Prior to the mid-sixth century B.C., Hebrew was the principal language of the Israelites. After this period, Aramaic increased in importance because it became the international language by virtue of its being the *lingua franca* of the Persian Empire. Under the Persians, Hebrew became less and less the common language, being replaced either by Aramaic or later, outside of Palestine, by Greek (after 333 B.C. through A.D. 325). Hebrew remained the official religious language and so remained the language of prayer and liturgy; generally all important religious matters were discussed in Hebrew. The Dead Sea Scrolls and literature written as late as A.D. 135 (e.g., Bar-kochbah literature) illustrate that Hebrew continued to be used outside of strictly rabbinical circles.

(2) *Aramaic:* Aramaic was spoken at least as early as the ninth century B.C. around the eastern Mediterranean fault called Levant and was used mostly in economic and diplomatic interaction (e.g., 2 Kgs 18:26). It probably originated with the Aramaeans (hence, "Aramaic") of northern Syria, thought to be among Abraham's ancestors (Gn 28:2-5; Dt 26:5). The Assyrians

conquered the Aramaeans, who pressed Aramaean scribes into scribal service. Eventually, Aramaic became the universal language of the ancient Near East from the eighth to fourth centuries B.C. Several Old Testament passages are written in Royal Aramaic (Ezr 4:8—6:18; 7:12-26; Dn 2:4—7:28; Jer 10:10-11; Gn 31:47). Jesus spoke Aramaic (and perhaps Hebrew); Aramaic appears in the New Testament (e.g., *Talitha koumi, Maranatha, Golgotha*).

(3) *Greek:* Parts of the Hebrew Old Testament were translated into Greek, beginning some time in the late fourth century and continuing until c. 200 B.C. The majority of the work appears to have been done in Alexandria, Egypt. The Greek dialect into which the Old Testament was translated and in which the twenty-seven books of the Greek New Testament were written is called *Koine* or Common Greek, so called because this was the version of Greek spoken and written after c. 325 B.C., following Alexander the Great's conquests of Europe and portions of the East as far as India. This Greek dialect is "common" in two senses: (1) "common" in that it was a universal language of international diplomacy and trade from around the fourth century B.C. to the sixth century A.D.; (2) "common" in the sense of its existence as a colloquial idiom spread by Alexander's colonies across his vast empire. Koine Greek is a simplified rendition of Attic Greek because of its lack of delicacy and refinement regarding use of particles, prepositions, participial constructions and the use of the moods. The uniqueness of this Greek in the Old and New Testaments lies mainly in its religious application and adaptation.

For further reading: John Huehnergard et al., "Languages," *Anchor Bible Dictionary*, 4:155-229.

Languages of the Church • There are many liturgical languages of the Church, including Ge'ez, Syriac, Greek, Arabic and Old Slavonic among the Eastern Churches, and Latin in the Roman Rite. Vatican II's Constitution on the Sacred Liturgy declared that the Latin language was to be preserved in the Latin Rites (n. 36), although it allowed for the use of the vernacular for the sake of the faithful. This has since become widespread in the Latin Church, and the Eastern Rites (which have always been open to the vernacular) have added new languages as well. Latin Mass, with its rich artistic and cultural heritage, is more frequently celebrated in Europe at cathedrals and monasteries than in the United States, where it is often difficult to find Latin Mass, Latin Gregorian or polyphony sung at all.

Lapsed • From the Latin *lapsi* (literally, those who have slipped away), lapsed has been used as early as the time of Cyprian of Carthage (d. 258) to refer to those Christian converts who had abandoned the Christian Faith and practice and returned to their pagan beliefs. The controversy in Cyprian's time centered on the question of whether or not the lapsed had in fact abandoned the Faith or did so only for the sake of appearance, so as not to commit a crime against the state. Emperor worship was required of all citizens for another fifty years; failure to participate was a capital offense, as is reflected in the Acts of the Christian Martyrs.

St. Cyprian writes of three classifications of *lapsi: thurificati,* who offered incense at pagan ceremonies; *sacrificati,* who participated in the pagan sacrifices; and *libellati,* who obtained legal documents stating that they had conformed to the required pagan practices. Frequently, Christians were able to obtain false documents attesting to their pagan conformity, when in fact they had remained faithful Christians. Unlike the unbending adherents of Novatian, Cyprian allowed the *lapsi*, if they had done penance for a long time and were in dangerous ill-health, to receive Reconciliation before death (*Epist.* 57:1). The question was finally resolved in line with Cyprian's reasoning at the First Council of Nicaea (A.D. 325).

More frequently in modern usage, a lapsed Catholic is understood to be one who has consciously abandoned the Catholic Faith, specifically by absenting oneself from the sacramental life of the Church, which is most clearly observable in the failure to make one's Easter duty. Penalties incurred by the lapsed are treated in the Code of Canon Law, Canons 1364-1369.

La Salette, Our Lady of • On September 19, 1846, the Blessed Virgin Mary appeared to two children, Mélanie Calvat and Maximin Giraud, in La Salette, a village near Grenoble, France. The message was only partially revealed by the children. Basically, the message was a plea for humility, prayer and penance, and a warning that a terrible punishment would be levied if people did not repent. In 1849 Mélanie revealed the other part of the message to the Holy See. However, it has not been revealed to the public.

Devotion to Our Lady of La Salette was approved by the bishop of Grenoble in 1851, and by the Popes since St. Pius X. Today there stands a large church on the site of the apparitions and nearby is the monastery of the Missionaries of La Salette, who administer the shrine.

Last Sacraments • These include Penance (or confession), Confirmation (when lacking), Anointing of the Sick (the preconciliar term

Last Supper site: St. Mary of Zion Church, Jerusalem

was Extreme Unction) and Viaticum (that is, the last reception of Communion for the journey from this life to eternity). In the evolution of the Church's practice, the order in which Penance and Anointing were administered was not uniform, largely because of the fact that Anointing of the Sick itself was regarded as celebrated for the forgiveness of sins. In the former and present Roman Ritual, many prayers and readings for the dying are offered, as well as the rubrics governing these sacraments.

The present ritual orders these sacraments in two ways. The "continuous rites of Penance and Anointing" include: Introductory Rites, Liturgy of Penance, Liturgy of Confirmation, Liturgy of Anointing, Liturgy of Viaticum and Concluding Rites. The "rite for emergencies" includes the sacrament of Penance, Apostolic Pardon, Lord's Prayer, Communion as Viaticum, Prayer before Anointing, Anointing, Concluding Prayer, Blessing, Sign of Peace.

Last Supper • We read about Christ's "Last Supper" at Matthew 26:20-29; Mark 14:17-25; Luke 22:15-20 and in Paul's letters at 1 Corinthians 11:22ff. In Jewish tradition, all meals were sacred and involved sacred ties among those gathered and between those gathered and God. Throughout Sacred Scripture, we learn that the giving of thanks to God was a normal part of the meal (2 Mc 1:11; 1 Thes 3:9; 1 Cor 1:14; Col 1:12), often expressed in the form of various prayers (Wis 16:28; 1 Thes 5:17; 2 Cor 1:11; Col 3:17).

The historical and religious antecedents of the Christian Eucharist are found in Jewish sacred meals, during which God is blessed and praised for His overflowing bounty, which (literally) sustains those gathered at the table. The food and meal together express God's providential care and faithfulness to His covenantal love and promise to care for Israel. The manna from God, quail from God, water from a rock (Ps 78:20-29) — all these anticipate and express a reality most clearly fulfilled in the Person of Jesus. He is the "Bread of Life" (Jn 6:26-52); His Flesh and Blood are our food and drink (Jn 6:51-58).

How does this work itself out? Jesus Himself gives us the answer in the Gospel accounts of the "Last Supper." In the Gospels, the Passover meal, the Garden of Gethsemane, Our Lord's crucifixion and resurrection are all of one piece, like an intricate tapestry creatively weaving a plethora of Old Testament images with the historical experience of Jesus' last few hours on earth prior to His glorification. By redefining the bread and wine as His Body and Blood which will be given up "for you," the Thursday night meal is inextricably connected to His Friday death on the cross, and to His Easter Sunday resurrection.

Bread and wine becoming Body and Blood means that the "Last Supper" cannot communicate their powerful salvific and redeeming message without reference to Christ's salvific and redeeming death on the cross. The breaking of the bread anticipates the violence of Jesus' death — the meal is simultaneously a meal and *the* sacrifice which brings about new life.

The new life is freedom not only from temporal captivity, but a deeper freedom — from the power of sin. In Judaism the sacrifice was burnt and then consumed and, through this action, the people were united to the oblation itself, as well as to God Who accepted it (1 Cor 10:18-21). For Jesus and His followers, union of Priest and Victim is more than a matter of connection; it is a matter of being incorporated into that new life, of which present experience is but a shadow (Heb 10:1; Col 2:17). Participation in this sacrifice is participation in the New Covenant which brings forth an eternal inheritance (Heb 9:15).

It is not correct to think about the memorial "Last Supper" strictly in terms of a *look back* into history to Christ's sacrifice, as if it were *only* a symbolic memorial of a sacred event. Rather, the "Last Supper"/death-resurrection of Jesus is at once universal, transcending all time and present to each successive generation, through the reenactment of Jesus' words and deeds; the Eucharist is our contact with the transformed and Risen Christ; the Eucharist is physical contact with that "new world," that "new creation" in the Person of the Risen Lord, Jesus Christ, Whose Body and Blood are now present to us under the guise of bread and wine; the Eucharist is our point of contact with the whole reality of the transformed world which received Mary's body in the Assumption and will receive all those who live in friendship with God.

For further reading: Robert F. O'Toole, S.J., "Last Supper," *Anchor Bible Dictionary*, 4:234-241.

Latae Sententiae • The Latin term for the automatic imposition or incurring of a canonical penalty as soon as the ecclesiastical crime has been committed. There are several crimes listed in the revised

Code which result in automatic or *latae sentinae* excommunications, interdicts or suspensions.

A *latae sentinae* penalty can be remitted by a bishop or other competent Church authority or by the Holy See alone if it is so reserved. In some cases, certain consequences of a *latae sentinae* penalty do not occur unless the penalty is formally declared by a Church authority. The law contains a process for declaring automatic penalties (cf. Canons 1314, 1318). The numerous factors which excuse or mitigate *latae sentinae* penalties, however, make them far less common in Church life than is popularly thought to be the case.

Lateran • The name of a prominent family in imperial Rome which has come to designate structures and events important in the history of the Church. The family lived in the "Lateran Palace" which was taken over by the Emperor Nero and subsequently given to the Church by the Emperor Constantine in A.D. 312. It then served as the residence of the Bishops of Rome, the Popes, until destroyed by fire in 1308. Adjacent to the papal palace, Pope St. Sylvester dedicated the Lateran Basilica to the Savior on November 9, A.D. 324, designating it the special church of the Bishop of Rome, thus the Cathedral of the Diocese of Rome. After restoration in the early tenth century, it was also dedicated to St. John the Baptist, and is to this day called "St. John Lateran."

From 1123 to 1215, four ecumenical councils were convened there, which history calls the Lateran Councils. Although the present basilica and palace date from the fourteenth century, the church is venerated as the *Mater et Caput*,

"Mother and Head," of all the churches in the world.

Lateran Church • This is one of the names by which the Pope's cathedral or principal church as Bishop of Rome is known. Found on the outskirts of ancient Rome and just within the walls of medieval Rome right inside the Lateran Gates, the Lateran Church was once a royal palace and basilica which belonged to Emperor Constantine and his family. Around the time of his conversion in A.D. 313, Constantine gave this palace and an adjacent church which he built from the basilica already standing, to Pope Miltiades. Its name derives from Plautinus Lateranus, a Roman senator executed under the Emperor Nero. As the Cathedral of the Pope, Supreme Pontiff and Pastor of the Universal Church, the Lateran Church or Basilica is the *caput et mater omnium ecclesiarum*, the head and mother of all churches. It is dedicated under the title of the Most Holy Savior, *Sanctissimi Redemptoris*, and also that of St. John the

The Lateran Basilica, Rome

Baptist. It is better known by this second title of St. John, its full proper name being the Patriarchal Basilica of the Most Holy Savior and Saint John the Baptist at the Lateran.

Lateran Councils • Those official councils convened at the Cathedral of the Diocese of Rome, the Lateran Basilica. From A.D. 313 to 1059, there were four local councils there: the first (313) condemned the Donatists; the second (649) curbed the Monothelite heresy; the third (769) warned against iconoclasm; and the fourth (1059) regulated procedures for electing Popes.

The term is usually associated with the four ecumenical councils which assembled at the Lateran between 1123 and 1512: Lateran I, the ninth ecumenical council (1123), considered questions of discipline, particularly clerical celibacy; Lateran II, the tenth ecumenical council (1139), discussed the antipope Anacletus, and healed that schism: Lateran III, the eleventh ecumenical council (1179), condemned the Albigensians and Waldenses, and reformed papal elections; Lateran IV, the twelfth ecumenical council (1215), sometimes referred to as the "Great Council," enacted reforms, established a truce and mandated the Easter duty.

Lateran Palace • Next to the Basilica of St. John Lateran is a large and beautiful palace which for many centuries served as the residence of the Pope. Having been the property of the Roman Senator Plautinus Lateranus, it passed along to the Emperor Constantine as part of his inheritance (or some say his dowry from the Empress Fausta, who had herself inherited it). When he was converted to and recognized Christianity in A.D. 313, the emperor wanted the Pope to have a residence befitting his exalted dignity, so he refurbished it and gave it to Pope Miltiades. Until recent times the Supreme Pontiffs have resided at the Lateran Palace.

At one time to say "the Lateran" was equivalent to saying "the Vatican" today. During the Avignon Papacy and the absence of the Popes from the Eternal City, the Lateran fell into ruins from lack of maintenance as well as from several earthquakes which ravaged it. So when the Popes finally returned, for practical reasons the Popes began to stay more at the private residence on the Vatican Hill. Little by little the Lateran, though rebuilt in reduced dimensions, was relegated more to the cardinal vicar whom the Pope named to govern his diocese in his name so he could devote more time to the universal Church. Since then, and in our day, the Lateran Palace houses the papal vicar for Rome and his household and offices, thus becoming the "chancery" of Rome. As such, it is commonly known today as *il Vicariato*, the Vicariate.

Lateran Treaty • On February 11, 1929, a treaty, financial agreement and concordat were signed by the Holy See and the Italian government, making Vatican City an independent state (about one hundred nine acres). Under the financial agreement, Italy agreed to compensate the Holy See for the loss of the Papal States by paying 750 million lire in cash and one billion lire in five-percent negotiable government bonds. The concordat regulated certain religious freedoms, including Catholic religious instruction in elementary and secondary public schools.

That treaty was renegotiated in the 1980s, resulting in the abolition of many of the Church's privileges, most notably the end to mandatory Catholic instruction in government schools and the cessation of government payment of clergy salaries. (Cf. Vatican State, City of.)

Latin • In ancient times Latin was the language of the inhabitants of the Italian province of Latium, whose capital was Rome. With the increased influence and power achieved by the Romans and their subsequent colonization of most of the then-known world, the Latin language also spread along with Roman customs and laws.

The Latin language was gradually adopted by Christians in the early Church as more and more Latin-speaking peoples were converted to the Faith. Curiously enough, this took place first in northern Africa, which in the first several centuries of the Church's existence was one of the most fruitful and influential Christian communities even before most of Europe was converted to Christianity. Though Greek remained the official language of the Roman Church until about the third century, when some of the first official documents and epistles from the Popes appeared in Latin, even in the second century the Scriptures and other documents for the faithful were being translated into Latin.

By the fourth century, St. Jerome (342-420) had translated the entire Bible into this, the then "vulgar" language of the people, which is why this particular translation, the official translation of the Church, is still known as the "Vulgate." Up to this time, Greek was not only the official language of the Church but the language used by the upper classes and the one used in learned circles, just as French was to become in modern times the language of the court and diplomacy. By the middle of the fourth century, the liturgy was also celebrated in Latin. Since then, up to our own day, Latin has been the official language of the Latin Rite of the Church.

Even though today the vernacular tongues may be used regularly in the liturgy, the Second Vatican Council, responsible in part for the introduction of the vernacular into official worship, nevertheless refers to Latin as the official language of the Latin or Roman Church and the Liturgy of the Latin Rite. Indeed, the Council even encourages its wide use by both the clergy and the faithful (cf. *Sacrosanctum Concilium*, nn. 36, 100; *Musicam Sacram* of March 5, 1967, by the Sacred Congregation of Rites, n. 41). Likewise, in regard to the laws of the Church, the Code of Canon Law, even today the only official version of the same is that to be found in Latin as promulgated in the Acts of the Holy See, the *Acta Apostolicae Sedis*.

As a language, of course, Latin has seen some variations in style and in usage, as with any other language, through the passage of time. Because of the great influence of the Roman Empire first, and then of the Church, for centuries the Latin language became the principal tongue spoken in the Western world and so it continued to develop, not as a dead language but as a living language, influenced by political, philosophical, theological, pastoral and other practical requirements of the passing ages. Church Latin has its own flavor as well, which has been influenced, of course, by the mind-set which comes along as a natural development of the following of the Faith.

Only in recent times, especially the last two hundred years, has Latin somewhat gone into practical disuse throughout the modern scholarly world. However, Latin retains its importance, not only because of its inherent beauty and usefulness (something that has always made it most useful for philosophy as well as for theology), but also because of its perpetual influence in most Western languages, even those not considered strictly Romance languages such as Italian, Spanish, French, Portuguese and Romanian.

In recent times the Popes have affirmed the necessity and importance of the Latin language for the Latin Church, as well as for the world's culture. Pope John XXIII wrote an encyclical on the matter, *Veterum Sapientia*, and Pope Paul VI established an association headquartered in the Vatican, Latinitas, for the promotion of Latin studies. Several voluminous dictionaries incorporating modern technological and scientific language have also been published.

Latin Mass • The official language of the Church has been Latin since around the third or fourth century. As such, the official language of Roman Catholic worship is Latin. This was not abolished by the Second Vatican Council when its Constitution on the Sacred Liturgy, *Sacrosanctum Concilium*, opened the doors to the use at Mass and other occasions of the vernacular tongue. Even though the originally intended occasional use of the vernacular has been almost universally adopted, Latin remains the point of reference for the Latin Rite. As such, any Mass celebrated in Latin — as happens every day in Rome and throughout the world — is a Latin Mass. For this, no permission is needed from anyone, and it is the privilege of any priest to exercise his option to celebrate in Latin, whether privately or publicly (in the latter case, it is strongly recommended that the parts of the Mass pertaining to the people, and the other principal parts of the Mass, be made available for the faithful to follow and participate more fully).

In recent times, many have equivocally termed Masses celebrated according to the former Roman Rite as codified by St. Pius V as the "Latin Mass." While this rite of the Mass is again available following Pope John Paul II's 1984 indult and then the promulgation of *Ecclesia Dei* in 1988 (and through the work of the commission bearing the same name in charge of its implementation), it is a confusing misnomer

to refer to it as *the* Latin Mass. The Ordo of Pope Paul VI of 1969 may be celebrated in Latin. (Cf. Latin Rite; Latin.)

Latin Rite • The Latin Rite of the Church, one of the many rites of equal dignity and rights, if not numbers of faithful, is that part of the Church which follows the Roman Rite in the liturgy. It also has its own laws and discipline, and is headed by the Patriarch of the West, the Bishop of Rome, who in addition is the Vicar of Christ, having divinely given authority and responsibility for the entire or universal Church. It is called "Latin" from the fact that since the fourth century its official language in discipline and liturgy is the language of the Roman Empire which proceeded from the Latins who ruled it from its Roman capital in the province of Latium. This latter geographical fact that the Supreme Shepherd and Patriarch of the West is the Bishop of the capital of Latium may also have had some place in the development of this name.

Since the Councils of Nicaea (A.D. 325), Constantinople (381), Chalcedon (451), the geographical area which fell under the Patriarchate of Rome or the West included the same area set up by Diocletian as the Prefectures of the West — Italy, Gaul, Illyricum. Since the discovery of the New World and with the improvements of the modern era in transportation and communication, the Latin Rite has seen a tremendous expansion in both territory and the number of its adherents. Indeed, today, with few exceptions, the entire New World area (North, Central and South America), as well as Australia and Oceania, belongs to the Latin Rite. Most of the Catholics on the African continent also are members of the Latin Rite.

Latria • This term is derived from a Greek root meaning "service," but in Christian thought, latria has come to denote specifically that kind and degree of praise which is reserved for God alone. It is thus firmly to be distinguished from dulia or hyperdulia.

It should also be observed that the ultimate form of veneration of God is adoration expressed in sacrifice, and that the Sacrifice of the Mass is the most perfect sacrifice which can be offered to God. This form of worship in sacrifice, then, is known as latreutic worship and falls under the strict regulation of Church authority.

Lauds • The traditional name for the Office of Morning Prayer of the Liturgy of the Hours, from the (still current) Latin title *Ad Laudes Matutinas* ("for morning praises"), the morning counterpart to Vespers (or, in the current English usage, Evening Prayer), with which it is considered by Vatican II's Constitution on the Sacred Liturgy to be a "hinge" Hour. In its present Latin Rite form, Lauds begins with the Invitatory verse (a "call to worship" antiphon) and Psalm 95 (several similar psalms are offered as alternatives), if it is the first Office of the day. If the Office of Readings (formerly "Matins" and in monastic communities "Vigils") precedes Lauds immediately, Lauds begins simply with the morning hymn. If a brief period of time intervenes between the Office of Readings and Lauds, the verse and response which commonly opens the Offices is used: "0 God, come to my assistance; 0 Lord, make haste to help me." After the morning hymn, Lauds continues with one psalm (referring in some way to the morning hour or the sanctification of the day), an Old Testament Canticle, and a "praise psalm." A brief Scripture reading follows (in communal celebrations a longer passage may be substituted and even followed by a homily), silent reflection, and a responsory, then the Gospel Canticle of Zechariah (the *Benedictus*) with its antiphon. A series of intercessions for the sanctification of the day's labors follows, concluding with the Lord's Prayer, a Collect, blessing and dismissal.

Lavabo • This term, which comes from the Latin verb for "I will wash," refers to the ceremonial washing of the hands by the celebrant at Mass, which takes place at the end of the Offertory or Preparation of the Gifts.

(1) In the Latin Rite before 1969 (the so-called "Tridentine Mass" or "Mass of St. Pius V"), the priest would recite part of Psalm 26: "I will wash my hands in innocence, and go about thy altar, O LORD." In Latin, it began with the word *Lavabo*, hence the name of the prayer and the action it accompanied. The washing that takes place during Mass today is principally a ceremonial washing, recalling the need to be purified before celebrating the sacred mysteries and the unworthiness of the priest to perform these *in persona Christi*, "in the Person of Christ," symbolized by the actual washing of the hands or fingertips. This washing may have had its origins in the fact that in the past the faithful brought their goods and the fruits of the fields and even animals for the Offertory for the support of the church and the priest. This meant, of course, that the celebrant's hands could become soiled and therefore needed to be washed before continuing with the Divine Sacrifice.

(2) As a secondary development, by association the receptacle into which the water is poured for the washing of the hands is often referred to as the lavabo. In sacristies there should also be a special sink provided for those who are about to engage in sacred actions to wash their hands, i.e., before Mass or distributing Holy Communion. This is also referred to as the lavabo.

L'Avenir: See Avenir, L'

Law • As defined by St. Thomas Aquinas, law is an ordinance of right reason, issued by one who has charge over the community, for the common good and publicly promulgated. Essentially, a law is a rule of conduct or being. Law may be divided into Divine law, which is ordered by the Creator; natural law, which is determined by the nature of a created being; and positive law, which is drawn up by human beings.

Law, Canon: See **Canon Law**

Law, Universal • Universal law is that law of the Church which binds the whole Church. Universal laws are passed either by the Roman Pontiff or by an ecumenical council with the Roman Pontiff. Universal laws bind all those for whom they were made. For instance, the universal law concerning the rights and duties of clerics or bishops binds all clerics and bishops (Canon 12).

Some universal laws are grounded in Divine law and therefore bind all people. Universal laws of ecclesiastical origin bind only those who have been baptized or received into the Catholic Church, unless the law itself makes express provision otherwise.

Law and Gospel • The relationship between law and Gospel is dependent on the definition of "law." The New Testament use of *nomos* ("law") covers a wide range of meaning, and only a small percentage of this actually refers to the law/Gospel relationship. There are New Testament instances in which the use of "law" sometimes parallels its general use in late Judaism as a technical referent to the Mosaic law or to the Old Testament as a whole. In this instance the term "law" has a positive connotation and approximates the notion of revelation, God's will, etc. The term can also simply refer to a principle or

dynamic and can have either a positive or a negative sense. For example, at Romans 7:21, the law is a power driving "me" toward sin; at 7:23, there is the law of sin and death; at Romans 8:2, the law of the Spirit of life in Jesus Christ. The New Testament reference to the law as Torah should not be viewed negatively; it is not a simple reference to hard rules and regulations of a distant and forgotten culture; rather, it is a reference to God and His will (e.g., cf. Ps 119).

There are four other important referents intended by "law" when used in the New Testament: (1) all commandments and stipulations which God gave to Moses; (2) the historical as well as juridical material in the Pentateuch; (3) all of the Old Testament which can collectively be regarded as "law"; (4) the oral traditions embodying the teachings of the great rabbinical figures. Jesus fulfills the law and thus surpasses it (Mt 5:17-20) because Jesus is the way to God (Mt 5:10-12). This "law" — as a referent to Old Testament as a whole — is comprehensive, revelatory, permanently valuable and consists of an intrinsic and indissoluble amalgam of moral, liturgical and juridical guidelines, some of which are fulfilled in the plan of salvation history.

Jesus' fulfillment of what these guidelines point to is available to all who have been incorporated into His death and resurrection. We might say that this is the Law of Life or the Law of Christ, in the sense of a positive, dynamic force which is an agent of the New Creation. The Gospel announces the Christocentric fulfillment of law, pointing out that contact with God is not by means of physical circumcision (Rom 2:28; 3:1; Gal 2:3, 7; 5:6) or observance of traditional applications of the Mosaic law (Gal 2:16; 3:2; 5:10; Rom 2:15; 3:20, 28). So, while the law is holy and good (Rom 7:12, 16) and an expression of God's will (Rom 2:27), it does not have the power to make holy, to transform, to renew. However, it does teach. Those "works" which are from faith — God's gift and action in us — can accomplish what Jesus now experiences (Rom 3:20, 28; Gal 2:16, 21; 3:11). Jesus is both the fulfillment of the law and the new Lawgiver, as Matthew's Sermon on the Mount makes clear. The Sermon is our best example of how law and Gospel relate: Jesus fulfills the law and teaches God's will in light of it *and* His salvific life, death and resurrection.

For further reading: Samuel Greengus et al., "Law," *Anchor Bible Dictionary*, 4:242-265.

Laxism • A seventeenth-century casuistic moral system, linked with probabilism and, like probabilism, developed to provide guidance for moral decision in matters about which a complete theological consensus did not obtain. Laxists taught that in cases where any doubts could be raised about the morality of a particular action normally considered wrong, the agent is free on that ground to undertake this course of action without incurring sin.

Blaise Pascal vigorously attacked laxism in his *Lettres provinciales* (1657). Laxism was condemned by Pope Alexander VII (in 1665 and 1666) and by Pope Innocent XI (in 1679). There is a growing consensus among moral theologians today that the entire approach represented by the casuistic moral systems was based on a faulty conception of the moral life in which the classical notions of virtue and character came to be displaced by obligation, decision and the study of cases.

Lay Baptism • The administration of the sacrament of Baptism by a non-ordained person. Ordinarily, the minister of Baptism is a bishop, priest or deacon. If a sacred minister is not available or is impeded, the local Ordinary can depute a lay catechist or

other person to perform Baptism. Finally, in case of necessity (such as possible danger of death, either remotely or proximately), any person (even a non-Christian) can administer Baptism, provided he has the intention of baptizing as the Church does and does so with the use of water and the minimal formula required (cf. Canon 861).

Lay Minister of Marriage • Under certain circumstances it is possible for a lay person to act as the official witness to the marriage of Catholics. To do so requires the favorable opinion of the episcopal conference followed by the permission of the Holy See. This having been done in the United States, a diocesan bishop can then delegate such a person to assist at marriages when a sacred minister is lacking (Canon 1112).

Lay People, Decree on the Apostolate of: See **Apostolicam Actuositatem**

Lay Reader • As early as the account of Justin the Martyr describing the celebration of the Sunday Eucharist in his *First Apology* (A.D. 150), the ministry of the person who proclaims the Scriptures at the liturgy (except the Gospel) has been specified; this person was named a "reader" or "lector." From the Middle Ages until the contemporary liturgical reform, it was customary for clerics to do the reading and to be ordained to the minor order of lector. Most often, in fact, readers at Mass were ordained priests (e.g., when they functioned as subdeacons or deacons at a Solemn High Mass).

The issuance of the *motu proprio Ministeria quaedam* on first tonsure, minor orders and the subdiaconate, by Pope Paul VI in 1972, effectively changed the understanding of the reader from one who received a minor order (one of the orders to be received as one progressed on the way to ordination to the priesthood, i.e., porter, lector, acolyte, exorcist) to one who would now be installed into the ministry of reader. One of the purposes for this change was to end the limitation of deputing only clerics to be readers at liturgical services. The text reads: "The above-mentioned ministries should no longer be called minor orders; their conferral will not be called *ordination*, but *institution*." It also says that "what were up to now called minor orders are henceforth to be called *ministries*. Ministries may be assigned to lay Christians; hence they are no longer to be considered as reserved to candidates for the sacrament of Orders."

The same document describes the ministry of the reader as one who reads the Scriptures (except the Gospel) at liturgy, recites the psalm between the readings (if there is no cantor), presents the intentions for the general intercessions (if there is no deacon) and "instruct[s] the faithful for the worthy reception of the sacraments." This latter task coincides with the description of readers in liturgical tradition as those who teach as well as proclaim the Scriptures.

Readers are instituted by the bishop or by the major superior of a clerical religious institute; the installation takes place during Mass. In *Ministeria quaedam* the installation of readers is reserved to men. In the absence of installed readers and acolytes, other lay persons may function as readers and acolytes, which is commonly done. The *General Instruction of the Roman Missal* states that "the conference of bishops may permit qualified women to proclaim the readings before the Gospel and to announce the intentions of the General Intercessions" (n. 70). In addition, the importance of this ministry is underscored when the *General Instruction* states that "the reader has his own proper function in the Eucharistic celebration and should exercise this even though ministers of a higher rank may be present" (n. 66).

Lay Trusteeism • The presumption by lay parish leaders of the prerogative, rightly that of the diocesan bishop, to regulate all parochial affairs, even that of appointing and dismissing the pastor. This abuse was perhaps the most severe challenge to the authority of the first bishop of the United States, John Carroll of Baltimore, and its curbing became a major goal of his successors through the middle of the nineteenth century. The dearth of clergy, European precedent, lack of hierarchy, democratic atmosphere and Protestant example all conspired to encourage early Catholics in America to exercise complete control over their own parishes, thus creating tension when properly appointed bishops and pastors came on the scene.

The first notable crisis caused by this insubordination occurred in St. Peter's Parish in New York City when, in 1786, the trustees voted to depose the rector, Charles Whelan, whom John Carroll, the prefect apostolic, had appointed, demanding that Carroll install Andrew Nugent, O.F.M. Cap., as the new rector. Although Carroll rejected their demands and pointed out that canon law gave them no right to dismiss or appoint pastors (the so-called "right of patronage"), the trustees so harassed Whelan that he left the parish. Nationalism and unruly clergy, especially at Holy Trinity Parish in Philadelphia, complicated the scene, and at times even led the independent trustees into actual schism from legitimate ecclesiastical authority. At the Cathedral of the Diocese of New Orleans, the trustees, there called *marguilliers*, refused to accept the priest whom Carroll had appointed their vicar general.

Problems continued to flare up through the 1820s. The beginning of the end of the trustee controversy came on August 24, 1822, when Pope Pius VII issued a brief, *Non Sine Magno*, reaffirming Church discipline that Church property is under the jurisdiction of the hierarchy, calling lay claims to the right of patronage ". . . quite unheard-of." Following the lead of John England, the first bishop of Charleston, the provincial councils of Baltimore enacted clear and decisive legislation curtailing trustee claims. Holdouts, especially at Holy Trinity in Philadelphia and St. Louis in Buffalo, continued to resist through the mid-1850s.

The crisis called "lay trusteeism" was a decisive phase in the accommodation of the Church to the American atmosphere.

Leader of Song: See **Song, Leader of**

Leadership, Pastoral • The guidance given by a minister of the Church in the exercise of his pastoral office. The Pope and bishops, due to their jurisdiction, have a special charism to lead and govern. Others have a special charism to lead and govern. Others also lead — priests, deacons, religious and the laity. Pastoral leadership inspires others to contribute their God-given gifts to the building up of the Body of Christ.

Leadership Conference of Women Religious • The association of the major superiors of women religious institutes in the United States. Its purpose is to foster the spiritual and apostolic well-being of those same institutes. Organized in the late 1950s, the conference was approved by the Congregation for Religious and Secular Institutes on June 13, 1962.

League for Religious and Civil Rights, Catholic: See **Catholic League for Religious and Civil Rights**

Lectern • The physical structure from which the Scriptures are read at liturgy. This may be a desk supported on a column of metal or wood, which column attaches to a base. In the Middle Ages it was common to construct lecterns with eagles or pelicans supporting the desk for the Bible, lectionary or Gospel Book. In contemporary liturgical documents, "ambo" is used interchangeably with lectern. In *Inter Oecumenici* (1964), the first Instruction from the Congregation of Rites on the orderly carrying out of the liturgy, it states that there should be a lectern "for the proclamation of the readings so arranged that the faithful may readily see and hear the minister" (n. 96). The *General Instruction of the Roman Missal* states that the readings, the Responsorial Psalm, and the Easter proclamation (*Exsultet*) are proclaimed from the lectern; it may be used also for the homily and the General Intercessions (Prayer of the Faithful). It is better for the commentator, cantor or choir director not to use the lectern (n. 272).

Lectionary • The liturgical book containing the Scripture readings (pericopes); to be distinguished from the Gospel Book, which contains the Gospel passages read at the liturgy. Originally, the lectionary meant a list of texts (a *cursus* of readings) which referred the reader to a text of the Bible itself, or to a Bible text in which the pericopes were marked (for example, by brackets). Eventually, in the Middle Ages, missals were published containing all the prayers, readings and chants needed for the celebration of Mass which were originally published in separate volumes: sacramentaries, lectionaries, Gospel Books, antiphonals and graduals. The present Roman Liturgy has restored the use of the lectionary as a proper ritual book. It contains all the Scripture readings (including the Gospels) which are needed for Mass, for the celebration of sacraments and for other ritual Masses (e.g., Masses for the blessing of an abbot, for the dedication of a church, etc.) and the intervening chants (i.e., Responsorial Psalms and Gospel Acclamations). The present, second edition of the *Ordo Lectionum Missae*, the Order for Mass Readings, contains an extensive General Instruction about the theology of the Word proclaimed at liturgy and the principles which govern the selection of the texts in the present lectionary arrangement.

Lector: See **Lay Reader**

Legate • An officially appointed representative or ambassador of the Pope. Legates may be appointed to act as papal representatives to secular nations, to the Catholic Church in a country, for a specific event or other reason determined by the Pope.

Legates *a latere* are representatives, always cardinals, who are sent as special personal representatives of the Pope for a specific event or to deal with an important matter. The legate *a latere* is a kind of *alter ego* of the Pope.

Nuncios are papal representatives chosen by the Pope to represent the Holy See in countries having full diplomatic relations with the Holy See. The papal nuncio is always the dean of the diplomatic corps in the country in which he serves. Countries that have a nuncio as their papal ambassador are those which recognize the agreement of the Congress of Vienna (1815), which sanctioned this ancient custom.

An internuncio is a representative of lesser rank than a nuncio, who represents the Holy Father in territories not having full diplomatic relations. He may also be called to represent the Holy Father in special matters.

A pronuncio is a papal representative in a country that has full diplomatic relations with the Holy See but where the Vatican or papal representative is not automatically the dean of the diplomatic corps.

An apostolic delegate is the personal delegate of the Holy Father to the Catholic Church in a country not having diplomatic relations with the Holy See.

The chargé d'affaires is a papal agent, usually a prelate without the episcopal character, sent to head a diplomatic mission that has not been raised to the status of a nunciature or apostolic delegation. While the appointment of a permanent chargé d'affaires is rare, in the absence of the head of a fully established mission, the ranking member of the diplomatic service on duty there is appointed chargé d'affaires by the nuncio or delegate.

Nuncios, pronuncios and apostolic delegates are nearly always titular archbishops, although the law does not stipulate that a papal legate be a cleric. A permanent legate to a country or particular church is not the head of the Church in the country of assignment. Papal representatives are to inform the Holy See of the conditions of the Church in that country, to foster relations between the hierarchy and the Holy See and to exercise any other faculties or carry out any instructions given by the Holy See. A major function of the legates in most countries is to investigate the suitability and to present candidates for the office of bishop to the Holy See.

For the most part, papal nuncios, pronuncios and apostolic delegates are career members of the diplomatic service of the Holy See. Prospective candidates are selected by their bishops after having been ordained a few years and, if accepted, are sent to a special school for diplomats in Rome, the Pontificia Accademia Ecclesiastica. Upon graduation, they are assigned as secretaries in the Vatican diplomatic missions throughout the world. Like many diplomatic services, that of the Holy See has a system of rank for its members. These include the ranks of secretary, auditor and counselor. Upward graduation in rank usually depends on years of service in the diplomatic corps. If deemed acceptable, a member will eventually be appointed a papal representative (cf. Canons 362-367).

Legate a Latere • A special envoy of the Pope, sent as his *alter ego* to a gathering of Catholics or to perform some special diplomatic mission for the Pope. Always a cardinal, the legate *a latere* receives his faculties and instructions directly from the Pope.

Legend, Golden: See **Golden Legend**

Legion of Decency • Responding to the need to promote morally high standards in the film media, the American Catholic bishops established a committee for this purpose in 1934. At first, the Legion of Decency did no more than appeal for moral decency in films and encourage all Catholics to be discriminating in the viewing of movies. Then, in 1935, several dioceses organized local boards to view movies and assess their moral quality. Finally, in 1936, a national ratings board was established in the Archdiocese of New York, with its recommendations published in all the American dioceses.

With the establishment of the United States Catholic Conference in 1965, the Legion of Decency became a division within the Department of Communication and is now called the Office of Film and Broadcasting with headquarters in New York City. Its purpose is to aid Catholics and other concerned Christians in forming a right conscience in selecting films for viewing.

The following rating classifications are used: A-I, suitable for general audiences; A-II, suitable for adults and adolescents: A-III, suitable for adults; A-IV, suitable for adults with reservations (i.e., films that are not morally objectionable but require

explanation to protect the uninformed against wrong interpretations of false conclusions); O, morally offensive. The USCC system of classification is not meant to coincide with the categories in use by the Motion Picture Association of America for rating current films (G, PG, PG-13, R, NC-17, X).

Legionaries of Christ • The Legionaries of Christ is a clerical congregation, founded in Mexico in 1941 by Marcial Maciel while he was still a seminarian. He continues as the general director of the congregation with headquarters in Rome. It began as a diocesan congregation (formalized in 1948 in Cuernavaca), and in 1965 became a congregation of pontifical right. The constitutions of the Legionaries received definite approval in 1983. There are about 100 houses of Legionaries in 12 countries worldwide, with 1,327 members and 288 priests. Since their first foundation in the United States in 1965, the Legionaries have established themselves in the archdioceses of Detroit, Hartford, Los Angeles, New York and Washington, and the dioceses of Dallas, Manchester, Madison and Providence. The congregation in the U.S. has 35 priests, 93 novices and 30 juniors.

The Legionaries place a major emphasis on the recruitment and formation of their seminarians. The founder, Father Maciel, has written a complete guide to priestly formation, entitled *The Integral Formation of Catholic Priests* (English edition, 1992). The congregation recruits its new members at a fairly young age (usually in high school), and enrolls them in a well-regulated formation program. Many of the congregation's seminarians are sent to Rome for a portion of their studies. Patterned on a traditional seminary model, Legionary formation stresses prayer, regular life and the wearing of clerical garb in order to cultivate a strong sense of priestly identity and mission. The apostolic work of the congregation centers on work with youth, education, family, missions, the poor, media and catechetics. A characteristic feature of the Legionaries' ministerial style is to invite and foster the collaboration of the laity in their apostolates.

Legitimation • The means by which a child, considered illegitimate in canon law, becomes legitimate. Legitimation takes place when the parents of a child born out of wedlock marry subsequent to the child's birth. Legitimation can also take place by rescript of the Holy See (cf. Canon 1139). For practical purposes, however, legitimacy has become a moot issue under canon law.

Lent • The forty-day liturgical season of fasting, special prayer and almsgiving in preparation for Easter. The name "Lent" is from the Middle English *lenten* and Anglo-Saxon *lencten*, meaning spring; its more primitive ecclesiastical name was the "forty days," *tessaracoste* in Greek. The pre-Easter fast in the first three centuries (observed especially by catechumens and sponsors) lasted only two or three days. It later developed into three or four weeks. The number forty is first noted in the Canons of Nicaea (A.D. 325), likely in imitation of Jesus' fast in the desert before His public ministry (with Old Testament precedent in Moses and Elijah). In some Eastern Churches this meant five fast days per week for seven weeks (Saturday and Sunday excepted), making the total only thirty-five; in Jerusalem in the fourth century, this meant five days' fast for eight weeks. In most of the West at the time, this meant six days' fast per week of six weeks; in the seventh century the days from Ash Wednesday through the First Sunday were added to make the number forty.

An important aspect of the Lenten Liturgy was the observance of the Station Masses whereby the Pope would celebrate Mass, preceded by a procession with a relic of the True Cross, in a different church in Rome for each day in Lent. The present sacramentary recalls this custom and then "strongly encourages the chief shepherd of the diocese to gather his people in this way. Especially during Lent, he should meet with his people and celebrate the liturgy with them." Another unique feature of the Lenten Liturgy is the present restoration of the Scrutiny Masses on the third, fourth and fifth Sundays of Lent for the catechumens (now called the "elect"), who will be initiated at the Easter Vigil.

Leopoldine Association • This outstanding missionary aid society was established in 1829 in Vienna chiefly through the efforts of Frederic Rése (later first bishop of Detroit) to channel financial support to the developing Church in the United States. It was named after Leopoldine, the daughter of Francis I of Austria, who died the empress of Brazil in 1826. The society was instrumental in helping with the capital costs of founding many new dioceses and parishes in America, and also contributed to the interest of many German-speaking immigrants and priests in coming to America. The activities of the society peaked in the early 1860s and declined thereafter, until they were suspended altogether in 1921. The *Berichte* (reports and papers) collected by the society over these years, however, remain an invaluable contribution to the recorded history of the Church in America during those formative years.

Lepanto, Battle of • After the fall of Constantinople in 1452, Turkish power continued to grow to the point where it seriously threatened European hegemony over the Mediterranean Sea. As an imminent invasion of Eastern Europe by Muslim forces loomed, Christian naval forces recruited primarily from Italy and Spain under Don Juan of Austria belatedly massed to face the considerably larger Turkish fleet then anchored in the Gulf of Corinth. In the predawn hours of October 7, 1571, Don Juan saw his opportunity to lead his 80,000-man fleet against the Turks' 120,000 (many of whom, incidentally, were Christian slaves captured by the Muslims in earlier battles), thus opening the last great naval battle between oared galleys.

After a near collapse of the Christian line of battle, Don Juan rallied his fleet and then inflicted severe losses on the Turkish fleet. The Turks bore nearly 30,000 killed and wounded, while Don Juan's loss of about 8,000 was softened by the rescue of at least that many Christian slaves. The value of following up on that victory was not recognized at the time, although the battle did mark the beginning of the decline of the Muslim military threat to Europe.

Pope St. Pius V, meanwhile, who had urged devotion to the Rosary as spiritual preparation for the battle to come, declared October 7 as the feast of Our Lady of the Rosary, in honor of the victory. The Battle of Lepanto was memorialized by the great Catholic author G. K. Chesterton in a poem of that name, rightly recognized as a masterpiece of Christian literature.

Leper Window • A low window in the chancel wall of a church which enabled lepers, who had to stay outside the church, to attend Mass and receive alms. Covered with bars or shutters, this window was found in medieval churches and is not presently used.

Lesson • Term more commonly replaced by "reading," referring to the texts, other than the Gospel, proclaimed at the liturgy. At the Office of Readings in the Liturgy of the Hours, two readings are given, one from Scripture, the other from a patristic author, a liturgical commentary or a Church teaching document (e.g., Vatican II). At Mass the lessons are any pericopes which precede the Gospel; sometimes common usage reserves the term "lesson" for the Old Testament only.

Levirate Marriage • The word "levirate" comes from the Latin word for brother-in-law (*levir*). A levirate marriage was one entered into by a widow and the brother of her dead husband. There are three texts in the Old Testament that one way or another make reference to this practice: Genesis 28; Deuteronomy 25:5-10; and Ruth 4. Each of these texts seems to give a different impression of the law, so that its nature remains unclear. Adding to the obscurity are texts such as Leviticus 20:21, which appears to rule out any marriage between a man and his deceased brother's wife. The law may have been aimed at preventing a widow from alienating any of the family's property by marrying outside the family. The law also guaranteed offspring to the deceased man. The firstborn son of a levirate union was given a patronymic. The New Testament reference to this law (Mt 22:23-33; Mk 12:18-27; Lk 20:27-40) probably should not be taken to mean that this practice was still followed in those times.

Leviticus • The third book of the Pentateuch takes its name from Levi, the son of Jacob from whom Jewish religious officials had descended. It is a collection of laws and rites regarding the worship of God.

What symbolic acts best express our human recognition of the excellence of God? Chapters 1-7 treat sacrifices: the holocaust, the immolation and oblation of animals, the appropriate victims and the appropriate representatives of the people. Leviticus says little about the interior religious spirit which these acts were supposed to reflect; it was left to the prophets to correct the aberration of externalism.

Chapters 8-10 contain regulations about the choice of priests, the prerequisites and the perquisites of the members of that class.

Chapters 11-16 discuss the required preparation of those taking part in various acts of divine worship. The emphasis is largely negative: various taboos render various classes of persons unclean and unable to participate. Some of these were perhaps useful to promote hygiene; others may have been intended solely to lift religious activity above the plane of ordinary actions and daily life.

Chapters 17-26 deal with some positive and negative laws of Jewish morality: kosher laws, illicit sexual conduct, the love of neighbor, the celebration of seasonal feasts and fasts, the observance of the sabbatical and jubilee years.

For further reading: Roland J. Faley, T.O.R., "Leviticus," *New Jerome Biblical Commentary*, 61-79; Baruch A. Levine, "Leviticus," *Anchor Bible Dictionary*, 4:311-321.

Liber Pontificalis • The Latin title of "the papal book" originating earlier but found for the first time in a text in the sixth century containing biographies of the Popes. There is a striking contrast between the biographies of early Popes (merest sketches through the fourth century) and those of the eighth and ninth centuries (each biography could be a volume on its own). The last known edition has information through the death of Martin V (1431).

Liber Usualis • A book containing Gregorian chants, edited by the Benedictines of Solesmes. This book, currently out of print, contains chants for the Ordinary and Propers of Masses, chants of Divine Office, chants of Masses of commons, chants for various rites and special Masses. It includes rules for interpretation according to the Solesmes method and rubrics for the chant at the Mass celebrated before Vatican II revisions. Besides being of tremendous historical value, the *Liber Usualis* chants can be used today at Mass, especially those parts included in the Ordinary of the Mass.

Pope Gregory XVI:
Condemned liberalism

Liberalism • The term connotes several meanings in various fields, e.g., politics, economics and ethics. In theology, liberalism is a broad body of doctrines described under names such as indifferentism, rationalism, positivism and modernism. Though it is a term which applies to many disparate ideas, theological liberalism was described succinctly by John Henry Cardinal Newman as "the doctrine that there is no positive truth in religion but that one creed is as good as another. . . . It is inconsistent with any recognition of any religion as true. It teaches that all are to be tolerated, for all are matters of opinion. Revealed religion is not a truth but a sentiment and a taste, and it is the right of each individual to make it say just what strikes his fancy. . ." (Wilfrid Ward, *The Life of John Henry Cardinal Newman*, London, Longmans, 1912, Vol. II, p. 460).

Liberalism precludes the possibility of the revelation of objective truth and makes individual experience, rather than authoritative teaching, the principal locus of theological knowledge. Liberalism usually denies that the Church is divinely instituted and insists that the Church of any given moment is merely the product of natural evolution and is therefore subject to substantial change according to the demands of the times.

Liberalism also generally collapses the distinction between nature and grace, thereby making even the transcendent God an object of human experience. And most characteristically, liberalism exalts subjective sincerity over objective truth to create a false opposition between individual conscience and the authority of the Magisterium.

In various forms and under different names, the doctrines of theological liberalism have been expressly condemned by Popes Gregory XVI, Pius IX, Leo XIII, St. Pius X, and Pius XII.

Dealing with many of the themes of liberalism in religion, the Fathers of the Second Vatican Council declared that Christ "himself explicitly asserted the necessity of faith and baptism, and thereby affirmed at the same time the necessity of the Church which men enter through baptism as through a door. Hence they could not be saved who, knowing that the Catholic Church was founded as necessary by God through Christ, would refuse either to enter it, or to remain in it" (LG 14).

Liberals, Catholic • Although the word "liberal" has a variety of political, economic, social, philosophical and theological meanings today, the term "Catholic liberal" is used precisely by historians to describe those nineteenth-century intellectuals who attempted to reconcile the progressive ideals of the French Revolution with traditional Catholic teaching. Because the revolution had resulted in outright persecution of the faithful, many Catholic leaders after the fall of Napoleon rejected everything associated with 1789, even contributions such as democracy, freedom of speech and the rights of the worker. Thus, in some circles, the Church was considered allied with the forces of reaction. Catholic liberals, especially in France, on the other hand, believed that while the revolution may have gone to extremes, many of the forces it unleashed, such as the liberties listed above, were positive, and should be blessed by the Church.

The three most celebrated Catholic liberals were a priest, Félicité de Lamennais (d. 1854), a layman, Count Charles de Montalambert (d. 1870), and a Dominican, Jean-Baptiste Lacordaire (d. 1861). These spokesmen founded l'Avenir (the Future), a newspaper with the banner "God and Freedom," urging the hierarchy to promote the reforms of 1789. "Let us not tremble before liberalism," Lamennais wrote, "let us catholicize it!" When the bishops of France condemned their approach, they appealed to Pope Gregory XVI (d. 1846), who also rejected their proposals in the encyclical Mirari Vos. Although this took away much of their steam, their ideas proved seminal and took root in Belgium, Ireland, England and the United States, where such ideas were not held guilty by association with revolutionary excesses.

Although today the term "Catholic liberal" has a much different meaning, essential to its definition is still the conviction that the Church flourishes in a free country, and that any movement which promotes responsible freedom and human dignity should be at home in the Church.

Liberation Theology • A contemporary theological movement launched in 1973 by the publication of A Theology of Liberation: History, Politics, and Salvation, by Gustavo Gutiérrez, a Peruvian Jesuit priest. In a wider sense, Gutiérrez gave direction and expression to the conclusions of the historic meeting of representatives of the Latin American Episcopal Conferences (CELAM) which took place in Medellín, Colombia, in 1968. At that meeting, made possible only in the climate of episcopal collaboration generated by Vatican II, the leaders of the various conferences gave important new emphasis to the historic commitment of the Church to help alleviate a full range of the problems of poor people. Gutiérrez's book gave the movement a name and immediately stimulated an immense number of theological works by scores of authors on what has since become known as "Liberation Theology." The sheer multiplicity of viewpoints, however, makes any general descriptions of the movement difficult.

On the one hand, the Liberation Theology movement, pluralistic as it is, is itself a reflection of the even broader postconciliar renewal of the Catholic Church and the recommitment of her resources to assist society, and poor members of the Church in particular, in their struggle against poverty. A reflex alignment of the Church in Latin America, especially the hierarchy, with the goals and strategies of persons of wealth, is no longer even a serious accusation.

On the other hand, Liberation Theology has become a popular vehicle of expression for all minority or disadvantaged groups, far transcending Latin America, and has influenced the thought of many within the Catholic Church and without, notably in Africa and India. Its analysis of the causes of poverty and wealth, its use of classist categories (division of society into economic "classes"), its advocacy of violence as a necessary catalyst for change, its assertion of the existence of society-wide "structures of sin" and the theocracy implicit in its core motivation for inducing political and economic reform as directly willed by Christ, "the Liberator," all of these are hotly contested points, both inside and outside the Liberation Theology movement.

Notwithstanding his enthusiastic endorsement of the rights of poor people, Pope John Paul II directed the Congregation for the Doctrine of the Faith to undertake a comprehensive study of Liberation Theology. The results of the study were published in two documents: the 1984 *Instruction on Certain Aspects of the Theology of Liberation* and the 1986 *Instruction on Christian Freedom and Liberation*. The first document expresses the ongoing serious reservations of the Holy See, especially in regard to the acceptance of many elements of Marxist class analysis by some exponents of Liberation Theology. The second emphasizes, in a more positive vein, the fundamental nature of liberation as an essential theme of Judeo-Christian theology and faith, and not the monopoly of any single group of thinkers or theologians.

In light of these statements of the Holy See, it is clear that a (if not "the") theology of liberation is critical for the Church in that the redemption, grace and divine forgiveness are inexplicable without reference to the liberation they are meant to convey to those to whom they are given. Moreover, the great biblical motifs exemplified by the Exodus event, the New Testament emphasis on the compassion of the Lord toward the poor and the Resurrection itself all are variations of ways in which the Sacred Scriptures repeatedly underscore the importance of liberation in Christian life.

As the movement relates to the issue of social justice as understood and taught by the Holy See, the immense and important body of doctrine contained in the great social encyclicals of the last hundred years must be kept in mind. Far from condoning injustice or inaction, the Magisterium has incessantly recalled the indispensability of a clear sense of social justice for Catholic orthodoxy; cf. *Rerum Novarum* (Leo XIII,

1891), *Quadragesimo Anno* (Pius XI, 1931), *Mater et Magistra* (John XXIII, 1963), *Populorum Progressio* (Paul VI, 1967), *Octogesima Adveniens* (Paul VI, 1971), *Evangelii Nuntiandi* (Paul VI, 1976) and *Laborem Exercens* (John Paul II, 1981).

Liberty, Religious • The doctrine that it is morally permissible for nations and states to permit individuals to worship and practice their religious beliefs in good conscience when these do not harm the common good. Because religion is itself a basic human good, practicing religion is not to be restrained by the state or society; only when religious practices or beliefs cause clear and express harm to states can it be limited or curbed.

The doctrine of religious liberty differs from that of religious freedom, which holds that all religions are essentially the same and therefore the state should be indifferent toward them. The doctrine of religious liberty, articulated by the Second Vatican Council's Decree on Religious Liberty, holds that not all religions have the same value, but that does not mean that some can be deliberately hindered if they cause no harm. Religious liberty holds that states have an interest in promoting religion because sound religion is an aid to the state.

Religious liberty is based on the doctrine that individuals have an obligation in conscience to search for the truth, and an aspect of this search is the quest for religious truth. Because they have this obligation, they must have the liberty to pursue those truths. The doctrine of religious liberty holds that individuals who sincerely pursue religious truths in accord with the dictates of conscience must be permitted to do so. The Decree on Religious Liberty, however, does hold that this liberty for the pursuit of religious truth must give special place to the teachings of the Catholic Church. (Cf. Dignitatis Humanae.)

Licentiate • This is the first of the two graduate-level degrees awarded by pontifical faculties in canon law, theology, philosophy and Sacred Scripture. It usually entails at least three years of post-collegiate study, passing a comprehensive examination and writing a satisfactory licentiate thesis. (Cf. also Abbreviations section.)

Licit • In canon law the term licit is used to describe an act which is done in full accordance with the law governing such actions. For example, the rubrics of the Mass require the celebrant to wear certain vestments. If the priest wears those vestments, he behaves licitly in the matter of liturgical attire. An illicit act, on the other hand, is one done in violation of one or more rules governing the action. A celebrant who omits, say, the chasuble in offering Holy Mass, to continue the example, acts illicitly.

The liceity of an action should be distinguished from the validity of the same action, for acts can be illicit yet valid in canon law. All things being equal, the improperly attired priest, while saying Mass illicitly, still says it validly. From the above, it can be seen that the terms "lawful" and "unlawful" must always be probed in order to determine whether they refer to the liceity or the validity of the act in question. More often than not, these terms refer to liceity, but confusion can be avoided by specifying whether one is speaking in terms of liceity or validity.

Lie • Any word, action or expression which deliberately and with free consent expresses what is known to be false and is done with a motive of deceiving or misleading others when they have a right to the truth.

Lies concerning grave material are contrary to justice and truth, for they deprive others of truths to which they have a right. But there are occasions when individuals have no right to a truth, and in those circumstances not communicating the truth is a lie, but its malice is minimal. Thus, to tell a lie to a member of the Gestapo searching for Jews may be immoral, but the malice of this "officious" lie is minimal. Lies done for humor, like the officious lie, are venially sinful, but like malicious lies which aim at bringing harm, they can become gravely sinful.

Life • The capacity to grow, respond to external and internal stimuli and cause either perceptual or conceptual mental states. In the Catholic Tradition life is the unique creation of God and it is to be revered because it is a unique gift of God.

Biologically, more is understood of the mysteries of life than has ever been the case in human history, and it is now possible to mimic through technology the creation of the basic structures of life. Manipulation of living beings, both human and nonhuman, is now possible for scientists, and radically new ethical problems have arisen because of these possibilities.

Catholic belief holds that nonhuman life exists to serve humanity, and that it is morally legitimate to use it to meet legitimate human needs. Nonhuman living beings are not strict rights-bearers, and strictly speaking, it is not possible to violate the rights of nonhuman living beings. This should not be construed to mean that they are to be abused or made the objects of cruelty, but "animal rights" are not strictly equivalent to human rights.

This means that it is not immoral to use animals as experimental subjects for legitimate human needs, and that, in fact, it is one of the ways in which humans are served by nonhuman life. Even though nonhuman life is not the object of moral obligations, it must be respected and treated honorably. As stewards of creation over which humans exercise dominion, we are to use non-human life with intelligence and reverence. This is not so much to respect the rights of animals, but to prevent corruption of the human person.

Human life, however, does bear rights because it has moral duties and responsibilities which it must execute to find fulfillment and completion. The basic human right is not to be deliberately killed when innocent of any willful threat against other innocent human beings. This moral absolute holds that it is always immoral deliberately to destroy a human person under such conditions because one has done nothing to merit the greatest of physical evils.

This prohibition applies not only to human life when it has achieved the fullness of its existence, but also as it is on a trajectory into and out of being. Thus, deliberately to prevent a potential human being from achieving the fullness of being by means of contraceptive practices is an assault on human life. Also, taking deliberate measures to speed a being out of existence in acts of mercy killing is also a violation of the rights of human beings to be free from deliberately lethal acts when innocent of deliberate attacks on others.

Life, Sanctity of: See **Sanctity of Life**

Life, Spiritual • The striving after Christian perfection, imitation of Christ, growth in holiness and perfection of love. Throughout the history of the Church, many different and complementary understandings of the spiritual life have developed. The spiritual life has consistently centered on Jesus Christ, and thus reflects the Christocentric character of Scripture.

The desire to strive after Christian perfection and enhance the life of the Spirit gave rise to various monastic forms of spirituality in both East and West. An apostolic thrust was united to this

Christocentric orientation of the spiritual life in the mendicant orders of the Middle Ages, and in modern times an impulse linking it to ministry in the secular world emerged. Modern approaches to spiritual life have sought to broaden its horizon by incorporating meditative elements from the great Eastern religions. Contemporary trends are seeking to confront modern secularism and humanism by developing a Christian spirituality that is more socially and politically active. This new spirituality aims at advancing and integrating contemporary dogmas of freedom and self-determination into a Christian spiritual context.

Ligamen • The Latin word which means a tie or bond. In canonical language, it refers to the bond of marriage (cf. Canon 1134).

Light • An important symbol of Christ, Who is described as the Light of the World. His teaching illuminates our hearts and minds, and thus drives out the darkness of sin and ignorance, by bringing us knowledge of God and God's promises and intentions for our salvation. When His light enters us, it transfuses us and transforms us into lights pointing to Christ. This symbolization is most stunningly enacted in the liturgy of the Easter Vigil when the light of the tall Paschal Candle serves as the representation of Christ risen and from this candle the individual candles of the faithful are lighted. This symbolism is repeated whenever the sacrament of Baptism is celebrated and whenever Baptism is recalled in the liturgical renewal of baptismal promises.

Lily • In Christian iconography, the lily has come to be used as the symbol for perfect chastity. Saints revered for their purity of life are often depicted holding a lily. This symbol figures most prominently in depictions of the Blessed Virgin Mary and St. Joseph, but also of St. Anthony of Padua, St. Catherine of Siena and St. Gertrude.

Limbo • The word comes from a Latin word meaning "border" or "edge." It is the state or place, according to some theologians, reserved for the dead who deserved neither the beatific vision nor eternal punishment. In medieval theology, limbo had two meanings: (1) the place where the pre-Christian just had to await the opening of heaven by Christ; (2) the place for unbaptized infants and children who, therefore, remained in original sin without ever incurring any actual sins.

Generally speaking, the latter is commonly associated with the idea of limbo. This belief was held by many throughout the Middle Ages and into the twentieth century. It should be noted, however, that no official teaching ever advocated this notion. (Cf. Baptism, Sacrament of.)

Literal Sense of Scripture • By "literal sense" (Latin, *sensus litteralis*) is meant the sense which the human author of Sacred Scripture intended to convey. The method for ascertaining the literal sense is principally grammatical and historical. Research at the level of grammar, vocabulary, syntax, semantics, literary structure, historical background and context, intended reader/hearer, etc., all play roles in determining the literal sense.

The traditional approach normally includes the following distinctions: explicit literal sense, implicit literal sense. *Explicit literal sense:* The literal sense of John 1:14, "The Word became flesh" is "Jesus Christ became man," as the context suggests. *Implicit literal sense:* If the Son of God was human, then it is correctly implied that He had a human soul (intellect/will), sexual identity (male), etc. The implicit sense never exceeds or contradicts the explicit sense.

In addition to the literal sense are the typological or mystical (which, when discussing manner of expression, can be distinguished as metaphorical or proper; when discussing subject matter as moral and allegorical) and the anagogical senses. In recent decades these principles of interpretation have either been abandoned or greatly revised. Most exegetical work still seeks the literal sense of a passage.

Literary Criticism • In the early decades of the twentieth century, literary criticism referred to methods used by biblical scholars to determine linguistic and historical features of a biblical work or a particular passage. The kinds of features generally examined were: authorship, occasion and purpose, date, literary form, context, literary structure in its sociological setting, etc. The term no longer refers to the above parameters of inquiry. The methods identified as "literary criticism" by biblical scholars include other critical or analytical categories as these emerge from literary criticism outside of biblical studies (e.g., comparative literature, English literature, linguistics, etc.).

This shift in methods is not so much a flight from the work of the historian as it is a question of raising philosophical questions about the nature of a "text" and the nature of "interpretation." The fruit of some of the philosophical and interpretive inquiries have led to a view of the text as an enclosed entity whose principal feature is self-contained meaning embedded within the linguistic/mental structure of the text (language-centered approach). The shortcoming of this approach can be the lack of appreciating the text's historical context. That is, the "text" is viewed not so much as a window which opens up the historical world of its author or reader/hearer, but as a medium which reflects a world existing in symbolic form within the narrative itself. In general, there are two modes of analysis which proceed from this "text as medium" method. (1) Text-centered approach: the text is viewed as a closed system of signals and signs which are decoded or which have meaning with reference to each other. The task of interpretation is fulfilled when the signal system has accounted for the major features of the text's deepest structures; (2) Audience-centered approach: the relationship between the "text" and the "reader/hearer" is what determines the text's meaning. The author's context and that of the reader are the keys to getting at the meaning of the text. These methods are still at the exploratory stages of discovery; it will probably take a generation or two of solid scholarly advances to understand clearly what is of lasting value for an improved understanding of Sacred Scripture.

Literary Qualities of the Bible • Like other great literary works, the Bible possesses distinctive literary qualities. It contains poetry, history, biography, prophecy, parables, epics and wisdom sayings. This in no way mitigates the divine authorship of Scripture; rather, as St. Jerome has said, the divine intention has been given human expression.

The Old Testament is called in Hebrew Tanak, an acronym that summarizes the three primary literary genres present there: *torah* (law), *nebiim* (prophets) and *ketubim* (writings). Similarly, the New Testament shows three basic literary forms: gospel (history), epistles (essay or teaching) and revelation (the prophetic or apocalyptic).

Little Office of the Blessed Virgin Mary • A devotion in honor of the Blessed Virgin Mary consisting of hymns, antiphons, psalms and collects arranged according to a single day's cycle of "canonical hours" in imitation of the Divine Office (now Liturgy of the Hours). Much simplified from the full Office, and, therefore, much easier to use, the "Little Office" was quite popular among layfolk in the Middle Ages, and many artistically beautiful editions of "Books of Hours" from this period are actually personal copies of the Little Office of the Blessed Virgin Mary. Some monastic communities, such as the Cistercians, added the Little Office as an extra devotion to their daily cycle of prayer found in the full Divine Office. Other communities used the Little Office as a Saturday Marian devotion. After the French Revolution, when many communities of religious women were founded for the active apostolate, the Little Office became their standard community prayer.

It was the desire of the Second Vatican Council that the official Liturgy of the Hours be prepared in such a way that not only priests but also religious and laity could use it as a common prayer. Accordingly, most communities and individuals who would have used the Little Office in the past, now use the official Liturgy of the Hours, or the one-volume edition without the Office of Readings (known in the United States as *Christian Prayer*). This would certainly seem to be in keeping with the mind of the Church as expressed in the Council's Constitution on the Sacred Liturgy and in Pope Paul VI's Apostolic Letter, *Laudis Canticum,* promulgating the new Liturgy of the Hours. It should be noted that the new Liturgy of the Hours provides for a Saturday memorial of the Blessed Virgin Mary during Ordinary Time, and the texts of this Saturday Office are drawn almost entirely from the former Little Office.

Nevertheless, a new and somewhat expanded edition of the Little Office of the Blessed Virgin Mary was published in England in 1986 and in the United States in 1988 for use by those who are not canonically bound to recite the official Liturgy of the Hours and who might find even the revised Liturgy of the Hours too expensive to purchase or too daunting to use.

Liturgical Art: See **Sacred Art and Furnishings**

Liturgical Books • The multiple volumes used in official celebrations of the Church's public worship. All vernacular liturgical books are translations or adaptations of the *editiones typicae* (or official, standard editions) of the Latin originals, prepared under the supervision of national conferences of bishops (or international commissions appointed by several conferences of bishops who share one language) and confirmed by the Holy See.

Among the more important liturgical books currently in use in the United States and Canada:

✧ Sacramentary (translation of the Roman Missal)
✧ Lectionary
✧ Book of Gospels
✧ Liturgy of the Hours (one-volume edition: Christian Prayer)
✧ Rituals:
  ▪ Baptism of Children
  ▪ Rite of Christian Initiation of Adults
  ▪ Confirmation
  ▪ Holy Communion/Worship of the Eucharist Outside Mass
  ▪ Rite of Penance
  ▪ Rite of Marriage
  ▪ Pastoral Care of the Sick: Anointing and Viaticum
  ▪ Order of Christian Funerals
✧ The Roman Pontifical: Rites of Ordination/Dedication of Church/ other ceremonies to be celebrated by bishops
✧ Book of Blessings

While not, strictly speaking, liturgical books, other volumes are customarily included in this listing, for instance, the *Ceremonial of Bishops* and the *Raccolta* (a collection of prayers and litanies sometimes used in popular devotions).

It is the responsibility of the pastor to see to it that the parish owns a full collection of the necessary liturgical books in up-to-date editions. The *Ceremonial* goes further in reminding cathedral sacristans that the liturgical books used in public ceremonies must be beautifully printed and bound. Such prescriptions are not simply an aesthetic opinion, but bear witness to the Catholic Church's belief in the dictum *lex orandi, lex credendi* (literally, "the norm of prayer is the norm of belief"). Since the liturgy enshrines our Faith, expresses it, and rekindles it, both the contents and appearance of the official liturgical books are of supreme importance.

Liturgical Commission • According to *Sacrosanctum Concilium*, the Constitution on the Sacred Liturgy of Vatican II, the competent, territorial ecclesiastical authority is to set up a commission "to regulate pastoral liturgical action throughout the territory, and to promote studies and necessary experiments whenever there is question of adaptations to be proposed to the Holy See" (n. 44). These commissions are to be assisted by "experts in liturgical science, sacred music, art and pastoral practice" and "as far as possible . . . [they] should be aided by some kind of Institute for Pastoral Liturgy. . . ." In the documents of liturgical implementation since Vatican II, commissions have been charged to insure proper catechesis about the *Ordo Missae*, the Order of Mass, with appropriate translations of Latin texts, and with consultation on music, art and the construction of churches. Diocesan commissions are distinguished from national commissions which have direct

relationship with the Concilium on the implementation of the reformed liturgy.

Liturgical Judgment: See **Judgment, Liturgical**

Liturgical Law • That body of Church law which pertains to the rites and ceremonies of the Sacred Liturgy. Most liturgical laws are not found in the Code but in the liturgical books, since their purpose, application and interpretation are different.

Liturgical laws are officially interpreted and changed only by the Holy See, except in those instances where either the episcopal conference or the bishop is empowered to do so (cf. Canon 2).

Liturgical Life • A chief characteristic of the liturgical movement of this century leading to *Sacrosanctum Concilium*, Vatican II's Constitution on the Sacred Liturgy, has been the concern that the celebration of the liturgy influence the daily lives of participants. A chief proponent of this theme internationally was Pius Parsch, the Canon of Klosterneuberg, near Vienna. His widely disseminated five-volume work *The Church's Year of Grace* contains commentaries about the celebration of the Mass and the Divine Office, as well as pastoral commentaries on the implications of the liturgy for daily life. In the United States the pioneering work of Dom Virgil Michel, O.S.B., of St. John's Abbey in Collegeville, Minnesota, in his founding editorials in *Orate Fratres* (now known as *Worship*), his catechetical writings and pamphlets, all attest to the same important union between the celebration of liturgy and life. Hence, "liturgical life" is a convenient term to describe the living of the liturgy in terms of exemplifying the union with Christ and the Church enacted in the liturgy and then fully assimilated into the whole of one's life.

Liturgical Movement • The influence of Prosper Guéranger in the late nineteenth century as well as the initiatives of Pope St. Pius X in the early years of this century in the revival of Gregorian chant as well as early and frequent Communion are clearly concerned in the early stages of this popular movement with the reform of the liturgy for the sake of the continual reform of the Church. The international conference held at Malines in Belgium in 1909, where the parish-priest-turned-Benedictine-monk Dom Lambert Beauduin drew attention to the central importance of liturgical reform and continual Church renewal, is often regarded as its watershed.

Among the many important Benedictine voices heard in reviving the importance of a theological appreciation of what occurs in liturgy was that of Odo Casel of Maria Laach in Germany in the 1930s in his editing of *Jahrbuch für Liturgiewissenschaft*, as well as his own key work *The Mystery of Christian Worship*. In the United States, Virgil Michel of Collegeville, the founder and the first editor of *Orate Fratres* (currently called *Worship*), often wrote of the importance of a liturgically inspired catechesis and of how a proper interpretation of the liturgy included ethics and social justice as constitutive aspects of the liturgical movement.

Historical liturgical scholarship was carried on by authors such as Jean Daniélou and Josef Jungmann. Pastoral concerns mark the writings and ministry of Pius Parsch. At Vatican II, the Council Fathers were aided by a number of *periti* (experts), among them Cipriano Vagaggini of San Anselmo, Bernard Botte and P. M. Gy of Paris, Balthasar Fisher of Trier in Germany, and Godfrey Diekmann of Collegeville.

In the United States, from the 1940s through the Council, pastoral initiatives such as the singing of Sunday Vespers and the Dialogue Mass presaged some of what would result in the contemporary reformed liturgy.

Liturgical Music Today: See **Music Today, Liturgical**

Liturgy • The liturgy is the Church's public worship. It includes all of the rites and ceremonies by which the Church expresses her worship of God. The celebrations of the liturgy are actions involving not only the sacred ministers but all of the people concerned. Liturgical prayer is not collective private prayer but the prayer of the assembly, joined together as God's People. In the liturgy the sacred ministers and those assisting them with more active roles do not perform while the congregation simply observes. All are called to participate in different ways.

The liturgy is to be carried out in the name of the Church by persons lawfully deputed to do so and according to ceremonies approved by Church authority. Lawful deputation in the broad sense means that liturgy is carried out or celebrated by the baptized. In the more technical sense it means that the offices and ministries of the liturgy are exercised by those with the power (Sacred Orders) and authority to do so (Canon 834).

The purpose of the liturgy is diverse. First and foremost, it is to give glory and honor to God through prayer. Second, it is to build up the faith of the people. Third, it is to teach and instruct the faithful in the meaning of Christ's word through the sacred mysteries. Liturgy is not simply an intellectual act but an act of the whole person. The intellect, senses, and emotions are involved. Liturgy is also an aesthetic and artistic expression of love for God. Liturgical actions include the spoken word, gestures, actions and the inclusion of symbols and material things, such as vestments, incense and candles. Sacred music also occupies a most important part of the liturgy.

The celebration of all the liturgical actions of the Church is ordered according to the liturgical norms promulgated by the Holy See. These are found in the various liturgical books and in the Code of Canon Law. Since the liturgy is the official public worship of the Church, and not the private domain of any one individual or group of individuals, the liturgical norms, ceremonies and texts are to be conscientiously observed by all.

First and foremost, the liturgy includes the celebration of the seven sacraments, especially the Holy Eucharist. Although individuals may be receiving certain sacraments at a liturgical action (e.g., Baptism, Matrimony, Confirmation, Holy Orders), the liturgy is celebrated not just for them but for and by the whole Church. In the sacramental liturgies, while certain elements and words are required for the canonical validity of the sacrament (e.g., water and the Trinitarian formula for Baptism; bread, wine and the Words of Institution for the Eucharist; imposition of hands for ordination), these canonical regulations cannot be isolated and viewed as all that is really necessary for the liturgy. The concept of validity can be broadened to include the overall intended effect of the liturgy: worship, increase in faith and instruction. Thus the concept of liturgy will not be seen as merely mechanical but as a fruitful celebration of the mysteries of Christ.

The supervision and regulation of the liturgy depends primarily on the Holy See. By virtue of the office of sanctifying, the diocesan bishop is primarily responsible for the liturgical life of his diocese. He has a regulatory authority according to the norms of law but can make changes and innovations only when allowed to do so by the universal law. Priests also share in the office of sanctifying, and although the bishop is the chief priest of his diocese, in reality it is the responsibility of the priests to see that the liturgy is properly carried out (Canon 835).

In addition to the liturgies of the sacraments, the official worship of the Church includes many non-sacramental liturgies such as Liturgies of the Word, the Liturgy of the Hours or Divine Office, numerous blessings and sacramentals.

Liturgy, Bishops' Committee on the: See **Bishops' Committee on the Liturgy**

Liturgy, Children's • This term refers to the wider phenomenon addressed in *Pueros baptizatos*, the *Directory for Masses with Children* published by the Sacred Congregation for Divine Worship in 1974. The directory marks the first time that an official Roman document of liturgical implementation deals with the presence of children at Mass and offers suggestions for adaptations to suit their needs. The document discusses ways in which children are to be introduced into the Eucharistic Liturgy (nn. 8-15), Masses with adults in which children also participate (nn. 16-19) and finally Masses with children at which few adults participate (nn. 20-54). This last section is the longest and is that which is more directly concerned with "children's liturgy." However, throughout the document, the ecclesiological principle that liturgy is for the whole community, with its variety of ages, nationalities and backgrounds, and not just for children, is upheld; children are to be trained and encouraged to enter the regular liturgical assembly.

Particular instances of adaptations for Masses with children have been the publication of three new Eucharistic prayers, first for a trial of three years and now extended indefinitely (*Postquam de Precibus*, decree approving the Eucharistic Prayers for Children and for Masses of

Reconciliation, Sacred Congregation of Divine Worship, November 1, 1974) and the issuance of lectionaries with Scripture readings accommodated for children according to the directory, which texts and commentaries are published at the initiative of local episcopal conferences.

Liturgy, Constitution on the Sacred: See **Sacrosanctum Concilium**

Liturgy, Divine • The Divine Liturgy is the name given to the Mass of the Oriental Rite.

Liturgy of the Hours • The official cycle of the Church's daily (and ideally public) prayer. Formerly this prayer was called the Divine Office and consisted of Matins (in monastic communities a nocturnal office and among the parish clergy frequently "anticipated" the afternoon or evening before), Lauds (at dawn), Prime (First Hour: around 6 A.M.), Terce (Third Hour: 9 A.M.), Sext (Sixth Hour: noon), None (Ninth Hour: 3 P.M.), Vespers (at dusk), Compline (before retiring).

The Second Vatican Council, "valuing highly this long-standing custom of the Church and wishing to renew it," provided a new form for the prayer, "revised so that it could more fittingly be used by the clergy and other members of the Church in the circumstances of modern life" (decree of promulgation, *Liturgy of the Hours*).

As noted, the revised work is called *The Liturgy of the Hours*, reflecting the purpose of the prayer, namely, to sanctify the entire course of daily life. In its new form, the Hours are these:

✧ Morning Prayer (Lauds) and Evening Prayer (Vespers): the "hinge Hours" upon which the whole cycle of daily prayer depends.

✧ The Hour of Prime (First Hour, around 6 A.M.) was suppressed for the universal Church as being an unnecessary duplication of the more ancient Lauds, although it may continue to be chanted in contemplative monastic communities.

✧ Midday Prayer: more brief than Morning and Evening Prayer, texts are provided for Midmorning (Terce), Midday (Sext) and Midafternoon (None) Prayer. Contemplative communities are to observe all three and, indeed, others are encouraged to do so. But it suffices to choose one Hour from the three to pray, using the texts appropriate to the particular time.

✧ Night Prayer (Compline): to be said before retiring, "even if this is after midnight." Previous legislation required that the entire cycle be accomplished before midnight.

✧ Office of Readings: three psalms or sections of psalms (which would have been one "nocturn" in the previous schema), followed by a scriptural reading and a patristic reading. In contemplative communities this is to retain its "nocturnal character," evoking the ancient Christian discipline of "keeping vigil" for the Lord's return. For parish priests (and for active religious and laity who choose to say this Office), it may be celebrated the evening before, early in the morning or any time in the course of the day conducive to prayer and spiritual reading.

Whereas the previous arrangement of this prayer presented all one hundred fifty psalms in a one-week Psalter (hence, the length of time needed for recitation), the Vatican II arrangement distributes the psalms over a four-week cycle ("the four-week Psalter").

Besides the official four-volume *Liturgy of the Hours* (in England and Ireland a three-volume version is entitled *The Divine Office*), numerous one-volume editions are available containing, usually, Morning, Evening and Night Prayer with a selection from Midday Prayer and Office of Readings. There are also "shorter" forms of Morning and Evening

Prayer available, maintaining the four-week Psalter but without full seasonal and sanctoral variations. In the United States there is a one-volume *Office of Readings* (Boston: Daughters of Saint Paul), which presents in a handy way the considerable wealth of patristic readings that is perhaps one of the revised Office's most important contributions to modern spirituality.

Lives of the Saints • Any of several collections of brief biographies of canonized saints. The purpose of such collections is to inform and edify the reader, and to inspire him to emulate the heroic virtue and faith of the saints, whether a particular saint be popular or obscure.

Such collections, the most notable in modern times being *Butler's Lives of the Saints*, can fill many volumes.

Loaves of Proposition: See **Showbread**

Local Ordinary • An Ordinary whose authority extends over a specific territory. By contrast, a personal Ordinary is an Ordinary whose authority extends over specific people.

Residential bishops, vicars and prefects apostolic, abbots and prelates nullius, vicars general and vicars episcopal are all local Ordinaries (Canons 134, 174).

Loci Theologici • This Latin term literally translates as "theological places," but more usually (with the Latin second word retained) as "theological *loci*." The term can mean either of two things, depending on the context. In its first sense, *loci* is equivalent to the "sources" which the theologian must consult in his account of Christian doctrines, chiefly Scripture, Tradition, the Magisterium (papal and conciliar teaching), the writings of the Church Fathers and Doctors, liturgy and canon law. The Dominican Melchior Cano (1509-1560)

provided an influential account of these *loci* or sources in his book *De locis theologicis* (1563).

In its second sense, *loci* is equivalent to the "topics" which the theologian addresses: the divine existence and nature, the Trinity, creation, grace, anthropology, Christology, ecclesiology, and so on. Whether *loci* refers to theological sources or theological topics can normally be determined from the context.

Logic • The branch of philosophy concerned with the study of reasoning and the methods of sound argumentation. Logic studies the basic elements of discourse — terms, propositions and arguments — in order to determine how they function in larger patterns of arguments in all fields of inquiry. Depending on the characteristics of the field and the nature of the premises, patterns of argument possess varying degrees of force. The domain of logic ranges as widely as the various fields of human inquiry extend.

In its more narrow sense, however, logic is often thought to be concerned chiefly with the strictest form of reasoning as represented in deductive arguments. In such arguments, a conclusion is advanced as compelling on the basis of true premises and valid reasoning. Much of the work of logic conceived in this narrow sense is to explore the forms of valid reasoning and to identify fallacies. It is assumed that training in logic, especially as a preparation for philosophical and theological studies, helps to cultivate patterns of sound reasoning in these areas.

Aristotle is generally credited with "founding" the systematic study of logic. His logical works have exerted a profound influence on both Eastern and Western theological traditions.

Logos • The Greek term *logos* can translate "word," "speech," "teaching," "thing" or "event." The term has a wide range of meaning in Hellenistic literature. Most of the ancient Semitic cultures shared the assumption that the spoken "word" was a distinct reality with its own power or dynamism, as is clear from the many Old Testament curses and the many blessings uttered at marriages, covenants, contracts, promises, etc. (e.g., Gn 20:7; Jos 6:26; 1 Kgs 16:34).

The New Testament authors share this basic understanding when they make use of *logos*. However, the term receives new meaning in light of the life, death and resurrection of Jesus Christ. (1) It can refer to the Word of God as spoken in the Old Testament (Acts 3:31; Lk 2:29; 3:2; Mk 7:13; Mt 1:22; 2:15; 15:6). In addition, God's Logos preexisted as wisdom (Prv 8:22ff.; Sir 24). (2) It can refer to particular sayings from Jesus (Mt 26:75; Lk 22:61; Jn 7:36; Acts 11:16; 20:35; 1 Thes 4:15; 1 Cor 7:10, 12, 25) or to His teachings as a whole (Mk 2:2; 4:33; Lk 5:1; Acts 10:36). (3) It can refer to the early Christian preaching about Jesus by the Apostles ("ministry of the word": Acts 6:4), that is, the proclamation of the Gospel (Acts 13:15; 15:36; 1 Cor 14:36; Eph 1:13, 1 Jn 1:5), centered on the Person and deeds of Jesus (Lk 1:2; Acts 1:1). (4) It can refer to Jesus Himself as the *Logos*. In the Johannine writings Jesus is God's Word (Jn 3:34; 8:47). Although He speaks of "my word" (Jn 5:24; 8:43, 51; 12:47-50; 14:23, 15:20), He actually speaks the *Logos* of the Father (Jn 8:55; 14:24; 17:6). Because of the wide semantic range of this term ("word," "saying," "teaching"), it is not surprising it was used to speak about Jesus' relationship to the Father. He is not just the Son of God; in His Person is the "teaching of God" or "the doctrine of God" or "the Word of God."

For further reading: Thomas H. Tobin, "Logos," *Anchor Bible Dictionary*, 4:348-356.

Lollards • The derisive term used to describe the followers of the early fifteenth-century Oxford priest John Wycliffe (or Wyclif). This heresy was strongly anticlerical and an early proponent of individual biblical interpretation. English bishops, however, effectively checked the spread of this heresy by suppressing the few influential supporters among the clergy of the now-condemned Wycliffe. When semiliterate laity then took over the notions for their own purposes, they were insultingly termed "mumblers," or lollards. Although the heresy was virtually extinct by the late 1500s, the rise of Luther in early sixteenth-century Germany breathed new life into the English Lollard movement for a time.

Longanimity • Related to the virtue of hope, this virtue gives one the capability to endure sufferings, trials, frustrations, failures and rejections incurred in the service of the Gospel with equanimity and balance. This is a necessary virtue for those who wish to grow in the spiritual life, as it leads one to greater maturity in the face of suffering and to deepen one's self-understanding.

Lord • In both ancient Greek literature and New Testament Greek, the word "lord" (Greek, *kyrios*) expresses a variety of meanings. The term was used more as an adjective than a noun in classical culture (prior to the New Testament period, c. 500-300 B.C.) and signified power and authority over the disposition of possessions, individuals or groups of people. Within this context, the term applies to emperors, monarchs, slave-owners, heads of families, masters of houses, military leaders, guardians over minors, etc.

The noun form appears around the first century B.C. in Egypt with reference to a goddess. After this time the noun appears with great frequency as a proper divine title in Syria and throughout Asia Minor. Its use in the Roman Empire is due to the influence of Hellenism on Roman civilizations. In concert with its Hellenistic pattern, the New Testament use of "Lord" can refer to sociological status or may have explicitly religious meaning.

In regard to sociological designations, "Lord" can mean "owner of possessions" (Mt 20:8; 21:40; Mk 12:9, etc.) or "of slaves" (Jn 13:16; Mt 10:24ff.; Lk 12:36). Ownership of substantial possessions and of slaves normally implies a person of high position, and thus in this case *Kyrios* could translate as "Sir" and therefore indicate the social and economic standing of the individual (Mt 27:63; 25:11; Jn 12:21; 20:15; Acts 16:30, etc.).

Romans 10:9 reads, "Jesus is Lord." The application of this title to Christ communicates His supreme authority, power and divinity. These two meanings would have been understood in their Hellenistic sense by any Greek. However, the term has a more specific meaning than that which emerges from its Hellenistic context. In the Old Testament God is often called "King" (1 Sm 8:7ff.; 12:12) and "Lord of Lords" (Dt 10:17; Ps 136:3). Such divine attributes are transferred to Jesus Christ when that term is applied to Him. Early in her life, the Church read various Old Testament passages in light of Jesus' teachings, the experience of His resurrected life and the experience of forgiving sins, healing, deliverance and community life. Within such a context, early Christians would read Psalm 110:1 which would "speak to them" in prophetic fashion about Jesus' royal humanity and His divinity.

Thus in light of the early Church's penetration of Sacred Scripture (the Old Testament), the attribution of Lordship to Jesus meant that He was King over all humans (Rom 14:9), over all His enemies (Col 2:10, 15) and even over death (1 Cor 15:24ff.; 1 Pt 3:22). This knowledge is consistent with the witness of Jesus' Lordship over the Church, which is not by force but by love (e.g., Col 3:18; Eph 1:20ff.; 4:15-16; 5:21-33). Not only the Church, but all of heaven, earth and hell give witness to Jesus' Lordship (Phil 2:10ff.).

In sum, His Lordship expresses His connection to the Davidic line, but more importantly, His divine status as absolute Lord against the forces of darkness and death and in love over the Church. Lordship should be understood as a power which enables by first breaking the stranglehold of sin, death and the forces of evil, and secondly by empowering, upbuilding and enlivening with resurrection life. The new creation, a transformed, wholesome and holy humanity centered and rooted in Christ, is what witnesses to the intended effects of Christ's Lordship over the Church.

For further reading: Gottfried Quell and Werner Foerster, "*Kyrios*," *Theological Dictionary of the New Testament*, 3:1039-1098.

Lord's Prayer • Usually called the "Our Father," this is the prayer which Jesus taught His disciples and is still the fundamental prayer of Christians today. Found in its fuller form in Matthew 6:9-13, the Lord's Prayer is in the center of Jesus' Sermon on the Mount. Luke 11:2-4 is a somewhat briefer version of the words of Christ.

The prayer is a beautiful combination of praise, petition and penitence. So significant is this prayer of Christ, it is offered every time the Eucharist is celebrated. At the beginning of the Communion Rite, priest and people together "pray with confidence to the Father in the words our Savior gave us."

It is also an integral part of Morning and Evening Prayer of the Liturgy of the Hours.

For further reading: J. L. Houlden, "Lord's Prayer," *Anchor Bible Dictionary*, 4:356-362.

Lord's Supper • Another name for the Last Supper (Mt 26:20-29, Mk 14:17-25, Lk 22:18, 1 Cor 11:23). It also may refer to Holy Thursday, the day of the Last Supper. In non-Catholic usage, too, it is commonly applied to a ritual reenactment of the Lord's Supper, as in a Communion service.

For further reading: Hans-Josef Klauck, "Lord's Supper," *Anchor Bible Dictionary*, 4:362-372.

Loreto, Holy House of • One of the principal Marian shrines throughout the world is that which is found in a small city off the Adriatic coast of central Italy and not far from the important port city of Ancona. The importance which this shrine has today and has enjoyed for many centuries lies in the fact that within the walls of a sumptuous basilica are to be found the relics of the house in which Mary is said to have conceived the eternal Word of God in her virginal womb at the message of the archangel Gabriel (Lk 1:26-38).

This house, or more precisely, room, is rich in history. Referred to by such trustworthy witnesses as St. Epiphanius (A.D. 315-403), St. Bede the Venerable (672-735) and St. Willibald (700-786), it was handed down by the first Christians as the house in which the Blessed Mother dwelt when she was visited by the angel.

St. Helen, in her concern for the preservation of the holy relics of the lives of Our Lord and Our Lady, built a large church or basilica over it. Even then it was a center of attraction of pilgrimages to the Holy Land. St. Louis IX of France was the last known saint to have visited it in 1251 before the fall of Jerusalem into Saracen hands. The basilica over it was destroyed by them in 1263, but the little house was miraculously spared. In 1289 a Christian pilgrim, Ricoldo di Montecroce, wrote in his "Itinerarium" that he and other pilgrims found this precious relic of the Annunciation and the Holy Family within the ruins of a large church.

A few years later in 1291, the same Holy House, as it was called, made its appearance in northern Italy near the present-day Yugoslavian border. Even to this day there are churches dedicated to this event and testifying to the devotion of the local citizens who considered themselves blessed by the presence of the Blessed Mother's house in their land. This was only a temporary move, as on December 10, 1294, the Holy House made its appearance in the region of the Marches of eastern Italy, found on a hill of laurels (hence, its name) near the cities of Recanati and Ancona.

According to an ancient tradition, it was brought by the ministry of angels to a field belonging to two brothers. When they became greedy and began to argue about the profits they were going to make from the concourse of people who would flock to behold this prodigy, the house vanished. The next day it was found atop a public road and by a ditch which crossed an uninhabited laurel hill nearby. This was to make clear that this relic of Christianity was for the edification of all the faithful and not for the profit of any individual. The house had no foundation, so the pilgrims who immediately began to appear on the scene built a wall of bricks around its circumference to preserve it.

In recent times documents hitherto unknown have been found which have given rise to theories which try to explain by natural means the movement of the Holy House from Nazareth to Loreto. Among the discoveries made is an undated but centuries-old letter which states that the expenses for the transfer of the Holy House were met by the Angeli (Angels) Family. Another dated 1294, the dowry of Margaret of Epirus, wife of Philip II of Anjou, lists in second place among the valuables given to Philip "stones of the House of Our Lady, the Virgin Mother of God." It is interesting that they list this after the relics of the True Cross but before a number of immensely valuable jewels and other properties, attesting to the esteem in which these stones were held.

Whether it was by the ministry of angels or by the ministry of the Angeli family, it can be ascertained today that the house found enshrined in the Basilica at Loreto is, indeed, the same house which early Christians held to be the place where Mary received the message of the angel and where tradition maintains that later she came with Christ and St. Joseph to live after their return from Egypt.

In the words of Pope Pius XI, "As far as the authenticity of the Holy House is concerned, there are many good reasons for acknowledging it, and no valid ones for denying it." Pope John Paul II, who has made two official pilgrimages as Pope to the Holy House, called it "the first temple, the first church on which shone the light of the maternity of the Mother of God." He also stated: "Beyond that which tradition narrates regarding the miraculous translation of the Holy House of Nazareth . . . that which strikes is the extraordinary concourse of peoples attested since the fourteenth century. . . . Devotion to the Madonna of Loreto is as ancient as the traditions about the circumstances of the translation of the small house of Nazareth to the hill of laurels near the city of Ancona." Indeed, over two million pilgrims flock annually to this shrine of the Holy Family and of the Incarnation to pay homage to Him Who deigned to be born of the Virgin.

Our Lady of Loreto is not only the patroness of homes but was also named patroness of aviators and air travelers by Pope Benedict XV (1914-1922).

L'Osservatore Romano: See **Osservatore Romano, L'**

Los-von-Rom Movement • This particular movement was a mixture of religious, ethnic and political ideas which combined against a perceived common enemy, the Church of Rome. Based primarily in Bavaria during the last years of the nineteenth century, the movement used ethnic and racial innuendo to attempt to draw German Catholics away from their affiliation with the Roman Church, which was accused of harboring anti-German sympathies for the Slavs, among other things. By the time the movement faded during the First World War (although it enjoyed some revival after that war), the Los-von-Rom or "away from Rome" movement had led some 75,000 Catholics into schismatic churches, with many others simply lapsing from the Faith.

Lourdes, Apparitions of • Eighteen appearances of Our Lady to Bernadette Soubirous, which occurred in 1858 at Lourdes in the Department of Hautes-Pyrenees, in the cave of Massabielle along the River Gave. In the final vision, Our Lady identified herself with the words, "I am the Immaculate Conception." She instructed Bernadette to drink from a spring under the rock of Massabielle. At first, Bernadette's efforts yielded nothing more than muddy water, but later that day, a spring began to flow from that spot down into the River Gave.

The visions, the unaccountable spring and reports of miraculous healings began to attract many pilgrims. After the Church officially approved Lourdes as a place of pilgrimage in 1862, it gradually became one of the most important pilgrimage sites (after the Holy Land) in the Christian world. A great basilica was dedicated in 1901 and a vast underground church in 1958. It is estimated that as many as six million pilgrims visit Lourdes every year, with a large and well-organized system of volunteer help drawn from all over the world. Since its beginnings, Lourdes has been the site of many reported miracles. A medical bureau and a hospital have been established to study and authenticate these miracles.

The local feast of the apparitions (February 11) was extended to the universal Church by Pope St. Pius X in 1907 and is now an optional memorial in the revised Calendar.

Love • Defining love broadly, it may be understood as any strong affection, closeness or devotion to things or persons. The Greeks distinguished four types of love: *storge, philia, eros* and *agape. Storge,* familial love, is a word for the bond that exists between one who loves and persons, animals and the things that surround him or her. It is compatible with quite a bit of taken-for-grantedness or even of hatred at times. *Philia* pertains to friends, freely chosen because of mutual compatibility and common values. *Eros* is passion, not only of a sexual nature, but also of an aesthetic or spiritual nature, for what is conceived of as supremely beautiful and desirable. Agapic love is manifested when one person has much to give to another more needy. It is generous self-donation without concern for reward.

Such distinctions become especially important in discernments about marriage, because the strength of *eros* love may blind one to the absence of other types of love needed to experience a good Christian bond that, with God's grace, can endure "till death do us part."

Love of God • The supreme Christian virtue, it is the virtue that informs and animates all Christian actions. Love of God can be an explicit and formal sort of action, or it can be the motive which underlies and animates all other Christian actions and thus perfects them. The command to love God without restriction is at the heart of Old Testament teachings, and the sort of love that is due to God is what is to be given to one's neighbor. The love of God which the Christian is to manifest to God is to be of the same character and intensity as that with which God has loved us.

Our capacity to love God ultimately derives from God's love for us, which is best exemplified in the passion and death of Jesus for the sins of all humanity. God loves us as Creator and Redeemer, and His love for us is the motive for His creation, while we love Him as created beings and from our debt to Him. Love of God that mirrors His love of us makes perfect love of neighbor possible as it sets the terms for this love. Because God loves us unreservedly and without restriction, He can demand this sort of love in return, and that it be expressed to our neighbor as well. God loves humanity universally as His special creation, and because His love is universal, He can demand this love of humanity by imparting His Spirit on it to make this possible.

Love of Neighbor • Catholic belief holds that it is a sin not to show love to all, even to enemies. It demands that unlimited love for all persons be shown, not only that those close to one be loved, but those afar, and it requires that Christians love not only their friends and those who do good for them, but also that enemies and those who do them harm be loved as well. This form of love is the sign *par excellence* of the Christian contradiction of the world with its hatred, selfishness and egotism.

Love of neighbor is the source of the unity of the Church and the clearest sign of the presence of the Holy Spirit, for the Holy

Spirit is the source of charity. True love of neighbor reveals God's love for us, is faithful, unselfish and a source of peace. Love of neighbor is grounded in the Eucharist and derives from it, for the love shown in that Sacrament is the model for love of neighbor. In loving one's neighbor, one formally encounters Christ, Who also loves the neighbor, causing a believer to love the neighbor as He does.

Low Sunday • The first Sunday after Easter, so called in contrast to the High Feast of Easter. This was called *Dominica in Albis* or Sunday in White Robes, because the newly baptized in the Early Church wore white robes as a sign of their putting on Christ in Baptism from Easter until the Sunday after. Low Sunday is now called the Second Sunday of Easter.

Ludwig Mission Association • Frederic Résé, a German priest active in the missions in North America and founder of the Leopoldine Foundation, established the Ludwig Mission Association in 1838 after nearly ten years of planning and preliminary efforts. The purpose of the Association was twofold: to assist the developing Church in the United States through financial grants to religious orders working there, and to help the Franciscans assigned to the shrines in the Holy Land. Over one million dollars was safely seen into the hands of American missionaries by the early 1920s, used in a wide variety of evangelical outreach programs.

Luke, The Gospel of • Luke's Gospel is the first of a two-volume work, the companion to the Acts of the Apostles (cf. Lk 1:1-4; Acts 1:1-2). The Gospel and Acts articulate a unified and systematic account of God's decisive and definitive acts of salvation — the fulfillment of His promises to Israel in the life of Jesus and the life of the Church. The two works are designed so that parallels exist between Jesus' life and the life of individuals in the early Church. For example, a comparison between Jesus' death (Lk 23:34, 46) with that of Stephen (Acts 7:59-60) illustrates how Jesus' mission to reconcile all of creation continues and develops in the Church. It is important to understand that the Gospel must be read in the light of Acts, and vice versa.

There is no scholarly unanimity as to the precise historical reason why Luke wrote his Gospel. The following theories are current: (1) Luke probably wrote for a Gentile Church (Lk 1:1-4) which found its universal mission to preach the Good News to all nations (Lk 24:47) rooted in its Jewish origins (e.g., Lk 1:68-79; esp. 2:32; Acts 10); (2) the Gospel clarified confusion about Jesus' true identity and nature (e.g., Lk 1:1); (3) Luke established that it is God's will to include Gentiles within the community of the redeemed (e.g., Acts 9; 15); (4) the Gospel defended Christianity in the eyes of educated citizens of the Roman Empire (Lk 23:13-16; Acts 16:37; 22:25-29).

What seems clear from Jesus' journey to Jerusalem (Gospel of Luke) and the Church's mission to "all nations" (symbolized by Paul's presence in Rome) and from other evidence is that: (1) God's great promises are fulfilled through Jesus' life, death and resurrection; (2) those promises are fulfilled in an ongoing and similar way in the life of the Church; (3) the promises fulfilled in Christ and fully present in the Church are accessible to all nations and peoples.

Major Themes: Luke presents the teachings of Jesus and the Apostles from the first century in Palestine to a largely Greco-Roman world. Luke shapes the narrative of salvation so that it has maximum impact on its reader. The Gospel's major themes are expressed in compact form within the infancy narratives (1:5—

2:52). These narratives are carefully crafted and of high theological quality and historical character. They connect Jesus' personal story with great salvific events in Israel's past. Thus the annunciation of Mary's impending pregnancy (1:28-33) recalls the annunciation passage found in Judges 13:2-5. Mary's canticle (1:46-55) carries the same melody as Hannah's song at 1 Samuel 2:1-10, but is transposed into a different "musical key" within the orchestration of salvation history. From Zechariah's prophecy over John, we learn of John's mission (1:76-77) which prepares us for learning about Jesus, Whose significance goes well beyond that of John. He is salvation for Israel (1:68-69) and for all people (2:29-32). These themes will recur and blossom into the early Church's mission, expressed first in Peter's life and then in Paul's as we read about them in Acts.

Contents:
A. Preface: 1:1-4
B. Fulfilling the Promises to Israel: 1:5—2:52
C. Before Jesus' Public Ministry: 3:1—4:13
D. Jesus Ministers in Galilee: 4:14—9:50
E. Jesus Journeys to Jerusalem: 9:51—19:27
F. Jesus Is Rejected in Jerusalem: 19:28—21:38
G. Jesus' Passion, Death and Burial: 22:1—23:56
H. Resurrection, Commission of Apostles and Ascension: 23:56—24:53

Authorship and Date: Both Church Tradition (e.g., Muratorian Canon, Irenaeus, Tertullian, Origen, Eusebius, Jerome) and some current scholarly opinion affirm the Lucan authenticity of the Gospel and Acts. The difficulties arise regarding a precise date for the two-volume work. The Gospel made use of material from Mark, which we can date just prior to or after the Jewish Wars of A.D. 66-70. Since Luke 21:5-38 seems to assume the destruction of Jerusalem, a date after 70 is reasonable. Luke/Acts gives no indication of any knowledge of the persecutions under Domitian's rule (85-96), nor of the intense struggles between the Church and emerging rabbinic Judaism c. 85-90. It is, therefore, reasonable to date Luke/Acts c. 70-85.

For further reading: Joseph A. Fitzmyer, S.J., *The Gospel According to Luke I-IX*, Anchor Bible 28A (Doubleday, 1981); Joseph A. Fitzmyer, S.J., *The Gospel According to Luke X-XXIV*, Anchor Bible 28 (Doubleday, 1985); Robert J. Karris, O.F.M., "The Gospel According to Luke," *New Jerome Biblical Commentary*, 675-721; Luke Timothy Johnson, *The Gospel of Luke*, Sacra Pagina 3 (Liturgical Press, 1991).

Lumen Gentium • Traditionally so called from the first words of its official Latin text, *Lumen Gentium*, the Dogmatic Constitution on the Church, was the third of the sixteen major documents issued by the Second Vatican Council. Called a "dogmatic constitution" in part to distinguish it from *Gaudium et Spes*, a "pastoral" constitution on the Church in the modern world, issued at the end of the Council, it was published on November 21, 1964.

A fuller commentary could show that *Lumen Gentium* was profoundly affected by its position, composed and debated and finally formulated in the early sessions of the Council, prior to the results of the discussions on the later documents. Its chapters show in outline its major points of emphasis: (I) The Mystery of the Church; (II) The People of God; (III) The Hierarchy; (IV) The Laity; (V) The Call to Holiness; (VI) Religious; (VII) The Pilgrim Church; and (VIII) Our Lady.

Lumen Gentium was written "for the benefit of the faithful and of the whole world, to set forth as clearly as possible, and in the tradition laid down by earlier Councils . . . [the] nature and universal mission" of the Church (n. 1).

The dogmatic constitution anticipates a subsequent development when it criticizes the division of the Church into an institutional body and a more spiritual association: "On the contrary, they form one complex reality which comes together from a human and a divine element" (n. 8).

"This is the sole Church of Christ which in the Creed we profess to be one, holy, catholic, and apostolic. . . . " "This Church, constituted and organized as a society in the present world, subsists in the Catholic Church, which is governed by the successor of Peter and by the bishops in communion with him" (n. 8).

The ecumenical interest of the Council is also emphasized: "Nevertheless, many elements of sanctification and truth are found outside its visible confines" (n. 8).

The continuing confusion regarding the distinction between the ministerial priesthood and the priesthood of the faithful is likewise an object of *Lumen Gentium's* concern (n. 10).

All the sacraments are essential to the Church's life, above all the Eucharist, "the source and summit of Christian life" (n. 11).

The college of bishops governs the whole Church. "One is constituted a member of the episcopal body in virtue of the sacramental consecration and by the hierarchical communion with the head and members of the college" (n. 22).

"Among the more important duties of bishops, the preaching of the gospel has pride of place" (n. 25).

The Magisterium of the Roman Pontiff is examined in a careful manner. Even when he does not pronounce a doctrine *ex cathedra* or solemnly, his teaching deserves a "loyal submission of the will and intellect," and three criteria for the interpretation of the Pontiff's "mind and intention" are listed:

(1) the character of the documents; (2) the frequency with which a doctrine is proposed; and (3) the manner in which the doctrine is formulated (n. 25).

Three criteria are also identified to determine the infallibility of the ordinary (i.e., non-solemn) Magisterium: (1) the bishops who teach it are in communion with each other and with the successor of Peter; (2) the doctrine has to do with faith or morals; and (3) the bishops are in agreement that the doctrine must be held definitively (n. 25).

The criteria established to determine the infallibility of the Roman Pontiff are repeated from the dogmatic constitution *Pastor Aeternus* of Vatican Council I (n. 25).

The diaconate as a third order of the hierarchy is described and a call is issued for its restoration, including a dispensation from the ordinary requirement of celibacy (n. 29).

The laity are defined as all the faithful, with the exception of those in Holy Orders and those who belong to a religious state approved by the Church (n. 31). "By reason of their special vocation, it belongs to the laity to seek the kingdom of God by engaging in temporal affairs . . . so that they may contribute to the sanctification of the world as from within, like leaven. . ." (n. 31).

No matter what their position in the Church, all are called to holiness (n. 39).

Because of a special grace from God and in order to contribute to the Church's mission of salvation, some people, clergy and laity, are called to the life of the consecrated religious (n. 43).

In an effort to increase the Church's devotion to the saints, *Lumen Gentium* describes her character as the Mystical Body of Christ and a Pilgrim People of God (n. 50) in union with those who have gone before us or who are yet being purified after their death (n. 51).

Far from neglecting the importance of Mary, the Mother of God, the entire last section of *Lumen Gentium* is dedicated to her. She occupies a "place in the Church which is the highest after Christ and also closest to us" (n. 54).

Essential for an integrated interpretation of *Lumen Gentium* are the numerous postconciliar documents of the Holy See, especially *Ad Pascendum* on the restoration of the diaconate (1973), *Ministeria Quaedam* on the ministries of lector and acolyte (1973), and the *Declaration of the Congregation for the Doctrine of the Faith Mysterium Ecclesiae*, on protecting the Catholic doctrine of the Church against certain errors of the modern day (1973).

Luna (also Lunette) • From the Latin for "moon," the lunette (or *lunula*) consists of two hinged pieces of metal in the form of a crescent, between which the Host is placed for use in the monstrance for solemn exposition of the Eucharist.

L'Univers: See Univers, L'

Lust • The disordered desire for sexual gratification. Lust is a particularly destructive vice because it clouds one's better judgments and makes a person vulnerable to particular forms of lust violence. This is borne out in Augustine's claim that lust quickly becomes cruel lust, which is seen in the fact that the consequence of lust is often abortion, the deliberate killing of an unborn child who results from lustful actions. This is also seen in the fact that lust often exhibits itself in forms of sexual violence.

Lust is different from the sexual attractions and afflictions that bind man and woman together in marriage, and it is most fully manifested in sexual activity outside the marriage bond. Lust is particularly harmful spiritually because it warps our perceptions of other persons, and this in turn compromises one's intimacy with others and deepens one's isolation. No other vice shows the intricacy and ingeniousness of human evil than lust, for the lustful person pursues pleasures with a ferocity and ingeniousness that is matched nowhere else in the animal kingdom. Lust is contrary to both charity and justice because it demeans the person who is made the object of lust.

It seems that the most effective antidote to lust is prayer, along with participation in the Eucharist and charitable works. Prayer draws one nearer to Christ, the ultimate Man of peace Who reconciles us to the Father and Who restores peace in our nature, and to charitable works that bring us to view others as more than mere instruments for self-gratification.

Lutheran-Catholic Dialogue • The current phase of officially sponsored Lutheran-Catholic dialogue at the national and international levels got underway almost immediately after the close of the Second Vatican Council and has continued without interruption since that time. The national Lutheran-Catholic dialogue has been particularly productive since its inception in 1965, when the National Lutheran Council and the Catholic Bishops' Commission for Ecumenical Affairs approved formal dialogue between the two communities. In fact, this is the longest continually functioning dialogue in America. In effect, the goal of the dialogue has been to discover the degree to which Lutheran-Catholic differences continue to constitute church-dividing disagreements.

In a succession of conversations, broad areas of doctrinal convergence have been discerned beneath the conflicting or simply different formulations that have emerged since the Reformation. The dialogue has been guided by a methodology that was geared to identifying such areas of convergence by beginning with the confession embodied in the Nicene Creed and espoused as normative by both communions. The published results of the Lutheran-Catholic dialogues indicate the range of issues considered to date: *The Status of the Nicene Creed as Dogma of the Church* (1965); *One Baptism for the Remission of Sins* (1966); *The Eucharist as Sacrifice* (1967); *Eucharist and Ministry* (1970); *Papal Primacy and the Universal Church* (1974); *Teaching Authority and Infallibility in the Church* (1980); *Justification by Faith* (1985); *The One Mediator, the Saints and Mary* (1992). The most recent round of dialogue sessions concerns Scripture and tradition.

The international Lutheran-Catholic dialogue has been similarly productive. Sponsored by the Lutheran World Federation and the Holy See, the Lutheran-Roman Catholic Joint Commission began its work in 1967. The Malta Report, *The Gospel and the Church* (1972), concluded the initial phase of dialogue, while the second phase saw the publication of common documents on *The Eucharist* (1978), *The Ministry in the Church* (1981), *Ways to Community* (1980), and *Facing Unity: Models, Forms and Phases of Catholic-Lutheran Church Fellowship* (1984). With the recent publication of *Church and Justification* (1993), marking the end of the third phase, the Joint Commission asked "whether, taken together, these documents constitute the sufficient consensus which would enable our churches to embark upon concrete steps toward visible unity."

Lutheranism • Refers to the distinctive cast given to traditional Christian belief and practice by the teachings of Martin Luther (1483-1546) and his first associates, and subsequently enshrined in a series of confessional statements gathered together in the *Book of Concord* (1580). Characteristic emphases of Lutheranism are the primacy accorded to Scripture over all other sources of doctrinal authority (*sola Scriptura*); justification by faith alone (*sola fide*); and the centrality of Christ's role as savior and mediator (*solo Christo*). These emphases were at first clearly intended to be corrective and reforming, but soon became constitutive and Church-dividing.

In the aftermath of the Reformation, Lutheranism assumed an institutional form, first as a state Church in countries that adopted Luther's reforming program (especially in various German principalities and in the Scandinavian countries) and then — with emigration from those countries throughout the following centuries — as a worldwide communion of local Lutheran churches. This communion was institutionalized on an international level with the establishment of the World Lutheran Federation in 1947.

In the United States, Lutheranism came to be organized along ethnic lines, depending on the countries of origin of the immigrant communities that constituted it. In 1987 three of the most important national groupings — the American Lutheran Church (ALC), the Lutheran Church in America (LCA) and the Association of Evangelical Lutheran Churches (AELC) — joined to form the Evangelical Lutheran Church in America, representing about sixty percent of the Lutherans in the United States. The fourth largest group, the Lutheran Church - Missouri Synod, remains independent. There are well over five million Lutherans in the U.S.

Lyons, Councils of • Two ecumenical councils, the thirteenth and fourteenth respectively, were held in the French city of Lyons. The first was called by the canonist Pope Innocent IV in June 1245. By that time, Frederick II had long been in conflict with the papacy; the affront of his recent capture of over one hundred bishops on their way to a Roman synod was heavy in the air of the First Council of Lyons. Frederick was excommunicated and then deposed by the council, which sat in three sessions and was attended by about one hundred fifty prelates. Other disciplinary matters were also treated by the council, and a call for volunteers to free the Holy Land was sent out.

The Second Council of Lyons was called by Pope Gregory X in 1274 and in many ways was more notable than the first. Although St. Thomas Aquinas, an invited *peritus* of the council, died before he could reach it, some two hundred bishops gathered and, in the course of four sessions, enacted thirty-one decrees touching on a wide variety of ecclesiastical affairs. The procession of the Holy Spirit, the mandatory use of unleavened bread in the Eucharist in the West, the doctrine of transubstantiation and the supremacy of the Roman Church over the other churches were all ratified in this council. The presence of St. Bonaventure (who actually died during the council) contributed, moreover, to a decree of reunion between the Eastern and Western Churches which was, however, only short-lived. Finally, several rules (some of them ingenious) on papal conclaves were established by the council, which in large part survive today.

St. Bonaventure: Lyons Council figure

Lyons, Rite of • A modification of the Roman Rite with elaborate ceremonial and numerous ministers (e.g., six priests, seven deacons, seven subdeacons, seven acolytes, all in full vestments assisting the bishop at a High Mass). Its origins are traced from Rome through Aachen (where Charlemagne adapted papal liturgical usages for his chapel), to Lyons at the beginning of the ninth century.

M

Maccabees, First and Second Books of • These books constitute the two canonical books of this name; there are also the apocryphal Third and Fourth Maccabees. The four books have little in common except their subject matter, which is Israel's resistance to Gentile domination and opposition to the influence of Hellenism. In fact, the Greek word for Judaism occurs for the first time in 2 Maccabees. Their title is derived from Maccabeus, the name assumed by Judas, son of Mattathias, protagonist of the account and leader of the Jewish insurrection (165-161 B.C.) against Antiochus Epiphanes. Historians depend on 1 Maccabees as the only extant document for the entire period it covers, from the accession of Antiochus in 175 B.C. to the death of Simon in 135 B.C. Though written before 1 Maccabees, 2 Maccabees gives little historical detail that is not already contained in 1 Maccabees. Its significance, however, lies in the great insight into contemporary religious beliefs that it provides, particularly belief in an afterlife and physical resurrection. Such ideas are recent in Jewish thought, found only in texts of the last two centuries of the pre-Christian era.

Written in Greek, 1 Maccabees and 2 Maccabees were likely the work of authors of the final quarter of the second century B.C.

For further reading: Hugh Anderson, "Maccabees, Book of," *Anchor Bible Dictionary*, 4:439-454; Neil J. McEleney, C.S.P., "1-2 Maccabees," *New Jerome Biblical Commentary*, 421-446; Uriel Rappaport, "Maccabean Revolt," *Anchor Bible Dictionary*, 4:433-439.

Italian Madonna (thirteenth century)

Macedonianism • A wide variety of Trinitarian heresies which once rocked the ancient Church. In A.D. 342 the

640

wicked Macedonius was set up in the See of Constantinople. As an Arian, Macedonius launched a persecution of both Novatians and Catholics which included torture and forced baptisms. Around 360, several Arian bishops, Macedonius among them, began to propagate the notion that there existed in the Trinity a hierarchy (instead of an equality) of Persons. This heresy, with many others, was condemned at the First Council of Constantinople. Macedonius, meanwhile, who had long since begun to wear on the patience of the populace and the emperor, was deposed, banished, and died presumably unreconciled in 364.

The magi (from a Canterbury panel)

Madonna • Literally, "my lady" in Italian, but in referring to the Blessed Virgin, it is equivalent to "Our Lady." Artistically, it refers to a representation of Mary in painting or sculpture and is more likely to be used of Western art than of Eastern icons. Early images of her are always with the Christ Child, as in a Nativity group, but after she was proclaimed *Theotokos* or Mother of God at Ephesus, the standard form of Mother and Child became common iconography.

In the West, naturalistic influences begun by Giotto tend to soften the features of the Madonna in painting. This also happens in French medieval sculptures of Our Lady. Many of the great Renaissance and Baroque masters have given us rich paintings of the Madonna, frequently reproduced as Christmas cards.

Magdalen • Descriptive title conferred originally upon a reformed prostitute (in imitation of St. Mary Magdalene) but later upon any penitent "public sinner" who sought admission to a religious community. Some communities have auxiliary congregations originally founded for this purpose. In times past, these sisters wore a distinctive and often penitentially colored habit, and lived apart from the other sisters, frequently in a cloistered setting.

Magi • The Greek word *magoi* at Matthew 2:1-12 refers to "wise men" who are said to be from "the East" (2:1), which could refer to Arabia, Mesopotamia or somewhere else east of Palestine. The fact that they were guided by the star (2:2) suggests they were learned in astrology or the science of navigation and time calculation by means of stellar configurations.

It was Origen who first proposed that there were three *magi* because of the three gifts offered to the Christ-Child (2:11). Tertullian is the first to suggest that they were kings (*fere reges* ["almost kings"], cf. *Adv. Jud.*, 9 and *Adv. Marc.*, iii.13). On the basis of the implied reference to Psalm 72:10, many speculated that they were royalty; by the sixth century it was a common assumption. The New Testament is silent concerning their number and relationship to royalty. By the Middle Ages these "three kings" are not only named (Caspar, Melchior, Balthasar), they are venerated as saints. A favorite theme in art dating from the late second century is the Magi adoring the Christ-Child. The fact that learned men, perhaps even of royal blood, come to worship the "King of the Jews" expressed the universal mission of Christianity — the Gospel or Good News from God is not just for the Jews but for all the nations of the world.

For further reading: Raymond E. Brown, S.S., *The Birth of the Messiah*, 165-201, Anchor Bible Reference Library (Doubleday, 1993).

Magic • Superstitious practices which claim to perform extraordinary wonders beyond human power by invoking hidden spiritual powers. Magic presumes that there are hidden intra-cosmic powers that can have extraordinary influences on natural phenomena if accessed in the proper manner. These intra-cosmic powers are discovered by the human will and can either control the life of the person or be controlled by the will of the person. Magic can be both "white" and "black." In the prior sort of magic, one seeks to communicate with these beings to gain special blessings and goods, while in the latter, one invokes these beings to bring extraordinary harm to others.

Despite these differences, the Church has condemned both as being contrary to the life of faith and the honor and respect due to God. Magical practices include divination, fortune-telling, interpretation of dreams, necromancy, ouija boards, ordeals to determine guilt or innocence, use of horoscopes, Devil worship and other similar practices. Magic was widely practiced in antiquity and among the Israelites, and there is some evidence that some early Christians practiced it as well. Church

teaching has condemned all forms of magical practices as being contrary to both faith and hope. Magic elevates to positions of preeminence the created realities of God, and thus dishonoring the Creator.

For further reading: *Catechism of the Catholic Church*, nn. 2110-2117.

Magisterium of the Church • The teaching office of the Church. To safeguard the real substance of faith in Jesus Christ and to prevent the individual from being entirely left on his own, the Magisterium of the Church was established by Christ.

The Magisterium captures the very heart and essence of the Church, which is to proclaim the Good News of Jesus faithfully. The Church takes the teachings of Christ and the doctrines taught by the Apostles, hands them down faithfully with the assistance of the Holy Spirit, and calls upon all to place their faith in these teachings. The New Testament attests to this in the formation of the apostolic college. The community of Apostles, when it taught as a unified body under Peter, attested to the truth of Christ, and they spoke authoritatively of Him. It was to the Apostles that the authoritative teachings of the kingdom were given in their fullness, and they were the closest eyewitnesses to Jesus. By the end of the apostolic era, it was the monarchical bishops appointed under the authority of the Apostles as their successors who were the final arbiters of faith and doctrine.

The limits of the Magisterium of the Church were gradually worked out at the Councils of Trent and Vatican I, and in the controversies with the Gallicans, Episcopalians and Conciliarists. The Magisterium exists to protect the authentic teachings of Christ until the end of time. The Magisterium proclaims the teachings of Christ infallibly, irreformably and without error when: (1) it teaches universally and without dissent; (2) when the failure to teach these doctrines would be considered negligent; (3) when the teaching concerns a grave issue necessary for faith or morality; and (4) when they are taught authoritatively.

In the extraordinary Magisterium, the Roman Pontiff and ecumenical councils, whose decisions are confirmed by the Pope, are able to proclaim certain matters of faith and morals necessary for salvation to be infallibly true. Such teachings must be proclaimed authoritatively and solemnly by either an ecumenical council or the Roman Pontiff and be consistently and universally held by the Church. They must be teachings that have never been tolerant of dissent.

The doctrine of the infallibility of the Magisterium does not mean that everything that is taught by the Church is proclaimed infallibly, but that its proclamation of Jesus Christ is faithful to Him and to what He taught. Through its authoritative teachings, the Magisterium truly leads to Christ, holiness and salvation, since the fullness of holiness and the gifts of the Holy Spirit can be found in the Catholic Church because of the guidance which the Holy Spirit gives the Magisterium.

Magnanimity • The virtue which prompts one to do morally good acts of exceptional quality. Magnanimous persons are disposed to perform actions of extraordinary generosity, kindness, fortitude and charity, not in order to gain fame, glory or recognition, but simply to do what is right, good, just or needed. Magnanimous actions are usually only possible for those who as a matter of habit and custom practice the other virtues with great regularity and ease. Magnanimity supports and enhances fortitude, and it is one of the highest forms of charitable self-sacrifice.

Magnanimous individuals trust in God's grace in their efforts to do what is exceptionally and extraordinarily good.

Magnanimity is different from brashness or impetuousness, in that it is restrained and directed by prudence. The opposite quality, pusillanimity, is a fear of doing these great and difficult deeds for fear of suffering deprivation or other such loss.

Magnificat • The Magnificat, Mary's song of praise, responds to Elizabeth's declaratory statements and questions by proclaiming the graciousness of God in fulfilling His promises to Israel (Lk 1:46-55). It is called the "Magnificat" because that is the first word of the hymn in its Latin version. In English, it begins, "My soul magnifies the Lord." The language of Mary's response to what God has done is strongly influenced by Old Testament hymnody, e.g., Psalm 30:8; 33:4. In fact, Mary's Canticle most closely resembles Hannah's Hymn of Praise (1 Sm 2:1-10) and may be the text which provides the basic framework for the Magnificat. Mary's hymn echoes the just response to God's great actions of salvation. Mary fully and clearly understood the events which were taking place, events in which she had an active role. In Luke's Gospel, Mary is the model of how each believer should respond to the deepest truths of the events of salvation of history, so as to perceive the hand of God at work. Storing up such events in one's heart and going over and over them in an inquisitive yet prayerful manner can bring us more deeply into an active knowledge of God's great plan of salvation and of eventual participation in it. Each day the Magnificat is prayed as part of Evening Prayer of the Liturgy of the Hours.

For further reading: Raymond E. Brown, S.S., *The Birth of the Messiah*, 330-366, Anchor Bible Reference Library (Doubleday, 1993).

Major Orders • Prior to the revision of orders which took place in 1972, major orders were the Sacred Orders of subdeacon, deacon, priest and bishop. The orders of deacon, priest and bishop have been traditionally considered sacraments, although a small minority of theologians believed that the subdiaconate was also a sacrament.

By contrast there were the minor orders, received in sequence prior to the reception of major orders. These were the orders of porter, lector, exorcist and acolyte. The minor orders were abolished as such in 1972, as was the subdiaconate. The orders of lector and acolyte were retained but reconstituted as ministries. The diaconate and priesthood are no longer called major orders but Sacred Orders.

In order to be valid, a bishop must ordain a man to the diaconate and priesthood. The ministries of lector and acolyte may be conferred by a priest other than a bishop. Laymen (males) now may receive the ministries, and all clerics destined for Sacred Orders must receive the ministries.

Major Superior • A superior of a religious institute or society of common life who has authority over all members in a territory or province of an institute or over some other grouping of members or communities. The superiors of entire institutes, as well as abbots, are also known as major superiors (Canon 620).

Makarisms • The Greek word usually translated into English as "Beatitudes."

Malabar Rites • A controversy similar to the Chinese Rites question arose in the sixteenth-century Jesuit Province of Malabar, whence the name. The great missionary Robert De Nobili, in converting Hindus to Christianity, tried to adopt as many of their customs as possible so that new Christians would not feel estranged from their culture. In this era of

inculturation, this seems obvious, but at his time, it was a revolutionary approach.

Although De Nobili took only those customs he considered to be civil (not religious), nonetheless the Dominicans and Franciscans felt that these practices would still carry Hindu significance and that many converts would see no difference between their former religion and their new Faith. The case was referred to Rome, which upheld De Nobili in 1623, but later in 1712 most of these adaptations were forbidden, as indeed were the parallel Chinese Rites of Matteo Ricci, another great Jesuit missionary in the Orient.

Malachi, Book of • This prophetic book was produced by a genuine religious reformer, perhaps a Jewish priest. The first verse introduces "the word of the Lord through my messenger (malaki)" and makes of it a proper name. The author has a high sense of the responsibility of priests for religious education (2:6-9) and for reverence in liturgical worship (1:12-13). He is confident that God will send His messenger to purge the people (3:1-5). In the New Testament times, John the Baptist is presented as one who fulfilled this role as an eschatalogical messenger. Malachi looks forward (1:11) to a universal and pure sacrifice, to be offered at all times and in all places. This verse is sometimes quoted by Catholic authors in reference to the Sacrifice of the Mass.

It is helpful to read this book against the background of Ezra 7-10 and Nehemiah 1-13. During the Persian period, after the rebuilding of the Temple, the priests began to be negligent about offering the sacrifices and instructing the people. Mixed marriages and divorce were also a serious problem.

For further reading: Aelred Cody, O.S.B., "Haggai, Zechariah, Malachi," *New Jerome Biblical Commentary*, 349-361; Andrew E.

Hill, "Malachi, Book of," *Anchor Bible Dictionary*, 4:478-485.

Malta, Knights of: See **Knights of Malta**

Mammon • The New Testament Greek word *mamonas* occurs at Luke 16:9, 11, 13 and Matthew 6:24. This word was "borrowed" from Aramaic and refers to material wealth and prosperity, especially property (Lk 16:9, 11). The word can be used to personify wealth (Mt 6:24; Lk 16:13) as a "master" at enmity against God.

For further reading: Max Wilcox, "Mammon," *Anchor Bible Dictionary*, 4:490.

Man • The word "man" is a generic word signifying the human person in male and female form. Philosophically, man or the human person is differentiated from lower creatures on the basis of reason and will. Self-consciousness and freedom mark the thoughts, feelings and actions of the human person as transcendent of the sometimes similarly appearing instincts and reactions of animals.

Catholic philosophy emphasizes the unity of soul and body in the human person. It refutes the errors of those who would, instead, eliminate soul altogether (materialists) and those who would make it seem that only the soul is the person, with the body a mere appendage (dualists and angelists). (Cf. Immortality of the Soul; Resurrection of the Body.)

Mandatum • The ceremony of washing the feet of twelve men at the Evening Mass of the Lord's Supper on Holy Thursday, in imitation of the Lord's action in regard to His Apostles. The term comes from the Latin text of the central phrase *mandatum novum*, "a new commandment," used in the Gospel acclamation that evening from John 13:34, "A new commandment I give to you, that you love one another; even as I have loved

you . . ." to introduce the Gospel text John 13:1-15; the phrase also appears as one of the optional antiphons to be sung during the washing of the feet itself. The ceremony of foot-washing also derives from monastic customaries in which the abbot would wash the feet of all the monks of the monastery once yearly. In some patristic literature the gesture of foot-washing is explained as an important symbolic gesture that effects reconciliation.

Mandyas • The distinguishing vesture of monks in the Byzantine Church covering the entire person. It varies in style from the simple short black cloak of the lower ranks to the more ornate and symbolic vesture of an archimandrite (plain black) or bishop (blue or purple), fastened at the neck and at the front hem, ornamented with four squares, two at each side, neck and hem, from which streamers of wide bands of red and white are attached, symbolizing the rivers of grace which flow from the dispensation of word and sacrament.

Manichaeism • A religious and ethical doctrine propounded by Mani (A.D. 216-277) or Manes (Latin form, Manichaeus), which held for an absolute dualism concerning God. Thus it holds that there are two equal, eternal principles: one of good, light and spirit; the other of darkness, matter, evil. It has affinities with a number of other religious and philosophical systems: Gnosticism (liberation of the soul from matter through enlightenment), Marcionism (distinction of the God of the Old Testament from the Father of Our Lord Jesus Christ), Mandeanism (dualism with Persian roots) and even Buddhism (concern for escape from the present world). It found a fertile field in those areas influenced by those forms of neo-Platonic thought which considered matter as "tainted." Mani argued that he was proposing a superior, universal religion whose previous messengers (Buddha, Zoroaster, Jesus) were concerned with only a part of the world and whose message was falsified since it was not put in writing.

Based on this belief in two fundamental principles of reality, the devout Manichee rejects anything that would link him to matter. He therefore should practice extreme asceticism, refrain from menial work (since it disturbs the fragments of light present in all visible things) and practice absolute sexual continence. Since in practice these demands are not fulfilled by most, a distinction is made between the *elect* and the *hearers*. The hearers serve the elect and hope in a future life to be born in the body of an elect and thus attain salvation.

Part of the success of Manichaeism was due to the fact that it was adapted to the prevailing religious culture in which it was preached. Thus in the Near East and Egypt, it was clothed in Christian imagery; in Persia, in the vocabulary of Zoroastrianism; in India, in Buddhist terms. It had a highly developed form of church organization and was found in many parts of the Roman Empire, especially in the eastern part. Opposition from Roman civil authorities limited the influence of these ideas, especially from the fifth century in the West and somewhat later in the East.

Pockets of Manichaeist or neo-Manichaeist thought were found in the Balkans in the medieval period. Groups with similar ideas — Albigensians or Cathari — were found in Western Europe in the twelfth to fourteenth centuries. It is not certain whether they have historic or only ideological links with the Manichaeans.

Manifestation of Conscience • The practice of disclosing one's conscience, in order to receive spiritual guidance. This practice is sometimes performed before a priest, but this is not necessary. These manifestations are purely voluntary, and religious superiors are forbidden to require them of their subjects; their sole purpose is to enhance the spiritual and moral life of the penitent.

Maniple • A napkin-like vestment worn over the left forearm by the priest, deacon and subdeacon in the Tridentine Mass. Its original purpose was practical, namely, to serve as a kind of handkerchief for the celebrant; eventually, it took on symbolic meaning.

Manna • The word is derived from the Hebrew *man*, which is used in the Old Testament to identify the miraculous nourishment provided by God for the Israelites in the desert (Ex 16:4-35; Dt 8:3-16 and elsewhere). The description of manna given in the Old Testament is couched in difficult language, making it difficult to envision manna in precise terms. According to popular etymology, the word is derived from two Hebrew words, *man hu* (What is this?) — words uttered by the Israelites upon first encountering the miraculous substance. It may be a resinous secretion emitted by the tamarisk tree and certain desert shrubs when punctured by a particular species of insect. It is edible and sweet to the taste. The miracle in manna consisted in the manner and quantity in which it was produced for the Israelites. There are several allusions to manna in the New Testament, viz., John 6:30f.; Hebrews 9:4f.; Revelation 2:17. By a natural symbolism, it has come to be regarded as a type of the Eucharist.

For further reading: Joel C. Slayton, "Manna," *Anchor Bible Dictionary*, 4:511.

Mantelletta • This Italian term, which means "small cloak," refers to the knee-length sleeveless garment (usually purple or scarlet, depending on the rank of the wearer and the liturgical season) worn by prelates over the rochet when in choir dress. As it was a symbol of limited jurisdiction, it was worn by bishops outside their territories, by domestic prelates everywhere, and (under the mozzetta) by cardinals when in Rome. Though Pope Paul VI discontinued its use in 1969 except for certain monsignori resident at Rome — and this abolition still applies for bishops and cardinals — it is used by the canons of the patriarchal basilicas. Thus the canons of St. Peter's wear a purple mantelletta, while gray is used by the canons of St. Mary Major.

Mantellone • A full-length sleeveless purple robe with long false sleeves hanging from the shoulder, worn (until 1969) by papal chamberlains, who were commonly known as *monsignori di mantellone*.

Mantum • Coming from the Spanish *manto* (cloak), this term refers to the great cope worn by the Pope on certain occasions. It is extra long and wide, and is either red or white (rose on Laetare Sunday). It is not to be confused with the *mantello*, which is the Holy Father's red winter cloak.

Manual of Prayers of the Council of Baltimore • Companion volume to the *Baltimore Catechism*, mandated by the same Plenary Council (Baltimore) of United States Bishops, and reprinted numerous times between the end of the nineteenth century and a final printing in the early 1950s. Deploring what they termed "a lamentable lack of knowledge of the Church's official prayer as contained in the Missal and Breviary," and regretting the multiplication of devotional manuals "of questionable theological and literary quality," the far-sighted prelates gathered at Baltimore wanted the emerging Catholic Church in the United States not only to know what to

believe (the Catechism) but how to pray (the Manual).

A survey of its contents shows how astute the compilers of the Baltimore *Manual of Prayers* were. In addition to the simple "Mass Devotions" common to the devotional manuals of the time, this official *Manual* contained the Ordinary of the Mass in Latin and English and, in a supplement, the proper texts (including the Scripture readings) for every Sunday and holy day of the year. In addition to devotional "morning and evening prayers," the entire Offices of Prime and Compline were excerpted from the Breviary and translated into English, along with Vespers in Latin and English for all Sundays and feast days (with an extensive collection of the classic Office hymns in Latin and English). The sacramental rites are given in full, together with a wide selection of litanies and indulgenced prayers. A helpful "Summary of Catholic Belief" and a solid "Guide to Christian Life" made the *Manual* one of the most complete and helpful books ever sponsored by the national episcopate. Judging from the number of copies still extant (and frequently found in private homes and used-book stores), the *Manual* was extremely popular, used as Sunday School prizes and Confirmation and wedding gifts. All subsequent and additional devotional books (*Blessed Be God*, *Key of Heaven*, etc.) were derived from this *Manual*, took their translations from it, but generally were not able to match the scope or quality of its presentation. The 1988 *Catholic Household Blessings and Prayers* is a modern attempt on the part of the United States bishops to provide a compendium of prayer similar to the *Manual* published so long ago by their predecessors.

Manuterge • Derived from the Latin words *manus* (hand) and *tergere* (to dry or wipe), this term refers: (1) to the white linen or cotton towel used by the celebrant during Mass to dry his hands at the lavabo at the Offertory or Preparation of the Gifts. This custom goes back to the early days of the Church and may have been a descendant of the ritual purifications performed by the Jews of old, as well as having practical use. The "manuterge" or *manutergium* was already mentioned in the rubrics of the fifth-century *Statuta Antiqua*, "The Ancient Statutes," which points to its antiquity even then; (2) to the towel reserved for the priests in the sacristy, used to dry their hands when they wash before Mass or before distributing Holy Communion.

The *manutergium* was also used in the preconciliar rite of priestly ordination to wrap the freshly anointed hands of the newly ordained priest. A pious custom grew up, whereby that linen was given to the new priest's mother and then placed in her casket for burial with her. The revised rite does not call for a *manutergium* as such, and so the subsequent practice has likewise fallen into desuetude.

Mappula • Latin for "small napkin," this term designates the linen gremial formerly used in the Dominican Rite of the Mass by the priest and his two assistants. Whenever the rites called for a period during which they had to sit, the mappula was placed over the lap; in turn, the celebrant and his assistant placed their hands palms down on the mappula. Its use probably developed as a practical way of keeping the sacred vestments from getting soiled. This is no longer used, since the Dominican Rite was allowed to fall into disuse at the time of Pope Paul VI's revision of the Roman Missal.

Marburg, Colloquy of • One of the first and most important attempts to achieve Protestant unity on matters of doctrine. It ended in failure, however, because the two main participants, Martin Luther and Ulrich Zwingli, could not agree on an understanding of the Eucharist. Luther pushed for a statement which would recognize the Real Presence of Christ in the Host along with the presence of bread, a theory known as consubstantiation. Zwingli, on the other hand, maintained that Christ's presence in the Eucharist was merely symbolic, which placed him even further outside the true doctrine of Transubstantiation. When it was clear that no accord would be reached, the Colloquy was disbanded by Prince Philip the Landgrave, the original engineer of the conference.

Margarita • Properly, a "pearl." In the Byzantine Rite, the name given to the smaller particles of consecrated Bread given at Communion. (Cf. Lamb.)

Marialis Cultus • Issued on February 2, 1974, the Apostolic Exhortation *Marialis Cultus* (*For the Right Ordering and Development of Devotion to the Blessed Virgin Mary*) was written by Pope Paul VI for the purpose of developing devotion to the Blessed Virgin within the context of the renewal resulting from the Second Vatican Council. Beginning with the revised Roman Liturgy, the exhortation points out the important place Mary has within the rhythm of the liturgical year, and how the various Marian themes relate to the mysteries of Christ and His Church. The document points out that Mary is "a model of the spiritual attitude with which the Church celebrates and lives the divine mysteries" in that "she is recognized as a most excellent exemplar of the Church in the order of faith, charity and perfect union with Christ. . . ."

Marialis Cultus calls for a renewal of devotion to Mary which is respectful of tradition and yet which is "open to the legitimate requests of the people of our time." It must reflect the proper Trinitarian and Christological aspects which form its foundation, and show the legitimate place Mary occupies in the Church. The document warns against those who would "scorn, *a priori*, devotions of piety which, in their correct forms, have been recommended by the Magisterium, who leave them aside and in this way create a vacuum which they do not fill," as well as those who "without wholesome liturgical and pastoral criteria, mix practices of piety and liturgical acts in hybrid celebrations." A renewed devotion to Mary has an important place in the ecumenical activities of the Church, since she has a concern for the reunion of Christians, and her faithfulness is to be seen as a model which is worthy of imitation in every age.

Marialis Cultus devotes a section to two important exercises of piety, the *Angelus* and the Rosary, both of which are seen as being grounded in the Gospel and are recommended to be used by the faithful. It closes with a reflection on the theological and pastoral value of devotion to the Blessed Virgin, pointing out its "effectiveness for renewing the Christian way of life."

Marian Year • The dedication of a particular year to the honor of the Blessed Virgin Mary has been a practice made prominent by twentieth-century Popes. This dedication has included the injunction of special prayers to the Blessed Virgin, special Marian observances, the practice of penance and the extension of generous indulgences to the faithful. Thus, on the occasion of the centenary of the promulgation of the doctrine of the Immaculate Conception, Pope Pius XII in the encyclical *Fulgens Corona* proclaimed that a special Marian Year would be observed throughout the universal Church. This was the first Marian Year. More recently, Pope John Paul II announced a fourteen-month-long Marian Year from Pentecost to the feast of the Assumption (June 7, 1987-August 15, 1988). In his encyclical *Redemptoris Mater*, the Pope specifically indicated that this Marian Year would be a preparation for the third millennium of Christianity.

Mariology • The study of the Blessed Virgin Mary in Christian theology, especially in the Roman Catholic Church. Mariology as such started in the sixteenth century when this study was separated from the rest of theology. Scriptural Mariology limits itself to the study of New Testament texts that refer to Mary (cf. Mt 1:16—2:23; 12:46-50; 13:55; Mk 3:31-35; 6:3; Lk 1:26—2:52; 8:19-21; 11:27-28; Jn 1:14; 2:1-12; 19:25-27; Acts 1:14; Rom 1:3; Gal 4:4). The study also concerns itself with the defined dogmas about Mary: her divine motherhood, her perpetual virginity, the Immaculate Conception (defined by Pope Pius IX in 1854) and the Assumption (defined by Pope Pius XII in 1950).

Vatican II's Dogmatic Constitution on the Church, in its final chapter (8), offered the first official Mariology of the Roman Catholic Church. It presented Mary in biblical, patristic, ecclesial and ecumenical perspective.

Maritain, Jacques • Born in 1882 to a wealthy French Protestant family, Jacques Maritain converted to Catholicism along with his wife Raïssa, the former becoming one of the most prolific Catholic writers of the twentieth century. Maritain lectured and taught at many universities in the United States and Europe. Maritain served as the French ambassador to the Holy See from 1945 to 1948, and represented his country in the United Nations Economic and Social Council. He died in Toulouse, France, in 1973, spending the last thirteen years of his life with the Little Brothers of Jesus of Charles de Foucauld.

Maritain deserves much recognition for his role in reviving the study of St. Thomas Aquinas (1225-1274). For his devotion to Aquinas, Maritain is indebted to the encyclical *Aeterni Patris* of Pope Leo XIII. Maritain dedicated his life to an examination of many areas in philosophy in the light of Aquinas, particularly in the areas of social ethics, art and theory of knowledge. Initially attracted to right-wing imperial groups in France, Maritain resigned from *Action Française* out of obedience to a general condemnation of that organization imposed by the Pope. In the process of maturing in his own work, and as a result of the influence his former student Yves Simon exerted on him, Maritain became an effective philosophical advocate of democracy and of human rights.

Maritain saw the creation of agreement about the tenets permitting the association of free persons to be a major challenge for modern democracy. Simple freedom and diversity cannot create the basis for a common life: "A genuine democracy implies a fundamental agreement between minds and wills on the basis of life in common"; a democracy must be "capable of defending and promoting its own conception of social and political life." Democracy declares to the world that it supports the common human creed of freedom (cf. *Man and the State*, pp. 109-110). The American and Canadian Maritain Associations, the Maritain Institute at the University of Notre Dame and the International Institute for Jacques Maritain promote the study of Maritain's work.

Mark, The Gospel of • The shortest, and generally thought of as the earliest, of the four Gospels. Mark's Gospel has a precise focus: the revelation of God's kingdom which comes to us through Jesus Christ, the Son of God (Mk 1:1). Jesus' identity, ministry and purpose, as well as the response of the disciples, all relate to this central theme of God's kingdom. God's kingdom is found in Jesus' preaching: "The time is fulfilled, and the kingdom of God is at hand; repent and believe in the gospel." God's kingdom arrives in power and might; it overtakes and breaks Satan's stronghold on "the world." Jesus uses the parables as an effective form of communicating various aspects of God's kingdom. Jesus is *the* parable of God's kingdom — He casts out demons, heals, forgives sins and is crucified and raised to resurrected life, all of which are signals that the age of salvation which the Jews awaited for centuries was "at hand."

St. Peter dictating to
St. Mark (eleventh century)

Jesus' titles illustrate His role in the coming of God's kingdom: the term "Christ" occurs throughout Mark (1:1; 8:29; 14:61; 15:32) and must be understood in terms of its Old Testament use, which was mainly for royal leaders who were anointed either to save Israel from an enemy or to restore the Davidic rule (e.g., 2 Sm 7:12-14). Jesus is God's anointed in the sense that He fulfills the Davidic rule but in a totally just, righteous and everlasting fashion, by bringing salvation, the power of God over sin, Satan and even death. Mark's Gospel is a "saving action" Gospel, with so many of Jesus' acts of power over the powers of darkness (e.g., exorcisms, healings, forgiveness of sins), all of which illustrate that the age of salvation (i.e., of being freed from the grasp sin has over the individual) is in fact present. The Gospel is written to draw out what this "age of salvation" means for the follower of Christ (discipleship).

Major themes: The key theme is the Person of Jesus, what He does and says. Jesus, Son of God, brings the kingdom of God in divine power and might: forgiveness of sins (2:10-12); dominion over the Sabbath (2:28; 3:1-5), authority over demons (1:27, 34; 3:11, etc.); knowledge of the kingdom secrets (2:8; 8:17; 12:15), etc.

Contents:

A. Prologue: 1:1-15

B. Jesus' Ministry in Galilee: 1:16—3:6

C. Jesus Rejected in Galilee: 3:7—6:6

D. Jesus Misunderstood by Disciples: 6:6—8:21

E. Jesus' Teaching and Journey to Jerusalem: 8:22—10:52

F. Jesus Teaches in Jerusalem: 11:1—13:37

G. Jesus Dies and Is Raised in Jerusalem: 14:1—16:20

Authorship and Date: The earliest explicit evidence that "Mark" wrote this Gospel is a reference to the remarks of Papias of Hierapolis (early second century) quoted by Eusebius (*Ecclesiastical History* 3.39, 15). The widespread affirmation that Mark wrote this Gospel is probably behind the title of the Gospel "According to Mark," which did not originate with the narrative. Scholars do not agree as to the exact historical identity of Mark (Acts 12:12, 25; 15:37, 39; Col 4:10; 2 Tm 4:11; Phlm 24; 1 Pt 5:13). Thus although the indirect evidence and traditional attestation point to Mark as the author of this Gospel, we are not yet certain of exactly who this person was. Tradition identifies this Mark as "Peter's interpreter," and situates this Gospel in Rome after Peter's death, c. A.D. 64-67.

For further reading: Paul J. Achtemeier, "Mark, Gospel of," *Anchor Bible Dictionary*, 4:541-557; Daniel J. Harrington, S.J., "The Gospel According to Mark," *New Jerome Biblical Commentary*, 596-629.

Marks of the Church • Characteristics or qualities of the Church which identify her as the true Church, belonging entirely to Christ, and serving as His instrument of salvation in the world. There are four marks, or signs, of the Church: She is "one, holy, catholic, and apostolic." The First Council of Constantinople (A.D. 381) used this phrase in formalizing the Nicene Creed. These four marks authenticate the Church. In brief, they may be understood as follows:

The Church is "one" — members are united in faith. They believe the same things, receive the same sacraments. They are united under the Pope.

The Church is "holy" — the Church is God-centered. Her teachings and worship are all of Christ and animated by the Holy Spirit. Members are called to live holy, sacramental lives, close to the Father.

The Church is "catholic" — the Church is for all peoples of every time and place. The word "catholic" means "universal," hence, the Church teaches to all people the entire doctrine of Jesus Christ.

The Church is "apostolic" — the Church presents the true, unchangeable doctrine of Jesus, as taught in the apostolic era and handed down through the Apostles' successors, the bishops. Bishops' authority is the same as that of the Apostles, to whom they trace their office of leadership.

While the Catholic Church alone enjoys the marks of the true Church, the teachings of the Second Vatican Council call Catholics to respond with respect and affection to those who belong to other Christian communities, who possess some or all of these marks in varying degrees.

For further reading: *Catechism of the Catholic Church*, nn. 811-870.

Maronites • The Maronite Church, an Eastern Catholic Church in communion with Rome, has a history reaching back to the fifth century. The monks of the monastery of St. Maron, from which the Church takes her name, were fierce opponents of the Monophysite heresy who learned to be independent during the violent theological struggle. At one point, the Monophysites killed three hundred fifty monks loyal to the teachings of the Council of Chalcedon. Correspondence of the time between St. Maron and Pope Hormisdas reveals that Rome recognized a degree of autonomy among the Maronites even then.

In the seventh century, during the conflict with the Arabs, the patriarchs of Antioch moved to Constantinople and were appointed by the emperor, thus leaving the Chalcedonians in Syria without a patriarch. In response, the monks of St. Maron and other local bishops elected the first Maronite patriarch in 685.

By the mid-eighth century, most Maronites had moved to Lebanon and established a tightly-knit Christian society presided over even in temporal affairs by the patriarch. The Crusades brought the Maronites into direct contact with the West, and in 1215 the Maronite patriarch participated in the Fourth Lateran Council and later received the pallium from Pope Innocent III.

From that time on, ties have been very strong between the Maronites and Rome, leading to a degree of Latinization of this Oriental Church. The use of Syriac, however, has been retained in the Maronite Liturgy.

Because of constant political turmoil and intermittent war with Muslims, many Maronites have left Lebanon. The Maronite patriarch still resides in Beirut but has jurisdiction over dioceses in Lebanon, Syria, Egypt, Australia, Brazil and the United States.

Marriage Encounter • A movement that began with Father Gabriel Calvo and twenty-eight Spanish Christian Family Movement couples in Barcelona, Spain, in 1958. It aims to deepen the husband and wife's relationship in order to realize their Christian potentiality. The Marriage Encounter Weekend offers conferences, private counseling, prayer, private reflection and interpersonal dialogue. The Mass is an important part of the program.

The first English-speaking Marriage Encounter took place in Miami, Florida, in January of 1968. Eventually, it spread to many areas of the United States and continues to grow and develop. Various programs have evolved from this movement, such as Encounters for divorced and widowed persons, engaged couples, Confraternity of Christian Doctrine programs and family weekend programs.

Marriage, Sacrament of • The institution of marriage was officially recognized as one of the sacraments of the Church at the Fourth Lateran Council in 1215. Prior to this time, it had always been considered a religious reality distinctly different from non-Christian forms of marriage. St. Paul referred to marriage as a *mysterion* or great mystery. Marriage was referred to by some of the early Christian writers, especially St. Augustine, as a sacrament, but the term had various meanings, all related to St. Paul's reference. Theologically, it is considered a sacrament because it images the union of Christ and His Church.

Unlike the other sacraments, marriage itself was not instituted by Christ. Since it predated Christianity, the Church teaches that Christ raised or elevated marriage to the dignity of a sacrament. This is so because He recognized something fundamentally good in the marital institution. This good is grounded in the complementary relationship of the man and the woman. In the creation account of the Book of Genesis, the male is created first but is incomplete. Man, in the generic sense, is completed with the creation of the female. The scriptural account states that the male could not find another creature that was fit to be his partner. This account goes on to state that the man and woman become one flesh. The "one flesh" union is a covenantal formula that refers not to the physical joining of the spouses but to the total human joining that comes about in marriage. This total relationship entails the giving of one spouse to the other for the purpose of aiding in the well-being of each other. This highest form of gift requires that the spouses be totally faithful to each other, a fidelity that is grounded in a special kind of love, referred to by St. Augustine as conjugal charity.

Marriage as an institution of nature is considered by Christian theology to be essentially good because it was founded by the Creator at the beginning of human history. It was subjected to the vicissitudes of history and experienced variations, some of which were contrary to God's plan (infidelity, concubinage, polygamy, among others).

As a sacrament, it is a means of encountering Christ in a special way and of bringing about the salvation of the spouses. The theology of Vatican II and the revised Code refer to marriage as a vocation (Canon 226.1), through which married persons work for the building up of the Body of Christ in a special way.

Marriage as a commitment or act is acknowledged in both civil society and law and Church society and law. This is primarily because of the role it plays in the welfare of Church and society. For this reason, both secular and religious institutions have enacted laws for the regulation of marriage. These laws treat of requirements for marriage as well as standards for the way spouses relate to and treat each other.

Closely related to the effect of marriage on the community is its fundamental purpose. For the sacrament, the purpose is twofold: marriage by its nature is ordered to the good of the spouses and the procreation and education of children (Canon 1055). Parents are instrumental not just in the physical procreation of children but are directly responsible for their natural and Christian nurture. This includes not simply their physical and material well-being but their training as Christians. The essential source of this training is the participation of the children in the total love relationship of the husband and wife for each other. By example, they learn the meaning of Christian charity and love of God.

The sacrament of Matrimony is also marked by certain unique attributes. These are total and perpetual fidelity and indissolubility. Once the marital covenant is entered into, the spouses are obliged to remain totally faithful to each other for life. Furthermore, after the consent has been consummated by sexual intercourse, it cannot be dissolved by any power on earth.

Marriage itself comes into being when the spouses express their consent to one another. This consent is no longer referred to exclusively as a contract but also as a covenant, since it is a reflection of the relationship of Christ to the Church, which is itself covenantal. By "covenant" is meant a relationship that recognizes the spiritual equality of the spouses and their capacity to enter into an agreement which demands a gift of the whole person, one to another. Once this covenant begins, the spouses are joined by the unique bond of marriage. If both are baptized, by the very fact that consent is expressed, the sacrament of Marriage is received. The ministers of the sacrament in the Latin Rite are the spouses themselves and not the official witnesses to the marriage. In the Eastern Rite, the blessing of the priest is also needed for validity. Sacramentality is not something added over and above the state of marriage. Rather, it is grounded in the very Baptism of the parties, by which they are deputed to be followers of Christ. It gives the opportunity of transforming their lives and directing them toward the Redeemer. The sacramentality of marriage is a result of Christ's action toward persons and not a response of the individual couple to Christ. Sacramentality does not objectively depend on the will of the spouses to receive the sacrament, for marriage itself is ordered to the perfection of charity.

In spite of these theological formulations, the sad fact remains that for countless people the sacramental reception of Baptism and Matrimony exist as mere ceremonies. Christ may reach out to people, but people are free to accept or reject Him. The Church has long presumed that those who marry do so as the Church wishes, with at least a fundamental acceptance of their Christian responsibilities.

Yet sociological facts indicate that this presumption is not as strong or well-founded in our contemporary society. We know that many Catholics, though baptized, do not lead the Christian life even on a minimal level. We also know that many who are married in a Catholic or otherwise Christian ceremony go through the ceremony with little if any commitment to the obligations of Christian marriage. The Church acknowledges the fact that many

men and women, products of a secular and materialistic society, enter marriage not believing in its sacramentality. In spite of this lack of faith, the Church teaches that these marriages are sacraments and not mere natural marriages.

Marriage is both a legal fact and a theological reality. The question of faith and its relationship to marriage is situated in the juridical as well as the theological order. If two free and capable, baptized Catholics exchange marital consent according to canonical form, the law presumes that the consent is valid and that a sacrament has come into existence. The law does not say that the spouses must have faith, yet the theological sources, including Vatican II, state clearly that the sacraments presuppose and require faith. Is there a contradiction between the two orders, juridical and theological?

The law speaks from a *presumption* that there is minimal faith. Theology states a *fact*: for a fruitful sacrament, faith must be present. A valid sacrament means that certain social and legal consequences follow upon its reception. If it is invalid, it does not exist, in spite of the sacramental ritual. A fruitful sacrament is one in which, in addition to validity, there exists the possibility of fulfilling the aims of the sacrament.

For the valid reception of the sacrament of Holy Matrimony, it is first necessary that both spouses be free of impediments. If an impediment exists, it must either be removed, if possible, or dispensed. Not all impediments can be dispensed. (Cf. Impediment.)

The spouses must also have the physical capacity for marriage, that is, the ability to complete the procreative sexual act. This is so because marriage is ordered to the procreation and education of children and because the sexual act, as a profound manifestation of conjugal love, is also essential to the total marriage relationship.

The mental capacity for marriage means that the spouses know what they are doing when they marry. They must also have the psychological capacity for fulfilling the fundamental marital obligations and the moral capacity for living out the demands of marriage as these are formulated by the Church.

It is also necessary that the spouses express consent in total freedom and this consent not have defects due to simulation. That is, the spouses must will to do what the consent implies and what the Church expects of them.

Finally, for Catholics it is required that consent be expressed according to canonical form, that is, before a sacred minister and two witnesses.

The theology of sacramental marriage has had a long and varied development throughout Christian history. Basically, it is grounded in the Old Testament account of creation, found in the Book of Genesis. The primary texts of the New Testament are found in the Gospels and in the epistles of St. Paul. Although several of the earliest Christian writers spoke of marriage, it was St. Augustine who provided the first systematic treatment of it as a Christian institution. After the Church acquired juridical or legal competence of a civil nature over marriage in the Middle Ages, the theological development shifted and became more juridical or canonical in nature, concentrating on the legal structure of marriage rather than the theological reality.

The renewal of the theological study of marriage came with the Second Vatican Council and is summarized in the statement on marriage found in *Gaudium et Spes* (Pastoral Constitution on the Church in the Modern World), nn. 47-52. Since that time, more attention has been given to the inner theological reality of marriage, the relationship of the faith of the spouses to the sacrament, and marriage as a vocation in the Church, among other things.

The 1980 Synod of Bishops was devoted to the study of marriage and the family in the contemporary world. Out of it came one of the most important sources for the theological meaning of the sacrament of Matrimony, namely the Papal Exhortation *Familiaris Consortio* (*On the Family*).

Martyr • Derived from the Greek word *martyria*, or witness (and originally used in reference to the giving of testimony in a legal or courtroom setting), in Christian usage the word martyr refers to one who gives a testimony or witness to his faith. This witness is not merely a verbal narration of one's beliefs, or even of events seen and experienced by the witness. Rather, it is the witness of an individual who willingly testified to his faith even in the face of suffering or death.

During the Apostolic and post-Apostolic Ages, the term "martyr" was reserved for one who actually died for his Faith. The deacon Stephen is considered the first martyr of the Church, having died for his confession of faith in Christ, at the hands of a Jewish mob presided over by Saul. Traditionally the Church has believed the Apostles were martyrs, witnessing by their deaths to the truth of Christ and the Church. The First Letter of Clement speaks of the testimony or witness of Sts. Peter and Paul in Rome as signs of their faith in Christ (I Clem. 5:4-7). Martyrdom is here a sign of one's faith in Christ.

Ignatius of Antioch, in his letters to the Ephesians, Romans and Smyrnaeans, written while he himself was being led to martyrdom in Rome in the early second century, wrote of his desire for martyrdom arising from his desire to resemble and imitate Christ most perfectly. Martyrdom is the most perfect imitation of Christ.

The *Passion of Perpetua and Felicity* relates the martyrdom in Carthage of Vibia Perpetua, a young, wealthy Catholic, and of her slave, Felicitas, in March, A.D. 202. The major portion of the work is composed of Perpetua's own diary, which relates the events up to the point of her own death. Martyrdom here is mentioned as a second Baptism for the witness martyred (18, 3; 21, 2. Cf. also Tertullian, "On Penance," 13).

The martyr, therefore, is one who dies in order to witness to the truth of Christ. It is not enough for an individual simply to be put to death in order to be considered a martyr. As St. Augustine wrote, "It is not the suffering, but the reason why [he suffers], that constitutes a martyr" (Epistle 89.2).

Throughout the history of the Church, thousands of the faithful have given up their lives to witness to Christ. Since opposition to Christ and His Church is a constant reality in the world, martyrdom is not simply a phenomenon isolated to the earliest centuries of the Church's history. The Second Vatican Council spoke of modern martyrs in *Lumen Gentium*, echoing the concepts of martyrdom of the early Church: "Martyrdom makes the disciple like his master, Who willingly accepted death for the salvation of the world, and through it he is conformed to Him by the shedding of blood. Therefore the Church considers it the highest gift and supreme test of love. And while it is given to few, all however must be prepared to confess Christ before men and to follow Him along the way of the cross amidst the persecutions which the Church never lacks" (LG 42).

St. Thomas More,
English martyr

Martyrology • To be distinguished from the accounts of the suffering and martyrdom of individual saints, this is a collection which lists all known Christian martyrs. The first examples are actually calendars, onto which saints' names are inscribed. Important martyrologies of local churches include those for Rome (fourth century) and Carthage (sixth century). The first martyrology proper is the so-called Hieronymian Martyrology of the mid-fifth century, named after St. Jerome, whose work it was purported to be. A new type of martyrology developed from the ninth century which added short descriptions of the life of each martyr, as well as names from Scripture, the writings of the Fathers and Church history, to fill out dates on which few martyrs had died. The compendium called the Roman Martyrology of the sixteenth century is derived from one such ninth-century example, that ascribed to Usuard. In some monasteries the martyrology was read at Prime (the first of the minor hours, suppressed at the reform of the Liturgy of the Hours after Vatican II); hence it is considered a liturgical book. In other monasteries and in many religious houses, it was read either before or after the main meal taken in common, a custom which survives in some places today.

Marxism • The movement which resulted from the writings of the philosopher and economist Karl Marx. As in all other social, political and economic movements, there are various factions within Marxism, right-wing, centrist and left-wing groups. Marxism arose in reaction to the philosophy of Feuerbach and Hegel, transforming many of their doctrines. Many Marxist philosophical, political and economic assertions have been discarded today as either obsolete or simply wrong.

Marxists generally rely on Marx's materialist analysis of reality and on his rejection of religion, but there is great divergence of opinion on his social, political and economic analyses. The gravest difficulty with Marxist philosophy is his anthropology and his predictions concerning the future of capitalism. Marx reduces the human person to an economic animal, which simply does not square with contemporary religious, psychological, sociological, political and scientific understandings of the human person.

While Marx's initial analyses of the person spurred great interest and research, contemporary findings cannot affirm his primitive claims. The most serious failure of the Marxist scheme has been the fact that proletarian revolutions did not occur in modern capitalist states, but in more backward feudal societies such as early-twentieth-century Russia and middle-twentieth-century China. No widespread revolutions occurred in capitalist countries, and the capitalist countries were able to adapt with much greater flexibility to changing conditions than Marx had predicted. Rather than disintegrating as a result of class struggle, capitalism was not only able to integrate the proletariat into its system of production better than imagined, but it has also shown itself far more capable of mobilizing economic resources than has Marxism.

Mary, Feasts of • The oldest Marian feasts are commonly agreed to be of Byzantine origin and to exemplify how the Church's reflection on the implications of

Ruins of the first church dedicated to Mary, in Ephesus, fifth century

Christological controversies influenced devotion to Mary. These celebrations and their dates include the feast of the Presentation of Our Lord on February 2 (sometimes termed the "Purification of Mary," as evidenced in the Roman Calendar after Trent; the original title has been restored in the present reform), the solemnity of the Annunciation of the Lord on March 25, the solemnity of the Assumption on August 15 and the feast of the Birth of Mary on September 8. These feasts passed into use in the Roman Liturgy through the Gelasian Sacramentary (seventh to eighth century). The oldest Marian feast native to Rome is the solemnity of Mary, Mother of God, celebrated on January 1. The commemoration of the Immaculate Conception on December 8 dates from the seventh century in the East (although the dogma was not defined until 1854). The commemoration of the Visitation seems to be dated in the late thirteenth century; it is observed on May 31.

Other Marian feasts of later development (largely as a result of popular devotion and the influence of local church practice) include the memorials of the Queenship of Mary on August 22, Our Lady of Sorrows on

September 15, Our Lady of the Rosary on October 7 and the optional memorials of Our Lady of Lourdes on February 11, Immaculate Heart of Mary on the Saturday after the Second Sunday after Pentecost, Our Lady of Mt. Carmel on July 16, the Dedication of the Basilica in Honor of St. Mary Major on August 5, the memorial of the Presentation of Mary on November 21 and the feast of Our Lady of Guadalupe on December 12. Many other feasts in honor of Mary were celebrated in the previous calendar, among them the Betrothal of Mary on January 23, Our Lady, Queen of Apostles on the Saturday after the Ascension, Our Lady, Mother of Grace on June 9, Our Lady of Perpetual Succor on June 27, the Humility of Our Lady on July 17, Our Lady, Mother of Mercy on the Saturday before the fourth Sunday of July, Our Lady, Refuge of Sinners on August 13, Our Lady, Health of the Sick on the Saturday before the last Sunday in August, Our Lady, Mother of the Divine Shepherd on September 3, Our Lady of Ransom on September 24, The Motherhood of Our Lady on October 11, the Purity of Our Lady on October 16, Our Lady, Mother of Divine Providence on the Saturday before the third Sunday in November, Our Lady of the Sacred Medal on November 27, the Holy House of Loreto on December 10 and Our Lady's Expectation on December 18.

Mary, Saturday Office of • Dated from the Middle Ages, this set of texts in the Divine Office paralleled the use of the Mass proper in honor of the Virgin Mary on Saturday, when no other obligatory commemoration was observed. In the Roman Breviary in use until the present reform, this Office combined special texts in honor of Mary with the current Psalter and daily readings. Additions to commemorate the Virgin Mary included the invitatory, twelve non-scriptural readings at Matins, one for each calendar month, and three sets of *Benedictus* antiphons and collects at Lauds, reflective of different liturgical seasons. In the present reform of the Liturgy of the Hours, this option is entitled the "Memorial of the Blessed Virgin on Saturday," containing two options for the invitatory, four non-scriptural texts for the Office of Readings, three Scripture readings and responsories at Morning Prayer, six *Benedictus* antiphons, two sets of sample intercessions and six options for the final prayer.

Mary, Virgin Mother of God: See **Deipara**

Maryknoll: See **Catholic Foreign Mission Society of America**

Marymas • Technically, this term refers to any feast of Mary, with the suffix *mas* derived from the Latin *missus* or the Anglo-Saxon *maessa* (from the verb *mittere* "to send"). Usually Marymas refers to the feast of the Annunciation of Our Lord on March 25, which date in liturgical history is obviously directly related to December 25, the celebration of the birth of Christ or Christmas. Hence, there is a terminological relationship between the two feasts in the use of "mas."

Masonry: See **Freemasonry**

Mass of the Catechumens • The first part of the Mass was known by this name until our own era, when Pope Paul VI revised the rites used in the Western Church. This began at the entrance antiphon or Introit and ended with the sermon, after which the dismissal of the catechumens (those adults preparing for Baptism), the *missa catechumenorum*, took place since the rest of the Eucharistic Sacrifice was jealously guarded by and for those who already belonged fully to the Body of Christ. As a result, just as the entire Eucharistic Liturgy curiously came to be known by the words used for the dismissal of the baptized, *Missa est* — "the assembly is dismissed" — so the first half of the Mass, now referred to as the Liturgy of the Word, became known by the words of dismissal of the catechumens. Eventually, the second half (the Liturgy of the Eucharist) became known as the *missa sacramentorum*, the Mass of the Mysteries (or Sacraments). These terms were already in use by the time of St. Augustine, who mentioned them in some of his sermons.

Master of Ceremonies • An altar server, usually a cleric, who supervises, directs and coordinates a religious ceremony and sees to it that it is properly celebrated. He especially guides the actions of the celebrant and his assistants according to the rubrics of the Sacred Liturgy. His proper attire is a cassock and surplice.

Master of Novices • A religious institute's canonical novitiate (usually lasting one or two years) is placed in the charge of a director or master of novices, who is a finally professed member of the community, appointed for this purpose and not impeded by other duties. The master/mistress of novices (and his or her assistant) must test and discern the authenticity of the vocations of those in one's charge, and cultivate in them the form of life characteristic of the religious institute.

Master of the Sacred Palace • The Pope's theologian and canonist. Legend has it that St. Dominic was the first to hold the office, and by immemorial custom it is still held by a Dominican priest. Formerly, he allowed or forbade the printing of all religious books. Presently, he has advisory functions in theological matters for the Pope, Secretariat of State and the rest of the Roman Curia. He resides in Vatican City.

Master of the Sentences • Peter Lombard (c. 1100-1160) was so named because of his most famous work, *Sententiarum libri quattuor*, called simply the "Sentences." This work was the standard textbook during the Middle Ages (superseded in the sixteenth century by Thomas Aquinas's *Summa Theologiae*) and the object of a vast commentatorial literature.

Mater et Magistra • The title of an encyclical issued by Pope John XXIII in 1963, meaning *Mother and Teacher*, which dealt with issues of human rights, political and economic development, and issues of justice and peace. It asserted that the individual is the basis of all social relationships and that social institutions must serve the legitimate needs and rights of the individual. The social teachings of the Church were based on the dignity of the human person, a dignity which derived from our relationship to God.

Materialism • The philosophical doctrine that only physical matter which can be touched, seen, felt and quantified exists in the cosmos.

Materialism first arose among the "older Epicureans" who attempted to account for the creation of the universe without invoking our doctrine of divine creation. There are various types of materialists, ranging from total to partial materialists. Materialism has gained its greatest impetus from science, which has achieved great successes in explaining events in the natural world by means of materialist concepts.

Infantile materialism has been rejected in large part, and today's materialism is highly technical and competent. Mechanistic explanations of the universe were in vogue in the eighteenth and nineteenth centuries, especially among the bourgeoisie and middle class, but this thoroughgoing materialism has fallen out of favor because of contemporary scientific developments.

Confidence that the entire cosmos could be explained by mechanistic principles has been shaken by the developments of acoustics, optics and thermodynamics, among other fields, because these have made it clear that other physical realities exist alongside matter. Gravitational and magnetic fields which are essentially different from matter have been discovered, and investigation of the atom and nuclear fields also challenge total materialism. Laws of physics once judged to be universal have now been rejected as incapable of providing explanations of the universe at the cosmic and atomic levels. And today, more than thirty elementary particles are known in the atomic nucleus, appearing and disappearing with great rapidity, changing into other particles. This suggests that matter might be best explained as a form of universal matter which is essentially energy, manifesting itself in different modalities.

Matins • From the Latin *tempora matutina*, "morning hours." Originally applied to the morning hour of Lauds (*laudes matutinae*), the term was later transferred to the preceding hour of Vigils, so called because in early Christian practice this office was properly sung around midnight. The practice of keeping vigil during the night in the early Church is mentioned in the Acts of the Apostles and is attested to by writers such as Tertullian (died after A.D. 220) and Hippolytus (215). These vigils became part of monastic practice and evolved into the hour of the Divine Office known as Matins. The main content of Matins consists of Psalm 95 (94) (the "invitatory," or invitation to prayer), a hymn, psalms, readings from Scripture, commentaries on Scripture (or, on feast days, a reading appropriate for the day),

responsories and a canticle on solemn feasts.

Matrimonial Court • A common name for a diocesan tribunal, so called because the great majority of cases heard in a diocesan tribunal are matrimonial in nature. Its most frequent function is to investigate and determine the validity of the marriage bond. A more accurate term for an annulment decision (which says that a marriage was invalid from its very beginning and therefore never really existed) is a decree of nullity. It is the task of this tribunal to investigate whether there has been a proven impediment to a valid marriage (Canons 1083-1094); an invalidating defect in the consent of either or both parties (Canon 1105); the fulfillment of the essential requirements for the external manifestation of matrimonial consent (Canon 108 and following Canons). The tribunal may also be employed in the processes of dissolution of a marriage that was not sacramental or not consummated (Canons 1141-1150). (Cf. Annulment.)

Matrimony: See **Marriage, Sacrament of**

Matthew, The Gospel of •
Unquestionably one of the Twelve Apostles, as St. Matthew's name occurs in all four lists of the New Testament. Prior to his calling, he had been a tax collector named Levi (cf. Mt 9:9-13 with Lk 5:27-32).

It is the unanimous tradition of Christian antiquity that he was the author of the first of the four Gospels. In the latter half of the twentieth century, this ascription has been challenged by a solid phalanx of Catholic commentators. The problem is compounded by the fact, admitted by conservative commentators as well, that we do not have a single fragment of the Aramaic original writing which antiquity ascribed to him. The trend of contemporary opinion is that the

Gospel "of St. Matthew" was written after and dependent upon the Gospel of St. Mark.

Certainly no one who is aware of the evidence could convincingly maintain that modern scholars have in hand a literal Greek translation of St. Matthew's original Aramaic work. Clearly, its Old Testament citations are from the Septuagint. Even the most skillful scholars find great difficulty in trying to retranslate this Greek into Aramaic. The parallel narratives in St. Mark are much more vivid and lifelike. At best, an informed conservative scholar would have to admit that the "translator" of Matthew has permitted himself considerable freedom.

On the other hand, contemporary exegetical fashions seem to treat too lightly the massive fact of the unanimous testimony of all those who were closer to the event itself. No one ascribes the book to anyone but St. Matthew. We have no reason to believe that their intelligence was less than ours; we know their access to written and oral sources was much greater than ours. Moreover, one must not ignore the forest while scrutinizing the trees: the strong Semitic flavor of the first Gospel is inescapable. It is clearly an apologetic work directed to the Jews, aimed at showing them that the teaching of Jesus is a genuine reform of their own venerable and beloved religion. It is incredible to think that it was first written after the collapse of Palestinian Judaism and yet fails to play the trump card of such an apologetic, the fall of Jerusalem in A.D. 70. The suggestion that it was written

St. Matthew (painting, circa 1285)

in Antioch, the home of Christianity's liberation from the law, seems rather baseless.

It is in Matthew's Gospel that Jesus says "every scribe who has been trained for the kingdom of heaven is like a householder who brings out of his treasure what is new and what is old" (Mt 13:52). This saying sets the tone of Matthew's Gospel, for we there find Jesus portrayed as the true teacher of the New Righteousness, the definitive teacher of God's Law, Who teaches with authority because of His own unique divine Sonship. Matthew presents five extensive sermons on Jesus:

1. The Sermon on the Mount (5-7)
2. The Missionary Sermon (10)
3. The Sermon in Parables (13)
4. The Community Sermon (18)
5. The Eschatalogical Sermon (23-25)

The basic outline of Matthew's Gospel, of which these five sermons are an integral part, include the following:

A. 1:1—4:16: The Origins: Jesus as the definitive revelation of God
B. 4:17—13:58: Jesus' ministry to Israel
C. 14:1—20:34: Jesus' ministry to His own disciples
D. 21:1—25:46: Jesus in Jerusalem
E. 26:1—28:20: The passion, death, resurrection and Great Commission

Matthew's perspective is predominantly Jewish Christian, but this Gospel is very much open to the Gentile mission. After all, it is in Matthew's Gospel that we find the Great Commission, in which the risen Jesus commands the eleven remaining Apostles to make disciples of all nations (Mt 28:16-20).

Matthew's Gospel places great emphasis on the mission of the Church and on the special role of Peter within the Church. It is in Matthew's Gospel that Jesus responds to Peter's confession of faith by saying, "I tell you, you are Peter, and on this rock I will build my church, and the powers of death shall not prevail against it. I will give you the keys of the kingdom of heaven, and whatever you bind on earth shall be bound in heaven, and whatever you loose on earth shall be loosed in heaven" (Mt 16:18-19).

For further reading: Daniel J. Harrington, S.J., *The Gospel of Matthew*, Sacra Pagina 1 (Liturgical Press, 1991); John P. Meier, "Matthew, Gospel of," *Anchor Bible Dictionary*, 4:622-641; Benedict T. Viviano, O.P., "The Gospel According to Matthew," *New Jerome Biblical Commentary*, 630-674.

Matthias, St. • The disciple chosen to take the place of Judas Iscariot among the Twelve after Judas's defection. From Acts 1:15-26, it may be inferred that Matthias had been a disciple of Jesus from the start of His public ministry. The name "Matthias" is a shortened form of *Mattathias* (*Mattathiah*), Hebrew for "gift of Yahweh."

For further reading: Thomas W. Martin, "Matthias," *Anchor Bible Dictionary*, 4:644.

Maundy Thursday • The term *mandatum* (whence "Maundy") means "commandment," taken from the first words at the ceremony of the washing of the feet, "A new commandment I give to you" (Jn 13:34), as well as from the commandment of Christ that we should imitate His loving humility in the washing of the feet of His Apostles (Jn 13:4-17). Therefore, the term *mandatum* has been applied to the rite of foot-washing on Thursday of Holy Week. (Cf. Holy Week, Liturgy of.)

Maurists • Those members of the French Congregation of Benedictines (O.S.B.), founded by St. Maur in 1618 but dissolved as a consequence of the anticlericalism of the French Revolution. Maurists are especially associated with hagiography by reason of their research in the lives of the saints. Their work survives the demise of their order in the continued publication of the *Acta Sanctorum*. From their ranks came Montfaucon and Mabillon, the founders of Greek and Latin paleography.

Means of Social Communication, Decree on the: See **Inter Mirifica**

Medals, Religious • Depictions of Christ, Our Lady or the saints in metal, wood or plastic — normally the size of a coin and worn around the neck. Medals are usually blessed and are thus sacramentals. They are intended to excite devotion and prayer, and in general to signify the Christian's commitment to a holy life or his commendation to the particular protection of the subject depicted. Their use in the Church is very ancient.

Mediator • The theological meaning of "mediator" is derived from its ordinary meaning: one who acts or speaks on behalf of others. Christ is the One Who exercises this role *par excellence*. "For there is one God, and there is one mediator between God and men, the man Christ Jesus" (1 Tm 2:5). Christ's mediatorship is based chiefly in the fact that He achieved our reconciliation with God through reparation for our sins. Through Him, we have a share in the divine life and are thus empowered to share in the work of our salvation.

Mediator Dei • A landmark encyclical letter issued by Pope Pius XII on November 30, 1947, it summarized the liturgical evolution in the Church from the Council of

Trent up to that point, while simultaneously initiating a discussion of a framework for future liturgical reforms. Its major provisions include: the primacy of interior worship; the centrality of the Eucharist in the Christian religion; the promotion of the Real Presence as an integral part of liturgical life; and the importance of the Divine Office in daily life. The document's survey of the Sacred Liturgy foreshadowed reforms to come later in the Second Vatican Council.

Mediatrix of All Graces • According to Vatican II, "the Blessed Virgin Mary is invoked by the Church under the titles of Advocate, Auxiliatrix, Adjutrix, and Mediatrix" because "by her maternal charity, Mary cares for the brethren of her Son who still journey on earth surrounded by dangers and difficulties." The Council insists that "this [title] . . . is so understood that it neither takes away anything from nor adds anything to the dignity and efficacy of Christ the one Mediator" (LG 62). Mary's role of mediatrix thus depends on Christ's mediatorship, to which she joins her own merits and love.

Meditation • A combined form of prayer and discursive reflection in which the person thinks about God by means of various images.

Meditation has as its aim the reflection on God, the economy of salvation, our call to discipleship and growth in intimacy with Christ. It aims at elevating the spirit of the person to God and, in so doing, advancing Christian holiness. Meditative prayer is prayer which links the human mind, heart and soul and is one of the fullest and most complete expressions of the inward person. Meditation is speaking to God, which implies that He answers, and it is speaking to God in a unity of mind, heart and soul. Meditation is essentially a response of the person to the grace given by God, a grace that calls forth our full and complete response of self-giving and self-offering. In meditation, the person's spirit encounters God and is an acceptance of God's response to ourselves, offered through Scripture and Tradition as understood in fidelity to the Magisterium of the Church. The highest, most mystical form of meditation is called contemplation. (Cf. Mysticism.)

Meekness • A virtue related to temperance, controlling anger and keeping one from losing one's temper on account of insignificant or trivial matters. It is the virtue which enables one to accept and tolerate the ordinary adversities of life with equanimity, balance and good humor.

Megalynarion • In the Byzantine Rite, the troparion of the Ninth Ode of the Canon of certain feasts. The Ninth Ode always corresponds to the Magnificat (in Greek, *Megalynei*). (Cf. Canon.)

Meletian Schism • Essentially a power struggle for control of the influential Church of Alexandria in the late fourth century, the Meletian Schism was unlike most other schisms of this type, in that its course involved so many notable personages of the day. Beginning about A.D. 360, one Meletius, former bishop of Sebaste, determined to take over the already-troubled see of Alexandria. The very complex machinations and polemics which followed (including the embrace of Nicaea by the Arian Meletius) involved such ecclesiastical giants as Sts. Basil, Jerome, Ambrose, John Chrysostom and Athanasius, to name a few. Eventually, Meletius was censured and exiled (although yet a third claimant to the see, Paulinus, was by then on the scene) and a reform-minded Meletian candidate, Flavian, was set up in the see. Meletius himself died reconciled in 381, and after extensive negotiations, Pope Siricius formally recognized Flavian as bishop in 398. The remaining schismatics lingered on until about 420.

Melkite (also Melchite) Rite • The division within the Eastern Church whose members descended from those who adhered to the Council of Chalcedon (A.D. 451), which condemned Monophysitism, the heresy that asserted that there was only one nature in Christ. The Melkites were united to the patriarch of Constantinople, who was involved in the Great Schism of the ninth to the eleventh centuries. However, the Melkites were reunited with Rome in the eighteenth century. The Melkite Liturgy is in Arabic, while the readings are in Greek. Arabic-speaking Catholics of Egypt, Palestine and Syria with the patriarchates of Alexandria, Antioch and Jerusalem comprise the Melkite Rite, which has some clergy in the United States.

Membership in the Church • A person becomes a member of the Catholic Church first and foremost through Baptism in the Church or by the Profession of Faith and reception into the Church if already baptized into another Christian denomination (cf. LG 14ff. and Canon 205).

Membership in the Church also means full communion with her. Those in full communion are joined to the Church by the specific bonds of faith in the Church, the sacraments and ecclesiastical governance.

Although a baptized Catholic always remains a member of the Church in some sense, it is possible for a Catholic not to be in full communion with the Church and therefore not subject to some of her laws and incapable of exercising some of the rights of Catholics.

Persons who embrace other religious denominations are no longer in full communion with the Church, nor are those who have left the Church by some public or notorious act. It is seriously questionable whether persons who refuse to accept ecclesiastical governance on a habitual basis and in serious matters are in full communion (Canons 204-205, 849).

Memento • Literally, "Remember. . . ," referring to the opening word of two sections of the Roman Canon (Eucharistic Prayer I), the first (before the consecration) for the living ("*Memento, Domine* . . . Remember, O Lord") and the second (following the consecration) for the faithful departed ("*Memento etiam, Domine* . . . Remember, also, O Lord"). From this derives the custom of using the word by itself and out of context to describe any "intention" or remembrance in prayer. It should be noted that the Roman Canon also contained remembrances for Church officials and for the worshiping assembly. Likewise the three additional Eucharistic prayers promulgated for the Roman Rite in 1970 contain "mementos" for the living and dead, the Church and the world. In addition to remembrances during the Eucharistic prayer, the Vatican II Rite prescribes extensive intercessory prayer in the restored Prayer of the Faithful or, as it is more precisely known, the General Intercessions.

Memorare • Literally, "Remember. . . ." Now the title, derived from the opening word, of a very popular prayer to the Blessed Virgin Mary, attributed to St. Bernard of Clairvaux (1090-1153) and made popular from the early seventeenth century on by a French priest, Claude Bernard. The complete prayer:

"Remember, O most gracious Virgin Mary, that never was it known
that anyone who fled to thy protection,
implored thy help
or sought thy intercession,
was left unaided.
Inspired by this confidence,

I fly unto thee, O Virgin of virgins, my
    Mother.
To thee do I come,
before thee I stand, sinful and sorrowful.
O Mother of the Word Incarnate,
despise not my petitions (in my necessity)
but in thy mercy (clemency) hear and
    answer me. Amen."

Memoria • Latin for memory, memorial or
remembrance, this refers to the lowest type
of feast formerly found in the liturgical
Calendar of the Church. In the present
Calendar there are found two different types
of memorial: the obligatory memorial which
must be celebrated, and the optional
memorial which may be celebrated
according to the priest's own choice, moved
perhaps by its practical value to the
assisting congregation or by its pastoral
value.

Memorial, Obligatory • Part of the
revision of the Liturgy after Vatican II
concerned the adjustment of the way the
seasons and feasts of the liturgical year were
ranked in importance. In order to simplify
the ordering of feasts of the Blessed Virgin
Mary, the martyrs and saints, the *General
Norms for the Liturgical Year and the
Calendar* (nn. 8-15) uses the terms
"obligatory memorial" and "optional
memorial." For "saints of universal
significance," whose feasts are required to
be celebrated, the term "obligatory
memorial" is used (nn. 8, 14). For the feasts
of saints who are revered by a "particular
Church, region, or religious family" (n. 9)
and are regarded as not having universal
significance, the term "optional memorial" is
used.

**Memorial, Optional: See Memorial,
Obligatory**

Menaion • The liturgical book of the
Byzantine Rite, containing the Propers of the
Saints and of the fixed feasts of the whole
year. From the Greek word meaning "month"
or the "monthly book."

Mendicant Orders • Term based on the
Latin *mendicare*, meaning "to beg," since
these groups of professed religious give up
the right to own any possession, therefore
depending completely upon God's
providence and the alms of the faithful. The
two charismatic leaders who promoted and
eventually founded orders incorporating this
ideal were Francesco Bernardone, St.
Francis of Assisi (1181-1216), the father of
the Franciscans, and Domingo Guzmán, St.
Dominic (1170-1221), the founder of the
Dominicans. Because this ideal of Gospel
simplicity and poverty arose at a time when
many in the Church, even her pastors, were
living in opulence, it had great appeal,
attracting thousands to the mendicant life,
and causing an internal reform in the life of
the Church.

Mene, Tekel, Upharsin • Three Aramaic
words inscribed on the plaster of the palace
wall during Belshazzar's feast (cf. Dn 5:25).
As found in the Hebrew text, the words run:
mene, mene, tekel, upharsin, but some judge
that the repetition of the first word, *mene*, is
a scribal lapse. The words, in fact, are
designations of three Babylonian measures:
a mina, a shekel and a half mina. In giving
his interpretation, Daniel makes a play on
words by taking the consonants of the three
words as those of three other word roots
which he then construes as: "He has been
measured," "You are weighed," and "[Your
kingdom] is divided." Daniel makes a further
play on the last word, *upharsin*, and renders
it "Persians."

Menology (also Menologion) • Especially
in the Eastern Church, a liturgical book

containing the lives of the saints arranged in the sequence of the ecclesiastical year. The Western counterparts of such menologies or "menologia" are the Martyrology and the Acta Sanctorum. In general usage, the term is also used to refer to nonliturgical personal collections of the lives of the saints.

Menorah • A Hebrew word for "candelabrum," used for the seven-branched candlestick which was one of the prominent appointments of the Jerusalem Temple. According to 1 Kings 7:49 and 2 Chronicles 4:7, Solomon furnished the Temple with ten such lamps made of gold. There is a Talmudic prohibition against making an exact replica of the menorah as used in the Temple. Though this prohibition has not always been strictly observed throughout Jewish history, it is generally heeded at present. The Hanukkah candelabrum with its eight branches is not in violation of the Talmud. The menorah has passed from being an item of Temple furniture to being a symbol of Jewish worship. It occurs frequently as a synagogue adornment in stained-glass windows, mosaics or wall painting.

For further reading: Efraim Gottlieb and Heinrich Strauss, "Menorah," *Encyclopedia Judaica*, 11:1355-1370.

Mensa • Term derived from the Latin *mensa* (table), to describe the flat stone which forms the top of the altar. Preconciliar legislation required that the mensa be constructed of a single piece of non-crumbling stone (Canon 1198). Present legislation reiterates this as proper custom but allows "even another material, worthy and solid" to be used, depending on the judgment of the conference of bishops (Canon 1236). The supports for the mensa may be of any material. The new canon also states that "a movable altar may be

constructed from any solid material appropriate for liturgical use."

Mental Reservation (or Mental Restriction) • The practice of giving one's words a meaning which does not disclose their full content in order to protect legitimately confidential, private or secret matters. Usually, the practice of mental reservation gives words a meaning different from what they ordinarily have; it is not simply lying or dissembling. In contrast to lying (strict mental reservation) the meaning of the words cannot be gleaned; but in loose mental reservation, an astute listener can ascertain the true meaning of the words. Mental reservation is morally permissible in those circumstances when it is the only means available to prevent others from learning what they have no right to know.

Mercy • In the Old Testament, mercy is predicated of God (Dt 7:9), and His attitude toward the repentant sinner is mercy rather than punishment. He calls upon all to show the same mercy to others that He shows to them. Mercy is an attitude which brings one to come to the aid of those in distress, and through the Incarnate Word, mercy is irrevocably present in the world (Heb 2:17). But the sinner should not presume that God will automatically or mechanically offer divine mercy, for it is only granted by God if the sinner assumes it to be incalculable and beyond measurement. Mercy does not override justice, but rather transcends it and converts the sinner into a just person by bringing about repentance and openness to the Holy Spirit.

Human mercy is an expression of divine mercy. Mercy sees the distress of others, identifies with it, and seeks to overcome it as one seeks to have one's own suffering, guilt and burdens overcome with the aid and assistance of others. Human mercy manifests divine mercy because of Christ's identification with our plight through His passion, death and resurrection. The Christian must forgive seven times seventy times, and Christian mercy is an expression of the double commandment to love God and neighbor. Mercy united with love fulfills the command of perfection (Col 3:14), showing the hospitality to others that is shown to Christ.

Mercy, Corporal and Spiritual Works of • Works of charity done out of compassion or concern for those in distress and suffering. The corporal works are feeding the hungry, giving drink to the thirsty, clothing the naked, sheltering the homeless, visiting the sick and imprisoned, ransoming the captive and burying the dead. The spiritual works are instructing the ignorant, correcting sinners, advising the doubtful, showing patience to sinners and those in error, forgiving others, comforting the afflicted and praying for the living and dead.

Merit • The Catholic doctrine of supernatural merit enshrines the deep truth that God brings about our salvation by establishing an order in which human freedom and action, under grace, contribute directly to the attainment and enjoyment of the benefits of eternal bliss. Human persons are not simply the inert and passive objects of a saving activity that bypasses the fundamental structures of human knowing, willing and acting. In the plan of divine wisdom, these very structures are taken up into and transformed in their very nature and exercise. Since Scripture and the writings of the Fathers are suffused with the teaching that eternal happiness in heaven is the reward for good deeds performed on earth, the Church has struggled to express this truth in such a way that it avoids the Pelagian mistake of thinking that grace itself can be merited by the creature. The succinct formulation of the Second Council of Orange

(A.D. 529) puts it thus: "The reward given for good works is not won by reason of actions which precede grace, but grace, which is unmerited, precedes actions in order that they be accomplished meritoriously." In opposition to the Lutheran denial of the reality of supernatural merit, the Council of Trent reaffirmed the truth that for the justified person eternal life is both a gift or grace promised by God and a reward for his own good works. In the divine order of grace, salutary works are at once the gift of God and the meritorious acts of the human person. Catholic Faith thus insists that justification changes our inherent nature, enabling us to perform acts of intrinsic saving value. We are thus made partners in our salvation with Christ. A distinction is generally drawn between merit based on justice (*meritum de condigno*) and merit based on equity (*meritum de congruo*). With condign merit, the reward is strictly earned, but with congruous merit, the reward far surpasses what is earned.

Messiah (also Messias): See **Christ**

Metanoia • The English term is a transliteration of the Greek *metanoia* and refers to a "change of thinking" based on a new horizon of understanding grounded in an act of God. Accompanying all authentic conversion is a change in lifestyle and of values (in varying degrees). The term occurs throughout the New Testament (Mt 3:8, 11; Mk 1:4; Lk 15:7; Acts 5:31; 20:21; 26:20; 2 Cor 7:9; Heb 6:1; 12:17). When one contemplates that, as in John's Gospel, we must be born again to enter the kingdom of God, it should be clear that some kind of radical change, shifts in thinking and in what controls the "heart" are necessary. The Pauline theme of "new creation" rightly implies that the "old person" must die; the "new creation" must emerge. The "new creation" involves being renewed by our understanding in the mind (and heart). Again this occurs at Baptism or through grace, but also by means of renewal of the mind (Rom 12:2; Eph 1:9ff.).

Metany • Properly speaking, penance. In the East, generally, an inclination of the head and shoulders (Lesser Metany) or a prostration to the ground (Greater Metany).

Metaphysics • That portion of philosophy concerned with the most fundamental aspects of being and existence. It reaches from consideration of the lowest forms of matter up to the reality of God. Some subdivisions of metaphysics include: *ontology*, about the nature of being itself; *rational psychology*, about the human soul; *natural theology*, about the reality and attributes of God.

The metaphysics of Catholic philosophy, as can be found in the writings of St. Augustine and St. Thomas and their contemporary followers, greatly differs in its emphasis on objective truth and substantial reality from that of some other prominent modern philosophers, who stress subjectivity or process instead.

Metempsychosis • Also referred to as reincarnation, the belief that the soul or character of one who dies is reborn in another appropriate, bodily individual. This belief usually involves a dualistic understanding of the human being, which treats the body and the soul as independently existing things (or non-things, as in Buddhism). The soul is the true self, and the body is the soul's temporary place of confinement, until the soul is purified of worldly attachments. Thus the soul or true "self" (or Buddhism's non-self) is not only distinct from the body but is so separable from the body that the soul loses nothing by being separated from the body. According to a dualistic view, when the soul is purified of worldliness, it is freed by death for the state of bliss. However, souls which are not purified are dragged, as it were, by their own "weight" and attachments, back into an available body which suits their character. This rebirth into a new body is reincarnation or metempsychosis. The character of the previous life's action determines the type of body into which the soul is reincarnated.

Doctrines of reincarnation appreciate the truth of the immortality of the soul, but misinterpret its character. In effect, such doctrines despair of the bodily world itself playing any role in the state of beatitude. Reincarnation is regarded in such doctrines as an unfortunate necessity until the soul is perfectly purified from any attachment to this world. Christian Faith holds that perfect purification is from sin, not from the bodily world as such, and the perfect overcoming of sin occurs not in being freed from our bodies in death, but only in our resurrection in the fullness of time, by God's grace, into our own glorified bodies.

Methodism • The doctrines, policy and worship of the Protestant denomination started in England by John Wesley. He and his brother Charles formed a group at Oxford that met for religious practices. From the way they conducted themselves by "rule and conduct," they were given the name "Methodists." In 1738, following a period of missionary work in America, Wesley became a religious leader in England. By the end of the eighteenth century, Methodism became strongly rooted in America.

The United Methodist Church, formed in 1968 by a merger of the Methodist Church and the Evangelical United Brethren Church, is the second largest Protestant group in the United States.

Methodists accept the Bible, Tradition, experience and reason as the four sources and guidelines. They reject the notion of praying to saints, priestly confessions, the Real Presence of Christ in the Eucharist, apostolic succession and purgatory. They recognize only two sacraments: Baptism and the Lord's Supper (Holy Communion).

The legislative power of the Methodist Church lies in a General Conference, which meets every four years and is composed of both clergy and laity, in equal numbers. The delegates to the General Conference are democratically elected by annual conferences, and on a proportional basis. The supreme judicial power of the Church rests in a judicial council, whose members and qualifications are determined by the General Conference of the Church.

Its liturgy has two parts: (1) the morning service has confession of sin, the Gloria or other hymn, the collect of the day, an Old Testament reading and/or an epistle, the Gospel, sermon, intercessions, Lord's Prayer; (2) the Lord's Supper has the Nicene Creed, an offertory with hymn, the thanksgiving, the breaking of bread, Holy Communion, final prayer, dismissal, and/or blessing.

Metropolitan • An archbishop who is the head of an ecclesiastical province is known as a metropolitan archbishop, and his archdiocese as the metropolitan archdiocese. The metropolitan is charged with seeing that the Faith and ecclesiastical discipline are observed in the suffragan dioceses of the province and notifying the Holy See of abuses. With permission of the Holy See, he can conduct a canonical visitation of an ecclesiastical institution if a suffragan bishop has neglected to do so. The metropolitan also has the right to appoint an administrator to a vacant see if the College of Consultors fails to elect one or if the one elected does not meet the canonical requirements.

Metropolitan archbishops are permitted to wear the pallium at liturgical services within the province (cf. Canons 435-438).

Mexican American Cultural Center • This institute, founded in 1971 by the Texas Catholic Conference, seeks to provide research, education, publications and leadership programs for Spanish-speaking Americans, especially those of Mexican origin. The center fosters cultural and spiritual development, the growth of leadership and a heightened awareness of rights and responsibilities among the Mexican-American people. Endorsed by the United States Catholic Conference, it also cooperates with two slightly more specialized groups: PADRES, an association of priests working with Spanish-speaking Americans, and Las Hermanas, an association of women religious working in the Spanish apostolate.

Micah, Book of • A contemporary of Isaiah, the sixth of the minor prophets, Micah (or Micheas) lived in Judah in the latter half of the eighth century. His name, an abbreviation of Micahiah, is akin to that of Michael.

He is a typical prophet, speaking for a God Who threatens disaster for the Jewish people because of their sins, and promising them freedom and prosperity under a new David in exchange for their repentance. Judah is called to take warning from the fall of Samaria. While Micah's chronology is not certain, it seems likely that the reform under Hezekiah was evidence of his success. He had a strong social conscience and felt solidarity with the oppressed poor (2, 3, 6:9-11). His most famous verse is 6:8, the definition of genuine religion: "To do justice, and to love kindness, and to walk humbly with your God."

For further reading: Marc Z. Brettler, "Micah," *Anchor Bible Dictionary*, 4:806-807; Delbert R. Hillers, "Micah, Book of," *Anchor*

Bible Dictionary, 4:807-810; Leo Laberge, O.M.I., "Micah," *New Jerome Biblical Commentary*, 249-254.

Middle Ages • The designation historians give to that period between the fall of Rome (A.D. 476) and the beginning of the Renaissance (roughly the late fifteenth century). Sometimes scholars prefer to date it from the coronation of Charlemagne (800). In any case, it refers to that "middle time" between the ancient and modern era. For some historians, it is used as a term of disparagement, since the great classics of the ancient world went into eclipse during these centuries, only to be rediscovered by the humanists on the eve of the Renaissance. The Protestant writers of early modern times agreed with this assessment, since the Middle Ages represent the zenith of a Europe united in a Christendom dominated by the papacy. However, achievements in theology, philosophy, art, architecture and literature demonstrate that this era was one of significant intellectual accomplishment.

Midrash • The noun *midrash* occurs only twice in the Hebrew text of the Old Testament (2 Chr 13:22; 24:27). It comes from the Hebrew *darash*, which has several Old Testament meanings, chief among them being "to seek, inquire," "to investigate" (Ps 119:10; 2 Chr 17:4; 22:9; 1 Sm 9:9; 1 Kgs 3:11; Jer 21:2; Jgs 6:29, etc.). Eventually, this term became associated with seeking and investigating the Scriptures. By the late second and first centuries B.C. and at Qumran, we find binding conclusions drawn from Scripture referred to as midrash. Because Scripture (Old Testament) was not just a historical record but rather the revelation of God and His Will, the texts of the Old Testament were pregnant with meaning to be uncovered through ever-deepening meditation and penetration of that meaning. Yet the new questions of each new generation were often confronted with the "silence" of the texts when read on a simplistic level.

Midrash served to relate possible meanings of a given passage to the contemporary world of the seeker. There were developed two sets of rules (*middoth*) to guide the interpreters. Three kinds of interpretation emerged: legal (called halakah), homiletic (called haggadah) and narrative (mostly legendary accounts). These bodies of literature are only now being dated with some historical accuracy. They offer a glimpse into the mind-set and religious values of many Jewish communities, and often they can shed light on the way New Testament authors interpreted Old Testament passages.

For further reading: Joseph Dan, "Midrash," *Encyclopedia Judaica*, 11:1507-1515; Gary G. Porton, "Midrash," *Anchor Bible Dictionary*, 4:818-822.

Migrant Ministries • Within the context of the total pastoral ministry of the Church special care is to be given to those with particular needs. In 1970, Pope Paul VI instituted a pastoral ministry under the supervision of the Congregation for Bishops to be directed toward migrants and other travelers. On June 28, 1988, this was made autonomous by Pope John Paul II, and was renamed as the Pontifical Council for Migrants and Travelers, with the purpose of providing priests with specialized abilities and language skills, and offering necessary services for the spiritual and temporal good of those faithful who are migrants, nomads, tourists or travelers of any kind.

Military Chaplains • Priests who minister to the spiritual needs of Catholic members of the military services and their families, or non-Catholics who seek their assistance. In the United States and many other countries, the priests are incardinated into dioceses or religious institutes but are released by their superiors to serve in the military. They then come under the primary jurisdiction of the military diocese of the country.

In the United States, chaplains are actually officers in the branch of the military in which they serve. As such, they must meet the criteria for commissioning as an officer and participate in special officer and chaplain training programs. They are assigned and transferred by the military authorities and not by the military diocese. Before being commissioned, a candidate for military chaplaincy must receive the endorsement of his own bishop or superior, as well as the endorsement of the military bishop. After entering the service, U.S. military chaplains (and those of most other countries) wear the military uniform while on duty and are subject to the regulation and discipline of the military authorities. In the U.S., each branch has a Chief of Chaplains (from any of the several denominations), with the rank of Major General or Rear Admiral.

The chaplains' primary responsibility is to serve the needs of the military personnel and their families. The ministry differs with each branch of the service. Navy chaplains spend a good deal of their time at sea, assigned to a ship or to a group of ships. Army chaplains minister on Army installations, and many accompany their units in the field. Air Force chaplains are routinely assigned to bases where they direct parishes while also spending a significant amount of their time with the service people.

Military chaplains receive faculties to exercise their Sacred Orders from the military bishop. As such, their jurisdiction is both personal, that is, applicable to their subject anywhere, and territorial, that is, applicable on military installations.

Military Ordinariate • A special diocese erected by the Holy See to serve the pastoral needs of the military personnel and their families of a particular country. The structure and jurisdiction of the military ordinariates is determined by the Apostolic Constitution *Spirituali militum curae*, issued in 1986, and by their own statutes, which are approved by the Holy See.

The clergy of a military ordinariate is made up of the military chaplains that serve the armed forces of the country. In some countries the chaplains are also military officers. A military ordinariate can have its own seminary and incardinate its own clerics. In many countries the priests who serve are not incardinated but are released by their bishops or religious communities to serve the military indefinitely or for a particular period of time.

The jurisdiction of a military ordinariate is both personal, extending to all of the members of the military and their families, and territorial, encompassing the territory of military installations in the country itself and throughout the world. The Ordinary of a military ordinariate may be either a bishop or an archbishop, depending on the decision of the Pope. If a military ordinariate is an archdiocese, it is not a metropolitan archdiocese since it has no suffragan dioceses.

Millenarianism • Virtually the same as chiliasm, and in fact the terms are frequently used interchangeably. The term "millenarianism" is derived from the Latin root for "one thousand," and refers to a belief that Christ will return to govern a temporal kingdom on earth for a thousand years. Like chiliasm, it is based on an excessively literalistic reading of the Book of Revelation, especially Chapter 20. Among modern sects professing more or less this belief are the Jehovah's Witnesses.

Millennium • A term drawn from Revelation 20 that refers to a period of grace. The idea that this period will last exactly one thousand years, however, or that it necessarily implies a temporal reign by Christ, has been censured by the Church in a number of documents as being an excessively literalistic interpretation of the passage. (Cf. also Chiliasm; Millenarianism.)

For further reading: J. Massyngbaerde Ford, "Millennium," *Anchor Bible Dictionary*, 4:832-834; Pope John Paul II, *Tertio Millennio Adveniente*.

Minister • Derived from the Latin word for servant, the term "minister" designates a wide variety of offices of service in the Church. Normally, its sense is liturgical: ministers are those who function in some capacity in the celebration of the Eucharist and the other sacraments. In these settings, the ministers include persons who are ordained (bishops, priests and deacons) and persons who are instituted in the ministries of lector and acolyte. Since Vatican Council II, the term has been applied more broadly to include roles of service of those who cooperate in the pastoral service of the parish priests — thus, for example, youth ministers and so on.

It should be noted, however, that both the Synod on the Laity of 1987 and Pope John Paul II's post-synodal reflection, *Christifideles Laici*, urged caution in applying the word "minister" to the unordained, lest confusion result about the uniqueness of the vocations of clergy and laity alike.

Ministries • The norm concerning liturgical ministries enunciated in *Sacrosanctum Concilium*, the Constitution on the Sacred Liturgy, that "in liturgical celebrations each person, minister, or layman who has an office to perform, should carry out and only those parts which pertain to his [her] office by the nature of the rite and the norms of the liturgy" (n. 28) reiterates the long-standing tradition that a diversity of roles and ministries is reflected in liturgical celebration. The *First Apology* of Justin the Martyr (c. A.D. 150) attests to the functioning of the reader, deacon, president and the people. *Ordo Romanus Primus*, the first of a series of descriptions of how the liturgy was carried out in the Middle Ages (the first is dated from the seventh century), attests to more than twenty ministers (including cantor, acolyte, etc.). The Roman Pontifical published after Trent attests to the ordination to both major (priest, canon and subdeacon) and minor orders (porter, lector, exorcist, acolyte), with all but porters and exorcists regularly functioning at liturgy. However, it was the custom in the preconciliar liturgy that ordained priests functioned as deacons and subdeacons at Solemn Masses and that they would proclaim the readings at Mass.

The contemporary reform of liturgical ministries restores the permanent deacon as a legitimate ordained (non-presbyterial) ministry, the roles of reader and acolyte (along with deacons) and the ministry of the "psalmist or cantor of the psalm" (*General Instruction of the Roman Missal*, n. 36) as integral to every liturgical celebration. The differentiation among these, for example, is that the deacon is ordained, readers and acolytes are installed, and cantors function without rites of installation. In addition, by custom, non-installed readers function ministerially at the liturgy, as well as those persons commissioned as extraordinary ministers of the Eucharist: both of these offices may be filled by women. The letter *Novit profecto* on new ministries to be established by the conferences of bishops (Sacred Congregation of Divine Worship, October 1977) opens the way for the development of additional ministries (which ministries, the document specifies twice, would be open to women) by conferences of bishops with the approval of the Apostolic See.

Ministry and Life of Priests, Decree on the: See **Presbyterorum Ordinis**

Ministry of the Word • In general terms the ministry of the word is the bringing of the Gospel message to the world through evangelization (instilling the beginning of faith in the hearts of individuals) and catechetics (which assists the individual to grow in the Faith, making it living and active). In the context of the Liturgy of the Eucharist, the ministry of the word includes the scriptural readings, the psalm and the homily. Theologians have a "ministry of the word" in their explorations of the doctrines of the Faith, insofar as they seek to illuminate for the faithful the magisterial teaching of the Church.

Minor Orders • The minor orders were the lesser degrees of ministry which candidates for the priesthood received prior to ordination to Sacred Orders. The minor orders of porter, lector, exorcist and acolyte were generally conferred by a bishop at various intervals in the first two years of theological training. The minor orders were abolished in 1972 and replaced by the ministries of acolyte and lector, which are conferred by a bishop or priest.

The minor orders were first mentioned in a letter of Pope Cornelius in A.D. 252. They included the subdiaconate, which was placed as the lower of the major orders by Pope Innocent III in 1207. The conferral of minor orders differed considerably from that of major orders. Essentially, the ritual consisted of a blessing and a handing over of the instruments required of the various offices. Historically, the minor orders came to be as an official recognition of some specific office in the Church or liturgy and given the status of a ministry or order.

Miracle • In Sacred Scripture a miracle occurs when an apparent law of nature has been altered, when an extraordinary and otherwise inexplicable event takes place and God is glorified. We could say that a miracle is a physical sign in this world from God. The event is prophetic, communicating God's salvific will and intent; the event is also salvific, in that all miracles advance God's great plan of reconciling to Himself a fallen cosmos. In Sacred Scripture the question of a miracle is always a matter of faith in God's existence and God's ability to manifest His love, care and plan of salvation. The miracle is God's self-communication in time and space, a revelation which builds faith and has the power to save. When the miracle restores health or even life, such an instance intrinsically manifests God's goodness and His overwhelmingly benevolent attitude toward humans. It thus reveals something of God's inner nature — abundant life to the overflowing, and love.

For further reading: Harold Remus, "Miracle (NT)," *Anchor Bible Dictionary*, 4:856-869; Zakovitch, Meir, "Miracle (OT)," *Anchor Bible Dictionary*, 4:845-856.

Miracle Plays (also Mystery or Morality Plays) • A popular dramatic genre in the Middle Ages, miracle plays presented the life of a saint, a religious historic event, a story from the Bible or some teaching of the Faith. They were intended primarily as teaching aids to convey some moral or religious principle to the uneducated who would not be exposed to the Faith in an attractive or understandable fashion otherwise. They were usually presented by touring troupes of players outdoors, often in the courtyard or square before a cathedral.

Miracle plays preceded mystery plays, which usually concentrated more on events from the Old Testament or New Testament. Many of the plays, in time, introduced verse, which remained the form of drama for centuries. (Cf. Morality Play.)

Miraculous Medal • It was on November 27, 1830, that the Blessed Mother appeared to a young sister, St. Catherine Labouré, in the motherhouse of the Daughters of Charity of St. Vincent de Paul in Paris. At this time Mary asked the Vincentian Sister to have a medal struck in honor of her Immaculate Conception, following the model she would show her: "Have the medal struck after this model. All who wear it will receive great graces. They should wear it around the neck." Following the period of testing which accompanies any such apparition, the medal was finally struck on June 30, 1832, with the permission of the Archbishop of Paris, Hyacinth Louis de Quelen. The many miracles that resulted after this gave it the popular name of the "Miraculous Medal." The devotion itself has been fostered and blessed by all the Popes since Pius IX. Indeed, the swift propagation of the medal may have had some not unimportant influence upon that Pontiff's infallible proclamation of the dogma of the Immaculate Conception in 1854.

On the front side of the medal may be seen the Blessed Mother standing on the globe of the earth and crushing the head of the evil serpent, Satan (cf. Gn 3:15). From

Miraculous Medal

her extended hands, rays of light stream forth upon the world, symbolizing graces which the good Mother procures from her Divine Son for her children. Around the edge of this side of the medal are inscribed the words: "O Mary, conceived without sin, pray for us who have recourse to thee." On the reverse side of the medal, the "M" of Mary is surmounted by the Cross of Christ, beneath which she stood and joined her sacrifice to the perfect sacrifice of her Son. Beneath this can be seen the Sacred Hearts of Jesus and Mary — together in the virginal womb during His gestation, together during life, together at Calvary and for eternity. Christ's Heart is surrounded by a crown of thorns and flames with a surmounted Cross atop it, to represent the burning love of Jesus for humanity testified unto by the shedding of His Blood at Calvary. Mary's heart is pierced by a sword, as Simeon the Prophet foretold (Lk 2:35), and surmounted by flames, her own burning love for humanity. This whole is surrounded by twelve stars around the edge of the medal, which refer to St. John's vision of the "woman clothed with the sun, with the moon under her feet and on her head a crown of twelve stars" (cf. Rv 12:1).

Mirari Vos • The encyclical of Pope Gregory XVI (1832) condemning the social and political doctrines of the l'Avenir group in nineteenth-century France, who were trying to reconcile some of the ideals of the French Revolution with Catholicism, especially freedom of the press or of worship. Lacordaire, the future Dominican, submitted, but Lamennais did not. Pius IX would condemn many of these same ideals in his *Syllabus of Errors* in 1864, but it can be argued that he was condemning extreme liberalism and not all democratic principles.

Miserere • Refers to the penitential Psalm 51 (50), which in Latin begins, *Miserere mei, Deus, secundum magnam misericordiam tuam* — "Have mercy on me, O God, according to thy great mercy." It was written by King David after he repented of his great sin of adultery and of having had Uriah the Hittite killed so that he could take his wife, Bathsheba, to himself (cf. 2 Sm 11 and 12). Though Psalms 55 (54) and 57 (56) also begin with *Miserere*, the prominence in the sacred liturgy, especially the canonical hours, and its great popularity have reserved this name exclusively for Psalm 51 (50). Formerly said as the first Psalm of Lauds in the ferial (weekday) office throughout the year and on many Sundays, it is now principally used on all Fridays to denote the penitential character of this day.

Missal: See Roman Missal

Missiology • The theological subfield, combining systematic and pastoral interests, concerned with the study and application of Christian doctrines commending the propagation of the Faith among those who do not know of it or adhere to it. Our Lord's teaching (Mt 28:19; Lk 24:47) provides the charter for the missionary enterprise and thus for the theological inquiry about it. In addition, as a perspective on the whole range of the Christian Faith, missiology considers particular Christian doctrines with a view to their communication in alien social and cultural settings. At the same time, it is part of the task of missiology to foster a sympathetic appreciation of these settings in order to discern their receptivity to the Christian message. Modern missiology seeks to cultivate this sympathetic encounter by fostering linguistic, historical and cultural anthropological studies. Finally, missiology extends to the study of the history of Christian missions and the analysis of missionary organization and methodology.

Mission cross from Sweden (tenth century)

Mission • The term "mission" has two distinct meanings in Christian usage. First, it refers to a central function of the Church, mandated by Christ Himself when He charged His Apostles to proclaim the Gospel and make disciples of all nations (Mt 28:19; cf. Mk 6:7-13). The Church's mission is thus central to its very identity as the community founded on the Apostles. From this basic sense of mission are derived several extended meanings. Mission designates the work of evangelization in localities where the Gospel has never been preached, or the actual territory itself where this work is performed, or an extension of a parochial church or the work of preaching renewal to the Christian people. Secondly, the term mission is used to describe the visible and invisible extensions of the processions of the Divine Persons or the Trinity. Thus, the incarnation of the Son is the mission of the Second Person, and the indwelling of the Spirit is the mission of the Third Person. These missions do not involve any actual movement or change in God Who is already everywhere. Rather, they involve a grace that produces a new way of being related to them in the ones to whom they are sent. It is not that God becomes more present to us, but that we become more present to Him.

Missionaries (also Missioners) • Religious or lay persons who are devoted to the propagation of the Christian Faith among non-Christian peoples or in places of markedly declining Christian Faith. Christ Himself provided the mandate for missionary activity when He commanded His disciples to proclaim the Gospel to all peoples (Mt 28:19; Lk 24:47). From the very beginning, engagement in mission has been seen to be fundamental to the identity of the Christian community. St. Paul and the other Apostles set the example and furnished the model for evangelization and for the establishment of core communities that would then take on the task of proclaiming the Gospel in their immediate environs. Many of the Church's great saints were missionaries, and often martyrs. Religious founders frequently organized their orders with missionary work as the principal if not exclusive objective.

Missionary Activity, Decree on the Church's: See **Ad Gentes**

Mitre (also Miter) • The liturgical headdress proper to all bishops of the Latin Rite, including the Pope. The word comes from the Greek *mitra*, which means "turban." It consists of two flaps, front and back, equal in size, which are joined at the bottom by a headband and which curve to a point at the top. A soft material also joins these two flaps together throughout, enabling the whole to be folded flat when not in use. There are two fringed lappets or "infulae" (Latin for "band"), which hang from the back. Oftentimes the coat of arms of the prelate is richly embroidered on the infulae. While remaining within this general description, the shape of the mitre has nevertheless changed throughout the centuries. Lately in some places, for instance, the medieval form of the mitre has gained popularity. This consists of a lower and softer version and is also very popular in the Anglican Communion and those associated with it. The Renaissance, or Roman, style of the mitre entails a much higher (even eighteen to twenty inches) version whose sides curve outwardly before they curve inwardly as it nears the top.

There are three kinds of mitres: the precious, or *mitra pretiosa*, adorned with gold and precious or semiprecious stones; the golden, or *mitra auriphrygiata*, made of plain gold cloth; and the simple, or *mitra simplex*, which is made of white linen or damask. Except for episcopal consecrations which he may confer, when in the presence of the Pope only the simple mitre may be worn. In the presence of the Pope only cardinals are allowed to wear the damask simple mitre, *mitra damasciata*. The simple mitre is that worn when the prelate assists or pontificates at funerals, during Lent and on Good Friday.

Though the mitre as we know it today did not make its appearance until the middle of the tenth century and was at first used only by the Pope at solemn liturgical functions, it goes back further in history. It developed from the conical head-covering or tiara worn by the Pope. This in turn may have developed from the headdress of the high priest of the Temple in Jerusalem, and more

Mitre of Cardinal Wiseman of England, 1850

likely than not from the head-covering worn by important civil officials in the Roman Empire, the *camelaucum*. Constantine had allowed the Pope and other bishops the use of this distinctive headdress as a sign of their new importance within his empire.

As with most other liturgical paraments, it developed from a particular everyday piece of secular clothing into a specifically clerical and liturgical vestment, in this case exclusively worn by the Popes to begin with and then gradually extended to others. As such, it became the custom for other bishops to use the mitre by the beginning of the twelfth century. This was later extended to other prelates, such as protonotaries apostolic and abbots. There were also some abbesses in the Middle Ages who were permitted the use of the mitre as a symbol only, not as a headdress. Today its use is mostly limited to bishops and abbots.

Mixed Marriage • A marriage between a Catholic and a non-Catholic. Marriages between a Catholic and an unbaptized person are known as disparity of cult marriages. Such marriages are invalid unless a dispensation has been received. Marriages between Catholics and non-Catholic Christians are known as marriages of mixed religion. These marriages require the permission of the bishop, but not a dispensation, to take place.

At one time, mixed marriages of either kind were severely prohibited and strongly discouraged. To emphasize this, they could not be celebrated with liturgical ceremonies but had to take place somewhere other than in a church. In 1966, the Holy See issued a new set of guidelines for mixed marriages allowing, among other things, their celebration with full liturgical ceremonies.

In order to receive a dispensation or permission for a mixed marriage, the Catholic party is to make a declaration and promise, either in writing or orally before a witness, that he or she will remove all dangers to the practice of the Faith and will do all in his or her power to see that any children born are baptized and raised in the Catholic Faith. The non-Catholic party no longer has to make any kind of promise but simply to be informed of the Catholic party's obligation (cf. Canons 1124-1129).

Modalism • In Trinitarian theology, the error of denying that the processions of the Son and of the Holy Spirit are the source of real distinctions among the three divine Persons. Modalism commonly understands the Father, Son and Holy Spirit to be roles, functions or modes adopted by the unipersonal Godhead for the purposes of the economy of salvation. In effect, modalism entails the absolute unknowability of the

Godhead itself: The unipersonal God appears only in the three (or more?) modalities displayed for the benefit of creatures.

While some version of this error always remains a logical possibility in Trinitarian theology against which the orthodox theologian must guard, it is identified in particular with the third-century heresies of Sabellianism (after its chief proponent, Sabellius), Monarchianism (which stressed the absolute unity of the Godhead to the point of excluding the distinction of the three Persons), and Patripassianism (which taught that in Christ it was the Father Who suffered and died). These heresies were vigorously opposed by Fathers of the Church and by the early councils in the course of the formulation of the orthodox doctrine of Blessed Trinity.

Moderator of the Curia • The moderator of the curia is a stable ecclesiastical office introduced after Vatican II. It is an administrative office that is to be held by a priest so appointed by the bishop. The duties of the moderator of the curia include the coordination of the administrative agencies of the diocese and the supervision of the members of the curia. The moderator of the curia should also be a vicar general (Canon 473).

Modernism • The term given a broad attempt by some thinkers at the beginning of the twentieth century to bring Catholic thought into line with the advances of current biblical, historical, philosophical and scientific finding. In the process, some "modernists" ended up altering Catholic doctrine in their attempt to make it more palatable to contemporary men and women, thus earning the condemnation of Pope St. Pius X in his decree, *Lamentabili* (September 8, 1907), and then his encyclical, *Pascendi Dominici Gregis* (September 8, 1907).

Prominent Modernists would include Maurice Blondel (1861-1949) in philosophy, Alfred Loisy (1852-1940) in Scripture, George Tyrrell (1861-1909) in theology and Frederick von Heigel (1852-1925) in a variety of fields, all bound by the belief that a questioning, critical, accommodating theology was necessary if the Church were to reach twentieth-century humanity. In its extreme form, it doubted the divinity of Christ, posited the Church as a purely sociological enterprise, viewed Scripture as mere literature and held that doctrines must change to suit the time. There is a question among historians as to whether Modernism was ever an organized, systematic movement or more of a tendency popular at the turn of the century. Whatever the case, St. Pius X attacked it with vigor, with some opponents of Modernism, called "integralists," reacting with such excess that the successor of St. Pius X, Benedict XV (1914-1921), had to urge moderation.

Modes, Gregorian: See **Gregorian Modes**

Modes of Responsibility • Also referred to as the requirements of practical reasonableness in the ethical and moral theological systems of John Finnis and Germain Grisez, these are the means by which one reduces basic obligations toward moral goods to practical action.

These modes of responsibility hold specifically, first of all, that human beings should cooperate with others in the achieving of human flourishing. Second, persons "who restrict all that is good will never make themselves a special case." Third, persons who are morally good will refuse to make choices directed against a basic good and will make efforts to promote that good even if they are not strictly bound to do so. Finally, those who respect all of the basic human goods will recognize that we have specific duties toward other persons, leading to cooperative activity that is organized by efforts of communities of individuals (*Life and Death with Liberty and Justice*, 370).

These modes of moral responsibility have been expressed in many different ways by these authors, resulting in some confusion about their precise character and function in the moral life.

Modesty • The virtue by which the individual exerts restraint over external actions, dress and conversation. The vices that are contrary to the virtue of modesty are lewdness, coarseness and boorishness on the one hand and excessive refinement and delicacy on the other hand. Modesty fosters social relations and charity, in that it facilitates our responses to one another because it promotes agreeable manners and harmonious relationships.

Mohammedanism: See Islam

Moicheia • The Greek noun *moicheia* occurs in the New Testament only in Matthew 15:19, Mark 7:22 and John 8:3, where it means adultery. Related to this word are the noun *moichalis*, meaning adulteress (Rom 7:3; 2 Pt 2:14; Jas 4:4; Mt 12:39; 16:4; Mk 8:38) and the verb *moichao*, meaning to commit or cause to commit adultery (Mt 5:32; 19:9; Mk 10:11ff.). The term refers to the breaking of the marriage one-flesh unity by means of sexual intercourse with a person not one's spouse. It should not be restricted to behavior alone, since one's intent is where the behavior initially begins (Mt 5:27-29).

For further reading: F. Hauck, "Moichao," *Theological Dictionary of the New Testament*, 4:729-735.

Moleben • A liturgical term derived from the Slavonic language to designate a service of prayer honoring a particular saint, the

Mother of God or Christ or a service of thanksgiving, petition or penance in the Byzantine Church.

Molech (also Moloch) • From the Hebrew *melek* (king) with the vowels of *boshet* (shame), Molech means literally king of shamefulness; it was a name given by the Israelites to the Canaanite god who presided over the realm of the dead. It appears related to other divine names such as Muluk and Milcom, found in the Mari texts and the Ugaritic tablets.

Under Assyrian influence, the cult of this king-god grew in Palestine (2 Kgs 23:10; Jer 32:35). The sacrifice of children was central to the pagan ritual in the worship of Molech and is attested to from the archaeological finds of infant remains placed under the entrances to Canaanite homes as propitiatory offerings to Molech; in fact, it is suggested that *molk* may have been the term for a votive offering. Most significant in this regard is the condemnation in Jeremiah 7:30-34 of the Canaanite practice of sacrificing children in the furnace of Topheth, in the Valley of Gehenna, west of Jerusalem.

For further reading: George C. Heider, "Molech," *Anchor Bible Dictionary*, 4:895-898.

Molinism • The theological doctrine proposed by Luís Molina that emphasized human freedom and diminished the efficacy and power of grace. Molina sought to resolve the theological problem of the relationship of grace and freedom: to protect human freedom, he held that God possesses sovereign authority in regard to human freedom.

Molina contended that without compromising human freedom, God can direct it as it pleases Him because of His knowledge of future possible conditionals. He knows what every free agent can and will bring about, and if He wishes to elicit a free choice by an agent, all that He must do is to bring about a situation in which He knows that the agent will make a certain choice, and it will come about. Logically prior to the free act, Molina claims that God directs the free action of the agent without coercing it. If one acts to promote salvation, the grace that brings this about is "efficacious" grace, even though it might be a different sort of grace from that which does not bring about the saving action.

The difficulty with Molinism is that it does not explain the origin of the conditionally free action which God foreknows. It is difficult to contend that God does not coerce human free action if this conditional action does not derive from Him, and if it does not derive from God, one must ask how God knows it.

Monarchianism • This term refers to a family of second- and third-century theological positions, led into Christological and Trinitarian heterodoxy by their otherwise legitimate concern to affirm a strict monotheism in the doctrine of God. Tertullian (d. A.D. 225) applied the term "monarchianism" to these positions because they stressed the unity or "monarchy" of the Godhead.

The principal forms of monarchianism were adoptionist and modalist. Adoptionism (associated chiefly with Theodotus and Artemon) secured the divine unity by contending that Jesus was a human being upon whom, at some point in His earthly life (possibly at His Baptism in the Jordan), God conferred a share in the divine power. Modalism (expounded notably by Sabellius) maintained that the internally undifferentiated Godhead adopted the successive roles of Father, Son and Spirit in executing the economy of salvation. Adoptionism thus denied the consubstantial divinity of the Son, and modalism the reality of the processions and relations within God.

Although the Council of Nicaea (325) did not put an end to the debate, it did supply the doctrinal rule for the historic mainstream by insisting on the true divinity of the Son and the reality of the doctrine of the Trinity. By insisting on the Trinity of Persons in one nature, the doctrine maintained the truth of monarchianism (affirmation of the unity of God) without prejudice to the reality of the divine self-identification as Father, Son and Holy Spirit.

Monastery • Originally the term for a cell in which a hermit lived or a cluster of cells. In popular and ecclesiastical usage, it applies to the dwelling place and community of men or women who live in seclusion. They lead a life of contemplation and recite the Divine Office in common. The physical property of a monastery differs, but in general each is composed of a church, chapter house, cloister, refectory, work area and

Monastery of Montserrat, Spain, ninth century

individual cells. Normally, these buildings form a quadrangle. Benedictines, Cistercians, Carthusians and Augustinians are some examples of monastic communities.

Monasticism • The mode of life followed by those who withdraw from society in order to devote themselves totally to God through prayer, penance and solitude. Throughout the history of the Church, it has usually taken two forms: the anchoritic style of monasticism, in which the monk lives completely by himself as a hermit, and the cenobitic, wherein the monks live in community. St. Anthony (d. A.D. 357) is usually considered the father of monasticism, although there is evidence of men and women withdrawing to the deserts of Egypt and Syria in the third century. Pachomius organized the first monastic communities in Upper Egypt, and the writings of Basil of Caesarea (d. 379) gave the monastic style of life much theological credibility.

Monasticism was slower to develop in the West, although Jerome, Martin of Tours, Augustine and John Cassian all contributed to its eventual prominence. It was St. Benedict of Nursia (d. c. 547) who gave monastic life a rule noted for its moderation, common sense and insistence upon structure and obedience, resulting in the spread of Benedictine monasticism in Europe. It is impossible to exaggerate the importance of monasticism to Western civilization, since the monks converted the Celt, German and Slav, preserved learning, founded schools and administered charity and welfare through the Middle Ages. However, even Benedictine monasticism needed periodic reform, which occurred by modifying the Rule, imposed renewal by civil or ecclesiastical leaders, or by forming new orders based on the monastic ideal. Examples of the latter would be the

Camaldolese, Carthusians, Cistercians and Premonstratensians.

Monism • The philosophical belief that underlying the apparent diversity of things, there is really just one being or one totality. This one totality includes within itself all apparent diverse things. Examples of monism may be found in the Hindu Vedantic thinker Sankara and in the modern philosopher Spinoza.

Monism is quite distinct from the monotheistic view of orthodox Christian, Jewish and Islamic thinkers. Orthodox monotheism holds that there is one God and that all beings other than God are created by God. Thus God is present in all beings by His creative love, but God is not their very substance or being; their being is really distinct from that of God. Monism in effect denies that beings other than God are really distinct from God. God's own power to create beings really distinct from Himself is also impugned in monism.

Monita Secreta • Secret instructions allegedly entrusted by the fifth general of the Society of Jesus to the Polish Jesuit Jerome Zahorowski. These "secret orders" concerned the expansion of the influence and power of the Society. Zahorowski was expelled from the Society in 1611 after the fraud was exposed.

Monk • Coming from the Greek word *monachos*, it means "one who lives alone," and refers to a member of a community of cenobites who live together under a rule and under an abbot with religious vows of obedience, poverty and chastity. Monks are distinguished from other orders of clerks or friars by their life in community, in a monastery, which is generally contemplative in nature. Today, the monks of the Roman Church in the West include Benedictines, Cistercians, Carthusians, Camaldolese and

Premonstratensians. In modern usage, the term "monk" has come to include both male and female members of monasteries, though the term most often refers to a man, whereas the term "nun" is used for his female counterpart.

Monogamy • The union of one man and one woman in a faithful, permanent, life-giving, publicly-contracted marriage, it is the only legitimate form of sexual union recognized by the Catholic Church.

According to the Church, this sort of union was given a sacramental character by Christ and is uniquely suited to the nature of the human person. It fulfills the human and personal needs of spouses for relational stability, intimacy and security. In addition, the monogamous, permanent relationship fulfills these needs of the child, who has a right to be reared by his or her own natural parents. Polygamy or polyandry, the taking of many wives or husbands, is contrary to monogamy and is in sharp decline today. But "serial polygamy," in which individuals take one wife or husband after another, is increasing rapidly with widespread acceptance of divorce and remarriage. Only monogamy fully protects the rights of all members of the family and enables all to achieve their own full human potential.

Monophysism (also Monophysitism) • This fifth-century Christological heresy has been attributed to Eutyches, but it probably had many contributors. It repudiated the two natures of Christ as expounded by the Council of Chalcedon, holding instead that Christ had but one composite nature. While a case can be made that the original dispute was perhaps merely terminological, the Monophysites became schismatic when they rejected the authority of councils to formulate any doctrine which was contrary to their thinking on the matter. Following their condemnation at the Second Council of Constantinople in 553, their formal sect fell into decline, although Monophysite sentiment lingered for nearly one thousand years, especially in the East.

Monotheism • As opposed to polytheism (belief in a plurality of divine beings) and pantheism (belief in the partial or complete identification of divine being with the world), monotheism affirms the existence of a single, personal and transcendent God. Monotheism should also be distinguished from henotheism (the belief, for instance, in a single tribal god). Judaism, Islam and Christianity are monotheistic religions. Against Judaism and Islam, the Christian community maintains that the doctrine of the Trinity is consistent with true monotheism in that it affirms not that there are three Gods (tritheism) but that there are Three Persons in one God.

Monothelism (also Monothelitism) • The theological proposal that since Christ is one Person, He has only one will. The view was proposed in the seventh century as a formula by which to reconcile those Monophysite (single-nature) Christians who felt that the unity of Christ was imperiled by the Council of Chalcedon's definition that Christ had two unmixed natures. The Council of Constantinople in 680 eventually defined Monothelism as a heresy. St. Maximus the Confessor (d. 662) had already helped draw the distinctions needed for orthodoxy by pointing out that the number of wills in Christ is a function of the natures of Christ rather than of His unity of person. Thus, in order to avoid injustice to the reality of both the divine and the human nature, it is necessary to acknowledge both a divine and a human will in Christ.

Monsignor • From the Italian *monsignore* which means "my lord," this term of address is one of honor for certain clerics in the

Catholic Church. All archbishops and bishops have a right to it, but it is most commonly used to refer to those having the titles of "Chaplain of His Holiness," "Prelate of Honor of His Holiness" or "Protonotary Apostolic." These are distinctions bestowed on certain priests as an elevation from among the general ranks of clergy. Monsignori are entitled to wear distinctive vesture similar to that of a bishop indicating that they have been given the honor of being part of the "papal household."

Monstrance • The sacred vessel used for exposition and adoration of the Blessed Sacrament, as well as solemn Benediction, is called a monstrance. Its name comes from the Latin verb *monstrare*, which simply means "to show." Another name for the monstrance is ostensorium, which, coming from the Latin *ostendere*, "to show," also denotes the same function for this vessel, since its primary purpose is to hold the Blessed Sacrament in such a way that It may be viewed and adored by the faithful. The general form and shape of the monstrance is that of a round glass or crystal-covered opening through which the Sacred Host can be seen while maintaining the proper care for the Sacred Species and the decorum that must accompany this most august Sacrament. This glass enclosure, or "luna," is oftentimes surrounded by rays or other decorations

Monstrance from
Louis XVIII's chapel

enhancing in a visible and artistic form the meaning of the spiritual graces conferred by the Holy Eucharist on those who believe, adore and participate. This is held by a stem resting on a base larger than, but not unlike, the base of a chalice. There are many styles and sizes of monstrances. Some are so large that for processions it took a cart to draw them along. Often a smaller monstrance, used for the Benediction, is incorporated into one of these majestic monstrances.

Montana Case • Among canon lawyers, the "Montana Case," or as it is more commonly known, the "Helena Case," refers to the first case in the United States of the Pope dissolving a marriage in favor of the Faith. The name refers to the case of an unbaptized man who had been married to a woman baptized in the Anglican Church. The man, after his divorce, wished to become a Catholic and marry a Catholic woman. In submitting the case to Rome, the bishop of Helena asked that the man be granted a papal dispensation from the obligations of the first marriage, in order to marry a Catholic. The response was favorable (decision of November 6, 1924).

This case was preceded by at least two other such cases, the first probably having been submitted by the Archbishop of Breslau and decided on April 2, 1924. Like the Montana Case, this marriage involved a baptized and an unbaptized person. In submitting the case, the archbishop asked that the woman petitioner be allowed to use the Pauline Privilege, which is the dissolution of a non-sacramental marriage between two unbaptized persons. The reply from the Holy Office simply stated that the woman could be permitted to contract a new marriage, but it did not give the reason for the dissolution. Canonists have questioned whether such cases are an application of the Pauline Privilege, since the marriages involved are certainly non-sacramental, or a use of the papal power to dissolve consummated but non-sacramental marriages.

Since these decisions were handed down, the Holy Office (later, the Congregation for the Doctrine of the Faith) routinely handled similar petitions. The process became known as the dissolution of marriage in Favor of the Faith or Privilege of the Faith cases. At first, all of the cases involved a baptized non-Catholic formerly married to an unbaptized person. One of the parties to the marriage had decided to convert to Catholicism and submitted the petition in order to be able to marry. In time, however, other types of cases were submitted.

In 1947, the so-called "Fresno Case" was decided. This was a marriage involving an unbaptized woman (the petitioner) who had been married to a Catholic with a dispensation from the impediment of disparity of cult. The marriage was dissolved by the Holy Father.

In 1959, a marriage between an unbaptized person and a baptized person was dissolved so that the unbaptized person, who had no intention of Baptism or conversion, could marry a Catholic. In the same year, the Holy Father dissolved a marriage of two unbaptized persons so that the second marriage of the unbaptized man and his Catholic wife could be rectified in the Church. In this case, the man refused to convert.

In all such cases, there is an evident favoring of the Faith of a Catholic person (the petitioner) who wishes to convert or a Catholic whom the non-converting petitioner wishes to marry.

Montanism • A heresy which first appeared in Phrygia in the mid-second century, one of the more serious and damaging threats to doctrine which plagued the early days of the Church. The Montanists would be termed "enthusiasts" many centuries later. Believing themselves to be oracles of the Holy Spirit and sole possessors of true charismatic qualities, the Montanists looked for an early Second Coming. Believing, moreover, that post-baptismal sins could not be forgiven, they practiced a severe asceticism and held themselves above the company of others. In A.D. 207, they accomplished perhaps their most significant act, the winning of the erudite and respected Tertullian to their sect. Pope Innocent I was the first of many Popes to score the Montanists, and following the excommunication of their leaders, the group fell into decline. It persisted, however, in small pockets through the sixth century, and in some places even until the ninth.

Montessori Method • The Montessori Method is a technique for educating children developed by Maria Montessori, an Italian physician and educator, and set forward in her book *The Montessori Method*, published in 1912. Montessori believed that each child has within himself the desire to learn and the ability to develop self-discipline by the exercise of personal freedom within an environment of trust and of limited control and direction. For Montessori, discipline is the end result of a good education, not a precondition for it.

In keeping with her ideas of child development, Montessori pioneered new techniques of education which relied upon specially designed curricula emphasizing cultural relevance, personal choice for students and a close, harmonious relationship between teacher and pupil. In the early twentieth century, Montessori opened schools in Italy based on these ideas, and later her method found adherents in the United States and Great Britain. Montessori's ideas were particularly compelling to American pragmatists such as John Dewey, whose own prominence in the United States ironically prevented wide dissemination of Montessori schools. Spurred by contemporary research in educational theory, however, there was a modest revival of interest in the U.S. during the 1950s and 1960s, and several Montessori schools were established around the country.

Month's Mind • Unofficial but still popular name for the anniversary Mass for a departed person offered on, or close to, the thirtieth day after death or burial. The custom of the month's remembrance arose from customs in monastic communities and among many ethnic groups to observe a full month of mourning. Hence, the pre-Vatican II Missal provided Mass formularies for the third, seventh and thirtieth days' remembrance. The Vatican II Missal provides texts for use on the day of burial, on the day news of the death is received or on the anniversary of death or burial (without specifying any numbers). Where the custom is preserved and fostered, such a celebration provides a good pastoral opportunity to visit the bereaved family, offering them the community's continued consolation and assistance. In some of the Eastern Churches (particularly those of Slavic heritage), the fortieth day is observed with a Divine Liturgy, followed by a

Panachyda (intercessory prayer service) for the departed.

Moral Person • The term that was used in the 1917 Code to designate what the revised Code refers to as a juridic person. Like the juridic person, a moral person was a kind of ecclesiastical corporation — a group of persons or things, duly constituted, that was subject to rights and duties. The phrase is still used in Canon 113 in reference to the Catholic Church and the Apostolic See.

Moral Theology • A field of theology which concerns the moral and ethical demands and requirements imposed by the Gospel for the full realization of holiness and union with Christ. Moral theology establishes the requirements of faith, hope and charity, and more specifically, it determines the rightness or wrongness, goodness or evil of actions according to the standards established by the Gospel and the Church. The norms of moral theology are not only those given by reason but also by faith, and it includes in the norm of faith the data given by the Tradition and Magisterium of the Church. The field of moral theology seeks to give a systematic and organized account of the requirements of Christian holiness and the demands of the Christian vocation.

What distinguishes moral theology from catechesis or apologetics is its systematic character. Moral theology has existed in continuous dialogue with the Church and the world which has led it to develop the field of casuistry enabling it to determine what one's precise moral obligations are, as well as maintaining a relationship to canon law which determined the gravity of actions. As a distinct field of learning, moral theology only arose after the Council of Trent, and few Christian theologians before that time thought of devoting independent treatises to Christian morality.

Moral theology has consistently developed in close union with canon law and civil law, as well as with faith and charity. It sought to facilitate the role of the confessor who had to determine the gravity of sinful actions and assign appropriate penances; moral theology also struggled hard to determine the relative gravity of various sorts of actions. In the contemporary era, moral theology seeks to give direction to believers in their struggle to deal with contemporary developments in medicine, society and politics.

Moral Virtues • The habits and powers perfected in a person by the performance of deliberate acts. These powers concern the basic human capabilities we have for doing moral good or evil, and they are contrasted to the intellectual virtues, which concern the development of our human power to know the truth, and also to the supernatural virtues, which orient the person toward God through sanctifying grace as an object to be possessed.

The four fundamental moral virtues are prudence, justice, fortitude and temperance, and the supernatural virtues are faith, hope and charity. All of the moral virtues are ultimately reduced to prudence, which is the virtue that enables one to accomplish good in the practical order. The aim of the moral life is the development of the moral virtues, for these are powers enabling the moral agent to accomplish what is good with ease and facility. Development of the virtues also brings about a reordering of our nature that places us more fully in the service of reason, love of God and love of neighbor.

The moral virtues are moral prerequisites for the supernatural virtues, and possession of the supernatural virtues through the gifts of grace enrich and enhance the moral virtues.

Morality • Often thought of as a matter of individual choice, or as conformity to the "correct" behavior learned in contact with family and society. For Christians, however, morality is the sum of true teachings about right and wrong, good and evil, as understood through natural reason and through fidelity to the teachings of Christ expressed in Scripture and Tradition.

In our times there is a strong contrast between what society says is correct as expressed in law, public school teaching and media presentation, and what is taught by the Catholic Church. This calls for a countercultural stance and formation of conscience based on a deep commitment to the good in the face of severe pressure.

Morality, however, is not simply a matter of following Church teaching without interior response. A Christian should be continually growing in love for the values of the kingdom of God, so that these become heartfelt responses to the good that can be achieved and rejections of the evil that is rampant not only in the world around but also as temptations in oneself. True Christian morality should be lived ultimately out of love for the beautiful good of Christ Himself and a desire to love others as He did. (Cf. Conscience.)

Morality Play • Plays that are so designated for the moral struggle between virtue and vice which figures at the core of this genre of religious drama. *Everyman* is an example of a morality play.

Moravian Church • The Moravian Church traces its history back to Jan Hus (or John Huss), a priest and rector of the University of Prague who was burned at the stake for heresy in 1415. Hus disputed the spiritual authority of the Pope and bishops and appealed to the Bible only. In 1457 a group of Hussites formed the Unitas Fratrum or Unity of the Brethren. By the end of the sixteenth century, the Unitas Fratrum became the largest Protestant Church in Bohemia. By the eighteenth century, the Moravians were sending missionaries to South America, Greenland, South Africa and the United States, particularly Pennsylvania.

This church follows the Church year and a liturgical form of worship, but Moravian Churches have no altars. They observe the Lord's Supper six or seven times a year. The church baptizes infants but does not admit children to Communion until they have been confirmed.

The power of Moravian bishops is spiritual rather than administrative. The orders of the Church also include presbyters, or elders, and deacons.

The Moravian Church in America is divided into two provinces, south and north, including Canada. It is governed by a synod made up of clergy and laity, forming a legislative assembly.

Morganatic Marriage • A union of a man of noble rank and a woman who is either of lesser rank or not a member of the nobility at all. In such marriages the woman could not accede to her husband's rank, nor could children of the marriage succeed to his property or dignities. Originally a German institution, the practice derives its name from the German *Morgengabe* or morning gift, because it was presumed that all the woman could expect was the *Morgengabe* or dowry. As far as the Church is concerned, a Morganatic marriage is no different from any other marriage.

Mormons • The Church of Jesus Christ of the Latter Day Saints, popularly known as the Mormons, was founded by Joseph Smith (1805-1844) in 1830 in Fayette, New York. According to Mormon belief, God revealed to Smith in a series of visions, beginning in 1820, that all existing churches had fallen into error and that Smith was to found the true church. He was led by an angel to Cumorah Hill near Manchester, New York, where he discovered golden tablets recounting the sacred history of America's ancient inhabitants (the Hebrew tribe, the Jaredites) and containing the word of God. Before being returned to the angel, the contents of these tablets were transcribed as the *Book of Mormon*, a scripture of equal authority with the Bible, "supporting but not supplanting" it.

Local opposition drove the Mormons from New York, first to Kirtland, Ohio, then to Independence, Missouri, then on to Nauvoo, Illinois (where Smith and his brother Hyrum were killed by a mob in 1844), and finally to Utah, where Salt Lake City became the headquarters of the church in 1847. As leader (president of the Quorum of the Twelve Apostles), Brigham Young (1801-1877) brought stability to the community, though not before the church was divided by schisms (from which the five denominations of Mormons arose).

Its basis in the Bible and the *Book of Mormon* gives Mormonism the flavor of conservative Protestantism. Mormons practiced polygamy until 1890, when, under pressure of the U.S. government, their leader advised conformity to the law (although excommunicated "Fundamentalists" continue to advocate the practice). Church teaching has a markedly Adventist bent in holding to the literal reign of Christ over the new earth. The church influences all phases of life and inspires deep loyalty. Mormons must devote eighteen months to full-time missionary work. Worldwide membership is about six and a half million.

Morning Offering • A prayer recited each day, offering the day in union with Christ's self-offering. The most common form is that used by the Apostleship of Prayer:

"O Jesus, through the Immaculate Heart of Mary, I offer You all my prayers, works, joys, and sufferings of this day, for all the intentions of Your Sacred Heart, in union with the Holy Sacrifice of the Mass throughout the world, in reparation for my sins, for the intentions of all our associates, and for the general intention recommended this month."

Morning Star • The expression "morning stars," in the plural, is found in Job 38:7, where the reference appears to be to the stars that are shining before sunrise. The word is used in Isaiah 14:12 to refer, in a rather unfavorable way, to the king of Babylon. In 2 Peter 1:19, it is used of Christ and is again so employed in Revelation 2:28 and 22:16.

By an odd twist of reference which combined Isaiah 14:12 with Luke 10:18, the Latin word for "light-bearer" or morning star, *lucifer*, has become a name for the Devil in the Latin Church. The expression *Stella matutina* (morning star) made its way into the Litany of Loreto as a title of Mary. This title may have evolved from a line of reasoning that sees Mary symbolized by the morning star — the last star visible in the sky before the rise of the sun. Mary heralded the dawning of the Sun of Justice, Jesus.

Mortal Sin • The deliberate, conscious and free transgression of a moral law, involving very serious matter, and resulting in the loss of grace and separation from God. Mortal sin is so grave that its punishment is eternal damnation in hell.

Three conditions must be present for the commission of a mortal sin: (1) the matter must be grave (e.g., murder, abortion, fornication, adultery, blasphemy); (2) there must be sufficient reflecting on the evil which one is contemplating; and (3) there must be full consent of the will. Various factors can limit these conditions, for example, lack of maturity, force of habit, etc. However, one must never presume to be incapable of such deadly sin.

Mortal sins are forgiven by God through the sinner's penitence and the sacramental absolution of a priest.

Mortal and Venial Sin: See **Sin, Mortal and Venial**

Mortification • The free and deliberate self-imposition of forms of suffering, pain or self-denial, in order to suppress immoral and sinful inclinations, thereby drawing closer to God and increasing one's holiness of life. Acts of mortification are acts in which the person turns against sinful tendencies and toward God as our security against them. Mortifying acts are part of our Christian life, for they enable us to participate vicariously in the sufferings of Christ: "[W]hoever wishes to be my follower must deny his very self" (Lk 9:23).

Mortification brings about a detachment from material and bodily goods, and it implies a deepened attachment to spiritual goods and higher moral values. Mortification turns the person to seek the joy that is related to charity, fraternal love and discipleship with Christ. Mortification is important because it gives us an awareness of the ever-present nature of sin. It conditions us to be able to bear the burdens of Christian life in the world, by striving for the salvation of the world and the building of the kingdom. It promotes the virtue of penance, by which we call upon God for His grace to make us strong in our weakness. (Cf. Asceticism.)

Mosaic Law • While the word "law" and particular laws are frequently mentioned both in the Old Testament and in the New Testament, God's revelation to Moses on Mount Sinai (Ex 19-24) is called the Law of Moses or the Mosaic law because of the privileged role assigned to Moses as mediator of that revelation to Israel.

The Mishnaic tractate *Aboth*, "The Fathers," begins, "Moses received the Torah from Sinai" (*Aboth* 1:1), — describing the unbroken line of oral and written tradition that stretches back to the Sinai revelation. Although the Hebrew word *Torah* means "instruction" or "teaching," its translation into Greek as *nomos* and into Latin as *lex* led to the English rendering of Torah as "law."

Biblical references to the Law of Moses generally refer to the whole Pentateuch, the first five books of the Bible, as distinguished from the Prophets and the Writings, which are the other two major divisions of the Hebrew Bible. References to the Pentateuch as the Law of Moses do not separate its legal prescriptions and prohibitions from other material found therein. The whole Torah constitutes the divine instruction which is the norm for Israel's life according to the covenant.

The traditional understanding that the entire Torah was revealed to Moses on Mt. Sinai is connected with the traditional conclusion that Moses was the author of the Pentateuch. Today it is commonly understood that Moses himself could not have been the author of the Pentateuch, but that the process of its composition was quite complex.

Michelangelo's Moses

The phrase "Law of Moses" and similar expressions are especially frequent in Deuteronomistic writings and in the work of the Chronicler (e.g., cf. Jos 1:7; 2 Chr 23:18; Ezr 7:6).

The New Testament also refers to the Law of Moses. In Luke 24:44, the risen Christ opens the minds of His disciples to understand the Scriptures, demonstrating that "everything written about me in the law of Moses and in the prophets and psalms must be fulfilled." Thus does the Lucan Jesus describe the entire Old Testament. Acts 28:23 uses the same expression in a similar way.

New Testament texts also present Moses in his role as lawgiver (e.g., Jn 1:17, 45; 7:19) and make reference to the prescriptive dimensions of the Mosaic law (e.g., Jn 7:23; Acts 15:5; 1 Cor 9:9).

For further reading: Michael D. Guinan, "Mosaic Covenant," *Anchor Bible Dictionary*, 4:905-909.

Moses • While the name "Moses" appears some 771 times in the Old Testament and a few more times in the New Testament, the figure or person we know as Moses appears for the first time in Exodus 2. Here the birth of Moses is recorded, along with his much-storied discovery by Pharaoh's daughter among reeds on the riverbank (Ex 2:3-10).

After growing up as the adopted son of Pharaoh's daughter, Moses killed an Egyptian (Ex 2:12). Knowing he would be the victim of Pharaoh's wrath, Moses fled to the land of Midian, where he married Zipporah. Together, they had a son whom they named Gershom.

While Moses was tending his father-in-law Jethro's flock, the Lord appeared to him in the form of a burning bush (Ex 3:2). At this point, God revealed His plan for Moses to lead the Israelites out of bondage in Egypt. But Moses considered himself a poor candidate to lead the Israelites to freedom; therefore, God gave Moses an assistant, his brother Aaron (Ex 4:16).

Under the direction of Moses, the Israelites crossed over the Red Sea and eluded the pursuit of Pharaoh's charioteers. Following their heroic escape, the Israelites made their way to the Promised Land. But, while out in the desert, Moses was summoned to the top of Mt. Sinai, where God gave him the Decalogue (Ex 20:1-17).

In the New Testament, Christ is presented as the New Moses, especially in St. Matthew's Gospel. Christ is the New Lawgiver, the One Who establishes the definitive covenant between God and man — a covenant sealed in the Blood of the Lamb.

For further reading: Florence Morgan Gillman, "Moses," *Anchor Bible Dictionary*, 4:909-920.

Moslems: See **Muslims**

Motet • Musical composition in polyphonic style. It is believed that the motet developed from Gregorian chant melodies being embellished with tropes and a process called organum. The original melodic line would be sung with Latin text. Gradually second and third lines were added above the original and either Latin or French words were sung. Some composers tried to include secular texts in the motet. These were not acceptable in the church service but found their way into the secular repertoire. The word "motet" is now used to refer to any choral work with religious words which are not part of the official liturgical texts.

Motive, Spiritual • The reason or purpose of an action, which for Catholics must ultimately be the love of God, promotion of holiness and the life of grace or the advancement of the moral virtues.

Motu Proprio • The common name given to a type of papal document which is written by the Pope on his own initiative and addressed to the entire Church, to a portion of it or to particular persons. A *motu proprio* may be administrative or doctrinal in nature or may contain a favor accorded by the Pope.

Movable Feasts • Those feasts of the liturgical calendar which are not assigned to a specific date, such as December 25 for Christmas, but which change because their celebration is based on another means of counting time, e.g., solstice and equinox, as opposed to chronological dates. The prime example is Easter, whose date changes annually based on the lunar calendar (it is celebrated on the first Sunday after the date of the first full moon occurring on or after March 21). Because this date changes annually, a number of "feasts" are movable annually: Ash Wednesday (forty days before Easter), Ascension and Pentecost (forty and fifty days after Easter, respectively), as well as the Sundays of the Lent and Easter Seasons. Similarly, because the First Sunday of Advent occurs on the Sunday falling closest to or on the feast of St. Andrew (November 30), the dates for the Sundays of Advent change annually.

Mozarabic Rite • One of the non-Roman Western liturgical rites proper to the Iberian

Peninsula, celebrated through the eleventh century. Early references to this kind of Iberian Liturgy derive from a letter of Pope Vigilius (c. 594) and Isidore of Seville's *De Ecclesiasticis Officiis*. Despite the efforts of Popes Alexander II and Gregory VII to abolish the Mozarabic Rites, pockets of this Moorish liturgical influence prevailed during the fourteenth and fifteenth centuries. Cardinal Ximénez, archbishop of Toledo from 1495 to 1517, secured papal approbation for its use in the Toledo cathedral and in six parishes according to a newly printed Missal and Breviary.

This Rite contained the customary Liturgy of the Word but retained the reading from the Old Testament as the First Reading at Mass, followed by a chant with clear Moorish influence. A series of nine prayers and rites followed, among which were two followed by the reading of names in the diptychs for intercessions, the kiss of peace, the *illatio* (or transition to the Eucharistic prayer, a chief characteristic of the Rite), and an epiclesis (invocation of the Holy Spirit, especially significant when this was absent from the Roman Rite). The fraction of the Host into nine pieces, seven of which were placed on the paten in the form of a cross, reflected Gallican and Celtic practices.

This Rite is now reserved to quasi-private celebrations in a chapel in the Cathedral of Toledo. Recent interest in research into this Rite has been sparked by the possibility of reviving some of its features for an indigenous Spanish Liturgy.

Mozzetta • An elbow-length cape buttoning down the front, worn by the Pope, cardinals, bishops, abbots and canons. It is worn over the rochet and the choir cassock. The Pope's mozzetta is of red satin, that of cardinals is scarlet wool and that worn by bishops is purple wool; abbots have one in the distinctive colors of their order, and

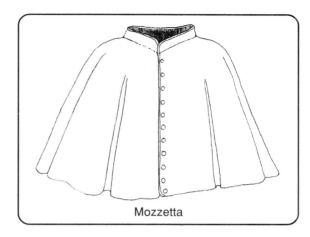

Mozzetta

canons wear gray or black with red or purple piping. A descendant of the almuce, the mozzetta gets its name from the Italian *mozzare*, "to cut off," a reference to its shortness. Before the reform of Pope Paul VI in 1969, the mozzetta was a sign of jurisdiction, but now any prelate entitled to wear it may wear it anywhere. It has been in use since the thirteenth or fourteenth century.

Muratorian Fragment • Also known as the Canon of Muratori. The oldest list of New Testament books, it was discovered in the Ambrosian Library in Milan by L. A. Muratori (1672-1750), after whom it is named. Muratori published his find in 1740. The manuscript is not older than the eighth century, but is believed to reproduce a listing of New Testament books drawn up, as it seems, in or near A.D. 180-190. St. Hippolytus is frequently thought of as the compiler of the list. The manuscript found by Muratori is fragmentary; its beginning is missing, and possibly its end as well. That part of the document that treats of Matthew and most of Mark is wanting. Further, there is no mention of Hebrews, James, 1 Peter, 2 Peter, or 3 John.

Music, Church • Music for use in the Church in both liturgical and paraliturgical services. Music in the Church can be traced back to Christ Himself, who sang psalms with His disciples at the Last Supper (cf. Mk 14:26). Church music with its Jewish tradition of psalms and canticles was gradually enlarged to include hymns and various chants, especially Gregorian chants. By the fifteenth century, polyphony was accepted for use in liturgical celebrations. The first Catholic hymn book was published in 1537. During the seventeenth century people were striving for new tunes which sounded fresh and somewhat worldly. Hymn books appearing in the mid-eighteenth century indicated their non-liturgical contents by their titles. One such book, *New Songs for Church and Home, Dedicated to God and the Lamb*, can be given as an example.

Church music became an ornament of worship and a means of providing artistic display. The notion that church music was an integral part of the liturgy was lost. With the rise of polyphonic choirs, the music *of* worship became the music *at* worship.

Today church music is a vital part of both liturgical and paraliturgical services. Since the Church is the guardian of the liturgy and the sacraments, she has the right and the obligation to legislate concerning all aspects of the liturgy and sacraments. Music for paraliturgical services retains great freedom, since these services do not reflect the entire Church but merely the particular worshipers present.

For music to be admitted into a liturgical celebration (e.g., Mass, Liturgy of the Hours, the sacraments, etc.), it must pass the triple judgment outlined in "Music in Catholic Worship."

It is important to note that the same piece of music may be acceptable for one liturgical service but not permissible in another. For example, *Salve Regina* sung at the close of the liturgy on the feast of the Immaculate Conception or at Night Prayer of the Liturgy of the Hours is certainly correct. The same hymn sung at the Communion of the Mass on Pentecost would be inappropriate and hence would not pass the triple judgment for that celebration.

Music Coordinator • Person responsible for all music in a parish. This person must be a competent musician and liturgist. He or she must make the musical and liturgical judgments on every piece of music used in the liturgical services of the parish. These include all Masses, Liturgy of the Hours and sacraments. The coordinator is responsible for the work of each group and makes the determination as to the appropriateness of each musical selection before it is admitted to the liturgy.

Music, Liturgical • Music intended and approved for use in liturgical services. Church music can be divided into two major parts, pieces accepted for use in liturgical services and those that are more appropriate for paraliturgical functions. In order for a piece of music to be approved for use in a liturgical service, it must pass the triple judgment test set forth in "Music in Catholic Worship." These judgments are the musical, the liturgical and the pastoral. A musical selection that fails in even one of these areas may not be used in a liturgical service but may be extremely useful to the congregation during a paraliturgical function. It should be noted that personal preference has no place in decision-making about the acceptability of music. Style is also not a measurement of supportable music. Each style is to be judged on its own merits in the context of the triple judgment.

Music in Catholic Worship • A 1972 publication of the Bishops' Committee on the Liturgy. It was presented as background and as a guideline for the proper role of music within the liturgy. The most noted section of the document deals with the three judgments that are to be made to determine the value of a given musical element before it is incorporated into the liturgy. These judgments are musical, liturgical and pastoral. (Cf. Musical Judgment; Liturgical Judgment; Pastoral Judgment.)

Music, Passion: See **Passion Music**

Music Today, Liturgical • A 1982 publication of the Bishops' Committee on the Liturgy. It reaffirms and elaborates the principles set down by the bishops' 1972 publication "Music in Catholic Worship." Between the Second Vatican Council and the publication of the 1972 document, not all of the rites of the sacraments had been revised. This later work, "Liturgical Music Today," expands on the directions found in the earlier paper, addresses some questions raised during the decade of its use, and deals directly with the celebration of the Liturgy of the Hours and the sacraments (except the Eucharist, which was treated exclusively in "Music in Catholic Worship").

Musical Judgment: See **Judgment, Musical**

Muslims • Muslims (or Moslems) are followers of Muhammad the prophet. They are believers in Islam (Mohammedanism), which originated in Arabia but today has followers all over the world. This last of the

Angelic musician (medieval illumination)

three great monotheistic religions to appear is the dominant religion throughout large areas of Asia, North Africa, the Middle East, Pakistan, Malaysia and Indonesia. Muslims revere their sacred book, the Koran, which they believe to contain revelations from God to Muhammad. The devout Muslim has five duties: (1) to recognize only one God; (2) to pray five times a day facing Mecca; (3) to give generous alms to the poor; (4) to maintain a fast in the month of Ramadan;

(5) to make a pilgrimage to Mecca at least once in a lifetime.

The positive attitude of the Catholic Church toward Islam is stated in the Vatican II document Declaration on the Relationship of the Church to Non-Christian Religions (*Nostra Aetate*), n. 3.

Mustum • Unfermented grape juice. It differs from ordinary grape juice in that it contains no additives. In 1974 the Congregation for the Doctrine of the Faith authorized Ordinaries to permit priests who were under treatment or had been treated for alcoholism to use mustum in place of regular wine at the celebration of Mass. In 1983 the same congregation revoked all general faculties relative to the use of mustum and decreed that celebrants may receive Communion by intinction and let another participant at the Mass consume the remainder of the consecrated Wine. Those priests who had received permission to use mustum before the revocation were not affected by this revocation and may continue to do so.

Myron • The Greek term means "perfumed or scented oil." Usually it refers to the chrism consecrated by a bishop on Holy Thursday during the Divine Liturgy and distributed to parishes and priests for the conferring of the mystery (sacrament) of chrismation (Confirmation). Myron, thus consecrated, is also used by a bishop (or designated priest) in the consecration of churches and altars. Myron may also refer to the oil which exudes from the bones of certain saints, for example, St. Nicholas of Myra, presently interred in Bari, Italy, or the oil which may appear streaming miraculously from the face of some holy icon, often bearing a sweet scent.

Myrrh • Gum resin used as an ingredient in incense. In ancient times it was used as a perfume and an embalmer. Myrrh was presented to the Infant Jesus by the Magi on the Epiphany as an acknowledgment of His future suffering and death.

Mysteries of the Rosary • Fifteen incidents in the life of Jesus or Mary which are meditated on during the recitation of the fifteen decades of the Rosary. Three sets of five mysteries each are assigned to different days of the week when all fifteen decades are not said together: joyful (Monday and Thursday), sorrowful (Tuesday and Friday) and glorious (Wednesday, Saturday and Sunday). The joyful mysteries are the Annunciation, Visitation, Birth of Our Lord, Presentation and Finding of Jesus in the Temple; the sorrowful are the Agony in the Garden, Scourging at the Pillar, Crowning with Thorns, Carrying of the Cross, Crucifixion and Death of Our Lord; the glorious are the Resurrection, the Ascension, Descent of the Holy Spirit, the Assumption and the Coronation of Mary as Queen of Heaven.

Mystery • In the theological sense, the term "mystery" refers to the whole plan by which God saves us in Christ. In this sense, mystery is a way of referring to God Himself: for the plan of our salvation is in the first place a plan conceived by God's loving knowledge. To be saved by Him is to be continually drawn into the mystery revealed in Christ. The term mystery, in the plural, refers then to the particular elements of the divine plan as we encounter it in faith and love, knowledge and experience. In its Christian sense, mystery transcends the ordinary meanings of the word associated with intellectual problems needing resolution or events requiring explanation. God's wisdom and plan are luminous in their intrinsic intelligibility. This luminosity only begins to become clear to the eyes of faith, and will be perfectly revealed only in the life of glory when we see God face to face.

Mystery, Paschal: See **Paschal Mystery**

Mystical Body of Christ • The notion that the Church forms the Mystical Body of Christ combines a number of important truths. In the first place, membership in the Church entails an intimate communion with Jesus Christ that He Himself described as the relationship of vine and branches (cf. Jn 15:5). The communion of life between Christ and His disciples gives rise to the Church. This communion in Christ is properly identified as: (a) "bodily," in that it is like the unity formed by the members, or parts, of a body; and as (b) "mystical," in that the reality of this unity is accessible, not to ordinary sense perception and knowledge, but to the eyes of faith. The Church forms a single body, united with Christ as the head, but with members who retain their diversity (1 Cor 12:1-11; Eph 1:18-23). The doctrine of the Mystical Body of Christ received a comprehensive formulation in the encyclical *Mystici Corporis* of Pope Pius XII (1943) and was reiterated at the Second Vatican Council (cf. LG 7).

Mystical Sense of Scripture • The "mystical sense" is sometimes called the typological meaning of a text. In biblical typology the figure, event or person of an Old Testament passage prefigures or anticipates a figure, event or person in the New Testament. That is, the type (Old Testament reference) foreshadows, anticipates or points to an antitype to be revealed at a future time (New Testament). An example or two might help to clarify matters. In the Old Testament we note that manna was sent by God to feed and nourish Israel in the Exodus-journey from slavery (Egypt) into freedom (Palestine). That manna became a type of the Eucharist and so anticipates Jesus as the deeper manna, the Bread from heaven. Manna is the type; Jesus is the antitype. Old Testament figures such as Adam, Melchizedek and David are types for Christ, Who is *the* antitype for the fulfillment of the deeper reality to which their lives pointed. The antitype is usually "organically" related to its type just as the Old Testament figures, persons or events blossom forth into full flowering in the New Testament. Thus the things *signified* by the Old Testament types refer to their immediate historical referents, as well as to their antitypes to be revealed later in the New Testament.

Mystical Theology • Since the seventeenth century there has been a tendency to distinguish the branches of theology in a way that was foreign to the unified vision of theology characteristic of classical medieval theology. Dogmatic theology (whose object is things to be believed) was distinguished from moral theology (whose object is things to be done), and moral theology itself was distinguished from ascetical theology and mystical theology. According to the latter distinction, moral theology is concerned with the basics of Christian life. Ascetical theology studies the dynamics of ordinary purification in the person who is beginning in the practice of virtue, while mystical theology is concerned with the higher states of prayer attained through the gifts of the Holy Spirit and the special grace conferred upon the person who is far advanced along the way of perfection.

Although these pragmatic divisions of the work of theology correspond to distinctions in the field of Christian belief and practice, they have contributed to a certain fragmentation in the unity of theology, to a marked intellectualization of dogmatic theology, and to the elevation of casuistry in moral theology. A more serious outcome of the division of moral, ascetical and mystical theology has been the implication that the call to perfect charity is a selective rather than a universal one. In order at least partly to compensate for this weakness, many recent theologians prefer to include ascetical and mystical theology under the more comprehensive rubric of spiritual theology. It can only be hoped that theologians will continue to seek and give expression to an integral vision of the Christian Faith and life, in which the profound unity of dogmatic, moral and spiritual theology will be clearly exhibited.

Mystici Corporis Christi • Published on June 29, 1943, *Mystici Corporis Christi* is the encyclical in which Pope Pius XII teaches about the Church as the Mystical Body of Christ. He builds upon that description, saying that the Church is a "body" because it is one, undivided and visible, with each member of the body having a proper role, drawing sustenance and being sanctified by the sacraments. He further teaches that the Church is the "Body of Christ" because it was Christ Who founded it through preaching, by His suffering on the cross, and in sending the Holy Spirit on the day of Pentecost. Christ is the Head of the body, His Church, by reason of His preeminence as God which gives Him the right to rule and govern the Church. This He does, invisibly in the hearts and minds of men, and visibly through the Pope and bishops. Through His governance Christ enlightens and sanctifies the Church, and by the graces which come from Him, He supports the Church in its mission of bringing His salvation to the world. The encyclical then teaches that the Church, the Body of Christ, is "mystical" because of that particular union which is between Christ and the Church, lifting it above any mere human society. This mystical union accomplishes many things in the lives of the faithful, bringing them closer to one another and to Christ through the virtues of faith, hope, and charity, with the indwelling of the Holy Spirit making their union more perfect.

After a brief teaching about the Holy Eucharist as the symbol of unity, *Mystici Corporis Christi* warns about certain errors which can endanger faith, such as false mysticism and quietism, and then exhorts the faithful to penance and prayer. In his conclusion, Pope Pius XII commends the Church to the protection of the Blessed Virgin Mary, that she "may never cease to beg from Him that copious streams of grace may flow from its exalted Head into all the members of the Mystical Body."

Mysticism • According to the apt definition of Jean Gerson (1363-1429), mysticism is the "knowledge of God arrived at through the embrace of unifying love." Mystical knowledge has the same object as the knowledge of faith and theology, but its method is more intuitive and direct than discursive and scientific. A disciplined life given over to long periods of contemplation sets the stage for, though it does not ensure, an intimate knowledge and experience of God that He bestows through a special grace. Detachment, purification and cultivation of stillness are fundamental in focusing the person's gaze on God. The struggle against distraction, sensuality and absorption in the concerns of simply bodily life prepare the mystic for the experience of mystical states.

Although the normal means by which human beings come to know God are through images and concepts, there is no reason to suppose that God could not bypass these ordinary vehicles in order to provide for a direct, spiritual intellection of Him that may be occasional or even permanent. Gerson's definition points to this harmonious ordering of the mystic's intellect and will toward the supremely perfect object of knowledge and love.

Christian mysticism is distinctive in the prominence it gives to the notion of union over that of absorption. The mystic retains his or her personal identity in the relationship of mystical knowledge and love. The mystical relationship is thus a truly personal relationship between a created person and the triunely personal Creator.

Hindu and Buddhist forms of mysticism, consistent with the pan-cosmic conceptions out of which they arise, stress the absorption of the mystic in the impersonal unity underlying all reality.

Myth • In ancient Greek literature (e.g., Homer, *Odyssey* 11.56) "myth" (Greek, *mythos*) designated a "word," "speech," later on "an account," "story" or "narrative" and eventually came to mean "rumor" or "fable." Contemporary scholars define myth as a symbolic form of thinking in the language, art and science of the day in which the mind attempts to understand that which is beyond sensible experience. Narratives and stories of this nature answer primary questions: Who am I? Who is "God"?/Who are the gods? What are the origins of the universe, the tribe? What is good?

In the New Testament the term invariably has a negative connotation. Typical use includes the notion that a story or teaching is unreliable, fanciful, of human origins alone or just plain false (1 Tm 1:4; 4:7; 2 Tm 4:4; Ti 1:14; 2 Pt 1:16). Some scholars consider any religious attempt to express the inexplicable as mythological in one way or another. Regardless of the merits or drawbacks of such a position, the presence of mythological images and other elements need not carry any pejorative meaning. Various images from ancient Greek mythologies (so prior to the pejorative use of the term) have found their way into New Testament passages expressing aspects of the Christian proclamation. In such instances, the New Testament authors are recasting or reshaping the conceptual material to fit the reality revealed to them.

For further reading: Robert A. Oden, Jr., et al., "Myth and Mythology," *Anchor Bible Dictionary*, 4:946-965.

Nag Hammadi • About sixty miles south of Luxor, Egypt, Nag Hammadi is the site of the discovery in 1945 of a collection of thirteen papyrus codices in an earthenware jar. These codices contained a Gnostic library written in Coptic. The discovery was of immense importance, since most of our knowledge of Gnostic ideas had come through the polemical writings of the Fathers of the Church. Scholars could now have the opportunity for direct study of Gnostic literature. An interesting outcome of this study has been the recognition of the general faithfulness of the patristic portrait of Gnostic ideas.

For further reading: Birger A. Pearson, "Nag Hammadi," *Anchor Bible Dictionary*, 4:982-993; James M. Robinson, ed., *The Nag Hammadi Library*, Revised Edition (Harper & Row, 1988).

Nahum, Book of • Late in the seventh century B.C., the Assyrian Empire was under attack by the Babylonians. Assyria had been such a cruel oppressor that the prospect of its fall evoked cries of joy from all those who had been its victims. This religious poet, Nahum, saw in the fall of Nineveh, "the bloody city," the hand of a just and avenging God. The three chapters of his book contain his triumphant orations and poems written as the end drew near.

For further reading: Kevin C. Cathcart, "Nahum, Book of," *Anchor Bible Dictionary*, 4:998-1000; Thomas P. Wahl, O.S.B., Irene Nowell, O.S.B., and Anthony Ceresko, "Zephaniah, Nahum, Habakkuk," *New Jerome Biblical Commentary*, 255-264.

Name, Christian • The former Code of Canon Law (1917) required that pastors saw to it that the name given a person at Baptism was a Christian name (normally that of a saint). The present Code states that "parents, sponsors and the pastor are to see that a name foreign to a Christian mentality" is not given at Baptism (Canon 855). This modification puts the burden on parents and sponsors and reiterates the mitigation already given in the Rite of Christian Initiation for Adults, where it states that in non-Christian territories "a Christian name or one in use in that part of the world, so long as it has a Christian meaning" (nn. 203, 205), may be chosen.

Name Day • The annual observance of one's patron whose memory is commemorated in the liturgical calendar. Feast days are reserved to deceased persons who have received the Church's approbation and been given the title "saint" or "blessed." Name days are for the living who have been named after such patrons.

Names of God • A host of names for God is found in the Old Testament: *El, Elohim, El Elyon, El Shaddai* and others. The proper personal for God is "Yahweh." Exodus 3:13ff. gives the impression that this name was first disclosed to Moses on the occasion of the burning bush, for him to pass on to the Israelites.

For further reading: Martin Rose, "Names of God in the Old Testament," *Anchor Bible Dictionary*, 4:1001-1011.

Nash Papyrus • Before the discoveries at Qumran, this was the only known ancient biblical manuscript in Hebrew. The Nash Papyrus is a fragment of papyrus purchased in 1902 from an Egyptian dealer by W. L. Nash. It dates from around 150 B.C. and contains the Ten Commandments, substantially in the form of Deuteronomy 5:6-21, and the Shema (Dt 6:4-5). Cambridge University Library houses this discovery. (Cf. Shema.)

National Assembly of Religious Women (NARW) • Originally founded in the spring of 1970 as the National Assembly of Women Religious (NAWR), a decade later it was changed to the National Assembly of Religious Women (NARW). It aims to be a voice for women who belong to different congregations and orders in the United States but are united by mutual concerns and goals, especially as they relate to social action programs. There are various classifications of membership in the National Assembly of Religious Women, even allowing for the admission of clergy and lay associates who share the concerns of the members. The headquarters of the NARW are in Chicago, Illinois.

National Association of Pastoral Musicians • Organization founded in 1976 to help foster deeper spiritual participation in liturgical functions through improved celebrations. The organization strives to improve the musical and liturgical caliber of all persons and materials involved in the liturgy. It allows for dual membership for clergy and musicians, arranges educational programs, conducts regional and national conventions and publishes materials dealing with musical and liturgical matters. The main office is located in Washington, D.C.

National Black Sisters' Conference (NBSC) • Developed in 1968, the conference seeks to identify and serve the needs of black Catholics in the United States and the offshore islands. Membership is composed of black sisters irrespective of their congregations or orders, along with other groups of women religious who are in agreement with the objectives and aspirations of the National Black Sisters' Conference.

Among the purposes of the National Black Sisters' Conference are the following: (1) to promote black Catholic vocations; (2) to act as a clearinghouse of information for black sisters; (3) to assist in the evaluation and execution of apostolic projects; (4) to improve black community schools; and (5) to aid in the reform of prisons.

The conference is headquartered in Oakland, California.

National Catholic Conference for Interracial Justice • This body provides programs and offers resources which contribute to an increased harmony and better understanding among the races. Originating in 1960, the national conference consists of more than sixty member councils encouraging Catholics to become more involved on the local level in fighting racial prejudice and discrimination. It has its headquarters in Washington, D.C.

National Catholic Educational Association (NCEA) • The largest private professional educational association in the world. Founded at St. Louis, Missouri, in 1904, it assumed the title of NCEA in 1929. Its membership represents more than 200,000 educators serving 7.6 million students in Catholic education at all levels, including preschools, elementary and secondary schools, religious education programs, universities and seminaries. Its mission is to respond to Christ's call to "go and teach all nations," by providing leadership and support to those in the educational apostolate of the Catholic Church.

Its specific aims are: (1) to promote improved means of teaching, administration and educational methods in Catholic schools, in keeping with the principles and philosophy of Catholic education; (2) to give assistance and encourage scholarly research in the fields of education and school administration; (3) to serve as an agency for the exchange of information through news releases and publications concerning programs, curricula, texts and general information for those engaged in teaching.

NCEA is composed of the following departments: Elementary Schools, Secondary Schools, Chief Administrators of Catholic Education, Religious Education, Catholic Colleges and Universities, and Seminaries.

Its annual convention, usually held in the week following Easter, draws over twenty thousand participants.

The NCEA is located in Washington, D.C.

National Catholic Welfare Conference (NCWC) • An "agency of the Archbishops and Bishops of the United States to organize, unify and coordinate Catholic activities for the general welfare of the Church," the NCWC succeeded the National Catholic War Council (1918-1919) on February 20, 1919. In 1967, after almost half a century of existence, its activities were taken over by the United States Catholic Conference and the National Conference of Catholic Bishops.

National Conference of Catholic Bishops (NCCB) • In response to the call of the Second Vatican Council for the formation of regional conferences of bishops, the National Catholic Welfare Conference (NCWC) was reorganized by the bishops of the United States in 1967. Under the bipartite reorganization, the public policy role previously exercised by the NCWC was continued under the United States Catholic Conference (USCC), while the new structure for the collegial exercise of the pastoral and teaching missions of the bishops was called the National Conference of Catholic Bishops. The NCCB and USCC express the two distinct areas of responsibility of the bishops for Church and society. The USCC is a civil, non-profit organization that shares administrative structures with the NCCB. (Cf. United States Catholic Conference.)

Headquartered in Washington, D.C., the staff of the NCCB/USCC operates under the direction of the general secretary and three associate general secretaries. The general secretary is elected by the bishops and serves a five-year term. The secretariats and departments of the NCCB/USCC serve as staff to the standing and ad hoc committees of the conference of bishops.

The principal standing committees of the NCCB are: Doctrine; Liturgy; Ecumenical and Interreligious Affairs; Pastoral Practices; Canonical Affairs; Priestly Life and Ministry; Vocations; Priestly Formation; Permanent Diaconate; Marriage and Family Life; Laity; Pro-Life Activities; Science and Human Values; Migration; Missions; Women in Society and in the Church; Hispanic Affairs; African-American Catholics.

National Council of Catholic Laity • Really a combination of two organizations, that is, the National Council of Catholic Men and the National Council of Catholic Women. Because it is an umbrella group, then, the National Council of Catholic Laity represents some fifteen smaller organizations of Catholic membership. To make known its programs and resources, the National Council of Catholic Laity publishes *People* (not to be confused with *People Magazine*). The organization is presided over by a national board of directors, elected officers and an executive secretary. The national headquarters are in Cincinnati, Ohio.

National Council of Catholic Men (NCCM) • Established in 1920 under the old National Catholic Welfare Conference (NCWC) and operating under the aegis of the American hierarchy, the National Council of Catholic Men exists to augment and extend the reach of the lay apostolate in the secular world. The National Council of Catholic Men is involved in liturgical and spiritual renewal, communications, social action, legislation, family life, youth work, public relations, international affairs and leadership training. One of the national council's most important functions is to represent American Catholic laymen at various international meetings. It is located in Annandale, Virginia.

National Council of Catholic Women (NCCW) • Coming into existence in 1920, the National Council of Catholic Women, like its counterpart, the National Council of Catholic Men, is a federation of service organizations for Catholic women in the United States. Through publications, conferences and sponsorship of events, the National Council of Catholic Women fosters a spirit of lay responsibility for the Church's mission in secular society. Although there is an important role for the National Council of Catholic Women to play on the domestic scene, it continues to exercise its greatest role on the international scene as a representative of Catholic women in the United States to the larger, universal Church. As such, it is an affiliate of the World Union of Catholic Women's Organizations. Its bimonthly publication is entitled *Catholic Woman*.

National Council of Churches • The National Council of the Churches of Christ in the U.S.A. was established in 1950 as the successor to the Federal Council of Churches, which had been organized in 1909. Its purpose is to encourage ecumenical and missionary endeavors, cooperation among the churches and more efficient use of resources. Its headquarters are in New York, New York.

National Federation of Priests' Councils (NFPC) • In 1968, the NFPC was founded to provide a national forum to address major issues affecting priestly life and ministry from the perspective of the lived experience of diocesan and religious priests. Its stated goals are to promote priestly unity and fraternity by facilitating communication among priests' councils, to assist priests' councils to reflect on and promote justice in light of the social teachings of the Church and to collaborate with the National Conference of Catholic Bishops.

The NFPC is directed by its House of Delegates, a national gathering of priests from member councils that sets the agenda for the year, and by an executive board. It is staffed by a president, an executive director and a program director. It is located in Chicago, Illinois.

National Parish • Although most parishes are territorial, it is possible to establish a personal parish that meets the pastoral needs of a specific group of people. For example, a national parish is one established for persons of a specific nationality or ethnic background. As a rule, national parishes are not territorial as such. Rather, they are comprised of all the people of a given nationality within a certain area and often are coextensive with one or more territorial parishes. Pastors of personal parishes exercise the care of souls and have jurisdiction over their subjects anywhere. As far as marriages are concerned, personal pastors of national parishes can validly witness them only if at least one of the parties is their subject.

National parishes were much more common in the last century and in the years prior to Vatican II. Since that time many of the ethnic groups who constituted national parishes have become more assimilated into the general population. Many national parishes no longer serve people of the original nationality but others (Canon 518).

Nationalism • Like certain forms of nativism, nationalism places undue stress on securing advantages for one's nation (or sometimes ethnic group) at the expense of the legitimate aspiration of others. It should not be confused with healthy expressions of patriotism or with the natural love of and pride in one's homeland or region. Historians agree, moreover, that the rise of excessively nationalistic theories in the late Middle Ages, theories which stressed political division rather than religious unity, were a major cause of the fracturing of Christianity which racked Europe and Western civilization in the sixteenth century and beyond.

Nativism • A school of political thought which holds that only those persons born within a political territory should be considered trustworthy enough for full political participation in that society. The American experience with Nativism, a recurring phenomenon, has been largely directed against Catholics and, consequently, those immigrants coming from predominantly Catholic countries. The irony of Nativism in a nation settled almost exclusively by immigrants has been noted by many but heeded by few. Nativism was particularly serious in colonial America, with many colonies and later early states enacting harsh restrictions on the foreign-born (especially Catholics), some of which disabilities persisted even into the mid-

twentieth century. The example of those states compares rather poorly with, for example, Maryland, once a heavily Catholic state which did not participate in Nativist paranoia.

Nativist political power reached its peak in the Know-Nothing movement during the mid-nineteenth century. Fading since that time, it seems to have died out on account of a variety of circumstances. At times, however, remaining Nativist sentiment is exploited within such otherwise legitimate issues as a nation's right and duty to police its borders or its policy regarding the basic regulation of immigration.

Natural Family Planning • Methods for pinpointing the fertile time in a woman's cycle. Current knowledge of this cycle is so great that careful use of the techniques available can considerably increase the chances of conceiving when there has been difficulty before, or highly reduce such chances when there is a very serious reason for postponing pregnancy. Natural family planning should not be confused with the older so-called rhythm method, which was much less effective than present methods.

Many couples study natural family planning because they find contraception repellent, dangerous to the health of the woman, and often abortifacient, i.e., flushing out the already formed human being at an early stage. (For moral reasons to avoid *all* contraceptives, cf. Birth Control.)

Couples can study natural family planning by reading manuals about it, but preferably by taking a course privately or with other couples where personal charting is done of an individual woman's cycle. Once understood, the present methods are very simple to use and have been known to increase communication and mutual love in marriage.

It should be noted that natural family planning is not merely a "Catholic" method of birth control; indeed, the underlying philosophy must be entirely different. And if it is not qualitatively different, the morality of the practice falls under the same judgment as artificial means of contraception.

More information on the technical, psychological and spiritual aspects of natural family planning is available from the Couple to Couple League in Cincinnati, Ohio.

Natural Law • The participation of human beings in the eternal law of God, it is the objective order established by God which determines the requirements for human fulfillment and flourishing. The natural law is fundamentally a work of divine reason and is promulgated by God. However, through practical reason, we are able to participate in the dictates of the natural law and promulgate for ourselves its dictates, so that the natural law is both a human and divine work. Through the dictates of conscience, all persons are able to know the requirements of the natural law.

The natural law is distinct from the law of nature which governs the actions of nonhuman creatures and which determines their requirements for fulfillment. Those who claim that the natural law alienates the person because it imposes a heteronomous morality fail to see that the human person is a co-promulgator of the natural law. For the person, seeking to know what must be done to attain self-realization, determines through practical reason what leads to human flourishing and the person issues a moral law from within his being. Besides being an autonomous moral law, it is also objective, in that it is promulgated not only by man, but also by God. Like the law of nature, it is a law in that violations of it bring punishments as a necessary consequence.

As human society develops through history, the specific requirements of the natural law increase in number to point the way to self-realization. This does not mean that the natural law is historically conditioned, but only that what was implicit in a previous era becomes explicit in a later and more socially developed one. This does not imply absolute relativism; rather, this development occurs because the increased potentialities of humanity through its history imply increased specific responsibilities. Primitive persons did not have a moral responsibility to care for the needy of the world because there were no social or political structures to realize that obligation.

The Catholic Church claims the power authoritatively to interpret the natural law and provide correct interpretations of its moral demands, where needed. The natural law exists prior to any positive human legislation, and is knowable to all human beings, even though the help of the Church might be necessary (DS 3875f.; 3892ff.).

Natural Rights • Inviolable, inalienable and universal rights attributed to human persons because they are personal beings of free will and intellect. Natural rights safeguard the human person from the inroads of state and society. The modern expressions of natural rights were first expressed formally in the Virginia "Bill of Rights" of June 12, 1776, and the Declaration of Independence of July 4, 1776. Since then, natural rights have become elements of almost all national constitutions.

St. Peter demanded that we obey God rather than men (Acts 4:19), and the tradition of natural rights was found in its seminal form in Origen, Lactantius and Gregory of Nyssa, who spoke against slavery and for the natural rights of persons. The Apostolic Constitutions permitted slavery but noted the essential equality of man. The Middle Ages did not abandon sight of the basic ideas of natural rights, as was seen in the Scholastic doctrines of the natural law. Notions of natural rights were later developed by modern Scholastics such as Vitoria, but the wars of religion and absolute monarchs soon overwhelmed what progress they had made. Only with the American Revolution and the Enlightenment did these ideas regain prominence, but the long-standing elaboration of human rights was undermined by the Enlightenment, which gave much more emphasis to the individual.

Pope John XXIII gave the first systematic Catholic account of natural rights in *Pacem in Terris* in 1963, but these doctrines were derived from teachings of Pope Pius XII. Generally, natural rights are considered to include a right to life, rights to certain moral and cultural values, a right to truth, a right to participate in social life, a right to the free exercise of religion, a right to free choice of one's state of life, economic and professional rights, a right to free association and assembly, a right to emigrate and immigrate, and a right to legal protection of personal rights. The Church considers the protection of the rights of the human person to be a solemn duty and rejects discrimination in any form (*Statement on Racism*, 1988). She rejects the use of force to bring about religious conversions and calls on Christians to respect the dignity and rights of others.

Natural Theology • The part of philosophy which treats the existence of God and the attributes of God by means of the natural light of reason without relying on the authority of God's revelation. Natural theology is not merely one part of philosophy among others, but is the peak to which all the others lead, and without which, sense cannot be made of the physical world or of the distinctiveness and dignity of human beings. Thinkers such as St. Augustine, St. Thomas Aquinas, St. Bonaventure or Duns Scotus clarify the contingency of the material world and of human life and thereby develop the contrast by which to characterize God as far as is possible by natural reason. St. Paul's statement, "since the creation of the world his [God's] invisible nature, namely, his eternal power and deity, has been clearly perceived in the things that have been made" (Rom 1:20), is often taken as the scriptural basis for development of a natural theology.

Natural theology involves some reasoning by which the existence of God is shown to be reasonable and by which the various objections to acknowledging God are overcome. Natural theology also clarifies the characteristics which we may reasonably attribute to God. For example, unity, truth, goodness and beauty are shown to be characteristic of all beings; they transcend the distinction of substantial and accidental being. Thus, once it is shown that God is infinite Being itself, there is reason to attribute each of these "transcendentals" to God. Thus God is unity itself, truth itself, goodness itself and beauty itself. A particular part of natural theology, theodicy, shows that the fact of evil in the world does not provide a reasonable basis for denying God's infinite goodness, knowledge and power.

Natural theology also clarifies the limited character of our knowledge of God. For the infinite difference between God and creatures implies that God's unity, truth, goodness or beauty is not exactly the same as our unity, truth, goodness or beauty. That such attributions are not univocal does not imply the opposite extreme, that they are meaningless, that existence or good in the case of God is utterly unlike human existence or goodness. Rather, natural theology shows that our knowledge of God is analogical.

The philosophical discipline of natural theology can provide apologetic reasons to aid nonbelievers to overcome obstacles to the Profession of Christian Faith. Likewise, it can clarify the preambles of the Faith upon which higher revealed theology builds by proceeding explicitly by the light of faith in considering what God has revealed.

Naturalism • Systems or styles of philosophical thinking which seek inner-worldly explanations for all phenomena are said to be "naturalistic." In line with such thinking, the existence of any ultimate reality transcending the universe of nature is either ruled out or regarded as irrelevant to the explanation of observable phenomena or to the legitimation of moral life. Naturalism is thus best seen less as a specific philosophical position than as an orientation in philosophical reflection that occurs in combination with a variety of other ideas, such as pantheism in philosophical theology, evolutionism in biology or reductionistic explanations of religion in psychology.

Nature • Sometimes this term refers to the entirety of the created order or, more technically, to the total system of material entities and events. However, in its properly philosophical sense, the term designates that which makes something to be the sort of thing it is, to operate the way it does and to seek the good that is its own — in short, a thing's essence as the source of its natural and purposeful activities. Two important theological uses of the concept occur in the doctrine of the Triune God (in discussing the Divine Nature common to the Father, Son and Holy Spirit) and in Christology (in

Nave of Salisbury Cathedral (circa 1220)

discussing the union of the human and divine natures in the Person of the Son).

The concept is also prominent in theological anthropology, where the relation between nature and grace in the human person's journey to God is considered. Here, "nature" designates the basic structure of the human person as a created bodily and spiritual being with various capacities for sense perception, emotion, knowledge, intention, decision and action, socially and interpersonally oriented, and in principle, morally perfectible through the free pursuit of the virtuous life that constitutes one of its most basic goods.

God has revealed that the destiny of human persons is to be united with Him in perfect love — a properly supernatural destiny, not only because it surpasses human capacities in their ordinary exercise and because it is an utterly free gift, but especially because it involves a participation in the divine life itself. Hence, although human persons are so constituted by nature as to be able to enter into relationships with other persons — including, in principle, God — it is only when human nature is elevated by grace that this possibility becomes a real one. In addition, grace heals the weakening and disruptive effects of original sin that impedes human nature in its pursuit of its perfect good.

Nave • The part of the church building between the front and the sanctuary where the body of the faithful assembles. The term either derives from the Latin *navis*, for "ship," which denotes the church as the body of believers in the ship of salvation, or it derives from a corrupt form of the Greek *naos*, for "temple," which denotes the church as the new temple of salvation.

Nazarite (also Nazirite) • From the Hebrew root *nezir*, the word originally designated someone set apart. In subsequent cultic rhetoric, it identified someone who had sworn a certain type of vow. Samson appears to be under such a vow for life (Jgs 13:5-7; 16:17). Later on, Paul and others in the New Testament have taken such a vow, but only for a set period of time (cf. Acts 18:18). The Nazarite, during the time the vow was binding on him, was held to refrain from using a razor to trim his hair and beard; he was further expected to abstain from intoxicating beverages, and he had to take care not to be defiled by contact with a corpse.

Nazorean (also Nazarene) • This term refers to a native of Nazareth, a small village in the territory of Zebulum. Jesus and His parents lived there until His public ministry (Mt 2:23). At Matthew 2:23, there is no clear indication as to which prophecies are being fulfilled. The ambiguity has led interpreters to speculate that Matthew may have intended the expression *nazoraios* to have a theological meaning drawn from an Old Testament text. If by *nazoraios* Matthew refers to the Semitic equivalent of "Nazorean" (e.g., Jgs 16:17), then the term means "holy to God." Such a reading of Matthew 2:23 is in line with Mark 1:24; Luke 4:34 and John 6:69. If by Nazarene is meant the Hebrew *neser* or "shoot," then reference to Isaiah 11:1 could be the referent. The term "Nazorean" was applied to Jesus' early followers in a pejorative sense (Acts 24:5).

Also a group of Judeo-Christians who lived in Aleppo, the Decapolis and Cochabe.

Although the historical evidence is not always consistent, it appears that they were doctrinally orthodox, had their own Gospel in Hebrew, practiced Jewish Law and, consonant with the Council of Jerusalem, acknowledged that Gentile Christians were not bound to follow the Jewish Law. They existed at least into the fourth century.

For further reading: Stephen Goranson, "Nazarenes," *Anchor Bible Dictionary*, 4:1049-1050; James F. Strange, "Nazareth," *Anchor Bible Dictionary*, 4:1050-1051.

Ne Temere • The name of a decree that was issued by the Holy See in 1908 which made the canonical form of marriage obligatory for all Latin Rite Catholics throughout the world, thus eliminating the last major exceptions to the requirements of canonical form established by the Council of Trent.

Necromancy • The practice of communicating with the souls of the dead by various magical and superstitious means, or in some instances the predicting of the future through this communication with the dead. The origins of necromancy seem to have been Egyptian, and some of the early Israelites practiced it to a certain degree. Saul consulted a necromancer and was severely punished for so doing (1 Sm 28:3, 8-14), and it was listed as one of the reasons why Yahweh destroyed Israel (2 Kgs 21:6). Also called the conjuring of spirits, it was a capital offense under the Mosaic code (Lv 19:31; 20:6).

Like other forms of astrology and occult practice, this is an extremely evil sort of action, as it challenges the entire world-order brought about by the redemptive actions of Jesus Christ. The proper relationship of Christians to the dead is to pray for those in need of our prayers and to invoke the intercession of the saints through prayer. And if Christians should seek to gain insight into the future, it should not be through communication with the dead, but through reading the "signs of the time" and through prayer for the gifts of the Holy Spirit, which can enable us to know the will of God more fully.

Nehemiah, Book of • The biblical book named for Nehemiah conserves the story of his efforts at restoring Jews to their homeland from the eastern captivity. He had been a faithful servant in the palace of Artaxerxes I, who was king of Persia from 464 to 424 B.C. When he heard of the sad condition of Jerusalem, with its walls and gates destroyed, he obtained the king's permission to go and rebuild it, using a Persian subsidy. Despite opposition from many Samaritans, in but a few months of 445 B.C., the walls were quickly rebuilt and the city was securely enclosed.

As governor, Nehemiah was concerned about the usury inflicted on the poor returnees and about the religious disunity caused by mixed marriages. In cooperation with the priest Ezra, he used his authority to abolish these abuses. He apparently returned to Persia in 433 B.C., but came back to Jerusalem shortly thereafter.

For further reading: Robert North, S.J., "Nehemiah," *Anchor Bible Dictionary*, 4:1068-1071; Robert North, S.J., "The Chronicler: 1-2 Chronicles, Ezra, Nehemiah," *New Jerome Biblical Commentary*, 362-398.

Neighbor • The biblical idea is one that is developed from the Old Testament concept of neighbor as a fellow member of the people of the covenant, with certain moral obligations and the guarantee of certain rights for each individual. This is outlined clearly in the Decalogue (Ex 20:16-17; Dt 5:20-21), and in Leviticus 19:18, "You shall love your neighbor as yourself." This Levitical injunction is repeated in the New Testament (Lk 10:27) and is received with approval by Christ, which then leads into the most important theological definition of neighbor, contained in the Lord's parable of the Good Samaritan (Lk 10:30-37). Christ teaches that the concept of neighbor is active, rather than passive, when He asks the lawyer, "Which . . . proved neighbor to the man who fell among the robbers?" and He receives the correct answer, "The one who showed mercy on him." It is the obligation of Christians to serve as compassionate neighbors in the world, and in this setting one's neighbors are those who seek to do him good, whether by offering needed help and encouragement, or by being openly in need and so allowing him to act in Christ's place. Jesus enlarges the term "neighbor" to mean all of mankind, and it is this interpretation which is found throughout the rest of the New Testament. Both St. Paul (Rom 13:9) and St. James (Jas 2:8) repeat the commandment, "You shall love your neighbor as yourself," with this wider meaning as the summary of all law.

Nemours, Edict of • The Protestant Reformation swept through Europe in the sixteenth century, with Calvinism and Catholicism fighting bitter battles in France. The Catholic League of France demanded that Henry III (1574-1589) outlaw Calvinism in France. He signed the document called the Edict of Nemours, which forbade Calvinists to impose their system of belief on the country.

Neo-Catechumenate • The Neo-Catechumenal Way, or simply the Neo-Catechumenate, is a Catholic renewal and catechetical movement founded in 1964 in Madrid by the layman Kiko Argüello, who continues as a chief catechist of the movement and who is currently a consultor to the Pontifical Council on the Laity.

With the encouragement of the Holy Father, the Neo-Catechumenal Way is located in dioceses whose bishops welcome it and in parishes whose pastors are committed to it. In 1990, the Neo-Catechumenate had 200,000 members worldwide, organized in 10,000 small communities in 80 countries. In the United States, they are represented in the archdioceses of Denver, Newark and Washington, as well as on the West Coast and in Texas.

Essentially, the Neo-Catechumenate is a movement providing a program of Christian formation. With its stress on exclusive fellowship, intense personal commitment, simplicity of life, communal sharing, and apostolic zeal, the Neo-Catechumenal Way takes its inspiration from the structure and ethos of the first Christian communities who were known as adherents of "the Way." Although it is fundamentally a lay movement, the commitment and leadership of the local pastor are crucial to its organization and activities. The Eucharist, celebrated by the pastor with great reverence in homes or in small groups, is the anchor of the Neo-Catechumenal Way. The Neo-Catechumenate is addressed to committed Catholics who want to deepen their faith and to fallen-away Catholics who want to rediscover it. Participants in the seven-year-long formation program are called "catechumens" in order to signal the fact that even the baptized person may not yet have attained a sufficient level of conversion and knowledge in the life of the faith. While continuing to live at home, catechumens participate in this formation as members of communities of fifteen to thirty members who meet at least twice a week for catechesis and to celebrate the Eucharist. Day-long meetings are held monthly, as well as occasional social gatherings and regular "scrutinies" and liturgies to mark the transition to a new stage of formation. Eventually, some members become "itinerants" and move on in order to establish Neo-Catechumenate communities elsewhere.

Neo-Scholasticism • This term designates a broad nineteenth- to twentieth-century movement of recovery of the works of the Scholastic masters for use in theology and philosophy. Within this movement, neo-Thomism refers particularly to the revival of study of the philosophical and theological works of St. Thomas Aquinas. The impetus for this revival came from many sources, but it was powerfully reinforced by Pope Leo XIII, who in his encyclical *Aeterni Patris* (1879) commended the study of Aquinas.

The energies of generations of scholars were devoted to the historical and systematic study not only of the works of Aquinas, but also of other great Scholastic masters such as St. Bonaventure and Duns Scotus. The movement stimulated a kind of intellectual renaissance in twentieth-century Catholic philosophy and theology, and inspired some of its greatest thinkers (e.g., Jacques Maritain). The intellectual renaissance was among the background factors that, along with the recovery of liturgical and patristic sources and the renewed study of the Scriptures, fostered the conditions that led to the Second Vatican Council.

Despite strong recommendations from the Council and from the Holy See, the immediate postconciliar period witnessed something of an eclipse of neo-Scholasticism and neo-Thomism, in favor of the adoption of more pluralistic philosophical and theological tools.

Nesteia • In the Eastern Churches and Rites, religious fasts and abstinences are known as nesteia.

Nestorianism • In A.D. 428, an Antiochene priest named Nestorius was installed as patriarch of Constantinople. Like other variations on an Arian theme, Nestorianism impugned the divinity of Christ and in particular the Marian title of *Theotokos*. It taught, moreover, that only Christ the man suffered death on Calvary. Nestorianism was condemned in 431 at the Council of Ephesus but persisted for many centuries. It was nearly eradicated, however, by military losses in seventh-century Persia.

In 1445 the Nestorians of Cyprus were reunited with Rome, and just over one hundred years later the Nestorian patriarch accepted Catholic doctrine. In 1559 the large (approximately 75,000 adherents) Nestorian Church of Malabar was reunited with Rome and since that time has remained in communion, celebrating a Syriac Liturgy.

New American Bible • The New American Bible (NAB) is the descendant of a long line of Catholic English-language translations of the Bible. It is the translation created especially for speakers of English in North America.

On September 30, 1943, Pius XII issued *Divino Afflante Spiritu*, which emphasized the necessity of textual criticism within Catholic biblical research. The emphasis meant that scholars would have to work directly with the original languages of biblical manuscripts. The authenticity of the Church's centuries-old Latin translation (Vulgate) was reaffirmed, as was the need for new translations into the vernacular, based on the original languages of Sacred Scripture. The work of Catholic biblical scholars and the impetus of DAS eventually led to the Episcopal Committee for the Confraternity of Christian Doctrine's sponsorship of an entirely new translation of Sacred Scripture for American Catholics. This work, including planning stages, spanned four decades (1944-1970). The text

of this translation was also intended for use at Mass and other liturgical celebrations. The first completed New American Bible was in 1970, a few years after the Second Vatican Council. This translation was based on reference to the original biblical languages, geared to the literary sensibilities of an American readership.

In 1987 a revised New Testament portion of NAB was published. This revision, like the original translation, was the fruit of much labor by members of the Catholic Biblical Association of America. Distinguishing this revision from the original are a significantly improved style and accuracy. In 1991, a revised translation of the Psalms appeared, raising some questions about accuracy and theological concerns — a definite judgment on which has yet to be made by ecclesiastical authority.

Nicaea, Councils of • The first ecumenical council of the Church was convoked by the Emperor Constantine toward the end of A.D. 324. It was held in the city of Nicaea in Bithynia and lasted from May to August of 325. The main purpose of the council was to decide the doctrinal question of the relationship between the First and Second Persons of the Trinity, with the discussion centering around the Greek word *homoousios*, which was open to various interpretations at the time. The Council also condemned the Arian heresy (cf. Arianism).

The Second Council of Nicaea was the seventh general council of the Church and was held in 787. It defined the Church's traditional teaching on the lawfulness of venerating images and praying to the saints. It was the last council to be recognized by the Eastern Orthodox Churches.

Nicene Creed • The original Nicene Creed was issued by the Council of Nicaea in A.D. 325, composed by the Council Fathers in response to the Arian heresy. However, the

Nicene Creed is more accurately the Nicene-Constantinopolitan Creed, a product of the First Council of Constantinople (381). Theologically, it is more sophisticated than the Apostles' Creed and the original Nicene Creed. The Nicene-Constantinopolitan Creed is the text used as the Profession of Faith in the liturgy and reads as follows in the presently authorized English translation:

"We believe in one God, the Father, the Almighty, maker of heaven and earth, of all that is seen and unseen. We believe in one Lord, Jesus Christ, the only Son of God, eternally begotten of the Father, God from God, Light from Light, true God from true God, begotten, not made, one in Being with the Father. Through him all things were made. For us men and for our salvation he came down from heaven: by the power of the Holy Spirit he was born of the Virgin Mary, and became man. For our sake he was crucified under Pontius Pilate; he suffered, died, and was buried. On the third day he rose again in fulfillment of the Scriptures; he ascended into heaven and is seated at the right hand of the Father. He will come again in glory to judge the living and the dead, and his kingdom will have no end. We believe in the Holy Spirit, the Lord, the giver of life, who proceeds from the Father and the Son. With the Father and the Son he is worshiped and glorified. He has spoken through the Prophets. We believe in one holy catholic and apostolic Church. We acknowledge one baptism for the forgiveness of sins. We look for the resurrection of the dead, and the life of the world to come. Amen."

Nihil Obstat • This Latin term, which literally means "nothing obstructs," refers to the approval granted by the officially appointed censor of books to a written work that requires the permission of Church authorities for publication. The *nihil obstat* precedes and is required for the *imprimatur*, which is the permission of the competent authority to publish (cf. Canon 830).

Nimbus • Coming from the Latin *nebula* for cloud, and the Greek *nephele*, which means vapor or cloud, this term has been inherited by the English language, especially in the fields of art and archaeology. In these areas the nimbus signifies a shining light implying great dignity. In Christian art, moreover, this refers to the holiness of God and of those who have been made holy by Him and have been faithful to Him. Thus the nimbus or halo, as it is often called in popular parlance, is used in conjunction with depictions of Christ, the Blessed Mother and the saints. It is usually placed behind or above the head of the subject being portrayed. Though it has varying shapes and sizes, it is commonly round and colored with white or gold. Sometimes it can also be square or rectangular. Christ is often depicted with a threefold or cruciform nimbus recalling the cross as well as the Trinity, thus His divinity. Frequently, the nimbus is depicted by a circlet over or behind the head of the subject. (Cf. Aureole.)

Ninety-Five Theses • A term associated with Martin Luther, who posted a series of statements of abuses in the Catholic Church. They were nailed to the main door of All Saints' Church in Wittenberg, Germany, on October 31, 1517. The date is, therefore, marked as the birthday of the Protestant Reformation. Written in Latin and translated into German, they received a wide circulation. Luther challenged papal authority, purgatory, indulgences, the relationship between faith and good works, and other points.

Eventually, Luther, Philip Melanchthon and Johannes Eck were responsible for what has come to be called Lutheranism, a Protestant form of Christianity. At the Diet of Worms in 1521, Luther was formally excommunicated from the Catholic Church by the Papal Bull *Exsurge Domine*. (Cf. Protestantism.)

Noble Guards • Formerly the highest ranking section of the papal military service, the Noble Guards were disbanded by Pope Paul VI in 1968. The members had been chosen from the Roman aristocracy. They attended the Pope at special ceremonies and were distinguished by their plumed helmets and elaborate military costume.

Nocturn • Liturgical term from the Latin *nocturnus* "of the night" (from *nox*, "night"), originally describing the night office in its entirety, formerly designated as Matins and Lauds. Later it came to specify a part of Matins, most usually divided into three nocturns on feasts (with three psalms and three readings in each) or one nocturn on ferias (containing nine, or formerly twelve psalms and three readings). In the monastic Breviary two nocturns were common, containing a greater number of psalms and readings (up to twelve each for the hour of Matins).

Nomocanons • The term used to describe various collections of legislation on ecclesial affairs which were gathered from both canonical and civil sources. Shortly after the Edict of Milan, but especially after the final transfer of the capital to Constantinople, the Roman emperors were seen by many to be competent to legislate on a variety of ecclesiastical matters which today would be seen as the province of the Church. These civil enactments on Church affairs were soon joined with canonical legislation on the same topics. By the seventh century, the canonical and civil provisions were thoroughly merged within these collections. The "Collection in XIV Titles," perhaps the most perfect example of a Nomocanon, was arranged anonymously during the reign of

Heraclius (610-640), and later revised, perhaps by Photius (cf. Eastern Schism). In many respects the Nomocanons contained prudent laws in a logical order. But because they seriously blurred the distinction between civil and ecclesiastical authority, some have suggested the Nomocanons to have been a contributing factor in the development of the Eastern Schism. (Cf. also Caesaropapism.)

Non-Christian Religions, Declaration on the Relationship of the Church to: See **Nostra Aetate**

Non-Consummation • The failure of a married couple to complete their marital consent by an act of heterosexual intercourse after consent had been exchanged. A non-consummated marriage between two baptized Catholics is considered sacramental, yet it can be dissolved by the Holy See.

The dissolution of non-consummated marriages first took place in the twelfth century under Pope Alexander III. Since it was not clear by what power this was done, the practice declined under successive Popes. It was revived in 1767 when Pope Benedict XIV declared that the Pope certainly had the power to dissolve non-consummated marriages.

The dissolution of a marriage because of non-consummation depends on the fact that complete sexual intercourse never took place or did not take place in a human fashion. The initial petition is prepared on the diocesan level and then submitted to the Congregation of the Sacraments for final disposition and submission to the Holy Father for decision (Canons 1142, 1697-1706).

Non Expedit • This Latin expression means "it is not expedient" and has been used many times in Church history to indicate that a certain action, while not intrinsically wrong, should not be performed at a certain time or under certain circumstances. Perhaps the most famous example of a *non expedit*, though, was that issued by Pope Pius IX which counseled against Catholics taking part in the Italian election of 1868, an election which was intended, in part, to pave the way for annexation of the rest of the papal states. Today, the expression is still used with some frequency, although usually within individual decrees and precepts, and only rarely in major pronouncements.

None • Literally, "ninth." From its Latin title, *ad [horam] nonam*, at the ninth [hour]. The canonical "Hour," or prayer service offered around the ninth hour of the day, i.e., 3 P.M.

Prior to the Second Vatican Council's revision of the Divine Office, None formed (together with Prime, Terce and Sext) one of the mandatory "little hours" of the daily cycle of prayer.

In the new *Liturgy of the Hours* the Hour is retained as mandatory in contemplative communities, and one of the three "little hours" from which one may choose: Midmorning (Terce), Midday (Sext) or Midafternoon (None).

Its present structure is similar to its previous form:

✧ the usual verse and response ("O God, come to my assistance. O Lord, make haste to help me.");

✧ a hymn (which in the official Latin refers to the day's labors drawing to a close and oncoming dusk as a reminder of life's end);

✧ three short psalms or three sections of a longer psalm;

✧ a brief Scripture passage;

✧ verse, response, collect;

✧ and the usual acclamations ("Let us bless the Lord. Thanks be to God").

North American College • Founded in Rome on December 8, 1859, by the bishops of the United States, the North American College serves as a residence and house of formation for American seminarians and graduate students. Only those individuals who have been designated by their bishop are admitted to the college, and theological studies take place at one of the Roman universities.

The ordination of the first alumnus took place in 1862, and since that time it has prepared more than two thousand men for the priesthood, including many bishops and cardinals. On October 25, 1884, Pope Leo XIII granted pontifical status to the college, and it has become a headquarters in Rome for Catholics from the United States.

North American Martyrs • The eight Jesuit missionaries who evangelized the native Americans in present-day upstate New York and southeast Canada, and who were tortured and martyred between the years 1642-1649. The martyrs and the years of their martyrdom are as follows: René Goupil, a lay medic and associate of the Society of Jesus, 1642; Isaac Jogues, a priest, who had returned to North America a second time after suffering terrible torture during his first stay, 1647; Jean Lalande, another lay associate of the Society of Jesus, 1647; Jean de Brébeuf, a priest, 1649; Antoine Daniel, priest, 1649; Gabriel Lalemant, priest, 1649; Charles Garnier, priest, 1649; Noël Chabanel, priest, 1649. Their witness and their writings continue to inspire people to follow the virtues of perseverance and fortitude. Bl. Kateri Tekakwitha received the Faith through the labors of these men and their collaborators. The martyrs are venerated at two shrines, one in Canada, one in Auriesville, New York; their feast is October 19.

North Door • That opening or portal of an iconostasis situated to the left of the celebrant as he stands facing the central altar or east in a church of the Byzantine Rite. The altar, whether it is actually geographic east or not, is considered the church's eastern point. Hence, all other points take their position from the altar. The door, then, to the celebrant's right would be the South Door; the nave, west; and the sanctuary, east. From the east rose Christ, the Sun of Justice. Facing east at prayer is a common element in many faiths and has been retained as an orientation for the church building in the Byzantine ritual. The central doors of the icon screen are called the Royal Doors, since Christ the King of Glory passes through in word and sacrament. Only a bishop, priest or deacon may use the central doors; the northern and southern doors are commonly used by the deacons, lower clergy and servers.

Bl. Kateri Tekakwitha

Nostra Aetate • This declaration begins with an affirmative statement of the unity and solidarity of the entire human race and concludes with a condemnation and repudiation of prejudice and ignorance in relationship to any people, individually or collectively.

Major religions are mentioned: Hinduism is praised for its search for God through asceticism and meditation; Buddhism is commended for its belief in the radical insufficiency of this temporal world and its search for enlightenment; Islam is complimented for its belief in God, its recognition of Christ as a prophet and its veneration of the Blessed Virgin Mary. The major burden and emphasis of the declaration, however, concerns the Jewish religion and its people.

Jewish-Christian Relationships in History: From the very beginning the Christian and Jewish communities were rivals and grew into antagonists. During the first three centuries A.D. "a vibrant and assertive Judaism" opposed the Christian Church, evoking a reciprocal response in which the seeds of anti-Semitism were sown.

In the fourth century charges of deicide, the killing of Christ, and the imputation of collective guilt on all the Jewish people received their pseudo-theological justification, particularly in the writings of St. John Chrysostom. His conclusions were contrary to the Tradition of the Church which held all sinners, thus all mankind, guilty of the death of Christ, and were contrary as well to the teaching of divine forgiveness.

In spite of the fact that anti-Semitism is not rooted in the Bible nor in orthodox Christian doctrine, it grew as a deadly virus in all of Europe, resulting in unjust persecutions down through the years even to Hitler and the Holocaust. This history hung like a specter over the Vatican Council.

Within a year after Pope John XXIII announced an ecumenical council, several groups in the Catholic Church sent recommendations to the Holy See for inclusion in the upcoming council. In April 1960 the Biblical Institute asked that anti-Semitism be condemned; in June, Seton Hall's Institute for Judaic Studies called for true reconciliation along paths charted by Pope Pius XI, who said, "Spiritually, we are Semites"; in August, the Apeldoorm Group from Holland suggested that the false contrasts between the Old and New Testaments be rectified.

In September of the same year Jule Isaac, a leading French Jewish scholar, made a personal appeal in a private audience with the Pope, who promised action. On September 18, 1960, Pope John XXIII commissioned Augustin Cardinal Bea to present a document to the Vatican Council.

The Council Document: The Council affirmed in a positive way that the Catholic Church finds its roots in the life and faith of the Jewish people as expressed in the Old Testament. At the same time, it pointed out that "Jerusalem did not recognize God's moment when it came" by Christ, and that the Apostles and the first Christians were Jews.

Very directly the Council rejected the charge that the Jews were guilty of deicide; that they were a race rejected by God; that there could be any collective guilt over the crucifixion of Christ, whether of those living at the time or in a later age: "Christ underwent His passion and death because of the sins of all men so that all might attain salvation."

The Council went a giant step further than the rejection of anti-Semitism only: "The Church reproves, as foreign to the mind of Christ, any discrimination against people or any harassment of them because of their race, color, condition of life or religion."

The Council Debate: There was opposition to the document, chiefly by those bishops who saw its political implications. Ironically, the Jewish groups in Europe and America argued that the document fell short precisely because it did not recognize the state of Israel. From Middle East countries such as Jordan and Syria, from Muslim and Orthodox religious leaders came strong voices in opposition, the Catholic bishops from those countries being put under very heavy pressure. In spite of the fact that Cardinal Bea had insisted in the Council that the document was entirely religious and utterly devoid of politics, many of the Council Fathers were not convinced.

Particularly poignant and compelling, on the other hand, was a statement that read: "We German bishops welcome the Council Decree on the Jews because we acknowledge the grave injustice done to the Jews in the name of our people."

The Council Vote: The final vote on the document *Nostra Aetate* was 2,221 in favor, with 88 contrary.

Pope Paul VI promulgated the declaration on October 28, 1965.

Novatianism • Novatian (born c. A.D. 200) was the first theologian of the Roman Church to write in Latin. He was a rigorist and the author of what has come to be called the Novatian heresy and schism, or Novatianism.

In his various writings, he taught that the Church was a society of saints in which no mortal sinner had a place, no matter how ready he might be to repent. He was especially hard on those who had fallen away from the Faith during times of persecution, believing that they could not be pardoned, since this would compromise

God's judgment — thus allowing no room for God's mercy.

With the election of Pope Cornelius in 251, Novatian established himself as essentially the first antipope. He was condemned by Pope Cornelius and a Roman synod and died in 258.

Novena • A term used to describe a continuous praying of a formula for personal devotion, either on nine consecutive days or once a week for nine weeks. Most often these prayers are for a particular intention and are in honor of a particular saint or aspect of the Person or mystery of Christ (e.g., Perpetual Help, in honor of the Sacred Heart). The practice derives only from the seventeenth century; however, the number nine derives from the time Mary and the Apostles waited for the coming of the Holy Spirit between Ascension and Pentecost.

Novice • According to the Code of Canon Law, novices (male or female) are those who begin a preparation and formation period in the novitiate of a religious institute under the direction of a master or mistress of novices. The time period is to be used by the candidates to discern their vocations, as well as to assist superiors in getting to know the candidates and, therefore, to pass correct judgment on their suitability for the religious life. This period must last for twelve months and may be extended to twenty-four months. At the end of it, novices either leave or are admitted to temporary vows of poverty, chastity and obedience (cf. Canons 646, 652).

Novitiate • This term can refer either to the period of formal probation of a person in a religious community or to the residence for novices. The residence may be the religious house itself or a part of it.

Nuclear Deterrence, Morality of • One of the most sharply debated questions in the Church, there is no consensus on the morality of the possession, threat to use, or use of nuclear weapons for only self-defense. While consistently calling for peace and reconciliation among the nations, the official teachings of the Church have not absolutely condemned nuclear deterrence as immoral.

There is a true dilemma involved in nuclear deterrence. Nations which do not possess these weapons can be blackmailed into submitting to the demands of a nation so equipped, which seems to lend justification to their possession. However, because these weapons kill so many with such swiftness, it seems that they are inherently indiscriminant and therefore immoral. This dilemma is seen further in the fact that some would hold that a state which did not use them to defend against unjust attack would be violating its duty to protect its innocent noncombatants who did not think them to be immoral. Yet using them would be considered by others to be the use of an immoral means for a good end.

The solution to this dilemma lies in the recognition that the deaths caused by the use of the last and only reasonably available means to defend innocent life are indirectly intended and are not morally culpable. This is why the physically indirect removal of an ectopic pregnancy or cancerous uterus is not immoral. This sort of action is the last means available of defending innocent life, and because the only option is to permit innocent life to be destroyed, the action is permissible. If such an action is permitted where innocent life is not under an intentional threat, there would be even stronger reasons for permitting this when innocent life is under an intentional threat.

As the technology of nuclear weapons develops, so also will the arguments concerning its moral permissibility, and thus, the debate concerning it will evolve and grow.

Numbers, Book of • The fourth book of the Pentateuch is so called because its first chapter contains the results of a census of the Jews who escaped from their slavery in Egypt. Additional enumerations are given later in the book, but they occupy a relatively minor space. Most of the book records additional legislation and history.

The census data given in the book is certainly an exaggeration, for it would indicate a total population in the desert of over two million. It has been suggested that the numbers have been multiplied a hundredfold.

The historical material dwells heavily on the rebellious behavior of the Jews — their failure to trust God and Moses.

For further reading: Conrad E. L'Heureux, "Numbers," *New Jerome Biblical Commentary*, 80-93; Jacob Milgrom, "Numbers, Book of," *Anchor Bible Dictionary*, 4:1146-1155.

Nun • Strictly, the title applies only to women who belong to a religious order with solemn vows. Popularly, this term refers to any religious woman, commonly called "sister."

Nunc Dimittis • Simeon's Canticle at the Presentation of Jesus (Lk 2:29-32), acclaiming Christ as a "light for revelation to the Gentiles, and for glory to thy people Israel" (v. 32). "Nunc dimittis" are the first words of this canticle in Latin. In the English translation used in the Liturgy of the Hours, Simeon's Canticle begins, "Lord, now you let your servant go in peace." It has been the customary New Testament canticle used toward the end of Night Prayer (formerly "Compline").

For further reading: Raymond E. Brown, S.S., *The Birth of the Messiah*, 456-460,

Anchor Bible Reference Library (Doubleday, 1993); Frederick W. Danker, "Nunc Dimittis," *Anchor Bible Dictionary* 4:1155-1156.

Nunciature • The official offices and residence of a papal legate with the status of nuncio, pronuncio or internuncio. It corresponds to an embassy. Even if not owned by the Holy See, a nunciature, by reason of international law, enjoys diplomatic exemption. In the United States, the Apostolic Nunciature is located in Washington, D.C., on Massachusetts Avenue across from the Naval Observatory (home of the Vice President of the United States).

Nuncio • A nuncio or apostolic nuncio is a papal representative or ambassador appointed by the Holy Father to be his representative to the government of one of the countries that was a signatory to the Convention of Vienna in 1815. A nuncio differs from a pronuncio or internuncio only in the fact that he is automatically the dean of the diplomatic corps in the country to which he is sent. He is usually an archbishop (cf. Canons 362-367).

Nuptial Mass and Blessing • The Nuptial Mass and blessing make up the liturgical service of the Roman Rite during which a couple confer on each other the sacrament of Matrimony. Until 1547 in some countries and 1909 in all countries, Catholics were not required to be married in the presence of a sacred minister for validity. However, from the Middle Ages on, the custom arose of Catholics exchanging their vows in the presence of a priest or bishop and then receiving his blessing. Even prior to this, it was customary for Catholics who had first exchanged their vows according to the civil customs of the time to go to the priest or bishop and ask his blessing. In time, the couple exchanged their vows before the priest *in facie ecclesiae*, literally "in front of the Church," and then entered the church for the celebration of Mass and reception of the priestly blessing. This led to the exchange of vows inside the church, followed by the celebration of the Mass.

Until 1969, the ceremonies of the Nuptial Mass remained essentially similar to those that were in place by the late Middle Ages. The couple entered the church and the wedding service itself was performed. This being done, the priest then began the celebration of the Mass itself. The nuptial blessing, a long blessing addressed specifically to the bride, was given after the recitation of the Lord's Prayer, shortly before Communion.

Before the liturgical reform, the Nuptial Mass and blessing could be celebrated only at marriages of two Catholics, but not during Advent and Lent, on Sundays or holy days of obligation.

By 1969, the liturgical revision of the marriage rite was completed. In the revised ritual, the spouses confer the sacrament upon each other not before the Mass but after the Gospel. The nuptial blessing is still given after the Lord's Prayer. The Nuptial Mass and blessing can now be celebrated at marriages of Catholics and non-Catholic Christians and even at marriages of Catholics with the unbaptized; however, the Nuptial Mass is discouraged in these latter cases. The nuptial blessing can now be given outside Mass and may be received more than once.

O

O Antiphons • Also known as the "major" or "great" antiphons chanted before and after the Gospel Canticle of the Blessed Virgin Mary (the Magnificat) on the last days of Advent, beginning with December 17. They are so called because each one begins with the vocative "O," chanted to a beautiful Gregorian melody. Invoking the coming Christ by appropriate titles derived from Old Testament prophecies, these antiphons are among the most popular of Advent prayer-texts, having been put in a metrical form to a hauntingly beautiful chant in France during the seventeenth century and translated into English by numerous people during the nineteenth century. Virtually every English-language hymnal contains "O Come, O Come, Emmanuel," the English metrical version which begins with a verse based on the antiphon which comes last in the original Latin Office text.

The O Antiphons are these: December 17 — O Sapientia (O Wisdom); December 18 — O Adonai (O Lord of Might); December 19 — O Radix Jesse (O [Flower of] Jesse's Stem); December 20 — O Clavis Davidica (O Key of David); December 21 — O Oriens (O Rising Dawn); December 22 — O Rex Gentium (O King of Nations); and December 23 — O Emmanuel.

O Salutaris • Literally, "O Saving . . ." from the first two words of the hymn *O Salutaris Hostia* ("O Saving Victim"), which is actually the two last verses of the Latin hymn *Verbum supernum prodiens* ("The heavenly Word proceeding forth"), attributed to St. Thomas Aquinas, who is said to have composed it as one of several hymns commissioned in 1264 by Pope Urban IV for the newly instituted feast of Corpus Christi.

The last two verses of this particular hymn are widely known among Catholics because of their long-standing association with Benediction of the Most Blessed Sacrament. Still frequently sung during the incensation which begins Eucharistic exposition, one popular English translation follows:

Pope Urban IV:
O Salutaris Hostia patron

"O Saving Victim,
op'ning wide
The gate of heav'n to men below:
Our foes press on from every side,
Thine aid supply, Thy strength bestow.
To Thy great Name be endless praise,
Immortal Godhead, One-in-Three,
O grant us endless length of days
In our true native land with Thee. Amen."

Oak, Synod of the •
Theophilus, the
patriarch of Alexandria
at the dawn of the fifth
century, had censured a
group of Origenist
priests. These priests
turned to St. John
Chrysostom, then
patriarch of
Constantinople, who
received them, but
withheld ecclesiastical
communion with them.
Incensed at even this
show of prudence by the
Constantinopolitan
prelate, however,
Theophilus organized
thirty-six bishops
(including more than
twenty of his suffragans
from Egypt) into a
canonically illegal synod
in a suburban area of
Constantinople known as The Oak.

After reciting a long (and at times comical)
list of crimes alleged against the saint, the
Synod Fathers demanded John's presence,
at which time John calmly denied the
charges. (His messengers, incidentally, were
beaten by Theophilus's Synod.)
Notwithstanding the clear illegality of their
proceeding, the Empress Eudoxia upheld
the base condemnation of Chrysostom and
ordered him into exile at the direction of the
Synod of the Oak. An earthquake, among
other things, convinced the authorities to
recall the saint sometime later, but it was
too late. The Greek Father had died in exile
from his beloved Church in A.D. 407.

Oath • A solemn invocation of God to
witness the truth of what one asserts to be
the case or the sincerity of one's
undertakings in regard to future actions.

King Henry VIII:
Oath of Succession creator

The Scriptures
discourage facile or
frequent oath-taking
(Mt 5:33-37; Jas 5:12).
Some Christians
(Quakers, Baptists,
Mennonites and
Waldensians) have
construed these texts
as constituting an
absolute prohibition
against the swearing of
oaths. However, most
Christians have
acknowledged the
importance and
appropriateness of
oath-taking on
occasions of great
importance.

Oath of Succession •
The Oath of Succession
is actually just one part
of a long and complex
series of events in the sixteenth century
which led to the martyrdoms of Sts. John
Fisher and Thomas More and to the schism
of the English Church which perdures to
this day. In outline form, the events were as
follows.

For personal and political reasons, King
Henry VIII of England decided that he
wished to "divorce" his wife, Queen
Katharine of Aragon. For this divorce (really
an annulment), he needed the approval of
the Pope. When it slowly became clear that
Rome was going to uphold the validity of
Henry and Katharine's marriage, Henry
began to search for a way around the Pope's
authority. Abetted by greedy barons, then,
Henry engineered the parliamentary
passage of a series of statutes which
supplanted the Pope's power over the
Church in England with Henry's own. Now
treated as the head of his own church,

Henry was granted his annulment and proceeded to "marry" his second wife, Anne Boleyn.

Earlier stages of Henry's legislative assault on papal authority had included, however, certain limiting language which, given the temper of the times, forestalled outright conflict. He was recognized by the Act of Supremacy as the head of the Church in England, but, at the insistence of Bishop Fisher, only "so far as the law of God allows." In the Acts of Succession, though, which were to guarantee that the offspring of Anne, and not those of Katharine, would rule England, this saving clause was omitted. When the accompanying Oath of Succession was then put to various national leaders, two (Fisher and More) refused. For this, both men were imprisoned. The presence of the holy preacher from Rochester and the former Lord Chancellor of England in the horrible Tower of London weighed heavily on public morale, of course, but legally Henry could not persecute them further. However, by means of trickery with Fisher and perjury for More, both men were convicted of denying the Boleyn succession and, more importantly, the statutes of supremacy (when actually both had been merely silent); they were put to death in late June and early July 1535. During the generations after Henry's death, the status of the Oath of Succession waxed and waned in inverse proportion to the status of Catholic rights and interests in England.

Obadiah, Book of • A short work of only twenty-one verses, this prophetic book is a diatribe against Israel's ancient enemy, Edom. In the fifth century B.C., the Edomites (descendants of Jacob's brother, Esau) took advantage of the fall of Jerusalem, migrated northward and invaded Judah.

Nothing is known of the prophet Obadiah other than his name, given at the very beginning of the book, which is entitled "The vision of Obadiah" (Ob 1). The first fourteen verses of the book are an oracle against Edom. Obadiah castigates the arrogance of the Edomites and predicts their downfall. The remaining seven verses focus on the Day of the Lord, a day of divine vengeance against the nations.

For further reading: Peter R. Ackroyd, "Obadiah, Book of," *Anchor Bible Dictionary*, 5:2-4; James M. Kennedy, "Obadiah," *Anchor Bible Dictionary*, 5:1-2; Elias D. Mallon, "Joel, Obadiah," *New Jerome Biblical Commentary*, 399-405.

Obedience • In its formal definition, "obedience" means action at the behest of or assent to a legitimate request from an authentic authority. Such a definition can mislead one to think in terms of oppressive constraints and passive responses. In Sacred Scripture we see a rather different meaning associated with obedience. In the pages of Scripture, we learn of obedience in terms of an individual and whole community response to God's self-disclosure and great plan of revelation. As such, the biblical notion of obedience has to do with responding to and entering into God's life itself (i.e., the goal of salvation history). The English word is from the Latin *ob-audire*, which expresses the meaning common to the Hebrew and Greek words in Scripture which mean "to hear." That is, in Sacred Scripture to obey is really to "hear" the expressed will of God by responding to it completely and without hesitation (e.g., Gn 22:18; Ex 15:26; Dt 5:31-33; Mt 7:21; Mk 3:35; Jn 12:47; Rom 2:13). Such a definition of "hearing" opens up new vistas in understanding the great Shema, the "creed" of Judaism: "Hear, O Israel, the Lord our God, the Lord is one" (Dt 6:5).

Elsewhere in Deuteronomy, Israel is exhorted to "hear" God's statutes and ordinances — meaning, they are exhorted to enter into what God has revealed to them (Dt 4:1-6). The Lord's requirement of obedience takes precedence over burnt offerings because with obedience there is a relationship with God within all of one's life and not just in the narrower liturgical ritual (1 Sm 15:22). Obedience is the means of fulfilling the human person by principles of logic and reason.

Obedience of Faith • At Romans 1:5, St. Paul speaks of his apostolic ministry to proclaim the Gospel of Christ, "through whom we have received grace and apostleship to bring about the obedience of faith for the sake of his name among all the nations." This expression, "the obedience of faith," is repeated in Romans 16:26. In Romans and elsewhere, this phrase refers to the dynamic revelation of God's sovereign will in time and space through Jesus Christ. That dynamic process inspires faith, so to speak, in the person seeking God. The response to God's sovereign act is, in effect, obedience. By that is meant a graced capacity to hear God and respond completely and without reservation.

The language of the Second Vatican Council's Dogmatic Constitution on Divine Revelation captures and further explicates the meaning of this expression from Romans. Obedience of faith "must be given to God as He reveals Himself. By faith man freely commits his entire self to God, making the 'full submission of intellect and will to God Who reveals,' and willingly assenting to the Revelation given by Him" (DV 5). That is, it is God's actions in and through Jesus which stir the heart, now filled with the gift of faith, to give all over to God completely and without hesitation; this is the core "experience" behind "the obedience of faith."

Oblates • Derived from the Latin *offerre, oblatus*, meaning to offer or be offered, this term has had several related though different applications throughout the centuries.

(1) Some religious orders go by this title of "oblates." These are communities of either men or women, not solemnly professed, who have nevertheless dedicated themselves to the service of God in religious life under the vows of chastity, obedience and poverty. Among these are the Oblates of Mary Immaculate, the Oblates of the Virgin Mary, the Oblates of St. Francis de Sales and the Oblate Sisters of Providence.

(2) In Benedictine monasteries it was the practice for young boys to be given over to the monastery by their parents to become vowed members of the community as they grew up. St. Benedict himself accepted this practice when, for instance, he received the oblation of the parents of both Sts. Maurus and Placidus when they were but very young boys. The Council of Toledo forbade this practice for children before the age of ten.

(3) The term "oblate" also denoted lay men or women who carried out the menial tasks in the monasteries and voluntarily subjected themselves to religious obedience and observance of the rule of the respective monastery as long as they remained in its service, which most often was for their entire lives.

(4) Finally, this title is still used today to refer to lay men or women who join themselves through the observance of part of the rule of a particular order, and under the guidance of a director belonging to the same order, to share in its apostolate, spiritual life and the spiritual benefits derived from belonging to it. These are the so-called third orders, or secular orders, which in this instance are referred to as oblates (as is the case with the Benedictines). Originally, the oblates lived on and cultivated the lands around the monastery and partook of its religious

services, that is, the Mass and the Divine Office. They also wore a simplified form of the habit of the order. Though this is no longer the case, they still try to live the religious life within their own particular state, in the world but not of it, and they also may still be buried in the respective habit.

Oblation • Derived from the Latin *oblatio* for offering or sacrificial offering, this term refers to the gift to be offered and the act of offering, as with the Mass. In this sense the Offertory or Preparation of the Gifts would be the oblation which the priest presents to God, in his name and on behalf of the whole Church; these are the gifts which, upon accepting them, God will give to us as the perfect oblation, Jesus Christ His Son, the Lamb of God slain for our sins. By extension, any other gift which is given unconditionally is termed an oblation.

Obreption • The statement of falsehood in a petition for a rescript of some kind. If the reason for the dispensation, favor or privilege which is being sought is based solely on a misstatement or falsehood, then the rescript itself and hence the favor requested is invalid. If, however, the petition is based on several reasons and one or more are false due to *obreptio* but other, equally foundational statements are true, then the rescript is valid (cf. Canons 59, 63).

Obscenity • Deriving from a Latin word meaning "repulsive," it refers to activities that are contrary to good manners, consideration for others, refinement and maturity. Usually dealing with written or visual material, it is difficult to define obscenity, but the standard for determining it should be the judgment of a mature, self-restrained person of strict, thoughtful and informed moral character.

It is not patently evident that obscenity is associated with any other vices or immoral actions, but it is rather clear that it promotes manipulation and exploitation of others, and it does not promote an appreciation of chastity and refinement of manners. Some recent studies have been done suggesting that obscene written and visual materials are associated with felonious crimes, but this is not certain. However, it would seem that there is a strong public interest in curbing obscene material as almost all rapists and child-abusers use obscene materials.

The public debate in many modern countries deals with whether it is legitimate to curb and limit obscene material without also curbing legitimate literary and artistic expression. But included in that debate should also be a discussion of the unrestricted exposure of obscene material to minors and adolescents who can be deeply impressed by it.

Obsession • A psychological illness characterized by involuntary and irrational preoccupation with external objects or persons, or internal states, ideas or emotions. Religious objects, persons or ideas can also become the focus of obsessions. These are usually best treated by a combination of spiritual direction and psychological therapy. In rare cases, obsessions can have a diabolical origin. But, just as in more full-blown cases of possession (of which diabolical obsession is a milder variety), the judgment of a competent priest must be sought before a determination of the existence of authentic diabolical obsession can be rendered and the rites of exorcism performed.

Occasion of Sin • Not simply a situation where the commission of a sin is a possibility, an occasion of sin is a person, place or thing which offers a positive enticement and attraction to sin. An occasion of sin can either be one which always and everywhere leads to sin, or one that usually brings one to commit sinful actions.

Avoiding occasions of sin is a counsel of prudence and should be done whenever and wherever possible. There are some occasions of sin which cannot always and everywhere be avoided, but in those cases, one has an obligation to resist the temptations presented by the occasion of sin.

Occult, Canonically • In canon law the term occult has the technical meaning of not provable by canonical standards or procedure (Canon 1074). As in other legal systems, the fact that something is unknown or unprovable generally precludes the competent authority from taking action on the matter. But because of the unique position of canon law (for it must be aware of both the external needs of governance in the Church and the internal exigencies of souls) the fact that something is occult does not always preclude Church authority from recognizing and responding to the situation.

For example, the matrimonial impediment of crimen might not be provable in the external forum at the time of the wedding. Therefore, the impediment is occult. Yet the impediment exists, and that putative marriage is nevertheless invalid. Likewise, Canon 1030 explicitly authorizes a bishop or major superior to deny a deacon promotion to the priesthood for any canonical reason, even if it be occult. Or again, the bribery of a Church official in order to obtain an ecclesiastical office under simony might be occult, say, by reason of the death of the bribed official. The office is for all that conferred invalidly. Note that these three examples involve very serious matters in the life of the Church, namely Christian marriage, priesthood and Church offices. It is understandable, then, that in such cases the Church be able to protect herself and the faithful from the dangers of fraud and invalidity in these areas.

Occult Compensation • The surreptitious taking of goods or other objects of value from another who has come into unjust possession of them when these goods are lawfully and justly owed you. This practice is legitimate when it is the only means available of coming into possession of what is rightfully one's own, but it is quite dangerous and open to abuse.

It is not morally acceptable for an employee to take goods or funds from an employer simply because the employee believes he or she is not being sufficiently paid, for these goods are not unjustly held by the employer. And it is not morally acceptable to take from another what he or she cannot afford to lose. Occult compensation tends to be infused with selfishness and rationalization, and it should be allowed only in the most extreme situations, when no other means is available to recover unjustly acquired goods. In most circumstances, it is more prudent and less fraught with danger to negotiate for higher compensation. Occult compensation is justified under the conditions of *epikeia*, but it is only to be permitted as the last resort.

Occultism • Signifying "concealed," these are theories or practices which aim at revealing the future or governing events of the future. Occultism includes such superstitious practices as astrology, ouija boards, palmistry, witchcraft, voodoo and satanism.

While admitting that there can be some diabolical influences in our world, the Church affirms the overwhelming power of grace over our lives. She is willing to admit that there are diabolical and evil forces in our world which can be invoked, but discounts the necessity of so doing and affirms that Christ is Lord over all of these powers. The Church rejects occult practices as demeaning the omnipotence and omniscience of God. Occult practices interfere with the communication of God's grace and with our response to that grace. Occultism refuses to place total faith, confidence and reliance on the One and Holy God, and it places undue trust in those powers that have been subordinated to Christ.

Occurrence • The falling of two feasts on the same day of the liturgical calendar, in which case, the higher-ranked feast is observed. If a solemnity is impeded by a liturgical day that takes precedence over it, it is transferred to the closest day which is free.

Octave • Literally "eight." In Roman Catholic liturgical usage, this is the practice of celebrating a major feast on the feast day itself and for seven days thereafter. The entire period is called an octave and the eighth day the octave day.

The practice originates in the Old Testament custom of prolonging a feast day (Passover, Tabernacles). Prior to a simplification ordered by Pope Pius XII in 1955, there were numerous octaves observed. This resulted in multiple prayers at Mass (prayers of the day plus prayers commemorating the feast whose octave was still on) and extensive duplications in the Divine Office. From 1955 until Vatican II, only three octaves were observed (Christmas, Easter and Pentecost).

In a desire to keep the Easter Season to the original "Great Fifty Days," the Vatican II Missal suppressed even the Pentecost Octave (though permitting the Mass of Pentecost to be offered again on the Monday and even on the Tuesday following, where the custom of octave was strong). During the Christmas Octave are celebrated those saints called the *comites Christi* (the retinue or companions of Christ: Stephen, John, the Innocents, Thomas Becket, Pope Sylvester I) and on the octave day itself, Our Lady under the title Genetrix (*Theotokos*), Mother of God. The Easter Octave is observed as a week of solemnities of the Lord to the exclusion of all other commemorations.

Liturgically, the celebration of an octave is marked by the use of the *Gloria* at Mass, the *Te Deum* at the Office of Readings, the use of the word "today" in some prayers and prefaces, and, in the case of the Easter Octave, by the addition of a double Alleluia to the dismissal and response, sung to a beautiful tone heard only during the Easter Octave and on Pentecost.

Ode • In the Eastern Churches, one of the nine sections of a Canon, composed of a Hirmos and a certain number of Troparia, the last of which is called a Theotokion or Megalynarion since it contains an invocation to the Mother of God. (Cf. Canon; Megalynarion.)

Offertory • The part of the Mass when the gifts of bread and wine (in addition to gifts of food or money for the poor) are collected and presented to the priest, who then places them on the altar for their transformation into the Body and Blood of Christ. In the former Missal (that of St. Pius V, the so-called "Tridentine"), this was considered one of the three principal parts of the Mass (along with the Consecration and the Communion of the priest). The five prayers accompanying this rite in the former Missal date only from the Middle Ages and reflect a duplication of parts of the Roman Canon. The ceremony of offering bread and wine developed and expanded from a very simple presentation rite to one that was expanded to the rather elaborate rite of the Missal of St. Pius V.

In the present Order of the Mass, the better term for this rite is the Preparation of the Gifts (*General Instruction of the Roman Missal*, nn. 49-53, 100-107). The gifts are preferably presented to the priest or deacon by the faithful (n. 49). "Money or other gifts for the poor or for the Church may be collected from the faithful and carried to the altar" (n. 49). The procession with gifts is accompanied by "the presentation song" which, if not sung, is omitted (n. 50). The gifts are placed on the altar to the accompaniment of the prescribed texts (n. 49). These texts are much briefer than those of the former Missal; both begin and end with acclamations of blessing derived from Jewish table prayers. First, the bread is presented on the altar on a paten; then the deacon (or in his absence, the priest) pours wine from a cruet into the chalice with a little water, while saying the prayer about our sharing "in the divinity of Christ who humbled himself to share our humanity" (placed at this point in the liturgy in the sixth century). The altar and the gifts may then be incensed; this is followed by the priest's washing of his hands (nn. 51-52). The presentation rite concludes "by an invitation to the people to pray with the priest, and by the Prayer over the Gifts which leads into the Eucharistic Prayer" (n. 53).

Offertory Collection • That action which takes place during Mass, at the time of the Offertory or Preparation of the Gifts, in which the congregation makes their offerings to the Church for her sustenance and that of the sacred ministers. In ancient times not only did the faithful bring money (usually this was done mostly by the wealthy), but they brought the fruits of their labor — cattle and sheep, chickens and eggs, cheese and bread, cloth and other materials necessary for daily life. This brought about the lavabo or washing of the hands of the priests and other ministers (only done by the principal celebrant today), whose hands became soiled from touching these offerings.

Today we are accustomed to give only money at this collection. The principle remains the same, however, for the good Lord has given us everything we have, life and health as well as all material goods. As such, each one of the faithful ought to be responsible to the church of which he or she is a member, for its propagation and sustenance as well as to share with those who have less than they. In fact, this is one of the Precepts of the Church, binding on all the faithful. (Cf. Tithe.)

Office • (1) The full cycle of canonical "Hours" called the Divine Office, the official daily, (and ideally) public prayer of the Church, now known as the Liturgy of the Hours; (2) any portion of the Liturgy of the Hours is often referred to simply as "the Office," (e.g. "the Morning Office"); (3) the entire day's liturgy, Mass and Liturgy of the Hours considered together; (4) more commonly in times past, any public celebration of ecclesial prayer (e.g., "the Office of the Churching of Women"), but still in Eastern usage (e.g., "the Office of Holy Anointing") and also in the Churches of the Reformation (e.g., "Book of Pastoral Offices"); (5) a ministry or function in the Church (e.g., "the office of reader").

Office, Ecclesiastical • A function or position in the Church, founded in either divine or ecclesiastical law and exercised in a stable manner for a spiritual purpose. The obligations, responsibilities and rights proper to individual ecclesiastical offices are defined either in the law by which the office is constituted or in the decree of the competent ecclesiastical authority by which an office is constituted and conferred.

An ecclesiastical office may be acquired either by appointment or election, but never by inheritance or self-conferral. Both lay persons and clerics can acquire ecclesiastical office; however, certain offices which require the care of souls cannot be conferred on those who do not have Sacred Orders. Most ecclesiastical offices presume certain requirements in the persons holding them. For instance, the office of ecclesiastical judge requires that the person have a doctorate or licentiate in canon law.

Certain offices acquired by election require the confirmation of an appropriate ecclesiastical authority, but others do not. A person can lose an ecclesiastical office through removal, resignation, transfer or privation of office as part of a canonical penalty incurred. An office can also be lost if the time limit attached to it lapses.

Some examples of ecclesiastical offices include the papacy, episcopate, pastor, local ordinary, vicar general, judge, defender of the bond (cf. Canons 145-196).

Office of the Dead • Prayers of the Divine Office, or Liturgy of the Hours, prayed for the repose of the souls of the deceased. The Office of the Dead consists of Readings, Morning, Daytime and Evening Prayer. Like the rest of the Liturgy of the Hours, it is composed primarily of Psalms, biblical and non-biblical readings, and intercessions.

The Office of the Dead is often prayed soon after a death, and on All Souls Day, November 2.

Official Catholic Directory of the United States • An annual Catholic and official publication of the Church, as its title denotes, in a particular country, such as the United States, containing: a list of all the Popes, notes on the hierarchy of the Church; the names of all the members of the College of Cardinals; the names of all the Congregations of the Vatican and other pertinent information concerning the administration of the Church in Rome; a list of the national colleges in Rome and of all pontifical universities throughout the world; lists of all the religious congregations and orders in the Church; all the dioceses and bishops of the respective country where it is published; a list of parishes and institutions in each diocese as well as the priests and religious in service there; and a necrology of bishops and priests who have died since the publication of the last directory. The directory also contains the latest census information on the number of baptisms, marriages and deaths within the particular territories principally involved.

Officialis • In the ecclesiastical arrangements of power and prerogatives mandated by canon law, the officialis is a judicial vicar or judge who, with a local bishop, constitutes a diocesan tribunal or court.

Historically, the officialis title was drawn from the early centuries of the Church, when bishops employed priests and deacons to attend to affairs both spiritual and worldly. The recruitment and education of seminarians and their presentation for Holy Orders were tasks traditionally performed by these episcopal representatives. They also maintained the Church treasury.

Eventually, however, the officialis evolved into the more independent status of archdeacon. Through the Middle Ages, these archdeacons ran synods, conducted courts, appointed pastors and disciplined clerics. Yet, by the twelfth century, their power was diluted by the widespread institution of rural deans.

Today the officialis is a priest who is at least thirty years of age and usually a doctor of canon law. In concert with the local ordinary, he sits on a tribunal which primarily investigates and rules on marriage and annulment issues.

Oil • The use of special oils for the anointing of priests and kings is described in the Old Testament (cf. Lv 8:12; 1 Sm 10:1; 1 Sm 16:13), and the practice of using oil for liturgical purposes continued after the founding of the Church. Traditionally oils are blessed by bishops on Holy Thursday for use in certain sacraments and blessings: the "oil of catechumens" (olive or vegetable oil) is used in the ceremonies of Baptism; "chrism" (olive or vegetable oil mixed with balm) is used also at Baptism, in Confirmation, at the ordination of a priest or bishop, and for the dedication of churches and altars; the "oil of the sick" (olive or vegetable oil) is used in the sacrament of Anointing of the Sick (cf. Jas 5:14).

Old Believers • Russian Orthodox Christians who dissented from the liturgical reforms carried out by Nikon, patriarch of Moscow (1605-1681). These reforms are generally regarded as having been necessary, in order to bring Russian practice into line with that of the Greeks and to eliminate corruptions. They were imposed, however, with the assistance of state power and provoked opposition. The Old Believers or "Raskolniki" (schismatics) were excommunicated in 1667 and during the next two hundred years were persecuted intermittently for their refusal to accept the reforms. One sect of Old Believers, the "Popovtsy," were finally able to establish a hierarchy when they were joined by the deposed Bishop Ambrose of Bosnia in 1846. They were recognized by the state in 1881.

Old Catholics • A title for several sects (Utrecht Holland Catholic Church, Polish National Catholic Church in the U.S., some German, Austrian and Swiss Catholics) who broke away from the Catholic Church because they objected to the dogma of papal infallibility defined by the First Vatican Council in 1870. They reject papal primacy, obligatory auricular confession, a celibate clergy, compulsory fast days, indulgences, veneration of the saints, relics and images, sacramentals, mixed marriages and pilgrimages. In general, they accuse the Catholic Church of deserting traditional Catholicism. For example, they accept only the first seven ecumenical councils as adequate statements of the Christian Faith.

Ombrellino • The small canopy formerly required to be held over the Blessed Sacrament when it was exposed in the monstrance and was moved from one place to another outside of processions, when a large canopy, supported by six pole-bearers, was used.

Omega Point: See **Teilhardism**

Omnipotence • Derived from the Latin word for all-powerful (*omnipotens*), the term "omnipotence" refers to an attribute that is proper to the Divine Nature: God can bring into existence anything that is conceivable. According to Christian Tradition, to ascribe omnipotence (also known as immensity) to God does not entail attributing to Him the ability to do absolutely anything (God cannot play the piano, for example), nor the ability to do the logically impossible (God cannot make a square circle). What this amounts to is that God cannot do things precluded by His nature (playing the piano demands having a body with fingers) or by the nature of the things He has made (a square circle is a contradiction). That God is omnipotent means that everything in the world was created by Him and that anything conceivable could be brought into existence by Him. It is especially through our creation (Gn 2:7) and redemption (Col 1:10-12) that God is recognized as omnipotent. Theologically, it is in connection with God's being the source of the existence of everything in knowledge and will that the doctrine of His omnipotence is expounded. In this way, Christian Tradition has avoided the suggestion that the divine omnipotence entails arbitrary or capricious action. God orders all things in wisdom and love for the fulfillment of His plan, revealed in Christ and at least obscurely discernible in the wonders of the natural order.

Omniscience • According to the Scriptures, the scope of God's knowledge is unlimited. It is in the first place a creative and redemptive wisdom. In wisdom, He brings all things into existence and orders the universe according to an intelligent and intelligible plan. In wisdom, He restores all

Pope St. Leo IV wearing a style of omophorion

things through Christ, Who reveals and accomplishes the divine plan of salvation. It follows that God's knowledge embraces everything in the world and penetrates into every human heart. What in the universe could escape the knowledge of the One Who creates, sustains and restores it? For God's knowledge of all things is not an addition to His knowledge of Himself. He knows all things as their creator and conserver, and thus He knows them in Himself. While creaturely knowledge is acquired and

sequential, God's knowledge is simultaneous and absolute. God timelessly knows what has happened, what is happening now and what will happen in the future. But He knows these events for what they are, in their very causes. For this reason, His knowledge of the future free actions of human beings does not destroy their freedom. His eternal knowledge does not impose necessity or determination on all future contingent events. He knows these future actions for what they are, precisely as freely performed actions.

Omophorion • A Byzantine liturgical vestment of the bishop, consisting in a broad strip of richly decorated cloth wrapped around the shoulders and falling in front over the left shoulder and in the back over the right. In character, it shares its origin with the pallium.

Only-Begotten One • Christ is the Only-begotten One Whom the Father has sent into the world because of His great love (Jn 3:16). The title "Only-begotten One" highlights several important aspects of Christ's identity. In the first place, He is the Son from all eternity, consubstantial with the Father, yet proceeding from Him in the eternal generation which implies no inequality. Then, He is the Incarnate Son, the Second Person of the Trinity Who becomes human in order to save the world by a perfect act of loving obedience. Finally, in our fellowship with Christ we have a unique access to the

Father's love, so that Christ becomes the first of many brothers and sisters.

Onomasticon • Compiled originally by Eusebius of Caesarea about A.D. 330, the onomasticon is a list in alphabetical order of over three hundred geographical names mentioned in the Bible. It was most commonly transmitted in its Latin translation, together with additions made by St. Jerome. Like the Medeba Map of Palestine, the mosaic floor of a church dating from the sixth century in modern Jordan, the onomasticon with its record of the traditional location of biblical sites is a valuable aid in the study of biblical geography and the science of biblical topography.

Ontologism • The philosophy that the human mind by its natural powers can intellectually intuit unlimited being, and thus God. This goes well beyond the Catholic view that by natural rational powers we can infer the existence of God as the cause of the world's beings. Many tenets associated with ontologism were condemned in the nineteenth century by the Holy Office.

The ontologist philosophy was developed by religious thinkers attempting to provide an alternative to the philosophy of Kant. Kant denied that the human intellect can possibly understand anything determinate about God's reality in itself; nor can we even rationally demonstrate that God exists. Kant insisted that each person has a rational idea of God, but that merely having such an innate idea yields no knowledge. The ontologists sought to overcome Kant by holding that we do have an innate, albeit confused, intuitive knowledge of unlimited being, rather than a mere idea which does not refer to anything objectively. Thus they defended our natural knowledge of God, Who is unlimited Being. And by our

intuitive understanding of being/God, we know all other things, at least implicitly.

Philosophers have challenged the ontologist claim that each of us as a matter of fact intuitively knows God. Such a claim seems to go beyond what is justified by the evidence of our own awareness. Ontologism can also suggest a pantheist view, according to which there is no difference between ourselves (who supposedly intuit God's being) and God (Who is intuitively present). Furthermore, knowledge by our natural rational power is thereby confused with supernatural knowledge. Several Catholic philosophers in the twentieth century, for example, the Thomists Jacques Maritain or Bernard Lonergan, have provided philosophical alternatives to Kant's agnosticism which do not rely on ontologism's postulate of an intuition of God.

Oplatki • A Polish word (o-PWAT-kee), meaning "thin disk, wafer." It is used among the Polish and some other Eastern European people as part of their Christmas customs. Some authors trace its derivation from the Jewish Passover meal observed in commemoration of the feast of Passover. It consists of a wafer-thin piece of unleavened bread in the form and size of a Mass host on which a picture of the Holy Family or of the Nativity has been impressed. This is then blessed, not consecrated, and distributed to members of the parish families and usually exchanged by one family with another. The breads are then broken into smaller pieces and shared with other family members and friends.

The custom seems to be more than a thousand years old and primarily symbolizes that the Body of Christ, through the sign of bread, becomes a part of each recipient and that Christ is welcomed into the lives of individuals by the sharing of His life; in a more extensive understanding, the exchange of even a small particle of bread reminds the recipient of the sustenance that comes from God the Father, Who provides for our daily needs. This simple sharing further recalls for the participants the common brotherhood of man and all mankind's needs, linking our past with our present.

Optatam Totius • Issued on October 28, 1965, *Optatam Totius*, the Decree on the Training of Priests, makes clear that the true renewal of the Church is dependent upon the training of priests so that they will be prepared for "a priestly ministry animated by the spirit of Christ. . . ." The decree deals with the fostering of priestly vocations, the importance of seminaries, the care which should be given to the spiritual formation of those preparing for the priesthood, the revision of ecclesiastical studies, training for pastoral work and the continuation of studies after ordination, all for the purpose of preparing priests to serve the Church in the spirit of renewal as outlined by the Second Vatican Council.

Opus Dei • Opus Dei, officially known as the Priestly Society of the Holy Cross and the Work of God, was founded in Madrid in 1928 by Bl. José María Escrivá de Balaguer. On November 28, 1982, Pope John Paul II established Opus Dei as a personal prelature. It had been a canonically recognized pious union from 1941, and in 1950 it became the first secular institute. On April 21, 1994, Msgr. Javier Echevarria was confirmed by the Holy Father as the new prelate of Opus Dei.

The goal of Opus Dei is to spread throughout all sectors of society a profound awareness of the universal call to holiness and the apostolate in the concrete circumstances of life. According to the constitutions of the prelature (1982 edition), the aim of Opus Dei is the personal sanctification of its members through the practice of Christian virtue in each one's state of life and profession "in the midst of the world." Prayer, sacrifice, humility, asceticism, assiduous study and fidelity to the Church's Magisterium are central to the ethos of Opus Dei. Intellectual and professional competence is seen to be crucial to the effectiveness of the members' Christian witness in the workplace, in society and culture and in the local church.

The prelature has about 1,500 priests, 350 major seminarians, and 77,000 lay men and women members in about 50 countries. The new leader of Opus Dei announced in 1994 that the prelature would extend its mission to post-communist Europe, with the establishment of branches in Lithuania, Ukraine, Croatia and Slovenia, Cuba, Angola and five other countries. The prelature would give priority to work with families, youth and cultural institutions. In the United States, Opus Dei operates corporate apostolic works (e.g., schools, retreat centers, campus ministries) in major cities in the East and Midwest, Texas and on the West Coast. In other parts of the world, Opus Dei sponsors universities, vocational institutes, training schools for farmers and numerous other apostolic activities.

Orange, Councils of • Two councils were held in Orange (in modern Southern France). The first was convened in A.D. 441 and attended by fifteen bishops, as well as by Hilary of Arles. Its thirty canons treated general matters of ecclesiastical discipline and reform. The second, called in 529, was directed against Semi-Pelagianism. The thirteen bishops in attendance, reacting to the heresy, framed a series of prudent responses, later approved by Pope Boniface II. Several of the canons, in fact, were carried into universal legislation by the

Council of Trent more than a thousand years later.

Orante • From the Latin *orans* (praying), *orante* is the term used for a figure depicted in early Christian art in the classical attitude of prayer; the *orante* has his or her hands lifted up, with palms facing outward, the elbows slightly bent. The physical demeanor of the *orante* is meant to convey an attitude of adoration and praise; as the hands are lifted up, so the *orante*'s mind and heart are raised to God. The palms are open to show an offering of thanks, but also to keep the sacred at a distance, lest the *orante* be guilty of profaning the presence of the sacred by approaching too closely. The most famous depiction of the *orante* is seen in the fresco painting of the three praying men in the Catacombs of St. Priscilla in Rome. In the Latin Rite, the celebrant assumes the posture of the *orante*, evoking similar religious sentiment.

Orarion • The stole of the deacon in the Byzantine Rite.

Orate, Fratres • The Latin words for "Pray, brethren" are the formal invitation to prayer recited by the celebrant to the congregation before the Prayer over the Gifts at Mass. The priest asks the people to pray that his sacrifice and theirs might be acceptable to God. This invitation is the oldest of the additions to the Mass made in the Roman Ordo in Frankish territory. It is first mentioned by Amalarius of Metz in the ninth century.

Oratory • A place set aside for divine worship by the bishop or a diocese for the celebration of all liturgical services unless the liturgical laws forbid them or the bishop (the Ordinary) limits them. Solemn public worship is not to be celebrated in it.

There are three types of oratories: (1) public, for religious communities, available to the public for special reasons; (2) semipublic, which may be used for some particular group; (3) private, which may be used for the particular use of a family or individual.

Order • The term "order" has several senses in Christian usage. In the first place, it has the philosophical sense of the structured and articulated interrelationship of the components that go together to make up any kind of whole. In theology, the term is used to designate certain levels of reality that, for some reason or other, need to be distinguished, notably, the natural order, the supernatural order and the moral order. The term also refers to the sacramentally conferred offices of deacon, priest and bishop. Another use of the term is to

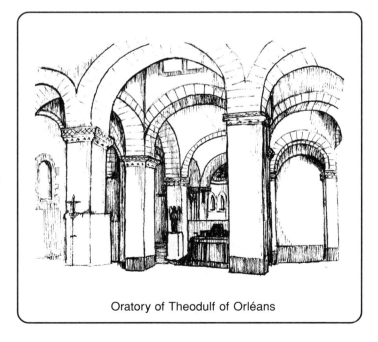

Oratory of Theodulf of Orléans

designate certain religious communities in the Church in which solemn vows are professed, for example, Franciscans (Order of Friars Minor), Dominicans (Order of Preachers), Benedictines (Order of St. Benedict), and the like. In another use, the term refers to the sequence of a religious service, as when one speaks of the Order of Worship or the Order of the Mass.

Order of Christian Funerals • Title of the revised English translation and pastoral rearrangement of the *Ordo Exsequiarum* (issued as the Vatican II revision of the burial rites in 1969), prepared by the International Commission on English in the Liturgy and authorized by the Holy See in 1989.

The "typical" Catholic funeral, as provided for in this Order, consists of three "moments" of prayer (*stationes* in Latin): (1) Vigil (or Wake) Service in the home of the deceased, funeral parlor or church; (2) Funeral Liturgy (usually with Mass, without Mass on liturgical days whose festal nature prohibits a funeral Mass, or when pastoral necessity or judgment counsel postponement); (3) Committal.

In addition, the new ritual provides for three additional times of prayer: (1) with the family (immediately after the occurrence or notification of death); (2) [First] gathering in the presence of the body (after it has been prepared for viewing before burial); (3) transferral to the church (before the coffin is closed and/or the time of vigil ended and as the procession is forming to bring the body to church for the liturgy).

The newly written pastoral notes set forth in great detail the various offices which the community (ordained and lay) is called upon to exercise on behalf of the bereaved at the time of death. Everything from liturgical roles to assistance with "the routine tasks of daily life" is considered in this vision of ministry to the bereaved.

The new ritual also contains complete rites for the burial of children, Morning and Evening Prayer for the Dead from the Liturgy of the Hours, an extensive collection of newly composed English prayers and the complete lectionary of Scripture selections for use in Masses and services for the dead.

Order of Mass, New • The present revision of the texts and rites for the celebration of the Eucharist in accord with the directives of Vatican II and promulgated by Pope Paul VI in 1969, which include the publication of a new lectionary and sacramentary for Mass (together these comprise what is often termed the new Missal of Paul VI). In the Apostolic Constitution *Missale Romanum*, approving the new Roman Missal, Pope Paul VI officially sanctioned this revision in accord with the demands of *Sacrosanctum Concilium*, Vatican II's Constitution on the Sacred Liturgy, and summarized its salient features.

Sacrosanctum Concilium stated that "both texts and rites should be drawn up so as to express more clearly the holy things which they signify" (n. 21), and that "the rite of the Mass is to be revised in such a way that the intrinsic nature and purpose of its several parts, as well as the connection between them, may be more clearly manifested, and that devout and active participation by the faithful may be more easily achieved" (n. 50). The Constitution also decreed that "the treasures of the Bible are to be opened up more lavishly, so that a richer fare may be provided for the faithful at the table of God's word" (n. 51). The Apostolic Constitution states that the rites in the Order of Mass have been "simplified, due care being taken to preserve their substance [and] parts which with the passage of time came to be duplicated, or were added with little advantage" (SC 50), have been eliminated, especially in the rites for the presentation of the bread and wine, the breaking of the bread and Communion.

The new lectionary contains a three-year cycle of readings for Sundays, a two-year cycle for weekdays and adjustments in the readings assigned for solemnities, feasts and memorials. In addition, the Missal "has also corrected and considerably modified other of its components": the Proper of the Seasons, the Proper of the Saints, the Common of Saints, ritual Masses, votive Masses, Mass texts for the major liturgical seasons of Advent, Christmas, Lent and Easter.

The decree *Ordine Missae*, promulgating the *editio typica* of the *Ordo Missae*, was published by the Sacred Congregation of Rites in 1969; this same document officially promulgated the *Institutio Generalis*, the *General Instruction of the Roman Missal*, which contains a detailed description of the nature of the changes in the Missal, the official text covering the various directives for the celebration of Mass, noting especially the active participation of the faithful and the roles to be exercised in celebration. Later, in 1969, the Sacred Congregation for Divine Worship published the Instruction, *Constitutione Apostolica*, on the gradual carrying out of the Apostolic Constitution *Missale Romanum*.

Orders, Holy • Holy Orders is the sacrament in which a bishop imposes hands upon a man, and uses the prescribed prayer, to confer spiritual power and grace to carry out the ordained ministry of the Church. Within this one sacrament there are the three sacramental orders of diaconate, priesthood and episcopate, each administered separately, with successively higher sacramental powers. Deacons are ordained to a ministry of service, and in communion with the bishops and priests they serve in the liturgy, in proclaiming the word and in works of charity. Priests are ordained with the power to celebrate the Holy Sacrifice of the Mass, give absolution to penitents, administer the sacraments, preach and teach the word of God, and fulfill the pastoral responsibilities given to them by their lawful superiors. Bishops receive the fullness of the priesthood, and are successors to the Apostles, and they alone have the sacramental power to ordain others. A bishop has the individual responsibility to care for the particular church which may have been put under his charge, and the bishops together have the collegial responsibility to care for the universal Church.

Any baptized male can validly receive the sacrament of Orders, although it would be illicit to ordain him before he had reached the age of reason. Because this sacrament confers an "indelible mark" upon the soul of the recipient, it can be received only once.

Orders, Major: See **Orders, Holy**

Orders, Minor: See **Minor Orders**

Ordinariate • Generally, an ordinariate may be considered as similar to a diocese, in that it has spiritual authority over a specific group of the faithful much as does a diocese, except that the jurisdiction of an ordinariate is personal and not usually limited by territory.

The best-known example of an ordinariate in the United States is the archdiocese for the Military Services, which oversees the religious welfare of Catholic service men and women, as well as their families, all over the world. Through its offices Catholic military personnel receive the sacraments, religious assistance and instruction in the Faith. The Military Archdiocese also operates its own tribunal and keeps sacramental records of its faithful, just like any territorial diocese. The main offices of the Archdiocese of the Military are located in Silver Spring, Maryland. (Cf. Canon Law; Jurisdiction.)

Ordinary • Canonical term for a person who has been placed in authority over a particular church or its equivalent, or any person who possesses ordinary executive power in a particular church or a community. By ordinary executive power is meant that power which is attached to an office.

The law refers to two types of Ordinaries. A local Ordinary is one who has authority over or in a particular church. All residential bishops are local Ordinaries, as are those who are comparable in law to bishops, namely, vicars and prefects apostolic and apostolic administrators. Those who hold vicarious ordinary power are also local Ordinaries. These include vicars general and episcopal vicars. To be a local Ordinary it is required that one be a priest, with the exception of the office of residential bishop, which requires the episcopate.

When a canon states that a certain act may be performed by a local Ordinary, it means that any local Ordinary, unless his powers have been restricted, may perform it. When a given act is to be performed only by the residential bishop, or another local Ordinary who is a bishop, the canon so states.

The superiors of clerical religious institutes and clerical societies of apostolic life are also called Ordinaries though not local Ordinaries. These include the supreme moderators of institutes and societies, as well as regional superiors, often called provincials (cf. Canon 134).

Ordinary Medical Treatments • Forms of care or medical treatment given under the authority of a physician which are: (1) not radically painful for the patient to receive;

(2) not extremely expensive; (3) readily available; and (4) expected to achieve their designated clinical objective. To refuse to receive ordinary medical treatments is not to be adequately committed to respecting the treasure and basic human good of one's life and is unjust toward oneself. What is morally required and ordinary is not determined simply by what physicians consider to be the customary procedure, for this standard does not take into account the financial or psychological capabilities of the patient to receive the treatments.

In some medical-ethical systems, ordinary medical treatments also include aspects of routine patient maintenance and basic nursing care such as feeding and hydrating patients, giving protection from exposure, sanitary care and psychological support.

Ordinatio Sacerdotalis • The apostolic letter of Pope John Paul II, issued in 1994 and addressed to the bishops of the Church, reaffirming the restriction of priestly ordination to men. In this letter, the Pope affirmed as the constant Tradition of the Catholic Church that she has no authority to confer ordination on women. This judgment is to be definitively held by all the faithful. The letter insists that the Church has no authority to do in this area what Christ Himself did not do, i.e., to choose and ordain women. According to the letter, the occasion for its issuance was the persistence of doubts about Church teaching on the matter of the proper recipient of the sacrament of Holy Orders, as well as the move toward the ordination of women in some branches of the Anglican Communion. The Pope insisted that this teaching does not entail the denial of the equality of men and women, nor the exclusion of women from a wide range of positions in the Church that do not, of their very nature, require ordination.

Ordination • The act of consecrating men to be the sacred ministers for the worship of God and for the sanctification of all people is known as ordination. The ministry of the Church has its origin in Christ Himself and traces its roots to His commissioning of the Apostles (Mt 10:1-5; Mk 3:13-19; Lk 6:12-16) and His appointment of the seventy (Lk 10:1) to work for the building up of the kingdom of God. When Our Lord instituted the Holy Sacrifice of the Mass, He conferred the fullness of the priesthood upon the Apostles as He said, "Do this in remembrance of me" (Lk 22:19), and on the first Easter day He added the power of forgiving and retaining sins (Jn 20:22-23). It is clear that Christ intended this to be a permanent possession of the Church which He founded, and so the power to convey it to others is an inherent part of His gift. After the ascension of Our Lord the Apostles took seriously their responsibility to carry on the ministry which they had received, and one of the first actions they took under the leadership of St. Peter was the selection of St. Matthias to take the place of the traitor Judas (Acts 1:15-26).

Although it is likely that Christ conferred the priesthood upon His Apostles without any special ceremony, the New Testament contains numerous passages mentioning the laying on of hands and prayer, which make up the external Rite of Ordination (Acts 6:6; 13:1-3; 1 Tm 4:14; 5:22; 2 Tm 1:6). There is one sacrament of Orders, but it has the three forms of diaconate, priesthood and episcopate. Although the New Testament sometimes uses the terms "bishop" and "priest" to refer to the same person, the threefold ministry is clear, with references to bishops (1 Tm 3:1-2; Ti 1:7), priests (elders or presbyters) (Acts 11:30; 14:23; 1 Tm 5:17; Jas 5:14) and deacons (Phil 1:1; 1 Tm 3:8).

The Catholic Church teaches that ordination can be performed validly only by a bishop, who is a successor of the Apostles, and that it can be received validly only by a baptized male. It is the episcopate which is the means of the transmission of grace in ordination, and is the guarantee that the Church of the Apostles is the same Church which exists today, carrying on the ministry identical to the one bestowed by Christ. (Cf. Orders, Holy; Women, Ordination of.)

Ordination of Women: See **Women, Ordination of**

Ordo • Technical term referring to the booklet published annually for a diocese or archdiocese or a group of dioceses, prescribing the dates of liturgical seasons and movable feasts, determining the rank, kind of festivity and liturgical colors to be used for all liturgical celebrations of the Mass and the Liturgy of the Hours. By custom these texts also summarize liturgical legislation about fasting and list the names of deceased priests of a given diocese or archdiocese.

Oriental Churches, Congregation for the • One of the several bodies of the Roman Curia concerned with the disciplinary matters of the Oriental Churches and structured in accordance with the norms provided for it by canon law (Canon 360). In addition to the assigned cardinal prefect, the various patriarchs, major archbishops and metropolitans of Eastern Catholic Churches are members by virtue of their positions, as is the president of the Council for Promoting Christian Unity.

Within the Congregation, there is a distinct office for each of the twenty Eastern Catholic Churches designated and divided into five Oriental ritual families: Alexandrian, Antiochene, Armenian, Byzantine and Chaldean. The Congregation has all the faculties that are exercised individually for Latin Catholics in separate congregations for bishops, clergy, religious and secular institutes, as well as Catholic education. Some matters particular to the administration of justice, such as matrimonial cases, are referred either to the Apostolic Signatura or the Rota.

Orientalium Ecclesiarum • The decree on the Eastern Churches of the Second Vatican Council, issued on November 21, 1964, setting forth the unequivocal equality, position and rights of the Eastern communities in the Catholic Church and reestablishing privileges and customs which may have been abrogated or fallen into disuse. The decree also exhibits great sensitivity to the Orthodox Churches, providing special consideration of the position of the patriarchs and collegial governance of the Churches. It clearly makes known the hope of the Council for the eventual reunion of the Eastern Churches now separated from the Church of Rome. The decree in particular enjoins Catholics of the Eastern Churches to know and preserve their lawful liturgical rites and their established way of life. It urges Catholics not of the Eastern Churches to become better acquainted with and knowledgeable about them.

The decree became law on January 22, 1965, and is composed of thirty articles and thirty-four footnotes. It redefines the love, admiration and respect which the entire Church has for the Churches of the East. It addresses the legal relationship of the various ritual Churches within the universal Church. Some of the articles which concern relationships between Catholic and non-Catholic Eastern Christians are the following:

✧ Article 18 declares valid all marriages between Eastern Catholic and non-Catholic Christians celebrated before a validly ordained priest.

✧ Article 24 urges Eastern Catholics to promote the unity of all Christians first by prayer, then by the example of their own lives, by religious fidelity to ancient Eastern traditions, by greater mutual knowledge, by collaboration and by a brotherly regard for sound attitudes.

✧ Article 25 permits individual Eastern non-Catholics, in joining the Catholic Church, to be accepted by a simple Profession of Faith and no other requirements.

✧ Articles 26-29 give principles to be utilized in acts of worship shared by Catholic and non-Catholic Eastern Christians. Article 27 specifically explains the circumstances which may allow the reception of sacraments by Catholics from non-Catholic Eastern priests, and non-Catholic Eastern Christians from Catholic priests.

The basis for this mitigation lies in the following considerations: (1) validity of the sacraments in non-Catholic Eastern Churches; (2) good faith and disposition; (3) necessity of eternal salvation; (4) the absence of one's own priest; (5) exclusion of the spiritual danger of scandal and of formal holding to dogmatic error.

Original Sin: See **Sin, Original**

Orléans, Councils of • Between 511 and 549, six national (not ecumenical) councils were held in this French city and enacted mainly disciplinary regulations. Among the results were canons structuring the Church in Gaul, encouraging charitable efforts by Christians and promoting clerical celibacy.

Orphrey • Coming from the Latin *auriphrygium*, meaning "gold embroidery," this signifies any one of a variety of ornaments with which vestments are decorated. More specifically, it is a long embroidered band — originally of gold cloth or embroidered in gold thread — which is used to decorate sacred vestments. This may range from the bishop's mitre to chasubles and copes, as well as burses and chalice veils. In recent times in Rome and other places, orphreys have also come to be used in decorating the alb. Originally, they may have been used not only as decoration but also to hide unsightly seams in the vestments. However, they have long since become a part of liturgical art and the decoration of vestments used in the Divine Liturgy.

Orthodox Church • That body of Eastern Christian believers identified as possessing and maintaining a valid sacramental and hierarchical system but separated from full communion with the Catholic Church by remaining independent of the Pope. Orthodoxy as a theological construct surfaced with the decisions of the early ecumenical councils, primarily Nicaea I (325), Ephesus (431) and Chalcedon (451), to distinguish Churches that accepted true teaching (orthodoxy) from the believers of false doctrine (heresy or heterodoxy).

The definitive date on which most historians agree marks the separation of the Orthodox and (Roman) Catholic Churches is July 16, 1054, when Cardinal Humbert, the head of a papal delegation in Constantinople, placed a document of excommunication on the altar of Hagia Sophia, the cathedral church of Constantinople. The official reasons for this were the removal of the *filioque* from the Creed; the practice of married clergy and some liturgical errors (for example, the use of leavened instead of unleavened bread for the Eucharist).

This historic act resulted in a schism between the Eastern and Western Churches which still exists. A symbolic gesture of reconciliation by the late Pope Paul VI and Patriarch Athenagoras I in 1966 lifting the anathemas of 1054 occurred and has advanced ecumenical dialogue. The patriarch of Constantinople remains the acknowledged, honored head of Orthodoxy, while for all practical purposes the Orthodox Church is now distinguished along national lines with many autonomous Churches. One can thus speak of the Greek, Russian, Bulgarian, Rumanian, Albanian, Ukrainian and Syrian Orthodox Churches, among many others.

Some important differences between the Orthodox and Catholic Churches include the acceptance by the Orthodox of only the first seven ecumenical councils, their rejection of any single supreme head of the Church, the remarriage of divorced individuals and the questioning of such Catholic dogmas as purgatory, papal infallibility and the Immaculate Conception.

There is a great richness of forms of the spiritual life in the Orthodox Church, exemplified in its monasticism and in its concept of complete renunciation of the life of this present world. Mysticism of the highest order marks the spiritual theology of the Orthodox. An important common element between the Orthodox and Catholic Churches is a shared and abiding love of the Mother of God.

Orthodoxy, Feast of • In the Byzantine Rite, this observance occurs on the First Sunday of Lent and marks the definition by the Second Council of Nicaea (787) of the proper doctrine concerning the veneration of images (icons) and relics. The teaching of this council marked the end of the heresy of iconoclasm or image-breaking. The council clearly distinguished between adoration which is paid to God alone and veneration which may be given to a sacred image or relic. The veneration tendered passes not to the image or object itself, but to the person or persons therein depicted. The iconoclastic conflict itself finally ended in the year 842 under the Empress Theodora.

Osservatore Romano, L' • The daily newspaper of the Holy See originally began publication in July 1861 under the leadership of four Catholic laymen. In 1890 Pope Leo XIII purchased the newspaper, which has been referred to as the "official newspaper of the Pope." Actually, the official news or announcements contained in its pages are under the heading *Nostre Informazioni*. The newspaper publishes the official policies, as well as the social and political attitudes, of the Holy See. A staff of reporters covers Rome news and foreign events.

A weekly English edition was inaugurated in 1968. Other weekly editions are printed in French, Spanish, Portuguese, German and Polish.

Ostiarius • Latin for "porter" or "doorkeeper," this refers to the ancient minor order of porter, he who was charged with taking care of the physical plant of the church building and thus the keys to the doors (hence the name). Formerly it was one of four minor orders conferred upon all candidates for the priesthood. The other three were the orders of lector, exorcist and acolyte. Pope Paul VI suppressed these, as well as the major order of subdeacon, by his Apostolic Letter, *Ministeria Quaedam*, of August 15, 1972. (Cf. Ministries.)

Ostpolitik • The Holy See's policy of openness toward the Communist governments of Eastern Europe, in an attempt to improve Church-state relations in those countries, thus gaining some religious freedom for their citizens. This conciliatory attitude, initiated by Pope John XXIII, developed by Paul VI and continued by John Paul II, differs from the more

confrontational style of Pius XII, who considered Communism to be so intrinsically evil that negotiation and dialogue with it were impossible. Its major architects have been Agostino Cardinal Casaroli, who became Secretary of State to His Holiness in 1979, and Franz Cardinal König, the Archbishop of Vienna from 1956 to 1985. The recent appointment of bishops in Eastern European countries, as well as signs of increased understanding between the Holy See and Communist governments (e.g., the visit of the Soviet President to John Paul II in November of 1989) would indicate that this approach is bearing fruit.

Our Lady • This title refers to the Blessed Virgin Mary. It is particularly common in Western Catholic writings and speech. Just as Christ, her divine Son, has been called since the earliest days of the Church by the title of "Lord" or "Our Lord," so she who shares so integrally in the mysteries of His incarnation, His birth and salvific work, and now in His glory in heaven, has been regarded as Lady and Mistress of all Christ's children in the order of grace. Though this title in reference to Mary is common to the majority of Western cultures and languages, it is most used in English and French. The latter, with which most Anglophones are familiar, is *Notre Dame*.

Oxford Movement • The Church of England (Anglicanism) has experienced throughout its history the tension between its more Catholic elements (e.g., emphasis on episcopacy, apostolic succession, sacramental life) and its more Protestant elements (e.g., presbyterial or congregational government, emphasis on the word). This tension was especially expressed in the Oxford Movement.

A group of Anglicans (including John Keble, R. H. Froude, John Henry Newman), concerned about the interference of the government in Church affairs and the loss of the significance of many elements of their religious heritage, began the publication of a number of tracts or short treatises on various aspects of Church life. Emphasis on the teaching of the Fathers of the Church was another way of conveying their ideas. Although the movement was occasioned, to some extent at least, by governmental action, it was theological rather than political in character.

There was strong reaction pro and con. New members joined the group (e.g., E. Pusey, R. Wilberforce), but others saw the movement as a thinly disguised Romanism.

The Oxford Movement's
Cardinal Newman

The publications of Newman's Tract 90 in 1841 (which tried to interpret the thirty-nine Articles in a more Catholic sense) brought forward a wave of criticism. It became clear to Newman and others that their notion of Anglicanism as a distinct but full expression of Catholic Faith was not correct. He and some others (e.g., W. G. Ward, F. Faber) left the movement and became Catholics.

As a distinct enterprise within Anglicanism, the Oxford Movement soon lost force. It had an enduring effect in the new attention given in some parts of Anglicanism to Catholic elements of Tradition, especially in liturgy.

𝒫

Pacem in Terris • An encyclical, whose title means *Peace on Earth*, issued by Pope John XXIII, in 1963, concerning the promotion of peace in the world. It set out the requirements of peace, security, liberty and human rights that are necessary for the establishment of enduring international peace. It emphasized that peace requires proper relationships between individuals, between individuals and states, and among states. One of many encyclicals on these issues, it asserted the traditional Christian claim that peace among individuals and communities requires the proper ordering of our own personal lives.

Pacifism • A modern doctrine which holds that war in all its forms is immoral and contrary to standards of humanity and decency, and that it is also contrary to the dictates of the Sermon on the Mount, especially Matthew 5:39. Pacifism rejects the claim that there can be a "just war," particularly in modern times because of the destructiveness of modern weapons; it also rejects the possibility of there being a just war in these times. It holds war to be immoral because it cannot be conducted without an evil heart and will.

Pope John XXIII, author of *Pacem in Terris*

Catholic theology, although sympathetic to the concerns of pacifism, has never accepted its final conclusions, preferring to call men and nations to peace while maintaining the morality of a just war under clearly defined conditions. (Cf. Just War Theory.)

Pactum Callixtinum • The Latin words for the agreement made between the Holy Roman Emperor Henry IV and Pope Calixtus II, more commonly known as the Concordat of Worms. This agreement essentially ended the practice of lay investiture, or the control which heads of state exercised over ecclesiastical appointments. The agreement was made in September of 1122 and confirmed by the First Lateran Council in March of 1123.

Paenitemini • Pope Paul VI issued this Apostolic Constitution changing the canonical requirements of fast and abstinence. Despite the revisions, the Pope restated the obligations of doing penance and made clear the changes were intended to strengthen the practice of penance among a greater number of the faithful. The Church "intends to ratify with her prescriptions other forms of penance . . . provided that it seems opportune to episcopal conferences to replace the observance of fast and abstinence with exercises of prayer and works of charity" (*Paenitemini, III*).

Paganism • In Christian usage, this term refers to all forms of polytheistic religions. It was first applied to the popular religions of the world of late antiquity, and subsequently to the religions that Christian missionaries encountered among the migratory peoples at the edges of the empire. The term continues to retain this primary sense and is never employed to describe monotheistic religions (such as Judaism or Islam) and not normally to refer to great world religions that are non-monotheistic (Hinduism) or non-theistic (Vedanta and some forms of Buddhism).

The term has an important extended usage in referring to libertine, hedonistic, irreligious and amoral forms of life.

Pain and Euthanasia • In an allocution to physicians and surgeons in 1957, Pope Pius XII answered a number of questions concerning the relief of pain and suffering, one of which dealt with whether it was morally permissible to give analgesic doses sufficient to overcome pain but which would "shorten" the life of the patient (Pope Pius XII, *Religious and Moral Aspects of Pain Prevention in Medical Practice*, February 24, 1957). Pope Pius XII argued that it was permissible to give such doses, provided that a number of conditions were met. Such lethal doses could be given provided: (1) the intention of the patient and physician was to alleviate pain and not to end life; (2) no other means were available to lower or alleviate the pain; (3) the patient explicitly requested the life-shortening analgesia, as it could not be given without patient consent; (4) the patient was free of any outstanding obligations to himself or others; (5) and the life-shortening analgesia was proportionate to the condition of the patient. This principle is now somewhat obsolete because there have been such remarkable advances in pain relief in recent decades that it seems unlikely to have situations where giving lethal doses of analgesia is medically necessary, and there are virtually no situations now when the alleviation of pain must be accomplished by the shortening of the patient's life.

Pain Bénit • French for "blessed bread," this designates any number of breads which, according to local customs and cultures, are blessed for distribution among and use of the faithful during certain times of the year, especially on Easter Sunday and during the Season of Easter, or Eastertide. This bread is then taken home by the faithful and eaten as a sacramental, with faith in and love for Jesus Christ, risen from the dead. In former times, wealthy patrons donated bread to be blessed after Mass and then distributed to the poor.

Palatine • In classical Rome, one of the seven hills that was sacred to Pallas Athena. This hill later became the site of the residence of the emperors and because of its original association was called the "palatine" hill. The word came to mean "palace." Eventually many offices associated with imperial or papal administration were called the "Palatine Guard." In addition, the Vatican Library was originally known as the "Palatine Library," a designation now applicable to only one section of its collection.

Palimpsest • From two Greek words meaning "to rub" and "again." The reference is to a piece of parchment (usually) which has been rubbed more or less clear of its original text, so that the same page of parchment could be used over again. Such parsimony was made necessary by the costliness of writing materials and made possible by the hardiness of such materials. With the advance of photographic technology, it has become possible to recover the original text with relative ease.

One of the more famous palimpsests is a copy of some of the writings of Ephrem the Syrian. These writings were set down in the twelfth century on pages of Scripture that had been erased. The sheets may have originally contained the complete text of the Old and New Testament. It was written down on these pages in the fifth century. Many of the pages of the original biblical text have been lost. The language of the text superimposed, as well as that of the original text, is Greek.

Pall • The term "pall" refers to two items used in the Liturgy, one for the Eucharist and the other for funerals. The pall used at the Eucharist is a piece of stiff linen, cardboard or even acrylic, covered with linen, usually between four and seven inches square, used to cover the chalice at Mass. It helps preserve the contents of the chalice from dust and flying insects that might fall into it. The upper part of the pall may be plain, or have an embroidered cross on it, or it may be lavishly ornamented with either embroidered or painted liturgical symbols or even depictions of Our Lord, the Eucharist or the Blessed Mother. Sometimes precious or semiprecious stones are incorporated in the embroidery. The

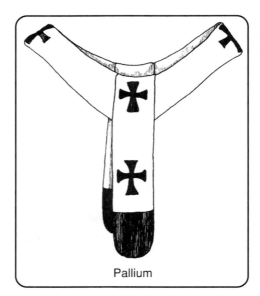

Pallium

bottom or lower part of the pall must be simple, of plain linen.

When used at the funeral liturgy the term "pall" refers to the cloth which is spread over the coffin at funeral Masses. This may be of the liturgical color proper to funerals, that is, black or violet, or in certain countries (such as the United States) white. In liturgical catechesis the funeral pall is often likened to the white garment one receives at Baptism. The use of the funeral pall, then, recalls being clothed in Christ at Baptism, while the funeral liturgy is understood as the sacramental completion of what was begun at Baptism.

Pallium • The circular band of white wool with two hanging pieces (front and back) decorated with six black crosses, worn over the shoulders by all metropolitan archbishops and by the Pope himself. Its origins are somewhat obscure. Prior to the ninth century, it was apparently a ceremonial garment granted to certain bishops as an honor; by the ninth century all metropolitans came to wear it at specific pontifical liturgies. The ceremony for blessing the lambs from whose wool the pallia are woven annually takes place on January 21, the feast of St. Agnes (mentioned in the Roman Canon) at the church of Santa Agnese Fuori le Mura (outside the walls of the city of Rome).

The *motu proprio* by Pope Paul VI on the pallium, *Inter eximia episcopalis*, abolished "any privileges and customs [then] applying either to particular churches or to certain bishops as a personal prerogative." The purpose of this *motu proprio* is stated to be the revision of "the privileges and practices related to the granting of the pallium in order that it might serve as a distinctive symbol of the power of the metropolitan."

Palm Sunday • The secondary title (in parentheses) for the Sunday before Easter, the day which opens Holy Week: Passion (or Palm) Sunday. Prior to the Second Vatican Council's revision of the Calendar, the last two weeks before Easter were designated "Passiontide," the first Sunday of which was "Passion" and the second "Palm" Sunday. Vatican II wished to restore Lent to its pristine prominence, hence the abolition both of the pre-Lent (Septuagesima) and post-Lent (or pre-Easter) "sub-seasons."

The new designation is more accurate, at any rate, since, in fact, in the former rite the Passion was *not* read on Passion Sunday. The revision likewise takes account of the fact that this Sunday before Easter combines — in one celebration — two traditions and themes: the Jerusalem custom (which came to Rome only in the twelfth century via Spain and Gaul) of the blessing and procession with palms (celebrating Christ's triumphant entry into Jerusalem) and the equally venerable Roman custom of the solemn proclamation of the Passion on the Sunday which ushers in the Holy Week commemoration of that mystery.

Palms, Blessing of • On the Sunday before Easter, designated by the Second Vatican Council's revised Calendar as "Passion (Palm) Sunday," Mass begins with a general introduction to Holy Week in the form of the celebrant's exhortation, and with the blessing of palm branches (other branches are used in areas where palms are not commonly available, e.g., olive and willow branches). Before the principal Mass, this blessing ideally takes place apart from the church, so that the congregation can go there in procession, singing hymns to Christ the Messiah and King, and so enter spiritually and physically (symbolically at least) into His entry into Jerusalem and ascent to the Temple and to His passion.

The Prayer of Blessing (two forms are provided) reminds the assembly that we are to welcome Christ into our own lives and bear faithful witness to His Lordship over us. The procession is preceded by the Gospel of the Lord's Entrance. At Masses without the procession, either a solemn or simple form of the entrance rite may be celebrated.

Panagia • Literally, the all-holy, the Mother of God, this image replaces the pectoral cross for a Byzantine Rite bishop. Also, the service of Blessing at Table in Eastern monasteries.

Pange Lingua • One of several Eucharistic hymns written by St. Thomas Aquinas, "Sing, my tongue, the Savior's glory," is performed at vespers on the solemnity of Corpus Christi. It is also used as a processional hymn on Holy Thursday, Corpus Christi, during the Forty Hours' devotion and generally in other rites honoring the Blessed Sacrament.

Pannykhidia • Literally, "the whole night" (Greek). In the Byzantine Rite, this term is used to designate a service for the departed. Originally, it was the vigil preceding a funeral. It may be celebrated as a separate memorial service as well.

Pantheism • The idea that the divine substance underlies and enters into composition with the non-divine, worldly realm. Pure pantheism would seem to entail the divine being's identification with the being of the worldly realm. Since it is not clear that anyone has ever proposed this blatant equation of the divine with the non-divine, the term "pan<u>en</u>theism" has recently been coined to express the more subtle idea that the divine enters into composition or relation with the non-divine such that its divine identity is intrinsically tied up with this connection, but not exhausted by it.

The following thinkers have been regarded as representative proponents of what seem to be panentheistic ideas or systems: the Hindu Vedantic philosopher Sankara, modern philosophers such as Spinoza, Fichte, Schelling, Hegel and Whitehead, and some Romantic poets like Goethe and the early Wordsworth.

Christianity, Judaism and Islam reject pantheism and panentheism. While the intention of such thinkers is a laudable one — countering materialistic and atheistic views of the universe — pantheistic ideas compromise the absolute distinction between the created and the uncreated. They make the divine being in some way dependent on the non-divine, and suggest that the divine is incomplete or imperfect except in conjunction with the non-divine. In Catholic theology, St. Thomas Aquinas has been prominent in his insistence that God's presence to all things — His "immanence" as it is called in theology — is a causal presence that creates and sustains things in existence. But God in no way enters into composition with things, for His existence transcends the participated or derived existence that He freely imparts in bringing a creaturely order into being *ex nihilo*.

Pantocrator • From the Greek, meaning ruler of all, pantocrator is the title given in the Eastern Church to Christ as the Ruler of Heaven and Earth; it corresponds to the Western title of Christ the King. In particular, the term is used of images of Christ depicted as Judge and Ruler; the most famous of these in the United States is the large mosaic of Christ the Judge behind the main altar and baldacchino of the National Shrine of the Immaculate Conception, Washington, D.C.

Papabile • A popular Italian term referring to the one most likely to be elected Pope after the death of a Pope.

Papacy • This term refers to the office of the Pope as head of the Church or as a civil ruler in the Vatican State. It also refers to the length or reign of any particular Pope or the collective listing of successive Popes since St. Peter.

Papal Blessing (Apostolic Blessing) • The blessing or benediction given by the Pope on certain occasions, such as the *Urbi et Orbi* blessing, and at the end of liturgical and even non-liturgical functions. In recent times it has been the custom to ask for a parchment containing testimony of the granting of such a blessing that may be sent to the faithful who have petitioned it for themselves or for loved ones. A small offering is given at this time, first, to pay for the materials used and the artists who paint them and letter them by hand, and second, to provide funds for the Apostolic or Papal Almoner for the poor. Others are empowered or delegated to give the apostolic blessing: cardinals, bishops and abbots may do so on certain solemnities; retreat masters can impart this blessing to the retreatants at the end of such a spiritual exercise; and all priests are to give this blessing to the sick at the hour of death. The papal blessing, in any of its forms, is accompanied by a plenary indulgence, i.e., the remittance of temporal punishment (cf. Purgatory).

Papal Chamberlain • Former title of a particular rank of honorary prelate, today known as Chaplain of His Holiness. Papal chamberlains actually exist as minor prelates in the papal household. The title is conferred as an honor upon priests at the request of their bishop. The title formerly had to be laid down at the death of the Pope who granted it, although in practice the newly-elected Pope always reappointed all honorary papal chamberlains. As of 1968, the title (and its present equivalent) is for life.

Papal chamberlains were styled "Very Reverend Monsignor" and wore a house cassock trimmed in purple with a purple sash; the church dress was a purple choir cassock with purple sash and mantellone, and the biretta had a purple tuft. Presently, Chaplains of His Holiness may wear only the house cassock, even in church, and the biretta should have a black tuft.

Papal Flag • The official flag of the Vatican. The flag has two equal vertical stripes of yellow and white. The yellow one hangs closer to the flagstaff. On the white half appear the insignia of the papacy — a triple tiara above two crossed keys, one silver and one gold. The tiara represents the teaching, sanctifying and ruling offices of the Holy Father. The keys symbolize the power of the keys given to St. Peter.

Papal Household • A prefecture of the Roman Curia, the papal household manages the living arrangements of the Holy Father, both in Rome and when he is traveling. The prefect of the papal household is a titular bishop who is assisted by a secretary and staff. The papal household arranges audiences with the Pope and supervises papal ceremonies other than liturgical services.

Papal Letters • Generic term for any kind of official but not necessarily public letter issued by the Pope. They are signed either by the Pope himself or issued with his

approval under the signatures of the prefect and secretary of a Roman Congregation or other agency. There are various kinds of papal letters, some concerning legal matters and others of a doctrinal or teaching nature. The most important form of papal pronouncement is the Apostolic Constitution, which is usually a statement of definitive legal or doctrinal nature. Second to it is the encyclical, always a teaching document. Other forms of papal letters are the *motu proprio*, papal epistle, exhortation and decree.

Papal States • These were the states under the civil authority of the papacy from 754 to 1870. The possession of these states made the Pope a sovereign. In the nineteenth century, a movement to unite Italy swept the Italian peninsula, and by 1870 all papal territory was lost. During the period of the papal states, pontifical administration was divided into two types, sacred and secular. With the loss of the papal states, the secular dicasteries fell into disuse, and only the sacred congregations still functioned. By the time of the Second Vatican Council, it was apparent the designation of all congregations as "sacred" was superfluous, and the adjective was dropped.

The independent State of Vatican City is comprised of about one hundred four acres of land within the city limits of Rome. Vatican City is governed by a special commission with several functions performed by the Apostolic Signatura. The Lateran Treaty of 1929 reestablished the temporal authority of the Pope.

Papal Theologian • The papal theologian, or theologian to the papal household, as he is formally known, is a theologian appointed by the Roman Pontiff who acts as his special adviser in theological matters. The office was formerly known as Master of the

Sacred Palace and is traditionally held by a Dominican.

Pappas • "Father" in Greek, the term is used in Greek-speaking Churches for all priests. From this is derived the popular "Papa" or Pope, that is, the Holy Father.

Parable • The term "parable" is from the Greek *parabole*, which means placing things side by side for comparison. In ancient rhetoric "parable" was a technical term for a particular figure of speech. For example, in Aristotle's *The Art of Rhetoric* (2.20), proofs from rhetoric can be divided into general statements used for deductive purposes (e.g., maxims and proverbs) or into stories written with specific points to make, for inductive purposes (e.g., historical or fictional narratives). Current theoretical analysis of New Testament parables suggests that although they are often written as similes (one thing compared to another, disciples sent out "as lambs in the midst of wolves" [Lk 10:3]) they function more like metaphors, in which a feature or quality of one thing is directly attributed to another ("You are the salt of the earth" [Mt 5:13]). Within such an understanding of "parable," one can include aphorisms, stories, proverbs, riddles, discourses, dialogues, when such are metaphorical or figurative.

Jesus' parables could be described as having been drawn from everyday life (Lk 11:5-8) and so have a sense of real life experience about them; they contain the novel and paradox (last hired is first paid, small amount of work gets a full day's pay [Lk 14:21, etc.]); and they contain a challenge which does not cease with initial accomplishment (e.g., Mk 4:9; Mt 20:15; 21:31; 13:45-46). They seem to have the effect of drawing the listener "into" the world of the content, in a sense communicating a knowledge of God and His kingdom not arrived at by principles of logic and reason. The meaning of the parable is without end because the reader who searches the parable always brings a fresh capacity to see more and more of the inexhaustible mystery of God's kingdom contained within it.

Paraclete • Our English term is a transliteration of the Greek term (*parakletos*) and literally means "called to the side of" and so can mean "advocate" (other translations are possible: counselor or comforter). The phrase occurs at John 14:16-17, 26; 15:26; 16:7-11. In the Fourth Gospel the Paraclete is the divine presence within the community after Jesus' ascent into heaven to be with the Father. The Paraclete is the Holy Spirit and is called the Spirit of Truth (Jn 14:17, 26) because He will continue Jesus' work (14:16-17), recall Jesus' teachings and lead believers to all truth (16:13). The Holy Spirit, the Paraclete, will bring Jesus' presence to perfection in the believer, for, like Jesus, the Paraclete is "in" them (14:17; 17:23) forever (14:16).

For further reading: John Ashton, "Paraclete," *Anchor Bible Dictionary*, 5:152-154.

Paracletikes • The Office of Consolation or Paraclisis, recited in honor of the Mother of God in the Byzantine Rite.

Paradise: See **Eden, Garden of;** also **Heaven**

Paraekklesia • Literally, "by the church." Structurally, this term designates any side chapel or addition to a church building in the Eastern Rites. A corresponding designation in the Roman Church would be a "winter chapel" or room attached to the main church where liturgical services could be celebrated for small groups.

Paraenesis • From the Greek *parainein* (to advise), paraenesis is, in general, any kind of advice or counsel. In particular, in biblical or patristic writers, it refers to the literary genre of preaching and exhortation. Examples include the Letter of James, the First Letter of Clement of Rome and the Shepherd of Hermas.

For further reading: Benjamin Fiore, "Paranesis and Protreptic," *Anchor Bible Dictionary*, 5:162-165.

Paraliturgical Actions • Those rites, prayers and ceremonies that are not strictly part of the liturgy but may be closely aligned with it as an overflow of its spirit, as, for example, exposition of the Blessed Sacrament is a contemplative extension of the Mass. Other devotions which tend to be more private in nature or which developed as substitutes for the liturgy are nonetheless warmly recommended by Vatican II's Constitution on the Sacred Liturgy.

Such practices as the Rosary, Stations of the Cross and novenas can prepare one for the Mass and carry its spirit into the rest of the day. The same document does, however, caution that "such devotions should be so drawn up that they harmonize with the liturgical seasons, accord with the sacred liturgy, and lead the people to it, since in fact the liturgy by its very nature is far superior to any of them" (n. 13).

Parallelism • The noun refers to a literary device frequently used in ancient literature. In 1753, R. Lowth published the first systematic analysis of Hebrew parallelism in the Old Testament. A parallelism contains expressions which are repeated and/or grammatical structures which are repeated in adjacent lines or phrases. An example which occurs frequently in Scripture is Psalm 103:10: "He does not deal with us according to our sins, nor requite us according to our iniquities." Here we have the first thought repeated, but with different vocabulary, an example of a synonymous parallelism. When the second thought contrasts with the first, we have an antithetical parallelism (e.g., Ps 20:9). When the first thought is extended and developed in parallel structure of vocabulary, we have a synthetic parallelism (e.g., Ps 2:2; Ps 19:8). The prologue of John's Gospel is an example of "staircase parallelism," so that one or two key words from one sentence are repeated in the next one, and two other words from that second sentence are repeated in the third, etc. The device is a powerful rhetorical tool which facilitates emphasis and accent of expression.

For further reading: Adele Berlin, "Parallelism," *Anchor Bible Dictionary*, 5:155-162.

Parapsychology • The study of extrasensory perception (ESP), psychokinesis and other psychic phenomena. Telepathy is ESP of subjective states or cognitive contents, while clairvoyance is telepathy of objective conditions. The focus of this field of study has been on the authenticity of claims that certain individuals possess special psychic powers which enable them to know beyond what ordinary sensory powers reveal to us.

Whether these extraordinary parapsychological powers actually exist is difficult to know. In studies done at Duke University in the 1930s, individuals were able to show remarkable consistency over a short period of time in predicting dice-throws, but usually these powers declined rapidly after a brief period of time. The attitudes of individuals toward these realities seem to have a profound effect on them, and this causes people to have doubts about their reality.

Catholic tradition has not placed much credence in these powers, and it holds that they are insignificant in comparison to the power of Christ to give rebirth and new direction to our lives.

Parenthood • The primary obligation of parents is to love, train and educate their children.

In the Old Testament, the first blessing uttered upon man was that of being fruitful and multiplying. In the Old Testament era, children were granted more rights in relation to their parents than was the case in pagan society, for many pagan societies allowed the father to reject and even kill an unwanted or deformed child by neglect. In Israelite society, this seems to have been prohibited, and it appears that infanticide was not practiced. God was regarded as the good Parent Who raised, loved and trained Israel (Dt 1:31).

In the New Testament, Christ presented the faith, hope and trust of a child as a model of faith for His disciples. The centurion who sought healing for his child is held as a model of Christian parenthood as well. The responsibilities of parenthood are modeled on the care which God gives to His people. The love and care which parents are to show their children is to imitate that of God (Mt 5:43-45).

The Second Vatican Council affirmed the solemn obligations of parents to children: "The family is, in a sense, a school for human enrichment. But if it is to achieve the full flowering of its life and mission, the married couple must practice an affectionate sharing of thought and common deliberation as well as eager cooperation as parents in the children's upbringing. The active presence of the father is very important for their training: the mother, too, has a central role in the home, for the children, especially the younger children, depend on her considerably; this role must be safeguarded without, however, underrating women's legitimate social advancement" (GS 52). The Council also affirmed that parents must be given the freedom by the state to educate their children as they see fit.

Modern criminology has shown with great force and clarity how the failure of parents to teach, care for and love their children adequately is associated with crime and poverty, and how governmental policies with anti-family effects only exacerbate these problems. Maintaining family life where both parents share responsibilities for the rearing of children is of critical importance for the social development of the children and the development of their potentialities. The family is the first school in the Faith for children, and the failure of families to educate their children in the Faith often destroys their faith.

Parents, Duties of • Parental obligations include providing for both the physical and spiritual needs of their children. Thus, it is the duty of parents (to the best of their ability) to see that their offspring receive adequate food, clothing, intellectual formation and anything else necessary for life. Also, they have a serious duty to provide a correct spiritual formation for their children by having them baptized as soon as possible after birth, by seeing that they receive the sacraments of Penance, Holy Eucharist and Confirmation at the proper time, by instructing them in the Faith and by training them to form a correct conscience in their moral conduct, taking advantage of any assistance which is available. Parents are to teach their children not only by word, but by their own example which is to be grounded in their faith.

Parish • A definite community of the faithful within a diocese. It is established on a stable basis by the bishop and entrusted to a pastor. For the first four centuries, parishes and dioceses were coextensive, being under the pastoral care of a bishop. With the end of the persecutions and the rapid increase of the Faith among people, it became necessary to establish communities of the faithful smaller than dioceses, since the bishop could not adequately tend to the spiritual needs of the large numbers of people. At first, bishops entrusted these smaller communities to the care of priests who were part of the cathedral clergy. During the Age of Feudalism, parishes were established in most of the villages and towns and were dependent on the support of the landowner. Up until the Council of Trent, parishes were, for the most part, territorial entities with loosely defined boundaries.

The Council of Trent decreed that parishes be established with definite geographical boundaries and that the pastor, or parish priest, have jurisdiction only over the faithful who resided within these boundaries.

In general, parishes are territorial in nature. The law also allows for the establishment of parishes based upon rite, nationality or language. Such parishes are often called personal parishes, since they are composed not of all persons in a territory but of persons having some similar quality.

Only a priest may be appointed pastor to a parish, and the practice of naming two or more priests as co-pastors in a single parish has been expressly forbidden by the 1983 Code (cf. Canon 526.2). In some places, however, because of shortages of priests, laypersons or religious are appointed to act as supervisors, but not administrators in the canonical sense, of parishes. The parish remains under the pastoral care of a pastor who visits it on a regular basis. In such parishes, the layperson or religious given charge of the parish may perform certain administrative

and even sacramental functions that do not require the power of Holy Orders.

Usually parishes are entrusted to diocesan priests. The bishop may, however, entrust a parish to a religious community. Prior to the revised Code, the local religious community itself was considered to be the pastor. At one time, the provincial superior or even the local superior could appoint a priest of the community to act as parochial vicar and function as actual pastor to the parish. The new Code does not allow this arrangement. With the consent of the competent religious superior, the bishop now entrusts a parish to a religious community and appoints a member of the community as its pastor. Usually the religious superiors present the candidates for pastor to the bishop for his appointment.

In some cases when parishes are entrusted to religious, the religious community itself actually founded the parish with the appropriate decree of erection from the local bishop. Ownership of the parish buildings depended upon the terms of the agreement with the bishop. In other cases, bishops have entrusted diocesan parishes to religious, usually because of a shortage of diocesan clergy (cf. Canons 515, 518, 520).

Parish Pastoral Council • A representative group of members of a parish who assist the pastor in fulfilling his ministry to the parish. The concept grew out of the Second Vatican Council's emphasis on expanding the role of the laity. Parish councils are not mandatory entities for every parish; however, the bishop can, if he judges it opportune, call for the establishment of parish councils in all of the parishes of his diocese.

Membership on the parish council is determined by norms determined or approved by the diocesan bishop. The most common form of obtaining membership is by election among the parishioners. The parish council is always presided over by the pastor. It is purely consultative in nature and has no legislative or decision-making power of its own (cf. Canon 536).

Parish Priest • The officially appointed pastor of a parish. The official Latin term for this is *parochus*, rather than *pastor*, as the latter term refers, in official canonical documents, to the bishop.

Parish Team • In the strictly canonical sense, a parish team is a group of priests who share the pastoral care of one parish or a group of parishes. Although no one of the priests is appointed as pastor, one of the group must be the moderator. The moderator is responsible for directing the joint action of the group and reporting to the bishop. All members of the parish team have ordinary pastoral jurisdiction, and all share in the obligation of celebrating the required Sunday and holy day Masses for the people of the parish (Canon 517.1).

The concept of a parish team predated the revised Code. It came into being in the years after the Second Vatican Council as an experiment in sharing the obligations and responsibilities of pastoral care. There were various models of parish teams, some including laypersons and religious as members. The parish team in the Code is the canonical entity that comprises the minimum required by law for a parish team. It simply says that the pastoral care (technically, the care of souls) is entrusted to several priests who share in the rights and obligations of the canonical role of pastor. It is possible to build on this basis and add to the team others who do not have Sacred Orders. The others, however, do not share in the canonical aspect and lack the jurisdiction of the priest-members of the team.

Parishioner • A member of a parish. Usually, one is a parishioner of the parish in which one has a domicile, although the possibility of having a simultaneous quasi-domicile makes it canonically possible, if rather impractical, for a person to have more than one parish (Canon 102). Under Canon 518 of the 1983 Code of Canon Law, moreover, provision is made for persons to belong to non-territorial parishes where they have been established.

Parishioners should recognize that parishes are more than simply administrative units within a diocese; indeed, most Catholics experience the life of the Church primarily as parishioners. Thus, from the point of view of ecclesiastical administration, as well as for a proper understanding of the local church, "parish-shopping" has always been frowned upon. Parishioners are bound, of course, to contribute a fair share to the support of their own parish.

Parochial Administrator • A priest appointed by the bishop to take the place of the pastor of a parish. An administrator is appointed if the pastor is impeded for any reason. Often parish administrators are appointed to direct parishes when the pastor dies or is hospitalized for a length of time. The administrator has the same rights and obligations as a pastor. He may not, however, do anything that would prejudice the rights of the pastor or cause harm to parish property (Canons 539-540).

Parochial Mass • Also called the *Missa pro populo* (Mass for the people), the parochial Mass is a Mass that the pastor is obliged to celebrate for all of the people entrusted to him. This obligation includes Mass on each Sunday and holy day of obligation. If the pastor is unable to celebrate the parochial Mass on the days appointed, he is to have another priest offer it for him or he is to offer the Mass on another day. If a priest is in charge of several parishes, he is bound to celebrate only one Mass on the proper days (Canon 534).

A diocesan bishop has a similar obligation to celebrate Mass on the same days for all of the people entrusted to him. Like the pastor, he may satisfy this obligation by having another priest celebrate the Mass, or he may celebrate it on another day (Canon 388).

Parochial Schools: See **Schools, Parochial**

Parochial Vicar • The new term for an assistant or associate pastor. It was chosen for inclusion in the revised Code because it reflects the role of the priest as a representative of the pastor rather than just an assistant.

A parochial vicar must be a priest and is always appointed or removed by the bishop. His duties are assigned and carried out under the authority of the pastor. The parochial vicar does not have ordinary jurisdiction. His jurisdiction is delegated, generally in the form of a grant of general delegation for all matters from the bishop when he receives his assignment.

The parochial vicar has no specific duties proper to his role. He generally shares in all the sacramental, pastoral and administrative tasks of the parish to which he is assigned (Canon 545).

Parousia • The term is from the Greek, *parousia*, and literally means "presence" or "arrival." In its secular use, the term refers to the arrival of the king or emperor in a city on a royal or imperial visit. The expectation of the coming of the messianic Lord from heaven to earth in all glory, power and might begins with the revelation of God's plan to His people Israel. The whole community of God looked for God's final presence and action as a people (Jer 23:6). They awaited the establishment of a kingdom of peace (Gn 49:8; Nm 23:21). Both destruction *and* salvation were expected, leading to the great judgment against all, Gentiles (Is 14:24ff.) and Jews (Is 10:1ff.).

These anticipations were fulfilled in Christ Jesus. In the New Testament, *parousia* refers to Christ's Second Coming, or "presence" at the end of history. At Matthew 24:27, 37, 39, Jesus mentions the *parousia* in terms of the Son of Man's return to earth. Paul writes about Christ's future *parousia* (1 Cor 15:23; 1 Thes 2:19; 3:13; 4:15; 5:23): first will come terrors from the lawless one (2 Thes 2:2ff.); then, the *parousia* will arrive amid cosmic travail (Mk 13:24ff.; Rv 8:7ff.; 9:1ff.; 2 Pt 3:6ff.); then, comes the Son of Man on the clouds shining with radiant light (Mt 24:30ff.). The salvific age is being completed. Christ's mere appearance obliterates Satan (2 Thes 2:8; Rv 20:9ff.), and the dead are raised (1 Thes 4:16; 1 Cor 15:52). The great judgment occurs (Mt 25:31ff.). The redeemed shall enter into resurrection and heaven. (Cf. the following texts for other New Testament uses of the term, e.g., 2 Thes 2:1, 8; 2 Pt 3:4; 1 Jn 2:28.)

For further reading: Christopher Rowland, "Parousia," *Anchor Bible Dictionary*, 5:166-170.

Particular Church • A term that came into being with Vatican II and is used to describe certain divisions within the universal Church, such as dioceses, vicariates, prelatures, territorial abbacies and prelatures. The Catholic Church exists in each particular Church and the universal Church is composed of all the particular Churches. Each particular Church is under the pastoral care of a bishop or his equivalent in law. The bishop has complete ordinary power in his diocese.

Describing a diocese as a particular Church more faithfully reflects the theology of the Church as the People of God. It also is more complementary to the renewed theology of the role of the bishop. Neither the diocese nor the bishop is an appendage of the Holy See. Rather, the one, holy, Catholic and apostolic Church exists and functions in each particular Church (Canons 368, 369).

Particular Councils • A gathering of all of the bishops of a given territory. There are two types of particular councils: plenary councils, which are made up of all the bishops of an episcopal conference; and provincial councils, made up of the bishops of an ecclesiastical province. Such councils are held whenever it seems advantageous, either to the conference of bishops or to the majority of the bishops of a province.

A plenary council is convoked by the episcopal conference with the approval of the Holy See. The conference also selects the site for the council, determines its dates, sets the agenda and terminates the council. The approval of the Holy See is also needed for the selection of the president, but not for the compilation of the agenda (Canons 440-441).

A provincial council is convoked by the metropolitan archbishop, with the consent of a majority of the suffragan bishops. The dates and place of the council as well as the agenda are also set by the metropolitan, with the consent of the majority of suffragan bishops. The provincial council is presided over by the metropolitan archbishop (Canon 442).

Participation and deliberative vote in particular councils are accorded to all diocesan, coadjutor and auxiliary bishops, as well as to other titular bishops who fulfill some special function in the territory.

Retired bishops can also be called to a particular council and have the right to a deliberative vote (Canon 443.1).

The law also requires that vicars general, episcopal vicars, elected representatives from among the major superiors of religious institutes and societies of apostolic life, rectors of ecclesiastical and Catholic universities and deans of ecclesiastical faculties of theology and canon law, and elected representatives from among the rectors of major seminaries likewise be included. Although these persons are present, they have only a consultative vote in the council (Canon 443.3).

The law also allows representatives of the priests and of the faithful to be called to a council, but only with a consultative vote (Canon 443.4).

Two representatives from the cathedral chapters, priests' councils and pastoral councils of each of the dioceses involved in the particular council can be invited to attend and given a consultative vote (Canon 443.5). Finally, the conference of bishops for a plenary council, and the metropolitan and his suffragans for a provincial council, can invite other guests to a particular council if they believe it will be advantageous.

Particular councils can enact legislation only if such provision is in the general law. The bishops gathered in particular councils do not enjoy infallible teaching authority, yet they are authentic teachers in the Faith. The faithful are called to give respect to the teachings that come out of a particular council.

Particular Law • A law which is enacted for all the persons of a diocese or some other territory or for all the persons of a specific group is known as particular law. It is not a law that binds the entire Church but one that binds only a specific segment of the Church. Legislation that a bishop enacts for his diocese is known as particular law, as is the legislation that is enacted either for members of religious institutes or for the members of a particular institute.

Particular law is presumed to be territorial unless the contrary is clear from the law itself. Particular law is promulgated in the manner determined by the legislator. It begins to bind one month from the date of promulgation, unless a different period is prescribed by the law itself.

Particular law that is territorial binds everyone who is in the territory: those with domicile or quasi-domicile there and those who do not but who are staying there temporarily (Canons 8, 12-13).

Pascendi Dominici Gregis • The encyclical issued by Pope St. Pius X on September 8, 1907, condemning the errors of Modernism, which the Pontiff termed "the synthesis of all heresies." In this document, the Pope reaffirmed the immutability of Revelation as expressed in the doctrines of the Church, the divine origins of the Church, the reliability of the Magisterium, and the truth of Sacred Scripture, all of which had

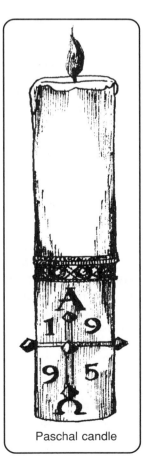

Paschal candle

been called into question by some thinkers at the turn of the century. Along with *Lamentabili*, a decree issued three months earlier, this encyclical sought to eliminate all modernist tendencies from Catholic life.

Pasch • From the Hebrew *Pesach*, Pasch was originally the first great feast of the Jewish liturgical year. It commemorates the passover of the Israelite homes by the avenging angel who killed only the firstborn of the Egyptians (Ex 11:1-10). The Pasch was celebrated at sunset on the fifteenth day of the month of Nisan (Dt 16:6), the first day of the Azymes, an agricultural feast of seven days. A lamb was sacrificed, roasted and eaten with bitter herbs and unleavened bread. The celebration of the exodus is symbolized by the garb and posture of the diners, who are to be ready for flight at any moment (Ex 12:1-28). Scholars suggest that the feast may have originated as a celebration of the birth of the kid goats in the spring, though this in no way denies the religious significance of the Passover. In patristic and medieval exegesis, the Pasch was considered as a symbolic type of Christ's sacrifice on the cross and the Eucharistic Sacrifice.

Paschal Candle • The large wax candle blessed after the Easter Fire during the Service of Light which begins the Easter Vigil, it symbolizes "the light of Christ rising in glory, which dispels the darkness of our minds and hearts." The paschal candle is usually adorned with a cross, alpha and omega, and numerals of the current year. Grains of incense and stylized wax "nails" are generally implanted at the ends of the cross-bars and in the center of the cross. These adornments may be carried out before the Vigil begins or as part of the lighting of the candle.

The deacon carries the paschal candle into the darkened church, pausing at three

Christ's Passion begins
(fifteenth-century painting)

stations to chant, "Christ our Light!" to which the assembly responds, "Thanks be to God!" From its flame, the smaller candles of the faithful are lighted; then the deacon places the paschal candle on a stand before the ambo or near the altar, and by its light chants the magnificent Easter Proclamation, the Exsultet.

The candle may be used during the Easter Vigil at the blessing of the font, and is customarily lighted at Mass as well as Morning and Evening Prayer throughout the fifty days of the Easter Season. Following the last service on Pentecost Sunday, the paschal candle is removed to the baptistery, and from its light the candles of newly-baptized children are lighted throughout the year. The paschal candle also stands at the head of the casket during Funeral Masses, as a reminder that in Baptism the deceased person was

incorporated into the death and resurrection of Jesus Christ.

Paschal Mystery • Christ's passion, death, resurrection and ascension into glory constitute the paschal or Easter mystery. The term "paschal" is derived from the word "Pasch," which refers to the feast of Passover — and not simply because the events from the Last Supper through the crucifixion and resurrection of Christ happened to coincide with Passover. The event celebrated by Passover — the deliverance of Israel from enslavement in Egypt — is itself the anticipation of the full deliverance won by Christ for the whole human race. The paschal mystery is thus the central mystery of the Christian Faith, celebrated at the Easter Triduum with a sublime and unique solemnity. Out of this mystery, the Church herself arises, and with her, the sacramental life. In particular, Baptism and the Eucharist recall the fullness of the paschal mystery and dispense its surpassing benefits to us.

Passion of Christ • The events from the Last Supper through the crucifixion and death of Christ are together described as His "passion." This word comprises two important related senses: a passive sense in which we refer to the sufferings Christ underwent, and an active sense in which we refer to the passage Christ embraced. It is clear that through His passion, Christ endured many sufferings for our sake: degradation, various forms of physical pain, deprivation, mockery, loneliness, death. But it is also true that these sufferings constituted a willingly embraced passage, from death to life, from apparent defeat to real victory, from the cross to glory.

Passion of the Martyrs • From the Latin *passio* (suffering), the passion of a martyr, also called martyr acts, is the written account of the events surrounding a martyrdom; it usually includes the court proceedings with the testimony against the martyr and a detailed description of the martyr's suffering, death and burial. It often ends with a depiction of the faithful who now come in pilgrimage to the tomb of the martyr; miracles obtained at the tomb are vividly described. The earliest such account in Latin is *The Acts of the Scillitan Martyrs* (A.D. 180); other notable passions include those of Perpetua and Felicity, Cyprian, Polycarp and the Forty Martyrs of Sebaste.

Passion Music • Musical form growing out of Gospel accounts of the suffering and death of Jesus. This musical form began with the simple antiphonal settings of the accounts of the Lord's passion sung during Holy Week. Soon different persons chanted various parts and there developed a more elaborate style with solo voices, chorus and instruments. After having fallen into disuse at liturgical celebrations, the form is enjoying a rebirth in the Church of the postconciliar years with settings composed in the vernacular being part of the prayer of Holy Week liturgies again.

Passion Sunday • Now the primary title of the Sunday before Easter, the Sunday which opens Holy Week: Passion (Palm) Sunday. Prior to the Second Vatican Council's revision of the Calendar, the last two weeks of Lent were designated "Passiontide," and the Second Sunday before Easter was thus "Passion Sunday." Although it is true that the Scriptures of the last two weeks of Lent did (and do) focus more intently on the Lord's conflict with the Jewish authorities and, therefore, on the approaching Passion, the term "Passion Sunday" was somewhat misleading, since, in fact, the Passion was not read on that Sunday but on the following Sunday, Palm Sunday.

Vatican II wished to eliminate the "subdivision" of Lent, Passiontide, and to emphasize the fact that on the Sunday that opens Holy Week two traditions are combined: the Jerusalem custom of blessing palms and the Roman custom of proclaiming Jesus' passion. Hence the new, visually awkward, but technically correct designation, Passion (Palm) Sunday.

Passion Week • Prior to the Second Vatican Council's revision of the Calendar, the last two weeks of Lent were designated as "Passiontide." The first Sunday of this "sub-season" was called Passion Sunday and the week following it, Passion Week. The second Sunday of Passiontide was called Palm Sunday, and the week following it, Holy Week.

In a desire not to obscure Lent, the designation "Passiontide" was suppressed, and the title "Passion Sunday" moved to and combined with "Palm Sunday." So the term "Passion Week" has passed out of use or, in some places, has been (mistakenly) applied to the week before Easter, which is more traditionally (and more accurately) called "Holy Week."

Passiontide • Prior to the Second Vatican Council's revision of the Calendar, this term was used as the designation for the last two weeks of the Lenten Season.

It is true that in these last two weeks, the focus of the Scriptures changes to a more intense consideration of the events leading to the Lord's passion and death. Nevertheless, the Council was concerned lest "sub-seasons" obscure the pristine prominence of Lent. Hence the abolition of the "pre-Lent" season of Septuagesima, and of the late-Lent or "pre-Easter" Passiontide. The Scriptures, with their shift of focus, remain virtually unchanged from the previous rite, the Preface of the Passion I is used, and provision is made for the (optional) veiling of crosses and images to indicate the approach of Holy Week. But the designation "Passiontide" is suppressed.

Passover • The English noun is derived from the Hebrew *pesach*, which occurs at Exodus 12:13. The term refers to the religious celebration commemorating God's deliverance of the Jews from slavery and bondage in Egypt. The feast is celebrated in the family (i.e., not at synagogue), at night, at the full moon of the vernal equinox, on the fourteenth of the month of Abib or of the corn, which after 587 B.C. was renamed the month of Nisan. A young lamb, born that year, is slain (Ex 12:3-6), with no bones broken (Ex 12:46; Nm 9:12), and his blood placed on the entrance of each household, preserving it from the angel of death (Ex 12:7, 22). The lamb's flesh is eaten in a manner reflecting someone rushed, about to leave on a journey.

The feast of the Unleavened Bread eventually rose to prominence within the Passover rite (Ex 12:15-20). Unleavened loaves were offered as first-fruits of the harvest (Lv 23:5-14; Dt 26:1f.). This tradition was associated with the exit from Egypt (Ex 23:15; 34:18), recalling the haste to depart out of Egypt — there was no time to let the leaven alter the bread. The practice of celebrating Passover was an important part of the life of Jesus and His disciples. The Synoptic Gospels describe Jesus' Last Supper as a Passover meal (Mk 14:12-16; Lk 22:15; etc.). The Jewish Passover celebrated by Jesus and His disciples is transformed and completed by what Jesus does and says at that meal.

The Passover, once focused on all of Israel, is now focused on Israel's greatest descendant, Jesus, God's only Son (Lk 2:41-51). Jesus' risen body will be the presence of God, the Holy of Holies, the definitive sanctuary (Jn 2:13-23; 1:14, 51; 4:21-24); His body is *the* bread offered in sacrifice (Jn 6), He is the new lamb Who passes from this world of sin into His Father's kingdom (Jn 13:1ff.). Christians celebrate Sunday as the fulfillment and completion of the long awaited liberation from sin and death, receiving and living in overflowing resurrection life, the new creation (Rom 6:4, 11; 7:4; Col 2:12ff.). Thus there is a new depth to the Passover which Jesus' life, death and resurrection reveal (1 Pt 1:13-21).

In Christian Baptism, believers come into contact with Christ, His life and being; they enter into that one great and final Passover from the bondage and slavery of sin into that freedom of being sons and daughters of God. The Lamb, Whose resurrected body still carries the wounds of sacrifice, lives, is in full glory and draws His witnesses and martyrs to Himself (Rv 5:6-12; 12:11) in the Eucharistic Passover we celebrate each Sunday and Easter, indeed every day until He comes in glory.

For further reading: Baruch M. Bokser, "Unleavened Bread and Passover, Feasts of," *Anchor Bible Dictionary*, 6:755-765.

Pastor • In the strictly canonical sense, a pastor is a bishop. In numerous places the law and related documents refer to the "sacred pastors" of the Church. This reference is to the bishops.

More commonly, the term "pastor" refers to what the Code calls the parish priest. Consequently, the pastor is a priest appointed by the bishop to exercise the care of souls for all the people of a particular parish. The pastor has authority over all the pastoral and educational ministry in his parish. He is also ultimately responsible for the proper administration of the parish buildings and finances.

A pastor is freely appointed by the bishop. Although the Code states that pastors should be appointed for indeterminate periods of time, in many North American dioceses, pastoral assignments are for a set term of years.

The responsibilities of the pastor, as set out in the Code, indicate a hierarchy of values to be applied in the ministry of a parish. First and foremost, the pastor has the obligation of seeing that the Word of God is proclaimed to the people of the parish through preaching, teaching and catechesis. Of equal importance is the pastor's obligation of making the Eucharist the center of the life of the parish. Thus the celebration of the Mass, especially on Sundays, is an essential and fundamental value in the life of a parish. Next is the celebration of the sacraments and other liturgical celebrations. The pastor is not only responsible for dignified and correct liturgical celebrations but for the catechesis, preparation and instruction that accompanies the celebration of certain sacraments (Canon 528).

The pastor is urged to get to know the people under his care, sharing in their lives, especially at moments of trial and tribulation (Canon 529.1). He is to recognize and promote the role of the laity (Canon 529.2). Finally, he is to see to the proper administration of the parish temporal goods. It is clear from a reading of the Code that the sacramental and educational dimension of parish life takes precedence over administration.

The pastor has several sacramental functions entrusted to him. In all these cases, he may allow other priests to exercise the function. These include administration of the following sacraments for the parishioners: Baptism, Confirmation in danger of death, Viaticum, Matrimony and the more solemn celebration of the Eucharist on Sundays and feast days. The pastor also has the right and obligation of conducting the funerals of his parishioners, blessing the baptismal font at Easter,

conducting processions and imparting more solemn blessings.

The pastor is considered the legal agent of the parish. Thus he represents the parish in all legal matters. The pastor is obliged to live in the parochial house near the church. He is to be present in the parish but may be absent for a total of one month a year as vacation time.

The pastor's office ceases when he resigns, is transferred or removed by the bishop, in accordance with the law.

Pastoral Care of the Sick • Subtitled, "Rites of Anointing and Viaticum," this ritual is the 1983 English translation and arrangement of the Latin *Ordo unctionis infirmorum eorumque pastoralis curae*, the Vatican II revision of all the pastoral rites celebrated for the sick. The ritual's introductory material contains Pope Paul VI's Apostolic Constitution by which he promulgates and confirms the revised rites. The Pope quotes Vatican II's Constitution on the Sacred Liturgy, which states: " 'Extreme Unction,' which may also and more fittingly be called 'Anointing of the Sick,' is not a sacrament for those only who are at the point of death. Hence, as soon as anyone of the faithful begins to be in danger of death from sickness or old age, the fitting time for [that person] to receive this sacrament has certainly already arrived." Further pastoral notes remind us that because anointing is properly a sacrament for the sick, "a prudent or reasonably sure judgment, without scruple, is sufficient for deciding on the seriousness of an illness." The sacrament specifically for the dying is the Holy Eucharist given as Viaticum, "food for the journey" to eternal life.

Part I of the ritual is entitled, "Pastoral Care of the Sick," and contains Offices for Visits to Sick Adults and Children, Communion of the Sick (in both ordinary circumstances and an abbreviated rite for use in hospitals or institutions) and Anointing of the Sick (outside Mass, during Mass — with a new set of Propers [including a magnificent Preface] and an abbreviated rite for use in a hospital or institution).

Part II is called "Pastoral Care of the Dying," and begins with a presentation of the rites as celebrated "when time is not a pressing concern, and the rites can be celebrated fully and properly." A separate chapter contains "Rites for Exceptional Circumstances," that is, a "continuous rite" (Penance, Anointing, Viaticum), Emergency Anointing and Christian Initiation for the Dying. Further chapters contain a complete Office for commending the dying, with fine translations or adaptations of the traditional prayers, and a separate chapter entitled "Prayers for the Dead," for use in those circumstances when death has already and certainly occurred, thereby precluding anointing, but when pastoral ministrations are in order for the consolation of the family and the repose of the departed.

Part III is a complete scriptural lectionary for all celebrations; the Rite of Penance is contained in an appendix.

Pastoral Counseling: See **Counseling, Pastoral**

Pastoral Epistles • The Pauline letters of 1 and 2 Timothy and Titus. The letters were originally designated "pastoral" by Berdot and Anton of Halle in the early eighteenth century. The letters share specific features which justify grouping them together: (1) they are addressed to individual pastors; (2) they are not directed to the local or universal Church; (3) their content, literary styles and theology are similar; (4) they deal with similar problems. These common features make it easy to group them together and to distinguish them from the other New Testament letters.

For further reading: Robert A. Wild, S.J., "The Pastoral Letters," *New Jerome Biblical Commentary*, 891-902.

Pastoral Judgment: See **Judgment, Pastoral**

Pastoral Ministry • The modern designation for the traditional *cura animarum* (care of souls) and refers to all those activities by which the ordained ministers of the Church provide for the spiritual well-being of the faithful. Those laity who are trained in pastoral specialties can assist and share importantly in this ministry. Pastoral ministry encompasses a wide variety of activities, chiefly the administration of the sacraments, preaching, catechesis, defense of the Faith, theological research and writing, pastoral counseling, spiritual guidance, education, communication, public witness, defense of the rights of the poor and oppressed, and socially constructive action.

Pastoral Provision for the Common Identity • In June, 1981, the Holy See approved a request which was made by the bishops of the United States on behalf of some clergy and laity of the Episcopal (Anglican) Church who were seeking full communion with the Catholic Church. A "Pastoral Provision" subsequently was established, whereby exceptions to the rule of celibacy were made for those former Episcopalian married clergy who were found to be eligible for ordination as Catholic priests, and also a liturgical use was approved for the parishes established to maintain an "Anglican common identity" within the full communion of the Catholic Church. The first of these parishes was canonically erected in San Antonio, Texas, on August 15, 1983, under the patronage of Our Lady of the Atonement. The Pastoral Provision, commonly called the Anglican

Use, worships according to the liturgical rites approved by the Holy See, called the *Book of Divine Worship*, which includes the orders for Baptism, Mass, Matrimony, Morning and Evening Prayer, Burial of the Dead and various other liturgical prayers. Each Pastoral Provision parish is under the jurisdiction of the local bishop.

Pastoral Theology • The branch of theology concerned with the theory and practice by which the entire pastoral mission of the Church is exercised. In its traditional sense — since pastoral theology was understood to comprise the knowledge required by the priest to carry out his ministry for the care of souls and the administration of the sacraments — it represented a synthesis of scriptural studies, dogmatic theology, spiritual theology and canon law. In recent years, pastoral theology has come to be understood more broadly. It now encompasses not only a practically oriented field of study for prospective priests, but also a global conception of the mission of the whole Church to proclaim the saving Gospel to the world.

The whole of theology is seen as potentially pastoral, in that the knowledge it seeks to cultivate is precisely the knowledge of salvation. In order to be effective, this knowledge must be linked with the experience of those who are to appropriate it. Modern pastoral theology thus comprises the study of the social and behavioral sciences, as well as that of history and anthropology, as it strives to develop a sense of the needs of those who are to be the object of the Church's mission of evangelization and sanctification.

Paten • The dish-like vessel used to contain the species of bread at Mass. Early in their evolution patens were large enough to hold the large loaves offered by the faithful to be distributed at Communion. As the numbers of the faithful who received Communion were reduced through the Middle Ages, so the size of the paten reduced, eventually to holding only the single host used by the priest for his own Communion. By custom, the paten was made of gold or silver. In the present reform of the liturgy, other suitable materials may be used, such as "ebony and certain hardwoods" (*General Instruction of the Roman Missal*, n. 292) or other "materials that do not easily break or deteriorate" (n. 290). "When consecrating bread for priest, servers and people, one may use a single large paten or communion bowl" (n. 293). The custom by which patens are blessed before liturgical use is reiterated in the Instructions in the *Rite of Dedication of a Church and an Altar* from the Sacred Congregation for Divine Worship (1977), Chapter 7, nn. 1-4.

Pater Noster • These are the first two words in the Latin version of the Lord's Prayer which, as with English, give it its common name — "Our Father." The prayer is found in St. Matthew's Gospel and in a slightly different version in that of St. Luke. In the early days of the Church, it was regarded so highly that catechumens were not taught it until after Baptism or just before. In many places both the priests at the altar and the congregation prostrated themselves when reciting it during Mass. As such, the words formerly used at Mass to introduce it (and now as an option according to the celebrant's pleasure) serve well to remind us of the sacredness of this prayer: "Taught by our Savior's command and formed by the Word of God, we dare to say . . ." The words of the Our Father in Latin are:

Pater noster, qui es in caelis: sanctificetur nomen tuum; adveniat regnum tuum;

fiat voluntas tua, sicut in caelo, et in terra.
Panem nostrum quotidianum da nobis
   hodie;
et dimitte nobis debita nostra,
sicut et nos dimittimus debitoribus nostris;
et ne nos inducas in tentationem;
sed libera nos a malo. Amen.

Patience • A part of the virtue of
fortitude, this virtue enables one to endure
suffering and evils over a long period of
time. While patience may seem to be a less
important moral quality, it is in fact quite
valuable for the life of charity. The presence
of this virtue does a great deal to enhance a
person's ability to act in accord with
charity, for many of the everyday sins
against charity derive from a lack of
patience.

The theological virtue of patience is an
infused virtue which enables one to endure
all sorts of ills and sufferings for the sake of
love of God and Christian love of neighbor
with a sense of composure and self-control.

Patriarch (Patriarchate) • The head of a
branch of the Oriental Church,
corresponding to a Province of the Roman
Empire. There are only five genuine
patriarchal sees: Rome, Constantinople,
Alexandria, Antioch and Jerusalem.

Patriarchs, Scriptural • Those nineteen
leaders of the Israelite tribes and heads of
prominent families who appear in Genesis
from Adam to Joseph. Honored as
especially significant patriarchs are
Abraham, Isaac and Jacob; the patriarchal
narratives in Genesis associated with them
constitute the prologue to Israel's salvation
history, and the period during which they
lived is known as the Age of the Patriarchs.
The title patriarch used for David (Acts
2:29) was simply one of honor.

Patrimony, Canonical • In the canonical
sense patrimony has two distinct
connotations, both appearing within the
field of temporal goods. The first and more
general sense of canonical patrimony is
used to describe those ecclesiastical goods
which, through canonical designation, are
considered the most important or stable
assets owned by a public juridic person
(Canon 1291). Common examples of such
goods would be land and buildings,
endowed funds, and so on. Goods
constituting the stable patrimony of a
juridic person may not be sold or otherwise
encumbered without following special
measures. Such rules are intended to
protect ecclesiastical institutions and
persons from the deleterious effects of
temporary mismanagement. (Cf. Alienation.)

The second sense of canonical patrimony
occurs in connection with entry into
religious life, and is the unofficial
designation of that property owned by a
member prior to entering religious life and
which, in certain institutes, the member is
able to retain legally, but generally not
control (cf., for example, Canons 668, 670).
Formerly, this property was frequently
styled a "dowry" and was intended to offset
the cost to the institute of supporting the
member. It rarely covered such expenses
completely, and in almost every case
became a token offering. It could not be
touched during the life of the member,
although the income derived therefrom did
belong to the institute. It was also intended
to serve as a financial cushion for the
member in the event that the member later
left the institute. These rules have been
simplified and incorporated into the canons
noted above. Finally, both senses of
canonical patrimony outlined here must be
distinguished from the spiritual patrimony
of an institute of consecrated life.

Patrimony, Spiritual • Canon 578 of the 1983 Code of Canon Law defines the spiritual patrimony of institutes of consecrated life as the "intention of their founders, along with their determinations on the nature, ends, spirit, and characteristics of the institute, as ratified by ecclesiastical authority, as well as its healthy traditions." Based on the directives of the Second Vatican Council as contained in its Decree on the Up-to-Date Renewal of Religious Life, *Perfectae Caritatis*, the spiritual patrimony of an institute is to be fostered and preserved by all. Many issues such as membership, apostolate, type of spirituality and prayer life, forms of governance, and so on, fall under the heading of spiritual patrimony. This use of the term "patrimony" is to be distinguished, however, from that referring to the canonical patrimony of various Church institutions, chiefly in the matter of temporal goods.

Patriotism, Christian • Respect for one's nation, its symbols and obligations, and fulfillment of one's legitimate duties to society. The state has traditionally been considered as a father, protector and life-giver, and because of that deserves respect. Christian patriotism recognizes that the authority of the state is morally legitimate when exercised for the well-being of all and that there is an obligation to respect its authority. *Gaudium et Spes* declared that "citizens should cultivate a generous and loyal spirit of patriotism, but without narrow-mindedness, so that they will always keep in mind the welfare of the whole human family which is formed into one by various kinds of links between races, peoples and nations" (n. 75). Patriotism is an aspect of the virtue of justice, and it is required of citizens in order to promote and protect the common good. Patriotism should be considered as a virtue

and is opposed by nationalistic chauvinism and disrespect for the state.

Patripassionism • This third-century heresy was derived from Sabellianism, in part through the writings of Tertullian, and held that because the Father was no different from the Son (obviously an error of the most profound sort), it must have been the Father, under the guise of the Son, Who actually suffered and died on the Cross. The term "Father's-passion" was actually coined by Western critics of the heresy.

Patrology • Otherwise known as patristics, this is the study of the Christian writers of antiquity who were accepted as orthodox or within the Great Church during their lives. The period ends with Isidore of Seville in the West (d. 636) and with John of Damascus in the East (d. 749). These writers are called the Church Fathers, and patrology studies the content of their thought. Patristic philosophy and theology were born from the creative intersection of Christianity, with its roots in Judaism and a biblical idiom, and Greek thought, especially Platonism.

Some of the better known Fathers in the East include: Clement of Alexandria, Origen, Gregory of Nyssa, Athanasius, Evagrius Ponticus, Ephrem of Syria, Basil the Great, Cyril of Jerusalem, Gregory of Nazianzus, Ignatius of Antioch, John Chrysostom, Maximus the Confessor, Tatian, Theodore of Mopsuestia, Eusebius of Caesarea and John of Damascus. In the West, to name but a few, are counted: Justin Martyr, Irenaeus, Hippolytus of Rome, Tertullian, Ambrose, Hilary of Poitiers, Benedict, John Cassian, Jerome, Lactantius, Leo the Great, Paulinus of Nola, Peter Chrysologus, Rufinus, Prosper of Aquitaine and Augustine of Hippo. Traditionally, the four marks of these writers are antiquity, orthodoxy, sanctity and Church approval.

Today, perhaps we might include a somewhat broader list for those who considered themselves orthodox on issues that were unclear at the time of their writing. The Fathers often wrote in a somewhat inconsistent, speculative and unsystematic way. They were struggling toward a dynamic synthesis between their faith and the thought-structures of classical civilization. If they sometimes lacked the scientific precision of the Middle Ages or later speculative Christian theology, they gained in a certain depth of insight and spiritual vision. A revival of interest in patristics has been strong since the middle of the nineteenth century. Recovery of patristic ways of seeing the Christian Faith formed the backdrop to the Second Vatican Council's efforts. On account of new critical editions of texts and archaeological work, the scholarship in this field is thriving today.

Patron • A benefactor or protector. In Church history patrons had been accorded various considerable rights and privileges in regard to the institutions of which they served as patron. (Cf. Iuspatronatus; Advowson.)

Today, patron is a non-technical term referring to one who offers substantial support to an ecclesiastical enterprise, but who does so without expecting or receiving any notable temporal return. (Cf. Patron Saints.)

Patron Saints • Saints who are acknowledged to be special protectors and intercessors for persons, churches, dioceses and the universal Church. The name taken at Baptism (and Confirmation) is most often that of a patron; the title of a parish church or diocesan cathedral is frequently that of a patron saint. Additional patrons for a diocese may be named, often in connection with the patron saints of a particular ethnic group in the diocese. The Third Eucharistic Prayer in the Roman Missal contains a place where "the saint of the day or the patron saint" may be named.

Patrology subject:
Pope St. Leo the Great

Patroness of the U.S.A. • The patroness of the United States of America is the Blessed Virgin Mary under her title of the Immaculate Conception. This was decided and decreed by the Sixth Provincial Council of Baltimore in 1846.

Paul, St. • Paul (Acts 13:9; 2 Pt 3:15; "Saul": Acts 7:58; 8:1, 3; 9:1) was perhaps the most dynamic missionary of the early Church and clearly a great champion of God's plan to spread Christianity to the ends of the earth. A chronology of his life can be constructed as follows: (1) Born circa A.D. 10; his father was a Roman citizen and a leather worker; raised in Tarsus with familial ties in Judaea (2 Cor 11:22; Phil 3:5). (2) He trained as a Pharisee in Jerusalem (Phil 3:5-6; Gal 1:14; 2 Cor 11:22). (3) Sometime after Christ's death, he actively persecuted the Jewish sect professing that Jesus of Nazareth was the Messiah and Son of God (Gal 1:13; 1 Cor 15:9), c. 31/33. Sometime around 33/35 Saul encountered Christ and experienced a radical reorientation in his life, a conversion (Gal 1:15-16; 1 Cor 15:8; Acts 9:4, 17; 22:7, 13; 26:14). (4) During 35-39, Paul preached in Arabia and Damascus. (5) Sometime during 37-39 Paul met with Peter and James in Jerusalem (Gal 1:18) and returned to Syria and Cilicia (Gal 1:21-22), probably for fourteen years or so. (6) During his missionary journeys he wrote letters to various communities which he either founded or taught. (7) We can date the rest of his life and works as follows: 50-52, Paul writes 1 and 2 Thessalonians from Corinth; 52-57, he continues missionary activity in Asia Minor and Greece; and he writes to the Galatians (c. 54), Philippians (c. 54-58), Philemon (c. 58 if during Paul's Caesarean imprisonment), 1 Corinthians (c. 55), 2 Corinthians (c. 55/56); he writes Romans from Corinth, c. 56/57. Paul takes a collection probably gathered from those Hellenistic churches he ministered to for the Jerusalem Church sometime between 56 and 57. Once there, he is eventually arrested and then imprisoned in Caesarea, c. 57/58. Prior to winter 59 or early spring 60, he is escorted to Rome and executed c. 62.

Paul's background was that of a Diaspora Jew, born a Roman citizen (Acts 22:25-29; 16:37; 23:27) in the Hellenistic city of Tarsus in the region of Cilicia (Acts 22:3, 6; 21:39). He was trained in Jerusalem in the Pharisaic tradition (Acts 22:3; 26:4-5; 23:6;

Phil 3:5-6; Gal 1:14; 2 Cor 11:22); hence, his extensive use of explicit Old Testament citations (at least ninety) and his familiarity with first-century Jewish interpretations of the Old Testament. Paul interpreted the Old Testament the same as the rabbis did, finding in it deeper meanings and teachings from the deeper meanings in the texts (Heb 2:4, Rom 1:17 and Gal 3:11; Gn 12:7 and Gal 3:16; Ex 34:34 and 2 Cor 3:17-18). Paul's life as a Jew prepared him to see that his Jewish Scriptures actually proclaim the Christian Gospel (Rom 1:2) and paved the way for Christ's coming (Gal 3:24).

But the Jewish Christian, the "Apostle to the Gentiles," was equally a "Greek" from the standpoint of culture. He was familiar with and made use of Hellenistic rhetorical skills. For example, he uses the *diatribe* (a Greek mode of argumentation which outlines or otherwise states an imaginary opponent's objections and refutes them) with skill and fluency (Rom 2:1-20 and 1 Cor 9). After his conversion to Christianity, he lived for approximately ten years in such great Hellenistic centers as Damascus, Tarsus and Antioch. Paul's mind constantly drew from his Hellenistic experience to explain the Gospel: Greek political language (Phil 1:27; 3:20; Eph 2:19); Greek athletic games (Phil 2:16; 3:14; 1 Cor 9:24-27; 2 Cor 4:8-9); Greek legal language (Gal 3:15; 4:1-2; Rom 7:1-4); and the jargon of slave traders (1 Cor 7:22; Rom 7:14).

Paul's message is grounded in what he received from God. The God of the Old Testament is the same God and Father of Jesus Christ. This God Paul served as a zealous Pharisee was the same God Who revealed His Son to Paul. He was the Creator, the Lord of Lords, the Lord of history, the Savior of His people Israel, the One faithful to His covenant with Israel. God showed Paul that He had to send His Son, the Messiah, to die on the cross so that with Christ, sin would die and so would all who are joined with Christ in Baptism. However, those who died in Christ would also live in Him. What the Jewish law, so good, righteous and holy (Romans; Ps 119), could not do, Jesus did, namely, break the power of Satan and death and bring new supernatural and everlasting resurrection life.

For further reading: Joseph A. Fitzmyer, "Paul," *New Jerome Biblical Commentary*, 1329-1337; Joseph A. Fitzmyer, "Pauline Theology," *New Jerome Biblical Commentary*, 1382-1416.

Pauline Privilege • A privilege in canon law whereby the marriage of two non-baptized persons is dissolved when, after their separation and divorce, one of the parties converts to Christianity and enters a subsequent marriage. The prior marriage is considered dissolved by the act of contracting the second marriage. The person who seeks the privilege must be baptized but not necessarily in the Catholic Faith. In such cases, the petitioner usually seeks to marry a Catholic. It is also permissible for the converted party to marry a non-Catholic Christian or a non-baptized person.

The Pauline Privilege is based on the teaching of St. Paul found in 1 Corinthians 7:12-15, whereby he allowed Christians to enter a second marriage if their non-Christian spouses had departed and refused to live peacefully with the Christian party.

The Pauline Privilege is handled on the diocesan level. The bishop has the responsibility of asking the former spouse of the person petitioning for the privilege if he or she wishes to receive Baptism or is at least willing to resume peaceful cohabitation with the petitioner. This is called "interpellation" of the departed spouse. The bishop may dispense with the obligation of interpellation. In actuality, the Pauline Privilege is requested by people who are already divorced with no reconciliation possible (cf. Canons 1143-1150).

Pax • The practice of exchanging a greeting of peace and unity after the Lord's Prayer and before the fraction rite in the Roman Eucharistic Liturgy. The custom is attested as early as the second century in the *First Apology* of Justin the Martyr. Most often in churches of the East, the sign of peace is exchanged before the Presentation of the Gifts, in accord with the dominical command in Matthew 5:23-24 about the requirement of mutual love before presenting gifts for sacrifice. Its place in the West as a part of the rites for Communion was known by St. Augustine and is firmly in place after the Lord's Prayer by the time of Innocent I (early fifth century). In the Middle Ages grew the custom of the priest celebrant kissing the altar first and then exchanging the peace gesture with the other ministers who, in turn, exchanged it with the people.

The *General Instruction of the Roman Missal* states: "By word and gesture the people pray for peace and unity in the Church and the whole human family, and express their love for one another before they share the one bread. Practical details of the way in which this is to be done are to be settled by the local Bishops' Conferences in accordance with the sensibilities and conventions of the people" (n. 56b). The *Appendix to the General Instruction for the Dioceses of the United States of America* leaves "the development of specific modes of exchanging the sign of peace to local usage. Neither a specific form nor specific words are determined" (n. 56b). According to the sacramentary, after the prayer for peace ("Lord Jesus Christ. . .") and the priest's verbal greeting of peace, "The peace of the Lord be always with you," the deacon or priest may say, "Let us offer each other the sign of peace."

Pax Christi • An international Catholic peace organization, started in March, 1945, to reconcile the French and Germans after World War II, particularly through prayers. However, it soon developed into an organization crusading for peace among all the nations. On July 3, 1947, Pope Pius XII gave the organization warm approval in a letter of commendation.

The explicit aim of *Pax Christi* is to promote "the unity and pacification of the world through the promotion of a new international order based on the natural law and on the justice and charity of Christ." It hopes to achieve this objective by promoting social, scientific and theological discussions and studies of peace. Its official monthly publication, *Pax Christi*, is explicitly religious, but it seeks the widest possible unity among various religious organizations. It does not take specific positions on issues of peace and war but only aims at promoting discussion and dialogue.

Peace • In the Old Testament "peace" (Hebrew: *shalom*) has a variety of meanings stemming from the notion of completeness; for example, one's strength is great when complete (Jb 9:4); the temple is said to be in good repair when it is complete (1 Kgs 9:25); peace can express the notion of a completed financial exchange (Ex 21:34), the fulfillment of a vow (Ps 50:14), etc. Peace is sometimes synonymous with good health (Ps 38:4); it can express what exists between good friends (Ps 41:10; Jer 20:10) or the content of a treaty between friendly nations (Jos 9:15; Jgs 4:17; Lk 14:32, etc.). In the New Testament "peace" (Greek, *eirene*) often occurs with "grace" (Greek, *kairis*) in the form of greetings to the recipients of letters or messages (1 Cor 1:3;

2 Cor 1:2; Gal 1:3; Eph 1:2; Phil 1:2; Col 1:2; 1 Tm 1:2; 2 Tm 1:2; Ti 1:4; Phlm 3). It can convey the absence of strife (Lk 11:21; 14:32; Rv 6:4). Absence of strife is a fitting beginning point to discuss the peace which comes from God, which is much more profound because it must be the basis for sociological, political or economic resolutions toward peace.

Peace describes the condition of the heart and mind — within our very soul and spirit — when renewed in Christ. Such a peace is deeper than our affections or intellect. It comes in and through Christ's work at the cross which destroys hostility to God, that which makes us "enemies of God" in our love of sin. Thus it is a characteristic feature of those who have received new life from God and entered into an eternal relationship with God; peace accompanies righteousness (Rom 14:17; Heb 12:11; Jas 3:18), grace (Phil 1:2; Rv 1:4), mercy (Gal 6:16; 1 Tm 1:2), love (Jude 2), joy (Rom 14:17; 15:13) and life (Rom 8:6). The cross is critical here because it has the power to break sin's grasp; once the hold is broken, so also is broken what separates us from God and from His peace. Peace with God — that is, life in friendship with God — is one of the characteristic features of the final age of salvation.

For further reading: Joseph P. Healey and William Klassen, "Peace," *Anchor Bible Dictionary*, 5:206-212.

Peace, Kiss of • Originally, the gesture of peace exchanged at the Eucharist was a kiss. It later developed into an embrace with a verbal exchange of a greeting of peace. The custom of the priest kissing the altar before exchanging the gesture was common in the Middle Ages. The present restoration of the sign of peace at Mass leaves the determination of this ritual gesture to the local conference of bishops.

Pectoral Cross • A cross, usually of precious metal (and sometimes ornamented with jewels) suspended by a chain around the neck, worn over the breast (hence, the name from *pectus*, "breast") by abbots, bishops, archbishops, cardinals and the Pope. It is worn over the cassock (or monastic habit) when the prelate is dressed in a cassock only (i.e., for non-liturgical functions), or over the mozzetta when he is in choir dress. It is worn over the alb and under the chasuble at the celebration at which a chasuble is worn (i.e., Mass, sacraments). The *Caeremoniale Episcoporum, Ceremonial of Bishops* (1984), states: "The pectoral cross is worn, suspended from a green cord intertwined with gold threads, under the chasuble (dalmatic) or cope, but over the mozzetta" (n. 43). It is also worn by prelates when dressed in a suit and collar; in this case the cross is usually placed in the vest pocket with the chain showing.

Pelagianism • A heretical theological position regarding grace and free will, it originated with the fifth-century British monk Pelagius who, like the Stoics, believed that every good could be gotten through prayer except virtue.

Specifically, Pelagius held that: (1) Adam was made mortal and would have died whether he had sinned or had not sinned. (2) The sin of Adam injured himself alone, and not the human race. (3) Newborn children are in that state in which Adam was before his Fall. (4) Neither by the death and sin of Adam does the whole race die, nor by the resurrection of Christ does the whole race rise. (5) The law leads to the kingdom of heaven as well as the Gospel. (6) Even before the coming of the Lord there were men without sin.

According to Pelagius, the gift of free will made it obligatory for the human person to make good use of prayer, and the person

was responsible for his or her actions. He understood the person as a free and created but autonomous individual who can observe the law of God by mere human powers, with no limits to the levels of sanctity that can be reached by unaided human powers. He held that there could be sinless men and because we were given existence by God that we had the obligation to sanctify ourselves. Pelagianism does not understand the social solidarity of sin or the Body of Christ.

Pelagius had a radically constricted concept of revelation, and he was unduly influenced by Stoic ideals. Today, we see new forms of Pelagianism in the Kantian emphasis on duties and the existentialist stress on the alienation of the person and the need for each person to shape his or her own destiny. But these new existentialist Pelagians are more dangerous because they do not believe in God and because they know no law except their own.

Pelvicula • This term, which is the Latin for "small basin," refers to the dish or plate on which the cruets for wine and water are placed and carried during the celebration of the Mass. Though the pelvicula is most often fashioned out of crystal or glass and matches the cruets, it may be of silver or gold, pewter, brass, ceramic or even carved wood.

Penal Laws • The Church has traditionally claimed the right to enact penal laws, that is, laws that determine crimes and impose punishments. The purpose of penal legislation is primarily the spiritual welfare of the community and of individuals in the community. The imposition of a penalty is a last resort; however, sometimes it is necessary in cases of grave offenses.

Book VI of the Code of Canon Law contains the penal laws of the Church. The canons therein explain the manner in which punishments are applied and removed. It explains the various kinds of punishments available in Church law. It also lists specific crimes for which a person is either punished automatically from the time the crime is committed, or punished by the imposition of a penalty by a competent authority. In addition, the canons treat in some detail of who can be punished and factors that either completely remove or diminish moral responsibility for an act considered to be an ecclesiastical crime.

There are two fundamental kinds of penalties in Church law: censures and expiatory penalties. Most of the punishments are censures. These are also called medicinal penalties, because their object is to bring about the reform and reconciliation of the offender. Expiatory penalties look more to restoring justice to the community because of the act of an offender and hence appear to be aimed more at punishing than healing.

Penal Process • The procedure outlined in the Code of Canon Law which must be followed when a person has been accused of an ecclesiastical crime and is being tried before a Church court.

The process begins with a preliminary investigation (Canons 1717-1719). If a superior receives a complaint, he is to investigate it before initiating a trial. If he believes that there is sufficient evidence to begin a judicial penal process, he is to pass the results of the investigation on to the promoter of justice, who acts like a prosecuting attorney and initiates the process by submitting a petition to the judge. The court is composed of at least three judges. The accused person must be notified of the allegation and the evidence. He must be represented by an advocate and is to be given an opportunity to defend himself.

In conducting a formal penal process, the procedural norms for all trials are followed unless exceptions are specifically mentioned in the particular section on the penal process. At the conclusion of the evidence-gathering phase of the trial, the promoter of justice studies the information brought forth and presents his arguments to the judges. The accused and his advocate have the right to speak last in the trial. In their deliberations the judges are to presume that the accused is not guilty. This presumption is overturned by arriving at moral certitude that the accused is guilty. This means that they must be certain beyond a reasonable doubt (as in common-law criminal trials). If they cannot reach this degree of certitude, which is much greater than the certitude produced by preponderance of evidence, then they cannot pronounce the accused guilty.

In the event of a finding of guilty, the accused has the right to appeal the decision to the court of second instance. Similarly, the promoter of justice has the right to appeal the decision (Canons 1721-1728).

The penal process also includes the possibility of proceeding by means of an extrajudicial administrative decree. In such cases, if the Ordinary believes that it is better to avoid a trial, he may issue a decree which includes a penalty. The accused must be notified of the allegation and the evidence and given the right of defense. The Ordinary studies the case with two assessors, and if he believes that the offense is certainly proven, he issues the decree which must contain, at least in outline form, the allegation, evidence and reasons in law and fact for the decision (Canon 1720).

Statutes of limitations exist in canon law. With specific exceptions, a criminal action may not be initiated if three years have passed from the date of the alleged offense or if it was a habitual offense, from the date it ceased. If the crime was an offense reserved to the Congregation for the Doctrine of the Faith or one of those specifically mentioned, the period is five rather than three years. The crimes for which a five-year statute of limitations exists are: attempted marriage by a cleric, concubinage or other public sexual crime by a cleric, grave mutilation, or murder and abortion (Canon 1362).

The various types of censures available in the law include suspension (clerics only), interdict and excommunication. Expiatory penalties include loss of ecclesiastical office, deprivation of residence and dismissal from the clerical state.

In its treatment of specific crimes, the penal-law section of the Code refers to crimes against religion and the unity of the Church, crimes against Church authorities, crimes committed in the exercise of ecclesiastical office, crimes against special obligations and crimes against human life and liberty (E. Peters, "Penal Procedural Law in the 1983 Code of Canon Law," *Studies in Canon Law* No. 537, Catholic University of America, 1991).

Penalty, Ecclesiastical • Broadly speaking, an ecclesiastical penalty is any deprivation of temporal or spiritual benefit imposed upon a delinquent as punishment for an ecclesiastical offense. Penal power exists in the Church both for the preservation of justice and good order and for the reform of the individual offender. These ends are reflected by the two great categories of penalties, or sanctions, in the Church: medicinal penalties or censures, which work for the reform of the person, and expiatory penalties, which protect justice and the needs of the community within the Church (Canon 1312). While the 1983 Code of Canon Law strongly emphasizes the "last-resort" nature of penalties (Canon 1341), and in fact has

greatly reduced and simplified earlier legislation on penalties, Canon 1311 affirms in no uncertain terms the Church's innate and proper right to impose penalties in the furtherance of her salvific mission.

Penalties can be enacted by those with legislative power in the Church, but only for the most serious reasons (Canons 1315, 1317). Particular penal law, moreover, should be as uniform as possible in the same regions (Canon 1316) and cannot provide for dismissal from the clerical state. Special restraint is to be used in enacting *latae sententiae* penalties (Canon 1318). And additional norms govern the issuing of penal precepts. Appeal from or recourse against a penalty is always in suspension of the obligation to observe the penalty (Canon 1353).

Ecclesiastical penalties should not be confused with penances or other spiritual exercises imposed in connection with the sacrament of Penance. These latter are part of the moral order and are issued for moral offenses, while penalties belong to the legal order. Where they might overlap in a certain case, the necessary distinctions must be carefully drawn in order that confusion in the observance or remission of the penalties be prevented.

Finally, Canon 1312 authorizes quasi-penal institutes known as penal remedies and penances (again, not to be confused with sacramental penances) which can be employed in certain cases. Penal remedies (usually formal admonition or rebuke) are used especially for the prevention of crimes, while penances (usually works of piety or charity) can be imposed where ordinary ecclesiastical penalties seem unwarranted or otherwise ill-advised (Canons 1339-1340). (Cf. Penal Process.)

Penalty, Vindictive • The 1917 Code used the term "vindictive penalties" to designate those canonical penalties which could be imposed for the most serious offenses. Vindictive penalties were not primarily medicinal in nature. Rather, they looked more to the punishment of the offender and the restoration of justice to the community.

The revised Code eliminated most of the legislation on vindictive penalties, including the name itself. The comparable entity in the canons is "expiatory penalty."

Penance • The virtue which enables human beings to acknowledge their sins with true contrition and a firm purpose of amendment. Confidence in God's mercy and forgiveness are fundamental to the Christian virtue of penance. Recognition of sin is complemented by the determination to practice the mortification that will erase the effects of sin and strengthen the resolve to turn away from sin in the future. This readiness to engage in works of penance or mortification is sustained by the knowledge that in this way we are more perfectly conformed to Christ, Who suffered and died for our sins.

Penance, Sacrament of • The sacrament of Penance, popularly called confession, is also referred to as the sacrament of Reconciliation (more accurately, it is the Rite of Reconciliation and the sacrament of Penance). The Church has always believed that Christ gave her the power to forgive sin (cf. John 20:23). In the course of history, she has exercised that power in various ways. Early sources (Jas 5:16 and the Didache 14:1) suggest that confession of sins for forgiveness may have been public, but if so, Poschmann maintains that this practice did not last long in the Church, for very early the confession of sins was secret and done individually to the bishop, while the medicinal penance was public and communal, as was the reconciliation or absolution after. Those guilty of the serious

and public sins of idolatry (apostasy), murder or adultery (sometimes fornication was included) had to enroll among the penitents for a period of time to do public penance. These wore sackcloth and ashes, could not receive Holy Communion and were the object of the Church's prayer while undergoing the penance (fasting, prayer and more severe penances), that the penance would change their lives. The penitents, having carried out the penance, would then be reconciled with God and the Church on Holy Thursday. Those committing less serious sins did not undergo this discipline, and it was believed that lesser sin could be forgiven through the traditional penitential practices of prayer, fasting and almsgiving.

In the eighth century, Irish monks, influenced by the Eastern custom of monks confessing their sins to each other, began to hear individual confessions of the laity in their care, not only for serious or mortal sin, but also for lighter or venial sin. They also granted the absolution immediately and left the penitent to do the penance later, a reversal of the earlier pattern. This new mode became very popular, though it was less ecclesial than the ancient practice. On the other hand, it was more approachable and less severe. The former method of public penance had the advantage of showing more clearly that sin alienated one not only from God, but also from the Church; yet because it was carried out so strictly, it had fallen off considerably in practice. The Irish monks revived the sacrament of Penance wherever they traveled and so bequeathed to us the form of the sacrament still in use today.

The Council of Trent defended Penance as a sacrament against the Reformers, who saw the priest as an unnecessary agent in granting God's forgiveness. Trent required Christians to confess all their mortal sins by species (type of sin) and number (approximate) to a priest, who would be able to absolve them in the name of Christ and His Church.

Vatican II's reform of the sacrament, while affirming the teaching of Trent, nonetheless stresses the medicinal and healing aspects of this sacrament. The new rite is either individually celebrated or offered for several penitents — designed to show more the communal ramifications of sin and the ecclesial dimensions of reconciliation; however, even in this new communal setting, the confession of sin and absolution is individual, i.e., between the priest and penitent alone. The present Code of Canon Law obliges all Catholics to confess all mortal sins by species and number at least once a year and encourages the practice of confessing venial sins as well.

Penance, Virtue of • The virtue including the proper attitudes of a sinner toward God and in respect to one's own sinfulness. The primary act of this virtue is contrition for sin, which is a total renunciation of sin from the motive of love of God. It also includes not only an attitude of turning away from sin and toward God, but also attitudes of atonement for sin, the courage to face one's own sinfulness and rejection of pharisaic self-righteousness.

The virtue of penance gives one the motivation to struggle against sin by prayer, mortification and acts of discipline. This virtue gives one the desire to struggle against the sin of the world and to seek forgiveness. Penance recognizes the absolute power of God to forgive sins and to restore to grace. The virtue of penance requires faith and hope and is not possible without those virtues.

Penitent • In liturgical tradition the term to describe the person seeking forgiveness of sins and reconciliation with the Church through sacramental absolution. In the early evolution of sacramental Penance, one who was guilty of serious sin was admitted into the Order of Penitents to perform prescribed ascetical practices for a specified time (e.g., Lent), in order to be readmitted to Eucharistic Communion through prayer, absolution and the sign of peace. In the present revision of the Rite of Penance, this term is used to denote the one seeking reconciliation and is also used in the titles of the three forms of sacramental Penance: Rite of Reconciliation of Individual Penitents, Rite of Reconciliation of Several Penitents with Individual Confession and Absolution, and Rite for Reconciliation of Several Penitents with General Confession and Absolution.

Penitential Books • The penitential books were sets of books that contained directions for confessors including prayers, questions to be asked of penitents and exhaustive lists of sins with appropriate penances. The penitentials originated in Ireland in the fifth century at the time when individual confession of sins was replacing public confession and penance. The earliest penitentials are ascribed to St. Patrick, but the best known were those probably written by Archbishop Theodore of Canterbury (seventh century). Although the use of the penitentials brought a degree of uniformity in discipline, they also contained conflicting information on the degree of gravity and assigned penance for certain sins and also conflicted with canonical legislation on certain points.

The penitentials reflected primitive customs to some degree, especially in regard to the administration of justice. Some reflect a curious mixture of Christian mercy, Roman legal enlightenment and primitive concepts of vengeance. Since they were written documents, they quickly took on an authority almost parallel to the canonical legislation, even though they were actually a kind of private law. By the end of the eighth century, Church authorities began to issue legislation condemning the penitentials because of the confusion caused by the apparent double standard of morality. They had totally faded from use by the eleventh century.

Penitential Psalms • Seven psalms which in one fashion or another give expression to sentiments of repentance and supplication. Specifically they are Psalms 6, 32, 38, 51, 102, 130 and 143. These psalms have been used liturgically from early Christian times (the designation "Penitential Psalms" dates from the seventh century A.D.). In the later medieval period they were prescribed for recitation after Lauds on the Fridays of Lent. Interestingly, they found a place in the English coronation ceremony up until the end of the sixteenth century.

Penitentiary, Sacred Apostolic • The first tribunal of the Church which has supreme authority over the sacrament of Penance. This tribunal governs the "internal forum" of the sacrament, and because of this, its deliberations are most secret. It grants absolution in reserved cases, issues instructions to confessors and considers secret cases such as private vows or secret matrimonial impediments. It also considers doctrinal aspects of certain prayers and liturgical formulations.

Pension • Under Canon 1429 of the 1917 Code of Canon Law, a bishop could impose a pension upon a parish for the support of retired or disabled pastors. The 1983 Code, however, has made other arrangements for the support of clergy, and thus this specific provision has been dropped. The mere existence of a priestly pension plan, however, does not guarantee that their rights under Canon 281.2 have been respected.

At the same time, dioceses and even parishes and religious institutes have recently come to appreciate the need for stable and well-planned pension provisions for their employees or members. Canon 231 specifically declares, in fact, that lay employees of the Church have the right to, among other things, a decent pension. In connection with this, Canon 222 reminds the faithful of their obligation to assist the Church in coping with the financial demands made on her for the support of ministers and employees.

Pentateuch • The first five books of the Old Testament are to Jews the most sacred part of it, called the Torah. In Greek, because of the fivefold division, they are called the Pentateuch. The convention of ascribing them to Moses, the liberator and lawgiver, is an ancient one, faithfully observed throughout the New Testament.

In the last few centuries critics have attacked the traditional thesis with growing success. More searching analysis has shown the hand of at least four or five distinct authors, each having his own vocabulary, style, historical and religious outlook. While Catholic authorities at first viewed this movement with suspicion and alarm, it seems to be more placidly accepted today. At the same time, it should be noted that more recent computer analyses suggest the hand of a single author.

The traditional form of the "four-source theory" hypothesized four documents: (1) the Yahwist document, of the ninth century; (2) the Elohist document, of the eighth century; (3) the Deuteronomist, made by seventh-century northern priests; (4) the priestly writer, a Jerusalemite priest of the fifth century. It claimed that our present Pentateuch is composed of selections from these four sources, J, E, D and P. Scholars have expended much energy in trying to show to the last detail what has survived from each of these supposed written sources. As more refined analysis entered, subdivisions came: two Elohists, two Yahwists and/or two Deuteronomists. The supposed history of Israel, political and cultural, is often used as a framework to justify the date given to the various fragments, of which the present Torah is composed.

More recent theory has been somewhat more skeptical about accepting any primitive documents as being the sources of the Pentateuch. It is more open to the hypothesis of differing oral traditions lying at the root of the written Torah and to accepting the core of this tradition as going back to Moses himself. There has likewise been a slight shift toward earlier dating of the first two written formulations of the fourfold source. But there is still ample support for explanations which correlate modifications of the text in response to historical developments within the Jewish community.

The Yahwist and Elohist are so called from their respective preference for these differing names for God. God, to the Yahwist, is a grandfatherly figure; to the Elohist He is more august and more remote. One emphasizes the immanence of God; the other, His transcendence. To the Deuteronomist, religion is obedience to law and respect for stipulated ritual. The priestly author is interested in genealogy and statistical matters. The ultimate redactor (who may have been Ezra the priest) showed his respect by striving to incorporate all that had been handed down to him.

For further reading: Roland Murphy, O.Carm., "Introduction to the Pentateuch," *New Jerome Biblical Commentary*, 3-7; Jerome Blenkinsopp, *The Pentateuch: An Introduction to the First Five Books of the Bible*, Anchor Bible Reference Library (Doubleday, 1992).

Pentecost
(from a Cluny Lectionary)

Pentecost • Leviticus 23:15-16 prescribes: "And you shall count from the morrow after the sabbath, from the day that you brought the sheaf of the wave offering; seven full weeks shall they be, counting fifty days to the morrow after the seventh sabbath; then shall you present a cereal offering of new grain to the LORD." In Hebrew, this "Feast of Weeks" is known as *Shavuot* (literally, "weeks"). "Pentecost" comes from the Greek meaning "fiftieth," as used to designate this feast in the Septuagint of Tobit 2:1 and 2 Maccabees 12:32. This Feast of Weeks or Pentecost was originally an agricultural festival during which an offering of the first fruits of the grain of the land was sacrificed to the Lord in thanksgiving for a successful harvest.

Exodus 23:14-17 specifies Passover (23:15), Pentecost (23:16) and Tabernacles (23:16) as the three pilgrimage feasts, commanding, "Three times in the year shall all your males appear before the Lord GOD" (23:17; cf. Ex 34:18-24; Dt 16:16; 2 Chr 8:13). The date of Pentecost is traditionally calculated as fifty days from the first day of the Passover observance.

In addition to its significance as an agricultural feast, the Jewish feast of *Shavuot* commemorates the revelation of the Torah to Moses on Mount Sinai. Although the association of this feast with the giving of the Torah is not found in the Old Testament, it is attested in early rabbinic literature. The feast is referred to as "the time of the giving of our Torah," the anniversary of the Sinai revelation. The Exodus account of the Sinai theophany (Ex 19:1—20:26) is the Torah reading for the first day of the feast, and the haftarah is the theophanic vision of Ezra 1—2.

For Christians, Pentecost acquires its significance from Acts 2:1-41, where this feast is the occasion on which the Holy Spirit descends on the assembled disciples in the appearance of "tongues as of fire, distributed and resting on each one of them" (Acts 2:3). Fire is associated with God's presence in the Sinai theophany: "Mount Sinai was wrapped in smoke, because the LORD descended upon it in fire" (Ex 19:18).

Peter's Pentecost discourse (Acts 2:14-36) explains the disciples' Spirit-prompted speaking in tongues as the eschatological outpouring of God's prophetic Spirit announced in Joel 3:1-5.

In the Church's liturgical Calendar, Pentecost is celebrated fifty days after Easter. The Preface for the solemnity of

Pentecost in the Roman Missal expresses well the liturgical focus of the celebration:
"Today you sent the Holy Spirit
on those marked out to be your children
by sharing the life of your only Son,
and so you brought the paschal mystery
to its completion.
Today we celebrate the great beginning of
your Church
when the Holy Spirit made known to all
peoples the one true God,
and created from the many languages of
man
one voice to profess one faith."
In the lectionary for Mass, the readings for the Vigil of Pentecost include Exodus 19:3-8, 16-20, from the Sinai theophany. The "Golden Sequence," *Veni Sancte Spiritus*, prays: "Come, Holy Spirit, and from heaven direct on man the rays of your light. Come, Father of the poor; come, giver of God's gifts; come, light of men's hearts." The ninth-century hymn *Veni Creator Spiritus* has been used since the tenth century as the hymn for evening prayer of Pentecost in the Liturgy of the Hours.

For further reading: Mark J. Olson, "Pentecost," *Anchor Bible Dictionary*, 5:222-223.

Pentecostal Churches • The label "pentecostal" applies to an assortment of assemblies, sects and churches that emerged in the aftermath of late nineteenth and early twentieth-century revivalistic preaching among American Methodist and Baptist congregations. The term derives from the charismatic phenomena — especially speaking in tongues and faith healing — that mark the gatherings of these groups. Pentecostal churches are generally conservative in doctrine, with particular emphases being the inerrancy of the Bible, the reality of the manifestations of the Holy Spirit and premillennialism (the belief that Christ's Second Coming will inaugurate his thousand-year reign on earth). Baptism and the Lord's Supper are the only sacraments commonly maintained.

A total membership of more than five million is estimated in the numerous Pentecostal churches, with the General Council of the Assemblies of God being the largest. Great emphasis is placed upon missionary activities.

Pentecostalism, Catholic • The adoption by Catholics — especially within the Charismatic Renewal — of communal practices and forms of prayer associated with the broader pentecostalist movement that spread from England to the U.S. and elsewhere early in the twentieth century. It is believed that the presence of the Holy Spirit in the Church gives rise to numerous gifts — such as those possessed by the early Christian community as described in the Acts of the Apostles and subsequently neglected in the Church. The movement stresses the recovery of the consciousness and experience of the Spirit-filled community. Notable among the practices adopted by Catholic pentecostal or charismatic groups is Baptism in the Spirit, speaking in tongues and healing by the invocation of the Spirit and laying on of hands. The movement has not given rise to sectarian division in the Catholic Church, since its leaders have insisted on remaining closely associated with local parishes and dioceses, and the American bishops have been careful to recognize the powerful force for renewal in the Church represented by the movement. In recent years, there has been less emphasis on the more spectacular manifestations associated with pentecostalism and greater stress on conversion and faithful living of the Christian life, usually in conjunction with loosely organized communities of Catholics.

Pentecostarion • In the Byzantine Rite, the book containing the propers of the movable feasts, from Easter to the week after Pentecost.

People of God • The designation for the Church, given new importance and currency by the Second Vatican Council's Dogmatic Constitution on the Church (*Lumen Gentium*), especially Chapter II, according to which the Church constitutes a people with Christ as its head, the Holy Spirit as the condition of its unity, the law of love as its rule and the kingdom of God as its destiny. Membership in the People of God is based not on racial or ethnic kinship, but on the call of God, His covenant of Grace, and His gift of the Spirit. Hence, Scripture speaks of a birth from above in water and the Holy Spirit. This people is the vanguard of the human race, for it is God's will to bring all human beings into this one people, united in Christ, overcoming all that now divides mankind.

Perfectae Caritatis • The Decree on the Up-to-Date Renewal of Religious Life, *Perfectae Caritatis*, was promulgated by the Second Vatican Council on October 28, 1965. This decree seeks to adapt religious life in all its manifold forms to the conditions of the modern world without changing anything essential to the consecrated life. This project, says *Perfectae Caritatis*, is to be directed according to five principles: (1) the Gospel must be the supreme rule; (2) each religious institute should recover and follow the intentions of its founder; (3) all institutes should participate in the work of the universal Church according to the degree allowed by their nature; (4) all religious should have a clear understanding of contemporary problems in order to help bring people to the Church; and (5) above all else, religious life must be understood not as activity, but as a way of life according to the evangelical counsels of poverty, chastity and obedience (PC 2).

Perfectae Caritatis recommends to all religious the traditional disciplines of fasting, mortification and custody of the senses (PC 12), and it requires of all religious a habit which "as a symbol of consecration, must be simple and modest, at once poor and becoming" (PC 17).

Widespread disagreement over the implementation of this decree led to the establishment of *Consortium Perfectae Caritatis*, which is described elsewhere in this work.

Perfection • The attainment of the fullness of Christian life, as Christ demanded (Mt 5:48). Full perfection is attained after the resurrection in union with Christ, but in this life, a relative perfection of love of God and neighbor can be attained. It is achieved by observance of the commandments of Christ, the practice of virtue, participation in the sacraments and growth in grace and charity. Growth in perfection aims at union with God, first through the Eucharist and finally with God in heaven. The Second Vatican Council urged all Christians to aim at spiritual perfection.

Pericope • From the Greek meaning selection (section) or extract. In early Christian times, it was used to refer to any passage in Holy Scripture. However, after the sixteenth century it came to be used to designate the particular portion of Scripture which is read on a given occasion during the liturgy. (Cf. Readings, Cycle of.)

Peritus • *Peritus* (plural: *periti*) is the technical term used to describe experts in various ecclesiastical fields. A peritus, obviously, in virtue of his or her special education or experience, can enrich the Church with information or advice. Numerous saints have distinguished themselves in part through their services as periti at various stages of Church history, for example, the work of the then-deacon, St. Athanasius, at the First Council of Nicaea. Periti were widely used at the Second Vatican Council and continue to serve as consultors to several Congregations of the Roman Curia. One's status as a peritus, naturally, is lived in filial service to the Church's divine guarantee of inerrancy in matters of faith or morals.

In canon law, peritus is the term used particularly to describe the expert witness called upon in ecclesiastical trials for special information, in much the same way that a civil court would make use of an expert (Canons 1574-1581). Several other canons of the 1983 Code of Canon Law, moreover, authorize or require the use of experts in ecclesiastical decision-making processes, such as Canon 1261, which calls for the use of liturgical and artistic experts before building or repairing a church.

Perjury • Deliberate and knowledgeable lying or withholding of the truth under oath. Perjury is a particularly malicious form of lying because it involves very grave issues, as one only takes an oath to tell the truth for the most serious of reasons.

Perjury is not only against the moral requirement to tell the truth, but is also against faith and religion. When one takes an oath, one calls upon God to be a witness to the truthfulness of one's statements. But when one commits perjury, one indirectly and implicitly makes God into a liar, which is a very grave offense against God Himself. Perjury can, according to circumstances, be a crime under canon law. (Cf., for example, Canon 1391.1.)

Permanent Deacon: See **Deacon, Permanent**

Perpetual Adoration • The practice of the continuous exposition of the Blessed Sacrament, usually in the monstrance, for the purposes of uninterrupted vigil and adoration on the part of the faithful. The devotion attained a great popularity — along with other forms of perpetual prayer, such as the perpetual recitation of the Rosary — in nineteenth-century France. During that period, many already existing communities of contemplative nuns adopted the devotion (notably Dominicans and Poor Clares), and other communities were founded for the purpose of engaging in perpetual adoration. In such communities, each nun takes an hour of "guard" before the Blessed Sacrament, so that adoration continues uninterruptedly throughout the day and night. Only during the daily celebration of the Eucharist is the Blessed Sacrament reposed.

Modified forms of the practice are found throughout the Church in the Forty Hours Devotion, Holy Hours of Adoration and day-long exposition of the Blessed Sacrament. Recently, however, the strictly perpetual adoration has been adopted by parish communities in which people volunteer for hours of vigil, so that the adoration of the Blessed Sacrament can continue without interruption. The practice of perpetual adoration has lately been adopted by several of the basilicas in Rome. Exposition and adoration of the Blessed Sacrament are seen by Catholics as profoundly effective means of focusing the heart and mind in prayer, with attention fixed on the central mystery of the Eucharistic presence of Christ in the Church. It is not that Christ becomes more present to us when the Blessed Sacrament is exposed for our adoration (than when in the tabernacle), but that we become more present to Him.

Persecutions • The Church was born in persecution, starting with the death of Jesus Christ on the cross. From the beginning, Christians have been the object of persecution in one form or another. We read in Acts 8:1-3, "And on that day a great persecution arose against the church at Jerusalem, and they were all scattered throughout the region of Judea and Samaria, except the Apostles. Devout men buried Stephen, and made great lamentation over him. But Saul laid waste the church, and entering house after house, he dragged off men and women and committed them to prison." Later, St. Paul admitted that he had been a persecutor (Gal 1:13).

Much has been made of the early martyrs in the Roman Empire. The persecutions under the emperors were uneven, and the motivations were sometimes local or particular. Both Peter and Paul were executed in Rome during the reign of Nero. In February A.D. 156 (the date is disputed), Polycarp was executed at Smyrna, along with eleven others. Under Junius Rusticus, Prefect of Rome (163-167), Justin Martyr and six others were condemned to death. Persecutions were also severe under the Emperors Decius, Diocletian and Julian the Apostate.

In the early centuries, persecutions of Christians also took place in Persia, and Christians persecuted each other, as when the Arian Vandals persecuted the Catholics. The barbarians on the fringes of the empire, and later within its territories, persecuted the Christians from time to time. One of the last to be converted were the Norsemen who lived in Scandinavia, and Christian Europe did not cease to fear them until the tenth and eleventh centuries.

The rise of Islam in the seventh century posed new threats for Christians, and the Crusades were inspired, at least in part, to avenge the Christians who were persecuted while on pilgrimage to the Holy Land. The theme of persecution becomes more complex when we see the Church persecuting heretics, as with the suppression of the Albigensians in the medieval era and the Hussites in Bohemia somewhat later. Needless to say, the Reformation period saw a good deal of persecution on the part of Lutherans, Calvinists and Catholics. The Huguenots in France and the recusant Catholics in England were special objects of persecution.

Closer to the modern period was the persecution of the Jansenists and their expulsion from France early in the eighteenth century, and the suppression of the Jesuits just before the French Revolution. The Revolution itself was the occasion for brutal and bloody persecution of the Catholic Church. The extermination of simple Catholic peasants in the suppression of the Vendée must be seen as religious as well as political persecution.

After the Council of Trent, an important missionary activity flowed from Catholic evangelical fervor. During the centuries after Trent, missionaries and their communities were persecuted, variously, in Asia, Africa and the Americas. The famous martyrs of Nagasaki in the sixteenth century are but one example.

The nineteenth century in Europe was a time of more subtle persecution. The rise of anticlerical parties in the Catholic countries, especially France, and Otto von Bismarck's anti-Catholic campaign in Germany were outstanding. Exile or social discrimination were more common than execution. All of this was leading up to the unprecedented events of the twentieth century, however.

Totalitarianism in this century, together with new technological possibilities for political and social control, opened a new age of persecutions. Catholics, and other believers, suffered unprecedented loss of life and property both in connection with the events following the Bolshevik coup d'état of 1917 and the Second World War. The introduction of Communism into Asia, notably China and Indochina, has had disastrous results. In the Roman Empire persecutions were sporadic, but in the changed circumstances of our times new levels of quantitative destruction have been achieved. The election of Pope John Paul II from a Poland which had known only persecution for most of this century has made the Church Universal especially aware of persecution and of the power of the Gospel to survive it.

Person • Church law applies for the most part to persons in the Church. Because this is so, it is necessary to include some precision in the concept of the person, for the law does not apply to all persons in the same way.

One becomes a member of the Church either by Baptism or by making a Profession of Faith. The ecclesiastical laws of the Church bind only those persons who are baptized or received into the Church and have not left it by a public act.

The law, as well as ecclesial rights and duties, also applies to persons in different ways because of age. An infant is a person who has not completed the seventh year of age, a minor is one who has not completed the eighteenth year, and an adult is one over the age of eighteen.

For the most part, law touches persons by reason of where they are living (Canons 96-112).

In addition to physical persons, canon law also makes provision for juridic persons (cf. Juridic Person).

Personal Prelature • An ecclesiastical entity established by the Holy See. It is similar to a particular Church, in that it is headed by a prelate appointed by the

Roman Pontiff. It is composed of clerics who are members of the secular clergy but incardinated into the prelature. The purpose of a personal prelature, which is defined in its statutes, is to carry out some special pastoral or missionary enterprise in different territories or for different social groups.

In many ways a Personal Prelature resembles an institute of consecrated life, although its members do not take vows. The first personal prelature (and only one to date) established by the Holy See is Opus Dei.

Lay people can be dedicated to the work of a personal prelature by way of special agreements made with it.

A personal prelature has the right to establish its own seminary and train its own clerics. It also could conceivably be entrusted with the pastoral care of parishes in much the same way that religious communities are given charge of parishes within dioceses (Canons 294-297).

Personalism • The philosophy that reality is basically personal in character, rather than basically impersonal. Beings are personal which are characterized by some power for intellectual knowledge and some power of will. Some forms of personalism suggest that nothing except persons is fully real. However, a philosophy is also personalist if the reality of nonpersonal beings such as trees, rocks or dogs is considered to be ultimately caused by and for the sake of persons.

Personalism is sometimes contrasted with individualism. Individualism treats reality as composed of individuals who are what they are independently of their relationships with other persons. Personalism insists that the relations of persons are not incidental to their being as persons; rather, personal being is inherently *being-with* other persons. Thus it would be impossible to have a universe composed solely of one person, in the personalist sense of person. The difference between individualism and personalism is especially clear in economic and political ethics. Individualism insists on an almost absolute individual freedom (for example, regarding private property) and acknowledges only the duty not to harm others and to avoid infringing on the freedom of other individuals. Personalism, on the other hand, insists that individual liberty is essentially freedom *for* community with others; thus there are several positive duties in strict justice toward other persons beyond the duty not to harm them unjustly. Catholic Faith implies a personalist way of thinking, since all worldly beings are created by God and God's reality is personal (or tri-personal to be exact). Furthermore, the purpose for which all parts of the world are created is ultimately to contribute to the glory of God through the reverent knowledge and love of God by created persons.

Though there are important non-Christian personalists (for example, the Jewish philosophers Martin Buber or Emmanuel Levinas) and even a few atheist personalists, most personalists tend to come from a Christian background. An impersonalist way of thinking is clearly in opposition to Christian Faith. Impersonalist philosophies treat reality as composed of some impersonal or blind-chance forces, rather than of persons. Impersonal attitudes toward reality imply ethical views which degrade the dignity of persons. Several twentieth-century Catholic intellectuals have made significant contributions to exposing the irrationality of impersonalist philosophies. Theist existentialists such as Gabriel Marcel, Emmanuel Mounier or Maurice Blondel, neo-Thomists such as Jacques Maritain, Yves Simon, Bernard Lonergan or Karol

Wojtyla (Pope John Paul II) and theologians such as Louis Bouyer or Hans Urs von Balthasar have clarified several implications of personal dignity in response to views which obscured or denied that dignity.

Peschitto, The • The word means "simple," in the sense of "common use," because it refers to the official Syriac-language Bible used by Syriac-speaking Christianity from at least the fifth century A.D. Syriac is the term under which many dialects of Aramaic are collected. It was a living language in the Middle East until the seventh century, after which Islamic conquests eventually made Arabic the common language of the people. The Peschitto manuscripts are of historical and theological value as witnesses to the Church's life of that period and in that group of Semitic cultures. Many manuscripts of this translation have survived; New Testament collections of manuscripts do not include 2 Peter, 2 and 3 John, Jude, and Revelation. The New Testament version appeared in the early fifth century; scholars are unsure of how or when the Old Testament manuscripts were produced. Several versions or translations exist (e.g., Philoxenian, Syro-Palestinian, Syro-hexapla, Syro-curetonian, Syro-Sinaitian).

For further reading: S. P. Brock, "Versions, Ancient (Syriac)," *Anchor Bible Dictionary*, 6:794-799.

Peter, First Epistle of • Two letters in the New Testament bear the name of St. Peter. Some deny the genuineness of both; most scholars accept the first.

The First Epistle of Peter was written from Rome (cryptically called "Babylon" in 5:13). The letter was sent by Silas (Silvanus, 5:12), known to have been the frequent companion of St. Paul. It contains many allusions to the thought of St. Paul. It was sent to various Eastern Churches (Galatia, Cappadocia, Asia, Bithynia and Pontus), which had been blessed with the apostolate of St. Paul. It was composed at a time when St. Peter thought there would be a persecution. All these items would favor dating it in A.D. 66, a year after the martyrdom of St. Paul and a year before the martyrdom of St. Peter. The Neronian persecution broke out after the fire at Rome in 64, and took the lives of "a huge number" of martyrs; its spread could well be feared.

St. Peter (painted panel)

The letter is a masterpiece of general spiritual direction. No class of Christians is left without some wise and gentle advice. The pagan slur against Christians as enemies of the state is rejected, and Christians are warned to be good citizens, to the extent that being good Christians demands and permits. While Christianity welcomed the slaves, no one should be permitted to say that it aimed to ruin the social order by forcing their immediate emancipation.

For further reading: William J. Dalton, S.J., "The First Epistle of Peter," *New Jerome Biblical Commentary*, 903-908; Karl P. Donfried, "Peter," *Anchor Bible Dictionary*, 5:251-263.

Peter, Second Epistle of • Stylistic differences from First Peter lead the generality of scholars to deny the authenticity of this second epistle. Certainly, the title and personal reminiscences (1:16-18; 3:1, 15) stand in its favor. Such evidence cannot be disregarded without casting aspersions on the general truthfulness of early Christians. It does appear (3:13-14) that it was written at the very end of the Apostle's life, perhaps while he was in prison, awaiting his martyrdom. If that were so, the aged Apostle could merely have expressed his thoughts to a trusted visitor, his final thoughts to the flock entrusted to his care, leaving his choice of phraseology to that person. Such a hypothesis would satisfy all the data.

As he showed his knowledge of St. Paul's letters in the first epistle, so here (3:15-16) he speaks of the Epistles of St. Paul and of the obscurity often found in them. During St. Paul's first imprisonment in Rome (A.D. 61-63), the Roman community had ample opportunity to get to know and love many of them, especially the Letter to the Romans, which does indeed challenge the best of interpreters. Even St. James (often tacitly cited in the First Epistle) found it "difficult to understand." St. Peter joins with St. Paul in warning Christians not to expect an imminent Second Coming of the Lord.

For further reading: Karl P. Donfried, "Peter," *Anchor Bible Dictionary*, 5:251-263; Jerome H. Neyrey, S.J., "The Second Epistle

of Peter," *New Jerome Biblical Commentary*, 1017-1022; Jerome H. Neyrey, S.J., *2 Peter, Jude*, Anchor Bible 37C (Doubleday, 1993).

Peter's Chains, Feast of • In the former Roman Calendar, ranked as a greater double feast, celebrated on August 1, a day which also celebrated the only Old Testament persons commemorated in the Catholic Calendar, the Seven Holy Maccabees whose sufferings are detailed in 2 Maccabees 7. Most of the Proper was taken from the texts of the feast of Sts. Peter and Paul (June 29) with three special Collects, secret prayers and Prayers after Communion, in honor of the release of St. Peter from the bondage of chains, in honor of St. Paul and in honor of the martyrdom of the Holy Maccabees. In the Middle Ages this date was called "Lammas Day," when it was customary to consecrate bread baked from the first grain harvest, or when the feudal tribute of lambs was paid annually.

Peter's Chair, Feast of • A feast attested to in Rome from the fourth century, presently celebrated on February 22 as the Chair of Peter, Apostle, formerly celebrated on January 18. In the previous Roman Calendar, the feast celebrated on February 22 was that of St. Peter's Chair at Antioch. The dominant theme of the celebration concerns the unity of the Church founded upon St. Peter. The present lectionary assigns 1 Peter 5:1-4 and Matthew 16:13-19 as the readings for Mass.

Peter's Pence • An annual collection, of a voluntary amount, taken up among all Catholics for the maintenance of the Holy See. It began in the eighth century as a tax of one penny on each household, hence the name. The amounts collected now are sent to Rome by the bishops and are sometimes part of the annual appeal of a bishop in his diocese.

Petrine Privilege • Another name for the Privilege of the Faith. This is the dissolution of a non-sacramental marriage by the Pope in favor of the faith of a Catholic person, either the petitioner for the privilege or one who hopes to marry a non-Catholic petitioner. It involves marriages between a baptized person and one who is not baptized. Such marriages may be dissolved since, although probably consummated, they are not sacramental.

Petitions for the Petrine Privilege are initiated on the diocesan level and then sent to the Holy See for the conclusion of the process and final decision. From the time of the establishment of this process in 1924 until 1989, the process was handled by the Congregation for the Doctrine of the Faith. It is now handled by the Congregation for Sacraments and Divine Worship.

Phantasiasm • A second-century variant on other similar heresies, phantasiasm saw only the appearance of divinity of Christ in His person. This aberration, in turn, was based upon Docetism, which held Christ Himself to be merely a phantom.

Pharisees • A Jewish religious party whose membership was largely lay, in contrast to the Sadducees, whose membership was mostly clerical. The name "Pharisee" may possibly derive from a Hebrew root meaning "to separate." The origins of the Pharisees remain obscure. Some scholars trace them back to the Hasideans,

a group that professed an intense devotion to the law; they flourished during the Maccabean period. Our principal sources of information about the Pharisees, apart from the New Testament, are Josephus and the Talmud.

Unlike the Sadducees, who regarded only the Torah as binding on the Jews, the Pharisees acknowledged the oral traditions of the elders as having binding power. They believed, as the Sadducees did not, in angels, spirits and the resurrection of the dead. In the New Testament they appear as the classic opponents of Jesus and in turn are censured by Jesus time and again for their merely external observance of the law. There is no warrant to think that every last Pharisee was guilty in this way. Indeed, the New Testament can on occasion make benign references to individual Pharisees, e.g., Nicodemus (Jn 3:1-21; 7:45-48) and Gamaliel (Acts 5:34). After the fall of Jerusalem, they pass from view, but their influence on subsequent Judaism was dominant.

For further reading: Anthony J. Saldarini, "Pharisees," *Anchor Bible Dictionary*, 5:289-303.

Phelonion (also Phenolion) • Ample outer vestment of the priest in the Eastern Rites. Corresponds to the Western chasuble.

Philemon, Epistle of Paul to • A convert of Paul's missionary work (v. 19?), Philemon apparently was the owner of the slave Onesimus. The slave escaped and seems to

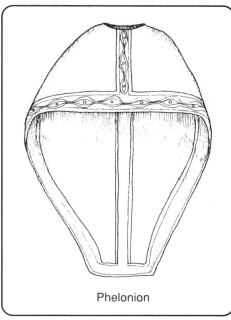

Phelonion

have inflicted some damage on Philemon (vv. 11, 18). Paul and Onesimus meet up in prison (Ephesus? Caesarea? Rome?). Onesimus converts and becomes an important part of Paul's mission (10). Paul wanted to keep Onesimus with him but realized Philemon's "right" over the slave and so sent Onesimus back to his master (14, 16), with a letter from Paul to Philemon.

Major Themes: This letter is a masterpiece of persuasion. It contains the classic form of the epistle: a greeting (1-3), thanksgiving (4-7), a body (8-20), final greeting (21-24) and a farewell section (25). Paul does not invoke his apostolic "rights over" Philemon — who owes Paul (8, 19); rather, Paul pleads with Philemon out of love (8-11, 21). As he does elsewhere (1 Cor 7:20-24; 12:13), Paul seeks to transform the master-slave relationship from within — the deeper reality of being "one body in Christ" driving the plea that Onesimus be forgiven and received back as an eternal brother (cf. also 1 Cor 7:22; Phlm 16).

Contents:

A. Introduction: 1-3
B. Thanksgiving: 4-7
C. An Appeal to Love: 8-20
D. Conclusions: 21-25

Authorship and Date: Almost all scholars agree that Paul wrote Philemon. Paul was in prison when he wrote this letter (1, 9-10, 13, 23), but it is not clear which one. If Paul wrote the letter during house arrest in Rome, then a date of A.D. 60-63 is possible; if he wrote while in prison at Caesarea, then 58-60; if at prison in Ephesus, then 56-57.

For further reading: S. Scott Bartchy, "Philemon," *Anchor Bible Dictionary*, 5:305-310; Joseph A. Fitzmyer, S.J., "The Letters to Philemon," *New Jerome Biblical Commentary*, 869-870.

Philippians, Epistle of Paul to the •

Paul's Letter to the Philippians is one of his warmest letters to have survived. Paul began his missionary journey west to Europe from Philippi. The account of the Church's beginnings at Philippi can be found in Acts 16:11-40. There was no synagogue there, so Paul preached at a "sacred center" by the river Crenides. He exorcised a slave girl, resulting in a loss of money for the owner; Paul in turn was arrested, whipped and imprisoned by the owner. Paul escaped, thanks to a providential earthquake. Paul probably wrote this letter from prison; references to the praetorium (1:13) and "Caesar's household" (4:22) lead to the conclusion that Paul wrote this while in prison in Rome.

The literary history of this epistle is complex, but a simple reading of its contents suggests the following purpose for its existence. Paul received money from the Philippians while in prison, probably from Epaphroditus (4:10-20). Scholars point out that the relationship between Paul and the Philippians was especially warm, "from the first day" (1:5; 4:15), and so the Philippians would have naturally wanted to send support to him while in prison. Paul learned that they were struggling with local inhabitants (1:28-30) and so wrote to encourage them. Furthermore, Paul's message engendered strong reactions against him in certain parties, whom he challenges, recognizing them as opponents (1:28): they are preaching out of rivalry and envy (1:15-28); they are mission workers in discord (4:2-3); they are enemies of the cross (3:18), "dogs" and "evil workmen" (3:2-4). Paul writes his letter to address these problems.

Major Themes: Paul's message included the urgency of doing God's will because the "Lord is at hand" (4:5). In passages such as 1:10; 2:16; 3:11, 20-21, Paul clearly expects the Lord to return and God's mercy to be addressed. That is, he looks forward to his "heavenly home" (3:20; cf. also 2 Cor 5:1-2; Eph 6:9; Col 1:5; 4:1). Christ is the humble servant God vindicated and glorified and made omnipotent over all (Phil 2:5-11; 3:21). Having the mind of Christ (2:5) is of utmost importance for dealing with problems which face the community from within and without.

Contents:

A. Introduction: 1:1-11

B. Paul's News: 1:12-26

C. Encouragement under Stress: 1:27—3:1

D. Exhortation against False Teachers: 3:1—4:1

E. Short Teaching on Unity, Joy and the Mind of Christ: 4:2-11

F. Thanks Offered for Gifts; Conclusions: 4:12-23

Authorship and Date: Paul's authorship has always been affirmed.

If Philippians was written from Rome, it should be dated sometime in the early A.D. 60s. If it was written during Paul's stay in Ephesus, date the letter c. 54-57.

For further reading: Brendan Byrne, S.J., "The Letters to the Philippians," *New Jerome Biblical Commentary*, 791-797; John T. Fitzgerald, "Philippians, Epistle to the," *Anchor Bible Dictionary*, 5:318-326.

Philosophy • Meaning "love of wisdom," philosophy is the body of truths known by reason concerning the most fundamental questions about the nature of reality. It includes wisdom about morality, beauty, the human person, the nature of matter and the Supreme Being: God.

True philosophy is an important ingredient in Catholic education, even though higher wisdom can come to us by faith, because true philosophy is a support for faith. In his encyclical *Aeterni Patris* (1879), Pope Leo XIII reaffirmed the constant teaching of the Church about the importance of genuine philosophy for the avoidance of error and the building up of a Catholic world-view. All candidates for ordination to the priesthood are required to study philosophy extensively.

Photius • A layman who became patriarch of Constantinople in 858. He was outstanding for his erudition, and perhaps his true stature is obscured by the political events surrounding his stormy career as patriarch. He was deposed from the patriarchal office in 867 by the unscrupulous Emperor Basil, but not before a series of events that have more import as historical precedent than anyone at the time might have guessed.

The patriarch got into a dispute with Pope St. Nicholas I and in 867 issued an encyclical defending the rights of Greek missionaries in Bulgaria, and in an astounding move proposed a charge of heresy in the matter of the *Filioque*. This addition to the Creed was not used in Rome but could be found in some parts of the Western Church. What is more, shortly thereafter, he "deposed" the Pope and declared him anathema.

Photius was reinstated as patriarch in 877, but was again overthrown in 886. The usual date given for his death is 891, but it is uncertain.

The affair of the "Photian Schism" brings to the surface the whole question of separate development between Eastern and Western theology. The notion of papal primacy and of a distinctly Latin theology seems to have been lost on Photius, as was the distinctly Byzantine ecclesiology implicit with Photius misunderstood in Rome and the West. Photius was perhaps concerned more for the political aspects of his insecure throne, but the fact that he accused the West of heresy and "deposed" the Pope was at least a model for later events, especially in 1054, when the schism between East and West occurred.

Pietism • A movement within German Lutheranism, originating in the teachings of the minister Philipp Jakob Spener (1635-1705), who sought to restore and enliven Christian practice within the state church. Dissatisfied with the level of religious life in the standard Lutheran orthodoxy of his time, Spener organized twice-weekly devotional meetings at his home, called *collegia pietatis*, with Bible reading and common prayer in order to foster the inner spiritual life of the participants. Although he frequently came into conflict with the Lutheran professoriate, his movement had wide appeal and often won him support among the German aristocracy.

When Frederick II founded the University of Halle in 1694, it became a pietist center. The movement flourished in a variety of forms and settings and influenced the emergence of similar developments elsewhere, notably the Methodism of John Wesley (1703-1791) in the Anglican Church. American movements of Pietist provenance are the Amana Church Society and a variety of Brethren Churches.

Piety • In this primary theological meaning, piety is one of the seven gifts of the Holy Spirit, along with understanding, counsel, wisdom, fortitude and fear of the Lord. These gifts make the Christian receptive to the prompting of the Holy Spirit. The gifts are further perfections of the infused theological and moral virtues and foster in the soul the readiness to follow the continuing divine tutelage that makes us able to participate more fully in the divine life. Each of the gifts pertains to a particular area of life. Ordinarily speaking, piety refers to the reverence in which we hold our parents and our homeland. As one of the gifts of the Holy Spirit, piety moves us to worship God Who is the Father of all, and also to do good to others out of reverence for God.

Pilgrim/Pilgrimage • A pilgrim is one who travels to a holy place to obtain some spiritual benefit; the purpose of the pilgrimage may be to venerate a sacred object or religious relic, to be in the presence of a holy person, to do penance or to offer thanksgiving in return for graces received.

There are scriptural foundations for a pilgrimage, where the people "sat . . . before God" (Jgs 21:2, 1 Sm 1:3). The Ark of the Covenant was taken on pilgrimage to Jerusalem by David and his men (2 Sm 6-7), ritually followed by the procession of the Ark to the Temple (1 Kgs 8:1-10). These pilgrimages were consciously likened to the journey from Egypt to Zion (Ps 68).

All this prefigured Christ's journey to Jerusalem (Lk 2:22, 19:28-38); Christ in turn leads an eschatological procession of all mankind to the heavenly kingdom (Rv

Pilgrim badge from Canterbury

7:1-12, Heb 11:8-16). Although the pilgrimage, in the common experience, has lost much of its religious significance, there remains the fact that all are called to journey to the Father through the Son.

Pious Foundation • An aggregate of goods intended for the pastoral apostolate, charitable apostolate or other work of the Church. A pious foundation may be autonomous and established as a juridic person. It may be non-autonomous, that is, given to another public juridic person such as a parish, diocese, religious community or religious house, for some express purpose related to the Church's mission. In return, there may be obligations incurred by the institution or entity receiving the foundation. These obligations may amount to spiritual exercises (such as the celebration of Masses), or they may be related to the use of the foundation for a specific purpose.

The permission of the religious superior or diocesan Ordinary is required to accept a pious foundation. This is so because the Ordinary must first determine that the entity (parish, religious house, etc.) is capable of fulfilling any obligations that come with the foundation.

In order to make radical changes in the disposition of pious foundations, such as changing the purpose for which they were given, the permission of the Holy See is required. Reduction or change in the way the obligation is satisfied can, in certain cases, be done by the Ordinary (Canons 1303-1310).

Pious Fund • The history of the Pious Fund begins in hope and generosity and ends in disappointment. In the seventeenth century, Catholic missionaries, especially the Jesuits, were granted permission by the Spanish crown to evangelize northwestern Mexico, today called Baja California. They were expressly cautioned, however, that the Crown had no funds to subsidize the enterprise. Undeterred, the Jesuits, under the illustrious Father Eusebius Kino, raised their own resources.

The bulk of these resources came in the form of donations of land and other properties which the Jesuits managed in such a way that the income from the properties would finance their missionary activities. For nearly a century, the fund grew and served its spiritual purposes well. In 1767, the Jesuits were expelled and the Spanish government took over administration of the Fund, also called by now the California Fund. For the most part, and to the credit of the Spanish government, it seems that the income of the fund was primarily directed to other missionary groups, notably the Dominicans and Franciscans.

However, in 1842, the Mexican government confiscated the properties and Santa Ana (also responsible for the massacre at the Alamo) appropriated the Fund to his own use for several years. In 1846, the bishop of California appealed under international law for return of the Fund, and an international arbitrator ruled in favor of the Church against the Mexican government, ordering Mexico to pay the Church one million dollars annually from the income of the properties. This Mexico did, more or less, until 1890.

New disputes arose, and this time (in 1903) the international court at The Hague ordered Mexico to pay certain back-interest and a new subsidy of just over $40,000 annually. In 1913, the anticlerical government of Mexico evaded its agreement and, notwithstanding protests of the Department of State, ceased all payments from properties donated to the Church. There the matter rested until 1967, when Mexico turned over $700,000 to the

Archdiocese of San Francisco in final "settlement" of the Church's claims.

Pious Will • A pious will (or pious disposition, as it is also known) is a donation of temporal goods, either in the form of money, securities or other objects, to the Church. A pious will differs from a simple donation, in that the donor makes some type of stipulation in return for the gift. This can consist of the offering of prayers or Masses for a specific cause, or it can consist in a stipulation that the donation or proceeds from the donations be used for a specific cause, such as the education of priests or missionary work.

Persons may make a pious will donation either when they are living or intend that the donation be made upon their death. The law stipulates that the Ordinary of the diocese or religious institute to which the donation is given is the executor of the pious will. If it is impossible for the religious entity to fulfill the obligations attached to the pious will, the Ordinary who is the executor, or his successor, can reduce or change the way the obligation is to be fulfilled after he has consulted those concerned, that is, someone connected with the party who made the pious will, as well as the diocesan finance committee.

If the obligation involves Mass obligations, as is often the case, the Holy See is competent to reduce the obligation, that is, the number of Masses that must be offered. If the pious will was solely for the purposes of Masses offered, the diocesan bishop or supreme moderator of the religious community has the power to adjust the obligation, in order to bring it into conformity with the level of offering current in the diocese. It often happens that a pious will made many years ago stipulates that a given number of Masses be offered each year and the offerings taken from the interest earned from the donation. In time, it becomes impossible or very difficult to satisfy the obligation because the number of Masses may be great and the offering minimal compared to contemporary standard. In such cases, only the Holy See can allow the obligation to be extinguished and the fund used for other purposes, but the bishop can adjust the number of Masses according to the current amount of the offering for a Mass (cf. Canons 1299-1302, 1308).

Pisa, Councils of • Two synods were called in the Italian city of Pisa in 1409 and 1411. Both were, unfortunately, lessons in making a bad situation worse. The bad situation was, of course, the Western Schism.

By 1409 there were two claimants to the See of Rome, Gregory XII and Benedict XIII, both commanding considerable support. Influential cardinals from both camps, however, joined forces and called a synod in Pisa with the aim of resolving the schism. The early days of this first synod boded well for the enterprise, for some two hundred bishops and seven hundred theologians attended. Both claimants were invited to the synod, though neither attended. Both were offered an opportunity to present their cases and were shown the utmost in legal and canonical due process, at least as far as the leaders of the synod understood it. However, when neither claimant appeared, both were declared contumacious and deposed. But the synod erred terribly when it went on to elect yet a third claimant to the papal throne, Alexander V.

The second and smaller Synod at Pisa two years later lacked even the procedural sense of the first and is generally considered thoroughly schismatic. The Fifth Lateran Council opened the next year and declared the Second Synod of Pisa void.

Piscina (also Sacrarium) • From the Latin *piscina* ("basin"), term to describe a niche in the right side wall of the church (or in the sacristy) for washing the priests' hands and the chalice and paten at Mass. The piscina dates from the Middle Ages; sometimes there are two set alongside each other (one for hands, the other for sacred vessels) and are decorated ornately.

Pistoia, Synod of • In 1768, the Jansenist bishop of Pistoia, Scipione de' Ricci, convened a diocesan synod which, under duress, enacted sixty-five decrees of a more or less heretical nature. Once the bishop had gathered his two hundred fifty priests in the synod, those who were less than enthusiastic about the proceedings received private notes of encouragement from the Grand Duke Leopold, who took up residence across the street from the assembly. Pope Pius VI, partially in response to the episode, issued the classic bull *Auctorem fidei* in 1794, which condemned, among other things, the Synod of Pistoia and Jansenism generally. Bishop de' Ricci, to his credit, submitted to the determinations of the Holy See.

Plainchant • Ancient monodic chant of the Church. Plainchant, also called plainsong, is a simple unaccompanied melodic line of music sung with Latin sacred texts. Many of the Ambrosian, Byzantine, Gallican, Gregorian and Mozarabic chants are plainchants. Although some erroneously call plainchant Gregorian Chant, the plainchant does have a much broader range than Gregorian alone.

Planeta (Pianeta) • This is the ordinary Roman, and Italian, name for the chasuble used by the priest at Mass. Derived from the Greek and Latin *planeta*, *planare* (to wander about), it refers to the fact that the full chasuble was seen to wander about the

body. Later on, the term came to refer more to the abbreviated style of the Roman, French or Spanish chasuble. In former times, this style of chasuble was folded during the ordination rites of a new priest. The term *pianeta piccata* (Italian) refers to the folded chasuble, which is no longer used.

Pleroma • In its properly Christian sense, "pleroma" refers first to the plenitude which is Christ Himself as the Son of God and the fullness of all things, and then to the fullness which encompasses all those who are in Him (Col 2:9-10; Eph 1:22-23). The term had a heretical sense in second-century Gnosticism, in that it referred to the primordial fullness of spiritual being from which the "creator" of the material world "lapsed" or fell, and to which all spiritual beings (now trapped in matter) must be returned.

Plumbator • A term derived from the Latin for metallic lead. A plumbator is the minor official whose task it is to affix the leaden seal to papal documents. Since the late nineteenth century, however, his services have been used only on the most solemn pontifical documents.

Pneumatomachi • This sect was part of, and basically indistinguishable from, the Macedonian heretics. Their strenuous opposition to the divinity of the Holy Spirit won them the title "enemies of the Spirit," hence the name. They were condemned at the First Council of Constantinople.

Polyglot Bible • An edition of the Bible which reproduces the text in several languages. During the sixteenth and seventeenth centuries, a number of polyglot versions were produced. Perhaps the best known of these is the Complutensian Polyglot (1522). It was issued under the patronage of Cardinal Ximénez. Its six volumes contain the Hebrew, Latin and Greek versions of the Old Testament and the Greek and Latin New Testament. The Complutensian Polyglot was followed by the Antwerp Polyglot (1569-1572), the Paris Polyglot (1639-1649) and the London Polyglot (1657). There is no evidence of earlier polyglots, although Diglot Bibles (two-language Bibles, e.g., Greek-Latin, Greek-Coptic, Coptic-Arabic) are known from the fifth century onward.

Pontiff (Supreme Pontiff) • Coming from the Latin *pontem facere*, "to build a bridge," the title of Supreme Pontiff was reserved in ancient Rome to the emperor, who as head of the principal college of priests in Rome was seen as the bridge or bridge-builder between men and the gods. The title was given to the Pope by Gratian in A.D. 375, and so rightfully he who is the Vicar of Christ on earth, the Supreme Pastor of the sheepfold of the Church, now bears this distinction of bridge-builder between God and man. As such, the Bishop of Rome, the Pope, is addressed as the Roman Pontiff or the Supreme Pontiff (in Latin, *Pontifex Maximus*, which is abbreviated "P. M." or "Pont. Max." and often written after the Pope's name).

This is not, however, the only title possessed by the Pope. Among his other titles are: Bishop of Rome; Vicar of Jesus Christ; Successor of St. Peter, the Prince of the Apostles; Patriarch of the West; Primate of Italy; Archbishop and Metropolitan of the Roman Province; Sovereign of the State of Vatican City; and Servant of the Servants of God.

Since a bishop in his own diocese is the "high priest" of that same diocese, technically he too is a pontiff. This title, however, is not used in English except when referring to the Roman Pontiff. Anything having to do with or pertaining to the Supreme Pontiff or to solemn ceremonies performed by him or any other bishop is referred to as "pontifical." (Cf. Annuario Pontificio.)

Pontifical Biblical Commission • Established with full pontifical rights and privileges by Pope Leo XIII, with the issuance of his Apostolic Letter *Vigilantiae* on October 30, 1902, the Pontifical Biblical Commission (PBC, called by its official Latin title *Pontificia Commissio de Re Biblica*) has as its stated purpose the assurance "that Holy Writ should everywhere among us receive that more elaborate treatment which the times require and be preserved intact not only from any breath of error but also from all rash opinions."

The character of the PBC became more interventionist under St. Pius X, when it adopted the practice of formulating and publishing "responsa" or replies to various contested questions in biblical studies. Between 1905 and 1914, the PBC replied to fourteen questions, such as the alleged authorship of the Pentateuch by Moses and the historical nature of the biblical narratives. These replies took on the quality of authoritative directions of the highest level.

The climate of Catholic biblical studies changed significantly in 1943 with the publication of Pope Pius XII's *Divino Afflante Spiritu*, sometimes called the Magna Carta of Catholic biblical research. Later, with the less defensive atmosphere generated by Vatican II, further changes for the PBC seemed to be indicated. In 1971, with his *motu proprio Sedula Cura*, Pope Paul VI reformed the PBC into a body of twenty prominent Catholic scholars (on the model of the International Theological Commission), no longer cardinals, and gave them the task of promoting biblical studies by the good example they themselves would provide, by the research they would conduct as a commission.

The Pontifical Biblical Commission comes under the direct authority and supervision of the Congregation for the Doctrine of the Faith. In addition to the Pontifical Biblical Institute in Rome and the École Biblique in Jerusalem, the Pontifical Biblical Commission itself has the faculties from the Holy See to grant both the pontifical license and doctorate in Sacred Scripture.

Significant documents issued by the Pontifical Biblical Commission include the response to Cardinal Suhard of Paris concerning the authorship of the Pentateuch and literary criticism of the Bible (1948), "Instruction on the Historical Truth of the Gospels" (1964) and its study on Christology (1983).

For further reading: Raymond E. Brown, S.S., and Thomas Aquinas Collins, O.P., "Church Pronouncements," *New Jerome Biblical Commentary*, 1166-1174.

Pontifical Biblical Institute • Founded at Rome in 1909, conducted by the Society of Jesus for the pursuit of higher biblical study. Together with the Pontifical Gregorian University and the Pontifical Oriental Institute, it forms part of the Gregorian University Consortium. Since 1927, the institute has also maintained a branch in Jerusalem. The scholarly periodical *Biblica* is published under the auspices of the Biblical Institute.

Pontifical Institutes of Higher Learning • There are eighteen universities and theological faculties in Rome with affiliation to the Holy See, thus designated as pontifical institutes. The universities offer general curricula in philosophy, theology, canon law and Church history. Aside from the institutes whose names indicate their specialized areas of study such as Scripture, church music and archaeology,

San Anselmo is noted for liturgical studies and the Salesianum for patristics. The pontifical institutes are empowered by the Holy See to grant one or several of the pontifical baccalaureate, license and doctoral degrees. The *Annuario Pontificio* lists these pontifical institutes (they are commonly called by the Latin or Italian names in parentheses):

(1) Pontifical Gregorian University

(2) Pontifical Biblical Institute (Biblicum)

(3) Pontifical Institute of Oriental Studies

(4) Pontifical Lateran University

(5) Pontifical Urban University (Propaganda Fide)

(6) Pontifical University of St. Thomas (Angelicum)

(7) Pontifical Athenaeum Salesianum

(8) Pontifical Institute of Classical Studies (Latinitas)

(9) Pontifical Athenaeum of St. Anselm (San Anselmo)

(10) Pontifical Athenaeum Antonianum

(11) Pontifical Institute of Sacred Music

(12) Pontifical Institute of Christian Archaeology

(13) Pontifical Theological Faculty of St. Bonaventure (Seraphicum)

(14) Pontifical Institute of Spirituality (Teresianum)

(15) Pontifical Theological Faculty of Mariology (Marianum)

(16) Pontifical Institute of Arabic and Islamic Studies

(17) Pontifical Faculty of Educational Sciences (Auxilium)

(18) Pontifical Athenaeum of the Holy Cross (Santa Croce)

Pontifical Mass • A Mass celebrated by a bishop. In the postconciliar liturgical reform the following documents deal specifically with what are now termed "episcopal liturgies" — the *motu proprio Pontificalia insignia*, on the use of pontifical insignia (1968), the *Instruction from the Sacred*

Congregation of Rites, Pontificalis ritus, on the simplification of pontifical rites and insignia (1968) and the *Caeremoniale Episcoporum,* the complete *Ceremonial of Bishops* (1984).

Pontifical Right • The term "pontifical right" refers to certain institutes of consecrated life which are under the authority of the Holy See, as opposed to being under the authority of a diocesan bishop. In order to become an institute of pontifical right, an institute must receive an appropriate decree from the Holy See through the Congregation for Religious and Secular Institutes.

Religious communities which are of pontifical right are required to submit their constitutions to the Holy See for approval. Other matters defined in the law must also be submitted to the Holy See for approval, such as confirmation of supreme moderators, dispensation of members in perpetual vows or promises, suppression of houses, etc.

Pontifical Secrecy • Moral theology generally distinguishes three types of secrets, namely natural secrets (those which concern one's private life or the lives of others, and which right reason determines should be kept so as to avoid embarrassment or harm), promised secrets (those which one has promised to keep after receiving confidential knowledge) and entrusted secrets (those which must be kept because of an agreement made prior to receiving the knowledge). Although all three types are binding, there are conditions under which the first two might be revealed; entrusted secrets, however, are sacrosanct, and include information given to professionals in both the Church and in secular society. Pontifical secrecy is governed by the principles surrounding entrusted secrets in those matters which, if disclosed, would cause injury to the Church and her mission to the world. Generally, those persons bound by pontifical secrecy are expressly informed of the same at the time from which they are bound. Occasionally, one may become bound by pontifical secrecy in some other less obvious way, such as by reading a document which is itself protected by pontifical secrecy.

Pontificals • The term "pontificals" refers to the special insignia worn by bishops during liturgical functions, including the mitre and crosier. A bishop has the unrestricted right to the use of pontificals in his own diocese, but may not do so in another diocese unless he has the express or at least reasonably presumed permission of the bishop of that diocese.

Poor and Needy (the Poor) • People who experience any of the various hardships resulting from the lack of life's necessities. In the material sense, the Church reaches out in compassion to help the poor. The charity to which all Christians are called by God finds its foundation in the words of Jesus to the rich young man: "If you would be perfect, go, sell what you possess, and give to the poor, and you will have treasure in heaven, and come, follow me" (Mt 19:21).

The first two Lucan Beatitudes console the poor: "Blessed are you poor, for yours is the kingdom of God. Blessed are you that hunger now, for you shall be satisfied" (Lk 6:20-21). Other similar encouragement abounds in the New Testament.

In biblical days there existed no middle class, and the great majority of people were poor. Thus the Church, from the beginning, was identified as the Church of the Poor. Still, as the Scriptures and many Church pronouncements make clear, the Christian is obligated to work toward alleviating the suffering and distress caused by poverty.

There is also "spiritual poverty," which refers to living in simplicity and detachment from possessions. This virtue is practiced in varying degrees by many. Religious communities voluntarily take vows of such poverty, in order to help members live in constant readiness and self-sacrificing love.

Pope • The Bishop of Rome, who exercises universal jurisdiction over the whole Church as the Vicar of Christ and the Successor of St. Peter. The term "pope" derives from the Latin for "father," *papa* (Greek, *pappas*), also used to refer to bishops and to priests in the Orthodox Churches. The Coptic Patriarch of Alexandria is also known by the title "pope." But in Western Christianity, this term refers exclusively to the Roman Pontiff, called His Holiness the Pope, who governs the universal Church as the successor to St. Peter. "The office uniquely committed by the Lord to Peter, the first of the Apostles, and to be transmitted to his successors, abides in the Bishop of the Church of Rome," who is "head of the College of Bishops, the Vicar of Christ, and the Pastor of the Universal Church," and who possesses "by virtue of his office, . . . supreme, full, immediate, and universal ordinary jurisdiction power in the Church" (Canon 331).

The Pope is assisted in carrying out his office by the bishops, the cardinals and the various offices of the Roman Curia. The Pope also has an enormously important international role, as visible symbol of the unity of the Church and as a universally acknowledged spokesman for justice, for world peace, for morality, for the dignity of the human person and for the transcendent meaning of all life on earth. In recent years, this role has been exercised in particular through pastoral visits to many countries of the world by Popes Paul VI and John Paul II.

Popes, List of • (Nationalities of non-Italian Popes given in parentheses; double dates refer to election and episcopal consecration or coronation)

St. Peter (Galilean) (d. c. A.D. 64 or 67)
St. Linus (67-76)
St. Anacletus or Cletus (76-88)
St. Clement I (88-97)
St. Evaristus (Greek) (97-105)
St. Alexander I (105-115)
St. Sixtus I (115-125)
St. Telesphorus (Greek) (125-136)
St. Hyginus (Greek) (136-140)
St. Pius I (140-155)
St. Anicetus (Syrian) (155-166)
St. Soter (166-175)
St. Eleutherius (Greek) (175-189)
St. Victor I (African) (189-199)
St. Zephyrinus (199-217)
St. Calixtus I (217-222)
St. Urban I (222-230)
St. Pontian (July 21, 230—September 28, 235)
St. Anterus (Greek) (November 21, 235—January 3, 236)
St. Fabian (January 10, 236—January 20, 250)
St. Cornelius (March 251—June 253)
St. Lucius I (June 25, 253—March 5, 254)
St. Stephen I (May 12, 254—August 2, 257)
St. Sixtus II (Greek) (August 30, 257—August 6, 258)
St. Dionysius (July 22, 259—December 26, 268)
St. Felix I (January 5, 269—December 30, 274)
St. Eutychian (January 4, 275—December 7, 283)
St. Caius (Dalmatian) (December 17, 283—April 22, 296)
St. Marcellinus (June 20, 296—October 25, 304)
St. Marcellus I (May 27, 308 or June 26, 308—January 16, 309)

St. Eusebius (Greek) (April 18, 309 or 310—August 17, 309 or 310)

St. Melchiades or Miltiades (African) (July 2, 311—January 11, 314)

St. Sylvester I (January 31, 314—December 31, 335)

St. Mark (January 18, 336—October 7, 336)

St. Julius I (February 6, 337—April 12, 352)

Liberius (May 17, 352—September 24, 366)

St. Damasus I (Spanish) (October 1, 366—December 11, 384)

St. Siricius (December 15 or 22 or 29, 384—November 26, 399)

St. Anastasius I (November 27, 399—December 19, 401)

St. Innocent I (December 22, 401—March 12, 417)

St. Zosimus (Greek) (March 18, 417—December 26, 418)

St. Boniface I (December 28 or 29, 418—September 4, 422)

St. Celestine I (September 10, 422—July 27, 432)

St. Sixtus III (July 31, 432—August 19, 440)

St. Leo I (the Great) (September 29, 440—November 10, 461)

St. Hilary (November 19, 461—February 29, 468)

St. Simplicius (March 3, 468—March 10, 483)

St. Felix III (actually II) (March 13, 483—March 1, 492)*

*Because St. Felix of Rome, a martyr, was erroneously considered by early historians to have been a Pope, Felix II and his successors were all incorrectly numbered.

St. Gelasius I (African) (March 1, 492—November 21, 496)

Anastasius Ii (November 24, 496—November 19, 498)

St. Symmachus (November 22, 498—July 19, 514)

St. Hormisdas (July 20, 514—August 6, 523)

St. John I (August 13, 523—May 18, 526)

St. Felix IV (actually III) (July 12, 526—September 22, 530)

Boniface II (September 22, 530—October 17, 532)

John II (January 2, 533—May 8, 535)

St. Agapitus I (May 13, 535—April 22, 536)

St. Silverius (June 1 or 8, 536—November 11, 537) (d. December 2, 537) (abdicated after being deposed March, 537)

Vigilius (March 29, 537—June 7, 555)

Pelagius I (April 16, 556—March 4, 561)

John III (July 17, 561—July 13, 574)

Benedict I (June 2, 575—July 30, 579)

Pelagius II (November 26, 579—February 7, 590)

St. Gregory I (the Great) (September 3, 590—March 12, 604)

Sabinian (September 13, 604—February 22, 606)

Boniface III (February 19, 607—November 12, 607)

St. Boniface IV (August 25, 608—May 8, 615)

St. Deusdedit or Adeodatus I (October 19, 615—November 8, 618)

Boniface V (December 23, 619—October 25, 625)

Honorius I (October 27, 625—October 12, 638)

Severinus (May 28, 640—August 2, 640)

John IV (Dalmatian) (December 24, 640—October 12, 642)

Theodore I (Greek) (November 24, 642—May 14, 649)

St. Martin I (July 649—September 16, 655) (exiled June 17, 655)

St. Eugenius I (August 10, 654—June 2, 657)

St. Vitalian (July 30, 657—January 27, 672)

Adeodatus II (April 11, 672—June 17, 676)

Donus (November 2, 676—April 11, 678)

St. Agatho (June 27, 678—January 10, 681)

St. Leo II (August 17, 682—July 3, 683)

St. Benedict II (June 26, 684—May 8, 685)

John V (Syrian) (July 23, 685—August 2, 686)

Conon (October 21, 686—September 21, 687)

St. Sergius I (Syrian) (December 15, 687—September 8, 701)

John VI (Greek) (October 30, 701—January 11, 705)

John VII (Greek) (March 1, 705—October 18, 707)

Sisinnius (Syrian) (January 15, 708—February 4, 708)

Constantine (Syrian) (March 25, 708—April 9, 715)

St. Gregory II (May 19, 715—February 11, 731)

St. Gregory III (Syrian) (March 18, 731—November 741)

St. Zachary (Greek) (December 10, 741—March 22, 752)

Stephen II (III) (March 26, 752—April 26, 757)*

*So named because after St. Zachary, a priest named Stephen was elected Pope but died four days later, too soon to be consecrated bishop (the official beginning of the reign in those times); however, in some lists, this Stephen appears as Stephen II, although technically he was not Pope.

St. Paul I (April [May 29] 757—June 28, 767)

St. Stephen III (IV) (August 1 [7], 768—January 24, 772)

Adrian I (February 1 [9], 772—December 25, 795)

St. Leo III (December 26 [27], 795—June 12, 816)

Stephen IV (V) (June 22, 816—January 24, 817)

St. Paschal I (January 25, 817—February 11, 824)

Eugenius II (February [May] 824—August 827)

Valentine (August 827—September 827)

Gregory IV (827—January 844)

Sergius II (January 844—January 27, 847)

St. Leo IV (January [April 10] 847—July 17, 855)

Benedict III (July [September 29] 855—April 17, 858)

St. Nicholas I (the Great) (April 24, 858—November 13, 867)

Adrian II (December 14, 867—December 14, 872)

John VIII (December 14, 872—December 16, 882)

Marinus I (December 16, 882—May 15, 884)

St. Adrian III (May 17, 884—September 885)

Stephen V (VI) (September 885—September 14, 891)

Formosus (October 6, 891—April 4, 896)

Boniface VI (April 896)

Stephen VI (VII) (May 896—August 897)

Romanus (August 897—November 897)

Theodore II (December 897)

John IX (January 898—January 900)

Benedict IV (January [February] 900—July 903)

Leo V (July 903—September 903)

Sergius III (January 29, 904—April 14, 911)

Anastasius III (April 911—June 913)

Landus (July 913—February 914)

John X (March 914—May 928)

Leo VI (May 928—December 928)

Stephen VII (VIII) (December 928—February 931)

John XI (February [March] 931—December 935)

Leo VII (January 3, 936—July 13, 939)

Stephen VIII (IX) (July 14, 939—October 942)

Marinus II (October 30, 942—May 946)

Agapitus II (May 10, 946—December 955)

John XII (December 16, 955—May 14, 964)*

Leo VIII (December 4 [6], 963—March 1, 965)

Benedict V (May 22, 964—July 4, 966)

* John XII was deposed by a council in Rome on December 4, 963. If this deposition was valid, Leo VIII was a legitimate Pope and Benedict V was an antipope; the reverse was the case if the deposition was invalid.

John XIII (October 1, 965—September 6, 972)

Benedict VI (January 19, 973—June 974)

Benedict VII (October 974—July 10, 983)

John XIV (December 983—August 20, 984)

John XV (August 985—March 996)

Gregory V (Saxon) (May 3, 996—February 18, 999)

Sylvester II (French) (April 2, 999—May 12, 1003)

John XVII (June 1003—December 1003)

John XVIII (January 1004—July 1009)

Sergius IV (July 31, 1009—May 12, 1012)

Benedict VIII (May 18, 1012—April 9, 1024)

John XIX (April [May] 1024—1032)

Benedict IX (1032—1044)*

* Benedict IX was forcibly removed in 1044; if this action was not legitimate, then Sylvester III was an antipope.

Sylvester III (January 20, 1045—February 10, 1045)

Benedict IX (second time) (April 10, 1045—May 1, 1045) (resigned; then removed at synod in December 1046)*

* If these actions were not legitimate, then Gregory VI and Clement II were antipopes.

Gregory VI (May 5, 1045—December 20, 1046)

Clement II (Saxon) (December 24 [25], 1046—October 9, 1047)

Benedict IX (third time) (November 8, 1047—July 17, 1048) (d. c. 1055)

Damasus II (Bavarian) (July 17, 1048—August 9, 1048)

St. Leo IX (Alsatian) (February 12, 1049—April 19, 1054)

Victor II (Swabian) (April 16, 1055—July 28, 1057)

Stephen IX (X) (French) (August 3, 1057—March 29, 1058)

Nicholas II (French) (January 24, 1059—July 27, 1061)

Alexander II (October 1, 1061—April 21, 1073)

St. Gregory VII (April 22 [June 30], 1073—May 25, 1085)

Bl. Victor III (May 24, 1086—September 16, 1087)

Bl. Urban II (French) (March 12, 1088—July 29, 1099)

Paschal II (August 13 [14], 1099—January 21, 1118)

Gelasius II (January 24 [March 10], 1118—January 28, 1119)

Calixtus II (French) (February 3 [9], 1119—December 13, 1124)

Honorius II (December 15 [21], 1124—February 13, 1130)

Innocent II (February 14 [23], 1130—September 21, 1143)

Celestine II (September 26 [October 3], 1143—March 8, 1144)

Lucius II (March 12, 1144—February 15, 1145)

Bl. Eugenius III (February 15 [18], 1145—July 8, 1153)

Anastasius IV (July 12, 1153—December 3, 1154)

Adrian IV (English) (December 4 [5], 1154—September 1, 1159)

Alexander III (September 7 (20), 1159—August 30, 1181)

Lucius III (September 1 [6], 1181—September 25, 1185)

Urban III (November 25 [December 1], 1185—October 20, 1187)

Gregory VIII (October 21 [25], 1187—December 17, 1187)

Clement III (December 19 [20], 1187—March 1191)

Celestine III (March 30 [April 14], 1191—January 8, 1198)

Innocent III (January 8 [February 22], 1198—July 16, 1216)

Honorius III (July 18 [24], 1216—March 18, 1227)

Gregory IX (March 19 [21], 1227—August 22, 1241)

Celestine IV (October 25 [28], 1241—November 10, 1241)

Innocent IV (June 25 [28], 1243—December 7, 1254)

Alexander IV (December 12 [20], 1254—May 25, 1261)

Urban IV (French) (August 29 [September 4], 1261—October 2, 1264)

Clement IV (French) (February 5 [15], 1265—November 29, 1268)

Bl. Gregory X (September 1, 1271 [March 27, 1272]—January 10, 1276)

Bl. Innocent V (French) (January 21 [February 22], 1276—June 22, 1276)

Adrian V (July 11, 1276—August 18, 1276)

John XXI* (Portuguese) (September 8 [20], 1276—May 20, 1277)

* Because of scribal errors in numbering the Popes named John, dating back to the time of John XV, the number XX was dropped in an attempt to bring the numbers into order.

Nicholas III (November 25 [December 26], 1277—August 22, 1280)

Martin IV* (French) (February 22 [March 23], 1281—March 28, 1285)

*The names of Popes Marinus I and II (above) were later misread as Martin. For this reason, Martin IV was really only the second Pope named Martin.

Honorius IV (April 2 [May 20], 1285—April 3, 1287)

Nicholas IV (February 22, 1288—April 4, 1292)

St. Celestine V (July 5 [August 29], 1294—December 13, 1294 [resigned]); d. 1296

Boniface VIII (December 24, 1294 [January 23, 1295]—October 11, 1303)

Bl. Benedict XI (October 22 [27], 1303—July 7, 1304)

Clement V (French) (June 5 [November 14], 1305—April 20, 1314)

John XXII (French) (August 7 [September 5], 1316—December 4, 1334)

Benedict XII (French) (December 20, 1334 [January 8, 1335]—April 25, 1342)

Clement VI (French) (May 7 [19], 1342—December 6, 1352)

Innocent VI (French) (December 18 [30], 1352—September 12, 1362)

Bl. Urban V (French) (September 28 [November 6], 1362—December 19, 1370)

Gregory XI (French) (December 30, 1370 [January 5, 1371]—March 26, 1378)

Urban VI (April 8 [18], 1378—October 15, 1389)

Boniface IX (November 2 [9], 1389—October 1, 1404)

Innocent VII (October 17 [November 11], 1404—November 6, 1406)

Gregory XII (November 30 [December 19], 1406—July 4, 1415 [resigned]); d. October 18, 1417

Martin V (November 11 [21], 1417—February 20, 1431)

Eugenius IV (March 3 [11], 1431—February 23, 1447)

Nicholas V (March 6 [19], 1447—March 24, 1455)

Calixtus III (Spanish) (April 8 [20], 1455—August 6, 1458)

Pius II (August 19 [September 3], 1458—August 14, 1464)

Paul II (August 30 [September 16], 1464—July 26, 1471)

Sixtus IV (August 9 [25], 1471—August 12, 1484)

Innocent VIII (August 29 [September 12], 1484—July 25, 1492)

Alexander VI (Spanish) (August 11 [26], 1492—August 18, 1503)

Pius III (September 22 [October 1, 8], 1503—October 18, 1503)

Julius II (October 31 [November 26], 1503—February 21, 1513)

Pope Pius VII

Leo X (March 9 [19], 1513—December 1, 1521)

Adrian VI (Dutch) (January 9 [August 31], 1522—September 14, 1523)

Clement VII (November 19 [26], 1523—September 25, 1534)

Paul III (October 13 [November 3], 1534—November 10, 1549)

Julius III (February 7 [22], 1550—March 23, 1555)

Marcellus II (April 9 [10], 1555—May 1, 1555)

Paul IV (May 23 [26], 1555—August 18, 1559)

Pius IV (December 25, 1559 [January 6, 1560]—December 9, 1565)

St. Pius V (January 7 [17], 1566—May 1, 1572)

Gregory XIII (May 13 [25], 1572—April 10, 1585)

Sixtus V (April 24 [May 1], 1585—August 27, 1590)

Urban VII (September 15, 1590—September 27, 1590)

Gregory XIV (December 5 [8], 1590—October 16, 1591)

Innocent IX (October 29 [November 3], 1591—December 30, 1591)

Clement VIII (January 30 [February 9], 1592—March 3, 1605)

Leo XI (April 1 [10], 1605—April 27, 1605)

Paul V (May 16 [29], 1605—January 28, 1621)

Gregory XV (February 9 [14], 1621—July 8, 1623)

Urban VIII (August 6 [September 29], 1623—July 29, 1644)

Innocent X (September 15 [October 4], 1644—January 7, 1655)

Alexander VII (April 7 [18], 1655—May 22, 1667)

Clement IX (June 20 [26], 1667—December 9, 1669)

Clement X (April 29 [May 11], 1670—July 22, 1676)

Bl. Innocent XI (September 21 [October 4], 1676—August 12, 1689)

Alexander VIII (October 6 [16], 1689—February 1, 1691)

Innocent XII (July 12 [15], 1691—September 27, 1700)

Clement XI (November 23, 30 [December 8], 1700—March 19, 1721)

Innocent XIII (May 8 [18], 1721—March 7, 1724)

Benedict XIII (May 29 [June 4], 1724—February 21, 1730)

Clement XII (July 12 [16], 1730—February 6, 1740)

Benedict XIV (August 17 [22], 1740—May 3, 1758)

Clement XIII (July 6 [16], 1758—February 2, 1769)

Clement XIV (May 19, 28 [June 4], 1769—September 22, 1774)

Pius VI (February 15 [22], 1775—August 29, 1799)

Pius VII (March 14 [21], 1800—August 20, 1823)

Leo XII (September 28 [October 5], 1823—February 10, 1829)

Pius VIII (March 31 [April 5] 1829—November 30, 1830)

Gregory XVI (February 2 [6], 1831—June 1, 1846)

Pius IX (June 16 [21], 1846—February 7, 1878)

Leo XIII (February 20 [March 3], 1878—July 20, 1903)

St. Pius X (August 4 [9], 1903—August 20, 1914)

Benedict XV (September 3 [6], 1914—January 22, 1922)

Pius XI (February 6 [12], 1922—February 10, 1939)

Pius XII (March 2 [12], 1939—October 9, 1958)

John XXIII (October 28 [November 4], 1958—June 3, 1963)

Paul VI (June 21 [30], 1963—August 6, 1978)

John Paul I (August 26 [September 3], 1978—September 28, 1978)

John Paul II (Polish) (October 16 [22], 1978—   )

Pope Speaks, The • Founded in 1954, *The Pope Speaks* is a quarterly journal which carries accurate English translations of the more important papal and, more recently, curial documents. Documents are identified by the official title drawn from the *editio typica*, an English title, subject matter and date of publication. *The Pope Speaks*, also provides a separate and comprehensive log of papal addresses (whether published in *The Pope Speaks* or not). *The Pope Speaks* is published by Our Sunday Visitor, Inc., and is available in most Catholic college and university libraries, as well as by individual subscription.

Popish Plot • The name given the fraud masterminded by two Englishmen, Titus Oates and Israel Tonge, who sought to discredit the Catholics in England. King Charles II (1665-1680) was thought to be sympathetic to the cause of Catholics, especially since he married Catherine, Catholic princess of Portugal. Giving in to pressure, however, he acceded to the demands of the Church's opponents that Catholics continue to be outlawed in the realm. At this point, Oates and Tonge, two malcontents who vehemently hated Catholics, brought false charges before Parliament, claiming that English Catholics, led by Jesuits, were conspiring to assassinate King Charles II, replacing him with his brother James, the Duke of York. Inflamed rumors of this plot exacerbated persecution of the Catholic community in England, even though by 1684 it had been exposed as a deception.

Populorum Progressio • The 1967 encyclical letter *On the Development of Peoples* by Pope Paul VI. The Pope reflects on the traditional Catholic teaching that economic goods are destined for all human persons and thus that the wealthy are bound in justice — not merely in charity — to help the poor meet their needs. He applies this teaching on a worldwide scope to show that wealthy nations are duty-bound to come to the aid of poor nations and to promote development of the poor nations to a full share in human community. He stresses that the needed development is not merely a matter of economic improvement, though that too is necessary. Authentic development helps human persons realize the integral fullness of their possibilities, especially their possibility of communion with God and of solidarity with all fellow human beings. Thus industrial growth and economic development plans should foster cultural, familial and religious growth rather than undercut them. Governmental bodies, both national and international, should take those steps which will promote this authentic integral development.

The Pope suggests several particular steps to be taken by the wealthier nations. There is a duty of direct aid from the wealthy nations to meet the immediate urgent needs of the poor. There is a duty of charitable outreach efforts by which human community among all peoples may be realized. And there is a duty to restructure trade relations between rich and poor nations, since the present free market structure yields inequitable results. The best means of determining just prices and promoting enterprise may well be a free market, when all traders enjoy the approximate equality which allows each to negotiate with true freedom. But the dire need of the poor nations does not give them the degree of equality within the world market to enter freely into equitable trade relations. Thus limits must be imposed on the competitive market so that it yields authentically free and just results between the rich and the poor nations, results which promote solidarity and equality among nations. Otherwise, international trade — without any particular acts of intentional injustice on the part of the rich — will inevitably lead to a widening gap between rich and poor nations.

The Pope concludes by pointing out the connection between a fully human and stable peace and the integral development in justice and solidarity of the whole human family: "The new name for peace is development" (n. 87).

Porter • The lowest ranking of the traditional minor orders, the office of porter or doorkeeper may have originated in the responsibility to exclude unauthorized people from entry into the Church during the celebration of the Eucharist. The order of porter was suppressed in 1972 with the revision of the sacrament of Orders mandated by Vatican Council II.

Portiuncula • At the beginning of the Franciscan adventure and family when St. Francis began to accept followers who wished to live his lifestyle of evangelical poverty and simplicity, the need arose for him to provide a place for them to live and worship. The word "portiuncula," similar to Italian for "a small portion," refers to the fact that at this time St. Francis accepted the generous offer made to him by the Benedictine monks of the nearby monastery of St. Benedict of a small portion of land. Also on the land was a small church, which was in ruins. This was about the year 1210. He accepted this offer on the condition that his friars would pay some type of rent in perpetuity, something done even to this day.

As with the church ruins at San Damiano where St. Francis received his initial call from the crucified Christ on the chapel's crucifix, he and his followers restored the little church. Today it stands in the midst of a glorious and sumptuous basilica, Our Lady of the Angels, and is a renowned place of pilgrimage. Along with the Basilica of St. Francis in Assisi, the Basilica of Our Lady of the Angels is a privileged papal basilica and belongs to the Holy See. Numerous Pontiffs have gone on pilgrimage there.

The Portiuncula Indulgence originated here when St. Francis received a vision of Our Lady, surrounded by angels, in which he was told that a special pardon, a plenary indulgence, could be obtained for the dead as often as a person would visit this chapel on August 2. This indulgence was first announced at the Portiuncula by St. Francis himself in 1216. (Though there is some doubt among scholars as to the veracity of this date, there is also sufficient evidence in its favor to support it.) At that time he announced the fact that Pope Honorius III had granted the plenary indulgence to those who visited this small church. This was later extended by ecclesiastical authority to all churches or public oratories belonging to the Franciscan Order(s). Nowadays any pastor may obtain the privilege of having the Portiuncula Indulgence in his parish from the Sacred Penitentiary in Rome and with his bishop's permission. It is obtained on the second of August. If this is a weekday, the indulgence may be transferred to the next Sunday. To obtain this indulgence, the usual conditions must be met and the Our Father, Hail Mary and Glory Be recited six times per visit for the Holy Father's intentions.

Positivism • The philosophy according to which the experimental method of modern science is the only source of definite, meaningful knowledge. Scientific method is understood always to proceed from "positive" data by induction to general conclusions; it never loses its base in positive data by engaging in the *a priori* armchair imaginations or speculations which are supposedly characteristic of earlier theological and metaphysical stages of human thought. In a thorough positivist analysis, reality is nothing more than what can be studied by scientific methods. Thus ideas about God, several absolute moral norms or other subjects which cannot be scientifically tested are nonsense.

The best known of positivists are perhaps the nineteenth-century French philosopher and reformer August Comte and the English utilitarian John Stuart Mill, as well as twentieth-century philosophers of science Bertrand Russell (in some works) and A. J. Ayer. Philosophy of science in the latter half of the twentieth century has tended to move beyond a positivist understanding even of what modern science is about. Catholic philosophers usually insist that positive sensory data compose a necessary component of human knowledge, but that it is by no means all that is required. For example, Bernard Lonergan, a Catholic transcendental Thomist philosopher, showed in *Insight* that an adequate understanding of scientific method does not close off questions transcending experience but rather opens out to them. With an adequate understanding of science and the human mind, the limitations which positivism placed on discussions of God and of morality are seen to be irrational.

Possession, Demonic • The condition of a person when control over mind and body is affected by a demon or demons. The New Testament records a number of instances of demonic possession (Mt 8:16; Mk 1:34; Lk 7:21; Acts 5:16). The essential remedy against possession, as well as against oppression and harassment from an evil spirit, is to cast out the evil entity in the Name of Jesus Christ. The authority of Christ's Name is related to God's power through Jesus Christ, which makes effective the victory of the cross over Satan and the kingdom of "this world." That action which casts out evil spirits is normally called exorcism, while that action which drives evil spirits away from a person who is not possessed is called "deliverance." It is a normal part of the Church's mission to free captives and liberate the oppressed — the deeper freedom coming from liberation from sin in the work of Christ on the cross. The popular and imaginative media portrayals of this phenomenon subject people to all kinds of naïve and false understandings of demonic possession.

Postcommunion • In the International Commission on English in the Liturgy's 1974 Roman Missal (and the latest U.S.

edition, sacramentary 1985), the title of this prayer of the Mass is "Prayer after Communion."

The Prayer after Communion is one of three variable "presidential" (or presiding priest's) prayers provided in each Mass "Proper" (or, on some saints' days, taken from "common" formularies), the other two being the Opening Prayer (traditionally called a "Collect") and the Prayer over the Gifts (formerly known as the "Secret" prayer because it was offered silently).

The Prayer after Communion is a brief prayer which concludes the period of silent thanksgiving or sung praise after the reception of Holy Communion. The classic Roman texts we have are exceedingly terse and generally offer, in a concise way, thanks for the sacrament received and intercession for the fruitfulness of the sacrament.

Postulant • A candidate for a religious order who has been accepted for admission but who undergoes a period of pre-novitiate formation to be prepared for entry into the more solemn formation period of the novitiate itself. The duration, format and religious garb of the period of postulancy vary widely from one community to another.

Postulation • A form of canonical election. It is the process whereby a person prohibited from being elected by a canonical impediment, from which a dispensation is possible and customary, is elected. A postulation requires a two-thirds majority from the electing body. After the required votes are received, the postulation is sent to the authority competent to grant the dispensation from the impediment, who then confirms the election. If the postulation is not confirmed, the electing body must hold another election (Canons 180-183).

Poterion • The Eastern Chalice.

Poverty • In its theological sense, poverty is the voluntary renunciation of the ownership and use of material goods for the sake of seeking a life of more perfect union with God. Traditionally, poverty is considered to be one of the evangelical counsels, along with chastity and obedience. The undertaking of a consecrated religious life in the Church usually takes the form of a public profession of the evangelical counsels. Poverty is thus one of the three "vows" normally professed by religious in canonically instituted orders, congregations and societies. Christ Himself and His common life with the Apostles provide the example of poverty, of life lived in dependence upon God and in communal sharing. In the tradition, this is often called the "apostolic life," particularly in that Christians sought to imitate the community described in the Acts of the Apostles in which all things were held in common. The replication of the apostolic life became the ideal for monks, nuns and religious throughout the centuries. Poverty is seen to be fundamental to this life in that it fosters dependence upon God, detachment from the goods of this world and communion with other Christians.

Power • The word "power" includes a large number of concepts which touch upon physical force, military strength, the ability to act/respond, to influence others or to wield power over others/things, as in dominion, majesty and lordship. Nature has or contains "power" (Gn 4:12; 49:3; Ps 19:2; 104; Wis 13:4; Rv 1:20), as do humans (Jgs 16:6; Prv 20:29) and animals (Jb 39:9-11; Prv 14:4). The biblical witness indicates that all power is from God (Ps 66:7; 147:5; Jer 10:6; Jb 36:22). God's power is depicted in terms of His redemptive and liberating action (Ex 15:6, 13; 32:11; Dt 3:24), which invigorates and enlivens the faint (Is 40:29) and is a refuge for the weary (Ps 28:7-8; Jer 16:19; Lk 1:49).

The ultimate manifestation of God's power is in the life and death of Jesus Christ (Mk 6:2, 5; Lk 4:14, 36; 5:17; 6:19), which power is transferred to the Church by and in the Holy Spirit (Acts 1:8; 4:33; Rom 15:19). It is important to note that the New Testament often refers to miracles as "power": The conception of Jesus in Mary's womb is by the power of God which overshadows her (Lk 1:35); Jesus is the Son of God "in power" (Rom 1:4) and is the power of God (1 Cor 1:24); the Gospel of Christ preached by the Apostles is the very power of God (Rom 1:16; 1 Cor 1:18); Jesus actually possesses the power of God (Mk 5:30; Lk 8:46). It is crucial to understand that "power" witnesses to God's greatness, to the means by which God destroys Satan, sin and death, and shows forth the means by which, through Christ, God restores humans to their original dignity.

For further reading: Clinton E. Arnold, "Power, New Testament Concept of," *Anchor Bible Dictionary*, 5:444-446.

Power of the Keys • In conferring the role of leadership upon Peter, Our Lord says: "I will give you the keys of the kingdom of heaven, and whatever you bind on earth shall be bound in heaven, and whatever you loose on earth shall be loosed in heaven" (Mt 16:19). The power of the keys thus refers to the supreme authority and jurisdiction vested by Christ in the Apostles and their successors.

Pragmatism • A philosophy or philosophical method which characterizes the truth or meaning of an area of reality in terms of its pragmatic impact on, or difference for, how we choose and act. The philosophers usually labeled pragmatists

are the Americans C. S. Peirce, William James and John Dewey. However, many other thinkers deserve the term equally, for example, the French Catholic philosopher Maurice Blondel.

Pragmatism can be developed in many — and even opposing — directions, of which some are compatible with Catholic Faith, whereas others are not. Opposed pragmatic developments are possible since thinkers have different understandings of our choice and action. This is critical since pragmatists characterize reality in terms of the difference it makes for our action. For example, if action is identified with experimental or technological control over an ongoing situation (as in the popularly received notion of John Dewey's thought), then reality cannot include anything which is inherently beyond our control. But if human action includes the attitudes of mind and will by which we hold ourselves open to things inherently beyond our control and without which we cannot be naturally or supernaturally fulfilled, then the correlative pragmatic notion of reality can include God. Maurice Blondel's *Action* (1893) developed a "pragmatic" account of reality which includes our dependence upon God and His grace, as well as a sacramental Church with a Magisterium. But in the usual secular sense of the term, a pragmatic philosophy casts doubt on the reality of that which cannot be produced or controlled by human activity — namely, God and Divine Revelation.

Prayer of the Faithful (also General Intercessions) • In liturgical tradition this term distinguished the intercessory prayers offered during the Eucharist by the already baptized from those offered by and for the catechumens which preceded them. Two main types of such intercessions have perdured in the West. The first is the litany form of petitions offered by the deacon (or by another minister, in his absence) with a sung or spoken response (such as, "Lord, hear us"). The petitions are introduced by an invitation to pray by the priest or bishop celebrant (a variation on "Let us pray") and completed with a concluding prayer. Examples for the seasons of the Church year and Ordinary Time are found in an appendix to the sacramentary.

The other kind is called the Roman type with the statement of the intention to be prayed for by the celebrant, a period of silence for personal prayer, and a concluding prayer by the celebrant. This latter type survives to this day in the afternoon liturgy of Good Friday, the Celebration of the Lord's Passion. In general, the intentions concern the needs of the whole Church, public authorities and the salvation of the world, those who are oppressed and the local community, including the sick and deceased (cf. *General Instruction of the Roman Missal*, nn. 45-46).

Prayer over the Gifts • One of the three "presidential" (or presiding priest's) prayers provided in each set of Mass Propers (or on some saints' days, taken from "common" formularies), the other two being the Opening Prayer (also known traditionally as the "Collect") and the Prayer after Communion.

In the pre-Vatican II Rite of Mass, this prayer was called the "Secret" prayer because the priest offered the text of the prayer silently, singing or saying aloud only the ending, "*per omnia saecula saeculorum* . . . for ever and ever."

The classic Roman texts which we use in translation are exceedingly brief, concise prayers. The theology manifested in them is pluriform. Some prayers ask that the Church's sacrifice be acceptable or that the gifts be transformed into Christ's sacrifice. Other prayers are proleptic in the sense that they speak about what is to be

accomplished through the Eucharistic gifts once they have become the Body and Blood of Christ, for example, that the unity and peace signified by the Eucharist might become realities in the Church.

The celebrant's invitation, "Pray, brethren . . ." and the people's response, "May the Lord accept . . ." represent an extended version of "*Oremus* . . . Let us pray," and serve as an introduction to the Prayer over the Gifts.

Prayer, Mystical: See **Mysticism**

Preaching • The oral communication of the Word of God that gives birth to or nourishes the faith of those who hear it. Preaching is a stable ecclesiastical office held by the Pope and bishops according to Divine law, and by others according to ecclesiastical law. The office of preaching has always been considered a preeminent ministry in the Church. Traditionally, it has been the fundamental means of instruction on the meaning of the Scriptures and other aspects of the Faith. Preaching can take several forms, including the sermon, missions, retreats and the liturgical homily. Throughout her history, the Church has regularly enacted legislation about preaching, especially in periods when there was laxity in this regard. In the Middle Ages, for instance, the lower clergy were generally not allowed to preach, considering the poor quality of their education. Although the bishops and abbots were the only ones allowed to preach, with the foundation of the mendicant orders and the Dominican Order in particular, papal permissions were given allowing the members of these orders to preach in the territories they visited.

Present legislation allows the Pope and bishops to preach anywhere. Priests and deacons possess the faculty, but not the inherent right, to preach anywhere with at least the presumed permission of the pastors or rectors of churches. This faculty can be restricted by a competent Church authority.

Laypersons may be permitted to preach if the episcopal conference of the country decides to allow it. As such, laypersons could be given permission to preach in most forms, with the exception of the homily, which is always reserved to sacred ministers (cf. Canons 762-772).

Precept • An order issued by an ecclesiastical superior to an individual under his or her authority (Canon 35). A precept is issued in the form of an administrative decree by which a person is enjoined to do or refrain from doing something (Canon 49).

A penal precept is a decree by which a superior threatens a subject with an ecclesiastical penalty if the terms of the precept are not obeyed (Canon 1320).

Precious Blood, Feast of the • Beginning in the nineteenth century, various religious orders in the Church celebrated feasts in honor of the Precious Blood. In 1859 Pope Pius IX decreed that such a feast was to be celebrated in the whole Church on the first Sunday in July; in 1914 Pope St. Pius X changed the date to July 1, the date kept until the postconciliar liturgical reform. The following texts were used: Introit from Revelation 5:9-10, Epistle from Hebrews 9:11-15, Gospel from John 19:30-35, Offertory from 1 Corinthians 10:16, Communion from Hebrews 9:28. This same Mass formula was also used in some places on the fifth Friday of Lent.

In the present reform of the liturgy, these same texts are used (with additional choices for readings) for the Votive Mass of the Precious Blood, which Mass replaces the feast date of July 1, which was dropped from the calendar.

Predella • Italian for "platform" or "stool," this is the floor of the platform on which an altar stands. On the old high altars the uppermost of the gradines where the candlesticks and flower vases rested was often referred to by this name.

Predestination • In the broad sense, predestination refers to every eternal resolve of the divine will. In the narrow sense, it refers to the divine resolve with respect to the supernatural destiny of creaturely persons. The doctrine of predestination affirms that, as part of the eternal plan of divine providence, God has predetermined certain persons to eternal bliss. This doctrine has a solid basis in Scripture. St. Paul wrote: "For those whom he foreknew he also predestined to be conformed to the image of his Son, in order that he might be the first-born among many brethren. And those whom he predestined he also called; and those whom he justified he also glorified" (Rom 8:29-30). (Cf. Mt 25:34; Jn 10:27; Acts 13:48; Eph 1:4.)

In grappling with the deep mystery of predestination, most Catholic theologians have taught that predestination is absolute, i.e., independent of any merits on the part of creatures (*ante praevisa merita*). On this account, God freely resolves from all eternity to call certain men to beatitude and therefore to endow them with the grace necessary for their attainment of salvation. Note that the phrase "certain men" does not imply a number such that some are chosen and some are not. It may indeed be true that some are predestined and some are not, but that is not the point of the doctrine of predestination. The point of the doctrine is that the supernatural end of beatitude can only be enjoyed by those (which could mean all, or many, rather than a few) whom God predestines. There is no creaturely enjoyment of beatitude without the eternal divine decree ordaining it — for a few, for many or for all creaturely persons.

Nor does the doctrine imply a positive act of reprobation on God's part. By reprobation is meant the eternal decree by which God predestines certain men, on account of their foreseen sins, to eternal rejection. Reprobation is best understood as a non-election to eternal bliss, according to which God declines to prevent (permits in a very weak sense) the moral failures and unrepentant guilt of certain persons. The point of the element of reprobation in the doctrine of predestination is to embrace the possibility of the actual failure of some creatures to attain the eternal beatitude which, in God's universal salvific will, is the divinely intended end of all creaturely persons. It cannot be known that any persons — except for the fallen angels — have been the object of this non-election.

The Church has consistently rejected all forms of heretical predestinationism, as represented, for example, by the teachings of Lucidus in the fifth century, reputedly by Gottschalk in the ninth and by John Calvin in the sixteenth. The Councils of Orange and of Trent condemned the predestinationist positions concerning a positive predetermination to sin, and an unconditional predestination to damnation (i.e., independently of foreseen sins and demerits). In insisting that only predestination to beatitude is absolute and unconditional, the Church thereby rejected the doctrine of so-called double predestination. To affirm an unconditional decree of reprobation implies that God causes sin or, in some strong sense, permits it in the way He permits physical evils or the pain of punishment — something that would directly contravene the divine goodness. In effect, the Church has insisted that an unconditional decree of reprobation would mean that God is at odds with Himself and that His purposes are contradictory. It may be taken as a sign of the error in the doctrine of double predestination that it has been the persistent source of contention and division within the ecclesial communities following the Reformed tradition of Calvin.

Preface • From the Latin, *praefatio*, a technical liturgical word, therefore denoting not what comes most readily to mind in English, preliminary, but rather a formal proclamation of praise by the presiding priest.

Originally any number of solemn prayers were designated *praefationes*, and chanted to the melody we now associate exclusively with the Preface (a surviving example, the second part of the Exsultet or Easter Proclamation and the Blessing of the Baptismal Font).

In current usage, the term Preface is restricted to that proclamation of praise and thanksgiving in the Eucharistic prayer which follows the opening dialogue ("Lift up your hearts, etc.") and leads into the *Sanctus* ("Holy, holy, holy Lord . . ."). Reacting to an inordinate proliferation of local texts (at one time close to three hundred), some of very dubious theological and literary quality, the Council of Trent suppressed all but eleven. The early twentieth century saw the introduction of a few more (for the Dead, St. Joseph, Christ the King, Sacred Heart). Then the Second Vatican Council's revised Missal for the universal Church dramatically increased the number of Prefaces to over eighty, with provision for national conferences of bishops to request additional texts. The United States, for example, received permission to add several texts for national celebrations (e.g., Thanksgiving Day, Independence Day).

With the publication of the Eucharistic Prayers for Masses of Reconciliation and Masses with Children, five more Prefaces made their appearance. The publication of the *Collection of Masses of the Blessed Virgin Mary* adds over forty more Prefaces to the Roman Rite, while the publication in every language (except English) of the so-called "Swiss Synod" Eucharistic Prayers (Eucharistic Prayer V-A through V-D in the new Italian, Polish and now Spanish language Missal for use in the United States) sets the number of Prefaces in more or less universal use at somewhere close to one hundred thirty.

Prefect, Apostolic (or Vicar Apostolic) • A priest or bishop who is given charge over a territorial division of the faithful which has not been directed as a diocese. Generally speaking, before a mission territory becomes a diocese, it is first erected as a prefecture; and when it attains an added degree of stability, it is made a vicariate. The basic difference between the two is that a prefecture is headed by one who is generally not a bishop but who possesses many of the juridical powers of a bishop. A vicar apostolic, on the other hand, is usually a bishop (cf. Canon 371).

Prefecture, Apostolic • A territorial division or jurisdiction of the Church that has been erected by the Holy See as such but which does not have the full canonical identity of a diocese. It is composed of several mission parishes. A mission territory is erected as an apostolic prefecture when the Holy See determines that it has a decree of stability and potential for growth. It is placed under the authority of an apostolic prefect, who is always a prelate but not necessarily a bishop, having many of the executive powers of a bishop (cf. Canon 371.1).

Prelate • A cleric who has some form of ordinary ecclesiastical jurisdiction. The term also refers to clerics who hold a major

or minor rank in the Church hierarchy. The Pope, cardinals and bishops are all prelates by reason of office. Prefects and vicars apostolic, abbots nullius, prelates nullius and apostolic administrators are also prelates by reason of their office, yet they cease to be prelates if they are not bishops when they lose the office held. Canons and certain of the officials of the Roman Curia are also considered prelates.

Religious who are either abbots, supreme moderators of their institutions or provincial superiors in clerical religious institutes or societies of apostolic life are likewise prelates.

There are also honorary prelates (Monsignori) who have no special jurisdiction or power. The various ranks of Monsignori are protonotaries apostolic, prelates of honor of His Holiness and chaplains of His Holiness.

The major prelates (the Pope, cardinals and bishops) all wear distinctive attire. Vicars and prefects apostolic, abbots and prelates nullius are permitted to dress as bishops. Honorary prelates wear a costume similar to that of bishops, and canons also have special dress.

Premoral Evil • In contemporary Roman Catholic proportionalist and consequentialist moral systems, an evil that is proportionate to the goods and evils effected by the act. When circumstances or realities intervene in an action to make this proportionate evil disproportionate to the goods and evils effected, the premoral evil then is transformed into a moral evil. Because of this feature, it is possible to assert both absolute moral prohibitions and requirements in some cases, and principles to which exceptions can be taken in other instances.

The difficulty with this doctrine of evil is that premoral evil has become an ill-defined and elusive reality that appears to be fluctuating and relative to the subjective assessments of the agent. Rather than being more in harmony with classical Catholic notions of the nature of evil, it appears to be closer to early modern voluntarist concepts of the nature of evil.

Presanctified, Mass of the • Term derived from the Greek (*leitourgia tou prohegiasmenou*), signifying a Eucharistic Liturgy without the consecration, with Hosts previously consecrated used for Communion. In the East it is attested from the late seventh century. It was used in the Byzantine Rite on most Lenten weekdays, eventually leading to its use only on the Wednesdays and Fridays of Lent. The theological rationale for this form of liturgy was that the Easter Season was the special time of the Paschal Eucharist and Lent was the time of Liturgies of the Word, looking toward the Easter celebration and its extension through the Easter Season. In the West it was used only on Good Friday, appearing first in the Gelasian Sacramentary; it was in use in Rome by the ninth century. The present Good Friday Liturgy is no longer associated with this term, although the Hosts for Communion at the afternoon liturgy, the Celebration of the Lord's Passion, are consecrated at the evening Mass of the Lord's Supper on Holy Thursday.

Presbyter • The word is from the Greek *presbyteros* and means "elder," with the connotation of one who oversees the life of a community. In the time of Jesus, the council of elders was an important feature in the organization and governance of Jewish communities. The practice of first-century Judaism is rooted in the Old Testament, where we learn that "elders" (Hebrew, *zaken*) represented the entire people (Ex 3:16; 4:29), acted on their behalf (Ex 17:5ff.; 18:13), and represented the

people when covenanting with David (2 Sm 5:3). The earliest Christian communities were composed mostly of converts from Judaism who simply adapted patterns and models of leadership from their Jewish sociological environments (e.g., synagogues). In Acts 11:30 and 15:23, we see that the Jerusalem Church was partially governed by the system of elders. In the early Church, pastoral responsibilities given to "elders" appear to overlap with those of "overseers" (Greek, *episcopoi* or "bishops"); in certain texts the two terms appear interchangeable (e.g., Acts 20:17ff.; Phil 1:1; Ti 1:5, 7). Eventually, by as early as A.D. 110, "bishop" became restricted to the leader of the elders; elders were representatives of the bishop and assisted in carrying out the bishop's increasing pastoral responsibilities. The elders eventually took on the roles which are today assumed by priests.

Presbyterian Churches • The term "presbyterian" refers to governance by presbyters, which is an important element in the polity of the Christian denominational bodies that have adopted this appellation. Although originally claiming this to be the authentic form of Christian polity as described in the New Testament, Presbyterians now generally admit the scriptural warrant and legitimacy of episcopal and congregational forms of church order. There is disagreement among churches of Presbyterian polity as to whether both ministers and elders are to be considered presbyters.

In doctrine, Presbyterian churches hearken to the teachings of John Calvin (1509-1564), although most of the American and British branches trace their origins to the Scottish Reformation led by John Knox (1513-1572). All Presbyterian churches take the Westminster Confession and Catechism (1643) as their rule of faith, although disagreements as to its proper interpretation have been the source of divisions within Presbyterianism. Sunday worship is simple in form, with emphasis upon the reading of the Bible and the sermon. Weekly celebration of the Lord's Supper is rare, and a quarterly or twice-yearly pattern of celebration is more common.

The Presbyterian Church (U.S.A.) is the largest body of Presbyterians in the U.S., comprised of northern and southern branches.

Presbyterorum Ordinis • Issued on December 7, 1965, *Presbyterorum Ordinis*, the Decree on the Ministry and Life of Priests, was written "with the aim of giving more effective support to the ministry of priests and making better provision for their life in the often vastly changed circumstances of the pastoral and human scene" (PO 1). Priests have been given a share in Christ's ministry, through their ordination by a bishop, to offer sacrifice and forgive sins, and "because it is joined with the episcopal order the office of priests shares in the authority by which Christ himself builds up and sanctifies and rules his Body" (PO 2). The priest is to be attached to his bishop with charity and obedience; he is to cooperate with his brother priests for the building up of the Church; and he is to promote the role of the laity in the mission of the Church. Because priests are consecrated to God not only by Baptism, but in a special way by their ordination, they are to use every means available to attain greater holiness so that their ministry will be more effective: they are to make the word of God part of their own lives; they are encouraged to celebrate the Eucharist daily; they are to give themselves to prayer and the administration of the sacraments, especially Penance; and they are to seek "not what is to their own advantage but what will benefit the many for salvation" (PO 13).

Priestly celibacy is to be "highly esteemed" (PO 16) as being particularly helpful to the mission of the priest. It is recommended by the example of Christ Himself, and it shows their willingness "to be dedicated with undivided loyalty to the task entrusted to them" (PO 16). This decree confirms the law of celibacy in the Latin Church, although it acknowledges that the nature of the priesthood does not demand it, and those priests who are lawfully married are exhorted "to persevere in their holy vocation and continue to devote their lives fully and generously to the flock entrusted to them" (PO 16).

Finally, priests are reminded that even in the midst of the difficulties they face in carrying out the ministry entrusted to them, "they are never alone but are supported by the almighty power of God," and "they have their brothers in the priesthood and indeed the faithful of the entire world, as allies" (PO 22).

Presbytery • This is derived directly from the Greek "presbyter" or elder. The early Christians did not want the priesthood which they had received from Christ to be confused with the Judaic priesthood of Aaron or Levi, nor did they want any connection whatsoever with the many types of pagan priests and priestesses which were found around them, so they adopted this word early in the life of the Church to refer to their priests (cf. Acts 15:2, 6; Jas 5:14).

(1) As such, the term "presbytery" refers to the part of the Church set aside for the exclusive use of the clergy. This is particularly so in cathedral churches where the priests gather around the bishop. (2) In ancient times, "presbytery" also used to designate the senate of priests which assisted the diocesan bishop in the

government of his diocese. (3) In some places this term is used to refer to the house where the clergy of a parish or institute live, what in the United States is usually referred to as a "rectory."

Prescription • A legal method of acquiring or losing a subjective right or means of freeing oneself of an obligation, primarily through the passage of time. Prescription has a number of applications in canon law (cf. Canons 197-199).

Prescription is accepted as a means of acquiring property. If property or goods are possessed in good faith for a period of time, the person possessing them can claim title of ownership. Since the Code does not stipulate how long a thing should be possessed, reference must be made to the civil law which governs acquisition of title by prescription (cf. Canon 1268).

Applied to criminal action in the Code, prescription means a statute of limitations. A criminal action is extinguished by prescription, that is, it cannot be pursued after three years have passed since the offense took place, or if in reference to a habitual or continuous offense, the day when it ceased. There are certain exceptions to this rule. These include offenses reserved to the Congregation for the Doctrine of the Faith, offenses not punished in common law but for which particular law has set a different period of time for prescription and four specific offenses mentioned in the canons (cf. Canon 1362).

The offenses of attempted marriage by a cleric (Canon 1394), concubinage or sexual relations with a minor by a cleric (Canon 1395), murder, abduction, kidnapping or mutilation (Canon 1397) and abortion (Canon 1398) have a prescription period of five years. This means that, in spite of any automatic penalties incurred which are not subject to prescription, additional penalties may not be imposed after the period of prescription has elapsed.

If a person is found guilty of an ecclesiastical crime but the judge has failed to notify him of the penalty within three years of the day upon which the sentence became a fully adjudged matter, the penalty cannot be applied (cf. Canon 1363).

Presence of God • Since everything depends for its continued existence on God Who is the source and conserver of all things in existence, God's presence in the universe is in the first place directly causal. The reality of this presence is captured in the term "omnipresence" which is attributed to God. The theological tradition has drawn a careful distinction between this universal causal presence of God and His personal presence to those who, through Jesus Christ, are His adopted sons and daughters in grace. By enabling human beings to live and function at a new level — the "supernatural" level — God makes possible a presence which is described as the indwelling of the Blessed Trinity. This is a strictly personal presence in which the Triune God makes Himself known and loved in His fully personal reality to the created human person.

"Divine indwelling" represents not a new presence on God's part over and above His "omnipresence," but a transformation of the human person who is then able to be engaged with God in His tripersonal reality. It is not that God becomes more present to us, but that we become more fully present to Him in knowledge and love. This presence of the Triune God in grace will give way to an even more intense form of presence to God in the beatific vision when we shall be perfectly united with the community of the Father, Son and Holy Spirit and drawn into the inner life of the uncreated, as fully as is possible for creatures.

Presence, Real • A doctrine of the Faith that the Body and Blood of Jesus Christ remain truly present under the consecrated species of bread and wine during and after the celebration of the Eucharist. This Real Presence of Christ in the Blessed Sacrament forms the basis of the practice of the reservation and the veneration of the sacrament in the tabernacle.

Presentation of the Blessed Virgin Mary • A feast celebrated on November 21, derived from the reference in the apocryphal Book of James describing the Presentation of Mary in the Temple when she was three years old. Origins of this feast can be traced to the East in the eighth century; in the West it made its appearance only in the Middle Ages. In 1585 Pope Sixtus V made it a feast of the universal Church. The Mass formula in the Missal of 1570 assigns a special Collect to the general Mass Proper of feasts of the Blessed Virgin, with the reference to the Presentation to be inserted into the Preface of Our Lady. In the present reform of the liturgy, this feast is ranked as a memorial, containing a special Collect (not from the previous Missal).

President • A current appellation for the celebrant of Mass, an unfortunate rendering of the Latin verb *praecedere* as a noun. The Missal of Paul VI often uses the word "priest" or "celebrant," to which some liturgists and theologians object, because they see all Christians as celebrants in the universal royal priesthood of all the baptized. Therefore, others offer the word "presider," which can also cover those celebrations which do not need a priest. However, the traditional term "celebrant" is normative, judging from the usage of Roman documents.

Presidential Prayers • The three principal prayers offered by the presiding priest celebrant in the name of the assembly, which are "proper" to each Mass, that is, taken from the special Mass formulary appointed for the day, as opposed to presidential prayers that form part of the "ordinary" of the Mass, e.g., the Eucharistic prayer, prayer for peace, invitation to Communion: all of which are also "presidential," in that they are recited by the presiding priest.

The three variable "presidential prayers" are the Opening Prayer (traditionally known also as the "Collect"), the Prayer over the Gifts (formerly known as the "Secret," because the celebrant prayed all but the ending silently), and the Prayer after Communion (or simply "Postcommunion").

Press, Catholic: See **Catholic Press**

Presumed Death • A common term for a process contained in the Code of Canon Law whereby a person is issued a decree of freedom to marry based on the presumed death of a spouse. This process is invoked when there is no official confirmation of the death. The decree is issued by a diocesan bishop after he has reached moral certitude from depositions of witnesses, hearsay or other indications that the person is dead. Unlike many civil law jurisdictions, the mere passage of a specified number of years does not constitute presumed death (Canon 1707).

Presumption • An affirmation of the truth or falsehood of a probable fact based on probable reasoning in the absence of actual certainty of the truth or falsehood of the matter at issue. There are two kinds of presumption in canon law: presumption of law and presumption of fact.

A presumption of law is a rule of law established by the law itself which holds that a specific matter be considered true or valid unless the contrary is demonstrated by objective evidence. Some presumptions of law allow proofs to the contrary. Perhaps the best known is the presumption favoring the validity of marriage. Once consent has been duly exchanged by persons capable of doing so, it is presumed that the marriage is valid. This presumption can be overturned by evidence to the contrary, which is precisely what happens in marriage tribunals when declarations of nullity are granted. Perhaps the most commonly known legal presumption of law is that a person accused of a crime is presumed innocent until proven guilty. Other kinds of presumptions of law admit no proof to the contrary. For example, if one party to a marriage has died, the law protects the marriage and allows no direct action against its validity.

A presumption of fact is a probable conjecture about an uncertain matter. Presumptions of fact are based on certain and determined facts which are directly related to the issue. As such, presumptions of fact are a vital source of proof in canonical and civil trials. In certain kinds of trials, for instance, the primary source of proof may be official documents. The judge presumes the truth of a duly signed and notarized public document, upon which he bases his decision. In other kinds of trials, testimony of witnesses is a major source of obtaining facts about the controversy. Depending on the credibility of the witnesses and their testimony, the judge (or jury) arrives at a presumption that the point of controversy is either true or that it cannot be proven to be true (cf. Canons 1584-1586).

Prevenient Grace • Prevenient grace stands at the beginning of our justification. It is the actual grace that stirs us to turn to God by inspiring us to recognize Him as our true good and salvation. Although justification cannot begin without

prevenient grace, the person to whom it is offered is free to accept or reject it. The mystery of grace is such that the failure to accept it is a human failure, while the capacity to accept it is a divine gift. In Christian teaching, support for the role of prevenient grace is found in the Scripture which teaches that even the beginnings of salvation are a free gift from God and in no way a human attainment (cf. Rom 8:30). The importance of this doctrine was seen vividly in the controversy provoked by the Pelagian heresy and the doctrine of prevenient grace was given its first theological formulation by St. Augustine.

Pride • In traditional Catholic moral teaching, the sin of pride is the first of the seven capital, mortal or deadly sins. As distinct from the holy recognition that one's self-worth is grounded in existence derived from God and His goodness, "pride" signals the taking or accepting of glory, attention, credit, honor, distinction not based on what is true or just. Pride involves a self-centered and perverse sense of self-love and self-esteem, even in its more subtle forms. Pride is believed to be the reason why angels rebelled from God and why humanity fell from original grace (Gn 3:1-9; Sir 3:17-28; Jb 21:14-16; Lk 19:1-10). As Sacred Scripture makes abundantly clear, in "pride" one rejects dependency on God (Sir 10:12-13; Prv 4:23; Jb 21:14-16; Mt 12:34).

Prie-Dieu • A bench found in many churches primarily intended for kneeling at private devotions. Resembling a wooden desk with armrests, its present form dates from the seventeenth century.

Priest • The priest, or presbyter, is a member of one of the three orders of ordained ministry in the Church (the others being the diaconate and the episcopacy). The chief role of priests is to offer sacrifice.

In the Eucharistic Sacrifice, they act in the person of Christ and thus join "the offerings of the faithful to the sacrifice of Christ their Head. . ." and "in the sacrifice of the Mass they make present again and apply . . . the unique sacrifice . . . of Christ offering himself once for all a spotless victim to the Father" (LG 28). This Vatican II document adds, "In virtue of the sacrament of orders, in the image of Christ the supreme and eternal priest. . . they are consecrated to preach the Gospel and shepherd the faithful, as well as to celebrate divine worship as true priests of the New Testament" (LG 28).

Priesthood, Ministerial: See **Priest**

Priesthood of the Faithful • By virtue of their Baptism, all Christians have a sacerdotal function and dignity. With Christ the Priest as their Head, they offer worship, sacrifice and glory to God. Their role in the Eucharistic celebration reflects their priestly function most clearly. Here they participate with the leader of the celebration — a member of the order of the priesthood — in joining themselves to the Sacrifice of Christ. This action embraces and draws up into itself all the sacrifices and offerings of their lives.

Along with Vatican II, it is important to note that while the ministerial priesthood and the priesthood of all believers are grounded in the one priesthood of Jesus Christ, "they differ essentially and not only in degree" (LG 10).

Priests, Decree on the Ministry and Life of: See **Presbyterorum Ordinis**

Priests, Decree on the Training of: See **Optatam Totius**

Priests' Associations • The Fathers of the Second Vatican Council, out of their concern for the brotherly bond and cooperation which should exist among priests, encouraged the formation of clerical associations in *Presbyterorum Ordinis*, the Decree on the Ministry and Life of Priests. As *Presbyterorum Ordinis*, n. 8, makes clear, this serves not only to strengthen the spiritual lives of priests, but also helps to build up the body of Christ.

While the right of clergy to form associations was implicitly recognized in the 1917 Code of Canon Law, that right is outlined specifically in the 1983 Code (Canon 278). The purposes of such associations include: "pursuing ends which befit the clerical state" (Canon 278, n. 1), and "to foster holiness in the exercise of the ministry by means of a suitable and properly approved style of life and by means of fraternal assistance, and which promote the unity of the clergy among themselves and with their own bishop" (Canon 278, n. 2). The third part of this canon cautions clergy to "refrain from establishing or participating in associations whose ends or activity cannot be reconciled with the obligations proper to the clerical state or which could hinder the diligent fulfillment of the duty entrusted to them by competent ecclesiastical authority."

Priests' Councils • Priests' councils, or presbyterial councils, as they are also known, are representative bodies of the presbyterate of the diocese, made up of *ex officio* members and members elected by the priests of the diocese. Priests' councils are mandatory for each diocese.

Those eligible to vote in priests' councils and to be elected as delegates include all secular priests incardinated in the diocese and other priests, including religious, who exercise some ministry in the diocese.

Although priests' councils are consultative in nature, in certain cases the bishop is obliged to consult them, e.g., on the advisability of calling a diocesan synod, modification of parishes, norms for parish councils, construction or sale of a church, fixing the amount of stole fees and the imposition of a diocesan tax. In one case only is the bishop to obtain the consent of his council, and that is the requirement that he submit a list of pastors to the priests' council, which in turn selects certain ones to serve as advisors to the bishop for cases of the removal of pastors.

Delegates to the priests' council serve for a set term. When the diocese becomes vacant, the council ceases to exist (cf. Canons 495-502).

Primacy of the Pope • The office, rank or character of the Pope, who has supreme and universal jurisdiction. He is the successor of St. Peter, the supreme legislator, ruler, judge and teacher.

Primate • At one time, a primate was a bishop or archbishop who had authority over all bishops and metropolitans of an area or nation. Usually the primate was the bishop or archbishop of the oldest diocese or archdiocese in the area covered.

At the present time, the only primate in the Catholic Church with such jurisdiction and authority is the Supreme Pontiff. The title is purely honorary in every other instance, and where it exists, it refers to the bishop or archbishop of the oldest see (cf. Canon 438).

Primatial Liturgy • At one time many of the primatial dioceses or archdioceses of the Latin Rite had their own unique liturgical uses. Most of these remain relatively insignificant in the context of the overall history of the Liturgy of the Latin Church. The rite associated with four primatial sees endured into the present century: Lyons (France), Braga (Portugal), Toledo (Spain) and Milan (Italy). The Rite of

Milan, also known as the Ambrosian Rite, is still in use in the churches in that city.

The liturgies of the primatial sees were actually variations on the Roman Liturgy, with certain differences in the rituals of the Mass and other sacraments.

Prime • Literally "first," from the Latin title of this section of the Divine Office, *ad (horam) primam*, "at the first (hour of the day). With Lauds as the principal and formal morning prayer sung at dawn, Prime developed in monastic communities as an additional prayer-community meeting held before the morning work period. Included in Prime was the reading of the martyrology (or saint of the day), a passage from the Holy Rule of the monastery and (presumably after the work assignments) a prayer that God "prosper for us the work of our hands." Prime was the morning counterpart of Compline, which added another "Hour" of prayer before bedtime to the daily cycle of monastic prayer, since the official evening office, Vespers (corresponding to Lauds) would have been sung at dusk.

In more recent times, especially among parish clergy and active religious, it was common to "anticipate" the nocturnal Office of Matins and the dawn Office of Lauds in the afternoon or evening of the day before, and begin the new day's cycle of prayer with Prime. In Vatican II's revision of the Divine Office, now called the Liturgy of the Hours, Prime was suppressed and its obligation abrogated for the universal Church as being an unnecessary duplication that detracted from the traditional importance of the more ancient Office of Lauds. Compline was retained, primarily as a private prayer to be recited before retiring. Some monastic groups continue to use the Office of Prime, and the newly issued *Psalterium Monasticum* (Monastic Psalter) makes provision for its celebration.

Principalities • In the New Testament, "principalities" refers to one of several metaphysical beings which are like angelic beings quite hostile to God and humans. Along with the "principalities" (Greek, *archai*; Rom 8:38; 1 Cor 15:24; Eph 1:21; 3:10; 6:12; Col 1:16; 2:10, 15) are the "powers" (Greek, *dynameis*; Rom 8:38; 1 Cor 15:24; Eph 1:21; 1 Pt 3:22; 2 Thes 1:7); "cosmological powers" (Greek, *exousiai*; 1 Cor 15:24; Eph 1:21; 3:10; Col 2:15); "dominions" (Greek, *kuriotes*; Eph 1:21; Col 1:16) and "thrones" (Greek, *thronoi*; Col 1:16). The clarity of the New Testament witness helps us see that these beings were created through Christ and for Him (Col 1:16). Given their hostility to God and humans due to sin, Christ's ultimate rule over them (1 Cor 15:28; 1 Pt 3:22; etc.) expresses the reign of the Lord over all that is in the cosmos — a witness grounded in Old Testament texts and completely reaffirmed in the New Testament. This Lordship of Christ, which reveals God's tremendous plan of salvation in the conquering of sin and death at the cross, now takes place in the Church (Eph 3:10).

It must be observed that the principalities discussed above are to be distinguished from the good angels which bear the same name, traditionally listed as one of the nine choirs of angels.

For further reading: Clinton E. Arnold, "Principalities and Powers," *Anchor Bible Dictionary*, 5:467.

Prior • The title of a superior in some religious houses. Benedictines and Cistercians distinguish among three types of prior: the claustral prior, or second in charge in an abbey, whose authority is delegated by the abbot; the simple or obedientiary prior, who rules a dependent priory and who is appointed by the motherhouse abbey; and the conventual prior, who is the independent superior of a monastery which does not have the status of an abbey. Some orders also use the title of prior to designate the superiors of their conventual priories, which are subject to a prior provincial and, ultimately, to the superior over the whole order, the prior general (called the master general in the Dominican Order). Carthusians have only conventual priors and a prior general.

Prioress • The title of a woman religious superior whose office corresponds in general to that of a prior of equal rank among monks or friars.

Priory • A term used to designate the houses of most monastic orders, some mendicant orders and some modern, that are governed by a prior or prioress. The priories of the Benedictines, their branches and some other orders may be conventual (i.e., autonomous, with the right to elect their own superior, but without the status of an abbey) or they may be simple or obedientiary (dependencies of abbeys).

Priscillianism • A fourth-century heresy, attributed to Priscillian, a leader of an ascetic movement in Spain. In its developed form, it blends Manicheanism, Docetism and Modalism, denying both the preexistence and the humanity of Jesus. Priscillian himself was executed for heresy in A.D. 386, although it took condemnations from both the Council of Toledo (340) and the Council of Braza (563) to eliminate his ideas.

Private Mass • Term customarily used to describe a Mass celebrated by the priest with the assistance of a server, or alone. The rationale for this kind of celebration would be the devotion of the priest himself or to satisfy the obligation required by having taken a stipend for a Mass. The postconciliar revision of the liturgy does not speak of a private Mass; instead, the sacramentary contains an Order of Mass Without a Congregation.

The sections of the *General Instruction of the Roman Missal* which deal with such Masses are nn. 209-231. Of the texts in the new canon law which speak of this kind of celebration of Mass, the following apply to this form of celebration. Canon 837 cites the principle from *Sacrosanctum Concilium*, n. 27, that liturgical actions are communal actions by their very nature and that they "are to be celebrated in common with the presence and active participation of the faithful." Canon 906 states that "a priest may not celebrate without the participation of at least some member of the faithful, except for a just and reasonable cause." This prohibition has been in Church legislation since the twelfth century; the requirement of a server was reiterated in the 1917 Code, Canon 813. The *General Instruction of the Roman Missal* (n. 210), states that in a Mass without a congregation "the server takes the people's part to the extent possible." Canon 902 states that "priests may concelebrate the Eucharist unless the welfare of the Christian faithful requires or urges otherwise but with due regard for the freedom of each priest to celebrate the Eucharist individually, though not during the time when there is a concelebration in the same Church or oratory." (The second part of this canon derives from *Sacrosanctum Concilium*, n. 57, about concelebration.)

Privation • According to Canon 184, ecclesiastical office can be lost, among other ways, through a legal process of privation. Canon 196 specifies that privation entails a particular form of removal from office, this in punishment for an ecclesiastical offense. The 1983 Code of Canon Law, in contrast with the 1917 Code, places additional limitations on the ability of ecclesiastical authorities to deprive a person of office. Strictly speaking, privation can take place only in accord with the general rules on the penal process. As such, privation is seen as a serious punishment but one which should not, however, be confused with the also serious but more restricted action of suspension. In addition, if the office in question is that of pastor, certain other norms might be applicable for the valid removal of the individual from office (Canons 1740-1752). (Cf. Penalty, Ecclesiastical.)

Privilege • The term privilege in canon law is derived from the Latin roots meaning "private law." A privilege, then, is a special grant by ecclesiastical authority by which a favor is bestowed (Canon 76). These favors may be granted to either physical or juridic persons by those possessing legislative power in the Church, or by their delegates. As a practical matter, such persons are diocesan bishops, religious superiors and various dicasteries of the Roman Curia.

Because privileges are exceptions to law, they are to be interpreted narrowly (cf. Canon Law, Interpretation of), but on the other hand, they should be interpreted in such a way that the beneficiary actually receives some favor (Canon 77). Privileges are presumed to be perpetual although personal privileges cease with the death of the beneficiary, and privileges attached to certain things or places (such as indulgences) generally cease with the destruction of the thing or place (Canon 78). Privileges do not cease when the one who issued them leaves office, unless the privilege was granted "only for so long as the grantor wills it," or words to that effect (Canon 81). Nor do they cease through non-use (Canon 82), and one is in no way bound to use a privilege if it was granted solely for that one's use (Canon 80).

Canon 79 of the 1983 Code of Canon Law specifies that privileges can be revoked by the issuing authority following certain formalities. It must be noted that privileges, because they are always favors, do not create a right in the beneficiary to have that favor continued against the will of the issuing authority. Canon 4 adds, however, that privileges granted by the Holy See, if they were still in use, remained in place after the promulgation of the new Code, unless they had been specifically revoked by the Code. Canon 83 is careful to emphasize, however, that any privilege ceases when the issuing authority determines that its continuation would become harmful. Canon 84 additionally directs that one who abuses a privilege is to be warned of the danger of such abuse and, that failing, the privilege may be revoked. If the privilege was granted by the Holy See, the same is to be notified of the abuse so that appropriate action can be taken.

Privileges should not be confused with dispensations, in part because the latter arise from executive, and not from legislative, authority in the Church. Dispensations generally tend to operate in a more restricted manner than do privileges. (Cf. Rescript.)

Privilege of the Faith • The dissolution of a marriage between a baptized person and an unbaptized person by the Holy Father is known as the Privilege of the Faith. This process is also known as the Favor of the Faith or the Petrine Privilege.

It is so called because the dissolution is granted in order to favor the faith of a Catholic person. Originally, dissolution by Privilege of the Faith was granted to a convert to Catholicism who had been married to an unbaptized person. The Holy Father was petitioned to dissolve the marriage by virtue of his vicarious power over the natural bond of marriage. The first

such dissolution took place in 1923. The Privilege can now be granted to persons who had been married in the Catholic Church with a dispensation from disparity of cult. It is granted to Catholic petitioners, as well as to non-Catholic and even unbaptized petitioners who wish to marry in the Catholic Church.

The process is initiated on the diocesan level and consists primarily of demonstrating that at least one party to the marriage was never baptized while the marriage lasted. The case is then sent to the Holy See for final processing and presentation to the Holy Father.

Privileged Altar • Term used in the 1917 Code of Canon Law (Canons 916-918) to describe an altar where a plenary indulgence can be gained for a soul in purgatory by the fact that a Mass is offered for that intention at that altar. Privileged altars were suppressed with the publication of the Apostolic Constitution *Indulgentiarum Doctrina*, of Pope Paul VI, on indulgences (1967), norm 20.

Probabiliorism • A moral system which held that the more probable opinion of a number of morally acceptable opinions concerning the binding character of a law was to be accepted and promoted. One was free from the obligations of a law if the reasons for being freed from it were more probably true and authoritative than were the reasons for abiding by the law. Probabiliorism was a harsher and more rigorous system than was probabilism, for it held that even if it was probable that a law did not bind, one still had to abide by it. Only if the opinion in favor of release from the requirements of a law was more probable than that holding the law to be valid would the probabiliorist allow one to be released from an obligation.

Probabilism • One of the many moral systems developed in the seventeenth century which held that a "probably" true, binding or correct law or moral viewpoint was to be permitted. The aim of probabilist reasoning was to give some relief to overburdened consciences, and it held that "a doubtful law does not bind in conscience." Probabilism asserted that liberty from a law was to be held in possession until the opposite was held to probably be the case. This opinion was considered to be too loose and ill-defined by systematic moral theologians later called rigorists, probabiliorists or equiprobabilists.

The difficulty with probabilism, a difficulty shared by all the moral systems, was that there was no objective criterion for determining whether a given law or moral obligation was probable, more probable or less probable. As a result, probabilism degenerated into voluntarism and experienced all of the problems involved in that system of moral analysis.

Pro-Cathedral • A church used as a temporary, or quasi-permanent, substitute for a diocesan cathedral, usually because the cathedral is too small or is in a location far removed from the majority of the diocesan population.

Process, Due: See **Due Process**

Process, Penal: See **Penal Process**

Procession, Divine • This term refers to the inner-Trinitarian origins of the Son and the Spirit. In its first and primary meaning, the term refers to the eternal procession of the Son from the Father (properly called generation) and the eternal procession of the Spirit from the Father and the Son (properly called spiration). According to Trinitarian doctrine, there is no distinction in God except that which arises by way of origin. So affirmation of the reality of divine processions remains fundamental to the Christian doctrine of the Trinity. Because of the processions there are relations, and the Persons are subsistent relations. Somewhat confusingly, the term "procession" has also come to refer to the attribute that distinguishes the Holy Spirit from the Father and the Son; their distinguishing attributes are paternity and filiation, respectively.

Processions • Sacred parades in which clergy and people move from one place to another. They may take place within a church or between churches, or outside a church or shrine. Reasons for processions vary from giving honor to God, the Blessed Mother or saints; to thank them; or to ask pardon for one's sins. Religious processions go back to the Old Testament times, recalling special events such as Passover. The clearest example of the use of processions as intrinsic to the Liturgy is during Holy Week. The procession with palm on Passion (Palm) Sunday from a location outside the church to the body of the church and the procession at the Easter Vigil from the blessing of the new fire to the proclamation of the *Exsultet* inside the church are prime examples of processions from outside to inside churches. The procession for the transfer of the Blessed Sacrament to the Repository on Holy Thursday, to venerate the Cross on Good Friday, or to and from the baptistery at the Easter Vigil, all exemplify processions from one part of the church building to another. According to Roman Catholic Church law, some liturgical processions are classified as ordinary, such as those for anniversaries or events. Still other processions are functional, such as funeral and offertory processions, or simply the entrance and recessional of the Mass.

Procurator • One who acts on behalf of another person or a group. The procedural law of the Church provides for the position of procurator to act on behalf of persons involved in judicial processes. To be appointed a procurator, a person must enjoy a good reputation and have attained his or her majority. It is not necessary that the person be a Catholic. In actual practice, the duties of the procurator are usually fulfilled by the advocate who represents a person (cf. Canons 1481-1490).

Procurator is also the title given to members of religious institutes and societies of apostolic life who are appointed by their superiors or elected to serve as representatives of their institutes or societies to the Holy See.

Profanity • Disrespectful use of the name of God. If this is done in anger or without thoughtfulness, it is venially sinful. But if deliberate or directed against God it can be seriously sinful, as it can be if it causes scandal.

Profession of Faith • A public act by which personal belief is outwardly manifested in the form of a recital of a creed giving witness to the community of the authentic belief by the person in the teachings of the Church. A common example familiar to all is the recitation of the Nicene Creed at Mass. By Divine law (the First Commandment) through the practice of the virtues of religion and piety arising from the gift and theological virtue of faith itself, one also professes one's faith by acting to defend it in the face of attack, insult toward God or the Church, contempt for religion or other serious moral derision. Failure to do so could readily convey the impression of assent and agreement with such attacks, leading to the sin of scandal to others and personal impiety.

The ultimate Profession of Faith is martyrdom, whereby an individual lays down his or her life to bear witness to the truth rather than deny it. Juridically, the Church specifies those who must make a Profession of Faith on occasion; for example, at Baptism, for or by the person to receive the sacrament; on the reception of a baptized non-Catholic into full communion as a Catholic; on the return to the Church by one who publicly renounced it.

Canon 883, in eight articles, provides a taxative list of those who are to make a Profession of Faith personally in accord with a formula approved by the Apostolic See. Among them are: those promoted to the cardinalatial dignity; all persons promoted to the episcopacy and those who are equivalent to a diocesan bishop; vicars general, episcopal vicars, judicial vicars and, at the beginning of their term of office: pastors, rectors of seminaries, and the professors of theology and philosophy in seminaries; those to be promoted to the order of diaconate; rectors of ecclesiastical or Catholic universities at the beginning of their term of office, as well as teachers, at the beginning of their term of office, who teach disciplines which deal with faith or morals in any university whatsoever. The law of the Church also specifies before whom the profession is to be made. The law does not oblige non-Catholics or those already holding offices or appointments at the time the revised Code of Canon Law went into effect.

Profession, Religious • By religious profession, the members of approved religious institutes in the Church undertake by public vow the observance of the three evangelical counsels (poverty, chastity and obedience) and thus are consecrated to God. Final or perpetual profession of vows constitutes one a full-fledged member of the religious institute. A period of temporary profession (usually three years, and no more than six, in duration) must precede perpetual profession.

Prokimenon • Versicles from the psalms chanted by the reader before the Epistle, in the Byzantine Rite.

Pro-life • The name for activities and attitudes that promote rather than negate life. The term was coined originally during the crisis caused by the 1973 Supreme Court decision legalizing abortion to describe opposition to such destruction of the life of the unborn child. Later, the term "pro-life" was expanded to include affirmation of life in all its stages and facets from conception to natural death.

Pro-life is the opposite of the view that only "quality" life is worthwhile and that any human life that is unwanted or likely to be severely painful should not be fostered by society but rather cut off, as in abortion and euthanasia. (Cf. Consistent Life Ethic.)

Promise of God • The term expressing the covenant which God established with the Israelites through Abraham and its subsequent fulfillment in the Person of Jesus Christ. The law is fulfilled in Christ, Who is the sole heir of the inheritance known as the "glory of God." If one wishes to inherit the kingdom, one must be united to Christ; hence, believers have the opportunity to become "coheirs" with Christ (Acts 20:32; Rom 8:17; Gal 3:26-29; 4:1-11). To share the promise of the kingdom is to be filled with the life of the Father through the Son in the Holy Spirit (2 Cor 1:22; Eph 1:14; Heb 9:15).

Promoter of the Faith (Adjutor Fidei) • The "Promoter of the Faith" is an older term for what today we would call the Promoter of Justice, or that official who acts in a sort of "district attorney" manner on behalf of the Church in matters affecting the common good of the diocese.

The term "Promoter of the Faith" is still encountered, moreover, when dealing with the causes of saints, and refers to that official whose task it is to assure the objectivity, integrity and balance of the investigation. Sometimes nicknamed therein "God's advocate," the Promoter of the Faith, because of his duty to raise all reasonable objections which could be lodged against the canonization of a particular Servant of God, has also been called the "Devil's advocate," giving rise to the popular secular expression of a similar connotation.

Promoter of Justice • An official of a Church tribunal. He acts as a kind of prosecuting attorney in all penal trials and in contentious trials if the public good is at stake. The promoter may be a cleric or layman with a doctorate or licentiate in canon law (cf. Canons 1430-1436).

Promulgation • The method whereby laws are made known to the community. The ordinary method of promulgation of general ecclesiastical laws is by publication in the *Acta Apostolicae Sedis*. Other methods of promulgation may be specified, however.

A law does not have force from the date of promulgation unless this is specified. Ordinarily, universal law goes into effect three months from the date it was published, and diocesan legislation takes effect one month from the date of its publication (cf. Canons 7-8).

Pro-Nuncio • A pro-nuncio is a papal legate or ambassador to a country that has diplomatic relations with the Holy See. The pro-nuncio represents the Holy Father to the secular government of the country. He also represents him to the Catholic Church in the same country.

A pro-nuncio differs from a nuncio only in that he is not automatically the dean of the diplomatic corps of the country to which he is assigned.

Proofs, Judicial • The procedural law of the Church, like that of secular legal systems, contains specific provisions for proofs or demonstrations of dubious or controverted facts. The law refers to the admissibility of different kinds of proofs and the weight to be given them. Full proof is that which demonstrates the issue at hand, and semi-full proof is that which does not completely demonstrate the issue but which must be joined with other sources of proof.

The basic sources of proof are the following: documents, declaration of the parties, testimony of witnesses, testimony of expert witnesses and presumptions. The judge has the discretionary power of admitting or rejecting proofs submitted by the parties.

The kind and amount of proof that is sufficient depends on the type of case. In cases involving the private good (property issues), a confession of one of the principal parties suffices. In cases involving the public good, however, that is, cases that have an effect on the community (e.g., marriage cases), more proof is necessary.

In some types of cases, documents alone are sufficient to establish proof of the controverted issue, e.g., invalidity of marriage due to an undispensed impediment.

The question of proofs is particularly important for those involved in marriage nullity proceedings. Since these cases are cases involving the public good and the status of persons, the declarations of the parties themselves cannot constitute full proof of nullity. These statements have probative force, however. To demonstrate full proof, the declarations of the parties or even of only one party must be thoroughly corroborated by other elements of proof. These other elements can constitute any type of proof admitted by the judge and are not restricted to testimony of witnesses. By using presumptions and other indicators, such as testimonials of the credibility of the party or parties, it is possible to arrive at full proof of nullity while having only the testimony of the principals as the primary source of proof.

The testimony of witnesses is usually required in cases involving the public good. There are different kinds of witnesses, depending on the type and source of their information. A witness *de scientia* is comparable to an eyewitness or a material witness. This person has first-hand knowledge of the matter under consideration. A character witness does not have this first-hand knowledge and may know nothing about it, but he or she is able to testify to the good character and credibility of the principal party or parties. Finally, there are witnesses who testify to what they heard about the controversy from either a third party or from public rumor.

An expert witness is one who studies the information in the case and offers his opinion or conclusions in the area of his expertise.

Finally, we come to presumptions, which are an important source of proof in any case. A presumption is a conjecture about an uncertain matter, arrived at by the judge because of his study of the facts and indicators in the case. For instance, if a man kept a mistress before his marriage and returned to the mistress on a regular basis after the marriage, the judge could rightly presume that the man had no intention of observing the obligation of fidelity. Similarly, if a person had been repeatedly committed by the courts to mental institutions, the judge, even without documentary proof of mental illness, could presume that the person suffered from some form of serious psychic disorder. An expert witness can be of great help in studying the circumstances of a case in order to assist the judge in arriving at a presumption (Canons 1526-1586).

Propaganda, Congregation of: See **Evangelization of Peoples, Congregation for the**

Propagation of the Faith and Sacred Congregation for the Evangelization of Peoples: See **Evangelization of Peoples, Congregation for the**

Propagation of the Faith, Society for the • This society is an international organization founded under the inspiration of Pauline Jaricot in Lyons, France, in 1822, with the goal of assisting missions and missionaries with prayers and financial aid. Today it serves as the organ of the Holy See for collection everywhere of alms and their distribution among all Catholic missions. Its United States headquarters are located in New York City.

Property, Ecclesiastical • Real or movable property or goods owned by an ecclesiastical juridic person. Ecclesiastical property can include land, buildings, works of art, vehicles and any other kind of material goods. It can also be nontangible goods, such as rights, leases, trusts and the like. Ecclesiastical property does not belong to any individual but to the juridic person. It cannot be disposed of or altered without following the process outlined in the canons, which includes permissions from certain authorities, depending on the nature of the property and its worth.

Prophecy • The expression and deliverance of a message from God which constitutes a true judgment of the present, in the light of the future, arrived at in obedience to the will and under the authority of God. In common parlance, "prophecy" is often synonymous with "prediction of the future." But in the Christian and scriptural sense, prophecy refers to any message from God. Sometimes the message may predict future events. But more often prophecy is a divinely inspired word about the present, in the light of God's purposes for the whole of history.

For further reading: H. B. Huffmon et al., "Prophecy," *Anchor Bible Dictionary*, 5:477-502.

Prophet • In the biblical sense, a prophet is an envoy of God, often critical of society's ungodly ways. Prophets are called by God to speak in His name (e.g., "The word of the LORD came to me. . ." [Jer 1:4]). Their office was publicly recognized in Israel. Their task was

The prophet Joel

to call people back to their Covenant with God, by proclaiming the commandments and identifying transgressions. They also challenged their hearers to repent and change their sinful ways, and interpreted the events of Israel's history in this light.

Typical of prophetic utterance would be moral corrections, threats of divine punishment and the element of hope for Israel's salvation. The prophets were aware of the dynamic element of life, and they knew that they must make the world holier, lest it and they become worse. They were more concerned with present reality than with predicting the future.

There are eighteen prophetic books in the Old Testament. The four "major prophets," so called because of the length of their books, are Isaiah, Jeremiah, Ezekiel and Daniel. The classic New Testament prophet is John the Baptist, whose ministry is described in each of the Gospels. Jesus Himself is called a prophet (e.g., Mt 16:14, Lk 7:16, etc.), and although He does not use it of Himself, He never refuses the title.

Both Old and New Testaments are replete with references to "false prophets," an expression often directed toward the cult or guild prophets presumably organized by the king as his court functionaries. Many of the true prophets met violent deaths, so difficult were their messages of repentance to hear.

Prophetical Literature of the Bible • The Hebrew Bible is divided into three parts: the Torah, the Prophets and the Writings. By far the longest of the three parts is the Prophets. The formation of all the parts was gradual. The prophetical section was completed and closed sometime between 400 and 200 B.C.

The prophetical literature is divided into the writings of the four major prophets (Isaiah, Jeremiah, Ezekiel and Daniel) and the twelve minor prophets (Hosea, Joel,

Amos, Obadiah, Jonah, Micah, Nahum, Habakkuk, Zephaniah, Haggai, Zechariah and Malachi). They are called major and minor prophets because of the length of their writings and not because of any distinction between them.

For further reading: Bruce Vawter, C.M., "Introduction to Prophetic Literature," *New Jerome Biblical Commentary,* 186-200.

Prophetism • In the first place, the special charism which God imparts to certain individuals and which thus empowers them to be spokespersons of His revelation. Thus, Moses, the prophets, John the Baptist, the Apostles and other singular figures in the Scriptures are the recipients of this gift. Although in many ways Christ resembles the prophets, His being and the character of His revelation utterly transcend these figures. Theologically speaking, the formal property of prophetism is that the prophet delivers not his own message but the word of God. Naturally, the prophet's gifts and character are not bypassed: They provide the vehicle by which God's word is communicated. But the substance of the message is of divine origin. Thus, it is in connection with the charism of prophetism that the divine inspiration of the human authors of the Scriptures is to be understood. With the conclusion of the apostolic revelation, manifestations of prophetic gifts must be judged with reference to Scripture, Tradition and the Magisterium.

Proportionalism • The moral theological doctrine which holds that the moral quality of an action is determined by whether the evils brought about by proposed action are proportionate to the goods the action effects. If the goods effected by the action are not in proportion to the evils caused, then the action is evil, but if they are, then the action is morally good, according to proportionalists. Proportionalism differs from consequentialism, in that it holds that the inherent moral quality of the action must be considered when determining the relevant proportions, and the intentions of the agent can have a bearing on the goods or evils effected by the act.

However, proportionalism shares many of the problems inherent to consequentialism and utilitarianism. The greatest problem is that of determining what effects are to be considered relevant to these judgments. Does one merely include short-range effects, or long-range ones as well? What level of value does one attribute to the act itself, its effects and consequences? Proportionalist theorists have yet to offer an objective criterion for determining when evils are proportionate or disproportionate, and some have admitted that this cannot be done. The result has been that proportionalism has lost intellectual credibility for many because it appears as a system of rationalizing one's subjective moral prejudices and biases.

Proportionalism legitimately aims at resisting deontological tendencies in moral analysis and promoting the role of prudence in these judgments. However, it does not give adequate consideration to the central role of the intrinsic nature of human acts, and it too readily subordinates this role to the role and importance of consequences of actions. Proportionalism also leaves little if any room for the development of the virtues, and some have criticized it for merely providing rationalizations for one's preferences and prejudices.

Propositions, Condemned • A set of eighty liberal and modernist propositions designated as contrary to the Catholic Faith by Pope Pius IX in the encyclical *Quanta Cura* in 1864. Included in this "Syllabus of Errors" were pantheism, naturalism, rationalism, latitudinarianism, socialism, communism and liberalism. Other condemned propositions concerned interpretation of the Bible, Church-state relations, papal temporal authority, Christian marriage and liberal political views.

Proselyte • The noun is from the Greek *proselytos*, literally "stranger" or "one who approaches." Claims about God's universal supremacy, as *the* Creator, the *only* God, etc., all naturally flow into the notion of mission to others. We find such convictions throughout the Old Testament (Is 42:6ff.; 45:14ff.; 56:1-8; 66:19; Jonah; etc.). Thus anyone who converts to the one true God and becomes a Jew in the full and legal sense is a proselyte. In classical Judaism, conversion included circumcision, a ritual bath and the offering of a sacrificial victim. From the second century B.C. to around the fourth century A.D., many Gentiles were attracted to elements of Judaism (e.g., monotheism, sexual ethics, Sabbath observance, knowledge of God through ancient writings, etc.). The New Testament offers limited evidence concerning Jewish attempts to convert Gentiles (Mt 23:15); many converts to Judaism became Christians (e.g., Acts 6:5).

For further reading: Paul F. Stuehrenberg, "Proselyte," *Anchor Bible Dictionary*, 5:503-505.

Proskomide • Literally, the credence, or table for offerings. In the Eastern Church, the same as the Altar of Prothesis. Also, the Office of Preparation performed at that altar.

Prosphora • The offering of the people for the celebration of the Divine Liturgy of the Byzantine Rite. In a more limited sense, the loaf out of which the priest will carve the portion to be consecrated. (Cf. Antidoron.)

Prostitution • The selling of one's body for sexual relations for either money or other goods. Prostitution is immoral because sexual relations find their moral meaning in marriage as an expression of permanent, faithful and life-giving love. Prostitution is contrary to the sacramental character of marriage because it is contrary to the good of marital fidelity. Prostitution is also contrary to the requirements of the common good, as the human person is biologically oriented toward monogamy.

Prostitution can increase the spread of sexually transmitted diseases, and to protect innocent members of society, prostitution can be legitimately prohibited by civil authorities. It also threatens marital unity and harmony, and to protect the rights of spouses and children, the state has the moral right to resist its spread.

Although prostitution by men is becoming more prevalent, it is usually practiced by women. Prostitution is more common, then, when it can exploit the disadvantages many women suffer in comparison to the physical and financial strengths of men.

Protestant • The name "Protestant" originated with the Second Diet of Speyer (1529), when several princes and cities drew up an objection to the reversal of a previous decision to allow each prince or city to decide between Catholicism and Lutheranism. The sense of "to protest" is not just negative but also means "to witness."

Because Protestantism, Roman Catholicism and the Eastern Orthodox Churches are expressions of Christian Faith, they agree in the essentials of Christian Faith, such as belief in Jesus Christ, the Trinity, the New Testament, salvation, resurrection and Christian love. However, Protestantism differs from Roman Catholicism in several ways, such as: (1) justification by faith alone; (2) grace alone as sufficient for salvation; (3) the primacy of the Bible; (4) the Lord's Supper; (5) the number of sacraments; (6) papal authority; (7) the position of the Virgin Mary.

Protestantism • The struggle for power between the spiritual and temporal authorities, aided by the growing spirit of nationalism in England, France, Germany and Bohemia, had created an anti-papalism and anti-clericalism in the late Middle Ages. The failure of the Church's general councils of the fifteenth century to reform Church abuses, such as the worldliness of the clergy, selling of indulgences and the decadence of monasticism, caused the Augustinian monk Martin Luther to post his ninety-five theses on the church door in Wittenberg, Germany, in 1517. Eventually others followed in their rebellion against the Roman Catholic Church, including John Calvin in France, Ulrich Zwingli in Switzerland and King Henry VIII of England. The position of the Catholic Church was set forth in the twenty-five sessions of the Council of Trent (1545-1563), which stated the Catholic position on doctrines denied by Protestants.

Today the major groups in Protestantism are: Baptists, Methodists, Lutherans, Presbyterians, Born-Again Christians, Episcopalians, Disciples of Christ and Quakers. (Cf. under separate listings.)

Prothesis • In the Eastern Church, the preparation of the offerings, performed on a side altar. Also, the side altar itself.

Protocanonical Books of Scripture • Those books which were admitted to the Canon of Scripture with little or no debate, having achieved canonical status early (called in the ancient tradition *homologoumena*, or agreed upon) and distinguished from the deuterocanonical books, which were under discussion for a while until doubts about their canonicity could be resolved (earlier called *antilogomena*, or disputed, *amphiballomena*, or doubtful).

Protoevangelium • The term refers to Genesis 3:15, where God promises Eve that the serpent who deceived her will be crushed by Eve's offspring. With the birth of Christ (Eve's offspring) and with Christ's victorious resurrection, there is a total defeat of the powers of darkness, and the promise of the "first gospel" (protoevangelium) is fulfilled.

Protomartyr • A title most often given to St. Stephen, the first martyr (Acts 7:60) or to the first martyr of a particular country. The feast of St. Stephen is celebrated in the Latin Church on the day after Christmas indicating the close relationship between Christmas as the feast celebrating "the beginning of our redemption" (Prayer over the Gifts, Vigil Mass) and the entrance of Christ's followers "into eternal glory" (Opening Prayer, feast of St. Stephen).

Protonotary Apostolic • A protonotary apostolic *de numero* is one of the seven minor prelates who form a college of notaries for the Roman Curia. Papal documents are signed by a protonotary apostolic.

The title of supernumerary protonotary apostolic is also conferred as an honor on priests who are not part of the Curia. As such, it is the highest honorary title that is awarded; the bearer is to be addressed as "Reverend Monsignor" (a protonotary *de numero* is "Right Reverend Monsignor"). A supernumerary protonotary apostolic is entitled to wear costume similar to that of a prelate of honor of His Holiness: a purple cassock and sash for choir dress, and a red-trimmed black cassock with purple sash and ferraiolone for nonliturgical dress. (Protonotaries *de numero* also wear a black biretta with a red silk tuft, but supernumerary protonotaries may only have a black tuft.)

St. Stephen, protomatyr

Prior to 1968, when the Holy See issued revised regulations concerning the use of pontifical insignia, priests holding this title were also allowed to wear a ring, pectoral cross, black skullcap with red piping and a white damask mitre (bordered in gold for *de numero* protonotaries) on certain occasions. The use of pontificals is no longer permitted, except to those protonotaries who received the title prior to the date of the revision.

Proverbs, Book of • The earliest of the Old Testament "Sapiential Books," the Book of Proverbs is traditionally attributed to King Solomon, who was renowned for his wisdom and good judgment (cf. 1 Kgs 4:29-34). A compendium of several smaller collections of moral and religious sayings, its present form can probably be dated in the sixth century B.C.

The proverbs do not follow any logical order. There are recurrent basic themes: the value of wisdom; knowledge of God's Law as the greatest wisdom; parents as a source of wisdom; religion, the key to wisdom; cautions against evil men and wicked women; warnings against idleness, greed, arrogance and gullibility. The initial verses of the book's first opening give an indication of its purpose. The book was written "That men may know wisdom and instruction, understand words of insight, receive instruction in wise dealing, righteousness, justice, and equity" (Prv 1:2-3).

The Book of Proverbs can be outlined as follows, mainly according to the headings of its various collections:

(1) "Proverbs of Solomon" — Wisdom Poems (1:1—9:18)

(2) "Proverbs of Solomon" — Wisdom Sayings (10:1—22:16)

(3) Admonitions (22:17—24:22)

(4) "Sayings of the Wise" (24:23-34)

(5) "Proverbs of Solomon" (25:1—29:27)

(6) "The Words of Agur" (30:1-33)

(7) "The Words of Lemuel" (31:1-9)

(8) Description of the Ideal Wife (31:10-31)

Perhaps the best known text of the book is Chapter 8, where Wisdom itself is personified, inviting hearers to be attentive to its counsels and describing its role in creation. As Wisdom says in 8:22, "The LORD created me at the beginning of his work, the first of his acts of old. . . . [T]hen I was beside him, like a master workman; and I was daily his delight, rejoicing before him always, rejoicing in his inhabited world and delighting in the sons of men" (Prv 8:22, 30-31). With these words, the Book of Proverbs describes the wisdom of God's design in the work of creation. This understanding, from the Old Testament Wisdom tradition, underlies the way in which the Gospel of John describes the role of the preexistent Christ in the Prologue, "In the beginning was the Word, and the Word was with God, and the Word was God. He was in the beginning with God; all things were made through him" (Jn 1:1-3).

For further reading: James L. Crenshaw, "Proverbs," *Anchor Bible Dictionary*, 5:513-520; Thomas P. McCreesh, O.P., "Proverbs," *New Jerome Biblical Commentary*, 453-461.

Providence of God • Divine providence is the plan by which God orders all things to their true end. While the plan itself is an act of divine wisdom, it presupposes the willing of an end or goal. Hence, in the first place, divine providence is itself eternal, identical with the knowledge and will of God. Its implementation occurs in time in divine conservation (whereby God preserves all things in existence) and governance (whereby He orders all things to their ends). Since God is the universal cause of all causes, nothing escapes His providence. Clearly, this is true of the created order, where natural processes follow their intricate course. Moreover, divine providence embraces the "hidden plan" that God made "in Christ as a plan for the fullness of time, to unite all things in him, things in heaven and things on earth" (Eph 1:9-10). Not even chance occurrences fall outside the scope of the universal cause. For events are said to occur by chance when they escape a particular causal ordering, but nothing escapes the ordering of the universal cause.

Although the plan itself and in all its detail is entirely the work of God, in its implementation God deploys the natural and free activity of many intermediary and secondary agents. Furthermore, even moral evils and physical defects, as permitted by God, cannot obstruct the consummation of the divine plan. Indeed, in the suffering, death and resurrection of His only Son, God Himself enters into and definitively overcomes the power of sin, suffering and death. Only in the end will the splendor of the divine plan be fully exhibited to His glory and for our worship, when God will be "everything to everyone" (1 Cor 15:28).

Providentissimus Deus • An encyclical issued by Pope Leo XIII in 1893. Sometimes described as the "Magna Carta of Biblical Studies," it began a new era in Catholic biblical theology. *Providentissimus Deus* upheld the Church as the only true interpreter of the Scriptures, but it also encouraged scholars to employ modern biblical critical methods, and to study the ancient languages in which the Scriptures were written.

Providentissimus Deus dealt with the divine inspiration of the sacred texts and asserted that God is the Author of the Bible because of His influence on the intellect and will of the human writers. This encyclical effectively opened for Catholic scholarship the tools of modern biblical research and textual criticism.

Leo XIII encouraged the faithful to read the Bible, "but always to approach the sacred writings with reverence and piety." Fifty years after *Providentissimus Deus*, Pope Pius XII issued a related document, *Divino Afflante Spiritu*, which ratified and further defined Pope Leo XIII's encyclical.

For further reading: Raymond E. Brown, S.S., and Thomas Aquinas Collins, O.P., "Church Pronouncements," *New Jerome Biblical Commentary*, 1166-1174.

Province • An ecclesiastical province is a grouping of two or more dioceses together with a metropolitan archbishop as the head. Usually, ecclesiastical provinces are made up of dioceses that border one another. In some countries or states, all of the dioceses of the territory form one province. In the U.S., most of the ecclesiastical provinces are co-extensive with the geographic boundaries of the state and include all of the dioceses within the state. There are some provinces that include dioceses in more than one state; in California, the dioceses of the state are divided into two ecclesiastical provinces (cf. Canons 431-433).

A religious province is a territorial division of the houses or institutions of the religious institute or society of apostolic life. The head of the province is usually called a provincial.

Provincial • In religious institutes made up of regional divisions or provinces, the provincial is the major religious superior of such regions. He or she is subject to the superior general of the institute, and exercises authority over the houses in the province. His or her chief function is to oversee the administration of the province, and particularly to foster fidelity to the constitutions of the institute by making regular visitations of the houses in his or her care. The office of provincial was an innovation introduced by the centrally organized mendicant orders in the Middle Ages. Provincials are normally elected, or at least designated for appointment, by provincial chapters; in some institutes, they are appointed by the superior general.

Provision, Canonical • The technical term applied to the formal filling of an ecclesiastical office. No Church office can be obtained validly without canonical provision (Canon 146). Usurpation or illegal retention of an office is, in fact, a crime in canon law (Canon 1381).

The 1983 Code of Canon Law establishes four basic ways in which an ecclesiastical office may be filled: (1) free conferral, that is, appointment to the office, which is, incidentally, the most common way of obtaining an office; (2) installation, whereby the competent authority selects a nominee from a list compiled by those with the canonical right to present such names (a rather rare event today); (3) confirmation, though only where necessary, of a duly elected candidate for a position, as is often the case with the election of a superior general in a religious institute; or finally (4) for simple election, where the mere acceptance of the election by the one elected is sufficient for the assumption of the office.

Canon 148 legislated a long-standing practice when it declared that the authority which can create, adapt or suppress an office is generally the one which can provide for, that is, fill, it. Such provision is to be made in writing (Canon 156). Offices which entail the full care of souls (for example, that of pastor) are to be filled promptly, and cannot be given to someone not in priestly Orders (Canons 150-151). Incompatible offices (to be so determined either by the law or in practice) are not to be entrusted to the same person, for the obvious reasons of efficiency and uprightness (Canon 152).

An officeholder is required to be in full communion with the Church, and must generally have those qualifications deemed necessary for the particular office (Canon 149). This latter requirement is to be read carefully, however, for only if the qualification in question was required for validity would the appointment of one without that qualification be rendered invalid. Under no circumstances, of course, can any office (even one not entailing the care of souls) be acquired validly under any degree of simony (cf. also Canon 1380).

Provisors, Statute of • In 1351, King Edward III of England, like many kings before and after him, passed a statute which purported to annul any episcopal appointments made in his realm by the Pope, unless the Holy See had first obtained the king's consent. The motivating cause behind this particular move was probably English irritation with the fact that the papacy was under heavy French influence, since this period was the height of the Avignon Papacy. In any event, the statute was forgotten soon after it was passed, until the time of Henry VIII, who found it a very useful device in his efforts to take control of the English Church.

Proxy Marriage • A marriage in which both parties to the marriage are not present to each other when consent is exchanged. One or both of the parties are represented by a proxy. The permission of the local Ordinary is required for such marriages.

The party or parties to the marriage must each sign a mandate for the proxy or proxies. The mandate must be drawn up in the manner of a document which is authentic in civil law. It must be signed by the person issuing the mandate and by the parish priest, by the local Ordinary, by a priest delegated to do so, by at least two witnesses (Canon 1105).

Prudence • Prudence, along with justice, fortitude (courage) and temperance (moderation), is a cardinal virtue. Greek and Roman philosophers, St. Augustine (A.D. 354-430) and St. Thomas Aquinas (1225-1274) regarded these virtues as the chief dispositions the moral person should acquire for his or her character. Persons acquire these virtues through the habitual choice of the right means and manner in all of their actions.

Prudence enjoys a special place in the moral life because it has qualities of both intellectual and moral virtue. As an intellectual virtue, prudence guides the doer in choosing a way of accomplishing something (a means and a manner) which keeps the entire good in mind. Thus prudence consults the demands of the other virtues in a situation of choice, making sure no aspect of the human good coming within the scope of the action is violated or neglected.

While prudence as an intellectual virtue guides the reason rightly, prudence as a moral virtue helps to control the will, or helps the doer of an action to make his or her choices in a reasonable way. The moral virtues direct the human will toward reasonable use by helping to control passions or desires. Each moral virtue controls a specific wrong tendency. Prudence enables a doer to avoid acting against justice because of his greed or favoritism; prudence prevents a doer from acting against temperance by striving to keep the necessary desires (such as the desire for some worldly goods and for food, drink and procreation) moderate and by rejecting inherently wrong desires (such as the desire for revenge, or for relations with another's spouse); and prudence helps the doer of an action to resist acts against fortitude by finding a way between excessive fear and recklessness.

Prudence, like art, operates on things that can change. But Aristotle (384-322 B.C.) and St. Thomas Aquinas point out that art and prudence differ in a very important respect. Art seeks to make or transform external things, and although an artist may be creative, arts have established ways of achieving results and the artist often can identify one best specific means. By contrast, prudence is about human action. Prudence involves doing something rather than making something, and this virtue draws on powers and capacities of the doer, including the doer's practical intelligence and virtue. Thus, when an artist wants to experiment and deliberately chooses a means that will not achieve the intended result, we do not consider him a bad artist. If the artist does not know what means will achieve his intended result, then he is ignorant of technique and is a bad artist. But in moral matters we blame an agent who willingly chooses a morally bad means, or a means which he knows will not produce the goal he seeks. On the other hand, we do not assign moral blame to a person who is simply a bad judge of

methods and consequences, although we would probably encourage the person who lacks practical knowledge to be guided by someone with more prudence.

Other aspects of prudence involve the command of the will to act once it has taken counsel on the moral choice, and solicitude to recognize and reject evil advice from other people.

An unfortunate development has occurred in modern moral philosophy. Immanuel Kant (1724-1804) identified prudence with calculations of self-interest in a very influential book entitled *Fundamental Principles of the Metaphysics of Morals*. Because other thinkers became attracted to Kant's ethics of duty, people often use "prudence" to mean "looking out for number one." Some moral philosophers consequently do not consider prudence a moral motive.

Ancient and Christian prudence is an openness of a doer choosing a way of performing an action which considers the entire human good. Catholics need to recover the idea of prudence in its fullest meaning.

Psalm, Responsorial • Psalm sung in response to the first reading of the Mass. The people listen to the first reading and respond to it with a psalm. Usually a cantor or the choir sings the psalm and the congregation sings a short refrain between the verses. Since it is a psalm, this part of the liturgy is properly sung.

Psalmody • The different methods and arrangements of singing the psalms during the liturgy is called psalmody and has its roots in the practice of the synagogue. There are three main types of psalmody: (1) responsorial, in which the leader sings the verse and the rest of the congregation counters with a simple refrain or response; (2) antiphonal, in which the congregation is divided into two groups and alternately sings the verses of the psalm; and (3) direct, in which all sing the psalm together. Monasteries most often use responsorial and antiphonal psalmody during the Liturgy of the Hours, while direct psalmody is used during the celebration of the Eucharist. Modern liturgy is witnessing a return to the psalms during Mass, where they are generally recited by the entire congregation.

Musical accompaniment of the psalms ranges from plain and Gregorian chant with their various modes to more modern renderings, the most popular of which is Father Joseph Gelineau's, published in 1953, which attempts to follow the rhythm of the Hebrew poetry. (Cf. Antiphon; Antiphonary; Psalms, Book of; Responsory; Divine Office; Liturgy of the Hours; Chant; Gregorian Chant; Gregorian Modes; Music, Church.)

Psalms, Book of • The Book of Psalms contains one hundred fifty of these religious songs, divided (like the Torah) into five books. The Vulgate numbering of the psalms, formerly used in the Catholic Church, differs slightly from that of the Hebrew Bible, now standard.

The psalms were originally composed by many authors, spanning perhaps a thousand years. The title of about half of the psalms names David as author, but Moses, Solomon or one of five minor sources are given for many of the rest.

They are songs, poems meant to be sung. In translation, however, whatever rhythm or assonance may have been in the original is sacrificed. Other features of Hebrew poetry (stanzas, anaphora [repeated openings], epiphora [repeated closings]) can still be easily recognized. They are meditative works, and we can often see the use of synonymous lines, antithetic lines, sequential thought.

As with all literature, knowledge of the historical and geographical background is indispensable for understanding and savoring the psalms. It has been well said that the best preparation for understanding the psalms is familiarity with the Bible as a whole.

Many of the psalms are hymns, songs of praise to God: examples are 100, 103, 104, 117, 148 and 150. Some of these take as their basis the power and goodness of God as seen in creation; others recall God's fidelity to His Chosen People in their tumultuous history.

There are also hymns of thanksgiving: 30, 107, 116, 118, 124, 138. The gratitude which they express springs from providential liberation from personal danger or national calamity. Many of these have a didactic purpose, that of perpetually reminding Israel of God's justice and mercy.

In times of imminent peril, there are hymns of petition: 12, 60, 80, 90, 123 envision danger for the nation; 5, 6, 7, 56, 57 and 98 are typical of the many personal pleas for help.

Seven psalms (6, 32, 38, 51, 102, 130 and 143) are the so-called penitential psalms, expressing the repentant sinner's cry for forgiveness and pardon.

The messianic aspirations of the Jewish people find expression in some of the most significant psalms: 2, 72, 110 and 132 are the most obvious examples. Christians should not deny that the most proximate and limited goal of these was to uphold the faith of the Jewish people in the special divine providence for the House of David, but it is clear that their full import is seen only in Jesus Christ.

This brief outline shows the broad scope of the psalms. From the beginning of Christianity, they were made the staple of Christian spirituality, particularly in the mandatory daily prayer of priests and religious.

For further reading: John S. Kselman, S.S., and Michael L. Barre, S.S., "Psalms," *New Jerome Biblical Commentary*, 523-552.

Psaltery • From the Latin *psalterium*. In the Middle Ages, it was the book of the psalms for recitation at the Divine Office. Psalteries, often containing canticles, hymns, litanies and ancillary prayers, fell into disuse when many of its elements were added to the Breviary.

Pseudo-Isidore • Writings attributed to Isidore Mercator (d. 850), but not likely his actual work, are distinguished from his genuine writings by the designation of Pseudo-Isidore.

Public Propriety • An impediment to marriage that arises when a couple lives together after an invalid marriage or are living in public concubinage. It exists between the man and the blood relatives in the first degree of the direct line of the woman, and vice versa. Consequently, a marriage between a man and the mother of the woman with whom he is living would be invalid, as would be a marriage between a man and the woman's daughter by another union. Since this is an impediment of ecclesiastical origin, it may be dispensed by the local Ordinary (Canon 1093).

Publican • A word of Latin origin which designates a man involved in the collection of taxes for the Roman government. The government farmed out, for a fixed yearly sum, the right to collect taxes. The amount charged for this right was reckoned on the basis of the estimated revenues. The fee charged was lower than the anticipated return. The tax collector was expected to pay the fixed price, whether he succeeded in collecting that amount or not. He could, however, keep any money above the amount established by the government. Those

engaged in this work were private businessmen. The agreement was struck between the government and the chief tax-gatherer, who in turn would employ tax-gatherers who would do the actual tax-gathering. As can be easily surmised, such a system was susceptible of abuses and corruption. That abuses did materialize is clear from the contempt in which publicans were held as a very general rule.

The Jews had further reasons to look down upon publicans. For one thing, publicans functioned in behalf of the foreign invaders, the Romans, which seemed disloyal. Besides, their role was reprehensible because it required Jewish publicans to be in close contact with Gentiles, an activity judged to be defiling. In New Testament times in Palestine, it was customary to farm out only customs duties, not regular taxes. Although publicans were, as a rule, bracketed with the lower elements of society, e.g., sinners, Gentiles (Mt 9:10f., 18:17), the New Testament does, on occasion, present publicans in a favorable light. It notes, for instance, that publicans were among those who came to be baptized by John the Baptist (Lk 3:12; 7:29), that Levi was a publican (Mt 9:9), and that Jesus told a parable which showed a publican in a good light (Lk 18:9-14).

Pulpit • Term derived from the Latin *pulpitum*, "platform," to describe the raised stand made of stone or wood which came into general use in the late Middle Ages, used by the preacher or reader to proclaim the homily or the Scripture readings during the liturgy. Traditionally, the bishop would preach from the *cathedra* (episcopal seat) in his cathedral; the ambo was also used for reading and preaching. In some places the pulpit is placed in the nave of the church, even in its middle, to allow for greater audibility. In the present *General Instruction of the Roman Missal*, it states that "the homily is given at the chair or the lectern" (n. 97). The revised *Caeremoniale Episcoporum, Ceremonial of Bishops,* states that the bishop "sits in his *cathedra* and gives the homily. . . . The homily may also be given from another, more suitable, place where the bishop can be seen and heard by all" (n. 120).

Purgatory • Based on the Judeo-Christian concept of the efficacy of prayers for the dead (2 Mc 12:42-45), purgatory is the condition or state for those who have not wholly alienated themselves from God by their sins, but who are temporarily and partially alienated from God while their love is made perfect and they give satisfaction for their sins. Catholic belief also holds that the prayers of the faithful on earth for those who are in purgatory are efficacious (DS 854, 1304, 1820). The official teachings of the Church do not specify the nature of the punishment of purgatory nor the duration of punishment of those in purgatory.

Catholic belief affirms that there are fires in purgatory, but these fires should be considered different from those of hell, as the consequence of the fires of purgatory is purification and ultimate union with God (DS 854). Those in purgatory are different from the damned because they are essentially in union with God, albeit an imperfect union, and purgatory makes their union perfect. Purgatory cleanses venial sins, imperfections, faults and flaws, and remits the temporal punishment of mortal sins that have been forgiven in the sacrament of Penance. Also, purgatory is a temporally limited condition, existing only until the Last Judgment.

The Reformers ultimately made a complete and total rejection of purgatory, and in so doing created significant problems in their accounts of the last things. Denying its existence forced them to hold that sins for which satisfaction had not been given were abolished without satisfaction. They were forced to hold either that sinners had their minor sins remitted with no satisfaction, or that this did not occur and that they were condemned for all eternity.

The Greek Orthodox reject the idea of there being a fire of purgatory or of there being an immediate retribution for one's sins. They regard the last universal Judgment as the only consummation, and individual judgments are either wholly rejected or are of minor importance for them. They believe that all (including the Virgin Mary and the Apostles) undergo the final fire, and they could only accept with reservation a particular judgment after death.

Purification of the Blessed Virgin Mary • The purification of the Blessed Virgin Mary according to the Jewish law of ritual cleansing after childbirth (Lv 12:1-8) is celebrated in the liturgical Calendar on February 2. It is also called the feast of the Presentation of Christ in the Temple. The popular name is Candlemas Day.

The feast was introduced into the Eastern Empire during the reign of Emperor Justinian (527-565). It is mentioned in the Gelasian Sacramentary for the Western Church in the seventh century. Candles are blessed on this day to commemorate Simeon's prophecy about Christ as "a light for revelation to the Gentiles, and for glory to thy people Israel" (Lk 2:32).

Purificator • A linen cloth used to dry the sacred vessels as they are cleansed after Holy Communion. It may also be used to catch any of the Precious Blood which may drip from the chalice during reception from the chalice.

Purim • According to popular etymology, the word derives from the Hebrew word for "lot" (*pur*, plural *purim*). The actual origins of the word, however, remain obscure; some suggest that it may have a Babylonian origin. The term designates a Jewish festival celebrated in the spring (February-March) on the 14th-15th of the Jewish month of Adar. The celebration commemorates the deliverance of the Jews in Persia from the persecution of Haman, as recounted in the Book of Esther. The feast seems to have more of a national and secular coloration than a religious one. It has also been suggested that Purim may represent an adaptation by the Jews of an original Persian or Mesopotamian holiday.

For further reading: Louis Jacobs, "Purim," *Encyclopedia Judaica*, 13:1390-1395; Carey A. Moore, "Esther, Book of," *Anchor Bible Dictionary*, 2:633-643; Irene Nowell, O.S.B., Toni Craven and Demetrius Dumm, O.S.B., "Tobit, Judith, Esther," *New Jerome Biblical Commentary*, 576-579.

Puritanism • A name applied to a variety of movements within the Church of England from the time of the Elizabethan Settlement (1559) to the Restoration (1660), by which time the term had lost its original meaning. The first Puritans objected that the reforms of Elizabeth I and her successors did not go far enough to eliminate all traces of Roman Catholicism. Advocating a return to a simpler, more fundamentalist church, they desired to "purify" the Church of England of all vestiges of the "old religion," especially vestments, any form of decoration and many practices of popular religion. They failed to bring a reform to suit their tastes, and many fled to Holland, later to found the Plymouth Colony in Massachusetts.

The term has come to mean anyone of very rigid and unyielding religious outlook. It is also used in a derisive fashion to denote anyone who adheres to a particularly high moral code.

Putative Father • This term which comes from the Latin word *puto*, for think or suppose, refers in Catholic Tradition to St. Joseph, who was thought to be the carnal father of Christ by those contemporaries who were not privy to the secret of the Incarnation. As such, since Joseph was esteemed to be the father of Jesus, the title clung to him even after this mystery was revealed and he has been known since then as the "putative father" of Our Lord.

Putative Marriage • A marriage that is actually invalid because of the presence of an undispensed impediment or defect in consent. Although the marriage is invalid, at least one if not both of the parties must have contracted it in good faith, unaware of the invalidating factors. Children born of a putative marriage are considered legitimate in canon law even if the marriage is subsequently declared invalid by competent Church authority (cf. Canon 1061).

Pyx • Term derived from the Greek *puxis*, denoting a box-shaped vessel originally made of wood, used as a receptacle for the Blessed Sacrament. By custom today it is a flat container made of metal (sometimes silver or gold) for bringing Communion to the sick, or it is a vessel in the tabernacle containing the large Host placed in a monstrance for Exposition and Benediction.

Q Document • This term refers to a hypothetical reconstruction of a common written source (German, *Quelle*) for both Matthew and Luke. The concept was first suggested by C. H. Weisse in 1838.

This theory is an attempt to explain the commonality between the Gospels according to St. Matthew and St. Luke. As it is generally proposed, this thesis suggests that various sayings of Jesus and other small literary units began to be written down and that this document became the source relied upon by Matthew and Luke, along with the oral tradition, when they came to commit their respective Gospels to writing.

The acceptance of the "Q Document" ran high in liberal Protestantism all through this century and experienced a significant degree of acceptance in Catholic circles from the 1950s on. Some recent scholarship, however, has questioned it for a variety of reasons, not least of which being that no one has ever found such a document and its supposition seems to cause as many problems as it solves. It should be noted that this theory in no way affects the historical truth of the Gospels, their divine inspiration, or their inerrancy.

For further reading: C. M. Tuckett, "Q (Gospel Source)," *Anchor Bible Dictionary*, 5:567-572.

Qoheleth: See Ecclesiastes, Book of

Quadragesima • A Latin term used to express the forty days of Lent, whose weekdays number forty. It is a penitential time for the Church.

Quadragesimo Anno • On the fortieth anniversary of Pope Leo XIII's epochal encyclical on social justice, *Rerum Novarum*, May 15, 1931, Pope Pius XI issued an encyclical letter known by this title. In essence, this teaching reaffirmed that of the earlier document, but had a sense of added urgency, coming as it did during the worldwide depression. Pius XI, echoing Leo, rejected both the economic extremes of unbridled, cut-throat capitalism, and collectivist, statist socialism. It also encouraged a restructured society, based on a respect for the trades, the laborer and the owner, holding up as a model the unified, organic society common to the Middle Ages. While supporting the right to private property, it also posited that government and the wealthy had the duty to ameliorate social evils, and that the worker had the right to a wage which would enable him to support his family "in reasonable and frugal comfort."

Quaestor • An antiquated term designating an individual charged with the collection of alms for distribution to the poor and needy.

Quakers • The nickname for the Religious Society of Friends, organized in England by George Fox (1624-1691) as a distinct Christian group in 1668 with the composition of his "Rule for the Management of Meetings." Persecuted in England as "nonconformist," his followers began emigrating to America early on. William Penn (1644-1718) founded the

Pennsylvania colony on Quaker principles in 1682. The central doctrine of the Friends involves the affirmation of the "Inner Light" of Christ. This Light represents the intrusion of the transcendent God into the soul, bringing with it freedom from sin, union with Christ and the ability to perform good works. The doctrine of the Inner Light has led to the rejection of the sacraments, ministry and all forms of liturgy normally associated with Christian Faith. The central communal activity of the Friends is the weekly meeting which begins in silence and expectation, broken only when a member is moved to speak. Quaker polity is democratic. While there are no formal ministers, elders and overseers do function as officers in the Society. The Friends, whose opposition to military service and the taking of oaths have at times brought them into conflict with civil society, are nonetheless widely respected for their moral integrity and generous philanthropy. American Quakers number about 112,000, organized in about 1,000 congregations. Reflecting their theological diversity, Quakers are grouped in several national bodies, the chief of which are the Evangelical Friends Alliance, the Friends General Conference and the Friends United Meeting.

Quanta Cura • The title of the encyclical issued by Pope Pius IX on December 8, 1864, promulgating the *Syllabus Errorum*, in which eighty characteristically liberal and modernistic theses are identified and condemned.

Quarantine • Originally the quarantine was a strict fast which lasted for forty days, and was a specific penance assigned by a confessor. The term came to be applied to partial indulgences, and the amount of temporal punishment which was removed by the particular penance. With the promulgation of Paul VI's *Indulgentiarum Doctrina* (Apostolic Constitution on the Revision of Indulgences) on January 1, 1967, this term ceased being used when referring to indulgences.

Quasi-Domicile • The same factors which make the determination of domicile an important consideration in canon law make the concept of quasi-domicile important, especially in a highly mobile society. Quasi-domicile, or temporary residence in a territory, is acquired by presence within that territory with the intention of remaining at least three months, or by mere presence in the territory for at least three months (Canon 102). One with quasi-domicile is called an *advena* (Canon 100) or temporary resident. A common example of temporary residents in canon law would be students away at college.

Persons with quasi-domicile are basically bound by the particular laws having force within that territory. It thus contributes to the good order of the Church, in that without the concept of quasi-domicile, many people would find themselves outside the normal avenues of ecclesiastical administration. As a general rule, though, the distinction between the effects of domicile and quasi-domicile for laity is slight, although it might be of some importance in establishing tribunal jurisdiction in marriage nullity cases (cf. Canon 1673).

Quasi-Parish • A quasi-parish is one that has not yet been erected to the full status of a parish. It is equivalent to a parish and has its own pastor but, because of special circumstances, it is not yet a parish (Canon 516).

Queenship of Mary, Feast of the • The Blessed Virgin was given the title of "Queen" by Pope Pius XII on May 31, 1954, during the Marian Year. In the new Calendar of the Church, there is a memorial of the Queenship of Mary, celebrated on August 22. Mary is honored as Queen of angels, patriarchs, prophets, apostles, saints, confessors and virgins, as well as Queen of peace and Queen of heaven and earth. (AAS 38 [1946], 266.)

Quiet, Prayer of
• Prayer, as man's response to God's presence, traditionally is divided into two types: vocal prayer and mental prayer. The prayer of quiet comes within the category of mental prayer. St. John Damascene (c. 675-c. 749) wrote of mental prayer as *ascensus intellectus in Deum* (the ascent of the mind to God). The use of the word *intellectus* is to be understood as the faculty of spiritual vision, and it is this which contributes to the prayer of quiet. During this prayer the mind is enlightened in a particular way by God's grace, leading to an internal peace and happiness in the divine presence. As a result of one's contemplative love for God, and as a fruit of the spiritual gift of wisdom, the prayer of quiet may be developed, through grace, as a constant state.

German statue representing the Queenship of Mary

The prayer of quiet is a form of contemplation which is a wholly gratuitous gift of God that cannot be achieved by human action. In this state, the soul's principal activity is affective, a motion of the will toward God, Who fills the soul with peaceful delight and an intimate awareness of His presence.

This form of contemplation, although a divine gift, usually presupposes a life of virtue and follows only after long practice of the prayer of recollection in which the intellect and memory are focused in meditation.

Quietism • A term broadly designating views that downplay the role of human activity and responsibility in the spiritual life. The clearest instance of a systematic spirituality along these lines is the Quietism of Miguel de Molinos (1640-1697), propounded in his *Spiritual Guide* (1675) but chiefly in his letters. Fundamental to the Quietism of Molinos is the notion that passive prayer constitutes the height of perfection. The attainment of this state demands total passivity, annihilation of the will, abandonment to God, and lack of concern for oneself and one's salvation. External works and the ordinary practices of Christian life are superfluous to one who has attained this state. The practice of nondiscursive mental prayer eliminates all desires, including those of faith, hope and charity which must be suppressed in order to achieve spiritual perfection. In such a state, actual sin is impossible, appearances to the contrary notwithstanding, since the will has been destroyed. The Quietism of Molinos was condemned by Pope Innocent XI in 1687.

Quinisextum Council • Known also as the Trullan Synod, this council of Eastern bishops was held in 691 in the banqueting hall (*in trullo*) of the Emperor Justinian II in Constantinople. The name "Quinisextum" (Fifth-Sixth) derives from the fact that the council was convoked in order to complete the work of the Fifth (553) and Sixth (680) General Councils. The canons of the council concerned such disciplinary matters as clerical marriage, ecclesiastical attire and the age of ordination. Pope St. Sergius I refused to accept the enactments of the Trullan Synod, not only because Rome had not been represented at its deliberations, but also because some of its canons directly conflicted with Roman practice (e.g., the allowance of clerical marriage). Justinian tried to enforce acceptance of the council by having Sergius kidnapped and brought to Constantinople. However, the Pope was successfully defended by the Roman populace. The dispute reflected the growing rift between the Eastern and Western Churches. In this connection, it is noteworthy that the Quinisextum Council enacted a canon that accorded equal status to the Pope and the Patriarch of Constantinople.

Quinquagesima • Literally, "the fiftieth." The Sunday before Lent, the fiftieth day before Easter. In the liturgical Calendar before the Second Vatican Council, this was the last of the "pre-Lenten" Sundays, the others being Septuagesima (seventieth), and Sexagesima (sixtieth). The reform of the Calendar mandated by Vatican II sought to highlight the importance of Lent as the traditional "forty-day fast," hence the elimination of this "pre-Lenten" season, which was considered to be an unnecessary duplication.

Quinque Viae • Literally, the "Five Ways," an expression that designates the celebrated five arguments for the existence of God advanced by St. Thomas Aquinas in his *Summa Theologiae*, part I, question 2, article 3. Each of the five ways begins with some feature of the observable structure of the cosmos, and moves to the conclusion that God acts causally in bringing this about. The First Way argues from the fact that there is motion and change in the world to an unchanged and unmoved Prime Mover. The Second Way has a similar logical structure: from the existence of series of subordinated agents in the world, it argues to a first uncaused Cause. The contingency or perishability of things is the starting point for the Third Way. Here it is argued that if everything were perishable or derivatively imperishable, then nothing would now exist — a patent falsehood. Thus there must be a cause whose imperishability or necessary existence is underived. This is God. In the Fourth Way, the various degrees of goodness and perfection in the universe feature prominently. The argument now is that there must be some unlimitedly perfect and good cause of which the limited goodness and perfection we observe are a reflection. The Fifth Way argues from the finality apparent in things, both rational and nonrational. That all things are clearly tending toward the good which is their own enjoyment of existence implies that there is some rational agent who has instilled this tendency in them. It is important to note that these arguments do not rest on the postulation of a methodological doubt or a suspension of belief in God's existence. Rather, presuming faith in God, the *Quinque Viae* argue that the God Whom we worship and confess as Christians is none other than the cause of the world.

Quinquennial Report • Every five years a diocesan bishop is required to submit a report on the state of his diocese to the Holy See. If the quinquennial report falls due during a diocesan bishop's first two years in the diocese, he is excused from making the report. The form of the report and the required information is provided by the Holy See. This report, known as the quinquennial report, contains information on all aspects of the diocese.

Unless he has been dispensed, the bishop is to submit this report personally to the Holy Father. If he is impeded, he may delegate his coadjutor bishop, an auxiliary bishop, or, if he has neither, a suitable priest. This is known as the quinquennial or *ad limina* visit. Such visits are generally arranged in such a way that all the bishops of a country or at least all of the bishops of regions within a country make them at the same time. In addition to the audience with the Holy Father, the bishops generally are received by the prefects of the various Roman Congregations to discuss matters of mutual concern (Canons 399-400).

Quirinal • The Quirinal is one of the seven hills of Rome. In the sixteenth century a papal palace was built there to serve as a summer residence for the Popes, taking advantage of the more salubrious air the hill offered. Numerous papal conclaves were held in this building. In 1870 it became the residence of the kings of Italy. Since the fall of the monarchy in 1946, it has been the residence of the presidents of the Italian Republic.

Qumran Community • A group of ascetical Jews, probably members of the Essene sect, who lived beside the Dead Sea at the Wadi Qumran between c. 150 B.C. and A.D. 70. Information about the Qumran community comes from three sources: (1) the Dead Sea Scrolls; (2) archaeological evidence from the ruins of the monastery; and (3) mention of the Essenes in the writings of Pliny the Elder and Philo Judaeus.

Members of the community, who thought of themselves as the remnant of Israel, met every day for prayers from the Psalter at evening and sunrise. They also performed two basic rituals: purificatory washings which symbolized repentance of sins and a religious meal of bread and wine presided over by a priest.

The community had both laymen and priests and apparently had both married and celibate members. Property was held in common, and daily life was rigorously ascetical. Because of their fervor, the community members were regarded by their contemporaries in Judea as fanatics.

Since the discovery of the Dead Sea Scrolls, there has been much speculation about the possible connection between the Qumran community and the early Church. It has been suggested, for example, that St. John the Baptist lived at Qumran or at least knew the community. From his exposure to them, continues the theory, St. John learned the ritual washing which became Baptism. So far, however, nothing of this sort has been demonstrated conclusively.

For further reading: Jerome Murphy-O'Conner, "Qumran, Khirbet," *Anchor Bible Dictionary*, 5:590-594.

Qumran Movement • The name given to a separatist movement in Palestinian Judaism after its library was discovered in 1947 in caves near the Wadi Qumran by the Dead Sea. This library of scrolls has come to be known as the Dead Sea Scrolls. The group lived as a community in this area until the time of the first Jewish revolt (A.D. 70) and is believed by many scholars to be the group known in ancient Palestine as the Essenes. This group saw itself as the true Israel, living a highly organized communal life, with a structure similar to that now associated with religious or monastic life.

Qumranites • A Jewish religious community that inhabited a site some seven to eight miles south of Jericho, near the Dead Sea. The location came to be known to the Arabs as Khirbet Qumran. It appears to have been the abode of the group roughly from 125 B.C. until about A.D. 66-70. In the opinion of most scholars, the members of this community were Essenes. The remains of their library (first found in 1947) have become known as the Dead Sea Scrolls.

Quo Vadis • An anecdote in the apocryphal Acts of Peter (c. A.D. 190) records the story of St. Peter fleeing the Neronian persecution in Rome.

According to the story, Peter meets Our Lord on the Appian Way and asks Him: *"Domine, quo vadis?"*, or "Lord, where are You going?" When Our Lord replies that He is going to Rome to be crucified, Peter turns around and returns to suffer martyrdom with his fellow Christians. The Acts of Peter also record that Peter was crucified head downward as a sign of his unworthiness to die as did Our Lord. A small chapel on the Appian Way commemorates this legendary occurrence.

The famous novel *Quo Vadis* was written by Henryk Sienkiewicz in 1895.

Rabat • A piece of material, generally black, attached to the Roman collar and worn under a suit or cassock as part of clerical garb. The rabat of a monsignor or a bishop is purple, that of a cardinal is red, and the Pope has a white rabat.

Rabbi • From an Aramaic root, literally, "my master," the term *rabboni* is an emphatic form of "rabbi." Originally, the word was employed as a respectful honorific form of address. In several of the Gospels, it is so used to address Jesus. This was the fashion in which students of a scribe would address their teacher. Right after the New Testament period, in the early Christian era, the word was used by Jews as a title and as such was combined with a scholar's name, thus: Rabbi Judah-ban-Nasi. At a still later time, the word "rabbi" began to be used as a common noun with the meaning, "a teacher." By this time, the force of the suffix "i" ("my") was no longer felt.

For further reading: Hayim Lapin, "Rabbi," *Anchor Bible Dictionary*, 5:600-602.

Rabdos • The Eastern bishop's staff or crosier.

Raccolta • An official Roman Catholic prayer book which contains the prayers, devotions and religious acts to which indulgences are attached. The first *Raccolta* was published in 1807 at Rome by Telesforo Galli. The conditions for gaining an indulgence and the amount of the indulgence, as well as the date of grant made by the Sacred Congregation of the Penitentiary, are listed with each prayer or devotion. Periodically, this book is published under the Latin title *Enchiridion Indulgentiarum* and updated with new indulgences for old prayers or for prayers newly composed.

Race • It is the teaching of the Church that the human race has an essential unity. This is expressed in *Gaudium et Spes*, the Pastoral Constitution on the Church in the Modern World, when it states that "all men are endowed with a rational soul and are created in God's image; they have the same nature and origin and, being redeemed by Christ, they enjoy the same divine calling and destiny; there is here a basic equality between all men and it must be given ever greater recognition" (GS 29). A statement or theory which says that any of the different races of the human family is superior or inferior to another denies this teaching, and is to be condemned as being incompatible with Catholic doctrine. *Gaudium et Spes*, n. 32, refers to Christ's command to the Apostles to "preach the Gospel to all peoples in order that the human race would become the family of God, in which love would be the fullness of the law." This the Church strives to do as a matter of justice, and in response to the command to love one's neighbor.

Racism • Prejudicial and/or discriminatory attitudes and beliefs about members of other racial groups.

In the twentieth century, as indicated in the encyclical of Pope John Paul II

Redemptor hominis, racism has become almost universal in our world. Racist attitudes violate justice, first of all, by denying the legitimate value and rights of others. And they are also contrary to the requirements of charity because they give justification for doing harm to one's neighbor.

Defining racism precisely is difficult. The Nazis were clearly racists in holding that the mythical Aryan race had a moral right to dominate and even suppress other races through genocide. But other more subtle forms of racial discrimination are more difficult to identify, and this is what makes it particularly hard to curb.

The requirements of justice demand that all persons be given an equal opportunity to acquire and possess goods. They also demand that goods and benefits not be denied individuals because of factors, such as race, over which they have no control. And they also require that the honor, respect and freedom due to persons not guilty of gross moral or serious criminal violations be accorded them.

Ransom • The term "ransom" has a strict meaning in its original sense — the cost for release from detention or incarceration. In the Old Testament, it expresses God's salvific response to Israel's predicaments; in the New Testament, it is God's response to the sinner who is in bondage or "incarcerated by sin" (Mt 20:28; Mk 10:45). The verb can refer to the action of paying the ransom (figuratively, 1 Pt 1:18) and means to set free, redeem or rescue (Lk 24:21; Ti 2:14; Acts 28:19). The noun means "redeemer," in the sense of one who effects freedom from slavery (e.g., Moses, Acts 7:35). The notion of ransom paid by a ransomer touches upon the very core of the mystery of salvation: we are dead to God, prisoners to the bondage of sin until we are freed, ransomed by Christ's precious Blood. His Blood communicates life to us (Jn

6:53ff.; 1 Cor 10:16); it is an offering for our sins (Rom 3:25), which "redeems" us (Eph 1:7) and draws us near to God (Eph 2:13), effecting eternal redemption (Heb 9:12).

Rapture • The "rapture" refers to the gathering up of the saved at the Second Coming of Christ. "And the dead in Christ will rise first; then we who are alive, who are left, shall be caught up together with them in the clouds to meet the Lord in the air" (1 Thes 4:16-17).

For further reading: Christopher Rowland, "Parousia," *Anchor Bible Dictionary,* 5:166-170.

Rash Judgment • An unfounded judgment — favorable or unfavorable — upon the moral states or actions of another. Our Lord Himself warned against rash judgment in the Sermon on the Mount (cf. Mt 7:1-2). These words cannot be taken as an absolute prohibition against judgment. There are many occasions when we are required to evaluate the activity or character of others — for example, when a religious community is called upon to attest to the fitness of one of its members for permanent profession or ordination. Such judgments must be reached in charity, with as complete a knowledge as possible of the particular circumstances of the person under evaluation, and with an awareness of the seriousness of the process and consequences of judgment. Rash judgment neglects these requirements and is thus a sin against the virtue of justice.

Ratio Studiorum • The plan of studies of a religious institute, usually published for the use of all the provinces. The Jesuit *Ratio Studiorum* comprises the entire system of education to be adopted not only for higher philosophical and theological studies for the members of the Society, but also for the curriculum of all levels of education in the schools under Jesuit sponsorship. The Dominican *Ratio Studiorum Generalis* lays out the plan of studies for its own members' intellectual formation as preparatory for ordination.

Rationalism, Theological • Broadly speaking, theological rationalism describes any position that champions the capacity of human reason to discover the full range of religious and ethical truth without benefit of Divine Revelation. Many such positions have been advanced in the history of Christian thought, stretching from medieval Latin Averroism, through Renaissance humanism, and on to nineteenth-century rationalism. Modern forms of rationalism have typically held that at the core of the mythological ideas taught in Christian revelation (creation, incarnation, redemption and the like) there lie the basic natural truths of religion and morality accessible to human reason and sufficient to guide persons in their relations with God and with each other.

Theological rationalists are inclined to view reason either as dispensing with or superseding properly religious faith. In the past two hundred years, bishops and theologians have frequently had occasion to challenge the adequacy of rationalist positions. The most authoritative Church teaching about this topic was propounded in the Constitution *Dei Filius* of Vatican Council I. Here the Church reiterated the traditional Catholic view expressing confidence in the scope of human reason, while at the same time acknowledging its limitations and the necessity of revelation.

Theological rationalism is correct in its emphasis upon the capacity of human reason to come to a knowledge of such truths as God's existence, the immortality of the soul, and the moral nature of man, and to explore and unfold the inner intelligibility of revelation. But the knowledge of the economy of salvation — the divine invitation to loving unity and the divine action that enables it — comes only in God's disclosure of His purposes in the revelation proclaimed by Christ and entrusted to the Apostles and the Church.

Readings, Cycle of • The Church calendar assigns a three-year cycle of Scripture readings for Sundays. A two-year weekday cycle, a one-year cycle for feasts of saints, and readings for ritual Masses and Masses for particular intentions are also designated. These readings are contained in a book called the lectionary.

The Constitution on the Sacred Liturgy of Vatican II decreed that "the treasures of the Bible are to be opened up more lavishly, so that a richer share in God's Word may be provided for the faithful. In this way, a more representative portion of Holy Scripture will be read to the people in the course of a prescribed number of years" (n. 51). Thus, the present *Lectionary for Mass* was issued in 1970, and a slight revision appeared in 1981 (whose General Instruction is a most valuable catechesis on the theological value of the Word as proclaimed in the liturgy). If three readings are required, the first is usually from the Old Testament, the second from the New Testament (Letters, Acts, Revelation) and the third reading is always a selection from a Gospel. If two readings are required, the first is from the Old Testament, Letters, Acts or Revelation; the second reading is a passage from one of the Gospels.

The Sunday lectionary arranges the texts in a three-year cycle. Thus the same text is read only once every three years. Each year is designated A, B or C. Year C is a year whose number is equally divisible by three. Thus 1995 is year C, 1996 is year A, 1997 is year B and so forth.

Reason, Age of: See **Age of Reason**

Recension • From the Latin *recensere* (to assess), a recension of a biblical text is a revision of the text based on critical examination of the sources. Clearly, from the significance of such a revision, there must be a substantial reason for a recension to be made, with the attempt always at transmitting the intended words of the inspired writer.

Rechabites • An order or group of people devoted to a seminomadic way of life. This group dwelt in the Judean desert in Jeremiah's time but during Nebuchadnezzar's campaign in Judah took refuge within the confines of the city of Jerusalem. The origins of the order remain obscure. In Jeremiah 35:6, they are reported as maintaining "Jonadab, the son of Rechab, our father." The ambiguity of the phrase does not quite make clear whether Jonadab or Rechab founded the order. Verse 19 asserts that Jonadab in fact was the founder, leaving unexplained why in that case they should be called Rechabites. The rule the Rechabites lived by was one of unadulterated nomadism. They eschewed wine and were not to build or live in houses. They lived in tents. Neither were they ever to sow seeds (Jer 35:6-7), for this was judged to be a degrading occupation for a man. This rule of life reflects the difference of outlook between those given to pastoral pursuits on the one hand and those engaged in agricultural enterprises on the other. It is a conflict that was encountered widely in the Near East of those times. In the literature of Sumer, the farmer is preferred to the shepherd; it is just the opposite in the Cain and Abel account, in which the shepherd is favored. Elsewhere in the Old Testament the naturalness and simplicity of the nomadic life is commended.

The Rechabites espoused the desert nomadic values as a religion. It has been remarked that the Rechabites could not have been very numerous, since Jeremiah assembles the whole group into a single room of the Temple. There is no sound basis for affirming the survival of the Rechabites beyond the Babylonian exile.

In the middle of the last century, the name "Rechabites" was assumed in New England by a society whose members were pledged to total abstinence from alcohol.

For further reading: Frank S. Frick, "Rechab," *Anchor Bible Dictionary*, 5:630-631.

Recidivist • One who repeatedly commits the same objectionable action and makes little improvement, despite continuous claims of repentance and sorrow.

Recidivism is contrary to the virtue of penance, which moves the individual to renounce sinful actions, tendencies and thoughts definitively. The recidivist's protestations of repentance are also contrary to the requirements of truthfulness, for the recidivist knows in his heart that claims of regret and sorrow are not sincere. Recidivists lack the virtue of patience and of fortitude, for such persons too often give in to temptation and cannot endure trials and sufferings over the long run for the sake of the Gospel.

Recollection • A term used by spiritual writers to refer to the concentration on God and spiritual things of those seeking spiritual perfection or the presence of God. A recollected person avoids distractions and activities that can turn one away from concentration on the Divine Presence in the soul and focuses on self-perfection.

Recollection also refers to a certain stage in spiritual growth where the person's memory, will and understanding are stilled by divine action, so that grace can work unimpeded.

Reconciliatio et Paenitentia • This apostolic exhortation, known in English as *Reconciliation and Penance*, was proclaimed by Pope John Paul II in December 1984 in the wake of the Sixth General Assembly of the Synod of Bishops.

Quite unsurprisingly, the Pope begins his discussion of reconciliation with a delineation of the sins and injustices of "a shattered world": global human rights violations; widespread religious oppression and discrimination; the increasing frequency of terrorist acts; a widening nuclear arms race; and growing populations suffering under chronic, trans-generational poverty. John Paul makes clear that all of these ills originate in "a wound in man's inmost self," i.e., Original Sin.

Changing these exterior conditions requires a transformation, or conversion in the hearts of individuals. In this way, doing penance and effecting such a conversion lead to reconciliation, or an "overcoming [of] that radical break which is sin."

With this backdrop, the Holy Father reappraises the Prodigal Son parable told by Jesus in the New Testament. "The story of the inexpressible love of a Father — God — Who offers . . . the gift of full reconciliation," the parable's fundamental lesson is that reconciliation among people is the fruit of the redemptive act of Christ. In other words, reconciliation originates with God the Father and finds its full expression in His Son's suffering, death and resurrection.

The Church is charged with a "ministry of reconciliation," even as it continually strives to be a community reconciled to itself. The Body of Christ, then, is a sacrament, or visible sign, of God's reconciliation in the world.

Sin, at bottom, the Pope instructs, is man's attempt to live without God. In its varying manifestations — personal and social, mortal and venial — sin is founded upon man's drive for radical independence.

This basic feature of sinfulness, both in particular acts as well as in a universal human condition, is expressed most clearly in the archetypal biblical stories of the Garden of Eden and the Tower of Babel.

What are the ways and means of promoting penance and reconciliation amid an enduring condition of alienation and fragmentation?

John Paul recommends a reinvigoration of ecumenical dialogue; a renewed emphasis on catechesis and repentance; a greater awareness of and sensitivity to opportunities of sinfulness and temptation, and, most importantly, a greater use of the sacrament of Penance, wherein an individual may experience a deeply personal and intimate encounter with a merciful God eager to heal a fractured humanity and a broken world.

Reconciliation • Given that sin destroys our relationship with God and undermines our relationships with other human beings, "reconciliation" designates that precise effect of Christ's redemption of the human race that restores our relationship with God and our human fellowship. Christ thus breaks down the barriers that sin raises between us and God, and within the human community. Since the full impact of Christ's salvation of the world is still taking hold in a struggle with the continuing power of evil and sin, the full reconciliation of the human race remains something to be consummated at the end of time. Precisely because our conversion from sin and our reception of divine mercy are continually renewed by confession, the Church has lately begun referring to this as the sacrament of Penance *and* Reconciliation. This designation also underscores the truths that serious sin separates us from the body of the Church and that sacramental Penance reconciles us with God and with the community of His people.

Reconciliation, Rite of: See **Penance, Sacrament of**

Reconciliation Room • The Second Vatican Council called for a revision of the Penitential Rite and formulae for the sacrament of Penance (SC 72). The sacrament's purpose is to "obtain pardon from God's mercy" and to be "reconciled with the Church which [sinners] have wounded by their sins, and which, by charity, by example, and by prayer, labors for their conversion" (LG 11).

Therefore, a new adaptation of the place of confession of sins, the reconciliation room offers an alternative to the confessional. The penitent is given the option of confessing anonymously behind a screen or conversing with the priest face-to-face. (Cf. Penance, Sacrament of; Counseling, Pastoral.)

Reconventio • In canon law a reconventio is the technical term generally applied to what, in civil law, would be known as a counterclaim. Canon 1482 states that the respondent has the right, within thirty days of the joinder of issues (Canon 1463), to file a counterclaim against the petitioner in an ecclesiastical case or controversy. The reconventio should have arisen from the same facts and conditions which led to the original case, and is generally tried by the same judge in the same proceedings as the original case. Its purpose is to avoid an unnecessary duplication of proceedings needed to resolve the disputes between parties. A counterclaim against a counterclaim is never allowed.

It can be argued, however, that the 1983 Code provisions on reconventio tend to blur the traditional distinctions between a reconventio, or a counterclaim, strictly speaking, and an "exception." Whereas a counterclaim usually arises between parties

based on similar facts, an exception, as developed in and borrowed from Roman law, is really an assertion of an affirmative defense for or justification of the respondent's action. It thus carries a necessarily much closer connection to the fact of the original case than would a reconventio and logically can be argued only within the context of that original controversy. Theoretically, a reconventio should be able to stand as the basis of an ecclesiastical trial on its own merits.

Records, Sacramental • Church law requires that certain official records be kept concerning the reception of sacraments by the faithful.

Sacramental records consist primarily of the baptismal register. This is a register kept at every parish church. In it the name of every person baptized there must be registered, together with the names of the minister of Baptism, the names of the parents and sponsors, and the date and place of the Baptism and the birth of the person baptized. The baptismal register is also to contain the date and place of marriage of the person, should this occur, along with the name of the spouse. If the marriage is subsequently dissolved or declared null, the date, place and protocol number of the pertinent document is also entered (Canons 1122-1123).

If the baptized person is confirmed, this information is also entered in the baptismal register (Canon 895), as is the fact of reception of Sacred Orders (Canon 1054).

The law also requires that a confirmation register be kept in parishes and in the diocesan curia (Canon 895). Similarly, a register for the reception of Sacred Orders is to be kept in the curia of the place of ordination (Canon 1053). Every parish is to have a marriage register that contains the names and addresses and religious affiliation of the spouses, the name of the official witness and other witnesses, and a notation of special permissions or dispensations granted. If a marriage is contracted with a dispensation from canonical form, it is to be registered in the parish church where the premarital investigation took place, as well as in the marriage register at the diocesan curia (Canon 1121).

Recourse, Hierarchical • A person who believes he or she has been injured or disadvantaged by an administrative decree or act of a superior has, in certain cases, the right to hierarchical recourse in order to have the decree amended or revoked. This means that the person has the right to appeal the decree to the superior of the person who issued it. In certain cases, while the matter is being considered by the hierarchical superior, the decree is suspended and does not go into effect until the recourse has been decided (Canons 1734-1739). Certain situations which have traditionally been sources of dispute, such as the removal or transfer of pastors, have over time been accorded their own specialized recourse procedures. Most other cases, however, require the administrators in recourse situations to apply the normal canons on juridical review, which judicial process, of course, does not always lend itself to easy use in administrative contexts. Although a series of proposed canons of general administrative recourse was dropped from the 1983 Code just before it was promulgated, it is clear that the Popes following the Second Vatican Council are concerned that administrative recourse be made viable in the Church, without denigrating Church leaders into squabble referees. It seems, for the time being, that the practical procedures of recourse will depend on the creative adaptation of canonical judicial procedures, along with clear and consistent praxis by the Roman Curia, to whom all canonists eventually look for guidance.

Rector • A priest to whom is entrusted the care of a church that is neither a parish church nor a church attached to a religious community. Because the rector is not a pastor in the canonical sense, he may not, without specific permission from the pastor of the parish within whose territory his church is situated, administer Baptism, Confirmation or the Anointing of the Sick (except in emergencies). Nor may he assist at marriages or conduct funerals.

Rector is also the title held by one who is in charge of a seminary or in some cases, a college (cf. Canons 556-563).

Recusants • From the Latin word meaning "to refuse," given those tenacious Catholics in England who refused to accept the Church of England during the reign of Elizabeth I (1558-1603) and beyond. A law of 1593 used the term as synonymous with traitor. Some recusants were martyred, some imprisoned, some harassed, some stripped of property and voting rights, and some forced into exile. One bright spot of centuries of oppression is that Catholic scholars established centers of learning at Douai and Rheims, where priests were formed and where the Scriptures were translated into English. Prejudice against the recusants came to an end during the reign of George II, when the Second Relief Act of 1791 repealed many anti-Catholic proscriptions.

Red Mass • The Mass of the Holy Spirit, so named from the red vestments used in celebrating the Mass and from the red robes traditionally worn by judges in the Middle Ages. This custom originated in Europe in the thirteenth century. Today the Catholic judges in England assemble at Westminster Cathedral for the celebration of the Red Mass. In France, it is celebrated at Saint Germain-l'Auxerrois. In Rome, the opening of the Sacred Roman Rota, the supreme judicial body of the Catholic Church, begins with a Red Mass. The inauguration of the Red Mass in the United States occurred in New York City on October 6, 1928, celebrated at old St. Andrew's Church on Duane Street with Patrick Cardinal Hayes. Since that time many groups of Catholic attorneys have continued to celebrate the Red Mass annually, offered to invoke the Holy Spirit, Who is the source of wisdom, understanding, counsel and fortitude.

Redditio of Creed • Literally, the "return" of the Creed, this expression refers to the acknowledgment or Profession of Faith during the baptismal rite. Here the Faith is professed through responses to questions which summarize the chief contents of the Creed.

Redemption of Man • Through Christ's passion, death and resurrection, the redemption of the human race was accomplished. This redemption is both the deliverance from sin and the restoration to the life of grace, or participation in the divine life itself. It is itself the free gift of God's mercy that our redemption was accomplished through the death of Christ. We cannot properly claim that this death was the necessary means for our redemption, though we can say it was fitting to employ the infinitely meritorious obedience of the God-Man, Jesus Christ, Who won redemption for us.

It is essential to understand that our redemption is won by the obedience of Christ, Who endured the ignominy and suffering of the cross in a perfect embrace of the divine will for our salvation. What God willed was our redemption; He permitted the betrayal, cowardice, malice and hatred that

brought about the conditions for Christ's death. Our redemption is accomplished by the obedient acceptance of a death brought about by human sin. In this way, Christ's resurrection from the dead demonstrates that the fateful power of sin and death is vanquished and neutralized forever. This redemption then opens the way to our new life in Christ. We become children of God, through Christ's grace, as the redemption He won for us once and for all takes hold in us through our justification and sanctification.

Redemptor Hominis • This encyclical (meaning *Redeemer of Man*) was issued early in the papacy of John Paul II. Dated March 4, 1979, and written in anticipation of the third millennium, the document surveyed the state of modernity and Christ's redeeming power to transform sinful humanity.

Expressing confidence in the Holy Spirit's unfailing guidance of the Church, the Pope began his discussion of the redemption of man by assessing the state of the Church, God's principal earthly instrument of redemption. The Church, he concluded, remains strong and unified in the face of "internal difficulties and tension." This strength and unity makes possible the important work of evangelization in a world sorely in need of the redemptive power of the Good News.

Christ is the "New Adam," he wrote, and recalling the words of the Second Vatican Council, John Paul reminded the faithful: "The truth is that only in the mystery of the Incarnate Word does the mystery of man take on light." The Church's role in this and in every age "is to direct man's gaze, to point the awareness and experience of the whole of humanity towards the mystery of God."

This mission, however, has been complicated by a condition of "fear" and "disquiet" afflicting modern man, as well as by an increasingly fashionable regard for theology as a "simple collection of [man's] personal ideas." Indeed, in the present age of technological progress and material wealth, certain realities threaten the very humanity of man, who is increasingly preoccupied with "having more" rather than "being more." Thus, the Pope concluded, a renewed devotion to the Eucharist, "the most perfect Sacrament" of the union between Christ and man, is required.

Redemptoris Mater • *The Mother of the Redeemer* is the sixth encyclical of Pope John Paul II. Released on March 25, 1987, in honor of the solemnity of the Annunciation and in celebration of the Marian year which was set to begin the following month, the Pope proclaimed the coming year an opportunity for a renewed reading of the Second Vatican Council's reflections on the Blessed Virgin Mary and her role in the Church and in salvation history. Mary, as a model of faith, is described as a beacon for the universal Church, and in a foreshadowing of John Paul's 1988 apostolic letter, "On the Dignity and Vocation of Women," the document also addresses Mary's "importance in relation to women and their status." The Blessed Mother's relationship to Jesus Christ and her role in forging a more fruitful ecumenism in the next Christian millennium are also noted.

Reformation • A complex movement of the sixteenth and seventeenth centuries that divided Christians into two distinct groups: Roman Catholics, marked by adherence to the Roman Pontiff and the historic formulations of the Faith; and a group of other Christian bodies, loosely united as "Protestants."

A number of factors had weakened the Church in the late medieval period: the decline of religious learning and fervor after the Black Death, the disruptions of the Avignon Papacy and the Schism of the West, conciliarism, the worldliness and corruption of many churchmen, nominalism and other unhealthy theological trends. Movements toward spiritual renewal, and even a renewal council (Lateran V, 1517) had limited influence.

The Reformation is generally dated from the publication of certain theses by Martin Luther on October 31, 1517. Central to Luther's teaching is the affirmation of original sin as sinful concupiscence that remains after Baptism (corruption of man) and an acceptance of man by God without interior regeneration of man (justification by faith alone, man at once sinner and justified). Opposition by Catholic theologians led Luther to harden his position, especially the rejection of any teaching authority of the Church, either papal or conciliar; and the rejection of traditional teaching on the sacraments. Luther held for a Real Presence of Christ in the Eucharist, but denied transubstantiation. Luther did not want to start a new church, but after the rejection at the Diet of Augsburg (1530) of the Protestant party's bid for acceptance as a valid form of Catholic life, Lutheranism became more clearly a separate denomination. It spread rapidly throughout much of Germany and throughout Scandinavia. Nonreligious factors also influenced the situation. Some German princes saw the new religion as a way of expressing independence from the Catholic emperor, and many were anxious to seize the wealth and lands of the Church.

Besides the Lutheran or Evangelical tradition, early Protestantism has several other strands. Ulrich Zwingli (1458-1531) began preaching about reform even before he was influenced by Lutheran teaching. He led the reform movement in Zurich and later in some other parts of Switzerland. His views, especially on the sacraments, were more extreme than Luther's. The groups led by Zwingli and his successor H. Bullinger eventually merged with those led by Calvin (1509-1564) at Geneva to form the Reform or Calvinistic tradition. A distinctive element of Calvin's thought (although not commonly held by modern Calvinists) is his teaching on predestination: that some humans are created for heaven, others for hell. His book, *Institutes of the Christian Religion*, in five versions between 1536 and 1559, is a kind of *Summa* of Calvinistic beliefs and helped assure him a significant place in the history of Western Christianity. Written in Latin and translated by Calvin into French, it soon appeared in other languages and helped fix the influence of the Reformed Tradition not only in Switzerland but also in parts of France, the Low Countries and Scotland.

The Anabaptists, the third Protestant tradition, are not an organized denomination but a loose association of more radical Protestants. They put great stress on inner religious experience, rejecting both ecclesiastical and civil authority. They reject infant Baptism as invalid, insisting on "believer's" Baptism: hence, their name Anabaptists, or "Re-baptizers." Fiercely persecuted and always small in number, they survive in a number of Mennonite and Amish communities.

The reform in England followed a complex course. Henry VIII broke with Rome but wanted to retain Catholic doctrine and worship. Under Edward VI, only nine years old when he succeeded his father, the regents introduced more Protestant elements. Mary Tudor (1553-1558) strove mightily — sometimes too mightily — to restore the old religion. The long reign of Elizabeth (1558-1603) saw the triumph of the new Anglicanism: some Catholic elements but more Calvinistic than the settlement of Henry VIII. These two elements — Catholicism and Calvinism — exist in a kind of tension in Anglicanism.

Sometimes Catholic forms seem to advance (e.g., under the Caroline divines); at other times, Calvinistic themes are more dominant (e.g., under Oliver Cromwell or after the Revolution of 1688).

Only in recent decades have the polemics of the Reformation era been muted, and the first tentative efforts at ecumenism begun.

Regina Coeli • These are the first words of the Latin version of the antiphon of the Blessed Mother which is chanted in the Divine Office or Liturgy of the Hours, after Compline, the last liturgical hour of the day, from Holy Saturday to the Saturday following Pentecost Sunday. The *Regina Coeli*, or Queen of Heaven, is recited during paschal time instead of the *Angelus* (since 1742 by decree of Pope Benedict XIV) at the prescribed hours three times daily, that is, at 6 A.M. or first thing in the morning, at 12 noon and at 6 P.M. It is recited standing.

Although legend attributes its composition to Pope St. Gregory the Great (590-604), who is said to have heard the angels singing it and who himself is said to have added the last line or versicle, it is now believed that the antiphon has later origins. First traces of it extant may be seen in the twelfth century. The Franciscans were the first to use it in their Office, after Compline. When Pope Nicholas III (1277-1280) replaced all the older Office books in the Churches of Rome with new ones following the Franciscan Ordo, its popularity increased and its place in later traditions was ensured. The words of the antiphon are as follows:

"Queen of Heaven, rejoice, Alleluia,
Because He Whom thou didst merit to
    bear, Alleluia,
Has risen as He said, Alleluia,
Pray to God for us, Alleluia."

(When the antiphon is recited instead of the *Angelus*, the following responsory and prayer are added:)

"Rejoice and be glad, O Virgin Mary, Alleluia,
The Lord has truly risen, Alleluia."
Let us pray. "O God, Who by the Resurrection of Thy Son, our Lord Jesus Christ, didst grant joy to the whole world: grant, we beseech Thee, that through the intercession of the Virgin Mary, His Mother, we may lay hold of the joys of eternal life. Through the same Christ our Lord. Amen."

Regulae Juris • The *Regulae Juris*, or Rules of Justice, is a series of ninety-nine canonical maxims which were developed over a period of centuries and which express in concise form the fundamental legal principles that helped to shape the practice of canon law.

Eleven of these rules appear at the end of St. Raymond of Peñafort's thirteenth-century *Liber Decretalium*, while eighty-eight are included at the end of Pope Boniface VIII's *Liber Sextus* some eighty years later (cf. Canon Law, History of). It was disputed though perhaps unnecessarily, whether the *Regulae Juris* were even officially recognized as law. For however one chose to resolve that question, it was clear that the wisdom and experience evidenced in the Rules guaranteed them a lasting place in the development of canonical practice. The great canonist Reiffenstuel, among many others, urged that "it is highly useful to read and reread them and, as far as possible, to commit them to memory." The Rules range over the whole field of jurisprudence, as this brief sampling taken from the *Liber Sextus* will demonstrate.

Rule 6 declares simply that "no one is bound to the impossible." "Odious matters are to be restrained," counsels Rule 15, "but favorable matters are to receive wide play." Rule 29 became a cornerstone of modern democratic theory when it declared that "What concerns all must be approved by all." Rule 30 prudently notes that "in obscure questions, only the minimum can be demanded." Rule 43 contains the famous maxim, "One who is silent seems to give assent," and Rule 49 benignly cautions that "in penal matters the gentler interpretation is to be made." "The crimes of the person," declares Rule 76, "must not be held against the Church." And Rule 3 taken from the *Liber Decretalium* upholds the idea that "the truth must not be hidden simply to avoid scandal."

None of the *Regulae* were intended to operate as autonomous razors in blind disregard for other laws. Indeed some Rules at times came into conflict with other Rules themselves, forcing an even greater reliance on the prudence of the ecclesiastical judge or legislator faced with making a decision in a particular matter. But in most cases, even to this day, the *Regulae Juris* are a reliable source of simple and sound direction in the difficult task of accommodating rights and responsibilities.

Reign of God, The • The term "reign" is synonymous with "kingdom." The "reign of God" thus includes the notion of kingship or the exercise of royal power and rule in a kingdom (Lk 19:12, 15; 1 Cor 15:24; Heb 8; Rv 1:6; 17:12). In particular, the kingdom or reign of God (or of heaven) communicates the salvation that has come with power and might, which we are to witness in the final days. Those who hear this message can find meaning for it in Jesus' parables (e.g., Mk 4:1-9, 10-12, 13-20; also, vv. 21-25; vv. 26-29 and especially vv. 30-32). (Cf. Kingdom of God.)

For further reading: Dannis C. Duling, "Kingdom of Heaven, Kingdom of God," *Anchor Bible Dictionary*, 4:49-69.

Reincarnation: See **Metempsychosis**

Reinstatement • A procedural act whereby a person injured by a judicial sentence that was unjust can, for reasons of equity, be restored to the status the person had before the sentence was issued. This is also known as *restitutio in integrum*. Reinstatement can only happen in a case where the sentence has become *res iudicata*. In such cases, since all appeals have been exhausted and the matter has become a closed judgment, the only redress is through reinstatement.

Reinstatement can be granted for five specific reasons: if the sentence is based on proofs later demonstrated to be false, so that without these proofs, the decision could not be sustained; if documents or proofs are found after the sentence which prove new facts demanding a contrary decision; if the sentence was pronounced because of fraud on the part of one party which harmed the other; if a prescription of a nonprocedural law was evidently neglected, or if the sentence is contrary to a preceding sentence which had become a closed judgment.

For the most part, reinstatement takes place when the proofs brought forward are discovered to have been false or when new information demands that a contrary decision be granted. In such cases involving the proofs or new information, the aggrieved person is to seek the reinstatement from the judge who made the original decision. If it is a question of one of the other reasons listed above, the person is to bring his case before the appeal tribunal of the court of first instance that handed down the sentence.

It should be noted that an action of reinstatement cannot be applied to marriage nullity cases. Such cases involve what the law refers to as "the status of persons." These cases never become a closed judgment but are always open to additional appeals, even after two concordant decisions are given (Canons 1645-1648).

Relativism • A broad term designating a wide range of views that have in common the denial of the possibility of determining the truth particularly in matters of philosophy, religion and morals. Relativistic views have been widespread in the twentieth century as a result of a prevailing epistemology according to which the belief systems and ethos of specific social groupings are said to be culturally and historically conditioned. The notion that the truth of these systems is located in their actual correspondence to reality is regarded as naive or illusory.

It is basic to modern forms of relativism to view truth and meaning as socially or psychologically constructed. Pragmatism and Marxism have exercised a powerful influence in the emergence of most modern forms of relativism, as has the application of sociological and psychological explanations to many aspects of contemporary thought and culture. The impact of relativist modes of thinking has been felt most strikingly in ethics, where the classical notion of universally valid moral norms has been undermined, and in religion, where the cognitive and truth claims thought to be embodied in doctrines have been reinterpreted in symbolic, linguistic and social terms.

Relativism poses an enormous challenge to all religious believers. Catholic leaders and thinkers have vigorously opposed it in the areas of philosophy, religion and morality. Without denying the influence of cultural, social and psychological factors, Catholics have upheld the ability of the human mind to arrive at the universally true in science, philosophy and morality, and to receive in faith a revelation that definitively discloses God's purposes for the eternal well-being of mankind.

Relics, Sacred • In Christian usage, the term applies to bodies or portions of the bodies of the saints after death, clothing or articles they used in life, or articles such as bits of cloth that have touched their remains or tombs. They may not be bought or sold. Those of martyrs are placed in the altar stone at the consecration of an altar. There are three classes of relics: the first is part of the saint's body and is the type placed in the altar stone; the second is part of the clothing or anything used during the saint's life; the third is any other object, such as a piece of cloth that has been touched to a first-class relic.

The earliest reference to relics is the account of the martyrdom of St. Polycarp in A.D. 156. The common belief that graces could be obtained through relics is mentioned by the Church Fathers of the fourth and fifth centuries. By the tenth century, relics were placed in shrines, and in reliquaries of churches which became centers of pilgrimage. Present regulations governing the veneration of relics are contained in Canons 1281-1289.

Relief Services, Catholic (CRS) • The association, funded by the contributions of American Catholics, dedicated to the assistance and development of needy countries. It was founded in 1943 by the bishops of the United States in order to aid war-stricken civilians in Europe and North Africa. Later, CRS assisted countries in Africa, Asia and Latin America. Seventy-four countries are helped by CRS through various projects. Dioceses in the United States, especially during Lent through the "Operation Rice Bowl" program, have contributed millions of dollars to CRS.

Religion • A term referring to any social, cultural and institutional forms of engagement with the transcendent reality that is believed to embrace the world and human existence. Religion can also be a "private" matter, in that a person constructs and follows a system of beliefs and practices that are analogous to the culturally and socially established religions. Commonly, scholars distinguish traditional (previously called "primitive") forms of religion from the major or world religions. The distinction is a relative one, in that it acknowledges the transcultural character of the worldwide religions and the high degree of institutional and intellectual development they evince. Thus, Native American religions are traditional religions, while Hinduism, Buddhism, Judaism, Christianity and Islam are major religions. Sometimes Taoism and Confucianism are added to the major religions, but these seem more like religio-philosophical systems.

Some scholars (e.g., Paul Tillich and Ninian Smart) cast the net further in order to include as quasi-religions or secular world-views the institutional embodiments of Marxism or National Socialism. Religion is not synonymous with theism, since some religions are nontheistic (e.g., forms of Buddhism). Prior to the Enlightenment period, religion referred to a part of the virtue of justice by which human beings pay due worship to God (e.g., Aquinas) and in particular to the proper way of undertaking this worship, the Christian Faith, *vera religio*. After the Enlightenment, the tendency arose to use the term "religion" to identify historical religions as social bodies, and to distinguish from these certain necessary beliefs and moral practices as the inner core of "natural religion," a basic endowment of human nature.

Religious Discourse • An umbrella term referring to the variety of uses to which ordinary language is put in the forms of speech by which particular religious communities commend and foster their distinctive patterns of life. The characteristic discourse of religious communities is found especially in their confessions, stories, prayers, invocations, blessings, poems, creeds and doctrines (conveying beliefs and practices). When in more highly developed religious traditions, this body of utterances begins to engender systematic reflection by theologians (and their counterparts in nontheistic communities), questions arise about the special character of the community's discourse as it bears on the reality of the transcendent object that is the focus of the community's life and worship.

How can human utterances apprehend or express the truth about that which completely surpasses ordinary experience? In the major world religions such as Judaism, Christianity, Islam, Hinduism and Buddhism, reflection about this question has given rise to various theories about the force of religious doctrines conveying beliefs. In the Christian community, reflection about this question is the domain of the specialty called philosophical theology, with apophantic theology and analogy and prominent topics.

In this century, especially in English-speaking philosophical circles, there was debate about the force of religious utterances (mainly with reference to Christian beliefs), with some philosophers espousing skeptical or emotive accounts of religious discourse. But such accounts have been largely superseded by more broadly conceived inquiries that attend not only to Christian discourse but to the discourse of other communities and that recognize the importance of truth claims in religion.

Reliquary from France
(thirteenth century)

Religious Institute: See **Institute, Religious**

Religious Liberty: See **Liberty, Religious**; also **Dignitatis Humanae**

Religious Life: See **Perfectae Caritatis**

Religious Life, Decree on the Up-to-Date Renewal of: See **Perfectae Caritatis**

Religious Orders: See **Orders, Holy**

Reliquary • A repository or receptacle for the preservation or display of a relic. Reliquaries vary in size and materials. Some are made with precious metals and ornamented with gems, enamels and paintings.

Among the famous reliquaries of the Church are the ivory casket-type reliquary in the museum at Brescia, Italy, which is decorated with Old and New Testament scenes; the bust reliquaries of the Apostles Peter and Paul at St. John Lateran Basilica in Rome; the silver shrine of the Three Kings at Cologne, Germany; and the enamel and jeweled table reliquaries containing a piece of the True Cross at the Cathedral in Limburg, Germany.

Modern reliquaries usually take a contemporary capsule form with a glass lid.

Remnant • The notion of remnant derives from several expressions used by the Old Testament to refer to those who are left as survivors of some calamity, especially the victims of military conquest. The concept of the remnant acquired its theological significance in Israel's prophetic literature from the interpretation of such disastrous events as manifestations of divine judgment.

Among the prophets, the idea of the remnant first appears in the forceful admonition found in Amos 5:15: "Hate evil and love good, and establish justice in the gate; it may be that the LORD, the God of hosts, will be gracious to the remnant of Joseph." The use of the word remnant here suggests that even though devastating woes are sure to come, the prophet holds out a possibility of hope for the survivors, while emphasizing that this hope depends on their conduct.

The symbolic name of Isaiah's son *Shear-Jashub*, "a remnant will return," highlights the negative and positive features inherent in the notion of the remnant. Negatively, it can imply that *only* a small portion of the people will escape destruction or return from forced deportation. Positively, it can imply that some *will* survive the coming distress, that not all are doomed, and that these survivors are those who place their trust in the Lord.

Isaiah 10:20-22 likewise illustrates both the negative and the positive implications of the remnant: "In that day the remnant of Israel and the survivors of the house of Jacob will no more lean upon him that smote them, but will lean upon the LORD, the Holy One of Israel, in truth. A remnant will return, the remnant of Jacob, to the

mighty God. For though your people Israel be as the sands of the sea, only a remnant of them will return. Destruction is decreed, overflowing with righteousness."

Divine justice decrees the decimation of Israel, yet among the surviving remnant this leads to renewed fidelity and a return to the Lord. In the interchange between King Hezekiah and Isaiah during the Assyrian crisis, the prophet offers hopeful words about the remnant, assuring the king that his prayers for help against the Assyrians have been answered: "And the surviving remnant of the house of Judah shall again take root downward, and bear fruit upward; for out of Jerusalem shall go forth a remnant, and from Mount Zion a band of survivors. The zeal of the LORD will do this" (2 Kgs 19:30-31).

Another hope-filled use of the remnant idea can be found in the book of the prophet Micah, who was Isaiah's eighth century B.C. contemporary (Mic 2:12; 4:7; 5:7; 7:18).

"The remnant of my flock" in Jeremiah 23:3 and "the remnant of Israel" in Jeremiah 31:7 are phrases which the prophet uses to designate those who have been deported to Babylon. These the Lord promises to gather and to bring "back to their fold" (Jer 23:3).

A bleaker picture of the remnant of Judah is presented elsewhere in the Book of Jeremiah. Urged to "pray to the LORD your God for us, for all this remnant" (Jer 42:2), Jeremiah returns with the divine message that the pitiful remnant of Judah is not to flee to Egypt out of fear of the king of Babylon and his armies. The remnant is to remain in the land, waiting there for God's restoring mercy (Jer 42:10-22). Jeremiah explains that the devastation of Jerusalem was divine punishment for Judah's sins of idolatry (Jer 44:3-6). When the remnant fails to heed these words and escapes to Egypt, the prophet utters God's grim sentence: "None of the remnant of Judah that have come to settle in the land of Egypt shall escape or survive" (Jer 44:13).

After the Babylonian exile, Haggai 1:12, 14; 2:2 and Zechariah 8:6, 11, 12 refer to the returnees from exile as the remnant of the people in hopeful terms that have to do with the resettlement of the land and with the project of rebuilding the Temple. In what Zechariah 8:12 calls "a sowing of peace," the remnant is heir to the promises which God made to the whole people.

In the New Testament, St. Paul employs the prophetic idea of the remnant. Romans 9:27 abridges Isaiah 10:22-23 as part of the series of Old Testament citations in Romans 9:25-29. In this citation, "Though the number of the sons of Israel be as the sand of the sea, only a remnant of them will be saved," both judgment and hope are drawn from the idea of the remnant into Paul's argument about the history of Israel's election by God. After Romans 11:1, "I ask, then, has God rejected his people? By no means!" Romans 11:5 emphasizes the steadfastness of God's grace toward the faithful remnant: "So too at the present time there is a remnant, chosen by grace."

For further reading: Lester V. Meyer, "Remnant," *Anchor Bible Dictionary*, 5:669-671.

Renewal, Charismatic: See Charismatic Renewal

Renunciation • Sacramentally, this term refers to the request made of the parent and godparent to renounce the Devil and his works, for becoming a Christian means that one is expected to reject all that is not in accord with Christ and His works.

Spiritually, renunciation implies sacrifice of material or human good, so that one can advance in the spiritual life. Renunciation implies rejection of goods or values to which one has a moral and legitimate claim and

right because these draw one away from God. This form of renunciation is a necessary part of spiritual growth because it purges one of harmful egotism and conforms the person more fully to the image of Christ. Christian renunciation does not romanticize suffering or deprivation but sees it as necessary for full participation in the paschal mystery. This spiritual renunciation fortifies the spirit, but if not properly directed toward charity and holiness, practices of renunciation can lead to pride and arrogance. The aim of these renunciations is to subject one's will more fully to that of the Father, and thus be more like Christ, Who was fully obedient to the Father by nature. Canonically, renunciation generally refers to an action whereby a litigant forgoes the right to seek justice in a given process. Very occasionally, one encounters the term renunciation as a form of resignation from ecclesiastical office.

Reparation • The religious meaning of reparation retains its ordinary meaning as the making of amends for harm or damage done to another person. Reparation is one of the four conditions of Penance in that it displays the determination to undo the harm caused by sins committed and forgiven. The efficacy of Christian reparation is rooted in the perfectly satisfying sacrifice of Christ Himself on the cross.

Repentance • A number of ideas are related to this concept, but generally it means sorrow for sins and turning to God, conversion, changing of attitude or intention. The theme of repentance is a major theme in the Scriptures. Even God shows repentance and change of heart, for He decides not to punish when His people turn from their sinful ways, and He "repents" of the punishments He had planned for them. Repentance is deeper than simple regret, for Judas regretted his betrayal of Jesus, but apparently he did not repent of it. He abandons hope of forgiveness and does not change his heart, and repentance includes not only turning from sin, but also turning toward God and a new life.

In the Old Testament, there were many liturgies of repentance, and the prophets condemned Israelites for not truly and deeply repenting during these rituals. True repentance is shown by helping the needy and by "turning" to God, His Law, righteousness, love and holiness, and away from sin and disobedience. The fruit of repentance is messianic salvation and deliverance from evil; for the Israelites, survival, prosperity, peace and union with God all ultimately come from repentance.

Repentance is at the heart of the New Testament teachings, and it was central to the preaching of John the Baptist and Jesus, who both demanded repentance because the kingdom of God was at hand in Jesus. Jesus claimed that the very reason for His coming was to call sinners to repentance. Repentance is shown by Baptism, faith, confession of sins and good works such as almsgiving. The unrepentant risk eternal damnation, and the greatest joy in heaven is for the repentant.

Hebrews 6:1-6 denies the possibility of second repentance, but it seems that this passage refers to apostasy from the Faith, rather than to the impossibility of being forgiven for sins. Forgiveness from God should not be presumed, but the person who is truly repentant should be aware of the grave seriousness of sin.

Reproductive Engineering • A term used to cover many different contemporary techniques concerned with fertility and conception such as *in vitro* fertilization, surrogate motherhood, sperm banks, etc. While understanding the legitimate and worthy desire of couples to become biological parents, Catholic teaching insists on submitting new techniques of reproductive engineering to ethical scrutiny. The basic principle for approval or disapproval concerns whether or not a given procedure deprives the unborn child of his or her right to be a result of marital love versus a product of technology.

Interventions which merely overcome a deficiency so as to increase fertility or facilitate implantation of a sperm and egg joined in the womb of the mother after an act of mutual sexual intercourse are licit. Interventions which supplant sexual love with masturbation or which join sperm and egg outside the nest of the womb are to be avoided. An explanation of the moral and spiritual reasons for Catholic teaching can be found in the Vatican Declaration published in 1987, *On Respect for Human Life in Its Origin and On the Dignity of Procreation.*

Requiem • Formerly (and, in some quarters, still) popular term denoting a Mass offered for the repose of the faithful departed. The expression came from the first word of the well-known and beautiful Gregorian (Latin) entrance chant (or Introit) at Masses for the Dead: "*Requiem aeternam dona eis, Domine* . . . Eternal rest grant unto them, O Lord." The current term is Funeral Mass or Mass of Christian Burial, or apart from the funeral rites, simply Mass for the Dead. (Cf. also Order of Christian Funerals.)

Reredos • An altar piece, that is, a screen of stone or wood at the back of the altar and connected to it by means of a predella. Reredoses became common in the twelfth century, when they were attached to altars containing relics. Some reredoses are fitted with richly decorated panels depicting religious scenes and narratives of the life of a saint to whom the altar is dedicated. In modern churches, any decorative panel may be replaced by a hanging, stained glass or a framed detail.

Rerum Novarum • An encyclical with the English title *On the Condition of Human Labor*, published on May 15, 1891, by Pope Leo XIII. The Pope wrote that overcoming the poverty he saw around him was the primary reason for its writing, and rather than calling for the overthrow of the capitalist order, he urged its renewal and transformation, so that justice could prevail in it. The encyclical articulated the principle of subsidiarity, which held that the law was to go no further than was necessary to remedy evils or remove dangers.

Pope Leo held that the ills of the world would be resolved by a return to the Church and her teachings. He defended a limited right to own private property, which right could only stand if just wages were offered to workers. However, the title to private property was not absolute and this right could be overridden for the common good. Workers should be allowed to organize and form labor unions, and they should be given a wage sufficient to allow the thrifty to work toward owning land.

This encyclical marked the beginning of the social-justice movement of the Catholic Church, and it had a profound impact on the involvement of the Church in these issues. As a result of this encyclical, the Church became firmly committed in the twentieth century to promoting social justice.

Res Iudicata • Literally, "judged thing," *res iudicata* refers to a definitive judicial sentence or decision that is so firm and final that it admits no further appeal. It can only be overturned by the canonical action of reinstatement. The decisions in only certain types of cases can become *res*

iudicata or closed judgments. Excluded are all cases concerning that status of persons, such as marriage nullity cases or cases that involve canonical penalties. Even after the normal appeal process has been completed, such cases are always open to additional appeals if new evidence is brought forward.

In those types of cases capable of having a closed judgment, the decision becomes irreversible in four cases: if there are two concordant or agreeing sentences in cases involving the same persons, the same petition and the same reasons for the final decision; if the appeal against the sentence has not been filed in the available time; if the prosecution of the case has been renounced or stopped at the appeal level; if a sentence has been rendered against which there is no available appeal, i.e., a sentence of the Supreme Pontiff himself or the Apostolic Signatura (Canons 1641-1644).

Rescript • Literally, a "writing back," a rescript is an administrative act issued in writing by a competent ecclesiastical superior, in response to a request for a privilege, dispensation or some other favor (cf. Canons 59-75).

Reservation of the Blessed Sacrament • Generally, the practice of keeping the Blessed Sacrament in a tabernacle in a prominent place in the sanctuary. This practice is based on the faith in the Real Presence of Christ under the consecrated species of bread and wine. Canon law stipulates that the Blessed Sacrament must be reserved in the cathedral church, in every parish church and in the chapels and churches attached to religious houses. The permission of the bishop is required in order to reserve the Blessed Sacrament in other chapels or oratories. Unless there is urgent pastoral need, the Church does not permit one to carry the Blessed Sacrament about on one's person. Normally, it is expected that the church in which the Blessed Sacrament is reserved would be open for at least part of the day for visits and prayer by the faithful. The term reservation is also applied more specifically to the conclusion of the Holy Thursday Mass of the Lord's Supper, at which point the Blessed Sacrament is removed from the tabernacle and reserved in a ciborium in a special repository chapel.

Reserved Censure • A reserved censure is one that can be absolved or remitted only by a specific authority in the Church. Although there are no longer any reserved sins in the revised Code, the penalties for certain ecclesiastical crimes are reserved to the Holy See. These include five of the seven automatic excommunications, namely: desecration of the Holy Eucharist (Canon 1367); laying violent hands on the Supreme Pontiff (Canon 1370.1); absolution of an accomplice in a sexual sin (Canon 1378.1); consecration of a bishop without a papal mandate (Canon 1382); violation of the confessional seal (Canon 1388).

The 1917 Code contained twenty-three automatic excommunications and an elaborate system of reservation of the penalties. The most serious were "most specially reserved to the Holy See." The remainder, depending on their seriousness, were "specially reserved to the Holy See," "simply reserved to the Holy See," "reserved to the Ordinary," or "reserved to no one."

Residence • The obligation assumed by certain officeholders in the Church that they will reside in the territory over which they have authority. A bishop is bound to reside in his diocese and not to be absent from it for more than one month unless he is attending a synod, council or other meeting recognized in the law (cf. Canon 395).

The pastor of a parish is required to reside in the parish. Like the bishop, he is not to be absent from the parish for more than one month (cf. Canon 533). An associate pastor is also bound to reside in the parish (cf. Canon 550).

Resignation • One way that a person can cease to hold an ecclesiastical office. Any ecclesiastical office, including the papacy, is subject to resignation. For validity, any resignation (except that of the Pope) must be accepted by a competent superior (cf. Canons 187-189).

Respondent • The commonly used term for the second party in a canonical trial. A trial is initiated by a petitioner. The other party, the respondent, is not presumed, even casually or unofficially, to be guilty or at fault because he or she did not enter the petition. The term is most often used in reference to marriage nullity cases.

The law protects the rights of a respondent by guaranteeing that he or she can submit evidence, have the services of an advocate, review the acts of the case upon completion of the evidence-gathering phase and, lastly, appeal the final decision.

Some erroneously believe that a case cannot be settled (especially a marriage case) without the consent of the respondent. This is not so. The purpose of contacting the respondent is to obtain information and facts about the matter under consideration. If the respondent refuses to participate in a case or simply ignores any and all communications from the ecclesiastical court, the judge has the power to continue processing the issue without the assistance and participation of the respondent. For that matter, a respondent need not even necessarily disagree or oppose the desires of the petitioner in a case and, provided there is no danger of collusion, he or she can even give evidence which advances the petitioner's claim. (Cf. J. Krol, "The Defendant in Ecclesiastical Trials," *Studies in Canon Law* No. 146, Catholic University of America, 1942.)

Responsibility, Modes of: See **Modes of Responsibility**

Responsorial Psalm: See **Psalm, Responsorial**

Responsory • Term taken from the Latin *responsorium* to denote a chant or spoken response to a liturgical reading whose text derives directly from the Scripture proclaimed or the season of the Church year. It originated in the Jewish synagogue service and is found (under the title *cantus responsorius*) in the writings of Tertullian (third century). At Mass, the Responsorial Psalm is one example of the cantor's singing verses of a psalm interspersed with the congregation's singing the refrain. In the former Mass the Gradual and Alleluia were examples. At the Liturgy of the Hours, the clearest examples follow the reading from Scripture and the nonbiblical reading at the Office of Readings. These responses are usually from Scripture (most often taken from the text just proclaimed), or they may be from another source. The first verse is followed by its being repeated by the congregation, the first part of the Glory Be, followed by the first verse repeated once again. The responsory had a particular application in the monastic office, as it provided the monks with a verse on which to focus their personal reflection. (St. Benedict's Rule attests to the use of the responsory.) Additional (usually shorter) responsories are presently found after the Scripture readings at Morning Prayer, Evening Prayer and Night Prayer (when the same responsory is always used).

Restitution • In moral theology, restitution is the act of "commutative justice" (i.e., between individuals), by which an injury which has been done to the property or person of another is repaired, either by return or compensation in the case of property, or by some proper means of reparation in the case of a person's reputation, health, life or chastity.

Restitution is included in the 1983 Code of Canon Law (Canon 981, Canon 982 and in numerous other canons), and receiving absolution from sin can be made contingent upon one's willingness to make restitution as a sign of sincere contrition and purpose of amendment.

Resurrection of the Body • The most central tenet of Catholic (and of all Christian beliefs) is the belief in the resurrection of the body. It is important to distinguish the biblical notion of resurrection from the Hellenistic concept of the soul's immortality. Greek philosophy and many religious movements within Hellenism held that the soul was incorruptible and "naturally" enters into divine immortality at death. The basic truth from Sacred Scripture is that the whole person (body, soul and spirit) will be resurrected on the "last day."

The Old Testament anticipates and prepares for the New Testament teaching on resurrection of the body in statements about God's great "power over life and death"; He brings "down to Sheol and raises up" (Wis 16:13; 1 Sm 2:6). God restores to life (Ps 30:3). The bringing back to life of dead children (1 Kgs 17:22; 2 Kgs 4:35; 13:21), as well as the above examples, prepare us for Christ's resurrection in the New Testament. Passages such as Isaiah 25:8 ("He will swallow up death for ever") and Isaiah 26:19 ("Thy dead shall live, their bodies shall rise") certainly anticipate something like the New Testament teachings on resurrection. A greater degree of explicitness concerning belief in the resurrection is achieved in passages such as 2 Maccabees 7:9-23; 12:41-45; Daniel 12:2-3. Except for the Sadducees, most Jewish groups believed in the resurrection of the body (e.g., Pharisees, Acts 24:15). The resurrection of the body is the preeminent sign that the final age of salvation has arrived. The general resurrection (Mt 11:22; 12:41, etc.) is consistent with such a belief. In John's Gospel, the teaching is clearer (Jn 5:28ff.; 6:39, 44, 54), and Paul is quite explicit about the resurrection of the body (e.g., 1 Cor 15:1-58), the hope of all who believe. In summary, those who live and die "in Christ" are hidden with Christ in God, but when Christ comes again they will appear with Him in glory (Col 3:3-4).

Resurrection of Christ • As a basic truth of the Christian Faith, the doctrine of the resurrection of Christ is an essential part of the teaching of the Church from the earliest days. The Gospels all give witness to Christ's resurrection (Mt 28:1-20; Mk 16:9-20; Lk 24:1-9; Jn 20:1-18), and it is professed in all the ancient Creeds. St. Paul proclaims that "if Christ has not been raised, then our preaching is in vain and your faith is in vain" (1 Cor 15:14).

Resurrection
(tenth-century manuscript)

On the third day after His death and burial, the Lord Jesus rose from the dead through His own power, because of the union of the human and divine natures in the one Divine Person of Christ. When Holy Scripture says that Christ was raised by God (Acts 2:24) or by the Father (Gal 1:1), it is to be understood that these statements refer to His human nature, but that the cause of the Resurrection was the hypostatic union of Christ's humanity with the Godhead.

The resurrection of Christ is objective in that He walked out of the tomb, still bearing the wounds of His suffering, but from the moment of the Resurrection His body was in a state of glory, which is attested to by the circumstances of His appearances recorded in the Gospels and in Acts, in which He is no longer bound by time or space.

Although our redemption comes through the merits of Christ's sacrificial death upon the cross, the resurrection of Christ is seen as the completion of the redemptive act and so is associated with His death as a complete whole. Also, the risen Christ is seen as the "first fruits of those who have fallen asleep" (1 Cor 15:20), and so is the model for the bodily resurrection of all the faithful on the last day.

For further reading: George W. E. Nickelsburg, "Resurrection (Early Judaism and Christianity)," *Anchor Bible Dictionary*, 5:684-691.

Retable • A structure placed at the back of an altar in the form either of a ledge or a frame for decorated panels. The ledge form is also known as a gradine, the frame form for panels as a reredos.

Retreat • A time taken by a priest, religious or lay person for the purpose of devotion, prayer and meditation, in order to advance in the spiritual life. A retreat also refers to a place of quiet where one can spend time in solitude to pray and reflect.

In essence, the practice of retreats is older than Christianity, and the forty days Christ spent in the desert serves as the model for Christian retreats. Retreats were widely and formally introduced during the Reformation era, and the Jesuits were the first to incorporate them into their rule of life. Sts. Francis de Sales and Vincent de Paul actively promoted retreats in the seventeenth century, and the practice of annual retreats became widespread in Roman Catholicism in the nineteenth century. The form and character of retreats has become more specialized and particular in recent decades, and they have been seen as a particularly effective means of advancing Christian life in specific areas.

Retribution • Although both the just reward or punishment due to good or sinful actions can be termed retribution, ordinary usage normally reserves this word for punishment. In the Christian understanding, the suffering is in part due to sin itself; in this sense, punishment is an intrinsic consequence of sin. The reward surpasses anything we could deserve or expect: the divine life itself.

Retroactive Force of Law • All ecclesiastical laws concern matters of the future and not the past. Hence, when a new law is passed, it does not have retroactive force unless this is specifically indicated. If an old law is replaced by a new law, the effects of the old law are canceled unless the new law is the same as the old law. Consequently, when the revised Code of Canon Law went into effect, the laws of the 1917 Code ceased to have force unless they were reproduced in the new Code (Canon 9).

Revelation • Revelation refers both to God's activity in making Himself and His purposes known to humankind through Christ, the prophets and Apostles, and to the content that is communicated and handed on.

Revelation has an interpersonal structure and point. God reveals to human beings His intention to draw them into union with Him. In the course of doing so, He discloses the mystery of His own inner trinitarian life and the true destiny of human beings. With revelation, therefore, comes a body of knowledge otherwise inaccessible to human discovery. The knowledge of God's own self-description and of His grace-filled purpose for human beings throws light on and draws to itself all the other knowledge that human beings can acquire by observation and inquiry. The divinely chosen vehicles of revelation are human beings who, through special grace, are inspired to speak and write on God's behalf. Paramount among these is Jesus Christ — the very Word of God — Who communicates, definitively and unsurpassably, all that the Triune God wants humankind to know about Himself and His saving purposes.

The normative source of revelation is the Scripture as encompassed within the living Tradition of the teaching and worshiping community of Christ's followers. The human response to revelation is faith chiefly in God Himself, and secondarily in the human bearers and sources of revelation.

By extension, the term "revelation" is also used to refer to what can be known about God through an understanding of His creation and through experience of human life in the world. Although this extended sense is commonly designated "general revelation," it should not be viewed as a genus with several species, of which revelation through Christ and the Apostles is one form (so-called "special revelation"). Revelation, properly speaking, is God's free, direct communication of Himself and His purposes, casting light on other putative revelations.

Revelation, Book of • This, the last book of the New Testament, has also been called by its Greek name, Apocalypse. The earliest Christian writers considered it to be the work of St. John the Apostle. Modern scholars, noting differences in style and vocabulary, are skeptical of this.

The Book of Revelation is composed of two main parts. In the first chapter, John is instructed to write seven messages to the churches in the Roman province of Asia (a portion of present-day Turkey): Ephesus, Smyrna, Pergamum, Thyatira, Sardis, Philadelphia and Laodicea. These messages, presented in the name of the risen Christ, combine encouragement and rebuke; when criticism is called for, it is expressed in such strong words as could only have come from one of high standing and authority. The messages to the seven churches, found in Chapters 2-3, exhort the churches to resist the challenges to their faith and to keep from yielding to the temptations that surround them. The messages never circulated independently of the Apocalypse as a whole, and there is nothing in any of them so specific that it could not be profitably read by the other churches.

The remaining nineteen chapters of the Apocalypse present a series of vivid eschatalogical visions. These begin in Chapters 4-5 with a vision of the heavenly throne room. There, Christ, presented as "a Lamb, standing as though it had been slain" (Rv 5:6), receives a sealed scroll from the hand of God, Who is seated on the throne. The opening of this scroll, sealed with seven seals, provides the structure for the visions that follow. With the unsealing of the scrolls, John's vision progresses. The series of seven scrolls is followed by two further sevenfold series, of trumpets and libation bowls. These sevenfold series present a sequence of eschatalogical tribulations, plagues modeled after those sent by God against the stubborn Egyptians in the Book of Exodus.

Written during the latter part of the reign of the Roman Emperor Domitian, probably in A.D. 95 or 96, the Apocalypse presents a message of firm resistance against the Roman imperial ideology, an ideology which was tremendously influential in Asia Minor. The Apocalypse insists strongly that Christ is the true ruler of the universe, and that every other power — including that of the Roman emperor — must submit to the sovereign power of Christ. Revelation 17 speaks of "Babylon the Great," a city built on seven hills. This is a clear reference to Rome, the *septimontium*. It is called "Babylon" in the Apocalypse, in contemporary Jewish documents and even in 1 Peter 5:13 because just as the Babylon of old had been responsible for the destruction of Jerusalem and the Temple, so too Rome was responsible for the destruction of the Holy City and the Temple in A.D. 70. The number 666, mentioned in Revelation 13:18 as "the number of the beast," is a reference to the Emperor Nero, whose persecution of Roman Christians in A.D. 64 made him the model villain and enemy of the Christian Faith. The

Apocalypse announces the imminent destruction of Babylon the Great, and looks forward to the advent of the New Jerusalem (Rv 21-22), the city where God and Christ His Son will dwell with the faithful. Christ will bring about the final and definitive victory, and the faithful are invited to participate in the combat that will result in that victory. That combat is not one undertaken by the force of arms, but rather through the paradoxical power of Christ's own cross. The Christ of the Apocalypse is the Lion of Judah in Lamb's clothing.

The Book of Revelation must be understood against the background of Jewish apocalypticism. That movement, which emerged from postexilic prophecy, emphasized both the immanence of divine judgment and the hope that God would transform created reality in the light of divine justice. Its vivid symbolism hints at the transcendence of God. Its scenes of heavenly worship call upon its readers to participate in the heavenly song of praise both in prayer and in their daily conduct.

Finally, the Jewish apocalyptic tries to view events as God sees them, simultaneously, without the historian's respect for time. This explains the montage that is frequently encountered in such writings. The woman of the Apocalypse, for example, can be understood by Jews as Israel and by Christians both as the Blessed Virgin Mary and Holy Mother Church. The woman in the heavens is crowned with twelve stars (Israel and the tribes, or the Apostles on Pentecost); she brings forth her Son (the Messiah), destined to shepherd the nations. The Devil tried in vain to devour her Son, and He ascended into heaven. The sufferings of Christ were prefigured in ancient Israel. The Church still suffers as she attempts to lead others to Christ's example. The Devil still resists those efforts, but he will not prevail.

For further reading: Adela Yarbro Collins,

"The Apocalypse (Revelation)," *New Jerome Biblical Commentary*, 996-1016; Wilfrid J. Harrington, O.P., *Revelation*, Sacra Pagina 16 (Liturgical Press, 1993).

Revelation, Dogmatic Constitution on Divine: See **Dei Verbum**

Reverential Fear • Fear is a condition that can invalidate a marriage. Common fear is that which is inspired by a force or agent hostile to the person. Canonical jurisprudence has also recognized a kind of fear known as reverential fear. This is a fear inspired not by a hostile agent, but by someone to whom the person is subject such as a parent or guardian.

Reverential fear is induced in a person when he fears the anger, disappointment or rejection that might result from a certain act. Reverential fear can occur in an unusually docile person who is controlled or influenced to an excessive degree by his parents or superiors. It most commonly occurs between parents and children and is such that the freedom of the will to choose is seriously diminished.

With regard to marriage, there are two operative jurisprudential principles. The fear must be grave and extrinsic, that is, from without, and it must be subjectively escapable only by marriage.

The most common example of a marriage invalid because of reverential fear is that of a marriage that takes place when the woman is pregnant. One or both of the parties consent to the marriage primarily as a means of escaping the disappointment, anger or rejection of the parents (Canon 1103).

Revivification • The belief that each sacrament, excepting the Eucharist and Penance, confer the grace available from the outset, once the obstacle shutting off grace is removed. For example, a person may want to receive the sacrament but lacks the proper disposition or state of mind, chiefly the condition of grace for sacraments of the living and sufficient contrition for sacraments of the dead. When one attains the state of grace or arrives at a suitable degree of contrition, the grace of the sacrament is "revived" without the repetition of the sacramental rite. The validity of Baptism, Confirmation, Matrimony and Holy Orders is invariably assured in these instances.

Rheims • The name of this town in France, noted for its magnificent Gothic cathedral, is also attached to a translation of the Bible into English, the so-called Douay-Rheims Bible, which was actually published in two parts in different cities at different times. The New Testament books were published in 1582 in the city of Rheims. The Old Testament was published between 1609 and 1610, in Douay, a city in northern France. The principal translators were Gregory Martin (d. 1582), Thomas Worthington, Richard Bristowe and William Allen, all from Oxford. The translation was to avoid the heretical tendencies found in other English language translations of the day (Protestant translations). The translation was not from the original Hebrew/Aramaic and Greek Old Testament texts, nor from the original Greek of the New Testament, but from the Latin Vulgate. This translation achieved a high standard of consistency and influenced the language found in the Authorized Version translation (1611). It remained the standard English-language Bible of Roman Catholics for three and a half centuries.

For further reading: F. F. Bruce, *History of the Bible in English*, 113-124 (Oxford University Press, 1978); Jack P. Lewis, "Versions, English (Pre-1960)," *Anchor Bible Dictionary*, 6:823.

Rheims Cathedral

Rights, Ecclesial • Rights that persons acquire by the very fact that they are members in communion with the Catholic Church. A right is something to which one is entitled, and in the Church there are certain rights common to all of the faithful, others common to the laity, and still others that are acquired because of the fact that a man is in Sacred Orders or because of an ecclesial office held.

The 1917 Code of Canon Law stated that Baptism constituted a person as a member of the Church with all of the rights and duties proper to Christians. It did not list what these rights and duties might be, with the exception of stating that Catholics had a right to the sacraments and were not to be denied them without just cause. This Code concentrated on the rights of certain groups in the Church (the clergy, religious, hierarchy) and certain office-holders.

The revised Code still contains the rights proper to certain groups and to office-holders, but before listing these, it enumerates several fundamental rights of all the faithful (Canons 208-223) and especially the laity (Canons 224-231). These rights are interspersed with various fundamental obligations. The enumeration of the rights and duties of the faithful was taken from the proposed *Lex Ecclesiae Fundamentalis* (Fundamental Law of the Church) which was studied but not included in the Code. The statements on rights in the *Lex* were, in great part, inspired by the documents of Vatican II.

The first canon in the section (Canon 208) states that by virtue of Baptism, there exists a true equality among all Christians. It distinguishes between fundamental spiritual equality and the fact that people differ in their capacities and in their roles in the life of the Church. Equality and capacity are not the same and the fact that some have authority roles in the Church and some do not does not mean that this differentiation is based on inequality.

Concerning the ecclesial rights of all the faithful, the following are found in the canons:

(a) The right to make known needs and desires, especially spiritual ones, to the pastors of the Church (Canon 212.2).

(b) The right and sometimes the duty to express one's opinion of matters pertaining to the good of the Church, both to Church authorities and other Christians (Canon 212.3).

(c) The right to spiritual assistance, especially the Word of God and the sacraments (Canon 213).

(d) The right to worship according to one's own rite and to follow one's own form of spiritual life (Canon 214).

(e) The right to found and govern associations for religious and charitable purposes and the right to assembly (Canon 215).

(f) The right to promote and sustain apostolic activity according to one's state and condition (Canon 216).

(g) The right to a Christian education (Canon 217).

(h) The right to academic freedom for those engaged in teaching and research in the sacred sciences, with due respect for the Magisterium (Canon 218).

(i) The right to choose freely one's state in life (Canon 219).

(j) The right to one's good reputation and the right to privacy (Canon 220).

(k) The right to defend and vindicate one's rights before a competent ecclesiastical court, the right to be judged, if called into court, according to the norms of the law and the right not to be punished by ecclesiastical penalties, except according to the norms of law (Canon 221).

These general ecclesial rights of all the faithful, clergy and laity alike, are to be understood within a specific context, that is, the fundamental obligation of all Catholics to build up the Church according to the teaching and discipline of the Magisterium.

Following the canons on the rights of all, the Code then considers specific rights of the laity. These are preceded by a statement of the fundamental obligation and right of the laity to participate in the mission of the Church (Canon 225). The first specific right pertains to married persons. Describing marriage as a vocation, the canon states that married couples have a special duty to build up the Body of Christ through their marriage. They have both the obligation and the right to educate children given them by God (Canon 226). The other rights pertain to the laity in general:

(a) The right to the same civil liberties enjoyed by all citizens (Canon 227).

(b) The capacity (rather than the right) to assume ecclesiastical offices and functions which they are capable of exercising according to the norms of law (Canon 228).

(c) The capacity of acting as experts and advisors to the bishops, provided they have been properly trained (Canon 228).

(d) The right to a Christian education and the right to study the sacred sciences at ecclesiastical institutions (Canon 229).

(e) The capacity to fulfill certain liturgical functions, including the distribution of Communion, presiding over the Liturgy of the Word and conferring Baptism when there is a need and they have been properly deputed (Canon 230).

(f) The right, for those employed in the service of the Church, to a decent remuneration, pension, social security and health benefits (Canon 231).

All of the canons on ecclesial rights are relatively broad in their approach. Their practical application and more specific meaning in real life hinges on the evolving understanding of the meaning of the Church as the "People of God," as well as on the development of tribunal structures and jurisprudence that will help spell out the meaning of these rights in actual situations.

Rights, Natural: See **Natural Rights**

Right to Die • The right to end one's life at the time of and in the manner of one's own choosing. Advocates of euthanasia assert that this right is justified by the right to privacy and claim it to be the ultimate expression of that right. They assert that included in this right is not only the right to end one's life by rejecting extraordinary painful, expensive and useless means of preserving life, but also those which are not. And some would even contend that this includes a right to end one's life by positive measures, such as by lethal injections or by refusal of simple, painless and effective means.

Catholic teaching holds that there is not a right to die, even though there is a right to refuse painful, useless or radically burdensome medical treatments. This right to refuse extraordinary medical treatments does not include a right to refuse treatments that are inexpensive, nonburdensome and effective. Catholic medical-ethical teaching contends that one cannot deliberately end one's life by positive measures. It does hold, however, that if a patient is in great pain and the only means available of relieving that pain is the giving of a dose of painkillers that will probably kill the patient, this can be done as long as the death is not intended. Whether this doctrine is in need of modification, however, is a subject of debate. (Cf. Pain and Euthanasia.)

Right to Life • The right of all innocent human beings not to be made the object of deliberate and intentional lethal acts by others. The demands of the right to life are equivalent in part to the ethical requirement to receive ordinary medical treatments, for it also includes a right to receive ordinary, nonburdensome, inexpensive and non-risky life-sustaining measures by others. The right to life is not vitalist and does not morally require that every possible life-sustaining measure be taken to prolong a person's life; thus, those which are expensive, of doubtful efficacy, risky and painful need not be utilized.

The right to life is based on the duty all have to preserve one's health and life. Because life is a gift of God and a treasure, it demands that we take at least minimal measures to preserve it. It is also based on the duty to take no directly lethal action against any innocent person. Assassination, direct abortion, dueling, euthanasia, infanticide, murder, terrorism, torture and unconsented nontherapeutic medical experimentation are all violations of the right to life.

Rights of the Human Person: See **Natural Rights**

Rigorism • The technical term in moral systems for "Tutiorism," which holds that the law must be followed unless it is "morally certain" that one may be freed from it. This opinion was condemned as being too harsh and restrictive of human freedom. Rigorism also connotes cults of extreme self-denial and asceticism, such as Puritanism or Montanism.

Ring • A ring is a circular band of metal, sometimes ornamented with gems, pearls or enamel.

The Christian use of wedding rings developed from the Roman custom of betrothal rings. Wearing the wedding ring on the third finger of the left hand seems to be connected originally with pronouncing the Trinitarian formula over the thumb and first two fingers, so that the "Amen" was pronounced on the third finger.

In the fifteenth century, rosary rings with ten beads for each decade came into use. This type of ring has been revived in modern times.

Episcopal rings are first mentioned as an official part of the bishop's insignia of office in the early seventh century. The bishop's ring is usually made of gold with an amethyst. Cardinals, abbots and abbesses also wear similar rings. Nuns' rings are conferred at solemn profession. Rules concerning the wearing of rings by clerics have been relaxed. Finally, the Pope's ring (the Fisherman's Ring) is a gold seal ring engraved with St. Peter in a boat fishing and the Pope's name around it. At the death of a Pope, it is ceremonially broken up by the Cardinal Camerlengo.

Ripidion • A fan used to ventilate the consecrated Species in the Byzantine Rite. When adorned with a six-winged cherub, it is called Hexapterygon.

Risorgimento • Echoed in the title of a newspaper founded in 1847 by Count Victor Cavour, the name *Risorgimento* ("Revival") applies to a political and intellectual movement devoted to the unification of Italy. The movement had papal support at first, but after the revolution of 1848, Pope Pius IX opposed it. Cavour sought to unite the Italian states in a confederation after eliminating foreign control.

Rite • The Latin word means religious custom, usage or ceremony. Therefore, it refers to the words and actions prescribed for a liturgical or sacramental act, such as Mass, Baptism, Confirmation, Holy Week services, religious orders and so forth. The origins of the various rites lie largely in the geographical, cultural and political diversity that accompanied the spread and development of the Church. In the Catholic Church there are nine rites: The Latin or Roman, Byzantine, Armenian, Chaldean, Coptic, Ethiopian, Malabar, Maronite and Syrian. In this sense the word "rite" is often considered synonymous with "liturgy." By Church law, Baptism initiates not only into the Church but also into a specific rite. Acquisition of rite is normally determined by the baptismal ceremony in the rite of the parents, or if parents belong to different rites, in the rite of the father. Baptized non-Catholics already have their rite prior to joining the Catholic Church and ordinarily must retain that rite. The unbaptized may choose their rite in joining the Church. Transfer from one rite to another generally requires the Holy See's permission. The one exception is an interritual marriage where the wife may transfer to the husband's rite and children under the age of puberty change rites with their father. (Cf. Eastern Churches.)

Rite, Alexandrian • The Liturgy of Alexandria is attributed to St. Mark and is the parent of all the Egyptian Liturgies. It was probably an adaptation of the Antiochene Rite (from Antioch), which was finalized by St. Cyril in the fifth century. The liturgy of St. Mark is no longer used, since it was used in Greek only by the Melkites, who later replaced it with the Byzantine Rite. It was adapted by the Copts and Ethiopians, who developed modified versions of it in their own languages (Coptic and Ge'ez). The present liturgy for the Catholic patriarchate of Alexandria is that of the Coptic Rite.

Rite, Antiochene • The rite of the early Christian community of Antioch (cf. Acts 8-11), which spread to Jerusalem and from there all over after it had been translated into Greek and Aramaic. As this rite crystallized in the patriarchate of Antioch, it had much influence on other rites (e.g., the Byzantine and Alexandrian). In ancient classic form, the outline of this rite can be found in Book 8 of the *Apostolic Constitutions*, a fourth-century Syrian source. The Liturgy of Antioch is sometimes called the West Syrian Rite, which developed after the condemnation of Nestorius (A.D. 431). Christians following this rite in union with Rome developed what is called the Chaldean Rite. The influence of the Antiochene Liturgy can be seen in India in both the Malankar and Malabar Rites, and the Liturgy of St. James, followed by the Christians in Iraq and Syria.

Rite, Armenian • When the Armenian Church was organized in the fourth century, the liturgical practice of Cappadocia was introduced, as were some Syrian customs, and this became the basis of the Armenian Rite. The lectionary reflects that of fifth-century Jerusalem. In the course of time, various influences have been felt on the rite: the Byzantine in the rite of preparation; Antiochene Syrian usage in the litany after the Epiclesis; and many Romanisms left by the Crusaders. This rite is used by Armenians united with Rome, who after Vatican II have purified their rite of most Roman usages.

Rite, Byzantine • One of several divisions or categories of Churches within the universal Church, specific to the East. The Byzantine Rite traces its origin to the ancient capital city of the eastern half of the Roman Empire, Constantinople, now Istanbul, formerly Byzantium. The Byzantine Rite shares its Tradition with the Churches of Antioch, Alexandria and Jerusalem. When Emperor Constantine moved his capital to Byzantium in A.D. 330, the city became the "New Rome," and its sphere of influence was secured. Next to the Roman, it is the second most used rite and is shared by Eastern Christians, both Catholic and Orthodox (since 1054, the time of the Great Schism between East and West).

The Byzantine Rite is more than ceremony. It has its own system of canonical legislation, cycle of liturgical feasts and saints, ethnic traditions and a unique patrimony. The liturgical year begins on September 1, and is punctuated by four periods of fasting: Pre-Christmas, from November 15 to December 24; the Great Fast or Lent preceding Easter; the Apostles' Fast preceding the Feast of Sts. Peter and Paul on June 29, observed from the Sunday after Pentecost until the Feast;

and the Dormition Fast, from August 1 through August 14 prior to the Assumption (August 15).

Traditionally, Baptism is administered by immersion, Confirmation (called chrismation) immediately follows and the Eucharist is given to the newly-baptized. Leavened bread is used for the Divine Liturgy, of which there are two, that of St. John Chrysostom and that of St. Basil the Great. An ancient Liturgy of St. James of Jerusalem is no longer used but reflects its roots from Jerusalem itself.

Rite, Celtic: See **Celtic Rite**

Rite, Chaldean: See **Chaldean Rite**

Rite, Coptic: See **Coptic Rite**

Rite, Georgian Byzantine: See **Georgian Byzantine Rite**

Rite, Latin: See **Latin Rite**

Rite, Malabar: See **Malabar Rites**

Rite, Melkite: See **Melkite (also Melchite) Rite**

Rite, Mozarabic: See **Mozarabic Rite**

Rite, Religious • A particular liturgical usage that was celebrated by the members of certain religious orders. Historically, several orders had their own rituals and liturgical calendars, which differed to a greater or lesser degree from the Roman liturgical usage. In some instances there is an interconnection between the rites of some religious orders, since they were patterned on or grew out of one another.

There was considerable variety in the liturgical practices of the various dioceses and geographic regions of the Church prior to the sixteenth century. Many of the religious orders founded in the eleventh to thirteenth centuries adopted the rites followed in the dioceses where they were founded and added, at times, their own practices. The liturgical rites included the ritual of the Mass, the ritual surrounding the solemn recitation of the Divine Office and the liturgical calendar. The Carthusian and Cistercian Orders, both monastic in nature, were founded in the eleventh century. Both orders initially followed the rite of the diocese wherein they were founded but eventually liturgical usages proper to each order emerged. The rites of both orders underwent occasional reforms throughout history. After the general reform of the liturgy in the 1960s, the Cistercians opted to adopt the newly revised Roman Rite. The Carthusians, however, have retained their own historic rite for the most part.

The Premonstratensian Order, a community of canons who led a common life and professed vows, was officially approved by Rome in 1124. At first, the order followed the liturgical practices of other canons regular, but in time a Norbertine (Premonstratensian) Rite developed and, like the monastic rites, experienced certain reforms as time went on.

The Dominican Order, founded in 1215, also followed local customs until a uniform liturgy was adopted in the middle of the century. The Dominican Rite is unique because it was adopted as the official Liturgy of the Roman Church in 1267. In the course of time, several other orders adopted the Dominican Liturgy as their own.

The Carmelites, the only other religious order with its own unique liturgy, claim their descent from Elijah, the Old Testament prophet. Although the order existed in the twelfth century, it was never officially approved until 1274. At first, its liturgy was that of the Holy Sepulcher; however, the Carmelites adopted the

Dominican Liturgy in 1259, while retaining some elements from other sources. The following century the rite was reformed and most of the Dominican usages were eliminated and replaced by the more historic Rite of the Holy Sepulcher.

During the postconciliar liturgical revision, the Premonstratensians, Dominicans and Carmelites all adopted the revised Roman Liturgy, although the rites of these three orders have never been officially suppressed.

Rite, Roman: See **Roman Rite**

Rite, Russian: See **Russian Rite**

Rite, Ruthenian: See **Ruthenian Catholics**

Rite, Syrian: See **Syrian Rite**

Rite of Christian Initiation of Adults (RCIA) • RCIA, the Rite of Christian Initiation of Adults, is the process by which adult converts are received into full communion with the Catholic Church. It takes place in four stages: (1) Pre-Catechumenate or Inquiry phase. (2) Catechumenate phase, which is a process of spiritual formation and introduction to Catholic life. (3) Election phase, the period just prior to sacramental initiation, during which the Lenten scrutinies occur. This phase begins with the rite of election on the First Sunday of Lent, leading to sacramental initiation (Baptism, Confirmation, First Holy Communion) at the Easter Vigil. (4) Mystagogy, the period after initiation during which the newly baptized receive additional catechesis on liturgy and sacraments and share most fully in the life of the Church. The rite itself envisions a period of up to three years for the Catechumenate, the Lenten season for the period of Election, and indeterminate time frames for both the Pre-Catechumenate and Mystagogy. Customarily, in the United States, the catechumenate lasts one calendar year.

The parish can start the renewal process all over again the following year. There is variation in the way the RCIA is used. Some parishes make a distinction between the unbaptized (catechumens) and those baptized in another Church (candidates for full communion); others do not. In other words, a parish may have two types of RCIA programs. The RCIA program was initiated by Pope Paul VI on January 6, 1972.

Rite of Constantinople • The largest of the four main patriarchal liturgical branches of the Eastern Churches, derived from the capital city of the ancient Byzantine Empire (formerly Byzantium). The Rite has its roots in ancient Antioch and is presently shared between Catholic and Orthodox Eastern Christians. Its principal liturgical languages are Greek and Church Slavonic, still in use largely by many Eastern-European Churches, many of whom are represented throughout the United States and the Western world. These national Churches have their own calendar of saints, canon law, system of theology and ritual rich in ceremony and a reverent sense of transcendent mystery. Catholic and Orthodox parishes of the Byzantine Rite can be found in most metropolitan areas, particularly in the northeastern region of the United States. American English has supplanted Greek or Church Slavonic for the most part in communities of this Rite. Istanbul is the modern-day name of ancient Constantinople.

Rites, Chinese • The term "Chinese Rites" refers to a variety of ancient practices on the part of the Chinese which were tolerated for a time by Catholic missionaries sent to evangelize them. The majority of these rites or customs involved Confucianism, ancestor worship and technical terms referring to God. In 1693, Roman authorities launched an extensive investigation into the practices to determine the degree to which they might be incompatible with Christian doctrine. Thus in 1715, Pope Clement XI issued the Apostolic Constitution *Ex illa die*, rejecting the practices and directing the missionaries to cease their toleration of them. Disputes continued over the implementation of the decision, however, until 1742, when Pope Benedict XIV put an end to the wrangling by affirming Clement's decision. There the matter rested, albeit uneasily, until the reign of Pope Pius XII, who indicated that the standing rejection of certain practices might be open to reconsideration.

Rites, Sacred Congregation of • The Sacred Congregation of Rites is now called the Congregation for Divine Worship. On March 1, 1989, it was joined to the Congregation for the Sacraments. It directs the ritual and pastoral aspects of divine worship for the Roman and other Western Rites. The worship life of the Church governs the Mass, the sacraments, and daily prayer life, such as the Liturgy of the Hours.

This Congregation was originally established by Pope Paul VI on May 8, 1969, to replace the Congregation of Rites instituted by Pope Sixtus V in 1588. It was then united with the Congregation for the Discipline of the Sacraments by Pope Paul VI in 1975, and then reestablished as a separate Congregation by Pope John Paul II on April 5, 1984.

Ritual • Ritual uses symbols, gestures, sacred objects, words and music to involve the community in liturgy. It also refers to an official authorized book called the Roman Ritual, periodically updated by the Holy See; it contains prayers and ceremonies used in the administration of the sacraments and other ceremonial functions.

Rochet • A white linen knee-length garment resembling a surplice but with tight sleeves. It is generally worn by the Pope and other prelates under the mozzetta or mantelletta. It is derived from the alb and until the fourteenth century was in use outside Rome for all clerics.

Rogation Days • Special days of penitential prayer marked liturgically with outdoor processions. Originally, these observances were acts of intercession for a fruitful harvest. Two sets of rogation days were kept since early Christian times: the major rogation on April 25, the feast of St. Mark; and the minor rogations on the Monday, Tuesday and Wednesday before Ascension Thursday.

With the Vatican II changes, the rogation days were replaced in 1969 by periods of prayer for the needs of people. The observance of these periods (one or several days) may take place at different times of the year. It is decided by conferences of local bishops. Suitable Masses are included in the 1970 Missal.

Rogito • The official collection of documents which certify the death and formal burial of the Roman Pontiff. They are stored in the Vatican Archives.

Roman Catholic • The name of the Church founded by Christ, whose members are named Catholic. The term "Roman Catholic" first appeared in the sixteenth century. This expression designates Christians who follow the Bishop of Rome, the Pope, who derives his supreme authority from the primacy of the Apostle Peter as Vicar of Christ. It is actually a misnomer, for one in union with the Bishop of Rome is a Catholic, without a further qualifier. It seems to have originated in one of two ways: First, from non-Catholic Christians who sought to justify their status as members of the Catholic Church (according to the so-called "Branch Theory"), all the while eschewing allegiance to the Pope; second, as a means of identifying Western Catholics. However, in the second instance, such Christians ought to be called Roman Rite Catholics, for "Roman" as a direct modifier of "Catholic" undermines the very catholicity intended.

In English-speaking countries, however, it has entered common parlance and is generally not intended negatively today.

Roman College • The Collegium Romanum was founded by St. Ignatius Loyola in 1551. Its buildings on the Piazza Collegio Romano were confiscated by the Italian Government in 1870. It then moved to the Via del Seminario. Now known as the Pontifical Gregorian University, it moved into its new location on Piazza della Pilotta in 1930.

The term is sometimes used to designate the other ecclesiastical universities in Rome, such as the Angelicum and the Lateran, as well as the various residential seminaries such as the North American College and the Bede the Venerable English College.

Roman Congregations • The highest ranking departments of the Roman Curia which assist the Pope in the government of the Church are called "congregations." Each is headed by a cardinal prefect and a secretary who is usually an archbishop. The congregations are: The Congregation for the Doctrine of the Faith, The Congregation for the Eastern Churches, The Congregation for Sacraments and Divine Worship, The Congregation for the Clergy, The Congregation for Religious and Secular

Institutes, The Congregation for the Evangelization of Peoples or "*de Propaganda Fide*," The Congregation for the Causes of Saints, and The Congregation for Seminaries and Catholic Institutions.

Collectively the congregations, together with the Secretariat of State and other commissions and councils, make up the Roman Curia. The most recent papal document governing the operation of Roman Congregations is *Pastor Bonus*, issued by Pope John Paul II on June 28, 1988.

Roman Law • In a general sense, "Roman law" refers to all the laws that prevailed in ancient Rome, from the earliest period, known as the Age of the Kings (fifth century B.C.) to the time of the Emperor Justinian (sixth century A.D.). In a more particular sense, Roman law is understood to refer to the compilation of laws known as the *Corpus Iuris Civilis* (Body of Civil Law). The latter is not simply a collection of all the various laws enacted by Roman kings, dictators, emperors and senates, but a systematic codification of the law that took place under the direction of the Emperor Justinian.

Roman law has had a profound effect on the development of nearly every legal system used in the civilized world, including the canon law of the Church. The *Corpus Iuris Civilis* had literally been lost from the time of the fall of Rome (fifth century A.D.) to the Middle Ages. At the time that feudalism was coming to an end and the political structure of Europe was changing, the *Corpus* was discovered. Since it was the only complete legal system in existence at the time, it was used in the construction of legal systems for the emerging European nation-states. It was at this time as well that the legal system of the Church was taking on a definite form. It too was influenced to a great extent both by the structure of Roman law and by many of the legal concepts contained therein.

One aspect of Roman law that has had a broad influence is the fact that it is a code system. All aspects of the law were placed into three categories: persons, things and actions. This type of division was used in the 1917 Code but not in the revised Code. In the 1917 Code the second and third books were called "Persons" and "Things," respectively. The third book contained the canons on the sacraments. The fourth and fifth books, concerned with processes and crimes and penalties, dealt with things.

The procedural law of the Church is directly related to that which grew out of Roman law. Cases are tried and decided by judges and not by juries, as is common in the Anglo-Saxon common law system.

Another inherited feature in canon law is the legal action that brings marriage into being. Roman law held that consent alone made marriage. When the Church acquired competence or jurisdiction over marriage in the Middle Ages, it had to be decided what legal act constituted a marriage, that is, when a marriage was really a marriage. Although there was a prolonged debate as to whether sexual consummation or consent made marriage, it was finally decided that consent alone constituted a true marital union.

The Roman law system provided the foundation of what is commonly called the civil law. This generic term refers to legal systems that are contained in a code and do not depend upon the judgments of courts. Most of the legal systems in the world today are civil law or code systems, the exceptions being Great Britain and certain of the countries that had been colonized by the English, the United States included.

Roman law remains a vitally important part of the study of law and of legal philosophy. Although it differs significantly from the common law system, many influencing elements of Roman law are found in this system. Law students in countries with civil law or code systems are still required to study Roman law as part of their overall preparation. Those preparing for pontifical degrees in canon law are also required to study Roman law.

Roman Missal • The literal translation of *Missale Romanum*, the title of the book containing the introductory documents and prayer-texts for the celebration of Mass according to the Roman Rite.

The Missal of the pre-Vatican II rite ("the Missal of Pope St. Pius V" or "Tridentine Missal," as it is sometimes called) contained all elements of the "propers" (Introit, Collect, Epistle, Gradual/Tract, Alleluia, Gospel, Offertory Verse, Secret, Communion Verse, Postcommunion) as well as the "Ordinary," or Order of Mass. The Roman Missal promulgated by Pope Paul VI in 1970, containing the revised liturgy of Mass, corresponding to the directives of Vatican II, actually consists of two books: (1) the Roman Missal properly so-called (in the United States and Canada, alone of all the nations, this book is entitled the sacramentary): containing the three proper "presidential prayers" for each Mass (Opening Prayer, Prayer over the Gifts, Prayer after Communion) and, for convenience, the Entrance and Communion Antiphons, as well as the complete Order of Mass; and (2) the Lectionary for Mass, containing the now greatly expanded selection of Scripture readings (a three-year cycle of Old Testament, New Testament, Gospel readings and intervenient chants for Sundays), and a two-year cycle of first readings with a daily Gospel for weekdays as well as readings for sanctoral, ritual and votive celebrations.

By a special indult of 1984, extended through the Apostolic Letter *Ecclesia Dei* of 1988, permission to use the former Roman

Missal (in its 1962 edition) has been granted by the Holy See under certain conditions.

Roman Missal, General Instruction of the • The introductory document which prefaces the Roman Missal (or sacramentary) and sets forth: (1) the historical context in which the Second Vatican Council mandated the revision of the Eucharistic Liturgy; (2) the theological orientation necessary to understand the Eucharist as the action of Christ within the community of His Church; (3) an extensive presentation of the various elements constituting the Eucharist and the rubrics governing its proper celebration.

An outline of the current English version (a translation of the Latin fourth edition, dated March 27, 1975) provides a summary of the scope and sequence of this important document, which, as much as the Second Vatican Council's Constitution on the Sacred Liturgy (*Sacrosanctum Concilium*) is foundational to any understanding of the liturgy of the Eucharistic Sacrifice as revised by the Council.

Introduction:
- ✧ a witness to unchanged faith
- ✧ a witness to unbroken tradition
- ✧ adaptation to modern conditions

Chapter I: Importance and Dignity of the Eucharistic Celebration

Chapter II: Structure, Elements and Parts of the Mass
- I. General Structure of the Mass
- II. Different Elements of the Mass
  - ✧ Reading and Explaining the Word of God
  - ✧ Prayers and Other Parts Assigned to the Priest
  - ✧ Other Texts in the Celebration
  - ✧ Vocal Expression of the Different Texts
  - ✧ Importance of Singing
  - ✧ Movements and Posture
  - ✧ Silence
- III. Individual Parts of the Mass
  - A. Introductory Rites
    - ✧ Entrance
    - ✧ Veneration of the Altar, Greeting the Congregation
    - ✧ Penitential Rite
    - ✧ Kyrie Eleison
    - ✧ Gloria
    - ✧ Opening Prayer or Collect
  - B. Liturgy of the Word
    - ✧ Scripture Readings
    - ✧ Chants Between the Readings
    - ✧ Homily
    - ✧ Profession of Faith
    - ✧ General Intercessions
  - C. Liturgy of the Eucharist
    - ✧ Preparation of the Gifts
    - ✧ Eucharistic Prayer
    - ✧ Communion Rite
  - D. Concluding Rite

Chapter III: Offices and Ministries in the Mass
- I. Offices and Ministries of Holy Orders
  - ✧ bishop, priest, deacon
- II. Office and Function of the People of God
  - ✧ assembly
  - ✧ choir
  - ✧ musicians
- III. Special Ministries
  - ✧ acolyte
  - ✧ reader
  - ✧ cantor
  - ✧ extraordinary ministers of Communion
  - ✧ altar boys
  - ✧ commentator
  - ✧ greeters
  - ✧ ushers

Chapter IV: The Different Forms of Celebration
- I. Mass With a Congregation
  - A. Basic Form of Celebration
    - ✧ Introductory Rites

The United States edition of the Roman Missal (sacramentary) contains an appendix of explanations, modifications and adaptations. Important related documents are also to be found in the front of the Missal after the General Instruction: Directory for Masses with Children, General Norms for the Liturgical Year and the Calendar (both the General Roman Calendar and the Proper Calendar for Dioceses of the United States).

Roman Rite • The manner of celebrating Mass, administration of the sacraments and sacramentals, recitation of the Divine Office and other ecclesiastical functions authorized for the Diocese of Rome and governed by the Roman Ritual. The Roman Rite is the dominant rite of Western Catholicism and the one most widely used throughout Christianity.

The Vatican II liturgical changes allowed the use of the vernacular language, the restoration of some ancient practices and cultural adaptation of the Roman Liturgy to fit the needs of various modern cultures and societies. (Cf. Rite, Religious.)

Romans, Epistle to the • Paul wrote his letter to the Christians in Rome at the point of realizing he had completed his evangelization mission in the eastern Mediterranean, having evangelized from Jerusalem to Illyricum (Rom 15:19). For years he had wanted to visit the believers in Rome and west of Rome, eventually all the way to Spain (1:13; 15:22, 24, 28). Paul did not establish the Church at Rome (Rom 1:10-13; Acts 28:15). He introduced himself as an Apostle to the Gentiles (11:13), which included a developed articulation of the Gospel he preached. He hoped this letter would introduce his message and so prepare the way for his eventual visit.

Major Themes: Paul outlined the message of the Gospel — salvation is through Jesus Christ and the cross, is rooted in God's righteousness and love, and is available to all humans who believe or come into faith. Justification and salvation before God is not attained by the working of the law's requirement but only through faith in Christ Jesus, God's Son. The Gospel is God's salvific work made known or revealed in Jesus Christ's Lordship (Rom 1:17; 10:9); access to salvation is by Baptism into Christ (Rom 6:3-11); the Gospel is a force, a power of God for the purposes of salvation (1:16); the Gospel should be welcomed, therefore, *and* obeyed (Rom 1:5); the Gospel contains the promises of God fulfilled (Rom 1:1 and Is 52:7; Rom 4:13-21; 9:4-13).

Contents:

A. Introduction: 1:1-15

B. Key Thematic Statement: 1:16-17

C. Justified by Faith: 1:18—4:25

D. Reception of Divine Life and Freedom from Sin: 5:1—8:39

E. Jews and Gentiles in God's Salvation Plan: 9:1—11:36

F. What the Gospel Implies for Renewed Life: 12:1—15:13

G. Conclusions and Final Greetings: 15:14—16:27

Authorship and Date: Pauline authorship of Romans is universally accepted. According to 15:24, Paul may have written Romans before he left for Jerusalem for the last time. He was probably either in Corinth or Cenchreae, in the winter of A.D. 57-58, when he wrote this letter, after evangelizing in Illyricum (15:19), Macedonia and Achaia (15:26; 1 Cor 16:5-7; Acts 20:3).

For further reading: Joseph A. Fitzmyer, S.J., "The Letter to the Romans," *New Jerome Biblical Commentary*, 830-868; Joseph A. Fitzmyer, S.J., *Romans*, Anchor Bible 33 (Doubleday, 1993); Charles D.

Myers, Jr., "Romans, Epistle to the," *Anchor Bible Dictionary*, 5:816-830.

Rome • The capital city of modern Italy, the seat of government and principal city of the ancient Roman Empire, Rome was inhabited, according to tradition, as early as 753 B.C.; in fact all Roman history was dated from the traditional year of the city's settlement (in Latin, *Ab Urbe Condita*), so that Christ is said to have been born A.U.C. 753. Actually, there were likely Etruscan settlers on the seven hills several centuries earlier, as is reflected in the very name of *Roma*, presumably derived from the Etruscan word for city, *Rom*. This etymology has an interesting parallel in Latin, since the Latin word for city, *urbs*, was also used with the specific meaning of Rome alone, as in the expression used for the blessing given by the Holy Father on special occasions, *Urbi et Orbi*, "to the city (i.e. Rome) and to the world."

Having ministered to the Christian communities of both Jerusalem and Antioch, St. Peter arrived in Rome in A.D. 42 and there established the Christian Faith and the Church; after making numerous converts, he suffered persecution and eventually a martyr's death. As Vicar of Christ, St. Peter enjoyed a most privileged position within the early Christian communities, and his immediate successors were recognized for the central role they played in Church governance (cf. Letters of Clement of Rome); hence, one understands the central place of Rome in the life of the Church today and the significance of the title, Roman Catholic Church, the Church that is universal, yet focused upon the ministry of the Bishop of Rome. Since the founding of the Church there by St. Peter, Rome has been the center of all Christendom.

The entire area of the sovereign Vatican City-State is confined within the city of

Rome. By way of the Lateran Pact with the Italian government of 1929, more recently reaffirmed by both sides, additional properties apart from Vatican City are also considered as territorial parts of the Vatican.

Rood-Screen • In Old English *rood* means "wood," and so wood of the cross; a crucifix usually with the figures of St. Mary the Virgin and St. John the Evangelist placed on each side. Usually, it was placed in medieval English churches on a rood beam laid across the front of the chancel arch. Below this was a rood-screen, beautifully carved and with paintings or carvings of Apostles, prophets and saints.

Rosary • According to tradition, the devotion of the Rosary was spread by St. Dominic in the thirteenth century. In the Roman Catholic Church, the feast of the Blessed Virgin Mary of the Rosary is observed on October 7.

The Rosary is a devotion to the fifteen mysteries in which fifteen decades of the Hail Mary are recited, each decade being preceded by an Our Father and followed by a Glory Be. The mysteries are divided into three groups of five as follows: The Joyful Mysteries (the Annunciation, the Visitation, the Nativity, the Presentation in the Temple, the Finding in the Temple); the Sorrowful Mysteries (the Agony in the Garden, the Scourging, the Crowning with Thorns, the Carrying of the Cross, the Crucifixion); the Glorious Mysteries (the Resurrection, the Ascension, the Descent of the Holy Spirit, the Assumption of Mary into Heaven, the Coronation of Mary).

Ordinarily, only one-third of the Rosary or chaplet is said on one occasion. It is a popular devotion among Catholics.

Rose Window • A stained-glass circular window with tracery radiating from the center. Gothic architecture employed the rose window in many churches. Usually the windows — which have gone through developments over the centuries — are in the transepts, behind the altar, or above the entrance to the church.

Rosh Hashanah • The Jewish New Year celebration observed each year on the first and second days of the Jewish month of Tishri (September-October). There is reason to think that the Semitic peoples in antiquity believed the New Year began at the time of the late harvest, in autumn. There appear to be a few broad references to this feast recorded in the Old Testament. Mowinckel has ventured the opinion that certain psalms make allusion to an autumn New Year celebration, during which God was symbolically enthroned as King.

Perhaps the most characteristic feature of this festival is the blowing of the shofar, which may be fashioned from the horn of any animal (except the cow). In time, the ram's horn became the shofar of preference. The blowing of the shofar has been judged to be allusive of a number of life situations, among them the sounding of trumpets at the coronation of a king and on the day God is acclaimed as King.

For further reading: Louis Jacobs, "Rosh Ha-Shanah," *Encyclopedia Judaica*, 14:305-310.

Rota, Sacred Roman • The highest appeal court in the Church. It is situated in Rome and is made up of judges, called auditors, who are chosen from countries around the world. The judges must be priests possessing a doctorate in canon law. There are also defenders of the bond and notaries attached to the Rota. Advocates who practice before the Rota must have a doctorate in canon law and, in addition, must be graduates of the special school operated by the Rota for their training. The majority of the Rota advocates are lay persons.

The Roman Rota is competent to hear cases on appeal as a court of second instance. It also acts as the court of third instance for all other diocesan courts. The Rota also hears, as a court of first instance, contentious cases involving bishops, abbots and the supreme moderators of religious institutes of pontifical right.

The Rota was founded in the thirteenth century and is said to take its name from the fact that the judges originally sat at desks arranged in a circle. In the fifteenth and sixteenth centuries, the Rota reached the peak of its power, handling both ecclesiastical and civil cases. By the nineteenth century, its work was largely confined to some civil cases, and with the loss of the Papal States in 1870 it ceased to function altogether. St. Pius X reconstituted it as a court in 1908. Since that time, its norms of competence have been changed on occasion. Most of the cases submitted to the Rota since its reconstitution have been appeals of marriage nullity cases from around the world (cf. Canons 1443-1444). The Rota publishes most of the sentences it issues, albeit after a delay of five to ten years. These sentences, however, do not bind lower Church courts, although they serve as good indicators of trends in the Vatican's canonical thinking.

Rubrics • They are the directive precepts or liturgical directives found in the Missal, including the sacramentary and lectionary, and in the Ritual, to guide bishops, priests and deacons in the Eucharistic Sacrifice, the administration of the sacraments and sacramentals, and the preaching of the Word of God. Rubrics are either obligatory or merely directive, as the context makes very clear. The word comes from the Latin for "red," since these directives are printed in that color to distinguish them from the text proper. (Cf. Order of Mass, New.)

Rule, Religious • The basic regulations of a religious institute are found in its rule. These regulations encompass the order of life and overall discipline of an institute, developed and amplified in its constitutions. The most influential religious rules were those composed by St. Basil, St. Augustine and St. Benedict. Many subsequent religious rules are based upon these early rules.

Russian Rite • A term meant to designate that usage of the Byzantine Rite proper to those national groups situated in Russia or tracing their ethnic origins thereto. Its main language remains Church Slavonic, since none of the "Russian" Churches has an extant contemporary translation of the liturgical services in the modern Russian vernacular. The vast majority of Russians are Eastern Orthodox. There is a Pontifical Russian College in Rome for the training of deacons and priests in the Byzantine Rite usages particular to Russian Christianity. Since 1968, the College has also been open to accept Russian Orthodox seminarians and clergy to reside and study there as well. An apostolic exarch resides in France for Russian Catholics throughout the world.

Ruth, Book of • This biblical book contains a charming short story of married love. The title character was a Moabite woman, left a widow, who faithfully remained with her Jewish mother-in-law. Having returned to the Holy Land, she took up residence in Bethlehem, encountered a kind Jewish landowner, won his heart and became his wife. By her, he became the father of Obed, the grandfather of David.

It is uncertain, and unimportant, whether the book contains a true story. Critical analysis would locate its composition sometime in the fifth century, 700 years after the supposed events; this is rather a long time for authentic history to be conserved by oral tradition.

The importance of the book is the glimpse it offers of the acceptance by good-hearted Jews of the righteous Gentile. The story is especially appealing to Christians, as it reveals more of the ancestry of Jesus, the Son of David.

For further reading: Alice L. Laffey, "Ruth," *New Jerome Biblical Commentary*, 553-557.

Ruthenian Catholics • Those Catholics of the Byzantine Rite who trace their ethnic origin to that geographical area which for the most part is designated the Transcarpathian Province of the former Soviet Union. Evangelized by the Greek brothers Sts. Cyril and Methodius in 863, this group of Eastern Christians lapsed into orthodoxy at the time of the Eastern Schism (1054) but returned to communion with Rome at the Union of Uzhorod on April 24, 1646.

In 1949, the Ruthenian Church in Eastern Europe was forcibly returned to the Russian Orthodox, but the majority of churches became restored to Catholic communion at the time of the Dubcek regime in Czechoslovakia in 1966. Hundreds of thousands of Ruthenian Catholics emigrated from the former Austro-Hungarian Empire at the turn of this century and were given their first bishop in 1925 in the person of the late Bishop Basil Takach, who resided in Pittsburgh.

Today the former diocese of Pittsburgh for the Ruthenians has become an archdiocese with a metropolitan archbishop residing there and suffragan sees in Passaic, New Jersey, Parma, Ohio, and Van Nuys, California. Within the jurisdiction of the Ruthenians also fall Hungarian and Croatian Catholics of the Byzantine Rite.

A separate jurisdiction for the Ukrainians was also established in 1925 with the late Bishop Constantine Bohachevsky as their first bishop in the United States. The Ukrainians trace their evangelization to Prince Vladimir in Kiev in the year 988. Following the schism of 1054, many Ukrainians resumed Catholic unity at the Synod of Brest-Litovsk in 1596. From August 1907 until his death on March 24, 1916, Bishop Soter Ortynsky served as the Ordinary common to both Ruthenian and Ukrainian Catholics in the United States. The Ukrainian Catholics today have a metropolitan archbishop residing in Philadelphia, Pennsylvania, with suffragan sees in Chicago, Illinois, Stamford, Connecticut, and Parma, Ohio.

Sabaoth • "Hosts" — plural of the Hebrew word *saba*. The word's most notable occurrence is in one of the divine names, "Yahweh of hosts" or "Yahweh, God of hosts." It is a title for God encountered most frequently in the prophets. The word "hosts" basically means an army prepared for war. When the word forms part of God's name, it is variously construed by scholars. Some understand it as referring to the armies of Israel, others feel that it indicates either angels or the heavenly bodies. Some have even suggested that it means all the cosmic forces, whether heavenly or earthly.

For further reading: C. L. Seow, "Hosts, Lord of," *Anchor Bible Dictionary*, 3:304-307.

Sabbatarianism • A largely seventeenth- and eighteenth-century movement, confined to Reformation churches in England and Scotland, and advocating public enforcement of rigorous observance of Sunday as a day of rest. Nicholas Bound's *True Doctrine of the Sabbath* (1595) marked the emergence of seventeenth-century Sabbatarianism with its advocacy of a strict enforcement of Sunday observance modeled on the Old Testament. A Puritan parliament, in a series of Acts (1644, 1650, 1655), succeeded in proscribing recreation of all kinds (including walking) on Sunday. The rigor of these enactments was mitigated in 1677, when Charles II's Act for the Better Observance of the Lord's Day failed to mention recreation among the activities prohibited (e.g., work and travel by horse or boat). At various points in the next century,

Sabbatarians were able to secure the prohibition of all recreation (including, in Scotland, non-religious reading and playing of musical instruments) and of all entertainments for which money was paid. By the late nineteenth century, Sabbatarian influence in public affairs eroded and secular imposition of strict Sunday observance was progressively mitigated in Great Britain and Scotland.

Sabbath • The seventh day of the Jewish week. The word is related to a Hebrew verb for "to cease" or "to rest." The beginnings of Sabbath observance remain obscure, although it seems clear that the practice of the Sabbath in its present form was established at least by the time of the monarchy in Israel. The Sabbath was observed by rest from work for slaves and animals as well as for the ordinary Israelite. The day was also marked by a religious and worship activity.

The details of the proper observance of the Sabbath came to be very minutely expressed. So, for example, the lighting of fire was forbidden, as was the carrying of loads, cooking and a host of other activities. The hyper-rigorous interpretation of the Sabbath became a source of contention between Jesus and the scribes and Pharisees (Mt 12:2-4, Mk 3:1-5, etc.). Jesus' attitude as represented in Mark 2:27 was that the Sabbath was made for man, and not vice versa.

In time, the early Christians took to celebrating the first day of the week rather than the seventh. They were mindful of the fact that the Resurrection had taken place on the first day of the week, as had the coming of the Holy Spirit at Pentecost.

For further reading: Moshe Greenberg et al., "Sabbath," *Encyclopedia Judaica*, 14:557-572; Gerhard F. Hasel, "Sabbath," *Anchor Bible Dictionary*, 5:849-856.

Sabellianism • This term is so named after its intellectual father, Sabellius, whose theory that Christ was no different from God the Father was an early variant on several similar heretical notions of the second and third centuries. After some initial overtures to Pope Callistus I, Sabellius was excommunicated in A.D. 217. Sabellius then returned to his native region, where Dionysius of Alexandria later attempted to engage him in discussion. By this time, however, Pope Dionysius was becoming concerned over the terms being used in the exchange by Dionysius of Alexandria, who thereupon submitted to the Holy See a clarification, which was accepted. There is no record indicating that Sabellius, meanwhile, was ever reconciled, and his notions apparently were submerged under the greater disputations of Tertullian. (Cf. Patripassionism.)

Sacramental • Sacred signs, bearing a certain likeness to the sacraments, by which spiritual effects are signified and obtained by the intercession of the Church (Canon 1166). Some sacramentals are objects (e.g., holy water, scapulars, medals, rosaries). Others are actions (e.g., blessings and exorcisms). Sacramentals differ from sacraments in several ways, chiefly in the manner of institution (Christ instituted the sacraments, whereas the Church institutes and can abolish sacramentals) and the manner of imparting grace (a sacrament imparts grace in virtue of the rite itself, while the grace of the sacramentals depends on the dispositions of the recipient and the intercession of the Church). The number of sacramentals is variable.

Sacramental Theology • The theological subfield that studies the sacramental belief and practice of the Church in order to articulate how the seven sacraments enhance the life of grace within us and empower us to engage in the worship of God and the ministerial service of others. The complexity of modern sacramental theology reflects the complexity of the sacraments themselves. As ritual activities, they comprise a range of elements: worship and invocation of God, rites, forms of words, formal gesture and movement, use of sacred texts, distinction of roles, use of physical objects, ruled actions, sacred place and vesture, particular occasions of communal and personal life, memorializations or imitations of Christ's actions, the enactment of intentions and purposes of the community with regard to itself as a whole or with regard to individual members, and the belief that this enactment realizes divine purposes and intentions. For this reason, study of the sacraments can take a variety of different points of view, focusing on one or another of these elements.

Such specialties as liturgiology, biblical studies, canon law, history, hermeneutics, the study of religion, sociology and psychology each contribute to an integrated understanding of the sacraments. The task of the sacramental theologian is to appropriate the results of these specialized studies in fielding an integrated understanding of the place of the sacraments within the Christian pattern of life as oriented to loving fellowship with God and with other human beings in Him. Theological appropriation and synthesis serves to balance the roles of specialized approaches to the sacraments and prevents the co-option of the field by one specialty, e.g., canon law (an error in the recent past) or liturgics (a temptation in the present).

Sacramentarians • The name Luther gave those Reformers (e.g., Zwingli) who held that the bread and wine of the Eucharist were only symbolically Christ, and therefore only in a metaphorical or "sacramental" sense. Luther himself always held for the Real Presence of Christ in the Eucharist, but only as consubstantiation or impanation, not transubstantiation, as defined by the Fourth Lateran Council and reiterated by Trent.

Sacramentary • A book of liturgical prayers, directives and rubrics used by the priest while offering Mass. Called the Roman Missal in the original, the sacramentary now in use was prepared in accord with the decrees of the Second Vatican Council and offers the prayers of the Mass in the vernacular. The biblical readings of the Mass are found in a separate book called a lectionary.

Though sacramentaries have been used regionally for many centuries, Pope St. Pius V promulgated the Roman Missal in 1570 by decree of the Council of Trent. This was in universal usage for four centuries. In promulgating the "new," current sacramentary, Pope Paul VI expressed the hope "that it will be received by all the faithful as a help and witness to the common unity of all. Thus, in the great diversity of languages, one single prayer will rise as an acceptable offering to our Father in heaven, through

Pope St. Pius V, "promulgator" of the 1570 Roman Missal

our High Priest Jesus Christ, in the Holy Spirit" (April 3, 1969).

Sacraments, Seven • Although in the broadest sense any external sign of the action of God's grace in the life of a believer has a sacramental aspect, there are seven sacraments instituted by Christ which actually confer the grace they signify, namely Baptism, Confirmation, the Eucharist, Penance, Orders, Matrimony and the Anointing of the Sick. Each of these sacraments is mentioned in the New Testament, and all seven are included in the writings of the early Fathers, but a complete list of the sacraments was not determined for several centuries. Most of the early references were made for the practical purposes of instructing the catechumens and guiding the faithful, and there was no real attempt to distinguish between what were productive signs of grace (sacraments) and what were simply signs (sacramentals). St. Augustine (d. A.D. 430) defined a sacrament both as "the visible form of invisible grace" and as "a sign of a sacred thing," and he even applied the word to the Creed and the Lord's Prayer. This broad application continued into the Middle Ages, with the theologian Hugh of St.-Victor (d. 1142) listing some thirty sacraments. As theological language became more precise, allowing for a clearer formulation of traditional teaching, so it was possible to develop a more exact sacramental theology. Peter Lombard, in 1148, was among the first to distinguish between those sacraments instituted by Christ and those which were simply sacramentals. This list of the seven sacraments was accepted by St. Thomas Aquinas (d. 1274), and was formally affirmed by the Council of Florence in 1439. On March 3, 1547, the Council of Trent defined as a matter of faith the number and names of the sacraments, and that these alone were instituted by Christ to produce grace "*ex opere operato*," meaning that, provided there is no obstacle placed in the way, every sacrament properly administered conveys the grace intended.

The fact that the seven sacraments were not defined earlier simply means that, although Christ had entrusted them to the Church and they were being used for the sanctification of the faithful, an actual inventory of them had not been made. Under the guidance of the Holy Spirit the Church grew in the knowledge of the truth, and with the development of systematic theology and philosophy, aided by a precision of language, was able to make a final definition.

Sacraments of Initiation • The three sacraments which bring the faithful to the "full stature of Christ," enabling them to carry out the mission of the Church in the world, are Baptism, Confirmation and the Eucharist, and they are known as the sacraments of initiation. Through Baptism, the faithful are reborn through Christ's paschal death and resurrection and are made members of the Church. Through Confirmation, they are strengthened in the gifts of the Holy Spirit. Through the Eucharist, they share in the Eucharistic Sacrifice which is their ongoing incorporation into the Body of Christ and the sacred meal of covenant renewal in Christ. Those who have received the sacraments of initiation are filled with divine grace, enabling them to grow in

perfection and in the fulfillment of Christ's command to the Church to "make disciples of all nations."

Sacred Art and Furnishings • The Church has from earliest times utilized external beauty as an expression of the invisible glory of God, whether in painting, sculpture, mosaics, architecture, vesture, etc. Even the catacombs were decorated with murals, as later basilicas were with mosaics, and medieval cathedrals with sculpture and stained glass. The arts in the service of the Church reached a great synthesis in the Middle Ages; however, surely another high point was achieved in the Baroque era, although such display is not always to contemporary taste.

Because much nineteenth- and twentieth-century art did not continue the high standards set by previous eras, the Vatican II Constitution on the Sacred Liturgy encourages Ordinaries to strive after "noble beauty rather than sumptuous display" (n. 124), probably a thrust at neo-historic styles copied in the last century. Unfortunately, this has often been misinterpreted, as if such simplicity excludes any art or images at all, even though the same Constitution says that sacred images are to be retained (n. 125). It would seem that, regardless of style (all architectural styles are permitted; cf. n. 123), a church edifice ought to have at least an image of the Crucified One over or near the altar, a Madonna and an image of the patron saint, with the possibility of other images, e.g., the life and teaching of our Lord, the mysteries of the Faith, the saints of the Church, and all or any of these depicted in such wise that they be recognized, i.e., not so abstract as to be meaningless. Of course, how much pictorial representation is possible would depend on the architecture of the structure, the financial resources to pay for good art, but this dimension of teaching and also of externalizing the glory of God ought not to be neglected.

The principal furnishings of the church discussed in the section "Arrangement and Decoration of Churches" of the *General Instruction of the Roman Missal* are, in order of importance, the altar, the chair, the lectern, the tabernacle and images. All of these items, as "signs and symbols of heavenly things, should be worthy and beautiful" (n. 253).

Sacred College of Cardinals: See **College of Cardinals**

Sacred Heart of Jesus • Devotion to the Sacred Heart consists primarily in attention to the inexhaustible source of mercy and love poured out for us by God through the pierced heart of Christ. The Sacred Heart of Jesus symbolizes God's love for us in a humanly concrete and profoundly attractive way. The devotion arose in the twelfth century. While theologians such as St. Bonaventure addressed the topic, it was propagated primarily through the experiences and writings of mystics such as St. Mechtilde of Magdeburg, Julian of Norwich and St. Catherine of Siena.

The seventeenth century witnessed a marked increase in the popularity of the devotion. Both St. Francis de Sales and St. John Eudes were drawn to it. The Visitandine nun St. Margaret Mary Alacoque experienced visions of the Sacred Heart (1673-1675) at Paray-le-Monial and received a set of twelve promises that would exert a strong influence on popular Catholic piety and devotion to the Sacred Heart. Liturgical observance of the feast of the Sacred Heart was authorized by the Church in 1765, and then extended by Popes Pius IX, Leo XIII and Pius XI. In response to the visions of Sister Droste-Vishering, Leo XIII in 1899 consecrated the whole world to the Sacred Heart of Jesus. In the renewed liturgy, the feast is celebrated as a solemnity on Friday of the second week after Pentecost. Devotion to the Heart of Jesus is not an exclusively Catholic one. English Puritan theologians such as Isaac Ambrose, Richard Baxter and Thomas Goodwin wrote about it. In the Catholic Church, the devotion has been fostered particularly by the Carthusians and the Jesuits.

Sacred Liturgy, Constitution on the: See **Sacrosanctum Concilium**

Sacred Meal • The gathering involving food which has a religious significance. In the Christian understanding, the sacred meal is the Last Supper of Jesus. The Holy Sacrifice of the Mass provides those present with the opportunity to participate in the Eucharistic Meal established by Christ on Holy Thursday. The notion of "meal" in reference to the Holy Eucharist, which connotes an aspect of "fellowship" (*koinonia*), must not be interpreted as opposed to the "sacrificial" or "sacramental" reality. On the contrary, the sacrifice of Christ completes the meaning of the meal, as the Lord's Holy Thursday promise of His Body to be given and His Blood to be poured out is fulfilled in His Good Friday sacrifice.

The *agape* was a fellowship meal which often preceded the celebration of the Eucharist in former times. Some ancient pagan cults offered food to the gods for the appeasement of their wrath. This meal, too, was called a "divine meal" because it was consumed by a god.

For further reading: Dennis E. Smith, "Greco-Roman Sacred Meals," *Anchor Bible Dictionary*, 4:653-655.

Sacred Places • Those places designated by Church authority for each divine worship or the burial of the faithful. Sacred places must be dedicated as such, usually by a diocesan bishop or a priest delegated by him. Once a place is dedicated, nothing contrary to or out of harmony with the purpose of the place may take place. In churches, however, the Ordinary can permit the use of the building for a purpose other than divine worship, provided this use is not contrary to the sacred character of the place.

A sacred place loses its dedication and therefore its sacred character if it has been in great part destroyed or if it has been given over to secular use either by decree of the Ordinary or simply in fact. A sacred place is desecrated when something is done in it which is so injurious and contrary to its nature that scandal is given. When the Ordinary determines that a sacred place has been desecrated, worship may not be held there until a special Penitential Rite has taken place (Canons 1205-1213).

Sacred places for divine worship include churches, oratories, private chapels, shrines and altars. No place may be set aside for divine worship without the permission of the diocesan bishop. Churches, which are the primary places for divine worship, may not be built, restored or given over to secular use without the bishop's permission. Furthermore, every church is to have a title which is not changed after its dedication.

An oratory differs from a church, in that it is set aside for the divine worship of a particular group to which the faithful in general have access. The chapels of many religious communities are classified as oratories. A private chapel is a sacred place which is designated for divine worship for one or more individuals but without regular access for the faithful in general.

A shrine is a church or other sacred place so designated by the local Ordinary where the faithful worship as pilgrims because of some special devotion.

All acts of worship may be conducted in churches, oratories, shrines and chapels. Certain of the sacraments may not be celebrated in oratories, chapels and shrines, however, unless permission from competent authority has been received. These include the administration of Baptism and Confirmation, the celebration of Matrimony and the conduct of funeral rites.

Cemeteries are also sacred places where the bodies of the faithful are buried. Parishes and religious institutes may have their own cemeteries. All the faithful are to be buried in cemeteries; only Popes, cardinals and diocesan bishops may be buried in churches (Canons 1205-1239).

Sacred Roman Congregations: See **Roman Congregations**

Sacred Times • The Sundays of the year, as well as feast days of obligation established by the Holy See. Sacred times also include days and seasons of penance (all Fridays, Ash Wednesday, Good Friday and the Season of Lent).

The faithful are obliged to participate in the celebration of the Eucharist on Sundays and feast days of obligation. They are obliged to abstain from eating meat on all Fridays of the year (unless dispensed by their episcopal conference) and are to both fast and abstain on Ash Wednesday and Good Friday.

Although the universal law specifies nine feast days of obligation (Christmas, Epiphany, Ascension, Corpus Christi, the Immaculate Conception, the Assumption, the feast of St. Joseph, the feast of Sts. Peter and Paul and All Saints), the episcopal conference, with the approval of the Holy See, can either suppress certain feasts or have them transferred to a

Sunday. In the same way, the episcopal conference can determine an alternate manner of observing the days and seasons of penance (Canons 1244-1253).

Sacred Vessels • The *General Instruction of the Roman Missal*, nn. 289-296, describes sacred vessels as those "requisites for the celebration of Mass" which "hold a place of honor, especially the chalice and paten" (n. 289). Other vessels described concern the celebration of the Eucharist or the worship of the Eucharist outside of Mass. Among these are the ciborium (the vessel which resembles the chalice with a cover containing the Eucharistic Bread), the pyx (the container for the large Host used in exposition from a monstrance), the monstrance (the large vessel for exposing the large Host for Exposition and Benediction) (n. 292). The *General Instruction* asserts that "for the consecration of hosts one rather large paten may properly be used; on it is placed the bread for the priest as well as for the ministers and the faithful" (n. 293). In preconciliar legislation, vessels for the Eucharistic Bread were to be made of precious metal (particularly gold or silver). The present *Instruction* states that they must be materials that are "solid . . . noble . . . and do not break easily or become unstable" (n. 290). "Vessels made from metal should ordinarily be gilded on the inside if the metal is one that rusts" (n. 294); other suitable materials for these vessels are those "that are prized in the region, for example, ebony or other hard woods" (n. 292). Chalices should "have a cup of nonabsorbent material" (n. 291).

The exact dimensions and design of sacred vessels are left to the artist's discretion and creativity: "The artist may

St. John, one of the sacred writers

fashion the sacred vessels in a shape that is in keeping with the culture of each region, provided each type of vessel is suited to the intended liturgical use" (n. 295). Following liturgical custom, such vessels are consecrated or blessed according to the prescribed rite. This may now be done by any priest and should be done for all such vessels, whatever their material (cf. n. 296).

Sacred Writers • The persons, inspired by the Holy Spirit, who wrote the books of Sacred Scripture. Specifically, the sacred writers are the four Evangelists — Matthew, Mark, Luke and John. The Dogmatic Constitution on Divine Revelation, *Dei Verbum*, from the Second Vatican Council stresses the importance of the contributions of these four men. "The sacred authors, in writing the four Gospels, selected certain of the many elements which had been handed on, either orally or already in written form, others they synthesized or explained with an eye to the situation of the churches, the while sustaining the form of preaching, but always in such a fashion that they have told us the honest truth about Jesus. Whether they relied on their own memory and recollections or on the testimony of those who 'from the beginning were eyewitnesses and ministers of the Word,' their purpose in writing was that we might know the 'truth' concerning the things of which we have been informed (cf. Lk 1:2-4)" (DV 19).

Sacrifice • The act of offering to God fruits or vegetables, animals, food, incense or some precious object (and possibly the immolation and ritual consumption of the offering). The practice is widespread in the history of religions, presumably stemming from deep sources in human nature. The first sacrifice recorded in the Old Testament is that of Cain and Abel (Gn 4:3-5). The celebrated substitution of a goat for the sacrifice of Isaac (Gn 22) shows that the Israelites were aware of human sacrifice and its repudiation in the biblical faith. The ratification of covenants by sacrifice is an important biblical theme. The Temple in Jerusalem was the principal site of sacrifice until its destruction in A.D. 70. Our Lord Himself identified His death as a sacrifice — a shedding of blood for a new covenant (Mk 10:45) — while the setting of the Last Supper clearly recalled the Passover sacrifice (Ex 24:4-8). The designation of Christ as the Lamb of God (Jn 1:29; Rv 22:1) implies that He is a sacrificial victim. Most important in the portrayal of Christ's sacrificial role is the Letter to the Hebrews. There Christ the High Priest's perfect obedience in self-offering constituted the permanently valid and definitive "single sacrifice for sins" (Heb 10:12). These ideas are fundamental to the Christian understanding of the redemption of humankind in the paschal mystery and of

our participation in its infinite benefits. The Eucharist is thus called the Sacrifice of the Mass; it is in this liturgical ritual that the one sacrifice of Christ is continually reenacted in an unbloody and sacramental manner.

Sacrifice of the Mass • It is a dogma of the Catholic Faith that the Mass or Eucharist is a true sacrifice and a representation in an unbloody manner of the sacrifice of Christ. According to traditional theology, the features constituting the nature of a true sacrifice are verified in the Mass: a sense-perceptible gift is offered and in some sense destroyed by an authorized minister for the purpose of worship of God. The Eucharist is a genuine sacramental sacrifice in that the Body and Blood of Christ, offered at His crucifixion and death, is now constituted the sacrifice of the Church by virtue of Christ's joining the liturgical offering to His own.

Sacrilege • Violent, contemptuous or disrespectful treatment of persons or objects dedicated to the service of God. Sacrilegious acts not only include violent or disrespectful actions toward persons, destruction of sacred objects, but also receiving sacraments unworthily and in a state of mortal sin. Many acts of sacrilege, such as desecration of the Eucharist, are ecclesiastical crimes under canon law (cf. Canon 1367).

Sacristan • Term to describe the person who is responsible for the contents of a church related to liturgical worship, such as vestments, vessels, books, etc. More generally, it can refer to the sexton who has the responsibility of the upkeep of the church building.

Sacristy • From the Latin *sacristia*, referring to a room adjacent to the sanctuary or near the main entrance to the church, containing requisite materials for the celebration of the liturgy; it is also where clerics vest prior to the liturgy. This room most often contains chests of drawers and closets for sacred vessels, liturgical books, vestments, etc. The sacristy would also normally contain a sink to supply water for liturgical use (Baptism, the Eucharist), as well as for washing soiled linens used at the altar. At times, the Eucharist was reserved in the sacristy for convenience in bringing it to the sick.

Sacrosancta • Sometimes referred to as *Haec Sancta*, this decree of the Council of Constance (1414-1418) is often called the Magna Carta of conciliarism, in that it proclaimed a general council to be the highest authority in the Church, to which even the Pope himself was subject. This notion was condemned by Pope Pius II (1458-1464) in his Bull, *Exsecrabilis*.

Sacrosanctum Concilium • The Constitution on the Sacred Liturgy, the first of the Second Vatican Council's official documents, was promulgated on December 4, 1963; known in the professional literature by its Latin title, it is named (as is the custom for official ecclesiastical documents) after its opening words, *Sacrosanctum Concilium*. Although commonly taken to be the mandate initiating the sweeping liturgical changes that took place at the time of the Council, this Constitution is better understood as the culmination of the liturgical research that had been underway for over a hundred years, and as the codification of various principles and practices that had been proposed and debated since the beginning of the twentieth century. For instance, it is possible to see the first tentative steps toward a more general liturgical renewal in

the various directives issued by Pope St. Pius X:

✧ his sweeping rearrangement of the Psalter for the Divine Office;

✧ the restoration of Sunday as the core of weekly liturgical observance (with a consequent reordering of sanctoral celebrations so as not to displace the Lord's Day);

✧ his restoration of the Roman chant books and fervent promotion of congregational participation in the Mass by means of music;

✧ and, perhaps the most popularly successful liturgical reform in history: early and frequent reception of Holy Communion.

After a hiatus of several decades, due in no small part to the chaos caused by two World Wars and the Holy See's necessary preoccupation with this, the work of liturgical renewal was taken up again by Pope Pius XII immediately following World War II. The two principal liturgical achievements of his pontificate are:

✧ the publication in 1956 of The Restored Order of Holy Week which gave the Paschal Triduum its present form and scheduled the major celebrations at their proper times;

✧ his encyclical letter *Mediator Dei*, which in many ways anticipated a number of the directives of Vatican II's Constitution on the Sacred Liturgy: Pius XII insisted on the supreme importance of the liturgy as the foundation of the Church's spiritual life and the centrality of Mass as the Church's principal prayer; encouraged congregational participation in the Sacrifice of the Mass by means of vocal prayer, song and frequent reception of Holy Communion (ideally from Hosts consecrated at the Mass being celebrated); presented the Divine Office as complementary to the Mass; and viewed the liturgical year as the framework for the spirituality of the faithful.

On the eve of the Council (1960), Pope John XXIII issued a decree simplifying a number of rubrics for the celebration of the Mass and Office. In this document, the Pope revealed that these minor changes were but the beginning of "a more general liturgical reform," envisioned by his predecessor but now to be set before the world episcopate at the forthcoming Council for input and deliberation.

The Constitution on the Sacred Liturgy, eventually promulgated by the newly-elected Paul VI (1963), consists of the following sections:

I. General Principles for Restoring and Promoting the Sacred Liturgy:
  1. Nature of the Sacred Liturgy and its importance in the Church's life;
  2. Promotion of liturgical instruction and active participation;
  3. Reform of the Sacred Liturgy:
    a) General principles;
    b) Principles drawn from the hierarchic and communal nature of the liturgy;
    c) Principles for adapting the liturgy to the culture and traditions of nations;
  4. Promotion of liturgical life in dioceses and parishes;
  5. Promotion of pastoral-liturgical action;
II. Mystery of the Holy Eucharist
III. Sacraments and Sacramentals
IV. Divine Office
V. Liturgical Year
VI. Sacred Music
VII. Sacred Art and Furnishings

The Constitution on the Sacred Liturgy was the subject of an Apostolic Letter of Pope John Paul II dated December 4, 1988, in celebration of the twenty-fifth anniversary of its promulgation. This Apostolic Letter provides a helpful reference point for understanding how the supreme teaching authority of the Church views the importance of the Constitution for the present and future life of the Church. The Constitution's program of liturgical renewal, says John Paul II, "was undertaken in accordance with the conciliar principles of fidelity to tradition and openness to legitimate development, and so it is possible to say that the reform of the liturgy is strictly traditional . . ." (n. 4). The Constitution was a seed that has sprouted and begun to bear fruit. Now "it is a matter of the organic growth of a tree becoming ever stronger the deeper it sinks its roots into the soil of tradition" (n. 23). The basic thrust of the Constitution, in Pope John Paul's view, is the clear enunciation of what the previous Popes of the twentieth century had been pointing to: the full, active and conscious participation of the baptized in the liturgy is "the primary and indispensable source of the true Christian spirit" (SC 14).

From the Constitution Pope John Paul derives three principles for the ongoing renewal of the faithful's liturgical life in our age. (1) The Reenactment of the Paschal Mystery: "The liturgy has as its first task to lead us untiringly back to the Easter pilgrimage initiated by Christ, in which we accept death in order to enter into life" (n. 6).

The liturgy is the privileged place of encounter between Christ and the members of His Body. The Holy Father echoes the Constitution in listing the ways in which Christ is encountered: Christ is present in the Church assembled at prayer in His Name; Christ is present and acts in the person of the ordained minister who celebrates; Christ is present in His Word; Christ is present and acts by the power of the Holy Spirit in the sacraments, especially in the Mass and in the Most Blessed Sacrament reserved for the Communion of the sick and the adoration of the faithful.

(2) The Reading of the Word of God: true, the Constitution mandated "a more lavish fare for God's people at the table of the

Word," and the new lectionary (so widely and unexpectedly adopted by non-Catholics) has provided the opportunity for this, but more needs to be done.

Pope John Paul urges "fidelity to the authentic meaning of the Scriptures . . . the manner of proclaiming the Word of God so that it may be perceived for what it is, the use of appropriate technical means, the interior disposition of the ministers of the Word so that they carry out properly their function in the liturgical assembly, careful preparation of the homily through study and meditation, effort on the part of the faithful to participate at the table of the Word, a taste for prayer with the Psalms, a desire to discover Christ — like the disciples at Emmaus — at the table of the Word and the Bread" (n. 8).

(3) The Liturgy Experienced as an "Epiphany" of the Church: the Church manifests herself most clearly when she is celebrating the liturgy.

In Pope John Paul's reading of the Constitution, the Church's unity, holiness, catholicity and apostolic nature are all rooted in the Sacred Liturgy and are to be clearly manifest in its celebration: in communion with the bishop (who in turn is in communion with the Pope), in the variety of ministries, in the people's participation through word, song, ritual and silence. In reference to this "ritual experience" of the reality of the Church John Paul II notes: "The revision of the rites has sought a noble simplicity and signs that are easily understood, but the desired simplicity must not degenerate into an impoverishment of the signs. On the contrary, the signs, above all the sacramental signs, must be easily grasped but carry the greatest possible expressiveness. Bread and wine, water and oil, and also incense, ashes, fire and flowers, and indeed almost all the elements of creation have their place in the liturgy as gifts to the Creator and as a contribution to the dignity and beauty of the celebration" (n. 10).

That the Constitution's program of liturgical renewal has encountered opposition and been subject to abusive interpretation could hardly be overlooked by the Pope in the year that witnessed a formal schism on the part of so-called "traditionalists" and ongoing, though fewer, liberties taken with official rites by self-styled "progressives." The Pope notes three faulty directions: indifference, outright rejection, outlandish innovations. The Pope rejects the charge that the liturgical renewal itself caused the problems and notes other factors that must be blamed: "An unfavorable environment marked by a tendency to see religious practice as something of a private affair, by a certain rejection of institutions, by a decrease in the visibility of the Church in society, and by a calling into question of personal faith" (n. 11). Then, too, the Pope admits, the transition from being "simply present" in an often passive and silent way to full and active participation has been too demanding for some.

While making pastoral provision for those deeply attached to the spirituality of the former rites, the Holy Father clearly sees the ongoing implementation of the Constitution (authentically interpreted by the competent Roman authorities in dialogue with the local conferences of bishops), what he calls "the pastoral promotion of the liturgy," as constituting "a permanent commitment" (n. 10). The most urgent task for the future, he says, is the ongoing biblical and liturgical formation of the People of God, both pastors and faithful, so that all may "grasp the meaning of the liturgical rites and texts, to develop the dignity and beauty of celebration . . . and to promote, as the Fathers did, a 'mystagogic catechesis' of the sacraments" (n. 21).

Sadducees • A Jewish group of the Second Temple period, the Sadducees are known on the basis of evidence from three sources: the writings of the first-century A.D. Jewish historian Josephus, the New Testament (Synoptic Gospels and Acts), and rabbinical writings. No extant writings can be traced to the Sadducees themselves.

Two main hypotheses predominate regarding the origin and meaning of the word "Sadducee." One hypothesis suggests that the term comes from the Hebrew word meaning "just" or "righteous," so that the Sadducees would be "the just ones" or "the righteous ones." Another hypothesis proposes that the group's name derives from Zadok, who served as priest during the reigns of David and Solomon (cf. 2 Sm 8:17; 15:24; 1 Kgs 1:32ff.), and whose descendants continued to function in the service of the Jerusalem Temple.

Josephus provides information about the Sadducees in his *Jewish Antiquities* (in book 13, dealing with the Hasmonean period; and in book 18, in which he treats events of the first century A.D.), and in book 2 of his *Jewish War*. He groups the Sadducees with the Pharisees and the Essenes, identifying them as three main Jewish schools of thought or sects. In his autobiography, the *Life*, Josephus writes of having firsthand experience of the ways of each group during the formative years of his youth.

From Josephus's description of successful efforts by Jonathan the Sadducee to convince the ruler-priest John Hyrcanus (134-104 B.C.) to redirect his favor from the Pharisees to the Sadducees, we can infer that the Sadducees were active in political and religious circles during the Hasmonean period. We also learn that they competed with the Pharisees for power and influence. It seems that while they themselves were not all part of the ruling class, the Sadducees were people who competed for influence and for the favor of the ruling class. Besides Jonathan the Sadducee, Josephus identifies only one other individual Sadducee, and that is Ananus the high priest, mentioned in book 2 of the *Jewish Antiquities*.

Because Josephus presents the Sadducees' beliefs only briefly, and by way of comparison and contrast with the beliefs of the Pharisees, it is difficult to form a complete picture from the evidence he provides. In the *Jewish War* 2.8.14, Josephus writes that the Sadducees ". . . do away with Fate altogether, and remove God beyond, not merely the commission, but the very sight of, evil. They maintain that man has the free choice of good or evil, and that it rests with each man's will whether he follows the one or the other. As for the persistence of the soul after death, penalties in the underworld, and rewards, they will have none of them" (*Loeb Classical Library* translation).

In these views the Sadducees are said to contrast with the Pharisees, for whom Fate is said to be quite important, and who believe in the imperishability of the soul.

Commenting on the social conduct of each group, Josephus notes that while the Pharisees "are affectionate to each other and cultivate harmonious relations with the community," on the other hand the Sadducees "are, even among themselves, rather boorish in their behavior, and in their intercourse with their peers are as rude as to aliens."

In the *Jewish Antiquities* (18.1.3-4), Josephus writes that the Pharisees act with deference and respect toward their elders, but that the Sadducees "dispute with the teachers of the path of wisdom which they follow." Further, Josephus notes that Sadducees "accept no observance apart from the laws," from which it can be understood that they did not accept the Pharisaic and rabbinic notion of the dual (written and oral) Torah, adhering only to the written Torah.

The Pharisees were "considered the most accurate interpreters of the laws," and they held "the position of the leading sect" (*Jewish War* 2.8.14). Though there were well-placed Sadducees in positions of power, the result of the Pharisees' influence was that Sadducees could "accomplish little in office because the masses force them to follow Pharisaic teaching" (*Jewish Antiquities* 18.1.4). In comparison with the Pharisees, the Sadducees seem to have constituted a numerical and ideological minority. Josephus reports that the relative few who adhered to the Sadducees' teaching were "those of the highest standing" (*Jewish Antiquities* 18.1.4), while the Pharisees enjoyed a broader base of popular support.

The New Testament evidence concerning the Sadducees complements the data Josephus provides. The pronouncement story found in Matthew 22:23-33/Mark 12:18-27/Luke 20:27-40 begins by identifying the Sadducees as a group of people "who say that there is no resurrection." There the Sadducees present Jesus with the hypothetical case of a woman whose seven successive husbands all die, and who eventually dies herself. When the Sadducees ask Jesus which of the seven will be her husband in the resurrection, Jesus answers in an unconventional manner by which the Pharisees come to understand that He agrees with their belief in the resurrection (Mt 22:34).

In Acts 23:8, we read that "the Sadducees say that there is no resurrection, nor angel, nor spirit; but the Pharisees acknowledge them all." This explanatory statement occurs in the context of a hearing before the Sanhedrin (Acts 23:1-11) at which St. Paul deflects attention from himself by inciting an argument between the two groups, both of which are represented in the Sanhedrin.

Paul does this by identifying his own background as a Pharisee and by stating that his Pharisaic hope in the resurrection of the dead is the charge of which he stands accused (Acts 23:6).

Besides describing some features of the Sadducees' beliefs, Acts 23 is one of several New Testament texts which suggest that at least some Sadducees held prominent positions of religious authority. More evidence of this social role is found in Acts 4:1-2, where a group composed of "the priests and the captain of the Temple and the Sadducees" confront Peter and John, "annoyed because they were teaching the people and proclaiming in Jesus the resurrection from the dead." Acts 5:17-18 then reports that the Apostles were jailed as a result of the jealousy of "the high priest . . . and all who were with him, that is, the party of the Sadducees."

The Sadducees and the Pharisees are mentioned together in Matthew 3:17, as members of both groups approached John the Baptist to be baptized. In Matthew 16:1, Pharisees and Sadducees appear together to test Jesus by seeking a heavenly sign from Him. Shortly thereafter, Jesus warns the disciples to "beware of the leaven of the Pharisees and the Sadducees" (Mt 16:6). When the disciples misunderstand, Jesus makes it clear "that he did not tell them to beware of the leaven of bread, but of the teaching of the Pharisees and Sadducees" (Mt 16:12). This suggests that the religious authority which these groups exercised involved teaching.

Besides the evidence from Josephus and from the New Testament, we also find references to the Sadducees scattered throughout the rabbinic literature. Because of the continuity of the rabbinic tradition with Pharisaism, the value of this material for information about the Sadducees is hard to assess. In this literature, positions held by Sadducees are presented in ways which demonstrate the convincing power of the contrasting Pharisaic positions.

For further reading: Gary G. Porton, "Sadducees," *Anchor Bible Dictionary*, 5:892-895.

St. Joseph's Oratory • St. Joseph, foster father of Jesus, was declared the patron saint of Canada on March 19, 1624. In recognition of his patronage, Brother André of the College of Notre Dame of the Holy Cross began, on July 20, 1896, construction of a small wooden chapel dedicated to St. Joseph near the summit of Mount Royal, overlooking the city of Montreal, Quebec. From its foundation, St. Joseph's Oratory quickly became a popular place of pilgrimage, largely by reason of its reputation as a place of miraculous cures. Many of them were attributed to Brother André, who has been beatified in recognition of the Church's acceptance of his miraculous powers. His constant good cheer belied the many fasts and penances which he endured, as is evidenced by his frequent response to admirers: "All this comes through St. Joseph's prayers; I am only St. Joseph's little dog."

Crowded with crutches and other testimonials of favors received through St. Joseph's intercession, the original chapel was enlarged three times. In 1918, work began on a considerably larger church; that year the crypt church was completed with its massive granite steps leading up the slope of Mount Royal. Today on the site of Brother André's humble shrine, there stands a magnificent church, in the neo-Classic style of the Renaissance. The faithful continue to come and testify to miracles received through the intercession of both St. Joseph and Bl. André. It is a further tribute to the patron of Canada and of the universal Church that there should be on the grounds of the shrine a library containing every book and major document concerning St. Joseph. Through its radio station and film production, the shrine fulfills the dream of its founder to promote devotion to St. Joseph.

St. Peter's Basilica • The largest church in the world, St. Peter's Basilica is built above the traditional site of the martyrdom and burial of St. Peter, Christ's appointed vicar and the first Pope of the Roman Catholic Church. Though within the modern city of Rome today, more specifically at the heart of Vatican City, the site of St. Peter's in ancient times was outside the city limits and, therefore, appropriate by Roman custom to serve as a burial ground, a fact confirmed only in recent years by the archaeological excavations beneath the Renaissance basilica.

The Piazza di San Pietro, with its still more ancient Egyptian obelisk at its core, is likely laid out over the site of Nero's forum, which, despite tradition, was a far more commonly used place than the Roman Colosseum for the persecution and martyrdom of the early Christians. The literary evidence suggests that St. Peter was martyred by crucifixion, head downward out of deference to the Lord, in this forum and that his body was quickly and discreetly removed to a nearby Christian burial place. After a brief removal of his remains to the Catacombs of St. Sebastian, they were returned to the burial place closer to his martyrdom, and here Constantine built the first basilica in the fourth century in honor of St. Peter, prince of the Apostles. Recent archaeological research confirms the belief that Peter's remains are in fact still entombed immediately beneath the high altar of the present basilica.

Because of its proximity to the papal palace of the Vatican, though not the cathedral of the Bishop of Rome (St. John

Lateran is the cathedral), St. Peter's Basilica is used for most of the major ceremonies of the Roman Catholic Church, the coronations or, more recently, the installations of Popes, their funerals, canonizations of saints and the Papal Masses on major feasts, such as Christmas and Easter. The last two of the twenty-one ecumenical councils of the Church have been held in St. Peter's Basilica.

Saints • In his Letter to the Colossians (1:2), St. Paul uses this word for Christians in general. Strictly speaking, saints are people whose lives were notable for holiness and heroic virtue. Through the process of beatification and canonization, the Church officially declares them saints. It means that these people are in heaven and may be publicly invoked for devotion.

Vatican II says that saints are those who are joined to Him "in sharing for ever a life that is divine and free from all decay" and "have found true life with God" (GS 18); they "share in his life and glory" (AG 2) and "share in his happiness" (GS 21).

Saints, Invocations and Veneration of • A praiseworthy practice which dates not just to the earliest days of the Church, but even to the example of the Old Testament. The veneration of the saints, as an expression of the communion of all the saints, is chiefly effected within the context of the liturgy, although private devotions, study and respect are frequently found and heartily encouraged. (Cf. Dulia; Hyperdulia.)

The invocation of the saints, likewise, has been proposed to the faithful in numerous councils, although the Councils of Nicaea, Trent and Vatican II deserve special mention. While always vigilant against abuse and superstition, the Church encourages the invocation of the saints in much the same way that one is encouraged to ask a skilled neighbor for help with a task. The saints, to be sure, do not perform their works willy-nilly or otherwise outside the plan of God's providence; rather, they join their highly meritorious prayers to ours and on our behalf. The invocation of the saints is an act of love both for the person of the saint and, ultimately, for the God Who created the saint and the petitioner alike.

Saints, Patron: See **Patron Saints**

Sakkos • The outer garment of a Byzantine bishop, over which the omophorion is wrapped.

Salt, Liturgical Use of • Most likely adopted for liturgical use because of its preservative qualities and as a sign of purity, and because of the New Testament references to salt representing Christian wisdom and integrity of life (Mt 5:13 and Col 4:6). Salt was customarily used during the scrutinies of catechumens or the Baptism of infants, which was likely a transformation of the pagan custom of placing salt on the lips of a newborn eight days after birth. Salt was also used in the blessing of holy water and in the rite of the consecration of a church and an altar. In the present reform of the liturgy, salt may be mixed with newly blessed holy water (cf. Rite for Blessing and Sprinkling with Holy Water); the salt is added to the water in silence after a prayer in which God is asked to bless the salt recalling the blessed salt "scattered over the water by the prophet Elisha," and invoking the protective powers of salt and water, that they may "drive away the power of evil." It is no longer used in initiation.

Salvation • Generally speaking, the concept of salvation involves three elements: a condition from which salvation is the release; the means of release; the state to be attained through salvation. Often the term refers especially either to the process by which release is gained or to the state to which it leads. The Christian meaning of salvation involves these three elements, but it is best to start with the last. Christianity teaches that we are called and destined by God to be in union with Him. Perfect love, or charity, is the goal of salvation. We are saved for this end, to enjoy the vision of God, the heavenly life and the consummation of our happiness as human beings.

The goal of salvation is thus both union with God and our own flourishing. The instrument or means of our salvation is in the first place Christ Himself. By His death and resurrection, our salvation is won. That our salvation requires these actions tells us something about our condition. Because of sin — the inherited sinful condition of the whole human race, and the multitude of personal sins — we need to be reconciled with God. Christ's action and the grace He wins for us both heal us and enable us to begin the journey of salvation in which we are purified and transformed. All the other means of salvation — revelation, the sacramental life, our membership in the Church — flow from Christ and from our communion with Him.

Salvation History • Refers to the whole "economy" of God's action in bringing about the consummation of His plan for the created natural and human orders, as recorded in the Old and New Testaments, and as continuing throughout history until the end of time. The modality and unfolding of God's saving action thus respect the character of the created order which He Himself brought into existence and designed. Human beings, as bodily and time-bound, are historical and social beings. God's plan thus unfolds in stages and through the instrumentality of chosen agents, communities and institutions. A particular people is set aside as the locus of God's saving actions: the people of Israel and the Church. God chooses and sends those who will accomplish His saving work: Christ, the prophets and Apostles.

The great occurrences and personages that make up salvation history are depicted in narratives and transmitted through generations of interpretation, recollection and proclamation. Through all these means, salvation history both takes place and is made known. Salvation and revelation together comprise a history of divine engagement in the human realm which has at its apex the incarnation, passion, death and resurrection of Jesus Christ. All this history takes place in order to bring human beings into fellowship with one another and with God forever.

For further reading: Gerald G. O'Collins, "Salvation," *Anchor Bible Dictionary*, 5:907-914.

Salvation Outside the Church • "Outside the Church, no one will be saved," wrote Origen. Cyprian concurred: "He who does not have the Church as his mother cannot have God for his Father." And these axioms are fully in keeping with St. Paul's doctrine which identifies the Church as the Mystical Body of Christ apart from which no one can have eternal life in God (cf. Eph 1:22-23, 4:4, 5:23; 1 Cor 12:27).

Several Popes have also addressed this matter. In *Unam sanctam*, Pope Boniface VIII taught that "outside this Church there is no salvation and no remission of sins." Making an even stronger statement in the allocution *Singulari quadam*, Pope Pius IX declared that "it must, of course, be held as a matter of faith that outside the apostolic Roman Church no one can be saved." And Pope Pius XII reinforced this doctrine in the encyclical *Humani generis*.

General councils have also taught on this subject. The Fourth Lateran Council declared that "there is but one universal Church of the faithful outside which no one at all is saved." Likewise, the Council of Florence taught that "no one remaining outside the Catholic Church . . . can become partakers of eternal life." And finally, the First Vatican Council, in a draft never formally adopted because of the Franco-Prussian War, stated that "it is a dogma of the faith that no one can be saved outside the Church."

From these authoritative teachings, it would seem clear that there is only one conclusion: anyone who dies without Baptism in the Roman Catholic Church is condemned to hell. For maintaining exactly this conclusion, however, Father Leonard Feeney, S.J., an American Jesuit at Boston College, was first expelled from the Society of Jesus and then excommunicated in the 1940s. After reading the teachings of the Fathers, the Councils and the Popes, Feeney could not see any other possible interpretation than the one for which he was condemned.

In the aftermath of the controversy, the Archbishop of Boston, Richard Cushing, received a letter of clarification from the Holy Office. This letter, dated August 8, 1949, is important for its explanation of the necessity of the Church: she is necessary for salvation by divine command, not by intrinsic necessity. The Church, as Christ's Mystical Body, is the sole ark of salvation, but direct membership in her through the sacraments is only the ordinary means of salvation. In other words, knowledge of the Church and of her Founder is required of anyone for whom direct membership in the Church is to be considered necessary for salvation.

This teaching is not a proclamation of religious indifferentism, nor is it an admission of universal salvation in the heretical sense. Rather, it is a carefully balanced understanding of the Church's role in salvation history and a recognition that ignorance of the true Church excuses one from culpability for not belonging to her.

In *Singulari quadam*, Pope Pius IX, in addition to teaching the necessity of the Church for salvation, also taught that "it must likewise be held as certain that those who are affected by ignorance of the true religion, if it is invincible ignorance, are not subject to any guilt in this matter before the eyes of the Lord. Now, then, who could presume in himself an ability to set the boundaries of such ignorance, taking into consideration the natural differences of peoples, land, native talents, and so many other factors?"

This understanding of the Church's place in the economy of salvation is also found in the Second Vatican Council. *Lumen Gentium* teaches that the Church is necessary for salvation and that anyone who knows the Church's true nature but remains outside her cannot be saved (LG 14). But *Lumen Gentium* also teaches that non-Catholic Christians, Jews, Muslims and all those who, in their ignorance, seek God with a sincere heart by obeying their consciences may in fact be saved (LG 15, 16). However, the possibility of salvation for such people, notwithstanding their ignorance of this fact, comes only from the grace of God through Jesus Christ and His Church.

The solution to this apparent contradiction is not equivocation. It is, rather, the Church's understanding of the whole Gospel of Christ. Such an understanding confesses that Jesus is the way, the truth and the life (Jn 14:6), and at the same time recognizes the infinite power and mercy of God, Who desires all men to be saved (1 Tm 2:4).

So, is there salvation outside the Church? No. Is a person who dies without Baptism in the Catholic Church condemned to hell by this fact? No. Is this a contradiction? No. A proper grasp of the Church's teaching allows an understanding of how this apparent antinomy is resolved.

Samuel, First and Second Books of • In the Vulgate, the first two of the four Books of Kings, the two Books of Samuel, were originally one writing. The title is taken from the name of the central character, the priest, prophet and judge Samuel, a most significant figure in this transitional period of Israel's history. In his lifetime, the twelve tribes became a unit, instituted under the one kingship (1 Sm 8:5-9). God led David to the heights of leadership and promised him a lasting "house." The basic religious idea of these books is "election," that God has chosen and made firm a people of His own and one in whom there would be carried out His salvific will toward the eventual salvation of all (cf. the Prophecy of Nathan in 2 Sm 7). As Samuel announced the new king of Israel, David, so St. John the Baptist is called the new Samuel who announced the King of all, the Messiah, the fulfillment of every messianic prophecy, such as that contained in 2 Samuel 7, Christ the Lord.

For further reading: Anthony F. Campbell, S.J., and James W. Flanagan, "1-2 Samuel," *New Jerome Biblical Commentary*, 145-159.

Sanation • Also called retroactive validation or healing, sanation is an administrative act whereby a competent ecclesiastical authority decrees that an act which was invalid for some reason is made valid without the necessity of repeating the formalities of the act. The more common form of sanation is that which takes place relative to marriages which were invalid through the presence of an impediment, lack of canonical form or defect of consent. Provided the invalidating reason has ceased and the original consent between the persons still exists, a sanation can be granted whereby the union is considered valid from the time of consent.

Sanation can also be used for other ecclesiastical acts which were, at the time they took place, invalid (Canons 1161-1165).

Sanctification • The whole process of the personal supernatural transformation by which we become intimates of the indwelling Trinity. Sanctification is thus nothing other than the perfection of the life of charity. The chief means of sanctification is the infusion of habitual grace which enables us to turn to God in faith, hope and love. The life of grace is continually enhanced in us through our membership in the Mystical Body of Christ and through our sharing in the sacramental grace that is at the very heart of the Church's life. First through Baptism when we are claimed by Christ, then preeminently through the Eucharist when we receive the food of our sanctification, through the sacrament of Penance as we receive forgiveness for our sins and the strength to respond to our high calling — in all these ways, the work of sanctification is underway throughout our lives. We become holy as God is holy so that we can be fit company for Him for all eternity.

Sanctifying Grace • According to Scripture, Baptism makes a person a new creation, through a rebirth and communication of the Holy Spirit (2 Pt 1:4). This abiding, interior, efficacious communication of the Divine Spirit with its effects is sanctifying grace. It belongs to the whole soul, mind, will and affections. It makes holy those who possess the gift by giving them a participation in the divine life. This grace produces a conversion, a transformation of one's predispositions. It is lost through mortal sin (but restored in the sacrament of Penance) and can be increased by good works and the reception of the sacraments.

Sanctity of Life • The theological doctrine that human life possesses a certain quality which draws it particularly close to God and which makes it inviolable to direct lethal attack when innocent of any deliberate and formal aggression. This doctrine was first propounded by Pope Pius XI in *Casti connubii*, probably in response to the horrible slaughter of World War I, the Russian Revolution and Civil War and the decision of the Lambeth Conference of 1930 of the Anglican Church to endorse the moral permissibility of contraception. Albert Schweitzer and other Protestant theologians of that era argued that reverence was to be given to all living beings, but Pius XI restricted the notion of the sanctity of life to human life.

Sanctity is properly ascribed to human life because it is created in the image of God and has a destiny to be re-created through grace in the likeness of God. Sanctity can be ascribed to human life because it alone has an ultimate destiny of direct participation in the divine life of the Three Persons of the Trinity. The spiritual nature of the person is derived indirectly and remotely from the Divine Nature, and this gives the human person a superiority to all other created beings and justifies predicating sanctity of it. Human beings alone are destined through grace to participation in the Trinity's divine life, which sets it apart from all other living beings.

Because the human person is more closely related to God than any other being on earth, deliberately attacking an innocent human being is a remote attack on God. Just as an assault on a nation's flag is an assault on that nation, so also is a deliberate attack on an innocent person, who is the image of God, a remote attack on God. The duty of all persons to refrain from such actions makes the deliberate killing of an innocent person immoral.

Sanctuary • The *General Instruction of the Roman Missal* states: "The priest and servers should have places in the sanctuary, that is, the part of the church which indicates what they have to do, whether presiding over the prayer, announcing the word of God or ministering at the altar" (n. 257). This area should be large enough to accommodate the celebration of all liturgical rites and "should be distinguished from the rest of the church by some feature such as a raised floor, special shape or decoration" (n. 258).

Sanctus • Literally, "Holy." The Latin title, popularly retained in all vernaculars, for the hymn of praise which concludes the Preface or the Eucharistic Prayer. The first part of the hymn is the song of praise offered by the angels before the throne of God in heaven (Rv 4:9-11, with reference also to Is 6:3, whence it entered the worship of the synagogue and Temple). The second part (*Benedictus qui venit* . . . Blessed is he who comes) echoes the praise offered to Christ upon His triumphal entry into Jerusalem (Mk 11).

In the pre-Vatican II Rite, the quiet recitation of this hymn by the priest was marked by a threefold ringing of bells. It was also very common at sung Masses using ornate musical settings of the hymn for the choir to separate the two parts of the hymn, singing the *Sanctus* before the Consecration, and the *Benedictus* afterward, while the priest prayed the Canon silently.

The Vatican II Rite restores the hymn to its integrity as a complete text and to the people as a song rightfully theirs (although it may be enhanced with the assistance of the choir). The priest, of course, cannot go on with the Eucharistic Prayer until the hymn is completed. Indeed, he is to join in singing it with the people.

The complete text:

"Holy, holy, holy Lord, God of power and might.
Heaven and earth are full of your glory.
Hosanna in the highest.
Blessed is he who comes in the name of the Lord.
Hosanna in the highest."

Sandals • These are the special ceremonial shoes which the Pope and other bishops formerly wore during Pontifical Solemn Masses. These *sandalia*, formerly also called *campagi*, were only used for the liturgy and were of the liturgical color of the day, except black. They developed from the footwear worn by the Roman senators and other persons of high rank. Later, the clergy were allowed to wear this particular style, but by the tenth century it had been reserved only to the hierarchy and some privileged abbots. The sandals were usually leather, soled with the upper part of the leather covered with silk.

After the thirteenth century it was normal for the upper part to be made solely of fabric, such as silk or damask which was often richly embroidered. While the earlier shape of the sandals was just that, with straps that were wound about the wearers' ankles, eventually they came to have the shape of slippers. Indeed, in the earliest days of the

Sandal of St. Andrew (reliquary)

Church, acolytes and subdeacons wore a type of sandal without straps, *subtalares*, and this style was eventually adopted by those to whom the sandals were to be reserved. There is no mention in the latest ceremonial books about the sandals, and using the Missal of Pope Paul VI they are not usually worn at all. Whenever the older, or Tridentine, Rite is celebrated (as is now available) the sandals would still be worn by a bishop or abbot for Solemn Pontifical Mass. Moreover, when sandals are worn, they must still be worn over the ceremonial stockings or buskins.

Sanhedrin • Coming from the Greek *synedrion* for "council," the term refers to the governing body or supreme council for the Jews, which functioned as a religious and civil court. There is no clear historical record regarding its origin, but it was most likely established in the second century B.C. In the time of Christ, it was composed of seventy-one elders, high priests and scribes. The venerated group met near the Temple in Jerusalem.

Referring to the Sanhedrin, Jesus warned His disciples that they would be hauled into court for preaching the Gospel (Mt 10:17). The Sanhedrin could mete out sentences, but in the case of a death sentence, the Roman procurator had to ratify and carry it out. At the Lord's trial, the "whole council" tried to produce "false testimony against Jesus that they might put him to death" (Mt 26:59). John 18:31

indicates that this body could put no one to death on its own authority.

After Pentecost, the Apostles encountered the Sanhedrin (e.g., Acts 4:5ff.), which tried in vain to stop their preaching of the Gospel. The Sanhedrin ceased functioning when Jerusalem fell in A.D. 70.

For further reading: Anthony J. Saldarini, "Sanhedrin," *Anchor Bible Dictionary*, 5:975-980.

Sapiential Books • Seven books of the Old Testament are generally classified as "wisdom literature." They are: Job, Psalms, Proverbs, Ecclesiastes (Qoheleth), the Song of Songs, Wisdom and Sirach. Each of these receives special treatment. Their purpose is instruction, the transmittal of those values which are the source of a truly good life.

In the ancient East, there is a great deal of this type of literature. It incorporates the results of human experience in facing life's problems. These are the problems that cross the path of everyone: our origin and destiny, our search for happiness, the problem of suffering, the use of pleasure, love and personal relationships, death and what lies beyond. In every civilization, loving elders, having learned from their own successes and failures, try to transmit to the young the fruits of their experience.

The divinely inspired sapiential literature of the Jews is profoundly religious and moral. Authentic wisdom is piety and morality. Ungodliness and immorality are folly. Christianity broadened this Old Testament view by holding up to the whole world the noble image of Jesus Christ (our Wisdom), as revealed in His life and death — foolishness in the eyes of the world, but everlasting wisdom in the eyes of God.

For further reading: Roland E. Murphy, O.Carm., *The Tree of Life: An Exploration of Biblical Wisdom Literature*, Anchor Bible Reference Library (Doubleday, 1990); Roland E. Murphy, O.Carm., "Wisdom in the Old Testament," *Anchor Bible Dictionary*, 6:920-931.

Sardica, Council of • Beginning probably in the fall of A.D. 343 at the urging of St. Athanasius and others, about one hundred Eastern and Western bishops convened in Sardica (in modern Bulgaria) to draft some twenty canons in Latin and Greek, intended to facilitate reforms necessitated by the Arian heresy. The norms so enacted chiefly worked to lessen the influence of meddlers in the affairs of local churches. Although there were indications that Pope Julius I intended the Council of Sardica to be an ecumenical one, it failed to attain such status, due in part to the small number of bishops in attendance and to the irregular and incomplete manner in which the canons of Sardica were later accepted in other churches. The well-balanced precepts of Sardica were, however, taken up with those of other similar councils and made part of universal law by the Second Council of Nicaea.

Sarum Use • The adaptation of the Roman Liturgy used at the cathedral of Salisbury, beginning in the thirteenth century, which spread to much of England, Wales and parts of Ireland prior to the Reformation. A first collection of services is ascribed to Richard le Poore (d. 1237), and a revision in the fourteenth century (including changes in the calendar) was called the New Sarum Use. The *Sarum Breviary* was imposed on the Province of Canterbury in 1543; the Sarum Use was a chief source for the *Prayer Book of Edward VI* (1549).

Satan: See **Devil**; also **Devil and Evil Spirits**

Satisfaction • In its theological meaning, satisfaction refers to the grace-inspired and supported endeavor to make reparation to God's goodness and holiness when He has been offended by sin. The concept refers supremely to Christ Himself, Whose enactment of our redemption is essentially one of satisfaction. Christ's human will is suffused with the fullness of love, and out of this love He enacts the original submission and subjection of humankind to God. In this way, He makes up for Adam's failure in this regard and becomes the first person bearing a human nature to enact this loving submission. In this way, Christ becomes the head of the human race. Thus it should be clear that the essence of Christ's satisfaction lies not in the intensity of the physical pain He endured for our sake, but in the perfectly obedient submission to the Father, stemming from love and responding in love.

Saul: See **Paul, St.**

Scala Sancta • In Rome, across from the Lateran Palace and St. John Lateran Basilica, there is a building with twenty-eight marble steps, covered with wood. They are believed to be the steps of Pilate's praetorium in Jerusalem which Christ walked up for His interrogation. They are alleged to have been brought from Jerusalem to Rome by St. Helena around A.D. 326.

Scamnum • Another name for the sedilia or bench on which the ministers sat during parts of the High Mass. This is now replaced by the celebrant's chair (presidential chair) and other seats for ministers in the sanctuary.

Scandal • Provoking immoral actions in others by either words or deeds. Direct scandal occurs when one deliberately and willfully seeks to draw another into sin, such as in deliberate seduction; indirect

scandal can occur when the sinful act of another is foreseen but not intended by one's sinful action. Scandal can also be given when one commits an action that is not sinful but which could lead another to sin, such as when a priest violates speed limits while driving his automobile.

Scapular • Coming to us from the Latin for shoulder blade (*scapula*), this is one of the Church's sacramentals and consists of a garment which is worn over the head and shoulders (hence its name), which covers the chest and the back of the wearer, reaching almost to the feet. Many religious orders have a scapular as part of their habit. Lay people, in modern times especially, wear a much abbreviated form of the scapular, consisting of two small pieces of cloth, about two and a half by two inches, connected by two long cords and worn over the head and resting on the shoulders like the regular-sized scapular. In order for persons to be invested in the scapular of a particular religious order or confraternity, they must be enrolled in that order and invested by a member of the order or another priest to whom this is delegated. Though in the last hundred years a small, more practical "scapular medal" has been approved for use instead of the small form of the scapular, the cloth scapular must be used at the investiture. It is only blessed at this ceremony and if a new one is obtained, it automatically becomes blessed once the wearer puts it on.

The most popular, most indulgenced and widely used scapular is that of the Carmelite Order, also popularly known as the "brown scapular," but there are eighteen different scapulars which have been approved by the Church for popular devotion. These are: the Scapular of Mount Carmel, the so-called "brown scapular"; of the Hearts of Jesus and Mary, white: of the help of the sick, black; of the Holy Face, white; of the Immaculate Conception, blue; of the Immaculate Heart of Mary, white surmounted on green, hence known as the "green scapular"; of the Mother of Good Counsel, white; of Our Lady of Ransom, the white of the Mercedarian Order; of the Passion, red; also of the Passion, the black scapular of the Passionist Congregation; of the Precious Blood, also red; of the Sacred Heart of Jesus, also referred to as the Badge of the Sacred Heart, red; of St. Benedict, black; of St. Dominic, white; of St. Joseph, violet or purple; of St. Michael, round and blue and black; of the Seven Dolors of the Blessed Virgin Mary, black; and that of the Most Blessed Trinity, white with the blue and red cross of the Trinitarian Order.

Schism • Derived from the Greek term for "tear" or "rent," schism is the formal and willful separation of a group from the unity of the Church and thus from ecclesiastical communion. Schism is to be distinguished from heresy in that the grounds for division are nondoctrinal, at least initially. The Second Vatican Council acknowledges that some bonds nevertheless exist between the Catholic Church and churches separated from her: Baptism, faith in Christ and the hope for future unity.

Schism, Eastern • This term refers to the fact that a group of Orthodox Churches, centered upon ancient patriarchal sees in the East — chiefly Constantinople — are no longer in communion with the Catholic Church under the Pope. The *de facto* separation was the outcome of centuries of growing tensions between Eastern and Western Christianity, in which deep-seated political, cultural and language differences played crucial roles.

While the break between Rome and Constantinople cannot be dated precisely, events in 1053-1054 are customarily regarded as decisive in causing a permanent rift. Michael Cerularius, patriarch of Constantinople, in response to what he perceived to be a threat to the Greek Churches in southern Italy, ordered that all Latin Churches under his jurisdiction adopt the Greek Rite. Mediation attempts collapsed when the papal legate, Humbert of Silva-Candida, laid a bull of excommunication against the Eastern Church on the altar of Santa Sophia in Constantinople. Cerularius responded with anathemas and an encyclical in 1054.

This split was in fact the culmination of long-standing tensions between the Latin and Greek Churches concerning such matters as papal primatial claims, the Latin insertion of *filioque* ("and from the Son") in the Nicene-Constantinopolitan Creed, and the coronation of Charlemagne with its implied challenge to the status of the Byzantine emperor. After 1054, the rift was accentuated by armed conflict between the Crusaders and Byzantine forces, resulting in the conquest of Constantinople and the installation of a Latin patriarch in that see (1204).

Reunion attempts at the Councils of Lyons (1274) and Florence (1438-1439) failed to produce long-term results. Although the Orthodox Churches still remain separated from Rome, the modern ecumenical movement has fostered renewed contacts and reconciliation between them and the Catholic Church.

Schism, The Great Western: See **Western Schism, The Great**

Schoenstatt Movement • An international movement founded at Schoenstatt, Germany, in 1914 by the Pallottine Father Joseph Kentenich, and giving rise to the formation of five secular institutes: one for laymen, two for women and two for priests. The movement seeks to cultivate the Christian life in its members through a highly developed and sophisticated process of formation. In addition, the movement stresses devotion to the Blessed Virgin Mary and fosters a dynamic spirituality. The secular institutes serve as the core and leader groups of the movement. The Schoenstatt Sisters of Mary, founded by Father Kentenich in 1926, is now the largest of the leader groups. The first foundations of the institute in the United States were made in 1949.

Schola Cantorum • School for singers and other liturgical musicians. It is believed that the Schola Cantorum was begun in the fifth century and continued in various areas of the world throughout the ages. It involves instruction in voice, instrument and composition. The name Schola Cantorum is also used for the group of singers who render more difficult pieces at a liturgical function.

Scholastic • A student of medieval philosophy favoring argumentation and discussion through a systematic use of logic. St. Thomas Aquinas, a philosopher of the thirteenth century, is often identified with Scholastic thought. This Angelic Doctor sought to reconcile the pagan philosophy of Aristotle with the Christian Faith. He held faith and reason to be the sources of knowledge. His teachings formed the basis for much of the theological formation provided in Catholic seminaries after the Council of Trent. His influence predominated until the recent conciliar emphasis on more scriptural and ecumenical considerations. However, Vatican II did call for a preeminent place to be assigned to St. Thomas in the academic formation of priests.

The term Scholastic is also used by the Society of Jesus to identify a member who has completed his novitiate and has entered into the preparatory stages for the priesthood.

Scholasticism • A method of theological and philosophical speculation which aims at better understanding and deeper penetration of revealed truths and Christian doctrine through the intellectual processes of analogy, definition, speculation, coordination and systematization of these materials.

The foundations for Scholasticism were laid by St. Augustine. In his *De Doctrina Christiana* he urged the use of dialectics to study Christian doctrine, and in his *De Praedestinatione Sanctorum* he claimed that belief was to ponder with assent. John Scotus Erigina was the first to put this plan into practice by making a distinction between *auctoritas* (Holy Scripture) and *ratio* (reason), holding that it was the duty of reason, illuminated by God, to investigate the data supplied by authority.

St. Anselm formulated the program of high Scholasticism by asserting the duty of reason to gain fuller understanding of what was given in faith. St. Anselm of Laon in the twelfth century gave impulse to this by arranging moral, ascetic and dogmatic issues under systematic headings. He expanded *auctoritas* to include Scripture and patristic sources, but was still rather shy about using reason. The development of the *quaestio*, with its assertions in behalf or against a point as a means of investigating the sources enhanced investigation. Peter Abélard perfected the investigative techniques of Scholasticism, and Hugh of St. Victor employed forms of secular learning to increase studies.

When Scholastic philosophers and theologians obtained translations from the Greek of Aristotle, the period of high Scholasticism began and its methods were developed most fully. Three schools developed from these translations. An

Augustinian branch sprang up which refused to accept anything from the Aristotelian corpus that was contrary to Augustine. The Latin Averroists under Siger of Brabant supported Aristotle, even though interpreted through the Arabian translators, against Catholic doctrine. And finally a Dominican branch surfaced which tried to harmonize Augustine and Aristotle. Under St. Albert the Great and St. Thomas Aquinas, lines were drawn between the declarations of faith and reason by the use of argument, counterargument and resolution of the dispute.

Their work was criticized most strongly by John Duns Scotus, who stressed in an Augustinian fashion the importance of the will. Drawing on his work, William of Occam dealt the death blow to Scholasticism by his Nominalist teachings, which in turn paved the way for the teachings of the Reformers. Scholasticism never entirely died, however, for in the seminaries of Latin countries it endured and was revived in the nineteenth and twentieth centuries by Pope Leo XIII. This "neo-Thomist" school found its best exponents in Jacques Maritain and Cardinal Mercier; since the Second Vatican Council, Scholasticism has enjoyed less prominence in Catholic thought.

Schools, Catholic • The tradition of U.S. Catholic schools dates to 1606, when the Franciscans opened a Catholic school in St. Augustine, Florida, to teach reading, mathematics and the principles of the Catholic religion. Catholic schools spread throughout the territories and were the first schools opened in Louisiana, California, Kansas, North Dakota, Ohio, Kentucky and the District of Columbia.

The U.S. Supreme Court's decision in "Pierce vs. Society of Sisters" (known also as the "Oregon Schools Case") of 1925 has been called the Magna Carta of Catholic schools — indeed, of all private schools — because it defended their right to exist and the fundamental right of parents to select the school of their choice.

In brief: "The state of Oregon claimed that the need for any other kind of school than that provided by the State has ceased to exist, that the existence of non-government schools was a fatal menace to the government school system and that religious schools were divisive and undemocratic. . . . The court ruled to the contrary."

Justice James McReynolds, representing a unanimous court, observed, "The child is not the mere creature of the State; those who nurture him and direct his destiny have the right, coupled with the high duty, to recognize and prepare him for additional obligations."

The average elementary school tuition (1992-1993) is $1,152 for the first child in the family and covers fifty-two percent of the average per-pupil cost. Parish support contributes $457 or forty percent, with the balance provided by local fund-raising and other income-producing activities. The average secondary school tuition (1993-1994) is $3,100 and covers seventy-five percent of the average per-pupil cost. Fund-

St. Albert the Great,
Scholasticism patron

raising and other income-producing activities contribute seventeen percent, while subsidies and other contributed services provide thirteen percent of an average high school's total income.

The Catholic community's expenditure of five billion dollars in tuition and contributions generates even larger savings for the civic community. Since Catholic schools operate on average at less than half the per-pupil costs of public education, which was estimated by the National Educational Association at $4,209 per pupil, Catholic schools represent a savings to U.S. taxpayers of more than ten billion dollars a year.

Catholic schools may be classified according to ownership and administration. Most elementary schools — about eighty-six percent — are operated by parishes. Secondary schools are administered and financed in several ways: by a single parish (fourteen percent); by several parishes (twelve percent); by a diocese (thirty-four percent); and by a particular religious community (forty percent).

In a diocese, the bishop is the traditional head of all schools and religious education programs. The superintendent and/or vicar of education represents the bishop, working with a diocesan school board. At the elementary level, the pastor and principal direct the school. Leadership at the individual secondary school depends on the administrative head — whether parish, diocese or religious community. Parent organizations and boards serve in an advisory capacity for both elementary and secondary schools.

Schools, Parochial • Elementary or secondary schools which are supported by the local parish or parishes. Unlike public school systems, the parochial school teaches the Faith and Catholic values to children. Traditionally noted for high standards of scholarship and discipline, parochial schools played an integral role in the education of droves of Catholic immigrants in the nineteenth and twentieth centuries. They have been and are relied on by millions of people seeking a Catholic education for their children.

In 1884, the Third Plenary Council of Baltimore mandated that every parish should have a school, if at all possible. In recent decades, some parochial schools have closed or consolidated with others, because of fewer vocations to the religious life, rising expenses, government regulations, etc. Still, around 7,800 parochial grammar schools exist in the United States, educating close to two million children. There are also over eight hundred diocesan and parochial high schools, which teach close to 400,000 students.

Scotism • The Franciscan Scholastic Doctor John Duns Scotus (1265-1308) was a philosopher and theologian of immense subtlety and erudition. In the history of Christian theology, he can be said to represent a reaffirmation of the Augustinian line in opposition to the nascent tradition emerging from the work of St. Albert the Great and St. Thomas Aquinas. At various points in philosophy and theology, Scotus took issue with Aquinas. It thus became customary to refer to his characteristic positions, as defended by his disciples, as Scotism in contrast to the Thomistic positions of Aquinas and his followers. In theology, the chief areas of contention between the two schools center on Scotism's adoption of the following positions: love as the essential identifying attribute in the Divine Nature; the primacy of the will; the centrality of the individual; the identification of justifying grace with love; and Christocentrism.

Bl. John Duns Scotus,
Scotism founder

Scribe • In Mesopotamia, Egypt and subsequently in Israel, professional scribes served the needs of those societies for persons with reading and writing skills. Since the scribes were virtually the only ones who had access to records and other written information, they played an important role in the community. During the Old Testament period of the monarchy, the term "scribe" (Hebrew, *sofer*) designated important officials in the royal court. Some scholars feel that David and Solomon used scribes not only to keep annals but to record Israel's beliefs and traditions as found in written and oral sources. It is probable that the actual writing down of the Old Testament began precisely in this way.

In time, the term "scribe" appears to be used to indicate a certain profession, namely one entailing the copying of Scripture. In the latter part of the Old Testament period, the term "scribe" designated a scholar in the area of Scripture study. In the New Testament, "scribe" was the name for a scholar, an expert in the law. He was given the title of "rabbi." Though a scribe as such was not automatically a member of a particular party, i.e., Pharisee or Sadducee, in point of fact most scribes were Pharisees.

The scribes as a group opposed Jesus, although it appears that individual scribes were open to Jesus and His teaching. For instance, Matthew 8:19 tells of a scribe who wished to join the company of Jesus. Mark 12:28-34 speaks of a scribe who asked Jesus what was the first and greatest commandment. Jesus told him he was not far from the kingdom of God. Luke 20:39 recounts how certain scribes praised Jesus for His rebuttal of the Sadducees. All this tends to show that the scribes were not, to a man, closed to Jesus and His teaching.

For further reading: Anthony J. Saldarini, "Scribes," *Anchor Bible Dictionary*, 5:1012-1016.

Scripture: See **Bible**

Scruples • Anxieties and concerns that a sin may have been committed when there is no justification for such concerns or anxieties. Scrupulosity often results from excessive exposure to rigorist or inappropriate ascetical teachings, but it often seems to be based in some psychological dysfunction in the person. Most often, scrupulous persons fear that they have consented to a sinful thought or desire when this was not in fact done. They also believe that an action concerns grave moral matter when this was not the case. It often makes penitents obstinate in confession and reluctant to heed the counsel of confessors. It is paradoxical that scrupulous persons often lapse into extreme self-indulgence, and they are usually advised to obey their spiritual director in everything. They should be treated with great gentleness and patience, and very minor penances should be given them in confession.

Scrutiny • The technical term which denotes the formal evaluation of a seminarian prior to ordination (Canon 1051), or more widely, a review of any candidate prior to selection for ecclesiastical office or membership in an institute of consecrated life. The obligation upon superiors to perform a thorough and careful scrutiny of candidates is a serious one and reflects the Church's concern that her ministers and officials exhibit the highest of qualities.

Used in the plural and in common liturgical usage associated with the RCIA, the scrutinies are celebrated after the Liturgy of the Word and before the General Intercessions on the Third, Fourth and Fifth Sundays in Lent. Although "scrutiny" in a secular context is often regarded exclusively as an examination, liturgical scrutinies ought to be viewed differently; one should think of the second verse of the classic Vespers hymn attributed to Pope Gregory the Great, *Audi Benigne Conditor*, in which God is referred to as *scrutator omnium cordium*, searcher of all hearts — but more than the examiner, the healer by Lenten discipline, of the hearts He searches.

The scrutinies are described by the official RCIA thus: "The scrutinies . . . are rites for self-searching and repentance and have, above all, a spiritual purpose. The scrutinies are meant to uncover, then heal, all that is weak, defective or sinful in the hearts of the elect [those to be baptized at the coming Easter Vigil]; to bring out, then strengthen, all that is upright, strong and good" (n. 141).

The structure of the scrutinies is as follows: celebrant's invitation to silent prayer; direction to the faithful to bow or kneel; a litany for the elect; a prayer of exorcism; the laying on of hands. In the rite fully celebrated, the elect are then dismissed since they are not permitted to join the baptized in the Creed or in the General Intercessions (which are, after all, also called the Prayer of the *Faithful*) until their own Baptism. For pastoral reasons in the United States, the elect are allowed to remain for the Liturgy of the Eucharist, but may not receive Holy Communion until their full incorporation into Christ's Church.

Seal (Lamb) • In the Eastern Church, the part of the Prosphora (the bread of offering) bearing the seal: "IC," "XC," "NI," "KA." Generally the same as the Lamb.

Seal of Confession • The obligation of never revealing anything told to the confessor during the act of sacramental confession. The confessor is strictly forbidden to betray a penitent by word or in any other way. He may not violate the seal either directly, by referring to a person and what the person said, or indirectly in such a way that there is even a remote chance that someone might be able to identify a penitent. The obligation to maintain absolute confidentiality supersedes any and all civil legislation by which a priest might be compelled to reveal what had been told to him in confession.

The obligation of the seal extends to interpreters who may be used in the hearing of confession, and to anyone else who may happen to overhear a confession (cf. Canon 983).

The confidentiality of the penitent is further protected by a canon which forbids the confessor from using any knowledge acquired in the confessional when it might be detrimental to a penitent. Furthermore, ecclesiastical superiors who are priests are forbidden from using information obtained in confession in the external exercise of their authority over persons (cf. Canon 984).

A priest who directly violates the seal is automatically excommunicated, with the lifting of the excommunication reserved to the Holy See. One who indirectly violates the seal does not incur an automatic penalty but is to be punished according to the gravity of the offense.

An interpreter or anyone else who violates the seal, e.g., someone who overheard a confession, is to be punished with a just penalty, not excluding excommunication (cf. Canon 1388).

Secret of the Mass • The term formerly used, in the pre-Vatican II Rite, for the Prayer over the Gifts, so called because the priest offered the prayer in silence, raising his voice only to say or sing the ending, "*per omnia saecula saeculorum* . . . for ever and ever" (or, literally, through all ages of ages). Now, of course, the prayer is offered aloud by the priest in the name of all, and is designated by its function, in Latin *super oblata*, in English "over the gifts." (Cf. Prayer over the Gifts.)

Secret Marriage • A marriage which is celebrated according to all the norms of law but which, for good reason, is celebrated without any of the usual publicity, so that it remains unknown to the public. Although marriage is always a matter of the external forum, the spiritual good of the parties may be better served by having the marriage celebrated in secret.

Only a local Ordinary can give permission for a secret marriage. All preparations are to take place in secret and all involved in the marriage, such as the official witness and the other required witnesses, are bound to observe the secrecy. Furthermore, the marriage is to be recorded only in the secret archives of the diocese.

Some examples of causes for secret marriages would be marriages contrary to civil law, if that law were itself contrary to natural law or ecclesiastical law (interracial marriages, for example) or marriages which take place in countries where the Church is persecuted and religious marriages are forbidden (Canons 1130-1133).

Secret Societies • Any organization whose beliefs, goals, ritual and membership are restricted to the initiated may be termed a "secret society." The most prominent secret society is the "Free and Accepted Order of Masons," which has existed in various forms for several centuries. In nineteenth-century America, a large number of secret societies developed. Many of these were similar to the Freemasons and espoused beliefs incompatible with membership in the Catholic Church. Others were fraternal orders which developed to advance the social welfare of the membership. A number of these had secret handshakes and passwords by which the members identified one another. In the case of societies of workingmen, secrecy was thought to be necessary to avoid infiltration of meetings by agents of employers.

The Holy See condemned secret societies in general, but the social character of some of these organizations brought about a mitigation of this condemnation. The outstanding example was the controversy over the Knights of Labor, an organization composed chiefly of Catholic laborers, whose goal was the social and material advancement of the members. After initial controversy, the situation was solved through the mediation of Cardinal Gibbons, who worked out a compromise satisfactory to the Holy See and the Knights, thus avoiding the alienation of the Catholic working class in the United States.

Secular Institute: See **Institute, Secular**

Secularism • A philosophical view and social movement according to which our world, space and time alone are apt for meaningful discussion and action. Since the world is treated as an absolute, its meaning is not dependent upon any other or non-worldly reality, specifically God. From a secularist perspective, the Jewish and Christian religious concern for God beyond this world appears vain. Those who hold a secularist philosophy attempt to organize culture, politics and economics so that worldly concerns receive all the time, energy and resources of people. Devoting resources to other worldly religious goals is regarded by secularists as wasteful and thus somewhat immoral.

The widespread contemporary appeal of secularism is perhaps a reaction to that mistaken religious attitude which seeks to do honor to God by degrading the world. It is one thing to be wary of the temptation to be overly concerned for worldly success and quite another to deny the basic goodness of the world of which God is the creator and in which God's Son became incarnate to restore and save.

The religious view which regards the world as inherently evil is heretical Manichaeism. Though the Church's faith and insistence upon social duties have always been opposed to that heresy, many secularists have seen in Christianity nothing more than Manichaeism or "Platonism" for the masses. At least to some degree, secularism is an effort — faulty, to be sure — to overcome world-hating false religiosity. But secularism fails to get to the root of the mistaken religion: with the evils of the world as they are, no one can reasonably affirm that world to be essentially good unless it is created by the infinitely good and powerful God, Whose grace can overcome our sins. The Christian response to secularism should include our Faith's affirmation of the basic goodness of the world, our love of neighbor as a cooperation in overcoming the effects of sin which mar our world and our witness to the God Whose Son became Incarnate.

Secularization • The canonical process whereby a member of a religious institute or society of devout life is separated from the institute or society. This can happen in three ways: by expiration of temporary vows, voluntary departure and involuntary dismissal.

First, a member in temporary vows can leave the institute upon the completion of the time of temporary profession of vows or promises. Actually this involves no canonical procedure because once the time limit has elapsed, the vows expire (cf. Canon 688.1).

A member who is bound by either temporary or perpetual vows or promises can petition for a dispensation from the same. Persons who are members of religious institutes of pontifical right may obtain such a dispensation from the supreme moderator, with the consent of their councils. Members who belong to religious institutes of diocesan right or who are cloistered nuns can obtain a dispensation in the same manner; however, it must be confirmed by the bishop of the diocese wherein the members are assigned. Societies of apostolic life are to determine in their own constitutions the manner with which a member in temporary profession can be dispensed (cf. Canons 688.2, 742).

Members of religious institutes of pontifical right who are under perpetual vows may obtain dispensation by first petitioning the supreme moderator. The supreme moderator then submits the petition, together with his or her opinion and that of the council, to the Holy See, which, acting through the Congregation for Religious and Secular Institutes, is the competent authority to grant the dispensation. A perpetually professed member of a society for apostolic life can be dispensed by the supreme moderator with the consent of his or her council unless the society's own constitution reserves the dispensation to the Holy See. Members of societies or religious institutes of diocesan right address their petitions to the supreme moderator and his or her council. The petition is then forwarded to the diocesan bishop who is competent to grant the dispensation (cf. Canons 691, 744).

A member of a religious institute or society of apostolic life is automatically dismissed if he or she has notoriously defected from the Catholic Faith or has contracted marriage or has attempted to do so. In all other cases, the canons specify that a process be followed in order to dismiss a member. This process includes an official warning to the member, the gathering of proofs and their study by the major superior (provincial) and his or her council, and the forwarding of the proofs and other information to the supreme moderator (cf. Canon 694).

The supreme moderator and the council study the information and vote on the issue. If a majority vote to dismiss the member, a decree of dismissal is drawn up and, together with all facts of the case, is sent to the Holy See for confirmation. For societies and institutes, as well as autonomous monasteries of nuns, the decree is to be confirmed by the local diocesan bishop (cf. Canons 695-700). The vows, promises or other sacred bonds and all rights and duties cease when a member is dismissed. If the member is a cleric, he may not exercise Sacred Orders until he finds a bishop who will accept him (cf. Canon 701).

Secularization is also a term sometimes used for a method of transfer of Church-owned institutions to secular or civil ownership. It refers to the process whereby a Church-owned institution that is incorporated with a board of directors, such as a school or hospital, is effectively given over to secular ownership by a change in the membership of the board. If the board is comprised of a majority of members who are not members of the religious institute or other Church organization that owned the institution, then the institution has been alienated. If no permission has been obtained for this action, the alienation is contrary to the law.

Sede Vacante • The Latin phrase *Sede vacante* refers to the period of time when the Apostolic See or a diocesan see is vacant. When the Apostolic See is vacant, the period is also known as an interregnum.

During the period that a diocesan see is vacant, the diocese is governed either by an apostolic administrator appointed by the Holy See or by a diocesan administrator elected by the College of Consultors. The Apostolic See is considered no longer vacant from the moment the newly elected Pope accepts the election. The diocese that is vacant is considered filled when the newly appointed bishop presents his letters of appointment to the College of Consultors, thus taking canonical possession of the diocese (cf. Canons 416-430).

Sedia Gestatoria • Originating from the Latin words *sedes* (chair) and *gestare* (to carry), this refers to the special portable throne used by the Popes throughout the centuries and on which they were carried during solemn processions and other public occasions. While serving a symbolic purpose, signifying the exalted dignity of the Supreme Pontiff, it also has served many practical uses. Oftentimes the Popes were elderly or sickly, and the use of the chair saved their much-needed strength. Also, when in large crowds, it made it possible for the persons standing at a

Pope Leo XII's *sedia gestatoria*

distance to see the Holy Father. Though he would have preferred not to use it, Pope John Paul I gave in to the numerous requests of the faithful to be carried on the *sedia gestatoria* so they could see him in his processions. The present Pontiff has chosen not to use it, however, despite the many requests for it, shying away from negative associations of worldly pomp associated with it.

Sedilia • Latin for seat or bench, this word refers to the special bench used in churches for the officiating clergy and their assistants. Usually, they accommodate three persons, the celebrant in the middle and the assistants at each side, but there are some with up to five seats. The first examples of the *sedilia* can be found in the catacombs. These were actually carved out of the south wall of the sanctuary, and in some places, such as England, this fashion may still be found where the *sedilia* is actually recessed into the thickness of the

south wall. Though the movable *sedilia* was formerly also placed at the south side of the altar or sanctuary, this is no longer necessary.

Semantics of Religion: See **Religious Discourse**

Semi-Arianism • As its name implies, Semi-Arianism was a derivative of Arianism, which tried to bridge the gap created by the latter. Fourth-century Semi-Arianism held the Son to be like the Father, though not His divine equal. It fell under condemnation at the First Council of Constantinople.

Semi-Pelagianism • A particular French form of Pelagianism, Semi-Pelagianism taught that the human will both deserved and made God's grace efficacious. It was chiefly developed by monks at the Abbey of St. Victor in Marseilles and was condemned by the Council of Orange.

Seminarian • One who attends an ecclesiastical seminary, a candidate for the priesthood. Vatican II declares: "In seminaries and religious houses, clerics shall be given a liturgical formation in their spiritual lives. They will also need to celebrate the sacred mysteries and popular devotions which are imbued with the spirit of the Sacred Liturgy. Likewise, they must learn to observe the liturgical laws so that life in seminaries and religious institutes may be thoroughly influenced by the liturgical spirit" (SC 17). One contemplating the priesthood may begin his studies in either high school or college, completing the program with four years of theology.

Seminary • An ecclesiastical institute of learning whose sole purpose is to train young men for the reception of Holy Orders.

Semite • Literally, a descendant of Sem (Gn 10:21-31). A member of a group whose language and culture have come to be known as Semitic. The adjective Semitic has been used since the time of A. L. Schlozer and J. G. Eichhorn (1781) to designate a language family and its speakers. Both Hebrew and Aramaic, which are used in the Old Testament, are Semitic languages. Arabic is also Semitic. The Semites originally inhabited the Fertile Crescent (so named by J. H. Breasted) — a stretch of arable terrain extending northwest from the Tigris and Euphrates to northern Syria, thence south along the coast of Syria, Lebanon and Palestine to, and, including the Nile Valley.

Senses of Scripture • The Bible, composed by men who were chosen by God, "is inspired by God and profitable for teaching, for reproof, for correction, and for training in righteousness, that the man of God may be complete, equipped for every good work" (2 Tm 3:16). The human authors of Scripture, writing what God wanted, nevertheless used their own intellectual and literary gifts. Therefore, as is taught in *Dei Verbum*, the Dogmatic Constitution on Divine Revelation, "it follows that the interpreter of sacred Scriptures, if he is to ascertain what God has wished to communicate to us, should carefully search out the meaning which the sacred writers really had in mind, that meaning which God had thought well to manifest through the medium of their words" (DV 12).

This *literal sense* is essential to the proper interpretation of Scripture, not as a word-for-word literalism, but as seeking the mind and intention of the inspired author. This includes a knowledge of the original languages of the Bible, literary forms, context, facts of culture, history, geography and other influences upon the writer. This literal sense of Scripture also encompasses the *sensus plenior* (plenary sense), whereby God sometimes intends a deeper sense than is evident from a solitary text; rather, the fullest apprehension of the truth is possible when later revelation is applied to that which came earlier, thus communicating something more profound than that which is apparent at first.

The *typical sense* of Scripture involves not only the meaning which a passage has in itself, but refers to some truth or event of which it is a "type" or "foreshadowing." This can be seen in such examples as the exodus of the Israelites from Egypt being a type of our deliverance from sin, or the bronze serpent on the rod of Moses foreshadowing Jesus Christ on the cross. This use of typology can be found in Scripture itself (for example, Jn 3:14; Rom 5:12-14; 1 Pt 3:20-21), and can show the unity of the Old and New Testaments in revealing God's plan for the salvation of mankind.

The *accommodated sense* of Scripture involves placing an interpretation upon a passage which has no strict connection to it. This may be done to make some moral or allegorical point, but if proper caution is not taken, it can distort the primary meaning of the words. An accommodation must never contradict the literal sense of the original text, nor can it be used as a proof of some particular doctrine.

Sentence • The written decision of a judge in a case presented to an ecclesiastical court. The sentence begins with the invocation of the Divine Name. Then follow the name of the tribunal, the judge or judges, the names and domiciles of the petitioner, respondent and procurators, as well as the names of the defender of the bond and promoter of justice if they took part in the case.

Next there is a brief explanation of the facts of the case and a summation of the proofs. The following section is known as the dispositive part of the sentence. It contains the reasons upon which the decision is based, as well as the law which is pertinent to the case. The sentence ends with the decision of the court. It must be signed by the judges and must indicate the date and place where judgment was made (Canons 1612-1613).

Separation • The physical separation of a husband and wife from each other for adultery or other serious causes is provided for in the Code of Canon Law. If one party to a marriage severs conjugal living because of adultery by the other, he or she can, after six months have passed, petition the competent ecclesiastical authority for permission to separate on a permanent basis. The competent authority is usually the local Ordinary or his delegate. When the reason for the separation ceases, the spouses are expected to resume conjugal cohabitation. There are no longer any canonical penalties for failing to observe the canons on separation.

Finally, a marital separation does not mean that the spouses are no longer bound by fidelity to each other (Canons 1151-1155).

Septuagesima • Literally, "the seventieth (day before Easter)." The third Sunday before Lent, the ninth Sunday before Easter. Before the Calendar revision of Vatican II, this was the first Sunday of a pre-Lent "subseason." The season marked a transition from the post-Epiphany Sundays to the Lenten observance. Violet vesture was worn, and the Alleluia was omitted from Masses and Offices (the remnant of a "farewell to the Alleluia" observance

survived in the chanting of the double Easter alleluia at the conclusion of Vespers on Septuagesima Sunday). On the other hand, there was no fasting.

The season seems to have come into the Roman Calendar under Eastern influence. Since the Eastern Church did not fast on Saturdays or Sundays, its Lenten period was somewhat extended to guarantee a literally full forty days of fasting. At the time of Vatican II's revision of the calendar, there was concern that this pre-Lent obscured the prominence of the Lenten observance itself, and that the confused rubrics of the season reflected this difficulty, and so the season, and hence the Sundays, were suppressed.

Septuagint • The Greek translation of the Hebrew Old Testament started in the third century B.C. in Alexandria, Egypt. The name Septuagint comes from the Greek word for "seventy"; hence the symbol LXX in Roman numerals. It refers to the seventy-two Jewish translators brought to Egypt by Ptolemy II Philadelphus (285-246 B.C.) to translate the Hebrew Bible for the non-Hebrew-speaking Jews. The translation was completed around 100 B.C. It differed from the Hebrew Bible in the arrangement of the books and included several books, later called deuterocanonical, which were not acknowledged as sacred by the Palestinian community. It should be noted, however, that the early Church used the Septuagint when citing Old Testament passages, as is evident from the New Testament and patristic sources.

For further reading: Melvin K. H. Peters, "Septuagint," *Anchor Bible Dictionary*, 5:1093-1104.

Seraph • The Hebrew word *seraph* (plural, *seraphim*) refers to a fiery supernatural being. In Numbers 21:6-9, we read of fiery (*seraph*) serpents who afflict the complaining Israelites in the desert. In Isaiah 6:1-7, they are attendants or guardians before God's throne. Seraphim are depicted as having six wings, with two covering their faces, two covering their feet (a Hebrew euphemism for genitals), and two for flying. They praise God, calling, "Holy, Holy, Holy is the Lord of Hosts." One of them touched Isaiah's lips with a live coal from the altar, cleansing him from sin. Later Jewish and Christian angelology ranked the Seraphim and the Cherubim as the two highest choirs of angels.

Sermon on the Mount • The discourse of Jesus found in Matthew 5:1—7:29 is traditionally known as the Sermon on the Mount. It is the first of five collections of Jesus' sayings arranged by Matthew into extended discourses. Each of these discourses begins with an introduction which indicates the circumstances of the discourse and the audience to which it is addressed. With each, there is a concluding formula which brings Jesus' word to a close. The five discourses are listed below, with an indication of where the concluding formula is found:

  5:1—7:29: Sermon on the Mount (7:28)
  10:5-36: Missionary Discourse (11:1)
  13:1-53: Parables Discourse (13:53)
  18:1-35: Community Discourse (19:1)
  23:1—25:46: Woes and Eschatological
    Discourse (26:1)

The Sermon on the Mount is a Matthean composition based mainly on the "Q" document, the sayings source common to Matthew and Luke. In broad terms, Matthew's text follows the outline of the much briefer Lucan "Sermon on the Plain" (Lk 6:20-49), with which it shares much common material. Both the Sermon on the Mount and the Sermon on the Plain begin with the Beatitudes (Mt 5:3-12; Lk 6:20-26) and end with the parable of the house built on rock and the house built on sand (Mt

7:24-27; Lk 6:46-49). To the material which both sermons share in common, Matthew adds other "Q" material (some of which is found elsewhere in Luke, such as the Lord's Prayer, found in Matthew 6:9-13 and Luke 11:2-4), as well as material from Matthew's own sources (such as the antitheses of Matthew 5:21-48).

The contents of the Sermon on the Mount can be outlined as follows:

  5:1-2: Narrative introduction
  5:3-12: The Beatitudes
  5:13-16: Salt of the earth and light of the
    world
  5:17-20: Jesus, the fulfiller of the law
  5:21-48: The Antitheses:
      5:21-26: Anger
      5:27-30: Adultery
      5:31-32: Divorce
      5:33-37: Oaths
      5:38-42: Retaliation
      5:43-48: Love toward enemies
  6:1-18: Genuine piety vs. exterior display:
      6:1-4: Almsgiving
      6:5-15: Prayer (6:9-13: The Lord's
        Prayer)
      6:16-18: Fasting
  6:19—7:12: Inappropriate concern vs.
    proper care:
      6:19-34: Treasure on earth vs.
        treasure in heaven
      7:1-5: On judging others
      7:6: Pearls before swine
      7:7-11: On prayer
      7:12: The Golden Rule
  7:13-27: Two ways
  7:13-14: The narrow gate
  7:15-20: By their fruits you will know
    them
  7:21-23: False disciples and true disciples
  7:24-27: The house built on rock and the
    house built on sand
  7:28-29: Narrative Conclusion

Some of the most familiar material in the New Testament is found in the Sermon on the Mount: the Beatitudes, the Lord's

Prayer, the Golden Rule, the command to turn the other cheek rather than retaliate against aggression. Understood across a broad spectrum of thought as everything from a new Torah proclaimed by Jesus as a new Moses to the new Israel, to a compendium of Christian moral doctrine, to a treasury of universal human values, the Sermon on the Mount has enjoyed a long and rich history of interpretation.

Biblical scholars identify three major currents in the history of interpretation of the sermon's meaning. The oldest is the ethical interpretation, typified by St. Augustine, who declared that the sermon contains "all the precepts by which the Christian life is formed" (*De Sermone Domini in monte*, 1, 1, 1. *PL* 34, 1231). According to the ethical interpretation, Jesus' Sermon on the Mount presents the disciples with a rule of life which they are directed to follow. The prescriptions of the sermon are the path by which Christians fulfill the command to "be perfect, as your heavenly Father is perfect" (Mt 5:48). The sermon provides an uncompromising moral standard which nevertheless remains attainable.

A second current of interpretation, represented by Martin Luther, understands the sermon's teaching not as a practicable code of conduct, but as an ideal which is impossible to fulfill. Still, the ideal serves a pedagogical function (as does the old law in Galatians 3), with radical demands which serve to highlight human sinfulness and faith's total dependence on God's grace. Confronted with the impracticability of the sermon's demands, believers realize that they cannot attain perfection by their own efforts.

A third current of interpretation emerged early in the twentieth century, represented by Johannes Weiss and Albert Schweitzer, around the thesis that Jesus preached the advent of God's kingdom as an event that would take place very soon. In the light of this eschatological urgency, the Sermon on the Mount offers an interim ethic, a morality demanding heroic effort for the short time remaining before the end. Given the imminence of the end, the Sermon on the Mount proposes a radical ethic suited to the severity of the crisis at hand.

Although many have attempted to tone down or domesticate the demands of the Sermon on the Mount, its authority is based on the supreme authority of its preacher, Jesus. This comes to a clear focus in the narrative conclusion: "When Jesus finished these sayings, the crowds were astonished at his teaching, for he taught them as one who had authority, and not as their scribes." It is Jesus, the eschatological herald of God's kingdom, Who bestows the blessedness of that kingdom on those who are named in the Beatitudes. According to Matthew's Jewish Christian perspective, it is Jesus, the fulfiller of God's law, Whose interpretation of the law rests on no authority besides His own. It is Jesus the true teacher Who calls disciples (Mt 5:18-22) who gather around Him to listen and to learn. Reminding the disciples that they are the salt of the earth and the light of the world, Matthew's Jesus provides them with an ethical standard which will make their conduct an example to others.

For further reading: Hans Dieter Betz, "Sermon on the Mount/Plain," *Anchor Bible Dictionary*, 5:1106-1112.

Servant of Yahweh • A number of individuals and groups in the Old Testament are described as servants of the Lord. For example, Moses is the servant of the Lord *par excellence* in the Deuteronomic writings (e.g., Dt 34:5; Jos 1:1-2; and cf. also Rv 15:3), and the title is extended to his successor Joshua (e.g., Jos 24:29; Jgs 2:8). Prophets collectively are the Lord's servants (e.g., 2 Kgs 17:13; 21:10; 24:2; and cf. also Rv 10:7), and individual prophets are identified as the Lord's servants (e.g., Elijah in 2 Kgs 9:36; Isaiah in Is 20:3). The king is also said to be the Lord's servant, and this is especially so in the case of David (cf. 2 Kgs 19:34: 20:6; Ps 18:1; 36:1; 78:70; 89:4, 21; 132:10; 144:10). Those who worship the Lord are His servants, both collectively (cf. Ps 134:1; 135:1) and as individuals who depend on the Lord and who place complete trust in Him (e.g., Ps 31:17).

The title "Servant of Yahweh," also called the "Suffering Servant of Yahweh," applies particularly to a figure found in four poetic texts of the Book of Isaiah. These four Servant songs or Servant poems are found in that portion of the Book of Isaiah (Chapters 40-55) attributed to an anonymous prophet who wrote during the Babylonian Exile and who is known as Second Isaiah or Deutero-Isaiah.

The distinctiveness of the Servant poems was first noted by Bernard Duhm (1847-1928), who observed that these poems appear to stand out from their context in Second Isaiah. Most scholars do not agree with Duhm's attribution of the Servant poems to someone other than the author of the rest of Isaiah 40-55. There is actually an increasing tendency to study these texts in the light of other texts in Second Isaiah which speak of servant(s) of the Lord. Even so, the distinctiveness of the four poems is broadly recognized.

The four Servant poems are: (1) Isaiah 42:1-7; (2) Isaiah 49:1-7; (3) Isaiah 50:4-11; (4) Isaiah 52:13—53:12.

Through the text of the Servant poems, the contours of the Servant's personality gradually take shape.

In the first Servant poem (Is 42:1-7), God calls the servant "my chosen," designating the Servant as the Spirit-anointed bearer of divine justice to the nations. It is the Servant's mission to open the eyes of the blind, to bring freedom and light to those in captivity and darkness.

The Servant himself speaks in the second poem (Is 49:1-7), confident that he has been called from his mother's womb for a mission "to raise up the tribes of Jacob and restore the preserved of Israel" (Is 49:6).

The third poem (Is 50:4-11) adds the dimension of suffering and opposition to the portrait of the Servant.

The Servant announces the purpose of his God-given, well-trained tongue: "That I might know how to sustain with a word him that is weary" (Is 50:4). The Servant willingly submits to those who subject him even to physical abuse (Is 50:6), confident that God will sustain and support him.

In the first three poems, the Servant carries out his mission by speaking. In the fourth poem (Is 52:13—53:12), the Servant accomplishes his mission by suffering on behalf of others, by whom he is despised and rejected. The Servant's self-sacrifice is the fulfillment of his God-given mission, and God alone recognizes and rewards the Servant's fidelity: "He shall see the fruit of the travail of his soul and be satisfied; by his knowledge shall the righteous one, my servant, make many to be accounted righteous; and he shall bear their iniquities" (Is 53:11).

In the quest for identification, the Servant of the poems has been subjected both to collective and individual interpretations. According to the collective interpretations, the Servant has been identified as the historical Israel, as an idealized Israel, and even as a pious remnant of Israel which has a mission to restore and renew the whole people. Corporate personality hypotheses have also been proposed as intermediate ground between collective and individual interpretations. Israel's identity is concentrated in the figure of the Servant, who acts for and on behalf of the whole people: one stands for all.

Hypotheses which identify the Servant as an individual have been wide-ranging. Some have suggested that the poems are autobiographical reflections by the otherwise anonymous author of Second Isaiah, or biographical poems by Second Isaiah about Isaiah of Jerusalem. Others have searched for the Servant's identity among the many historical figures who might be viewed as servants of the Lord. Still others see in the figure of the Servant an ideal or even messianic figure, with some hypotheses focusing on the prophetic character of the Servant, and others on royal aspects of the Servant's characterization.

It is perhaps Duhm's insistence on the distinctiveness of the Servant poems from the rest of Second Isaiah that has led twentieth-century scholars to pursue the task of identifying the Servant of the poems as an individual to be distinguished from other servants of the Lord in Second Isaiah. Besides the author of Second Isaiah himself and the eighth-century B.C. prophet Isaiah, candidates proposed have included Moses, Ezekiel, Jeremiah, Hezekiah, Uzziah, Jehoiachin, Zerubbabel and Cyrus, king of Persia.

The poems themselves say little that might lead to a clear determination of the Servant's identity. In the first poem, the Lord points him out as "my servant, whom I uphold, my chosen, in whom my soul delights" (Is 42:1). The figure is also called "my servant" in the second poem (49:3, 6) and in the fourth (52:13; 53:11). Outside the Servant poems themselves, it is clear in texts of Second Isaiah that Israel in exile is the Lord's chosen servant, whom the Lord Himself strengthens and upholds (Is 41:8-9; 44:1-2, 21; 45:4). Within the poems, in Isaiah 49:3 the Servant is called "Israel, in whom I will be glorified," though Isaiah 49:4-6 complicates this identification by indicating that the Servant has a mission to Israel. The identification is further complicated by the opposition which the Servant faces and the oppression to which he is subjected, especially in the fourth poem (Is 52:13—53:12).

Very early on, Christians came to recognize Jesus as the fulfillment of the Servant poems, understanding Jesus as the Servant of the Lord.

In Luke 22:37, Jesus announces His fulfillment of Isaiah 53:12, part of the fourth Servant poem: "For I tell you that this scripture must be fulfilled in me, 'And he was reckoned with transgressors'; for what is written about me has its fulfillment." Matthew 8:17, a fulfillment citation, draws a connection between Jesus' healing and exorcising and Isaiah 53:4, a verse from the fourth Servant poem: "He took our infirmities and bore our diseases."

The longest Matthean citation of the Old Testament is the Matthew 12:17-21 citation of Isaiah 42:1-4, part of the first Servant poem. Jesus withdraws from the scene after His healing of the man with the withered hand causes the Pharisees to plot against Him. This is explained as the fulfillment of the prophecy about the Servant according to which "He will not wrangle or cry aloud, nor will any one hear his voice in the streets; he will not break a bruised reed or quench a smoldering wick. . ." (Mt 12:19-20; cf. Is 42:2-4).

As Philip meets the Ethiopian court official on the road from Jerusalem to Gaza, he finds the official puzzling over Isaiah 53:7-8, a portion of the fourth Servant poem (Acts 8:30-35). When the official asks about the identity of the one about whom it is said, "As a sheep led to the slaughter. . . ," Philip explains that the text refers to Jesus.

The First Letter of Peter (2:21-25), a text used in the Liturgy of the Hours as the New Testament canticle for Sunday Evening Prayer during Lent, cites Isaiah 53:9, part of the fourth Servant poem: "He committed no sin; no guile was found on his lips" (1 Pt 2:22). Here the Righteous Sufferer of the Servant Poems provides the model for understanding the passion and death of Jesus.

Server, Altar • Also known as Mass server, the altar server is one who is privileged to assist the bishop or priest at the Eucharist and other liturgical rites. It is customary for servers to be vested in cassock and surplice, to take part in the processions at the beginning and end of the rite by bearing the processional cross, candles, incense and thurible, to accompany the priest or deacon at the proclamation of the Gospel, to assist with the wine and water at the preparation of the gifts and the lavabo, and in general to add to the solemnity and tone of the celebration by a reverent comportment and attention to the action of the rite. Although the altar server is sometimes called an "acolyte," the two roles are distinguished, properly speaking, by the fact that acolyte is the title of an instituted ministry in the revised arrangement of ministries and orders mandated by Vatican Council II.

Customarily, this liturgical role was reserved to males only, largely because of the association of this ministry with the minor order of acolyte which one would receive on the way to sacramental ordination. In June 1994, the permission was given for diocesan bishops to allow female servers (reiterating that this ministry is no longer a minor order and that women cannot be ordained to the priesthood).

Service • (1) The performance of one's duty toward God and neighbor. The first three commandments are concerned with man's duties toward God. A person serves God by acts of prayer, virtue and worship. The remaining seven commandments deal with man's responsibilities toward others.

He fulfills this obligation through the corporal and spiritual works of mercy. Jesus emphasized the necessity of service when He summed up the Ten Commandments into two: "You shall love the Lord, your God, with all your heart, and with all your soul, and with all your mind. . . . You shall love your neighbor as yourself" (Mt 22:37, 39). The word "deacon" — the title of those ordained men who are not bishops or priests — is derived from the Greek *diakonia*, which means "service."

(2) The name given to a religious ceremony. In the Catholic Tradition, "service" refers to a ceremony without the Mass, e.g., the Good Friday Liturgy, a prayer vigil before a funeral, etc.

Servile Work • Occupations that rely primarily on physical activity for material gain. Church law forbids servile work on Sundays and holy days of obligation, but exceptions are made for those functions that are necessary for the well-being of society, or for those who must support their family or to maintain their livelihood.

These precepts against servile work on Sundays and holy days are primarily intended to foster the practice of religion and devotion to God. They also aim at protecting those who earn a livelihood by servile labor from being exploited by others. Unfortunately, in many secularized and advanced societies, these prohibitions now go largely unheeded, and as a result, Sundays have become the most profitable business days of the week for merchants. Thus, not only have Sundays and holy days had their sacred character compromised, but workers are more exploited as well.

Seven Joys of the Blessed Virgin • The practice of gathering series or chains of scriptural passages referring to particular moments in the life of Christ and Our Lady for the purpose of prayer and meditation goes back to the Middle Ages. This practice is in fact in the background of the development of the Fifteen Mysteries of the Rosary. Thus the Seven Joys of Mary are: the Annunciation, the Visitation, the Birth of Christ, the Adoration of the Magi, the Finding of Jesus in the Temple, the Apparition of the Risen Christ to his Mother, and the Assumption and Coronation of the Blessed Virgin.

Sex and Christianity • In the context of Scripture and Catholic Tradition, sexuality only finds its fullest expression in either the dedicated celibate lifestyle or sacramental marriage.

Scripture is quite clear that the Christian should not even entertain lustful thoughts in one's heart. Adultery was condemned as immoral by Jesus, even though He forgives those who repent of it. Sexuality is to be used to give life to children and to bind man and woman into a life-giving, permanent, faithful union. Thus, to engage in sexual actions for other purposes is to degrade human sexuality and compromise its integrity, alienating it from its destiny.

Chastity is imperative for stability in marital relationships as it promotes respect for the spouse. It also symbolizes one's dedication and moral integrity better than almost all other virtues.

Sexuality can readily become "deified" as the history of fertility cults shows, for sexual pleasure is the highest of natural pleasures. And because sexual pleasure is so intense, it can readily appear to be a panacea. It is not clear if this is as much a danger as human sexuality's being devalued by reduction to simple and straightforward recreation. This seems to be the greatest danger posed by the "sexual revolution," which turns sexual communication into a sport with no greater human meaning and value than athletic competitions. The development of contraceptive drugs and modern antibiotics has made promiscuous and recreational sex appear safe, but this is more than doubtful. For in recent years new forms of social diseases, such as AIDS and penicillin-resistent gonorrhea, have made promiscuous sex quite dangerous.

Sexagesima • Literally, "the sixtieth" (day before Easter). The second Sunday before Lent and the eighth Sunday before Easter. The second Sunday of a pre-Lenten season suppressed in the calendar revision after Vatican II in a desire to restore Lent to its pristine prominence and to remove the possible obscuring caused by this transitional "subseason." (Cf. Septuagesima.)

Sexism • A word used to describe discrimination against individuals on the basis of sex. It is a parallel to racism or classism or ageism. Coined by feminists, it is used as an appellation to describe attitudes and behaviors, such as brutality, exploitation, discrimination and ridicule, based on a theory that one sex, usually the male sex, is inherently superior to the other.

There is much controversy within the Catholic Church concerning what attitudes and actions constitute sexism and which may reflect a traditional role differentiation that is legitimate and even positive. For example, whereas all agree that brutality is sinful, not all would agree that an exclusively male priesthood is an example of sexism. In fact, Catholic teaching affirms differences in roles, especially in regard to motherhood and priesthood.

Sext • From the Latin *hora sexta*, "sixth hour," i.e., 12 noon. One of the "little hours" of the Divine Office, recited midday.

Sexuality • A term used to designate the entire experience that a man or woman may have of living as a male or female person in a particular society. For instance, psychologists speak of experiencing one's sexuality in a positive or negative manner. The topic of sexuality in this broader sense to include more than strictly biological sexual identity has become a popular topic also in Catholic spirituality, as individuals wrestle with tensions concerning femininity and masculinity.

Beginning with appreciation for creation "male and female," a Catholic will ponder the plan of God in one's being created as a man or woman and seek to develop a Christian mode of living as male or female in a world where sexual identity is questioned and subject to constant immoral pressure concerning sexual activity and rejection of natural roles.

Shedding of Blood • A term used down through the ages to describe the sacrifices made by various saints and martyrs of the Church in defense of the Faith.

Shema • The name and first Hebrew word of the Jewish declaration of faith found in the Pentateuch (Dt 6:4). It reads, "Hear, O Israel! The LORD our God is one LORD." By the second century A.D., the Shema prayer consisted of Deuteronomy 6:4-9; 11:13-21; and Numbers 15:37-41. In traditional Jewish practice, the Shema is written on the phylacteries and mezuzah. Jesus identified the Shema as the First Commandment in the law (cf. Mk 12:29).

Shepherd, Good • Jesus identifies Himself as the Good Shepherd in John 10:11-18, specifying in verse 11: "The good shepherd lays down his life for the sheep," adding in verse 14 that as the Good Shepherd, "I know my own and my own know me."

The Good Shepherd metaphor in John 10:11-18 is but part of the pastoral imagery presented in John 10. The chapter begins with the parable of the sheepfold (10:1-6), where Jesus distinguishes between the true shepherd, who enters the sheepfold through the gate to lead out the sheep he knows by name, and the thieves and robbers who climb into the sheepfold by another way and are not recognized by the sheep. Explaining this imagery, Jesus first identifies Himself as the gate through which the sheep are safely led to pasture (10:7-10), and then by identifying Himself as the Good Shepherd.

The imagery of John 10 has its background in the pastoral imagery of the Old Testament. In a society where the care and feeding of sheep and other domesticated animals was a matter of everyday economic importance involving a significant portion of the population, metaphors involving sheep and shepherding were immediately accessible and easily understandable.

The Old Testament metaphorically refers to human leaders as shepherds, and the prophets employ the metaphor to criticize leaders who are ineffective and unfaithful (cf. Jer 23:1-4). Because a shepherd is one who carefully tends and protects the flock under his care, the Old Testament refers to God as the shepherd of His people (cf. Gn 49:24; Ps 23:1-4; Ps 80:1).

In Ezekiel 34, God speaks through the prophet to denounce the "shepherds" who are Israel's leaders, to decree their punishment and to announce that God Himself will take charge of shepherding His own flock. This contrast between the ruthless shepherds who "have fed themselves and have not fed my sheep" (Ez 34:8) and God as the vigilant and provident Shepherd provides a background for John 10. In John 10, it is Jesus Who assumes the role of the Good Shepherd, while the "thieves and robbers" are the Pharisees of John 9.

John 10 is an effective vehicle of Johannine Christology. The description of the Good Shepherd as one Who knows His sheep and Who is known by them is connected in John 10:14-15 to the mutual knowledge which exists between Jesus and the Father. That communion of knowledge underlies the mutual knowledge of the sheep and the Good Shepherd, for it stems from Jesus' loving fulfillment of the Father's command (10:17-18). Thus the Good Shepherd is the One Who willingly lays down His life for the sheep.

For further reading: Jack W. Vancil, "Sheep, Shepherd," *Anchor Bible Dictionary*, 5:1187-1191.

Showbread • The twelve loaves of bread which, set in two piles of six, were placed on the golden table "before the LORD" as prescribed in Leviticus 24:5-9. On each pile was sprinkled a quantity of pure frankincense. These loaves or cakes, each made from two-tenths of a measure of flour, were set out each Sabbath. Each Sabbath the priests consumed the cakes (loaves) which had been set in place the preceding Sabbath. This usage appears to be a holdover of an ancient pagan practice of putting out food and drink for the god, who, it was thought, required nourishment in the same way that humans do. Among the Hebrews this practice was not construed in such crassly material terms but was rather seen as symbolic.

Mark 2:26 makes reference to an incident recounted in 1 Samuel 21:2-7 which tells of Achimelech allowing David and his troops to eat the showbread since no other food was available at the time.

The English expression "showbread" appears to have been taken over by William Tyndale from Martin Luther's word *Schaubrot*. When the Temple was razed by the Romans in A.D. 70, among the Temple treasures which were carried off was the golden table upon which the showbread rested. This is prominently sculpted into the Arch of Titus in Rome, which commemorates the successful sack of Jerusalem by the Romans.

For further reading: Carol Meyers, "Bread of the Presence," *Anchor Bible Dictionary*, 1:780-781.

Shrine • Canon 1230 of the 1983 Code of Canon Law defines a shrine as a church or other sacred place approved by the local Ordinary to which the faithful go to make pilgrimages. Two points stand out: shrines must be approved by ecclesiastical authority and they are intended primarily for pilgrimages. Canon 1231 regulates the particular designation of shrines as national (to be determined by a national conference of bishops) or as international (determined only by the Holy See). These same authorities have the right to approve the norms governing the operation of such shrines. Shrines are also intended to foster an active liturgical life, especially through the Holy Eucharist and Penance, and may be invested with special privileges, for example, indulgences (Canons 1233, 1244). (Cf. Basilica of the Immaculate Conception, National Shrine of the.)

Shroud, Holy • In the Cathedral of St. John the Baptist in Turin, Italy, stands the black marble Royal Chapel, which houses the linen cloth (fourteen and a half feet long and three and a half feet wide) alleged to be the burial cloth of Jesus. The image of a man is imprinted on the cloth, and many scholars believe that this image is of Jesus' Body. The Gospel accounts describe the burial preparation of Jesus' Body: He was wrapped in a linen shroud (Mt 27:59; Mk 15:46; Lk 23:53; Jn 19:40), after His Body was anointed with myrrh, aloes and scented oil (Jn 19:39-40). Prior to the fourteenth century, the shroud seems to have been in

Edessa (now Urfa, Turkey); Istanbul (Constantinople), Turkey; and France. From the fourteenth century, the shroud can be traced to Lirey and Chamery, France. Eventually, it went to Turin in the sixteenth century, where it is today. In 1983 the former king of Italy, Umberto II, willed the shroud to the Vatican. However, the Holy See allows the shroud to remain in Turin. Tests in 1988 seemed to indicate the cloth is of medieval origin, but further testing has been suggested, and no tests could rule out a miraculous origin. The official position of the Roman Catholic Church is that the shroud is not a matter of faith, so that Catholics may accept or reject its authenticity as they wish.

Shrovetide • Originally confined to Shrove Tuesday, the day before Ash Wednesday, as a day for "shriving," that is, for telling one's sins in confession and receiving absolution, this period has been variously calculated in liturgical commentaries and devotional manuals as lasting from one to six days before Ash Wednesday to prepare Christians for the discipline of Lent.

Sick, Sacrament of the Anointing of the: See **Pastoral Care of the Sick**

Sign • One of the general principles governing the contemporary liturgical reform concerns revived emphasis on the nature of liturgy as a central means of communicating redemption through the use of sacred signs. *Sacrosanctum Concilium*, Vatican II's Constitution on the Sacred Liturgy, states: "The liturgy . . . involves the presentation of man's sanctification under the guise of signs perceptible by the senses and its accomplishment in ways appropriate to each of these signs. . ." (n. 7). The central core of all liturgical symbolism is found in sacraments, which classical

theology regards as celebrations that effect change and cause grace by the act of signifying *(significando causant)*.

One of the purposes of the contemporary liturgical reform in revising liturgical rites is to enhance the power of their constitutive signs in terms of experiencing salvation and in terms of a theology drawn from the liturgy that uses signs as an important source for interpreting sacred rites. The *Liturgy Constitution* states that "in this restoration both texts and rites should be drawn up so as to express more clearly the holy things which they signify" (n. 21). One way for this to occur, as envisioned in *Sacrosanctum Concilium*, is to remove unnecessary accretions in the liturgy that have prevented appreciation of the central signs of the liturgy: "The rites should be distinguished by a noble simplicity . . . within the people's powers of comprehension and normally should not require much explanation" (n. 34). Thus the didactic function of the liturgy is understood to derive from signs, as well as texts, and the act of liturgy is oriented toward engagement of the whole person through the use of many signs, not only an appeal to the mind.

Liturgical signs include gestures (such as standing, kneeling, bowing, sitting, prostration, walking in procession, facing east), actions (sign of the cross, elevation and extension of hands, immersion or infusion for water Baptism, anointing with oil or chrism for sacraments), the use of vestments (alb, chasuble, cope, etc., in their varied colors), vessels (chalice, paten, water font, etc.), material elements (light, incense, bread, wine, water), church buildings and art (building itself, altar, lectern, baptistery, place of tabernacle, cross, icons, stained glass, bells, decorated lectionary and Gospel Book). Contemporary discussion of liturgical signs is usually done in conjunction with liturgical symbolism (this being the term more broad than sign).

Sign of the Cross • The ritual gesture used principally at Baptism, Confirmation and the Eucharist reflecting the conjunction, of the paschal mystery with invoking the Trinity. As early as the third century, Tertullian (c. A.D. 230) attests to the tracing of the sign of the cross on the forehead as a personal gesture of piety to sanctify the actions of daily life. From their earliest development, initiation rites attest to the tracing of the sign of the cross on the forehead during the catechumenate and at sacramental initiation. At present, this form is used in the rite of becoming a catechumen, at the rite of welcome of children to be initiated (traced by celebrant, parents and godparents), and during Confirmation (the bishop or priest traces the sign of the cross with chrism on the forehead with the formula, "N., be sealed with the Gift of the Holy Spirit"). It developed as a Mass gesture somewhat later, in the form of placing the right hand on forehead, breast, then both shoulders, to accompany the celebrant's speaking the formula invoking the Father, Son and Holy Spirit. It is now used in two places in the *Ordo Missae*, the Order of Mass: before the greeting after the entrance procession and at the end of the liturgy to accompany the final blessing. This form is customarily used when one begins or ends prayers of personal devotion (e.g., the Rosary, grace at meals).

Sign of Jonah • In Mark 8:11-12, the Pharisees' demand that Jesus produce a sign from heaven to lend credibility to His claims is met with Jesus' reply that "no sign shall be given to this generation." In Matthew 12:38-42, 16:1-4 and Luke 11:29-32, Jesus responds to the demand for a

sign by declaring that no sign will be given "except the sign of the prophet Jonah."

The sign of Jonah episode is drawn from "Q," the sayings source common to Matthew and Luke. Although the "men of Nineveh" and the "queen of the south" are mentioned in different order in Matthew 12:41-42 and Luke 11:31-32, the wording of the sign of Jonah episode in Matthew and Luke is virtually identical. The principal difference between the Matthean and Lucan versions lies in the additional material found in Matthew 12:40: "For as Jonah was three days and three nights in the belly of the whale, so will the Son of Man be three days and three nights in the heart of the earth."

For "Q" and for Luke, the sense of the sign of Jonah is found in Luke 11:32 (parallel to Matthew 12:41): "The men of Nineveh will arise at the judgment with this generation and condemn it; for they repented at the preaching of Jonah, and behold, something greater than Jonah is here." The sign of Jonah, the prophet come to pagan Nineveh from afar, was his preaching, which led the Ninevites to repentance and conversion. The sign of Jesus, the "one greater than Jonah," is Jesus' own preaching, a sign which "this generation" failed to recognize.

To the material found in "Q," Matthew adds an allegorization of Jonah 2:1 to indicate that Jesus' death and resurrection, together with His preaching, constitutes the "sign of Jonah." This is so, despite the fact that the preaching of the biblical Jonah makes no reference to that prophet's sojourn in the belly of the fish. Jonah's announcement is quite brief: "Yet forty days, and Nineveh shall be overthrown!" (Jon 3:4).

The order of Luke 11:31-32, the queen of the south rising in condemnation followed by the men of Nineveh rising in condemnation, is more likely to represent the original order of "Q" than the order found in Matthew 12:41-42. Because the mention of the queen of the south seems not to fit into the explanation of the sign of Jonah, Matthew mentions the men of Nineveh first and the queen of the south only subsequently.

The later mention in Matthew 16:4 of the sign of Jonah is brief and without explanation, clearly because the explanation offered in Matthew 12:40-42 is presupposed.

Simon, Yves R. • Yves René Simon is one of the most important contemporary Catholic philosophers in the tradition of St. Thomas Aquinas (1225-1274). Born in Cherbourg, France, in 1903, Simon studied philosophy and medicine at Paris universities, earning a doctorate in philosophy in 1934. During his university years, Simon became a follower and friend of Jacques Maritain. In 1938, Simon brought his family with him to assume a visiting professorship at the University of Notre Dame in Indiana. Yves and Paule Simon were the parents of six children. The fall of France to German military defeat prevented their return to Europe during the war, and Simon adopted the United States as his country in 1946 when he became a citizen. In 1948, Simon joined the faculty of the University of Chicago, where he taught eleven years before illness forced his retirement. He died in 1961.

Simon wrote broadly in philosophy, combining a keen understanding of Aristotle, Aquinas and the thinkers of the Catholic Counter-Reformation with a rigorous and enlightening analysis of concepts. Simon's writings contributed to the philosophy of being and knowledge, ethics and political philosophy. Simon's political writings were both practical and theoretical. He deplored anti-Semitism, inquiring into the falsehoods which nourished it. Simon also reflected on the tragedy of the Italian Ethiopian invasion, the options which Christians had when confronted with the Fascist overthrow of the Spanish republic in 1936, and the mistakes which took the French down the road to Vichy. Called "the philosopher of the fighting French," Simon applied his theoretical ability to a quest for a durable freedom. In works on prudence, authority, democratic government and freedom of choice, he brought to light a compelling reading of the Catholic intellectual tradition. Simon shows how this tradition can guide today's democratic citizenry in its design of workable institutions and in its cooperation or constructive resistance toward governing personnel who seek the common good of society. After a period of some neglect, scholars are rediscovering the importance of Simon as a philosopher and democratic theorist. The Yves R. Simon Institute is located in Mishawaka, Indiana. (Cf. Prudence; Maritain, Jacques.)

Simony • Biblically, this term can be traced to Simon, the magician of Samaria converted by the preaching of the Apostles. He wished to purchase from them their spiritual gifts (Acts 8:9-24). From him the vice of simony, commercial traffic in sacred things, takes its name. Both the law of God and that of the Church forbid the buying or selling of something spiritual such as grace, a sacrament (cf. Canon 1380), a relic, and so forth.

Simple Feast • The least important grade in the ranking of feasts in the preconciliar Western Liturgy, which term was adjusted by decree of the Sacred Congregation of Rites, effective January 1, 1961, "feasts that were formerly of simple rite are now merely commemorated." In the present reform of the Calendar, most of these feasts are now ranked as optional memorials. Examples include the feast of Sts. Vincent and Anastasius, martyrs, on January 22, ranked as "simple" in the former calendar, now the optional memorial of St. Vincent; the (simple) feast of St. Martina, formerly assigned to January 30, has been dropped from the present Calendar.

Simulation • The falsification of a canonical or liturgical act. It is usually applied to the sacraments and especially to marriage.

For a marriage to be valid, the internal consent of the mind and will must be in conformity with the external expression of consent. If a person pronounces the marriage vows while at the same time positively excluding marriage itself or an essential element or property of marriage, then the person is said to have simulated consent. In such cases, the marriage is invalid.

Simulation entered the judicial arena in the thirteenth century, when the Pope upheld a decision of a diocesan court that held a marriage to be invalid because the man had not intended to be married. The decision, contained in the *Decretals of Gregory IX* (*Tua nos*) was followed by a general decretal (entitled *Si Conditiones*), which stated that if conditions are placed, the consent could be invalid. This decretal gave three examples of conditions contrary to the three goods of marriage. Since that time, simulation has traditionally involved a positive exclusion of the obligation of fidelity, the right to children or the obligation of marital permanence.

Since simulation involves a mental act, it is difficult but not impossible to prove in the external forum. Over the course of time, the jurisprudence on simulation has evolved particularly with respect to the proofs required. Prior to the promulgation of the 1917 Code, required proof involved a contrary condition or intention that was expressed as part of consent. After the

Code, a mentally contained contrary intention was accepted as proof. The fact of such an intention was determined by statements the simulator might have made prior to or even after the marriage to the effect that he or she intended to simulate. It also was determined by testimony of witnesses and the actions themselves of the simulator both before and after the wedding.

In order to prove simulation, it is necessary to show that a person knew what was required for consent and intentionally excluded an essential element.

The essential properties of marriage to which the canon refers are unity (that is, one man and one woman together with the obligation of total fidelity) and indissolubility. The essential elements of marriage are its ordination to the good of the spouses and to the procreation of children. Exclusion of the element of procreation includes both the right to the conjugal act and the procreation and education of children.

It is possible also to exclude marriage altogether. This occurs when a person or a couple go through a wedding ceremony for purposes other than establishing a marital community, e.g., in order to obtain immigration papers (Canon 1101).

Other examples of sacramental simulation could be pretending to confect the Eucharist when one is not a priest or purporting to confer absolution when one does not have proper faculties (cf. Canons 1378-1379). Simulated sacraments are, of course, invalid.

Sin • Sin is the deliberate transgression of the divine law. Since the divine law is given so that human persons can choose the ultimate good which is God Himself, sin constitutes a disordered or bad choice. In a particular thought, word or deed, or in a pattern of thoughts, words and deeds, a person fails to discern and choose the perfect good by which he is made good and grows in goodness. In contravening the divine law, the sinner deliberately prefers some created good to the ultimate or perfect Good. Since this transgression must involve sufficient knowledge and free consent of the will, it is a personal action. The sole cause of sin is the personal agent himself. The sole remedy for sin is the passion, death and resurrection of Christ, in virtue of which the infinite offense of sin is atoned for and the individual sinner who turns to God for mercy is forgiven. (Cf. Actual Sin; Evil; Sin, Mortal and Venial; Sin, Original.)

Sin, Actual: See **Actual Sin**

Sin, Mortal and Venial • The distinction between mortal and venial sin is grounded in logic and in the Sacred Scriptures, wherein one finds: "All wrongdoing is sin, but there is sin that is not deadly" (1 Jn 5:17). A mortal sin is a violation of the law of God that concerns grave moral matter and is done with full knowledge, deliberation, freedom and consent. Such an action concerns serious moral transgressions and not light or insignificant issues. The agent must know what the action is and also that the action is gravely immoral. The action must be chosen in full freedom, which means that the agent had the opportunity to refrain from performing the action, but chose not to do so. One mortal sin alters one's "fundamental option" in relation to God because it destroys the love of God in our hearts. On the other hand, a venial sin either involves light moral matter or is done without adequate knowledge, full consent or adequate freedom.

Unlike venial sin, mortal sin destroys the love of God within us. Mortal sin can only be absolved through the sacrament of Penance, and all mortal sins must be confessed in that sacrament according to their number and kind. A penance assigned by the confessor must be performed, and true contrition or attrition is required for their absolution. Confessing one's sorrow for mortal sins to God privately, or confessing these sins at the Penitential Rite at the Eucharist is not sufficient for their absolution.

Sin, Occasion of: See **Occasion of Sin**

Sin, Original • Refers to two things that must be kept distinct: first, the actual personal sin of the first human beings; second, the consequences of that action for all subsequent human beings. The seriousness of the actual sin of the first human beings arises from the interrelational character of God's purposes in creating personal beings. Whatever the precise nature of their sin, it must never be conceived of as the transgression of a purely arbitrary divine command. Rather, it was a failure of the first human beings to respond to God's love and offer of friendship. The seriousness of the consequences of this first sin for the condition of subsequent human beings arises from the status of the first beings as generators of humankind. Whether *homo sapiens* emerged from a single primate population ("monogenism" — a view increasingly favored by recent evidence) or from several geographically separated populations ("polygenism"), Catholic doctrine insists that revelation teaches that the first human beings who were the antecedents of the present human race fell into sin. By resisting God's offer of love, these first humans lost the original justice with which God had endowed them.

Although the state of original justice involved certain exceptional human traits, its chief property was the grace-endowed perfect ordering of the person to God and the resultant harmony and integrity of the person's inner life. By their sin, the first human beings lost the state of original justice and the ability to transmit this state — along with all the other traits of human nature — to their progeny. Hence, original sin in us is not a positive inclination to moral evil (as some have thought), but a lack of facility in doing the good. As a consequence of the first sin properly so-called, original sin in us is the lack of original justice, the absence of the ordering of our persons to God and the interior harmony which such an ordering brings with it (concupiscence). This lack of harmony is evident in our own personal sins. Through the merits of Christ's redemption, only Mary of all human beings (by her Immaculate Conception) is preserved from this consequence of the first sin.

Sin, Reserved • The 1917 Code of Canon Law gave bishops the power to reserve the absolution of certain sins to themselves. This meant that a person confessing such a sin had to be absolved by the person who reserved the sin, by one delegated by him, or in danger of death, by any priest. The only sin as such that was reserved to the Holy See was the sin of false denunciation of a confessor of the crime of solicitation for sexual favors in the confessional. The entire section on reserved sins has been dropped from the revised Code.

There remain, however, certain ecclesiastical crimes, always objectively sinful, whose penal remission is reserved to certain authorities.

Singing • Adding another dimension to audible texts. Throughout history mankind has included singing in its praises to God. St. Augustine has usually been credited with saying, "He who sings, prays twice." However, part of almost every sacred ritual from prehistoric and ancient times to our own have included some song. Vatican Council II certainly encouraged singing at liturgy, especially in *Sacrosanctum Concilium*. This singing may include parts for the celebrant, cantor and choir, but should also include singing for the entire congregation.

Singing, Congregational • Sung participation in a liturgical or paraliturgical service by all members of the congregation. Music adds a second dimension to the words of a prayer. While the music must be simple so as to allow for participation of all worshipers, it must also be of a caliber to add to the spiritual experience of the total congregation. Before being admitted into the liturgy, each musical piece must be judged by liturgical, musical and pastoral criteria. The singing of a cantor or a choir is truly encouraged; but this does not take the place of congregational singing, except in a very rare situation, such as a special "Gloria" at a particular liturgy. The cantor or choir must not usurp the parts of the liturgy reserved for the congregation.

Sins Against the Holy Spirit: See **Holy Spirit, Sins Against the**

Sirach, Book of • A lengthy (fifty-one chapters) sapiential book of the Old Testament, also called Ecclesiasticus, was written in Hebrew at the beginning of the second century B.C., then translated into Greek shortly after 132 B.C. It is a deuterocanonical book, not accepted as inspired by Jews and Protestants, but included in the Catholic canon. The author is actually a descendant of Sirach, who identifies himself (50:27) as "Jesus, the son of Sirach, son of Eleazar." Perhaps many of the author's counsels had come from his father and grandfather.

It contains the most complete and systematic presentation of the ideals of Jewish spirituality. In a paternal but not paternalistic way, it shows loving concern for the well-being of the coming generation. It offers guidance in almost every area of life.

For further reading: Alexander A. Di Lella, O.F.M., "Sirach," *New Jerome Biblical Commentary*, 496-509; Alexander A. Di Lella, O.F.M., "Wisdom of Ben-Sira," *Anchor Bible Dictionary*, 6:931-945.

Sisters: See **Perfectae Caritatis**

Sistine Chapel • Often referred to as the Pope's Chapel, it is the principal chapel of the Vatican palace. It is most noted for its ceiling murals by Michelangelo and Raphael which depict the creation epic and religious aspirations of man. The Sistine Chapel is also where the consistory of cardinals meets to elect a new Pope.

Sistine Choir • Singers who perform at functions presided over by the Pope. The choir has been given credit for spreading the use of *a cappella* singing in the sixteenth century. The official title of the group is "*Il Collegio dei Capellani Cantori della Capella Pontificia.*"

Situation Ethics: See **Ethics, Situation**

Slander • Knowingly uttering, communicating or attributing falsehoods about another for the purpose of bringing harm. The most common form of slander is the spreading of stories that are partly true and partly false. Often slander involves omitting details, so that the reputation of the person is blackened by the story. Slanderous acts impose an obligation in justice to restore the good name of the person defamed; this is usually done by explicit retraction of the slanderous remarks. The bitterness of the person slandered can be rectified by an outright apology, and the person guilty of slandering another must do what is reasonable to prevent the spread of further harm. Slander is often excused as being necessary in some circumstances, but the classical Catholic tradition has held that it cannot be justified or rationalized (cf. Canons 128, 220).

Slavorum Apostoli • Sts. Cyril and Methodius, the Greek brothers who brought Christianity to the Slavic populations of Central and Eastern Europe, are celebrated as "the authentic precursors of ecumenism" in the fourth encyclical written by Pope John Paul II. The document, dated June 2, 1985, and issued the following month to coincide with the eleventh centenary of the death of Methodius (885), celebrated the evangelists as "connecting links or spiritual bridges between the Eastern and Western traditions, which both come together in the one great tradition of the universal Church." The evangelization which they carried out continues to serve as a model for current efforts at propagating the Faith among native cultures and as a reminder of the catholicity of the Church, John Paul concluded.

Social Communication, Decree on the Means of: See **Inter Mirifica**

Social Encyclicals: See **Encyclicals, Social**

Social Justice • The virtue which moves one to cooperation with others in order to render social institutions better servants of the community and better facilitators of the common good. The Church has always taught that while the responsibilities of social justice fall upon the individual, a person cannot fulfill them alone.

Social Sin • The inherent sinfulness of the community into which a person is born, the term is founded on the premise that modern social relations and collectivism have enmeshed everyone in others' values and choices to a previously unparalleled degree.

Socialism • A collective term for a number of different social movements and systems of thought critical of contemporary society. They all oppose individualism and selfishness, and they unite in encouraging responsibility for one's duties and obligations to others.

Communism is the most striking example of socialism which so exalts the collectivity over the individual that it denigrates human dignity. Most forms of socialism derive from non-Christian sources, and Marxism has been aggressively hostile to religion from the beginning. For the working class, socialism was virtually a religion, often seeing the Church as inimical to their interests.

However, socialist intellectual elites have in recent years become spokespersons for what are virtually national movements that transcend economic classes. Many contemporary African nations consider themselves to be "socialist," but this usually means that they are aiming at more of a middle way between Marxism and capitalism than did classical socialism. It is not clear that contemporary socialism has any unitary philosophical basis, as various nationalist socialist movements claim to be based on different philosophical presuppositions.

Society • The totality of interactions among individuals. In the Middle Ages and Reformation era, the aim of the Christian community was to subordinate the aims and objectives of society to those of the Church. In those periods, the aim of society was to promote "true religion" and the life of holiness of individuals. With the emergence of the Enlightenment and liberal democracy, the Church came to accept the claim that society had an end independent of the Church. Society exists to promote the common good of all its members, which is the set of public conditions that enable the members to achieve human flourishing. Society existed no longer to promote the specific doctrines and practices of a given religion, but to protect the autonomy and integrity of religion in general.

For its part, religion is to aid society in achieving its goals. Religious communities are to educate in moral and spiritual values, as these enhance and promote social living. These are functions which can be uniquely performed by religious bodies, and they should pursue them as a means of promoting the well-being of society.

Society of Apostolic Life • An entity comparable to an institute of consecrated life. The members live together in common and pursue some apostolate. They do not, however, take vows. In some societies the members oblige themselves to the evangelical counsels by some form of sacred bond, such as a promise.

Societies have their own statutes and constitutions which determine their internal governance. In clerical societies, the members are incardinated into the society unless the constitutions provide otherwise (Canons 731-746).

Society, Religious: See **Congregation;** also **Order**

Socinianism • One of a family of Unitarian positions that affirm the unipersonality of God and deny the doctrine of the Trinity and the doctrine of the divinity of Christ. The term derives from *Socinus*, the Latinized version of the surname of Lelio

Sozzini (1525-1562) and his nephew Fausto (1539-1604), both of whom propagated moderate Unitarian views among the Reformed communities in Geneva, Italy and Poland.

Sociology • The systematic study of society, its institutions and relationships. This study focuses particularly on the development, structure and function of human groups, on their interaction, on their characteristic patterns of organization and on the ideational structures that maintain them. From its very beginnings in the nineteenth century, sociology has been preoccupied with the study of religion, both in its place as an important segment of the institutions and ideas of a society, and also in itself. Both the great founders of scientific sociology — Emil Durkheim and Max Weber — applied their methods to an interpretation of the social structures of religion. Religions have continued to attract the attention of subsequent generations of sociologists. Insofar as the Church is a human society, she is susceptible of study by these methods. Social theory, when properly integrated into a sound theological perspective, can be of great assistance in understanding the internal functioning of the Christian community and enhance its ability to interact creatively with the surrounding society.

Sodality • The common name given to an organization which generally promotes pious or charitable acts (Canon 298). A wide variety of sodalities exists in the Church today, while the postconciliar decline in the size and numbers of sodalities seems to have leveled off. It should be noted that, especially in the nineteenth and early twentieth centuries, sodalities were very active in the development of religious vocations, with a few sodalities actually petitioning for and

being granted transformation into religious communities. (Cf. Associations of the Christian Faithful.)

Sodepax • The Joint Commission on Society, Development and Peace was an agency both of the World Council of Churches and the Pontifical Commission for Justice and Peace. As a product of the desire for increased ecumenical cooperation, it was established in 1968, and was replaced by another agency on December 31, 1980.

Solesmes • Village in France. The Benedictine monks in the abbey at Solesmes undertook the tremendous task of researching the Gregorian chant melodies and restoring them to their original form and rhythmic structure. Prosper Guéranger, the first abbot, directed the work. These monks are responsible for the publication of the *Liber Usualis*, which includes the chants and rules for interpretation according to the Solesmes research. Though most musicologists agree with the work of the monks, there are some who argue with the Solesmes interpretation. Prosper Guéranger himself was responsible for a great deal of liturgical writing, including the multivolume series (*The Liturgical Year*) which served as an important catechesis on liturgy from the 1930s up to Vatican II. As abbot of Solesmes, he emphasized the celebration of communal liturgy as a chief aspect of the cenobitic monastic vocation.

Solitude • The practice of permanent or temporary withdrawal from social intercourse in order to pursue a more intense relationship with God and cultivate a deeper inner life, free from the distractions of conversation, exchange and involvement with other people. For Christians, the paradigm for such withdrawal is Christ's sojourn in the desert before taking up His public ministry. The great tradition of spiritual reflection in the Church, stretching from the earliest monastic writers, stresses the necessity of periods of silence and solitude for the development of an authentic Christian life.

The practical wisdom and concrete legislation of almost all religious communities in the Church contain provision for solitude. Some contemplative communities — such as the Cistercians, or the Carmelite, Dominican and Poor Clare nuns — withdraw into the communal solitude of the monastic enclosure. In addition, other religious orders have emerged in the Church in which a permanent state of solitude is adopted in such a way as to reduce contact even within the enclosure to an absolute minimum. Prominent examples of such "eremitical" orders are the Carthusians and the Dominicans.

Sollicitudo Omnium Ecclesiarum • Pope Paul VI's June 1969 letter delineating the official duties of the representatives of the Bishop of the Rome and the Holy See. The practical intention of the apostolic document is a recasting, in more contemporary terms, of the roles and functions of the many and varied delegates of the Roman Pontiff around the world.

Sollicitudo Rei Socialis • The 1987 encyclical letter *On Social Concern* by Pope John Paul II, reflecting on Pope Paul VI's encyclical *Populorum Progressio*, which dealt with the moral duty to promote fully human development on a worldwide scope. Pope John Paul stresses the ongoing duty for members of all nations, but especially of the rich nations, to take into account in their personal and political decisions the worldwide interdependence of all peoples, the desperate need of many people for basic necessities and the widening gap between rich and poor, with the consequent lack of solidarity among all.

Citizens of well-off nations are reminded that their nations' leadership in the world is morally justified only by promoting the common good of the entire human family, and by respecting the transcendent dignity of all human beings as images of God. The Pope highlights the moral and religious roots of the failure to promote development or to approach development adequately from a more than merely economic perspective.

The Church's teaching is clearly distinguished from both classical liberal capitalism and Marxism; a sound social order can be built neither on the basis of the avaricious pursuit of profit nor of collectivized power. Not only the raw materials but even industrially processed goods are destined by God for the satisfaction of the basic needs of all humans, and for the integral development of each toward freedom in solidarity with each other and ultimately in religious communion with God (n. 39). International economic and legal institutions must be designed to encourage human solidarity in the fully personal development of every human person. The Pope warns against failure to act for worldwide social development through fear, indecision or cowardice. Personal sins, often sins of omission, are the root of the problems.

All persons of good will, and particularly religious people, are called upon to promote just development according to their gifts and abilities. The goodness of the world — especially as renewed by the grace of Christ, made present in the sacraments, and interceded for by Mary — is held out as a sure motive for such devotion.

Solomon • His name means "peaceful" or "beloved by Yahweh." He was the youngest son of King David and Bathsheba. Besides being noted for his wisdom, he is remembered for his writings, including poems (psalms) and proverbs, wealth, commercial success, magnificent buildings, including the Great Temple in Jerusalem, palaces and other structures. During his forty-year reign (961-922 B.C.), his efforts at centralization of the government failed, leading to the division of the kingdom upon his death. The story of Solomon is told in 1 Kings 1-14, and 2 Chronicles 1-13.

The sole New Testament reference to Solomon is made by Jesus: "Consider the lilies of the field, how they grow. . . . I tell you, even Solomon in all his glory was not arrayed like one of these" (Mt 6:28-29).

For further reading: Tomoo Ishida, "Solomon," *Anchor Bible Dictionary*, 6:105-113.

Son of Man • A New Testament title for Christ, occurring almost without exception only in the Gospels and only in self-reference to Christ. Perhaps the most significant uses of the title occur in sayings that refer to or predict Christ's future suffering. According to traditional interpretation, "Son of Man" refers to the emptying or humility of Christ, in particular, whereas "Son of God" refers to His glory as divine.

For further reading: George W. E. Nickelsburg, "Son of Man," *Anchor Bible Dictionary*, 6:137-150.

Song, Leader of • A person who encourages active participation during liturgical celebrations by leading the congregation in sung prayer. The voice of the leader should never dominate or overpower but must be strong enough to give support and direction, when needed. The leader of song may use hand signals and conducting patterns when this would be helpful, but he or she must become

almost transparent so as to lead in prayer, always directing the congregation's attention toward the Deity, and not toward the leader of song. At times the cantor may assume the role of song leader.

Song of Songs • Known also as the Canticle of Canticles and the Song of Solomon, a clutch of long songs and fragments of love songs apparently not the composition of one author. Through the mouths of lovers, the book praises love in courtship and in marriage. The goodness and propriety of marriage is celebrated through a series of rich images drawn from a blend of nature and love. The book reveals the warm and innocent satisfaction the ancient Hebrews drew from the physical and emotional relationships of man and woman. There was some reluctance to receive the Song of Songs into the canon of Jewish scriptures, but it was eventually accepted as ceremonial. Beginning with the Jewish period and onward, there has been the almost irresistible tendency to allegorize the work. For the Jews, Yahweh was seen as the lover, the beloved, Israel. For some of the Fathers and other Christian commentators, the bride was the Church. At times the figure of the bride has been felt to have layered meaning: Israel, the Church, the Virgin Mary and the individual believer. In recent times the urge toward allegorical interpretation of the Song of Songs seems to have abated.

For further reading: Roland E. Murphy, O.Carm., "Canticle of Canticles," *New Jerome Biblical Commentary*, 462-465; Roland E. Murphy, O.Carm., "Song of Songs, Book of," *Anchor Bible Dictionary*, 6:150-155.

Songs of Ascent • The designation of a particular grouping of psalms (120-134) in the Psalter. It is not entirely clear why these psalms should be so named. The explanation frequently offered is that they were psalms chanted in the processions held during the New Year celebration. "Ascent" would allude to the pilgrims' "ascent" to Jerusalem or to a procession's "ascent" to the Temple.

Sorrows of the Blessed Virgin Mary • Also called the Seven Dolors of Our Lady, the Seven Sorrows are an expansion upon the five Sorrowful Mysteries of the Rosary. Traditionally, they include the prophecy of Simeon (Lk 2:35) that a sword would pierce Mary's heart by reason of her Son being a sign of contradiction to the world, the flight into Egypt (Mt 2:13) and the loss of the child Jesus in the Temple (Lk 2:46). The final four involve Mary in her Son's passion and death: the *via dolorosa* (or way of the cross), the crucifixion, the descent from the cross and the entombment in the Holy Sepulcher. The Latin Rite chapel in the Church of the Holy Sepulchre in Jerusalem has as its focus a very moving sculpture which portrays Mary with her heart pierced by seven small swords. The liturgical calendar celebrates the memorial of Our Lady of Sorrows on September 15, appropriately the day following the feast of the Exaltation of the Cross.

Soteriology • Derived from the Greek word for savior (*soter*), the term "soteriology" designates the theological subfield that focuses on the central Christian mystery that, through the passion, death and resurrection of Christ, the redemption of humankind is accomplished. It falls under soteriology to consider the nature of the atonement itself and the manner in which Christ's saving grace is imparted to human beings. In this way, it considers the principles of both our justification and our sanctification. At least implicitly, soteriology also must give an account of the human condition (Why is salvation necessary?) and human destiny (What is the goal of salvation?).

Soul • Together with the body, the soul constitutes the substantial unity of the human being. It is the immaterial, immortal, directly created principle that constitutes a particular individual as human. The distinguishing feature of the human soul is that it is rational or intellective. The immortality of the soul arises from its simplicity or lack of composition: unlike material things, there are no components into which the human soul can break up. Incorruptibility is thus one reason for the soul's immortality. Another is that man evinces unlimited spiritual capacities. Thus, although the soul and the body are a substantial unity, the soul is intrinsically independent of matter both in being and in origins. The soul endures after biological death. Further, the soul cannot be generated out of material conditions. According to Christian teaching, each soul is directly created by God. Human identity is nonetheless constituted by the unity of soul and body. The relation of the soul to the body is not an instrumental one, but a real, substantial one.

Spiritism • The attempt to communicate with departed souls. These practices often involve the use of ouija boards, seances, table-tapping and various forms of witchcraft. Even though there is some record of communication with the dead, this action is a sin against the respect that is owed God as Creator.

The earliest example of spiritism in Scripture is found in 1 Samuel 28:8, and modern forms of spiritism date from the Fox family, who, in reaction to the materialism of their era, claimed to be able to communicate with the dead in 1848. Some recognized scholars have professed their belief that such communications are possible, and the Society for Psychical Research was founded in England in 1822 to study these phenomena. These researchers ruled out various forms of fraud and naturally-occurring phenomena in these purported communications and concluded that there seemed to be some substance to claims of a power to communicate with the dead.

Some Christian theologians argue that such communications result from the interventions of demons and spirits, as their message is usually hostile to Christian doctrine and is of no moral or spiritual value. The cult of communicating with the dead has been highly exploited in the U.S. for its commercial value and has served only to obscure the issue.

Spiritual Communion • The conscious burning desire to receive Holy Communion when unable to do so physically. According to the Catechism of the Council of Trent, the faithful who receive the Body of Christ in such a spirit partake of "very great benefits" [*On the Eucharist*].

Spiritual Exercises of St. Ignatius Loyola • Written by St. Ignatius Loyola (d. 1556), the founder of the Society of Jesus (Jesuits), the *Spiritual Exercises* were intended primarily as a guide for his spiritual sons in making their annual month-long religious retreat. Directed to the amendment of one's life and the achievement of personal sanctification, the Exercises develop a particular point of meditation and resolution for each of the four weeks: (1) the consequences of sin; (2) Christ as exemplar for the Christian; (3) amendment in imitation of Christ; and (4) the reward of eternal life.

Given their great practicality and sound psychology, the *Spiritual Exercises* of St. Ignatius have long had an appeal beyond the confines of Jesuit life; in fact, many non-Jesuit spiritual directors today employ the principles of the Ignatian Exercises in directing retreats.

Spiritual Works of Mercy: See **Mercy, Corporal and Spiritual Works of**

Spirituality • Simply and basically, the response of the individual, by the grace of the Holy Spirit, to Christ's ongoing invitation to "repent and believe the Gospel." This personal conversion (in the Greek, *metanoia*) expresses itself in an ever-deepening communion of faith, hope and love with one's fellow believers in the community of the Catholic Church, and an ever more faithful witness to Christ, the values of His Gospel and the teaching of His Church in one's daily life in the world.

While the history of the Catholic Church is replete with a wide variety of "spiritualities" (Ignatian, monastic, etc.), there is in the final analysis one only and all-embracing Catholic spirituality: the rootedness of the individual both in the paschal mystery of Christ's death and resurrection and in the community of the Catholic Church brought to birth by that paschal mystery. This spirituality is common to cleric and layperson alike, to every member of the Church from the Pope to the newest of the baptized. It is a life of grace anchored in the rhythm of the liturgical year's celebration of the mystery of Christ, His mother and His saints; nourished by the food of the Eucharist, sustained by the grace of the other sacraments and deepened by communal participation in the daily public prayer of the Church and the private devotion to which the individual soul is attracted.

The Second Vatican Council, in its Decree on the Apostolate of Lay People, says as much, in other words, and seems to echo the wisdom of *the* saint of (lay) spirituality,

Francis de Sales, who spoke in his classic *Introduction to a Devout Life* of a basic spirituality common to all Christians, doing violence to no one's station or status, but rather enriching and enhancing all of one's relationships and endeavors because of its wholeness, balance and rootedness in Christ and His Church.

The Council states: "Family cares should not be foreign to their spirituality, nor any other temporal interest; in the words of the apostle, 'Whatever you are doing, whether speaking or acting, do everything in the name of the Lord Jesus Christ, giving thanks to God the Father through him' (Col 3:17). . . .

"This lay spirituality will take its particular character from the circumstances of one's state of life (married and family life, celibacy, widowhood) . . . from one's professional and social activity. Whatever the circumstances, each one has received suitable talents and these should be cultivated, as should also the personal gifts he has from the Holy Spirit" (AA 4).

Sponge • A compressed pad of natural sponge material approximately two inches or more, usually oval-shaped or circular, used in the ritual of the Eastern Churches as a tool to brush the diskos clean of any blessed or consecrated particles of the Precious Body as It is placed into the chalice for distribution in Holy Communion. A sponge is also sometimes used to cleanse any excess oils remaining from the anointings of Baptism, chrismation (Confirmation), the sacrament of the Anointing of the Sick, or the solemn consecration of an altar, church or sacred vessel.

Sponsors • An ancient institution in the sacramental history of the Church. In canon law, a sponsor is a person who will give special assistance to one about to be baptized or confirmed in the Faith to lead a life in harmony with that Faith (Canon 872). A sponsor must be a Catholic who has already participated in the sacraments of initiation, is firm in the practice of the Faith and should generally be at least sixteen years old (Canon 874). Especially in the case of the Baptism or Confirmation of children, the sponsor is to be an aide to the parents in raising the child as a Catholic; thus parents may not serve as their child's sponsor. The old rule, however, of prohibiting a spouse from so serving has been abrogated by the 1983 Code of Canon Law. So too, the "spiritual affinity," which arises from serving as a baptismal sponsor, is no longer an impediment to the marriage of those two persons. A similar impediment for Confirmation sponsors ceased with the promulgation of the 1917 Code.

Although a sponsor is not necessary for the valid celebration of Baptism or Confirmation, it is required for the licit celebration of the same. The preference of Canon 893 is that the person who served as baptismal sponsor also serve as sponsor at the Confirmation. The minister of the sacrament has the duty to assure himself that sponsors of candidates for Baptism and Confirmation are themselves suitably prepared for their responsibilities. The 1983 Code is clear that one sponsor of either sex, and at most two sponsors of opposite sex, are to be used at Baptism (Canon 873). There is no prohibition against clerics, religious or persons of the opposite sex serving as sponsors at either Baptism or Confirmation.

Spoon, Liturgical • In the Byzantine Rite, a spoon is used by the priest to dip the particle of consecrated Bread into the chalice, and to give Holy Communion to the faithful.

Spouse of Christ • As St. Paul develops in his Letter to the Ephesians, the Church is especially understood as the spouse of Christ (Eph 5:22-33). A professed religious woman, by reason of her vowed chastity, is also called a bride of Christ, the symbolism of which was traditionally emphasized by the elaborate ceremony reminiscent of a wedding used for the entrance into convent life. The nun would dress as a bride on that day and would continue to wear a wedding ring symbolic of her intimate union with the Lord.

Spouses of the Blessed Virgin Mary • St. Joseph, as the betrothed of Mary, is described in the Gospel as "her husband . . . and a just man unwilling to put her to shame" (Mt 1:18-19; cf. Lk 1:27, 2:5), who decided in view of her pregnancy "to send her away quietly." Through angelic intervention, it was made clear to Joseph that it was "by the Holy Spirit she had conceived this child" (Mt 1:20). With that assurance, Joseph lived with Mary in a chaste and virginal relationship and is justifiably called the spouse of the Blessed Virgin Mary. In the Gospels, Jesus is typically called the carpenter's son, in recognition of Joseph as the human foster-father of the Son of God.

By reason of the Annunciation and Incarnation, the Holy Spirit is also considered the Spouse of the Blessed Virgin Mary, since it is by Him that she conceived her Child.

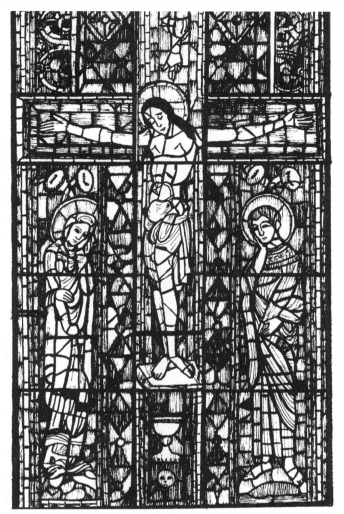

Stained-glass window (circa 1190, Rheims Cathedral)

Stained Glass • An art form used to decorate churches, buildings and homes. The use of stained glass, dating to the twelfth century, provides for a silent but demonstrative expression of the presence of God. The Cathedral of Chartres is one example of a church which has become famous, in part, due to its enormous stained-glass window. The color of the pieces of glass and their arrangement make this art form appealing and full of meaning.

State of Grace • Grace involves the transformation of the soul, so that it lies and functions at an entirely new interpersonal level, knowing and loving God and other persons in Him. This grace is called habitual or sanctifying: it qualifies the existence of the one who possesses it. A soul so qualified is said to be in the state of grace. According to Tradition, the state of grace can be lost because of serious sin and regained by repentance and sacramental confession.

Stations of the Cross • A devotional practice involving tracing Jesus' journey from the trial before Pilate to Calvary, first observed in all likelihood in the city of Jerusalem itself by processing from place to place, stopping at each point for reflection, silence and prayer. The devotion spread in the Middle Ages (largely through the Franciscans) to other churches where a series of fourteen images or small plain crosses marked the walls of the inside of the church. People would walk from station to station for prayer and reflection centered on the person(s) or place imaged in the station. Indulgences are attached to observing this devotion.

The selection of the fourteen stations was likely not finally settled until the eighteenth century. The Stations observed are: Jesus is condemned, Jesus carries His cross, Jesus falls the first time, Jesus meets His Mother, Simon of Cyrene helps carry the cross, Veronica wipes Jesus' face, Jesus falls a second time, Jesus meets the women of Jerusalem, Jesus falls the third time, Jesus is stripped of His garments, Jesus is nailed to the cross, Jesus dies on the cross, His body is taken down from cross, and His body is laid in the tomb.

Stations, Roman • Churches in the city of Rome where (mostly the early) Popes would celebrate the liturgy at least on special days; eventually, this came to be observed principally as a Lenten devotion. Usually the stational observance would begin with clergy and congregation gathering at one place (*collecta*) and processing with accompanying litanies and prayers to the day's station (*statio*) for the Eucharist. During Lent, at the head of these processions, a relic of the True Cross was carried aloft. Today a list is published in Rome at the beginning of Lent proclaiming what churches will be stational and on what day, a necessary practice because of scholarly debate about the historical precedent of using some of the churches and also because some Roman churches are closed for periodic repairs.

More famous examples of stational observance include St. Mary Major at Midnight Mass on Christmas and St. John Lateran for Easter (with the large baptistery building used at the Easter Vigil for initiation). The Lenten station days are carried on in a modified fashion today, although the Pope normally celebrates Ash Wednesday only by processing from the Church of San Anselmo on the Aventine (home of the Benedictines) to the home of the Order of Preachers at Santa Sabina (also on the Aventine) for Mass.

Status Animarum • This Latin term means "status of the souls" and is the official designation of an annual report filed with the Holy See by each diocese reflecting the overall condition of the Church within that territory. Basic statistics are included (for example, numbers of parishes, priests, baptisms, marriages and so forth), as well as explanatory notes on special diocesan projects and concerns. The report is intended to serve as an update for the much more extensive quinquennial report required every five years in conformity with Canon 399 of the 1983 Code of Canon Law. There is also available (usually in Latin, French and English) a similar type of annual report for the universal Church known as the *Annuarium Statisticum Ecclesiae* published by the Vatican Polyglot Press.

Quinquennia, because they frequently include confidential material, are not to be available to the public, except perhaps in a condensed form. The *Status*, on the other hand, is usually treated under the general rules governing diocesan archives, which implies somewhat greater accessibility. The *Annuarium*, finally, is widely available in Catholic college and university libraries.

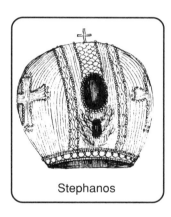

Stephanos

Stephanos • The episcopal mitre in the East. Also, the crowns used in the ceremonies of marriage.

Sterilization • An operation, medication or procedure undertaken by a male or female to prevent the begetting of children. Sterilization is usually done to free intercourse from anxiety about conceiving offspring. This century has also seen the emergence of eugenic sterilization. With the rapid advances of technology in recent years, a variety of forms of sterilization are now possible. Through several types of contraceptive devices, such as the pill or the condom, it is possible to sterilize individual conceptive acts. Contraceptive drugs make it possible to sterilize the conceptive act for either a short or a more extended period of time. Surgical procedures such as what is now misleadingly called a "uterine isolation" can make conception impossible, and with new drugs such as RU 486 it is possible to make conceptive acts that were fertile infecund by chemically killing off the offspring, either prior to or immediately after implantation.

All of these actions, devices, procedures and potions are considered to be sterilizing and if taken for no therapeutic end are considered gravely immoral by the Church. All forms of sterilization have been condemned in the official teachings of the Church, especially in the encyclical *Casti Connubii* in 1933, and laws to permit this practice were condemned as well. The encyclical *Humanae Vitae* said of direct sterilization that "[E]qually to be excluded, as the teaching authority of the Church has frequently declared, is direct sterilization, whether perpetual or temporary, whether of the man or of the woman" (n. 14).

Therapeutic sterilizations, if they are the last and only means available of curing, remedying or palliating a pathological condition, are permissible. But direct, deliberate and nontherapeutic sterilization is immoral because it is a nontherapeutic mutilation; and it is against justice because it denies the human life-to-be the opportunity to realize its full being. And not only is the act of sterilization sinful, but the subsequent marital acts undertaken after a sterilization to avoid serving life are also sinful. However, if the guilty party repents, normal relations may be resumed for legitimate reasons.

Stewardship • A biblically-based concept which implores Christians to use what they have — money, time, talent and service — in such a way that it honors God as the Creator of all things visible and invisible and contributes in a conscious way to the building of God's kingdom on earth. In imitation of the wise steward of the Gospel

(Lk 12:42; 16:2), Christians ought to exercise a responsible administration over resources, personal and corporate, because these resources are ultimately not theirs but the Lord's. The practice of stewardship, then, means that Christians forsake a self-aggrandizement and prefer instead a glorification of the One Who is over all, and an ardent attention to the common good. This is especially true when the rich, in whatever sense it may be applicable, are getting richer at the expense of the poor or poorer.

Padre Pio,
modern-day stigmatic

Sticharion • In the Eastern Churches, a silk or linen embroidered vestment worn by the priest under the phelonion. It corresponds to the alb of the Western Church.

Stichon • In the East, a quotation from Holy Scripture, particularly from the psalms. A prayer inspired by such a quotation.

Stigmata • The plural of the Greek noun *stigma* (mark or tattoo), "stigmata" is used in English as a collective noun for the scars that correspond to the wounds suffered by Christ in His passion and crucifixion and appear as abrasions of the skin on certain individuals of unusual personal holiness. The majority of stigmatists experience great pain accompanying this phenomenon, which is usually external and visible. The stigmata most often consist of wounds to the forehead, hands and feet, which bleed profusely; sometimes there is also a wound in the person's side. Equally painful invisible stigmata can also occur, as was the experience of St. Catherine of Siena.

The Church considers the three hundred recorded manifestations of the stigmata as a sign of particular favor by the Lord, Who allows the stigmatist in this life a physical participation in His suffering. Perhaps the most famous stigmatic is St. Francis of Assisi; in this century stigmatics have included Theresa Neumann of Germany and the Italian Padre Pio.

Stipend • In canon law, stipend is the term formerly applied to offerings given by the faithful to the priest in connection with the celebration of the Eucharist. Although the term stipend has been dropped in the 1983 Code of Canon Law, it is still in common usage and might occasion some misunderstanding.

The custom of offering bread and wine to be used for the celebration of the Eucharist can be traced to the earliest days of the Church. Over the centuries, monetary offerings came to be substituted for bread and wine, and the excess in these offerings was used for the support of the poor and, in time, for the support of ministers. In the face of frequent challenges to the appropriateness of the practice, the Church upheld the right of sacred ministers to receive Mass stipends, provided that any hint of coercion, simony or trafficking in the same was avoided (cf., for example, Canon 1385).

By the time the 1917 Code appeared, the legislation governing stipends had become quite complex, in large part as a check against abuses in the practice. Regulations on the number of stipends which could be accepted, how the intention of the donor was to be safeguarded, norms on the ability of priests and bishops to transfer or reduce Mass obligations and careful classifications of stipends based on their sources were marks of this earlier legislation. For the most part, it seems that the legislation was successful in preventing abuse in the system, at least in the United States.

Some impatience with the complexity of the regulations on stipends, however, coupled with continuing concern over the public perception of stipends in some areas, led to some significant revisions of and reductions in the law on stipends in the 1983 Code. Notably, however, the Code explicitly recognizes that such offerings by the faithful are praiseworthy because, among other things, they evidence concern for the Church and the work of her ministers (Canon 946). Indeed, throughout much of the developing world, Mass stipends remain the primary source of support for clergy.

As indicated above, the term stipend (which suggested to some ears a mandatory exchange of money for special remembrance in the Mass) was dropped in favor of the more explicit term "offering." This new term leaves no doubt that any offerings given in connection with the celebration of the Eucharist must be freely given (Canon 945). Nor does the law require the priest to accept such offerings, although obviously if he does accept he is bound in justice to offer the Mass in accord with the intention of the donor (Canons 948-950).

The usual amount of the offerings is to be determined by the bishops of the province. A priest may nevertheless accept an offering which is larger than this amount, provided it was freely offered. Canon 848 is careful to note, moreover, that the poor and needy are never to be denied access to the sacraments because of their inability to provide the customary offerings. The diocesan bishop, or religious superior, as the case may be, has the duty to see to it that the priests subject to him are fulfilling their Mass obligations. Stipends, or more accurately Mass offerings, should also be distinguished from stole fees.

Stole • The liturgical vestment in the form of a long narrow strip of cloth worn by deacon, priest or bishop around the neck, under the deacon's dalmatic and the priest's or bishop's chasuble. The *General Instruction of the Roman Missal* prescribes that "the priest [or bishop] wears the stole around his neck and hanging down in front. The deacon wears it over his left shoulder and drawn across the chest to the right side, where it is fastened" (n. 302). The color of the stole matches that of the liturgical color of the day.

The origins of the stole are difficult to trace with precision. The deacon's stole is in evidence in

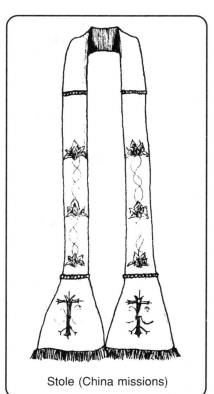

Stole (China missions)

Spain by the sixth century and in Rome by the eighth century. The priest's stole is mentioned in the statutes of the Synod of Mainz (813), and its use appears to have spread throughout Gaul and then into Italy by the eleventh century. Today it is worn by priest and deacon at Mass, at other sacraments and when preaching. In the rite for concelebration, clear preference is given in the liturgical directives for all concelebrants to wear "amice, alb, cincture, stole and chasuble" (*Introduction on the Rite of Concelebration of the Sacred Congregation for Rites*, 1965, n. 17,b). However, the wearing of the chasuble by all concelebrants is not strictly required, which practice draws greater attention to the stole.

Stole Fee • A voluntary offering given on the occasion of the administration of certain sacraments and sacramentals. The stole fee is voluntary and not a right of the sacred minister who performs the ceremony. Customarily, the faithful make offerings on the occasion of Baptism, Confirmation, marriages and funerals.

Although stole fees are voluntary, the diocesan bishop, after consulting with the priests' council, has the authority to regulate the amount of stole fees to be expected, as well as their allocation. The revised law suggests that all stole fees be put into a parish account unless it is the explicit will of the donor that they be given to the cleric or unless diocesan regulations state otherwise (Canon 531).

Stone, Altar: See **Altar Stone**

Stylite • From the Greek *stylos* (pillar), a stylite was a hermit whose particular form of asceticism consisted of his removal from society by living atop a pillar. Food and other necessities were usually obtained by way of a basket maneuvered by ropes and pulleys. Stylites were most common in the Eastern Church and the most famous of them was Simon Stylites. Their way of life did not survive beyond the early centuries of the Church.

Subdeacon • In the development of orders and ministries in the Western Church, that of the subdeacon appears as early as the third century both in Rome and in Africa, although it was only in the thirteenth century that it was finally regarded as one of the major orders (the others being deacon and priest). At his ordination, the subdeacon promised obedience to the bishop and faithful recitation of the Divine Office. Dressed in amice, alb, tunic and maniple at a Solemn Mass, the subdeacon would chant the Epistle, assist the deacon with the bread, wine and water at the Offertory and remove the vessels from the altar after Communion. By the *motu proprio Ministeria quaedam* (1972) on first tonsure, the minor orders and the subdiaconate, Pope Paul VI suppressed the subdiaconate: "The functions heretofore assigned to the subdeacon are entrusted to the reader and the acolyte; consequently, the major order of subdiaconate no longer exists in the Latin Church." However, the *motu proprio* also adds that "there is no reason why the acolyte cannot be called a subdeacon in some places, at the discretion of the conference of bishops."

Subdelegation • The act whereby a person who has delegated power of governance allows someone else to act on this power. A subdelegated person must be capable of exercising ecclesiastical jurisdiction. Power can only be subdelegated for individual cases and may not be again subdelegated unless this was expressly provided for by the person with ordinary power who originally delegated this power (cf. Canon 137).

Subpedaneum (Suppedaneum) • Latin for "footstool" or, literally, "that which goes under the feet." This refers to the footstool, platform or pillow which traditionally has been placed beneath the feet of the Holy Father when seated on his throne or on the *sedia gestatoria*, in order to make it more comfortable, since these are very large chairs serving more a symbolic than a functional purpose. Though the present Pontiff has not regularly used this, it was used a great deal by most of his predecessors, including Popes Paul VI and John Paul I.

Most commonly, however, *suppedaneum* refers to the predella, or platform upon which a priest stands when officiating at the altar.

Subreption • In canon law subreption is the concealment of certain truths or other information from ecclesiastical authority (Canon 63). It is usually discussed in connection with petitions for rescripts wherein subreption, whether deliberate or unintentional, renders a rescript invalid, where the information withheld was such that it should have been expressed for the valid issuance of a rescript. An example would be, in seeking permission for the alienation of certain ecclesiastical properties, the failure of the petitioner to mention that the property has previously been subdivided and is being sold in lots.

Because some rescripts are effective immediately while others are effective only upon their execution, the possible presence of subreption is to be judged, not at the time the rescript was actually petitioned, but rather when it is to become effective. Subreption in canon law should be distinguished from the canonical conception of obreption and from the notion of subreption in connection with the sacrament of Penance.

Subsidiarity • The principle by which the state acknowledges the rights of the members in a political community, i.e., those in higher authority respect the freedoms and prerogatives of those in lower authority. Catholic social theory has traditionally maintained that political and social action ought not be taken on by a higher authority when a lower level of competence would suffice.

Suburbicarian Dioceses • The seven dioceses nearest to Rome whose bishops are designated cardinal-bishops. Each works on one or more of the Congregations or Commissions of the Vatican. The dioceses are Albano, Frascati, Ostia, Palestrina, Porto, Santa Rufina and Velletri.

Suffering and Euthanasia • It is a fundamental Christian conviction that the suffering that often accompanies a final or chronic illness can never be terminated by the positive administering of any agent or the withholding of the basic nutrients in such a way that the death of the dying person is the direct result. "Euthanasia" (literally, "easy death") refers to the painless ending of the life of persons who are actually dying in great suffering, or who anticipate this outcome on the basis of a current diagnosis, or who want to avoid the reduced "quality of life" entailed by future senescence and illness.

According to Christian moral teaching, euthanasia in any form is never permissible. However, there is no requirement in Christian moral teachings that extraordinary treatments be provided in order to prolong life. Decisions about what constitutes extraordinary treatment depend on the circumstances surrounding the illness, the medically indicated care for the patient suffering from it and the application of Christian moral principles. Euthanasia is excluded as a course of action, not only because it involves the usurpation of the divine authority over life and death, but also because it curtails unforeseen and unpredictable opportunities for grace and transformation for the person who is dying or just terribly ill. At the heart of the Christian rejection of euthanasia and its supporting ideology is the mystery of our participation in the suffering of Christ, Whose example and Whose direct aid makes our suffering bearable and assures our victory over all suffering and death.

Suffragan Bishop • A bishop of a diocese of a province other than the metropolitan is called a suffragan bishop.

Suffrages • Required prayers or Masses said for special intentions, particularly for the dead.

Summa Theologiae • The major work of systematic theology done by St. Thomas Aquinas (1225-1274). This renowned theologian and scholar was given the title "Angelic Doctor" by the Church. He applied Aristotelian philosophy in the systematic and rational explanation of dogma and morals, without any substantial modification of the traditional teaching of the Catholic Church. Its main theme is God, considered in three parts: (1) God is studied as Creator; (2) God is seen as the Good, that is, as the end of created beings, and especially of angels and men; (3) God is studied as the Way Who is needed to redeem the fallen world. (Cf. Scholasticism.)

Sunday • Term deriving from the pagan Latin *dies solis* used to describe one of the days of the week, the "day called after the sun"; it was then reapplied to Jesus, Who is acclaimed the "Sun of Righteousness" (in light of Mal 4:2). The more direct Christian origins of this day derive from terming it the day of the Lord (from Rv 1:10), *Dominica* in

Latin (and in various modern-language derivations). Sunday replaced the Jewish Sabbath in observance beginning in the New Testament, with this first day of the week noted as the day "to break bread" (Acts 20:7) and in theology, since this was the day to commemorate the Resurrection (specified in the letters of Ignatius of Antioch).

Other subsequent theologies added to this day concern it as the first day of creation (Justin the Martyr and St. Isidore of Seville) and the day of the coming of the Spirit (commemorating His descent at Pentecost). This latter led to Trinitarian associations which governed the prescribed use of the Preface of the Trinity on Sundays in the former Roman Missal prescribed by St. Pius V. As it was the "day of the resurrection," fasting or kneeling were traditionally not observed. Its observance as a day of rest came about in the fourth century, first by ecclesiastical encouragement (Council of Elvira, c. A.D. 306) and then by civil edict (of Constantine), which specified it as a day when no work was to be done. Subsequent Church legislation combined required attendance at the Sunday Eucharist with abstaining from servile work.

Liturgically, Sunday was focused on the celebration of the Eucharist, noted as requisite on this "first day of creation," or on this "eighth day," one day added to the seven-day week to signify perfection. One entered into the kingdom of God through the Eucharist on Sunday, a day both in and "out of time," the day to experience what will be realized fully only in the kingdom. The present sacramentary rite for blessing and sprinkling with holy water, reserved to Sunday, contains references to the rich theology of Sunday. The present *General Norms for the Liturgical Year and the Calendar* state that "the Church celebrates the paschal mystery on the first day of the week, known as the Lord's Day or Sunday [and that] Sunday must be ranked as the first holy day of all" (n. 4). "Because of its special importance, the Sunday celebration gives way only to solemnities or feasts of the Lord" (n. 5).

A particular feature of the present sacramentary is the choice from eight Sunday Prefaces for proclamation on the Sundays of Ordinary Time to replace the previously required Preface of the Trinity on Sundays. The present Code of Canon Law (Canon 1247) states that on Sundays the faithful are bound to participate in the Mass and are "to abstain from those labors and business concerns which impede worship to be rendered to God, the joy which is proper to the Lord's Day, or the proper relaxation of mind and body."

Sunday Obligation • The faithful are obliged to participate in the celebration of Mass on all Sundays and holy days of obligation. This is a grave obligation, and willfully to neglect it can constitute a serious sin.

The revised Code has made some significant changes in the manner in which this obligation may be fulfilled. First, participation at Mass may be at the Eucharist in the Latin or Oriental rites and may be in any church, oratory, shrine or chapel and not just one's parish church. Furthermore, the obligation may be fulfilled either on Sunday or the feast itself or at a Mass celebrated on the eve of the day.

If there are no priests available or if a person cannot participate at Mass for grave reason, a person can participate in a Liturgy of the Word, or if this is not possible, the obligation can be satisfied by engaging in either group or private prayer.

A bishop or pastor can dispense from the obligation in individual cases for a just reason (Canons 1245, 1248).

Supererogation, Works of • Works that are not required by morality, but which are beneficial for the development of the spiritual and moral life of the individual. Such works include the counsels of perfection and works of charity as the corporal works of mercy and actions done purely for the love of God.

Suppedaneum: See **Subpedaneum**

Suppression • Certain ecclesiastical institutions or actions, whatever their original value and fruitfulness, can over time become unnecessary or even counterproductive. The term "suppression" is a wide one which refers broadly, then, to any situation in which an organization, action, devotion or the like is foreclosed by the proper Church authority. As a general rule, the authority capable of issuing the original authorization for an institute or action is also the one capable of suppressing it, as well as making provision for its remaining members and property, if any.

In making the decision to suppress, Church authorities are to consider such things as the present usefulness and appropriateness of continuing the project, the costs or demands entailed in maintaining the effort and whether the goals served by it can be better accomplished in another way. Furthermore, in suppressing an institute or action, ecclesiastical authority is to take care that the rights of persons are not unduly compromised by the suppression. It may be observed, finally, that perhaps the most controversial act of suppression occurred when the Jesuits were temporarily suppressed at the end of the eighteenth century.

Supreme Moderator • The highest superior of a religious institute or society of apostolic life. The supreme moderator has ordinary authority over all members of the institute or society, exercised according to the constitutions. All supreme moderators are elected to this position, and in any instance the election must be confirmed by the Holy See or the diocesan bishop (Canon 622).

Surplice • From the Latin *superpelliceum* (over a fur garment), the surplice was originally a loose choir vestment substituted for the closer-fitting alb, because it was to be worn over the fur coats which were customary in the cold northern countries. Made of linen or cotton, by the twelfth century it came to be the distinctive dress of the lower clergy and to be used by priests (except when celebrating Mass) to administer the sacraments. Originally the surplice reached the feet, but it began to be made shorter, until in the eighteenth century it reached just below the hips, with the sleeves also being reduced in size. This form of the surplice came to be known as the cotta.

The looser, more graceful form of the surplice has regained favor, and is worn by clergy in choir, in processions or when administering sacraments, and often is used by laymen when serving at liturgical functions. When the surplice is used, it is always worn over the cassock or religious habit.

Suspension • An ecclesiastical penalty that can only be applied to clerics. A

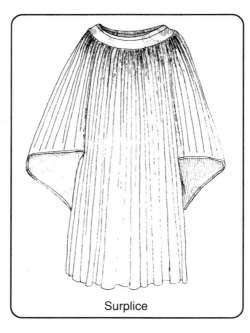

Surplice

suspension can prohibit all or some of the act of the power of Sacred Orders (such as the administration of the sacraments and the celebration of Mass), and it can prohibit all or some of the power of governance. A suspension can also prohibit the exercise of all or some of the rights or functions attached to an ecclesiastical office held by the person suspended. The extent of a suspension is determined either by the law itself, by a precept issued or by the decree or judgment whereby the penalty is imposed (cf. Canons 1333-1334).

A cleric who performs acts of the power of Orders contrary to a prohibition does so validly but illicitly. If the cleric witnesses a marriage, however, and lacks the jurisdiction to do so, the marriage is invalid. As far as acts of the power of governance are concerned, the law or precept can stipulate that such acts are either invalid or valid but illicit.

A suspension may be incurred in three ways: automatically by the law itself, by administrative decree of a competent superior or by imposition after a valid penal trial.

A suspension is automatically incurred by a cleric in the following cases: physical attack upon a bishop (Canon 1370.2); a deacon pretending to offer Mass or grant sacramental absolution (Canon 1378.2); a bishop ordaining a man who is not his subject without the proper dimissorial letters from the man's competent superior (Canon 1383); being ordained deacon or priest without the proper dimissorial letters (Canon 1383); a cleric falsely accusing a priest of solicitation in the confessional (Canon 1390.1); a cleric who attempts marriage (Canon 1394.1).

If an ecclesiastical superior judges that there are just causes for doing so, he may suspend a cleric by administrative decree. The superior is first required by law to warn the cleric to cease his offensive behavior. Only if he has not done so may the superior proceed. The decree of suspension must contain a summary of the reasons for the action and must stipulate the limits of the suspension. It is to be signed by the superior, notarized and then given to the cleric. If the decree is communicated orally, it must be done by the superior in the presence of two witnesses. The cleric retains the right of administrative recourse against the decree. A suspension by administrative decree cannot be imposed perpetually but only for a limited period of time.

Finally, a suspension can be imposed by a judicial (penal) process. This involves a full trial before three judges. The accused cleric must be given an advocate and is allowed to submit evidence. If he is found guilty, he has the right to appeal the sentence to a court of second instance.

A suspended cleric may not be deprived of his right to residence (Canon 1333.3.2). Nor may a suspended cleric be deprived of whatever is needed for his decent support (Canon 1350).

Suspension is a type of canonical penalty known as a censure. The purpose of a censure is not so much to punish as to prompt the accused person to rectify his ways. As with all other penalties, the superior is not to consider imposing a suspension unless fraternal correction and other similar methods have failed to repair scandal caused, restore justice and bring about the reform of the accused (Canon

1341). Suspension should not be confused with canonical irregularity, which latter state does not necessarily imply delictual behavior or suspected delictual behavior.

Swedenborgianism • This system of speculative mystical theology derives its name from its founder, Emanuel Swedenborg (1688-1772). Born in Sweden, he was the son of Sara Behm, wealthy heiress of a prominent mining family, and Jesper Swedberg, who at various times served as professor of theology, dean and rector of the Uppsala University, and later the Swedish Lutheran bishop of Skara. Swedenborg clearly grew up in a well-to-do and thoroughly religious household. Bishop Swedenborg showed an unusual and, by modern standards, relatively unhealthy proclivity toward the primeval spirit forms of the Nordic imagination; he was not reluctant to invoke spirits, good and evil alike, in his typically florid fashion from the pulpit.

Stephen Larsen, in *Emanuel Swedenborg* (Paulist Press, 1984, p. 4), provides this telling description of the father and son: "Jesper Swedberg was a Christian shaman who healed, not only by prayer, but by the laying on of hands and even casting out spirits. He well believed in his own (God-given, to be sure) personal power. The presence of other worlds was taken for granted in the Swedberg household. When Emanuel said he was with other children but was obviously alone, it was thought he played with angelic companions; and when out of his mouth came very precocious sayings, his parents thought angels must be speaking through him. But perhaps his pre-Christian ancestors might have thought him fey and companioning with the elves."

Out of this environment, Emanuel Swedenborg developed his theories of the basic spiritual structure of the universe. He claimed to have had a number of visions in

1745 wherein Christ instructed him in the spiritual sense of Scripture and then commissioned him to share this privileged knowledge with others, not unlike the heretical Gnostic traditions with which the early Church Fathers were forced to contend. Combining pantheism and theosophic concepts, Swedenborg attempted in his *Arcana Coelestia* (1756) to propose the basic tenets of his "New Church," which was intended eventually to supplant Christianity itself. He refused to acknowledge a belief in the Trinity, original sin, Christ's resurrection and the sacraments, except Baptism and the Eucharist.

Remnants of his religious system still survive in various New Church groups and the Church of the New Jerusalem. In the United States, such congregations are found primarily in southeastern Pennsylvania, where William Penn's policy of religious tolerance made allowance for many diverse religious groups, and in Delaware, where Swedenborg's thought found a natural reception among the Swedish colonists. The Swedenborgian Cathedral for the United States is located in Wilmington, Delaware.

Swiss Guards • Although papal armies had included Swiss mercenaries even earlier, it was in 1505 that Pope Julius II organized a distinctive body of Swiss men to protect him. This original group of two hundred men arrived in Rome in 1506. They have been charged with the personal safety of the Popes since that time. The most famous military event involving the Swiss Guards was their defense of Pope Clement VII during the sack of Rome in 1527. One hundred and forty-seven Swiss Guards were killed, and only forty-two reached safety with the Pope in Castel Sant'Angelo.

The Swiss Guards wear bright red, yellow and blue uniforms designed by Michelangelo more than four hundred years ago. Recruits must be Swiss, practicing Catholics and less than twenty-five years of age.

Syllabus of Errors • A set of eighty propositions representing erroneous positions, identified by Pope Pius IX as inconsistent with the Catholic Faith and promulgated on December 8, 1864, with the encyclical *Quanta Cura*. The errors were classified and presented under ten headings: I. Pantheism, naturalism, extreme rationalism (1-7); II. Moderate rationalism (8-14); III. Indifferentism and latitudinarianism (15-18); IV. Socialism, communism, secret societies, Bible associations, and liberal clerical groups (with references to previous papal documents); V. Rights of the Church (18-38); VI. Church-state relations (39-55): VII. Morality (56-64); VIII. Christian marriage (65-74); IX. Papal temporal authority (75-76); X. Liberalism (77-80).

Publication of the *Syllabus of Errors* provoked considerable controversy in secular and ecclesiastical circles. The First Vatican Council's Dogmatic Constitution, *De Fide*, incorporated many of the fundamental points of the *Syllabus*.

Symbol • Term derived from the Greek *symbolon*, meaning literally a token, pledge or sign through which one infers or can come to experience something else. Hence, it has been customary in liturgical literature to refer to the symbolic nature of the liturgy, meaning that symbols are privileged means through which Christ's paschal mystery is experienced. The direct and immediate encounter with Christ's saving passion, death, resurrection and continuing intercession experienced in the liturgy is only able to come to sensible expression through the use of symbols. At the Eucharist, for example, the bread and wine are presented, transformed into the Body and Blood of Christ and shared in a meal that nurtures contemporary congregations on the very same redemption won once for all in Jesus' dying and rising.

The background provided by the Greek verb *symballein*, a combination of *syn*, meaning "together," and *ballein* meaning "to throw," is important here in that it assumes interactive communication through the use of symbols. To appreciate symbols as used in the liturgy is to understand their value as means of divine self-communication requiring our attentive response. To "throw together" here would signify, first, a sacred object put before the congregation as conveying and containing the reality of Christ's salvation. Second, as a symbol this sacred object requires acceptance, appropriation and response. Hence the important value placed on active participation as a hallmark of the contemporary liturgical reform. The theological truth here is that symbols make us partakers in the mystery of Christ; through them we take part in and become contemporaneous with His dying and rising. Liturgical symbols have effects upon us; through them, Christ acts among us. To participate in liturgy also invites a conscious and faithful active response on the part of participants.

This understanding of symbol holds true for the proclamation of the Word. The proclaimed Word at liturgy is symbolic in the sense that it, too, requires an appreciation that through it we become partakers in Christ and that, as an effective announcement of salvation, it requires our faithful appropriation and response. As symbol, the Word is announced and offered to the congregation at liturgy. It is for their sakes that through the Word the chief events of redemption are recalled, recounted and effected. Active ratification of the proclamation by the congregation restores the proclamation of the Word to its rightful position as a symbolic rehearsal of salvation that effects again and again the good news of redemption.

Other important liturgical symbols besides the Word, bread and wine, include water, oil of the catechumens and chrism for initiation, oil of the Anointing of the Sick, etc. Often in liturgical literature the notion of "symbol" is identical with that of "sign." However, the contemporary revival of interest in symbol generally separates sign from symbol. In this case, sign means a one-to-one correspondence between sign and the reality signified; symbol means a multivalent means of communication, interaction and appropriation of the mystery of Christ as experienced in the act of liturgy.

Symbolism • Term that can mean a system of symbolic usage at the liturgy, and the practice of using symbols in relation to one another as a group. Symbolism can mean the reflective understanding of the meaning behind the use of signs and symbols, particularly as these relate to an overall vision of symbol in the liturgy. Unlike signs, which generally have a one-to-one correspondence, symbols disclose many layers of meaning (they are "multivalent"); one of the functions of the blessing prayers during the liturgy (e.g., prayer for blessing water at Baptism) is to specify something of the symbolic richness and theology there. Contemporary studies of symbolism in liturgy frequently stress the role of imagination in engaging oneself in liturgical symbols. When this occurs, then symbols are most effective since they function to draw others into the mystery celebrated. The symbol and the congregation are literally "thrown together" in the use of symbols.

Synagogue • From a Greek word (*synagoge*) meaning "a gathering place" or "assembly." The word is used in the New Testament to indicate a religious meeting place of the Jews. The beginnings of the synagogue can be traced at least as far back as the time of Ezra.

It is believed by some to have originated even earlier, during the Babylonian Exile. The destruction of the Temple in 587 B.C. had left the Jews without an official place of worship. In any case, the dispersion of the Jews abroad kept them at a distance from Jerusalem and the Temple. All of this created a need for an alternative place of worship.

In the beginning, the synagogues may have been little more than private meetings in private homes. Synagogue worship consisted in readings from the Torah and the prophets, along with prayers and hymns; it was and is a non-sacrificial form of worship. The synagogue was not viewed as the dwelling place of God among His people but was seen rather as a study house and a place to meet and pray. The synagogue played an important role in the beginning and early spread of Christianity. Jesus Himself attended the synagogue regularly, as is noted in Luke 4:15-16. Paul started as a preacher of the Gospel in the Damascus synagogue (Acts 9:20). In Paul's travels it was his custom to go first to the synagogue of the place he was visiting, where, as a guest, he would be invited to preach.

For further reading: Eric M. Meyers, "Synagogue," *Anchor Bible Dictionary*, 6:251-263.

Synapte • A succession of prayers resembling a litany in the Byzantine Rite. There are two in the celebration of the Divine Liturgy.

Synaxis • From the Greek term denoting an assembly or congregation, commonly used by Christian writers to describe any assembly for liturgy, e.g., hours and sacraments, with the Eucharist most often understood by this term in the Eastern Churches. An aliturgical synaxis can also refer to a liturgical assembly that consists of a celebration of the Word as distinct from the Eucharist.

Synderesis (also Synteresis) • This term has two meanings. In its more common meaning — in moral theology — synderesis refers to our knowledge of the first principles of moral action. It is an instinctive disposition of the practical intellect indicating that good should be done and evil avoided. Strictly speaking, as an instinctive disposition, synderesis is distinguished from conscience, which is a judgment on the particular moral choice confronting a particular act. Mystical theology provides the second sense of the term. Here it refers to the mysterious center or ground in the soul where mystical union occurs.

Synod • A gathering of clergy and/or laity. In the revised Code of Canon Law there are two types of synod: the Synod of Bishops and the diocesan synod. Although not called by the name, ecumenical and particular councils are also synods.

The Synod of Bishops is a gathering of representatives from the episcopal conferences around the world. All representatives are bishops. The synod is usually held every three years. The purpose is to foster unity with the Roman Pontiff, to assist him with their counsel and to consider questions concerning the Church's activities in the world. Membership in the synod consists in large part of elected representatives. Certain bishops attain membership by the law itself, and others are appointed by the Pope. There are also representatives of certain of the clerical religious institutes.

The Synod of Bishops has a permanent

secretariat in the Roman Curia. The secretariat provides staff services to the synod while it is in session; in between synods, it canvasses bishops around the world for potential topics for future synods.

The Pope himself sets the topic of discussion for each synod. Although the synods from 1971 onward have focused on one major topic, discussions on other topics take place. The major themes of the synods have been: 1967 — dangers to the Faith, revision of Canon Law, seminaries, mixed marriages; 1971 — ministerial priesthood and justice in the world; 1974 — evangelization; 1977 — catechetics; 1980 — the role of the family; 1983 — reconciliation; 1987 — the laity. Apostolic Exhortations have been issued after several of the synods, based on the discussions that took place (Canons 342-348).

The diocesan synod as a canonical institute dates from the fourth century, although its composition and purpose have evolved considerably since then. In the early centuries, synods were gatherings of bishops, priests and abbots from the same region. The earliest Church law came from the synods and councils in the form of canons enacted to deal with various problems facing the Church. In time the diocesan synod came to be a gathering of the priests of a diocese with their bishop to discuss needs of the diocese. The 1917 Code mandated that a diocesan synod be held at least once every ten years; however, the synod fell into desuetude in many areas of the world and actually became an exception rather than a rule.

In the revised Code, the synod is a gathering of representatives of the clergy, religious and faithful of a diocese for the purpose of assisting the bishop in leading the entire diocese. The synod is convoked by the diocesan bishop whenever he deems it necessary. Participation in the synod is mandatory for certain diocesan officials and the members of the presbyterial council. At least one priest from every vicariate is to be selected. Representatives of the religious communities and from among the laity are also designated to participate. This designation is usually by election, although the bishop has the right to appoint other participants from among the clergy, religious and faithful.

The diocesan synod, like the Synod of Bishops, is consultative in nature. Any legislation enacted must be ratified and promulgated by the bishop (Canons 460-468).

Synod of Bishops • This assembly of bishops chosen from throughout the world, which meets in Rome every few years under the direction of the Pope, was chartered by Pope Paul VI on September 15, 1965, in the document *Apostolica sollicitudo*. Its description is included in *Christus Dominus*, the Decree on the Pastoral Office of the Bishops in the Church, which says, "Bishops chosen from different parts of the world in a manner and according to a system determined or to be determined by the Roman Pontiff will render to the Supreme Pastor a more effective auxiliary service in a council which shall be known by the special name of Synod of Bishops. This council, as it will be representative of the whole Catholic episcopate, will bear testimony to the participation of all the bishops in hierarchical communion in the care of the universal Church" (CD 5). Although the Synod exercises its duties only occasionally, its nature is permanent. The Pope, as president of the Synod, has the authority to assign the agenda, to call it together and (although it is normally a consultative body) to give it deliberative power. The 1983 Code of Canon Law deals with the Synod of Bishops in Canons 342-348, incorporating much of the content of *Apostolica sollicitudo*, and reflecting the experience gained from the synodal assemblies which began in 1967. In general, the quality of the material generated by episcopal synods since the Second Vatican Council has been regarded as very high. (Cf. J. Johnson, "The Synod of Bishops: An Analysis of its Legal Development," *Studies in Canon Law* No. 518, Catholic University of America, 1986.)

Synoptic Gospels, The • There is an impressive agreement — verbal and sequential — among the first three Gospels: Matthew, Mark and Luke. For purposes of comparison, these Gospels can be put into parallel columns. This ordering of materials is known as a "synopsis." As a result, Matthew, Mark and Luke have come to be known as the Synoptic Gospels. The extensive similarity of content and arrangement among these Gospels, alongside some notable dissimilarities which they exhibit vis-à-vis one another, gives rise to what has become known as the Synoptic Problem or the Synoptic Question.

Synoptic Question, The • Since the time of J. Griesbach (1776), the first three Gospels, Matthew, Mark and Luke, have been called the Synoptic Gospels because they provide a "synoptic" view of the life and teaching of Christ. That is, they offer a presentation of these materials from a more or less similar point of view. The "question" or "problem" arises when these Gospels are compared with one another. Such a comparison reveals a notable concordance in form and content but a surprising divergence in details. Several explanations for this situation have been proposed. Among these, the explanation that is most widely accepted is the two-source hypothesis. According to that understanding of the relationship among the Synoptic Gospels, Mark's was the earliest Gospel, and the Gospels of Matthew and Luke rely on Mark's Gospel for much of their material. The second of the two sources is called "Q" (the initial of the German word *Quelle*, meaning "source"), from which Matthew and Luke draw material they hold in common which is not found in Mark's Gospel. In addition, Matthew and Luke relied on their own particular sources (commonly designated as "M" and "L"), oral and/or written, for some of the material preserved in their Gospels. It must be acknowledged, however, that no explanation rises above the level of hypothesis.

For further reading: Frans Neirynck, "Synoptic Problem," *New Jerome Biblical Commentary*, 587-595; C. M. Tuckett, "Synoptic Problem," *Anchor Bible Dictionary*, 6:263-270.

Synteresis: See **Synderesis**

Syrian Rite • In the early evolution of worship structures in the Churches of the East, this family of rites refers to those having the same basic structures and some formularies in common. Some of these originated in Syria proper, with strong Antiochene influence; others derived from Upper Mesopotamia (Chaldea), with stronger Semitic characteristics. Syrian liturgies are divided into the East-Syrian (Syro-Mesopotamian) and the West Syrian type. The East Syrian type of liturgies has strong Semitic roots. The anaphora of Addai and Mari, whose original text may derive from the third century, reflects this influence. The two anaphoras of Theodore of Mopsuestia and the Aramaic Anaphora of the Apostles are rooted in the Antiochene example of this Rite. The West Syrian Rite contains the following four subgroups: the Syro-Antiochene (so-called "Jacobite" Rite), the Maronite Rite, the Byzantine Rite and the Armenian Rite.

Tabernacle • The prominently placed and suitably adorned receptacle in which the Blessed Sacrament is reserved in churches, chapels and oratories. It should be "immovable, made of solid or opaque material, and locked so that the danger of profanation may be entirely avoided" (Canon 938). Usually, the contents of the tabernacle are ciboria containing consecrated Hosts and a lunette (or luna) holding a large consecrated Host for insertion into the monstrance for exposition and Benediction of the Blessed Sacrament. The tabernacle is no longer located on the altar of sacrifice (as was customary in the past), but is placed either at the center of the sanctuary or in a side chapel suitable for prayer and adoration. A burning sanctuary lamp is kept near the tabernacle to signal the presence of the Blessed Sacrament. *Tabernaculum* — the Latin word for tent from which the term tabernacle is derived — reminds us of the Old Testament and Jewish origins of this sacred receptacle. Under the direction of Moses, the tabernacle was constructed to house the Ark of the Covenant (cf. Ex 25-31; 35-40). In the Jewish liturgical year, the feast of Tabernacles (*Succot*) is a great, eight-day celebration coinciding with harvest time and recalling Israel's dwelling in tents during the forty years in the desert (Lv 23:42).

Talitha Koum (Koumi) • Aramaic words found in Mark 5:41, as having been spoken by Jesus to the dead daughter of Jairus. The words are translated as "Little girl, get up." The word *talitha*, here construed as "little girl," derives from a word meaning literally "ewe lamb," but used in Aramaic as a term of endearment when addressing a little girl.

For further reading: Max Wilcox, "Talitha Cumi," *Anchor Bible Dictionary*, 6:309-310.

Talmud • A noun formed from the Hebrew verb meaning "to learn." The word in general means "learning" or "teaching," primarily teaching about the Torah. More specifically, the term designates a collection which contains the Mishnah (oral Jewish teaching on the Torah) and the Gemara (discussions of the Mishnah). There are two versions of the Talmud: the Jerusalem Talmud, which contains the teaching of the Palestinian rabbis but is incomplete; and the Babylonian Talmud, which is the larger of the two. This latter derives from Babylon and is generally regarded as the more important of the two. Both works stem from the early centuries of the Christian era. The language of both Talmuds is Aramaic: the Jerusalem Talmud is composed in Palestinian Aramaic, the Babylonian in Eastern Aramaic.

For further reading: Gary G. Porton, "Talmud," *Anchor Bible Dictionary*, 6:310-315.

Tametsi • The title of the decree issued by the Council of Trent (1563) concerning the form of marriage. According to this decree, which had the force of law, a marriage between two baptized persons, including non-Catholics, was valid only if contracted in the presence of the parish priest, the local Ordinary, or another priest delegated by one of these, and two witnesses. The terms of the decree were problematic because they would have reduced the marriages of all Protestants to illicit cohabitation. In addition, it was stated that the decree was to have force only in those places where it was first officially promulgated.

Tametsi was never promulgated in predominantly Protestant countries nor in mission countries. Hence, the obligation of canonical form did not affect all Catholics. In order to clarify matters and end the confusion, the Holy See issued another decree on the form of marriage in 1908. By the terms of this decree, called *Ne temere*, the obligation to marry before a priest and two witnesses applied only to Catholics. Furthermore, Catholics were not obliged to marry before their parish priest but before any properly delegated priest. Finally, *Ne temere* obliged all Catholics of the Latin Rite throughout the world.

Tantum Ergo • The final two verses of the Eucharistic hymn, *Pange Lingua*, composed by St. Thomas Aquinas for the Office of the feast of Corpus Christi. Increasingly, it is known in an English translation beginning with the line, "Down in adoration falling." Along with the *O Salutaris Hostia*, this hymn is customarily sung kneeling at Benediction of the Most Blessed Sacrament.

Te Deum • An ancient Latin hymn, "*Te Deum Laudamus*" traditionally is attributed to St. Ambrose but almost certainly was not composed by him. In fact, scholars do not agree on its origins. Some favor St. Niceta of Remesiana (d. A.D. 414), others an essentially liturgical provenance — perhaps the Paschal Vigil. In any case, its early incorporation into Matins (now Office of Readings) of the Liturgy of the Hours is attested by the Rule of St. Benedict (c. 540). The *Te Deum* is sung now at the conclusion of the Office of Readings on Sundays,

solemnities and feasts. The hymn is particularly associated with joyful occasions of thanksgiving, e.g., the successful conclusion of warfare, the election of a prior, and so on. Thus, for instance, at the liberation of Paris by the Allied forces in 1945, General Charles de Gaulle went to the Cathedral of Notre Dame to participate in the singing of the *Te Deum*.

Teilhardism • A religio-scientific synthesis advanced in the posthumous philosophical and theological works of the French Jesuit paleontologist Pierre Teilhard de Chardin (1881-1955), notably *The Phenomenon of Man* (1955) and *The Divine Milieu* (1957). The Teilhardian synthesis is characterized chiefly by a vision of the universe as an evolutionary process unfolding in the direction of systems of increasing complexity, primary among which is the movement toward higher levels of consciousness. Crucial advances, or leaps, in this process have occurred with the emergence of life on earth and the development of human consciousness. The latter advance implies that human intelligence now joins with natural processes in directing the progress of evolution.

The powerful eschatological or futuristic pull exerted by the *divinus terminus* (the "Omega Point") of this process gives Teilhardism a markedly optimistic cast. Indeed, since the Incarnation, it is possible to describe the vast evolutionary movement as a kind of "Christification." In the aftermath of the lively controversy provoked by Teilhardism, the prospects for a calmer assessment of these ideas have improved. It now seems clear that what Teilhard de Chardin presented in these works was not a strictly scientific, philosophical or theological account of science and religion, but a powerful mystical vision of the evolutionary process moving inexorably toward its consummation in God.

Teilhardism may thus be understood as endeavoring to exhibit the striking affinities between the Christian and modern scientific views of the universe and to dispel the deeply seated impression that these views are in irreconcilable conflict.

Temperance • A cardinal virtue which encourages moderation of our instincts and drives for pleasure. Temperance enables the person to establish a proper spiritual relationship with God because it properly orders our drives.

Temperance is an important virtue for our era because it not only moderates our drive for pleasure but also our drive for violence. Philosophers such as Schoepenhauer noted that pleasure and violence are mysteriously intertwined; this is represented by the Buddhist god Shiva, who is both the god of violence and of pleasure. Schoepenhauer argues that to restrain our love of violence, we must also restrain our love of pleasure. Temperance enables us to pursue only those pleasures which do not lead to death. The Christian virtue of temperance argues that to control violence we must control our love for pleasure.

For Catholics, the Virgin Mary expresses temperance superbly, for she is the model of both peace and chastity. Precisely because she is perfect in chastity is she perfect in

Paris statue
representing temperance

peace, and this is because she perfectly orders her loves, desires and passions. The virtue is a sorely needed virtue because it does more to bring peace into our lives than perhaps any other virtue.

Temple in Jerusalem, The • The Second Book of Chronicles (3:1) speaks of the revelation to King David of the site in Jerusalem upon which the Temple of the Lord was to be built. Mt. Moriah was believed to have been the spot upon which Abraham prepared to sacrifice Isaac (Gn 22:2); the threshing floor of Ornan where David encountered the angel, poised to exterminate the people of Jerusalem in payment for David's sins; and the location of David's altar upon which holocausts and peace offerings were made (2 Kgs 24). There David's son, Solomon, erected the first of three temples, all now destroyed, replaced by the Mosque of Omar, commonly known as the Dome of the Rock, which enshrines a large outcropping of rock, long believed to have been the foundation for the Temple altar, and the site of Muhammad's ascent to heaven.

Solomon built the first Temple, employing materials and treasure amassed for the purpose by King David. Skilled workmen from Tyre and unskilled men from the vicinity of Jerusalem labored for seven years to complete the main structure (1 Kgs 5-6). Not much detailed information has come down to us concerning the exterior, except the basic measurements and general description of the structure.

The building was rectangular in shape, constructed of local stone, decorated with carved wood, cast bronze, hammered gold and other precious metals. The structure rose to a height of approximately fifty-four feet, from foundational plinth to the top of the roof cornice. It was fronted by a staircase, flanked by two monumental bronze pillars or stelae, detached from the façade (1 Kgs 7:21). The function of these pillars is unclear, but may simply have harked back to earlier Canaanite cult.

Situated in front of the building, on each side of the main staircase, were the "Altar of Bronze" (2 Kgs 16:14) and the "Sea of Bronze," a large basin of cast bronze supported by twelve bronze oxen, used by the priests for ritual purification (1 Kgs 7:23-26). Other smaller lavers of bronze were mounted on wheels, used to purify the sacrificial animals.

The Temple, which, according to the Book of Wisdom, was designed according to the specifications of the original Meeting Tent erected in the desert by Moses (Wis 9:8), consisted of three areas: a vestibule (*Ulam*), the Holy Place or Sanctuary (*Hekal*) and the Holy of Holies (*Debir*). The chambers were all thirty feet in width, varying only in their length, with the vestibule measuring fifteen feet, the sanctuary, sixty feet, and the Holy of Holies, thirty feet. Storerooms ran the length of the sanctuary and the Holy of Holies on both sides of the building.

The sanctuary housed the Altar of Incense, the Table of Showbreads, or Loaves of Proposition, and the ten lampstands. Here various cultic actions were performed by the priests. At the far end of the sanctuary was a smaller staircase which rose to the Holy of Holies.

The Holy of Holies enshrined the Ark of the Covenant and two gilded Cherubim, whose outstretched wings formed the Throne for Yahweh. This was the most sacred area of the Temple, which remained in darkness throughout the year and was separated from the sanctuary by a veil of heavily embroidered, rich material.

Solomon's Temple was destroyed in the year 587 B.C. by Babylonian forces, its treasures and sacred vessels looted and carted away by the conquering army. It was not until the return of the Jewish exiles in 538 B.C. that the prospect of reconstruction existed. However, not until Zerubbabel and Jeshua urged the people on did work begin in earnest to rebuild the sanctuary in 520 B.C.

Little is known of this second temple, attributed to Zerubbabel, but it is imagined that it followed the same general plan of Solomon's work, if not so rich and elaborately decorated as the original (Ezr 5:8). This temple was plundered in 169 B.C. by Antiochus Epiphanes, and further profaned in 167 B.C. by the worship of Zeus Olympios (1 Mc 1:44-59). Only in 164 B.C., following the victory of the Maccabees, was the temple reconsecrated and true worship once again offered within its precincts. In 20 B.C., Herod the Great began the work of extensive reconstruction and embellishment of the Temple. Enthroned by Rome as the puppet ruler of Judah, Herod sought to win the support of the Jewish populace by his work on the Temple. Herod extended the Temple Mount to nearly twice its original size and constructed an enormous wall to enclose the entire area, measuring nearly thirty-six acres. He followed the basic structural design of Solomon's edifice, yet was determined that his work should outstrip the original in size and magnificence. He succeeded, creating one of the most impressive buildings of antiquity. He completed work on the main portion of the temple complex in approximately ten years. Work on the courtyards, annexes and secondary structures continued, however, well into the decades of the first millennium, and was completed about A.D. 63.

Various gateways and porticoes pierced the enclosure wall, leading into the Court of the Gentiles. Across the court, a large stone wall or barrier surrounded the entire temple precinct, clearly marking out the area where non-Jews were permitted. Beyond this initial court no non-Jew could pass, under pain of death. The temple precinct was within the confines of this barrier and was entered by the Beautiful Gate. The temple area was divided into two areas. The first was composed of the large Court of the Jewish Women, which was gained directly by the Beautiful Gate, and the smaller Court of the Jewish Men. The second area was composed of the Court of the Priests, surrounding the temple proper. There were numerous other structures, storerooms and chambers, besides these major courtyards, cultic area and the Holy of Holies. On the north side of the Temple was located the Fortress or Tower Antonia which afforded the Roman forces an easy vantage point and access to the temple area. Josephus describes the Temple and its precincts in detail, as well as the political machinations involved in the construction of the sanctuary (*The Antiquities of the Jews*, 15.11; *The Wars of the Jews*, 5.5).

The Temple of Herod was the place in which Zechariah offered incense and was struck dumb for his disbelief of the angel's words concerning the conception of John the Baptist. It was here that Simeon and the prophetess Anna met the Infant Jesus, His Mother Mary and Joseph. Here too did Jesus and His Apostles visit, pray and preach during Our Lord's public ministry. It was the veil of this temple that was torn in two by the death of the Lord, and it was this temple that the Apostles and early members of the Church visited daily for prayer, and in which they wrought miracles in the name of the Lord.

Following the Jewish revolt against Roman rule, the Temple and the surrounding enclosure area (except for the Western Wall) was totally destroyed in A.D. 70 by the Emperor Titus (Josephus, *The Wars of the Jews*, 5.5—6.7; Tacitus, *The History*, 5.8-12).

For further reading: Carol Meyers, "Temple, Jerusalem," *Anchor Bible Dictionary*, 6:350-369.

Temporal Goods • The Church, insofar as she is an earthly society, uses material things to aid in the pursuit of her salvific mission. The canonical term "temporal goods" generally denotes that property belonging to the Church, but technically encompasses only that property belonging to a proper juridic person. Such property is thereby designated "ecclesiastical property." Thus, for example, the land and buildings, together with cash, stocks and bonds, automobiles, artistic works, personal property and intangible but non-spiritual assets, all constitute the temporal goods of ecclesiastical entities such as dioceses, parishes, religious and secular institutes, and the like. Temporal goods are regulated by Book V of the 1983 Code of Canon Law.

At various stages of Church history, forces both within and outside the Church have attacked her right to own and administer property in her own name. From her earliest days, however, the Church has upheld the appropriateness of her owning worldly property as a temporal necessity for the fulfillment of her divine mission. Canon 1254, which opens the modern canonical treatment of temporal goods, offers both a declaration of this right and an outline of the purpose behind the Church's use of property: namely, "to provide for divine worship, the decent support of ministers and works of the apostolate, and for the purposes of charity especially toward the needy." Moreover, while ownership (both canonical and civil) of temporal goods is usually vested in some level of the Church lower than the Roman Pontiff, Canons 1256 and 1273 affirm the final authority of the Holy See over all ecclesiastical property.

The Catholic Church acquires property through a variety of means. The largest single source of income is free-will offerings of the faithful, both offerings made in justice under Canon 1262 and those made in gift under Canon 1261. In many nations the Catholic Church receives some governmental support in virtue of concordats, although such has not been the practice in the United States. The Church and her ministers also receive income from fees associated with various services and from donations made upon the celebrations of sacraments. Beyond this, the Church is the recipient of income from investments and endowments of various sorts and is the beneficiary of bequests under wills and similar documents. Canon 1263, finally, legislates on the right of the Church to enact certain forms of canonically binding taxes where necessary for the support of her mission. (Cf. also Cathedraticum.) Each of the above sources of income is subject to specific regulations of the Code of Canon Law.

The canons governing the administration and disposal, that is, alienation, of ecclesiastical property are also complex, but certain aspects are especially noteworthy. Building upon the canonical distinction between the ordinary and the extraordinary administration of temporal goods, the Code of Canon Law places rather stricter controls on the discretion of ecclesiastical superiors in regard to transactions which are designated extraordinary. For example, transactions which involve the canonical patrimony of an institution or which exceed certain sums require more in the way of checks and reviews before such a transaction is canonically valid. Other canonical institutes, such as mandatory diocesan and parish finance councils and independent finance officers, also reflect a heightened concern on the part of ecclesiastical authority that the goods of the Church be used in the most efficient manner. It may also be observed that negligence or corruption in the administration of the Church's temporal affairs can result in both canonical penalties and the obligation of restitution upon those responsible.

Temporal Power • A description sometimes used in ecclesiastical parlance to designate the jurisdiction or authority a Church official enjoys in civil or secular concerns. Such authority is invested, for example, in pastors and parochial administrators over the material goods, properties and functioning of a parish or school. Temporal power is distinguished from spiritual power, which is the authority invested in Church officials over spiritual matters such as the administration of the sacraments, the celebration of liturgical services and certain juridical areas such as the resolution of the validity of marriage by a tribunal.

By virtue of his office as Head of the Vatican City State, the Pope is sovereign of the secular matters in that tiny nation, as well as the supreme spiritual authority over the Catholic Church. His dominion over the Papal States ended in 1870, when they were seized by the kingdom of Italy. In 1929, a concordat was reached between the Holy See and the Italian government, resolving the status of the Church's temporalities. (Cf. Lateran Treaty.)

The Church assumes a role in society, nonetheless, to indicate and teach those conditions beneficial to promoting mankind's spiritual and temporal welfare alike. The Church acknowledges the duties citizens have to submit to rightful laws and to act in accordance with the decisions of the state in secular and legal matters. The Church also has the right to exert her influence in the realms of political life through her moral teaching and proper direction of souls (cf. Mt 22:15-22; Rom 13:7; 1 Tm 2:1-2; Ti 3:1; Acts 4:19; 1 Pt 2:13-17).

The Second Vatican Council instructs the laity to infuse a Christian spirit into the mentality, customs and laws as well as the structures of the community in which a person lives by the example of his or her life.

"Laymen ought to take on themselves as their distinctive task this renewal of the temporal order. Guided by the light of the Gospel and the mind of the Church, prompted by Christian love, they should act in this domain in a direct way and in their own specific manner. As citizens among citizens they must bring to their cooperation with others their own special competence, and act on their own responsibility; everywhere and always they have to seek the justice of the kingdom of God. The temporal order is to be renewed in such a way that, while its own principles are fully respected, it is harmonized with the principles of the Christian life and adapted to the various conditions of times, places and peoples. Among the tasks of this apostolate Christian social action is preeminent" (AA 7).

Temptation • In Christian usage, any incitement to sin arising from the world (the actions or inducements of others), the flesh (our own weaknesses and desires) and the Devil (suggestions by the fallen angels). According to Scripture, God allows us to be tempted, but never beyond our powers to resist. In this way, the basic etymological sense of temptation — as a trial or testing — is preserved in the Christian usage. The trial represented by temptation provides the occasion for moral and spiritual growth as the soul's desire for God and His goodness becomes the chief motive for freely turning away from sin and doing the good. In a certain sense, fidelity to the practices and discipline of the Christian life and, above all else, perseverance in prayer provide the chief means by which one is strengthened against the pressures of temptation. Failure is never the last word, for divine forgiveness is forthcoming whenever we turn to God and implore His mercy. For the Christian, temptation is basic to the struggle to be conformed to Christ, a struggle coming from the world, especially today in the form of temptations to materialism, secularism and atheism, a struggle which His own powerful presence in grace makes bearable and fruitful.

Tenebrae • Term from the Latin for "darkness," used to signify the combination of Matins and Lauds for Holy Thursday, Good Friday and Holy Saturday in the former Divine Office, which were celebrated on the evening before these days. The term *tenebrae* refers to the evening setting for these services of the Word and the progressive extinguishing of the church lights during them. In the Middle Ages this custom became stylized, so that a candle stand (often termed a "hearse") for fifteen candles (the number of the psalms prayed each day) was used, one candle being extinguished after each psalm was sung. The main focus during these services was on Christ's suffering, death and descent among the dead. The *tenebrae* custom is technically suppressed in the present edition of the Liturgy of the Hours; however, it is possible to celebrate a combination of the Office of Readings and Morning Prayer on Good Friday and Holy Saturday mornings.

Terce (also Tierce) • From the Latin *tertius*, "third (hour)," i.e., 9 A.M. One of the "little hours" of the Divine Office, recited mid-morning.

Ternus • The Latin term for the list of three names of possible candidates for the office of bishop. The *ternus* (plural, *terna*) is usually drawn up by the papal representative of the country and submitted to the Holy See. If the appointment is for a Latin Rite bishop, the matter is handled by the Congregation for the Bishops or the Congregation for the Evangelization of Peoples for Latin Rite bishops in mission territories. If the appointment is for an Oriental Rite bishop, it is handled by the Congregation for the Oriental Churches.

Some dioceses have the approved custom whereby the chapter of canons of the diocese selects the candidates whose names will be placed on the *ternus*.

In any case, the composition of the *ternus* is preceded by a thorough and strictly confidential investigation into the suitability of each candidate. A complete report of the investigation is sent with the *ternus* to the Holy See. The appropriate congregation completes the investigation and makes its own recommendation to the Holy Father, who then makes the final decision (cf. Canon 377).

English-speakers often refer to this document as a *terna*, perhaps confusing the presence of three names with a plural form. The correct usage for the singular, however, is *ternus*.

Tertiaries • Members of associations, sometimes called "Third Orders," who "lead an apostolic life and strive for Christian perfection while living in the world and who share the spirit of some religious institute under the higher direction of that same institute" (Canon 303). Tertiaries are not religious, but they may be full-fledged members of a religious order, subject in their life of perfection to the superior general of the institute. The following religious institutes have Third Orders: Augustinians, Benedictines, Carmelites, Dominicans, Franciscans, Premonstratensians, Servites and Trinitarians.

Testament • From the Latin *testamentum*, a word used to translate the Greek *diatheke*, which means an agreement or last will. When *diatheke* is used in the Bible, it is often a synonym for "covenant." That is the sense in which "Old Testament" and "New Testament" are to be understood. The books of the Old Testament (the Torah, the Prophets and the Writings, according to their Jewish designation) give testimony to the covenant between God and Israel. The books of the New Testament (the Gospels, the Epistles, the Apocalypse of John) bear witness to the definitive covenant established in and through the person of Jesus Christ, the Son of God.

For further reading: G. E. Mendenhall, "Testament," *Interpreter's Dictionary of the Bible*, 4:575.

Tetragrammaton • A term of Greek origin, meaning literally, "four letters." It refers to the four consonants (YHWH) of God's proper name, Yahweh, disclosed by God to Moses out of the burning bush (Ex 3).

Thaumaturgus • This Greek term stands for "wonder-worker." It is a title conferred on some saints due to the number and magnitude of the miracles attributed to them. The one most known by this name is St. Gregory Thaumaturgus (also spelled Taumaturgus), A.D. 213-268. He is said to have moved objects around at command, to have dried up a lake and done other wonderful works. Other saints on whom this title has been conferred are Sts. Cosmas and Damian (d. c. 303); St. Achilles (330); St. Bessarion (450); St. Nicholas of Bari (350); St. Dimitrios (306); St. Anthony of Padua (1231); and St. Vincent Ferrer (1419).

Theodicy • The term widely used to designate that branch of philosophical theology concerned with the problem of evil. As the term itself suggests (derived from the Greek words for God [*theos*] and for right [*dik*]), theodicy concerns the vindication of the divine omnipotence and goodness in the face of the existence of physical and moral evils in the world God created and sustains. Although he was by no means the first thinker to address this problem, the philosopher G. W. Leibniz (1646-1716) is credited with coining the term "theodicy" to designate this aspect of the work of philosophical theology. (Cf. Evil.)

Theologian • A person who possesses formal training in theology, usually certified by the acquisition of a doctoral or licentiate degree from a recognized faculty or university. Although theologians ordinarily devote their professional lives to teaching, research and publication in one or another area of theological specialization, Catholic tradition has commonly expected them to have a grasp of the whole of the contents of the Faith and to be able to expound these contents in their inner intelligibility and coherence. Since theology arises out of faith as well as the impulse to understand, the theologian's vocation is both academic and ecclesial: the application of a rigorous and critical scientific methodology to the study of Christian doctrines must be combined with a lively faith, a strong communal commitment and a profound respect for the privileged role of the Magisterium in the articulation of the contents of revelation.

The term is also employed to refer to a seminary student aspiring to Holy Orders who is pursuing theological studies as part of his priestly formation. (Cf. Theology.)

Theological Notes • The degrees of certainty attaching to propositions of faith and theological opinions, along with the corresponding censures for their denial. The highest degree of certainty pertains to truths immediately revealed by God and to such truths as the Church certifies as contained in revelation by the ordinary (*fides catholica*) or extraordinary Magisterium (*de fide definita*). The denial of such a truth is called heresy. Next are truths proximate to the faith (*sententia fidei proxima*) which are regarded by theologians as truths of revelation but have not been officially defined as such by the Church. The denial of such a truth is called proximate heresy. Third in order of certainty is a truth that pertains to the Faith (*sententia ad fidem pertinens*) that is theologically certain because of its intrinsic connection to revelation but has not been defined by the Church. The denial of such a truth incurs the suspicion of heresy. Next is a doctrine, which in itself remains a matter of free opinion but which is generally accepted by theologians (*sententia communis*). The denial of such a doctrine is called erroneous, while the denial of a dogmatic fact is called a false proposition. Theological opinions of lesser grades of certainty are called probable, more probable, or well-founded (*sententia probabilis, probabilior, bene fundata*), while those in agreement with the consciousness of the Faith are called pious opinions and those not contrary to Faith but not well-warranted by it are called tolerated opinions. Censures of less seriousness pertain to propositions which can be described as follows: temerarious (one that deviates without reason from the general teaching); offensive to pious ears (one that contravenes religious feeling); badly expressed (*male sonans* — one that is open to being misconstrued by reason of lack of precision); captious (one that is intentionally ambiguous); scandalous (one that excites scandal).

Theological Virtues • The virtues of faith, hope and charity are the three theological virtues. Faith is a divinely infused virtue which enables us to assent with conviction to the truths of salvation revealed by God. Because it enables us to do this, we are obliged to make acts of faith and to foster the growth of faith in our lives through prayer and worship. Hope is the infused virtue that enables us to rely on God's grace and salvation to look forward to achieving eternal salvation and fulfillment in Him. Charity is the infused virtue which enables us to love God for His own sake and oneself and others for His sake as well. Acts of charity are necessary to attain salvation and, like acts of faith and hope, they are required for growth in the likeness of Christ. Growth in the theological virtues is the ultimate aim of Christian life, for their perfection opens the Christian fully to the movements of the saving grace of God.

Theology • Literally, the word "theology" means "science of God." In practice, it has come to designate the disciplined reflection upon the whole body of revealed and human knowledge in the light of God's self-described nature and purposes and under the guidance of faith in Him. Hence, theology has been aptly termed *fides quaerens intellectum*, "faith seeking understanding."

Theology has a rightful place among other disciplined intellectual inquiries, in that it turns its attention to the body of knowledge generated by Divine Revelation. Employing all the tools of other fields of inquiry (especially logic, hermeneutics, history, philosophical analysis), theology seeks to discern and exhibit the inner intelligibility of revelation and its connection with other areas of knowledge and experience. Traditionally, mastery of sound biblical exegesis and of the history of doctrine has been presupposed to the mature practice of theology. But with the rapid expansion of knowledge in exegesis and doctrinal history, there have emerged the scholarly specializations of biblical theology and historical theology alongside systematic and dogmatic theology.

Concentration on particular areas of Christian doctrines gives rise to further specialties such as moral theology, Christology, ecclesiology, sacramentology, liturgics, and so on. The potential fragmentation of theology into these subfields can be avoided if the orientation of all theological inquiry toward the wisdom of God is systematically retained and continually underlined. The results of theological inquiry and reflection are submitted in faith, with the understanding that they are subject to appraisal by those in the community who are authorized to preserve and transmit the authentic apostolic tradition of the Christian community. In this way, theologians and the Magisterium collaborate in the study and proclamation of Divine Revelation.

Theophany • From the Greek word *theophaneia*, meaning the manifestation of God. Properly speaking, theophany refers either to an actual appearance of God in His glory, or to the medium in which God appears. Thus, in the first sense, God appeared to Moses on Mt. Sinai (Ex 19:1-25); Christ appeared in His glory in the Transfiguration (Mt 17:1-9). In the second sense, various forces of nature are said to be the vehicles of God's manifestation (e.g., storms, fire and wind), as are human likenesses and angelic apparitions. At the end of the world, a final theophany is promised in the Second Coming of Christ (Rv 21:22).

It is also the word of choice in the Eastern Churches for the feast of the Lord's Baptism, commemorated on January 6 (when the Western Church celebrates the Epiphany to the Magi).

For further reading: Theodore Hiebert, "Theophany in the Old Testament," *Anchor Bible Dictionary*, 6:505-511.

Theotokion • A Troparion in which the Mother of God is exalted or called upon in the Byzantine Liturgy.

Theotokos • The Mother of God, the principal title of the Virgin Mary in the Oriental Church. Its use in liturgical prayer is very prominent. The title can be traced at least as far back as the third century and was first sanctioned at the Council of Ephesus (A.D. 431). The Latin term *Deipara* closely approximates the original Greek ("Birth-giver of God").

Thessalonians, First and Second Epistles to the • New Testament epistles written to the Church at Thessalonica, a major city of Macedonia. Thessalonica was founded c. 316 B.C. and named after a half-sister of Alexander the Great by one of his generals who was her husband. Through the apostolic preaching of St. Paul, first-century A.D. Thessalonica became home to a church that included both Jewish and Gentile Christians.

Written by St. Paul in A.D. 50, perhaps only a few months after his departure from Thessalonica, 1 Thessalonians is the earliest of the New Testament epistles. It represents Paul's first effort to adapt the form of the Greco-Roman letter to his own apostolic purposes. By means of this letter, Paul maintained contact with the Christian community he founded in Thessalonica and addressed their concerns.

Some evidence of Paul's initial contact with the Thessalonians is found in the stylized account of Acts 17:1-9, according to which Paul preached in the synagogue at Thessalonica over the course of three weeks

(three sabbaths), during his second missionary journey, while a guest at the house of Jason. The success of Paul's preaching caused jealousy and rioting, so that Paul and his co-worker Silas were forced to flee to Beroea. From Beroea, Paul moved on to Athens and then to Corinth, where Silas and Timothy rejoined him. From Athens, Paul sent Timothy to Thessalonica to strengthen and encourage the Christian community there (1 Thes 3:1-3). Timothy's report upon rejoining Paul provided the occasion for Paul's writing to the Thessalonians and suggested the concerns which are addressed in the letter.

First (or 1) Thessalonians can be outlined as follows:

1. Salutation: 1:1
2. Thanksgiving: 1:2-10
3. Body of the Letter: 2:1—5:11
    a) Paul's initial ministry among the Thessalonians: 2:1-12
    b) Paul's further involvement with the Thessalonians: 3:1-13
    c) Exhortations: 4:1-12
        i. Concerning sexual conduct: 4:1-8
        ii. Concerning charity: 4:9-12
    d) Eschatology: 4:13—5:11
        i. Christian death: 4:13-18
        ii. The day of the Lord: 5:1-11
4. Concluding Exhortations: 5:12-22
    a) Order and authority in the community: 5:12-13
    b) A series of brief exhortations: 5:14-22
5. Closing: 5:23-28
    a) Closing prayer: 5:23-25
    b) Final greeting: 5:26-28

Doctrinally, the eschatological teaching of 1 Thessalonians is especially significant, for it is the earliest extant articulation of the salvific meaning of Christ's death, resurrection and return in glory. It is likely that the material presented in 1 Thessalonians 4:13—5:11 responds to Thessalonian Christians' concerns conveyed to Timothy and reported to Paul. The deaths of some community members produced anxiety among the believers, and Paul deals with this by writing about the significance of Jesus' death and resurrection. In hopeful terms Paul could refer to dead Christians as "those who have fallen asleep," so that "since we believe that Jesus died and rose again, even so, through Jesus, God will bring with him those who have fallen asleep" (1 Thes 4:14).

It is important to recognize that 1 Thessalonians 4:13—5:11 does not provide a literal account of the events which are to take place at the end of time. Paul uses the expressive symbolism of apocalyptic imagery to console the Thessalonians in their anxiety about the imminence of the day of the Lord. Because the day of the Lord is to be the *parousia*, the glorious return of the crucified and risen Jesus, it is the fulfillment of Christian hope. The Thessalonians' anxiety "concerning times and seasons" regarding the coming of the day of the Lord was to yield to an attitude of constant vigilance animated by faith, hope and love, "For God has not destined us for wrath, but to obtain salvation through our Lord Jesus Christ" (1 Thes 5:9).

The faith, hope and love which characterize the Thessalonians' eschatological vigilance are also to animate the day-to-day conduct of the members of the Church. Besides the teaching on eschatology found in 1 Thessalonians, the letter provides an exhortation on the conduct of Christian life in the community. It is the eschatological hope of Christians which sets the standards for their daily living in faith and love. Thus, Paul's instructions to the community regard the holiness that is to characterize sexual morality (1 Thes 4:3-8) and the mutual charity members of the community are to observe toward one another (1 Thes 4:9-12). Likewise, Paul's instructions inviting the

Thessalonians to respect those in authority over the Church (1 Thes 5:12-13) and the series of brief exhortations in 1 Thessalonians 5:14-22, aim at giving shape to the eschatological vigilance according to which the community is to live.

Remarkable similarities in structure, vocabulary and themes exist between 1 Thessalonians and 2 Thessalonians.

Second (or 2) Thessalonians can be outlined as follows:

1. Salutation: 1:1-2
2. Thanksgiving: 2:3-12
3. Body of the Letter: 2:1-17: Warning against misinformation concerning the day of the Lord
4. Concluding exhortations: 3:1-16
   a) Request for prayers: 3:1-5
   b) Against disorder in the community: 3:6-16
5. Closing: 3:17-18

This second letter to the same community is hard to date and even harder to locate in terms of context and situation. Similarities aside, 2 Thessalonians takes on a very different tone from 1 Thessalonians almost from the very beginning, suggesting that the situation faced by the community underwent considerable change.

While the thanksgiving of 1 Thessalonians cites with joyful recollection the Thessalonians' conversion as a result of Paul's initial preaching (1 Thes 1:9), the thanksgiving of 2 Thessalonians offers words of encouragement to a community undergoing persecution and suffering.

The main concern of 2 Thessalonians is to correct misinformation concerning "the day of the Lord" which disturbed the community and threatened its faith. The Thessalonians are warned in 2 Thessalonians 2:1-17 "not to be shaken out of your minds suddenly, or to be alarmed either by a 'spirit,' or by an oral statement, or by a letter allegedly from us to the effect that the day of the Lord is at hand" (2 Thes 2:2). Using apocalyptic imagery that remains quite obscure, the letter invites its readers to maintain steadfast confidence that Christ will defeat "the mystery of lawlessness" (2 Thes 2:7) that is already at work in the world.

Second Thessalonians 2:2 points out the possible sources of the confusions which troubled the community. These are "a spirit," some ecstatic pseudo-charismatic utterance; "an oral statement," a sermon or discourse of some sort; or "a letter allegedly from us," a forgery. Each of these three is identified as a possible source of the information that the day of the Lord had already arrived. To counteract this, the community is urged to "stand firm and hold fast to the traditions that you were taught, either by an oral statement or by a letter from us."

Second Thessalonians 3:17 guarantees the reliability of this letter as a source of true teaching for the community: "I, Paul, write this greeting with my own hand. This is the mark in every letter of mine; it is the way I write." Similar personal notes appended to letters are found in 1 Corinthians 16:21 and Galatians 6:11, reflecting the longstanding practice of dictating correspondence to a scribe or secretary and then adding an autograph closing. The emphatic way in which 2 Thessalonians 3:17 is phrased serves as protection against the sort of forgery mentioned in 2 Thessalonians 2:2.

In recent times, some scholars have voiced the suggestion that Paul himself was not the actual author of 2 Thessalonians, but that the letter is a pseudepigraphical document written authoritatively in Paul's name to preserve authentic apostolic teaching and to correct misconceptions and misperceptions which had arisen; 2 Thessalonians 2:15 communicates this concern for authentic tradition. Arguments in favor of considering 2 Thessalonians pseudepigraphical include its close literary relationship with 1 Thessalonians, the contrast between the tone and content of the eschatological material in 1 Thessalonians 4:13—5:11 and 2 Thessalonians 2:1-17, and the use of vocabulary in 2 Thessalonians which is not characteristic of Paul's other letters. The contrasting arguments in favor of the Pauline authenticity of 2 Thessalonians stress the continuity of consistent development from 1 Thessalonians to 2 Thessalonians, and that the differences in tone and content can be explained in terms of the changing circumstances which gave rise to the need for clarification and development.

For further reading: Raymond F. Collins, "The First Letter to the Thessalonians," *New Jerome Biblical Commentary*, 772-779; Charles Homer Giblin, S.J., "The Second Letter to the Thessalonians," *New Jerome Biblical Commentary*, 871-875; Edgar M. Krentz, "Thessalonians, First and Second Epistles to the," *Anchor Bible Dictionary*, 6:515-523.

Thomas, Gospel of • The so-called Gospel of Thomas was discovered in 1945 as part of the twelve-volume Gnostic library of papyri found near the town of Nag Hammadi in upper Egypt. Like the other Nag Hammadi texts, the extant version of the Gospel of Thomas is a translation into Coptic of a Greek original. Fragments of the original Greek text, only identified as part of the Gospel of Thomas subsequent to the discovery of the Nag Hammadi collection, are found in Oxyrhynchus papyri 1, 654 and 655.

Although it is difficult to provide a precise date and location, scholars have suggested that the Gospel of Thomas was written no later than A.D. 140, and that it may have been written in Syria, since the Syrian Church preserved traditions concerning Judas Thomas, to whom they referred as "the brother of Jesus."

The Gospel of Thomas begins by claiming, "These are the secret sayings which the living Jesus spoke and which Didymos Judas Thomas wrote down." "Didymos" and "Thomas" both mean "twin." Not a gospel according to the literary genre of the four canonical gospels, the Gospel of Thomas is a collection of one hundred fourteen sayings of Jesus, many of which have parallels in the Synoptic Gospels and in John. The Gospel of Thomas can be likened to "Q," the hypothetical sayings source on which both Matthew and Luke may depend.

Most of the sayings are introduced by the phrase, "Jesus said." While the arrangement of the one hundred fourteen sayings does not appear to follow any clear plan, they can be classified according to the following broad categories, presented below with an example of each:

Parables: "The disciples said to Jesus, 'Tell us what the kingdom of heaven is like.' He said to them, 'It is like a mustard seed. It is the smallest of all seeds. But when it falls on tilled soil, it produces a great plant and becomes a shelter for birds of the sky' " (Saying 20).

Proverbs: "Jesus said, 'If a blind man leads a blind man, they will both fall into a pit' " (Saying 34).

Prophecies (Eschatological sayings): "Jesus said, 'Two will rest on a bed; the one will die, and the other will live' " (Saying 61).

Rules for Disciples: "The disciples said to Jesus, 'We know that You will depart from us. Who is to be our leader?' Jesus said to them, 'Wherever you are, you are to go to James the righteous, for whose sake heaven and earth came into being' " (Saying 12).

With its emphasis on the possession of knowledge which leads to salvation, the Gospel of Thomas would receive a sympathetic hearing in Gnostic circles. According to Saying 1, "Whoever finds the interpretation of these sayings will not experience death." Even so, the discovery of the Gospel of Thomas among Gnostic texts does not necessarily lead to the conclusion that this text itself is Gnostic. It may be seen to reflect themes and concerns from the Jewish wisdom traditions.

For further reading: Ron Cameron, "Thomas, Gospel of," *Anchor Bible Dictionary*, 6:535-540.

Thomism • A system consisting particularly of philosophical positions, but also comprising theological theses, drawn from and dependent upon the works of St. Thomas Aquinas (1225-1274) and his principal commentators. Chief among the latter were: Joannes Capreolus (1380-1444), Thomas Cajetan (1469-1534), and John of St. Thomas (1589-1644).

The synthesis achieved by Aquinas has had an immense influence on Catholic thought. In the century after his death, the chief Thomists were to be found among his fellow Dominican friars, and this has remained generally true throughout history. A tremendous flowering of Thomistic thought — often called "second Thomism" — occurred in the sixteenth century and was centered among the Dominicans and Jesuits of the University of Salamanca in Spain. Among the widely acknowledged accomplishments of this group of thinkers was the founding of the field of international law, largely as a response to the cruel treatment of the Amerindians by the Spanish conquistadors.

In the nineteenth century and continuing into the twentieth, a movement known as "neo-Thomism" emerged as a powerful force in the renewal of Catholic thought and education in response to the challenges posed by modernity. The movement was inspired by Pope Leo XIII (through *Aeterni Patris* in 1879) and encouraged by Pope St. Pius X (through his insistence that Thomism provide the basis for Catholic seminary education). Neo-Thomism produced a tremendous outpouring of historical and speculative work, and contributed to a revival of interest in other major figures of medieval scholastic thought like St. Bonaventure and St. Albert the Great. Many of the greatest Catholic thinkers of the twentieth century — Etienne Gilson, Jacques Maritain, Karl Rahner, and Pope John Paul II among them — either were Thomists or were profoundly influenced by Aquinas's thought.

Characteristic elements of Thomism in its varied historical embodiments are an affirmation of the integrity and interrelation of the realms of faith and reason, a marked confidence in the ability of the mind to determine the truth and in the effectiveness of sound reasoning and argumentation in philosophy and theology, and an emphasis on the primacy of grace in all phases of justification and salvation. Thomists commonly insist on the real distinction between essence and existence in the created order, on the substantial unity of the body and soul in human beings, on the importance of bodiliness as an essential element of human existence, on the centrality of virtue and grace in moral life, and on the possibility of arguing for the existence of God on the basis of starting points in experience. Perhaps the most significant feature of Thomism lies in its serene projection of an integral vision of philosophy and theology leading the human mind to contemplate the truth of God Himself.

Thomism, Transcendental • A twentieth-century philosophical movement which attempts to develop philosophical themes from Thomas Aquinas into a philosophy which meets the "transcendental" demand of modern philosophers — especially Kant — for self-critical awareness of the limited character of human intellect. Kant demanded that philosophers refrain from defining reality until they had realized self-critically what he argued in his *Critique of Pure Reason*: that the human mind cannot possibly know anything determinate about reality in itself. According to Kant's philosophy, many tenets of Catholic Faith exceed what humans can think about meaningfully.

Some Catholic thinkers since Kant have totally repudiated his claim that metaphysics (philosophy of being) be based in a "critical" account of knowledge. Unlike such thinkers, transcendental Thomists do not reject Kant's claim without an examination. They attempt to show that Kant's own philosophy contains uncritical and self-defeating claims and that his basic philosophical question rests on faulty philosophical assumptions. They make these points in the course of their attempt to develop a constructive and self-critical account of human knowing which meets the philosophically defensible portion of Kant's basic demand. They show that a proper understanding of human knowing does allow us meaningfully to raise definite questions about beings themselves and God. They develop a metaphysical understanding of being which is generally regarded as a development of St. Thomas Aquinas's thought.

The Jesuit Joseph Maréchal (as influenced by Maurice Blondel and Pierre Rousselot) is usually regarded as the founder of the transcendental development of Thomism. The late Karl Rahner (perhaps the single most important theologian during the Second Vatican Council), Emerich Coreth and Bernard Lonergan are the foremost transcendental Thomists in the second half of the twentieth century.

Throne • The seat of the bishop, behind the Holy Table, or main altar, in a cathedral church of the Eastern Churches.

Thurible • A metal vessel for the ceremonial burning of incense, also known as a censer. It is usually suspended on chains, so that it can be swung while incensing at Mass, Divine Office or Benediction of the Blessed Sacrament.

Tiara • The crown or ceremonial headdress proper to the Supreme Pontiff of the Catholic Church. Shaped much like a beehive, it is made of silver cloth (sometimes gold) with three golden crowns ornamented with precious stones. A small cross sits on its highest point. The three crowns or diadems give the tiara its other name, *triregnum* or "threefold rule." The first coronet may be taken to symbolize the Vicar of Christ's universal episcopate, the second his supremacy of jurisdiction and the third his temporal influence.

The tiara traces its origin, like the mitre, to the ancient *phrygium*, which was given to the Popes as a privilege by Constantine and later given to other bishops. However, as with the mitre, it owes its ultimate origin to the Old Testament priesthood. It simply developed in a different direction because of the universal and supreme authority conferred by Christ on Peter and his successors. Though it was in use centuries before, the word "tiara" first appears in official documents from around the year 1100 in the *Liber Pontificalis* of Pope Paschal II. By the middle of the fourteenth century, it had its present form with the

Thurible

three coronets (Boniface VIII is said to have added the second one, and Benedict XII the third one).

Though the tiara at present has fallen into disuse (Paul VI stopped wearing it after Vatican II, and Popes John Paul I and John Paul II were never even crowned with it), any future Pope is free to be crowned with it and wear it if he should so choose. It was never a liturgical vestment and was worn to and from Mass, during the proclamation of a dogma or a canonization and on other solemn occasions.

Time • According to Aristotle, time is defined as "the measure of change," involving the system of relationships which change entails, such as past, present and future. He builds upon Plato's concept by maintaining that numeration is essential to time, and considers whether time could exist without the soul, since there cannot be anything to count unless there is someone to count it. He says also that some things are eternal, in the sense of not being in time, such as numbers.

St. Augustine (A.D. 354-430) is perhaps the first theologian and philosopher to attempt to discuss the concept of time in Christian terms. He parts company with the Greek view that creation out of nothing is impossible, and accepts the truth of Genesis, which says that God did create substance *ex nihilo*. He asserts that time came into being when the world was created, and that God is eternal (in the sense of being timeless). God's eternity is exempt from the relation of time, and all time is present to Him at once. This harmonizes with that part of the Greek concept which speaks of time as the measure of change: God is unchangeable and is therefore outside of time; the creation is changing and is therefore measured by time. St. Augustine puts forth the theory that neither past nor future, but only the present, really *is*; the present is only a moment, and time can be measured only while it is passing. The past must be identified with memory and the future with expectation, and memory and expectation are both present facts. "My soul yearns to know this most entangled enigma," he writes in his *Confessions*, and goes on to say, "I confess to Thee, O Lord, that I am as yet ignorant what time is." His solution, unsatisfactory even to him, is that time is subjective and in the human mind, which "expects, considers, and remembers." His conclusion is that there can be no time without a created being, and that to speak of time before the creation is meaningless.

Much of St. Augustine's philosophy about time was accepted by St. Thomas Aquinas (1225-1274) and incorporated into his system of thought. In his letter to Abbot Bernard of Monte Cassino, he writes, "Because we are subject to mutation and time, in which there is a before and after, we know events successively — we remember the past, see the present, and foretell the future. But God, who is immune from all change . . . is beyond the passage of time, nor is there found in him past or future, for everything is present before him."

Time, Computation of • Since the law often establishes periods of time with respect to canonical processes, terms of office, fulfillment of obligations and the like, it is necessary also to have general norms on how time is calculated, in order to avoid confusion and doubt.

Continuous time is understood to be that which is not subject to interruption. The day on which a specific computation of time begins is not counted in the total time; however, the last day of the period is counted in the total.

Available or useful time is an important concept, especially with regard to time limits set in the procedural law of the Church. Available time is that time which a person has to exercise or pursue a right. Available time does not begin until the person is aware of the situation and does not run when he or she is unable to act. Thus if a person has fifteen days to appeal a decision, the computation of this period begins on the day the person becomes aware of the right to appeal. Sundays and holidays are not computed in the total period, because it is presumed that the person is unable to communicate with the proper authorities on those days (Canons 200-203).

Timothy, First Epistle to • Paul's First Letter to Timothy (1 Tm) belongs with 2 Timothy and Titus. They are called the "Pastoral Letters" (since the mid-1700s) because they are all addressed to individual elders and not to local churches or the universal Church; in addition, their pastoral nature is evident in the relationship between doctrine and life, which leads to establishing Church practice and governance. In order to reconstruct the purpose of each letter, we shall consider these letters together and draw out data accordingly. What follows is the setting inferred from evidence internal to the letters themselves. Paul was in Crete and left Titus there, apparently departing for Ephesus (Ti 1:5). Paul then traveled to Macedonia and wrote 1 Timothy (1 Tm 1:3), then on to Nicopolis where he remained during the winter season (Ti 3:12). He then went to Rome, presumably with Titus (Ti

St. Timothy
(twelfth-century window)

(1:1-20) and to instruct Timothy about public worship (2:1-7), women's roles (2:8-15) and the selection of ministers (3:1-16). The letter develops exhortations and encouragements (4:1-16) and outlines pastoral duties (5:1—6:2), with renunciation as a pastoral guide (6:3-10). The letter closes with a reminder to Timothy of his call (6:11-16) and other concerns (6:17-21).

Contents:

A. Address and Greetings: 1:1-2
B. Introduction to the Key Themes: 1:3-20
C. Worship in Public and Ministers: 2:1—3:13
D. Order for God's Household: 3:14-16
E. Affirming the Goodness of God's Creation: 4:1-10
F. Exhortation to Govern and Teach: 4:11-16
G. Church Order Outlined: 5:1—6:2
H. Summary and Conclusions: 6:3-21

Authorship and Date: Since the late eighteenth or early nineteenth century some scholars have questioned Pauline authorship due to the letter's heavy style, the apparent insertion of hymnic and confessional passages uncharacteristic of Paul's style in the undisputed letters (e.g., 1 Tm 3:16; 2 Tm 2:11-13), the listing of lengthy Church rules and the clear guidelines concerning the appointment of ministers. The evidence, however, can be interpreted in ways supportive of Pauline authorship. The debate continues. If Paul actually wrote this letter, then it can be dated in the early A.D. 60s. If the letter was written after Paul's death, we could date this letter c. 90, since the persecutions mentioned may have occurred under Emperor Domitian (c. 90).

For further reading: Jerome D. Quinn, "Timothy and Titus, Epistles to," *Anchor Bible Dictionary*, 6:560-571; Robert A. Wild, S.J., "The Pastoral Letters," *New Jerome Biblical Commentary*, 891-902.

3:12; 2 Tm 4:10), where others joined him (2 Tm 4:10-12), perhaps during his imprisonment and trial (2 Tm 4:16-18). Believers in Ephesus rejected Paul (2 Tm 1:15), except for one named Onesiphorus who joined Paul in Rome (2 Tm 1:16-17). Paul sent Tychicus (who also joined Paul in Rome) back to Ephesus (2 Tm 4:12). The pastorals, then, are written from Paul's missionary activity and his final two years on earth, imprisoned in Rome. Paul writes to Timothy who has responsibilities over the Churches in Macedonia and Titus over the Church at Corinth.

Major Themes: Paul wishes to warn Timothy of false teachers who would teach false doctrines regarding the authentic role of the Old Testament law in Christianity

Timothy, Second Epistle to • *Major Themes:* In Paul's First Letter to Timothy, Paul outlines the problems encountered in certain false teachings; he continues this line of thought in 2 Timothy. Suffering, endurance, steadfastness, the charism of strength and love all work to sustain the believer (1:6—2:13). True teaching should and can be distinguished from heretical dogma (2:14-26). Pastoral directives for living in "these last days" are timely helps for remaining faithful to what Paul taught — the Gospel (3:1-17). (For background and introductory comments, cf. First Epistle to Timothy.)

Contents:

A. Address and Greetings: 1:1-2

B. Introduction of Key Themes: 1:3-7

C. Suffering and Those Chosen by God: 1:8—2:26

D. Heresy, Prophecy and Tradition: 3:1—4:5

E. Conclusions and Final Greeting: 4:6-22.

Authorship and Date: See 1 Timothy for a brief outline of objections to Pauline authorship for the Pastoral Epistles. This document can be dated within one year after the writing of 1 Timothy (either c. A.D. 60s or 90s).

For further reading: Jerome D. Quinn, "Timothy and Titus, Epistles to," *Anchor Bible Dictionary*, 6:560-571; Robert A. Wild, S.J., "The Pastoral Letters," *New Jerome Biblical Commentary*, 891-902.

Tithe • A percentage of one's income, usually ten percent, given as an offering to God. Israelite law (Lv 27:30) prescribed that a tenth of all produce, animals and plants be designated for the Lord God. Similarly, in Christian usage, a tithe is usually a tenth of one's gross income given to a church by a parishioner for the fiscal support and maintenance of that church and its life, as well as to other works of religion.

For further reading: J. Christian Wilson, "Tithe," *Anchor Bible Dictionary*, 6:578-580.

Titulus • In classical times, titulus referred to an inscription which might denote a boundary line or indicate the ownership of a particular building. Various homes in Rome used for Christian worship in the early centuries were indicated by the titulus. Cardinals' churches in Rome are today designated by this term, as, for example, "Cardinal of the title of Sant Onofrio." This term is also applied to the sign placed on the cross above Our Lord which said in Latin, Greek and Hebrew, "Jesus of Nazareth, King of the Jews."

Titus, Epistle to • Paul wished to solidify the life of the Christian community in Crete and so focused on opposing the false teachers who were perverting the Gospel he brought (1 Tm 1:4-7). He wrote this letter to address the problems. (For background and introductory comments, cf. First Epistle to Timothy.)

Major Themes: The false teachers advocate circumcision (Ti 1:10) and "Jewish myths" (1:14). Members of the Church are encouraged in how to live with one another (2:1-10); finally, general ethical instructions are drawn from the reality of baptized Christianity and legitimate religious practices (2:11—3:15).

Contents:

A. Address and Greeting: 1:1-4

B. The Character of the Leader: 1:5-9

C. False and True Teachers and Teachings: 1:10—3:8

D. Moral Exhortations: 3:9-11

E. Personal News and Closing: 3:12-15

Authorship and Date: (Cf. this section in the entry on First Epistle to Timothy for argument regarding authorship and date.)

For further reading: John Gillman, "Titus," *Anchor Bible Dictionary*, 6:581-582; Jerome D. Quinn, "Timothy and Titus, Epistles to,"

Anchor Bible Dictionary, 6:560-571; Jerome D. Quinn, *The Letter to Titus*, Anchor Bible 35 (Doubleday, 1990).

Tobit, Book of • Sometimes this book is called Tobias. Probably written between the third and first centuries B.C., it exists in the ancient Greek, Latin, Aramaic and Syriac manuscripts. Tobit is a story of the tribulations of life in the Diaspora (non-Palestinian areas inhabited by Jews) with the message that God will protect and heal those who are pious and compassionate. While Tobit is written in the form of a narrative, it is questionable whether it can be historical, except perhaps the names of some of the characters. The historical situation of Tobit corresponds to nothing that is known of the period in which the story is placed.

The angelology of Tobit is considerably advanced beyond the angelology of older books of the Old Testament. It is accepted in the canon of the Catholic Church but does not appear in Jewish and Protestant canons.

For further reading: Carey A. Moore, "Tobit, Book of," *Anchor Bible Dictionary*, 6:585-594; Irene Nowell, O.S.B., Toni Craven and Demetrius Dumm, O.S.B., "Tobit, Esther, Judith," *New Jerome Biblical Commentary*, 568-571.

Tones • A system of eight standard melodies with variations used in plain chant in the Eastern Churches sung in continuous cycle throughout the liturgical year.

Tonsure • Custom of shaving part (or all) of the hair of the head, derived from monastic observance originating in the fourth and fifth centuries and formerly observed by all clerics until the revision of the minor orders after Vatican II. The custom of shaving the whole head, or leaving an outside ring of hair on the scalp (representing a crown of thorns) became common for clerics in the sixth and seventh centuries. Through the Middle Ages, the style of tonsure was different for religious clergy (more obvious) than it was for secular clergy (often only a small space on the crown of the head). The rite of tonsure signified one's entrance into the clerical state.

The customary rite after Trent was for the bishop to cut some hair at five places (sometimes deliberately in the form of a cross) and to invest the candidate with the surplice. In 1972 Pope Paul VI officially suppressed tonsure. The *motu proprio Ministeria quaedam*, on first tonsure, minor orders and the subdiaconate, states that "first tonsure is no longer conferred; entrance into the clerical state is joined to the diaconate."

The *motu proprio Ad pascendum*, laying down norms regarding the Order of Diaconate, states: "Since entrance into the clerical state is deferred until diaconate, there no longer exists the rite of first tonsure, by which a layman used to become a cleric. But a new rite is introduced [termed 'Candidacy'] by which one who aspires to ordination as a deacon or presbyter publicly manifests his will to offer himself to God and the Church, so that he may exercise a sacred order."

Torah • A word from a Hebrew root meaning "to instruct." By a natural evolution of meaning, it came to be used of the written collection of the law, that is, the Pentateuch, the first five books of the Hebrew Scriptures.

For further reading: Richard Elliott Freedman, "Torah (Pentateuch)," *Anchor Bible Dictionary*, 6:605-622.

Totalitarianism • A theory of government in which the state claims complete control of the life and conduct of its citizens. It is contrary to Catholic teaching, not only because of the official atheism and restricted religious practice usually associated with totalitarianism, but also because it violates the rights of individuals and families to pursue their own good ends within the general principle of seeking the good of society.

Totemism • A phenomenon that is partly religious, medicinal and magical, found among primitive peoples where members believe themselves to be associated with a special species of plant or animal. Sometimes the totem is held to be sacred or to have special powers and is therefore untouchable, except at tribal feasts. But at other times, the totemic object is purely secular. Some have speculated that totemism is found in all religions in their primitive roots and have even asserted that the Israelites had totemic origins. Because Leah means "wild cow" and Rachel means "ewe," this has been suggested, but there is too little evidence to confirm this view.

Toties Quoties • Literally "as often as," this Latin expression meant that particular plenary indulgences could be gained as often as the necessary conditions were fulfilled. According to present Church law, a plenary indulgence can be gained only once a day.

Tower of Babel: See Babel, Tower of

Tract • The chant sung in the former liturgy in place of the Alleluia on penitential days. Originally it was the psalm sung after the second reading, but when this reading was suppressed, it took the place of the Alleluia during Lent. It is no longer used in the current liturgy, except occasionally at Latin Mass before the Gospel during Lent.

A tract is also a pamphlet on a religious topic. Most famous were those of the Anglicans of the Oxford Movement of the nineteenth century, whose tracts describing Anglican belief with a very Catholic interpretation earned the authors the name Tractarians, and brought many into the Church, most notably John Henry Newman.

Tradition • The word comes from the Latin meaning "handing over." In the religious sense, it is the teachings and practices handed down, whether in oral or written form, separately from but not independently of Scripture. Tradition is divided into two areas: (1) Scripture, the essential doctrines of the Church, the major writings and teachings of the Fathers, the liturgical life of the Church, and the living and lived faith of the whole Church down through the centuries; (2) customs, institutions, practices which express the Christian Faith.

The Council of Trent (1546) affirmed both the Bible and Tradition as divine sources of Christian doctrine. Vatican II states, "It is clear . . . that, in the supremely wise arrangement of God, sacred Tradition, sacred Scripture and the Magisterium of the Church are so connected and associated that one of them cannot stand without the others. Working together, each in its own way under the action of the one Holy Spirit, they all contribute effectively to the salvation of souls" (DV 10).

Traditionalism • Largely a nineteenth-century phenomenon, traditionalism held that metaphysical and ethical truth can be known only by Divine Revelation. According to important proponents of this theological and philosophical position — notably Louis de Bonald (1754-1840) and Félicité de Lamennais (1782-1854) — knowledge of these basic truths was originally imprinted on the human mind by God and subsequently transmitted in linguistic form. Thus, tradition and faith play an indispensable role in the transmission not only of supernatural truths but also of natural truths (hence the tag "traditionalism").

This view ran counter to traditional Catholic doctrine, which construed Scripture (especially such important passages as Wis 13:1-9 and Rom 1:19-21) as teaching that certain so-called "natural" truths could be known by the proper exercise of reason. But traditionalists denied that unaided intellectual inquiry could come to a knowledge of the existence of God, the immortality of the soul, the natural moral law and the concept of being.

In part, traditionalists can be understood as reacting to the prevailing rationalism of their times and countering it with a marked, but finally un-Catholic, pessimism about human nature and its reasoning capacities. Traditionalist positions were repeatedly repudiated by local Church authorities (especially in France) and by the Holy See throughout the nineteenth century. Partly in response to traditional views, Vatican Council I in its Constitution on Divine Revelation, entitled *Dei Filius*, laid out the proper Catholic understanding of the relation between reason and revelation.

Traditores • From the Latin *tradere* (to hand over or betray), *traditores* (literally, in this context, "traitors") was the technical term first applied at the Council of Arles (A.D. 314) for those priests and other clerics who willingly surrendered sacred vessels and biblical and liturgical texts over to the pagan authorities who threatened persecution for noncompliance.

Traducianism • The erroneous teaching of the fifth century which held that individual human souls originated by derivation from the souls of their parents, in a way analogous to the generation of individual bodies. The heretical proponents of traducianism maintained that God does, in fact, create individual souls, but with reliance on the parents' souls which provide the matter for this divine activity, just as the bodies of the parents provide the matter for the divine creation of the body of their offspring. Heresy enters with the denial of God's creation of the soul *ex nihilo*, whereby His divine activity presupposes no prior object upon which He works.

Both Tertullian and St. Augustine at times subscribed to theories of traducianism, although ultimately St. Augustine, judging that Scripture does not give an adequate answer to the questions posed by traducianism, refused to endorse the traducianist theory of creation. Pope Anastasius (d. A.D. 498) condemned traducianism as a heresy, while St. Gregory the Great (d. 604) pronounced the question unresolved.

Training of Priests: See **Optatam Totius**

Transcendence • From the Latin *transcendere*, it literally means to go beyond or to surpass. It describes the relationship between two things when one is superior and surpasses the other.

All living things, with their power to grow and reproduce, transcend the nonliving. Man transcends other animals by his power to know and love. The act of knowing allows man, in a sense, to transcend himself.

The most important sense of transcendence is how it describes God as surpassing the universe. In the Scriptures, God reveals Himself as the Creator of the universe and thus in no way dependent upon it. This revelation brought a new insight to the Greek world, which had always conceived the gods, while above us, as part of the universe. Thus the universe was always to be accepted as a given because there was no God Who stood apart from the universe to create it. The truth of God's transcendence must be understood along with His immanence, His utter closeness to us.

Transfiguration • According to the accounts in the first three Gospels (Mt 17:1-13; Mk 9:2-13; Lk 9:28-36), the Apostles Peter, James and John witnessed an unveiling of the divine glory of Christ, and the appearance with Him of Moses and Elijah. This event has come to be called the "Transfiguration" on the basis of the scriptural report, "He was transfigured before them." According to Tradition, the Transfiguration occurred on Mt. Tabor, but some believe it may have taken place on Mt. Hermon or even the Mount of Olives.

Various reasons for the Transfiguration have been offered by the Fathers of the Church and subsequent theologians. The most significant are: (1) that Christ wanted to bolster the faith of the Apostles prior to His crucifixion and death, so they would recognize that, just as His divine glory is hidden beneath His human appearance, so too a real victory would be concealed in the apparent defeat of the cross; (2) that the disciples would know that Christ is truly divine, with Moses and Elijah bearing witness to Him, and the voice of God speaking from the cloud; (3) that all Christians would learn to hope for their own glory, as they are being transformed by Christ's grace.

Transitional Deacon: See Deacon, Transitional

Transubstantiation • The "change of substance" of bread into the Body of Christ and wine into the Blood of Christ at the Consecration of the Mass. Although this fundamental doctrine of the Catholic Church was held by the faithful since apostolic days, the term "transubstantiation" was adopted by the Fourth Lateran Council in 1215, to describe the Eucharistic mystery. This was reinforced by the Council of Trent (1545-1563), which spoke of "a wonderful and singular conversion" of the Eucharistic elements.

Only a validly ordained priest can confect the Eucharist. Because of the reality of transubstantiation, reference to the Eucharistic Species as "bread and wine" is wrong. They are properly called the Body and Blood of Christ.

Tree of Jesse • This expression is based on the messianic prophecy of Isaiah, "There shall come forth a shoot from the stump of Jesse, and a branch shall grow out of his roots" (Is 11:1). The family tree of Jesus Christ is called the Tree of Jesse since it traces His lineage to Jesse, father of King David (cf. 1 Sm 16:18-22), thereby establishing Christ as the proper fulfillment of messianic prophecy (2 Sm 7). In medieval art and in the stained-glass depictions of the Jesse-Window, the various biblical ancestors of the Lord are frequently shown seated on the branches of the tree, while Jesse forms the very roots and Jesus is seated with Mary on the highest branches.

During the season of Advent, the antiphon for Evening Prayer of the Liturgy of the Hours on December 19, one of the "O Antiphons," invokes Christ: "O Flower of Jesse's stem, you have been raised up as a sign for all peoples; kings stand silent in your presence; the nations bow down in worship before you. Come, let nothing keep you from coming to our aid."

Trent, Council of • The nineteenth ecumenical council of the Catholic Church was summoned by Pope Paul III several times between 1537 and 1542. Unsettled political conditions forced delays until a small body of bishops was finally able to convene at Trent on December 13, 1545. Plagued by interruptions, the Council ran to twenty-five sessions — with the last one concluding in December, 1563. Its decrees were confirmed by Pope Pius IV on January 26, 1564 and required many years to implement.

The council was convoked to address the spread of the Protestant Reformation and to institute a range of ecclesiastical reforms long recognized as urgently needed.

Pope Paul III:
Summoned Council of Trent

the formation and education of the clergy, and insistence on the residence of bishops in their dioceses. The council had an immense impact on all aspects of Catholic life and thought.

Tribunals • The ecclesiastical courts of the Church. By law, every diocese must have a tribunal. The tribunal is composed of judges, defenders of the bond and a promoter of justice. Advocates and procurators represent and assist persons bringing cases to the tribunals.

The council's doctrinal decrees addressed the principal points controverted by the Reformers: the legitimate role of Tradition along with Sacred Scripture in the Church's proclamation of the truth of Revelation; the understanding of grace, sin and merit in justification and sanctification; and the theology of the sacraments. The last mentioned topic received sustained attention throughout the council, with the reaffirmation of the legitimacy of the traditional seven sacraments and extensive teaching concerning the nature of individual sacraments.

In particular, many aspects of the doctrine of the Eucharist received official formulation at the council. The hope that these doctrinal decrees would bring about the reconciliation of Reformation leaders went largely unfulfilled in the end. The objective of ecclesiastical reform produced many important decrees, among them the reform of the liturgy (implemented by Pope Pius V), the establishment of a seminary system for

Tribunals are supposed to decide cases concerning disputes over Church law. To do so, the Code of Canon Law contains certain processes to be followed. These include the ordinary contentious process, penal process and special processes for the nullity of Christian marriage, the nullity of Holy Orders, and marriage separation cases. In actual practice, most tribunals handle marriage nullity cases almost exclusively.

Since the revised Code contains what amounts to a bill of rights for the faithful (Canons 208-223), including provision for the vindication and defense of these ecclesial rights (Canon 221), the tribunals face a new challenge.

Tribunals, Roman • There are three tribunals or courts in the Roman Curia. The Roman Rota and Apostolic Signatura handle cases in the external forum, while the

Roman Penitentiary handles cases in the internal forum.

The Roman Rota tries cases in the third or fourth instance (appeal) from all over the world. It is also empowered to try cases in the second instance from any other tribunal.

The Signatura handles cases involving complaints of nullity and exceptions of suspicion involving decisions of the Roman Rota. It also decides questions of competence or jurisdiction concerning lower tribunals as well as administrative controversies.

The Penitentiary handles internal forum cases that are referred to it. These are usually cases of censures incurred which are reserved to the Holy See (Canons 1442-1445).

Triduum • This ecclesiastical term draws its meaning from its Latin roots, *tres* (three) and *dies* (day[s]). Thus it refers to a period of three days. Particularly, it stands for a three-day period of prayer or devotion, whether private or public, held specifically in preparation for some feast, solemnity or event (such as ordination, First Holy Communion, Confirmation), or in petition for the conferral of some grace or benefit.

Triduum, Paschal • The period of three days beginning with the evening Mass of the Lord's Supper and concluding with Vespers on Easter Sunday. As Sunday is the preeminent day of the week, so the Paschal Triduum is the celebration *par excellence* of the entire liturgical year. These three days recall Christ's institution of the sacraments of the Holy Eucharist and Holy Orders, His passion and death, and His triumphant resurrection from the dead.

Trination • The faculty for priests to celebrate Mass "three times on Sundays and holy days of obligation, provided there is genuine pastoral need," listed among the faculties given to residential bishops according to the 1964 *motu proprio Pastorale munus,* of Pope Paul VI, on the powers and privileges granted to bishops.

Trinity, The Most Holy • The central mystery of the Christian Faith is that the one God is Father, Son and Holy Spirit, Three Persons sharing one nature. Although the term "Trinity" does not appear in Scripture, the reality of the Triune God is unmistakably present in Christ's references to the Father and the Spirit. For example, Christ says: "When the Counselor comes, whom I shall send to you from the Father, the Spirit of truth, who proceeds from the Father, he will bear witness to me" (Jn 15:26). The central conviction of historic mainstream Christianity — hammered out over the course of three centuries of doctrinal controversy against modalism and subordinationism — is that Christ is describing not merely the external relations of God but the very inner life of the Triune God.

The procession of the Word from the Father (called "generation") and the procession of the Spirit from the Father and the Son ("spiration") are eternal and immanent. The only distinctions in the otherwise perfectly undifferentiated Divine Nature are those that arise by reason of the two processions. If the processions are real, then the relations to which they give rise must be real. However, since whatever is real in God is identical with the Divine Nature, the relations, though distinct from each other, are not distinct from God. The Three Persons of the Trinity are subsistent relations, each fully divine, each consubstantial with the other.

Thus, the inner life of the Triune God is a life of pure mutual interrelation in knowledge and love. The astonishing destiny of every created being (human and angelic) is to share in this union both through love of other persons and consummately in the Trinitarian life itself. This is mystery in the strictest sense, knowable only through the revelation of the Triune Godhead.

Triodion • The liturgical Book of Three Odes in the Byzantine Rite containing the variable parts for the daily services proper to Great Lent and Holy Week. The Triodion actually opens twenty-two days before Lent begins with the Sunday of the Publican and the Pharisee (so-called from the Gospel reading of the day) and closes with the midnight Office on the night of Holy Saturday. The book is termed "three odes," since many of the Lenten canons contain only three rather than the customary nine odes.

Triple Candle • A threefold candle used in the Holy Saturday Liturgy for the *Lumen Christi* from the Middle Ages through 1955, when the Paschal Candle was returned to its ancient and privileged position.

Triple Judgment: See Judgment, Triple

Triptych • Three painted panels joined by hinges; usually the central panel is the largest and depicts the most important scene of the painting, often a significant event from the life of Our Lord, Our Lady or one of the saints. The side panels often portray other participants in the central event, angels in adoration or the patrons of the artwork, or sometimes a combination of them. In the Middle Ages, triptychs were frequently placed above the high altar of a church. During Passiontide, the side panels were closed to bring a more somber atmosphere to the sanctuary or chancel and to deny the congregation the joy derived from the artwork, which would be inappropriate during that penitential season.

Trisagion • In the Byzantine Rite, the Thrice-Holy Hymn recited during the Divine Liturgy: "Holy God, Holy and Mighty, Holy and Immortal, have mercy on us."

Triumph of the Cross (also Exaltation of the Cross) • This feast is kept on September 14 to commemorate the time when the True Cross was exposed for veneration in Jerusalem in 629 by the Emperor Heraclius, after his recovery of it from the Persians. Actually, the event described above took place in the spring, and what is commemorated on September 14 was the dedication of the Basilica of the Resurrection, built by Constantine over the Holy Sepulcher, but in the course of time, the celebration of the cross became fixed on September 14. (Cf. Cross, Veneration of the.)

Triumphalism • The notion that one is saved, not fundamentally through one's faith, prayer, discipleship and obedience to Christ and His grace that He offers not only to the Church but to all, but by means of the graces that He gives exclusively through the Church. This can be a dangerous view as it leads to the belief that one need not strive to advance in the spiritual life or respond to Christ's grace and because it narrows the scope of divine grace and unreasonably excludes others from it. This latter doctrine has been rejected by the Church as clearly erroneous.

This form of triumphalism is contrary to Christian humility and is actually a form of pride. Even though the Catholic Faith possesses the fullness of truth, the core of that truth is the cross, its shame, humiliation and degradation. It was through the humility, shame and lowliness of the cross that salvation was won, and this central reality argues with force against Christian triumphalism.

Troparion • In the East, a short prayer of ecclesiastical origin, generally drawn from the Bible and referring to the feast of the day. (Cf. Hirmos; Idiomelon; Kontakion; Theotokion.)

Truce of God • Enacted by the Council of Elne in 1027, the Truce of God is one of the more interesting examples of the influence for peace wielded by the medieval Church. Under the terms of the truce, combatants were forbidden from waging war on the Lord's Day (or from Saturday evening until early Monday morning). Violation of the truce carried spiritual, and then political, consequences. Later, the Synod of Clermont extended the effects of the truce in some areas from the beginning of Advent until eight days after the feast of the Epiphany. Other such Church-inspired cessations of conflict, though perhaps less notable in their effectiveness, have been proposed and exercised at various stages in history.

Trullo, Council of • The Second and Third Councils of Constantinople were dogmatic in character and enacted no disciplinary or implementing decrees. Ten years after the latter, then, in October of 691, Emperor Justinian II (and not Pope Sergius I) convened a synod of Eastern bishops which met under the Trullo dome of the imperial palace. This synod enacted just over one hundred disciplinary canons, which were generally accepted throughout the Eastern Church (cf. Canon Law, Eastern). Because the ecumenical councils which Trullo meant to implement were the Fifth and Sixth respectively, the Council of Trullo is also known as the Fifth-Sixth, or Quinisext, Synod.

It was not until 878, however, that Pope John VIII cautiously ratified the canons of the Synod of Trullo (most likely during the Synod of Troyes) and approved them "insofar as they are not opposed to other canons of the pontiffs or, of course, to good morals." Several canons of the Synod of Trullo were cited more than 1,200 years later by Pope Pius XII in his codification of the Eastern canon law on marriage.

Trusteeism • The system used to administer property belonging to dioceses and individual parishes. Bishops frequently choose a group of persons who, together with an ecclesiastical superior, form an administrative council to manage and protect possessions, property and finances. This group must regularly account for its stewardship and can in no way infringe upon the spiritual administration of the parish or diocese. The Holy See has approved such councils, stating that the vesting of church property in a duly chosen board of trustees is a permissible procedure. The Church, however, prohibits an exclusively lay board of trustees or any arrangement by which the authority of a bishop of a diocese or pastor of a parish might be circumvented.

Historically, the Church in the United States suffered from the extremes of this approach to administration, such that even into the early part of this century disgruntled laity refused to accept pastors assigned by bishops, sought to sell parish property without episcopal approval, and even brought legitimate Church authority into civil courts to press their claims.

Tunic • The outer liturgical vestment, formerly worn by the subdeacon. By custom in the West, this garment was worn by the bishop with the dalmatic under the chasuble. Some trace its origins to an ordinary overgarment (the *tunica*) of the empire. St. Gregory the Great suppressed it, but it reemerged at Rome around 1000. At times during its evolution, the tunic was distinguished from the dalmatic in terms of ornamentation, but eventually these garments became very similar. The tunic is no longer listed among vesture to be used by the bishop (only the dalmatic is noted in the *Caeremoniale Episcoporum*, n. 38); with the suppression of the subdiaconate, it is no longer in evidence in the Western Liturgy, except where worn by instituted acolytes for greater solemnity.

Tutiorism • The moral principle that only the most certain moral opinion may be morally followed when there is doubt as to whether a moral law is binding or not. In an absolute tutiorist system, one must choose only the most certain opinion, but in a mitigated tutiorist system, one may choose the opinion that is not just more probable, but most probable.

Typikon • The book containing the rubrics of all liturgical ceremonies for the Churches of the East.

Typological Sense of Scripture • This phrase refers to a way of reading the Bible as a unified whole, with Christ at the center. Christians discern in Old Testament persons and events prefigurements or "types" of persons and events that occur in the new dispensation. Thus, King David points to Christ, the King of the New Israel; the passage of Israel to Egypt points to the passover of Christ; and so on. Indeed, the employment of the typological reading of Scripture implies that the "real" meaning of earlier events is to be found in those consummations in the later events and persons to which they point. This standard way of reading Scripture as a typologically and narrationally unified book, with Jesus Christ at its center, is clearly reflected in the organization of the lectionary and, indeed, in the very pattern of the liturgy itself. The contemporary community is thus taken up into an overarching narrative of cosmic significance, embracing everything that has happened in the history of salvation from the very beginning and moving under God's providential care to its consummation.

At the same time, typology should not be used in a way which might suggest that the Old Covenant has been rendered void or useless.

For further reading: John E. Alsup, "Typology," *Anchor Bible Dictionary*, 6:682-685.

U

Ubiquitarianism • The view, propounded by Martin Luther and for a time by his followers, that Jesus Christ is present everywhere in His human nature. Luther appealed to this notion in his writings on the Eucharist in order to defend the Real Presence of Christ. The doctrine is not normative for the Lutheran confessions.

Ultramontanism • The term coined in the seventeenth century from the Latin roots meaning "on the other side of the mountains." The mountains were, in this case, the Alps, beyond which lay Rome. Ultramontanism, then, was a movement which stressed, occasionally in an exaggerated form, devotion to and service for the Holy See. It was chiefly aligned against Gallicanism and its many intellectual cousins which sought to establish national churches independent of the Roman Pontiff.

Of the many proponents of Ultramontanism, none was perhaps more striking than the nineteenth-century French writer and editor Louis Veuillot. After assuming the editorship of the stagnating *L'Univers* from the great Abbé Migne, the layman Veuillot transformed the paper into an immensely influential defender of papal rights over and responsibilities for the Church. Veuillot, a gifted writer himself, was particularly devoted to the cause of Catholic education, which he saw as increasingly threatened by the rise of unduly nationalistic states. At times, it must be admitted, Louis Veuillot injured his cause by his acerbic style, which won for him entanglements in numerous lawsuits and even a stint in prison. But when the archbishop of Paris ordered his newspaper to be suppressed, Pope Pius IX intervened on behalf of Veuillot, and *L'Univers* once again flourished.

Ultramontanism, it may be said, carried the day at the First Vatican Council, which defined papal infallibility and supremacy, although one must be very cautious in ascribing to any particular movement results which had been in long development under the inspiration of the Holy Spirit.

Umbanda • A cult that arose in Rio de Janeiro in the 1920s, with an estimated twenty million members today, Umbanda is one of the largest and most influential of the Afro-Brazilian mediumistic religions whose beliefs and practices are an amalgam of African, native Indian, Roman Catholic and spiritualist elements. Umbanda's social organization is hierarchical, with the *pai de santo* occupying the highest position and the mediums subject to him. Although Umbanda, like the other cults, is nominally monotheistic, its rituals are held at *centros* which are dedicated to deities of West African origins — called *orixas* — who are associated with Roman Catholic saints. The central ritual of these cults is the *consulta* (consultation), in which mediums provide assistance to those who have come for help. At Umbanda *consultas* the mediums, attired completely in white, dance in a circle and go into trances, and then prescribe remedies for the specific evils afflicting those seeking help. As might be expected, Umbanda and the other cults pose enormous pastoral

Pope Boniface VIII:
Promulgated *Unam Sanctam*

of France, who was threatening interference in ecclesiastical affairs.

Unam Sanctam develops the theory of the two swords (one spiritual, one temporal), which together rule the world. The Church's supremacy is a moral one, thus, on matters touching morals, the temporal sword must yield to the spiritual. Boniface makes clear, however, that he is not arguing for a unity of authority (cf. Caesaropapism), but that he is affirming unambiguously the right and duty of the Church to pass judgment on the political arena in matters of morals. The final sentence of the bull contains the only formal declaration in the document: "We declare, state and define that for salvation it is altogether necessary that every human creature be subject to the Roman Pontiff."

The successors of Pope Boniface also affirmed that *Unam Sanctam* did not change any existing relations between the Church and the state. The final sentence, of course, has given rise to one of the most intensely studied theological issues in the history of the Church, an inquiry which continues to this day.

problems for the Church in Brazil — not the least of which is that many of the people who practice Umbanda continue to consider themselves Catholics.

Unam Sanctam • *Unam Sanctam* (One, Holy) is the title of perhaps the most significant, or at least controversial, Papal Bull of the High Middle Ages. Promulgated by the canonist Pope Boniface VIII in November 1302, *Unam Sanctam* was the Holy See's formal response to Philip the Fair

Unction • Derived from the Latin verb *ungo* (to smear or anoint) and the noun *unctio* (anointing), this word was also formerly used in the English language to signify the same. It is more of an archaism today, however. Formerly the sacrament of the Sick or of the Anointing of the Sick was called "Extreme Unction" since it was administered only in very serious illness or in danger of death. It was also described because of this as the "Last Rites" performed on a person — i.e., before death.

There are several other sacraments in which anointing or unction plays an important part. These include Baptism, during which the person being baptized is anointed first with the oil of catechumens on the chest and then with sacred chrism on the crown of the head, and Confirmation, during which one is anointed on the forehead with sacred chrism. Finally, in the sacrament of Holy Orders, the newly ordained's hands are anointed with sacred chrism. An extension of this occurs at the consecration of a bishop, whose head is also anointed with sacred chrism.

The word "unction" may also refer to the oils used to anoint.

Uniate Churches • Those ecclesial communities of Eastern Christians who have resumed communion with the Catholic Church and recognize the Pope as their legitimate head. In the eyes of most Orthodox Churches and believers, such a return constitutes a surrender to Latinism and a sacrifice of one's native religious heritage for an artificial unity. The term "Uniate," then, is defamatory and is best relegated to dictionaries and encyclopedias for reference purposes, since in the view of non-Catholic Eastern Christians, Oriental Catholicism is a superficial amalgam of certain Oriental accidentals by people who are in fact simply Latins in spirit. Any trend, however, toward Latinization has largely been reduced by the effects of the Decree on the Eastern Catholic Churches of the Second Vatican Council, *Orientalium Ecclesiarum*, and the Eastern Catholic Churches are recovering their vast spiritual, cultural, theological and canonical Eastern treasures and patrimony.

Uniformity, Acts of • The Uniformity Acts were, as their name suggests, intended to bring about a uniformity of practice concerning, in this case, English religious conduct following Henry VIII's catapulting of the English Church into schism. This series of laws, passed under the sickly Edward and his sister Elizabeth from the late 1540s to the early 1560s, commanded the use of the Book of Common Prayer, required attendance at Anglican services and forbade Roman Catholic Liturgies or affiliation. As such, these laws were an integral part of the Elizabethan Settlement. In 1791, however, and again in 1846, the laws were revised, but not repealed, in such a way as to lessen their discrimination against Catholics.

Unigenitus • On September 8, 1713, Pope Clement XI published his constitution *Unigenitus*, in which he condemned one hundred one propositions contained in the *Réflexions* of Pasquier Quesnel (1634-1719). Quesnel's work, based upon previously condemned Jansenist theology, asserted that no grace is given outside the Church, that grace is irresistible, that without grace man is incapable of any good and that all acts of a sinner, even prayer and attendance at Mass, are sins. Quesnel never accepted Clement's condemnation, and although he asked for and received the Last Sacraments of the Church, he appealed to a "future Council" to vindicate his teaching. Even though no such vindication was forthcoming, the spirit of Jansenism continued to give rise to various false teachings, all of which have been condemned by the Church.

Union Mystical: See **Mysticism**

Unitarianism • The term refers broadly to positions that assert the unipersonality of God against the doctrines of the Trinity and the divinity of Christ. The early Church knew a form of unitarianism in Monarchianism, but modern Unitarianism as a form of religious belief and observance dates from seventeenth-century England, with precursors in Reformation movements like Socinianism.

Despite its rejection of the Nicene-Constantinopolitan faith that is fundamental to all forms of Christianity, Unitarianism began to take shape as a kind of Christian denomination in England and America. In America, King's Chapel in Boston and the Divinity School at Harvard University became centers of Unitarian thought and practice. William Ellery Channing (1780-1842) and Ralph Waldo Emerson (1803-1882) played influential roles in expounding the philosophical and theological elements of American Unitarianism.

According to Unitarian belief, practical religion is summed up in love of God and love of neighbor. Unitarians insist on the absolute unicity of God, the strict humanity of Christ, the perfectibility of human character, and the ultimate salvation of all persons. They generally reject the doctrines of original sin, atonement and eternal punishment. However, in the absence of a formal Unitarian creed, there is wide latitude in actual belief. Unitarianism is typically liberal in its espousal of social causes and universalist in its attitude to other religions.

The Unitarian Universalist Association dates from 1961 and has about 170,000 members in loosely organized local churches with congregational governance. (Cf. Socinianism.)

Unitatis Redintegratio • The Decree on Ecumenism, *Unitatis Redintegratio*, was promulgated by Vatican Council II on November 21, 1964. It contains three chapters which discuss Catholic principles and the practice of ecumenism and the status of ecclesial communities separated from Rome. *Unitatis Redintegratio* makes clear that overcoming the scandalous divisions among Christians requires recognition that "Christ the Lord founded one Church and one Church only" (UR 1) and then refers to *Lumen Gentium*, which declares that "the sole Church of Christ . . . constituted and organized as a society in the present world, subsists in the Catholic Church, which is governed by the successor of Peter and by the bishops in communion with him" (LG 8). This truth is the foundation of the Council's teaching on ecumenism.

Toward overcoming divisions among Christians, the decree admits that the responsibility for the schisms of the sixteenth century lies with both Catholics and Protestants and that "one cannot charge with the sin of separation those who at present are born into these communities and in them are brought up in the faith of Christ, and the Catholic Church accepts them with respect and affection as brothers" (UR 3). This recognition is significant, but the decree goes one more step and teaches that the life of grace, the theological virtues and the other gifts of the Holy Spirit are available to Christians outside the visible boundaries of the Catholic Church (UR 3).

Lest this be interpreted as indifferentism, however, *Unitatis Redintegratio* immediately reminds us that "it is through Christ's Catholic Church alone, which is the universal help towards salvation, that the fullness of the means of salvation can be obtained" (UR 3).

The decree urges all Christians to pray for the unity of the Church and to work toward that goal according to the mind of Christ (UR 7). But while identifying unity as one of the principal concerns of the Council, exhorting all to promote dialogue, and urging all Christians to avoid bitterness and polemics, the decree also proclaims that "nothing is so foreign to the spirit of ecumenism as a false irenicism which harms the purity of Catholic doctrine and obscures its genuine and certain meaning" (UR 11).

This theme of balancing ostensibly irreconcilable positions is present throughout *Unitatis Redintegratio* and shapes the general approach to ecumenism desired by the Council. The decree concludes by pointing out that the reconciliation of Christians is an objective beyond human power and by placing the hope for true unity in the prayer of Christ for His Church.

United States Catholic Conference (USCC) • The public policy agency of the American Catholic hierarchy. It is a civil, nonprofit organization incorporated in the District of Columbia. The USCC shares administrative structures with the National Conference of Catholic Bishops (NCCB) and is organized around five committees: Communications, Education, Campaign for Human Development, Domestic Policy and International Policy. Unlike the NCCB committees, whose members are bishops exclusively, the USCC committees include clergy, religious and lay people. Their chairmen and one other bishop-member are elected by the bishops. The USCC committees develop policy and programs for approval by the bishops. Approved policies are then implemented by the departments of Communications, Education, and Social Development and World Peace, and also by the Campaign for Human Development and by Migration and Refugee Services.

Unity • The attribute of a thing whereby it is undivided in itself and yet distinct from other things. In properly metaphysical terms, unity is one of the transcendental properties of being, along with truth and goodness. (Sometimes beauty is added to the list.) The transcendentals are coextensive with being and given with it. The point here is that everything that exists, insofar as it exists, is one, true (known and knowable) and good (desired and desirable). The concept of unity has many theological uses. Perhaps the most significant is the doctrine of God. Christians affirm the divine unity against all forms of polytheism: there is only one God, the Creator of the Universe, and the One Who has made Himself known as the Three. It is fundamental to the Christian Faith, as proclaimed in the Scriptures and in the earliest creeds, that God is Three Persons Who are one in substance, one in being God. The doctrine of the Trinity involves no fracturing of the unity of God.

Univers, L' • The nineteenth-century French newspaper, edited by the fiery Louis Veuillot, which led the opposition to Catholic liberals. Through this publication, Veuillot urged Catholic leaders to condemn the principles of the French Revolution. The editor and his followers believed that the Church should seek an intimate alliance with any regime that would unite Church and state and return to the more authoritarian, structured society of prerevolutionary Europe.

Universal Law: See **Law, Universal**

University, Pontifical • A pontifical university is one erected by the Holy See and under its direct supervision. It has its own constitution and statutes, which must be approved by the Holy See. A pontifical university differs from a Catholic university, in that the latter is not necessarily erected by the Holy See.

There are several pontifical universities throughout the world. They specialize in the teaching of the sacred sciences of theology, canon law and philosophy. The most prominent are the pontifical universities in Rome.

Urbi et Orbi • Latin phrase meaning (literally) "to the city and to the world," used to describe the papal blessing given twice annually from the balcony of St. Peter's, at Christmas and Easter. In practice, this blessing is preceded by the Pope's delivering a message to the world (e.g., about world peace) and his offering Christmas and Easter greetings in numerous foreign languages.

Urim and Thummim • The Israelite priests used two objects of unspecified material to obtain divine answers to their questions. They were kept in the high priest's breastplate (Ex 28:30). It is thought that each of these objects must have had "yes" and "no" sides, since the inquirer asked questions in that form (1 Sm 14:41; 28:6). The biblical scholar H. H. Rowley suggested that the Thummim was the "yes" symbol and the Urim was the "no."

For further reading: I. Mendelsohn, "Urim and Thummim," *Interpreter's Dictionary of the Bible*, 4:739-740.

Ursacrament (also Ursackrament) • A German expression recently introduced by some theologians (e.g., Karl Rahner) to signal the doctrine that the Church is the original (*ur*) or fundamental sacrament and that the seven sacraments flow from her sacramental nature. The doctrine of the Incarnation lies in the background of this idea. The presence of grace in the Church and under the sacramental form is seen to parallel the incarnate presence of the divine in the human form. These ideas proved fruitful for fielding a more comprehensive sacramental theology in postconciliar thought and practice.

Usury • The demanding of excessive interest for the loaning of money. It is forbidden by the natural law; it is a violation of justice and may also violate charity.

Originally, in Jewish and Christian Tradition, usury meant taking any interest for a loan. In the early Church, Christians were forbidden to take interest on money from a poor or needy person. The Councils of Carthage (A.D. 345) and Aix (789) declared it reprehensible to make money by lending at interest. This reasoning continued into the Middle Ages. Eventually the Church in the eighteenth century recognized the legitimacy of loans with a fair interest.

Ut Unum Sint • Holding that the authority of the papacy is absolute and supreme, Pope John Paul II invites leaders of other Christian denominations into a discussion of the role of the papacy in *Ut Unum Sint*, the twelfth encyclical of his pontificate. Released in May 1995, the papal letter, whose English translation is *That They May Be One*, calls for an examination of an ecclesiastical office which "constitutes a difficulty for most other Christians." At the same time, the document voices one of John Paul II's oft-stated hopes: a reunification of a Christian community splintered many times over during the past one thousand years.

An assessment of the papacy is an "immense task, which we cannot refuse and which I cannot carry out by myself," the Pope writes. Calling on "Church leaders and their theologians to engage with [him] in a patient and fraternal dialogue. . . , leaving useless controversies behind," John Paul seeks an understanding of how the primacy of the Bishop of Rome was accepted in the first Christian millennium and how it might once again be accepted by the beginning of the third.

The Pope notes that some progress toward this end has been made in the three decades since the Second Vatican Council's call for a renewed ecumenism. Improved relations with the Orthodox Church, which split from Rome in 1054, receives particular attention. However, five major stumbling blocks to full and authentic Christian unity remain: (1) the relationship of Scripture and Tradition; (2) the Eucharist; (3) priestly ordination; (4) the Roman Church's teaching authority; and (5) the place of the Virgin Mary in salvation history.

Utraquism • The term has its origin in the Latin phrase *sub utraque specie* ("under both forms") and identifies the Hussite doctrine insisting on Communion under both kinds. According to this doctrine, the integral reception of Holy Communion requires consumption of both the consecrated Bread and the Wine. At the time, only the priest was permitted to drink from the cup. Although John Huss (1372-1415) did not himself make a point of pressing the case, his followers insisted on Communion under both kinds. Jacob of Mies was the first to advocate the doctrine at the University of Prague in 1414. Utraquism was condemned at the Councils of Constance (1415) and Basle (1432).

Vagi • The Latin term for "wanderers." These are people who have neither a domicile nor a quasi-domicile, that is, no fixed residence. The law makes several provisions for wanderers. Since they have no fixed residence, they are bound by the universal and particular laws of the place where they are actually present (Canon 13). The proper pastor and Ordinary of a wanderer is the pastor and Ordinary of the place where he is actually present at the time (Canon 107).

Wanderers are not to be allowed to enter into marriage, except with the permission of the bishop (Canon 1071). The reason for this is that vagi often face a variety of personal and situational difficulties which can place added strains on a marriage.

Vaison, Councils of • Two synods, one disciplinary and the other liturgical, were held near Avignon, France, in the city of Vaison. The first, in A.D. 442, formulated rules on, among other things, the use of Holy Chrism and the adoption of children. The second synod, held in 529, is the better known, chiefly for its liturgical legislation concerning the triple use of the *Kyrie* at Mass, and its requirement that the words "as it was in the beginning," etc., should be added to the Glory Be. The synod was historically mistaken, however, in claiming that this certainly beautiful conclusion to the prayer was already in wide use in the East, since it was not.

Valentinianism • This Gnostic heresy arose in Egypt during the second century. It is believed that one Valentinus, after being denied episcopal consecration, turned against the Church and developed this very complex, heavily Platonic heresy. It divided mankind into three categories, of which only the first group (which included the Valentinians) were assured of salvation. The intricate formulations of Valentinus, however, are difficult to determine because his followers, to a very considerable degree, apparently reworked and adapted his original theories. Although Valentinianism attracted a rather wide following, it was notably short-lived, especially after refutations from St. Irenaeus.

Valid • A valid legal, canonical, sacramental or administrative act is one that is real, that is, it has legal, spiritual or social consequences. Canon law stipulates that a law must specify whether or not an act can result in nullity or invalidity (Canon 10). Therefore, an act is to be presumed valid and a person capable of validly acting unless the contrary is proven. The legislative, executive or judicial acts of a person are valid if that person actually has the power of jurisdiction which empowers him to act.

The acts of the power of Sacred Orders are valid if the cleric actually possesses the order and, in some cases, has fulfilled any other legal requirements for validity. For example, for the valid absolution of sins, it is required that the minister be at least a priest and have the faculty or permission to absolve (Canon 966). Similarly, a cleric acts invalidly if he lacks jurisdiction to witness a marriage. In this case, the administration of the sacrament by the spouses is itself invalid because the presence of a duly authorized cleric is required for validity (Canon 1108).

In some cases, acts that are invalid can be "sanated" or made valid retroactively by a decree of the competent authority. In other cases, an invalid act must be repeated correctly to have validity.

Validation of Marriage: See **Convalidation**

Vandalism • The destruction or damaging of goods from a perverse pleasure in destruction. Psychologically, vandalism results from immaturity, and it is similar to a temper tantrum in a child. The object of anger in an act of vandalism is misplaced, and the act has the characteristics of impotent fury.

Vandalism is a sin against justice, and absolution requires restitution or compensation for the damage done. It is also in violation of the demands of charity as it alienates its victims.

Vatican • Since the end of the Avignon captivity in 1377, the chief residence of the Pope is located in the Vatican. Over a period of several centuries, beginning especially with the building program of Pope Nicholas V in 1447, the Popes initiated various construction projects to bring the Vatican to its present form. Most of the offices of the Papal Curia are located in the Vatican, as well as the residences of several cardinals and the site of the renowned Vatican Museums and Library. The Vatican is located within the Vatican City State, the last remnant of the Papal States, and recognized as an independent sovereignty by the Lateran Treaty of 1929. The word "Vatican" often serves as shorthand for denoting the papal provenance of Church policies or pronouncements.

Vatican Council I • The twentieth ecumenical council, but the first actually held within the Vatican, was convoked by Pope Pius IX on December 8, 1869, with over eight hundred prelates attending at least some of the sessions. A wide variety of issues was addressed in the four major sessions of the Council, and nearly ninety meetings were held before the Council was forced into permanent suspension by the entrance of Garibaldi's troops into Rome in July, 1870, during the Italian Revolution.

Among the several decrees promulgated by the Council, besides pronouncements on revelation and natural religion, the best known are those defining papal supremacy and the infallibility of the Pope when formally addressing matters relating to faith or morals. Many other pressing concerns, however, had to be abandoned when the safety of the Council Fathers was threatened by the presence of Garibaldi's troops. Perhaps most notable among these losses were plans to organize the first codification of canon law, a project which was subsequently delayed for nearly fifty years.

Vatican Council II • The twenty-first ecumenical council of the Catholic Church was announced by Pope John XXIII on January 25, 1959, and held its opening session on October 11, 1962, at St. Peter's Basilica in Rome. The Pope's stated objectives in calling the Council were to seek the renewal of the Church and to modernize its forms and institutions. Central to Pope John's overall hopes for the Council was the fostering of unity among Christians. This threefold mandate — renewal, modernization and ecumenism — was reaffirmed by Pope Paul VI (who succeeded Pope John on June 21, 1963) and continued to shape the Council's deliberations over the next three years. About twenty-five hundred bishops participated, with a complement of Catholic and non-Catholic observers.

The dramatic transformation which the Council would stimulate was signaled by its first-promulgated Constitution on the Sacred Liturgy. The other constitutions were those on the Church, on Divine Revelation, and on the Church in the Modern World. The wide range of topics treated during the Council is apparent from the list of its remaining documents: Declaration on Christian Education; Declaration on the Relations of the Church to Non-Christian Religions; Decree on Religious Liberty; Decree on the Means of Social Communication; Decree on the Eastern Catholic Churches; Decree on Ecumenism; Decree on the Up-to-Date Renewal of Religious Life; Decree on the Training of Priests; Decree on the Apostolate of Lay People; Decree on the Church's Missionary Activity; Decree on the Ministry and Life of Priests; Decree on the Pastoral Office of the Bishops in the Church.

Over the years since the Council's closing session in 1965, implementation of its actions has been a challenge to the Church. Debate over the Council's meaning has been a source of tension, especially where its discontinuity with the preceding Tradition has been exaggerated.

Vatican State, City of • It is properly called the Papal State and includes the Vatican Palace, its gardens, the Basilica and Piazza of St. Peter's and other official buildings on a plot of land approximately one square mile, with about one thousand residents, all of whom are citizens. It is governed by the Pope as the sovereign ruler with executive, legislative and judicial powers exercised through commissions and delegated groups.

Vaudois: See **Waldenses**

Veils • In the celebration of the Divine Liturgy of the Byzantine Rite, the Offerings are covered with three veils: the chalice veil, the veil over the diskos and the aer, which covers them both.

Venerable • The title given to one who, although not yet proclaimed saint or even blessed, has been judged to have lived the cardinal and theological virtues to a heroic degree. If the individual was a martyr, the fact of the martyrdom is also confirmed by the title of venerable. A private cult is permitted for one who has been ranked as venerable. (Cf. Heroic Virtue.)

Veneration of the Saints • Devotion to and invocation of the saints are practices as ancient as Christianity itself. Already in the Old Testament, there are signs of a conviction of the importance of holy ones who pray for the community on earth (2 Mc 15:12). This idea is echoed in the Letter to the Hebrews, which refers to the holy people of the Old Testament as a "cloud of witnesses" (Heb 12:1). Fundamental to the theological understanding of veneration of the saints is the Pauline doctrine of the Mystical Body of Christ. The earliest expression of such veneration is the reverence accorded to the martyrs in the early Church. Especially from the fourth century, veneration of the saints became widespread and has continued unabated to the present day.

Traditional theology has sharply distinguished the reverence accorded to the saints ("dulia") from the worship and adoration that are due to God alone ("latria"). The praise of the saints is in fact the rendering of thanks and praise to God, Whose triumphant grace has become fully and unambiguously effective in the lives of these holy ones. In their stunning diversity, the saints offer an inexhaustible source of imitation and inspiration to Christians still on their pilgrim way. Invoking the intercession and patronage of the saints is perfectly appropriate; just as in life they prayed unceasingly for their fellows, so now they join their prayers to those of the Blessed Virgin Mary and to the uniquely powerful intercession of Christ as they stand before the Father imploring His mercy and grace on our behalf. A rich and creative tradition of iconography and hagiography serves to keep these blessed ones before our minds and hearts.

Veni, Creator Spiritus • Hymn addressed to the Holy Spirit. This hymn has long been associated with the sacraments of Holy Orders and Confirmation, as well as Church elections and special meetings. True authorship is unknown, but over the years it has been attributed to St. Ambrose, St. Gregory the Great, Charlemagne and Rabanus.

Veritatis Splendor • The encyclical letter of Pope John Paul II, issued in 1993, concerning fundamental questions of the Church's moral teaching. Unlike much previous magisterial teaching in the area of morality, this encyclical undertook to expound the basic principles of the moral life rather than address specific moral issues. A vision of the Christian moral life as a transfigured life in Christ infuses the encyclical with a high spiritual tone. The Pope is critical both of classical forms of legalism and of modern forms of relativism. The goal of moral life is not simply to obey moral commands, but to become good in seeking the ultimate Good which is God Himself. The encyclical rides the crest of the post-Vatican II renewal in moral theology by deploying scriptural, patristic and scholastic resources with creativity and passion. At the same time, the Pope cautions against and corrects certain trends in contemporary moral theology — chiefly consequentialism and proportionalism, and certain theories of the fundamental option — that are theologically erroneous and pastorally harmful.

Versicle • The first part of a pair of phrases or sentences commonly taken from the Psalter, joined together and sung or said antiphonally at the liturgy. The classic opening versicle and response to Morning and Evening Prayer are: "God, come to my assistance," "Lord, make haste to help me," the versicle sung by the leader and the response sung by all. A series of versicles and responses follow the *Te Deum* when this is included in the Office of Readings. In the revised *Caeremoniale Episcoporum, Ceremonial for Bishops*, the "Second Form" of episcopal blessing offered is introduced by two versicles with responses: "Blessed be the name of the Lord," "Now and for ever." "Our help is in the name of the Lord," "Who made heaven and earth."

Vespers • From *vesper*, Latin for "evening." The evening prayer of the Church and, along with Lauds, one of the two most important hours of the Divine Office. Vespers of the present Roman Rite consists of an introductory verse, a hymn, two psalms and a New Testament canticle, with their antiphons, a reading from Scripture, a response, the *Magnificat* with Antiphon, intercessions, the Lord's Prayer, the concluding prayer and final blessing.

Vestments • Term derived from the Latin *vestimentum* from the verb *vestire*, meaning "to clothe," signifying the garments worn by the clergy at liturgy and other religious functions. In the Catholic Church their design and color have been prescribed in liturgical and canonical legislation. Their origins from customary secular usage trace back to the fourth century, with a fairly stable usage in place by the ninth century.

All liturgical services have prescribed vesture for the ministers, a chief example of which is the new Order of Mass.

The *General Instruction of the Roman Missal* (n. 297) states that the diversity of liturgical roles is demonstrated by the diversity of liturgical vestments. "These signify the role proper to each person who has a special part in the rite, and they help to make the ceremonies beautiful and solemn" (n. 297). The vestment common to all ministers at Mass is the alb (with cincture and amice, if needed) (n. 298). The chasuble is the vestment proper to the priest celebrant; it is worn over the alb and stole (n. 299). The dalmatic, worn over the alb and stole, is the proper vestment of the deacon (n. 300). Priests wear the stole around the neck, hanging down; deacons wear the stole over the left shoulder fastened on the right side (n. 302). A cope is worn by the priest "in processions [e.g., with palms on Passion Sunday] and certain other liturgical actions when this is indicated in their respective rubrics" (n. 303).

"The beauty and dignity of liturgical vestments is to be sought in the excellence of their material and the elegance of their cut, rather than in an abundance of adventitious ornamentation. Any images, symbols or figures employed should be sacred in character and exclude anything inappropriate" (n. 306) The *Instruction* states that traditional colors for vestments are retained in the present reform: white for the seasons of Easter and Christmas, feasts of the Lord, of Mary, angels, most saints, All Saints, John the Baptist, John the Evangelist, Chair of St. Peter Apostle, Conversion of St. Paul; red on Passion Sunday, Good Friday, Pentecost, birthday feasts of other Apostles and evangelists, celebrations of martyrs; violet for the seasons of Lent and Advent, offices for the dead; black is optional for Masses for the dead, and rose is optional on Laetare and Gaudete Sundays. In addition, "Bishops' Conferences may determine and propose to the Holy See changes in these customs if they judge that a different selection of colors would better suit the needs and tastes of their people" (n. 308).

Viaticum • The administration of the Holy Eucharist to those about to die. The present *Rites of Anointing and Viaticum* contain a special chapter on the "Celebration of Viaticum" (Chapter 5, nn. 175-211), which is introduced by the statement: "The celebration of the Eucharist as Viaticum, food for the passage through death to eternal life, is the sacrament proper to the dying Christian. It is the completion and crown of the Christian life on this earth, signifying that the Christian follows the Lord to eternal glory and the banquet of the heavenly kingdom" (n. 175). Two rites are provided for Viaticum, one within Mass and the other outside Mass (containing Introductory Rites, Liturgy of the Word, Liturgy of Viaticum, Concluding Rites).

Vicar • A person who takes the place of another and performs acts of authority in an ecclesiastical office in the name of another. Vicars general and vicars episcopal act in the name of the residential bishop. Vicars who are clerics are also known as ordinaries because they possess power that is attached to their office, even though this power is not personal to them but exercised in the name of another.

Vicar, Judicial • Second only to the diocesan bishop, the judicial vicar is the chief judge and judicial officer of a diocese. He has ordinary jurisdiction to judge any ecclesiastical matter, except those cases which have been reserved or which the bishop calls to himself (Canon 1420). Frequently styled the "officialis," the judicial vicar must be a priest, have at least a licentiate in canon law and be at least thirty years old. Of course, he must have a high reputation for honesty and prudence. He is to make a Profession of Faith before assuming office (Canon 833) and is bound by all canonical and professional obligations of confidentiality and integrity (Canon 1454). If circumstances warrant, assistant judicial vicars can also be appointed.

Judicial vicars differ significantly from and should not be confused with vicars general or episcopal vicars. The primary task of the judicial vicar is to see to the efficient administration of the diocesan tribunal, for example, by assigning judges to particular cases (Canon 1425), and so on. Judicial vicars should be appointed to a definite term of office (cf. Office, Ecclesiastical) and cannot be removed prior to the completion of that term, except for serious reasons.

Vicar of Christ • A title meaning "one who takes the place of Christ," often used of the Bishop of Rome in particular, but used to refer to bishops in general as well. It was first used by the Roman Synod of A.D. 495 to refer to Pope Gelasius. It was introduced into Roman Curial usage, to refer to the Bishop of Rome, during the reign of Eugene III (1145-1153). Innocent III (1198-1216), while employing the title to refer to bishops and even priests, explicitly asserted that the Pope is the Vicar of Christ. It remains in Roman Curial usage to this day.

The Council of Florence in its famous *Decree for the Greeks* (1439) defined the Pope as the "true Vicar of Christ," which language was repeated verbatim by Vatican Council I (1870) in *Pastor Aeternus*, n. 3. Vatican Council II, in *Lumen Gentium*, n. 27, calls bishops in general "vicars and legates of Christ," showing that the title is not used exclusively of the Roman Pontiff.

The central point is that *all* bishops are vicars of Christ for their local Churches, as the Pope is for the universal Church, in their ministerial functions of priest, prophet and king. While bishops are likewise called successors of the Apostles, the title "Vicar of Christ" denotes that they receive their power not by delegation from any other person, ecclesiastical or civil, but from Christ Himself in virtue of their reception of the sacrament of Holy Orders.

Vicar of Peter • Literally, "one who takes the place of Peter." It was never an official papal title and was even explicitly rejected by Innocent III. The title of "vicar" is not synonymous with "successor," since it implies that the vicar holds his office at the behest of Peter. Thus construed, it could be held to contradict the office of Vicar of Christ, since it would suggest that the papal authority was not of divine but human origin. "Successor" denotes that there has been a transfer of office and authority but does not imply how the transfer was accomplished.

Vicariate, Apostolic • A territorial division of the Church that does not have the full status of a diocese. When a mission territory has been established in a country that does not have an established hierarchy and shows potential for stability and growth, it is first erected as an Apostolic Prefecture under the authority of a prelate. Continued growth may result in the change of the entity's status from Apostolic Prefecture to Apostolic Vicariate, the difference being that an Apostolic Vicariate is governed by a titular bishop (Canon 371.1).

Vice-Chancellor • According to Canon 482, a diocesan bishop can appoint vice-chancellors to assist the chancellor when the bishop feels it expedient. Given the general trend toward increasing the duties of chancellors, such a policy is often adopted.

Vienne, Council of • The fifteenth ecumenical council was convoked by Pope Clement V in 1311 and lasted about nine months. In its three sessions, the Council of Vienne enacted at least thirty-eight canons, of which nearly twenty were included in the *Clementinae* collection of Canon law (cf. Corpus Iuris Canonici). It is possible that more canons were passed, but by historical accident, all of the original documents of this council have been lost, perhaps as a result of the confusion surrounding the opening of the Avignon Papacy, of which Clement was the first member. Among the significant issues faced by the council were the suppression of the Knights Templar, unrest in the Holy Land and Franciscan disputes concerning the practice of poverty.

Vigil • Liturgical services consisting of psalms, readings and silent prayer were common in earliest Christianity, as attested to in Pliny's Letter to Trajan (c. A.D. 112) and in Egeria's Diary (late fourth century); often the vigils lasted all night and ended with the Eucharist. Vigils of particular importance were those for Easter and Pentecost. A connection between keeping vigil and the Liturgy of the Hours is clear in the evolution of Matins and preserving a Saturday evening Vigil of the Resurrection, which looked toward the Eucharist on Sunday, the day of

St. Vincent de Paul

the Resurrection. The present revision of the Liturgy of the Hours contains an appendix for "Canticles and Gospel Readings for Vigils." The Gospel texts provided are the accounts of the post-Resurrection appearances from the four evangelists (Mt 28:1-20, Mk 16:1-20, Lk 24:1-53, Jn 20:1-31, 21:1-14).

Another meaning of the term signifies the celebration of Mass on evenings preceding important feasts. Those which perdure in the present liturgy are vigils for Christmas, Easter, Pentecost, Birth of John the Baptist, Sts. Peter and Paul, and the Assumption.

Vigil Light • A candle burned in a church or at a shrine for a particular intention, or in honor of God or a saint. The burning flame "keeps vigil" when the individual cannot be present. Long a very popular tradition, vigil lights may burn for merely a few hours or as long as a week.

Vincent de Paul, St. • French saint (1581-1660). Born of peasants, Vincent was ordained a priest in 1600 after theological studies in Toulouse. Noted as a preacher of missions, and with the assistance of several Paris priests, Vincent set up charitable organizations, or "conferences," wherever he preached. He likewise started hospitals for convicts, and was most instrumental in giving rise to French seminaries at a time when vocations to the priesthood were low in France. His ten-day conferences for ordination candidates gradually inspired the concept of extending formal training in seminaries. In 1625 he established his Congregation of Priests of the Mission, whose purpose it was to evangelize the poor country people. Beginning in 1633, Vincent held his famous weekly Tuesday Conferences for priests, infusing in the French clergy a new Christian enthusiasm and, through them, in the French people.

Most notable in the life of this priest were his love of and care for the poor. In 1633 he established the Daughters of Charity, who helped in supplying food and shelter to thousands of men and women. It is estimated that his service to the poor benefited sixteen thousand people daily on soup lines, and nine hundred women in shelters.

The process of Vincent's canonization began in 1705; he was canonized by Pope Clement XII in June 1737. Pope Leo XIII declared Vincent the patron saint of charitable works and organizations dedicated to serving the poor. His feast day is September 27, the day of his death.

Vindictive Penalties: See Penalty, Vindictive

Virgin Birth of Christ • According to the Scriptures (Mt 1:18-25; Lk 1:26-38) and the consistent teaching of the Church, Jesus Christ was conceived by the Blessed Virgin Mary by the Holy Spirit and had no human father. This mystery is accessible only to the eyes of faith. Nonetheless, it has always seemed appropriate to Christians that the birth of Christ should have taken place in this way. For one thing, the eternal origin of the Son is His procession from the Father: Jesus Christ has but one Father. Furthermore, it is fitting that the principle of the new creation, the Holy Spirit, should inaugurate it through the virginal conception of Christ in the Blessed Virgin Mary. The virginal conception, in addition, begins something radically new: the adoption by God of all those born anew in Christ.

For further reading: Raymond E. Brown, S.S., *The Virginal Conception and Bodily Resurrection of Jesus* (Paulist, 1973).

Virgin Mary • The Mother of Jesus, who conceived the Son of God by the Holy Spirit. The angel Gabriel announced to Mary, "You will conceive in your womb and bear a son, and you shall call his name Jesus. He will be great, and will be called the Son of the Most High (Lk 1:31-32). When Mary asked, "How shall this be, since I have no husband," the angel informed her, "The Holy Spirit will come upon you, and the power of the Most High will overshadow you; therefore the child to be born will be called holy, the Son of God" (Lk 1:35-36).

The Church has consistently taught the perpetual virginity of Mary: she was a virgin before, through and after the conception and birth of Christ (*ante partum, in partu, et post partum*, according to an ancient formula). The objection that Jesus had brothers and sisters (cf. Mk 3:31-35) and that Mary must therefore have had children after giving birth to Him has never been credited in the Church. The persons referred to in the Scriptures were close relations, possibly cousins. Jesus Christ is the only Son of Mary. Still, her maternity extends to encompass all those who are born again in Christ, the "first-born among many brethren" (Rom 8:29).

According to the *Catechism of the Catholic Church*: "The deepening of faith in the virginal motherhood led the Church to confess Mary's real and perpetual virginity even in the act of giving birth to the Son of God made man" (n. 499).

"Jesus is Mary's only son, but her spiritual motherhood extends to all men whom indeed he came to save" (n. 501).

Virginity • An evangelical counsel, virginity entails the practice of perpetual sexual abstinence for the sake of the kingdom (Mt 19:10). The root of Christian virginity is the motive of love: in order to seek the perfect love of God alone, the virgin forgoes the sexual expression of love for fellow human beings. Christian teaching has been resolute in affirming the fundamental good of married sexual love. Virginity is not the avoidance of something evil, but the voluntary renunciation of something intrinsically good. Thus, it entails a quite concrete form of self-denial, and in this way conforms the virgin to the death of Christ. It is understood that such a way of life must be, strictly speaking, a vocation to which God calls some persons and for which He supplies the grace. Virginity attests to the radical character of the love of God, a love that transcends human understandings and categories at the same time that it transforms them.

Virtue • A habit or power which enables one to perform an action with facility and competence. Virtues are either developed by practice, such as the virtues of prudence, temperance, justice or fortitude, or are infused by God, such as the virtues of faith, hope and charity. The virtues are the fullest expression of the person, for they manifest the precise powers and capabilities of the individual.

Virtues, Moral: See Moral Virtues

Virtues, Theological: See Theological Virtues

Visions • A revelation of some aspect of the personal mystery of God, sometimes through the mediation of the Mother of God or another saint, to an individual or group of individuals. Such a favor is the free gift of God, though a person may be predisposed and prepared for such a gift by a life of prayer, penance and spiritual dedication.

The Church is, understandably, extremely reluctant to pass judgment on the authenticity of any such claims, although, in the face of obvious fraud (for instance, alleged visions accompanied by messages in which Our Lady repudiates liturgical practices or ecclesial discipline approved by the Magisterium of the Church), she will at times render a negative judgment, a pastoral warning or even a formal repudiation for the spiritual good of her children who might otherwise be deceived.

Such occurrences, even if judged authentic, however, remain in the realm of "private revelation," as opposed to the "public revelation" of Scripture and Tradition, and as such can make no claim to be binding upon the Church as a whole or upon individual members of the Church.

Visitation, Episcopal • An official visit by the diocesan bishop to all diocesan institutions, to be made at least every five years.

Visitation of Mary • Following the angel Gabriel's announcement of Jesus' birth to Mary (Lk 1:26-38), Luke presents Mary's journey to a town in the Judean hills to visit her pregnant relative Elizabeth (Lk 1:39-56). The annunciation scene prepares the way for the visitation scene. During the annunciation (1:36-37), Gabriel announces Elizabeth's unusual pregnancy to Mary as a sign that "with God nothing will be impossible."

Mary's response to Gabriel's words is twofold. First, she declares her willingness to cooperate with God's word as "the handmaid of the Lord." Second, she goes to the assistance of Elizabeth, whose pregnancy has been announced by angelic revelation.

The Lucan timetable of Elizabeth's pregnancy is carefully traced through the narrative. First, Elizabeth conceives and spends five months in seclusion (1:24). Next, the annunciation to Mary takes place during the sixth month of Elizabeth's pregnancy (1:36). Third, Mary spends three months with Elizabeth, departing not long before the birth of John the Baptist (1:56). Once Mary leaves the scene, the narrative turns to the account of the birth and naming of John the Baptist (1:57-66). The text does not tell us of any contact between Mary and Elizabeth before the visitation, making it clear that Mary learns of Elizabeth's pregnancy from the angel.

The encounter between the two women is also the first encounter between their two unborn sons, Jesus and John the Baptist. Just as Mary learned of Elizabeth's condition by divine mediation, Elizabeth learns of Mary's pregnancy through the first prophetic act of John the Baptist, who leaps in his mother's womb at the sound of Mary's greeting (Lk 1:41, 44). In this way the Baptist fulfills the prediction of Luke 1:15, "he will be filled with the Holy Spirit even from his mother's womb." An Old Testament analogue for the Baptist's leaping in the womb can be found in Genesis 25:22, where the jostling of Esau and Jacob in Rebekah's womb anticipates the quarreling of the peoples who are their descendants.

Filled with the Holy Spirit, Elizabeth blesses Mary in words that are taken up later in Luke. Luke 1:42, "Blessed are you among women and blessed is the fruit of your womb," and Luke 1:45, "Blessed is she

The Visitation
(sixteenth-century painting)

who believed that there would be a fulfillment of what was spoken to her from the Lord," look ahead to Luke 8:19-21 and 11:27-28. In Luke 8:19-21, Jesus responds to the notice, "Your mother and your brethren are standing outside, desiring to see you" by declaring that attention and obedience to God's word are the basis for relationship with Him: "My mother and my brethren are those who hear the word of God and do it" (cf. Mt 12:46-50; Mk 3:31-35). In Luke 11:27-28 a woman calls out to Jesus, "Blessed is the womb that bore you and the breasts that you sucked." Jesus replies, "Blessed rather are those who hear the word of God and keep it!" The connection between these texts and Elizabeth's words to Mary clearly indicates that Mary is among those who hear and observe God's word.

Elizabeth's words to Mary are followed in Luke 1:46-55 by Mary's Canticle, the *Magnificat*, which is framed by Elizabeth's words to Mary in 1:45 and the conclusion of the visitation episode in 1:56.

Visitator, Apostolic • An apostolic visitator (or visitor) is a special legate of the Holy Father assigned to visit and report on a diocese, ecclesiastical territory, religious community or some other ecclesiastical institution. A visitator is given specific instructions and guidelines and, if necessary, may also be given authority to take certain actions or make decisions concerning the institution visited. Such appointments are quite unusual in modern times.

Vitalism • The contemporary moral and medical-ethical doctrine which holds that all human life must be preserved no matter what expense, pain or burden is involved. It is not clear if any responsible ethicists or moral theologians hold this doctrine, and it is ethically objectionable because it would force dying patients to accept expensive and futile treatments. The charge of "vitalism" is often issued by infanticide and euthanasia advocates against those who object to the denial of beneficial care and treatments for the disabled, burdensome, sick or dying which they perceive to be inexpensive, non-burdensome and effective. Rather than being a coherent philosophical position,

vitalism is more of a rhetorical term used against more conservative moral positions in contemporary debates.

Vitandus • The 1917 Code of Canon Law made a distinction between two types of excommunicated persons: one who was *vitandus*, that is, to be avoided, and one who was *toleratus*, that is, to be tolerated. A person declared *vitandus* was not to be associated with in any way by other members of the Church. The status of *vitandus* had to be expressly stated in the decree of excommunication. Furthermore, it could only be imposed on persons excommunicated by name by the Holy See. It was automatically incurred, however, by those who laid violent hands on the Roman Pontiff.

The revised Code did not retain the distinction nor the possibility of imposition of the status of *vitandus*. The closest similarity is the regulation that one who has had a declared or imposed excommunication be prevented from attending liturgical services (Canon 1331.2).

Vocation • In the Christian life, the divine calling to follow a certain course of action in life, especially with regard to the choice of a state in life (married, single or religious) is spoken of as a vocation. In practice, although the term has this broad meaning, it has come to refer in a special way to the call to the religious and/or priestly life. Hence, it is common to speak of a religious vocation, and also of the signs of a religious vocation. Here, the Church seeks to discern whether the call to a priestly or religious life is authentic in the young persons who experience or sense it. In its broadest meaning, the term refers to the universal call of God to all to a life of grace and union with Him. This is the great vocation, the call that gives human life its supernatural destiny and meaning.

Voluntarism • Philosophical and theological positions that give primacy to the will in the explanation of human behavior and divine activity are often said to be voluntaristic. But there is a wide range in the applicability and meaning of the term. Voluntarism in the theology of God commonly signifies an emphasis on the divine will, as opposed to the divine wisdom, in explaining divine activity in creating and redeeming the world. The difficulty that can arise in such explanations is that they leave little room for the intrinsic intelligibility of divine action. Voluntarism in moral theology discovers the good or evil of an action in the agent's will or intention rather than primarily in the nature of the moral object itself. Here voluntarism can lead to subjectivism in the evaluation of conduct.

Von Balthasar, Hans Urs • Swiss Catholic theologian (1905-1988), founder of the *Communio* journal for Catholic scholarship, honored by Pope John Paul II for constructive theological service in the Church and, a month prior to his death, named to the Cardinalate.

Von Balthasar entered the Jesuits after earning a doctorate in German humanities in the 1920s. In the next two decades he made noteworthy scholarly contributions with his studies on patristic figures such as Origen, Gregory of Nyssa and Maximus the Confessor. He translated many works of Catholic literature, for example, poetry and drama by Paul Claudel, and ecumenically related Catholic thought to the work of the Protestant theologian Karl Barth as well as that of the Jewish thinker Martin Buber.

He left the Jesuits in the late forties and worked to foster the secular institute form of Christian community. He was the spiritual director of Adrienne von Speyer, a contemplative whose reflections on the Scriptures and Christian life became influential in von Balthasar's own theology.

In the sixties he began publishing his multivolume *magnum opus*, which was completed in the eighties. This work is organized into three parts: (1) *The Glory of the Lord: A Theological Aesthetic*; (2) *Theodrama*; and (3) *Theologic*.

Von Balthasar's theology is so rich as to defy summary. Nevertheless, a few central themes may be mentioned. First, he takes pains to identify the distinctiveness of what God has done in Christ; thus he stresses how Christ goes beyond anything humans have hoped for or even dreamed of in their most spiritual religions, philosophies and arts.

Second, he shows that one misses Christ's distinctiveness if Christ is divorced from His Bride, the Church with her ministries (for example, the priestly and the papal Petrine ministry). Because the very being of a person is constituted by the person's relationships, Christ is Christ-ing in His in-Spirited glorifying of the Father in communion with the members of His Bride the Church, and in His working through those who are commissioned to special office (e.g., as Peter was commissioned to the Petrine or papal ministry).

Thirdly, von Balthasar's reflections on the Church lead to Mary as the one whose consent to God's word is at the very heart of the Church. Mary's prayerful consent to God manifests better than any of the specialized and visible offices of priest, bishop or even Pope, the innermost role Christians play within the Church.

Finally, von Balthasar can help us understand the concrete sense in which creation is designed by God from the beginning for the sake of His deed in Christ. Thus for example, the natural difference of the sexes and their marital intercourse foreshadow the difference between Christ and His Bride the Church and their Eucharistic Communion. In such a context von Balthasar shows that the Church's inability to ordain women to the office of priest (one who acts in the role of Christ) is based on reverent respect for the created role of men in their difference from and relation to women and for the distinctive and thus irreplaceable role of Christ as different from and related to the Church.

By identifying in detail the significance of worldly natural realities for God's supernatural works of grace, von Balthasar contributes greatly to moving beyond the residual Platonism (the tendency to regard religion as a flight from the world rather than as our share in God's restoration and supernatural fulfillment of the world) in some Christian thought.

In short, von Balthasar's works are wholly devoted to highlighting the fundamental and distinctive character of what God is doing in Christ and then using that understanding to clarify the "signs of the times," the concrete life of the Church and contemporary culture.

Votive Mass • In general, this term refers to Mass formularies in the Roman Missal for special occasions or in honor of aspects of the mystery of God or the saints. In the present sacramentary, "Masses and Prayers for Various Needs and Occasions" are divided into three types: ritual Masses (celebration of certain sacraments), various needs and occasions (as the need arises), and "votive Masses of the Mysteries of the Lord or in honor of Mary or a particular saint or of all the saints, which are options provided for the faithful's devotion" (n. 329). The priest may choose to use these texts when no other solemnity, feast or memorial occurs on that day. The sacramentary contains the following Mass formulas: Holy Trinity, Holy Cross, Holy Eucharist, Holy Name, Precious Blood, Sacred Heart, Holy Spirit, Blessed Virgin Mary, Angels, St. Joseph, Apostles, Peter, Paul, One Apostle, All Saints.

Votive Offerings • From the Latin *votum*, meaning a wish or a vow, votive offerings are freewill offerings of money or goods presented as an expression of piety and devotion in light of a particular request or need. In church construction and renovation, sometimes the term refers to major art works, artifacts or sacred vessels given to signify the need of the donor. Votive offerings are also the donation offered for the lighting of candles or vigil lamps to pray for an intention (e.g., restoration to health of the donor or another).

Votive Office • Similar to votive Masses in the sense that these can substitute for the regular daily office on particular occasions. The *General Instruction of the Liturgy of the Hours* states that "for a public cause or out of devotion [except on solemnities and certain feasts] . . . a votive office may be celebrated, in whole or in part: for example, on the occasion of a pilgrimage, a local feast, or the external solemnity of a saint" (n. 245). The clearest example in the present edition of the Liturgy of the Hours is the Office for the Dead.

Vow • A free and deliberate promise made to God concerning a possible and better good to be fulfilled by the person making the vow by reason of the virtue of religion.

A public vow is one that is accepted in the name of the Church by a legitimate superior; otherwise, it is private. A vow is solemn if it is acknowledged as such by the Church. Other vows are termed simple vows. Another distinction is between perpetual vows and temporary vows.

Private vows may be dispensed by the Roman Pontiff and by local Ordinaries, pastors and superiors of clerical religious institutes for their respective subjects. Perpetual public vows are dispensed only by the Holy See. Public temporary vows may be dispensed by the supreme moderators of religious institutes.

All members of religious institutes take vows to observe the evangelical counsels of poverty, chastity and obedience. The 1917 Code distinguished between solemn vows, taken by members of religious orders, and simple perpetual vows, taken by members of congregations. The difference between the two consisted in the effects of the vows of chastity and poverty. The solemn vow of chastity invalidated an attempted marriage, while a simple vow rendered the marriage illicit. With the solemn vow of poverty, the religious gave up the right of radical ownership of goods. The right to radical ownership was retained with the simple vow; however, the religious gave up the right to use goods owned. In the revised Code, the distinction between solemn and simple vows for religious is not found. Vows are either perpetual or temporary. The perpetual vow of chastity renders all attempted marriages invalid. As to the law of poverty, the Code leaves it to the particular law of each institute to determine how the goods of members are used, owned and disposed of.

Since the revised Code still speaks of solemn vows, it follows that those religious orders that had solemn vows prior to its promulgation still have them (Canons 1191-1198).

Vulgate • This term refers to that version of the Bible translated from the Greek and Hebrew into the Latin language by St. Jerome between A.D. 390 and 405. Since at that time the nobility still spoke Greek, and Latin was considered the vulgar language or the language of the common people (*vulgus* in Latin), St. Jerome's translation of the Scriptures was called the "Vulgate." Ironically, this Vulgate became the only official text of the Sacred Scriptures used by the Church even to this day. Under the direction of Popes Paul VI and John Paul II, a new version of the Vulgate has been prepared and published, and it is known as the *Nova Vulgata*.

For further reading: D. C. Parker, "Vulgate," *Anchor Bible Dictionary*, 6:860-862.

Waldenses • Also known as "Vaudois" or the "Poor Men of Lyons," this small Christian sect still has about 20,000 members, centered chiefly in the Piedmont region of northern Italy. They were founded by Peter Valdes (incorrectly known as "Waldo"), a rich merchant of Lyons who, around 1173, gave away his possessions and became an itinerant preacher. Valdes and his followers preached against clerical worldliness and Catharist heresy, sought ecclesiastical approval from the Third Lateran Council (1179) and won the permission of Pope Alexander III to preach only in regions where they were welcomed by the local clergy. The Pope's condition was not always respected, and despite their complete orthodoxy, the Waldenses were excommunicated (along with the Cathari) by the Council of Verona (1184). Subsequently, they began to organize themselves outside the Church, spreading from southern France to Spain, Germany, Piedmont and Lombardy, especially among the lower classes.

Their increasingly heterodox views — concerning the number and understanding of the sacraments, the invalidity of sacraments administered by unworthy clergy, rejection of purgatory and devotion to the saints, and their refusal to swear oaths — made them objects of persecution both by the Church and by the secular authorities. Their "proto-Protestantism" brought them into contact with Reformation movements in the sixteenth century. With their adoption of a formal Confession of Faith and their repudiation of the Catholic Church at the Synod of Chanforans (1532), the Waldenses in effect became a Reformed Protestant sect. Until 1848, when the Waldensian community in Piedmont won religious freedom from Duke Charles Albert of Savoy, they had been the object of intermittent and sometimes severe persecution.

War, Morality of • There are occasions and circumstances in which a war can be moral. War can be conducted morally if the following conditions are met: (1) the intention of the agent is just; (2) the means used is proportionate, discriminate and just; (3) it is resorted to only as a last means to resolve the conflict; (4) there is a proportion between the goods being protected by the war and the evils the war brings about; (5) there is a reasonable prospect for success; and (6) the cause of the war is just. On close analysis, one sees that these conditions are very difficult to meet, and the classical criteria held that a war could be considered just only if it was *morally certain* that these conditions were met. Because of this, one must wonder if there can be a just war today, particularly because it is not evident that the weapons used in virtually all wars today can meet the criteria of discrimination and proportionality.

Water • The symbolic use of water is found throughout Old Testament religious practice in such ceremonies as the setting apart of priests (Ex 29:4; Lv 8:6; Nm 8:7) before offering sacrifice (Ex 30:17-21), in the formal accusation of adultery (Nm 5:17-28), and in the ablutions before meals (Mk 7:3).

The Church, by the command of Christ, has always used water as the essential matter for the sacrament of Baptism (Jn 3:5), and in imitation of His example, maintains the devotional practice of the washing of feet with water on Holy Thursday (Jn 13:5).

Through His Baptism by St. John the Baptist in the Jordan, Christ sanctified water for the Christian sacrament of Baptism, and confirmed this symbolically when water and blood flowed from His wounded side.

Western Schism, The Great • This sad event in ecclesiastical history centers around rival claimants to the papacy after its return from Avignon to Rome. The period of 1378-1417 was one of confusion for the Church, and these are the usual dates given for the schism. The canonical election of Urban VI in Rome in 1378 was followed by a second election when many of the cardinals doubted the mental stability — and, perhaps more accurately, the governing style — of Urban. Clement VII was then elected, and he returned to Avignon in France. The schism became a reality in 1378. Various national groups supported one side or the other, symbolized by the factions of cardinals who had grown powerful in this era. Many plans were put forth to correct the matter, including the election of a third Pope, Alexander V (1409-1410), at the Council of

Pisa. His successor, John XXIII, was repudiated as an antipope in 1958 when a new Pope took this name again.

There were now three lines — the Roman, the Avignonese and the Pisan. Most efforts to end the schism failed, and bitter politics were involved the whole time. The University of Paris had submitted diplomatic and canonical counsel, but none of its remedies seemed to work easily or quickly. Theologians then debated the source of authority in the Church. Was it the College of Cardinals, the will of the Pope or a general council? The theory of conciliarism was utilized to help the situation, but its placing superiority of council over Pope would only undermine papal supremacy in the long run. It was formally condemned by Pope Pius II (1458-1564) in the Bull *Exsecrabilis*, and later by the First Vatican Council (1869-1870).

Finally, the Council of Constance (1414-1418) elected Oddo Cardinal Colonna, who was immediately ordained a priest, consecrated bishop and finally crowned as Pope Martin V on November 21, 1417. Thus ended the schism. The other rivals either resigned or eventually died. But the destabilization it produced and the lack of respect for the papacy which it engendered were to form a significant part of the background for the Reformation in the next century.

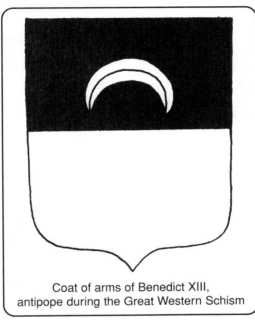

Coat of arms of Benedict XIII, antipope during the Great Western Schism

Wine, Liturgical Use of • In the Old Testament, the abundance of wine is often seen as a symbol of God's bountiful grace (e.g., Joel 2:24). Its liturgical use, however, is rooted in the uniquely symbolizing role which Our Lord attaches to it when, at the Last Supper, He compares it to His own blood. In combination with another staple of the human diet — bread — wine symbolizes a food in a comprehensive sense. Bread and wine together, transformed into the Body and Blood of Christ at the Eucharist, offer the perfect Food which strengthens us for full participation in the divine life.

In accord with the example of Christ, unleavened bread and grape wine are used in the celebration of the Eucharist. The *General Instruction of the Roman Missal* states, "The wine used to celebrate the Eucharist must be made of the fruit of the vine (cf. Lk 22:18), natural and pure, unmixed with anything else" (n. 284). The 1983 Code of Canon Law reiterates this prescription and says that the Eucharist "must be offered with bread and wine, with which a small quantity of water is to be mixed" (Canon 924.1). "The wine must be natural wine of the grape and not corrupt" (Canon 924.3).

With regard to the distribution of the Eucharist under both species, the Code states: "Holy Communion is to be given under the form of bread alone or under both kinds in accord with the norm of the liturgical laws or even under the form of wine alone in case of necessity" (Canon 925).

Wisdom • In its ordinary meanings, wisdom refers either to the perfection of knowledge or to the accumulated information in a certain field, in ancient sources or in human experience. The term also has more than one theological meaning. In the Scriptures, it refers to the personification of God's wise dealings and plan for the world and the human race, manifest in both creation and redemption. The term also refers to one of the seven Gifts of the Holy Spirit, along with understanding, piety, counsel, knowledge, fortitude and fear of the Lord. The gifts are further perfections of the infused theological and moral virtues and cultivate in the soul the readiness to respond to the divine guidance that makes us able to participate fully in the divine life. All the gifts pertain to particular areas of the Christian life. Along with knowledge, wisdom is a gift perfecting the use of judgment. Knowledge perfects the judgment of practical reason, while wisdom perfects the judgment of speculative reason.

Wisdom, Book of • The last of the seven sapiential books in the Old Testament is the deuterocanonical Book of Wisdom, written in Greek by a Jew of Alexandria about 100 B.C. The tone of the book indicates how the Hellenistic mentality had begun to change the Hebrew mind and choice of language. No reader could fail to recognize that it was written by a good and faithful Jew. But it is equally unmistakable that the author had some contact with the more abstract and speculative manner of thinking which we associate with the great Greeks.

The author speaks in the name of Solomon, and it is thought that he addresses those Jews who were so enamored of Greek science and philosophy that they were tempted to abandon their own religion. In contrast with Sirach, who is mostly concerned with the practical problems of daily life, this author takes a more transcendental view. The first wisdom is in God; human beings participate in it; its first manifestation in them is their recognition of God.

Three doctrines of Christian importance begin to emerge here: (1) that the true God can be naturally known to exist by pondering the origin of the universe; (2) that the human soul is immortal and survives the death of the body; and (3) that with God there is divine wisdom, through which He made the universe.

Witness • In its ordinary meaning, witness refers to the attestation of testimony concerning some state of affairs or action of which one has direct knowledge or acquaintance. In its specifically Christian sense, it refers in the first place to the testimony of those who knew Our Lord and who bear witness to His resurrection. The Apostles and the first disciples of Christ are the chief witnesses in the Christian community. Subsequently, however, all who are followers of Christ are called to bear witness to the hope that He imparts to Christians and to the whole world. In this sense, the shape of the Christian's daily life is a living witness to His faith and hope in Christ. The Christian may also be called upon to bear witness to Christ in words, in exhortation, in encouragement, in preaching, in defending the Faith, and so on.

Women, Ordination of • It has been the constant tradition and teaching of the Church that women are ineligible to receive the sacrament of Orders, not as a reflection of their dignity and holiness, but because of the relationship between Christ as Spouse and the Church as Bride. The exclusion of women from ordination is found in the expressed will of Christ, Who called men alone to be His Apostles. With the rise of feminism there are some who have sought to reopen the question of the ordination of women; however, both Pope Paul VI and Pope John Paul II have reaffirmed the unbroken teaching of the Church as being in conformity with the mind of Christ. In 1976, the declaration of the Congregation for the Doctrine of the Faith, *Inter Insigniores*, dealt with this matter in a detailed and authoritative manner. (Cf. Ordinatio Sacerdotalis.)

World Council of Churches (WCC) • An international organization representing one hundred forty-seven Protestant and Orthodox churches, established in 1948 with headquarters in Geneva, Switzerland. Its establishment was the outcome of discussions underway throughout the preceding decades and stimulated by an increasingly influential ecumenical concern in the various branches of Christianity. The First Assembly (held at Amsterdam) stated that its chief objective was to "hasten international reconciliation through its own members and through the cooperation of all Christian churches and of all men of good will." Although, generally speaking, the World Council of Churches has been a force for social good, its doctrinal positions have sometimes provoked considerable controversy and criticism. And although the Catholic Church has not joined the World Council of Churches, it has permanent cooperative relationships with the WCC, especially in the area of social justice.

Wreath, Advent • A popular, though not strictly speaking liturgical, custom whereby a circlet made of evergreen boughs and adorned with four candles is suspended from the ceiling, or placed on a stand, with the candles lighted in succession to mark the passage of the four weeks of Advent. By tradition, but not of necessity, the candles are of the color of the Advent vestments: usually three purple and one rose (for the third Sunday, "Gaudete . . . Rejoice" Sunday).

Originally a focal point for prayer in the home, and still placed in the refectory of many monastic and religious communities, the Advent Wreath has become a standard decoration of the worship space during this preparatory season for Christmas.

The new *Book of Blessings* provides for a formal blessing of the Advent Wreath as part of the General Intercessions on the First Sunday of Advent. The Spanish *Bendicional* has an alternative approach, in which the Blessing of the Wreath and Lighting of its First Candle take place at Vespers or at the beginning of the Vigil Mass of the First Sunday of Advent. In both rituals, the lighting of the subsequent candles on the following weeks takes place in silence or during the opening hymn with no further words or ceremonies.

A form for blessing the Advent Wreath at home, and prayers to be used at the candle-lighting each evening, are given in *Catholic Household Blessings and Prayers*.

Yahweh • The vocalization of the four consonants of the covenant name for God, which is believed to approximate the original pronunciation of the word. There is a welter of opinion about the basic, etymological meaning of the word and about its original form as well. In biblical tradition, "Yahweh," God's proper name, was disclosed to Moses during the Exodus (Ex 3). In this moment of revelation, Israel came to know more precisely the identity of God as the One Who snatched His Chosen People from slavery in Egypt.

The Yahwist tradition cites people using the name of Yahweh in the time of Enosh, grandson of Adam (Gn 4:26). This tradition seems eager to show Yahweh as the God of the whole human race and not just of Israel. According to the Priestly tradition, though God appeared to Abraham, Isaac and Jacob, He did not identify Himself to them by this name (Ex 6:2-3). The Elohist tradition appears to confirm this by not using the word "Yahweh" in Genesis, that is, before it is revealed to Moses in Exodus 3:11ff. All the traditions, however, are one in maintaining that Moses did not encounter a new God in the burning bush. The God of the bush was the "God of the fathers."

Originally, God's name appeared in Hebrew as a four-consonant word, YHWH, not displaying any vowels, which were added at a much later time. Hence, the original Hebrew pronunciation can only be conjectured. The abbreviated form "Yah" occurs twenty-five times in the Old Testament text. It appears, for example, in the aspiration "hallelu-Yah," i.e., "Praise Yah." Sometimes the abbreviated forms "Yahm" or "Yo" are found in proper names (Isaiah: "Yahm is salvation"; Joel: "Yo is God.")

The basic linguistic meaning of the word has not to date been established beyond doubt. Some of the possible meanings that have been put forward are: "He Who is," "He Who acts passionately" (this latter suggestion does justice to the vigorous, dynamic image of God as detailed in the Old Testament), "He Who speaks" (this emphasizes the revealing character of God), "sustainer." One suggestion that has attracted special attention is one that derives the meaning from a form of the verb "to be," in the sense of "to come into being." In this case, "Yahweh" would mean "The One Who causes to be whatever comes to be." Obviously, there is a stress here on God as Creator and Sustainer. Still another appealing suggestion is that the word means "I am" in the sense, "I am here standing by, ready to be of assistance." In the end, it must be observed that Israel's faith in God was not based on or much affected by the etymology of His name but by His mighty deeds.

For further reading: Henry O. Thompson, "Yahweh," *Anchor Bible Dictionary*, 6:1011-1012.

Yom Kippur: See **Atonement, Day of**

Youth, Impediment of • Canon 1083 of the 1983 Code of Canon Law establishes that boys must be at least sixteen years old and girls at least fourteen years old to enter sacramental marriage validly. In Roman law, and throughout much of the history of canon law, the minimum ages for marriage were fourteen for boys and twelve for girls, which are roughly equivalent to the ages of puberty. The 1917 Code raised the minimum ages as above. They would have been raised higher still with the appearance of the 1983 Code, except for the great difficulty in arriving at a suitable universal age, given the fact that the Code of Canon Law operates in a wide variety of cultures and economic conditions. Because the minimum ages were determined by ecclesiastical law, it is within the power of the diocesan bishop to dispense from this matrimonial impediment. On the other hand, the conference of bishops may establish a higher age for the licit celebration of marriage.

The Church's concern for the marriage of the very young extends considerably beyond the establishment of the impediment of youth. Canon 1072, for example, directs pastors to discourage persons from marrying when they are merely younger than the customary age for marrying in that area or community. The good sense behind this canon is self-evident. Canon 1071 requires the pastor (or other official witness) for a proposed marriage to seek the permission of the diocesan bishop when it is a question of marrying persons who are under eighteen if their parents are unaware of the marriage or are reasonably opposed to it. And more broadly yet, Canon 1063 urges pastors to develop a system of marriage preparation suitable for young people, among others, in order to help them grow in their understanding of the fullness of Christian marriage. Warning of the dangers of weddings contracted by the immature should be an integral part of such preparation programs.

Youth Organization, Catholic: See **Catholic Youth Organization**

Zeal • The motive of love and the resulting action that prompts one to serve God, a motive which can be inhibited by scrupulosity. Zeal for the Faith comes from a realization of the great blessings received through faith, and it expresses itself in a desire to proclaim and live in its fullness the Catholic Faith. It arises from a concern that so many suffer on account of their lack of faith or poor instruction in the Faith. Zeal is misguided when it believes that people will be lost if they do not explicitly profess the Catholic Faith, but it does not compromise the Faith for the sake of harmony. Zeal also stems from the obligation to promote and protect the Faith.

Zechariah, Book of • To the eleventh of the twelve major prophets is attributed a book of fourteen chapters. The first eight are generally considered authentic, and would locate the author toward the end of the sixth century, making him a contemporary of Haggai. The last six chapters are not regarded as belonging to this author, and their origin and date are most uncertain; scholars allot them to "Deutero-Zechariah."

In the first and authentic part, we have eight carefully dated (520-518 B.C.) nocturnal visions, to encourage the maintenance of the messianic hope among the people. They had recently returned from exile in Babylon, and were attempting to rebuild their lives, the city and the temple. Hostility from neighboring inhabitants made this a discouraging task. Zechariah urges them to do this with the promise that the coming of the Messiah will bring great blessings. As a religious educator, his pedagogical technique is to exhibit a mysterious symbol, and then to explain it.

The second part continues to emphasize the messianic theme. Gentile oppression will come to an end when God fulfills His promises and the Messiah comes. Although a son of David, He will be poor; it is this feature that Jesus Himself emphasized.

For further reading: Aelred Cody, O.S.B., "Haggai, Zechariah, Malachi," *New Jerome Biblical Commentary*, 349-361; Carol Meyers, Eric M. Meyers and Henry O. Thompson, "Zechariah, Book of," *Anchor Bible Dictionary*, 6:1061-1068.

Zelanti • From the Latin *zelantes* (literally, eager ones), the *Zelanti* (or Zealots) were those Franciscans in the Franciscan Controversy of the thirteenth century who opposed any modification of the Franciscan Rule as it was established by St. Francis of Assisi in 1221 and revised by him in 1223. They were opposed in their zeal by the *Relaxati* (or Lax), who favored a relaxation of the rigors of their rule.

Zeon • In the East, warm water which the priest pours in the chalice immediately before Communion.

Zephaniah, Book of • The message of the seventh-century B.C. prophet Zephaniah is best viewed against its historical background. The Scythians invaded Palestine, and this disaster elicited from Zephaniah the interpretation found in his book that these barbarian hordes served as the instrument of God's judgment on Judah and in a sense on the whole world (1:2-3). Zephaniah puts his finger on the root cause of Jerusalem's and Judah's offense: the pagan rituals to which the people had become addicted (1:8-9). The prophet also censures the people's blithe unconcern for ethical standards in their day-to-day transactions. He concentrates sharply — perhaps more than any other prophet — on the Day of the Lord and its punishing fallout of ruin and devastation. Zephaniah also depicts God's action as it impinges on the neighboring nations with which Judah was in contact: Philistia, Egypt, Assyria (2:4-15). Finally, Jerusalem is censured and threatened for not heeding the warnings issued to it, for not turning to God.

Zucchetto
(worn by Pope Pius IX)

There is an optimistic ending to the book. We are told about a faithful nucleus in Judah. God will renew this remnant and will rejoice over them (3:9-20). There is some scholarly opinion that the book has been deeply edited, with sections added from a later time. The influence of Amos and Hosea is noticeable at different points in the work.

Zephaniah the man was a prophet of Judean origins. He is listed ninth among the minor prophets and is thought to have been born not much before 660 B.C. He is a lineal descendant of King Hezekiah of Judah.

For further reading: John S. Kselman, S.S., "Zephaniah," *Anchor Bible Dictionary*, 6:1077-1080; Thomas P. Wahl, O.S.B., Irene Nowell, O.S.B., and Anthony R. Ceresko, O.S.F.S., "Zephaniah, Nahum, Habakkuk," *New Jerome Biblical Commentary*, 255-258.

Ziggurat • A word of Assyrian origin, meaning "pinnacle" or "height." It came to indicate a temple tower of the Assyrians and Babylonians. In form, the structure was a terraced pyramid with each level smaller than the level just below it. (Cf. Babel, Tower of.)

Zimarra • This Italian term, which comes into English as "simar," refers to the cassock-like attire formerly used by all prelates, but which is now reserved to bishops, cardinals and the Pope. It resembles the house cassock (i.e., black with red or purple piping, according to rank), but it has a small shoulder cape (*pellegrina*) attached to the collar. It was regarded as informal dress until Pope Pius IX decreed that, when worn with a ferraiolone, it would be standard attire for prelates at papal audiences.

Until 1969, the simar also had false half-sleeves that reached to the elbow, slit and fastened with a row of buttons. Now that this has been abrogated, many prelates today find it convenient to buy a detachable shoulder cape to wear over the house cassock. The Pope's everyday dress is the white simar, with white silk buttons, piping and white watered-silk cuffs.

Zone • Belt worn by an Eastern-Rite priest over the sticharion.

Zucchetto • Derived from the popular Italian idiom *zucca*, meaning a pumpkin, which was used for "head," the zucchetto is a small skullcap which at one time was worn by any number of persons as a head covering, especially in the winter cold. It has come to mean the skullcap worn by ecclesiastics, in particular prelates. The Pope wears a white zucchetto of watered silk. The cardinals use scarlet, and bishops, purple. Monsignori may wear black with purple piping. All others may use simple black, including abbots who are not endowed with the episcopal dignity.

Zwinglianism • Ulrich Zwingli (1484-1531), the Swiss Protestant reformer, was a parish priest at Glarus, Switzerland. By 1524 he, like Luther, attacked fasting, clerical celibacy and the Mass. He preached predestination, advocated a married clergy and denied the authority of the Pope, free will, purgatory and the forgiveness of sins by priests. Baptism and the Eucharist were the only sacraments acknowledged by him. While Luther affirmed a Real Presence of Christ in the Eucharist, Zwingli believed it to be symbolic. In 1525 he published his *Commentary on True and False Religion*. In a battle at Kappel between Protestant and Catholic Swiss cantons, he was killed in 1531. Although in Switzerland the Reformation gradually became Calvinistic, Zwingli had a great influence on Protestant theology.

List of Entries

Aer
Aesthetics
Aeterni Patris
Aetianism
Affectio Maritalis
Affections
Affective Prayer
Affinity
Africa, Church in
Agape
Age, Canonical
Age, Impediment of
Age of Reason
Aggiornamento
Aggressor, Unjust
Aglipay Schism
Agnosticism
Agnus Dei
Agony of Christ
Agrapha
AID
AIDS
AIH
Aisle
Aitesis
Akeldama
Akolouthia
Alais, Treaty of
Alamo
Alb
Albania, The Church in
Albigensianism
Alcantara, Knights of
Alcoholism and Related Drug Problems,
    National Catholic Council on
Aleph
Alexandria, Church of
Alexandria, School of
Alexandrian Rite
Alexandrine Liturgy
Alienation
Alimentation
Aliturgical Days
All Saints, Solemnity of
Allah
Allatae Sunt
All Souls Day
Allegorical Interpretation (Biblical)
Allegory
Alleluia
Allocution
Alma (Almah)
Almanac, Our Sunday Visitor's Catholic
Almighty, The
Almoner

Alms
Almuce
Alpha and Omega
Alphabetic Psalms
Altar
Altar Bread
Altar Cards
Altar Cloths
Altar, Consecration of an
Altar, Gregorian
Altar Linens
Altar Societies
Altar Stone
Altar, Stripping of the
Ambo
Ambrosian Chant
Ambrosian Hymnography (also Ambrosiani)
Ambrosian Liturgy
Ambry: See Aumbry
Ambulatory
Amen
Amendment, Purpose of
American Board of Catholic Missions
American Cassinese Congregation
American Protective Association
Americanism
Amice
Amish
Ammonian Sections
Amos, Book of
Amovability
Ampulla
Amula
Amulet
Anabaptism
Anagni
Anagnostes
Anagogical Sense
Analecta
Analogy
Anamnesis
Ananias
Anaphora
Anastasis
Anathema
Anchor
Anchor-Cross
Anchorhold
Anchorite
Ancient of Days
Andrew, St.
Angel
Angel, Guardian: See Guardian Angels
Angels, Names of the
Angelic Salutation: See Ave Maria

Angel-Lights
Angels, Evil: See Devil and Evil Spirits
Angels of the Churches
Angelus
Anger
Anglican, Anglicanism
Anglican Orders
Anglo-Catholics
Anima Christi
Animals in Church Art
Anne de Beaupré, St., Shrine of: See
    Canadian Shrines
Anniversary
Annuario Pontificio
Annulment
Annunciation of Mary
Anointing
Anointing of the Sick
Anointing of the Sick, Rite for
Anomoeans
Antediluvian
Antependium
Anthem
Anthropomorphism
Anti-Catholicism (in America)
Anticamera
Antichrist
Anticipate
Anticipated Mass
Anticlericalism
Antidicomarianites
Antidoron
Antigonish Movement
Antilegomena
Antimension
Antinomians
Antioch
Antioch, Patriarchate of
Antioch, School of
Antiochene Rite: See Rite, Antiochene
Antiphon
Antiphonal
Antiphonal Chants
Antiphonary: See Antiphon
Antipopes
Anti-Semitism
Antistes
Antitrinitarians
Antitype
Apocalypse: See Revelation, Book of
Apocalypticism
Apocalyptic Number
Apocatastasis
Apocrisarius
Apocrypha — New Testament

Apodeipnon
Apodosis
Apollinarianism
Apologetics
Apologist
Apology (or Apologia)
Apolusia
Apolysis
Apolytikion
Apostasy
Apostle
Apostles' Creed
Apostles of Places and Peoples
Apostleship of Prayer
Apostolate
Apostolate of Lay People, Decree on the: See
    Apostolicam Actuositatem
Apostolate of Suffering
Apostolic Canons
Apostolic Constitution
Apostolic Datary
Apostolic Delegate
Apostolic Fathers
Apostolic Ministry
Apostolic Prefecture: See Prefecture,
    Apostolic
Apostolic See
Apostolic Signatura
Apostolic Succession
Apostolic Union
Apostolic Vicariate: See Prefect, Apostolic;
    also Prefecture, Apostolic
Apostolicae Curae
Apostolicam Actuositatem
Apostolici
Apostolicity
Apostolos
Apparel (Paratura)
Apparitions
Appeal
Appellant Controversy
Appellants
Appetite
Appropriation
Apse
Apsidole
Aquamanile
Aquarians
Aquileian Rite
Aramaic
Arca
Arch
Archaeology, Christian
Archaeology, Commission of Sacred
Archangel

Archbishop
Archbishop, Titular
Archbishop-Elect
Archconfraternity
Archdeacon
Archdiocese
Archetype
Archiepiscopal Cross (Patriarchal Cross)
Archimandrite
Architecture
Archives
Archivist
Archpriest
Arcosolium
Arcula: See Arca
Areopagite
Areopagus: See Areopagite
Arianism
Ariel
Ark
Arles, Councils of
Armageddon
Armagh, Book of
Armenian Church
Armenian Rite: See Rite, Armenian
Arms of Christ, The
Art, Christian
Art, Liturgical
Art, Sacred
Artoklasia
Artos
Arts, The Liberal
Ascension of Christ
Ascetical Theology
Asceticism
Aseity
Ash Wednesday
Ashes
Asperges
Aspergillum (Aspergill)
Aspersion
Aspersory (Aspersorium)
Aspirations
Ass
Assessor
Assist at Mass
Assistant at the Pontifical Throne
Assistant Priest
Associate Pastor
Associations of the Christian Faithful
Assumption of the Blessed Virgin Mary
Assumptionists
Asteriskos
Astrology
Asylum, Right of

Athanasian Creed: See Creed, Athanasian
Atheism
Atonement
Atonement, Day of
Attention
Attributes of God: See God, Attributes of
Attrition
Audience, Papal
Auditor
Augsburg, Diet of
Augsburg, Peace of
Augustinian Fathers
Augustinism
Aumbry (also Ambry)
Aureole
Auricular Confession
Auriesville
Aurifrisium (Apparel)
Aurora, Mass of
Austerities
Australia, Christianity in
Authenticity, Biblical
Authority of Scripture
Authorized Version
Autocephalous
Auto-da-Fé
Autonomous Religious House
Autonomy
Auxiliary Bishop
Avarice or Covetousness
Ave Maria
Avenir, L' (Future, The)
Aversion
Avignon Papacy
Azrael
Azyme
Azymites

B

B.C.
Baal
Babel, Tower of
Babylon, The Patriarch of
Babylonian Exile
Bachelor
Bad Faith
Baha'i
Baianism
Baldacchino
Balm (or Balsam)
Baltimore
Baltimore Catechism
Baltimore, Councils of

Banner
Banneux, Apparitions of
Banns
Baptism of Bells
Baptism of Blood
Baptism of the Dead
Baptism, Lay
Baptism, Sacrament of
Baptismal Font
Baptismal Name
Baptismal Robe
Baptismal Vows or Promises
Baptismal Water: See Baptismal Font
Baptistery (also Baptistry)
Baptists
Barefoot Friars
Barnabas
Baroque Art and Architecture
Bartholomew
Baruch, Book of
Basel, Council of
Basic Teachings for Catholic Religious
    Education
Basil, Liturgy of
Basilian Fathers
Basilian Rule
Basilica
Basilidians
Bay Psalm Book
Beatific Vision
Beatification
Beatitude
Beatitude of Heaven
Beatitudes, The
Beatus or Beata
Beauraing, Our Lady of
Beautiful Gate
Beelzebub
Befana
Beguines and Beghards
Being
Belfry
Belial
Belief
Bell, Book and Candle
Bells
Bema
Benedicite
Benedict, The Holy Rule of
Benedictines
Benediction
Benediction of the Blessed Sacrament
Benediction, Apostolic
Benediction with a Ciborium
Benedictional

Benedictus
Benefice
Benefit of Clergy
Benemerenti Medal
Benjamin
Berakoth
Bestiaries
Bethel
Bethlehem
Betrothal
Betting
Bible
Bible, English Editions
Bible Reading
Bible Societies and Study Groups
Bible Studies, Catholic
Bible Vigil
Biblia Pauperum
Biblical Chronology
Biblical Commission, Pontifical: See
    Pontifical Biblical Commission
Biblical Institute: See Pontifical Biblical
    Institute
Biblical Institute of Jerusalem: See École
    Biblique
Biblical Revival
Bigamy
Bigot
Bilocation
Bination
Biretta
Birth Control
Birth Control Pill
Bisexual
Bishop
Bishop, Auxiliary
Bishop, Coadjutor: See Coadjutor Bishop
Bishop, Suffragan
Bishop, Titular
Bishop of Rome
Bishops, Collegiality of
Bishops in the Church, Decree on the
    Pastoral Office of the: See Christus
    Dominus
Bishops' Committee on the Liturgy (BCL)
Black
Black Fast
Black Friars
Black Legend
Black Monks
Black Pope
Blaise, Blessing of St.
Blasphemy
Bless Oneself
Blessed

Capital Sins (also Capital Vices or Deadly Sins)
Capitulary
Cappa
Cappa Magna
Cappa Pluvialis
Captivity Epistles
Cardinal Legate
Cardinal Protector
Cardinal Vicar
Cardinal Virtues
Care of Souls
Caritas Internationalis
Carmel, Mount
Carnival (also Carnivale)
Carolingian Schools
Carthage, Councils of
Carthusians
Cases of Conscience
Cassock (also Soutane)
Castel Gandolfo
Casuistry
Catacombs
Catafalque
Catechesis
Catechetics
Catechism
Catechism of the Catholic Church
Catechist
Catechumens
Categorical Imperative
Cathari
Cathedra
Cathedral
Cathedraticum
Catholic
Catholic Action
Catholic Church
Catholic Communications Foundation
Catholic Epistles
Catholic Foreign Mission Society of America
Catholic Household Blessings and Prayers
Catholic League for Religious and Civil Rights
Catholic Press
Catholic Press Association (CPA)
Catholic Truth Society
Catholic University of America, The
Catholic Worker Movement
Catholic Youth Organization
Catholicos
Catholics in Statuary Hall
Cause
Causes, Four
Cautiones

Celebrant
Celebret
Celestial Hierarchy
Celibacy
Cell
Cellarer
Celtic Cross
Celtic Rite
Cemetery
Cenacle
Cenobite
Censer
Censor of Books
Censure
Centesimus Annus
Cerecloth (Chrismale)
Ceremonial of Bishops
Ceremony
Certitude
Chains of St. Peter
Chair: See Cathedra
Chair of St. Peter
Chalcedon, Council of
Chaldean Rite
Chalice
Chalice Veil (also Peplum and Sudarium)
Chamberlain
Chambre Ardente
Chancel
Chancellor
Chancery
Chancery, Papal (Apostolic)
Chant
Chant, Ambrosian: See Ambrosian Chant
Chant, Gregorian: See Gregorian Chant
Chantry
Chapel
Chapel of Ease
Chaplain
Chaplet
Chapter, Cathedral
Chapter, Conventual
Chapter House
Chapter of Faults
Character
Charismata (also Charisms)
Charismatic Renewal, Catholic
Charity
Charity, Heroic Act of
Charity, Works of
Chartres, Cathedral of (Notre Dame de Chartres)
Chartreuse, The Great
Chastity
Chasuble

Cherubikon
Cherubim
Chevet
Child of Mary
Childermas
Children, Duties of
Children, Mass for
Children's Communion
Children's Crusade
Chiliasm
Chinese Rites: See Rites, Chinese
Chi-Rho
Chirograph
Chirotony
Chivalry
Choir
Chrism
Chrismal (also Chrismatory)
Chrismarium
Chrismation
Christ
Christ, Supreme Order of
Christ of the Andes
Christening: See Baptism, Sacrament of
Christian
Christian Brothers
Christian Democrats
Christian Doctrine
Christian Doctrine, Confraternity of: See
    Confraternity of Christian Doctrine
Christian Education, Declaration on: See
    Gravissimum Educationis
Christian Family Movement
Christian Philosophy
Christian Science
Christian Socialism
Christianity
Christifideles Laici
Christmas
Christology
Christophers
Christus Dominus
Chronicler
Chronicles, Books One and Two of
Chronista
Chronology, Biblical: See Biblical
    Chronology
Church
Church, Early
Church, Dogmatic Constitution on the: See
    Lumen Gentium
Church History
Church Militant, Suffering, Triumphant:
    See Communion of Saints
Church Property: See Temporal Goods

Church and State
Church in the Modern World, Pastoral
    Constitution on the: See Gaudium et Spes
Churching of Women
Churchyard
Ciborium
Cilicium: See Hair Shirt
Cincture
Circumcellions
Circumcision
Circumincession (Divine Perichoresis)
Cistercians
Citation
City of God
Civil Allegiance
Civil Law
Civil Marriage
Civory
Clandestinity
Clapper (also Clepper or Crotalum)
Clementine Instruction
Clergy
Clergy, Byzantine
Cleric
Clerical Dress: See Dress, Clerical
Clerical Obligations
Clerical Privilege
Clericalism
Clerks Regular
Clinical Baptism
Cloister (also Close)
Clothing
Cluny
Coadjutor Bishop
Coat-of-arms
Co-Consecrators
Code of Canon Law
Codex
Codex, Canonical
Coelibatus Sacerdotalis
Coenobium
Collateral
Collation
Collect
Collection, Offertory: See Offertory
    Collection
Collection of Masses of the Blessed Virgin
    Mary
Collections, Canonical
Collectivism
College
College of Cardinals
College of Consultors
Collegiality
Collegiate Church

Collegiate Tribunal
Collegium Cultorum Martyrum
Colors, Liturgical
Colossians, Epistle to the
Commandments of the Church
Commandments of God
Commemoration
Commemoration of the Living and the Dead
Commendation of the Soul
Commentaries, Biblical
Commissary
Commissions, Ecclesiastical
Commixture, Liturgical
Common Life
Common Prayer, Book of: See Book of
    Common Prayer
Common of the Saints
Common Teaching of Theologians
Communicatio Idiomatum
Communicatio in Sacris
Communications, Decree on the Means of
    Social: See Inter Mirifica
Communications Foundation, Catholic: See
    Catholic Communications Foundation
Communion, Holy
Communion of the Mass
Communion of Saints
Communism
Community
Comparative Religion
Competence
Complaint of Nullity
Compline (Complin)
Compostela, Pilgrimage of
Comunione e Liberazione
Concelebration
Conciliar Theory (also Conciliar Movement)
Conclave
Concomitance
Concord, Formula of
Concordance
Concordat
Concordat of Worms
Concupiscence
Concursus
Condign Merit
Conditional Administration of the
    Sacraments
Conferences, Clergy
Conferences, Episcopal
Confession
Confession of a Martyr (also Confessio)
Confessional
Confessor
Confirmation, Sacrament of

Confirmation Name
Confiteor
Confraternity
Confraternity of Christian Doctrine (CCD)
Congregation
Congregational Singing: See Singing,
    Congregational
Congregationalism
Congresses, Eucharistic
Congruism
Consanguinity
Conscience
Consecration
Consecration Cross
Consent, Marital
Consequentialism
Consistent Life Ethic
Consistory
Consortium Perfectae Caritatis
Constance, Council of
Constancy
Constantine, Donation of
Constantinople, Councils of
Constantinople, Patriarch of
Constantinople, Rite of: See Rite of
    Constantinople
Constitutional Clergy
Constitutions
Consubstantial
Consubstantiation
Consultors
Consummation
Contemplative Life
Contentious Trials
Continence
Contract
Contrition
Contumacy
Contumely
Convalidation
Convent
Conventual Mass
Conversion
Convert
Cope
Copt
Coptic Rite
Cor Unum
Coram Cardinale (Episcopo)
Corinthians, First Epistle to the
Corinthians, Second Epistle to the
Cornette
Corona
Coronation of the Blessed Virgin Mary
Coronation of the Pope

Corporal
Corporal Works of Mercy
Corpus Christi
Corpus Iuris Canonici
Cosmology
Costume, Clerical
Cotta
Council
Councils, Ecumenical
Counseling, Pastoral
Counter-Reformation
Courts, Ecclesiastical
Covenant
Cowl
Creation
Creationism
Creator
Crèche
Credence
Creed
Creed, Athanasian
Cremation
Crib: See Crèche
Crimen
Criticism, Biblical
Crosier (also Crozier)
Cross
Cross, Relics of the True
Cross, Veneration of the
Crown, Episcopal
Crown, Franciscan
Crown of Thorns
Crucifix
Crucifixion
Cruet
Crusade, Children's: See Children's
    Crusade
Crusades
Crypt
Cubiculum
Culpability
Cult (also Cultus)
Cult, Disparity of
Curate
Curator
Curia, Diocesan
Curia, Roman
Cursillo
Cursing
Cursing Psalms: See Imprecatory Psalms
Custom
Custos
Cycle: See Calendar
Cycle of Readings

D

Dalmatic
Dance, Liturgical
Daniel
Daniel, Book of
Dark Ages
Dark Night of the Senses
Dark Night of the Soul
David
Day of Atonement: See Atonement, Day of
Day Hours
Day of Indiction
Day of the Lord
Days of Prayer
De Condigno
De Congruo
De Profundis
Deacon, Permanent
Deacon, Transitional
Deaconess
Deacons, First Seven
Dead Sea Scrolls
Dean
Deanery
Death
Deborah, Song of
Decade
Decalogue
Declaration
Decorations, Pontifical
Decree
Decretalist
Decretals
Decretals, False
Decretist
Decretum Gratiani
Dedication of a Church
Defect, Irregularity of
Defect of Form
Defender of the Bond
Defender of the Faith
Defensor Ecclesiae
Definition, Papal
Definitors
Defrocking
Degradation
Dei Verbum
Deification
Deipara
Deisis
Deism
Delator
Delegation
Delict

Deluge
Demiurge
Demon
Demoniac
Denunciation
Deontological Ethics
Deposing Power, Papal
Deposit of Faith
Deposition
Deposition, Bull of
Desecration of a Church
Desire, Baptism of
Despair
Detachment
Detraction
Deuterocanonical Books
Deuteronomy, Book of
Development of Doctrine
Development of Peoples
Devil
Devil and Evil Spirits
Devil's Advocate
Devolution
Devotion
Diabolical Possession
Diakonikon
Dialogue Mass
Diaspora
Diatesseron
Dicastery
Didache, The
Didascalia Apostolorum
Dies Irae
Diet of Augsburg: See Augsburg, Diet of
Diffinitor: See Definitors
Dignitatis Humanae
Dimissorials
Diocesan Administrator
Diocesan Clergy
Diocesan Pastoral Council (also
    Archdiocesan Pastoral Council)
Diocesan Right
Diocese
Diptychs
Direct Line
Directorium: See Ordo
Diriment Impediment: See Impediment,
    Diriment
Discalced
Discernment of Spirits
Disciple
Disciplina Arcani
Discipline
Discrimination
Diskos

Dismissal
Disparity of Worship: See Cult, Disparity of
Dispensation
Dissidio
Dissolution of Marriage
Dives in Misericordia
Divination
Divine Comedy
Divine Office
Divine Praises
Divine Revelation, Dogmatic Constitution
    on: See Dei Verbum
Divine Worship, Congregation for: See Rites,
    Sacred Congregation of
Divinity of Christ
Divino Afflante Spiritu
Divorce
Divorce From Bed and Board
Docetism
Doctor
Doctor Angelicus
Doctor Communis
Doctor Gratiae
Doctor Marianus
Doctor Mellifluus
Doctor Seraphicus
Doctor Subtilis
Doctor Universalis
Doctrine of the Catholic Church
Documentary Process
Dogma
Dogmatic Theology
Dom
Domestic Prelate
Domicile
Dominations
Dominic, St.
Dominicans (also Order of Preachers)
Dominum et Vivificantem
Donation of Constantine: See Constantine,
    Donation of
Donatism
Doorkeeper: See Porter
Dormition of the Blessed Virgin Mary
Dossal (also Dorsal)
Douai Bible (also Douay or Doway Bible)
Double
Doubt of Law, of Fact
Dove
Doxology
Dreams
Dress, Clerical
Drug Education, Catholic Office of
Dualism
Due Process

Duel
Dulia
Duties
Duties of Parents
Dying, Prayers for the

E

Early Church: See Church, Early
Easter
Easter Controversy
Easter Duty
Easter Season
Easter Water
Eastern Churches
Eastern Churches, Decree on the Catholic:
    See Orientalium Ecclesiarum
Eastern Monasticism
Eastern Studies, Pontifical Institute of
Ebionites
Ecce Homo
Ecclesia
Ecclesiam Suam
Ecclesiastes, Book of
Ecclesiastic
Ecclesiastical
Ecclesiastical Law
Ecclesiastical Regions
Ecclesiastical Titles
Ecclesiasticus: See Sirach, Book of
Ecclesiology
École Biblique
Economic Affairs, Prefecture of
Economics
Economy, Divine
Ecstasy
Ecthesis
Ecumenical Councils: See Councils,
    Ecumenical
Ecumenical Theology
Ecumenism, Decree on: See Unitatis
    Redintegratio
Eden, Garden of
Edict of Milan
Edict of Nantes
Edict of Restitution
Edification, Christian
Editio Typica
Education, Declaration on Christian: See
    Gravissimum Educationis
Efficacious Grace
Eileton
Ejaculation
Ekphonese

Ektene
Elect
Election, Canonical
Election, Papal
Eleemosynary Office
Elevation at Mass
Elizabethan Settlement
Elkesaites
Elne, Council of
Elvira, Council of
Ember Days
Emblems of Saints
Embolism
Eminence
Emmanuel (also Immanuel)
Empire, Holy Roman
Enchiridion
Enclosure (also Cloister)
Encratism (or Encratites)
Encyclical
Encyclical Epistle: See Encyclical
Encyclicals, Social
Encyclopedists
End
End of Man
End of the World
Endowment
Ends of the Mass
Energumen
English Martyrs
Enkolpion
Enlightenment, The Age of
Entelechy
Enthronement of the Sacred Heart
Enthusiasm, Catholic
Entrance Antiphon/Song
Envy
Eparch
Eparchy
Ephesians, Epistle to the
Ephesus, Council of
Ephesus, Robber Council of
Epiclesis (also Epiklesis)
Epigonation
Epimanikia
Epiphany
Episcopacy
Episcopal Vicar
Episcopalians
Episcopalism
Epistle
Epitaphion
Epitrachelion (also Epitakhelion)
Equality
Erastianism

Feasts of the Church
Febronianism
Federation of Diocesan Liturgical
    Commissions (FDLC)
Feminism, Christian
Ferendae Sententiae
Feria
Ferraiolone
Festival of Lights: See Hanukkah
Fetishism
Feudalism
Fides
Filioque
Final Perseverance
Finance Council
Finance Officer
Finding of the Cross
Fire, Blessing of the
First Friday Devotions
First Fruits
First Holy Communion
First Saturday Devotion
Firstborn
Fiscal Procurator
Fish
Fisherman's Ring
Fistula
Five Wounds
Flabellum
Flagellation
Flat Hat
Flectamus Genua
Flock
Florence, Council of
Florida Pascua
Focolare Movement
Fontes
Form
Form, Canonical
Form Criticism
Fortitude
Fortune-Telling
Forty Hours Devotion
Forum
Foundation Masses
Four Causes: See Causes, Four
Fraction
Franciscan Controversy
Franciscans
Frankfort, Council of
Frankincense
Fraternal Correction
Fraud in Marriage
Freedom

Freedom, Religious: See Liberty, Religious;
    also Dignitatis Humanae
Freemasonry
Friar
Friary
Friends of God
Friendship
Fruits of the Holy Spirit
Fruits of the Mass
Fundamental Articles
Fundamental Option
Fundamental Theology
Funeral Mass

G

Gabbatha
Gabriel
Galatians, Epistle to the
Galilee
Galileo Affair
Gallican Liturgies
Gallican Psalter
Gallicanism
Gambling
Garden of Eden: See Eden, Garden of
Gaudete Sunday
Gaudium et Spes
Ge'ez (also Gheez)
Gehenna
Genealogy of Christ
General
General Absolution
General Chapter
General Confession
General Instruction of the Roman Missal:
    See Roman Missal, General Instruction of
    the
General Intercessions: See Prayer of the
    Faithful
Genesis
Genocide
Gentile
Genuflection (also Genuflexion)
Georgian Byzantine Rite
Gethsemane
Ghibellines: See Guelfs and Ghibellines
Gifts of the Holy Spirit, The Seven
Gifts, Preternatural
Gifts, Supernatural
Gift of Tongues
Glagolithic Alphabet
Gloria in Excelsis Deo
Gloria Patri

Glorified Body
Glory
Glossator
Gloves, Episcopal
Gluttony
Gnosis
Gnosticism: See Gnosis
God
God, Attributes of
God, Presence of
Godparents
God-spell
Gold
Golden Bull
Golden Legend
Golden Rose
Golgotha
Good Faith Solution
Good Friday
Good Shepherd
Goodness
Goods, Temporal: See Temporal Goods
Goods of Marriage
Gospel
Gospel, The Fifth
Gospel, The Last
Grace
Grace, Actual: See Actual Grace
Grace, Efficacious: See Efficacious Grace
Grace, Habitual: See Habitual Grace
Grace, Sanctifying: See Sanctifying Grace
Grace at Meals
Gradine
Gradual
Gradual Psalms
Graduale Romanum
Graffito
Grail, The Holy
Grail Movement, The
Gravissimum Educationis
Greater Double
Greca
Greek Church
Greek Church, United
Greek Corporal
Greek Fathers
Gregorian Calendar
Gregorian Chant
Gregorian Masses
Gregorian Modes
Gregorian Reform
Gregorian Sacramentary
Gremial (also Gremiale)
Grille
Guadalupe, Our Lady of

Guardian
Guardian Angels
Guelfs and Ghibellines
Guilds
Guilt
Gyrovagi

H

Habakkuk, Book of (also Habacuc)
Habit
Habit, Religious
Habitual Grace
Haceldama: See Akeldama
Haggai, Book of (also Aggai or Aggaeus)
Hagia
Hagiography
Hail Mary
Hair Shirt
Halo: See Aureole
Hampton Court Conference
Hanukkah
Happiness
Harmony, Biblical
Hasmoneans
Hatred
Hearse
Heart of Mary, Immaculate
Heaven
Hebdomadarius
Hebrew-Catholic
Hebrew Feasts
Hebrew Language
Hebrew Poetry: See Psalms, Book of
Hebrews, Epistle to the
Hedge Schools
Hedonism
Hegoumenos
Hell
Hellenism
Henotikon
Heortology
Heptateuch
Heresy
Heretic
Hermeneutics
Hermesianism
Hermit
Heroic Virtue
Hesperinos
Hesychasm
Hesychasts
Hexaemeron (also Hexahemeron)
Hexapla

Hexapteryga
Hexateuch
Hierarch
Hierarchy
Hieratikon
Hierodeacon
Hieromonk
Hierurgia
High Priest
Hirmos
History, Church
Hogan Schism
Holiness
Holiness Churches
Holiness, Mark of the Church
Holocaust
Holy Alliance
Holy Communion
Holy Days
Holy or Royal Doors
Holy Family
Holy Father
Holy of Holies, The
Holy Hour
Holy Name of Jesus
Holy Office, Congregation of the
Holy Oils
Holy Places
Holy Roman Empire
Holy Saturday
Holy See
Holy Sepulcher in Jerusalem, The
Holy Sepulcher, Knights of
Holy Souls: See Purgatory
Holy Spirit
Holy Spirit, Sins Against the
Holy Thursday
Holy Water
Holy Water Font
Holy Week, Liturgy of: See Triduum, Paschal
Holy Year
Home-Schooling
Homiletics
Homily
Homoousios and Homoiousios
Hood
Hope
Horologion
Hosanna
Hosea, Book of
Host
Hosts: See Sabaoth
Hours, Book of
Hours, Little
Huguenots

Human Acts
Human Dignity
Human Life International
Humanae Vitae
Humani Generis
Humanism
Humanitarianism
Humeral Veil
Humiliati
Humility
Hylics
Hymn
Hymnal
Hymnody
Hymnology
Hyperdulia
Hypostasis
Hypostatic Union
Hyssop

I

Icon (also Ikon)
Iconoclastic Controversy
Iconostasis (also Ikonostasis)
Ideology
Idiomelon
Idioms, Communication of: See
    Communicatio Idiomatum
Idol
Idolatry
Ignorance
IHS
Illegitimacy
Illuminative Way
Image of God (also Imago Dei)
Images
Imitation of Christ
Immaculate Conception
Immaculate Conception, National Shrine of
    the
Immanence
Immanuel: See Emmanuel
Immensae Caritatis
Immersion, Baptism by
Immortality of the Soul
Immovability of Pastors
Immovable Feasts
Immunity
Immutability
Impeccability
Impediment
Impediment, Diriment
Impediments, Hindering

Imperfections
Imposition of Hands
Impotence
Imprecatory Psalms
Imprimatur
Improperia (or Reproaches)
Impurity
Imputability
In Articulo Mortis
Incardination
Incarnation, The
Incense
Indefectibility
Index of Forbidden Books
Indifferentism
Indissolubility
Individualism
Indulgences
Indult
Indwelling of the Holy Spirit
Inerrancy
Infallibilists
Infallibility
Infamy
Infidel
Infinite
Infused Virtues
Infusion: See Baptism, Sacrament of
Inopportunists
Inquisition
Inquisition, Spanish
I.N.R.I.
Inspiration of Scripture
Installation
Institute, Religious
Institute on Religious Life
Institute, Secular
Instruction, Canonical
Intellect
Intention
Intercession
Intercommunion
Interdict
Inter Mirifica
Internal Forum
International Committee (or Commission)
   on English in the Liturgy, Inc. (ICEL)
International Theological Commission (ITC)
Internuncio
Interpretation, Scriptural
Interpretation of Law
Interregnum
Interstices
Intinction
Introduction, Biblical

Introit
Investiture
Invincible Ignorance
Invitatory (also Invitatorium)
"In Vitro" Fertilization
Ipso Facto
Ipsum Esse
Irenicism
Irregularity, Canonical
Irremovability of Pastors
Isaac
Isaiah
Islam
Israel
Itala Vetus
Iuspatronatus

J

Jacob
Jacobins
Jacobite Church
James, Epistle of
James the Greater, St.
James, Liturgy of St.
Jansenism
Januarius, Miracle of St.
Jehovah
Jehovah's Witnesses
Jeremiah, Book of
Jerusalem
Jerusalem, Council of
Jerusalem, Patriarchate of
Jesse-Window
Jesuit Reductions
Jesuit Relations, The
Jesuits
Jesus Seminar
Jewish Canon of Scriptures
Jews
Jews for Jesus
Job, Book of
Jocists
Joel
Joel, Book of
John, First, Second and Third Epistles of
John, The Gospel of
John the Baptist
Joinder of Issues
Jonah, Book of
Jonah, Sign of
Joseph, St.
Josephism (also Josephinism)
Joshua, Book of

Joy
Joys of the Blessed Virgin Mary
Jubilee
Judaism
Judaizers
Jude, Epistle of
Judges
Judges, Book of
Judges, Synodal
Judgment, General
Judgment, Liturgical
Judgment, Musical
Judgment, Particular
Judgment, Pastoral
Judgment, Triple
Judica Psalm
Judith, Book of
Juridic Person
Jurisdiction
Jurisprudence
Jus Patronatus: See Iuspatronatus
Just War Theory
Justice
Justification

K

Kanon: See Canon
Kantism (also Kantianism)
Kathisma
Katholikon
Katholikos
Kenosis
Kerygma
King James Version
Kingdom of Christ
Kingdom of God
Kings, First and Second Books of
Kingship of Christ
Kinonikon
Kiss, Liturgical Use of
Knights of Columbus
Knights of Malta (Hospitallers)
Knights, Orders of
Knights, Papal
Knock, Our Lady of
Knowledge
Know-Nothingism
Knox Version of the Bible
Koimesis
Koinonia
Kontakion
Koran
Ku Klux Klan

Kulturkampf
Kyriale
Kyrie Eleison

L

Labarum
Labor
Laborem Exercens
Lady Chapel
Lady Day
Laetare Medal
Laetare Sunday: See Gaudete Sunday
Laic Laws
Laicism
Laicization
Laity
Laity, Institutions of
Lamb (Eucharist)
Lamb of God
Lambeth Conference
Lamentations, Book of
Lamp-Lighting
Lamps
Lance, Holy
Languages, Biblical
Languages of the Church
Lapsed
La Salette, Our Lady of
Last Sacraments
Last Supper
Latae Sententiae
Lateran
Lateran Church
Lateran Councils
Lateran Palace
Lateran Treaty
Latin
Latin Mass
Latin Rite
Latria
Lauds
Lavabo
L'Avenir: See Avenir, L'
Law
Law, Canon: See Canon Law
Law, Universal
Law and Gospel
Laxism
Lay Baptism
Lay Minister of Marriage
Lay People, Decree on the Apostolate of: See
    Apostolicam Actuositatem
Lay Reader

Lay Trusteeism
Leader of Song: See Song, Leader of
Leadership, Pastoral
Leadership Conference of Women Religious
League for Religious and Civil Rights,
    Catholic: See Catholic League for
    Religious and Civil Rights
Lectern
Lectionary
Lector: See Lay Reader
Legate
Legate a Latere
Legend, Golden: See Golden Legend
Legion of Decency
Legionaries of Christ
Legitimation
Lent
Leopoldine Association
Lepanto, Battle of
Leper Window
Lesson
Levirate Marriage
Leviticus
Liber Pontificalis
Liber Usualis
Liberalism
Liberals, Catholic
Liberation Theology
Liberty, Religious
Licentiate
Licit
Lie
Life
Life, Sanctity of: See Sanctity of Life
Life, Spiritual
Ligamen
Light
Lily
Limbo
Literal Sense of Scripture
Literary Criticism
Literary Qualities of the Bible
Little Office of the Blessed Virgin Mary
Liturgical Art: See Sacred Art and
    Furnishings
Liturgical Books
Liturgical Commission
Liturgical Judgment: See Judgment,
    Liturgical
Liturgical Law
Liturgical Life
Liturgical Movement
Liturgical Music Today: See Music Today,
    Liturgical
Liturgy

Liturgy, Bishops' Committee on the: See
    Bishops' Committee on the Liturgy
Liturgy, Children's
Liturgy, Constitution on the Sacred: See
    Sacrosanctum Concilium
Liturgy, Divine
Liturgy of the Hours
Lives of the Saints
Loaves of Proposition: See Showbread
Local Ordinary
Loci Theologici
Logic
Logos
Lollards
Longanimity
Lord
Lord's Prayer
Lord's Supper
Loreto, Holy House of
L'Osservatore Romano: See Osservatore
    Romano, L'
Los-von-Rom Movement
Lourdes, Apparitions of
Love
Love of God
Love of Neighbor
Low Sunday
Ludwig Mission Association
Luke, The Gospel of
Lumen Gentium
Luna (also Lunette)
L'Univers: See Univers, L'
Lust
Lutheran-Catholic Dialogue
Lutheranism
Lyons, Councils of
Lyons, Rite of

M

Maccabees, First and Second Books of
Macedonianism
Madonna
Magdalen
Magi
Magic
Magisterium of the Church
Magnanimity
Magnificat
Major Orders
Major Superior
Makarisms
Malabar Rites
Malachi, Book of

Malta, Knights of: See Knights of Malta
Mammon
Man
Mandatum
Mandyas
Manichaeism
Manifestation of Conscience
Maniple
Manna
Mantelletta
Mantellone
Mantum
Manual of Prayers of the Council of
  Baltimore
Manuterge
Mappula
Marburg, Colloquy of
Margarita
Marialis Cultus
Marian Year
Mariology
Maritain, Jacques
Mark, The Gospel of
Marks of the Church
Maronites
Marriage Encounter
Marriage, Sacrament of
Martyr
Martyrology
Marxism
Mary, Feasts of
Mary, Saturday Office of
Mary, Virgin Mother of God: See Deipara
Maryknoll: See Catholic Foreign Mission
  Society of America
Marymas
Masonry: See Freemasonry
Mass of the Catechumens
Master of Ceremonies
Master of Novices
Master of the Sacred Palace
Master of the Sentences
Mater et Magistra
Materialism
Matins
Matrimonial Court
Matrimony: See Marriage, Sacrament of
Matthew, The Gospel of
Matthias, St.
Maundy Thursday
Maurists
Means of Social Communication, Decree on
  the: See Inter Mirifica
Medals, Religious
Mediator

Mediator Dei
Mediatrix of All Graces
Meditation
Meekness
Megalynarion
Meletian Schism
Melkite (also Melchite) Rite
Membership in the Church
Memento
Memorare
Memoria
Memorial, Obligatory
Memorial, Optional: See Memorial,
  Obligatory
Menaion
Mendicant Orders
Mene, Tekel, Upharsin
Menology (also Menologion)
Menorah
Mensa
Mental Reservation (or Mental Restriction)
Mercy
Mercy, Corporal and Spiritual Works of
Merit
Messiah (also Messias): See Christ
Metanoia
Metany
Metaphysics
Metempsychosis
Methodism
Metropolitan
Mexican American Cultural Center
Micah, Book of
Middle Ages
Midrash
Migrant Ministries
Military Chaplains
Military Ordinariate
Millenarianism
Millennium
Minister
Ministries
Ministry and Life of Priests, Decree on: See
  Presbyterorum Ordinis
Ministry of the Word
Minor Orders
Miracle
Miracle Plays (also Mystery or Morality
  Plays)
Miraculous Medal
Mirari Vos
Miserere
Missal: See Roman Missal
Missiology
Mission

Missionaries (also Missioners)
Missionary Activity, Decree on the
  Church's: See Ad Gentes
Mitre (also Miter)
Mixed Marriage
Modalism
Moderator of the Curia
Modernism
Modes, Gregorian: See Gregorian Modes
Modes of Responsibility
Modesty
Mohammedanism: See Islam
Moicheia
Moleben
Molech (also Moloch)
Molinism
Monarchianism
Monastery
Monasticism
Monism
Monita Secreta
Monk
Monogamy
Monophysism (also Monophysitism)
Monotheism
Monothelism (also Monothelitism)
Monsignor
Monstrance
Montana Case
Montanism
Montessori Method
Month's Mind
Moral Person
Moral Theology
Moral Virtues
Morality
Morality Play
Moravian Church
Morganatic Marriage
Mormons
Morning Offering
Morning Star
Mortal Sin
Mortal and Venial Sin: See Sin, Mortal and
  Venial
Mortification
Mosaic Law
Moses
Moslems: See Muslims
Motet
Motive, Spiritual
Motu Proprio
Movable Feasts
Mozarabic Rite
Mozzetta

Muratorian Fragment
Music, Church
Music Coordinator
Music, Liturgical
Music in Catholic Worship
Music, Passion: See Passion Music
Music Today, Liturgical
Musical Judgment: See Judgment, Musical
Muslims
Mustum
Myron
Myrrh
Mysteries of the Rosary
Mystery
Mystery, Paschal: See Paschal Mystery
Mystical Body of Christ
Mystical Sense of Scripture
Mystical Theology
Mystici Corporis Christi
Mysticism
Myth

N

Nag Hammadi
Nahum, Book of
Name, Christian
Name Day
Names of God
Nash Papyrus
National Assembly of Religious Women
  (NARW)
National Association of Pastoral Musicians
National Black Sisters' Conference (NBSC)
National Catholic Conference for Interracial
  Justice
National Catholic Educational Association
  (NCEA)
National Catholic Welfare Conference
  (NCWC)
National Conference of Catholic Bishops
  (NCCB)
National Council of Catholic Laity
National Council of Catholic Men (NCCM)
National Council of Catholic Women (NCCW)
National Council of Churches
National Federation of Priests' Councils
  (NFPC)
National Parish
Nationalism
Nativism
Natural Family Planning
Natural Law
Natural Rights

Natural Theology
Naturalism
Nature
Nave
Nazarite (also Nazirite)
Nazorean (also Nazarene)
Ne Temere
Necromancy
Nehemiah, Book of
Neighbor
Nemours, Edict of
Neo-Catechumenate
Neo-Scholasticism
Nesteia
Nestorianism
New American Bible
Nicaea, Councils of
Nicene Creed
Nihil Obstat
Nimbus
Ninety-Five Theses
Noble Guards
Nocturn
Nomocanons
Non-Christian Religions, Declaration on the
    Relationship of the Church to: See Nostra
    Aetate
Non-Consummation
Non Expedit
None
North American College
North American Martyrs
North Door
Nostra Aetate
Novatianism
Novena
Novice
Novitiate
Nuclear Deterrence, Morality of
Numbers, Book of
Nun
Nunc Dimittis
Nunciature
Nuncio
Nuptial Mass and Blessing

O

O Antiphons
O Salutaris
Oak, Synod of the
Oath
Oath of Succession
Obadiah, Book of

Obedience
Obedience of Faith
Oblates
Oblation
Obreption
Obscenity
Obsession
Occasion of Sin
Occult, Canonically
Occult Compensation
Occultism
Occurrence
Octave
Ode
Offertory
Offertory Collection
Office
Office, Ecclesiastical
Office of the Dead
Official Catholic Directory of the United
    States
Officialis
Oil
Old Believers
Old Catholics
Ombrellino
Omega Point: See Teilhardism
Omnipotence
Omniscience
Omophorion
Only-Begotten One
Onomasticon
Ontologism
Oplatki
Optatam Totius
Opus Dei
Orange, Councils of
Orante
Orarion
Orate, Fratres
Oratory
Order
Order of Christian Funerals
Order of Mass, New
Orders, Holy
Orders, Major: See Orders, Holy
Orders, Minor: See Minor Orders
Ordinariate
Ordinary
Ordinary Medical Treatments
Ordinatio Sacerdotalis
Ordination
Ordination of Women: See Women,
    Ordination of
Ordo

Oriental Churches, Congregation for the
Orientalium Ecclesiarum
Original Sin: See Sin, Original
Orléans, Councils of
Orphrey
Orthodox Church
Orthodoxy, Feast of
Osservatore Romano, L'
Ostiarius
Ostpolitik
Our Lady
Oxford Movement

P

Pacem in Terris
Pacifism
Pactum Callixtinum
Paenitemini
Paganism
Pain and Euthanasia
Pain Bénit
Palatine
Palimpsest
Pall
Pallium
Palm Sunday
Palms, Blessing of
Panagia
Pange Lingua
Pannykhidia
Pantheism
Pantocrator
Papabile
Papacy
Papal Blessing (Apostolic Blessing)
Papal Chamberlain
Papal Flag
Papal Household
Papal Letters
Papal States
Papal Theologian
Pappas
Parable
Paraclete
Paracletikes
Paradise: See Eden, Garden of; also Heaven
Paraekklesia
Paraenesis
Paraliturgical Actions
Parallelism
Parapsychology
Parenthood
Parents, Duties of

Parish
Parish Pastoral Council
Parish Priest
Parish Team
Parishioner
Parochial Administrator
Parochial Mass
Parochial Schools: See Schools, Parochial
Parochial Vicar
Parousia
Particular Church
Particular Councils
Particular Law
Pascendi Dominici Gregis
Pasch
Paschal Candle
Paschal Mystery
Passion of Christ
Passion of the Martyrs
Passion Music
Passion Sunday
Passion Week
Passiontide
Passover
Pastor
Pastoral Care of the Sick
Pastoral Counseling: See Counseling,
    Pastoral
Pastoral Epistles
Pastoral Judgment: See Judgment, Pastoral
Pastoral Ministry
Pastoral Provision for the Common Identity
Pastoral Theology
Paten
Pater Noster
Patience
Patriarch (Patriarchate)
Patriarchs, Scriptural
Patrimony, Canonical
Patrimony, Spiritual
Patriotism, Christian
Patripassionism
Patrology
Patron
Patron Saints
Patroness of the U.S.A.
Paul, St.
Pauline Privilege
Pax
Pax Christi
Peace
Peace, Kiss of
Pectoral Cross
Pelagianism
Pelvicula

Penal Laws
Penal Process
Penalty, Ecclesiastical
Penalty, Vindictive
Penance
Penance, Sacrament of
Penance, Virtue of
Penitent
Penitential Books
Penitential Psalms
Penitentiary, Sacred Apostolic
Pension
Pentateuch
Pentecost
Pentecostal Churches
Pentecostalism, Catholic
Pentecostarion
People of God
Perfectae Caritatis
Perfection
Pericope
Peritus
Perjury
Permanent Deacon: See Deacon, Permanent
Perpetual Adoration
Persecutions
Person
Personal Prelature
Personalism
Peschitto, The
Peter, First Epistle of
Peter, Second Epistle of
Peter's Chains, Feast of
Peter's Chair, Feast of
Peter's Pence
Petrine Privilege
Phantasiasm
Pharisees
Phelonion (also Phenolion)
Philemon, Epistle of Paul to
Philippians, Epistle of Paul to the
Philosophy
Photius
Pietism
Piety
Pilgrim/Pilgrimage
Pious Foundation
Pious Fund
Pious Will
Pisa, Councils of
Piscina (also Sacrarium)
Pistoia, Synod of
Plainchant
Planeta (Pianeta)
Pleroma

Plumbator
Pneumatomachi
Polyglot Bible
Pontiff (Supreme Pontiff)
Pontifical Biblical Commission
Pontifical Biblical Institute
Pontifical Institutes of Higher Learning
Pontifical Mass
Pontifical Right
Pontifical Secrecy
Pontificals
Poor and Needy (the Poor)
Pope
Popes, List of
Pope Speaks, The
Popish Plot
Populorum Progressio
Porter
Portiuncula
Positivism
Possession, Demonic
Postcommunion
Postulant
Postulation
Poterion
Poverty
Power
Power of the Keys
Pragmatism
Prayer of the Faithful (also General
    Intercessions)
Prayer over the Gifts
Prayer, Mystical: See Mysticism
Preaching
Precept
Precious Blood, Feast of the
Predella
Predestination
Preface
Prefect, Apostolic (or Vicar Apostolic)
Prefecture, Apostolic
Prelate
Premoral Evil
Presanctified, Mass of the
Presbyter
Presbyterian Churches
Presbyterorum Ordinis
Presbytery
Prescription
Presence of God
Presence, Real
Presentation of the Blessed Virgin Mary
President
Presidential Prayers
Press, Catholic: See Catholic Press

Q

R

Ring
Ripidion
Risorgimento
Rite
Rite, Alexandrian
Rite, Antiochene
Rite, Armenian
Rite, Byzantine
Rite, Celtic: See Celtic Rite
Rite, Chaldean: See Chaldean Rite
Rite, Coptic: See Coptic Rite
Rite, Georgian Byzantine: See Georgian
    Byzantine Rite
Rite, Latin: See Latin Rite
Rite, Malabar: See Malabar Rites
Rite, Melkite: See Melkite (also Melchite) Rite
Rite, Mozarabic: See Mozarabic Rite
Rite, Religious
Rite, Roman: See Roman Rite
Rite, Russian: See Russian Rite
Rite, Ruthenian: See Ruthenian Catholics
Rite, Syrian: See Syrian Rite
Rite of Christian Initiation of Adults (RCIA)
Rite of Constantinople
Rites, Chinese
Rites, Sacred Congregation of
Ritual
Rochet
Rogation Days
Rogito
Roman Catholic
Roman College
Roman Congregations
Roman Law
Roman Missal
Roman Missal, General Instruction of the
Roman Rite
Romans, Epistle to the
Rome
Rood-Screen
Rosary
Rose Window
Rosh Hashanah
Rota, Sacred Roman
Rubrics
Rule, Religious
Russian Rite
Ruth, Book of
Ruthenian Catholics

S

Sabaoth
Sabbatarianism

Sabbath
Sabellianism
Sacramental
Sacramental Theology
Sacramentarians
Sacramentary
Sacraments, Seven
Sacraments of Initiation
Sacred Art and Furnishings
Sacred College of Cardinals: See College of
    Cardinals
Sacred Heart of Jesus
Sacred Liturgy, Constitution on the: See
    Sacrosanctum Concilium
Sacred Meal
Sacred Places
Sacred Roman Congregations: See Roman
    Congregations
Sacred Times
Sacred Vessels
Sacred Writers
Sacrifice
Sacrifice of the Mass
Sacrilege
Sacristan
Sacristy
Sacrosancta
Sacrosanctum Concilium
Sadducees
St. Joseph's Oratory
St. Peter's Basilica
Saints
Saints, Invocations and Veneration of
Saints, Patron: See Patron Saints
Sakkos
Salt, Liturgical Use of
Salvation
Salvation History
Salvation Outside the Church
Samuel, First and Second Books of
Sanation
Sanctification
Sanctifying Grace
Sanctity of Life
Sanctuary
Sanctus
Sandals
Sanhedrin
Sapiential Books
Sardica, Council of
Sarum Use
Satan: See Devil; also Devil and Evil
    Spirits
Satisfaction
Saul: See Paul, St.

Sorrows of the Blessed Virgin Mary
Soteriology
Soul
Spiritism
Spiritual Communion
Spiritual Exercises of St. Ignatius Loyola
Spiritual Works of Mercy: See Mercy,
  Corporal and Spiritual Works of
Spirituality
Sponge
Sponsors
Spoon, Liturgical
Spouse of Christ
Spouses of the Blessed Virgin Mary
Stained Glass
State of Grace
Stations of the Cross
Stations, Roman
Status Animarum
Stephanos
Sterilization
Stewardship
Sticharion
Stichon
Stigmata
Stipend
Stole
Stole Fee
Stone, Altar: See Altar Stone
Stylite
Subdeacon
Subdelegation
Subpedaneum (Suppedaneum)
Subreption
Subsidiarity
Suburbicarian Dioceses
Suffering and Euthanasia
Suffragan Bishop
Suffrages
Summa Theologiae
Sunday
Sunday Obligation
Supererogation, Works of
Suppedaneum: See Subpedaneum
Suppression
Supreme Moderator
Surplice
Suspension
Swedenborgianism
Swiss Guards
Syllabus of Errors
Symbol
Symbolism
Synagogue
Synapte

Synaxis
Synderesis (also Synteresis)
Synod
Synod of Bishops
Synoptic Gospels, The
Synoptic Question, The
Synteresis: See Synderesis
Syrian Rite

T

Tabernacle
Talitha Koum (Koumi)
Talmud
Tametsi
Tantum Ergo
Te Deum
Teilhardism
Temperance
Temple in Jerusalem, The
Temporal Goods
Temporal Power
Temptation
Tenebrae
Terce (also Tierce)
Ternus
Tertiaries
Testament
Tetragrammaton
Thaumaturgus
Theodicy
Theologian
Theological Notes
Theological Virtues
Theology
Theophany
Theotokion
Theotokos
Thessalonians, First and Second Epistles to
  the
Thomas, Gospel of
Thomism
Thomism, Transcendental
Throne
Thurible
Tiara
Time
Time, Computation of
Timothy, First Epistle to
Timothy, Second Epistle to
Tithe
Titulus
Titus, Epistle to
Tobit, Book of

Tones
Tonsure
Torah
Totalitarianism
Totemism
Toties Quoties
Tower of Babel: See Babel, Tower of
Tract
Tradition
Traditionalism
Traditores
Traducianism
Training of Priests: See Optatam Totius
Transcendence
Transfiguration
Transitional Deacon: See Deacon,
    Transitional
Transubstantiation
Tree of Jesse
Trent, Council of
Tribunals
Tribunals, Roman
Triduum
Triduum, Paschal
Trination
Trinity, The Most Holy
Triodion
Triple Candle
Triple Judgment: See Judgment, Triple
Triptych
Trisagion
Triumph of the Cross (also Exaltation of the
    Cross)
Triumphalism
Troparion
Truce of God
Trullo, Council of
Trusteeism
Tunic
Tutiorism
Typikon
Typological Sense of Scripture

U

Ubiquitarianism
Ultramontanism
Umbanda
Unam Sanctam
Unction
Uniate Churches
Uniformity, Acts of
Unigenitus
Union, Mystical: See Mysticism

Unitarianism
Unitatis Redintegratio
United States Catholic Conference (USCC)
Unity
Univers, L'
Universal Law: See Law, Universal
University, Pontifical
Urbi et Orbi
Urim and Thummim
Ursacrament (also Ursackrament)
Usury
Ut Unum Sint
Utraquism

V

Vagi
Vaison, Councils of
Valentinianism
Valid
Validation of Marriage: See Convalidation
Vandalism
Vatican
Vatican Council I
Vatican Council II
Vatican State, City of
Vaudois: See Waldenses
Veils
Venerable
Veneration of the Saints
Veni, Creator Spiritus
Veritatis Splendor
Versicle
Vespers
Vestments
Viaticum
Vicar
Vicar, Judicial
Vicar of Christ
Vicar of Peter
Vicariate, Apostolic
Vice-Chancellor
Vienne, Council of
Vigil
Vigil Light
Vincent de Paul, St.
Vindictive Penalties: See Penalty, Vindictive
Virgin Birth of Christ
Virgin Mary
Virginity
Virtue
Virtues, Moral: See Moral Virtues
Virtues, Theological: See Theological Virtues
Visions

W

XYZ